P9-DWX-960

Managerial Accounting

Second Edition

HOUGHTON MIFFLIN COMPANY BOSTON

Dallas Geneva, Illinois Palo Alto Princeton, New Jersey

Managerial Accounting

Second Edition

Don Ricketts

D.B.A., M.B.A.
Arthur Andersen Alumni Fellow
Professor of Accounting
University of Cincinnati

Jack Gray

Ph.D., M.B.A., CPA
Ernst & Young
Professor of Accounting
Michigan State University

This book is written to provide accurate and authoritative information concerning covered topics. It is not meant to take the place of professional advice.

Cover artwork by Gary Eldridge. Artist Gary Eldridge has created a cover image to convey some of the key topics in this second edition. The just in time philosophy, the influence of computers, the international economy, and the human element of managerial decision making are highlighted to illustrate their growing importance in the field of managerial accounting.

Printed in the U.S.A.

Library of Congress Catalog Card Number: 90-80351

ISBN: 0-395-43362-2

ABCDEFGHIJ-RM-9987654320

Contents

Preface

The first edition of *Managerial Accounting* was based on a systematic evaluation of the needs of managerial accounting students and teachers. We used extensive market research and analyzed over 100 course syllabi. The second edition benefits from the feedback from many users and nonusers in all parts of the United States and Europe. Many instructors and students shared their experiences with the first edition. The authors used their combined 41 years of experience in teaching managerial accounting to write the second edition.

The success of the first edition showed the importance of a balance of contemporary content, flexible organization, attention to problem solving, and student-oriented pedagogy. The text illustrates the application of managerial accounting in a variety of organizations, including service and retail in addition to manufacturing. We continue our commitment to a complete and comprehensive array of high quality student and instructor learning and teaching aids beyond the textbook itself.

Flexible Organization and Content

Managerial Accounting, Second Edition, is divided into five flexible parts. Entire sections can be reordered or left out with no loss of continuity. The manuscript was class tested and proven to be an effective teaching tool.

Part 1: Fundamentals of Managerial Accounting. This section covers the major definitions and concepts of managerial accounting. Chapter 1 makes a clear distinction between cost and managerial accounting topics. Chapter 2 discusses the concepts most fundamental to managerial accounting: cost classification and flow. Chapter 3 shows how fixed, mixed, and variable costs are estimated for both cost and managerial accounting.

Part 2: Cost Accounting Systems. These two chapters succinctly cover the essentials of cost accounting: job order (chapter 4) and process costing (chapter 5). The two costing methods are defined, and numerous examples of their appropriate uses in both service and manufacturing companies are illustrated. Part 2 can be taught as a unit at any point in the course.

Part 3: Accounting in Managerial Planning Decisions. These three chapters show students how managers successfully use accounting information in planning decisions. Chapter 6 shows how to use cost-volume-profit analysis to develop plans for reaching target profits. Chapter 7 explains how to develop a master budget that ensures that resources are available to reach those targets. Identifying and analyzing costs relevant to nonrecurring decisions is discussed in chapter 8.

Part 4: Accounting in Managerial Control Decisions. This part shows students how to prepare and analyze the reports that managers use to control organizations. Chapter 9 discusses responsibility accounting. Chapter 10 covers control of direct materials and direct labor costs through use of standard cost accounting systems. Chapter 11 comprehensively discusses using flexible budgets to control overhead costs. The final two chapters of Part 4 cover control reporting for managers of revenue and profit centers (chapter 12) and investment centers (chapter 13).

Part 5: Advanced Topics in Managerial Accounting. This section of the text covers capital expenditure analysis (chapters 14 and 15), including the Tax Reform Act of 1986, and cost allocation (chapter 16). The last two chapters, Analysis of Financial Statements (chapter 17) and the Statement of Cash Flows (chapter 18), may be covered at any point during the course.

Appendix. Appendix A, Present Value Tables, includes tables for the present value of $1 and the present value of an annuity. Examples of the use of each table are provided.

Throughout the text, we have included examples from service, nonbusiness, and manufacturing organizations in order to accurately reflect the economic trends and job markets of the 1990s and beyond.

Content Improvements in the Second Edition

Managerial accounting is a discipline in transition. Current research, business innovation, the increased use of the microcomputer and the impact of the global economy of the 90s have mandated that new information be introduced into the traditional structure of the managerial accounting course. During the revision process, many changes were made to the existing chapters, integrating and updating current information. There are, however, some specific changes that the authors bring to your attention. The most important expansions of the subject matter include coverage of the Just in Time manufacturing philosophy, ethics, and international issues.

The text integrates Just in Time into the text at various points, particularly in Chapter 7 where the text discusses planning and the master budget. Ethics is introduced in Chapter 1 with discussion of the *Code of Ethics* published by the National Association of Accountants. The discussion of ethics is followed with several cases raising ethical issues. Finally, the authors' experiences teaching in China, Thailand, Indonesia, France, and Morocco help them introduce the appropriate issues in international accounting. For example, see the international transfer pricing discussion in Chapter 13.

Problem-Solving Approach in the Second Edition

We have taken a comprehensive approach to the problem-solving aspects of managerial accounting. Each chapter begins with examples of the kinds of issues real-world managers must face. Then, within the chapter, step-by-step examples highlight the methods used to analyze these issues. The end-of-chapter review problems, questions, exercises, problem sets, and cases test student comprehension of the chapter. We carefully designed the problem sets to include multiples of frequently assigned problem types, many of which deal with the use of managerial accounting by managers in retail and service organizations. For this edition, 175 questions, exercises, and problems were added and 43 new cases have been included.

For the second edition, we developed a unique use of illustrative review exercises. In each chapter, a short in-text exercise and its solution are given immediately after each major computational step illustrated in the chapter discussion. This new feature expands on the idea of the comprehensive review problem included at the end of the chapters by providing students with the opportunity to work through a new illustration and check their solutions immediately. This corrects any errors in thinking and provides positive reinforcement of what the student has learned. The review exercises are linked to specific assignments at the end of each chapter via references given at the end of the exercises. Either the student or instructor can choose similar assignments to further reinforce the learning.

New to this edition, a series of Lotus 1-2-3 templates for selected chapter exercises and problems are available. These are partially completed templates to be used in solution of problems. The student less familiar with spreadsheet programs can use these quite easily to produce solutions to the selected assignments. They are also easily used for "what if" analysis. For example, in the chapter on capital expenditure analysis, it is a simple matter to change the discount rate and see what effect it has on the net present value. This method can be used to determine the time-adjusted rate of return on an investment.

Students with more familiarity with the spreadsheet programs, in general, may find it interesting to study the logic of the spreadsheet formulas and can modify the templates to solve other similar exercises and problems with some guidance from the instructor.

Permission has been granted by the American Institute of Certified Public Accountants to adapt selected problems from various CPA exams. These problems are noted as (AICPA). Permission has also been received from the Institute of Certified Management Accountants of the National Association of Accountants to adapt questions from past CMA exams. These problems are noted as (CMA). The assistance of these organizations is appreciated.

A Student Oriented Text

The text also uses a learning-by-objective pedagogical approach that directly relates materials in the end-of-chapter assignments and teaching and study aids to the relevant sections of the text's exposition. At the beginning of each chapter, carefully written learning objectives preview chapter content. The objectives are repeated next to the related text material in the chapter. They provide the organizational framework for the chapter summary. The learning objectives are used throughout the Study Guide, Instructor's Handbook, and Test Bank to reinforce comprehension of the text material and aid instructors in designing their courses.

Managerial Icons

A unique feature of the second edition is a system of managerial icons that has been carefully designed to help students and instructors focus on managerial decision making and the emerging trends. They are located in the margins throughout the second edition text and problem sets.

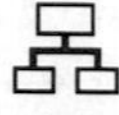
Managerial uses of accounting information

International examples

The role of the computer and assignments that can be solved using the Lotus templates

Just in Time and automation

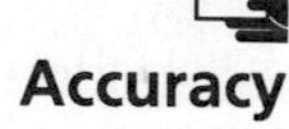
Examples from service and nonbusiness organizations

Accuracy

Accuracy is most important in accounting texts, since the ability to solve the problems is key for student understanding. Both the students and the instructor must be assured that the solution to each problem is complete, accurate, and consistent. The authors and the publisher of this text have taken a five-step approach to ensure an accurate text.

First, we developed and solved many of the problems ourselves using the LOTUS® spreadsheet program. Next, these solutions were evaluated for consistency in format and accuracy of content by a professional reviewer. A task force of managerial accounting professors actively teaching the course read through page proofs for the entire text and worked all the problems again. Finally, we compared the task force's solutions with those previously prepared as a final check.

It is also important to note that the capital expenditure analysis chapter was evaluated by the firm of Ernst & Young to ensure that topical coverage of the Tax Reform Act of 1986 was complete and consistent. Chapter 18, Statement of Cash Flows, was written using the most up-to-date information available from the Financial Accounting Standards Board regarding the format and content of this statement.

Comprehensive Ancillary Package

A wide variety of ancillaries is available to adopters and students using *Managerial Accounting*, Second Edition.

For Students

Study Guide. By Bobbe Barnes, University of Colorado at Denver. The Study Guide systematically reviews chapter content with summaries, objective questions, and additional exercises and problems. It is organized by the text's learning objectives. In addition, each chapter includes an acrostic puzzle and a what-if scenario, in which students can apply their decision-making skills to real-life situations.

LOTUS Assignment Templates. Lotus 1-2-3 spreadsheet templates are available for selected exercises and problems. They are highlighted in the text with a computer icon.

LOTUS® Problems for Managerial Accounting. Using the power of LOTUS® 1-2-3 software, students solve managerial accounting problems from the text and explore "what-if" scenarios in a detailed manner.

Working Papers. These provide preprinted forms that correspond to all text problems. Also included are forms for cases and selected blank forms that can be used with the exercises.

The Windham Company, 2/e. By Henry R. Anderson, University of Central Florida. This practice set is really two sets in one. The first set requires students to prepare the worksheet and financial statements for a manufacturer using a periodic inventory system. The second set covers the same tasks for a manufacturing firm using a perpetual inventory system. This practice set is available in workbook format and requires about 10 hours.

McHenry Hotels: A Practice Case in Management Decision Analysis. By Henry R. Anderson, University of Central Florida and Sandra VanTrease, Price Waterhouse, St. Louis. McHenry Hotels focuses on the operations of the Dallas branch of a chain of luxury hotels. Students analyze internal accounting data and prepare a final report to the board of directors.

Callson Industries, Inc. Also by Henry R. Anderson and Sandra VanTrease. This managerial accounting decision case concerns a company that has converted its manufacturing facilities to a JIT environment but has not yet changed its management accounting approach to include new procedures and reports that give managers relevant and timely information about operations. The required analysis of the case provides a step-by-step conversion process for this fastener manufacturer. Students deal firsthand with the development of an internal accounting and reporting system involving the new manufacturing environment.

Polyform, Inc.: A Computerized Decision Case for Cost and Managerial Accounting. By Kirk L. Tennant, Southern Methodist University and Galen Rupp, Pittsburg State University, Kansas. Using the microcomputer, students make cost and/or managerial accounting decisions for a plastics manufacturer. This decision case covers the major topics of a managerial accounting course. Its modular format enables instructors to pick and choose those assignments most appropriate to their courses.

For Instructors

Instructor's Solutions Manual. This contains step-by-step solutions for all questions, exercises, problems, and cases in *Managerial Accounting*.

Instructor's Handbook. This provides suggested course outlines, lecture outlines and chapter summaries, teaching strategies, reviews of key terms, lists of problems by learning objective with difficulty and time charts, and check figures for the problems and cases. The Instructor's Handbook also includes a 10 minute quiz for each chapter.

Test Bank. The expanded test bank contains over 2,000 items including true-or-false statements, multiple-choice questions, and problems. All items are keyed to the text's learning objectives. A microcomputer version and a call-in test service are also available.

Solutions Transparencies. High-quality mylar reproductions of the solutions for all exercises and problems. The type size has been increased substantially.

Teaching Transparencies. Seventy two- and three-color mylar transparencies are available for selected text illustrations.

A.S.S.E.T.: Presentation Software for Managerial Accounting. This innovative microcomputer program combines instructor lecture outlines, selected illustrations, figures, and exhibits from the text and LOTUS based templates and solutions to selected exercises and problems. A.S.S.E.T. may be used to prepare customized lecture outlines, syllabi, etc., for classroom distribution, or when used with a liquid crystal display device, complete lectures that can be displayed.

Acknowledgments

Many fine people have been involved with the development of this text. For their assistance in developing the ancillaries, we would like to thank Virginia Clark, University of Cincinnati; Diane Matson, University of Minnesota; Margaret McCullough, University of Louisville; and Tim Sale, University of Cincinnati.

We would also especially like to thank the following for their work on the second edition.

For Accuracy:

Professor Virginia Clark
University of Cincinnati

Harry Falk, CPA

Professor Thomas Hoar
Houston Community College

Professor Anne Kotheimer
Widener University

Professor Shirley Polejewski
College of St. Thomas

For Reviews:

Professor Penne Ainsworth
Kansas State University

Professor N. Lee Baker
Alvin Community College

Professor Neil C. Bassano
William Patterson College

Professor Samuel Battaglia
University of Denver

Professor Marvin L. Bouillon
Iowa State University

Professor Don Call
California State University—Northridge

Professor Bobby J. Carmichael
East Texas State University

Professor Michael A. Casey
University of Toledo

Professor Ricky Casey
University of the Ozarks

Professor Arthur V. Corr
University of Wisconsin—Parkside

Professor Stephen J. Dempsey
University of Vermont

Harry Falk, CPA

Professor Jerry W. Ferry
Pittsburg State University

Professor David Franz
San Francisco State University

Professor Harlan J. Fuller
Illinois State University

Professor Joseph Garlic
Syracuse University

Professor Dennis Geyer
Golden Gate University

Professor Edward S. Goodhart
Shippensburg State University

Professor Charles F. Grant
Skyline College

Professor Rosalie C. Hallbauer
Florida International University

Professor Ennis Hawkins
Sam Houston State University

Professor Thomas Hoar
Houston Community College

Professor Royal E. Knight
University of North Alabama

Professor Anne Kotheimer
Widener University

Professor Paul Krause
California State University—Chico

Professor Robert Landry
Massasoit Community College

Professor Donald R. Law
Augusta College

Professor Martha Marshall
University of North Carolina—Ashville

Professor Marvin Morris
University of Nebraska

Professor Chaim Mozes
Baruch College

Professor Brian O'Doherty
East Carolina University

Professor Paul Parkison
Ball State University

Professor Eileen Peacock
Oakland University

Professor Denis E. Raihall
Drexel University

Professor Lynn Rans
California State University—Los Angeles

Professor Alfredo Salas
El Paso Community College

Professor Vicki Shipley
Ball State University

Professor Carl S. Smith
University of Hartford

Professor Monte Swain
Michigan State University

Professor Nancy Tang
Portland State University

Professor Howard Toole
San Diego State University

Professor Sue Van Boven
Paradise Valley Community College

Professor Paul Waite
Niagara County Community College

Professor Richard B. Watson
University of California—Santa Barbara

Professor Wallace Wood
University of Cincinnati

Professor Robert Zimmer
University of Denver

Professor Gilroy J. Zuckerman
North Carolina State University

Publisher's Preface

This text uses a learning-by-objectives pedagogical approach that directly relates material in the end-of-chapter assignments and selected teaching and study aids to the relevant sections of the text's exposition.

This system was pioneered and elaborated for accounting texts by Belverd E. Needles, Jr., Henry R. Anderson, and James C. Caldwell in collaboration with Houghton Mifflin Company.

Managerial Accounting

Second Edition

Part 1

Fundamentals of Managerial Accounting

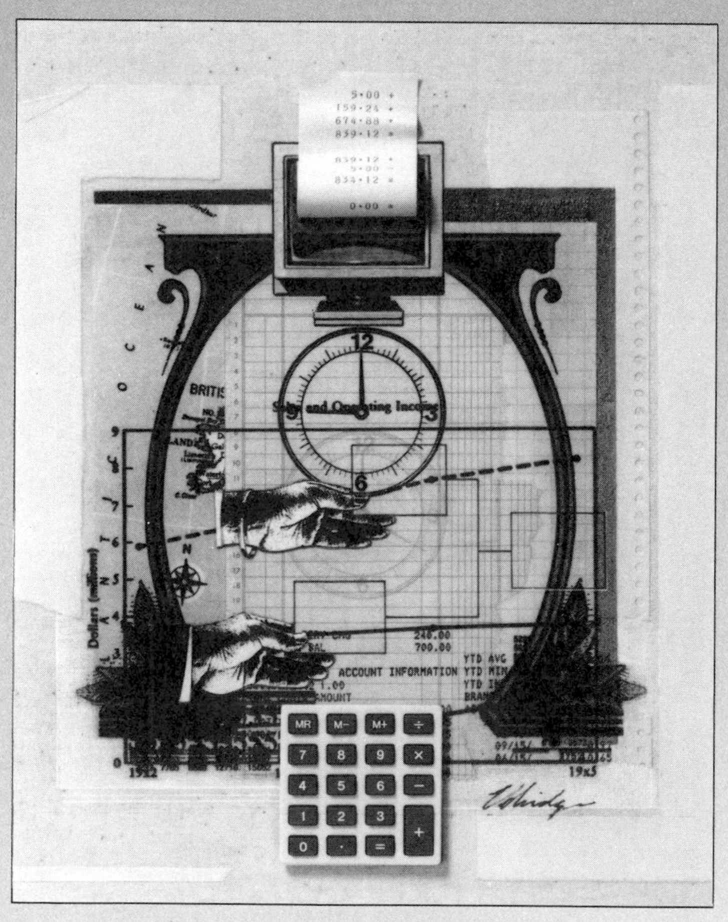

The primary aim of managerial accounting is to help managers make decisions that support the achievement of an organization's financial goals and objectives. Part 1 gives an overview of the concepts basic to managerial accounting. It introduces some fundamental terms and discusses how costs change as the volume of operations changes.

■

Chapter 1, Accounting and the Management Process, covers the management process, the accounting process, and the ways in which accountants assist managers in planning and control of operations.

■

Chapter 2, Cost Classification and Flow, covers those cost concepts that are most fundamental to managerial accounting. It introduces different types of costs, and two methods of accounting for them.

■

Chapter 3, Cost Behavior and Estimation, shows how fixed and variable production costs are estimated for use both in cost accounting and in the planning and control of an organization's operations. Cost accounting reports manufacturing costs for preparing balance sheets and income statements. Managerial accounting estimates future costs for planning and control.

■

1

Accounting and the Management Process

LEARNING OBJECTIVES

After studying this chapter you should be able to:

1. Define management's role in an organization
2. Define objectives and goals and explain how they vary between profit-seeking and not-for-profit organizations
3. Name and describe the four basic activities of the management process
4. Describe the accountant's role in the organization and list the duties of the controller and treasurer
5. Distinguish between financial and managerial accounting
6. Discuss the ethical concerns of managerial accountants
7. Describe how managerial accountants are certified and list the professional objectives of the CMA program

Accounting provides reliable information on an organization's economic activities to interested people, both inside and outside the organization. Managerial accounting is the branch of accounting primarily concerned with reporting to internal managers for decision-making purposes. Managers establish an organization's objectives and coordinate the resources to attain these objectives. The role of managerial accounting is to provide information that helps managers fulfill their role.

■

Organizations: Their Objectives and Goals

An **organization** is a group of people working together to achieve a common goal. A college or university is an organization whose goal is to provide educational services. A town or city government is an organization whose goal is to provide fire and police protection, water, and other services to its residents.

Organizations may exist within organizations. For example, a major auto manufacturer has five automobile divisions. A separate division provides loans to dealers and customers. Still another division provides data processing services to businesses. Each of these divisions is an organization. The common factor in each of them, as in the other organizations, is people working together toward a common purpose. The company owns buildings, machinery, and vehicles throughout the world, but without people those properties would be empty shells. It is the people who give the organization life — who get the automobile from the factory to the showroom and to the consumer.

OBJECTIVE 1
Define management's role in an organization

Management's role within the organization is to establish objectives and goals, to develop plans for achieving those objectives and goals, and to implement plans so the organization's resources are used wisely. It is the responsibility of managers to ensure that plans are successfully implemented. This involves initiating corrective action when results deviate from plans.

OBJECTIVE 2
Define objectives and goals and explain how they vary between profit-seeking and not-for-profit organizations

In order to function effectively, the people in an organization need **objectives** — guidelines prepared by top management to establish the long-range direction of the organization. Objectives vary, depending on whether the organization is profit-seeking or not-for-profit, such as a city government. An objective of profit-seeking organizations is to provide goods and/or services that will earn an acceptable rate of return on the owners' investment. If profits fall below a certain level, investors will withdraw their funds and place them in a more lucrative venture. Another major objective of most organizations is to maintain financial solvency, or the ability to pay employees and creditors on time. If a business generates insufficient cash from selling its products or services, it risks bankruptcy and the sale of its assets to satisfy its obligations. Consequently, a primary concern of most businesses is a strong cash flow. Other objectives of a profit-seeking organization might include maintaining or improving the company's market share, developing new products or services, and modifying production methods to conserve resources or lower costs.

Not for profit organizations, on the other hand, generally seek to provide high-quality goods and services at the most reasonable cost. Major objectives of a city government, for instance, might include delivery of high-quality police, fire, and water services at the most reasonable rate. Major objectives of charitable organizations, such as the United Appeal, might be to raise a given amount of money and distribute it at minimum cost.

Objectives tend to be broad, general statements. At best, they can only guide managers in developing more specific goals. **Goals**, on the other hand, are concrete targets to be achieved within a definite time period. Generally, goals are quantified, so progress toward them can be measured. For example, General Motors' goal might be to obtain 40 percent of the small-car market by 1992. The United Appeal of Freeport might set a fund-raising target, or goal, of $5 million for 1994.

■

The Management Process

An organization just doesn't run smoothly without management. Except in the smallest companies, smooth operations are achieved by people, generally many people, whose activities are carefully planned. Say, for example, that one of an American automobile manufacturer's major objectives in recent years was to become competitive in the small-car market. To accomplish that objective, the board of directors needed to approve design and production funds for a new model. Next, the company president had to delegate design responsibility to the design group, in which individuals were chosen to develop engineering plans. Once a design was accepted, the location and structure of the manufacturing facilities had to be determined. The timing, cost, and market acceptability of all these activities had to be coordinated by top management.

OBJECTIVE 3
Name and describe the four basic activities of the management process

The management process is commonly thought to include these four basic activities:

- Planning and budgeting
- Organizing
- Implementing
- Controlling

These activities are performed more or less simultaneously throughout the year.

Planning and Budgeting

Planning is the process of identifying alternative courses of action, evaluating those alternatives, and choosing the alternative that will best attain the organization's objectives and goals. For example, West Grocery Company, a large, national food retailer, aspires to gain the highest market share in grocery stores. It also aspires to provide its shareholders with an acceptable rate of return. To achieve these objectives, West might plan to open a new store in each of its territories every two years. According to estimates, such an investment would increase the company's market share by 5 percent. Another of West's goals might be to reduce operating costs by 5 percent.

Having established objectives and goals, management must devise plans to accomplish them. For example, West might commission a market research study to determine the location of each new store and the products to stock. To reduce its operating costs, the company might analyze its purchasing and distribution methods. In fact, all of management's decisions — that is, which services to offer, how much staff to hire, and what marketing and advertising plans to adopt — must be made with overall objectives and goals in mind.

Once product, staffing, and marketing and advertising plans are made, managers must express those plans in financial terms. **Budgeting** is the quantification of plans to guide future operations and measure performance. A **budget** is the document that communicates management's plans for the organization; it is the standard against which the organization's performance is measured. (Budgeting will be discussed in Chapter 7.)

Organizing

Organizing is the process by which managers delegate responsibility for using human, financial, or physical resources. Top management delegates authority to use specific resources to middle managers, who then delegate authority to their subordinates. Each individual is responsible for efficiently using resources at his or her disposal to achieve the firm's objectives.

Figure 1–1 shows the organization chart of West Grocery Company. Such charts specify the formal relationship between individuals in the organization and the level of authority and responsibility delegated to each one. These charts also show which positions are line positions and which are staff. **Line positions** are those involving direct responsibility for creating and delivering the organization's goods and services to customers. West's primary objective is to sell groceries and related products. Consequently, its line positions include the president, the vice president of operations, the territory managers, and the store managers. **Staff positions** are those that support line positions. Purchasing, market research, and financial and managerial accounting services are staff positions at West. For example, since West's purchasing department buys in bulk for the entire company, it obtains better prices than each territory or store could on its own. Nevertheless, purchasing activities merely support the sale and delivery of products. On the other hand, managers in line positions decide what products to sell and therefore what products need to be purchased at what prices.

Notice that in Figure 1–1, there are two levels of staff at West Grocery Company. The corporate level includes purchasing, market research, the controller, and the treasurer. At the territory level there are separate human resources and controller's offices for each of the four territories. Having human resources

Figure 1–1
Organization Chart for West Grocery Company
Line positions are represented by the red shade.

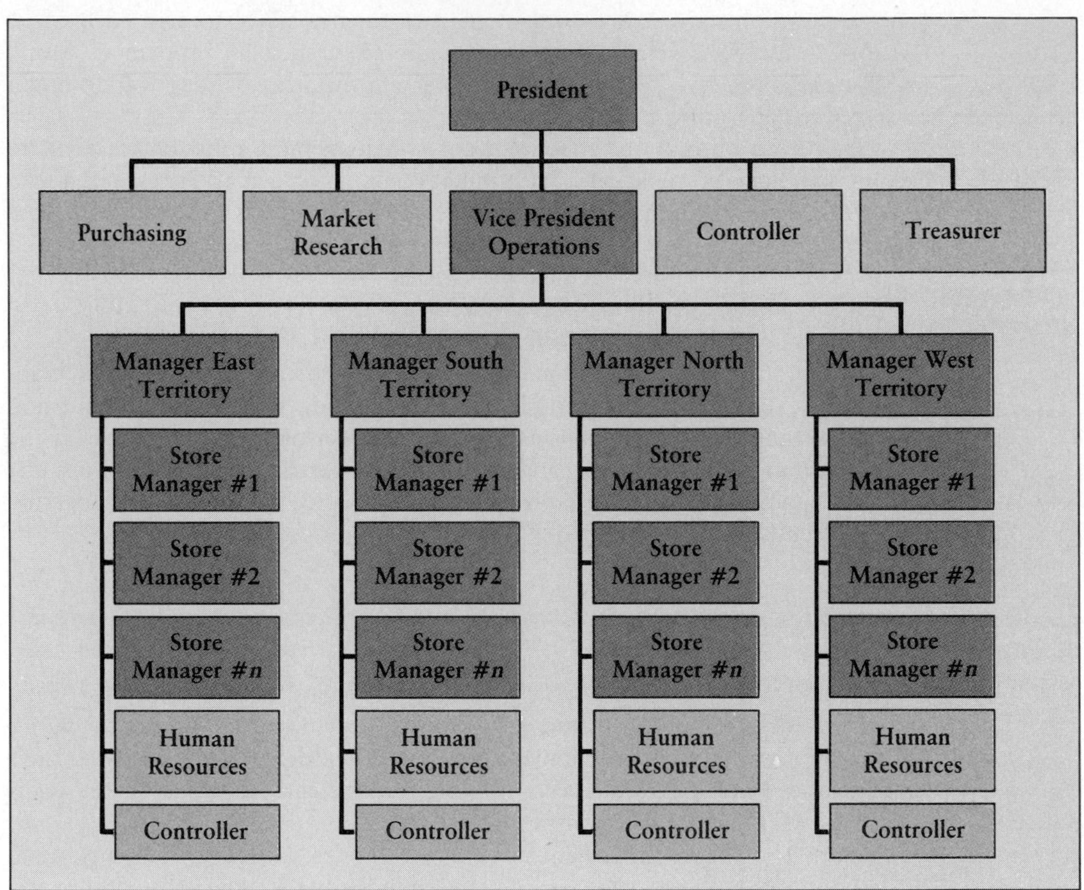

at the territory level is convenient because most of the company's hiring and training occurs in communities where there are West stores. Likewise, much of the company's accounting work is generated in the territories by the stores. Both human resources and accounting are considered staff positions because they support rather than direct the sale and delivery of merchandise.

Implementing

Implementing is the process of motivating people to work together efficiently and effectively. Once managers have developed a plan and delegated responsibilities, they must see that day-to-day operations proceed accordingly. Each employee must be assigned a specific job, and his or her progress must be monitored regularly. New employees must be trained, work must be scheduled, and resources needed to keep the organization going must be acquired. All these tasks must be accomplished to fulfill the company's objectives and goals. Management's role is to ensure that each employee accomplishes these tasks in an efficient manner.

For example, one of West's goals is to increase its market share by 5 percent. To implement this goal, the vice president of operations must convert the planned 5 percent market share increase into sales dollars and assign it to West's four territories. Territory managers must then divide their share of the increase among their store managers. Finally, store managers must apportion the store's assigned increase to the store's revenue-producing departments. Specific dollar increases are assigned to produce, meats and poultry, frozen vegetables, canned goods, dairy goods, bakery items, and household products. Store managers must hire, train, schedule, and motivate workers in such a way that these dollar goals are realized.

Controlling

Controlling is the process of ensuring that management's plan is successfully implemented. Accounting reports play an important part in this process by providing feedback on how well operations are progressing. Such reports compare the company's actual revenues, costs, and profits with its planned results. The difference, called a **variance**, tells managers whether operations are under control. Remember that plans are translated to budgets that show emphasis on the financial results of the company's objectives. In controlling, emphasis is on keeping actual financial results in line with planned financial results.

The control process is continual. After plans are implemented, results are observed and compared with the plan. If necessary, changes are made and implemented. Then, new results are observed and compared with the plan. For example, assume that West Grocery Company originally planned to achieve an annual sales increase of $2 million in the Cincinnati region. At the end of the first quarter, however, the actual sales increase was only $100,000. As a result, the bulk of the sales increase — $1,900,000 — must by realized in the last three quarters. At this point, management must decide on how to ensure higher-than-planned sales in the last three quarters. Some possible actions might include:

- Lowering prices to increase sales volume
- Increasing advertising to increase sales volume

Managers might also consider lowering their targeted increase in sales volume if it seems unrealistic.

To help managers, West's accountants will estimate the financial consequences of each alternative. Management will then evaluate each option and select the one with the highest probability of success. Once an action has been selected, it must be implemented and the results monitored to determine whether additional action is warranted.

The management process is summarized in Figure 1–2. Notice its circular nature. The process begins by selecting a plan that fits the organization's objectives and goals. This plan is expressed financially in the form of a budget. In the second stage, organizing, management delegates authority to use resources to accomplish

Figure 1–2
The Management Process
Notice the circular nature of the management process. Management is continually reviewing results, revising plans and budgets, organizing, implementing, and controlling.

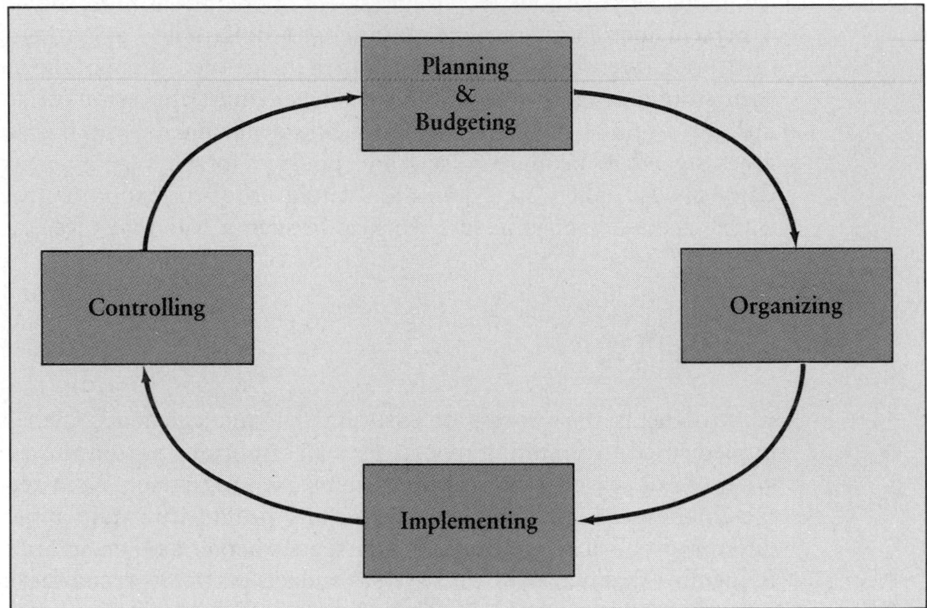

the plan. In the third stage, implementing, managers must ensure that the organization's goals are pursued in day-to-day activities, such as hiring, training, and scheduling. In the final stage, controlling, actual results are compared with planned results, so actions can be taken to correct differences.

Accountants play a major role in the first and last stages of the management process. In the planning and budgeting stage, they translate the consequences of a plan into budgeted financial statements. In the control stage, they prepare performance reports, which compare actual results with planned results.

■

The Accountant in the Organization

OBJECTIVE 4
Describe the accountant's role in the organization and list the duties of the controller and treasurer

Refer again to the organization chart of the West Grocery Company in Figure 1–1. Notice the two staff positions at the corporate level, controller and treasurer. Both positions involve working closely with accountants at the company. The controller has primary responsibility for accounting reports and systems. The treasurer is primarily responsible for financing the organization's activities and managing the cash resources.

The Controller's Office

The **controller** is in charge of accounting services. Duties generally assigned to this position include the following:

- Designing, installing, and maintaining an accounting system, including a data processing system
- Preparing financial reports for external users, including shareholders, banks, and government regulatory agencies
- Designing, installing, and maintaining a system of internal control
- Establishing and administering procedures for complying with federal, state, and local tax policies
- Auditing internal operations, except when internal audit reports to an audit committee composed of members of the board
- Designing, installing, and maintaining a budgeting system
- Monitoring, analyzing, and reporting the results of operations in performance reports
- Providing special information requested by management

Figure 1–3 shows the organization chart for the controller's office in West Grocery Company. Responsibility for performing most of the controller's functions is delegated to two assistant controllers. One is responsible for financial accounting and systems analysis; the other, for planning and budgeting.

One responsibility of the assistant controller for financial accounting and systems analysis is general accounting. Designing and implementing a system for reporting to external parties, such as shareholders, banks, and government agenceis, is one of those functions. The general accounting group in the assistant controller's office prepares the company's annual report, which contains an income statement, a balance sheet, a statement of retained earnings, and a statement of cash flows. This group also prepares additional reports required by government agencies, such as the Securities and Exchange Commission (SEC), or company banks.

Another group, the internal audit group, reviews the organization's records and operations to evaluate the quality of management's performance in carrying out assigned responsibilities in an economical and efficient manner. The internal audit also audits the company's books, division by division, to verify the integrity of the internal control system. An **internal control system** is a firm's organizational plan plus all methods and measures the firm takes to safeguard its assets, to ensure the accuracy and reliability of its accounting data, to promote operational efficiency, and to encourage compliance with company policy. The importance of internal control and internal auditing was recognized in 1977, when Congress passed the Foreign Corrupt Practices Act. That act requires organizations to maintain an adequate system of internal controls, so corrupt practices, such as bribery, can be discovered and stopped. To give auditors more independence, many companies have recently removed internal auditing from the controller's office. In such cases, a special audit committee, whose members are from the board of directors, oversees internal auditing.

Figure 1–3
Organization Chart for West Grocery Company Controller's Office

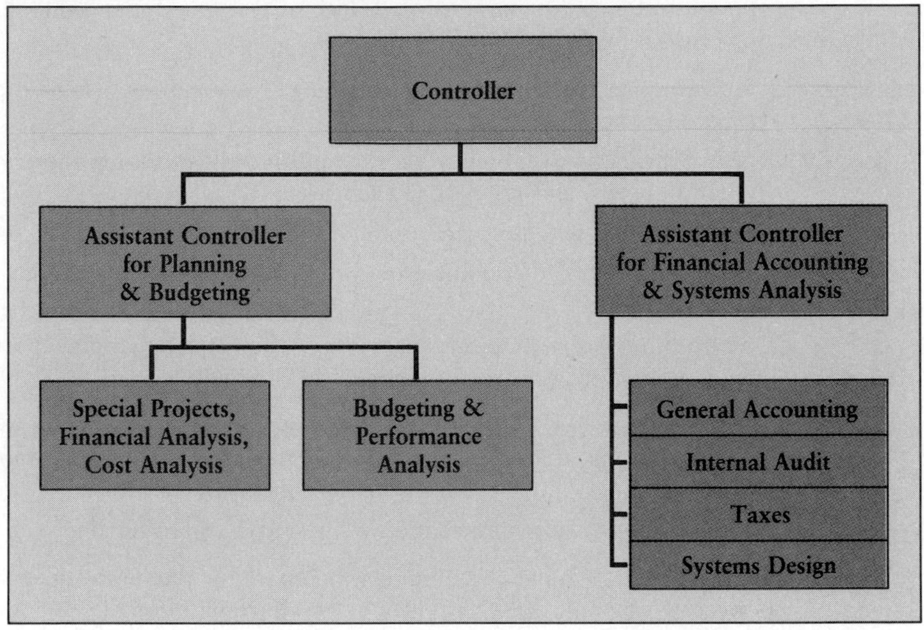

The tax department prepares all federal, state, and local tax returns for the West Grocery Company. The systems design group helps design and implement the data processing systems used by the general accounting, tax, and budgeting and performance groups. It also helps design, install, and maintain the internal control system.

The second assistant controller's position, assistant controller for planning and budgeting, is responsible for designing, installing, and maintaining a budgeting system and for preparing budgets and performance analyses for West's managers. Once top management has prepared the year's plan, the accountants in the budgeting and performance group must express this plan financially in the form of a budgeted balance sheet, a budgeted income statement, and a cash budget. They must also prepare monthly performance reports to inform management whether the plan is being achieved. Managers then make control decisions based on these reports.

Accountants in the special projects, financial analysis, and cost analysis group advise management on the financial effect of nonroutine decisions. For instance, should the company close its Pittsburgh stores to escape the city's high union wages? Should it manufacture its own paper products or continue to purchase them from suppliers? To help answer such questions, accountants in the special projects group prepare cost and revenue projections for proposed alternatives. Managers then choose the most desirable one.

The Treasurer's Office

The treasurer is another staff position closely related to accounting.[1] The **treasurer** is responsible for a company's financing activities. The major duties of this position include the following:

- Providing operating capital (long-term financing)
- Maintaining shareholder relationships
- Obtaining short-term financing
- Receiving, disbursing, and keeping custody of the organization's cash
- Establishing sound credit and collection policies — people who report to the treasurer implement the policies set
- Investing the organization's funds
- Maintaining adequate insurance coverage

The treasurer is the primary decision maker when choosing between *financial* alternatives. For example, the treasurer is the one to decide whether the West Grocery Company should finance its expansion by offering additional shares of stock, negotiating a long-term bank loan, or selling long-term bonds. The treasurer is also a primary decision maker in establishing a firm's credit policies.

■

The Accounting Process

OBJECTIVE 5
Distinguish between financial and managerial accounting

Accounting systems serve people both inside and outside an organization. The different needs of internal and external users require different approaches to reporting information. As a result the accounting profession has two distinct branches. **Financial accounting** deals with information reported to people outside an organization. **Managerial accounting** deals with information collected and analyzed for people inside an organization.

Financial Accounting

Outside users want to know the results of last year's operations and their effect on the organization's current financial position. Since many people and organizations need this information, the reports must be prepared in a standard format. Since these reports contain financial results of entire organizations, the infor-

[1]In some organizations the controller and treasurer's functions are combined into one position called vice president of finance.

mation is highly summarized, providing limited details about the performance of specific divisions.

External reports must conform to generally accepted accounting principles. In the United States a number of professional groups influence standards for external reports: the Financial Accounting Standard Board (FASB), the American Institute of Certified Public Accountants (AICPA), the Securities and Exchange Commission (SEC), the American Accounting Association (AAA), the Internal Revenue Service (IRS), the Government Accounting Standards Board (GASB), the National Association of Accountants (NAA), and the Financial Executives Institute (FEI). The most influential groups are the FASB and the SEC. The FASB issues Statements of Financial Accounting Standards. The SEC is a U.S. government agency with the legal power to establish accounting practices for companies whose securities are offered for sale to the public. Adherence to generally accepted accounting principles ensures that financial statements are prepared objectively and consistently from year to year. Subjective judgments of either the accountants or management are minimized in external financial statements.

External reports prepared by an organization's accountants are audited by independent certified accountants. The purpose of an audit is to express the auditor's professional opinion about whether the organization's financial statement fairly report its financial position and operating results. Independent certified public accountants (CPAs) are licensed by each state, in much the same manner as physicians and attorneys. They are independent in the sense that they are not employees of the organizations whose statements they audit. When performing an audit, a CPA carefully studies an organization's accounting and control systems, checks and tests its accounting records, observes inventories, and verifies amounts owed by customers. The CPA then expresses an opinion about the fairness of the organization's financial statements.

Managerial Accounting

Managerial accounting is the process of identification, measurement, accumulation, analysis, preparation, interpretation, and communication of financial information used by management to plan, evaluate, and control within an organization and to assure appropriate use of and accountability for its resources. In the context of this definition, financial information includes any information, financial and nonfinancial, necessary to interpret the effect of economic events or the consequences of business decisions.

Identification involves the recognition and evaluation of economic events and business transactions for appropriate accounting action. Measurement is the quantification of economic events and business transactions that have occurred or may occur. Accumulation is the recording and classifying of business transactions and other economic events. Analysis is the determination of the reasons for the reported activity and the relationships between various activities and economic events. Preparation and interpretation is the meaningful coordination of data to provide information to managers and to draw conclusions from the data. Communication is the reporting of relevant information for internal or external use.

Managerial accounting is used by management to plan and control the activities of an organization. Planning is the process of identifying alternative courses of action, evaluating those alternatives, and deciding which one will best achieve an organization's objectives and goals. Controlling is the process of ensuring that management's plan is successfully implemented. A large part of managerial accounting is to design the managerial accounting system to provide information to the managers so that the organization's objectives and goals can be achieved.

Managerial accounting assists managers in making planning and control decisions. Recall that planning involves establishing objectives and goals as well as strategies for accomplishing them. Some planning decisions requiring managerial accounting information include:

- What price to charge for a product
- How many units of product to manufacture
- Whether to expand production facilities
- How much money to spend on advertising
- Whether to rely solely on cash receipts from operations to cover cash expenditures

All these decisions require estimates of future revenues and/or costs. In fact, managerial decisions concern the financial effect of future actions and thus must be based on forecasted rather than historical information. Financial accounting generally reports past financial performance; managerial accounting estimates future financial outcomes.

Control decisions involve adjusting implemented plans to achieve desired results. Control decisions are made only when actual results differ significantly from expected results. Thus, the first step in making control decisions is to compare actual and expected results.

Some typical control decisions requiring managerial accounting information include:

- What action to take to bring actual sales in line with expected sales
- Whether to authorize overtime to make up for lost production volume
- Whether to increase advertising to improve sales

Again, these are decisions requiring estimates of future revenues and/or costs.

Whereas financial accounting reports tend to cover a company's activities as a whole, managerial accounting reports tend to cover specific product lines, divisions, sales territories, or customers grouped by dollar volume of orders. Indeed, most operating decisions are made at the division or territory level. And unlike financial accounting reports, managerial accounting reports are not subject to externally imposed reporting standards. Thus, they may include subjective information. For example, in setting monthly sales targets, management is more interested in the sales managers' subjective estimates of future sales than the objective value of past sales. That is not to imply that last month's sales are unimportant. Often, last month's sales are the best estimate of next month's sales. However, forecasted sales figures are more important than past statistics when setting targets.

Table 1–1
Summary of Differences Between Financial and Managerial Accounting

Financial accounting
Information is meant primarily for external users. Information summarizes the financial effects of past events. Decisions on what to report are guided by generally accepted accounting principles. Data are based on objective observations. Reports cover whole organizations and provide few details. Reports are designed for general use.
Managerial accounting
Information is meant primarily for internal users. Information forecasts the financial effects of future events. Decisions on what to report are guided by the information's relevance to managers' needs. Data are based partially on subjective judgments. Reports cover product lines, divisions, and sales territories in detail. Reports are designed for special purposes.

Managers may actually make bad choices if they use financial accounting data to make decisions. For example, marketing and production managers want to be informed of sales orders as they are received, that is, before products are shipped. Such information helps the production manager decide which products to produce and in what quantities. Yet, financial accounting reports only the revenues and costs of orders shipped. Production must be scheduled based on orders to be shipped this month and the next. Table 1–1 summarizes the significant differences between financial and managerial accounting.

Given the variety of information that might be reported to managers, how does an accountant decide what to report and to whom? To make those decisions, an accountant must consider the specific uses a manager has for the information. In other words, it is up to the accountant to decide which information is relevant. **Relevant information** is information that will affect the accomplishment of objectives or the choice of one alternative over another. Such information always differs between alternatives.

For example, assume the purchasing manager of the Acme Manufacturing Company is considering a long-term contract to purchase sheet metal. Two suppliers have quoted the same price for the sheet metal. In this case price is irrelevant to the decision. If, however, the suppliers' price differed, then price would be relevant. The relevant information in this example also includes the supplier's reliability in meeting delivery dates, the quality of the sheet metal supplied, and the supplier's financial stability. (Information on the supplier's financial stability would come from an analysis of its financial statements.)

Accounting Information as an Economic Commodity

Accounting information is an economic commodity. Just like televisions, washing machines, golf clubs, and food, it costs money to produce. Thus, when managers ask an accountant to provide information for internal use, they must first perform a **cost-benefit analysis** of that information. A cost-benefit analysis shows whether the potential benefit of the expenditure is worth its estimated cost. In other words, will the accounting information improve the manager's decision by saving or earning the organization more money than it costs the accountant to prepare the information? For example, the supervisor of the assembly department is considering (a) adding a second shift or (b) working the first shift overtime to meet production schedules. Should the supervisor request a special study from the accounting department to determine which alternative is less costly? That decision depends on the cost of the study and its expected benefits.

All managers who purchase services, such as market research, efficiency engineering, and managerial consulting, designed to help their organization become more productive must examine the cost and benefit of the service. For example, if a company seems to be incurring high electricity costs, management might hire an engineering firm to monitor use by department, perhaps by installing meters. The company is buying information whose cost, the cost of the study and of metering use, is offset by the benefit of learning where conservation efforts would be most likely to produce the greatest savings. A secondary benefit might be more accurate product cost estimates. Product costing is discussed in Chapters 4 and 5.

Usually the accountant and the manager decide together what type of services and information should be bought, based on their costs and benefits. In general, services and information are considered beneficial if they can potentially change a decision.

■

Standards of Ethical Conduct

Managerial accountants have a responsibility to management to provide relevant and timely information for planning and control decisions. They also have responsibilities to their profession, individuals outside their organization, and themselves. Managerial accountants in their role of collecting, analyzing, and reporting information must exercise good judgment in determining what and how information should be reported.

OBJECTIVE 6
Discuss the ethical concerns of managerial accountants

One of the objectives of managerial accounting is to assist managers in increasing the profits of the organization. Because of the profit objective, managers might attempt to manipulate accounting data to increase profits or to commit the organization to actions that are not in the best interest of society or customers. Managerial accountants have the responsibility to ensure the

Table 1–2
Standards of Ethical Conduct

Competence*

Management accountants have a responsibility to:

- Maintain an appropriate level of professional competence by ongoing development of their knowledge and skills.
- Perform their professional duties in accordance with relevant laws, regulations, and technical standards.
- Prepare complete and clear reports and recommendations after appropriate analyses of relevant and reliable information.

Confidentiality

Management accountants have a responsibility to:

- Refrain from disclosing confidential information acquired in the course of their work except when authorized, unless legally obligated to do so.
- Inform subordinates as appropriate regarding the confidentiality of information acquired in the course of their work and monitor their activities to assure the maintenance of that confidentiality.
- Refrain from using or appearing to use confidential information acquired in the course of their work for unethical or illegal advantage either personally or through third parties.

Integrity

Management accountants have a responsibility to:

- Avoid actual or apparent conflicts of interest and advise all appropriate parties of any potential conflict.
- Refrain from engaging in any activity that would prejudice their ability to carry out their duties ethically.
- Refuse any gift, favor, or hospitality that would influence or would appear to influence their actions.
- Refrain from either actively or passively subverting the attainment of the organization's legitimate and ethical objectives.
- Recognize and communicate professional limitations or other constraints that would preclude responsible judgment or successful performance of an activity.
- Communicate unfavorable as well as favorable information and professional judgments or opinions.
- Refrain from engaging in or supporting any activity that would discredit the profession.

Objectivity

Management accountants have a responsibility to:

- Communicate information fairly and objectively.
- Disclose fully all relevant information that could reasonably be expected to influence an intended user's understanding of the reports, comments, and recommendations presented.

integrity of the accounting data so that unethical behavior is reported to the proper individual. For example, a divisional sales manager of a large organization was under pressure to reach the targeted sales figure so he shipped unordered products to the division's distributors. This was accomplished by reentering a previous order, increasing the amount of an order, and shipping unordered products when the ordered product was not in stock. When the distributors complained of the overshipments, the sales manager offered special discounts, the opportunity to exchange the goods for other goods, or the distributor could store the goods at the manufacturer's expense. This tactic increased sales by millions of dollars, and consequently profits were also increased. In another company the purchasing department bought both machinery and parts from the same supplier. The cost of the machinery was capitalized and expensed over the life of the machine, while the cost of the parts would be expensed when the product was sold. By negotiating with the supplier, the purchasing agent was able to have some machinery billed to the company at a higher price and the parts at a lower price. This resulted in an increase in profits for the year due to the decrease in the price of parts.

Other examples of unethical actions by managers could be discussed, but these two serve to illustrate how unethical actions can be taken to influence the profits of an organization. In an organization, senior management sets the tone for ethical behavior. This is done by personal behavior and written policies. Most large companies have written policies related to ethics, conflict of interest, and insider trading. These policies are usually communicated to the managers annually. The managers are required to sign a statement that they have read and are in compliance with the policies.

The managerial accounting system is used for planning and controlling the operations of an organization. The managerial accounting system should not be used to support unethical behavior. In addition to examining the profitability of alternative courses of action in planning and controlling the operations, management should examine the social and ethical consequences of these actions.

Before implementing any questionable action, managerial accountants should ask whether the standards of ethical conduct would be violated. The National Association of Accountants adopted the standards of ethical conduct shown in Table 1–2 on June 1, 1983, to help managerial accountants assess ethical dilemmas.

When a managerial accountant is confronted with an ethical dilemma, the accountant should follow the policies of the organization. If organizational policies do not resolve the problem, the managerial accountant should first discuss the problem with his or her supervisor, unless the supervisor is involved in the problem. If the supervisor is involved in the problem, the next level of management should be contacted. If the ethical dilemma cannot be resolved within the organization, the managerial accountant should seek a confidential discussion and analysis of all options with an objective individual. If the issue is significant, the managerial accountant may have no other option than to resign and present a written document to a representative of the organization. Except where prescribed by law, it would not be considered appropriate to communicate the ethical issue to individuals outside the organization.

■

Certification in Managerial Accounting

OBJECTIVE 7
Describe how managerial accountants are certified and list the professional objectives of the CMA program

Managerial accountants may become a **Certified Management Accountant** (CMA) through the Institute of Certified Management Accountants (ICMA). The CMA program requires candidates pass a series of examinations and meet educational and professional standards to qualify for and maintain this certificate. According to a booklet distributed by the National Association of Accountants (NAA), the objectives of the CMA program are:

- To establish managerial accounting as a recognized branch of the accounting profession by identifying the role of the managerial accountant and the knowledge demanded for that role
- To foster higher educational standards in managerial accounting and outline a course of study through which the necessary knowledge can be acquired
- To establish an objective measure of one's knowledge and competence in managerial accounting

The CMA exam has four parts, covering the following topics: (a) economics, finance, and management; (b) financial accounting and reporting; (c) management reporting, analysis, and behavioral issues; and (d) decision analysis and information systems.[2] The ICMA, by including basic management topics on the CMA exam, has emphasized the dual role of the managerial accountant — that of businessperson and accountant.

Chapter Review

Review of Learning Objectives

1. Define management's role in an organization.
An organization is a group of people working together to achieve a common goal. Organizations may be either profit-seeking or not-for-profit. Managers must set objectives and goals against which an organization's performance can be measured. Managers formulate and implement plans and take corrective action when actual results deviate from planned results.

[2]For more information on the CMA exam, write to the Institute of Certified Management Accountants, 10 Paragon Drive, P.O. Box 433, Montvale, New Jersey 07645.

2. **Define objectives and goals and explain how they vary between profit-seeking and not-for-profit organizations.**
Objectives are guidelines prepared by top management to establish the long-range development of an organization. Profit-seeking organizations generally aim to provide goods and services that will earn an acceptable return on the owners' investment. Not-for-profit organizations generally seek to provide high-quality goods and services at the most reasonable cost. Goals are concrete targets to be achieved in a specific period of time. A profit-seeking organization might set a goal of increasing profit at a rate of 10 percent per year. A not-for-profit organization, such as the Boys Club of Cincinnati, might set a goal of raising $1 million in 1992.

3. **Name and describe the four basic activities of the management process.**
The management process consists of planning and budgeting, organizing, implementing, and controlling. Planning and budgeting is the process of establishing objectives and goals and translating them into financial plans. Organizing is the process by which top management delegates responsibility for ensuring that all human, financial, and physical resources are obtained and used properly to achieve the organization's objectives. Implementing is the process of motivating and assigning employees to day-to-day activities and monitoring their work. The final step, controlling, compares actual results with planned results to determine whether corrective action or revised plans are needed. These four activities are performed continually throughout the year.

4. **Describe the accountant's role in the organization and list the duties of the controller and treasurer.**
Accountants generally report to the controller, a top-level staff position. The controller's duties include the preparation of reports for external and internal use. Accountants who prepare external reports are known as financial accountants. Those who advise managers inside an organization are managerial accountants. The treasurer is responsible for financing a company's activities, cash management, establishing sound credit policies, and investing funds.

5. **Distinguish between financial and managerial accounting.**
Because financial accounting reports must cover the performance and current financial position of entire organizations, they are highly summarized and provide few details about specific divisions. Financial accounting reports must be objectively prepared according to generally accepted accounting principles and examined by independent certified public accountants. Managerial accounting reports, on the other hand, are prepared for managers to use in the planning and control process. They concentrate on information relevant to specific managerial decisions. The manager and the accountant must decide which information is relevant to a decision and whether the information should be purchased.

6. **Discuss the ethical concerns of managerial accountants.**
Ethical issues such as deliberate misclassification of accounting data to improve profits must be dealt with by managerial accountants. Managerial accountants have a responsibility to management, their profession, individuals outside the organization, and themselves to provide relevant and timely data for planning and control decisions. To guide the managerial accountant, the National Association of Accountants developed the Standards of Ethical Conduct for Management Accountants. The standards cover competence, confidentiality, integrity, and objectivity.

7. **Describe how managerial accountants are certified and list the professional objectives of the CMA program.**
Accountants may become Certified Management Accountants by taking an examination administered by the Institute of Certified Management Accountants. The professional

objectives of the CMA program are to establish managerial accounting as a recognized branch of the accounting profession, to foster higher educational standards in managerial accounting, and to establish an objective measure of one's knowledge and competence in managerial accounting.

Review of Key Terms

Budget The document through which management communicates its plans for the organization and measures the organization's performance. As a quantification of planned revenues and expenses, the budget is used to communicate goals for revenues, expenses, assets, liabilities, and other business activities.

Budgeting The quantification of plans to guide future operations and measure performance.

Certified management accountant (CMA) One who holds a certificate of professional competence obtained by passing a four-part exam given by the Institute of Certified Management Accountants.

Controller The person in charge of all accounting services in an organization.

Controlling The process of ensuring that management's plan is successfully implemented.

Cost-benefit analysis A comparison of the benefits of an action with its cost.

Financial accounting The branch of accounting that deals with information reported to people outside an organization.

Goals Concrete targets to be achieved within a definite time period.

Implementing The process of motivating people to work together efficiently and effectively to achieve an organization's objectives and goals.

Internal control system An organizational plan plus all methods and measures taken to safeguard assets, verify the accuracy and reliability of records, encourage efficiency, and ensure compliance with company policy. An internal control system is generally evaluated through internal audits.

Line position An employment position with direct responsibility for creating and delivering an organization's goods and services to customers. Sales and product management are line positions.

Managerial accounting The branch of accounting primarily concerned with information collected, analyzed, and reported to people inside an organization for planning and control purposes.

Objectives Guidelines prepared by top management to establish the long-range direction of an organization.

Organization A group of people working together to achieve a common goal.

Organizing The process by which managers delegate responsibility for using an organization's human, financial, and physical resources.

Planning The process of identifying alternative courses of action, evaluating those alternatives, and deciding which one will best achieve an organization's objectives and goals.

Relevant information Information that affects the accomplishment of objectives and that differs between alternatives.

Staff position A position that indirectly supports creation and delivery of goods and services to customers. Jobs in purchasing, market research, and financial and managerial accounting services are staff positions.

Treasurer The person responsible for a company's financing activities, including financing, cash management, establishing sound credit policies, and investment of funds.

Variance The difference between actual revenues, costs, and profits and planned, or budgeted, results, expressed numerically.

Chapter Assignments

Questions

1. (L.O. 1, 2) Define an organization. Why do organizations need objectives and goals?
2. (L.O. 1, 2) Explain the difference between an objective and a goal.
3. (L.O. 2) Assume you are a manager in the soap division at a major consumer products company. Formulate a goal for your division and devise a plan to achieve it.
4. (L.O. 2) List three examples each of profit-seeking and not-for-profit organizations.
5. (L.O. 3) What are the four basic activities of the management process?
6. (L.O. 3) What purpose do budgets serve?
7. (L.O. 3) What information can be obtained from an organization chart?
8. (L.O. 3) Distinguish between line and staff positions.
9. (L.O. 3) "Control may be thought of as replanning." Do you agree with this statement? Discuss it.
10. (L.O. 4) What duties do in-house accountants perform?
11. (L.O. 4) Is the controller's position responsible for financial accounting functions, managerial accounting functions, or both?
12. (L.O. 4) Why do internal auditors frequently report to a special audit committee rather than the controller?
13. (L.O. 4) What is the treasurer's role in an organization?
14. (L.O. 4) Distinguish between financial accounting and managerial accounting. What principles determine whether information is reported in each.

15. (L.O. 5) Define relevance and its relationship to accounting information. Is the concept of relevance more important in managerial accounting or financial accounting? Why?

16. (L.O. 5) What are generally accepted accounting principles? Of what significance are they to financial accountants? To outside users of financial accounting reports? To users of managerial accounting reports?

17. (L.O. 5) What is an audit by a CPA, and what is its purpose?

18. (L.O. 5) Explain the importance of forecasting in managerial accounting.

19. (L.O. 5) Explain how cost-benefit analysis applies to accounting information.

20. (L.O. 6) Discuss the ethical considerations of managerial accountants.

21. (L.O. 6) What should a managerial accountant do when confronted with an ethical dilemma?

22. (L.O. 7) Distinguish between a Certified Public Accountant and a Certified Management Accountant.

Case 1
Ward Corporation (L.O. 6)

Ward Corporation is a manufacturer of cleaning products with three wholly owned subsidiaries that are operated as separate divisions. Ward's corporate headquarters are located in an industrial park in a Chicago suburb. The Industrial Products Division is located in the same industrial park but in its own building. The other two divisions are located in Milwaukee and Indianapolis.

The corporation's operating and financial records are maintained on a mainframe computer at corporate headquarters. Each division has a small accounting department that submits operating and financial data to corporate headquarters on a regular basis.

The profit planning department at corporate headquarters is responsible for preparing special analyses and reports for Ward. To facilitate its work, the profit planning department has linked a microcomputer to the mainframe to download data. The special analyses are prepared using these data and a purchased spreadsheet software package.

Beth Simons recently joined the Industrial Products Division as an accounting analyst. Simons is proficient in the use of microcomputers and spreadsheet software. She has been given an assignment to work with Doug Laird, marketing manager of the Industrial Products Division, to develop analyses and reports. One week into the assignment, she suggested that the microcomputers used in the marketing department for word processing could be valuable analytical tools if spreadsheet software were acquired. Laird knows little about computers, but he has received some of the special analyses prepared by the profit planning department at corporate headquarters. Laird wants Simons to try her idea but has suggested that she first borrow the software from the profit planning department.

Simons has approached Tom Field, manager of profit planning, regarding the use of the software package. Field was very sympathetic to Simons' request, but the software is used extensively in his department. Therefore, he did not want to loan the original system disk. Furthermore, the software was copy-protected. However, Field did have a utility program that allowed him to make back-up copies of most copy-protected software. Since there was no back-up of the spreadsheet software, Field decided to make a copy and give it to Simons for her use. Simons indicated that she planned to use the software during regular business hours.

Upon giving the copy to Simons, Field said, "This is my only copy but you may borrow it for your use only. Don't give it to anyone else. Once you have tried the software for your assignment, you must return this copy to me. Industrial Products' accounting or marketing department will have to purchase its own copy."

Field did not give Simons a copy of the licensing agreement that accompanied the original software package. The license agreement reproduced below was affixed to the original sealed disk package. While Simons was not aware of the specific provisions of the licensing agreement that pertained to the borrowed software, she knew that they accompanied computer software packages.

Software License Agreement

IMPORTANT: Please read this agreement before opening the envelope. Opening the disk envelope indicates the user's acceptance of the agreement to abide by these terms.

1. The software may be used on any compatible hardware that the purchaser owns or uses.
2. Back-up copies of the software can be made provided that these copies are for exclusive use of the purchaser and only one copy of the software is in use at any one time.
3. No alterations to the software or the documentation are permitted.
4. The software may not be distributed to others on a permanent or temporary basis.
5. This license and the software may be transferred to another party provided that all copies of the software and documentation are transferred and the original party ceases to use the software after the transfer.

Required

1. Based upon the stipulations enumerated in the license agreement for the spreadsheet software, did Tom Field violate the agreement when he
   a. Made a copy of the software disk using the utility program?
   b. Gave Beth Simons the copy of the software disk he had made?
   Explain your answer in each case.
2. Without prejudice to your answer in *1* above, assume that Tom Field did violate the license agreement when he copied the software disk and gave it to Beth Simons. Identify the alternatives that Tom Field could have employed to determine the applicability of the spreadsheet software to the application of the marketing department of the Industrial Products Division without violating the license agreement.

3. Management accountants are expected to abide by "Standards of Ethical Conduct for Management Accountants." Were any provisions of this Statement violated by
   a. Tom Field when he copied the software disk and gave Beth Simons the copy for her use?
   b. Beth Simons when she used the copy of the software to determine its usefulness in the applications for the marketing department of the Industrial Products Division?

   Explain your answer in each case being sure to identify the standard(s) that is(are) violated or explaining why the statement was not violated. (CMA)

Case 2
Earth Products, Inc. (L.O. 6)

Victoria Addison is the assistant director of financial reporting for Earth Products, Inc., a large processor of ores and minerals. The finance department is in the final stages of compiling the financial statements for the fiscal year ended April 30, 19x1, and Addison is working late to complete the footnotes pertaining to long-term contracts. Addison has gathered several files that contain the information she needs to complete her work.

Among the contracts and other documents in the files, Addison has found a copy of a report from the procurement manager of Earth Products to the division manager of the company's coal cleaning plant regarding the procedures for disposing of plant wastes. Addison noticed some penciled calculations and notes on the bottom of the report. According to these notes, Earth Products has been using a nearby residential landfill to dump toxic coal cleaning fluid wastes, and the dump site is nearing saturation making it necessary to locate a new disposal site for these toxic wastes. The calculations indicate that significant amounts of toxic cleaning fluids have been mixed with residential refuse over the past two years.

Determined to learn more about this situation, Addison kept the report. Uncertain how she should proceed, Addison began to ponder her options by outlining the following three alternative courses of action:

- Seek the advice of her boss, the director of financial reporting.
- Anonymously release the information to the local newspaper.
- Bring the information to the attention of an outside member of the board of directors with whom she was acquainted.

Required

1. Discuss why Victoria Addison has an ethical responsibility to take some action in the matter of Earth Products, Inc., and the dumping of toxic wastes.
2. For each of the three alternative courses of action that Victoria Addison has outlined, explain whether or not the action is appropriate.
3. Without prejudice to your answer in 2 above, assume that Victoria Addison sought the advice of her superior, the director of financial reporting, and discovered that the director was involved in the dumping of toxic wastes. Describe the steps that Victoria Addison should take in proceeding to resolve the conflict in this situation. (CMA)

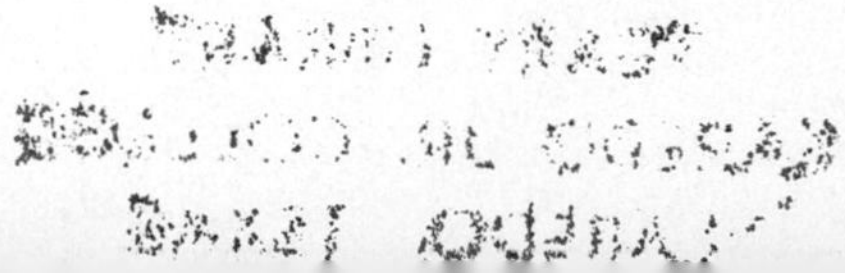

2

Cost Classification and Flow

LEARNING OBJECTIVES

After studying this chapter you should be able to:

1. Distinguish between product and period costs
2. Explain how product costs are treated differently in merchandising, service, and manufacturing firms
3. Classify manufacturing product costs as direct materials, direct labor, or manufacturing overhead costs
4. Classify manufacturing product costs as prime or conversion costs
5. Distinguish between total and unit manufacturing costs, and explain how unit manufacturing costs are used to prepare financial reports
6. Trace the flow of manufacturing costs through manufacturing accounts to the Cost of Goods Sold account
7. Understand the cost of goods manufactured and cost of goods manufactured and sold statements
8. Distinguish between job order costing and process costing

Chapter 1 outlined the differences between financial accounting, which is primarily concerned with external reporting, and managerial accounting, which is primarily concerned with internal reporting. Although the two branches differ in their objectives, they share a common data base as well as some basic concepts. In this chapter you will study some of the basic cost classification schemes used in both financial and managerial accounting.

Accounting costs are classified in numerous ways. To prepare financial statements, accountants must associate costs with specific time periods. The classification of costs into product and period costs allows accountants to do that. Costs are also classified differently depending on the type of organization involved, that is, merchandising, service, or manufacturing. The most complex cost classification systems are found in manufacturing organizations, where a special statement must be prepared to determine the cost of goods sold. Among manufacturing firms, product costing systems have been developed to suit two types of manufacturing: process and job order.

There are still other ways to classify costs. This chapter concentrates on only the most basic cost classifications — those needed to prepare financial statements. Data from income statements and balance sheets are the basis for many managerial planning and control decisions. As further types arise, additional cost classification schemes will be introduced.

■

Product Costs Versus Period Costs

In both financial and managerial accounting, costs are related to time periods. In financial accounting, income statements and balance sheets are prepared quarterly and annually for shareholders. In managerial accounting, reports comparing actual results to expected, budgeted results are prepared monthly, quarterly, and annually. Most planning and control decisions are also related to time periods. Actual results are compared with budgeted results at the end of each month, and corrective action is taken as needed.

OBJECTIVE 1
Distinguish between product and period costs

Costs related to time periods are either product costs or period costs. **Period costs** are selling and administrative costs that usually cannot be associated with a product or sale. For example, the president's salary is an administrative cost not directly associated with particular products. General liability insurance is an administrative cost applicable to all activities rather than to particular ones. Accountants charge these expenses against revenues for the periods in which they were incurred. Hence, they are called *period costs.*

Any period cost assigned to an unconsumed item or unexpired contract is classified as an asset rather than an expense. This cost is referred to as a **prepaid expense.** For example, assume that on January 1, 19x8, a company purchases a three-year insurance policy for $6,000. At the end of the year, one year of the

three-year policy has expired. Hence, $2,000, the cost of insurance for 19x8, must be deducted from the year's revenues. The remaining, unexpired cost of $4,000 is treated as a prepaid expense and is not deducted from revenues until it expires.

A **product cost,** on the other hand, is a cost incurred to acquire or manufacture finished goods inventory. A department store purchases finished inventory items from a supplier for sale to its customers. An automobile producer manufactures its finished inventory. Thus, for a merchandising company, product cost is the purchase price of goods acquired for resale. For a manufacturing company, product cost is the cost of materials plus the sum of all costs incurred to convert those materials into finished products. That includes not only the cost of the materials but also the cost of labor, equipment, and buildings used to produce the finished product.

Like period costs, product costs are used by both financial and management accountants. Financial accountants use product costs to find the cost of inventories and the cost of goods sold. Managerial accountants use product costs to evaluate the profitability of products or services.

Like unexpired period costs, product costs are treated as assets until the products are sold. Product costs that are assigned to units of inventory are sometimes referred to as **inventoriable costs.** When products are shipped to customers, these costs become expenses and are deducted from sales revenues. Thus, the expense of earning revenues is reported in the same period as the revenues.

For example, assume that on January 1, 19x8, Compco acquired ten microcomputers at a wholesale cost of $900 each. Compco planned to sell these machines for $1,500 each. But during the year only one microcomputer was sold. The product cost of $900 for that one microcomputer will be charged against the $1,500 in revenue from its sale. The $8,100 in product costs for the remaining nine microcomputers will be deferred until the machines are sold. This process of associating product costs with the period in which a product is sold (and period costs with the time period in which the costs expire) is called **matching.**

Sometimes an accountant must divide a single cost between a product cost and a period cost. For example, assume a manufacturing company has a warehouse that is used to store materials and finished products. Since the cost of storing the materials is a manufacturing cost, it should be treated as a product cost. But because the cost of storing finished products is a selling cost, it is treated as a period cost. If warehousing costs for the year are $400,000 and 30 percent of warehousing activity is associated with materials, then $120,000 (30% × $400,000) of the cost would be charged to product costs. The period cost would be $280,000 (70% × $400,000). The $120,000 in product costs are inventoriable and chargeable against revenues when the goods are finished and sold. That may not be until next year. But the $280,000 in period costs will be charged against revenues in the same year the cost is incurred, regardless of whether the finished goods in storage are sold.

Figure 2–1 summarizes the differences between product costs and period costs. Product costs are treated slightly differently in merchandising, service, and manufacturing companies. In the next three sections, the reasons for those differences will be explained.

Figure 2–1
Product and Period Costs

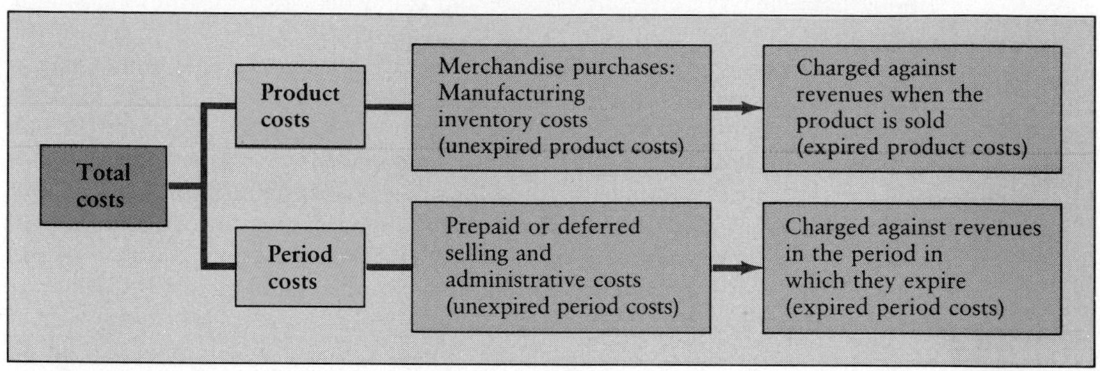

Review Exercise 2–1

Calculate Product and Period Costs

Colleen Company purchased 200 dresses for $100 each. Colleen planned to sell the dresses for $200 each. During the year, Colleen sold 150 dresses for $200 each. Also at the beginning of the year, Colleen paid $2,000 for a two-year insurance policy.

Required

Calculate the product and period costs that will be included in Colleen Company's income statement for the year.

Solution

Product cost calculated:

150 dresses at $100 each = $15,000

Period cost calculated:

$2,000 for 2-year insurance policy/2 years = $1,000

(see Exercise 18)

■

Cost Classification in a Merchandising Company

OBJECTIVE 2
Explain how product costs are treated differently in merchandising, service, and manufacturing firms

Merchandising companies, such as computer stores, department stores, drugstores, and retail outlets, purchase the merchandise they sell to customers. Their product costs are the purchase price of the merchandise. When products are purchased, their costs are recorded as assets on the balance sheet under **Merchandise Inventory.** This account includes all goods purchased for resale that were not sold by the end of the accounting period. When products are sold, their costs are removed from the balance sheet and charged against sales revenues in the income statement.

Exhibit 2–1 on page 30 shows the income statement and the current assets section of the balance sheet for Compco. Notice how product costs are used to compute the cost of goods sold in the income statement. The cost of the beginning merchandise inventory, \$120,000, is added to the cost of recent **purchases of inventory,** \$490,000, to obtain the total cost of goods available for sale, \$610,000. From this total the cost of the ending inventory, \$150,000, is deducted to obtain the cost of goods sold for the year, \$460,000. This cost of goods sold is then deducted from sales revenues, \$987,000, to obtain the gross margin, \$527,000. Note that selling and administrative expenses are separately deducted from gross margin. These expenses are expired period costs — that is, the price of resources consumed in operating the business during the past year.

Also notice how product costs in Exhibit 2–1 are shown in the current assets section of the balance sheet. The \$150,000 for merchandise inventory represents the cost of the merchandise purchased but not sold during the year. This amount is the ending inventory figure that was deducted from the cost of goods available for sale in the income statement. The cost of this unsold inventory will not be deducted from revenues until the inventory is sold. Again, period costs are listed separately. The \$50,000 in prepaid expenses represents the cost of resources

Figure 2–2
Classification of Total Costs in a Merchandising Company

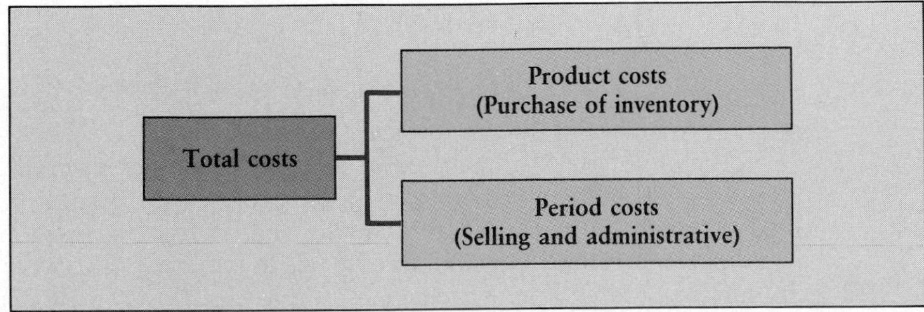

Exhibit 2–1

Income Statement and Current Assets of a Merchandising Company

The highlighted lines represent the product costs section of the income statement and balance sheet.

Compco
Income Statement
For the Year Ended December 31, 19x8

Sales revenues		$987,000
Product costs		
Merchandise inventory, Jan. 1, 19x8	$120,000	
Purchases of inventory	490,000	
Total goods available for sale	$610,000	
Merchandise inventory, Dec. 31, 19x8	150,000	
Cost of goods sold		460,000
Gross margin		$527,000
Selling and administrative expenses		
Period costs		
Salaries	$ 60,000	
Sales commissions	98,700	
Rent	110,000	
Advertising	58,000	
Utilities	20,300	
Insurance	15,000	
Supplies	18,000	
Total selling and administrative expenses		380,000
Operating income		$147,000

Compco
Current Asset Section of Balance Sheet
December 31, 19x8

Current assets	
Cash	$120,000
Accounts receivable	90,000
Merchandise inventory	150,000
Prepaid expenses	50,000
Total current assets	$410,000

purchased but not consumed in 19x8. This cost will be matched with revenues in future years when the resources are consumed.

The information summarized in these financial statements is routinely reported to shareholders and other interested people, such as bankers. But it is also used by company managers for planning and control purposes. In many companies, income statements similar to the one in Exhibit 2–1 are prepared for each product or product line. Managers use these specialized statements to evaluate the profitability of a product and to compare actual results with budgeted results.

Review Exercise 2–2

Classify Product and Period Costs

Hanes Retail Company incurred the following costs during their first year of operation:

a. Sales salaries
b. Rent for retail space
c. Heat, light, and power costs
d. Purchases of merchandise for resale
e. Interest on a bank loan
f. Purchases of office supplies

Required

Classify the costs for Hanes Retail Company as product or period costs.

Solution

a. Period	*c.* Period	*e.* Period
b. Period	*d.* Product	*f.* Period

(see Exercise 28)

To summarize: In a merchandising company, product costs are the cost of acquiring inventory for sale. All selling and administrative costs are classified as period costs, as shown in Figure 2–2.

■

Cost Classification in a Service Company

Service companies, such as accounting and consulting firms, auto repair shops, health maintenance organizations, and banks and brokerage houses, produce services rather than products. Services are generally delivered when they are produced. Therefore, in service industries there is no product (service) inventory, and all costs are related to the time period in which they expire. Thus, the distinction between product and period costs is not useful to service companies. Instead, costs are customarily divided into direct and indirect costs.

Direct costs are costs physically traceable to a specific product or service, such as salaries paid to accountants and mechanics. These costs are similar to the product costs of merchandising companies. They are the cost of providing a

Exhibit 2–2

Income Statement and Current Assets of a Service Company

The highlighted costs represent direct costs in the income statement. The unbilled services, at estimated billable rates, are based on the direct costs of services unfinished at year-end.

AAA Consulting Company
Income Statement
For the Year Ended December 31, 19x8

Fees for professional service		$500,000
Employee compensation and fringe benefits	$245,000	
Rent of office facilities	30,000	
Training and research	20,000	
Personnel recruiting	10,000	
Professional insurance and litigation	6,000	
Other	25,000	
Total expenses		336,000
Operating income		$164,000

AAA Consulting Company
Current Asset Section of the Balance Sheet
December 31, 19x8

Current assets	
Cash	$ 25,000
Accounts receivable	63,000
Unbilled services, at estimated billable rate	50,000
Prepaid expenses	14,000
Total current assets	$152,000

salable product (service) to a customer. Direct costs for performing specific services are matched with the revenues they generate.

Indirect costs are costs that cannot be traced to a particular product or service, such as insurance or office rent. Like period costs in a merchandising company, indirect costs are generally deducted from revenues in the period in which the costs expire.

At the end of an accounting period, some services are usually incomplete. The expected revenues associated with these services must be estimated, for they constitute an asset. Generally, service companies estimate the amount of such revenues by multiplying the ratio of incurred direct costs to total expected direct costs by total expected revenues when the service is completed.

For example, assume at the end of the year, AAA Consulting Company has incurred $15,000 of direct costs on a consulting engagement that is expected to cost $45,000. The anticipated revenues for the consulting engagement amount to $90,000. The revenue to be recognized for the year is calculated as follows:

$$\frac{\text{incurred direct costs}}{\text{expected direct costs}} \times \text{expected revenues}$$

$$\frac{\$15{,}000}{\$45{,}000} \times \$90{,}000 = \$30{,}000$$

Exhibit 2–2 shows the income statement and current assets of AAA Consulting Company. The first expense listed, employee compensation and fringe benefits, is a direct expense of earning revenue. All other expenses, such as rent, are indirect expenses. Notice that the balance sheet contains no entry for inventory. Instead, there is an account for services not billed. This amount represents the expected revenues for services performed as of December 31 but not yet billed to clients. This amount was estimated on the basis of direct service costs incurred.

To summarize: Service companies have no need to classify costs as product or period costs. Instead, they divide costs into direct and indirect costs. They match the direct costs of providing their services against the revenues they earn for their services. They charge their indirect costs against revenues in the period in which the costs expire.

Review Exercise 2–3

Calculate Service Company Revenue

Holder Consulting Company is in the process of preparing their annual financial statements for 19xx. At the end of the year, the company had one uncompleted contract. The expected revenues from the contract are $100,000. The total expected direct costs are $50,000. As of year-end, $30,000 of direct costs had been incurred on the contract.

Required

Calculate the revenue that Holder Consulting Company should recognize on the uncompleted contract for 19xx.

Solution

Calculation of revenue for 19xx:

$$\frac{\text{incurred direct costs}}{\text{expected direct costs}} \times \text{expected revenues}$$

$$\frac{\$30{,}000}{\$50{,}000} \times \$100{,}000 = \$60{,}000$$

(see Exercise 21)

■

Cost Classification in a Manufacturing Company

A **manufacturing company** is an organization that converts materials into products for sale. Like merchandising companies, manufacturing companies divide their expenses into product and period costs. Computing period costs is done similarly in both types of companies. But because manufacturing companies make rather than buy the products they sell, their product costs are more complicated than those of a merchandising company. For example, manufacturing companies, such as steel companies, convert materials, such as iron ore, into finished products, such as sheet metal. The company's product costs include not only the cost of purchasing but also the cost of converting materials into salable products. Product costs include the cost of the materials, the cost of the labor used in processing those materials, and the cost of occupying and operating the facilities in which the product is made. These product costs are counted as assets until the product is sold and the revenue from the sale is recorded on the income statement.

Exhibit 2–3 shows the income statement for ABC Manufacturing Company. On the surface, this document is similar to that of Compco (Exhibit 2–1). The only difference is in the section on product costs. Unlike a merchandising company, which refers to the value of goods ready for sale as merchandise inventory, a manufacturing company uses the term Finished Goods Inventory. And instead of referring to purchases of inventory, a manufacturing company refers to the **cost of goods manufactured.** This term means the value of goods completed and transferred from Work in Process Inventory to Finished Goods Inventory during the quarter or year covered by the statement.

The manufacturing company's balance sheet is also similar to that of a merchandising company, except for the product costs section. A merchandising company's balance sheet contains only one product account, Merchandise Inventory (Exhibit 2–1). A manufacturing company's balance sheet has three inventory accounts: Direct Materials Inventory, Work in Process Inventory, and Finished Goods Inventory (Exhibit 2–3). All three inventory accounts represent company assets. **Direct Materials Inventory** includes the cost of materials purchased but not yet used in the manufacturing process. **Work in Process Inventory** includes the cost of direct materials, direct labor, and manufacturing overhead invested in the manufacture of products not yet finished. **Finished Goods Inventory** includes the cost of goods that are finished but unsold. Once sold, the cost will be transferred from the balance sheet to the Cost of Goods Sold account on the income statement.

OBJECTIVE 3
Classify manufacturing product costs as direct materials, direct labor, or manufacturing overhead costs

Table 2–1 lists comparable accounts in merchandising and manufacturing companies.

Computing the cost of goods manufactured is more difficult than accounting for purchases in a merchandising company. The accountant must be able to identify all product costs and follow their flow through various manufacturing accounts. To make the job more manageable, manufacturers divide product costs into three

Exhibit 2–3

Income Statement and Current Assets of a Manufacturing Company

The highlighted costs represent the product costs. Notice that in the balance sheet, a manufacturing company has three inventory accounts, whereas a merchandising company has only one.

ABC Manufacturing Company
Income Statement
For the Year Ended December 31, 19x8

Sales revenues		$1,140,000
Product costs		
Finished goods inventory, Jan. 1, 19x8	$140,000	
Cost of goods manufactured	520,000	
Total goods available for sale	$660,000	
Finished goods inventory, Jan. 1, 19x8	120,000	
Cost of goods sold		540,000
Gross margin		$ 600,000
Selling and administrative expenses		
Period costs		
Salaries	$ 60,000	
Sales commissions	98,700	
Rent of sales offices	110,000	
Advertising	58,000	
Utilities	20,300	
Supplies	18,000	
Insurance	15,000	
Total selling and administrative expenses		380,000
Operating income		$ 220,000

ABC Manufacturing Company
Current Asset Section of the Balance Sheet
December 31, 19x8

Current assets	
Cash	$150,000
Accounts receivable	220,000
Inventories	
Direct materials	40,000
Work in process	60,000
Finished goods	120,000
Prepaid expenses	60,000
Total current assets	$650,000

Table 2–1
Comparable Accounts in Manufacturing and Merchandising Companies

	Name of account	
	In merchandising company	In manufacturing company
Materials purchased for manufacture	—	Direct materials inventory
Goods processed but not finished	—	Work in process inventory
Cost of inventory acquired to sell	Purchases of inventory	Cost of goods manufactured
Goods ready for sale to customers	Merchandise inventory	Finished goods inventory
Goods sold	Cost of goods sold	Cost of goods sold

subcategories: direct materials, direct labor, and manufacturing overhead. These subclassifications are used in both financial and managerial accounting.

Financial accountants use documents and cost collection techniques based on these categories to assign costs to products. Managerial accountants recognize that the planning and control of manufacturing product costs rests with many managers. For example, the foreman of the fabricating department can influence the material and labor costs in that department. But to fully control those costs, he or she must work with the purchasing and human resources departments. The purchasing department influences the price of materials through the selection of suppliers. The human resources department influences the labor cost by establishing the labor rate. A major task of a managerial accountant is to identify costs within the control of managers, so steps may be taken to control those costs as necessary.

Direct Materials

Direct materials are materials that can be physically traced to a particular job or product. In any manufacturing facility, one can see direct materials being converted into finished products. For example, one can observe sheet metal being shaped into automobile bodies or silk and cotton fabrics being made into clothing. These direct materials become a physical part of the product, and there is a direct relationship between the input of direct materials, two yards of fabric, and the output, one shirt. The cost of direct materials would include the price paid for the materials plus any cost of shipping to obtain the materials and sales tax. Although other materials, such as thread and screws, are used in the production process, they are not accounted for as direct materials because their cost is small relative to the high cost of keeping records on them. Instead, these miscellaneous items are classified as **indirect materials,** a subdivision of manufacturing overhead.

Direct Labor

Direct labor is work that can be physically traced to a particular product. Like direct materials, direct labor can be observed. One can walk into a factory and actually see employees working on the production line. The people who assemble automobiles, cut fabric for clothing, or lay bricks are all performing direct labor. Their wages are classified as direct labor costs. The direct labor cost would include allowances for nonproductive time that is normal and unavoidable. For example, personal time and coffee breaks are included as direct labor time. The cost of direct labor would also include the direct payments to the employee plus the cost of normal fringe benefits. Fringe benefits are a significant part of the total cost of labor, accounting for almost 40 percent of the total labor cost. Fringe benefits include the cost of health insurance, life insurance, holiday pay, pension costs, and unemployment compensation insurance. Costs such as overtime premiums and additional pay for working the evening shifts (shift premiums) are generally not considered a direct labor cost. The reason for this is that usually it is not clear which product caused the overtime or is scheduled for a shift with a premium. The cost of overtime pay and shift premiums is usually classified as manufacturing overhead. An exception would be where a particular product is directly responsible for the overtime or shift premium. In this case, the additional cost would be considered direct labor. This might occur due to a rush order by the customer.

Factory work not performed directly on a particular product is classified as **indirect labor.** The work of factory supervisors, janitors, and materials handlers, who transport materials and partially finished products, belongs in this category. Like indirect materials costs, the cost of indirect labor is included in manufacturing overhead.

Manufacturing Overhead

Manufacturing overhead includes all manufacturing costs other than direct materials and direct labor. Besides indirect materials and indirect labor, manufacturing overhead includes: (a) depreciation of plant and equipment, (b) maintenance and insurance of plant and equipment, (c) property taxes on plant and equipment, (d) overtime premiums and shift premiums, for production employees, and (e) the cost of utilities used in the production process plus any other cost associated with operating or maintaining the manufacturing plant. None of these overhead costs are traceable to a particular product. The electricity that lights the factory, for example, illuminates many work areas as well as nonproduction-related areas, such as the lunchroom.

The sum of applied manufacturing overhead, direct materials, and direct labor costs is a manufacturing firm's **total manufacturing cost.** Figure 2–3 summarizes the classification of product costs in a manufacturing company.

Figure 2–3
Summary of Total Costs in a Manufacturing Company

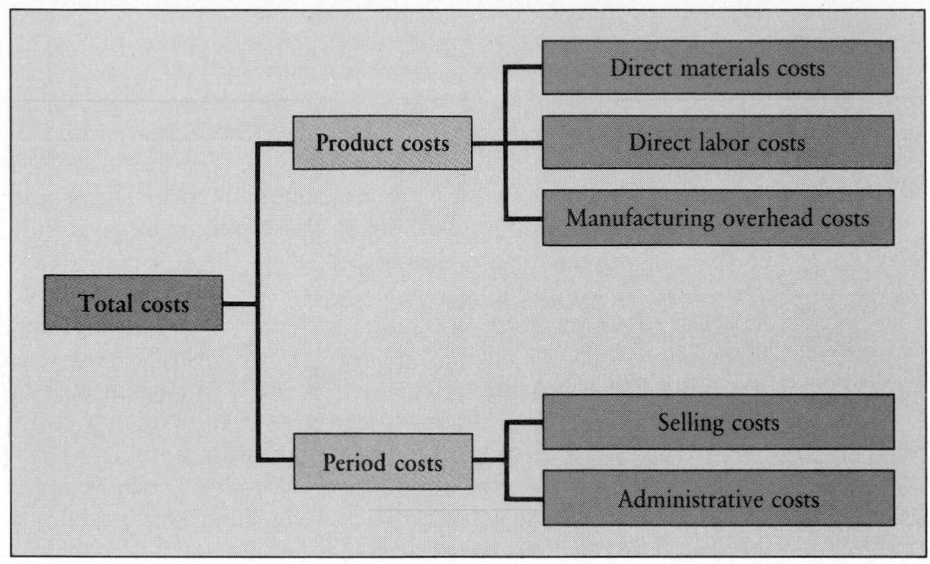

Prime Costs and Conversion Costs

OBJECTIVE 4
Classify manufacturing product costs as prime or conversion costs

Accountants sometimes find it convenient to divide manufacturing product costs into two additional categories, prime costs and conversion costs. **Prime costs** are the sum of direct materials and direct labor costs. The term probably derives from when firms began analyzing manufacturing product costs. At that time, direct materials and direct labor comprised the major portion of manufacturing costs, and plant and equipment represented a relatively small investment. Later, firms automated their production processes and invested more in heavy equipment. Manufacturing overhead then became a more important part of a product's total cost, and firms analyzed it more closely.

Conversion costs are the sum of direct labor and manufacturing overhead costs. These are the costs an organization incurs to convert direct materials into finished products. In some industries, such as the chemical industry, direct labor and overhead costs are incurred uniformly throughout the production process, and direct labor represents only a small portion of the total cost. In such industries, accountants generally prefer to deal with direct labor and manufacturing overhead together as conversion costs. The task of accounting for the two separately is not worth the effort.

Figure 2–4 summarizes the difference between prime costs and conversion costs. Notice that the two categories overlap. Prime costs and conversion costs should never be added together, for that would cause a double counting of direct labor costs.

Figure 2–4
Computation of Prime Costs and Conversion Costs
Notice that prime costs and conversion costs are not added together, since this would cause direct labor costs to be double-counted.

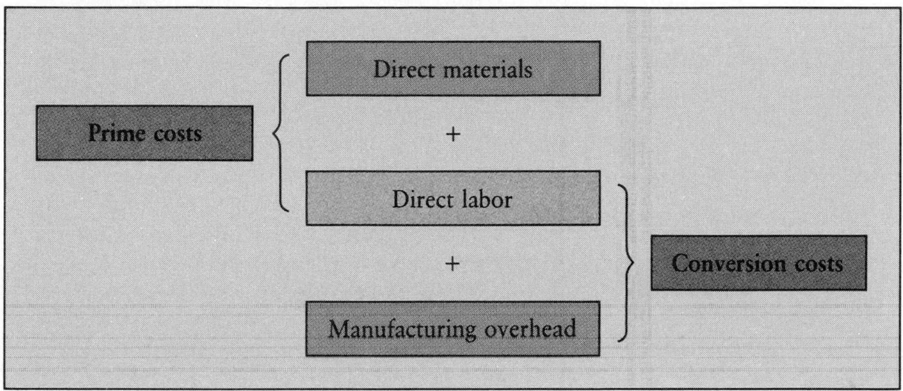

Review Exercise 2–4

Classify Costs

The following costs are for the AER Perfume Company.

a. Wages for the mixing process operator
b. Insurance on the manufacturing facilities
c. Overtime premiums to production workers
d. Rental cost for manufacturing office space
e. Plastic bottles for packaging the product
f. Labels for the bottles
g. Wages for the plant supervisor

Required

Classify the above costs as

1. Direct materials
2. Direct labor
3. Manufacturing overhead

Solution

Cost classification:

a. Direct labor
b. Manufacturing overhead
c. Manufacturing overhead
d. Manufacturing overhead
e. Direct materials
f. Direct materials
g. Manufacturing overhead

(see Exercises 24, 31)

Total Manufacturing Costs Versus Unit Manufacturing Costs

OBJECTIVE 5
Distinguish between total and unit manufacturing costs, and explain how unit manufacturing costs are used to prepare financial reports

One more cost category, **unit manufacturing costs,** is required in manufacturing companies. These costs are the average manufacturing cost per unit. They are used to determine how much of total manufacturing costs should be assigned to the Cost of Goods Sold account and how much to the ending inventories. Assume, for example, that a firm's yearly production costs are

Total manufacturing cost	$400,000
Total units started and completed	100,000
Unit cost ($400,000 ÷ 100,000)	$4

Assume also that 80,000 of the 100,000 units started and completed were sold to customers. This situation leaves 20,000 units in finished goods inventory. The unit cost of $4 is used to divide total manufacturing costs between the Cost of Goods Sold and the ending Finished Goods Inventory accounts as follows:

Cost of goods sold (80,000 units × $4)	$320,000
Ending finished goods inventory (20,000 units × $4)	80,000
Total manufacturing costs	$400,000

Of course, in the real world, all units would probably not be started and completed in the same period. The costing of partially completed units in work in process is covered in Chapters 4 and 5.

Manufacturing Cost Flows

OBJECTIVE 6
Trace the flow of manufacturing costs through manufacturing accounts to the Cost of Goods Sold account

Figure 2–5 illustrates the flow of manufacturing costs through manufacturing accounts. Notice that costs move from one account to another in the same sequence as products flow through the factory to the customer. The starting point is the purchase of direct materials, which is recorded as an asset in the Direct Materials Inventory account. As materials are used, their cost is removed from the Direct Materials Inventory account and placed in the Work in Process Inventory account. The cost of direct materials still on hand in either account at period end will appear as an asset in their respective accounts on the balance sheet.

Unlike direct materials, direct labor costs are recorded as they are consumed. Direct labor expires with time and cannot be stored for use in a latter accounting

Figure 2–5
Manufacturing Cost Flows on a Balance Sheet and Income Statement
The Direct Materials Inventory, Work in Process Inventory, and Finished Goods Inventory accounts are asset accounts shown on the balance sheet. Cost of Goods Sold is an expense account shown on the income statement.

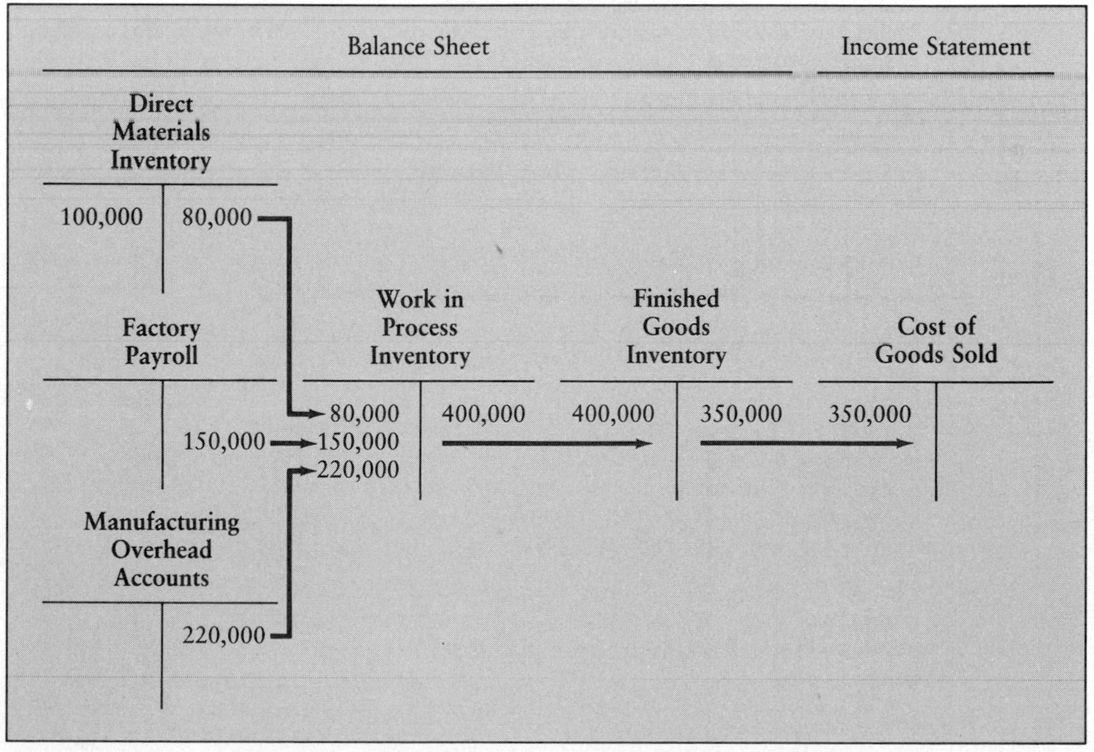

period. As direct labor is used, the cost is placed in the Work in Process Inventory account and the Factory Payroll account. Manufacturing overhead is placed in the Work in Process Inventory account from depreciation charges, use of indirect labor, expiration of insurance premiums, and use or expiration of other factors necessary for manufacturing operations. The manufacturing overhead costs are recorded in accounts such as Accumulated Depreciation, Prepaid Insurance, or Accounts Payable on the balance sheet. In Figure 2–5, these accounts are in the T account labeled Manufacturing Overhead Accounts.

As products are completed and moved from the factory to the storeroom, the accountant moves direct materials, direct labor, and manufacturing overhead costs from the Work in Process Inventory account to the Finished Goods Inventory account. Finally, when the products are sold, their total cost is transferred from the Finished Goods Inventory account to the Cost of Goods Sold account.

Statement of Cost of Goods Manufactured

At the end of the accounting period, information previously passed through the manufacturing accounts is summarized in a statement of cost of goods manu-

Exhibit 2–4

Statement of Cost of Goods Manufactured

The cost of goods manufactured represents the cost of a product completed during the year and transferred to Finished Goods Inventory.

ABC Manufacturing Company
Statement of Cost of Goods Manufactured
For the Year Ended December 31, 19xx

Direct materials		
Direct materials inventory, Jan. 1, 19xx	$ 30,000	
Purchases of direct materials	110,000	
Total direct materials available	$140,000	
Direct materials inventory, Dec. 31, 19xx	40,000	
Direct materials used		$100,000
Direct labor		150,000
Manufacturing overhead		
Factory utilities	$ 20,000	
Factory supervision	60,000	
Property taxes on factory equipment	20,000	
Factory maintenance and repairs	10,000	
Depreciation of plant and equipment	90,000	
Total manufacturing overhead		200,000
Total manufacturing costs		$450,000
Work in process inventory, Jan. 1, 19xx		130,000
Total		$580,000
Work in process inventory, Dec. 31, 19xx		60,000
Cost of goods manufactured		$520,000

factured. Exhibit 2–4 shows such a statement for ABC Manufacturing Company. This document is unique to manufacturing companies because it includes the three manufacturing accounts for recording manufacturing product costs.

The first section of Exhibit 2–4 summarizes activity in the Direct Materials Inventory account. Purchases of direct materials amounting to $110,000 were added to a beginning inventory of $30,000, resulting in an available supply of direct materials worth $140,000. Since $40,000 worth of direct materials are still on hand at year-end, $100,000 worth of direct materials must have been used in production. To this $100,000 cost is added the cost of direct labor, $150,000, and the sum of manufacturing overhead costs, $200,000. The resulting figure, $450,000, represents total manufacturing costs incurred during 19xx.

To determine the cost of goods completed in 19xx, one must adjust this total manufacturing cost for beginning and ending work in process. The $130,000 in beginning work in process is added to total manufacturing costs of $450,000. Next, the ending work in process figure of $60,000 is subtracted, leaving a total of $520,000. This total, called the cost of goods manufactured, is the value of the goods transferred to finished goods. You may recall that the cost of goods manufactured is used in the income statement to calculate the cost of goods sold (Exhibit 2–3).

Statement of Cost of Goods Manufactured and Sold

OBJECTIVE 7
Understand the cost of goods manufactured and cost of goods manufactured and sold statements

Some manufacturing companies expand their statement of cost of goods manufactured to include the **cost of goods sold,** that is, the cost of goods manufactured after adjustments for beginning and ending finished goods inventories. (Compare Exhibits 2–4 and 2–5.) Notice that Exhibit 2–5 is basically the same as the statement of cost of goods manufactured shown in Exhibit 2–4. The difference is in the final section. In Exhibit 2–5, the value of the beginning Finished Goods Inventory, $140,000, is added to the cost of goods manufactured to obtain the value of the total goods available for sale, $660,000. Then, the value of the ending Finished Goods Inventory, $120,000, is deducted to obtain the cost of goods sold, $540,000.

Refer back to Exhibit 2–3, the income statement for ABC Manufacturing Company. Notice that the cost of goods sold is the same as in Exhibit 2–5. The same figures were used in both computations. If a manufacturing firm prepares a separate statement of cost of goods sold, it need not include details on the cost of goods sold in the income statement. A single line for the cost of goods sold is sufficient.

You have seen how manufacturing costs are classified and how they flow through a firm's accounts before being matched against revenues. But you have not seen how these costs are obtained. There are two systems for collecting manufacturing product costs: job order cost accounting and process cost accounting. Job order cost accounting is covered in depth in Chapter 4 and process cost accounting in Chapter 5. Here we will provide an overview of both systems.

Exhibit 2–5
Statement of Cost of Goods Manufactured and Sold

ABC Manufacturing Company
Statement of Cost of Goods Manufactured and Sold
For the Year Ended December 31, 19xx

Direct materials		
Direct materials inventory, Jan. 1, 19xx	$ 30,000	
Purchases of direct materials	110,000	
Total direct materials available	$140,000	
Direct materials inventory, Dec. 31, 19xx	40,000	
Direct materials used		$100,000
Direct labor		150,000
Manufacturing overhead		
Factory utilities	$ 20,000	
Factory supervision	60,000	
Property taxes on factory equipment	20,000	
Factory maintenance and repairs	10,000	
Depreciation of plant and equipment	90,000	
Total manufacturing overhead		200,000
Total manufacturing costs		$450,000
Work in process inventory, Jan. 1, 19xx		130,000
Total		$580,000
Work in process inventory, Dec. 31, 19xx		60,000
Cost of goods manufactured		$520,000
Finished goods inventory, Jan. 1, 19xx		140,000
Total goods available for sale		$660,000
Finished goods inventory, Dec. 31, 19xx		120,000
Cost of goods sold		$540,000

Review Exercise 2–5

Prepare a Statement of Cost of Goods Manufactured and Sold

West Company had inventories at the beginning and end of 19xx as follows:

	Jan. 1, 19xx	Dec. 31, 19xx
Direct materials inventory	$60,000	$80,000
Work in process inventory	75,000	65,000
Finished goods inventory	90,000	75,000

During 19xx, the following costs were incurred:

Purchases of direct materials	$100,000
Direct labor	120,000
Manufacturing overhead	240,000

Required

Prepare the statement of cost of goods manufactured and sold for West Company.

Solution

Statement of cost of goods sold prepared:

West Company
Statement of Cost of Goods Manufactured and Sold
For the Year Ended December 31, 19xx

Direct materials		
Direct materials inventory, Jan. 1, 19xx	$ 60,000	
Purchases of direct materials	100,000	
Total direct materials available	$160,000	
Direct materials inventory, Dec. 31, 19xx	80,000	
Direct materials used		$ 80,000
Direct labor		120,000
Manufacturing overhead		240,000
Total manufacturing costs		$440,000
Work in process inventory, Jan. 1, 19xx		75,000
Total		$515,000
Work in process inventory, Dec. 31, 19xx		65,000
Cost of goods manufactured		$450,000
Finished goods inventory, Jan. 1, 19xx		90,000
Total goods available for sale		$540,000
Finished goods inventory, Dec. 31, 19xx		75,000
Cost of goods sold		$465,000

(see Exercise 19)

■

Two Product Costing Systems

Manufacturing costs are assigned to products by using one of two costing procedures, job order cost accounting and process cost accounting. The choice depends on the nature of the firm's production process.

Job Order Cost Accounting

OBJECTIVE 8
Distinguish between job order costing and process costing

Job order cost accounting was designed for companies whose products or services are produced in distinct batches, often to customers' specifications. It is the major cost accounting system in home construction, printing, furniture and machine-tool manufacturing, management consulting, and public accounting. In all these industries, products and services differ between clients, and each job has a definite beginning and end. For example, in the home construction industry, each home is built a little differently. One might be colonial in style; the next, contemporary. Likewise, in a printing company, the presses might be used to print an accounting book on Monday, Tuesday, and Wednesday and a magazine on Thursday and Friday.

It would make little sense for a building contractor to calculate an average price per house or a printing company to calculate the average cost of printing both magazines and textbooks. The houses might differ in square footage and materials used. A book and a magazine would certainly differ in the quality and quantity of paper used and the number of copies gathered and bound. For this reason, companies providing products and services based on customers' specifications collect separate cost data for each job. In the home construction industry, a job would consist of a single house; in the printing industry, a single 10,000-copy printing of a textbook. In an accounting firm, the job might be an audit or the design of a new management information system. Since costs are assigned to individual jobs, unit cost is calculated after each job is completed.

Process Cost Accounting

Although job order costing is suitable for customized production, it is unsuitable for mass production of identical products on a continuous assembly line. For that type of production, **process cost accounting** works better. Chemical and oil refining, paint manufacturing, beer brewing, and meat packing are all industries that use process cost accounting.

In process cost accounting, costs are accounted for by department instead of by job. Accountants collect costs department by department, either weekly or monthly. To calculate the average cost per unit at the end of the accounting period, accountants divide total costs by the number of units produced in each department. These unit costs are then used to assign departmental costs to finished products.

Job order costing and process costing are extremes of the cost accounting continuum. Few products are costed exclusively by job order or process procedures. Instead, many manufacturers use a blend of the two, applying both at various phases of the production process. For example, an automobile manufacturer applies process costing to the production of such basic parts as shock absorbers, which are manufactured continuously in its parts division. Engines and air conditioning units are also costed, using process procedures. But finished automobiles are accounted for as separate jobs, since each must be fitted with options to meet customers' orders. Some receive air conditioning and some AM/FM radios, whereas others require deluxe interiors. Thus, the cost of each completed car off the assembly line will be different. Even when a special run of a hundred identical cars is made, job order costing is used. The job is one hundred cars.

Chapter Review

Review of Learning Objectives

1. **Distinguish between product and period costs.**
Total costs may be divided into two broad categories, period costs and product costs. Period costs are general costs that usually cannot be associated with a product or sale. They are charged against total revenues in the period in which they expire and include all selling and administrative costs. Product costs are costs incurred to acquire or manufacture finished goods inventory. When finished goods inventory is acquired, its cost is recorded as an asset. When sold, its cost is deducted from revenues generated by its sale. Product costs are matched against product revenues in the period in which the revenues are recognized.

2. **Explain how product costs are treated differently in merchandising, service, and manufacturing firms.**
Product costs are incurred and matched against revenues at different times in different types of companies. In merchandising companies, product costs are incurred at the time of purchase. In service companies, product costs, or direct costs, are incurred as services are provided, and charges for these services are billed almost immediately. In manufacturing companies, product costs are incurred over the period in which products are manufactured. These products may or may not be sold. If sold, their costs are matched against revenues from their sale in the period the sale occurred.

3. **Classify manufacturing product costs as direct materials, direct labor, or manufacturing overhead costs.**
All manufacturing product costs may be divided into direct materials, direct labor, and manufacturing overhead. Direct materials costs include the cost of all important materials that can be physically traced to a product. Direct labor costs include the cost of all important labor that can be physically traced to a product. All other costs of production

— minor direct material and labor costs plus indirect materials and indirect labor — are considered part of manufacturing overhead.

4. **Classify manufacturing product costs as prime or conversion costs.**
Prime costs are the sum of direct materials and direct labor costs for a product. Conversion costs are the sum of direct labor and manufacturing overhead costs for a product.

5. **Distinguish between total and unit manufacturing costs, and explain how unit manufacturing costs are used to prepare financial reports.**
Total manufacturing costs are the sum of all costs to manufacture a product. Unit manufacturing costs are total manufacturing costs divided by total units started and completed. The unit manufacturing cost is used to determine how much of total manufacturing costs should be assigned to units sold and how much to the units still in ending inventory.

6. **Trace the flow of manufacturing costs through manufacturing accounts to the Cost of Goods Sold account.**
Manufacturing product costs are recorded first in the Direct Materials Inventory, Factory Payroll, and Manufacturing Overhead accounts. As work is performed, these costs are transferred to the Work in Process Inventory account. When the product is completed, its costs are totaled and transferred from the Work in Process Inventory account to the Finished Goods Inventory account. Finally, when the product is sold, its costs are transferred from the Finished Goods Inventory account to the Cost of Goods Sold account and reported on the firm's income statement.

7. **Understand the cost of goods manufactured and cost of goods manufactured and sold statements.**
The statement of cost of goods manufactured summarizes yearly activity in the Direct Materials Inventory, Direct Labor, Manufacturing Overhead, and Work in Process Inventory accounts. The statement of cost of goods manufactured and sold contains the same information as the statement of cost of goods manufactured plus a summary of the activity in the Finished Goods Inventory account.

8. **Distinguish between job order costing and process costing.**
There are two systems for collecting manufacturing product costs, job order cost accounting and process cost accounting. Job order costing is used to record costs for products produced in batches to customers' specifications. Process costing is used to collect costs for mass-produced identical products.

Review of Key Terms

Conversion costs The sum of direct labor and manufacturing overhead costs.

Cost of goods manufactured In a manufacturing company, the total cost of all good units completed during a period and transferred from Work in Process Inventory to Finished Goods Inventory during the quarter or year covered by the income statement. Obtained after adjusting total manufacturing costs by beginning and ending work in process inventories. Equivalent to purchases in a merchandising company.

Cost of goods sold The total cost of all products sold during the accounting period. In a manufacturing company, the cost of goods sold is obtained by adjusting the cost of goods manufactured for the beginning and ending finished goods inventories.

Direct costs Costs physically traceable to a specific product or service.

Direct labor Work that can be physically traced to a particular product.

Direct materials Materials that can be physically traced to a particular job or product.

Direct Materials Inventory An account that includes the cost of materials purchased but not yet used in the manufacturing process.

Finished Goods Inventory In a manufacturing company, an account that represents the cost of products finished but not sold by the end of the accounting period. Equivalent to merchandise inventory in a merchandising firm.

Indirect costs Costs not directly traceable to a product or service.

Indirect labor Factory work that is not performed directly on a particular product. Accounted for as a part of manufacturing overhead.

Indirect materials Miscellaneous materials of small value used in a factory. Accounted for as part of manufacturing overhead.

Inventoriable costs Costs incurred to acquire or manufacture finished goods inventory for sale. Also called *product costs.*

Job order cost accounting A cost accounting system designed for companies whose products or services are produced in distinct batches, often to customer specifications.

Manufacturing company An organization that converts materials into products for sale.

Manufacturing overhead All manufacturing costs other than direct materials and direct labor necessary to manufacture a product. Also called *factory overhead.*

Matching The process of associating product costs with the period in which a product is sold and period costs with the time period in which the costs expire.

Merchandise Inventory A merchandising company account that includes all goods purchased for resale that were not sold by the end of the accounting period. Equivalent to finished goods inventory in a manufacturing company.

Merchandising companies Companies that purchase merchandise for resale.

Period costs Selling and administrative costs that usually cannot be associated with a product or sale.

Prepaid expense An unconsumed or unexpired period cost classified as an asset on the balance sheet.

Prime costs The sum of direct materials and direct labor costs.

Process cost accounting A cost accounting system designed for companies that mass-produce identical products on a continuous assembly line.

Product cost A cost incurred to acquire or manufacture finished goods inventory. Also called *inventoriable cost.*

Purchases of inventory In a merchandising company, the cost of inventory purchases made during a specific accounting period. Equivalent to cost of goods manufactured in a manufacturing company.

Service company A company that provides services rather than products to customers. Accounting firms are service companies.

Total manufacturing cost The sum of manufacturing overhead, direct materials, and direct labor costs incurred during an accounting period.

Unit manufacturing costs The average manufacturing cost per unit, found by dividing total manufacturing costs by the number of units manufactured. Also called *average cost per unit.*

Work in Process Inventory An account that represents the cost of direct materials, direct labor, and manufacturing overhead invested in the manufacture of products not yet finished.

Review Problem

The following data pertain to the operations of Brockett Company for the year 19xx:

Sales revenues	$1,000,000
Direct materials inventory, Jan. 1, 19xx	15,000
Direct labor, wages	300,000
Depreciation, plant	60,000
Depreciation, equipment	40,000
Cutting tools used	10,000
Indirect labor, wages	5,000
Heat, light, and power, plant	10,000
Supervisors' salaries, plant	50,000
Indirect materials	5,000
Property taxes, administrative offices	10,000
Finished goods inventory, Jan. 1, 19xx	30,000
Work in process inventory, Dec. 31, 19xx	20,000
Supplies, administrative offices	10,000
Property taxes, plant	15,000
Finished goods inventory, Dec. 31, 19xx	40,000
Direct materials inventory, Dec. 31, 19xx	25,000
Sales representatives' salaries	250,000
Work in process inventory, Jan. 1, 19xx	30,000
Purchases of direct materials	110,000
Supplies, plant	5,000
Depreciation, administrative offices	50,000

Required Prepare a statement of cost of goods manufactured and an income statement for Brockett Company.

Solution to Review Problem

Brockett Company
Statement of Cost of Goods Manufactured
For the Year Ended December 31, 19xx

Direct materials		
Direct materials inventory, Jan. 1, 19xx	$ 15,000	
Purchases of direct materials	110,000	
Total direct materials available	$125,000	
Direct materials inventory, Dec. 31, 19xx	25,000	
Direct materials used		$100,000
Direct labor		300,000
Manufacturing overhead		
Depreciation, plant	$ 60,000	
Depreciation, equipment	40,000	
Cutting tools	10,000	
Indirect labor	5,000	
Heat, light, and power, plant	10,000	
Supervisors' salaries, plant	50,000	
Indirect materials	5,000	
Property taxes, plant	15,000	
Supplies, plant	5,000	
Total manufacturing overhead		200,000
Total manufacturing costs		$600,000
Work in process inventory, Jan. 1, 19xx		30,000
Total		$630,000
Work in process inventory, Dec. 31, 19xx		20,000
Cost of goods manufactured		$610,000

Brockett Company
Income Statement
For the Year Ended December 31, 19xx

Sales revenues		$1,000,000
Cost of goods sold		
Finished goods inventory, Jan. 1, 19xx	$ 30,000	
Cost of goods manufactured	610,000	
Total goods available for sale	$640,000	
Finished goods inventory, Dec. 31, 19xx	40,000	
Cost of goods sold		600,000
Gross margin		$ 400,000
Selling and administrative expenses		
Supplies, administrative offices	$ 10,000	
Sales representatives' salaries	250,000	
Depreciation, administrative offices	50,000	
Property taxes, administrative offices	10,000	
Total selling and administrative expenses		320,000
Operating income		$ 80,000

Chapter Assignments

Questions

1. (L.O. 1) Distinguish between a product cost and a period cost. Give examples of each for a merchandising company.
2. (L.O. 2) What is a product cost? State its components in a manufacturing company.
3. (L.O. 1) Before a prepaid fire insurance policy on administrative facilities expires, is the cost considered an asset or a liability? After it expires, is it considered a product cost or a period cost?
4. (L.O. 2) How does accounting for product costs differ between a merchandising and a manufacturing company?
5. (L.O. 6) Explain how costs flow in a manufacturing company.
6. (L.O. 2) "In a service company direct costs may be called product costs; indirect costs, period costs." Explain.
7. (L.O. 3) Define each of the following terms:
   a. Direct labor cost
   b. Direct material cost
   c. Manufacturing overhead
8. (L.O. 3) When manufacturing furniture, the cost of moving furniture from one work station to another is classified as manufacturing overhead. Why?
9. (L.O. 3) Explain the difference between the following:
   a. Direct costs and indirect costs
   b. Direct labor and indirect labor
   c. Direct materials and indirect materials
10. (L.O. 8) What are the basic differences between job order costing and process costing?
11. (L.O. 8) State the conditions under which it is appropriate to use the following:
    a. Job order costing
    b. Process costing
    c. A blend of job order and process costing
12. (L.O. 1) All unexpired costs are inventoriable costs. Do you agree? Discuss.
13. (L.O. 4) What are prime costs? Conversion costs?
14. (L.O. 3) The screws used in assembling a VCR are classified as indirect materials even though their cost can be directly traced to the VCR. Explain.
15. (L.O. 5) Explain how the unit manufacturing costs are used in the preparation of financial statements.
16. (L.O. 7) Define cost of goods manufactured and cost of goods sold.

Exercises

17. (L.O. 2) AAA Consulting Company's total fees for professional services were $800,000 in 19x9. In earning these fees, the company incurred the following costs:

Salaries	$350,000	Training	$25,000
Rent, office space	100,000	Supplies	10,000
Professional insurance	50,000		

Required Prepare an income statement for 19x9.

18. (L.O. 2) Ace Merchandising Company incurred the following costs during 19xx:

Purchases of merchandise	$150,000
Sales salaries	60,000
Rent, sales facility	40,000
Utilities	10,000
Supplies	5,000
Advertising	15,000

Ninety percent of the merchandise purchased was sold in 19xx.

Required Calculate the product and period costs that will be included in Ace Merchandising Company's income statement for 19xx. (see Review Exercise 2–1)

19. (L.O. 2, 7) Ajax Company had inventories at the beginning and end of 19xx as follows:

	Jan. 1, 19xx	Dec. 31, 19xx
Direct materials inventory	$55,000	$65,000
Work in process inventory	96,000	80,000
Finished goods inventory	50,000	85,000

During 19xx, the following costs were incurred:

Direct materials purchased	$400,000
Direct labor	200,000
Manufacturing overhead	330,000

Required Prepare the statement of cost of goods manufactured and sold for Ajax Company. (see Review Exercise 2–5)

20. (L.O. 1) The following costs were taken from the accounting records of the Macklin Company:
    a. Wages for employees working in the assembly department
    b. Wages for the employees delivering the product to the customers
    c. The cost of materials used in the production process
    d. Interest on notes payable
    e. Rent for the sales outlet in New York City
    f. State income taxes

g. Depreciation expense on delivery trucks
h. Wages for the sales staff
i. Insurance on the manufacturing facilities
j. The cost of merchandise purchased for resale
k. Travel expenses for sales staff
l. Cost of electricity for manufacturing equipment

Required Classify each of the above costs as product or period costs.

21. (L.O. 2) The accountants at XYZ Consulting Company are in the process of preparing the end of the year financial statements. The company has one uncompleted contract as of December 31, 19xx. On the uncompleted contract the company has incurred $30,000 of direct costs on a consulting engagement that is expected to cost $100,000. The anticipated revenues for the consulting engagement amount to $200,000.

Required Calculate the revenue to be recognized for the year 19xx. (see Review Exercise 2–3)

22. (L.O. 4) Eberly's Elegant Earings Incorporated incurred the following costs for the period ended December 31, 19xx:

Assembly-line workers	$ 7,000
Production managers	15,000
Beads used in production	4,000
Cleanup crew salaries	1,000
Storage cost of finished goods inventory	1,200
Glue used in production	500
Gold wire used in production	8,000
Electricity, factory	1,200
Secretary salary, administration	13,000
Depreciation of manufacturing equipment	7,500
Factory rent	8,000

Required From the above expenses, determine prime cost and conversion cost for the year ended December 31, 19xx.

23. (L.O. 3) The following manufacturing costs are associated with ABC Manufacturing Company. The company produces two products.
    a. Rent for the factory building
    b. Salary of the casting department supervisor
    c. Salary of the machine operator
    d. Fire insurance on the factory equipment
    e. Labor cost for materials handling
    f. Cost of power to operate plant machinery
    g. Storage costs for materials
    h. Major materials used to manufacture the product
    i. Lubricants for machinery

Required Classify the above costs as direct or indirect product costs.

24. (L.O. 3) The following costs are for XYZ Manufacturing Company:
    a. The company president's salary
    b. Oil for a drill press
    c. Salary of the milling machine operator

d. Salary of the assembly department supervisor on Products X and Y
e. Depreciation on the factory building
f. Federal income tax expense
g. Plastic case for the product
h. Depreciation on administrative office building
i. Rent on finished goods warehouse
j. Rent on sales office
k. Insurance on truck used to deliver finished goods sold
l. Gasoline for truck used to transfer work in process inventories between departments
m. Cost of batteries installed in an electronic calculator used by the sales manager
n. Contribution to the United Fund
o. Interest on notes payable.

Required Classify the above costs as:

1. Direct materials
2. Direct labor
3. Manufacturing overhead
4. Nonmanufacturing expense

(see Review Exercise 2–4)

25. (L.O. 5, 7) Beatty Corporation incurred the following costs for the period ending December 31, 19xx:

Janitorial staff, factory	$ 12,000
Secretarial staff, administration	30,000
Foreman's salary	30,000
Assembly-line workers	10,000
Electricity, office	1,600
Electricity, factory	3,600
Packaging crew	500,000
Office supplies	3,000
Packaging materials	25,000
Materials	300,000
Miscellaneous materials	150,000
Sales staff	150,000
Depreciation, office equipment	20,000
Depreciation, factory equipment	40,000

During the period, 100,000 units were started and completed, 60,000 units were inventoried, and the remainder were sold.

Required

1. Determine the unit manufacturing cost.
2. Determine the cost of the ending inventory and the cost of the units sold.

26. (L.O. 8) Below are some manufacturing operations:
a. Producing industrial chemicals
b. Constructing a new housing development
c. Producing an automobile
d. Printing a college textbook
e. Manufacturing custom-made furniture
f. Refining crude oil

g. Manufacturing videocassette recorders (VCRs)
h. Manufacturing jet engines
i. Producing home telephone equipment
j. Manufacturing toaster ovens
k. Distilling whiskey

Required Classify each one as requiring job order costing, process costing, or a blend of the two. Briefly discuss your answer for each operation.

27. (L.O. 7) Durer Publishing Company incurred the following production costs for the period ended December 31, 19xx:

Property tax	$ 3,600
Sales salaries	75,000
Advertising expense	125,000
Purchases of direct materials	500,000
Production workers' salaries	100,000
Foreman's salary	40,000
Depreciation, manufacturing equipment	225,000
Depreciation, office equipment	22,000
Payroll tax, office	8,000
Direct materials inventory, Jan. 1, 19xx	250,000
Direct materials inventory, Dec. 31, 19xx	300,000
Electricity, factory	9,000
Electricity, office	4,000
Secretaries' salaries, office	29,000

The company produced 90,000 units during the period. Sales price per unit was $20.

Required Prepare an income statement including a detailed cost of goods sold section for the period ended December 31, 19xx.

28. (L.O. 1) The following costs were incurred by Sam Retail Company:

Sales salaries	$30,000
Sales expenses	9,000
Delivery truck maintenance	1,500
Depreciation, delivery trucks	2,890
Delivery staff salaries	20,000
Rent, retail space	8,600
Utilities, retail space	2,500
Office rent	4,000
Office utilities	1,200
Office supplies	3,000
Purchase of merchandise for resale	190,000

Required Classify the above costs as product or period costs. (see Review Exercise 2–2)

29. (L.O. 6) D. P. Venkatesh Manufacturing Company, located in downtown Hong Kong, produces men's high-quality clothing. During June 19xx, the company purchased 10,000 yards of fabric at a cost of $10 per yard. During the month, 6,000 of these yards were withdrawn from inventory and placed into production. Of the clothes in production during the month of June, 80 percent were completed and

transferred from Work in Process Inventory to Finished Goods Inventory. Of the clothes completed during the month, 50 percent were sold to retailers.

There were no inventories on hand at June 1, 19xx.

Required

1. Determine the cost of direct materials (fabric) that would appear in each of the following accounts at June 30, 19xx.
   a. Direct Materials Inventory
   b. Work in Process Inventory
   c. Finished Goods Inventory
   d. Cost of Goods Sold
2. Specify whether each of the above accounts would appear on the balance sheet or income statement at June 30, 19xx.

30. (L.O. 7) Carter's Carvers, manufacturers of fine furniture, incurred the following costs for the period ended July 31, 19xx:

Direct materials inventory, July 1, 19xx	$ 20,000
Direct materials inventory, July 31, 19xx	10,000
Work in process inventory, July 1, 19xx	30,000
Work in process inventory, July 31, 19xx	40,000
Finished goods inventory, July 1, 19xx	56,000
Finished goods inventory, July 31, 19xx	41,000
Indirect materials	4,000
Indirect labor	29,000
Direct labor	90,000
Purchases of direct materials	130,000
Depreciation, office equipment	2,000
Depreciation, factory	6,500
Rent, factory	17,000
Rent, office	3,000
Advertising expense	10,000

Required

Prepare a statement of cost of goods manufactured and sold for the period ended July 31, 19xx.

31. (L.O. 3) Some costs associated with operating a manufacturing facility are given below.

a. Maintenance of robots used to heat treat steel
b. Depreciation of robots used in welding
c. Janitors' salaries
d. Rent on a manufacturing facility
e. Electricity for operating machinery
f. Production manager's salary
g. Plastic used in automobile bodies
h. Storage cost of direct materials
i. Cloth used to manufacture suits
j. Machine lubricants
k. Screws used to assemble VCRs
l. Fiber glass used to produce skis
m. Metal used to manufacture automobile engines
n. Wages for assembly employees
o. Glue used to assemble wood tables

Required Classify each cost as a direct product cost or an indirect product cost. (see Review Exercise 2–4)

32. (L.O. 5) The following information pertains to Ping Company for the year 19x9:

Sales	$126,000
Cost of goods manufactured	70,000
Selling and administrative expenses	30,000
Beginning finished goods inventory	-0-
Actual production	8,000 units
Ending finished goods inventory	2,000 units
Beginning and ending work in process inventory	-0-

Required Calculate the unit manufacturing cost and prepare an income statement for Ping Company for the period.

33. (L.O. 1) Bryant Manufacturing Company has a single warehouse for storing materials and finished products. Total warehouse space is 500,000 square feet. Direct materials occupy 200,000 square feet. The remainder of the warehouse is used to store finished goods. During 19x0, warehouse operations cost $1,250,000.

Required Calculate the amount of warehousing costs that should be classified as product cost and as period cost.

Problems

34. (L.O. 7) Ajax Company produces a line of men's clothing. During 19x9, the company incurred the following costs:

Factory rent	$100,000
Direct labor	300,000
Utilities, factory	30,000
Utilities, sales office	5,000
Advertising	80,000
Sales salaries	250,000
Purchases of direct materials	450,000
Indirect materials	80,000
Maintenance of factory equipment	45,000
Indirect labor, factory	60,000

Inventories during the year were

	January 1	December 31
Direct materials inventory	$ 80,000	$ 60,000
Work in process inventory	100,000	110,000
Finished goods inventory	130,000	110,000

Required Prepare a statement of cost of goods manufactured and sold for the Ajax Company.

35. (L.O. 4) Westin Company had the following inventories at the beginning and end of March 19x9:

	March 1, 19x9	March 31, 19x9
Direct materials inventory	$36,000	$20,000
Work in process inventory	18,000	12,000
Finished goods inventory	54,000	72,000

The following manufacturing cost data on March were available:

Purchases of direct materials	$ 84,000
Direct labor	60,000
Cost of goods sold	270,000

Required Calculate prime costs and conversion costs for March.

36. (L.O. 2) The following information is from the accounting records of the Johnson Retail Store:

	Case 1	Case 2	Case 3
Sales revenues	40,000	?	?
Merchandise inventory, Jan. 1	5,000	10,000	15,000
Purchases	25,000	10,000	30,000
Merchandise inventory, Dec. 31	?	5,000	?
Cost of goods sold	20,000	?	35,000
Gross margin	?	15,000	?
Selling and administrative expenses	?	5,000	25,000
Operating income	5,000	?	20,000

Required For each case listed, calculate the unknowns indicated by a question mark. Treat each case independently.

37. (L.O. 7) The following data are from the accounts of Watson Manufacturing Company. Figures are for the month of July 19x9 or as of July 30, except when stated otherwise.

Accounts receivable	$19,000
Sales	89,000
Direct labor	21,000
Heat and power, factory	4,000
Factory superintendent	1,000
Finished goods inventory, July 31	6,000
Property taxes, factory	1,000
Income taxes	10,000
Direct materials inventory, July 1	8,000
Direct materials inventory, July 31	10,000
Finished goods inventory, July 1	17,000
Work in process inventory, July 1	17,000
Factory maintenance	3,000
Advertising expense	2,000
Direct materials purchases	19,000
Sales commissions	4,000
Selling expenses	11,000
Administrative expenses	9,000
Work in process inventory, July 31	7,000
Depreciation, plant and equipment	5,000

Required From the data prepare a statement of cost of goods manufactured.

38. (L.O. 5, 7) Burns Company manufactures wood television cabinets. During 19xx, Burns Company incurred the following costs:

Purchases of lumber	$ 80,000
Direct labor	110,000
Indirect materials	10,000
Indirect labor	20,000
Rent, factory	30,000
Utilities, factory	20,000

Inventories for the year were as follows:

	January 1	December 31
Lumber	$20,000	$10,000
Work in process inventory	–0–	–0–
Finished goods inventory	–0–	?

During the year, Burns Company completed 1,000 cabinets. Because the company sold only 800 of these cabinets, there were 200 in ending inventory.

Required

1. Prepare a schedule of total manufacturing costs.
2. Calculate unit production cost for 19xx.
3. Prepare a statement of cost of goods manufactured and sold for 19xx.

39. (L.O. 7) Gann Company manufactures one product. Beginning and ending inventories for the current year's production are given below along with actual manufacturing costs.

Inventories	Jan. 1, 19xx	Dec. 31, 19xx
Direct materials	$53,576	$47,860
Work in process	75,650	62,420
Finished goods	84,250	75,600

During the year, the company purchased $250,000 of direct materials and used 36,500 hours of direct labor at $6.75 per hour. Actual manufacturing overhead costs for the year are summarized as follows:

Supervisors' salaries	$ 45,000
Indirect labor	60,000
Lubricants	40,000
Depreciation	200,000
Property taxes, plant	80,000
Other manufacturing expenses	160,000
Total	$585,000

Required Prepare a statement of cost of goods manufactured for 19xx.

40. (L.O. 7) The following information was taken from the accounting records of XYZ Manufacturing Company. Unfortunately, some of the data was destroyed by fire.

	Case 1	Case 2	Case 3
Sales	$20,000	$30,000	$?
Finished goods inventory, Jan. 1, 19x1	?	4,000	2,000
Finished goods inventory, Dec. 31, 19x1	3,000	5,000	?
Cost of goods sold	9,000	?	12,000
Gross margin	?	16,000	3,000
Selling and administrative expenses	5,000	?	1,000
Operating income	?	8,000	2,000
Work in process inventory, Jan. 1, 19x1	1,000	?	4,000
Direct materials used	3,000	4,000	3,000
Direct labor	4,000	5,000	3,000
Manufacturing overhead	?	7,000	?
Total manufacturing costs	?	?	14,000
Work in process inventory, Dec. 31, 19x1	1,000	4,000	?
Cost of goods manufactured	10,000	?	12,000

Required For each case listed above, calculate the unknowns indicated by a question mark. Treat each case independently.

41. (L.O. 5) K. Kaiser Company manufactures no-slice golf balls. During 19xx, the company incurred the following costs.

Direct materials used	$100,000
Direct labor	100,000
Indirect labor	140,000
Factory supplies	60,000
Factory depreciation	30,000
Electricity, factory	30,000
Other indirect costs, factory	20,000
Sales salaries	260,000
Advertising	100,000
Other selling expenses	30,000
Total	$870,000

During the year, 50,000 packages of one-dozen golf balls were produced and 45,000 dozen sold. The selling price is $24 per dozen. The company maintains no direct materials inventory, and because of the production process, no work in process inventories are maintained. Beginning Finished Goods Inventory was zero.

Required

1. Calculate unit production costs.
2. Calculate the dollar value of the ending inventory and cost of goods sold.
3. Prepare an income statement for 19xx.

42. (L.O. 6) The following inventory data relate to Shirley Company:

	Beginning	Ending
Finished goods inventory	$110,000	$95,000
Work in process inventory	70,000	80,000
Direct materials inventory	90,000	95,000

Costs incurred during the period are as follows:

Cost of goods available for sale	$754,000
Total manufacturing costs	654,000
Manufacturing overhead	167,000
Direct materials used	193,000

Required Calculate direct materials purchased, direct labor costs, and cost of goods sold. (AICPA)

43. (L.O. 7) Helper Corporation manufactures one product. You have obtained the following information for the year ended December 31, 19x3, from the corporation's books and records:

Total manufacturing costs during 19x3 were $1,000,000 based on direct materials, direct labor, and factory overhead.
Cost of goods manufactured was $970,000, also based on direct materials, direct labor, and factory overhead.
Factory overhead was 75 percent of direct labor dollars. Factory overhead for the year was 27 percent of total manufacturing costs.
Beginning work in process inventory on January 1 was 80 percent of ending work in process inventory on December 31.

Required Prepare a statement of cost of goods manufactured for Helper Corporation for the year ended December 31, 19x3. Show supporting computations. (AICPA)

44. (L.O. 1, 7) The following cost and inventory data were taken from the records of Franks Widget Factory as of June 30, 19xx:

Costs incurred

Rent, factory	$ 65,000
Direct labor	50,000
Customer service crew salaries	40,000
Purchases of direct materials	150,000
Indirect labor	10,000
Utilities, factory	8,000
Advertising expense	10,000
Indirect materials	5,000
Sales salaries	45,000

Inventories

	June 1, 19xx	June 30, 19xx
Direct materials	$15,000	$10,000
Work in process	21,000	26,000
Finished goods	40,000	32,000

Sales for the period amounted to $500,000.

Required

1. Classify the costs as product or period costs.
2. Prepare a statement of cost of goods manufactured and sold.
3. Prepare an income statement for the month of June 19xx.

45. (L.O. 7) The books of Steve's Sailboat Manufacturing Company reflected the following costs for the period ended December 31, 19xx, and the beginning and ending inventory balances.

Direct materials inventory, Jan. 1, 19xx	$500,000
Direct materials inventory, Dec. 31, 19xx	450,000
Work in process inventory, Jan. 1, 19xx	125,000
Work in process inventory, Dec. 31, 19xx	200,000
Finished goods inventory, Jan. 1, 19xx	950,000
Finished goods inventory, Dec. 31, 19xx	950,000
Indirect materials	250,000
Direct labor	75,000
Purchases of direct materials	300,000
Depreciation, manufacturing facility	125,000
Depreciation, manufacturing equipment	50,000
Depreciation, general office	20,000
Depreciation, general office equipment	8,000
Janitorial staff, manufacturing facility	12,000
Secretarial staff, office	30,000
Foremen's salaries	60,000
Utilities, manufacturing facility	100,000
Utilities, general office	1,200
Indirect labor, manufacturing facility	25,000

During the period, 600 sailboats were sold. Each boat retails for $2,000.

Required

1. Prepare a statement of cost of goods manufactured and sold.
2. Prepare an income statement for the period ended December 31, 19xx, in good form.

46. (L.O. 5, 7) Donna Company manufactures widgets using a just-in-time manufacturing process that allows the company to eliminate all work in process inventories and to maintain minimal finished goods inventory. During the year 19xx, the company incurred the following costs:

Direct materials used	$200,000
Direct labor	200,000
Indirect labor, factory	140,000
Factory supplies	120,000
Rent of delivery trucks	40,000
Factory depreciation	60,000
Electricity, factory	60,000
Other indirect, factory	40,000
Sales salaries	520,000
Advertising	200,000
Other selling costs	60,000

During the year, 100,000 widgits were produced, and 90,000 widgets were shipped to the customers at a sales price of $25 each.

Required

1. Classify the costs for Donna Company as product or period costs.
2. Calculate the total manufacturing costs.
3. Calculate the unit manufacturing costs.
4. Calculate the cost of goods sold.
5. Prepare an income statement.

Case 1
ABC Manufacturing Company (L.O. 7)

The managerial accountants at ABC Manufacturing Company were in the process of preparing the statement of cost of goods manufactured and sold for the year ended December 31, 19xx, when an explosion on the right side of the accounting office (next to the windows) destroyed all of the information relating to the credits associated with the inventory accounts. Fortunately, the debit information was available and is listed below.

Purchases of direct materials	$125,000
Total manufacturing costs	600,000
Cost of goods manufactured	650,000
Cost of goods sold	700,000

While the debit information is useful, Jeri, one of the older and wiser managerial accountants, reminded everyone that this was insufficient to prepare a statement of cost of goods sold. Jim, a recently hired managerial accountant, finally realized that he was sitting on some important data, last year's annual report. He realized that the beginning inventory values would be on the balance sheet. Jim opened the report and read the balance sheet information relating to inventories. The inventory values for January 1, 19xx, are listed below:

Direct materials inventory	$100,000
Work in process inventory	150,000
Finished goods inventory	200,000

Jeri, the old and wise managerial accountant, again reminded the staff that this was insufficient data to prepare a statement of cost of goods sold. Julie, a recently hired managerial accountant, had been working on the manufacturing overhead costs for 19xx and remembered that manufacturing overhead amounted to 50 percent of the total manufacturing costs and was 150 percent of the direct labor costs. Jeri finally smiled and said: "This might be sufficient information to prepare the statement of cost of goods sold." Jim said "What about the ending inventory values?" Jeri responded "You can calculate those!"

Required Calculate the ending inventory values for ABC Manufacturing Company.

■

3

Cost Behavior and Estimation

LEARNING OBJECTIVES

After studying this chapter you should be able to:

1. Name the four cost behavior patterns and explain how changes in business activity cause costs to vary
2. Describe the concept of the relevant range and explain its importance when analyzing cost behavior
3. Explain how management decisions influence cost behavior
4. Describe the engineering and historical data approaches to estimating costs
5. Plot cost and activity data on a scattergraph and visually fit a line to the plotted points
6. Analyze a mixed cost using the high-low approach
7. Perform simple regression analysis without a computer
8. Prepare an income statement using the contribution format, and explain why that format is sometimes preferable to the functional format

Understanding the difference between product and period costs helps managers in the planning and control process. Understanding how costs vary with changes in business activity is even more helpful. If sales volume is expected to increase, management must estimate the cost of increased output. To make such estimates, one must first know the type of cost involved and the way it behaves, or changes, as activity changes.

In this chapter, four cost behavior patterns and their possible causes will be examined. Several approaches to estimating costs are based on those patterns, and you will learn to use three of them. Finally, you will be introduced to a special format used in preparing income statements. This format reveals the effects of different cost behavior patterns on profits.

Cost estimates are used primarily in managerial accounting. However, because they are also used to calculate predetermined overhead rates, cost estimates are also used in financial accounting (see Chapter 4).

■

Cost Behavior Patterns

Not all costs vary with changes in activity nor do those that vary change in the same way as other costs. To estimate expected changes in a cost, the accountant must first identify the **cost behavior pattern,** the relationship between a cost and the level of business activity. Four cost behavior patterns are listed below.

- Variable costs
- Fixed costs
- Mixed costs
- Step costs

Once an accountant understands the behavior pattern of each category and has an estimate of changes in business activity, he or she can estimate future costs.

Variable Costs

OBJECTIVE 1
Name the four cost behavior patterns and explain how changes in business activity cause costs to vary

Variable costs are costs whose total changes in direct proportion to changes in business activity. Variable cost *per unit,* however, is constant as activity changes. For instance, assume that production of one unit requires $3 of direct labor. Table 3–1 shows the total direct labor cost at three activity levels. Notice that even as the total cost goes up, the unit cost remains the same.

The same concept is illustrated in Figure 3–1. Notice there that the total cost increases uniformly as the number of units produced increases. If 1,000 units are produced, the total cost is $3,000. If 2,000 units are produced, the total cost is $6,000. If 3,000 units are produced, total cost is $9,000. Nevertheless, the cost per unit remains at $3 per unit.

Table 3–1
Variable Cost

Number of units produced	Total direct labor cost	Direct labor cost per unit
1,000	$3,000	$3
2,000	6,000	3
3,000	9,000	3

For a cost to be a variable cost it must change with a change in business activity. The measure of business or production activity that causes the cost to change is called a **cost driver,** or *activity base* or *measure.* In the example given above, the cost driver is number of units produced. The more units produced, the greater the direct labor cost. Direct materials such as the battery installed in each completed automobile would be a variable cost. The cost driver for direct materials would be the number of units produced. In a retail organization that pays its employees using sales commissions, the sales commissions would be a variable cost with respect to sales dollars. The sales dollars are the driver causing the variation in sales commissions. In a hospital, the cost of laundry would be a variable cost. The number of patients would drive the cost of the laundry.

Sales commissions and the cost of goods sold in merchandising companies are other examples of variable costs. In manufacturing companies, the cost of direct materials, such as parts, and direct labor, such as product assembly, are examples of variable costs. For each unit produced, the unit cost of direct materials and direct labor remains the same. Only the total cost of these items varies,

Figure 3–1
Variable Cost Behavior
Notice that total cost increases in direct proportion to increases in output. This is because the variable cost per unit remains constant.

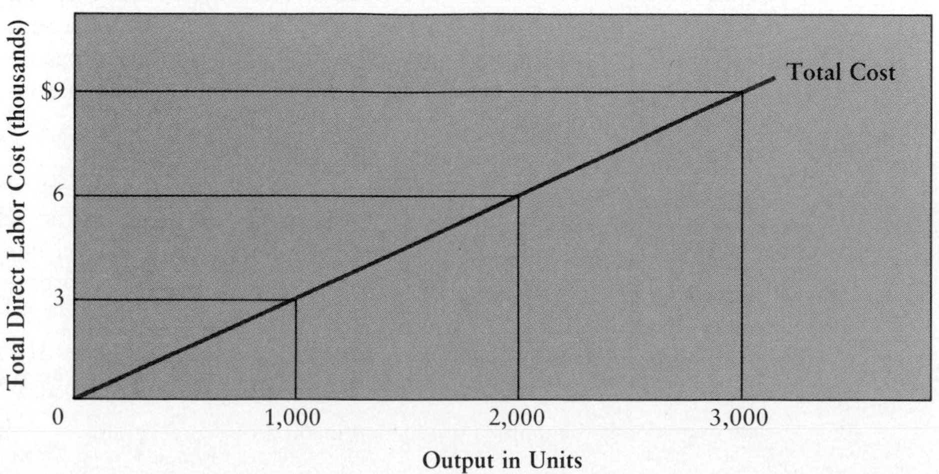

Figure 3–2
Fixed Costs and the Relevant Range
Notice that from 0 to 40,000 units, total depreciation cost is $70,000. To produce more than 40,000 units, additional equipment must be purchased, increasing total depreciation costs to $90,000. The relevant range for $70,000 in depreciation is 0 to 40,000 units. The relevant range for $90,000 in depreciation is 40,001 to 80,000 units.

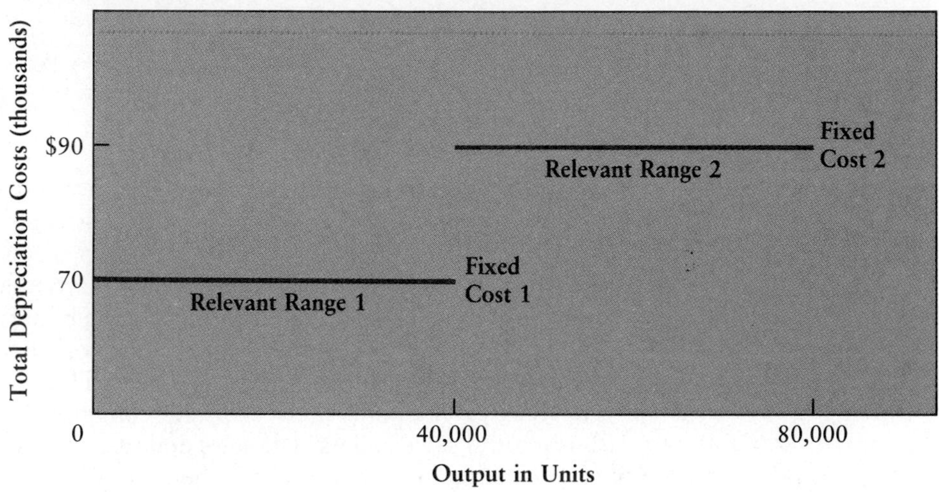

depending on the number of units produced. Other examples of variable costs include indirect materials, indirect labor, lubricants for equipment, factory supplies, freight-out, and sales commissions.

Effective operational control requires managers to know how costs vary with changes in business activity. This information allows managers to estimate the increase or decrease in cost as a result of changes in business activity.

Fixed Costs

Fixed costs are costs whose total remains constant over a wide range of business activity. Within that range fixed costs can change, but not because of changes in business activity. Insurance, depreciation,[1] and property taxes are examples of fixed costs. Other examples include costs for administrative salaries, research and development, professional development, supervisors' salaries, and facilities and equipment.

OBJECTIVE 2
Describe the concept of the relevant range, and explain its importance when analyzing cost behavior

The range of business activity over which fixed costs do not change and cost estimates are valid is called the **relevant range.** Figure 3–2 shows depreciation costs over two relevant ranges. Notice that between 0 and 40,000 units, total depreciation costs are constant at $70,000. If production rises above 40,000 units, however, depreciation costs increase to $90,000. This is because additional equipment must be purchased to achieve the higher pro-

[1]The exception is the units of production method of depreciation.

Table 3–2
Calculating Fixed Costs per Unit

Number of units produced	Total fixed costs	Fixed costs per unit
20,000	$70,000	$3.50
30,000	70,000	2.33 (rounded)
40,000	70,000	1.75

duction level. This change in costs does *not* mean, however, that depreciation is a variable cost, for total costs remain constant over a wide range of activity. Depreciation costs are fixed at $70,000 whether management produces 15,000 units or 40,000 units.

Although total fixed costs remain constant, fixed costs *per unit* vary with the number of units produced. The more that is produced, the lower the fixed costs per unit. Table 3–2 illustrates this concept. Note that as production increases, fixed costs per unit decrease from $3.50 at 20,000 units to $1.75 at 40,000 units.

This variation in unit cost can cause difficulties in both financial and managerial accounting. Assume, for example, that management uses fixed costs per unit in product pricing. If 20,000 units are produced in January and 40,000 units in March, should the accountant cost inventory at $3.50 per unit in January and $1.75 per unit in March? Obviously, the answer is no. Consumers would not pay more for a product simply because it was produced in January. To avoid this type of situation, accountants have developed special procedures for dealing with fixed costs, which will be discussed in Chapter 4. For now, you should simply note that accountants and managers must be careful about how they present and use data when dealing with fixed costs per unit.

Mixed Costs

In practice, many costs cannot be classified as either variable or fixed. They are a combination of the two. Costs that contain both a variable element and a fixed element are called **mixed costs,** or **semivariable costs.** The compensation of a sales representative who receives a base salary of $10,000 per year plus a 10 percent commission on each sales dollar he or she generates is a mixed cost.

Figure 3–3 illustrates this concept. Notice that the line representing total costs for the sales representative's work starts at $10,000 on the vertical axis. This amount is the fixed part of the representative's compensation. Even if the representative sells nothing, he or she will receive $10,000. The variable part, however, increases at a rate of 10 percent for each dollar of sales generated. Thus, if $150,000 worth of goods are sold, the representative's total compensation will be $25,000 ($10,000 fixed salary + 10% × $150,000).

Figure 3–3
Mixed Cost Behavior
The sales representative's base salary of $10,000 is represented by the fixed cost of $10,000. The variable cost is 10 percent of sales dollars. When sales are $150,000, the sales representative receives a base salary of $10,000 plus (10% × $150,000) $15,000 in commissions for a total salary of $25,000.

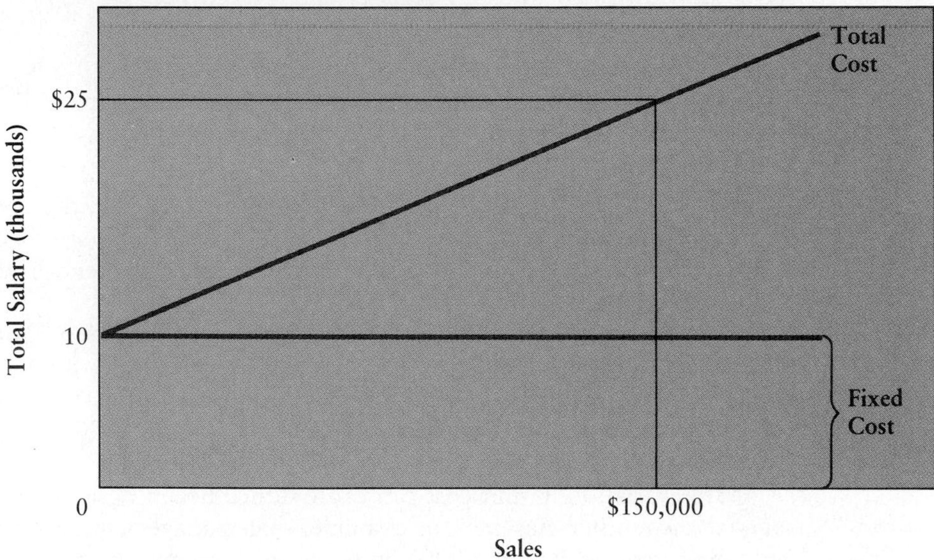

In a manufacturing environment, electricity is an example of a mixed cost. A certain amount of electricity is needed to light work areas and provide security after dark. The cost of electricity for these purposes is fixed, since the total cost does not change with changes in business activity. The cost of electricity for running equipment does change with changes in business activity, however. If sales increase, production will be stepped up. Machinery will be operated for longer periods of time, and the total cost of electricity will increase. Another example of a mixed manufacturing cost is maintenance. A certain amount of maintenance is needed to keep equipment running properly regardless of the level of business activity. But as activity increases, equipment is used more, and more maintenance is required.

Step Costs

Another common cost behavior pattern is the step cost. A **step cost** is a cost that is fixed over a short range of business activity, but then rises abruptly and remains fixed over another short range.

Supervision costs fit nicely into the step cost category. Assume, for example, that a factory is operated with one supervisor for each eight-hour shift. The number of shifts per day depends on product demand. Assume further that total production is limited to 10,000 units a month per shift and that each supervisor

Figure 3–4
Step Cost Behavior
At discrete points in output, supervision costs rise by a constant amount. This happens because supervisors are added.

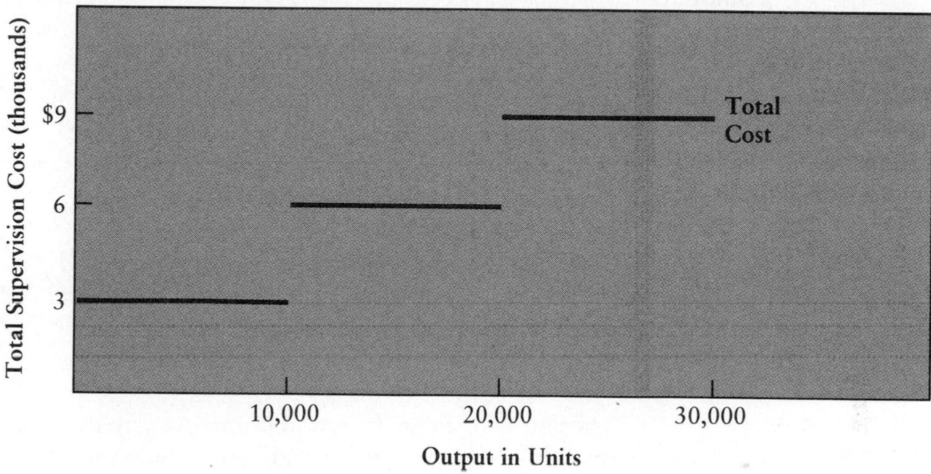

is paid $3,000 per month. If demand for the product is 10,000 units a month, only one shift will be needed, and monthly supervision costs will be $3,000. If demand rises to between 10,000 and 20,000 units a month, two shifts will be needed, and supervision costs will increase to $6,000. To produce 20,000 to 30,000 units, three shifts will be required at a supervision cost of $9,000 per month. Figure 3–4 shows these abrupt changes in cost.

Review Exercise 3–1

Classify Fixed and Variable Costs

Christ Hospital has incurred the following costs during the current year:

a. Nursing care for patients
b. Housekeeping for patient rooms
c. Housekeeping for reception areas
d. Administrative staff salaries
e. Surgical supplies
f. Depreciation for ambulances
g. Heat, light, and power
h. Medical staff for the emergency room

Required

Classify the above costs as fixed or variable costs.

Solution

a. Variable	*c.* Fixed	*e.* Variable	*g.* Fixed
b. Variable	*d.* Fixed	*f.* Fixed	*h.* Fixed

(see Exercises 15, 22)

■

Causes of Cost Behavior Patterns

OBJECTIVE 3
Explain how management decisions influence cost behavior

The nature of an organization's business activity significantly affects its cost structure. Electric and water companies tend to have high fixed costs because they require heavy capital investments. Historically, manufacturing companies have had high variable costs because the production process requires many materials and extensive labor. But as more and more companies automate their production facilities, fixed costs are substituted for variable costs. A prime example of this is the textile industry, which was once labor intensive (having high variable costs and low fixed costs). But because of automation, it is now capital intensive (having high fixed costs and low variable costs).

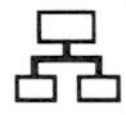

The nature of the company's business as well as the product being manufactured or sold will also affect the level of variable costs. For example, a toy manufacturer and a camera manufacturer must both decide whether to make their products out of plastic or metal. Their decisions will be based both on the product's design and marketability and the price of materials. The toy manufacturer, operating in a trendy, price-conscious market characterized by throwaway products, might well opt for a low-priced plastic. The camera manufacturer, faced with a demand for quality and durability, might select an expensive metal over plastic. In both cases, the nature of the business and the product determine the allowable level of variable costs.

The trend in today's manufacturing environment is toward greater fixed costs and less variable costs. As manufacturing companies are implementing flexible automation environments through computer-assisted manufacturing, the fixed machine-related costs are increasing and the variable labor-related costs are decreasing. In a computer-assisted environment, numerous pieces of equipment can be operated by a single individual. Through the use of computer technology, machines can be reprogrammed for different products without any direct labor.

Casualty insurance, property taxes, depreciation of plant and equipment, and salaries of key employees tend to be fixed, since they are based on facilities and needs not easily changed. Such costs are often referred to as **committed fixed costs,** for they represent the cost of the basic facilities and organizational structure necessary to a business. Committed fixed costs are usually established during long-range planning, when the organization's objectives and goals are set. These costs cannot be changed over the short run without modifying the organization's objectives and goals. Because of their potential effect on the organization, proposed changes in committed fixed costs are usually evaluated carefully.

Some fixed costs, such as middle managers' salaries, research and development costs, and advertising expenses, may be reduced or even eliminated in a relatively short time. These fixed costs are called **discretionary fixed costs,** since management can partially control their level at any time. Discretionary fixed costs are usually budgeted at the beginning of the year when management decides on the levels of research and development, advertising, and employee training needed to achieve the company's goals. Once budgeted, these costs are fixed in the sense that they will not change unless management alters its planning decisions. Unlike committed fixed costs, these costs can be changed within a short time horizon. At a minimum, these costs are reviewed annually and a decision is made concerning whether they should be eliminated or continued. And if continued, at what level?

Some variable costs are discretionary, since the per unit rate can be changed on short notice. For example, some manufacturing companies pay wholesalers an advertising allowance based on the number of units sold. These allowances behave like variable costs. Their total cost increases with the number of units sold. If, however, the manufacturer changes the per unit rate paid for advertising because of changes in demand for the product, it is exercising discretion over a variable cost. Commissions paid to sales representatives are also a discretionary variable cost. In many companies, per unit sales commissions are even changed to encourage sales representatives to push some products more than others.

■

The Engineering Approach to Cost Estimation

In industries that produce large quantities of a product, total costs for direct materials and direct labor are high. They are therefore carefully planned and controlled. Certainly, companies in such mammoth industries as automobile manufacturing want to know precisely how much material and labor should go into the 10 or 11 million vehicles they produce each year in the United States. Therefore, these companies put great effort into studying and analyzing the production process to determine the most efficient use of handling labor and materials. A lot of engineering talent is used to develop accurate estimates of these major variable costs.

OBJECTIVE 4
Describe the engineering and historical data approaches to estimating costs

The **engineering approach to cost estimation** is based on the physical relationship between manufacturing activity and costs. Industrial engineers observe each step of the production process, both to measure the time needed to perform a task and to determine the most efficient way of doing it. Based on these time and motion studies, the engineers determine the average amount of time needed per task. The direct labor cost is then estimated by multiplying the average labor time by the labor rate, which is usually determined by a labor-union contract. Time and motion studies are also used to estimate the cost of certain repetitive selling and administrative tasks. In warehousing, for example, labor time may be estimated on the basis of pounds of product moved. In computer data entry, labor time may be related to the number of orders processed.

The approach to estimating direct materials costs is slightly different. In this case, the engineer studies the materials and machines used to produce a product and identifies the quantity and quality of direct materials needed. Allowances are made for normal spoilage, and prices are estimated by using quotes from suppliers.

The engineering approach generally produces reliable cost estimates. And since it involves a complete analysis of the direct labor and direct materials required, it may also suggest alternate manufacturing procedures to reduce costs. The engineering approach is a **normative approach** rather than a predictive one; that is, it is used to determine what costs *should* be rather than how high they actually will be. Also, because this approach relies on identifying a physical relationship between the production task and cost, it is difficult to apply to such indirect costs as supplies and office expenses. the engineering approach is an expensive method for estimating costs. Therefore, it is appropriate only for major manufacturing costs.

■

Cost Estimation from Historical Data

When the engineering approach is too expensive, accountants use the **historical data approach** to estimate future costs. The basic assumption behind this approach is that future costs will behave the same as past costs. Such is usually the case unless the production or administrative process has changed. In that case, costs recorded in the accounting records will not be useful in estimating future costs. Changes in manufacturing equipment or materials, employees' skills, or compensation methods can all render historical costs unreliable for estimating purposes.

When the production process has changed, accountants must either omit historical data from their analysis or adjust the data to reflect the changes. For example, if a utility company has recently raised its electric rate, accountants might use a firm's old electric bills. Using data on the quantity of electricity used, the accountants could then calculate the firm's future electricity costs using the new rate. Or, if there is enough data on costs after the rate change, they could base their estimates on those figures.

To develop a cost estimate using historical data, the accountant must obtain two sets of data. The first set covers costs incurred in prior accounting periods, such as the cost of electricity per month. The second set shows the monthly measure of activity directly related to a cost. This measure is called the cost driver, or *activity base* or *measure*. The selection of the appropriate cost driver is crucial.

It must cause a change in the cost being estimated. Since electricity is consumed when machines are operated, machine-hours might be an appropriate activity measure in a manufacturing company. If so, the accountant would note both the cost of electricity and the number of machine-hours worked each month.

Selection of a Cost Driver

As you have seen, the engineering approach to estimating costs uses physical observation to identify the cost driver causing costs to vary. Although observation is the best procedure for identifying the appropriate cost driver, the relationship between cost and cost driver is frequently indirect and not readily observable. The cause-and-effect relationship must be inferred based on an understanding of how the cost was incurred. Here, the accountant must rely heavily on the experience of those who regularly observe the production process. Engineers and

Table 3–3
Typical Costs and Related Cost Drivers

Cost	Cost driver
Repairs, maintenance	Repair hours or machine-hours
Cafeteria	Number of employees
Electric power plant	Kilowatt-hours generated or machine-hours
Purchasing	Number of vendors
	Number of parts received per month
	Number of products
Materials handling	Pounds of materials moved
	Number of materials moved
Production scheduling	Number of orders processed
	Number of products
	Number of parts in a product
	Number of process change orders
	Number of units scrapped
Personnel management	Number of employees served
	Number of labor transactions
Warehousing activities	Pounds or crates handled
Packing of finished goods	Units processed
	Number of products
Delivery of products	Miles driven
	Number of products
Order entry	Orders processed
	Number of customers
	Number of products
Billing	Lines typed or bills processed
Selling costs	Units sold or sales in dollars
Administrative costs	Units sold or sales in dollars

managers, for instance, might explain how an activity will cause a cost to vary and suggest a cost driver. Its reliability can then be tested by statistical analysis.

Cost drivers useful for estimating manufacturing overhead costs include direct labor hours, direct labor dollars, machine-hours, and units of production. Table 3–3 lists typical costs and their related cost drivers.

Once a cost driver has been selected, the accountant must choose one of three approaches for analyzing historical data: the graphic approach, the high-low approach, or regression analysis.

The Graphic Approach

OBJECTIVE 5
Plot cost and activity data on a scattergraph and visually fit a line to the plotted points

The first step in analyzing cost data when using the **graphic approach** is to plot data onto a graph. This approach is also referred to as the **scattergraph method.** Exhibit 3–1 shows data on monthly selling and administrative expenses, or costs, as a function of sales dollars, the cost driver. This same information is shown on the graph in Figure 3–5 (Part A). Once the data have been plotted, the accountant visually draws a straight line either through or as close as possible to the majority of points. This procedure is also known as *fitting a line to the plotted points*. Personal judgment is involved. Each person will draw a slightly different line. As long as the line is reasonably close to most points, however, it will suffice.

The next step is to use the line to estimate the fixed expense per month and the variable expense per sales dollar. Once the line has been drawn, the plotted

Exhibit 3–1
Historical Data: Sales Versus Selling and Administrative Expenses (in Thousands)

Date	Sales dollars (*X* axis)	Selling and administrative expenses (*Y* axis)
January	$ 425	$ 135
February	450	136
March	565	166
April	625	177
May	838	214
June	746	195
July	713	187
August	698	193
September	643	184
October	586	166
November	520	156
December	490	149
Total	$7,299	$2,058

Figure 3–5
Graphic Representation of Data in Exhibit 3–1

A.

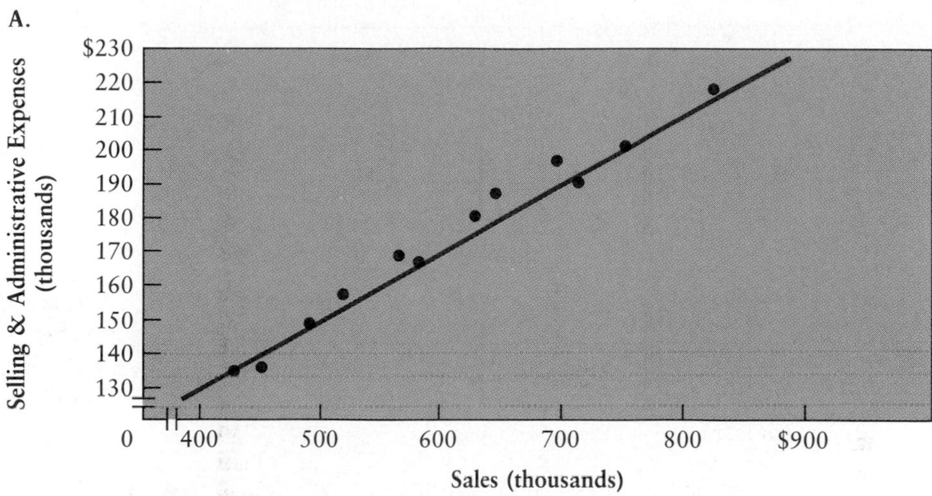

B.

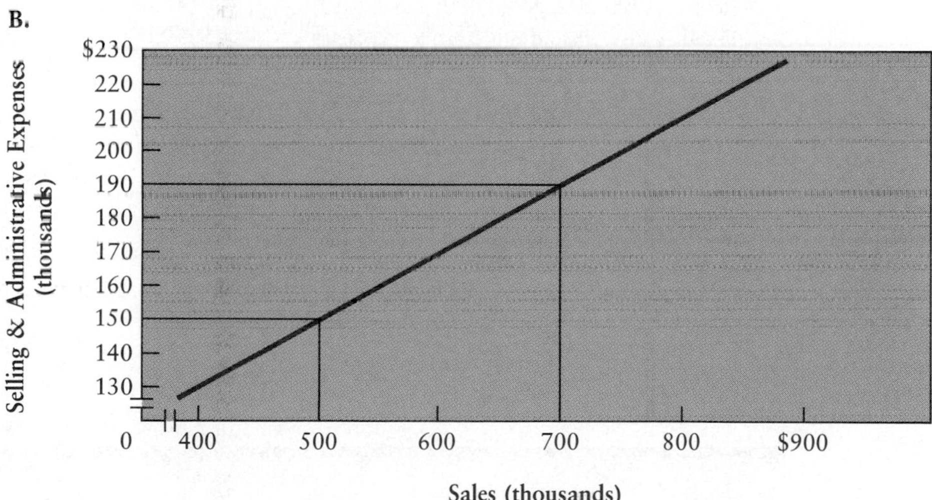

points are ignored. To estimate the fixed and variable expense, the accountant chooses two points on the activity (X) axis and uses the line drawn in Part A to read the corresponding expense amounts on the opposite (Y) axis (see Part B of Figure 3–5). Assume, for example, that an accountant chooses the $500,000 and $700,000 points on the horizontal (sales) axis. The corresponding points on the vertical (selling and administrative) axis are $150,000 and $190,000.

In Figure 3–5 you may recognize that line as a mixed cost. Compare it with the line in Figure 3–3. The next step is to find the **cost formula,** or mathematical equation, describing the line. The accountant finds the variable cost by dividing the change in total cost (selling and administrative expenses) by the change in activity (sales dollars). The computations are as follows:

$$\text{Variable cost} = \frac{\text{change in total cost}}{\text{change in activity}}$$

$$= \frac{\$190{,}000 - \$150{,}000}{\$700{,}000 - \$500{,}000}$$

$$= \frac{\$40{,}000}{\$200{,}000}$$

$$= \underline{\underline{\$0.20}} \text{ per sales dollar}$$

The variable selling and administrative expense is $0.20 per sales dollar.

To find the fixed cost, the accountant must take the total cost at any volume of activity and estimate the variable cost included in the total. Then, he or she must subtract the variable cost from the total cost. If $700,000 sales volume is chosen:

Total cost at $700,000 sales dollars	$190,000
Less variable cost ($700,000 × $0.20)	140,000
Fixed selling and administrative expenses	$ 50,000 per month

The fixed selling and administrative cost is $50,000 per month. It is $50,000 *per month* because the graph was based on monthly data (Exhibit 3–1).

Finally, the accountant must put the variable and fixed costs together to obtain the cost equation for total selling and administrative expenses:

Total selling and administrative expenses
= $50,000 per month + $0.20 per sales dollar

Review Exercise 3–2

Compute Costs with Graphic Approach

Interstate Bank is attempting to determine the costs of its data processing operation. The following costs and processing hours have been collected for the past six months of operation:

Month	Costs	Processing hours
January	$22,500	1,600
February	24,320	1,700
March	21,500	1,500
April	24,900	1,750
May	26,100	1,900
June	22,200	1,550

Required

Using the graphic approach, compute the fixed and variable costs of the data processing operation.

Solution

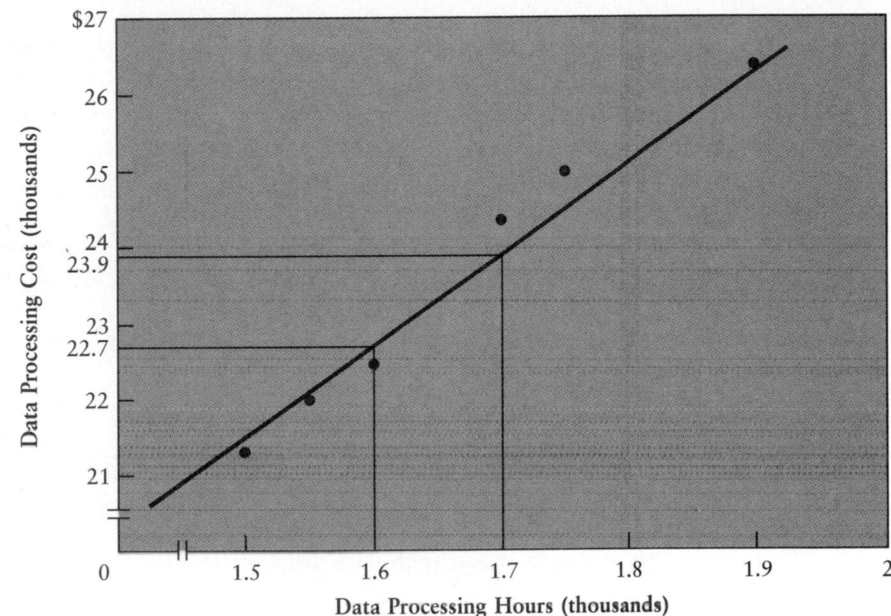

$$\text{Variable cost} = \frac{\text{change in total cost}}{\text{change in activity}}$$

$$= \frac{\$23{,}900 - \$22{,}700}{1{,}700 - 1{,}600}$$

$$= \frac{\$1{,}200}{100}$$

$$= \underline{\underline{\$12}} \text{ per processing hour}$$

Fixed cost computation

Total cost at 1,700 processing hours	$23,900	
Less variable cost (1,700 × $12)	20,400	
Fixed data processing costs	$ 3,500	per month

Total data processing costs

= $3,500 per month + $12 per processing hour

(see Exercises 18, 20)

The High-Low Approach

OBJECTIVE 6
Analyze a mixed cost using the high-low approach

The **high-low approach** crudely resembles the graphic approach. The accountant selects two extreme activity figures from the historical data, one high and the other low. In some firms the very highest and lowest activity figures are used. Such a practice simplifies the process so people with little training can do it. If the points selected are nonrepresentative of the underlying process, however, unsatisfactory estimates result. Some judgment is required to use this method effectively. *Nonrepresentative* means that the costs are the result of some unusual event, such as increased overtime costs due to the loss of finished goods in a fire. It is not anticipated that the event causing the costs will occur on a regular basis.

To illustrate this approach, data from Exhibit 3–1 will be used again. The extreme activity figures occurred in May ($214,000 at $838,000 sales dollars) and in January ($135,000 at $425,000 sales dollars).

Using these two figures, one calculates variable and fixed costs as follows:

$$\text{Variable cost} = \frac{\text{change in total cost}}{\text{change in activity}}$$

$$= \frac{\$214{,}000 - \$135{,}000}{\$838{,}000 - \$425{,}000} = \frac{\$79{,}000}{\$413{,}000}$$

$$= \underline{\underline{\$0.19}} \text{ per sales dollar}$$

Total costs at $425,000 sales dollars	$135,000
Less variable cost at $425,000 sales dollars ($0.19 × $425,000)	80,750
Total fixed costs	$ 54,250 per month

Total selling and administrative expenses
= $54,250 per month + $0.19 per sales dollar

Notice that the cost formula obtained by using the high-low approach is different from the one obtained by using the graphic method.

High-low approach

Total selling and administrative expenses
= $54,250 per month + $0.19 per sales dollar

Graphic approach

Total selling and administrative expenses
= $50,000 per month + $0.20 per sales dollar

Only two observations were used with the high-low approach, as opposed to the 12 that were used with the graphic approach. Generally, the more observations used to construct a cost formula, the better the cost estimates. Thus, the graphic approach is more valid.

Figure 3–6
Comparison of High-Low and Graphic Methods

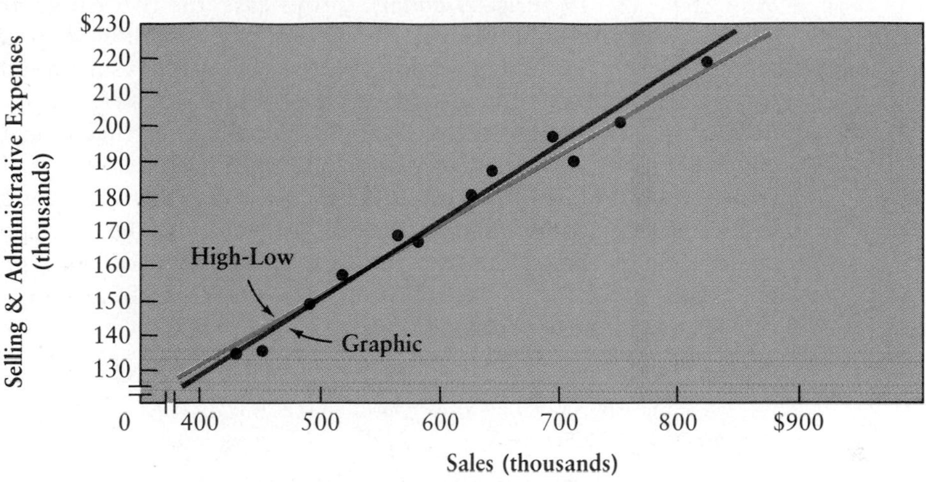

Figure 3–7
Influence of Outliers on Accuracy of High-Low Method
The colored line is fitted using the high-low method. The gray line is fitted using the graphic method and ignoring the outliers.

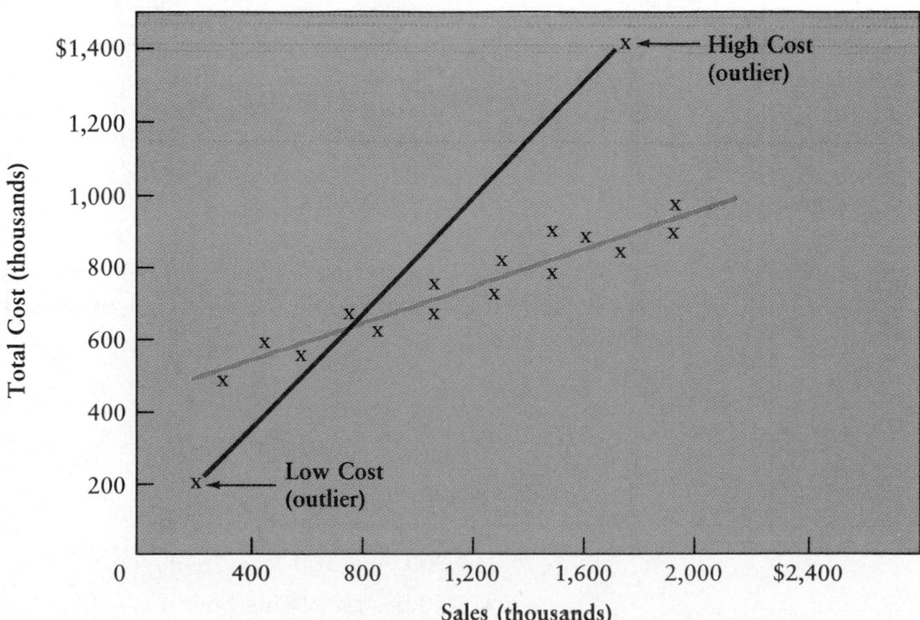

Figure 3–6 compares the total cost line obtained by the graphic approach in Figure 3–5 with a total cost line plotted by using the high-low formula above ($54,250 + $0.19 per sales dollar). In this case, the two curves are reasonably close, and not much accuracy is lost by using the high-low approach.

The advantages of the high-low approach are that it is simple and inexpensive. But if either of the two points selected represent an **outlier**, a cost influenced by unusual events, then the high-low approach will be unreliable. Figure 3–7 is an example of data where both the high and low points are outliers. Thus, the line representing the high-low cost estimate is considerably different from the line drawn using the graphic approach. In this situation the high-low approach is very inaccurate. The two points on which it is based simply do not represent normal operations. With the graphic approach, these points are immediately recognizable as outliers and therefore ignored.

Review Exercise 3–3

Compute Costs with High-Low Approach

Interstate Bank is attempting to determine the cost of its data processing operation. The following costs and processing hours have been collected for the past six months of operation:

Month	Costs	Processing hours
January	$22,500	1,600
February	24,320	1,700
March	21,500	1,500
April	24,900	1,750
May	26,100	1,900
June	22,200	1,550

Required

Using the high-low approach, compute the fixed and variable costs of the data processing operation.

Solution

$$\text{Variable cost} = \frac{\text{change in total cost}}{\text{change in activity}}$$

$$= \frac{\$26{,}100 - \$21{,}500}{1{,}900 - 1{,}500} = \frac{\$4{,}600}{400}$$

$$= \underline{\underline{\$11.50}} \text{ per processing hour}$$

Fixed cost computation:

Total cost at 1,900 processing hours	$26,100
Less variable cost (1,900 × $11.50)	21,850
Fixed data processing costs	$ 4,250 per month

Total data processing costs

= $4,250 per month + $11.50 per processing hour

(see Exercises 17, 23)

■

Regression Analysis

OBJECTIVE 7
Perform simple regression analysis without a computer

Regression analysis is a more accurate version of the graphic approach because the human judgment involved in drawing a line close to a series of plotted points is eliminated. Instead, algebraic equations are used to position the line precisely. A line drawn in this way is called a **regression line,** or **least squares line.** Figure 3–8 shows such a line. Notice that the space between the regression line and the plotted points is measured vertically. Regression analysis minimizes the sum of the squared deviations between the plotted points and the total cost line — thus, the term *least squares.* This method is more time-consuming than the graphic approach, but it is objective and uses all the data.

Simple Regression Analysis **Simple regression analysis** is based on the algebraic equations for a straight line

$$Y = a + bX$$

In this equation a represents fixed costs, and b represents variable costs. Y is the dependent variable, which in the example is total selling and administrative expenses. X is the independent variable, sales dollars. Using this basic equation, mathematicians have developed two equations that can be solved simultaneously

$$\Sigma XY = a\Sigma X + b\Sigma X^2$$

$$\Sigma Y = an + b\Sigma X$$

where

a = fixed costs per time period
b = variable costs per activity measure
n = number of observations
X = value of the independent variable
Y = value of the dependent variable
X^2 = value of the independent variable squared

Figure 3–8
A Graphic Illustration of Regression Analysis
The objective of regression analysis is to fit a line to the data so the sum of the squared deviations between the line and the data points is minimized.

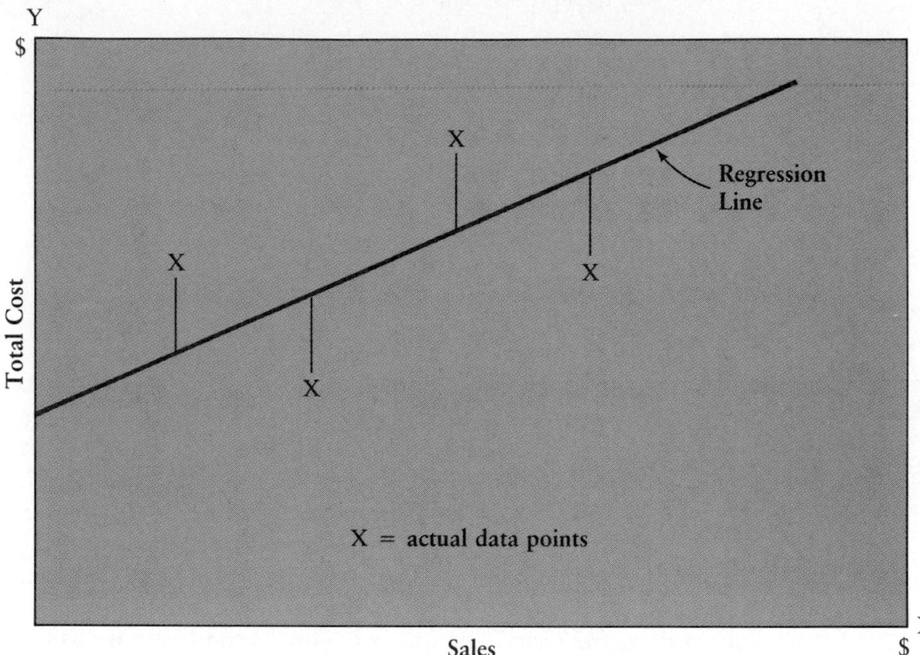

XY = product of X times Y
Σ = sum of

If these two equations are rearranged to solve for a and b, they are stated as follows:

$$b = \frac{n\Sigma(XY) - \Sigma X \Sigma Y}{n\Sigma X^2 - (\Sigma X)^2}$$

$$a = \frac{\Sigma Y - b(\Sigma X)}{n}$$

Using data from Exhibit 3–1, in which selling and administrative expenses where the dependent variable (Y) and sales dollars the independent variable (X), the values of a and b are calculated as in Exhibit 3–2. Notice that to obtain the basic values substituted into the equations, you must first calculate the values for X^2 and XY and total them. Then, you must find the value for b, since it is needed to calculate a. Next, using the value obtained for b, $0.19297, you must find the value of a: $54,126. Finally, by substituting values for a and b into the formula for a straight line, $Y = a + bX$, you can obtain the cost formula Y = $54,126 + 0.193X$. That is, total selling and administrative expenses (Y) equals $54,126 per month in fixed costs plus $0.193 per sales dollar.

Exhibit 3–2
Regression Analysis (Quantities in Table in Thousands)

Date	Sales dollars (X)	Selling and administrative expenses (Y)	X^2	XY
January	$ 425	$ 135	$ 180,625	$ 57,375
February	450	136	202,500	61,200
March	565	166	319,225	93,790
April	625	177	390,625	110,625
May	838	214	702,244	179,332
June	746	195	556,516	145,470
July	713	187	508,369	133,331
August	698	193	487,204	134,714
September	643	184	413,449	118,312
October	586	166	343,396	97,276
November	520	156	270,400	81,120
December	490	149	240,100	73,010
Total	$7,299	$2,058	$4,614,653	$1,285,555

$$b = \frac{n\Sigma(XY) - \Sigma X \Sigma Y}{n\Sigma X^2 - (\Sigma X)^2}$$

$$= \frac{12(\$1{,}285{,}555) - \$7{,}299(\$2{,}058)}{12(\$4{,}614{,}653) - (\$7{,}299)^2}$$

$$= \frac{\$15{,}426{,}660 - \$15{,}021{,}342}{\$55{,}375{,}836 - \$53{,}275{,}401} = \frac{\$405{,}318}{\$2{,}100{,}435}$$

$$b = \underline{\underline{\$0.19297}} \text{ per sales dollar}$$

$$a = \frac{\Sigma Y - b(\Sigma X)}{n}$$

$$= \frac{\$2{,}058 - \$0.19297(\$7{,}299)}{12}$$

$$= \frac{\$649{,}512}{12}$$

$$a = \underline{\underline{\$54{,}126}} \text{ per month}$$

If you compare the cost formula just obtained with those from the high-low and graphic methods, you will see that it falls between the first two:

Technique	Cost formula
High-low	$54,250 + $0.19 per sales dollar
Regression analysis	$54,126 + $0.193 per sales dollar
Graphic method	$50,000 + $0.20 per sales dollar

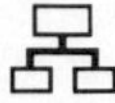

Of the three techniques, regression analysis is the most reliable. Without a computer, however, it is more time-consuming than the other two methods. In selecting a technique, the accountant must weigh the costs against the potential benefits. If a manager's decision might be changed by small errors in estimated costs, then the accuracy of regression analysis is probably worth the extra effort. If that decision will not be particularly affected by costs, however, then the high-low or graphic method is appropriate. If a computer is available, however, regression analysis is easier than the other two methods.

Notice that in this illustration, the answer obtained by using the high-low technique more closely resembles the one obtained by using regression analysis than the one obtained by using the graphic technique. In this case, the highest and lowest cost observations were exceptionally close to the regression line, so the high-low method produced an estimate more accurate than usual. Generally, the graphic method is more valid, especially if the cost data include outliers, as in Figure 3–7.

Multiple Regression Analysis The example you have been studying involved only one independent variable, sales dollars. Not all cost formulas are so simple, however. In some organizations a cost might be driven by several variables. For example, selling costs can be driven by the sales of individual products. **Multiple regression analysis** estimates costs using more than one independent variable. For example, in a firm with many products, management might need to know the variable selling and administrative costs associated with each product. In that case, the total cost formula might be expressed as shown below. The firm in this case has three products.

$$Y + a + b_1X_1 + b_2X_2 + b_3X_3$$

where

Y = total selling and administrative cost

a = fixed cost per month

b = variable cost per product

X = sales revenue per product

$_1$ = Product 1

$_2$ = Product 2

$_3$ = Product 3

Such equations are called **multiple regression equations,** since they have more than one independent variable.

To estimate total fixed costs and variable costs for each product, the accountant uses basically the same procedure used in simple regression analysis. Again, the objective is to minimize the sum of the squared deviations between the cost data and the line fitted to it. Because of the complexity of the calculations, multiple regression analysis is most always done by computer.

Exhibit 3–3
Historical Data: Sales Versus Selling and Administrative Expenses (in Thousands)

	Sales			Total selling and administrative expenses
Month	Product X_1	Product X_2	Product X_3	(Y axis)
January	$2,000	$400	$600	$450
February	1,940	430	610	445
March	1,950	380	630	445
April	1,860	460	620	438
May	1,820	390	640	433
June	1,860	440	580	437
July	1,880	420	570	438
August	1,850	380	580	434
September	1,810	390	580	430
October	1,770	290	610	425

As a way of understanding this concept, assume the data in Exhibit 3–3 have been collected from the sales and expense records for the three products.[1] Using a computer program with selling and administrative expenses as the dependent variable (Y) and product sales as the independent variables (X_1, X_2, and X_3), accountants obtained the following results:

$$Y = \$228{,}000 + \$0.098X_1 + \$0.025X_2 + \$0.024X_3$$

These results indicate that management can expect $228,000 in fixed selling and administrative expenses each month plus variable expenses equal to $0.098 per sales dollar on Product 1, $0.025 per sales dollar on Product 2, and $0.024 per sales dollar on Product 3.

■

Using Cost Behavior in Reporting Income: The Contribution Format

Once total costs have been separated into fixed and variable costs, how do managerial accountants use that information? One important use involves the construction of a special income statement, one that differs from the functional

[1]Adapted from *The Accounting Review* Supplement to vol. XLVI (Evanston, Illinois, American Accounting Association, 1971), pp. 229–231. Used by permission.

Exhibit 3–4
Comparison of Functional Income Statement with Contribution Income Statement

A. Functional income statement		
Sales revenues		$955,000
Cost of goods sold		597,500
Gross margin		$357,500
Selling and administrative expenses		276,000
Operating income		$ 81,500
B. Contribution income statement		
Sales revenues		$955,000
Variable costs		
Cost of goods sold	$477,500	
Selling and administrative expenses	191,000	668,500
Contribution margin		$286,500
Fixed expenses		
Manufacturing	$120,000	
Operating	85,000	205,000
Operating income		$ 81,500

OBJECTIVE 8
Prepare an income statement using the contribution format, and explain why that format is sometimes preferable to the functional format

income statements illustrated in Chapter 2. Those statements are referred to as **functional income statements**, since they group expenses by business functions such as production and selling and administration. Examine the income statement in Part A of Exhibit 3–4. Notice how the cost of goods sold is deducted from sales revenues to obtain gross margin. Then, the selling and administrative expenses are deducted to obtain operating income. Neither expense category is separated into fixed and variable expenses.

Now, examine Part B of Exhibit 3–4, which shows a **contribution format income statement.** Notice how variable expenses are first deducted from sales revenues to obtain what accountants call the **contribution margin.** Next, fixed expenses are deducted from the contribution margin to obtain operating income. In a contribution income statement, expenses are grouped by cost behavior pattern rather than business function.

The contribution margin is the crucial figure. It tells management the amount sales contributed toward fixed expenses and toward operating income. In this example, sales revenues of $955,000 contributed $286,500 toward fixed costs and left $81,500 worth of operating income. The contribution format is used extensively in business for internal planning and control. It is useful in analyzing cost-volume-profit relationships as well as product profitability and sales and managerial performance. (All these topics are covered in later chapters.)

Review Exercise 3–4

Prepare Functional and Contribution Income Statements

Holmes Company produced and sold 40,000 units during the current year. There was no beginning Finished Goods Inventory, and the company maintains no materials inventory. Following is a summary of the activity:

Selling price per unit	$25
Materials (per unit)	6
Direct labor (per unit)	10
Total fixed manufacturing cost for the period	$80,000

Administrative expenses = $30,000 + $0.60 (sales units)
Selling expense = $24,000 + $2 (sales units)

Required

1. Prepare an income statement using the functional format.
2. Prepare an income statement using the contribution format.

Solution

1. Functional income statement

Sales revenues (40,000 units @ $25)		$1,000,000
Cost of goods sold (40,000 units @ $18)*		720,000
Gross margin		$ 280,000
Operating expenses		
Administrative ($30,000 + 40,000 @ $0.60)	$ 54,000	
Selling ($24,000 + 40,000 @ $2)	104,000	
Total	$158,000	
Operating income	$122,000	

2. Contribution income statement

Sales revenues (40,000 units @ $25)		$1,000,000
Variable costs		
Cost of goods sold (40,000 @ $16)	$640,000	
Operating expenses		
Administrative (40,000 @ $0.60)	24,000	
Selling (40,000 @ $2)	80,000	744,000
Contribution margin		$ 256,000
Fixed expenses		
Manufacturing	$ 80,000	
Administrative	30,000	
Selling	24,000	134,000
Operating income		$ 122,000

$*\$10 + \$6 + \frac{\$80,000}{40,000} = \$18$

(see Exercise 19 and Problems 30, 34)

■

Chapter Review

Review of Learning Objectives

1. **Name the four cost behavior patterns and explain how changes in business activity cause costs to vary.**
Costs are classified by the way they vary with business activity. The four major cost behavior patterns are variable costs, fixed costs, mixed costs, and step costs. Variable costs change in direct proportion to changes in business activity. Fixed costs remain constant over a wide range of business activity. Mixed costs contain elements of both variable and fixed costs. A step cost remains fixed over a short range of business activity.

2. **Describe the concept of the relevant range and explain its importance when analyzing cost behavior.**
Relevant range is the range of business activity over which a cost behavior pattern can be expected to hold. This is the activity level over which reliable cost estimates can be made.

3. **Explain how management decisions influence cost behavior.**
Costs are influenced by the nature of a business; the nature of the product; the basic facilities and personnel required for a business; and the contractual arrangements management makes with employees, suppliers, and customers. Therefore, changes in management decisions affect the way costs behave.

4. **Describe the engineering and historical data approaches to estimating costs.**
The engineering approach to estimating costs is based on the physical relationship between the manufacturing activity and costs. By doing time and motion studies of the manufacturing process and analyzing material requirements, industrial engineers develop estimates of production costs. When the engineering approach is too expensive, accountants estimate future costs based on historical data.

5. **Plot cost and activity data on a scattergraph and visually fit a line to the plotted points.**
In the graphic approach, historical cost and activity data are plotted on a graph that shows total costs on the *Y* axis and the activity base on the *X* axis. A straight line is then visually fitted to the data points. Using two points on the line, the accountant computes the variable and fixed costs mathematically, as in the high-low method. Because this approach uses all the data, outliers can be readily identified and eliminated from the analysis.

6. **Analyze a mixed cost using the high-low approach.**
The high-low approach crudely resembles the graphic approach. Only two cost figures, the highest and lowest, are used. The accountant calculates variable costs by dividing changes in total costs by changes in activity. Then, he or she computes the variable cost at one of the two points. Next, that variable cost is subtracted from total costs to obtain fixed costs. Although this approach is simple, if the two points used are nonrepresentative, the results will be inaccurate.

7. **Perform simple regression analysis without a computer.**
Regression analysis uses algebraic equations to fit a line to a set of cost and activity data. This line is drawn visually in the graphic method. The objective of regression analysis is to minimize the sum of the squared deviations between this line and the data points. Exhibit 3–2 shows the formulas and sample calculations involved in this kind of analysis. Although the calculations are lengthy, the results are highly accurate.

8. **Prepare an income statement using the contribution format, and explain why that format is sometimes preferable to the functional format.**
The contribution format for income statements separates variable from fixed expenses. Variable expenses are subtracted from sales revenues to obtain the contribution margin, which shows the amount sales contributed to fixed expenses and operating income. Then, fixed expenses are subtracted from the contribution margin to obtain the operating income. The contribution format is used extensively for internal planning and control because it indicates which costs will change with activity level and which will remain constant.

Review of Key Terms

Committed fixed costs The cost of the basic facilities and organizational structure needed for a business.

Contribution format income statement An income statement in which expenses are grouped by cost behavior. Variable expenses are totaled and deducted from sales revenue to obtain the contribution margin. Fixed expenses are then totaled and deducted from the contribution margin to obtain operating income.

Contribution margin Sales revenues less variable expenses. Represents the amount sales has contributed toward fixed expenses and operating income.

Cost behavior pattern The relationship between a cost and the level of business activity.

Cost driver A measure of business or production activity, such as machine-hours or miles driven, that causes a cost to change. Also called *activity base* or *measure.*

Cost formula A mathematical equation describing the fixed and variable components of a cost. The cost formula is generally expressed as $Y = a + bX$ (total costs = fixed costs + variable costs × activity measure).

Discretionary fixed costs Fixed costs over which management can exercise some control at any time during the fiscal year.

Engineering approach to cost estimation A cost estimate based on the physical relationship between manufacturing activity and costs, as measured by time and motion studies and materials estimates.

Fixed cost An operating cost whose total remains constant over a wide range of business activity.

Functional income statement Income statements in which expenses are grouped by business functions. Fixed and variable costs are not listed separately under each functional expense category.

Graphic approach A method of estimating costs by plotting historical cost and activity data onto a graph. A line is then fitted visually onto the data. Also called the *scattergraph method.*

High-low approach A method of estimating costs by using only the high and low points of historical costs and activity data.

Historical data approach An approach to estimating costs that is based on historical data of costs and business activity.

Least squares line A line fitted to a series of plotted points by means of statistical analysis. Also called a *regression line.*

Mixed costs Costs composed of both variable and fixed elements. Also called *semivariable costs.*

Multiple regression analysis A statistical approach to estimating costs by using more than one independent variable.

Multiple regression equations Regression equations with more than one independent variable.

Normative approach An approach to estimating costs that prescribes what future costs ideally should be based on engineering estimates.

Outlier A cost observation that is influenced by unusual events and, thus, is nonrepresentative of the true cost of business activity.

Regression analysis A more accurate version of the graphic approach to estimating costs. Using this approach, one fits a line to cost and activity data by means of statistical analysis.

Regression line A line fitted to a series of plotted points by means of statistical analysis. Also called a *least squares line.*

Relevant range The range of business activity over which fixed costs do not change and cost estimates are valid.

Scattergraph method See *Graphic approach.*

Semivariable costs Costs composed of both variable and fixed elements. Also called *mixed costs.*

Simple regression analysis A statistical approach to estimating costs by using only one independent variable.

Step cost A cost that is fixed over a short range of business activity, then rises abruptly and remains fixed over another short range.

Variable costs Costs whose total changes in direct proportion to changes in business activity. (Cost per unit remains constant.)

Review Problem

Acme Company has collected the following data concerning sales dollars and sales and administrative expenses (S&A) for the year 19x9:

Month	Sales dollars (*X* axis)	S&A expenses (*Y* axis)
January	$35,000	$20,500
February	41,000	22,600
March	49,000	25,800
April	50,100	26,800
May	50,500	26,900
June	48,700	25,600
July	45,000	23,700
August	47,900	26,300
September	46,900	23,900
October	50,000	26,400
November	52,000	27,500
December	52,500	28,800

Required

1. Using the high-low approach, determine the relationship between administrative expenses and sales dollars.
2. Using the graphic approach, determine the relationship between administrative expenses and sales dollars.
3. Using regression analysis, determine the relationship between administrative expenses and sales dollars.

Solution to Review Problem

1. High-low approach

$$\text{Variable cost} = \frac{\text{change in total cost}}{\text{change in activity}}$$
$$= \frac{\$28{,}800 - \$20{,}500}{\$52{,}500 - \$35{,}000}$$
$$= \frac{\$8{,}300}{\$17{,}500}$$
$$= \underline{\underline{\$0.47}} \text{ per sales dollar}$$

Fixed cost computation:

Total cost at $52,500 sales dollars	$28,800
Less variable cost ($52,500 × $0.47)	24,675
Fixed S&A expenses	$ 4,125 per month

2. Graphic approach

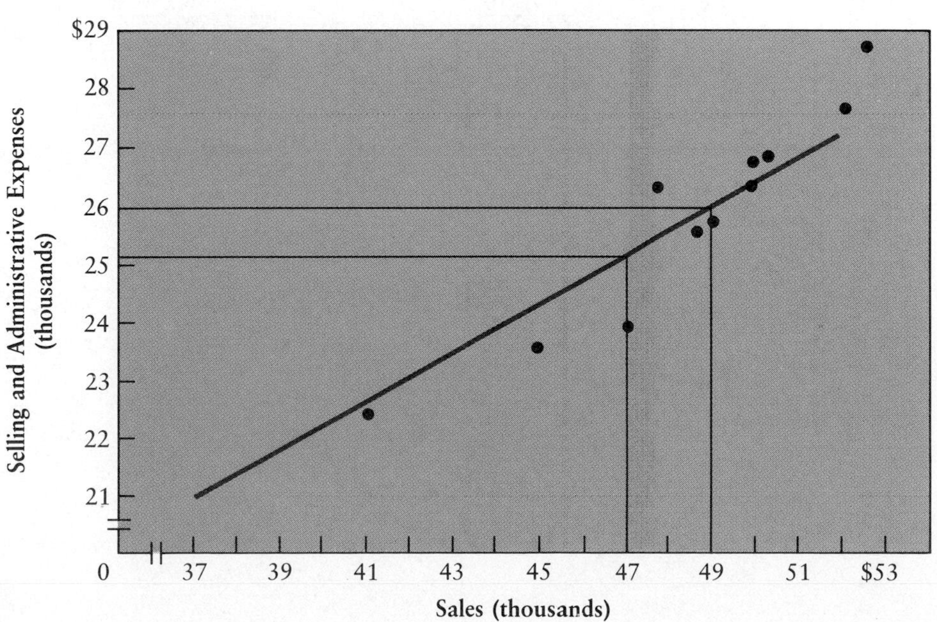

$$\text{Variable cost} = \frac{\$26.00 - \$25.20}{\$49.00 - \$47.00}$$

$$= \frac{\$0.80}{\$2.00}$$

$$= \underline{\underline{\$0.40}} \text{ per sales dollar}$$

$$\text{Fixed cost} = \$25{,}200 - \$0.40 \times \$47{,}000$$

$$= \$25{,}200 - \$18{,}800$$

$$= \underline{\underline{\$6{,}400}} \text{ per month}$$

3. Regression analysis

Months	Sales dollars (*X*)	S&A expenses (*Y*)	X^2	*XY*
January	$ 35,000	$ 20,500	$ 1,225,000,000	$ 717,500,000
February	41,000	22,600	1,681,000,000	926,600,000
March	49,000	25,800	2,401,000,000	1,264,200,000
April	50,100	26,800	2,510,010,000	1,342,680,000
May	50,500	26,900	2,550,250,000	1,358,450,000
June	48,700	25,600	2,371,690,000	1,246,720,000
July	45,000	23,700	2,025,000,000	1,066,500,000
August	47,900	26,300	2,294,410,000	1,259,770,000
September	46,900	23,900	2,199,610,000	1,120,910,000
October	50,000	26,400	2,500,000,000	1,320,000,000
November	52,000	27,500	2,704,000,000	1,430,000,000
December	52,500	28,800	2,756,250,000	1,512,000,000
Total	$568,600	$304,800	$27,218,220,000	$14,565,330,000

$$b = \frac{n\Sigma(XY) - \Sigma X \Sigma Y}{n\Sigma X^2 - (\Sigma X)^2}$$

$$= \frac{12(\$14{,}565{,}330{,}000) - (\$568{,}600)(\$304{,}800)}{12(\$27{,}218{,}220{,}000) - (\$568{,}600)^2}$$

$$b = \underline{\underline{\$0.44516}} \text{ per sales dollar}$$

$$a = \frac{\Sigma Y - b\Sigma X}{n}$$

$$= \frac{\$304{,}800 - \$0.44516(568{,}600)}{12}$$

$$= \frac{\$51{,}682}{12}$$

$$a = \underline{\underline{\$4{,}307}} \text{ per month}$$

Chapter Assignments

Questions

1. (L.O. 1) Define a fixed cost, variable cost, mixed cost, and step cost. Give examples of each.
2. (L.O. 2) "Depreciation is a fixed cost." What qualifications should be attached to this statement? Why?
3. (L.O. 1) What happens to variable costs per unit and fixed costs per unit as volume increases?
4. (L.O. 3) "Discretionary fixed costs are nothing but variable costs." Is this statement true? Give the reasons for your answer.
5. (L.O. 3) What is the difference between committed fixed costs and discretionary fixed costs?
6. (L.O. 4) Describe the process of estimating direct labor costs using time and motion studies.
7. (L.O. 4) What are the drawbacks of using historical data to estimate future costs? What precautions must be taken when using this approach?
8. (L.O. 5, 6) Compare the graphic approach to estimating costs with the high-low approach. What are the advantages and disadvantages of each?
9. (L.O. 7) Why is regression analysis superior to the graphic and high-low methods of estimating costs?
10. (L.O. 8) How would you compute operating income using the contribution approach? What information does the contribution approach provide, and how is it useful to managers?
11. (L.O. 7) What is multiple regression analysis? How does it differ from simple regression analysis?
12. (L.O. 4) In selecting a cost driver for estimating costs, what criteria should the accountant use?
13. (L.O. 4) Why is the engineering approach to estimating costs generally not useful when analyzing indirect costs?
14. (L.O. 8) What is the major difference between a functional income statement and a contribution income statement? Explain.

Exercises

15. (**L.O. 1**) The following costs were incurred by Wood Manufacturing Company.

a. Sales representatives' salaries (annual wages and commissions)
b. Factory wages, direct labor
c. Advertising expenses based on sales volume
d. Depreciation, straight line
e. Direct materials
f. Management salaries
g. Wood in a furniture factory
h. Carpenters' wages
i. Glue used to produce furniture
j. Rent, production facilities
k. Insurance premium, factory
l. Electricity, factory

Required Classify the above costs as fixed, variable, or mixed. (see Review Exercise 3–1)

16. (**L.O. 1**) The following costs are from the XYZ Company:

a. Depreciation, straight line
b. Salary, company president
c. Electricity and lighting for manufacturing activity during June
d. Telephone bills with minimum monthly charge
e. Expenses for car fuel

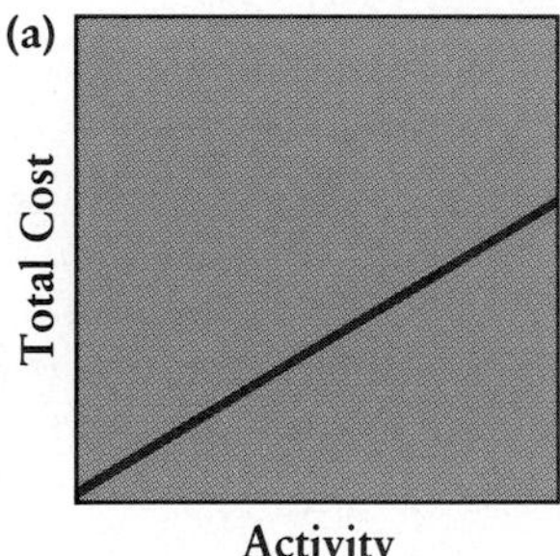

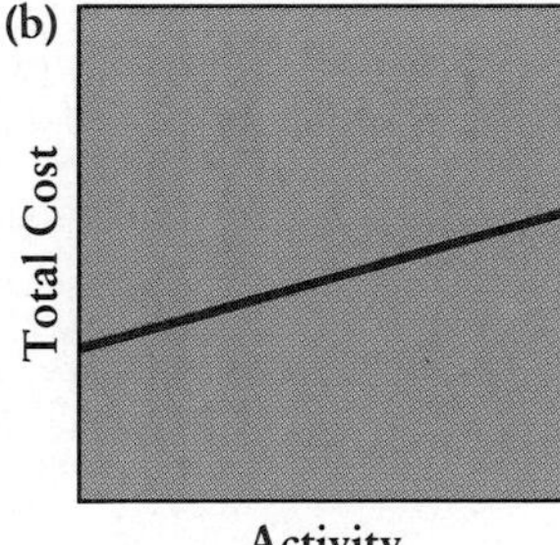

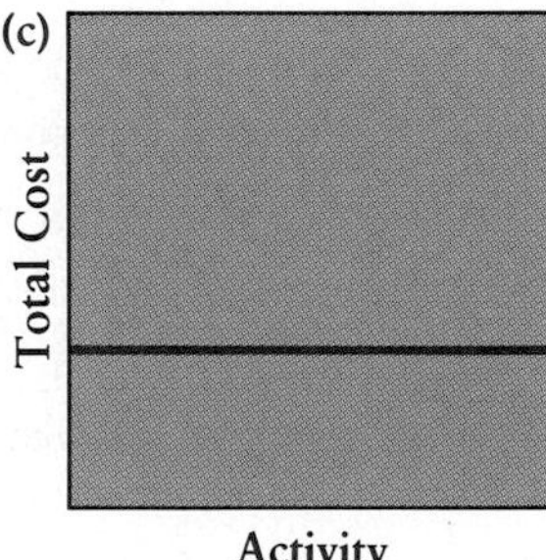

Required Identify the costs with the above graphs.

17. (**L.O. 6**) Maryville Corporation has collected the following data on the cost of electricity used and direct labor hours worked for the past six months:

Month	Cost of electricity	Direct labor hours
July	$15,600	3,000
August	13,400	2,050
September	16,900	2,800
October	19,800	3,650
November	17,300	2,620
December	18,200	2,590

Required Using the high-low method, calculate fixed and variable costs. (see Review Exercise 3–3)

18. (L.O. 5) Konstance Company has collected the following data from their manufacturing operations over the past eight months:

Period	Units	Total costs
1	2,200	$10,500
2	3,100	12,750
3	5,600	18,500
4	1,700	9,250
5	6,300	20,750
6	8,100	25,250
7	5,050	17,625
8	3,000	12,500

Required Using the graphic approach, find the fixed cost and variable cost in the above data. (see Review Exercise 3–2)

19. (L.O. 8) ABC Company manufactured and sold 12,000 units during 19xx. There were no inventories at the beginning or end of the year. Selected cost data are as follows:

Direct Materials	$12 per unit
Direct Labor	$3 per unit
Selling Price	$25 per unit
Fixed Factory Expenses	$12,000 per year
Fixed Administrative Expenses	$1,000 per month
Variable Administrative Expenses	$500 per 100 units
Fixed Selling Expenses	$5,000 per year
Variable Selling Expenses	$1,000 per 1,000 units sold

Required Prepare a contribution margin income statement. (see Review Exercise 3–4)

20. (L.O. 6) Eberly Retail Company incurred the following selling and administrative expenses and revenues during the last six months of 19xx:

Month	S&A Expenses	Sales revenues
July	$ 90,000	$170,000
August	120,000	220,000
September	130,000	250,000
October	100,000	186,000
November	95,000	176,000
December	110,000	190,000

Required

1. Using the high-low approach, calculate the fixed and variable costs.
2. Using the graphic approach, calculate the fixed and variable costs.
3. If the estimated sales for the month of January are $190,000, what are the expected selling and administrative expenses?

(see Review Exercise 3–2)

21. (L.O. 6) The number of rolls of film developed and related costs over the last nine months for the Scholes Film Developing Company are as follows:

Month	Number of rolls developed	Development cost
January	5,000	$28,000
February	7,500	30,000
March	6,525	28,700
April	4,500	26,000
May	5,025	28,000
June	7,500	29,000
July	8,000	31,000
August	6,500	26,500
September	4,000	25,000

Required

1. Using the high-low method, determine the formula for film developing costs.
2. What developing cost would you expect to be incurred during a month in which 5,500 rolls of film were developed?

22. (L.O. 1) The following costs were incurred by Kaufman Corporation:
    a. Marketing Costs (based on sales volume)
    b. Factory Production Line Wages, Direct Labor
    c. Depreciation
    d. Direct Materials
    e. Managerial Salaries
    f. Nails Used in Production
    g. Insurance expense, Factory
    h. Rent, Factory
    i. Utilities, Factory
    j. Sales Salaries (annual wages + commissions)

Required Classify the above costs as fixed, variable, or mixed. (see Review Exercise 3–1)

23. (L.O. 6) Garry's Delivery Express monitored delivery information over a two-year period and determined that if a delivery vehicle was driven 150,000 miles during a year, the operating cost was 10.5 cents per mile. If a truck was driven only 125,000 miles during a year, the operating cost increased to 12 cents per mile.

Required

1. Using the high-low method, determine the variable and fixed cost elements of the annual cost of truck operations.
2. Express the expected cost in the form of $Y = a + bX$.
3. If a delivery vehicle were driven 130,000 miles during a year, what total cost would you estimate?

(see Review Exercise 3–3)

24. (L.O. 6) Sanger Retail Company incurred the following selling and administrative expenses and revenues during the last six months of 19x9:

Month	S&A expenses	Sales revenues
July	$45,000	$ 85,000
August	60,000	110,000
September	65,000	125,000
October	50,000	93,000
November	48,000	88,000
December	55,000	95,000

Required

1. Using the high-low approach, calculate the fixed and variable costs.
2. Using the graphic approach, calculate fixed and variable costs.

25. (L.O. 5, 6) Boston Company has collected the following data concerning materials-handling costs for the past six months:

Period	Materials-handling costs	Direct labor hours
1	$4,180	1,510
2	4,500	1,750
3	3,480	1,450
4	4,000	1,500
5	4,600	1,850
6	4,800	1,800

Required

1. Plot the data on materials-handling costs onto a graph, showing the costs as a function of direct labor hours.
2. Visually draw a line through the data and compute the fixed and variable components of the cost.
3. Use the high-low method to compute the fixed and variable components of the cost.

Problems

26. (L.O. 5, 6, 7) XYZ Company sells computers. Sales representatives, who are paid a fixed salary plus commissions, are responsible for 95 percent of company sales. Data on units sold and compensation for six months are shown below.

	Units sold	Compensation
January	500	$2,825
February	700	2,955
March	600	2,760
April	300	2,695
May	1,000	3,150
June	600	2,890

Required

Using the graphic approach, the high-low approach, and the regression analysis approach, compute the fixed and variable costs in the compensation.

27. (L.O. 5) The following data was obtained from the Barrett Manufacturing Corporation. The data relates to the cost of operating one of the corporations processing facilities at various levels of production.

Month	Units produced	Total costs	Month	Units produced	Total costs
January	6,000	$14,500	July	9,000	17,000
February	8,000	15,000	August	7,000	15,500
March	7,000	15,000	September	6,000	16,000
April	4,000	13,000	October	5,000	15,000
May	5,000	14,000	November	3,000	12,000
June	6,500	14,500			

Required

1. Prepare a scattergraph by plotting the above data on a graph. Plot cost on the vertical axis and activity on the horizontal axis. Fit a regression line to the plotted points by visual inspection.
2. Calculate the expected cost at 6,000 units of production.

28. (L.O. 8) Mandel Manufacturing produced and sold 150,000 units during 19xx. There were no inventories at the beginning or end of the year. At December 31, 19xx, the books reflected the following costs:

Direct labor	\$ 5.00/unit
Direct materials	10.00/unit
Variable expenses	
Selling	10.00/unit
Administrative	1.00/unit
Fixed expenses	
Factory	\$250,000 per year
Selling	150,000 per year
Administrative	10,000 per month
Selling price	\$50.00/unit

Required Prepare a contribution margin income statement for the period ended December 31, 19xx.

29. (L.O. 8) Boner Company plans to sell 100,000 record albums at \$12 each. Fixed costs are \$280,000.

Required At what level must Boner keep total variable costs in order to realize a \$200,000 operating income? Hint: Prepare an income statement using the contribution margin format and fill in variable costs as the last item.

30. (L.O. 8) The following information is available for Keller Corporation's new product line for the year 19x8:

Selling price per unit	\$ 15
Variable manufacturing costs per unit of production	8
Total annual fixed manufacturing costs	25,000
Variable administrative costs per unit of sales	3
Total annual fixed selling and administrative expenses	15,000

There were no inventories at the beginning of the year. During the year, 12,500 units were produced and sold.

Required Prepare income statements, using the functional and contribution formats. (see Review Exercise 3–4) (AICPA adapted)

31. (L.O. 8) SWB Advertising Agency has presented you with the following information for 19x7:

Sales revenue	\$3,000,000
Sales commissions	1,000,000
Supplies for preparing artwork	500,000
Rent, office, space	250,000
Salaries, office staff	500,000
Office supplies	80,000

Required Prepare an income statement using the contribution margin format.

32. (L.O. 7) Dailey Corporation has collected the following data:

Month	Units produced	Manufacturing costs
July	800	$10,195
August	600	10,216
September	300	10,157
October	200	10,138
November	1,000	10,290

Required Using regression analysis, determine the fixed and the variable cost elements of the manufacturing costs.

33. (L.O. 6) Rich Company has presented you with the following data:

Year	Units	Total costs
19x1	3,000	$ 6,000
19x2	5,000	8,000
19x3	6,000	7,500
19x4	7,000	10,000
19x5	6,000	9,200
19x6	6,500	?

Required Using the high-low and the graphic approaches, estimate total manufacturing costs for 19x6.

34. (L.O. 8) Singer Company produced and sold 20,000 units during the year 19x8. There was no beginning finished goods inventory, and the company maintains no direct materials inventory.

Selling price per unit	$20
Direct materials per unit	3
Direct labor per unit	5
Total fixed manufacturing costs for the period	$40,000
Administrative expense	15,000 + $0.30 (units sold)
Selling expense	24,000 + $1.00 (units sold)

Required Prepare an income statement using (a) the contribution format and (b) the functional format. (see Review Exercise 3–4)

35. (L.O. 8) Grady Company began operations on January 1. The single product it produces sells for $10 per unit. During the year, 100,000 units were produced and sold. Manufacturing costs and selling and administrative expenses for the year were as follows:

	Fixed costs	Variable costs
Direct materials	$ –0–	$2.00 per unit produced
Direct labor	–0–	1.25 per unit produced
Manufacturing overhead	120,000	0.75 per unit produced
Sales and administration	70,000	1.00 per unit sold

Required Prepare income statements using the functional and contribution formats.

36. (L.O. 5) CPB Company incurred the following manufacturing overhead costs during the past four months.

Month	Direct labor hours	Manufacturing overhead costs
April	2,000	$20,000
May	2,500	22,500
June	4,000	30,000
July	3,500	27,500

Required

1. Using the graphic method, calculate the fixed and variable costs per direct labor hour.
2. If the company expects to work 3,000 direct labor hours in August, what are the estimated total manufacturing overhead costs?

37. (L.O. 8) Costable Manufacturing Company manufactures and sells champagne glasses. The relevant range for manufacturing normally is within 500,000 to 1,000,000 units produced and sold per year. A partially completed schedule of the company's total and per unit costs over this range is given below.

	Units produced and sold		
	500,000	800,000	1,000,000
Total variable costs	$200,000	?	?
Total fixed costs	350,000	?	?
Total costs	$550,000	?	?
Cost per unit			
Variable costs	?	?	?
Fixed costs	?	?	?
Total costs per unit	?	?	?

Required

1. Complete the schedule of the company's total and unit costs.
2. Assume the company produces 800,000 units during the year. The selling price per unit is $0.95. Prepare an income statement in the contribution format for the year.

38. (L.O. 6, 8) The books of Howard Manufacturing Company, producers of hand-held calculators, reflected the following revenues and expenses for various dates during the year ended June 30, 19xx.

	August	December	May
Sales in units	10,000	15,000	12,000
Sales revenues	$100,000	$150,000	$120,000
Cost of goods sold	(20,000)	(30,000)	(24,000)
Gross margin	$ 80,000	$120,000	$ 96,000
Operating expenses			
Advertising	(15,000)	(15,000)	(15,000)
Commission salaries	(30,000)	(45,000)	(36,000)
Selling expenses	(6,000)	(7,500)	(6,600)
Operating income	$ 29,000	$ 52,500	$ 38,400

Required

1. Identify the above expenses as either variable, fixed, or mixed.
2. Separate each mixed expense into variable and fixed expense by using the high-low methods. State the cost formula for each mixed expense.
3. Prepare a contribution income statement using the data for the month of December.

39. (L.O. 6) Newland, Inc., of London, England, producers of computer keyboards and accounting books, reflected the following information at December 31, 19x1, 19x2.

	12/31/x1	12/31/x2
Production	50,000 units	100,000 units
Cost of goods manufactured	£800,000	£1,570,000
Work in process inventory, beginning	£20,000	£40,000
Work in process inventory, ending	£10,000	£30,000
Direct materials inventory, per unit	£5	£5
Direct labor, per unit	£10	£10
Manufacturing overhead, Total	?	?

Manufacturing overhead consists of both variable and fixed cost elements. Management wants to determine the overhead breakdown between variable and fixed cost per year.

Required

1. For both years, determine total manufacturing overhead costs. (Hint: Use a cost of goods manufacturing schedule.)
2. Determine the cost formula for manufacturing overhead by means of the high-low method of cost analysis. Express the variable portion in terms of variable cost per unit of production.
3. If 80,000 units are produced during a period, what would be the total manufacturing cost?

40. (L.O. 6) Nathan Company's sales volume and expenses for the past six months were as follows:

Month	Selling expense	Sales dollars
January	$ 876	$4,400
February	1,112	6,123
March	1,100	5,284
April	1,200	6,500
May	1,300	6,700
June	870	4,300

Ms. Nathan wants to know what selling expenses will be for the next six months.

Required

1. Using the high-low method, determine a formula for a line so selling expenses can be forecasted.

2. Use the formula from *1* above to forecast selling expenses for each of the next six months. Assume sales forecasts are as follows:

July	$7,200	October	$6,300
August	6,500	November	7,500
September	8,100	December	7,300

3. What should be your main concern about the forecast you made in 2 above for September? Should you have similar concerns about other months?

41. (L.O. 5, 6) Barby Company has selected the following information from their accounting records:

Month	Labor hours	Overhead costs
January	6,000	$1,800
February	4,800	1,630
March	7,080	1,750
April	8,000	1,900
May	4,000	1,400
June	6,070	1,690
July	6,050	1,710
August	6,200	1,740
September	8,100	1,960
October	10,100	2,200
November	13,000	3,200
December	12,900	2,800

Required

1. Using the high-low method, estimate a cost function for the overhead cost.
2. Plot the data and visually draw a line through the data. Calculate the cost functions for the overhead cost.
3. Evaluate the function computed in *1* above when compared with the results of *2* above.

42. (L.O. 7) Labor hours and production costs for the past four months of 19x9 are shown below. You believe these costs are representative for the year.

Month	Labor hours (*X*)	Total production costs (*Y*)
September	2,500	$ 20,000
October	3,500	25,000
November	4,500	30,000
December	3,500	25,000
Total	14,000	$100,000

$\Sigma XY = \$360{,}000{,}000$

$\Sigma X \Sigma Y = \$1{,}400{,}000{,}000$

$\Sigma X^2 = 51{,}000{,}000$

$(\Sigma X)^2 = 196{,}000{,}000$

Required Based on the above information, select or provide the best answer to the following questions:

1. The equation(s) required to compute fixed and variable production costs are
   a. $\Sigma XY = a\Sigma X + b\Sigma X^2$
   b. $\Sigma Y = an + b\Sigma X$
   c. $Y = a + bX^2$ and $\Sigma Y = an + b\Sigma X^2$
   d. $\Sigma XY = a\Sigma X + b\Sigma X^2$ and $\Sigma Y = an + b\Sigma X$

2. Monthly production costs could be expressed as
   a. $Y = aX + b$
   b. $Y = a + bX$
   c. $Y = b + aX$
   d. $Y = \Sigma a + bX$

3. Using the least squares method, the variable production cost per labor hour is
   a. $6
   b. $5
   c. $3
   d. $2

4. Using the least squares method, the fixed monthly production cost is
   a. $10,000
   b. $9,500
   c. $7,500
   d. $5,000

(AICPA adapted)

43. (L.O. 8) Alpha Company plans to introduce a new product, which it will sell for $6 a unit. The following estimates cover the manufacturing costs for producing 100,000 units in the first year:

Direct materials	$50,000
Direct labor	40,000
Labor rate, $4 per hour	

Overhead costs for the new product have not been estimated yet. Monthly data on total production and overhead costs for the past 24 months have been analyzed, however, using simple regression analysis. The following results, derived from that analysis, will provide the basis for estimating overhead costs in the new product:

	Computed values: manufacturing overhead cost estimates
Fixed cost	$40,000 per month
Variable cost	$2.10 per direct labor hour

Required

1. Calculate total overhead costs for an estimated activity level of 20,000 direct labor hours.
2. Calculate the total expected contribution margin to be earned during the first year if 100,000 units of the new product are sold.

3. Calculate the expected per unit contribution margin during the first year if the 100,000 units of new product are sold. (CMA)

Case 1

Ramon Co. (L.O. 6, 7)

The Ramon Co. manufactures a wide range of products at several different plant locations. The Franklin Plant, which manufactures electrical components, has been experiencing some difficulties with fluctuating monthly overhead costs. The fluctuations have made it difficult to estimate the level of overhead that will be incurred for any one month.

Management wants to be able to estimate overhead costs accurately in order to plan its operation and financial needs better. A trade association publication to which Ramon Co. subscribes indicates that for companies manufacturing electrical components, overhead tends to vary with direct labor hours.

One member of the accounting staff has proposed that the cost behavior pattern of the overhead costs be determined. Then overhead costs could be predicted from the budgeted direct labor hours.

Another member of the accounting staff suggested that a good starting place for determining the cost behavior pattern of overhead costs would be an analysis of historical data. The historical cost behavior pattern would provide a basis for estimating future overhead costs. The methods proposed for determining the cost behavior pattern included the high-low method, the scattergraph method, simple linear regression, multiple regression, and exponential smoothing. Of these methods Ramon Co. decided to employ the high-low method, the scattergraph method, and simple linear regression. Data on direct labor hours and the respective overhead costs incurred were collected for the past two years. The raw data are as follows:

19x1	Direct labor hours	Overhead costs
January	20,000	$84,000
February	25,000	99,000
March	22,000	89,500
April	23,000	90,000
May	20,000	81,500
June	19,000	75,500
July	14,000	70,500
August	10,000	64,500
September	12,000	69,000
October	17,000	75,000
November	16,000	71,500
December	19,000	78,000

19x2		
January	21,000	86,000
February	24,000	93,000
March	23,000	93,000
April	22,000	87,000
May	20,000	80,000
June	18,000	76,500
July	12,000	67,500
August	13,000	71,000
September	15,000	73,500
October	17,000	72,500
November	15,000	71,000
December	18,000	75,000

Using linear regression, the following data were obtained.

Fixed cost = $39,859 per month
Variable cost = 2.1549 per direct labor hour

Required

1. Using the high-low method, determine the cost behavior pattern of the overhead costs for the Franklin Plant.
2. Using the results of the regression analysis, calculate the estimate of overhead costs for 22,500 direct labor hours.
3. Of the three proposed methods, (high-low, scattergraph, linear regression), which one should Ramon Co. employ to determine the historical cost behavior pattern of Franklin Plant's overhead costs? Explain your answer completely, indicating the reasons why the other methods should not be used.

(CMA)

■

Case 2

Alma Plant (L.O. 3, 7)

The Alma Plant manufactures the industrial product line of CJS Industries. Plant management wants to be able to get a good, yet quick, estimate of the manufacturing overhead costs which can be expected to be incurred each month. The easiest and simplest method to accomplish this task appears to be to develop a cost equation for the manufacturing overhead costs.

The plant's accounting staff suggested that simple linear regression be used to determine the cost behavior pattern of the overhead costs. The regression data relating overhead cost to direct labor hours can provide the basis for the cost equation. Sufficient evidence is available to conclude that manufacturing overhead costs vary with direct labor hours. The actual direct labor hours and the corresponding manufacturing overhead costs for each month of the last three years were used in the linear regression analysis.

The three-year period contained various occurrences not uncommon to many businesses. During the first year, production was severely curtailed during two months due to wildcat strikes. In the second year, production was reduced in one month because of material shortages and materially increased (overtime scheduled) during two months to meet the units required for a one-time sales order. At the end of the second year, employee benefits were raised significantly as the result of a labor agreement. Production during the third year was not affected by any special circumstances.

Various members of Alma's accounting staff raised some issues regarding the historical data collected for the regression analysis. These issues were as follows.

a. Some members of the accounting staff believed that the use of data from all 36 months would provide a more accurate portrayal of the cost behavior. While they recognized that any of the monthly data could include efficiencies and inefficiencies, they believed these efficiencies/inefficiencies would tend to balance out over a longer period of time.

b. Other members of the accounting staff suggested that only those months which were considered normal should be used so that the regression would not be distorted.

c. Still other members felt that only the most recent 12 months should be used because they were the most current.

d. Some members questioned whether historical data should be used at all to form the basis for a flexible budget formula.

The accounting department ran two regression analyses of the data—one using the data from all 36 months and the other using only the data from the last 12 months. The information derived from the two linear regressions is shown below.

Least Squares Regression Analyses

	Data from all 36 months	**Data from most recent 12 months**
Fixed cost	\$123,810	\$109,020
Variable cost per direct labor hour	\$1.6003	\$4.1977

Required

1. From the results of Alma Plant's regression analysis which used the data from the most recent 12 months:

a. Formulate the cost equation that can be employed to estimate monthly manufacturing overhead costs.

   b. Calculate the estimate of overhead costs for a month when 25,000 direct labor hours are worked.

2. How would the four specific issues raised by the members of Alma's accounting staff influence your willingness to use the results of the statistical analyses as the basis for the flexible budget formula? Explain your answer.

(CMA)

■

Part 2

Cost Accounting Systems

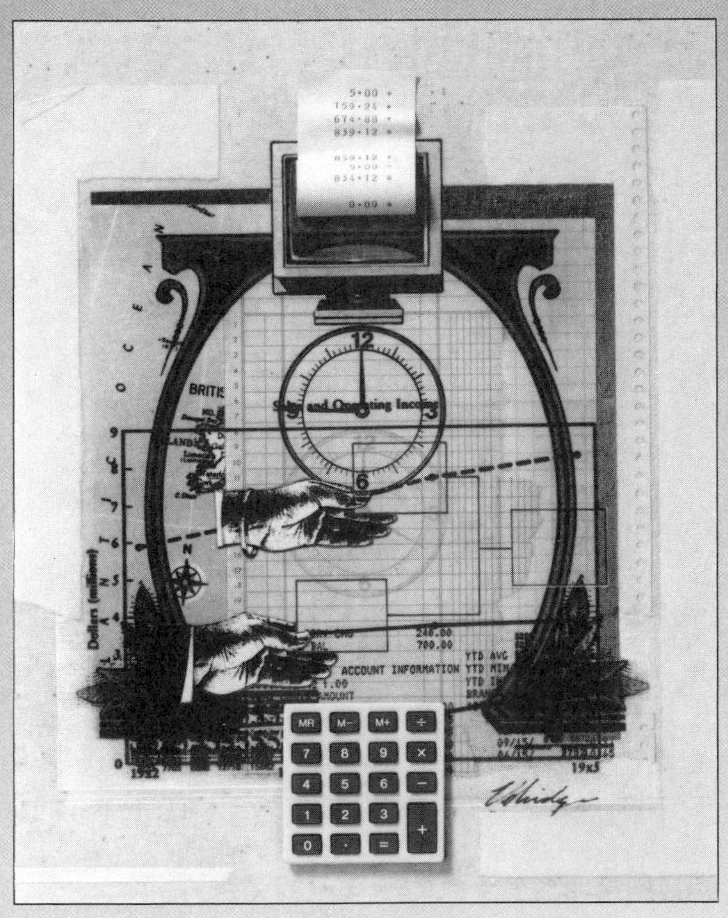

Part 2 describes two different methods of accounting for production costs, job order costing and process costing. It discusses the methods used to calculate production costs and journal entries used to record those costs.

■

Chapter 4, Job Order Costing, explains how costs are accounted for in a batch production system. Since each job, or batch, is distinct from other jobs and has a definite beginning and end, direct material and direct labor costs can be traced to individual jobs. Manufacturing overhead costs are divided among jobs using a ratio called the predetermined overhead rate. Once the job is complete, the cost for units in the job is found by dividing the total costs for the job by the number of units in the job.

■

Chapter 5, Process Costing, describes the method used to account for the cost of goods produced on a continuous, production-line basis. Since there are no distinct jobs in this type of production, costs are accounted for by activity, on a monthly basis. At month end, the cost of units processed in an activity is found by dividing total costs for the activity by the number of units processed by the activity during the month.

■

4

Job Order Costing

LEARNING OBJECTIVES

After studying this chapter you should be able to:

1. Explain the difference between job order and process costing
2. Complete a job cost sheet and calculate the average cost per unit of a job
3. Record the purchase and issue of materials with journal entries
4. Record labor costs with journal entries
5. Calculate a predetermined overhead rate and use it to assign overhead costs to a job
6. Record applied manufacturing overhead costs with journal entries
7. Record actual manufacturing overhead costs with journal entries
8. Compute over- and underapplied overhead
9. Calculate cost of goods manufactured and cost of goods sold

"What does it cost?" That is one of the most frequently asked questions in business. The cost of production is of particular concern to managers, for it determines whether a product or service will be profitable. Following are some illustrations of business activities where the cost of a product or service will influence a decision.

- Dynan Corporation's product is custom-made electrical generators for use in boats, campers, at remote construction sites, and as standby systems in hospitals. The company offers several basic models, including gasoline, natural-gas, and diesel-powered units, in various sizes. Customers may also choose from various control systems. In fact, each year Dynan produces thousands of generators made to customers' specifications. The company's distributors must be able to quote a price on any generator and compare it with others. How much more does a diesel-fueled generator cost than a natural gas-fueled generator? What does a 100-kilowatt generator cost versus a 1,000-kilowatt generator? What is the cost of a control system that automatically switches the system on if power fails?
- The manager of an advertising agency wants to know the cost of providing various services to clients. The amount of money a client pays depends on the amount of advertising bought. A client is profitable if revenues from the client are greater than the cost of serving the client. Which clients are most profitable for the agency? Why? Is the agency losing money on some of its clients?
- A consulting firm bills some clients at an hourly rate, which is intended to cover the cost of the service and provide a profit. Does the hourly rate actually achieve these objectives? Or are some of the firm's services unprofitable?
- A bank offers checking and savings accounts, loans, credit investigations, safe-deposit boxes, and various other services to customers. Different customers use different combinations of services. Are all combinations profitable for the bank, or are some combinations unprofitable?
- A home construction firm prepares fixed-price estimates for potential customers. The managers of the firm want to know the cost of building similar models in the past, since those costs can serve as a basis for other estimates.

In all these situations, managers need information on the cost of producing a job or service. To fulfill that need, they require a cost accounting system designed for the products and services they offer and the production methods they used. How such a system is designed and used is the subject of this chapter.

■

Designing a Cost Accounting System

In designing any cost accounting system, accountants are required to make four decisions:

1. Will the system use historical costs or standard costs? **Historical costs** are actual costs incurred in the past. **Standard costs** are estimates of what unit costs should be, based on past costs and engineering estimates. The system described in this chapter uses historical costs. Standard costs are discussed in Chapters 10 and 11.

2. Will the system be a job order or a process cost accounting system? The answer to this question depends on whether the product is produced in distinct batches or in a continuous process. This chapter describes a job order cost accounting system used for batch production. Process cost accounting is described in Chapter 5.
3. Will the system be based on full absorption or direct costing of inventory? The choice will determine whether fixed manufacturing overhead is included in the unit cost of inventory. **Full absorption costing** includes fixed manufacturing overhead whereas direct costing treats fixed manufacturing overhead as a period cost rather than an inventory cost. In this chapter a full absorption costing system is described. Direct costing is discussed in Chapter 9.
4. What system will be used to assign overhead costs to products? Will the company use plantwide or activity-based predetermined overhead rates? What and how many cost drivers should be used? This chapter describes plantwide overhead rates and cost driver selection. Activity-based overhead rates are discussed in Chapter 16.

Cost accounting systems can vary greatly depending on these decisions. For example, a standard process costing system might be based on full absorption costing and a plantwide overhead rate. A standard job order costing system might be based on direct costing and a departmental overhead rate. Some combinations are more common than others. But to completely describe a cost accounting system, all four decisions must be made.

■

Choosing Between Job Order and Process Costing

OBJECTIVE 1
Explain the difference between job order and process costing

Products are produced either in batches or in a continuous process. Although some departments in an organization may produce in batches and others continuously, the production method of a single department does not vary. Since costs are normally accounted for at the departmental level, a choice is made between job order and process costing when designing a cost accounting system.

Job Order Costing

A **job order cost accounting system** is used to assign costs to a product or service produced in distinct batches. A **job** or batch, has two important characteristics:

1. A definite starting and completion point
2. Distinct separation from other batches, so the direct materials and labor used in one batch can be distinguished from those used in others

The first characteristic is important because the cost of a job cannot be calculated without definite starting and completion points. The second characteristic is important because materials and labor must be identified with particular jobs. Otherwise, the cost of each job cannot be calculated.

In all the examples listed in the opening of this chapter, the products being produced are made in distinct batches. Dynan Corporation, for example, makes its generators in batches of one, each produced according to customer specifications. If a customer occasionally orders more than one generator, a batch might then consist of three or four identical units.

Other types of companies make products in larger batches. Cloth is woven from a certain color thread into a particular pattern and size. A batch of cloth might consist of 500 bolts of one pattern and weave. Wood products, such as picnic tables and boat docks, might be manufactured in batches of a thousand each. The number of units in each batch is unimportant. What is important is that they are produced in batches, each with a clear starting and completion point. Job order is also appropriate when a company waits to produce until after orders have been received from customers.

Organizations that produce services may also use job order costing. In advertising agencies and consulting firms, a batch is a particular service provided to a particular customer. An advertising campaign for a product or installation of a client's new data processing system are both batch jobs for accounting purposes.

Process Costing

A **process cost accounting system** assigns costs to large quantities of identical products produced more or less continuously. Recording the quantities of material and labor used for each order is impractical when large numbers of units are produced. And because the units are identical, there is no reason to cost each unit separately. All units produced in a given period, usually monthly, are assumed to have the same cost. Process costing is the topic of Chapter 5.

Process costing is appropriate for companies that mass-produce products. Imagine a production line in which toasters are produced continuously in large quantities. Some have fancier trim than others; some operate on 220 rather than 110 volts. Still they are enough alike that management has safely assumed that all units produced in the same month have the same cost. This concept is important. The products need not be completely identical for the purposes of process costing. All that is required is that the units be similar enough for management to assume they have the same cost.

When the differences between similar products become so great that management needs to distinguish between their costs, a job order costing system must be used. If a company produces standard toasters on an assembly line for three weeks, then switches to producing toaster ovens, it must use job order costing for both products. Toaster ovens require different components from toasters, and the assembly process is more complex. Thus, management would not want to assume that toasters and toaster ovens cost the same to produce. Although both are produced on an assembly line, they are still produced in batches. All toasters produced without interruption of the assembly line are regarded as one batch. The toaster ovens produced next are considered another batch. Were the firm to set up a second production line and produce both toasters and toaster ovens continuously throughout the year, separate process costing systems could then be used for each production line.

The rest of this chapter is devoted to job order costing. The illustrations show how to calculate the cost of a product. The same steps may be used to calculate the cost of services, even though journal entries differ from those made for products.

■

Calculating the Average Cost per Unit

Managers must know the cost of producing various products or services to determine which are profitable. They must also know a product's **average cost per unit** in order to report the inventory cost on the firm's balance sheet. Generally accepted accounting principles require that inventories be reported at cost.[1]

In a merchandising organization, inventory cost is easy to determine. It is the purchase price adjusted for freight costs and quantity discounts. In a manufacturing organization, determining the cost of inventory is more complicated. Products are not purchased ready-made. Instead, materials are bought and direct labor, manufacturing equipment, and other resources are used to produce finished products. The total cost of the finished product is a combination of direct materials, direct labor, and manufacturing overhead costs.

OBJECTIVE 2
Complete a job cost sheet and calculate the average cost per unit of a job

To calculate the average cost per unit, the total manufacturing cost of a job is divided by the number of units produced. Although the formula is simple, the accuracy of the answer depends on whether all costs have been carefully accounted for. Since most organizations produce many products, all costs of production must be correctly charged to the units produced. That is why the concept of a batch or job is so useful.

In a job order cost accounting system, care is taken to accurately record the quantities of direct materials and direct labor used on each job. Then the accountant **allocates** or **applies** a portion of manufacturing overhead costs to the job. That is to say, manufacturing overhead costs are divided among all jobs for the period. The average cost per unit is found by dividing the total cost of the job (direct materials, direct labor, and applied manufacturing overhead costs) by the number of good finished units produced in that job, as shown below.

$$\text{Average cost per unit} = \frac{\text{total manufacturing cost of job}}{\text{total number of good finished units in job}}$$

[1]When obsolescence, physical deterioration, or changes in supply or demand lower the market value of inventory below cost, inventory will be reported at market value. But even in this case, management needs to know the cost to apply the lower-of-cost-or-market rule.

Figure 4–1
Job Cost Sheet for Woodland Products Company
A job cost sheet is used to record the cost of producing each job. Once the job has been completed and all costs entered, the cost per unit is calculated, as shown in the lower right corner. A separate job cost sheet is maintained for each job.

Customer or department ordering ____________ Job number ____________
Date ordered ____________
Date started ____________ Product ____________
Date completed ____________ Number of units ____________

Direct Materials

Date	Department	Requisition Number	Total Cost

Direct Labor

Date	Department	Timecard Number	Total Cost

Applied Overhead

Date	Department	Base of Application	Units of Base	Rate	Total Cost

Total Manufacturing Cost ____________
Units Produced ____________
Unit Cost ____________

The total manufacturing cost is obtained from the **job cost sheet**, a document for recording all costs of a given job. Figure 4–1 shows a job cost sheet for Woodland Products Company. Notice the following features:

1. An identification section with space for the customer's name, the job number, the name of the product, and the number of units requested. The date of the order and the dates the product was started and completed are also recorded here.

2. A section for recording the cost of direct materials used.
3. A section for recording the cost of direct labor used.
4. A section for recording the amount of manufacturing overhead applied to the job.
5. A summary, showing total manufacturing costs, number of good units completed, and average cost per unit. The number of units requested and the number of good units completed may differ slightly. The company may have produced extra units to allow for spoilage that did not occur or it may have experienced abnormally high amounts of spoilage.

The next several sections will explain the sources of the cost information entered on the job cost sheet.

■

Accounting for Materials Costs

Purchase of Materials

OBJECTIVE 3
Record the purchase and issue of materials with journal entries

Purchasing materials is the first step in the production cycle. As an example, this section will use the Woodland Products Company, which makes picnic tables, boat-dock sections, and other outdoor products. Woodland records the purchase on account of both **direct materials** and **indirect materials** (production supplies and minor parts, such as nails and sandpaper) by increasing the Materials Inventory and Accounts Payable accounts. **Materials Inventory** is an asset account on the balance sheet. It shows the value of direct and indirect materials on hand for use in production. The journal entry for one such purchase is as follows:

	Debit	Credit
(1) Materials Inventory	17,800	
Accounts Payable		17,800
To record the purchase of 4,000 board feet of lumber from Forest Lumber Company		

Throughout the month, similar entries are made as additional materials and production supplies are purchased. When financial statements are prepared, the cost of unused materials is shown as an asset (Materials Inventory) on the company's balance sheet.

Journal entries are used both to update the Materials Inventory account and to fill in **materials stock cards**. Figure 4–2 shows a materials stock card. Notice that it contains three sections, one for the receipt of materials from the supplier, one for the issue of materials to production, and one for the balance of materials available for production.

A separate stock card is maintained on each type of material used. When the balances on all stock cards are totaled, they should equal the total in the Materials Inventory account.

Figure 4–2
Materials Stock Card for Woodland Products Company
The materials stock card shows the balance of units received and issued, which reflects the amount of material in inventory not yet put into production. A materials stock card is kept for each type of material.

Item Name **Item Number**

	Receipts				Issued				Balance		
Date	Invoice Number	Quantity	Unit Cost	Total	Requisition Number	Quantity	Unit Cost	Total	Quantity	Unit Cost	Balance

Issue of Materials

Accounting for the issue of materials is a complicated process. Assume, for example, that Woodland has received an order for 100 picnic-table kits from a large building supply company. Woodland produces these kits by cutting lumber to the appropriate size and packaging it with the bolts, nails, and other supplies needed for assembly. In the first step of the process, the production manager prepares **materials requisition forms** for each item needed to produce the tables. Figure 4–3 shows a materials requisition form for 155 feet, part of the lumber needed for the kits. Because the requisition was for direct materials, Woodland wrote a job number in the lower left corner. Had the requisition been for indirect materials, there would have been an Actual Manufacturing Overhead account number written in the lower left corner. No job number is written for indirect materials.

When production is about to start, the manager presents the forms at the storeroom to obtain the materials. Once the materials are issued, a copy of the materials requisition form is sent to the accounting department. Accountants use these forms in three ways:

- To record the issue of materials and reduce the balance on the materials stock card (Figure 4–2)
- To assign costs to specific jobs or to actual manufacturing overhead
- To make journal entries that record materials costs on a companywide basis

To accurately assign costs, an accountant must enter a job number or an Actual Manufacturing Overhead account number at the bottom of each materials requisition form. The job number is used to record the cost of direct materials in the direct materials section of the job cost sheet (Figure 4–1). In the case of

Figure 4–3

Materials Requisition for Woodland Products Company

The materials requisition form is a record of materials issued from the storeroom. It is used to charge the cost of direct materials to particular jobs and the cost of indirect materials to Actual Manufacturing Overhead

Date April 12, 19×1 Requisition number M 3401
Inventory item name 2×4 redwood Inventory item number L2410

Quantity	Unit Cost	Total Cost
1,200 feet	$10.33 per hundred feet	$ 124.00

Job number MP 135 Issued by Fred
Actual manufacturing overhead account number Received by Mike
Department Cutting

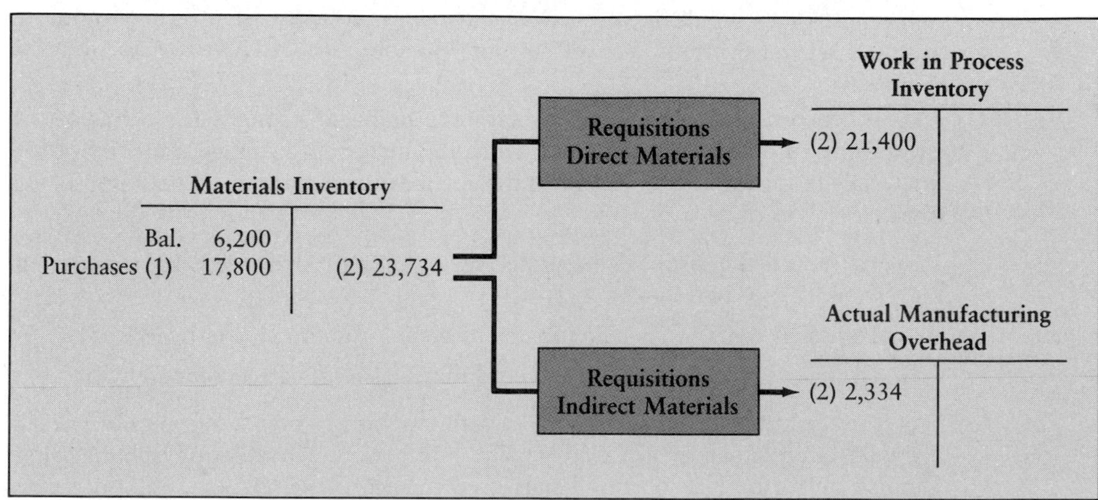

Figure 4–4

T Accounts for Materials at Woodland Products Company

Woodland's T accounts show the flow of its materials costs. An entry on the left side of an account represents an increase. An entry on the right side represents a decrease. The numbers in parentheses refer to Woodland's journal entries.

indirect materials (supplies and parts of minor value), the Actual Manufacturing Overhead account number is entered on the materials requisition form.

At least once a month, all requisitions are totaled. One journal entry is then made. This entry reduces the Materials Inventory asset account and increases two other accounts, Work in Process Inventory and Actual Manufacturing Overhead.

(2) Work in Process Inventory	21,400	
Actual Manufacturing Overhead	2,334	
Materials Inventory		23,734
To record issue of materials for April on requisitions numbered M3390 to M3456		

Figure 4–5
Uses for the Materials Requisition Form

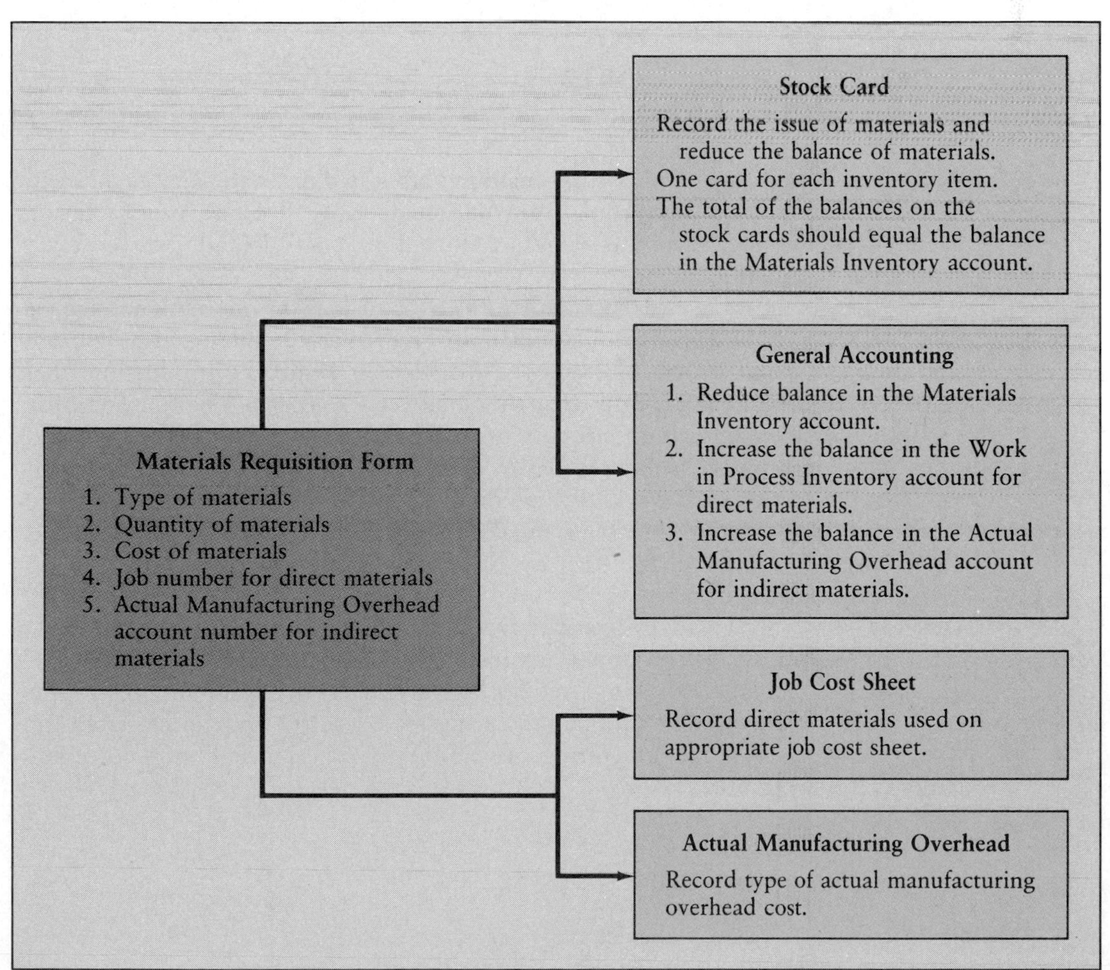

Work in Process Inventory is an account that represents the cost of partially completed units of product. Found only in manufacturing companies, it appears as an asset on a firm's balance sheet.

Figure 4–4 shows how materials costs follow through Woodland's accounts (all of Woodland's journal entries for April are summarized in Figure 4–12, page 140). The purchase of $17,800 in materials is shown as entry **1** on the left side of the Materials Inventory account. This entry indicates an increase in the inventory balance. The issue of $21,400 worth of direct materials and $2,334 worth of indirect materials is shown in total—$23,734—on the right side of the Materials Inventory account as entry **2**. This entry also records increases in the Work in Process Inventory account and the Actual Manufacturing Overhead account. Later, overhead will be applied to Work in Process Inventory, using a predetermined overhead rate.

Figure 4–5 summarizes the three uses for the materials requisition form.

■

Accounting for Labor Costs

Like materials, some labor used in manufacturing is direct and some is indirect. **Direct labor** is labor performed on a particular job. All other manufacturing labor—supervising, materials handling, inventory control, and even cost accounting—is **indirect labor.**

Labor costs are recorded on daily time cards such as the one shown in Figure 4–6. A **timecard** shows the hours an employee worked each day and how those hours were spent. When an employee works directly on the production of a product, the job number is entered on the employee's timecard. When an employee works in maintenance or on cleanup, or is idle, an Actual Manufacturing Overhead account number is entered. From these cards the payroll department calculates the cost of each worker's time on a job or on an overhead activity. The figures on daily labor costs are eventually totaled to calculate the payroll. Timecards are also used to charge the cost of direct labor to specific jobs on the job cost sheet (Figure 4–1).

OBJECTIVE 4
Record labor costs with journal entries

Finally, timecards are used to make journal entries for labor costs. For example, suppose Woodland's timecards show $12,500 in labor costs incurred for last month. Of that amount, $8,300 was direct labor on manufacturing jobs; $4,200 for indirect labor, an actual manufacturing overhead cost. The journal entry to record these costs would read

(3) Work in Process Inventory	8,300	
Actual Manufacturing Overhead	4,200	
Wages Payable		12,500
To record manufacturing labor costs for April		

Figure 4–6

Daily Timecard for Woodland Products Company

The daily timecard is used to prepare the payroll and to charge labor costs to the appropriate account. Direct labor costs are charged to specific jobs; indirect labor costs, to actual manufacturing overhead.

Name ____________________
Date ____________________ Department __________

Job number or Actual Manufacturing Overhead account number	Start time	Stop time	Hours

Total hours for the day __________
Pay rate per hour __________
Total pay for the day __________

Figure 4–7

T Accounts for Factory Labor at Woodland Products Company

Woodland's labor costs for the month are first entered as an increase in Wages Payable. The cost is then split between the Work in Process Inventory account (for direct labor) and the Actual Manufacturing Overhead account (for indirect labor).*

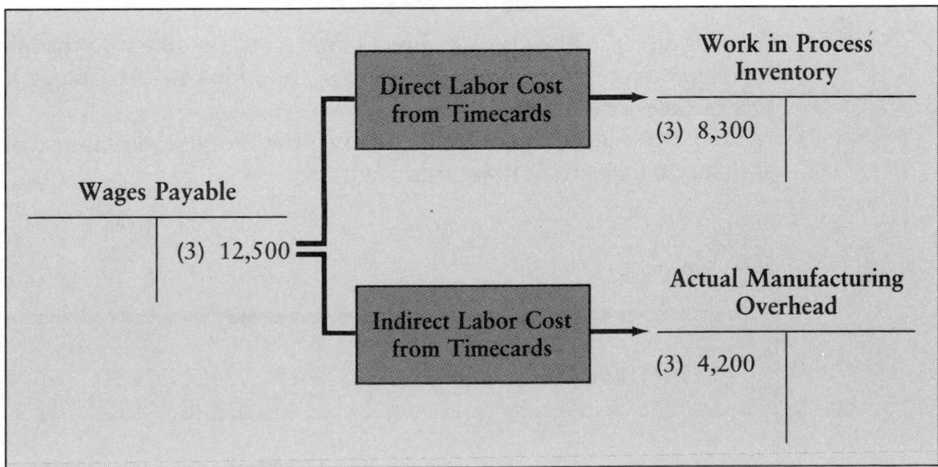

*To emphasize the main concepts and simplify the journal entries, we assume that no withholdings for taxes or other items were made from the payroll.

Figure 4–8
Uses for the Timecard

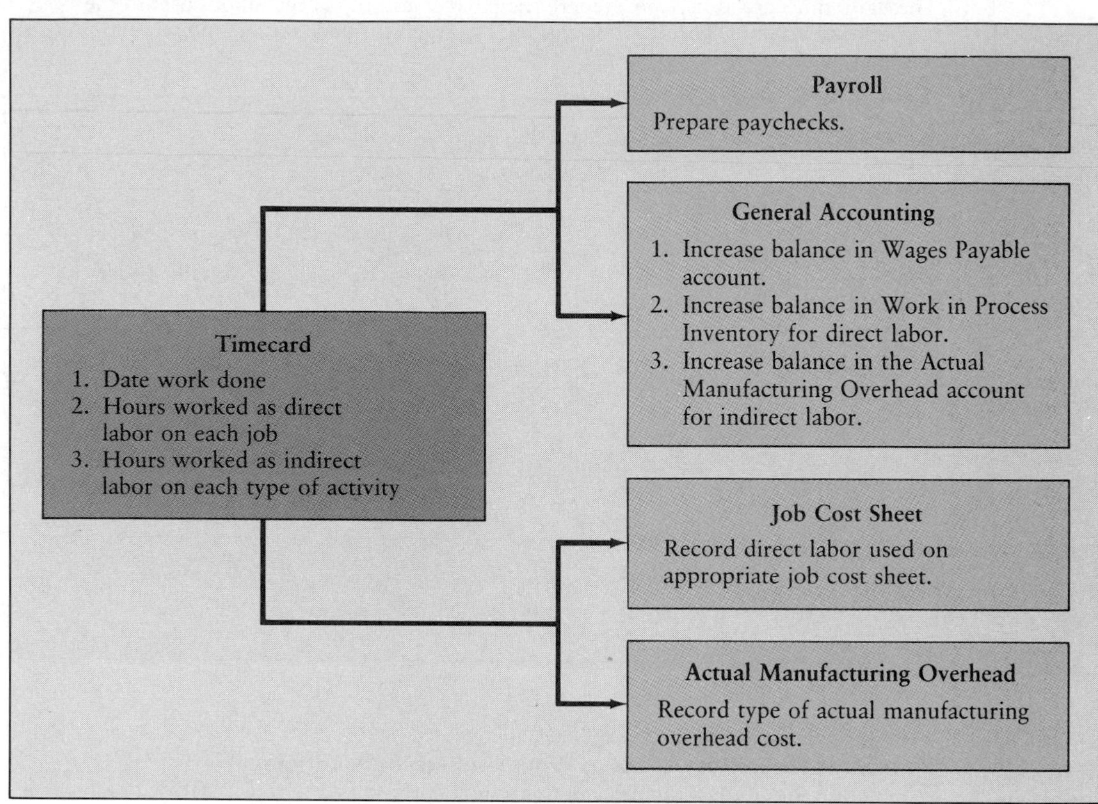

As with direct material costs, direct labor costs are added to the Work in Process Inventory account. Indirect labor costs are added to the Actual Manufacturing Overhead account.

Figure 4–7 uses T accounts to show how Woodland's labor costs flow. Figure 4–8 summarizes how timecards are used.

Review Exercise 4–1

Prepare a Job Cost Sheet and T Accounts

Vento Corporation prints small books. They use a job order costing and treat each book as a job. The following activity occurred during the month of January:

Jobs started
Job 9001
Job 9002
Job 9003

Costs incurred

Cost of materials purchased on account			$35,000
Materials requisitions			
Requisition R931	Job 9001	January 2, 19x3	$11,000
Requisition R932	Job 9002	January 11, 19x3	8,000
Requisition R934	Job 9003	January 21, 19x3	2,000
Requisition R933	Indirect	January 18, 19x3	7,000
Total			$28,000
Cost of labor in printing department			
Timecard L193	Job 9001	January 8, 19x3	$ 4,300
Timecard L293	Job 9002	January 15, 19x3	2,500
Timecard L393	Job 9003	January 22, 19x3	1,000
Timecard L493	Indirect	January 29, 19x3	4,000
Total			$11,800

Required

1. Prepare a job cost sheet for Job 9002. Enter the direct materials and direct labor cost of job. Job 9002 was for 2000 cookbooks ordered by Dakota Bookstore on December 12, 19x2. The job was started January 11, 19x3 and is not yet completed.
2. Prepare T accounts for Materials Inventory, Work in Process Inventory, and Actual Manufacturing Overhead. Make entries in the T accounts for materials costs and labor costs for January.

Solution

1. Job Cost Sheet Prepared

Customer *Dakota Book Store* Job number *9002*
Date ordered *December 12, 19×2*
Date started *January 11, 19×3* Product *Books*
Date completed Number of units *2,000*

Direct Materials

Date	Department	Requisition Number	Total Cost
January 11, 19×3		*R 932*	*$ 8,000*

Direct Labor

Date	Department	Timecard Number	Total Cost
January 15, 19×3		*L 293*	*$ 2,500*

Applied Overhead					
Date	Department	Base of Application	Units of Base	Rate	Total Cost

Total Manufacturing Cost ______
Units Produced ______
Unit Cost ______

2. T Accounts Prepared

Accounts Payable	
	(1) 35,000

Materials Inventory	
(1) 35,000	(2) 28,000

Work in Process Inventory	
(2) 21,000 (3) 7,800	

Wages Payable	
	(3) 11,800

Actual Manufacturing Overhead	
(2) 7,000 (3) 4,000	

■

Accounting for Manufacturing Overhead Costs

Manufacturing overhead costs are all costs other than direct materials and direct labor necessary for the manufacture of a product. Examples of manufacturing overhead costs include production supplies, electricity and heating costs of the factory, depreciation, insurance, and property taxes on factory and production equipment. To help management estimate and control future costs, each type of manufacturing overhead cost is recorded in a separate account. For instance, factory electricity will be recorded in one account, factory heating in another account. Each account has a number. The number of the Production Supplies Account appears on materials requisition forms in the place of the job number. The account number for Factory Janitor Salaries appears on the janitor's timecards.

Assigning direct materials and direct labor to jobs is relatively easy because the physical link between direct materials, direct labor, and product makes it possible to measure precise quantities used on each job. Factory materials that do not become part of the product and factory labor not performed directly on the product are harder to assign to jobs. The same is true of all manufacturing overhead costs. Although manufacturing overhead is part of the cost of making products, it is not physically linked to particular units. Repairing a machine, for instance, benefits all products produced on that machine, not just products in a single job. Similarly, the plant manager's attention benefits production generally and his or her salary cannot be identified with particular jobs.

Another way of stating the difference between direct materials and direct labor and overhead is to say that overhead costs are generally common costs, which benefit several products (jobs) rather than a single job. In addition to indirect materials and indirect labor, manufacturing overhead costs include rent, depreciation, and insurance on plant and equipment; fringe benefits and payroll taxes; maintenance of factory equipment; and utilities, such as electricity, used in the factory. **Actual manufacturing overhead costs** are really a pool of these common costs, which must somehow be assigned to jobs for product costing purposes.

Without a physical link between common manufacturing overhead costs and units of product, the accountant must find another way of assigning overhead costs to products. Generally overhead costs are *applied*, or *allocated*, among the products produced throughout the year according to a ratio called the predetermined overhead rate.

■

The Predetermined Overhead Rate

Overhead is applied to units of product according to some **cost drivers** that measure production activity. The cost drivers chosen should cause, at least indirectly, the overhead costs. Direct labor cost is the most widely used cost driver. It causes such overhead costs as supervision, payroll accounting, fringe benefits, training, and similar costs. Machine-hours is a popular cost driver in automated factories because automation increases machine-related costs. Machine-related costs include machine depreciation, electricity to operate the machines, machine maintenance, and similar manufacturing overhead costs. As production becomes more automated, companies are more likely to use machine-hours as a cost driver. In some factories, direct labor cost has become less than 10 percent of total production cost. These factories are likely to drop direct labor cost as a cost driver and use machine-hours or some other cost drivers. Another cost driver that is important for many companies is the amount of materials handled. This cost driver causes materials storage expenses, costs of conveyors and lift trucks, and wages of people who move the materials from one work station to another in the factory.

OBJECTIVE 5
Calculate a predetermined overhead rate and use it to assign overhead costs to a job

Once the cost drivers are chosen, the predetermined overhead rates can be established. A **predetermined overhead rate** is simply a ratio that relates total estimated manufacturing overhead costs for the year to expected manufacturing activity for the year. A predetermined overhead rate based on direct labor costs is expressed as a percentage of direct labor costs. Suppose the predetermined overhead rate is 120 percent for each $1.00 of direct labor costs charged to a job. The accountant uses the daily timecards to apply $1.20 worth of overhead to the job for each dollar of direct labor used on the job. The procedure for estimating the predetermined overhead rate is as follows:

1. Choose cost drivers that cause major categories of overhead cost.
2. Estimate output for the coming year in units of product. Calculate the amount of each cost driver that will be needed to produce next year's estimated units of product. For example, if direct labor is chosen as a cost driver, calculate the number of direct labor hours that will be required to produce next year's estimated output. This provides the estimated activity level of this cost driver for next year.
3. Divide the overhead costs for next year into pools of cost that are caused by each cost driver. For each pool, estimate the total fixed and total variable manufacturing overhead for the coming year.
4. Divide the total estimated overhead cost in each pool from *3* above by the estimated activity level of its cost driver for next year from *2* above.

Woodland Products Company has decided that they have two important overhead cost pools and related cost drivers. One relates to materials-handling costs. It includes the costs of receiving, inspecting, and storing materials until they are needed. It also includes the costs of moving the materials from storage to the work stations and finally to the shipping department and shipping costs. The cost driver associated with this pool is board feet of lumber used. The other overhead cost pool are costs caused by direct labor. Woodland uses this cost driver because its production process is not very automated.

Woodland next estimated the fixed and variable expenses for each cost pool for next year. Woodland's accountants reviewed overhead costs from last year and adjusted them as necessary for the coming year. Woodland's production capacity is adequate for the coming year's estimated output. However, they expect changes in supervisors' salaries, insurance and other fixed manufacturing overhead costs. Allowing for these changes, Woodland estimated the fixed manufacturing costs for each pool for the coming year to be the following:

Fixed materials handling overhead	$31,960
Fixed labor related overhead	50,760

Materials-handling variable costs consisted mainly of supplies and indirect labor. They had been $0.20 per board foot last year. Since no changes were foreseen, Woodland estimated they would be $0.20 per board foot in the coming year. Labor-related variable expenses were mainly fringe benefits. These had been 10 percent last year, but increases in payroll taxes lead Woodland to estimate that they would be 12 percent in the coming year.

Woodland next estimated the amount of the cost drivers they could expect next year. From the estimated output of product, the accountant could estimate the number of board feet of lumber that would be used for the coming year. The estimate was 399,500 board feet. Woodland's accountant estimated the direct labor cost by a similar method. Those calculations are illustrated in Exhibit 4–1. Exhibit 4–1 shows how the accountant took estimated demand from the

Exhibit 4–1
Woodland Products Company
This exhibit shows how Woodland estimates direct labor cost for the coming year based on estimated demand for products

Estimated output in units	Estimated direct labor costs per unit	Total estimated direct labor costs per year
2,200 picnic-table kits	$8	$17,600
3,400 dock sections	6	20,400
12,000 landscaping timbers	3	36,000
5,000 other	4	20,000
		$94,000

marketing department and the estimated direct labor costs per unit of different products and estimated the total direct labor cost to be incurred in the coming year.

These calculations permit the estimation of the total manufacturing overhead costs for the coming year. They are shown below.

Materials-handling overhead costs
$31,960 fixed + ($0.20 per board foot × 399,500 board foot)
= $111,860

Labor-related overhead costs
$50,760 fixed + (12% × $94,000 direct labor cost)
= $62,040

With these estimates and the annual estimates of the cost drivers, we can calculate Woodland's two predetermined overhead rates.

Predetermined overhead rate for materials-handling costs

$$= \frac{\text{estimated materials-handling overhead for the year}}{\text{estimated board feet of lumber used for the year}}$$

$$= \frac{\$111{,}860}{399{,}500 \text{ board feet}}$$

$$= \underline{\underline{\$0.28}} \text{ per board foot of lumber}$$

Predetermined overhead rate for labor-related costs

$$= \frac{\text{estimated labor-related overhead for the year}}{\text{estimated direct labor cost for the year}}$$

$$= \frac{\$62{,}040}{\$94{,}000 \text{ direct labor cost}}$$

$$= \underline{\underline{66}} \text{ percent of direct labor cost}$$

Applied Overhead Costs

Woodland will use its new predetermined overhead rates throughout the year to calculate its **applied manufacturing overhead costs,** the estimated total manufacturing overhead costs assigned to each job or product. For job MP135, the order for 100 picnic tables discussed earlier in the chapter, suppose timecards showed that $225 worth of direct labor costs were charged to that job during April.

Other production records showed that 1,269.64 board feet of lumber had been used on the job. Using Woodland's two predetermined overhead rates, accountants applied overhead to Job MP135 as follows:

Applied materials-handling cost	
= $0.28 per board foot × 1,269.64 board feet =	$355.50
Applied direct labor-related costs	
= 66% × $225 direct labor cost =	148.50
Total overhead cost applied to Job MP135	$504.00

This would be done by entering the figure in the Applied Overhead section on the job cost sheet (Figure 4–1). Similar entries would be made on job cost sheets for other jobs worked on during the month of April.

OBJECTIVE 6
Record applied manufacturing overhead costs with journal entries

In addition to recording applied overhead on the job cost sheets, accountants must also enter it in the company accounts. Woodland's total direct labor costs for April were $8,300 (see journal entry 3, page 122). In addition, Woodland used a total of 16,007 board feet of lumber. The applied overhead for April is therefore:

Material handling	16,007 × $0.28 =	$4,482
Labor	$8,300 × 66% =	5,478
Total applied overhead		$9,960

To record the total applied overhead for April, the accountant makes the following journal entry:

(4) Work in Process Inventory	9,960	
Applied Manufacturing Overhead		9,960
To record applied manufacturing overhead for April		

Actual Overhead Costs

OBJECTIVE 7
Record actual manufacturing overhead costs with journal entries

The use of a predetermined overhead rate results in jobs being charged with a portion of the year's estimated cost. However, it does not eliminate the need to record data on actual manufacturing costs incurred during the year. Indirect materials and indirect labor are recorded in the Actual Manufacturing Overhead account based on requisition forms and timecards, as illustrated in journal entries 2 (page 121) and 3 (page 122). Other actual overhead costs may be summarized in a journal entry involving several accounts. Depreciation of factory equipment increases Accumulated Depreciation. Expired insurance on factory and equipment reduces Prepaid Insurance. Such items as electricity, heat, and rent increase Accounts Payable. To avoid complicating the illustration, all actual manufacturing overhead costs will be recorded in a single account rather than the individual accounts for depreciation, electricity, heat, and the other usual manufacturing overhead accounts.

Woodland's actual overhead summary entry for April is as follows:

	Debit	Credit
(5) Actual Manufacturing Overhead	2,579	
Accumulated Depreciation		850
Prepaid Insurance		650
Accounts Payable		1,079
To record actual overhead costs for April		

Figure 4–9 summarizes the flow of manufacturing overhead costs. Actual manufacturing overhead costs include indirect materials and indirect labor. Other

Figure 4–9

T Accounts for Manufacturing Overhead at Woodland Products Company

Overhead costs are applied to jobs by using a predetermined overhead rate. The Work in Process Inventory account is increased by the total amount of applied overhead. Actual Manufacturing Overhead includes indirect materials, indirect labor, and other factory costs. They are not charged to specific jobs.

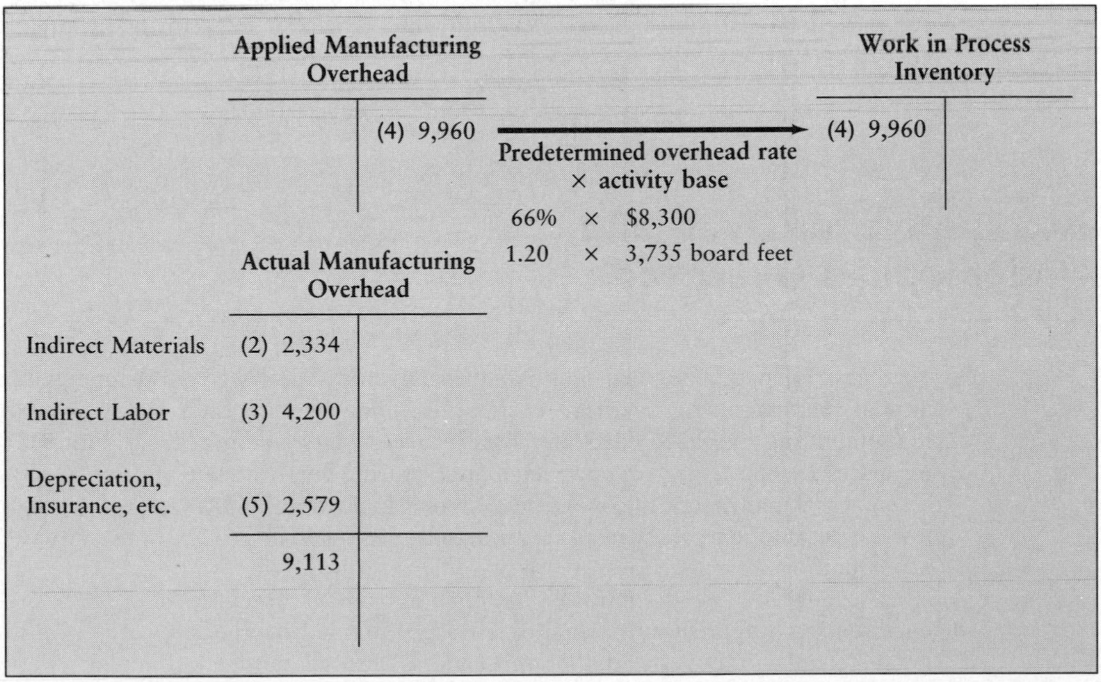

Applied Manufacturing Overhead

	(4) 9,960

→ **Predetermined overhead rate × activity base**

66% × $8,300

1.20 × 3,735 board feet

Work in Process Inventory

(4) 9,960	

Actual Manufacturing Overhead

Indirect Materials	(2) 2,334	
Indirect Labor	(3) 4,200	
Depreciation, Insurance, etc.	(5) 2,579	
	9,113	

Figure 4–10
Documents Used to Record Actual Manufacturing Overhead Costs
Actual manufacturing overhead costs are obtained from various sources.

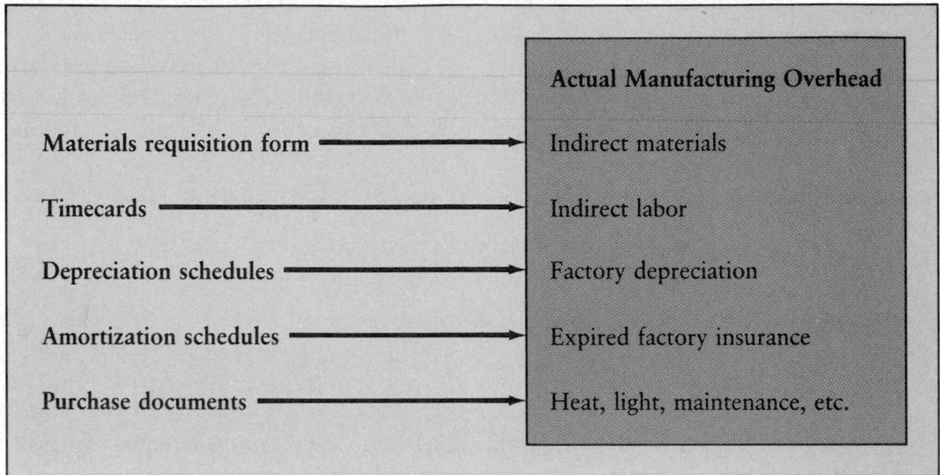

factory costs, such as factory depreciation, insurance, maintenance, heating, and lighting, are also actual manufacturing overhead costs. Accountants do not attempt to divide these costs among jobs. Instead, overhead costs are applied to jobs by using a predetermined overhead rate. At the end of the month, one entry increases Work in Process Inventory for the total amount of applied overhead costs. Figure 4–10 shows the sources from which actual manufacturing overhead costs are recorded.

■

Accounting for Over- and Underapplied Overhead

You have seen that applied manufacturing overhead is based on estimates of annual manufacturing overhead costs and annual production volume. Actual manufacturing overhead costs are costs incurred in any month. If accountants' estimates are good, the year's applied manufacturing overhead will approximately equal actual manufacturing overhead. For any single month, however, one should not expect applied overhead to equal actual overhead. In fact, they usually are not equal.

Accountants use the terms *overapplied* and *underapplied* to refer to differences between applied and actual overhead. If applied overhead for a period is greater than actual overhead, the overhead has been **overapplied**. If applied overhead for a period is less than actual manufacturing overhead, it has been **underapplied**. In the case of Woodland, the applied manufacturing overhead for April was \$9,960, whereas actual manufacturing overhead costs were only \$9,113. Therefore, overhead was overapplied in April by \$847.

There are several causes of difference between applied and actual overhead costs. Each cause will be briefly covered before going into the procedure for reporting over- or underapplied overhead.

Causes of Over- and Underapplied Overhead

The four causes of over- or underapplied manufacturing overhead are summarized as follows:

1. Some actual overhead costs vary by season.
2. Some actual overhead costs are not incurred evenly throughout the year.
3. Production volume often varies by season.
4. Estimates of total manufacturing overhead or total production may be incorrect.

The first three causes may produce differences between applied and actual overhead at month end, but these differences will average out over the year. No action is necessary. But the last cause, faulty estimates, can produce over- or underapplied overhead at year-end as well. When this situation occurs, the predetermined overhead rate should be revised.

Seasonal Overhead Variations Some examples will help illustrate the effect of each cause. Seasonal variations in actual overhead costs are fairly common. One example is heating costs in cold climates and air conditioning costs in warm climates. Another example is the cost of lighting, which varies with the length of the day. In the North, then, actual overhead costs tend to be higher in December and lower in April or May, when the weather is milder and the days longer. But applied overhead averages costs over the year. So all units of product are allocated an average amount of heating and lighting costs, regardless of the month in which the units were produced. The result: underapplied overhead in December and overapplied overhead in May. Because these variations are expected, however, they should be ignored. Management is interested only in unexpected cost variations.

Costs Not Incurred Regularly Maintenance is an example of irregular costs. Routine maintenance may occur regularly, but its *cost* is not necessarily regular. If a machine requires new parts or other maintenance after operating 1,000 hours and average monthly operating time is 500 hours, the cost of replacing parts is included in actual overhead costs only every other month. Other types of maintenance occur randomly, such as when a machine breaks down. Although breakdowns may be expected on the average every 5,000 hours, they may occur between 3,000 and 7,000 hours. Differences between actual and applied overhead caused by such irregularly incurred costs are expected and therefore, require no special attention. If the expected amount of maintenance is performed at some time during the year, actual overhead will be the same as applied overhead for the whole year.

Production Volume Variations Sometimes overhead is under- or overapplied not because overhead costs vary but because production levels vary. Many manufacturing overhead costs are fixed. If volume changes, actual fixed costs per unit change as well (see Chapter 3, page 68). A simple example will illustrate this concept.

Suppose a company expects actual fixed manufacturing overhead to be $30,000 for the year: $15,000 in the first six months and $15,000 in the second. The company expects to incur $20,000 worth of direct labor costs in meeting its annual production volume. Its predetermined fixed overhead rate is 150 percent of direct labor costs.

The first half of the year is the slow season. During this time, the company incurs only $8,000 in direct labor costs. In the second half, volume increases, and the company incurs $12,000 in direct labor costs. In this situation, actual fixed overhead costs remain the same, but applied fixed overhead differs from one half to the other:

First half	Second half
$8,000 × 150% = $12,000	$12,000 × 150% = $18,000

The result is $3,000 in underapplied overhead during the first half ($15,000 − $12,000). In the second half, there is an equal amount of overapplied overhead ($15,000 − $18,000).

In this illustration, variable costs, seasonal cost variations, and irregularities in fixed costs were omitted for simplicity. But the result would have been similar if those complications had been included.

Incorrect Overhead Estimates The fourth case of over- or underapplied overhead, incorrect estimates of either total annual manufacturing overhead or total annual production volume, is by definition an unexpected departure from plan. And management would want to know about it in order to decide whether corrective action is needed. Incorrect estimates could be due to a change in production process. If the company purchases a new major machine, the estimated annual overhead is likely to be incorrect.

If a company discovers that its estimates are off by a significant amount, the appropriate response is to recalculate the predetermined overhead rate based on revised estimates of overhead costs and production volume. This procedure requires revision of the entries charging applied overhead to the Work in Process Inventory account. It also means that each job cost sheet as well as each job cost must be recalculated. Because of the work involved, the predetermined overhead rate is revised only when there is a major change in annual estimates.

How does management know whether annual estimates are wrong? For errors in estimates of production volume, management must usually rely on the marketing manager, since the major input into the estimate of production volume is the estimated sales volume. For errors in estimates of actual overhead costs, variances from budgeted costs are the best indicator. For now, you should simply note that an unfavorable variance from budgeted overhead costs is a sign that actual overhead costs are above those expected. There is no reason to assume that an unfavorable variance will be offset by a favorable variance in future months. If anything, the opposite is true. A significant unexpected cost variance means that actual overhead costs may be out of control and should be analyzed by management. Such management decisions will be discussed in Chapter 11.

If one assumes that the differences between actual and applied overhead costs are small and require no revision of the predetermined overhead rate, how should the accountant go about reporting them?

Reporting Over- or Underapplied Overhead

OBJECTIVE 8
Compute over- and underapplied overhead

Calculating over- and underapplied overhead is simple. The amount of over- and underapplied manufacturing overhead is the difference between two accounts, Actual Manufacturing Overhead and Applied Manufacturing Overhead. If applied overhead exceeds actual overhead, overhead has been overapplied. If applied overhead falls short of actual overhead, overhead has been underapplied.

In April, actual manufacturing overhead costs for Woodland Products Company totaled \$9,113, whereas applied manufacturing overhead was \$9,960. Therefore, overhead was overapplied by \$847, as shown below.

Over- or underapplied overhead
= actual manufacturing overhead − applied manufacturing overhead
= \$9,113 − \$9,960 = \$−847

The minus sign is unimportant. The important issue is whether applied overhead is *greater* than actual overhead (overapplied) or *less* than actual overhead (underapplied).

How over- or underapplied overhead is treated depends on its cause. No accounting is required when it stems from seasonal variations in cost or volume or irregularly incurred costs. Since these variations are expected and will average out by year-end, they should not affect a firm's net earnings. Including them in monthly income statements tends to be misleading.

In this case, the accountant reports over- or underapplied overhead on the balance sheet. Usually it is added to or subtracted from Work in Process Inventory. The drawback to this approach is that as a balance sheet item, over- or underapplied overhead has little meaning. It is neither an asset nor a liability in the usual sense. Of course, by year-end the difference between the two accounts should be so small as to be immaterial and, thus, how it is reported is of little concern.

In practice, over- and underapplied overhead is usually reported on monthly income statements, despite the fact that it can be misleading. Underapplied overhead is added to the cost of goods sold and decreases net earnings. Overapplied overhead is subtracted from cost of goods sold and increases net earnings.

As you have seen, when over- or underapplied manufacturing overhead is caused by an incorrect predetermined overhead rate, a new rate should be calculated and accounting for the year redone. Besides changing entries to the Work in Process Inventory account and on the job cost sheets, one must change entries to the Finished Goods Inventory and Cost of Goods Sold accounts as well. Ideally, these changes should be made as soon as the inaccurate rate is discovered. If the revised predetermined overhead rate is correct, there will be no over- or underapplied overhead by year-end.

When estimating errors are small and the predetermined overhead rate will not be revised, over- or underapplied overhead is reported on the yearly income statement. It is shown as either an addition to or subtraction from the cost of goods sold. Since the amounts are small, the effect of these additions and subtractions is insignificant.

Review Exercise 4–2

Calculate Predetermined Overhead Rate

At the start of the year, Vento Corporation, a book printer, estimated that its total overhead expense for the year would be $1,800,000. Vento applied overhead to products based on the number of pounds of paper in each book produced. It estimated that it would produce 600,000 pounds of books during the year.

Vento used 55,000 pounds of paper for books produced during January. It incurred actual overhead costs of $162,300 during January.

Required

1. Calculate Vento's predetermined overhead rate for the year.
2. Calculate how much overhead Vento would apply to Work in Process Inventory during January.
3. Is overhead over- or underapplied during January? By what amount?
4. What are the possible ways of reporting January's over- or underapplied overhead? Explain briefly.

Solution

1. Predetermined overhead rate $= \dfrac{\text{estimated total manufacturing overhead for the year}}{\text{estimated total pounds of paper used for the year}}$

$$\text{Predetermined overhead rate} = \frac{\$1,800,000}{600,000 \text{ pounds}}$$
$$= \underline{\underline{\$3}} \text{ per pound of paper}$$

2. Applied overhead = predetermined overhead rate
× pounds of paper used in January
= $3 per pound × 55,000 pounds
= $165,000

3.

Applied overhead	$165,000
Actual manufacturing overhead	162,300
Overapplied overhead	$ 2,700

The overhead is *over*applied because the applied overhead is greater than the actual manufacturing overhead.

4. Overapplied overhead may be subtracted from Work in Process Inventory in the balance sheet. Alternatively, it may be subtracted from Cost of Goods Sold in the income statement. These are appropriate if there is no evidence that the year's total manufacturing overhead or total pounds of paper to be used have been misestimated.

If there is evidence that the year's total manufacturing overhead or the total pounds of paper to be used have been misestimated, a new rate could be calculated and used. This would divide the overapplied overhead between Work in Process Inventory and Cost of Goods Sold and reduce both of them.

The small amount of overapplied overhead in this problem does not suggest that the predetermined overhead rate has been misestimated. Management would therefore choose between the alternatives suggested in the first paragraph. In practice, overapplied overhead is most often subtracted from Cost of Goods Sold in the income statement.

(see Exercises 13–17)

■

Accounting for the Cost of Finished Goods and the Cost of Goods Sold

Up to this point you have been concerned with accounting for direct materials, direct labor, and applied and actual manufacturing overhead. In terms of production, the needed materials have been purchased, the necessary labor hired, and production begun. The next step is to complete the job; the final step, to sell the finished units.

Figure 4–11
Job Cost Sheet for Woodland Products Company
Once a job has been completed and all costs entered, they are totaled. The cost per unit is then calculated. Both figures are entered in the lower right corner. A separate job sheet is maintained for each job.

Customer or department ordering ________ Job number MP 135
Date ordered March 28, 19×1
Date started April 12, 19×1 Product Picnic table kits
Date completed April 15, 19×1 Number of units 100

Direct Materials

Date	Department	Requisition Number	Total Cost
April 12, 19×1	Cutting	M3401	$ 124.00
April 12, 19×1	Cutting	M 3402	37.00
April 12, 19×1	Cutting	M 3403	82.00
April 15, 19×1	Packing	M 3445	84.00

Direct Labor

Date	Department	Timecard Number	Total Cost
April 12, 19×1	Cutting	C 412	$ 48.00
April 13, 19×1	Cutting	C 418, C 423	96.00
April 15, 19×1	Packing	P 776	81.00

Applied Overhead

Date	Department	Base of Application	Units of Base	Rate	Total Cost
April 12, 19×1	Cutting	DLC	$ 48.00	66%	$ 31.68
April 12, 19×1	Cutting	Bd. ft.	296.25	$1.20	355.50
April 13, 19×1	Cutting	DLC	96.00	66%	63.36
April 15, 19×1	Packing	DLC	81.00	66%	53.46

Total Manufacturing Cost $1,281.00
Units Produced 100
Unit Cost $ 12.81

Cost of Finished Goods

Once a job has been completed and the finished goods moved from the production area into storage, the accountant totals the items on the job cost sheet. These items include all direct materials and direct labor costs as well as applied manufacturing overhead. Figure 4–11 shows the completed job cost sheet for Woodland's Job MP135. The total cost of the job and the total cost per unit are shown in the lower right corner.

The total job cost figure is then subtracted from the Work in Process Inventory account and added to the **Finished Goods Inventory** account by a journal entry similar to the one shown below.

(6) Finished Goods Inventory	1,281	
Work in Process Inventory		1,281
To record the completion of 100 picnic-table kits in Job MP135		

Eventually this total job cost figure will be used to calculate the **cost of goods manufactured**, the total cost of all the good units completed during the accounting period.

Cost of Goods Sold

When some or all of the finished goods are sold, the accountant computes their cost and transfers it from the Finished Goods Inventory account to the **Cost of Goods Sold** account. This is the final step in accounting for a manufactured product. Suppose that out of the 100 picnic-table kits in Job MP135, 60 are sold and shipped. Woodland must now reduce the Finished Goods Inventory account by the cost of the 60 units and increase the Cost of Goods Sold account by the same amount.

Calculating the cost of goods sold is quite simple. The lower right corner of the job cost sheet shows the cost per unit, $12.81. Since 60 kits were sold, their cost is $768.60 ($12.81 × 60). The transaction is recorded as follows:

(7) Cost of Goods Sold	768.60	
Finished Goods Inventory		768.60
To record the cost of 60 picnic-table kits sold from Job MP135		

If the manufacturing costs of all products Woodland sold during the accounting period were totaled, they would equal the cost of goods sold. But instead of totaling all costs, Woodland's accountants can simply adjust the cost of goods manufactured for the beginning and ending Finished Goods Inventories by using the formula:

  Cost of Goods Manufactured
+ Beginning Finished Goods Inventory
− Ending Finished Goods Inventory
= Cost of Goods Sold

The resulting figure should then be reported on Woodland's income statement. Finally, revenue from selling the kits must be recorded and included on Woodland's income statement. Sales records show the kits were sold on account for $22.50 each. The entry to record the revenue would be as follows:

(8) Accounts Receivable	1,350	
Sales		1,350
To record the sales revenue from 60 picnic-table kits sold from Job MP135		

Figure 4–12

Flow of Manufacturing Costs Through T Accounts at Woodland Products Company

Woodland's manufacturing cost flow begins with the purchase of materials (entry **1**) and continues with the addition of direct materials, direct labor, and applied manufacturing overhead to Work in Process Inventory (entries **2**, **3**, and **4**). Indirect materials, indirect labor, and other actual manufacturing overhead costs are recorded in the Actual Manufacturing Overhead account (entries **2**, **3**, and **5**). Once the job has been completed, manufacturing costs are transferred to Finished Goods Inventory (entry **6**). Finally, when goods are sold, their cost is transferred to the Cost of Goods Sold account (entry **7**). These entries were explained in the text starting on page 118.

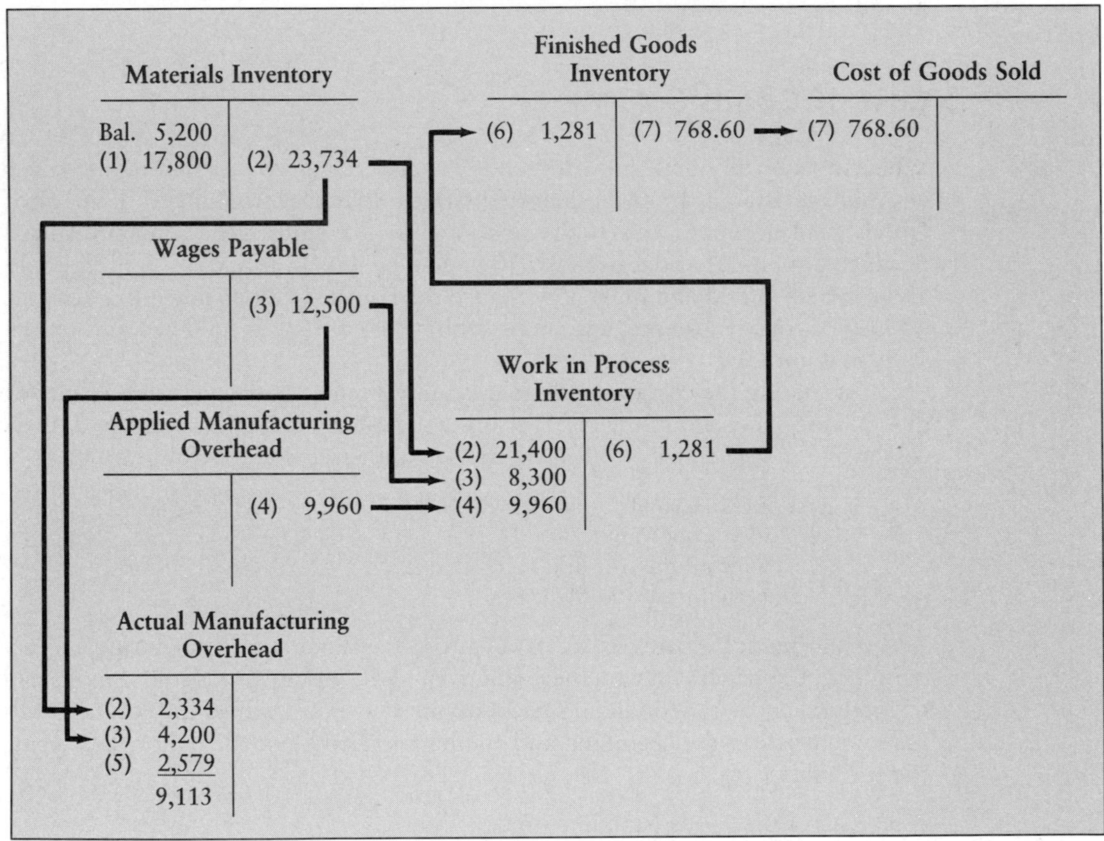

Figure 4–12 shows the complete flow of manufacturing costs for one job in the Woodland Products Company. Other jobs that were started or completed in April would be similarly accounted for. Study the figure carefully, tracing the costs through each step of the production process, from the purchase of materials to the start and completion of production and finally the sale of the finished product.

■

Preparing Statements of the Cost of Goods Manufactured and Sold

The basic format for a statement of the cost of goods manufactured and sold was shown in Chapter 2. The information on that statement was gathered from the manufacturing accounts described in this chapter. That basic format will now be expanded and used to prepare two statements, the cost of goods manufactured and the cost of goods manufactured and sold.

The Statement of Cost of Goods Manufactured

The statement of cost of goods manufactured is a record of the cost of goods completed during a period of time. It is also a report of activity in the Work in Process Inventory account. Preparing a statement of cost of goods manufactured is an organized way of calculating the cost of goods manufactured.

OBJECTIVE 9
Calculate cost of goods manufactured and cost of goods sold

When preparing a statement of cost of goods manufactured, one usually begins the month with a balance in Work in Process Inventory. That balance represents the cost of units partially completed at the beginning of the month. The cost of direct materials and direct labor used during the month is then added to this balance, along with applied overhead. Finally, the ending Work in Process Inventory balance is subtracted to obtain the cost of goods manufactured or completed. Exhibit 4–2 shows a cost of goods manufactured statement for Sample Company. The process of preparing the statement and calculating cost of goods manufactured is summarized below.

  Direct Materials Used
\+ Direct Labor
\+ Applied Manufacturing Overhead
\= Total Manufacturing Costs
\+ Beginning Balance, Work in Process Inventory
\− Ending Balance, Work in Process Inventory
\= Cost of Goods Manufactured

To obtain the beginning balance for Work in Process Inventory, total the costs on the job cost sheets for jobs started but not completed at the beginning of the month. To obtain the ending balance for Work in Process Inventory, total the costs on the job cost sheets for jobs started but not completed at month end. To find the cost of direct materials, total the requisitions for direct materials made during the month. And to find the cost of direct labor, total the costs on the month's timecards.

Use the predetermined overhead rate to calculate applied overhead. The **total manufacturing cost** is equal to the sum of direct materials, direct labor, and

Exhibit 4–2
Statement of the Cost of Goods Manufactured for Sample Company

Direct materials used	$ 9,116
Direct labor used	6,414
Applied overhead	9,621
Total manufacturing costs	$25,151
Beginning work in process inventory	4,151
Total	$29,302
Ending work in process inventory	$ 1,129
Cost of goods manufactured	$28,173

applied manufacturing overhead costs. To check the cost of goods manufactured, total the costs on the job cost sheets for jobs completed during the month.

Assume Sample Company worked on five jobs during the month but completed only four. The total manufacturing costs from the job cost sheets for the five jobs is shown below.

	Total manufacturing cost
Job 543	$8,450
Job 544	6,565
Job 545	3,650
Job 546	9,508
Job 547	1,129

The other way of calculating the cost of goods manufactured uses the total manufacturing cost from the job cost sheets. Cost of goods manufactured is the total manufacturing cost of all jobs *completed* during the month. Sample Company completed Jobs 543, 544, 545, and 546. We therefore add together the total manufacturing costs of these jobs ($8,450 + $6,565 + $3,650 + $9,508) which gives us the same $28,173 cost of goods manufactured shown in Exhibit 4–2. Notice, that Job 547, which is not completed at month end, has a cost of $1,129, the same as the ending Work in Process Inventory shown in Exhibit 4–2.

The Statement of Cost of Goods Sold

Accounting for finished goods in a manufacturing company is the same as accounting for inventory in a merchandising company, except the cost of goods manufactured is substituted for the cost of goods purchased. Preparing a statement of cost of goods sold is a way to easily organize calculating cost of goods sold.

Just as the statement of cost of goods manufactured can be thought to report activity in the Work in Process Inventory account, the statement of cost of goods sold can be thought to report activity in the Finished Goods Inventory account. The statement of cost of goods sold takes the cost of goods manufactured from the statement of cost of goods manufactured. The cost of goods manufactured is added to the beginning Finished Goods Inventory. Then, the ending Finished Goods Inventory is subtracted from that total to obtain the Cost of Goods Sold. Exhibit 4–3 shows a sample statement of cost of goods sold for Sample Company. The process of preparing such a statement and calculating cost of goods sold may be summarized as follows:

Cost of Goods Manufactured
\+ Beginning Finished Goods Inventory
= Total Goods Available for Sale
− Ending Finished Goods Inventory
= Cost of Goods Sold

To double-check this calculation, one multiplies the number of units sold in each job by the average cost per unit for that job.

Suppose that during the month, Sample Company had sold all of the units in Jobs 543 and 544, and 80 percent of the units in Job 545. We could calculate the cost of goods sold directly as follows:

Job 543 (100%)	$ 8,450
Job 544 (100%)	6,565
Job 545 (80%)	2,920
Cost of goods sold	$17,935

The Finished Goods Inventory consists of 20 percent of the cost of Job 545 and 100 percent of the cost of Job 546 ($730 + $9,508 = $10,238). These numbers correspond to the amounts in Exhibit 4–3.

Sometimes the statement of cost of goods manufactured is combined with the statement of cost of goods sold, as in Exhibit 2–5, page 44.

Exhibit 4–3
Sample Statement of Cost of Goods Sold

Cost of goods manufactured	$28,173
Beginning finished goods inventory	-0-
Total goods available for sale	$28,173
Ending finished goods inventory	10,238
Cost of goods sold	$17,935

Chapter Review

Review of Learning Objectives

1. **Explain the difference between job order and process costing.**
Job order and process costing are both used to find the cost of manufactured products. The choice of method depends on the production situation. When a product or service is produced in batches, job order costing is appropriate. Each batch must have recognizable starting and completion points. For products produced in one continuous process, process costing is appropriate. A soap manufacturer or an oil refiner would use process costing; a home builder, job order costing.

2. **Complete a job cost sheet and calculate the average cost per unit of a job.**
The cost of direct materials used, direct labor, and applied overhead is recorded on job cost sheets. When a job is completed, these costs are totaled. The average cost per unit is determined by dividing the total cost of the job (from the job cost sheet) by the number of good units produced.

3. **Record the purchase and issue of materials with journal entries.**
To record the purchase of materials, the accountant increases both the Materials Inventory and Accounts Payable accounts. To record the issue of direct materials, the accountant reduces the Materials Inventory account and increases the Work in Process Inventory account by the amount shown on the materials requisition form. To record the issue of indirect materials, the accountant reduces the Materials Inventory account and increases the Actual Manufacturing Overhead account.

4. **Record labor costs with journal entries.**
To record direct labor costs, the accountant increases the Work in Process Inventory and Wages Payable accounts by total direct labor costs on a job. This total is calculated from workers' timecards. Indirect labor is recorded as an increase to the Actual Manufacturing Overhead account and an increase to Wages Payable.

5. **Calculate a predetermined overhead rate and use it to assign overhead costs to a job.**
Because manufacturing overhead costs are common costs that benefit more than one job, the manufacturing overhead costs incurred on a specific job cannot be measured. Instead they must be assigned according to a ratio called the predetermined overhead rate. The predetermined overhead rate is the ratio of total estimated manufacturing overhead costs for the year to the expected manufacturing activity for the year, measured according to some cost driver, such as direct labor costs. To assign, or apply, overhead costs, the accountant multiplies total monthly output per job, measured by the chosen cost driver, by the predetermined overhead rate.

6. **Record applied manufacturing overhead costs with journal entries.**
To record applied overhead, the accountant increases the Work in Process Inventory and Applied Manufacturing Overhead accounts by the amount of overhead assigned to jobs, using the predetermined overhead rate.

7. **Record actual manufacturing overhead costs with journal entries.**
To record actual manufacturing overhead costs, the accountant adds these costs to the Actual Manufacturing Overhead account. Actual overhead costs include the cost of indirect

materials and indirect labor as well as other indirect costs, such as insurance and utilities. Thus, expired factory insurance simultaneously reduces the Prepaid Insurance account and increases the Actual Manufacturing Overhead account. Factory depreciation would increase the Accumulated Depreciation account; utilities costs, the Accounts Payable account.

8. **Compute over- and underapplied overhead.**
Because applied overhead costs are an average amount each month, whereas actual overhead costs follow seasonal or irregular patterns, actual manufacturing overhead often differs from applied overhead. To find the amount by which these costs were over- or underapplied, the accountant compares total applied overhead costs to total actual overhead costs.

When applied overhead is greater than actual manufacturing overhead, the overhead is referred to as overapplied. When applied overhead is less than actual manufacturing overhead, the overhead is underapplied. Over- or underapplied overhead costs are usually subtracted from or added to the cost of goods sold on the monthly income statement.

Manufacturing overhead may be over- or underapplied at month end because of seasonal variations in actual overhead costs, an irregular occurrence of actual overhead costs, seasonal variations in production volume, or inaccurate estimates of total manufacturing overhead or total production output.

Although the first three causes will produce differences between actual and applied overhead on a monthly basis, by year-end the differences will average out. No corrective act is needed. The last cause, faulty estimates, can also produce over- or underapplied overhead at year-end as well as at month end. If the differences are large, the predetermined overhead rate should be revised.

9. **Calculate cost of goods manufactured and cost of goods sold.**
You find the cost of goods completed during the month, called the cost of goods manufactured, by analyzing activity in the Work in Process Inventory account over the past month. The process for preparing the statement and calculating cost of goods manufactured is as follows:

  Direct Materials Used
+ Direct Labor
+ Applied Manufacturing Overhead

= Total Manufacturing Costs
+ Beginning Balance, Work in Process Inventory
− Ending Balance, Work in Process Inventory

= Cost of Goods Manufactured

The cost of goods manufactured is used in preparing the statement of cost of goods sold. Cost of goods manufactured can also be calculated by summarizing the cost of all jobs completed during the period.

The statement of cost of goods sold can be considered an analysis of the Finished Goods Inventory account. Preparing a statement of cost of goods sold and calculating cost of goods sold is done as follows:

  Cost of Goods Manufactured
+ Beginning Finished Goods Inventory

= Total Goods Available for Sale
− Ending Finished Goods Inventory

= Cost of Goods Sold

The cost of goods sold can also be calculated by multiplying the number of units sold times the per unit cost shown on the job cost sheets. Cost of goods sold is used in preparing the income statement.

Review of Key Terms

Actual manufacturing overhead costs All manufacturing costs except direct labor and direct material costs necessary for the manufacture of a product. Includes the cost of indirect materials, indirect labor, expired factory insurance, depreciation on factory equipment, utilities, and other costs of operating the factory.

Allocate To divide a general cost of production among products, departments, or divisions.

Applied manufacturing overhead costs The estimated total manufacturing overhead costs assigned to a job or product. Calculated by using a predetermined overhead rate.

Apply To divide the manufacturing overhead cost of production among products, using a predetermined rate based on activity measure or usage.

Average cost per unit The unit manufacturing cost of a product; used in valuing inventory on the balance sheet. In a job order costing system, average cost per unit is calculated by dividing total costs of the job by number of units in the job.

Cost driver A measure of business or production activity, such as direct labor cost, machine-hours, or miles driven, that causes changes in the manufacturing overhead cost. Also called *activity base or measure.*

Cost of goods manufactured The total cost of all good units completed during a period and transferred from the Work in Process Inventory to the Finished Goods Inventory during the quarter or year covered by the income statement. Obtained by adjusting the total manufacturing cost for the beginning and ending work in process inventories.

Cost of Goods Sold An account that represents the total cost of all products sold during the accounting period. In a manufacturing company, the cost of goods sold is obtained by adjusting the cost of goods manufactured for the beginning and ending finished goods inventories.

Direct labor Work that can be physically traced to a particular product.

Direct materials Materials that can be physically traced to a particular job or product.

Finished Goods Inventory An account that represents the cost of products that have been finished but not sold by the end of the accounting period.

Full absorption costing A cost accounting system that includes fixed manufacturing overhead costs in the unit cost of inventory.

Historical costs Actual costs incurred in the past.

Indirect labor Factory work that is not performed directly on a particular product. Accounted for as a part of manufacturing overhead.

Indirect materials Miscellaneous materials of small value used in a factory. Accounted for as part of manufacturing overhead.

Job A batch of products with a definite starting and completion point and with a distinct separation from other batches. May consist of one or more units of product.

Job cost sheet A form for recording the direct materials, direct labor, and applied manufacturing overhead costs of a job as well as the number of units produced.

Job order cost accounting system A cost accounting system designed for use in companies whose products or services are produced in distinct batches, often to customer specifications. See *Job*. Each job has a clear starting and completion point.

Manufacturing overhead All manufacturing costs other than direct materials and direct labor necessary to manufacture a product.

Materials Inventory A balance sheet asset account that shows the value of direct and indirect materials on hand for use in production.

Materials requisition forms Forms used to request materials for use in production. Indicates where materials were used in the factory and for what purpose, either job or overhead.

Materials stock cards Records the quantity and cost of materials used in production. A separate card is maintained on each type of material used. Includes receipts for the materials, issues of the materials to production, and the balance of materials available for production.

Overapplied overhead The amount by which applied overhead for a period is greater than actual manufacturing overhead.

Predetermined overhead rate A ratio that relates total estimated manufacturing overhead costs for the year to expected manufacturing activity for the year. Used to assign manufacturing overhead costs to batches of product or to departments. Calculated by dividing estimated total manufacturing overhead costs for the year by estimated amount of cost driver for the year.

Process cost accounting system A cost accounting system designed for companies that mass-produce identical products on a continuous assembly line.

Standard costs Estimates of what unit costs should be, based on past costs and engineering estimates

Timecard A record of the total hours an employee worked on any one day and how those hours were spent.

Total manufacturing cost The sum of the direct materials, direct labor, and applied manufacturing overhead costs incurred during the accounting period.

Underapplied overhead The amount by which applied overhead for a period is less than actual manufacturing overhead.

Work in Process Inventory An account that represents the cost of direct materials, direct labor, and manufacturing overhead that has been invested in the manufacture of as yet unfinished products.

Review Problem

Sample Company manufactures products in batches and uses a job order costing system. The company normally works on three or four jobs a month. Recent data are summarized below.

Annual Data

At the beginning of the year, Sample Company's marketing department estimated annual sales. Based on that estimate the production manager estimated the year's total direct labor costs to be $69,800. Finally, the accounting department and the production manager estimated the year's total manufacturing overhead costs to be $104,700. Since most of Sample's overhead costs, such as fringe benefits and supervision, are labor related, Sample Company used direct labor costs as its cost driver.

Data for this Month

Work in Process Inventory, Beginning of Month	
Job 222	$2,442
Job 223	1,270
Job 225	439
Total	$4,151

Direct Materials Used This Month	
Job 223	$ 369
Job 225	4,773
Job 226	3,435
Job 227	539
Total	$9,116

Note that all materials needed for Job 222 were added last month.

Direct Labor Used This Month	
Job 222	$1,444
Job 223	748
Job 225	2,102
Job 226	1,884
Job 227	236
Total	$6,414

Actual manufacturing overhead costs for the month were $9,211. At month end, jobs 222, 223, 225, and 226 had been completed. Unit sales for the month are summarized below.

Job number	Units in job	Units sold
222	80	80
223	65	65
225	125	100
226	90	

There was no Finished Goods Inventory at the beginning of the month.

Required

1. Calculate Sample Company's predetermined overhead rate.
2. Calculate the total cost of each job worked on during the month. Include any beginning inventory costs. For jobs completed during the month, calculate the cost per unit for each job.
3. Calculate the cost of goods manufactured during the month. Some of your calculations for 2 above will help in answering this question.
4. Calculate the Cost of Goods Sold for the month. Some of your calculations for 2 above will help in answering this question.
5. Calculate the balance of Work in Process Inventory at month end.
6. Prepare a statement of cost of goods manufactured.

7. Prepare a statement of cost of goods sold.
8. Calculate the amount of over- or underapplied overhead for the month.

Solution to Review Problem

1. The predetermined overhead rate is found by dividing estimated overhead for the year by estimated direct labor costs.

$$\text{Predetermined overhead rate} = \frac{\text{estimated total manufacturing overhead costs for the year}}{\text{estimated total direct labor costs for the year}}$$

$$= \frac{\$104{,}700}{\$69{,}800}$$

$$= \underline{\underline{150}} \text{ percent}$$

2. Total costs on each job and cost per unit for completed jobs are summarized below. The direct materials and direct labor costs were given in the problem. The applied overhead was found by multiplying direct labor costs for the month by the 150 percent predetermined overhead rate.

Job number	Beginning balance	Direct materials	Direct labor	Applied overhead	Total costs
222	$2,442	$ —	$1,444	$2,166	$ 6,052
223	1,270	369	748	1,122	3,509
225	439	4,773	2,102	3,153	10,467
226	—	3,435	1,884	2,826	8,145
227	—	539	236	354	1,129
Total	$4,151	$9,116	$6,414	$9,621	$29,302

Job number	Total costs	Completed units	Costs per unit
222	$ 6,052	80	$75.6500
223	3,509	65	53.9846
225	10,467	125	83.7360
226	8,145	90	90.5000
227	1,129	(not completed)	

3. The cost of goods manufactured for the month is the cost of jobs completed during the month. Jobs 222, 223, 225, and 226 were completed during the month. The total cost of each job is taken from the answer to 2 above.

Job number	Total costs
222	$ 6,052
223	3,509
225	10,467
226	8,145
Cost of goods manufactured	$28,173

4. The cost of goods sold can be found by multiplying the number of units sold from each job by the cost per unit calculated in *2* on preceding page. Units from Jobs 222, 223, and 225 were sold this month.

Job number	Costs per unit	Units sold	Cost of goods sold
222	$75.6500	80	$ 6,052
223	53.9846	65	3,509
225	83.7360	100	8,374
Cost of goods sold			$17,935

5. Since Jobs 222, 223, 225, and 226 were completed during the month, the only job remaining uncompleted at month end is Job 227. Calculations in *2* on preceding page show the cost to date of Job 227 is $1,129. Therefore, the Work in Process Inventory balance at month end is $1,129.
6. The statement of cost of goods manufactured is shown as Exhibit 4–2. In *3* above, you found the cost of goods manufactured by calculating the total cost of each job completed during the month and adding these cost together. The statement of cost of goods manufactured shows the other approach, analysis of the Work in Process Inventory account. Of course, both methods give the same result.
7. The statement of cost of goods sold is shown as Exhibit 4–3. In *4* above, a direct calculation was used to find the cost of goods sold (unit costs × number of units sold). Exhibit 4–3 follows the approach of analyzing the Finished Goods Inventory account. Again, both methods give the same result.
8. Over- or underapplied overhead is the difference between applied overhead and actual manufacturing overhead costs. Applied overhead costs, which were calculated in *2* above, are shown in the next to last column. They are $9,621. The basic data of the problem told you that actual manufacturing overhead costs were $9,211. Since applied overhead is greater than actual manufacturing overhead, overhead is *over*applied by $410.

Chapter Assignments

Questions

1. (L.O. 1) Why are managers interested in knowing the cost of a product or service?
2. (L.O. 1) What four decisions must a management accountant make when designing a cost accounting system?
3. (L.O. 1) Describe the physical characteristics of a production process that would cause management to choose a job order costing system. A process costing system.
4. (L.O. 2) What is the function of the job cost sheet in a job costing system?

5. (L.O. 3) What information is contained on a materials requisition form? What four ways does an accountant use the information on a materials requisition form?

6. (L.O. 4) What information is contained on a timecard? What four ways does an accountant use the information on timecards?

7. (L.O. 7) List five types of documents that provide information about actual manufacturing costs for a period.

8. (L.O. 5) How is manufacturing overhead allocated to jobs?

9. (L.O. 8) What four conditions may result in over- or underapplied overhead at month end?

10. (L.O. 8) Ideally, how should over- or underapplied overhead be accounted for at month end if it is *not* caused by errors in estimating total manufacturing overhead or total production for the year? In practice, how is it usually accounted for?

11. (L.O. 9) Using job order costing, how would you determine the cost of goods manufactured?

Exercises

12. (L.O. 2) Elliott Company manufactures tools to customers' specifications. The following data pertain to Job 1501 for February:

Direct materials used	$4,200
Direct labor hours worked	300
Direct labor rate per hour	$8
Machine-hours used	200
Predetermined overhead rate	$15 per machine-hour

Required Calculate the total manufacturing costs of Job 1501 for February. (AICPA adapted)

13. (L.O. 5, 8) Woodman Company applied factory overhead on the basis of direct labor hours. Budget and actual data for direct labor and overhead for the year are as follows:

	Budget	Actual
Direct labor hours	600,000	550,000
Factory overhead costs	$720,000	$680,000

Required Calculate the over- or underapplied overhead. (see Review Exercise 4–2) (CMA adapted)

14. (L.O. 5, 8) At the beginning of the year, Carl Company budgeted Department A's annual overhead at $255,000, based on a budgeted annual volume of 100,000 direct labor hours. At year-end the Actual Factory Overhead account for Department A had a balance of $270,000. Actual direct labor hours for the year were 105,000.

Required Calculate the over- or underapplied overhead for the year. (see Review Exercise 4–2) (AICPA adapted)

15. (L.O. 5, 8) Cannon Cannery, Inc., estimated its factory overhead at $510,000 for 19x4, based on an expected production level of 100,000 direct labor hours. Actual direct labor hours for 19x4 totaled 105,000, whereas actual manufacturing overhead totaled $540,000 at year-end.

Required Calculate the over- or underapplied factory overhead for 19x4. (see Review Exercise 4–2) (AICPA adapted)

16. (L.O. 8) Select year-end balances from Worley's accounting records were as follows:

Sales	$1,200,000
Cost of goods sold (before adjustments)	720,000
Applied manufacturing overhead	315,000
Actual manufacturing overhead	324,000

Worley adjusts the Cost of Goods Sold for any over- or underapplied overhead at year-end.

Required Prepare a schedule showing Worley's gross margin for the year. (see Review Exercise 4–2)

17. (L.O. 9) At the end of the past fiscal year, Barter Company had the following account balances:

Applied overhead	$ 211,000
Actual manufacturing overhead	210,000
Cost of goods sold (before adjustment)	980,000
Sales	1,432,000

Barter adjusts the Cost of Goods Sold for any over- or underapplied overhead at year-end.

Required Prepare a schedule showing Barter's gross margin for the year. (see Review Exercise 4–2)

18. (L.O. 2, 5, 9) Richin Company manufactures special-order products. They use a job order cost accounting system. The predetermined overhead rate applies overhead at the rate of 185 percent of direct labor costs. Data for production and sales activities for October are given below. There was no beginning Work in Process Inventory. At the end of October, all jobs had been completed except Job 4. The beginning Finished Goods Inventory consisted of 600 units completed in earlier months, costing $28.90 per unit. All beginning Finished Goods Inventory was sold during the month for $48.50 per unit.

Job	Units	Direct materials per unit	Direct labor hours per hour	Direct labor rate per unit	Units sold	Selling price
1	800	$5	0.7	$12	800	$46
2	900	4	0.8	12	700	49
3	400	9	1.2	15	200	99
4	900	6	0.8	12	-0-	

Required

1. Calculate the cost of Jobs 1–4 and per unit costs for all completed jobs.
2. Calculate the Cost of Goods Sold for October.
3. Calculate the Finished Goods Inventory at October 31.
4. Calculate the Work in Process Inventory at October 31.

19. (L.O. 2, 5, 9) Bricker Company manufacturers electrical components to customers' specifications. It uses a job cost accounting system with a predetermined overhead rate. Data for production and sales activities for January are given below. There was no beginning Work in Process or Finished Goods Inventory at the beginning of January. At the end of January, all jobs had been completed except Job 104.

Job	Units	Total direct materials costs	Total direct labor costs	Machine-hours per unit	Units sold	Selling price
101	10,000	$20,020	$42,500	0.30	8,000	$40
102	5,000	24,000	37,000	0.26	4,000	36
103	6,000	35,040	54,000	0.38	1,000	60
104	8,000	27,000	43,000	0.31	-0-	

The company's predetermined overhead rate is $32 per machine-hour.

Required

1. Calculate the cost of Jobs 101–104 and per-unit cost for all completed jobs. Round per unit cost to the nearest cent.
2. Calculate the Cost of Goods Sold for the month.
3. Calculate the Work in Process Inventory at month end.
4. Prepare a statement showing gross margin for the month.
5. Prepare a journal entry to record the cost of goods transferred to Finished Goods Inventory during the month.
6. Prepare a journal entry to record the Cost of Goods Sold.

20. (L.O. 8, 9) Hamilton company uses job order costing. Manufacturing overhead is applied to production at a predetermined rate of 150 percent of direct labor costs. Any over- or underapplied factory overhead is closed to the Cost of Goods Sold account at month end. Additional information is available as follows:

    a. Job 101 was the only job in process on January 31, 19x4. Accumulated costs were as follows:

Direct materials	$4,000
Direct labor	2,000
Applied manufacturing overhead	3,000
	$9,000

    b. Jobs 102, 103, and 104 were started during February.
    c. Direct materials requisitions for February totaled $26,000.
    d. Direct labor costs of $20,000 were incurred for February.
    e. Actual factory overhead was $32,000 for February.
    f. The only job still in process on February 29, 19x4, was Job 104. Cost for direct materials were $2,800; for direct labor, $1,800.

Required

1. Prepare a statement of cost of goods manufactured for February.
2. Calculate the over- or underapplied overhead. (AICPA adapted)

21. (L. O. 2) Flawless Word Processing Services specializes in large word processing orders such as textbooks. Flawless uses a job cost accounting system to record costs of each order. Its main reasons for knowing job costs is to determine the profitability of each order and to bid better on future orders.

    A summary of costs on order 11-350 are as follows:

Computer disks	$211
Paper	150
Computer hours	110 hours
Printer hours	40 hours

    Typing labor costs Flawless $15 per hour. Typing hours are equal to computer hours. Printing labor costs Flawless $10 per hour. One-half hour of labor is required for each printer hour since one person can supervise two printers at the same time. Flawless uses an overhead rate of 70 percent of direct labor cost to cover supervision, office, and administrative costs; $6 per hour for computer time; $4 per hour for printer time.

Required

1. Prepare a job cost sheet for order 11-350. Use the format of Exhibit 4–1 to the extent you have the data.
2. Suppose that Flawless bid $5,600. What is the dollar amount of their profit on order 11-350? What was the profit as a percentage of selling price?

22. **(L.O. 2, 8)** Martin Frenzel provides part-time lobbying services to a variety of clients. Frenzel uses a job order costing system and regards each lobbying engagement as a job. Frenzel worked on only two jobs during April.

	Job number	
	S41	**H42**
Direct lobbyist hours	20	30
Direct typing and clerical hours	10	8
Direct entertainment expense	$ 600	$ 870
Direct lobbyist salary cost	2,400	3,000
Direct typing and clerical cost	180	140

Frenzel has two overhead cost pools, one for typing and clerical costs and one for other overhead costs. The cost driver for the typing and clerical costs is direct typing and clerical cost. The cost driver for the other overhead costs is based on direct lobbyist hours.

The predetermined overhead rate for typing and clerical is 150 percent of direct typing and clerical cost. The predetermined overhead rate for other overhead costs is $125 per direct lobbyist hour. The actual overhead cost incurred in April was $7,170.

Required

1. Calculate the cost of each job for April.
2. Calculate the cost per lobbyist hour for each job.
3. By what amount is the overhead cost over- or underapplied for April?

23. **(L.O. 5)** Tillman Corporation uses a job order costing system. Budgeted manufacturing costs in 19x4 are

Direct materials	$ 800,000
Direct labor	1,000,000
Manufacturing overhead	1,000,000

Actual material and labor costs charged to Job 432 during 19x4 were as follows:

Direct materials	$25,000
Direct labor	20,000

Tillman applied manufacturing overhead to production orders on the basis of direct labor costs, using rates predetermined at the beginning of the year. These rates were based on the annual budget.

Required Calculate total manufacturing costs associated with Job 432 for 19x4. (AICPA adapted)

24. **(L.O. 5)** Advertiser Printing Company (APC) prints advertising supplements for inclusion in Sunday newspapers and for distribution to homes. There are three main

activities in preparing and printing an advertising supplement. These correspond to the following overhead pools, each with its cost driver:

Pool	Cost driver
Composing, layout, and design	Composing, layout, and design labor hours
Printing and assembly	Tons of paper
Distribution	Delivery miles

APC's accounting system records most overhead costs according to these three activities. There is a small amount of general overhead that cannot be assigned directly to these activities. This general overhead is assigned to printing jobs according to their total direct labor cost.

In planning for next year, management has estimated the following:

	Estimated costs in the pool	Estimated amount of cost driver
Composing, layout, and design	$240,000	8,000 labor hours
Printing and assembly	300,000	20,000 tons of paper
Distribution	150,000	300,000 delivery miles
General overhead costs	90,000	$225,000 direct labor cost

Required

1. Calculate predetermined overhead rates for each activity and for the general overhead for next year.
2. Assume that one of next year's jobs will have the following characteristics.

Job 1154 15 composing, layout, and design hours
70 tons of paper
1,200 delivery miles
$425 other labor cost

Calculate the amount of overhead cost which will be assigned to the job using the rates you determined in *1* above.

Problems

25. (L.O. 5, 9) Kanodia Company manufacturers models to customers' specifications. The company uses a job order cost accounting system with a predetermined overhead rate based on direct labor costs. Data for production and sales activities for March are given below. There was no beginning Work in Process Inventory. The ending Work in Process Inventory consisted of Job 304, which was not completed during March. The beginning Finished Goods Inventory consisted of 60 units, each one costing $289. The units sold in March for $485 per unit.

Job	Units	Direct materials per unit	Direct labor hours per unit	Direct labor rate per hour	Units sold	Selling price
301	80	$40	7	$12	80	$460
302	90	44	8	12	70	490
303	40	60	12	15	20	990
304	90	35	8	12	-0-	

At the beginning of the year, Kanodia estimated that total overhead for the year would be $521,100. Total direct labor costs for the year were estimated to be $270,000.

Required

1. Calculate Kanodia's predetermined overhead rate.
2. Calculate the cost of Jobs 301–304 and the overhead rate. Round per unit cost to the nearest cent.
3. Calculate the Cost of Goods Sold for the month.
4. What is the cost of the Work in Process Inventory at month end?
5. Prepare a statement showing gross margin for March.

26. **(L.O. 2, 5, 9)** Carter Company manufactures special tools in batches. The company uses a job order cost accounting system with a predetermined overhead rate based on machine-hours. Production and sales activities for November are summarized below. In addition to the costs shown, $24,000 in costs were incurred on Job 1101 during October. At the end of November, the Work in Process Inventory consisted of Job 1104, which had not yet been completed. There was no Finished Goods Inventory on November 1.

Job	Units	Total direct materials costs	Total direct labor costs	Machine-hours per unit	Units sold
1101	10,000	$ —	$12,500	0.70	10,000
1102	9,000	17,000	16,000	1.20	7,000
1103	7,000	25,000	18,000	0.65	4,100
1104	12,000	14,000	12,000	0.31	-0-

The company's predetermined overhead rate is $5.70 per machine-hour.

Required

1. Calculate the total cost of Jobs 1101–1104 and the per-unit cost of completed jobs. Round per unit cost to the nearest cent.
2. Calculate the Cost of Goods Sold for the month.
3. What is the cost of the Work in Process Inventory at month end?
4. Prepare a journal entry to record the cost of goods manufactured, the transfer of costs from Work in Process Inventory to Finished Goods Inventory.
5. Prepare a journal entry to record the Cost of Goods Sold.

27. **(L.O. 3, 4, 9)** The Summit Company provided the inventory balances and manufacturing cost data shown below for the month of January.

	Inventories	
	January 1	January 31
Direct materials	$30,000	$40,000
Work in process	15,000	20,000
Finished goods	65,000	50,000

	Month of January
Applied manufacturing overhead	$150,000
Cost of goods manufactured	515,000
Direct materials used	190,000
Actual manufacturing overhead	144,000

Under Summit's cost system any over- or underapplied overhead is closed to the Cost of Goods Sold account at the end of the calendar year.

Required Set up T accounts for Materials Inventory, Work in Process Inventory, Finished Goods Inventory, Cost of Goods Sold, Applied Manufacturing Overhead, and Actual Manufacturing Overhead. Enter the data given into the T accounts. Then, use the T accounts to find the following and write journal entries for each.

1. Direct Materials Purchased on Account
2. Direct Labor Costs Incurred
3. Cost of Goods Sold

(AICPA adapted)

28. (L.O. 3, 4, 9) Selected cost data (in thousands) concerning operations for the past fiscal year at Televans Manufacturing Company as presented below.

	Inventories		
	Beginning		**Ending**
Materials	$75		$ 85
Work in process	80		30
Finished goods	90		110
Direct materials used		$326	

Total manufacturing costs charged to production during the year, including direct materials, direct labor, and manufacturing overhead applied at a rate of 60 percent of direct labor cost	$686
Cost of goods manufactured plus beginning finished goods inventory	826
Selling and general expenses	25

Required Prepare T accounts for Materials Inventory, Work in Process Inventory, Finished Goods Inventory, and Cost of Goods Sold. Enter the data into the appropriate T accounts. Use the T accounts to find the following. Write journal entries for each.

1. Materials Purchased on Account
2. Direct Labor Costs Incurred
3. Cost of Goods Manufactured
4. Costs of Goods Sold

(CMA adapted)

29. (L.O. 5, 9) Worrell Corporation has a job order costing system. The following amounts appear in the Work in Process Inventory account for March 19x4:

Balance, March 1	$ 12,000
Direct materials used	40,000
Direct labor	30,000
Transferred to finished goods	100,000

Worrell applies overhead to production at a predetermined rate of 90 percent based on direct labor costs. Job 232, the only job still in process at the end of March 19x4, has been charged with factory overhead of $2,250.

Required

1. Calculate the balance in Work in Process Inventory at March 31.
2. Calculate the amount of direct materials charged to Job 232.

(AICPA adapted)

30. (L.O. 3, 4, 5, 9) Rayburn Company produces custom-made educational toys. Because the toys are designed to meet each customer's needs, they are produced in batches.

Rayburn uses a job order cost accounting system with a predetermined overhead rate based on direct labor hours. March production data and sales activities are as follows:

Job	Direct materials per job	Direct labor hours	Direct labor rate per hour	Units sold	Selling price
765	$ —	40	$15	80	$3,560
766	440	50	16	70	3,840
767	600	100	14	20	7,890
768	350	70	16	-0-	—

Job 765 was already in process at the beginning of the month, and $550 had already been spent on that job during February. All jobs except Job 768 were completed by the end of March. The beginning Finished Goods Inventory consisted of 10 units of Job 764, each costing $149. These units were sold during the month for $385 per unit. Jobs 765, 766, and 767 were special order work. All units were sold at the agreed contract price.

At the beginning of the year, Rayburn estimated that total manufacturing overhead for the year would be $140,000. Accountants estimated that total direct labor hours for the year would be 5,000.

Required

1. Calculate Rayburn's predetermined overhead rate.
2. Calculate the cost to date of Jobs 765–768.
3. Calculate the Cost of Goods Sold for the month.
4. Calculate the cost of the Work in Process Inventory at month end.
5. Prepare a statement showing the gross margin for March.
6. Prepare journal entries to record costs added to Work in Process Inventory during March.
7. Prepare a journal entry to record the cost of goods manufactured for March.
8. Prepare a journal entry to record the Cost of Goods Sold for March.

31. (L.O. 3, 4, 8) Roja Corporation manufacturers aluminum fasteners. Among Roja's 19x4 manufacturing costs were:

Wages and salaries	
Machine operators	$ 80,000
Factory supervisors	30,000
Machine mechanics	20,000
Aluminum	400,000
Machine parts	18,000
Lubricants for machines	5,000
Other manufacturing overhead	40,000
Applied manufacturing overhead	110,000

Required

1. Calculate direct materials and direct labor costs.
2. Calculate the over- or underapplied overhead. (AICPA adapted)

32. (L.O. 2, 5) Blackwood uses a job order costing system and applies manufacturing overhead to production orders on the basis of direct labor costs. The overhead rate for the year is 225 percent. Job 123, started and completed during the year, was charged with the following costs:

Direct materials	$ 30,000
Direct labor	?
Applied factory overhead	108,000

Required Calculate total manufacturing costs on Job 123.

33. (L.O. 2, 3, 4, 5, 6, 8, 9) Baehr Company is a manufacturing company that uses a job order accounting system for production costs. The company's predetermined overhead rate is based on direct labor hours. Before the start of the year, Baehr estimated its manufacturing overhead costs at several volumes of output for 19x3.

Volume in direct labor hours	50,000	60,000	70,000
Variable overhead costs	$325,000	$390,000	$455,000
Fixed overhead costs	216,000	216,000	216,000
Total overhead	$541,000	$606,000	$671,000

Company officials expect to operate at 60,000 direct labor hours capacity for 19x3. Actual operating results for November 19x3 are presented below. Jobs 83-50 and 83-51 were completed during November.

Inventories, November 1, 19x3	
Materials and supplies	$ 10,500
Work in process (Job 83-50)	54,000
Finished goods	112,500
Purchases of materials on account	150,000
Materials and supplies requisitioned for production	
Job 83-50	$ 45,000
Job 83-51	37,500
Job 83-52	25,500
Supplies	12,000
	$120,000
Factory direct labor hours	
Job 83-50	1,750
Job 83-51	1,500
Job 83-52	1,000
	4,250
Labor costs	
Direct labor wages (4,250 hours)	$ 51,000
Indirect labor wages (2,000 hours)	15,000
Supervisory salaries	6,000
	$ 72,000
Building occupancy costs (heat, light, depreciation, etc.)	
Factory facilities	$ 6,500
Sales offices	1,500
Administrative offices	1,000
Total	$ 9,000
Factory equipment costs	
Power	$ 4,000
Repairs and maintenance	1,500
Depreciation	1,500
Other	1,000
Total	$ 8,000

Required

1. Calculate the predetermined overhead rate to be used during the year.
2. Calculate total costs incurred on Jobs 83-50, 83-51, and 83-52.
3. Prepare a statement of cost of goods manufactured for November.
4. Calculate the total amount of over- or underapplied overhead for November.
5. Prepare journal entries to
   a. Record the purchase of materials.
   b. Record the direct and indirect materials used
   c. Record the direct and indirect labor
   d. Record applied overhead costs
   e. Record cost of goods manufactured (CMA)

34. (L.O. 2, 3, 4, 6) United Rocker Company makes rocking chairs. It has six popular models. Normally, it manufactures only one model of rocker at a time. It accumulates orders for a particular model of rocker and then builds enough to satisfy the orders. Usually about two models are built each month.

United has two cost pools, cutting and other. It keeps the costs of the cutting pool separate because some rockers are quite complicated and require a lot of cutting, while other rockers are simple and require only a little cutting time. The cost driver for the cutting cost pool is hours of cutting time. The cost driver for the other cost pool is board feet of wood in a job. For the coming year, United estimated that it would incur $380,000 cost in the cutting cost pool and $560,000 in the other cost pool. They also estimated 20,000 hours of cutting time and use of 280,000 board feet of wood.

United had no Work in Process Inventory or Finished Goods Inventory at October 1. In October, United worked on two jobs, Job 54 and Job 55. Job 54 consisted of 120 modern-style rockers. Job 55 consisted of 50 oriental rockers.

During April, United had the following transactions:

a. Purchased 18,000 board feet of wood for $25,200. United is to pay the invoice next month.
b. Requisitioned 4,800 board feet of wood for Job 54 costing $10,180, 15,000 board feet of wood for Job 55 costing $12,000, and $3,400 of supplies.
c. Incurred $9,500 of direct labor cost on Job 54, $8,500 hours of direct labor cost on Job 55, and $8,000 of indirect labor cost.
d. Applied overhead costs using cost drivers. Job 54 required 240 hours of cutting time, and Job 55 required 250 hours of cutting time.
e. Job 54 was completed during the month. Job 55 was not finished by the end of the month.
f. 100 units from Job 54 were sold on account for $400 each.

Required

1. Calculate the cost per unit of rockers in Job 54.
2. Prepare journal entries to record events a through f.
3. Calculate the cost of Work in Process Inventory and the cost of Finished Goods Inventory at the end of April.

35. (L. O. 5) Sabo Repair Shop has three overhead cost pools. The first includes materials-handling costs. Its cost driver is number of parts used. The second cost pool includes machine-related costs. Its cost driver is machine-hours. Finally, the last cost pool includes all other costs. Its cost driver is direct labor costs.

For the coming year, Sabo has made the following estimates:

Number of parts used	11,340
Number of machine-hours worked	7,000

Number of direct labor hours worked	12,000
Materials-handling costs	
Fixed	$13,608
Variable	$0.40 per part
Machine-related costs	
Fixed	$16,100
Variable	$0.20 per machine-hour
Other overhead costs	
Fixed	$21,600
Variable	$0.75 per direct labor hour

Required

1. Calculate Sabo's three predetermined overhead rates.
2. Give two examples of costs which might be found in each overhead pool.
3. Explain briefly which of each cost driver might be a logical choice for its cost pool.

Case 1
Sauer and Sauer CPA

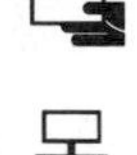

The Sauer and Sauer CPA firm requires each of its employees to complete a weekly timecard specifying the hours they worked on each job, the hours spent on professional development, and the unassigned hours. This information is then transcribed to job cost sheets for each of the clients and used for costing and billing purposes. The timecards for the past week are summarized below.

Employee	Rank	Client	Hours
P. Maska	Junior	101	10
		102	20
B. Bucks	Junior	101	10
		102	20
		104	5
T. Whitehall	Junior	103	10
		104	15
Q. Faxon	Junior	102	10
		103	5
		104	25
P. Bills	Junior	101	15
		103	10
		104	10
J. Jones	Senior	101	15
		102	25
S. Send	Senior	103	20
		104	20

From Jack Gray and Don Ricketts, *Cost and Managerial Accounting* (New York: McGraw-Hill Book Company, 1982), pp 122–123. Reproduced with permission from McGraw-Hill, Inc.

Employee	Rank	Client	Hours
P. Rabit	Manager	101	10
		102	15
		103	5
		104	20
J. Sauer	Partner	101	10
		104	15
S. Sauer	Partner	102	16
		103	15

The weekly pay rates for the employees are

Junior	$ 520	Manager	$1,000
Senior	600	Partner	1,400

These rates represent the pay for 40 hours. To allocate the salary cost to the clients an hourly rate is calculated and used to assign the salary cost to the clients. Any professional development time and unassigned time is charged to an Overhead account. The overhead cost is allocated to the client at a rate of 200 percent of the salary cost.

The clients are billed for the services based on the following rates:

Junior	$ 40 per hour	Manager	$ 80
Senior	60	Partner	100

Required

1. Calculate the salary and overhead cost assigned to each client.
2. Assuming the audit is completed for clients 102 and 104, calculate the amount of each bill that will be submitted to the client.
3. Comment on the use of the job cost data calculated in *1* above for estimating the cost of future audits.

Case 2
Morgan Manufacturing Company

Morgan Manufacturing Company has two departments, fabricating and assembly, for the production of automotive parts. The overhead in each department is applied to the jobs using direct labor hours (DLH) as the cost driver. The cost of the beginning work in process and a summary of the direct materials and direct labor cost for the month of June 19x9 are provided below. A schedule for the estimated annual overhead for each department is provided. During the month, all Jobs were completed except job X765.

From Jack Gray and Don Ricketts, *Cost and Managerial Accounting* (New York: McGraw-Hill Book Company, 1982), pp 123–125. Reproduced with permission of McGraw-Hill, Inc.

Beginning Work in Process

Job	Direct materials	Direct labor	Applied overhead	Total
X751	$2,000	$3,050	$6,200	$11,250
X761	3,000	4,755	9,500	17,255

Summary of Direct Materials Requisitions

Requisition	Job	Quantity	Cost per unit	Total
R1008	X762	100 lbs	$3.50	$350
R1009	X763	120 lbs	4.20	504
R1010	X763	60 lbs	4.20	252
R1011	X764	85 lbs	5.00	425
R1012	X764	70 lbs	1.00	70
R1014	X765	160 lbs	4.00	640
R1013	X762	30 lbs	3.50	105

Direct Labor Data Summary—Fabricating

Work order	Job	Hours	Cost per hour	Total
F 75	X751	8	$14.00	$112
F 76	X762	45	14.00	630
F 77	X763	70	14.00	980
F 78	X764	45	14.00	630
F 79	X765	20	14.00	280
F 80	X762	10	14.00	140

Direct Labor Data Summary—Assembly

Work order	Job	Hours	Cost per hour	Total
A 96	X751	10	$10.00	$100
A 97	X761	15	10.00	150
A 98	X762	30	10.00	300
A 99	X763	45	10.00	450
A 100	X764	25	10.00	250
A 101	X765	15	10.00	150

Annual Budgeted Overhead

	Department	
Item	Fabricating	Assembly
Supervision	$18,000	$15,000
Indirect labor	7,500	5,000
Depreciation	20,000	6,000
Miscellaneous supplies	4,000	2,000
Total	$49,500	$28,000
Estimated cost driver (DLH)	2,500	1,600
Predetermined overhead rate	$19.80 per DLH	$17.50 per DLH

The production and shipping records for the month provided the following information:

Completed Jobs

Job	Units Produced	Units Shipped
X751	100	80
X761	150	150
X762	100	60
X763	160	160
X764	150	70

Required

1. Calculate the total cost of producing each job.
2. Prepare schedules showing the cost of the ending work in process, finished goods, and cost of goods sold.

Case 3
Offset Press Company (L.O. 8)

Tom Savin has recently been hired as a cost accountant by the Offset Press Company, a privately held company that produces a line of offset printing presses and lithograph machines. During his first few months on the job, Savin discovered that Offset has been underapplying factory overhead to the Work in Process account, while overstating expense through the general and administrative account. Underapplying overhead reduces the value of inventory because not enough overhead is being applied to each job. If the underapplied overhead is reported as general and administrative expense, it increases expense and understates net income.

This practice has been going on since the start of the company, which is in its sixth year of operation. The effect in each year has been favorable, having a material impact on the company's tax position. No internal audit function exists at Offset, and the external auditors have not yet discovered the underapplied factory overhead.

Savin had pointed out the practice and its effect to Mary Brown, the corporate controller, and had asked her to let him make the necessary adjustments. Brown directed him not to make the adjustments. Savin, however, believes that the adjustments should be made and that the external auditors should be informed of the situation.

Since there are no established policies at Offset Press Company for resolving ethical conflicts, Savin is considering following one of the three alternative courses of action listed on page 165.

1. Follow Brown's directive and do nothing further.
2. Attempt to convince Brown to make the proper adjustments and to advise the external auditors of her actions.
3. Tell the audit committee of the board of directors about the problem and give them the appropriate accounting data.

Required

1. For each of the three alternative courses of action that Tom Savin is considering, explain whether or not the action is appropriate. Hint: Review Ethics Section of Chapter 1.
2. Without prejudice to your answer in *1* above, assume that Tom Savin again approaches Mary Brown to make the necessary adjustments and is unsuccessful. Describe the steps that Tom Savin should take in proceeding to resolve this situation. (CMA adapted)

■

5

Process Costing

LEARNING OBJECTIVES

After studying this chapter you should be able to:

1. Describe how process costing accumulates costs and calculates cost per unit
2. Write journal entries to record manufacturing costs and transfers
3. Calculate equivalent units when resources are added uniformly
4. Calculate equivalent units when resources are added in a lump
5. Using equivalent units, calculate the unit cost for all types of costs and record them on a cost summary
6. Calculate unit cost using the moving average method, and use it to compute the cost of completed units and ending work in process
7. Calculate unit cost using the FIFO method, and use it to compute the cost of completed units and ending work in process

As discussed in Chapter 4, **process costing** is the cost accounting system used by companies that produce large amounts of nearly identical products more or less continuously. Soap, paint, chemicals, and small appliances are examples of mass-produced products that lend themselves to this approach. Although a few services, such as routine medical tests, may be done in so large a volume that process costing is justified, process costing is mainly applicable to factory production lines.

The main difference between process costing and job order costing is that in process costing, costs are recorded and the cost per unit is calculated by department or activity rather than by batch. Firms that use process costing usually maintain an inventory of finished product out of which orders are filled. There simply are no batches on a production line. Production is continuous. Without the convenient starting and stopping point of a job, accountants must record costs and units and calculate unit cost for a period such as a month. Instead of measuring and recording direct materials and direct labor used on a job, they must measure and record them by activity. Manufacturing overhead costs are allocated to departments rather than to jobs.

Once direct materials, direct labor, and manufacturing overhead for the month have been identified with activities, the per unit cost can be calculated in the usual way. That is, an activity's monthly costs can be divided by the number of units the department processed that month. The key to process cost accounting is to match costs with activities and to correctly measure the number of units processed in each activity each month.

■

A Simple Illustration of Process Costing

OBJECTIVE 1
Describe how process costing accumulates costs and calculates cost per unit

To illustrate **process costing**, we will look at the way that Stoney Point Canning Company accumulates costs by activity and calculates cost per unit for the month of July 19x1. For two months each summer, Stoney Point Canning Company uses one of its factories to can green beans. Although this factory cans several foods, only one food is canned at a time. The factory is therefore treated as a single activity for accounting purposes. Since the machinery is cleaned each day at the end of the last shift, there are no partially canned units at the start or the end of the day and thus none at the start or end of the month.

During July, accountants recorded the following data:

Direct materials purchased	$22,845
Direct materials used	20,000
Indirect materials used	3,227

Figure 5–1
Flow of Costs
This figure shows how costs flow through accounts. Notice that the flow is the same for process costing and job order costing.

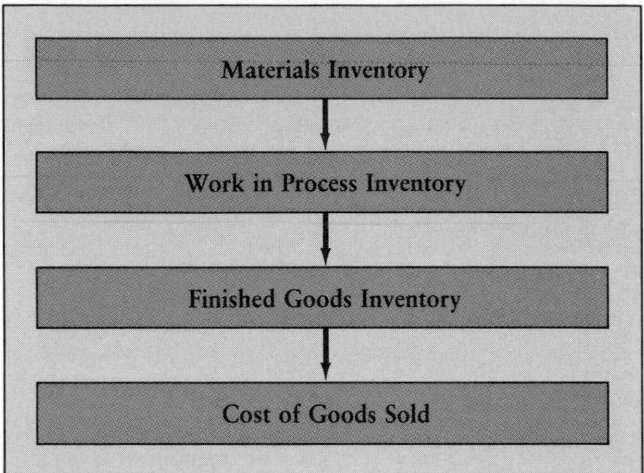

Figure 5–2
Stoney Point Canning Company Flow of Costs Through Accounts, July 19X1
In process costing and job order costing, costs flow through accounts in the same way. The major difference between the two systems is that in process costing, costs are recorded by department rather than by job.

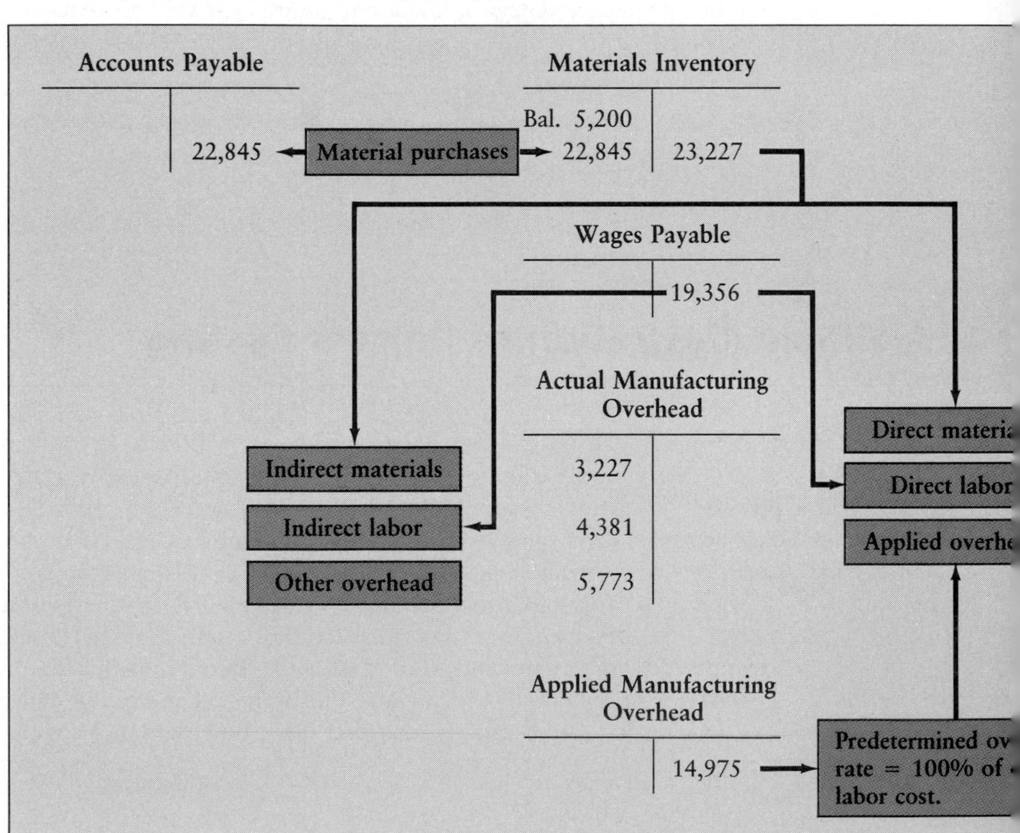

Direct labor	14,975
Indirect labor	4,381
Other actual manufacturing overhead costs	5,773
Cases of beans produced	15,000
Cases of beans sold	2,000

Stoney Point's **predetermined overhead rate** is 100 percent of its **direct labor costs.** Costs per unit are calculated just as in job order costing except that one month's production in the plant (department) is substituted for one job, as shown below.

$$\text{Cost per unit} = \frac{\text{direct materials} + \text{direct labor} + \text{applied manufacturing overhead}}{\text{units produced}}$$

$$= \frac{\$20{,}000 + \$14{,}975 + \$14{,}975}{15{,}000 \text{ cases}}$$

$$= \frac{\$49{,}950}{15{,}000 \text{ cases}}$$

$$= \underline{\underline{\$3.33}} \text{ per case}$$

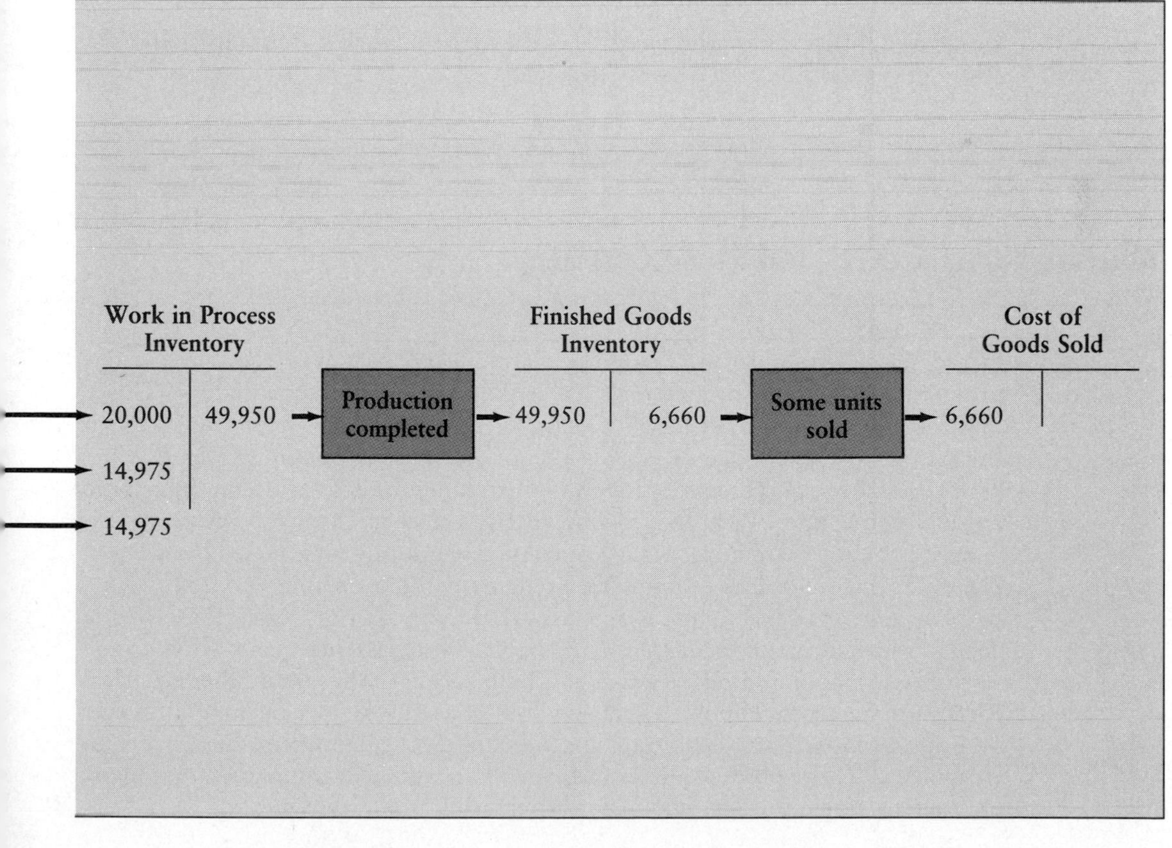

In process costing, use of **direct** and **indirect materials** is recorded by activity on materials requisition forms. Use of **direct** and **indirect labor** is recorded on timecards. Direct labor is recorded by activity, and indirect labor is charged to manufacturing overhead accounts that show the nature of the indirect labor, for example, supervision or time keeping. **Actual manufacturing overhead** is recorded as incurred, just as it is in job order costing. **Manufacturing overhead** is applied to activities and is used to calculate the cost per unit. As in job order costing, over- or underapplied overhead usually occurs at month end. By year-end, actual manufacturing overhead should approximately equal applied manufacturing overhead, assuming annual estimates are accurate. There are no job cost sheets in process cost accounting, since there are no jobs.

Costs flow through accounts in process costing and in job order costing in the same way (Figure 5–1). Direct materials used, direct labor, and applied overhead costs are added to work in process. At month's end, Work in Process Inventory is reduced by the cost of units completed. Finished Goods inventory is increased by the same amount. In Stoney Point's case, since all units worked on were completed, 15,000 cases valued at $3.33 per case are transferred to Finished Goods Inventory. Since 2,000 cases were sold in July, Finished Goods Inventory is decreased by 2,000 cases times $3.33 per case. The Cost of Goods Sold account is increased by the same amount.

Figure 5–2 summarizes how costs flow through Stoney Point's accounts. Journal entries will not be illustrated until the next example. You can see from Figure 5–2, however, that the journal entries are the same as those for **job order costing** because the cost flows are the same.

■

Identifying Costs with Activities

In the simple example just discussed, only one product was produced in one production activity. More often several activities must be accounted for. This is the case with Drumm Safety Light Company, which produces safety-light kits for small trailers. The finished product is a set of plastic cases containing lights, wire, wire connectors, and mounting screws—everything needed to mount lights onto a trailer and connect them to a towing vehicle's electrical system. The product is packed in a cardboard box, which is open on one side and wrapped in transparent plastic so customers can examine the contents without opening the box.

Drumm's product requires the use of three activities. First, the molding department makes plastic cases for the lights. Next, assembly cuts wires to the appropriate length and places purchased bulb sockets, wires, and other electrical parts into the cases. Finally, packaging completes the sets by packing all pieces into the cardboard box and wrapping it. Figure 5–3 summarizes the process. In Drumm's case, the product passes through all activities. In companies with many products, a single product may pass through only some activities.

Figure 5–3
Drumm Safety Light Company
In process costing, costs are added to the production process as the product flows through production activities.

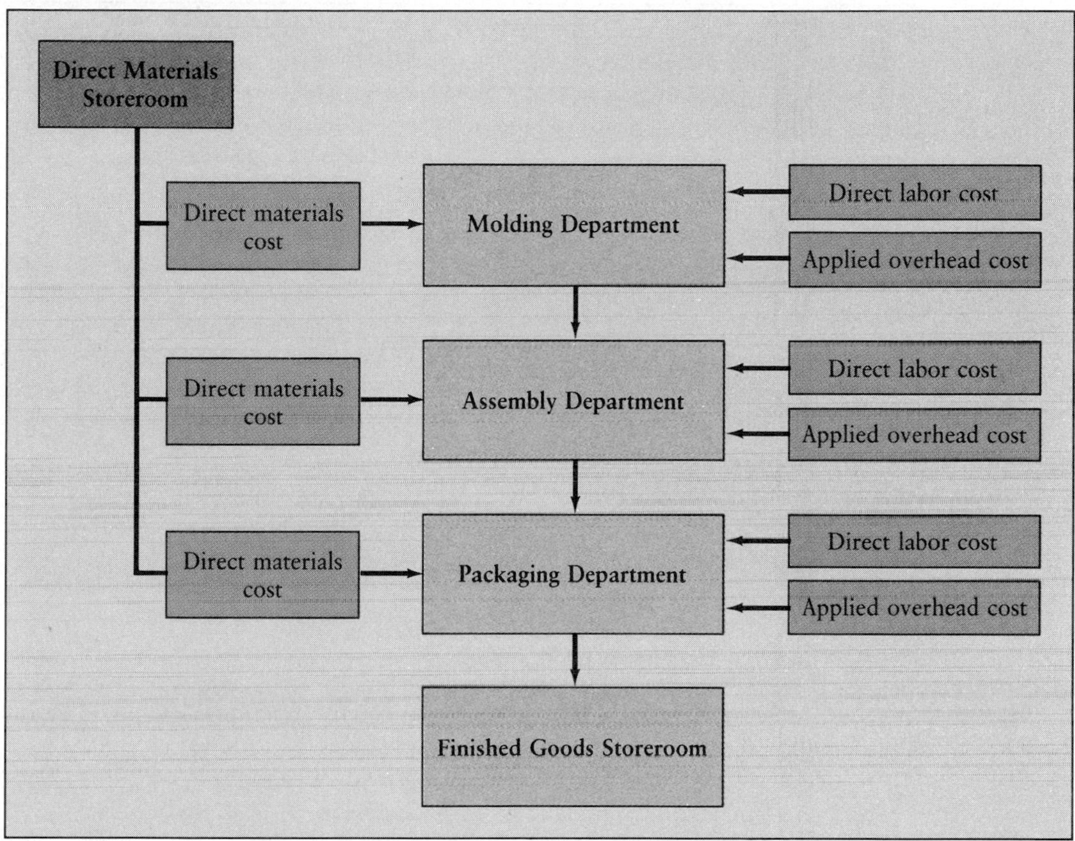

Drumm's light set accumulates costs as it flows through each activity. The cost of the plastic, direct labor, and applied overhead is added in the molding activity. The cost of the metal sockets, bulbs, wire, wire connectors, more direct labor, and applied overhead is added in the assembly activity. In the packing activity, the cost of the packaging, more direct labor, and applied overhead is added to the other costs. The cost of a completed package is the sum of the costs incurred in each activity (Figure 5–4).

With this understanding of the general process, you are now ready for a detailed look at how costs are accounted for in each activity. In order to illustrate further aspects of process cost accounting, the example above will become progressively more complex for each of Drumm Safety Light's activities. Therefore, assume the molding activity of Drumm Safety Light began March with no partially completed units on hand. During the month, direct materials necessary to complete 40,000 plastic cases were added to production. By month end, all 40,000

Figure 5–4
Drumm Safety Light Company
In process costing, the cost of a finished product is the sum of the costs incurred in each production activity.

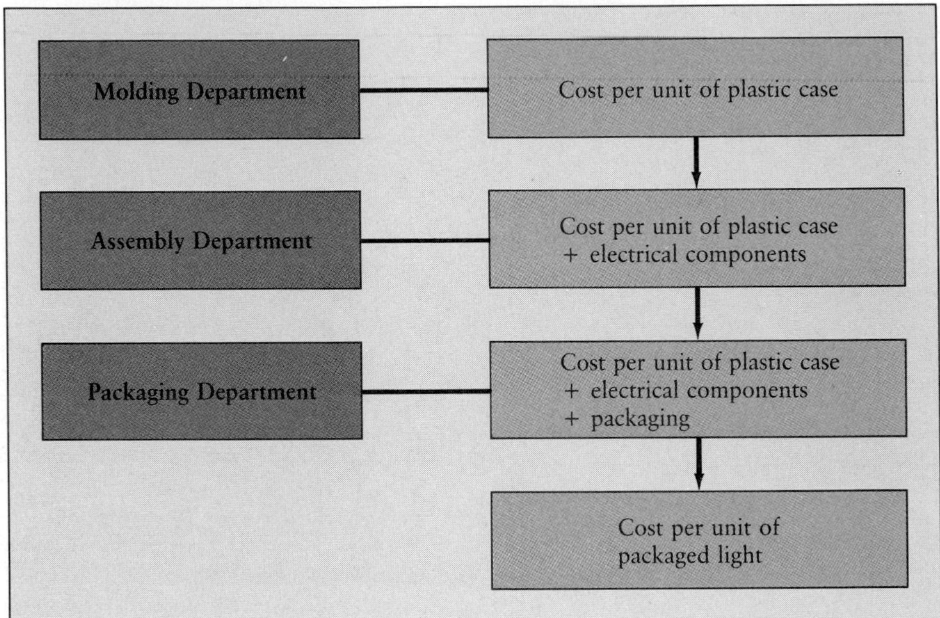

units had been completed and transferred to the assembly activity. Unit production figures and total costs for the month are summarized as follows:

Units	
Beginning work in process	-0-
Units started	40,000
Units completed	40,000
Ending work in process	-0-
Costs added in March	
Direct materials	$ 2,000
Direct labor	4,000
Applied manufacturing overhead*	6,000
Total	$12,000

*Predetermined overhead rate = 150 percent of direct labor cost.

Such monthly production costs are reported in a cost summary (Exhibit 5–1). The summary has four major sections: **Units to account for, Units accounted for, Costs to account for,** and **Costs accounted for.** Study the format of the cost summary carefully. This summary is used for all process costing calculations. The

Exhibit 5–1

Drumm Safety Light Company—Molding Activity Cost Summary for March

This exhibit shows (1) the number of units the molding activity was responsible for during March and (2) where the units were at the end of the month. It also shows (3) costs charged to the molding activity in March and (4) where those costs were at month end.

1. Units to account for	Physical units		
Beginning work in process	-0-		
Units started	40,000		
Total	40,000		
2. Units accounted for	**Physical units**		
Completed	40,000		
Ending work in process	-0-		
Total	40,000		
3. Costs to account for	**Current period cost**	**Units**	**Average cost per unit**
Direct materials	$ 2,000		
Conversion	10,000		
Total	$12,000	40,000	$0.30
4. Costs accounted for	**Total cost**		
Completed and transferred to assembly activity 40,000 @ $0.30	$12,000		

calculations become more complicated as production methods become more complex, but the format of the summary remains the same.

Total units to account for must always equal total units accounted for. Likewise, total costs to account for must always equal total costs accounted for. The computations in Exhibit 5–1 involve round numbers that yield an **average cost per unit** of exactly $0.30 ($12,000 ÷ 40,000), so units and costs balance perfectly. In other cases, computations must be carried to enough decimal places to avoid rounding errors. With computers this task is easy. Four decimal places is usually a reasonable compromise for working problems. Rounding errors may still result, but they should be small. For now, you should be primarily concerned with the logic of the process anyway.

OBJECTIVE 2
Write journal entries to record manufacturing costs and transfers

The costs added to Work in Process Inventory in the molding activity are recorded in journal entries. Usually, separate entries are made for direct materials, direct labor, and applied manufacturing overhead, but they are summarized here as one entry:

(1) Work in Process Inventory, Molding	12,000	
Materials Inventory		2,000
Wages Payable		4,000
Applied Manufacturing Overhead		6,000
To record the molding total costs for March		

By month end, all 40,000 plastic cases had been transferred to assembly for the next step in the production process. The completion of the units is recognized by the following journal entry:

(2) Work in Process Inventory, Assembly	12,000	
Work in Process Inventory, Molding		12,000
To transfer the cost of 40,000 completed cases at $0.30 per unit from molding to assembly		

So far, the accounting process at Drumm Safety Light has paralleled Stoney Point's (pages 167–170). Because there were no partially completed units in the molding department at the beginning or end of the month, the calculations have been simple. In real life, however, the manufacturing process is hardly ever so neat.

In the next section you will see how partially completed units are accounted for, using Drumm's assembly activity as an example. You will also see how partially completed units at both the beginning and end of the month are handled when the accounting for the packaging activity is illustrated. The assembly activity begins the month with a clean slate (no beginning inventory of partially completed units). By month's end, however, there are partially completed units to account for.

■

Accounting for Partially Completed Units in Ending Inventory

Frequently, a department has some partially completed units on hand at month end. These unfinished units complicate the accounting process. Try visualizing a production line with some units just started and other units near completion. The

Figure 5–5
Allocation of Manufacturing Costs to Partially Complete Units and Fully Complete Units
In process costing, costs incurred in an activity during a month are divided between fully completed units transferred out and the ending inventory of partially completed units.

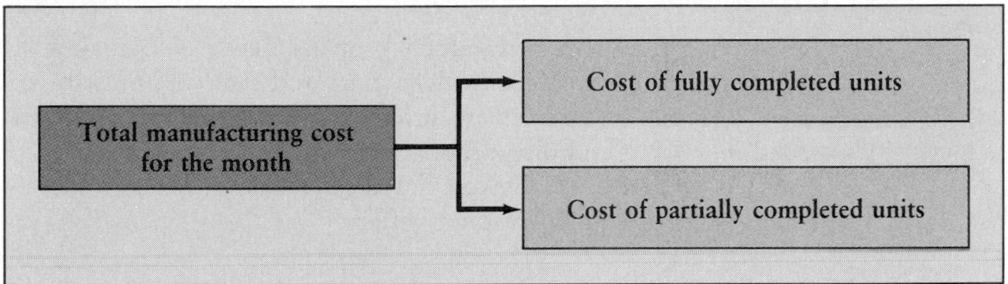

work done on the partially completed units has cost something, but not as much as the work on the fully completed units. Estimating the cost of these partially completed units is what complicates the process.

In the last section you calculated that units produced in the molding activity cost $0.30 each ($12,000 ÷ 40,000 units = $0.30 per unit). Had some of those units been only partially completed in that activity, some of the molding activity's $12,000 in operating costs would belong to those units (Figure 5–5). But since those units were only partially complete, you cannot assume that they cost $0.30 to produce. In April, additional costs would have to be added to complete production of the units that were unfinished at March 31.

When an activity has partially completed units on hand, the cost per unit is calculated as usual. Total cost of production is divided by total units produced. But the number of units produced must be adjusted to make the effort and cost required to produce the partially completed units equivalent to the effort and cost required for fully completed units. These adjusted units, called **total equivalent units**, are a measure of the effort and cost put into both the partially completed and the fully completed units processed during an accounting period. Before equivalent units can be computed, the accountant must determine when and how materials, direct labor, and applied manufacturing overhead are used in production. Resources are generally used in one of two ways:

1. Uniformly throughout the production process
2. In lumps at specific points in the production process

Direct labor, machinery use, and manufacturing overhead items are examples of resources normally used uniformly during processing. Direct labor is most often added uniformly from the start to the end of production. Similarly, manufacturing facilities tend to be used more or less continuously. In contrast, direct materials tend to be added in lumps at specific points in the production process. Some material is always added at the start of production. Otherwise there would be nothing for laborers to work on. Other materials may be added later. For example, an upholstered chair would begin with wood for constructing a frame. Later, the springs, padding, and fabric would be added. In the manufacture of concrete, however, cement is added uniformly as the concrete is mixed. Generally, materials are added in lumps, whereas direct labor and manufacturing overhead are added gradually.

Adding resources to production at different points makes it harder to calculate equivalent units. Equivalent units and unit cost must be calculated separately for resources added in different ways. Since materials costs are usually added in a lump and direct labor and manufacturing overhead costs uniformly, materials costs are usually calculated separately from the other two costs. This is because their equivalent units differ.

Calculating Equivalent Units for Resources Added Uniformly

Equivalent units are easy to calculate for resources that are added uniformly. If a unit is 50 percent complete, one assumes it contains 50 percent of the effort and cost of a fully completed unit. If a unit is 30 percent complete, one assumes it contains 30 percent of the cost of a fully completed unit.

To illustrate the use of equivalent units in calculating cost per unit, return to the example of the Drumm Safety Light Company. In order to compute the cost of production for March in Drumm's assembly activity, the following facts are needed:

1. At the start of March, there were no partially completed units in inventory in assembly.
2. During March, assembly received 40,000 cases from molding. These were the same cases that came out of the molding activity in March.
3. By the end of March, assembly had completed 38,000 units and transferred them to packaging. Two thousand partially completed units remained in assembly at month end.
4. Direct materials are added in a lump at the start of the production process. Direct labor and manufacturing overhead are added uniformly throughout production.
5. The 2,000 partially completed units are 100 percent complete in terms of materials and 70 percent complete, on average, in terms of direct labor and manufacturing overhead.

Although the assembly activity completed 38,000 units in March, one cannot say that its output was only 38,000 units. Most of the activity's efforts were expended on the completed units, but some effort was also made on the partially completed units. Since you cannot assume that the effort and cost expended on a partially completed unit was the same as the effort and cost expended on a fully completed unit, you use an estimate of the percentage of completion of the partially completed units.

Recall that in Chapter 2, direct labor and manufacturing overhead were identified as **conversion costs.** Since both resources are added uniformly in the assembly activity, their equivalent units and cost per unit calculations are the same. Therefore, they can be combined, making separate computations for direct labor and manufacturing overhead unnecessary. In the next section you will compute the equivalent units for direct materials costs when materials are added in a lump.

OBJECTIVE 3
Calculate equivalent units when resources are added uniformly

So far, you know that in March, conversion costs were expended on 38,000 fully completed units and 2,000 other units, which were on average 70 percent complete at month end. Notice that not all 2,000 units are 70 percent complete. Some are more than 70 percent complete. Some are less than 70 percent complete. On average, however, the units are 70 percent complete. The equivalent units of conversion costs for the partially completed units may be found by multiplying the number of partially completed units by their percentage of completion, as shown below.

Equivalent units
in ending inventory
= physical units × average percentage of completion
= 2,000 × 70%
= 1,400 equivalent units

This answer means that the 2,000 partially completed units would use the same effort and cost as 1,400 fully completed units. The 38,000 fully completed units used 38,000 equivalent units of conversion costs.

For purposes of computing unit conversion costs, the total output of the assembly activity in equivalent units is as follows:

Units completed	38,000
+ Equivalent units (2,000 units × 70% complete)	1,400
= Total equivalent units	39,400

Later, this figure will be used to calculate March conversion costs per unit for the assembly activity.

Calculating Equivalent Units for Resources Added in a Lump

You have just calculated the equivalent units for conversion costs in the assembly activity at Drumm Safety Light Company. The equivalent units for Drumm's materials costs will be different, since materials are added in a lump at the start of the production process rather than uniformly throughout. That is, when the

Figure 5–6

Diagram of the Flow of Physical Units for Drumm Safety Light Company — Assembly Activity

In the assembly activity of Drumm Safety Light Company, 40,000 units were started and 38,000 finished during March. Ending work in process was 100 percent complete for direct materials; 70 percent complete for conversion costs.

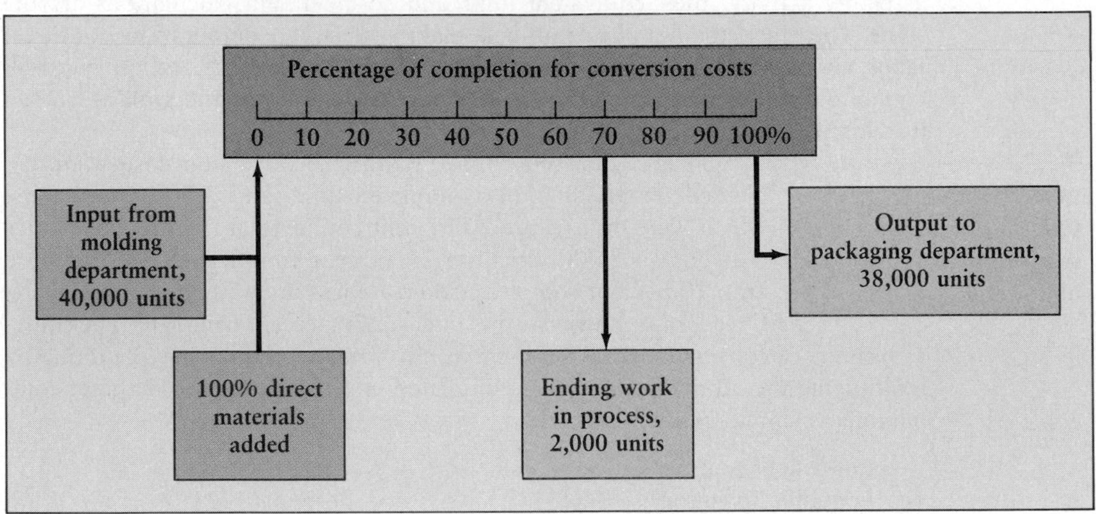

assembly of a unit is started, all needed materials are added at once. If 40,000 units are started, then enough direct materials for 40,000 units must be added. In fact, *when materials are added at the start of production, the number of equivalent units for materials always equals the number of units started.*

A more general rule for resources added in a lump, regardless of the point at which they are added, is

> The equivalent units for resources added in a lump equal the number of physical units passing the point at which the resource is added.

OBJECTIVE 4
Calculate equivalent units when resources are added in a lump

For resources added in a lump at the start, one simply counts the number of units started. For resources added at the end of production, one counts the number of units finished. For resources added at the 40 percent mark in the production process, one counts the number of units that passed the 40 percent mark.

In Drumm's assembly activity in March, 40,000 units were started. Since materials were added in that activity at the start of production, the equivalent units for materials is 40,000.

Figure 5–6 summarizes how units flowed through the assembly activity in March. Knowing the equivalent units for both materials and conversion costs, you are now ready to compute March unit costs for the assembly activity.

■

Using Equivalent Units to Calculate Unit Costs and Total Costs

OBJECTIVE 5
Using equivalent units, calculate the unit cost for all types of costs and record them on a cost summary report

When a product is produced in several activities, units enter each activity except the first, with costs assigned to them in earlier activities. Costs assigned to units in activities through which they were processed are called **prior department costs.** For all practical purposes, prior department costs are accounted for as material costs, even though they are listed separately on cost summary reports. Once a product has progressed through more than one activity, all prior department costs are combined, regardless of the activity from which they came.

You already know that $12,000 worth of prior department costs were transferred from molding to assembly in March. These prior department costs were recorded earlier in journal entry 2 (page 174). To these costs, assembly added the cost of electrical connectors and wires and the direct labor and manufacturing overhead needed to assemble them. An accountant totaled the materials requisitions for assembly and found that direct materials costs for the month were $22,400. Conversion costs totaled $26,004: $11,820 worth of direct labor (totaled from timecards) and $14,184 worth of applied manufacturing overhead (based on assembly's predetermined overhead rate of 120 percent of direct labor cost).[1] Adding these costs to assembly is recorded in summary journal entries as follows:

(3) Work in Process Inventory, Assembly	22,400	
Materials Inventory		22,400
To record the cost of direct materials used in assembly in March		
(4) Work in Process Inventory, Assembly	11,820	
Wages Payable		11,820
To record the cost of direct labor used in assembly in March		
(5) Work in Process Inventory, Assembly	14,184	
Applied Manufacturing Overhead		14,184
To apply manufacturing overhead to assembly at a rate of 120 percent of direct labor cost		

With these costs and equivalent units for the activity's monthly production, you can calculate the activity's unit costs in the usual manner. (Since prior department costs are added in a lump at the start of the activity's process, equivalent

[1]The assembly activity's predetermined overhead rate is lower than the molding activity's rate because the molding activity is more highly automated and uses less direct labor.

units for prior department costs are the same as the number of units started: 40,000.) We earlier calculated equivalent units for conversion costs to be 39,400. The calculations are as follows:

Prior department costs

$$\text{Unit cost} = \frac{\text{total costs}}{\text{equivalent units}} = \frac{\$12{,}000}{40{,}000 \text{ units}} = \$0.30 \text{ per unit}$$

Direct materials costs

$$\text{Unit cost} = \frac{\text{total costs}}{\text{equivalent units}} = \frac{\$22{,}400}{40{,}000 \text{ units}} = \$0.56 \text{ per unit}$$

Conversion costs

$$\text{Unit cost} = \frac{\text{total costs}}{\text{equivalent units}} = \frac{\$26{,}004}{39{,}400 \text{ units}} = \underline{\$0.66} \text{ per unit}$$

Total costs per completed unit $\underline{\underline{\$1.52}}$ per unit

Once you know total unit costs for the activity for the month, you can compute the value of finished units transferred out of the activity. Simply multiply the number of completed units by unit cost:

$$\begin{aligned}\text{Cost of completed units} &= \text{number of completed units} \times \text{unit cost}\\ &= 38{,}000 \times \$1.52\\ &= \underline{\underline{\$57{,}760}}\end{aligned}$$

The journal entry to transfer this cost to packaging would read as follows:

	Debit	Credit
(6) Work in Process Inventory, Packaging	57,760	
Work in Process Inventory, Assembly		57,760
To transfer the cost of 38,000 units completed in March at a cost of $1.52 per unit from assembly to packaging		

You know that at the start of the month, assembly had no inventory. During the month, $60,404 worth of costs were added to the activity for prior department costs, direct materials, direct labor, and applied manufacturing overhead (journal entries 2 through 5). Journal entry 6 reduces the balance in Work in Process Inventory, assembly activity, by $57,760. This reduction leaves $2,644, the cost of the 2,000 partially completed units in the ending inventory. You can calculate the cost of the ending inventory directly to verify the ending balance. Recall that these units contain 100 percent of prior department and direct materials costs and 70 percent of the activity's conversion costs.

Exhibit 5–2

Drumm Safety Light Company—Assembly Activity Cost Summary for March

This cost summary shows the number of units worked on in the assembly department during March and where they were at month end. It also shows costs charged to the department in March and the units to which they belong. Because the assembly department had partially completed units at month end, the format is more complex than that in Exhibit 5–1. Equivalent units and separate unit costs are included for three costs: prior department, direct materials, and conversion.

1. Units to account for	Physical units				
Beginning work in process	-0-				
Received from molding	40,000				
Total	40,000				

2. Units accounted for	Physical units	Equivalent finished units: Prior department	Direct materials	Conversion
Completed	38,000	38,000	38,000	38,000
Ending work in process	2,000	2,000	2,000	1,400
Total	40,000	40,000	40,000	39,400

3. Costs to account for	Current period cost	Total equivalent units	Average cost per unit
Prior department	$12,000	40,000	$0.30
Direct materials	22,400	40,000	0.56
Conversion	26,004	39,400	0.66
Total	$60,404		$1.52

4. Costs accounted for	Total equivalent units		Average cost per unit	Cost of ending Work in Process Inventory	Total costs
Completed and transferred to packaging	38,000	@	$1.52		$57,760
Ending work in process					
Prior departments	2,000	@	0.30	$ 600	
Direct materials	2,000	@	0.56	1,120	
Conversion	1,400	@	0.66	924	2,644
Total					$60,404

Prior department costs (2,000 @ $0.30)	$ 600
Direct materials costs (2,000 @ $0.56)	1,120
Conversion costs (2,000 × 70% @ $0.66)	924
Total cost of ending Work in Process Inventory	$2,644

The assembly activity's costs can be summarized in a cost summary statement similar to the one shown in Exhibit 5–1. However, the assembly activity's cost summary is a bit more complicated than the one in Exhibit 5–1 because of the partially completed units in ending inventory. The calculation of equivalent units and cost per unit for prior department costs, direct materials, and conversion costs must be shown. Nevertheless, the format of both statements is basically the same.

Exhibit 5–2 shows the cost summary statement for Drumm's assembly activity. The first section, **Units to account for**, indicates that during March the activity had no beginning inventory, but that 40,000 units were transferred in from molding. As in Exhibit 5–1, the first column of the second section, **Units accounted for**, shows what happened to those units. Of the 40,000 units, 38,000 were completed and transferred to packaging. The remaining 2,000, only partially completed, remained in assembly's ending Work in Process Inventory.

The next three columns in the second section are new. They show equivalent units for three types of costs: prior department, direct materials, and conversion. Since prior department costs and direct materials are added at the start of the assembly process, all units, even incomplete ones, carry 100 percent of these costs. So the amounts in those columns and in the first column, physical units, are the same. Conversion costs are added uniformly. However, as you know, a completed unit must carry a full share of the activity's conversion costs. So in the last column, equivalent units equal physical units *for the completed units*. The units left in ending work in process are only 70 percent complete with regard to conversion costs, so the equivalent units for those are 70 percent of the amount shown in the first column:

$$2{,}000 \times 70\% = 1{,}400$$

The third section of Exhibit 5–2, **Costs to account for**, is similar to the same section in Exhibit 5–1. Because of partially completed units, the units column changes to equivalent units. The number of equivalent units may be different for prior department costs, direct materials costs, and conversion costs. The average cost per unit is found by dividing each cost by *total equivalent units*, rather than physical units.

In the fourth section, **Costs accounted for**, the average cost per unit is used to calculate the amount of costs transferred out of the assembly department and the amount remaining at the end of March. The 38,000 completed units are transferred out at full cost (prior department costs + direct materials and conversion costs). The remaining 2,000 units must be costed, using equivalent units, since on average they carry only 70 percent of conversion costs. Entry 6, shown earlier, transfers the cost of completed units from assembly to packaging.

Review Exercise 5–1

Prepare a Cost Summary — No Beginning Inventory

Vernon Corporation makes film. There was no Work in Process Inventory of film at January 1. During January, they started 100,000 meters of film. They completed 99,200 meters during the month. Base material is added at the start of the production process. Chemical materials and conversion costs are added uniformly during the production process. The ending Work in Process Inventory was 60 percent complete as to chemical materials and conversion costs. Overhead is applied at a rate of $0.75 per meter. During January, Vernon used $11,000 of base material, $59,808 of chemicals, and $14,952 of direct labor.

Required

Prepare a cost summary similar to Exhibit 5-2 for Vernon's film-making activities for January.

Solution

Vernon Corporation
Cost Summary for January

1. Units to account for	Physical units
Beginning work in process	-0-
Started during January	100,000
Total	100,000

2. Units accounted for	Physical units	Equivalent finished units: Base material	Chemical materials	Conversion
Completed	99,200	99,200	99,200	99,200
Ending work in process	800	800	480	480
Total	100,000	100,000	99,680	99,680

3. Costs to account for	Current period cost	Total equivalent units	Average cost per unit
Base material	$ 11,000	100,000	$0.11
Chemical materials	59,808	99,680	0.60
Direct labor	14,952	99,680	0.15
Applied overhead ($0.075 × 99,680)	74,760	99,680	0.75
Total	$160,520		$1.61

4. Costs accounted for	Total equivalent units	Average cost per unit	Cost ending Work in Process Inventory	Total costs
Completed and transferred to finished goods	99,200 @	$1.61		$159,712
Ending work in process				
Base material	800 @	0.11	$ 88	
Chemical materials	480 @	0.60	288	
Direct labor	480 @	0.15	72	
Applied overhead	480 @	0.75	360	808
Total				$160,520

(see Exercises 21, 26, 27 and Problem 29)

■

Accounting for Partially Completed Units in Beginning Inventory

You just followed the flow of units produced in March through the first two activities of Drumm Safety Light Company. The same 40,000 units were processed in both activities during that time. The next step is to account for activity in the packaging activity during March.

The packaging activity had partially completed units on hand at both the beginning and the end of the month. The flow of units through the activity is therefore more complicated than in the first two activities. The activity started the month with 5,000 units in Work in Process Inventory. During March, it completed 42,000 units, with 1,000 partially completed units on hand at month end. Figure 5–7 shows this flow of units.

This type of diagram is useful in solving problems, especially when some data on the flow of units are missing. For example, the data in the last paragraph

Figure 5–7

Flow of Physical Units for March for Drumm Safety Light Company — Packaging Activity

Diagrams like this one are helpful in analyzing the flow of physical units through an activity. Because they show physical rather than equivalent units, they can be used for either moving average or FIFO calculations. The data in this figure is taken from Exhibit 5–3, page 186.

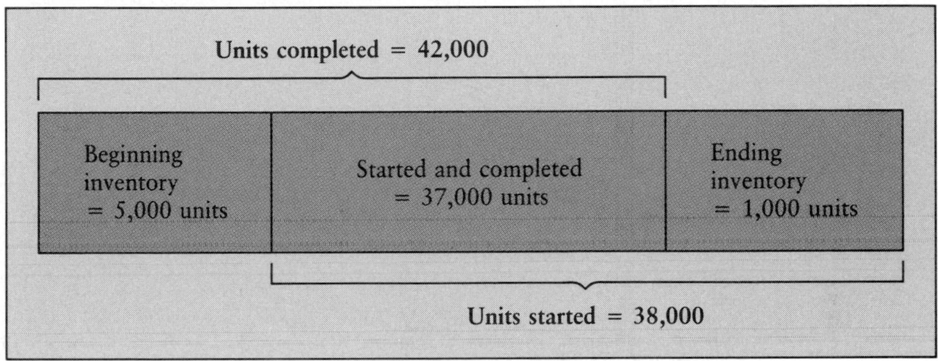

did not include how many units were started and completed in March. But by drawing the diagram, you can see that of the 42,000 units completed, 5,000 were in beginning inventory at the start of the month. Therefore, 37,000 units must have been started *and* completed during the month. And since logic tells you that the ending Work in Process Inventory must also have been started during the month, the total number of units started must be 38,000 (37,000 started and completed + the additional 1,000 still in process at month end). This number corresponds to the number of units known to have been completed in assembly and transferred to packaging during March.

A diagram of the physical flow of units is useful in all process costing problems, but particularly when there are partially completed units in both beginning and ending inventory. We will use the diagram in Figure 5–7 in the cost summary for Drumm's packaging activity in Exhibit 5–4. You might find it helpful to draw such a diagram for any process costing problem you must solve.

With this understanding, turn to the choice of a cost flow assumption used to determine the unit cost of inventories. A cost flow assumption is required when there is beginning inventory of partially completed units. Because production costs vary from month to month, accountants need a method of blending the costs of one month with slightly different costs of another month. The two main methods of doing this are the moving average cost flow assumption and the FIFO cost flow assumption. The **moving average cost flow assumption** will be discussed first, followed by a discussion of the FIFO cost flow assumption. You should notice that the assumption affects only how costs are assigned to units, not the physical flow of units. This is the reason the diagram on the physical flow of units is the same for either assumption.

Exhibit 5–3

Drumm Safety Light Company—Packaging Activity Data Needed to Calculate a Moving Average Unit Cost for March

To calculate a moving average unit cost, the accountant needs information from various sources. Beginning inventory costs were calculated at the end of the previous month. The costs for the present month must be taken from company cost accounting records. Applied manufacturing overhead is calculated by using the predetermined overhead rate. Finally, the number of units transferred out of the activity or left in inventory at month end are taken from company records.

Beginning inventory, March 1		
Units, 5,000		
Prior department costs, 100%		$ 7,170
Direct materials, 80%		740
Conversion costs, 30%		
Direct labor	$ 554	
Applied manufacturing overhead	831	1,385
Total		$ 9,295
Activity in packaging during March		
Units started, 38,000		
Units completed, 42,000		
Prior department costs (from Exhibit 5–2)		$57,760
Direct materials		4,074
Conversion costs		
Direct labor	$3,876	
Applied manufacturing overhead	5,814	9,690
Total costs added		$71,524
Ending inventory, March 31		
Units, 1,000		
Prior department costs, 100%		
Direct materials, 80%		
Conversion costs, 60%		

The Moving Average Cost Flow Assumption

OBJECTIVE 6
Calculate unit cost using the moving average method, and use it to compute the cost of completed units and ending work in process

A **moving average** is the weighted average of the cost of beginning inventory plus costs from the current period. To calculate a moving average, an accountant must combine total units completed in the current period, regardless of when they were started, with equivalent units of ending Work in Process Inventory. Costs incurred in the current period are then combined with the costs of beginning Work in Process Inventory. Using these total costs and equivalent units, the accountant then calculates the moving average cost per equivalent unit. Finally, this cost is used to calculate (1) the total cost of the units transferred out of the activity and (2) the cost of the work still in process at month end. As illustrated earlier in this chapter, when equivalent units differ in their cost category (direct materials, conversion, or prior department), separate equivalent units and unit cost calculations must be made for each category. Stated as formulas, the four steps are:

Step 1: Total equivalent units for each cost category
= total units completed in the current period
+ equivalent units in ending work in process

Total costs for each category
= costs of beginning work in process
+ costs incurred in current period

Step 2: Moving average cost per unit

$$= \frac{\text{total prior department costs}}{\text{total prior department equivalent units}} + \frac{\text{total direct materials costs}}{\text{total direct materials equivalent units}} + \frac{\text{total conversion costs}}{\text{total conversion equivalent units}}$$

Step 3: Cost of units completed
= moving average cost per unit
× total units completed

Step 4: Cost of ending Work in Process Inventory
= (prior department costs per unit
× prior department equivalent units in ending work in process)
+ (direct materials costs per unit
× direct materials equivalent units in ending work in process)
+ (conversion costs per unit
× conversion equivalent units in ending work in process)

To find the moving average cost for Drumm's packaging activity, one needs additional information. Recall that Drumm's safety lights were packaged in a box covered with a tight plastic wrap. The wrap not only kept the parts in the box but it also kept the parts clean. The wrap also allowed customers to see inside the box without opening it. Exhibit 5–3 shows the number of units in beginning Work in Process Inventory at the start of the month and their costs, as computed at the end of the previous month. It also shows the number of units started and completed in the activity and the costs incurred in March. Finally, it shows the number of units in Work in Process Inventory and their percentage of completion in each cost category at month end. No costs are shown for ending inventory, since they must be calculated on the basis of the March data.

Before finding the activity's moving average, the accountant records the costs added to packaging during the month. The transfer of costs from assembly was shown earlier in journal entry **6**. The addition of new costs is recorded as follows, using data taken from Exhibit 5–3:

	Debit	Credit
(7) Work in Process Inventory, Packaging	4,074	
Materials Inventory		4,074
To record the cost of direct materials used in packaging in March		

(8) Work in Process Inventory, Packaging	3,876	
Wages Payable		3,876
To record the cost of direct labor used in packaging in March		
(9) Work in Process Inventory, Packaging	5,814	
Applied Manufacturing Overhead		5,814
To record the cost of manufacturing overhead applied to packaging in March		

With costs recorded, the moving average cost can be calculated. The steps that follow expand on the four formulas given on page 187.

Step 1: Calculate total equivalent units. The easiest way of doing this is to fill out a cost summary. Exhibit 5–4 shows a completed summary for Drumm's packaging activity. Section 2 shows the calculation of the total equivalent units for each cost category. This is the first part of step 1 listed on page 187. During the month, 42,000 units were completed, each carrying 100 percent of direct materials costs. The ending Work in Process Inventory included 1,000 units, 80 percent complete as to direct materials. Thus, the number of equivalent units for direct materials was 42,800.

Notice that for the completed units, equivalent units and physical units are the same, even though beginning inventory units were already 80 percent complete in terms of direct materials when the month began. When calculating a moving average, you always assume that units in beginning work in process were 100 percent processed this month. The effect of this assumption is offset when cost per unit is calculated. To perform that calculation, one adds beginning inventory costs to costs incurred during the month. This averages the costs of the beginning inventory with costs incurred during the month.

In Exhibit 5–4, the first two columns of section 3 show the cost of beginning Work in Process Inventory as well as costs for the current month. Packaging began the month with $740 worth of direct materials in beginning inventory. An additional $4,074 were incurred over the month. The third column shows total materials costs of $4,814. This is the second part of step 1 on page 187.

Step 2: Calculate the moving average cost per unit. A per unit cost must be found for each of the three cost categories: (1) prior department, (2) direct materials, and (3) conversion. In Exhibit 5–4, these computations are shown in the last two columns of section 3. Total equivalent units, taken from section 2 of the cost summary, are copied into section 3. Then, total cost, shown in the previous column, is divided by total equivalent units to obtain the average cost per unit. For direct materials, the $4,814 in total costs are divided by the 42,800 total equivalent units to obtain a direct materials cost of $0.11248 per unit. (Normally computations need not be carried to five decimal places. In this case, it is done to eliminate rounding differences.) The computations for prior department costs and conversion costs are done similarly (see section 3 of the summary).

Step 3: Calculate the cost of units completed. This step is illustrated in section 4 of the cost summary statement. The cost of units completed ($79,063) is simply

Exhibit 5–4

Drumm Safety Light Company—Packaging Activity Cost Summary for March Using the Moving Average Cost Flow Assumption

Because packaging had partially completed units at both the beginning and the end of the month, this cost summary is more complicated than the one shown in Exhibit 5–2. The format is basically the same, however.

1. Units to account for	Physical units				
Beginning work in process	5,000				
Received from assembly	38,000				
Total	43,000				
			Equivalent finished units		
2. Units accounted for	Physical units		Prior department	Direct materials	Conversion
Completed	42,000		42,000	42,000	42,000
Ending work in process	1,000		1,000	800	600
Total	43,000		43,000	42,800	42,600
3. Costs to account for	Cost of beginning Work in Process Inventory	Current period costs	Total costs	Total equivalent units	Average cost per unit
Prior department	$7,170	$57,760	$64,930	43,000	$1.51000
Direct materials	740	4,074	4,814	42,800	0.11248
Conversion	1,385	9,690	11,075	42,600	0.25998
Total	$9,295	$71,524	$80,819		$1.88246
4. Costs accounted for		Total equivalent units	Average cost per unit	Cost of ending Work in Process Inventory	Total costs
Completed and transferred to finished goods		42,000 @	$1.88246		$79,063
Ending work in process					
Prior department		1,000 @	1.51000	$1,510	
Direct materials		800 @	0.11248	90	
Conversion		600 @	0.25998	156	1,756
Total					$80,819

Exhibit 5–5

Drumm Safety Light Company—Packaging Activity T Account for Work in Process Inventory for March Using the Moving Average Cost Flow Assumption

Additions to and transfers out of the Work in Process Inventory, Packaging, account for Drumm Safety Light Company are summarized in this exhibit in the form of a T account. The beginning inventory and current month's costs come from Drumm's accounting records (Exhibit 5–3). The costs transferred out and the balance in ending work in process come from section 4 of the cost summary statement (Exhibit 5–4). The beginning balance plus the additions minus the costs transferred to finished goods equal the ending inventory balance. The ending balance matches the amount calculated in section 4 of Exhibit 5–4.

Work in Process Inventory, Packaging			
Beginning inventory	9,295	79,063	(10) Transfer to finished goods
(6) Prior department	57,760		
(7) Direct materials	4,074		
(8) Direct labor	3,876		
(9) Applied overhead	5,814		
Ending inventory	1,756		

the total unit cost shown in section 3 ($1.88246) times the number of units completed and transferred out of the activity (42,000 units).

Recall that the 42,000 units completed consisted of 5,000 units in beginning inventory plus 37,000 units started and completed. In the calculation of cost of units completed, no distinction is made between the units in beginning inventory and the 37,000 started and completed during the month. All units completed in March are assigned the same moving average cost.

Step 4: Calculate the cost of ending Work in Process Inventory. To calculate the cost of ending Work in Process Inventory, one multiplies the average cost of each cost category (prior department, direct materials, and conversion) by the *equivalent* units in ending inventory for each category. This step is shown in section 4 of the cost summary statement. All three types of costs must be computed separately, since the number of equivalent units differs for each one. For example, the bottom of Exhibit 5–3 shows 1,000 equivalent units for prior department costs, 800 for direct materials, and 600 for conversion costs.

The journal entry to transfer the cost of completed units from packaging to Finished Goods Inventory uses the figure from the first line of section 4 of the cost summary:

	Debit	Credit
(10) Finished Goods Inventory	79,063	
Work in Process Inventory, Packaging		79,063
To transfer the cost 42,000 completed units to Finished Goods Inventory at an average cost of $1.88246 per unit		

No journal entry is required for the packaging department's ending Work in Process Inventory. If the correct costs have been transferred in and transferred out, the inventory balance will agree with that shown in the cost summary report: $1,756. The activity in the packaging activity can be summarized in a T account, as shown in Exhibit 5–5.

Review Exercise 5–2

Prepare a Cost Summary—Moving Average Assumption

Baker Company makes bricks. On March 1, the company had 5,000 bricks in process. These bricks were 60 percent complete as to conversion cost. During March, Baker started 120,000 bricks. The company completed 112,000 bricks during March. All materials are added at the start of the production process. Conversion costs are added uniformly. March 31 work in process was 30 percent complete as to conversion costs. Overhead is applied at a rate of $0.06 per brick. During January, Baker used $1,250 of materials and $3,477 of direct labor. Baker uses the moving average cost flow assumption.

Required

Prepare a cost summary similar to Exhibit 5–4 for Baker's brick-making activities in March.

Solution

Baker Company — Cost Summary for March

1. Units to account for	Physical units
Beginning work in process	5,000
Started during January	120,000
Total	125,000

		Equivalent finished units	
2. Units accounted for	Physical units	Direct Materials	Conversion
Completed	112,000	112,000	112,000
Ending work in process	13,000	13,000	3,900
Total	125,000	125,000	115,900

3. Costs to account for	Cost of beginning Work in Process Inventory	Current period cost	Total costs	Total equivalent units	Average cost per unit
Direct materials	$ 50	1,200	$ 1,250	125,000	$0.01
Direct labor	90	3,387	3,477	115,900	0.03
Applied overhead ($0.06)	180	6,774	6,954	115,900	0.06
Total			$11,681		$0.10

4. Costs accounted for	Total equivalent units		Average cost per unit	Cost of ending Work in Process Inventory	Total costs
Completed and transferred to finished goods	112,000	@	$0.10		$11,200
Ending work in process					
Direct materials	13,000	@	0.01	$130	
Direct labor	3,900	@	0.03	117	
Applied overhead	3,900	@	0.06	234	481
Total					$11,681

(See Exercises 15, 16, 17, 24, 25 and Problem 32)

■

The FIFO Cost Flow Assumption

FIFO stands for first in, first out. In process cost accounting, it means that the units in work in process at the beginning of the month are the first ones completed and transferred out of the department during the month. The FIFO cost flow assumption is similar to the FIFO method of accounting for direct materials and finished goods inventories. For most organizations, it follows the actual flow of materials through production.

As you have seen, when the moving average method is used, the costs and equivalent units of beginning work in process are merged with the current month's costs and equivalent units. Under the **FIFO cost flow assumption**, beginning work in process is accounted for separately from units started and completed in the current period. Not mixing the costs of the two periods may be more useful for control decisions. The FIFO cost flow assumption differs from the moving average assumption only in how it accounts for *beginning* Work in Process Inventory. Since most companies have beginning work in process inventories, the two assumptions give slightly different results. The results of the two methods usually differ little. Since the moving average method is a bit simpler, most companies prefer it, but you should be familiar with both approaches.

All process costing requires dividing costs into the three cost categories when they exist: prior department, direct materials, and conversion. Like the moving average assumption, there are four steps in making FIFO cost flow calculations. For simplicity, we will illustrate the four steps using only the conversion cost information for the packaging activity of Drumm Safety Light Company. The cost summary will add direct materials costs and prior department costs to the illustration. You should notice that the four steps do not correspond to the four sections of the cost summary illustrated in Exhibit 5–6. Earlier we used this same department to illustrate the moving average method. Figure 5–7 gives the basic data concerning physical units. Exhibit 5–3 provides cost data and percentages of completion.

OBJECTIVE 7
Calculate unit cost using the FIFO method, and use it to compute the cost of completed units and ending work in process

Step 1: Calculate total equivalent units for each cost category. To perform this computation, one must first calculate: (a) the number of equivalent units needed to *complete* beginning work in process, (b) the number of equivalent units in units started and completed during the month, and (c) the number of equivalent units in ending work in process. These units are then added together as follows:

Total equivalent units for each cost category
= equivalent units needed to complete beginning work in process
+ units started and completed this month
+ equivalent units in ending work in process

Figure 5–7 shows that for the Drumm's packaging activity, there were 5,000 units in work in process at the beginning of the month, that 37,000 units were started and completed during the month, and that there were 1,000 units in the ending work in process. Exhibit 5–3 shows that the beginning work in process was 30 percent completed at the start of the month and that the ending work in process was 60 percent complete at month end. This gives us the data needed to perform step 1.

Total conversion cost equivalent units	
= equivalent units needed to complete beginning work in process, 70% × 5,000	3,500
+ units started and completed this month	37,000
+ equivalent units in ending work in process, 60% × 1,000	600
Total conversion cost equivalent units	41,100

Step 2: Calculate the current month's cost per unit for each cost category. This step requires you to divide the current month's prior department costs, direct materials costs, and conversion costs by equivalent units obtained in step 1 as follows:

$$\text{FIFO cost per unit} = \frac{\text{current prior department costs}}{\text{total prior department equivalent units}} + \frac{\text{current direct materials costs}}{\text{total direct materials equivalent units}} + \frac{\text{current conversion costs}}{\text{total conversion equivalent units}}$$

$$\text{FIFO conversion costs per unit} = \frac{\text{current conversion costs}}{\text{total conversion cost equivalent units}}$$

Exhibit 5–3 gives total conversion costs for the month at $9,690.

$$\text{FIFO conversion costs per unit} = \frac{\$9{,}690}{41{,}100 \text{ units}} = \$0.23577 \text{ per equivalent unit}$$

Step 3a: Calculate the cost of completing the beginning work in process for each category and add it to costs already incurred. To calculate the cost of completing beginning work in process, multiply the FIFO cost per unit *for each cost category* by the percentage remaining to complete by the number of physical units. That is, use the following formula first to figure out the cost of completing prior department costs; then direct materials costs; and then conversion costs.

Cost of completing beginning work in process for a specific cost category
= (FIFO cost per unit for a specific cost category)
× (1 − percentage of completion at the start of the month)
× number of physical units

Then, to the cost figures you have obtained, add costs incurred in the previous month, as follows:

Total cost of beginning inventory
= prior department cost to complete beginning inventory
+ direct materials costs to complete beginning inventory
+ conversion costs to complete beginning inventory
+ costs incurred in previous month

Conversion cost of completing beginning inventory	
$0.23577 × (1 − 30%) × 5,000	$ 825
Conversion cost in previous month	1,385
	$2,210

Step 3b: Calculate the cost of units started and completed in the current month. To calculate the cost of units started and completed, multiply the number

of units started and completed by the total cost per unit obtained in step 2 as follows:

Cost of units started and completed in this period
= total FIFO cost per unit
× number of physical units started and completed in the current period

Conversion cost of units started and completed this month	
$0.23577 × 37,000 units	$8,723

Step 3c: Calculate the cost of goods transferred out of the department. To calculate this cost, add the total cost of beginning inventory to the cost of units started and completed as follows:

Cost of goods transferred out of department
= total cost of beginning inventory
+ costs of units started and completed in the period

Conversion cost of goods transferred out of department	
Conversion cost of completing beginning inventory	$ 2,210
Cost of units started and completed this month	8,723
Total conversion cost transferred out	$10,933

Step 4: Calculate cost of ending Work in Process Inventory. For each cost category multiply the FIFO cost per unit for that cost category (obtained in step 2) by the number of physical units in ending inventory by the percentage of completion for that cost category. Then add those costs together as follows:

Cost of ending work in process for specific cost category
= FIFO cost per unit for a specific cost category
× physical units in ending work in process
× ending inventory percentage completion

Total cost of ending Work in Process Inventory
= prior department cost of ending work in process
+ direct materials cost of ending work in process
+ conversion cost of ending work in process

Conversion cost of ending Work in Process Inventory	
$0.23577 × 1,000 units × 60% complete	$141

The easiest way to organize the computations is to fill out a cost summary. Because FIFO is simply a different method of accounting for the same economic activities, the FIFO method will now be illustrated by using the same data as that used for the moving average assumption.

Exhibit 5–6 shows the new cost summary for Drumm Safety Light Company's packaging activity. The summary was redone according to the FIFO cost flow assumption, using the same format as that of earlier cost summaries.

Section 1 of Exhibit 5–6 reports the physical units for which packaging is responsible. The first section is exactly the same as it was for the moving average assumption. The number of physical units is not changed by the accounting for the cost of those units. Notice that sections 2 through 4 of the cost summary contain the four cost calculation steps we have just illustrated.

The number of equivalent units necessary to complete beginning work in process (the first part of step 1) is calculated on the first line of section 2. Because prior department costs are carried over from the last period, the units to which these costs are attached are, by definition, finished. (Were they not finished, they would never have been transferred.) Therefore, zero equivalent units of prior department costs are required to complete the units. Since beginning inventory of 5,000 physical units is 80 percent complete as to direct materials (Exhibit 5–3), they must be 20 percent incomplete. To finish them, packaging needs 1,000 equivalent units (20% × 5,000 units) of direct materials, as shown in part 2 of Exhibit 5–6. Similarly, these 5,000 physical units that are 30 percent complete as to conversion costs require 70 percent more conversion effort, or 3,500 equivalent units, to be finished.

Exhibit 5–6

Drumm Safety Light Company—Packaging Activity Cost Summary for March Using the FIFO Cost Flow Assumption

This exhibit is based on the same data as Exhibit 5–4. However, the computations were done by using the FIFO rather than the moving average cost flow assumption. Compare the two exhibits. Notice the differences in the calculations.

1. Units to account for	Physical units
Beginning work in process	5,000
Received from assembly	38,000
Total	43,000

		Current period equivalent finished units		
2. Units accounted for	Physical units	Prior department	Direct materials	Conversion
To complete beginning work in process	5,000	-0-	1,000	3,500
Started and completed	37,000	37,000	37,000	37,000
Ending work in process	1,000	1,000	800	600
Total	43,000	38,000	38,800	41,100

3. Costs to account for	Costs	Current period equivalent units	Current period cost per unit
Beginning work in process	$ 9,295		
Prior department	57,760	38,000	$1.52000
Direct materials	4,074	38,800	0.10500
Conversion	9,690	41,100	0.23577
Total	$80,819		$1.86077

4. Costs accounted for	Total equivalent units		FIFO cost per unit	Cost of ending Work in Process Inventory	Total costs
Completed from beginning work in process					
Beginning inventory, 5,000 units				$9,295	
Current period costs to complete					
Direct materials (5,000 × 20% × $0.10500)				105	
Conversion costs (5,000 × 70% × $0.23577)				825	
					$10,225
Started and completed (100 percent) from current production	37,000	@	$1.86077		68,849*
Total costs transferred to finished goods					$79,074
Ending work in process					
Prior department	1,000	@	1.52000	$1,520	
Direct materials	800	@	0.10500	84	
Conversion	600	@	0.23577	141	1,745
Total					$80,819

*$1 rounding error.

For the 37,000 units started and completed during March (Exhibit 5–3), equivalent units must equal physical units, since all work on those units was done this month. Thus, these units require 37,000 equivalent units of prior department, direct materials, and conversion costs to be complete. The equivalent units for ending work in process are computed in the same way as when the moving average cost flow assumption is used. Namely, the number of physical units is multiplied by their percentage of completion at month end. Since the 1,000 units left in ending inventory are 80 percent complete as to direct materials, they have already used 800 equivalent units (1,000 × 80%) of direct materials.

You may have noticed that the only difference between the moving average cost flow assumption and the FIFO cost flow assumption is the treatment of beginning work in process. The moving average method merges units in beginning inventory with those started and completed in the current period. The FIFO cost flow assumption separates the beginning inventory units from the started and completed units.

The costs to account for (*step* 2) are listed in the first column of section 3 of Exhibit 5–6 of the cost summary statement. Since the equivalent units in section 2 differ, depending on the type of cost, the per unit cost must be figured separately for each category. To perform that calculation, one divides prior department costs, direct materials costs, and conversion costs for the current period listed in the second column by their total equivalent units, listed in the third column. The resulting unit costs are shown in the fourth column: $1.52000 for prior department costs, $0.10500 for direct materials costs, and $0.23577 for conversion costs. The computations are carried to five decimal places here to avoid rounding differences. In most instances, rounding to four decimal places is adequate.)

The calculation (in *step* 3) for the cost of completing beginning work in process and starting and finishing units begun in the current month is shown in section 4 of Exhibit 5–6. Recall that in Exhibit 5–3, beginning inventory was valued at $9,295. Direct materials were listed as 80 percent complete; conversion costs, 30 percent complete. To finish these units, therefore, 20 percent more direct materials costs and 70 percent more conversion costs must be added. As you know from section 2, there are 5,000 physical units in beginning inventory. And as you know from section 3, material costs per equivalent unit are $0.10500. Therefore, the cost of completing direct materials is $105.

$$5{,}000 \times 20\% \times \$0.10500 = \$105$$

Similarly, the cost of completing the conversion of direct materials is $825.

$$5{,}000 \times 70\% \times \$0.23577 = \$825$$

Therefore, the total cost of beginning work in process, when completed, will be $10,225 ($9,295 worth of costs from the last month plus the current month's costs of $105 added for direct materials and $825 for conversion).

The cost of units started and completed during the month is the total cost per unit, $1.86077 (section 3), times the 37,000 units started and completed during the month, or $68,849 (includes $1 rounding error). By adding this figure to the total cost of the completed beginning inventory, which was just calculated, one finds that total costs are $79,074. These costs are then transferred out of Work in Process Inventory to Finished Goods Inventory during March ($68,849 + $10,225 = $79,074). The journal entry to transfer the costs would be:

		Debit	Credit
(10a)	Finished Goods Inventory	79,074	
	Work in Process Inventory, Packaging		79,074
	To transfer the cost of completed units to Finished Goods Inventory at FIFO cost of $1.88271 per unit		

Notice that the total cost transferred to finished goods is slightly higher than when the moving average cost flow assumption was used (journal entry **10**, page

Exhibit 5–7

Drumm Safety Light Company—Packaging Activity T Account for Work in Process Inventory for March Using the FIFO Cost Flow Assumption

A T account summarizes activity in Work in Process Inventory, Packaging Activity for March. Compare the figures in this exhibit, based on the FIFO cost flow assumption, with those in Exhibit 5–5, based on the moving average cost flow assumption. Notice that the beginning inventory and current month's costs are the same in both exhibits. Only the cost of the units transferred to Finished Goods Inventory and of the ending Work in Process Inventory differ.

Work in Process Inventory, Packaging			
Beginning inventory	9,295	79,074	(10a) Transfer to Finished Goods Inventory
(6) Prior department	57,760		
(7) Direct materials	4,074		
(8) Direct labor	3,876		
(9) Applied overhead	5,814		
Ending inventory	1,745		

190). This is so because beginning inventory units were quite costly, averaging more than \$2 per unit (\$10,225 ÷ 5,000 units = \$2.045). With the FIFO cost flow assumption, this high beginning inventory cost was entirely transferred to finished goods at month end. With the moving average cost flow assumption, a small portion of that high cost was left in ending inventory in the packaging department.

The cost of ending work in process (*step* 4) is calculated by multiplying the number of equivalent units in the ending inventory (section 2) by the current month's costs per unit (section 3). (These computations are shown in the last part of section 4.) This calculation method is exactly the same as that used in the moving average cost flow assumption except the numerical results are slightly different. Again, the FIFO cost flow assumption determines the cost of the ending inventory solely on the basis of the current month's processing costs. In Drumm's case, they are lower than the previous month's costs. To confirm the calculations for the costs transferred to finished goods, check that the costs to account for equal the costs accounted for, as they do here (\$80,819 = \$80,819).

The entire FIFO costing process is summarized in Exhibit 5–7, which shows the activity in Work in Process Inventory, Packaging Department account in the form of a T account for March. By comparing Exhibit 5–7 with Exhibit 5–5, you find that the difference between the FIFO and moving average cost flow assumptions is small. In this case, the difference for ending work in process is just \$11 (\$1,745 versus \$1,756). Because the differences between the two methods are small and moving averages do not require the cost of beginning work in process be kept separate from other costs, most companies use the moving average method.

Chapter Review

Review of Learning Objectives

1. **Describe how process costing accumulates costs and calculates cost per unit.**
Process costing is used when products are produced continuously, that is, when there are no distinguishable starting and stopping points in the production process. When using this method, you accumulate costs by activity and calculate cost per unit by activity at the end of a specified time period, usually a month. Cost per unit is calculated by dividing activity costs by units processed.
A cost summary summarizes costs and units for an activity when process costing is used. An example of the most complex form of a cost summary is shown in Exhibit 5–6. If you understand the complex form from your study of this Chapter, you will also understand the simpler forms. As you can see from this example, a cost summary reconciles the number of units an activity processed (section 1, Units to account for) with the number of units transferred out of or remaining in ending inventory (section 2, Units accounted for). Section 2 also shows how equivalent units were calculated for each cost category. The last two sections of the summary reconcile the costs transferred in and out of the activity. Section 3 lists the costs of beginning inventory as well as the costs added in each cost category during the month. To obtain the unit costs for each category, the costs in section 3 are divided by the equivalent units for each category (obtained from section 2). In section 4 the unit costs from section 3 are used to calculate the cost of units transferred out of the activity and the cost of ending inventory. The costs of beginning inventory plus the costs from section 3 should equal the costs transferred out plus the cost of ending inventory.
The cost summary is a useful tool, especially when computations are complex, such as when partially completed units must be accounted for.

2. **Write journal entries to record manufacturing costs and transfers.**
The journal entries used to transfer costs between activities in process costing are basically the same as those used in job order costing. The way you calculate the unit costs needed to make the journal entries, however, is different.
Journal entries transfer separate costs from one production activity to another and to Finished Goods Inventory. Other journal entries are required to add direct materials costs, direct labor costs, and applied manufacturing overhead to each production activity.

3. **Calculate equivalent units when resources are added uniformly.**
Partially completed units are often in inventory at the end of a period. Since some of the period's production costs belong to those partially completed units, their cost must be calculated according to equivalent units rather than physical units.
Prior department costs are rarely added uniformly. Instead, they are added at the start of the process. Conversion costs, however, are almost always added uniformly. And direct materials are usually added in a lump at some point in the production process, but are sometimes added uniformly, as in a mixing process. When resources are added uniformly throughout the production process, equivalent units are found by estimating the percentage of completion or effort put into the partially completed units. That percentage is then multiplied by the number of physical units. Since direct materials costs, prior department costs, and conversion costs may differ in their percentage of completion, equivalent units must be calculated separately for each cost category.

4. **Calculate equivalent units when resources are added in a lump.**
When a resource is added in a lump, 100 percent of the resource is added at a specified time in the production process, often at the start. Prior department costs and direct materials costs are usually added this way. When they are, equivalent units equal the number of physical units that have passed this point. For resources added in a lump at the start, equivalent units equal the number of units started. For resources added in a lump at the end of the production process, equivalent units equal the number of units completed.

5. **Using equivalent units, calculate the unit cost for all types of costs and record them on a cost summary report.**
The first step in calculating unit cost is to analyze the flow of physical units. This task can be done by using a bar diagram similar to the one shown in Figure 5–6 (page 178). Next, equivalent units must be calculated for each cost category. This is done by multiplying the number of physical units by the percentage of completion in each category. The same process is used for units started and completed and for ending inventory, whether the moving average or the FIFO cost flow assumption is used. Equivalent units of beginning inventory are treated differently under each assumption, however. Finally, the cost per unit is found by dividing the total monthly cost of each cost category by equivalent units for that category.

6. **Calculate unit cost using the moving average method, and use it to compute the cost of completed units and ending work in process.**
When an activity using a moving average has partially completed units on hand at both the beginning and end of the month, the costs of the beginning inventory are averaged with the current month's production costs. This average unit cost is then used to calculate the cost of goods transferred to finished goods and the cost of ending work in process.

7. **Calculate unit cost using the FIFO method, and use it to compute the cost of completed units and ending work in process.**
When the FIFO method is used, the costs of beginning work in process are separated from current costs. Using the current month's costs and equivalent units, a unit cost is calculated for each cost category. The unit costs are used to calculate (1) the cost of completing beginning work in process and (2) the cost of units started and completed during the month. Finally, unit costs are used to calculate the cost of partially completed work in process at month end.
Because the moving average method is slightly easier and yields almost the same result as FIFO, most companies use a moving average.

Review of Key Terms

Actual manufacturing overhead costs All manufacturing costs except direct labor and direct materials costs necessary for the manufacture of a product. Includes the cost of indirect materials, indirect labor, expired factory insurance, depreciation on factory equipment, utilities, and other costs of operating the factory.

Applied manufacturing overhead costs The estimated total manufacturing overhead costs assigned to a job or product. Calculated by using a predetermined overhead rate. (Calculations explained in Chapter 4.)

Average cost per unit The unit manufacturing cost of a product; used in valuing inventory on the balance sheet. In a process costing system, average cost per unit is calculated by dividing the total cost of processing in an activity by the number of units processed in a particular month.

Conversion costs The sum of direct labor and applied manufacturing overhead costs.

Costs accounted for Section 4 of the cost summary, which shows the cost of units completed and transferred out of the activity and the cost of units in the ending inventory. The sum of these costs should equal the month's costs to account for (see section 3 of the cost summary).

Costs to account for Section 3 of the cost summary, which shows the cost of the activity's beginning inventory and the cost of units started or transferred into the activity during the month. The sum of these costs should equal the month's costs accounted for (see section 4 of the cost summary).

Direct labor cost The cost of work that can be physically traced to a particular job or product.

Direct materials Materials that can be physically traced to a particular job or product.

Equivalent units See *Total equivalent units.*

FIFO cost flow assumption A method of accounting for beginning work in process inventories. The cost of beginning work in process is separated from the cost of units started and completed during the period. For contrast, see *Moving average cost flow assumption.*

Indirect labor Factory work that is not performed directly on a particular product.

Indirect materials Miscellaneous materials of small value used in a factory. Accounted for as part of manufacturing overhead.

Job order costing A cost accounting system designed for use in companies whose products or services are produced in distinct batches, often to customers' specifications. Each job has a clear starting and completion point.

Manufacturing overhead All manufacturing costs other than direct materials and direct labor costs necessary to manufacture of a product.

Moving average A weighted average of the cost of the beginning inventory (partially completed in the last period) and costs from the current period.

Moving average cost flow assumption A method of accounting for beginning work in process inventories. The cost of beginning inventories is averaged with the cost of other units worked on during the period. For contrast, see *FIFO cost flow assumption.*

Predetermined overhead rate A ratio that relates the total estimated manufacturing overhead costs for the year to the expected manufacturing activity for the year. Used to assign manufacturing overhead costs to batches of product or to activities. Calculated by dividing estimated total manufacturing overhead cost for the year by estimated amount of cost driver for the year.

Prior department costs Costs assigned to a product by activities through which it was processed earlier.

Process costing A cost accounting system designed for companies that mass-produce large amounts of nearly identical products on a continuous assembly line.

Total equivalent units A measure of the effort and cost put into both partially completed and fully completed units processed during an accounting period.

Units accounted for Section 2 of the cost summary, which shows the number of physical units completed and transferred out of the activity and the number of units in the ending inventory. The sum of these units should equal the month's units to account for (see section 1 of the cost summary).

Units to account for Section 1 of the cost summary, which shows the number of physical units in an activity's beginning inventory and the number of units started or transferred into the activity during the month. The sum of these units should equal units accounted for (see section 2 of the cost summary).

Review Problem

Information on the finishing activity at Toby Company is as follows:

	Units
Beginning work in process	700
Units transferred in (started)	2,600
Ending work in process	400

	Costs			
	Prior department	Direct materials	Conversion	Total
Work in process, May 1	$ 3,150	$ —	$ 1,848	$ 4,998
Units transferred in	12,195	23,490	10,618	46,303
Total	$15,345	$23,490	$12,466	$51,301

The finishing activity receives partially processed units from the assembly activity. After finishing, the units are ready for sale and are transferred to the finished goods storeroom. On May 1, finishing's Work in Process Inventory was 70 percent complete as to conversion costs. On May 31, it was 60 percent complete as to conversion costs. Prior department costs were added at the start of production. Materials were added at the end.

Required

1. Prepare a bar diagram similar to Figure 5–7 showing the total units completed and total units started.
2. Assume the Toby Company uses the moving average cost flow assumption. Prepare a cost summary similar to the one in Exhibit 5–4 for the finishing department.
3. Assume Toby uses the FIFO cost flow assumption. Prepare a second cost summary similar to the one in Exhibit 5–6 for the finishing department.

Solution to Review Problem

1. The hand-written numbers shown in the figure on page 204 are calculated for Toby Company from the data.

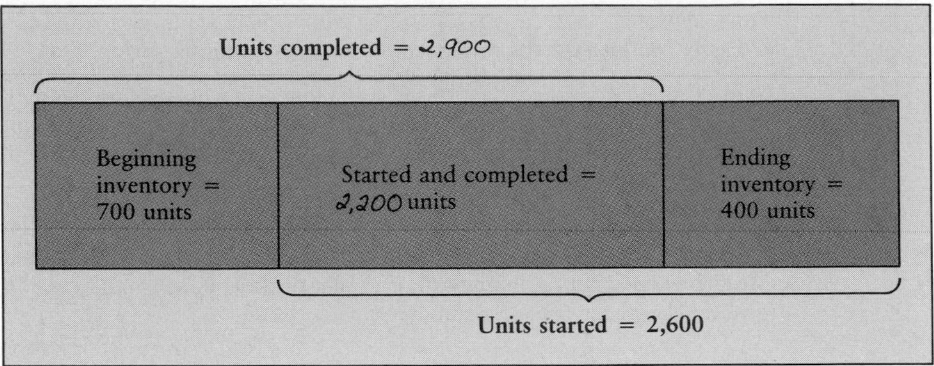

2. Cost summary — moving average method:

Toby Company
Cost Summary—Moving Average Method
For the Month of May

1. Units to account for	Physical units
Beginning work in process	700
Received from assembly	2,600
Total	3,300

		Equivalent finished units		
2. Units accounted for	Physical units	Prior department	Direct materials	Conversion
Completed	2,900*	2,900	2,900	2,900
Ending work in process	400	400	0†	240
Total	3,300	3,300	2,900	3,140

3. Costs to account for	Cost of beginning Work in Process Inventory	Current period cost	Total	Total equivalent units	Average cost per unit
Prior department	$3,150	$12,195	$15,345	3,300	$ 4.65
Direct materials	-0-	23,490	23,490	2,900	8.10
Conversion	1,848	10,618	12,466	3,140	3.97
Total	$4,998	$46,303	$51,301		$16.72

*Taken from diagram in 1 above.
†Zero because materials are added at completion of production, and these units are not yet completed.

4. Costs accounted for	Total equivalent units		Average cost per unit	Cost of ending Work in Process Inventory	Total costs
Completed and transferred to finished goods	2,900	@	$16.72		$48,488
Ending work in process					
Prior department	400	@	4.65	$1,860	
Direct materials	0	@	8.10	-0-	
Conversion	240	@	3.97	953	2,813
Total					$51,301

3. Cost summary — FIFO method:

Toby Company
Cost Summary — FIFO Method
For the Month of May

1. Units to account for	Physical units
Beginning work in process	700
Received from assembly	2,600
Total	3,300

		Current period equivalent finished units		
2. Units accounted for	Physical units	Prior department	Direct materials	Conversion
To complete beginning work in process	700	-0-	700	210
Started and completed	2,200	2,200	2,200	2,200
Ending work in process	400	400	-0-	240
Total	3,300	2,600	2,900	2,650

3. Costs to account for	Costs	Current period equivalent units	Current period cost per unit
Beginning work in process	$ 4,998		
Prior department	12,195	2,600	$ 4.6904
Direct materials	23,490	2,900	8.1000
Conversion	10,618	2,650	4.0068
Total	$51,301		$16.7972

4. Costs accounted for	Total equivalent units		FIFO cost per unit	Cost of ending Work in Process Inventory	Total costs
Completed from beginning work in process					
Beginning inventory, 700 units				$ 4,998	
Current period costs to complete					
Direct materials	700	@	$ 8.1000	5,670	
Conversion	210	@	4.0068	841	
					$11,509
Started and completed (100% from current production)	2,200	@	16.7972		$36,954
Total costs transferred to finished goods					$48,463
Ending work in process					
Prior department	400	@	4.6904	1,876	
Direct materials	-0-	@	8.1000	-0-	
Conversion	240	@	4.0068	962	2,838
Total					$51,301

Chapter Assignments

Questions

1. (L.O. 1) What types of manufacturing companies use process cost accounting systems?
2. (L.O. 1) What are the major differences between job order costing and process costing?
3. (L.O. 3) Define total equivalent units.
4. (L.O. 3) Why are there no equivalent units in job order costing?
5. (L.O. 5) Briefly explain the meaning of prior department costs.
6. (L.O. 5) How do prior department costs differ from direct materials costs?
7. (L.O. 3) Why are equivalent units for direct materials costs usually different from equivalent units for conversion costs?

8. (L.O. 1) List the four major sections on a cost summary.

9. (L.O. 6) Distinguish between the FIFO and moving average cost flow assumptions.

10. (L.O. 7) If a department has no beginning work in process, both the moving average and FIFO cost flow assumptions will produce the same cost per unit. Explain.

Exercises

11. (L.O. 3) Casting A is the first stage of the production cycle at S. Mann Company. The following information on conversion costs for April is available:

	Units
Work in process, April 1	-0-
Started in April	340,000
Completed in April and transferred to Grinding	320,000
Work in process, April 30 (40% complete)	20,000

Required Calculate total equivalent units for conversion costs, using the moving average cost flow assumption.

12. (L.O. 3, 4) Records at Ace Company show the following data for the cutting activity for April:

	Units
Work in process, April 1	2,000
Units completed during April	30,000
Work in process, April 30	8,000

Materials were added at the beginning of the process. Work in process at April 1 was 40 percent complete as to conversion costs. Work in process at April 30 was 60 percent complete as to conversion costs.

Required

1. Using the moving average cost flow assumption, calculate total equivalent units for both direct materials and conversion costs.
2. Using the FIFO cost flow assumption, calculate total equivalent units for both direct materials and conversion costs. (AICPA adapted)

13. (L.O. 3, 4) Greenwood Company uses a process costing system. It had no Work in Process Inventory at the beginning of September. During September, 5,000 units were started. On September 30, there were 1,000 units in work in process. They were 70 percent complete as to conversion costs and 90 percent complete as to material costs.

Required

1. Using the moving average cost flow assumption, calculate total equivalent units for both direct materials and conversion costs.
2. Using the FIFO cost flow assumption, calculate total equivalent units for both direct materials and conversion costs.

14. (L.O. 3, 4, 6) Richardson Company computed the flow of physical units completed for the grinding activity in March as follows on page 208.

Units completed	
From work in process, March 1	15,000
From March production	45,000
Total	60,000

Materials were added at the beginning of the process. Work in process on March 1 was 90 percent complete as to conversion costs. Work in process on March 31 consisted of 12,000 units, which were 70 percent complete as to conversion costs. The cost of the beginning work in process included $18,600 direct materials and $45,900 conversion costs. During March, $67,800 of direct materials was used and $190,080 of conversion costs were incurred.

Required

1. Prepare a bar diagram similar to the one in Figure 5–7.
2. Using the moving average cost flow assumption, calculate total equivalent units for both direct materials and conversion costs.
3. Calculate the cost per unit for direct materials and conversion costs.

15. (L.O. 3, 4, 6) Machining is the first stage in Drucker Company's production cycle. The following information on conversion costs is available for April:

	Units	Direct materials	Conversion costs
Work in process, April 1	40,000	$90,000	$16,800
Started in April	320,000		
Work in process, April 30	20,000		

Direct materials were added at the start of the production process. The April 1 inventory was 40 percent complete as to conversion costs. The April 30 inventory was 60 percent complete as to conversion costs. Direct materials used during April cost $738,000. Conversion costs incurred in April were $370,400.

Required

1. Prepare a bar diagram similar to the one in Figure 5–7.
2. Using the moving average cost flow assumption, calculate total equivalent units for both direct materials and conversion costs.
3. Calculate per-unit direct materials and conversion costs for April.

(see Review Exercise 5–2)

16. (L.O. 3, 4, 6) Walden Company uses a process costing system. All materials are added in production at the beginning of the process. The following information is available for January:

Work in process, January 1 (40% complete as to conversion costs)	500 units
Completed and transferred to Department 2	2,100 units
Work in process, January 31 (25% complete as to conversion costs)	400 units
Cost of beginning work in process	
Direct materials	$5,700
Conversion costs	2,950
Costs incurred during January	
Direct materials	22,550
Conversion costs	29,610

Required

1. Prepare a bar diagram similar to the one in Figure 5–7.
2. Using the moving average cost flow assumption, calculate total equivalent units for both direct materials and conversion costs.
3. Calculate the direct materials and conversion costs per unit.

(see Review Exercise 5–2)

17. (L.O. 3, 4, 6) Sussex Corporation began November with Work in Process Inventory of $144,000 direct materials cost and $142,000 conversion costs. The production cycle at Sussex Corporation starts with the mixing activity. Materials are added at the beginning of the mixing process. For November the following information is available:

Work in process, November 1 (50% complete)	40,000 units
Started in November	240,000 units
Work in process, November 30 (60% complete)	25,000 units

During November, Sussex used direct materials costing $836,000 and incurred $2,342,000 conversion costs.

Required

1. Prepare a bar diagram similar to the one in Figure 5–7.
2. Using the moving average cost flow assumption, calculate total equivalent units for both direct materials and conversion costs.
3. Calculate the direct materials and conversion costs per unit.
4. Calculate the total cost of the units transferred to finished goods.

(see Review Exercise 5–2) (AICPA adapted)

18. (L.O. 3, 4, 7) On January 1, Bronson Company had 6,000 units in work in process, which were 60 percent complete as to conversion costs. During January, 20,000 units were completed. On January 31, 8,000 units remained in work in process, 40 percent complete as to conversion costs. Materials were added at the beginning of the process. The cost of the beginning inventory of work in process included $24,900 of direct materials and $24,300 conversion costs. During January, $92,400 direct materials were used and $131,320 conversion costs were incurred.

Required

1. Prepare a bar diagram similar to the one in Figure 5–7.
2. Using the FIFO cost flow assumption, calculate total equivalent units for both direct materials and conversion costs.
3. Calculate the direct materials and conversion costs per unit for January production and the cost of Work in Process Inventory at January 31. (AICPA adapted)

19. (L.O. 3, 4, 7) AZ Company uses a process costing system. Materials are added at the beginning of the process in the forming activity. Conversion costs are incurred uniformly throughout the process. On October 1, work in process in forming consisted of 50,000 units, 30 percent complete as to conversion costs. During October, 150,000 units were started in forming, and 160,000 units were completed and transferred to finishing. Forming's work in process on October 31 was 20 percent complete as to conversion costs. Forming's beginning Work in Process Inventory had $94,000 direct materials and $80,250 conversion costs. During October, forming used $285,000 direct materials and incurred $826,200 conversion costs.

Required

1. Prepare a bar diagram similar to the one in Figure 5–7.

2. Using the FIFO cost flow assumption, calculate total equivalent units for both direct materials and conversion costs.
3. Calculate the per unit direct materials and conversion costs for October production and the cost of units transferred to finished goods.

20. (L.O. 2, 6) Information for January on Ogden Corporation's production is shown below:

	Direct materials		Conversion costs
Work in process, January 1	$ 8,000		$ 6,000
Costs incurred in January	40,000		32,000
Total costs	$48,000		$38,000
Total equivalent units, using moving average method	100,000		95,000
Units completed		90,000 units	
Work in process, January 31		10,000 units	

Materials were added at the beginning of the process. The ending Work in Process Inventory is 50 percent complete as to conversion costs. Notice that equivalent units were calculated for you.

Required

1. Calculate total costs transferred from work in process to finished goods.
2. Calculate the cost of the Work in Process Inventory on January 31.
3. Prepare a journal entry for January to transfer the cost of Work in Process Inventory to finished Goods Inventory. (AICPA adapted)

21. (L.O. 6) Martin Testing Company has an activity that tests the contents of water samples. The process is routine, and Martin makes many of these tests each month. Martin completes all tests on the day they are started. Thus, Martin has no beginning or ending Work in Process Inventory. The tests use no direct materials. Required supplies are considered part of overhead. The following data is available on March activities:

Tests completed	5,240
Direct labor cost	$14,148
Applied overhead	36,784

Required

Calculate the cost per test for March. (see Review Exercise 5–1)

22. (L.O. 2) Vartval is a soap manufactured by Major Products Company. Major produces the soap in a process that operates 24 hours per day. Production starts in blending and is completed in cooking and packing. The T accounts below show the costs recorded in Major's two activities during March.

Work in Process Inventory, Blending

Balance, March 1	4,600	Transferred out	440,800
Direct materials used	229,000		
Direct labor	?		
Applied overhead	127,000		
Balance, March 31	3,400		

Work in Process Inventory, Cooking and Packing

Balance, March 1	18,200	Transferred out	?
Transferred in	440,800		
Direct materials used	17,000		
Direct labor	59,300		
Applied overhead	118,600		
Balance, March 31	14,900		

Required

1. Prepare journal entries to record the March cost flows shown in the T accounts.
2. The predetermined overhead rate in the cooking and packing activity is based on direct labor cost. What was the rate used in the cooking and packing activity?

23. (L.O. 2) Johnson Canning Company cans fruit and vegetable juices. Since they operate 24 hours per day during their busy season, there is often a beginning and ending Work in Process Inventory. Production starts in the preparation activity and is completed in the cooking and canning activity. The T accounts below show the costs recorded in their two activities during July.

Work in Process Inventory, Preparation

Balance, July 1	1,500	Transferred out	?
Direct materials used	85,000		
Direct labor	24,000		
Applied overhead	32,000		
Balance, July 31	1,800		

Work in Process Inventory, Cooking and Canning

Balance, July 1	3,400	Transferred out	?
Transferred in	140,700		
Direct materials used	72,000		
Direct labor	36,000		
Applied overhead	76,000		
Balance, July 31	4,800		

Required Prepare journal entries to record the July cost flows shown in the T accounts.

24. (L.O. 3, 4, 6) Newton Steel Company is a small producer of a special steel used in automobiles. Newton adds direct materials at the start of the production process, and conversion costs are incurred uniformly throughout production. Data relating to April production are given below.

		Percentage Completion	
	Tons of steel	Direct materials	Conversion costs
Work in process, April 1	800	100%	40%
Work in process, April 31	700	100	30
Completed during April	12,000		

Work in process, April 1, included $22,000 direct materials costs and $13,376 conversion costs. During April, Newton Steel used $333,600 of direct materials and incurred conversion costs of $536,824.

Required

1. Draw a bar diagram similar to Exhibit 5–7. How many tons of steel did Newton start during April?
2. Calculate the cost per ton of steel processed in April using the moving average cost flow assumption.

(see Review Exercise 5–2)

25. (L.O. 3, 4, 6) Paper Products Company produces cardboard used in boxes. Data relating to one of their production lines for July is given below.

	Tons of paper	Percentage completion: Direct materials	Percentage completion: Conversion costs
Work in process, July 1	5,000	100%	55%
Work in process, July 31	4,000	100	45
Started during July	800,000		

Work in process, July 1 included $204,000 direct materials and $189,750 conversion costs. During the month, Paper Products used $3,289,500 of direct materials and incurred conversion costs of $5,581,410. Direct materials are added at the start of production, and conversion costs are added uniformly during production.

Required

1. Draw a bar diagram similar to Exhibit 5–7. How many tons of paper did Paper Products complete during July?
2. Calculate the cost per ton of paper processed in July using the moving average cost flow assumption.

(see Review Exercise 5–2)

26. (L.O. 3, 7) Wilmar Paint Company uses a process costing system. The company follows the FIFO cost flow assumption. Its mixing activity used $67,735 of direct materials and incurred $53,010 conversion costs in May. There was no Work in Process Inventory at the start of May. During May, the company started 30,000 gallons and had 1,000 gallons in work in process at May 31. Both direct materials and conversion costs are added uniformly throughout production. The ending work in process was 45 percent complete as to both direct materials and conversion costs.

Required

1. Calculate the cost per gallon produced during May and the cost of gallons transferred out of the mixing activity during May.
2. Calculate the cost of the Work in Process Inventory on May 31.

(see Review Exercise 5–1)

27. (L.O. 6) Speedy Car Wash uses a process cost accounting system. All washes are completed at the end of the day so the company has no beginning or ending Work in Process Inventory. The washes use no direct materials. Required supplies are considered part of overhead. The following data are available for October and November activities:

	October	November
Cars washed	4,480	4,850
Direct labor cost	$ 5,824	$ 6,360
Applied overhead	12,870	12,846

Required

1. Calculate the cost per wash for October.
2. Calculate the cost per wash for November.
(see Review Exercise 5–1)

Problems

28. (L.O. 6) At Maurice Company, forming is the first stage of a two-stage production cycle. Materials are added at the beginning of the cycle. Information on materials used in forming during May is as follows:

	Physical units	Direct materials
Work in process, May 1	12,000	$ 6,000
Units started during May	100,000	51,120
Units completed and transferred to next activity during May	88,000	

Required Using the moving average method, calculate materials costs for both goods completed and work in process on May 31. (AICPA adapted)

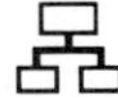

29. (L.O. 5, 6) Blye, Inc., instituted a new process in October. In that same month, 10,000 units were started. Of the units started, 8,000 were completed, and 2,000 remained in work in process on October 31. The work in process was 100 percent complete as to materials costs and 50 percent complete as to conversion costs. Materials costs of $47,000 and conversion costs of $40,000 were incurred during October.

Required

1. Prepare a cost summary similar to the one in Exhibit 5–2. Use the moving average method.
2. Would your answer change if you used the FIFO method? Why or why not?
(see Review Exercise 5–1)

30. (L.O. 3, 4, 7) The wiring activity is the second stage of Flem Company's production cycle. On May 1, work in process contained 25,000 units, which were 40 percent complete as to conversion costs. During May, 100,000 units were transfered in from the prior activity. On May 31, work in process contained 20,000 units, which were 30 percent complete as to conversion costs. In wiring activity, materials were added at the end of the process.

Required

1. Prepare a bar diagram similar to the one in Figure 5–7.
2. Using the moving average cost flow assumption, calculate (a) total equivalent units for prior department costs, (b) total equivalent units for direct materials, and (c) total equivalent units for conversion costs.
3. Using the FIFO cost flow assumption, calculate (a) total equivalent units for prior department costs, (b) total equivalent units for direct materials, and (c) total equivalent units for conversion costs. (AICPA adapted)

31. (L.O. 3, 4) Jorcano Manufacturing Company uses a process costing system to account for costs on Product Z. Production begins in fabrication, where material is added at the start of production. Fabrication makes sets of parts. Once complete, all sets are immediately transferred to assembly, where the parts are connected to finished units.

No material is added in assembly. Once assembly is complete, all sets are immediately transferred to packaging, which places materials around the sets. Packaging completes the production process.

At the beginning of the year, Joranco had no inventory on hand. Production and inventory data are given below:

Unused direct material or packaging material: 0

Fabrication:
  Beginning inventory, 100 units
  Ending inventory, 300 units
100 percent complete as to material; 50 percent complete as to conversion costs.

Assembly:
  Beginning inventory, 800 units
  Ending inventory, 1,000 units
100 percent complete as to prior department costs; 40 percent complete as to costs.

Packaging:
  Beginning inventory, 200 units
  Ending inventory, 100 units
75 percent complete as to packaging material; 25 percent complete as to packaging department conversion costs.

Units completed and transferred out of packaging: 5,000

Required

1. For each activity, prepare a bar diagram similar to the one in Figure 5–7. Label the physical units. Hint: Do packaging first.
2. For each activity, calculate the number of equivalent units of direct materials and conversion costs in ending Work in Process Inventory. (CMA adapted)

32. (L.O. 3, 4, 5, 6) ABC Company provided the following information on one of its production activities:

	Units
Work in process, June 1	5,000
Units transferred in from prior department	35,000
Units completed	37,000

	Prior department	Direct materials	Conversion costs	Total costs
Work in process, June 1	$ 2,900	$ —	$ 3,400	$ 6,300
Current period costs	17,500	25,500	15,000	58,000
Totals	$20,400	$25,500	$18,400	$64,300

Beginning Work in Process Inventory was 20 percent complete as to conversion costs. Ending Work in Process Inventory was 40 percent complete as to conversion costs. Prior department costs were added at the start of production. Materials were added at the end of production. Assume ABC uses the moving average method.

Required

1. Prepare a bar diagram similar to the one in Figure 5–7.

2. Prepare a cost summary similar to the one in Exhibit 5–4 for this activity. (see Review Exercise 5–2)

33. (L.O. 3, 4, 5, 7) Use data from Problem 32 but assume ABC Company uses the FIFO cost flow assumption rather than the moving average cost flow assumption.

Required

1. Prepare a bar diagram similar to the one in Figure 5–7. (Skip this requirement if you prepared the diagram as part of your answer to Problem 32.)
2. Prepare a cost summary similar to the one in Exhibit 5–6 for the production activity described in Problem 32.

34. (L.O. 3, 4, 5, 6) Roy Company manufactures Product X in a two-stage production cycle, involving machining and finishing. This problem concerns only finishing. Materials were added at the beginning of the process in finishing. On February 1, finishing had 6,000 units in work in process, 50 percent complete as to conversion costs. On February 28, there were 8,000 units in work in process, 75 percent complete as to conversion costs. During February, 12,000 units were completed and transferred out of finishing. Costs relating to finishing's production activity and beginning Work in Process Inventory were as follows:

	Prior department	Direct materials	Conversion costs
Work in process, February 1	$12,000	$2,500	$1,000
February costs incurred	29,000	5,500	5,000

Required

1. Prepare a bar diagram similar to the one in Figure 5–7.
2. Assume that Roy Company uses the moving average cost flow assumption. Prepare a cost summary for finishing similar to the one in Exhibit 5–4.

35. (L.O. 3, 4, 5, 7) Use data from Problem 34 but assume Roy Company uses the FIFO cost flow assumption.

Required

1. Prepare a bar diagram similar to the one in Figure 5–7. (Skip this requirement if you prepared the diagram as part of your answer to Problem 34.)
2. Prepare a cost summary similar to the one in Exhibit 5–6 for finishing.

(AICPA adapted)

36. (L.O. 3, 4, 5, 6) Barnett Company adds materials at the beginning of the process in assembly. The 8,000 units in work in process on May 1 were 75 percent complete as to conversion costs. The 6,000 units in work in process on May 31 were 50 percent complete as to conversion costs. During May, 12,000 units were completed and transferred to assembly. The cost of Work in Process Inventory on May 1 and production costs for May are as follows:

	Direct materials	Conversion costs
Work in process, May 1	$ 9,600	$ 4,800
Costs incurred during May	15,600	14,400

Required

1. Prepare a bar diagram similar to the one in Figure 5–7.
2. Assume that Barnett Company uses the moving average cost flow assumption. Prepare a cost summary similar to Exhibit 5–4 for assembly. (AICPA adapted)

37. (L.O. 3, 4, 5, 7) Use data from Problem 36 but assume Barnett Company uses the FIFO cost flow assumption.

Required

1. Prepare a bar diagram similar to the one in Figure 5–7. (Skip this requirement if you prepared the diagram as part of your answer to Problem 36.)
2. Prepare a cost summary similar to the one in Exhibit 5–6 for assembly.

(AICPA adapted)

38. (L.O. 3, 4, 5, 6) On April 1, Collins Company had 6,000 units of work in process in molding, 50 percent complete as to conversion costs. The costs of these 6,000 units were as follows:

Prior department costs	$12,000
Direct materials	2,500
Conversion costs	2,000

Materials were added at the beginning of the process in molding. During April, 14,000 units were transferred in from mixing. When the units arrived in molding, they carried $27,000 in costs from mixing. During April, direct materials added in molding cost $3,500. Conversion costs of $3,000 were also added. On April 30, molding had 5,000 units of work in process, 60 percent complete as to conversion costs.

Required

1. Prepare a bar diagram similar to the one in Figure 5–7.
2. Assume that Collins Company uses the moving average cost flow assumption. Prepare a cost summary similar to Exhibit 5–4 for molding. (AICPA adapted)

39. (L.O. 3, 4, 6, 7) Flynn Earth Sciences, Inc., designs foundations for large buildings. In designing foundations, the company must drill with hollow drills into the earth to take cores of the soil. Soil composition, as revealed by these tests, guides the engineers in designing the foundations. A single activity does the routine tests. The drilling usually takes several days, so Flynn normally has several incomplete tests at the end of a month.

Flynn uses process cost accounting for this testing activity. At the beginning of the year, they estimated that the activity's overhead would be $126,700. They also estimated that the activity would do 101,360 drilling hours during the year. Materials costs are small enough that they are included as part of overhead cost.

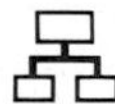

The following data are available on October activities:

	October 1		October 31
Tests in process	15		10
Percentage completion	60%		70%
Work in process balance	$1,394.90		?
Tests completed during October		240	
Drilling hours during October		8,420	
Direct labor cost		$25,056	

Required

1. Calculate the cost per test for October assuming that Flynn uses the moving average cost flow assumption.
2. Calculate the cost of the Work in Process Inventory on October 31, assuming that Flynn uses the moving average cost flow assumption.
3. Calculate the cost per test for October assuming that Flynn uses the FIFO cost flow assumption.
4. Calculate the cost of the Work in Process Inventory at October 31, assuming that Flynn uses the FIFO cost flow assumption.

5. Flynn's new controller is considering the use of a job cost system for accounting for the cost of this activity. Discuss briefly the advantages and disadvantages of job order costing.

40. (L.O. 2, 3, 4, 7) Haslow Company produces battery cases in molding and finishing. The company uses a process costing system with the FIFO cost flow assumption. Direct materials are added at the start of molding. Conversion costs are incurred uniformly throughout the molding process. Molded cases are transferred to finishing.

Molding started September with 500 units in work in process with a total cost of $860. These units were 100 percent complete in materials and 60 percent complete as to conversion cost. During the month, 125,000 units were completed and 300 units remained in ending work in process. The ending work in process was 100 percent complete in direct materials cost and 30 percent complete in conversion cost. During the month, molding used $99,840 direct materials. Molding incurred $74,874 in direct labor cost during September and used a predetermined overhead rate of 150 percent of direct labor cost.

Finishing started September with 800 cases in process which had a total cost of $2,184. These cases were complete as to transferred in costs but only 40 percent complete as to direct labor and applied overhead. During September, finishing received 125,000 cases from molding. At the end of the month, finishing had 1,000 units in process which were 70 percent complete as to conversion costs. Finishing used no direct materials. It incurred $106,403 of direct labor cost. Its applied overhead for September was $43,813.

Required

1. Calculate the cost of goods transferred from molding to finishing during September.
2. Prepare a T account for molding work in process. Enter the beginning balance, the activities for September, and the ending balance.
3. Calculate the cost of the ending Work in Process Inventory in finishing.
4. Make the journal entries to account for the activity in finishing for September.

41. (L.O. 3, 4, 5, 7) Use data in Problem 38 but assume Collins Company uses the FIFO cost flow assumption.

Required

1. Prepare a bar diagram similar to the one in Figure 5–7. (Skip this requirement if you prepared the diagram as part of your answer to Problem 38.)
2. Prepare a cost summary similar to the one in Exhibit 5–6 for molding.

Case 1

Ralla Brinkley (L.O. 6)

Ralla Brinkley looked with dismay at the array of papers on her desk. She had a report on May production due early next morning. Since she had been too busy to do the report that day, she brought home the necessary information. While eating supper, Ralla's cat jumped on the desk and chewed her notes.

Sorting through the papers, Ralla was able to make out the following information on page 218.

Total costs to account for	$189,000
Equivalent units for conversion cost	59,200
Total cost per unit	$3.15
Costs transferred to finished goods	$173,250
Ending work in process, materials	6,300
Equivalent units of materials in ending work in process	7,000

Ralla was aware that all materials were added at the start of the company's single production process and that the company used the moving average cost flow assumption.

Required To prepare her report, Ralla needed the following additional information. Help her find it.

1. Cost per unit for materials and conversion costs.
2. Total conversion cost for May (beginning inventory plus conversion costs incurred in May).
3. Total materials cost for May (beginning inventory plus current materials used).
4. Equivalent units for materials for May.
5. Number of units completed and transferred to finished goods.
6. Equivalent units of conversion costs in May 31 Work in Process Inventory.

Case 2
Dexter Products Company (L.O. 3, 4, 5, 6)

Dexter Products Company manufactures a single product. Its operations are a continuous process carried on in machining and finishing. Materials are added at the start of production in each activity.

For the month of June, company records show the following production data:

	Machining	Finishing
Materials	$240,000	$ 88,500
Labor	140,000	141,500
Overhead	130,000	25,700

Cost records show the following costs for June:

	Units	
	Machining	**Finishing**
Work in process, June 1	-0-	-0-
Transferred from prior activity	-0-	60,000
Started in production	80,000	-0-
Completed and transferred out	60,000	50,000
Work in process, June 30	20,000	10,000
Percent of completion of units in process on June 30		
Materials	100%	100%
Labor	50	70
Overhead	50	70

Dexter uses the moving average cost flow assumption.

Required For both machining and finishing, prepare bar diagrams and cost summaries similar to the one in Exhibit 5–4. Notice that the cost of units completed in machining during June becomes a prior department cost for finishing.

(AICPA adapted)

■

Part 3

Accounting in Managerial Planning Decisions

Part 3 shows how to compile and use accounting information in managerial planning decisions. To ensure that an organization achieves its goals, managers must develop detailed profit plans. To implement their profit plans, managers must marshal the required resources. Any managerial planning decisions, like budgeting, must be made on a regular basis. But in the course of implementing business strategies, managers must sometimes make nonrecurring decisions.

■

Chapter 6, Cost-Volume-Profit Analysis, explains how managers plan costs, volume, and sales price to develop a plan that will earn the organization its targeted profit.

■

Chapter 7, Planning the Master Budget, shows how to develop a master plan to assure that the necessary resources will be available as needed to accomplish the profit plan.

■

Chapter 8, Relevant Costs and Management Decisions, shows how managers identify and analyze the costs that are relevant to nonrecurring decisions. Special orders, decisions on whether to make or buy parts, to add or drop products, or to sell a product with or without further processing are all nonrecurring decisions.

■

6

Cost-Volume-Profit Analysis

LEARNING OBJECTIVES

After studying this chapter you should be able to:

1. List the assumptions behind cost-volume-profit analysis
2. Express algebraically the relationship among total costs, total revenues, and profit
3. Calculate contribution margin per unit and the contribution margin ratio
4. Graph cost, volume, and profit data to analyze breakeven, profit, and loss
5. Calculate the margin of safety and explain its use
6. Calculate the effect of cost and revenue changes on profit
7. Calculate breakeven sales volume and total profit in a multi-product firm, and estimate how changes in sales mix affect profit
8. Calculate contribution margin per unit of a scarce resource
9. Describe how cost-volume-profit equations are used to build computerized financial planning models

A key factor in almost any business decision is its effect on the organization's operating income. Managerial accountants are daily asked to answer questions such as these:

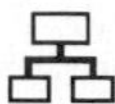

- How would a 5 percent increase in the sales price affect operating income?
- If variable manufacturing costs are reduced 7 percent, how many units of product must be sold to earn $200,000 operating income?
- If Midwest Airline offers a special fare between New York and Miami, how will it affect revenues, costs, and operating income?
- If Fast Food, Inc., increases its advertising budget by $1 million, how many hamburgers must it sell to cover the increase in fixed expenses?
- If the campus bookstore extends its hours, how much additional revenue must it earn to cover the increased operating expense?

To answer these and similar questions, the accountant turns to cost-volume-profit analysis.

Cost-volume-profit analysis is a method of estimating how changes in the following variables will affect profit: unit variable cost, unit sales price, total fixed costs per period, sales volume, and sales mix. As the name implies, cost-volume-profit analysis is an examination of how total revenues and total costs (and therefore profits) vary with changes in sales volume. In this chapter, cost classifications and their uses, which were discussed in Chapter 3, are expanded. Separating total costs into fixed and variable components is vital to cost-volume-profit analysis. The basic assumptions of cost-volume-profit analysis are discussed first. Basic approaches to cost-volume-profit analysis are then illustrated. Next, some managerial uses of cost-volume-profit analysis are discussed and illustrated. Emphasis is on how the accountant can develop information to help managers make decisions. The chapter concludes by illustrating how basic cost-volume-profit analysis can be computerized so management can quickly assess how changes in variables affect profits.

■

Basic Assumptions of Cost-Volume-Profit Analysis

OBJECTIVE 1
List the assumptions behind cost-volume-profit analysis

Cost-volume-profit analysis is based on the following assumptions:

1. A firm's total revenues change in direct proportion to changes in its unit sales volume. That is, the average sales price per unit of product is constant.
2. Total costs can be separated into fixed costs and variable costs.

Exhibit 6–1

A Contribution Income Statement

The contribution margin per unit is the dollar amount contributed toward fixed costs and then to operating income by the sale of one unit of product.

Holder Company
Contribution Income Statement
For the Year Ended December 31, 19x7

	Total	Per unit
Sales revenues (200,000 units)	$800,000	$4.00
Variable costs	500,000	2.50
Contribution margin	$300,000	$1.50
Fixed costs	100,000	
Operating income	$200,000	

3. Total variable costs change in direct proportion to changes in sales volume. That is, the average variable cost per unit remains constant over the relevant range.
4. Total fixed costs (per month or per year) remain constant over the range of sales volume being considered.
5. Sales mix remains constant over the range of sales volume that is being considered.
6. Sales volume equals production volume. That is, inventory levels remain constant.

To the extent that any of these assumptions are not true, the analysis would be more complex. For example, nonlinear functions could be modeled to represent revenues and costs. However, for most organizations these assumptions hold, and the analysis produces useful information.

In Chapter 3, you saw that separating total costs into fixed and variable components is required for a contribution income statement. Over the relevant range only total variable costs change with changes in sales volume. A contribution income statement makes it easy to see how changes in volume affect profit. Exhibit 6–1 shows a contribution income statement similar to the one in Chapter 3 in Exhibit 3–4, page 88. In fact, the only difference between Exhibit 6–1 and Exhibit 3–4 in Chapter 3 is the inclusion of per unit information in the right column. In cost-volume-profit analysis, changes in sales price or variable costs are often stated on a per unit basis. As the exhibit shows, for each unit of product sold, $1.50 first goes toward covering fixed costs. Once fixed costs have been covered, $1.50 per unit goes toward operating income.

Cost-volume-profit analysis can be accomplished either graphically or mathematically. In this text, mathematical approaches are considered first.

■

Basic Approaches to Cost-Volume-Profit Analysis

There are three basic approaches to cost-volume-profit analysis: (1) the equation approach, (2) the contribution margin per unit approach, and (3) the contribution margin ratio approach.

Equation Approach

The first step in the **equation approach** is to separate total costs into fixed and variable components. Once this is done, profit (operating income) can be represented in terms of the following equations:

Sales revenues − variable costs − fixed costs = profit

or

Sales revenues = variable costs + fixed costs + profit

Notice that the first equation follows the sequence of the contribution income statement. The second equation simply moves variable and fixed costs to the right of the equal sign. This format is easier to work with for some computations. However, either version can be used for any set of computations.

OBJECTIVE 2
Express algebraically the relationship among total costs, total revenues, and profit

Now, return to Holder Company's income statement in Exhibit 6–1. Assume that for the next year, 19x8, Holder expects its sales price to remain \$4.00 per unit and its variable costs to remain \$2.50 per unit. Because of increases in rent and administrative salaries, fixed costs are expected to increase to \$150,000. Using this information, one can express Holder's expected profits as follows. X represents sales volume in units.

Sales revenues − variable costs − fixed costs = profit

$$\$4.00X - \$2.50X - \$150{,}000 = \text{profit}$$

In this equation, total sales revenues are expressed as the product of the selling price times the number of units sold ($\$4.00X$). Total variable costs are expressed as the variable cost per unit times the number of units sold ($\$2.50X$). Total fixed costs are expressed simply as \$150,000 per year, since fixed costs are not expected to change with sales volume.

To calculate expected profits, you need only an estimate of expected sales volume, or X. Holder expects its sales volume for 19x8 to equal sales in 19x7. To calculate Holder's expected profit, substitute the value 200,000 for X as follows:

$$\text{Profit} = \$4.00(200{,}000) - \$2.50(200{,}000) - \$150{,}000$$

$$\text{Profit} = \$800{,}000 - \$500{,}000 - \$150{,}000$$
$$= \underline{\underline{\$150{,}000}}$$

As you can see, if fixed costs increase and Holder sells the same number of units as last year, profits will be $50,000 lower.

A question many managers ask is: "How many units must we sell to break even?" The **breakeven point** is the sales volume at which total sales revenue equals total costs and there is no profit or loss. To calculate the breakeven point, the accountant assigns profit a value of zero and finds the necessary sales volume, X, needed to cover only the fixed costs. For Holder, the breakeven point is calculated as follows:

$$\begin{aligned} \text{Sales revenues} &= \text{variable costs} + \text{fixed costs} + \text{profit} \\ \$4.00X &= \$2.50X + \$150{,}000 + \$0 \\ \$1.50X &= \$150{,}000 \\ X &= \underline{\underline{100{,}000}} \end{aligned}$$

Holder must sell 100,000 units to break even.

The breakeven point can be expressed in dollars by multiplying breakeven units by the estimated sales price per unit. For Holder:

$$\begin{aligned} \text{Breakeven sales dollars} &= \text{breakeven units} \times \text{sales price per unit} \\ &= 100{,}000 \text{ units} \times \$4 \text{ per unit} \\ &= \underline{\underline{\$400{,}000}} \end{aligned}$$

Contribution Margin per Unit Approach

OBJECTIVE 3
Calculate contribution margin per unit and the contribution margin ratio

The **contribution margin per unit** is the dollar amount contributed by the sale of one unit to fixed costs and, after covering fixed costs, to the company's operating income. It is found by subtracting the variable cost per unit from the sales price per unit. For Holder Company, the calculations are as follows:

Sales price per unit	$4.00
− Variable costs per unit	2.50
= Contribution margin per unit	$1.50

In other words, for every unit Holder sells, $1.50 is contributed to fixed costs and operating income.

To find the number of units Holder must sell to cover fixed costs, the accountant divides fixed costs by the contribution margin per unit as follows:

$$\begin{aligned} \text{Breakeven sales volume (in units)} &= \frac{\text{fixed costs}}{\text{contribution margin per unit}} \\ &= \frac{\$150{,}000}{\$1.50 \text{ per unit}} = \underline{\underline{100{,}000}} \end{aligned}$$

Exhibit 6–2

Computation of Operating Income for the Sale of One Unit Above the Breakeven Point

Holder Company
Contribution Income Statement
For the Year Ended December 31, 19x8

Sales revenues	
(100,001 units @ $4.00 per unit)	$400,004.00
Variable costs	
(100,001 units @ $2.50 per unit)	250,002.50
Contribution margin	$150,001.50
Fixed costs	150,000.00
Operating income	$ 1.50

This answer agrees with the one arrived at by using the equation approach. If a specific profit figure is included in the computation, the sales volume needed to generate the profit is calculated as follows:

$$\text{Sales volume} = \frac{\text{fixed costs} + \text{profit}}{\text{contribution margin per unit}}$$

Once the breakeven point is reached and fixed costs are covered, each additional unit sold increases Holder's operating income (profit) by $1.50. If 100,001 units are sold, operating income (profit) increases from zero to $1.50. As proof, one need only check the contribution income statement for 100,001 units (shown in Exhibit 6–2) or use the following equation:

$$\begin{aligned}\text{Sales volume} &= \frac{\text{fixed costs} + \text{profit}}{\text{contribution margin per unit}} \\ &= \frac{\$150{,}000 + \$1.50}{\$1.50} \\ &= \underline{\underline{100{,}001}} \text{ units}\end{aligned}$$

Review Exercise 6–1

Calculate Expected Profit and Breakeven Sales Volume

Brockett Fast Food Company is in the process of developing a strategic plan for the year 19xx. The company sells gourmet hamburgers. During the coming year, management expects to sell 200,000 hamburgers. The hamburgers sell for \$2.50 each. The variable costs of selling the hamburgers are \$1.25. This includes the cost of all ingredients. The company expects to incur rental costs of \$125,000 for the year and salary costs of \$75,000. Management would like to know the expected profits and the breakeven sales units for the year 19xx.

Required

1. Calculate the expected profit if Brockett Fast Food Company sells 200,000 hamburgers.
2. Calculate the number of hamburgers the company must sell to break even.

Solution

1. Expected profit calculated:

Sales revenues − variable costs − fixed costs = profit

$$\begin{aligned}\text{Profit} &= \$2.50(200{,}000) - \$1.25(200{,}000) - \$200{,}000\\ &= \$500{,}000 - \$250{,}000 - \$200{,}000\\ &= \underline{\underline{\$50{,}000}}\end{aligned}$$

2. Breakeven sales volume calculated:

$$\begin{aligned}\text{Breakeven sales volume (in units)} &= \frac{\text{total fixed costs}}{\text{contribution margin per unit}}\\ &= \frac{\$200{,}000}{\$1.25\text{ per unit}}\\ &= \underline{\underline{160{,}000}}\text{ units}\end{aligned}$$

(see Exercises 18, 23, 24)

■

Contribution Margin Ratio Approach

The **contribution margin ratio** indicates the percentage of each sales dollar contributed toward fixed costs and, after covering fixed costs, to the company's operating income. The contribution margin ratio is calculated as follows:

$$\text{Contribution margin ratio} = \frac{\text{contribution margin}}{\text{sales dollars}}$$

The contribution margin ratio approach differs from the contribution margin per unit approach in that sales volume is expressed in dollars rather than units. This is an important distinction because a major segment of the business community produces services rather than units of product. Plumbers, electricians,

Exhibit 6–3

Calculation of the Contribution Margin Ratio

The contribution margin ratio is the percentage of each sales dollar available to cover fixed costs and then operating income.

Jay's Advertising Agency
Contribution Income Statement
For the Year Ended December 31, 19x8

	Dollars	Ratio
Sales revenues	\$2,000,000	100%
Variable costs	1,400,000	70
Contribution margin	\$ 600,000	30%
Fixed costs	300,000	
Operating income	\$ 300,000	

CPAs, consulting firms, and advertising agencies all measure their services in sales dollars rather than units. In addition, most manufacturing companies produce more than one product. In that case, total sales volume is expressed better in dollars than in units. Consider a major consumer products company that produces hundreds of products for industrial and consumer markets. Would it make sense for them to express their breakeven point in units? No, because a unit of industrial chemicals is far different from a unit of toothpaste.

Consider the income statement for Jay's Advertising Agency shown in Exhibit 6–3. The dollars column shows the contribution margin in dollars. The ratio column shows the same information as a ratio. That is, the ratios of variable costs and contribution margin to total sales are shown as percentages—70 percent for variable costs to sales and 30 percent for contribution margin to sales. Or to put it another way, for every sales dollar, \$0.70 goes toward variable costs and \$0.30 to fixed costs and operating income.

To calculate the breakeven point in sales dollars, you can use the contribution margin ratio to solve the equation for sales revenues. As before, profit at the breakeven point is represented as \$0. Variable costs are represented as 70 percent of sales revenues, as follows:

$$\text{Sales revenues} = \text{variable costs} + \text{fixed costs} + \text{profit}$$

$$X = 0.70X + \$300{,}000 + \$0$$

$$0.30X = \$300{,}000$$

$$X = \frac{\$300{,}000}{0.30}$$

$$X = \underline{\underline{\$1{,}000{,}000}}$$

Jay's Advertising Agency requires sales revenues of \$1 million to break even.

Notice that in the third step of these computations, fixed costs (\$300,000) are divided by the contribution margin ratio (0.30). Computing the breakeven point can be simplified by skipping to that point in the calculations as follows:

$$\text{Breakeven sales dollars} = \frac{\text{fixed costs}}{\text{contribution margin ratio}}$$

If a specific profit is desired, the sales revenue needed to generate that profit can be calculated as shown below.

$$\text{Sales revenues} = \frac{\text{fixed costs} + \text{profit}}{\text{contribution margin ratio}}$$

Review Exercise 6–2

Calculate Expected Profit and Breakeven Sales Dollars

Jay's advertising agency is in the process of developing a bid for an advertising campaign for the Greater Cincinnati Chamber of Commerce. Historically, the variable costs for this type of campaign have been 70 percent of the sales dollars. The fixed costs have averaged about $40,000. Jay is considering a bid of $200,000.

Required

1. Calculate the expected profit if Jay is successful with the $200,000 bid.
2. Calculate the bid price that would allow Jay to break even.

Solution

1. Expected profit calculated:

$$\begin{aligned} \text{Sales revenues} &= \text{variable costs} + \text{fixed costs} + \text{profit} \\ \$200{,}000 &= 0.70(\$200{,}000) + \$40{,}000 + \text{profit} \\ \text{Profit} &= \$200{,}000 - \$140{,}000 - \$40{,}000 \\ &= \underline{\underline{\$20{,}000}} \end{aligned}$$

2. Breakeven sales dollars calculated:

$$\begin{aligned} \text{Breakeven sales dollars} &= \frac{\text{fixed costs}}{\text{contribution margin ratio}} \\ &= \frac{\$40{,}000}{(1 - 0.70)} \\ &= \underline{\underline{\$133{,}333}} \end{aligned}$$

(see Exercises 19, 27)

■

The Graphic Approach to Cost-Volume-Profit Analysis

OBJECTIVE 4
Graph cost, volume, and profit data to analyze breakeven, profit, and loss

Cost-volume-profit data can be represented on a graph by plotting total revenues and total costs against sales volume. A **cost-volume-profit graph** shows the relationship between revenues, costs, profit, and volume over a wide range of sales activity. It therefore provides more information than the equation or contribution margin approach, which represents costs and profit at only one level of activity.

To illustrate the graphic approach, this text will use data on Holder Company. For 19x8, Holder's projected sales price is \$4.00 per unit; its variable costs, \$2.50 per unit; and its fixed costs, \$150,000. These revenue and cost data are plotted in Figure 6–1. The total sales revenue line is constructed by multiplying the sales price per unit by sales volume. Since the relationship between sales revenue and sales volume is a straight line, only two points are required to locate that line on the graph. Multiplying the unit sales price, \$4, by sales volume at points 0 and 100,000 yields the following results:

$$\$4 \times 0 = \$0 \qquad \$4 \times 100{,}000 = \$400{,}000$$

Figure 6–1
Cost-Volume-Profit Graph
This cost-volume-profit graph illustrates the relationship between sales volume and revenues and between sales volume and costs. The difference between the total costs and total revenues lines is the profit or loss at each sales level. The breakeven point is the point at which the total revenues line and the total costs line intersect.

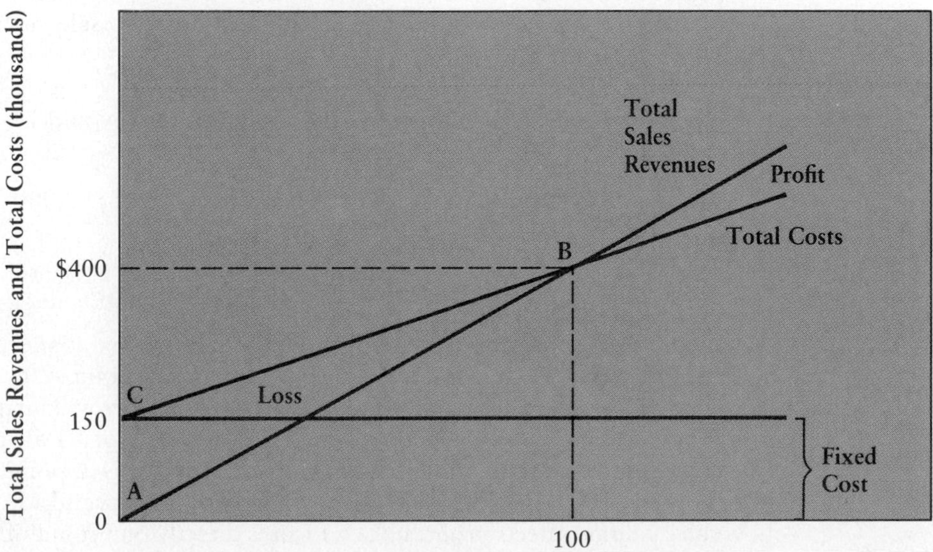

The two points are plotted onto the graph as points A and B, and a straight line is drawn between them to obtain the total sales revenues line.

The total costs line is similarly obtained. The total costs formula is TC = \$150,000 + (\$2.50 per unit × number of units). Any two unit amounts can be substituted in the cost formula. The results are plotted onto the graph, and the two points are connected by a straight line. Assuming sales volumes of zero and 100,000, you can calculate total costs as follows:

$$\$150{,}000 + (\$2.50 \times 0) = \$150{,}000$$

$$\$150{,}000 + (\$2.50 \times 100{,}000) = \$400{,}000$$

Figure 6–1 shows the total costs line obtained from these calculations. The total costs line was drawn by connecting points C and B.

Once the total revenues and total costs lines are drawn, the graph can be interpreted. The vertical distance between the total sales revenues line and the total costs line is the profit or loss at each sales level. The breakeven point is the point at which the total revenues line and total costs line intersect, or point B in this case. At any sales level greater than the breakeven point, total sales revenues are greater than total costs. The company will then earn a profit. At any sales level below the breakeven point, total sales revenues are less than total costs. The company will then sustain a loss.

Cost-volume-profit data can also focus on changes in profit rather than in revenues, and costs. Compare the cost-volume-profit graph in Figure 6–1 with the profit-volume graph in Figure 6–2. In the cost-volume-profit graph, the profit or loss is the difference between the total revenues and total costs lines. In the **profit-volume graph,** profit is shown by the profit line. The sales revenues and total costs lines are omitted.

Because total sales revenues and total costs are represented by straight lines, the profit line plotted against sales volume is also a straight line. Therefore, only two points are required to construct a profit-volume graph. And these points can be obtained by solving the following equation at any two sales volume levels:

$$\text{Profit} = \text{sales revenues} - \text{variable costs} - \text{fixed costs}$$

For Holder Company, profit at zero and 100,000 units would be calculated as follows:

$$\text{Profit} = \$4.00(\text{sales units}) - \$2.50(\text{sales units}) - \$150{,}000$$

$$\$4.00(0) - \$2.50(0) - \$150{,}000 = -\$150{,}000$$

$$\$4.00(100{,}000) - \$2.50(100{,}000) - \$150{,}000 = \$0$$

Figure 6–2 shows the resulting profit line, drawn by connecting points A and B. Notice that the line intersects the vertical axis at point A, or −\$150,000. This intersection indicates that if zero units are sold, Holder will incur a \$150,000 loss. The line then moves upward to the right at a rate of \$1.50 per sales unit (the contribution margin) and intersects the horizontal axis at point B, the breakeven point of 100,000 units. The profit-volume graph is useful for summarizing how sales volume affects profit, since it focuses directly on profitability and shows the contribution margin as the slope of the line.

Figure 6–2
Profit-Volume Graph
A profit-volume graph illustrates the relationship between sales volume and profit or loss. The contribution margin per unit can be found by calculating the slope of the profit line.

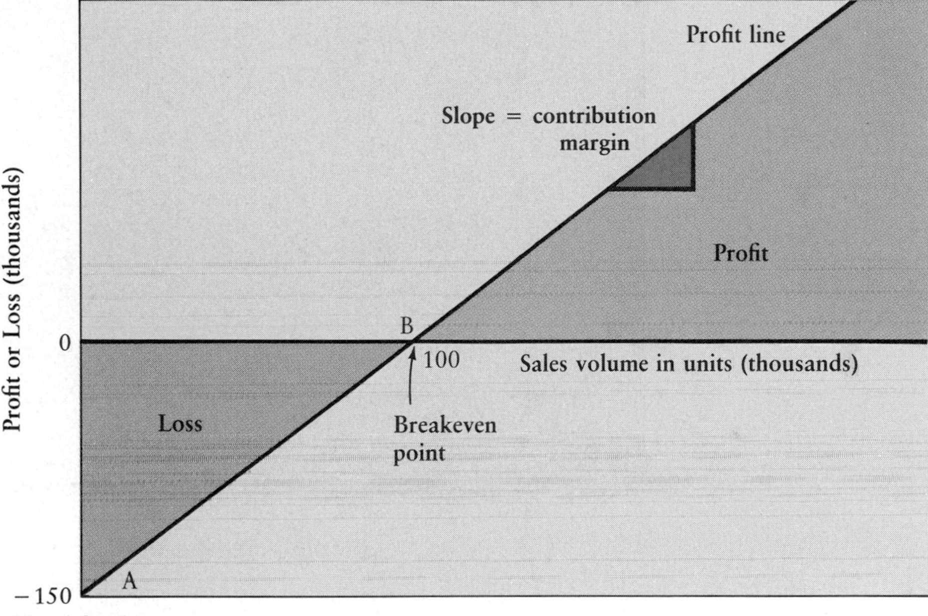

Review Exercise 6–3

Prepare a Profit-Volume Graph

Jay's advertising agency is in the process of developing a bid for an advertising campaign for the Greater Cincinnati Chamber of Commerce. Historically, the variable costs for this type of campaign have been 70 percent of the sales dollars. The fixed costs have averaged about $40,000. Jay is considering a bid of $200,000.

Required

Prepare a profit-volume graph for Jay's Advertising Agency. The *X* axis should use sales dollars to measure volume.

Solution

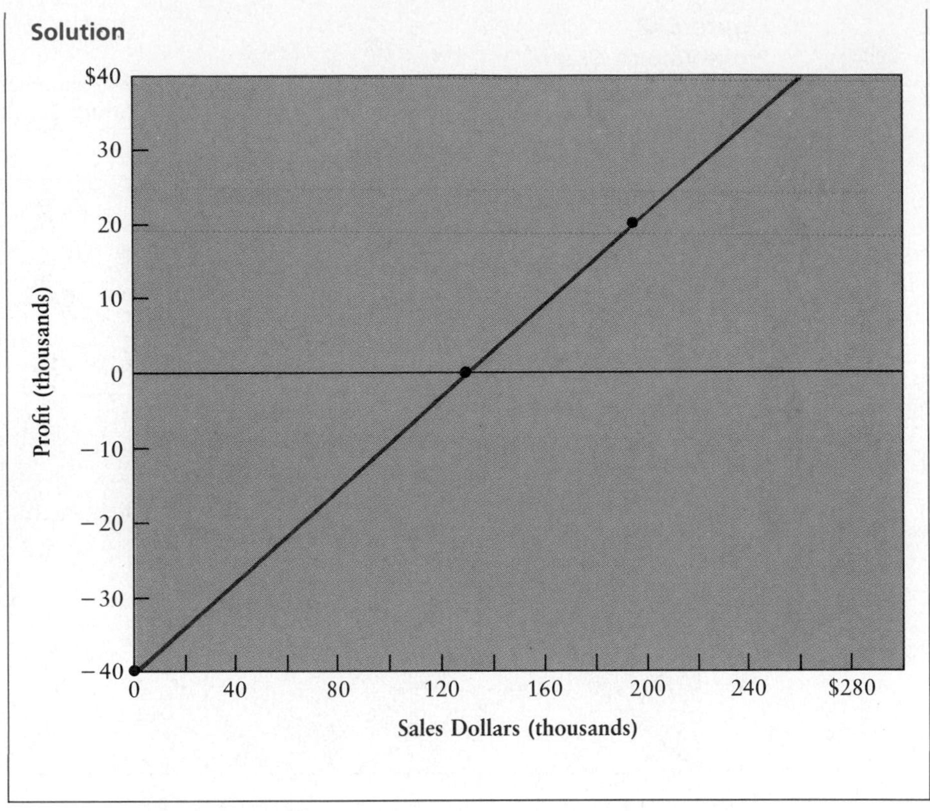

Some Managerial Uses of Cost-Volume-Profit Analysis

Cost-volume-profit analysis helps accountants provide information for managerial planning and decision making. With this tool the accountant can easily calculate the sales volume needed to achieve a specific profit. He or she can also determine how a change in price, sales volume, variable costs, or fixed costs will affect profits. Furthermore, the method can be used to estimate the acceptable leeway between expected sales volume and breakeven sales volume. Each of these uses will now be examined individually.

Target Profit

Having made an investment in a project or business, an investor expects to receive some level of profit. The amount of profit expected by investors is often referred to as **target profit.** Cost-volume-profit analysis can be used to determine the number of units that must be sold or sales dollars that must be earned for a company to achieve its target profit.

Return to the example of Holder Company (pages 224–227). The basic figures for this company are:

Sales price	$4.00 per unit
Variable costs	2.50 per unit
Fixed costs	$150,000 per year

Assume the owners invested $200,000 in the company and desire a 25 percent annual return on their investments. This means Holder has a target profit of $50,000 (25% × $200,000 = $50,000). To find the number of units that must be sold to earn this profit, the accountant substitutes the required profit ($50,000) into the cost-volume-profit equation. He or she then calculates the number of sales units (X) as shown below.

$$\text{Sales revenues} = \text{variable costs} + \text{fixed costs} + \text{profit}$$

$$\$4.00X = \$2.50X + \$150{,}000 + \$50{,}000$$

$$\$1.50X = \$200{,}000$$

$$X = \underline{\underline{133{,}333}}$$

Holder must sell 133,333 units to earn a $50,000 profit. Or stated in dollars, sales must total $533,332 ($4 × 133,333).

You can also find the target profit by using the contribution margin per unit. The formula for breakeven sales volume can be adapted to include a target profit as follows:

$$\text{Sales volume} = \frac{\text{fixed costs} + \text{target profit}}{\text{contribution margin per unit}}$$

$$= \frac{\$150{,}000 + \$50{,}000}{\$1.50}$$

$$= \underline{\underline{133{,}333}}\text{ units}$$

Generally, this approach is easier and more direct than using the cost-volume-profit equation.

Margin of Safety

OBJECTIVE 5
Calculate the margin of safety and explain its use

Sometimes management wants to know the amount actual sales volume can drop before its firm will incur a loss. Called the **margin of safety,** this amount is the difference between the expected sales volume and the breakeven point in units divided by expected sales volume. Generally expressed as a percentage of expected sales volume, it is computed as follows:

$$\text{Margin of safety} = \frac{\text{expected sales volume} - \text{breakeven sales volume}}{\text{expected sales volume}} \times 100$$

Assume Holder Company's expected sales are 133,333 units and its breakeven sales are 100,000 units. Holder's margin of safety is

$$\text{Margin of safety} = \frac{133{,}333 - 100{,}000}{133{,}333} \times 100$$
$$= \underline{\underline{25}} \text{ percent}$$

Holder's margin of safety is 25 percent. That is, if actual sales drop to 25 percent below expected sales volume, the firm will only break even.

Managers use the margin of safety to indicate the risk inherent in a sales plan. The larger the margin, the less the risk. If the planned margin of safety is unacceptably low, management will consider increasing sales activity or decreasing costs to improve the margin.

Effect of a Change in Sales Price

OBJECTIVE 6
Calculate the effect of cost and revenue changes on profit

Managers must constantly decide whether to change sales prices. Consumers tend to resist price increases by buying less of a product. This can offset the effect of a price increase. Sometimes, competition forces management to consider a price reduction. Using cost-volume-profit analysis, the accountant can determine the amount that sales volume must change after instituting a price change in order to yield the target profit.

Assume that Holder Company is considering a price increase of $0.25 per unit. How many units must be sold at the new price to break even? To achieve a $50,000 profit? The computations, when cost-volume-profit analysis is used, are shown below.

	Original data	$0.25 increase in sales price
Sales price per unit	$4.00	$4.25
Variable costs per unit	2.50	2.50
Contribution margin per unit	$1.50	$1.75
Total fixed costs	$150,000	$150,000
Target profit	50,000	50,000
Breakeven sales units	= $150,000 / $1.50 = 100,000	= $150,000 / $1.75 = 85,714
Sales units to earn a $50,000 target profit	= $200,000 / $1.50 = 133,333	= $200,000 / $1.75 = 114,286

These computations indicate that a $0.25 increase in sales price would reduce the breakeven point from 100,000 units to 85,714 units. The number of units that must be sold to earn a $50,000 profit has been reduced from 133,333 units to 114,286 units.

Should Holder increase its sales price? The answer depends on whether management thinks the company can sell 114,286 units at $4.25 per unit as easily as it can sell 133,333 units at $4.00 per unit. If the price is raised, Holder can sustain a 19,047 decrease in sales volume (133,333 − 114,286) and still earn a $50,000 profit. If sales decline less than 19,047 units, profits will exceed $50,000.

Effect of a Change in Variable Costs

The products in some business environments are so competitive that managers cannot increase sales prices. Competition is too strong to allow it. In such cases, managers attempt to decrease costs rather than increase sales prices. Costs can often be reduced by using less expensive materials, by installing laborsaving equipment, or by purchasing materials in bulk at quantity discounts. To estimate the effect of these cost reductions, you must again use cost-volume-profit analysis.

Assume Holder Company has the opportunity to reduce variable costs by $0.20 per unit by purchasing material in bulk. Also assume that Holder's target profit remains at $50,000. How many units must Holder sell to break even? To earn a $50,000 profit? The computations are as follows:

	Original data	$0.20 decrease in variable costs
Sales price per unit	$4.00	$4.00
Variable costs per unit	2.50	2.30
Contribution margin per unit	$1.50	$1.70
Total fixed costs	$150,000	$150,000
Target profit	50,000	50,000
Breakeven sales units	= $150,000 / $1.50	= $150,000 / $1.70
	= 100,000	= 88,235
Sales units to earn a $50,000 target profit	= $200,000 / $1.50	= $200,000 / $1.70
	= 133,333	= 117,647

The decrease in variable costs of $0.20 per unit reduces the breakeven point from 100,000 units to 88,235 units. The number of units that must be sold to earn a $50,000 profit is reduced from 133,333 to 117,647 units.

Effect of a Change in Fixed Costs

Generally, fixed costs are not expected to change during the year, at least not over the relevant range. In the annual planning process, however, managers reassess the company's level of discretionary fixed costs. Recall from Chapter 3 that discretionary fixed costs can be changed in a relatively short time.

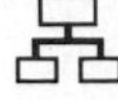

For example, managers can increase fixed cost items such as advertising or research and development to increase sales volume or develop new products for the future. Or they might decrease training costs in order to raise the current year's operating income. Any increase or decrease in fixed expenses changes the breakeven point and the sales volume necessary to achieve a target profit.

Assume the managers of Holder Company are considering a $20,000 increase in advertising expenditures. How many units must be sold to break even, given this cost increase? To earn a profit of $50,000?

	Original data	$20,000 increase in fixed costs
Sales price per unit	$4.00	$4.00
Variable costs per unit	2.50	2.50
Contribution margin per unit	$1.50	$1.50
Total fixed costs	$150,000	$170,000
Target profit	50,000	50,000
Breakeven sales units	= $150,000 / $1.50	= $170,000 / $1.50
	= 100,000	= 113,333
Sales units to earn a $50,000 target profit	= $200,000 / $1.50	= $220,000 / $1.50
	= 133,333	= 146,666

The $20,000 increase in fixed costs has increased the breakeven sales volume by 13,333 units and raised the sales volume needed to achieve the target profit by 13,333 units.

Should Holder increase its advertising expenditures? That depends on the additional sales volume it can realize from the additional cost. If the advertising is expected to increase sales volume by at least 13,333 units, Holder should probably buy the additional advertising.

Another way to arrive at this answer is to calculate the additional units that must be sold to recover the increase in advertising costs. To do so, divide the increase in fixed costs by the contribution margin per unit as shown below:

Increase in fixed costs	$20,000
Contribution margin per unit	$1.50
Sales units to cover the increase in fixed costs	= $20,000 / $1.50
	= 13,333

Effect of Simultaneous Price and Cost Changes

Thus far, you have considered only changes in one variable at a time. In reality, price and costs often change at the same time. Variable costs change frequently, and businesses react by changing their prices. Return to the Holder Company example. Assume that managers are considering a $20,000 increase in advertising costs. They hope to cover this increased cost by raising sales prices by $0.25 per unit. How many units must Holder sell to break even? To earn a $50,000 profit? The computation method is the same. The only difference is that you must allow for two changes instead of one:

	Original data	$0.25 increase in sales price and $20,000 increase in fixed costs
Sales price per unit	$4.00	$4.25
Variable costs per unit	2.50	2.50
Contribution margin per unit	$1.50	$1.75
Total fixed costs	$150,000	$170,000
Target profit	50,000	50,000
Breakeven sales units	= $150,000 / $1.50	= $170,000 / $1.75
	= 100,000	= 97,143
Sales units to earn a $50,000 target profit	= $200,000 / $1.50	= $220,000 / $1.75
	= 133,333	= 125,714

The increase in the sales price of $0.25 coupled with the added $20,000 fixed expense reduces the breakeven point to 97,143 units. It also reduces the number of units that must be sold to earn the target profit to 125,714 units.

Should management implement the proposed changes? Again, that depends on their expectations for sales volume, which cannot be forecasted with complete accuracy. If Holder can sell more than 125,714 units at a price of $4.25, then the expected profit would be greater than $50,000. But if the increased price will force demand for the product below 125,714 units, the proposal should not be implemented.

Review Exercise 6–4

Calculate Expected Profits

Brockett Fast Food Company is in the process of developing a strategic plan for the year 19xx. The company sells gourmet hamburgers. During the coming year, management expects to sell 200,000 hamburgers. The hamburgers sell for $2.50 each. The variable costs of selling the hamburgers are $1.25.

This includes the cost of all ingredients. The company expects to incur rental costs of $125,000 for the year and salary costs of $75,000. This plan produces a profit of $50,000. Management is looking for alternatives to increase profits for the coming year. They are considering increasing the sales price, reducing the variable cost, or increasing the advertising.

Required

1. Calculate the expected profits if the sales price is increased by $0.20 per hamburger and 200,000 hamburgers are sold.
2. Independent of *1* above, calculate the expected profits if variable costs are reduced by $0.25 per hamburger and 200,000 hamburgers are sold.
3. Independent of *1* and *2* above, calculate the expected profits if management spends $20,000 on advertising and sales increase to 220,000 hamburgers.

Solution

1. Expected profits if the sales price is increased by $0.20.

   Sales revenues − variable costs − fixed costs = profit

   Profit = $2.70(200,000) − $1.25(200,000) − $200,000
   = $540,000 − $250,000 − $200,000
   = $90,000

2. Expected profits if the variable cost is reduced by $0.25.

   Sales revenues − variable costs − fixed costs = profit

   Profit = $2.50(200,000) − $1.00(200,000) − $200,000
   = $500,000 − $200,000 − $200,000
   = $100,000

3. Expected profits if $20,000 is spent on advertising and sales increase to 220,000 hamburgers.

   Sales revenues − variable costs − fixed costs = profit

   Profit = $2.50(220,000) − $1.25(220,000) − $220,000
   = $550,000 − $275,000 − $220,000
   = $55,000

(see Exercise 31 and Problem 44)

Multiproduct Cost-Volume-Profit Analysis

Until now, you have been dealing with cost-volume-profit analysis in a firm that produced only one product. Under those circumstances the major factors to be considered are sales price, variable costs, fixed costs, and sales volume of a single product. When cost-volume-profit analysis is applied to a multiproduct firm, managers must still consider the price, costs, and sales volume of each product. But the firm's overall profitability also depends on the sales mix. A **sales mix,** sometimes called the **product mix,** is the proportion of total sales volume contributed by each product. For example, if a firm sells 40,000 units of Product A and 60,000 units of Product B, its sales mix is 40 percent A and 60 percent B. Sales mix is important because the contribution margin of products often differs.

Consider a firm whose sales mix consists mostly of products with a relatively high contribution margin per unit. If sales shift toward products with a relatively low contribution margin per unit, the firm's total profits will drop. This assumes that only the mix of units sold changes, not total sales units. Profits might drop even if total sales increase. This is because the total contribution margin, not sales revenues, determines a firm's profitability. For this reason, some firms compensate sales representatives according to the contribution margin of the products they sell rather than their total sales in dollars.

An example will illustrate how sales mix influences an organization's profits. Hathaway Company sells two products, X and Y. Their price, costs, and contribution margins are as follows:

	Product X	Product Y
Sales price per unit	$8	$10
Variable costs per unit	4	7
Contribution margin per unit	$4	$ 3
Total fixed costs	$400,000	

Notice that Product X's contribution margin per unit ($4) is one dollar greater than Product Y's. Other things being equal, management would rather sell one unit of Product X than one unit of Product Y, since it has a higher contribution margin per unit.

If during the coming year, Hathaway expects to sell 60,000 units of Product X and 60,000 units of Product Y, the company's expected profit can be calculated as follows:

	Product X	Product Y	Total
Sales units	60,000	60,000	120,000
Sales revenues	$480,000	$600,000	$1,080,000
Variable costs	240,000	420,000	660,000
Contribution margin	$240,000	$180,000	$ 420,000
Fixed costs			400,000
Operating income			$ 20,000
Contribution margin ratio	50%	30%	38.9%

OBJECTIVE 7
Calculate breakeven sales volume and total profit in a multiproduct firm, and estimate how changes in sales mix affect profit

The expected profit from selling 60,000 units of Product X and 60,000 units of Product Y is $20,000. The breakeven point can be calculated using the average contribution margin ratio, as follows:

$$\text{Breakeven sales dollars} = \frac{\$400{,}000}{0.389} = \underline{\underline{\$1{,}028{,}278}}$$

This breakeven sales figure depends on a 50/50 unit sales mix of Products X and Y. Notice that neither Product X nor Product Y has a contribution margin ratio of 38.9 percent. X has a 50 percent contribution margin ratio; Y a 30 percent ratio. If the sales mix changes, the average contribution margin ratio changes, along with the breakeven point and the firm's overall profitability.

To illustrate the effect of changes in the product mix, assume that Hathaway's projected sales are 50,000 units of Product X and 70,000 units of Product Y. The expected profits from this slightly different sales mix are calculated as follows:

	Product X	Product Y	Total
Sales units	50,000	70,000	120,000
Sales revenues	$400,000	$700,000	$1,100,000
Variable costs	200,000	490,000	690,000
Contribution margin	$200,000	$210,000	$ 410,000
Fixed costs			400,000
Operating income			$ 10,000
Contribution margin ratio	50%	30%	37.3%

Notice that total sales units have remained the same, but sales revenue in dollars has increased slightly. This change reflects the shift toward greater sales of the more expensive Product, Y. Total contribution margin has decreased significantly, however. Although Product Y has a higher sales price than Product X, it has a lower contribution margin ratio. As you can see, the shift toward greater sales of Product Y has lowered Hathaway's total contribution margin.

This shift in sales mix has also affected Hathaway's breakeven point. Since the company depends more on the higher-priced product whose contribution margin ratio is lower, the breakeven sales volume in dollars has increased, as the following computations show:

$$\text{Breakeven sales dollars} = \frac{\$400{,}000}{0.373} = \underline{\underline{\$1{,}072{,}386}}$$

Although total sales units have not changed, the breakeven sales volume in dollars has risen from $1,028,278 to $1,072,386.

In the examples just discussed, the contribution margin ratio was used in the computations. The same figures can be computed by using the average contribution margin per unit. To do so, return to the original data on the Hathaway

Company. Now, substitute the contribution margin per unit for the contribution margin ratio, as shown below.

	Product X	Product Y	Total
Sales units	60,000	60,000	120,000
Sales revenues	$480,000	$600,000	$1,080,000
Variable costs	240,000	420,000	660,000
Contribution margin	$240,000	$180,000	$ 420,000
Fixed costs			400,000
Operating income			$ 20,000
Contribution margin per unit	$4.00	$3.00	$3.50

Notice that the average contribution margin per unit of $3.50 is based on the projected 50/50 unit sales mix. Neither Product X nor Product Y has a contribution margin per unit of $3.50. The breakeven point is computed as follows:

$$\text{Breakeven sales units} = \frac{\$400{,}000}{\$3.50}$$

$$= \underline{\underline{114{,}286}} \text{ units}$$

This breakeven point represents total sales units of Products X and Y. To determine how many units of each product must be sold to break even, you must use the sales mix that produced the average contribution margin per unit of $3.50. The mix is 60,000 units of Product X and 60,000 units of Product Y, or a 50/50 mix. Using these proportions, divide the total breakeven sales figure into two product breakeven sales figures as follows:

Breakeven sales of Product X = 50% × 114,286 = 57,143 units

Breakeven sales of Product Y = 50% × 114,286 = 57,143 units

Review Exercise 6–5

Calculate Expected Profit and Breakeven Point

Westend Company wholesales two products, Product A and Product B. The sales price, variable cost, and fixed cost are given below.

	Product A	Product B
Sales price	$10	$12
Variable costs	5	9
Contribution margin per unit	$ 5	$ 3
Total fixed costs	$300,000	

Westend Company plans to sell 40,000 units of Product A and 60,000 units of Product B.

Required

1. Calculate the expected profit for Westend Company if the company sells 40,000 units of Product A and 60,000 units of Product B.
2. Calculate the breakeven point if Westend Company sells 40,000 units of Product A and 60,000 units of Product B.

Solution

1. Expected profit calculated:

	Product A	Product B	Total
Sales units	40,000	60,000	100,000
Sales revenues	$400,000	$720,000	$1,120,000
Variable costs	200,000	540,000	740,000
Contribution margin	$200,000	$180,000	$ 380,000
Fixed costs			300,000
Operating income			$ 80,000

2. Breakeven sales units calculated:

$$\text{Average contribution margin} = \$380{,}000/100{,}000 = \$3.80$$

$$\text{Breakeven sales units} = \frac{\$300{,}000}{\$3.80}$$

$$= \underline{\underline{78{,}947}} \text{ units}$$

(see Exercises 15, 32)

■

Maximizing the Contribution from Scarce Resources

OBJECTIVE 8
Calculate contribution margin per unit of a scarce resource

When attempting to maximize a company's contribution margin, managers cannot rely solely on the contribution margin per unit or the contribution margin ratio. Managers need to know the **contribution margin per unit of a scarce resource** particularly when a firm must use scarce resources in its production or distribution. In a manufacturing company, direct labor hours, machine-hours, and materials can qualify as scarce resources. In a merchandising company, display space and sales personnel, which might be in short supply, can be considered scarce resources.

When faced with a shortage of resources, managers must decide which product to produce or sell based on the amount of the resource going into each product or sale.

Consider the revenue and cost data for the two products listed below.

	Product Y	Product Z
Sales price per unit	$8	$10
Variable costs per unit	4	8
Contribution margin per unit	$4	$ 2
Contribution margin ratio	50%	20%

As you can see, Product Y has a contribution margin of $4 per unit and a contribution margin ratio of 50 percent. Product Z has a contribution margin of $2 per unit and a contribution margin ratio of 20 percent. The materials costs of Product Z are substantially greater than those for Product Y. On the surface, Product Y appears more profitable. Assume, however, that the company has only 3,000 labor hours per month. Also assume that Product Y takes three hours to produce, whereas Product Z takes only one hour. Thus, the firm can produce 1,000 units of Product Y or 3,000 units of Product Z. The contribution margin for these two alternatives would be:

Contribution margin for 1,000 units of Y = 1,000 × $4 = $4,000

Contribution margin for 3,000 units of Z = 3,000 × $2 = $6,000

Because labor hours are limited and three units of Z can be produced for only one unit of Y, Product Z is more profitable. To maximize the company's total contribution margin, managers should choose to produce Product Z, even though Product Y has a higher contribution margin per unit and a higher contribution margin ratio.

This same answer could have been found by computing the contribution margin per unit of scarce resources. If labor hours are the scarce resource, the contribution margin per labor hour is calculated as follows:

Product Y's contribution margin per labor hour
= $4 per unit ÷ 3 labor hours per unit
= $1.333 per labor hour

Product Z's contribution margin per labor hour
= $2 per unit ÷ 1 labor hour per unit
= $2 per labor hour

Since Product Z has the highest contribution margin per labor hour, Product Z should be produced.

To check your answer, multiply the contribution margin per labor hour by total labor hours, as shown on page 246.

Contribution margin for 3,000 manufacturing hours for Product Y
= 3,000 × $1.333 = $3,999

Contribution margin for 3,000 manufacturing hours for Product Z
= 3,000 × $2 = $6,000

Notice that when the effects of rounding are allowed for, these figures agree with those obtained by using the contribution margin per unit.

This basic concept has been used effectively by discount food stores and discount department stores. Even large discount stores lack the display space to show all products in all sizes. In order to accept a lower markup on their merchandise, and therefore a lower contribution margin per unit, such stores must achieve a high turnover rate of their stock. By moving products off the shelves as quickly as possible, they maximize the contribution margin per square foot of their scarce resource, display space.

The computations are simple enough when only one resource is limited. Often, however, management must deal with more than one limited resource. In such cases, a method called **linear programming** is used to determine the combination of products or merchandise that will maximize the total contribution margin. Linear programming is discussed in Appendix 6 (pages 270–276).

Review Exercise 6–6

Calculate Contribution Margin

Martha Company produces and sells two products, J and F. The sales price, variable cost, and contribution data are given below.

	Product J	Product F
Sales price	$10	$12
Variable costs	5	9
Contribution margin per unit	$ 5	$ 3
Contribution margin ratio	50%	25%

Both products are produced on the same machine which is capable of running 6,000 hours per year. Product J requires two machine-hours, and Product F requires one machine-hour. The additional material and labor requirements are readily available in the local market.

Required

Assuming Martha could sell all of either product she could produce, which product should she produce and sell to maximize the total contribution margin?

Solution

Computation of the contribution margin per machine-hour:

Product J's contribution margin per machine-hour = \$5.00/2
= \$2.50

Product F's contribution margin per machine-hour = \$3.00/1
= \$3.00

Since Product F has the highest contribution margin per machine-hour, Martha should produce and sell Product F. The total contribution margin for 6,000 machine-hours with Product F is

6,000 machine-hours × \$3 = \$18,000

(see Exercises 37, 38)

Computerized Cost-Volume-Profit Analysis

OBJECTIVE 9
Describe how cost-volume-profit equations are used to build computerized financial planning models

The cost-volume-profit equations just discussed can be used to develop computerized financial planning programs. These programs quickly calculate the effects of changes in price, costs, and volume on an organization's profits. They answer such what-if questions as those listed in the beginning of the chapter. Such programs vary in complexity. Some simple programs can include only those variables discussed. Other, more complicated programs can include an organization's complete budget.

Many firms use interactive programs of basic cost-volume-profit equations on their microcomputers to analyze data they have collected and entered. These program's interactive capabilities allow managers to enter and change their inputs easily, and also make the analysis of the financial effects of various alternatives simpler.

Recall that Hathaway distributes two products, with the following expected sales prices and costs:

	Product X	Product Y
Sales price per unit	\$8	\$10
Variable costs per unit	4	7
Contribution margin per unit	\$4	\$ 3
Total fixed costs	\$400,000	

This information, along with the projected sales figure of 60,000 units per product, was entered into a spreadsheet program. A program was developed to calculate breakeven volume and expected operating income at given sales levels.

The results for Hathaway Company are shown in Exhibit 6–4. The top half of the exhibit represents results from the first set of data entered into the computer.

Exhibit 6–4

Hathaway Company—Spreadsheet Example of Multiple Product Breakeven Analysis and Simulation

Original data

	Product X	Product Y
Sales units	60,000	60,000
Sales price	$8.00	$10.00
Variable costs	4.00	7.00
Contribution margin per unit	4.00	3.00
Fixed costs	$400,000	

Contribution margin statement

	Product X	Product Y	Total
Sales revenues	$480,000	$600,000	$1,080,000
Variable costs	240,000	420,000	660,000
Contribution margin	$240,000	$180,000	$ 420,000
Fixed costs			400,000
Operating income			$ 20,000
Contribution margin ratio	50%	30%	38.9%
Breakeven sales dollars			$1,028,278

Hathaway Company — proposed changes

	Product X	Product Y
Sales units	70,000	65,000
Sales price	$7.20	$9.50
Variable costs	4.00	7.00
Contribution margin per unit	3.20	2.50
Fixed costs	$450,000	

Contribution margin statement

	Product X	Product Y	Total
Sales revenues	$504,000	$617,500	$1,121,500
Variable costs	280,000	455,000	735,000
Contribution margin	$224,000	$162,500	$ 386,500
Fixed costs			450,000
Operating income			$ (63,500)
Contribution margin ratio	44%	26%	34.5%
Breakeven sales dollars			$1,304,348

However, management changed some of the data so it could see how these changes might affect breakeven volume and operating income. The changes increased the advertising budget by $50,000 and lowered the selling prices of Products A and B to $7.20 and $9.50, respectively. The changes also increased expected sales of the two products to 70,000 and 65,000. These changes are highlighted in the bottom half of Exhibit 6–4. As shown, the breakeven sales dollars increased from $1,028,278 to $1,304,348. The expected operating income decreased, causing a $63,500 loss.

These computations require only a few seconds when a spreadsheet program is used. The beauty of such programs is that they allow managers to repeatedly experiment until a combination of inputs providing the desired operating income is found.

Chapter Review

Review of Learning Objectives

1. **List the assumptions behind cost-volume-profit analysis.**
Cost-volume-profit analysis is based on certain basic assumptions about price, costs, sales mix, and sales volume. The most important assumption is that total costs can be separated into fixed and variable components. Thus, this type of analysis also provides input to contribution income statements.

2. **Express algebraically the relationship among total costs, total revenues, and profit.**
The basic concept of cost-volume-profit analysis can be expressed algebraically as follows:

    Sales revenues = variable costs + fixed costs + profit

3. **Calculate contribution margin per unit and the contribution margin ratio.**
The contribution margin per unit is the difference between sales price per unit and variable cost per unit. It represents the dollar amount that each unit sold contributes to covering fixed costs and then to the company's operating income. The contribution margin ratio is the percentage of each sales dollar available to cover fixed costs and to contribute to operating income. It is calculated by dividing contribution margin by sales revenue.

4. **Graph cost, volume, and profit data to analyze breakeven, profit, and loss.**
Total costs and total revenue can be portrayed on either a cost-volume-profit graph or a profit-volume graph (Figures 6–1 and 6–2). Such graphs visually summarize how sales volume affects total costs, total revenues, and total profits over a range of sales. The breakeven point is the point at which the total costs line intersects the total revenues line. At volumes greater than the breakeven point, the area representing profit is the vertical distance between the total revenues and total costs lines. At volumes below the breakeven point, the loss is represented by the same vertical distance.

5. **Calculate the margin of safety and explain its use.**
The margin of safety is the difference between the expected sales volume and the breakeven point in units divided by expected sales volume. It represents the percentage by which actual sales volume can drop below expected sales volume and still allow the firm to break even.

6. **Calculate the effect of cost and revenue changes on profit.**
The basic equation of cost-volume-profit analysis is

Sales revenues = variable costs + fixed costs + profit

This equation can be used to predict how profit will change with changes in sales volume, selling price, variable costs, and fixed costs. (This approach is also useful in determining the sales level needed to achieve a target profit.) An alternate approach is to use the contribution margin per unit or the contribution margin ratio to predict changes in profit.

7. **Calculate breakeven sales volume and total profit in a multiproduct firm, and estimate how changes in sales mix affect profit.**
In a multiproduct firm, the mix of products sold will affect the firm's profitability. In such cases, breakeven sales volume and estimated profit are calculated based on an assumed sales mix. If the sales mix changes, there will also be shifts in the breakeven volume and profit.

8. **Calculate contribution margin per unit of a scarce resource.**
The availability of resources must be considered in most business decisions. If any of the resources used in production or distribution are scarce, a firm must base its decisions on the contribution margin per unit of the scarce resource. The contribution margin per unit of a scarce resource is calculated by dividing the unit contribution margin by the amount of the scarce resource needed to produce or distribute one unit of product.

9. **Describe how cost-volume-profit equations are used to build computerized financial planning models.**
The basic equations of cost-volume-profit analysis can be built into interactive computer programs, which allow management to experiment with changes in price, costs, and volume. These programs are especially valuable to managers who must consider multiple changes in price, costs, and volume for several products simultaneously.

Review of Key Terms

Breakeven point The sales volume at which total sales revenue equals total costs and there is no profit or loss.

Contribution margin per unit The dollar amount contributed by the sale of one unit to fixed costs and, after covering fixed costs, to the company's operating income. Calculated by subtracting the variable cost per unit from the sales price per unit.

Contribution margin per unit of scarce resource For each product, the contribution margin generated by one unit of the scarce resource. Calculated by dividing the contribution margin per unit by the quantity of scarce resource required to produce one unit of product.

Contribution margin ratio The percentage of each sales dollar contributed toward fixed costs and, after covering fixed costs, to the company's operating income. Calculated by dividing contribution margin by revenues.

Cost-volume-profit analysis A method used to estimate how changes in the following variables will affect profit: fixed costs, unit sales price, sales volume, unit variable costs, and sales mix.

Cost-volume-profit graph A graph showing the relationship between revenues, costs, profit, and volume over a range of sales activity. At any volume, profit or loss is the vertical distance between the total revenues, and total costs lines.

Equation approach An approach to analyzing cost-volume-profit relationships based on this equation:

Sales revenues − variable costs − fixed costs = profit

Margin of safety The difference between the expected sales volume and the breakeven point in units divided by expected sales volume. Expressed as a percentage of expected sales volume, it is used as a measure of the risk inherent in a sales plan.

Product mix See *Sales mix.*

Profit-volume graph A graph showing the relationship between profits and volume. Profits are shown by a profit line, which intersects the horizontal axis at the breakeven point.

Sales mix The proportion of total sales volume contributed by each product. Also called the *product mix.*

Target profit The amount of profit expected by investors in a business.

Review Problem

The following projections were made for the Full Ton Company for 19x4. Full Ton produces one product, Product USA.

Full Ton Company
Financial Projection of Product USA
For the Year Ended December 31, 19x4

Sales revenues (100 units at $100 a unit)			$10,000
Manufacturing cost of goods sold			
Direct labor	$1,500		
Direct materials used	1,400		
Variable manufacturing overhead	1,000		
Fixed manufacturing overhead	500		
Total manufacturing cost of goods sold			4,400
Gross margin			$ 5,600
Selling expenses			
Variable	$ 600		
Fixed	1,000	$1,600	
Administrative expenses			
Variable	$ 500		
Fixed	1,000	1,500	
Total selling and administrative expenses			3,100
Operating income			$ 2,500

Required

1. How many units of Product USA must be sold to break even?
2. What would be the operating income if projected sales units increased by 25 percent?
3. What would sales dollars be at the breakeven point if fixed overhead increased by \$1,700? (AICPA adapted)

Solution to Review Problem

1.

Sales revenues (100 units @ \$100 a unit)		\$10,000
Variable costs		
Direct labor	\$1,500	
Direct materials	1,400	
Manufacturing overhead	1,000	
Selling	600	
Administrative	500	
Total variable costs		5,000
Contribution margin		\$ 5,000
Fixed costs		
Manufacturing overhead	\$ 500	
Selling	1,000	
Administrative	1,000	
Total fixed costs		2,500
Operating income		\$ 2,500

Contribution margin per unit = \$5,000 ÷ 100 = \$50 per unit

$$\text{Breakeven sales units} = \frac{\text{fixed costs}}{\text{contribution margin per unit}} = \frac{\$2,500}{\$50} = 50 \text{ units}$$

2.

Sales revenues (125 units @ \$100)	=	\$12,500
Variable costs (125 units @ \$50)	=	6,250
Contribution margin		\$ 6,250
Fixed costs		2,500
Operating income		\$ 3,750

3.

$$\text{Breakeven sales dollars} = \frac{\text{total fixed costs}}{\text{contribution margin ratio}} = \frac{\$4,200}{\$5,000 \div \$10,000} = \$8,400$$

Chapter Assignments

Questions

1. (L.O. 1) On what assumptions are cost-volume-profit analyses based?
2. (L.O. 2, 3) What are the three basic approaches to cost-volume-profit analysis? Discuss each briefly.
3. (L.O. 2) What is the breakeven point? Why is it important?
4. (L.O. 3) What is the contribution margin per unit? How is it computed?
5. (L.O. 4) On a profit-volume graph, what do the following indicate:

   a. The point of intersection with the vertical axis
   b. The point of intersection with the horizontal axis
6. (L.O. 6) Explain how cost-volume-profit analysis can help a manager decide whether or not to increase a sales price.
7. (L.O. 3) How does an increase in variable costs per unit affect the following:

   a. The breakeven point, assuming the sales price and fixed costs remain constant.
   b. The contribution margin per unit, assuming the sales price remains constant.
8. (L.O. 7) Define sales mix. Explain how a change in the sales mix can cause the breakeven point to increase and operating income to decrease.
9. (L.O. 5) Define margin of safety. How is it computed and used?
10. (L.O. 6) For what purposes is cost-volume-profit analysis used?
11. (L.O. 3) Which choice from the list below best completes this sentence? The contribution margin ratio always increases when:

    a. Variable costs as a percentage of sales revenues decrease
    b. Variable costs as a percentage of sales revenues increase
    c. The breakeven point decreases
    d. The breakeven point increases
12. (L.O. 3) To find the unit sales level needed to earn a target profit, the accountant sets up an equation in the form of a fraction as outlined below. Select the proper combination from the table below.

Contribution margin per unit	Projected profit	Fixed cost
a. Denominator	Denominator	Numerator
b. Denominator	Numerator	Numerator
c. Numerator	Denominator	Denominator
d. Not used	Numerator	Denominator

13. (L.O. 3) If sales price and variable costs remain constant and fixed costs increase, what will happen to the breakeven point and the contribution margin? Select the proper row from the table below.

Breakeven point	Contribution margin
a. Decrease	Increase
b. Increase	No change
c. Increase	Decrease

14. (L.O. 3) To calculate expected sales level in units, when an operating loss is predicted, the loss would be:
a. Added to fixed costs in the numerator
b. Subtracted from fixed costs in the numerator
c. Added to fixed costs in the denominator
d. Subtracted from fixed costs in the denominator

Exercises

15. (L.O. 7) Clifton Hardware sells nuts and bolts. For each bolt, they sell two nuts. The contribution margin is $1.00 for a bolt and $0.50 for a nut. Fixed costs are $80,000 per year.

Required How many nuts and bolts must the store sell to break even? (see Review Exercise 6–5)

16. (L.O. 3, 5) Conrad Company expects to sell its product at $40 per unit. Variable costs are $28 per unit; manufacturing costs are $22 per unit; and selling costs of $6 per unit. Fixed costs are incurred uniformly throughout the year and amount to $800,000: manufacturing costs are $500,000 per year; and selling and administrative costs are $300,000 per year.

Required

1. Calculate the breakeven point in units for this product.
2. Calculate how many units must be sold to earn income of $60,000 for the year.
3. Calculate the margin of safety, using your answer to 2 above as expected sales.

17. (L.O. 3, 4, 5) Maxi Company is contemplating an expansion program that will result in the following budget for the next year:

Expected sales	$1,200,000
Variable costs	800,000
Fixed costs	120,000

Required

1. What is the amount of breakeven sales dollars?
2. What is the margin of safety?
3. Prepare a cost-volume-profit graph for Maxi Company. Their product sells for $1 per unit.

18. (L.O. 3) Guppies at Gus' Guppy Store now sell for $9 each. Only 40 percent of that selling price is available to cover fixed costs and to provide profit. The fixed costs of running the fish store are $18,000 per year.

Required How many guppies must be sold to break even this year? How many to make a $9,000 profit? (see Review Exercise 6–1)

19. (L.O. 3) In planning its operations for 19x9, Skiline Chili prepared the estimates shown below. They are based on a sales forecast of $6 million.

	Variable costs ($6 million sales)	Fixed costs per year
Direct materials	$1,600,000	
Direct labor	1,400,000	
Manufacturing overhead	600,000	$ 900,000
Selling expenses	240,000	360,000
Administrative expenses	60,000	140,000
	$3,900,000	$1,400,000

Required What is the total amount of sales revenues at the breakeven point? (see Review Exercise 6–2)

20. (L.O. 7) Thomas Company sells Products X, Y, and Z. Thomas sells three units of X for each unit of Z and six units of Y for each unit of Z. The contribution margins are $1.00 per unit of X, $1.50 per unit of Y, and $3.00 per unit of Z. Fixed costs are $600,000 per year.

Required Calculate the units of X, of Y, and of Z that Thomas must sell at the breakeven point. (AICPA adapted)

21. (L.O. 7, 8) Insula Corporation produces and sells two products, D and W. Insula generally sells two units of D to every three units of W sold. The contribution margin is $4 per unit for D and $2 per unit for W. Insula has fixed costs of $420,000 per year.

Required

1. Calculate total units sold at the breakeven point.
2. Assume that total labor hours available for production are 2,000. Product D requires 0.75 hours to produce, and Product W requires 0.25 hours. Which product should Insula produce to maximize the total contribution margin? (AICPA adapted)

22. (L.O. 3, 6) The University of Cincinnati Business Association is planning a spring break canoe outing. The social committee has assembled the following budget proposal for the event:

Canoe rental (per person)	$ 6
Food and beverage (per person)	10
Bus rental	90
Advertising expense	15

The Committee members have decided to charge $20 per person for the event.

Required

1. Compute the breakeven point for the canoe outing in terms of number of participants.
2. If the organization would like to make a $200 profit, how many participants must attend the spring break event?

23. (L.O. 2, 6) Rasta Manufacturing Company manufactures and sells beaded necklaces. Each necklace sells for $50 and has a contribution margin of 25 percent per unit sold. The company's fixed expenses are $500,000 per year.

Required

1. Determine the amount of variable expense incurred per unit.
2. Using the equation method, determine the following:
   a. Breakeven point in units and dollars.
   b. Required number of unit sales to earn a profit of $800,000.
   (see Review Exercise 6–1)

24. (L.O. 3, 6) Huseman Manufacturing Company incurs $400,000 in fixed cost uniformly throughout each year of production. Variable costs are $25 per unit, and the product sells for $150 per unit.

Required

1. Calculate the breakeven point in units.
2. Calculate the required number of units Huseman must sell in order to make $500,000 operating income for the year.
   (see Review Exercise 6–1)

25. (L.O. 7) Kilby's Computer Wholesalers sells transistors for $4 and diodes for $2. For every transistor sold, they sell three diodes. The contribution margin is $2.50 for a transistor and $0.75 for a diode. Fixed costs are $150,000 per year.

Required

1. Calculate the number of units that must be sold to break even.
2. Calculate the number of sales dollars to break even.

26. (L.O. 3, 6) Davis Manufacturing Company, producers of fine leather clothing, has designed a new leather jacket sure to sweep the market during the coming back-to-school season. Based on research studies conducted by an independent marketing research firm, Davis Company estimates first-year sales will be 50,000 jackets. The selling price per jacket will be $250. Variable costs are estimated to be 50 percent of the selling price. Fixed costs are estimated at $750,000 per year.

Required

1. What is the breakeven point in units?
2. What is the breakeven point in dollars?
3. How many jackets must Davis Company sell in order to earn an operating income of $300,000?

27. (L.O. 3) Garry Publishing Company prints and sells college textbooks. The company's income statement for the most recent year-end appears as follows:

Sales Revenues	$1,500,000	100%
Variable Costs	900,000	60
Contribution Margin	$ 600,000	40%
Fixed Costs	200,000	
Operating Income	$ 400,000	

Required

1. Calculate the breakeven sales.
2. Compute the total variable costs at the breakeven point.

28. (L.O. 2, 3) At a breakeven point of 400 units sold, variable costs were $400 and fixed costs were $200.

Required

What will the 401st unit sold contribute to operating income?

29. (L.O. 7) Venus Company plans to produce Comets and Asteroids. It plans to sell 200,000 Comets at $4 a unit and 300,000 Asteroids at $3 a unit. Variable costs are 70 percent of sales for Comets; 50 percent of sales for Asteroids.

Required To realize a $200,000 profit using this plan, how high can total fixed costs be?

30. (L.O. 3, 5) Bonzat Company plans to market a new product. Based on its market studies, Bonzat estimates it can sell 6,000 units in 19x6. The selling price will be $4 per unit. Variable costs are estimated at 70 percent of the selling price. Fixed costs are estimated at $6,000 per year.

Required

1. What is the breakeven point in units?
2. Calculate the expected operating income if sales are 6,000 units.
3. Calculate the margin of safety if expected sales are 6,000 units.

31. (L.O. 3, 6) Kanen Company prepared the following tentative forecast for Product B in 19x4:

Sales revenues	$250,000
Selling price per unit	$2.50
Variable costs	$150,000
Fixed costs	$ 75,000

A study made by the sales manager disclosed that a unit selling price increase of 20 percent would decrease expected volume by only 10 percent.

Required

1. Assuming Kanen incorporates these changes into its 19x4 forecast, what should the 19x4 operating income from Product B be?
2. Calculate the operating income if Kanen does not incorporate these changes.

(see Review Exercise 6–4)

32. (L.O. 6, 7) Taylor, Inc., produces two products, Acdom and Belnom, which account for 60 percent and 40 percent of the total sales dollars, respectively. Variable costs are 60 percent of sales dollars for Acdom and 85 percent for Belnom. Total fixed costs are $150,000 per year.

Required

1. What is Taylor's breakeven point in sales dollars?
2. Assuming Taylor's total fixed costs increase by 30 percent, how many sales dollars are needed to generate $15,000 of income? (AICPA adapted)

(see Review Exercise 6–5)

33. (L.O. 3) In 19x3, the contribution margin ratio of Lambert Company was 30 percent. In 19x4, fixed costs are expected to be $120,000, the same as in 19x3. Sales are forecasted to be $550,000, a 10 percent increase over 19x3.

Required Calculate the contribution margin ratio that Lambert will need if it wants to increase income by $30,000 in 19x4.

34. (L.O. 6) Pittsburgh Company is considering a proposal to replace machinery used to manufacture Product A. The new machines are expected to increase annual fixed costs by $240,000. Because of reduced direct labor hours and more efficient use of direct materials, variable costs should decrease to 50 percent of sales. If this change is not made, Pittsburgh's budgeted sales and costs for Product A for 19x4 will be as follows:

Sales revenues	$4,000,000
Variable costs	70% of sales
Fixed costs	$ 800,000

Required How much will budgeted operating income increase for Product A for 19x4 if Pittsburgh replaces the machines on January 1, 19x4?

35. (L.O. 3, 4, 6) Meredith Company plans to sell Product T for $10 a unit. Variable costs are $6 a unit, and fixed costs are $100,000 per year.

Required

1. What must total unit sales be to break even?
2. Prepare a cost-volume-profit graph.
3. Prepare a profit-volume graph. (see Review Exercise 6–3)
4. Assume that fixed costs have increased to $150,000 and that variable costs are $5 per unit. Plot this change onto the graph you prepared in *3* above.
5. Were you the owner of Meredith Company, which cost structure would you prefer? Explain your answer briefly.

36. (L.O. 4) Study the following graph for Ann Company.

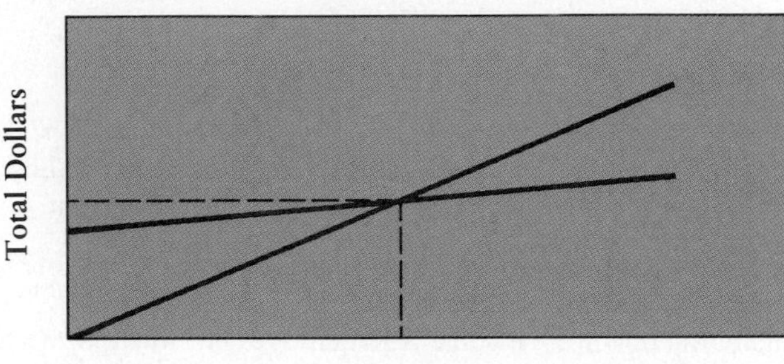

Required Identify the items below by placing the item letter at the appropriate point on the graph.

A Total fixed costs
B Total costs line
C Total revenues line
D Breakeven point
E Sales volume in dollars to break even
F Sales volume in units to break even

37. (L.O. 8) Aru Company produces and sells two products, D and E. The sales price, variable costs, and contribution data are given below.

	Product D	Product E
Sales price	$20	$24
Variable costs	10	18
Contribution margin per unit	$5	$3
Contribution margin ratio	50%	25%

Both products are produced on the same machine which is capable of running 6,000 hours per year. Product D requires two machine-hours, and Product E requires one machine-hour. The additional material and labor requirements are readily available in the local market.

Required Assuming Aru could sell all of either product she can produce, which product should she produce and sell to maximize the total contribution margin? (see Review Exercise 6–6)

38. (L.O. 8) Gunning Company sells two products, Q and Z. The sales of the two products are directly related to the advertising dollars spent promoting them. Mr. Gunning has $200,000 of advertising available for the coming year with no opportunity to increase the advertising expenditure.

The sales price, variable costs, and contribution margin for Product Q and Product Z are given below.

	Product Q	Product Z
Sales price	$80	$100
Variable costs	60	70
Contribution margin per unit	$20	$ 30
Contribution margin ratio	25%	30%

Based on an analysis of past sales and advertising, for every $10 spent on promoting Product Q two units were sold and for every $10 spent on promoting Product Z one unit was sold.

Required

1. Determine how Gunning should spend his advertising dollars.
2. Calculate the total contribution margin based on your answer to *1* above.

(see Review Exercise 6–6)

Problems

39. (L.O. 3, 4, 5, 6) XAnn Company operates a sweater shop in the eastern part of the United States. Sales personnel receive base salaries plus commissions. All sweaters sold by XAnn have the same selling price and unit cost. The financial results for 19x2 are given below.

XAnn Company
Operating Income Statement
For the Year Ended December 31, 19x2

Sales revenues (6,000 units @ $30)		$180,000
Variable costs		
Purchase price (6,000 units @ $10)	$60,000	
Sales commissions (6,000 units @ $4)	24,000	84,000
Contribution margin		$ 96,000
Fixed costs		
Rent	$20,000	
Salaries	35,000	
Utilities	5,000	60,000
Operating income		$ 36,000

XAnn is preparing a plan for 19x3. They have asked you to assist in the analysis.

Required

1. Assume expected sales will be 6,500 sweaters in 19x3 with no changes in sales price or costs. Calculate the expected operating income for 19x3. What is the unit breakeven point? Calculate the margin of safety using units to measure sales volume.
2. Ann, the president of the company, may decide to eliminate base sales salaries of $20,000 in 19x3 and pay all sales personnel a commission of $7 per sweater sold. Assuming an expected sales volume of 6,500 sweaters and no other changes in costs, calculate expected operating income for 19x3. What is the unit breakeven point? Calculate the margin of safety using units to measure sales volume.
3. Prepare a profit-volume graph, comparing how the results in *1* and *2* above will affect profits.

40. (L.O. 6) Wilson Company prepared the preliminary forecast on Product G for 19x4 as shown below. Assume there are no expenditures for advertising.

Selling price per unit	$10
Unit sales	100,000
Variable costs	$600,000
Fixed costs	$300,000

Based on a market study in December 19x3, Wilson estimated that if $100,000 were spent on advertising, the unit selling price could be increased by 15 percent; the unit sales volume, by 10 percent.

Required Assuming Wilson spends $100,000 on advertising in 19x4, what will its operating income from Product G be? (AICPA adapted)

41. (L.O. 3, 6) In a recent period, Zero Company had the following experience:

	Fixed	Variable	Total
Sales revenues (10,000 units @ $200)			$2,000,000
Costs			
Direct materials	$ —	$ 200,000	
Direct labor	—	400,000	
Manufacturing overhead	160,000	600,000	
Administrative expenses	180,000	80,000	
Other expenses	200,000	120,000	
Total costs	$540,000	$1,400,000	1,940,000
Operating income			$ 60,000

Required

1. Calculate the breakeven point for Zero in units and sales dollars.
2. What sales volume is needed to generate an operating income of $96,000?
3. What is the breakeven point in units if fixed advertising costs increase by $18,000?

(AICPA adapted)

42. (L.O. 7) Rain Company, Inc., manufactures and sells wet weather fashion apparel. Among the many quality items produced, Rain Company produces two grades of umbrellas, standard and deluxe. Selected information on the umbrellas is as follows:

	Standard	Deluxe
Selling price per umbrella	$15	$20
Variable costs per umbrella		
Production	8	10
Selling	1	2

Company records indicate that the following fixed costs are associated with the umbrella division:

	Per month
Fixed production costs	$10,000
Advertising expense	2,000
Administrative salaries	75,000
Total	$87,000

Sales per unit for the last quarter were as follows:

	Standard	Deluxe
April	25,000	30,000
May	20,000	27,000
June	12,000	14,000

Required

1. Compute the Umbrella Division's breakeven dollars for the month of April.
2. Prepare an income statement, using the contribution approach, for the last quarter (April–June). Break the income statement information down according to the following headings:

Standard		Deluxe		Total	
Amount	Percent	Amount	Percent	Amount	Percent

43. (L.O. 3, 6) Hewitt Manufacturing Company produces hand-held scientific calculators. Price and cost data on Hewitt's product and operations are as follows:

Sales price per unit	$25
Variable costs per unit	
Direct labor	$ 6
Direct materials	10
Manufacturing overhead	3
Selling expenses	1
Total variable costs	$20
Annual fixed costs	
Selling and administrative	$ 500,000
Manufacturing overhead	300,000
Total fixed costs	$ 800,000
Projected yearly sales	$2,500,000

Required

1. Calculate breakeven in units.
2. Calculate the required number of units Hewitt must sell in order to recognize an operating income of $500,000.
3. If direct materials cost increases by 10 percent, what will be the breakeven point?

44. (L.O. 3, 6) Maxwell Company manufactures and sells a single product in Toronto, Canada. Price and cost data on Maxwell's product and operations are

Selling price per unit	$25.00		
Variable costs per unit		Annual fixed costs	
Direct materials	$11.00	Manufacturing overhead	$192,000
Direct labor	5.00	Selling and administrative	276,000
Manufacturing overhead	2.50	Total fixed costs	$468,000
Selling expenses	1.30		
Total variable costs	$19.80		
Forecasted annual sales volume		(120,000 units)	$3,000,000

Required

1. Calculate Maxwell's breakeven point in units.
2. Calculate how many units Maxwell must sell to earn $156,000 of operating income.
3. Maxwell estimates that its direct labor costs will increase by 8 percent next year. How many units must Maxwell sell next year to reach the breakeven point?

4. If Maxwell's direct labor costs increase by 8 percent, what must the selling price per unit of product be to maintain the same contribution margin ratio? (AICPA adapted) (see Review Exercise 6–4)

45. (L.O. 3, 6) The income statement for Davann Company presented below represents operating results for the fiscal year just ended. Davann had sales of 1,800 tons of product during 19x0. The manufacturing capacity of Davann's facilities is 3,000 tons of product.

Davann Company
Income Statement
For the Year Ended December 31, 19x0

Sales revenues		$900,000
Variable expenses		
Manufacturing	$315,000	
Selling	180,000	
Total variable expenses		495,000
Contribution margin		$405,000
Fixed expenses		
Manufacturing	$ 90,000	
Selling	112,500	
Administrative	45,000	
Total fixed expenses		247,500
Operating income		$157,500

Required Treat each of the following questions independently:

1. Calculate the breakeven volume in tons of product for 19x0.
2. If sales volume is estimated at 2,100 tons for next year and prices and expenses stay at the same levels and amounts, how much operating income can Davann expect for 19x1?
3. Davann's potential foreign customer has offered to buy 1,500 tons of product at $450 per ton. Assume all of Davann's variable expenses per unit and fixed expenses per year are at the same levels and rates as in 19x0. How much operating income will Davann make if it takes this order and accepts only 1,500 tons of business from its regular customers (accepting more would exceed capacity)?
4. Davann plans to market its product in a new territory. Davann estimates that it needs additional advertising and promotion, which will cost $61,500 annually. An additional sales commission of $25 per ton is needed for the sales force in the new territory. How many tons must be sold in the new territory to maintain Davann's current operating income of $157,500.
5. Davann may replace a labor intensive process with an automatic machine. This change would increase annual manufacturing fixed expenses by $58,500. Variable manufacturing expenses would decrease by $25 per ton. What is the new breakeven volume in tons? (AICPA adapted)

46. (L.O. 3, 4, 6) Mr. Calderone started a pizza restaurant in 19x0. He rented a building for $400 per month. He hired two people to work full time at the restaurant at fixed salaries. An outside accountant was engaged to provide tax and bookkeeping services for $300 per month. The necessary restaurant equipment and delivery cars were purchased with cash. Mr. Calderone has noticed that expenses for utilities and supplies have been fairly constant.

Mr. Calderone increased his business between 19x0 and 19x3. Profits have more than doubled since 19x0. Mr. Calderone does not understand why his profits have increased faster than his sales volume.

A projected income statement for 19x4 was prepared by his accountant. The average pizza sells for $5.

Calderone Company
Projected Income Statement
For the Year Ended December 31, 19x4

Sales revenues		$95,000
Cost of food sold		28,500
Gross margin		$66,500
Salaries and employee benefits of restaurant help	$25,450	
Rent	4,800	
Accounting services	3,600	
Depreciation, delivery equipment	5,000	
Depreciation, restaurant equipment	3,000	
Utilities	2,325	
Cleaning supplies	1,200	
Total operating expenses		45,375
Operating income		$21,125

Required

1. How many pizzas must be sold to break even?
2. Mr. Calderone would like an operating income of $28,000. How many pizzas must be sold to earn the target profit?
3. Briefly explain why Mr. Calderone's profits have increased at a faster rate than his sales. (Preparing a graph may help.) (CMA adapted)

47. (L.O. 3, 6) Pawnee Company operated at normal capacity during the current year producing 50,000 units of its single product. Sales totaled 40,000 units at an average price of $20 per unit. Variable manufacturing costs were $8 per unit, and variable marketing costs were $4 per unit sold. Fixed costs were incurred uniformly throughout the year and amounted to $188,000 for manufacturing and $64,000 for marketing. There was no year-end Work in Process Inventory.

Required

1. Calculate Pawnee's breakeven point in sales dollars for the current year.
2. Calculate the number of units required to be sold in the current year to earn an operating income of $180,000.
3. Pawnee's variable manufacturing costs are expected to increase 10 percent in the coming year. Calculate Pawnee's breakeven point in sales dollars.
4. If Pawnee's variable manufacturing costs do increase 10 percent, what selling price would yield the same contribution margin in the coming year. (CMA adapted)

48. (L.O. 3, 6) Donnelly Corporation manufactures and sells T-shirts imprinted with college names and slogans. Last year, the shirts sold for $7.50 each, and the variable cost to manufacture them was $2.25 per unit. The company needed to sell 20,000

shirts to break even. The operating income last year was $8,400. Donnelly's expectations for the coming year include the following:

- The sales price of the T-shirts will be $9.
- Variable cost to manufacture will increase by one-third.
- Fixed costs will increase by 10 percent.

Required

1. Calculate the selling price that would maintain the same contribution margin rate as last year.
2. Calculate the number of T-shirts Donnelly must sell to break even in the coming year.
3. Sales for the coming year are expected to increase by 1,000 units. If this occurs, calculate the expected sales volume.
4. Calculate the dollar sales volume Donnelly Corporation needs to earn $37,500 of operating income. (CMA adapted)

49. (**L.O. 3, 6**) All-Day Candy Company is a wholesale distributor of candy. The company services grocery, convenience, and drugstores in a large metropolitan area.

Small but steady growth in sales has been achieved by the All-Day Candy Company over the past few years while candy prices have been increasing. The company is formulating its plans for the coming fiscal year. Presented below are the data used to project the current year's operating income of $184,000.

Average selling price	$4.00 per box	
Average variable expenses		
Cost of candy	$2.00 per box	
Selling expenses	0.40	
Total	$2.40 per box	
Annual fixed expenses		
Selling	$160,000	
Administrative	280,000	
Total	$440,000	
Expected annual sales volume (390,000 boxes)		$1,560,000

Manufacturers of candy have announced that they will increase prices of their products an average of 15 percent in the coming year due to increases in materials (sugar, cocoa, peanuts, etc.) and labor expenses. All-Day Candy Company expects that all other expenses will remain at the same rates or levels as the current year.

Required

1. What is All-Day Candy Company's breakeven point in boxes of candy for the current year?
2. What selling price per box must All-Day Candy Company charge to cover the 15 percent increase in the cost of candy and still maintains the current average contribution margin per box?
3. What volume of sales in dollars must the All-Day Candy Company achieve in the coming year to maintain the same operating income as projected for the current year if the selling price of candy remains at $4 per box and the cost of candy increases 15 percent? (CMA adapted)

50. (**L.O. 3, 6**) R. A. Ro and Company, maker of quality handmade pipes, has experienced a steady growth in sales for the past five years. However, increased competition has led Mr. Ro, the president, to believe that an aggressive advertising campaign will be necessary next year to maintain the company's present growth.

To prepare for next year's advertising campaign, the company's accountant has prepared and presented Ro with the following data for the current year, 19x2:

Variable expenses	
Direct labor	$ 8.00 per pipe
Direct materials	3.25
Variable overhead	2.50
Total variable expenses	$13.75 per pipe
Fixed expenses	
Manufacturing	$ 25,000
Selling	40,000
Administrative	70,000
Total fixed expenses	$135,000
Selling price per pipe	$25.00
Expected sales, 19x2 (20,000 units)	$500,000

Ro has set the sales target for 19x3 at a level of $550,000 (or 22,000 pipes).

Required

1. What is the projected operating income for 19x2?
2. What is the breakeven point for 19x2 in units?
3. Ro believes additional advertising expense of $11,250 in 19x3, with all other expenses remaining constant, will be necessary to attain the 19x3 sales target. What will be the operating income for 19x3 if the additional $11,250 is spent and 22,000 pipes are sold?
4. What will be the breakeven point in dollar sales for 19x3 if the additional $11,250 is spent for advertising?
5. If the additional $11,250 is spent for advertising in 19x3, what is the required sales level in dollar sales to equal 19x2's operating income?
6. At a sales level of 22,000 units, what is the maximum amount that can be spent on advertising if an operating income of $100,000 is desired? (CMA adapted)

51. (L.O. 7) Hewtex Electronics manufactures two products, tape recorders and electronic calculators. It sells them nationally to wholesalers and retailers. Hewtex's management is pleased with the company's performance for the current fiscal year. Sales for 19x7 were 70,000 tape recorders and 140,000 electronic calculators.

The tape recorder business has been fairly stable the past few years, and the company does not intend to change the price of this product. However, competition among manufacturers of electronic calculators has increased. Hewtex's calculators have been popular with consumers. But to sustain this interest and to meet price reductions expected by competitors, management will reduce its wholesale price from $22.50 to $20.00 per unit, effective January 1, 19x8. During fiscal year 19x8, the company plans to spend an additional $57,000 on advertising. Consequently, management estimates that 80 percent of its total revenue will be derived from calculator sales, as compared with 75 percent in 19x7. The sales revenue mix is assumed to be the same at all volume levels.

Total fixed manufacturing overhead will remain unchanged in 19x8, as will variable overhead per unit. However, the cost of materials is expected to change. Hewtex estimates that in 19x8 materials costs will drop 10 percent for the tape recorders; 20 percent for the calculators.

Hewtex Electronics
Earnings Statement
For the Year Ended December 31, 19x7
(dollars in thousands)

	Tape recorders		Electronic calculators		
	Total amount	Per unit	Total amount	Per unit	Total amount
Sales revenues	$1,050	$15.00	$3,150	$22.50	$4,200
Production costs					
Direct materials	$ 280	$ 4.00	$ 630	$ 4.50	$ 910
Direct labor	140	2.00	420	3.00	560
Variable overhead	140	2.00	280	2.00	420
Fixed manufacturing overhead	70	1.00	210	1.50	280
Total production costs	$ 630	$ 9.00	$1,540	$11.00	$2,170
Gross margin	$ 420	$ 6.00	$1,610	$11.50	$2,030
Fixed selling and administrative expenses					1,040
Operating income					$ 990

Required

1. How many tape recorders and electronic calculator units did Hewtex have to sell in 19x7 to break even?
2. How many tape recorder and electronic calculator units must Hewtex sell in 19x8 to break even?
3. What volume in sales dollars is needed for Hewtex Electronics to earn a 15 percent higher operating income in 19x8 than in 19x7? (CMA adapted)

Case 1

Columbus Hospital (L.O. 3, 6)

Columbus Hospital operates a general hospital but rents space and beds to separate entities for specialized areas such as pediatrics, maternity, psychiatric, etc. Columbus charges each separate entity for common services to its patients such as meals and laundry and for administrative services such as billings, collections, etc. All uncollectible accounts are charged directly to the entity. Space and bed rentals are fixed for the year.

For the entire year ended June 30, 19x3, the pediatrics department at Columbus Hospital charged each patient an average of $65 per day, had a capacity of 60 beds, operated 24 hours per day for 365 days, and had revenue of $1,138,800.

Expenses charged by the hospital to the pediatrics department for the year ended June 30, 19x3, were as follows:

	Basis of Allocation	
	Patient days	Bed capacity
Dietary	$ 42,952	
Janitorial		$ 12,800
Laundry	28,000	
Laboratory, other than direct charges to patients	47,800	
Pharmacy	33,800	
Repairs and maintenance	5,200	7,140
General administrative services		131,760
Rent		275,320
Billings and collections	40,000	
Bad debt expense	47,000	
Other	18,048	25,980
	$262,800	$453,000

The only personnel directly employed by the pediatrics department are supervising nurses, nurses, and aides. The hospital has minimum personnel requirements based on total annual patient days. Hospital requirements beginning at the minimum, expected level of operation follow:

Annual patient days	Aides	Nurses	Supervising nurses
10,000–14,000	21	11	4
14,001–17,000	22	12	4
17,001–23,725	22	13	4
23,726–25,550	25	14	5
25,551–27,375	26	14	5
27,376–29,200	29	16	6

The staffing levels above represent full-time equivalents, and it should be assumed that the pediatrics department always employs only the minimum number of required full-time equivalent personnel.

Annual salaries for each class of employee follow: supervising nurses, $18,000; nurses, $13,000; and aides, $5,000. Salary expense for the year ended June 30, 19x3, for supervising nurses, nurses, and aides was $72,000, $169,000, and $110,000 respectively.

The pediatrics department operated at 100 percent capacity during 111 days for the past year. It is estimated that during 90 of these capacity days, the demand averaged 17 patients more than capacity and even went as high as 20 patients more on some days. The hospital has an additional 20 beds available for rent for the year ending June 30, 19x4, increasing bed capacity cost by $151,000 for the year.

Required

1. Calculate the minimum number of patient days required for the pediatrics department to break even for the year ending June 30, 19x4, if the additional 20 beds are not rented. Patient demand is unknown, but assume that revenue per patient day, expense per patient day, expense per bed, and employee salary rates will remain the same as for the year ended June 30, 19x3.

2. Assuming for purposes of this problem that patient demand, revenue per patient day, expense per patient day, expense per bed, and employee salary rates for the year ending June 30, 19x4, remain the same as for the year ended June 30, 19x3, should the pediatrics department rent the additional 20 beds? Show the annual gain or loss from the additional beds. (AICPA)

Case 2

Pralina Products Company (L.O. 7)

Pralina Products Company is a regional firm that has three major product lines — cereals, breakfast bars, and dog food. The income statement was prepared by product line using a functional format.

Pralina Products Company
Income Statement
For the Year Ended April 30, 19x8
(000 omitted)

	Cereals	Breakfast bars	Dog food	Total
Sales in pounds	2,000	500	500	3,600
Revenue from sales	$1,000	$400	$200	$1,600
Cost of goods sold				
Direct materials	$ 330	$160	$100	$ 590
Direct labor	90	40	20	150
Factory overhead	108	48	24	180
Total cost of goods sold	$ 528	$248	$144	$ 920
Gross margin	$ 472	$152	$ 56	$ 680
Operating expenses				
Selling expenses				
Advertising	$ 50	$ 30	$ 20	$ 100
Commissions	50	40	20	110
Salaries and related benefits	30	20	10	60
Total selling expenses	$ 130	$ 90	$ 50	$ 270
General and administrative expenses				
Licenses	$ 50	$ 20	$ 15	$ 85
Salaries and related benefits	60	25	15	100
Total general and administrative expenses	$ 110	$ 45	$ 30	$ 185
Total operating expenses	$ 240	$135	$ 80	$ 455
Operating income	$ 232	$ 17	$(24)	$ 225

Other data:

1. *Cost of goods sold* The company's inventories of direct materials and finished products do not vary significantly from year to year. The inventories at April 30, 19x8, were essentially identical to those at April 30, 19x7.

The actual factory overhead costs for the 19x7–19x8 fiscal year were as follows:

Variable indirect labor and supplies	$ 15,000
Variable employee benefits on factory labor	30,000
Supervisory salaries and related benefits	35,000
Plant occupancy costs	100,000
	$180,000

2. *Advertising* The company has been unable to determine any direct causal relationship between the level of sales volume and the level of advertising expenditures. However, because management believes advertising is necessary, an annual advertising program is implemented for each product line. Each product line is advertised independently of the others.
3. *Commissions* Sales commissions are paid to the sales force at the rates of 5 percent on the cereals and 10 percent on the breakfast bars and dog food.
4. *Licenses* Various licenses are required for each product line. These are renewed annually for each product line.
5. *Salaries and related benefits* Sales and general and administrative personnel devote time and effort to all product lines. Their salaries and wages are allocated on the basis of management's estimates of time spent on each product line.

Required

1. The controller of Pralina Products Company has recommended that the company do a cost-volume-profit analysis of its operations. As a first step the controller has requested that you prepare a revised income statement for Pralina Products Company that employs product contribution margin format which will be useful in cost-volume-profit analysis. The statement should show the profit contribution for each product line and the operating income for the company as a whole.
2. Calculate the breakeven point in sales dollars for 19x8.
3. What volume of sales dollars is necessary to achieve a 19x9 operating income 20 percent higher than in 19x8 assuming the revenue, cost, and product mix patterns as in 19x8? (CMA adapted)

Case 3
Seco Corp. (L.O. 7)

Seco Corp., a wholesale supply company, engages independent sales agents to market the company's lines. These agents currently receive a commission of 20 percent of sales, but they are demanding an increase to 25 percent of sales made during the year ending December 31, 19x9. Seco had already prepared its 19x9 budget before learning of the agents' demand for an increase in commissions.

The following pro forma income statement is based on this budget:

Seco Corp. Pro Forma Income Statement For the Year Ending December 31, 19x9		
Sales revenues		$10,000,000
Cost of sales		6,000,000
Gross margin		$ 4,000,000
Selling and administrative costs		
Commissions	$2,000,000	
All other costs (fixed)	100,000	2,100,000
Operating income		$ 1,900,000

Seco is considering the possibility of employing its own salespersons. Three individuals would be required, at an estimated annual salary of $30,000 each, plus commissions of 5 percent of sales. In addition, a sales manager would be employed at a fixed annual salary of $160,000. All other fixed costs, as well as the variable cost percentages, would remain the same as the estimates in the 19x9 pro forma income statement.

Required

1. Compute Seco's estimated breakeven point in sales dollars for the year ending December 31, 19x9 based on the pro forma income statement prepared by the company.
2. Compute Seco's estimated breakeven point in sales dollars for the year ending December 31, 19x9, if the company employs its own salespersons.
3. Compute the estimated volume in sales dollars that would be required for the year ending December 31, 19x9 to yield the same operating income as projected in the pro forma income statement, if Seco continues to use the independent sales agents and agrees to their demand for a 25 percent sales commission.
4. Compute the estimated volume in sales dollars that would generate an identical operating income for the year ending December 31, 19x9, regardless of whether Seco employs its own salespersons or continues to use the independent sales agents and pays them a 25 percent commission.

(AICPA adapted)

■

Appendix 6 — Linear Programming

Acme Company manufactures three products in a single factory. Total production volume is limited to 30,000 units per year. Acme's managers must decide which product mix will maximize the total contribution margin.

Burns Company has $2 million to spend on advertising for 19x9. The advertising budget is divided among radio, television, and newspaper promotions.

Burns's advertising manager wants to know how best to spend its advertising budget so total sales revenues are maximized.

Sale Company has three factories and six warehouses in the United States. Based on regional demand for the company's product, the production manager must decide which factories should supply which warehouses in order to minimize total shipping costs.

OBJECTIVE 1A
Formulate and use linear programming to solve a profit planning problem

In the discussion on the contribution from scarce resources on pages 244–247, you considered the possibility that production, distribution, or sales resources might be limited. Furthermore, demand for a product is usually limited by competition in the marketplace. When more than one resource is limited, a technique called **linear programming** can determine the quantity of each product to produce and sell.

The objective of linear programming is either to maximize or minimize some variable. Consider the examples at the start of this appendix; for the Acme Company, the objective is to maximize the total contribution margin; for the Burns Company, it is to maximize total sales revenues; and for the Sale Company, the objective is to minimize total shipping costs. When expressed algebraically, these objectives are called **objective functions.**

Linear programming problems have constraints as well as objectives. In the case of Acme, the constraint was limited production capacity. Burns Company had a limited budget for advertising, and Sale Company had a limited number of warehouses for supplying customer demand. Usually, a company also has additional constraints. Like objectives, constraints can be expressed algebraically. Such equations are known as **constraint equations.**

In summary, all linear programming problems are characterized both by the objective of maximizing or minimizing some variable and by constraints limiting the size of some variables. In linear programming, these objectives and constraints are expressed algebraically. Then, the problem is solved by using either a graph or a computer. You can solve any practical problem using a computer. A graphic solution helps you understand what the computer does.

As an example, consider the case of West Company. West Company produces two products, which will be referred to as Product X and Product Y. Product X's contribution margin is $4 per unit; Product Y's contribution margin is $6 per unit.

A single piece of equipment is used to fabricate both of West's products. Product X requires two hours of machine time; Product Y, five hours. Each year, 2,000 hours of machine time are available.

The same work force assembles both products. West can obtain about 3,000 labor hours per year. Product X requires five hours to assemble; Product Y, six hours.

West's managers estimate that West can sell a maximum of 500 units of Product X this year. Given this information, they want to know how many units of Product X and how many of Product Y should be produced and sold in order to maximize West's total contribution margin.

How would an accountant translate the facts given above into algebraic equations?

Formulation of the Problem

As seen earlier, each linear programming problem consists of an objective and one or more constraints. West's objective is to maximize its total contribution margin. Now, suppose unit sales of Product X are represented as *X* and unit sales of Product Y as *Y*. Since Product *X*'s contribution margin is \$4 per unit, the total contribution from sales of Product X is \$4 times *X*. And since Product Y's contribution margin is \$6 per unit, the total contribution from sales of Product Y is \$6 times *Y*. If the contribution margins for West's two products are added together, they express West's objective as shown below:

$$\text{Total contribution margin} = \$4X + \$6Y$$

Remember that the objective is to maximize West's total contribution margin. Were there no limits to West's resources, management could simply decide to produce and sell as many units of Product Y as possible, since it offers the higher contribution margin per unit. But there are several constraints on production and sales that must be considered.

Constraint 1 West's yearly machine capacity is 2,000 hours, and Product X requires only two hours of machine time, whereas Product Y requires five. Using this information, you can formulate the following equation:

$$2X + 5Y \leq 2{,}000$$

where $\leq$ means less than or equal to

That is, the total number of machine-hours used in production must be less than or equal to West's 2,000 machine-hour limit. This kind of relationship is referred to as an **inequality**.

Constraint 2 West's assembly department is limited to 3,000 labor hours. Product X requires five labor hours, whereas Product Y requires six. Again, you can formulate an equation to state this constraint:

$$5X + 6Y \leq 3{,}000$$

Constraint 3 Sales of Product X are limited. Recall that West's managers estimated no more than 500 units of Product X could be sold. This constraint can be represented as follows:

$$X \leq 500$$

Constraints 4 and 5 West cannot produce and sell a negative quantity of products. That is, *X* and *Y* must be equal to or greater than zero:

$$X \geq 0$$

$$Y \geq 0$$

These constraints might seem so obvious as to be unnecessary to the solution. And indeed, if this problem were solved on paper, such constraints would probably be taken for granted. But most linear programs are solved by computer. And as anyone working with computers knows, you must be very explicit when defining parameters in a computer program.

A summary of West's linear program is as follows:

Objective function	Equation
Maximize total contribution margin	$\$4X + \$6Y$

Subject to:	Equation	Constraint number
Machine constraint	$2X + 5Y \leq 2{,}000$	1
Labor hours constraint	$5X + 6Y \leq 3{,}000$	2
Demand constraint, Product X	$X \leq 500$	3
Nonnegative output constraint	$X \geq 0$	4
Nonnegative output constraint	$Y \geq 0$	5

■

Graphic Solution of a Linear Program

Since West Company produces only two products, X and Y, its linear program can be solved graphically as well as by computer. To do so, an accountant must first develop a graph to display all possible product mixes. Then, he or she must identify the **area of feasible solutions** by plotting the program's constraint equations onto the graph. Finally, the accountant must select the solution that maximizes the program's objectives from the possibilities within that area. The process is illustrated in Appendix Figure 6–1.

In Part A of Appendix Figure 6–1, Product X's potential production volume is displayed on the horizontal axis, Product Y's, on the vertical axis. The graph shows only positive values of *X* and *Y*, since constraints 4 and 5 limit the area of feasible solutions to nonnegative numbers. The dark area represents the values of *X* and *Y* that will satisfy constraints 4 and 5. These constraints state that *X* and *Y* must be equal to or greater than zero.

In Part B of Appendix Figure 6–1, constraint 1 has been added and greatly restricts the dark area of feasible solutions. This constraint states that only 2,000 hours of machine time are available. Product X requires two machine-hours per unit; Product Y, five hours. The maximum number of units of Product X that West can produce is 1,000 (2,000 ÷ 2); the maximum number of Y, 400 (2,000 ÷ 5). The graph shows this constraint as a line connecting those points

Appendix Figure 6–1
West Company — Graphic Solution to a Linear Program
The numbers 1–5 in graph d refer to the corner coordinates calculated on page 275.

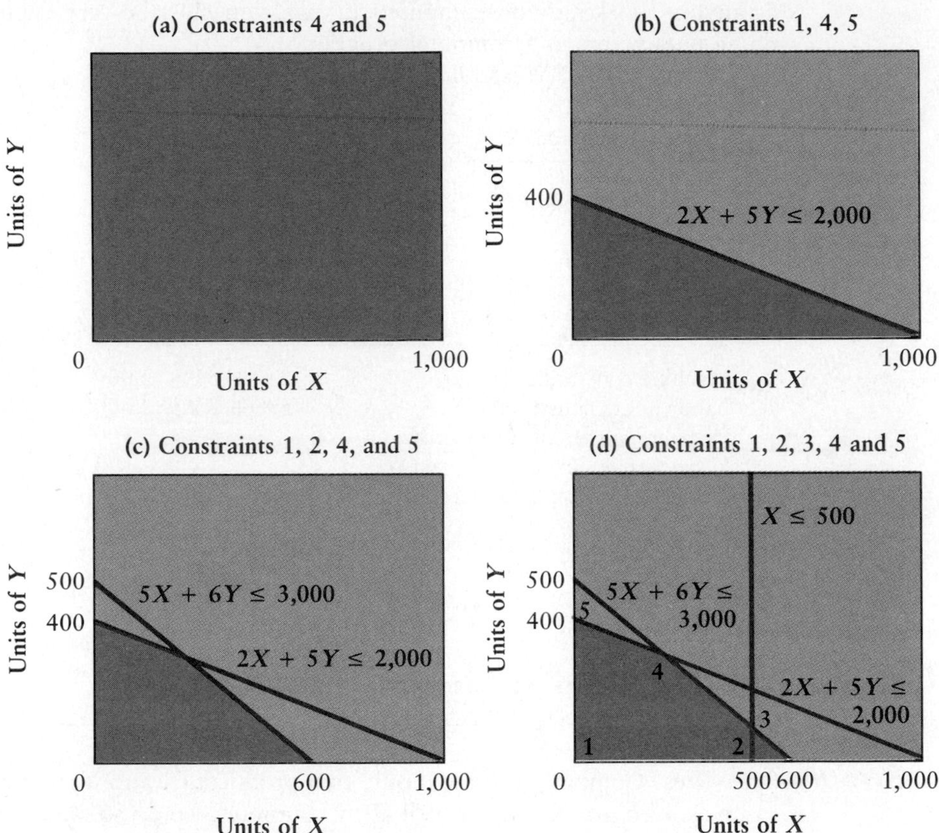

on the horizontal and vertical axes. Since this is a less-than-or-equal-to constraint, any point on the line or in the shaded area below and to the left will satisfy the constraint.

In Part C of Appendix Figure 6–1, constraint 2 further reduces the dark area of feasible solutions. Finally, in Part D of Appendix Figure 6–1, constraint 3 reduces the dark area so that all of West's constraints are satisfied.

It has been proven that the **optimal solution** to a linear program, that is, one that maximizes a program's objective function, lies at a corner of the area of feasible solutions. To determine the optimal solution, you must therefore calculate the coordinates at each corner of the area of feasible solutions and compute the total contribution margin at each corner. The corner that produces the largest contribution margin represents the optimal solution.

The coordinates of each corner and the total contribution margin at each one are as follows:

Corner	Production in units X	Y	Total contribution margin $4X + $6Y
1	-0-	-0-	$ -0-
2	500	-0-	2,000
3	500	83.3	2,500
4	230.8	307.7	2,769
5	-0-	400	2,400

Since the optimal solution is the one that maximizes total contribution margin, corner 4 represents the best production plan. West should produce and sell approximately 230.8 units of *X* and 307.7 units of *Y*, which will generate the maximum total contribution margin of $2,769.

Appendix Review

Review of Appendix Learning Objective

1A. **Formulate and use linear programming to solve a profit planning problem.**
Linear programming problems are characterized both by an objective of maximizing or minimizing some variable, and by constraints limiting the size of some variables. These objectives and constraints are expressed algebraically. The problem can then be solved using either a graph or a computer.

Review of Appendix Key Terms

Area of feasible solutions On a linear program graph, the area bounded by constraint equations.

Constraint equation An equation representing a limitation on the production, distribution, or demand for a company's product. Used in linear programming.

Inequality A relationship between two numbers that indicates those numbers to be of unequal value.

Linear programming A method for determining the quantity of each product that should be produced and sold in order to maximize or minimize some objective. In this chapter, the objective is to maximize total contribution margin. Used when more than one resource is limited.

Objective function An algebraic representation of a company goal that is to be maximized or minimized by a linear program. An example is to maximize total contribution margin.

Optimal solution In linear programming, the solution that maximizes the program's objective function. Generally found at one corner of the area of feasible solutions.

Appendix Assignments

Problems

1. (L.O. 1A) Random Company manufactures two products, Zeta and Beta. Each product must pass through two processing operations. All materials are introduced at the start of the first process. There are no work in process inventories. Random may produce either one product exclusively or various combinations of both products, subject to the following constraints:

	Process 1	Process 2	Contribution margin per unit
Hours required to produce 1 unit of			
Zeta	1 hour	1 hour	$4.00
Beta	2 hours	3 hours	5.25
Total capacity in hours per day	1,000 hours	1,275 hours	

Assume all relationships between capacity and production are linear.

Required Graphically determine the optimal solution to maximize the total contribution margin.
(AICPA adapted)

2. (L.O. 1A) Patsy, Inc., manufactures two products, X and Y. Each product must go through three departments: assembly one and two and finishing. The hours needed to produce one unit of product and the maximum possible hours per department are as follows:

	Production hours per unit		
Department	Product X	Product Y	Maximum capacity in hours
Assembly 1	2	2	500
Assembly 2	2	3	600
Finishing	2	1	420

Other constraints are as follows:

$X \geqslant 50$

$Y \geqslant 50$

The objective function, which is to maximize total contribution margin, is:

$\$4X + \$2Y$

Required Graphically determine the output of X and Y that will maximize the total contribution margin.
(AICPA adapted)

7

Planning the Master Budget

LEARNING OBJECTIVES

After studying this chapter you should be able to:

1. Explain why a company prepares a master budget
2. List the components of a master budget and explain their interrelationship
3. Prepare a master budget for a manufacturing company
4. Explain the difference between a master budget in a manufacturing company and a master budget in a merchandising company
5. Prepare a master budget for a merchandising company
6. Explain the role of computerized financial planning models in the budgeting process
7. Discuss the impact of the new manufacturing environment on production planning.

If you are serious about achieving something, you must sooner or later establish a goal and a plan to reach it. Without such direction there is no clear basis on which to make day-to-day decisions. For example, should you enroll in a managerial accounting course, or should you take intermediate golf lessons? The answer depends on whether you want to pursue a business career or become a professional golfer. If you choose to go to college and have no idea of why you are doing so or what goal education will help you achieve, then you will have a hard time choosing your courses.

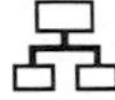

Managers face the same problem. They must develop a plan to guide them in day-to-day decisions. In this chapter you will see how projected data on revenues and costs are used to develop such a plan, called a budget. A budget is a quantification of marketing, production, and financial plans, which is used to establish goals for revenues, expenses, assets, liabilities, and other business activities. It consists of a series of documents that communicate expected results of operations to managers at all levels and in all business functions. Periodically the budget is used to compare actual results of operations with forecasted results to see how well managers have met their objectives.

In this chapter you will first look at the purposes of a master budget. An overview of the master budget follows. In the next two sections, the mechanics of preparing a master budget are discussed and illustrated by looking at both a manufacturing company and a merchandising company. The final section covers the use of computerized financial planning models.

■

Purposes of the Master Budget

The **master budget** is a series of interrelated **budgets** that quantify management's expectations about the company's revenues, expenses, net income, cash flows, and financial position. As the final product of the planning process, it details in financial terms how the company will achieve its goals and objectives for the coming year. The master budget includes, among other documents, an income statement, a balance sheet, and a cash budget. Depending on a company's size and complexity, the statements may be accompanied by supporting schedules.

Preparing a master budget requires a lot of time and effort from all members of an organization. Indeed, managers frequently complain that they are too busy to prepare a budget. Another common complaint is that a business is so complex or uncertain that a formal budget would be outdated by the time it was finished. Yet on closer examination, one finds that managers making such comments are usually making informal plans. They are always trying to anticipate what might happen next and then prepare for it. In fact, most managers have fairly well-defined ideas about what they want to accomplish and how to do it. Budgeting merely formalizes those ideas, enabling managers to communicate those ideas to others.

OBJECTIVE 1
Explain why a company prepares a master budget

There are four major advantages to preparing a master budget:

1. It helps in implementing a strategic plan that efficiently and effectively achieves an organization's objectives.
2. It coordinates activities among various segments of an organization.
3. It provides a means of communicating the plan throughout the organization.
4. It provides a standard for evaluating managers' performance.

Each of these uses for the master budget will now be discussed.

Strategic Planning

A major advantage of budgeting is that it requires managers to periodically think about what they want their departments to accomplish. That is, they must try to anticipate the operating conditions they will face and how they should react. They must analyze their operations and estimate how future events, including new product lines, new environmental control laws, labor force changes, and competitors' reactions to old and new products, will affect operations. When necessary, current operations must be adjusted to allow for such changes. For example, management at a large consumer products company recently decided to sell the company's toy business and concentrate on the food business. This decision caused many changes in their plans and budgets the following year.

Coordination of Activities

In most large organizations, production, marketing, and financial services are managed by different people. The budgeting process allows these people to exchange ideas about the best way to achieve an organization's objectives. For example, coordination between marketing and production managers helps ensure the availability of products at the appropriate time and place at minimum cost to the organization. The production manager relies on the marketing department's forecast of annual sales volume when ordering raw materials, hiring labor, and leasing or buying production equipment. The treasurer uses both the sales forecast and the production plan to determine the company's cash needs for the year. Will sufficient cash be available each month to meet the cash outflows of the production department, or must the company borrow to satisfy its cash needs? The budgeting process helps answer such questions and resolves inconsistencies in plans between departments.

Communications of Plans

Once a master budget has been prepared, it reminds managers of the goals they have agreed to achieve. The master budget also informs managers of the resources at their disposal. For example, this budget not only informs the marketing manager about expected sales volume but also about the money available for advertising and selling expenses. Besides informing the production manager of the monthly production requirements, the master budget identifies the resources available. Finally, the master budget anticipates the company's cash flows so the treasurer can negotiate loans or invest excess cash.

Performance Evaluation

Because the master budget is a quantitative expression of management's expectations, it is a better basis for evaluating an employee's performance than past performance. Although this year's sales may be 20 percent higher than last year's, that does not necessarily mean the sales manager has done an outstanding job. Indeed, an increase in advertising and market demand may make even a 30 percent increase unremarkable. Likewise, a drop in sales may not mean poor performance, particularly if it was expected and shown in the master budget.

Uses and Abuses of the Master Budget

The manner in which top management establishes and uses the master budget will influence how middle managers respond to it. When used properly, this budget can help motivate managers to achieve their objectives. It can also help identify matters needing investigation. However, if top management uses the master budget to punish employees for poor performance, the budgeting process will become a game in which middle managers pad their budgets to protect themselves. Such a result, of course, defeats one fundamental reason for developing a budget: to provide a standard for measuring managers' performance in changing economic conditions.

The personal dimension of budgeting is as important as the mechanical aspects. To effectively implement a budget, the managers responsible for this process must accept its basic premises. Budgets imposed by upper management on managers lower in the organization are generally not as successfully implemented as those developed with active participation at all management levels.

■

An Overview of the Master Budget

OBJECTIVE 2
List the components of a master budget and explain their interrelationship

The master budget can be divided into two major parts, the operating budget and the financial budget. The **operating budget** represents expected results of operations. In a manufacturing company, it contains the following documents:

1. Sales budget

2. Production budget[1]
   a. Direct materials budget
   b. Direct labor budget
   c. Manufacturing overhead budget
3. Ending inventory budget
4. Selling and administrative expense budget
5. Budgeted income statement

The **financial budget** details capital expenditures and summarizes how operations affect a company's cash balances and expected financial position. The financial budget contains:

1. Capital expenditure budget (see Chapters 14 and 15)
2. Cash budget
3. Budgeted balance sheet

All of the above budgets are strongly interrelated, and some must be prepared before others.

Figure 7–1 shows the interrelationship between components of the operating and financial budgets. The sales budget (top, center) is the starting point for the entire process, since all other budgets are related to it. It is based on forecasted sales for the coming year. Notice that the sales budget has a reciprocal relationship with the selling and administrative expense budget. This is because the level of sales depends partly on the amount of money available for advertising and promotion.

Once the sales budget is established, a production budget for expected sales volume can be developed. This budget determines the direct materials, direct labor, and manufacturing overhead budget. All three budgets feed into the budgeted income statement, which is then used to prepare the financial budgets (bottom row in Figure 7–1).

The **capital expenditure budget** (bottom, left in Figure 7–1) lists all approved long-range expenditures planned to improve the firm's operating capacity or efficiency. The capital expenditure budget is based on the sales forecast and other information (see Chapters 14 and 15). Both it and the budgeted income statement are then used to prepare the budgeted balance sheet (bottom, right).

The **planning period** is the time period for which detailed budgets are developed from managers' plans. The planning period for the master budget can vary from one month to several years. Capital budgets, discussed in Chapters 14 and 15, may affect planning periods up to twenty years into the future. Such budgets represent major expenditures for buildings and equipment whose expected useful life is more than a year. Many organizations, however, prepare budgets for a year, then break them down month by month. By doing so, an organization can compare actual results with budgeted results at month end. This process allows managers to monitor the organization's progress toward achieving its objectives.

[1]Purchases budget in a merchandising company (see pages 305–307).

Figure 7–1
Master Budget Relationships

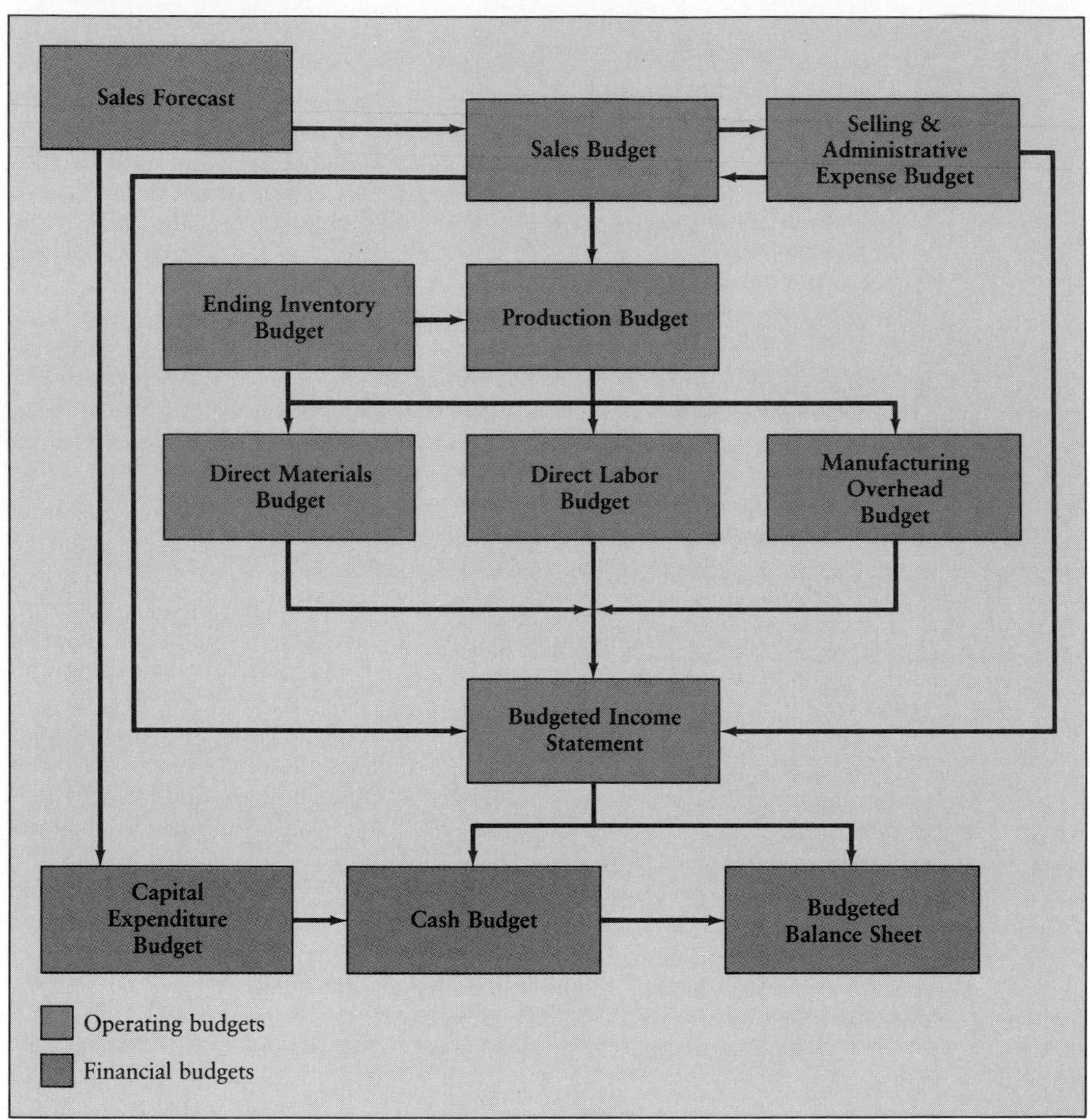

Traditionally, budgets are used for planning and control decisions during the fiscal year. Only major economic changes will cause a company to change a budget once it is established. At the end of the fiscal year, a new budget is prepared for the coming year.

An alternative to the traditional budget is the **continuous budget.** In continuous budgeting, a future time period is added as the one just ended is completed and dropped. Sometimes called a *rolling budget*, the continuous budget is revised at the end of each period to add one new period. Thus, if the period is a quarter, the new, revised budget covers the next three quarters plus one additional quarter. That is, each quarter the budget rolls forward one quarter to replace the quarter just gone. The major advantage of a continuous budget is that it makes planning a continual activity. This forces managers to continually assess the future.

■

Preparing a Master Budget

OBJECTIVE 3
Prepare a master budget for a manufacturing company

To illustrate the step-by-step development of a master budget, this chapter will follow that process at the fictional Beta Corporation. Although most companies prepare a master budget by the month, for simplicity's sake this illustration will cover only four quarters of 19x9. The basic computations are the same regardless of the length of the period covered.

Beta Corporation produces and sells a single product, called Alpha, in a single factory. Because the production process requires little time, the work in process inventory is negligible and can be omitted from the budgeting process.

Based on engineering studies, product specifications, and managerial estimates, the following cost estimates for direct materials, direct labor, and variable overhead were compiled by Beta's accountants:

Direct materials

1 pound of material #103 × $2 per pound = $2 per unit

Direct labor

0.25 hours of labor × $20 per hour = $5 per unit

Variable overhead

$0.80 per direct labor dollar × $5 per unit = $4 per unit

Beta's balance sheet as of December 31, 19x8, is shown in Exhibit 7–1. Given this general information, how does the accountant prepare the master budget? The first step, as you have seen, is to develop the sales budget.

Sales Budget

A **sales budget** is an estimate of the unit sales and sales revenue expected during the budget period as well as an estimate of cash receipts. To prepare a sales budget, the accountant needs a sales forecast. Usually, the sales manager prepares this forecast, using one of several approaches. The qualitative approach is based on expert opinions about economic trends that influence product demand. For

Exhibit 7–1
Balance Sheet for a Manufacturing Company

Beta Corporation Balance Sheet December 31, 19x8		
Assets		
Cash		$ 200,000
Accounts receivable		300,000
Materials inventory (5,000 pounds × $2)		10,000
Finished goods inventory (15,000 units × $11)		165,000
Plant and equipment	$1,000,000	
Accumulated depreciation	(350,000)	650,000
Total assets		$1,325,000
Liabilities and Equity		
Accounts payable, purchases		$ 50,000
Federal income taxes payable		-0-
Common stock		550,000
Retained earnings		725,000
Total liabilities and equity		$1,325,000

new products, market surveys and test marketing are two tools that may be used. If available, relevant historical data may also be considered.

Another approach, time series analysis, relies totally on historical data. The analyst looks for seasonal variations in demand as well as cyclical patterns over several years. Sales forecasts are adjusted accordingly.

A third and broader approach combines the results of market surveys and time series analysis with information on other variables that might influence sales. Such variables include (a) competitors' reactions; (b) impact of planned advertising campaigns; (c) possible strikes; (d) changes in pricing policies or government taxes and regulations; and (e) economic conditions, both general and industry-wide. All of this information is combined into a causal model to forecast sales.

The choice of forecasting technique depends on many factors: the availability of data, the desired degree of accuracy, the time period of the forecast, and the costs and benefits of the forecast. Generally, managers choose the method that makes the best use of data while providing the desired degree of accuracy. Although sales forecasting has traditionally been heavily qualitative, most companies rely to some degree on the other approaches. More and more companies now start with quantitative information and modify it based on their salespeoples' feel for the market.

Beta Corporation's sales forecast was developed by using information collected from sales representatives. At a sales price of $25 per unit, estimated sales

Exhibit 7–2
Sales Budget for a Manufacturing Company

Beta Corporation
Sales Budget
For the Year Ended December 31, 19x9

Schedule 1	Quarter 1	Quarter 2	Quarter 3	Quarter 4	Year
Sales units	55,000	60,000	45,000	50,000	210,000[1]
Sales price per unit	$ × 25	$ × 25	$ × 25	$ × 25	$ × 25[2]
Total sales	$1,375,000	$1,500,000	$1,125,000	$1,250,000	$5,250,000
Schedule 2					
Cash collections					
Last quarter's sales	$ 300,000	$ 550,000	$ 600,000	$ 450,000	$1,900,000[3]
This quarter's sales	+825,000	+900,000	+675,000	750,000	+3,150,000[4]
Total collections	$1,125,000	$1,450,000	$1,275,000	$1,200,000	$5,050,000

Source of Data
[1]Management's estimates.
[2]Management's estimates.
[3]40% × last quarter's sales.
[4]60% × this quarter's sales.

for the next five quarters[2] are

Quarter	Sales in units
1	55,000
2	60,000
3	45,000
4	50,000
5	50,000

Schedule 1 of Exhibit 7–2 shows Beta's sales budget. Notice that it includes the expected sales volume in both units and dollars. The dollar figures were calculated by multiplying sales units for each quarter by unit sales price, $25. In the fifth column, yearly sales in units and dollars have been calculated by adding the quarterly figures.

The sales budget is usually accompanied by quarterly estimates of cash collections. Beta expects all sales to be credit sales. Of those sales, 60 percent will be collected the same quarter in which the sale is made; 40 percent, the quarter following the sale. Since Beta collects 40 percent of its sales in the following

[2]The estimate for the fifth quarter will be needed later, for preparation of the production budget.

quarter, 40 percent of sales from the last quarter of 19x8 will be collected in the first quarter of 19x9. The accountant obtains this amount — $300,000 — from Beta's balance sheet of December 31, 19x8 (Exhibit 7–1). There, this amount is shown as Accounts Receivable ($300,000). Notice that this figure is placed in Schedule 2 of Beta's 19x9 sales budget (Exhibit 7–2, column 1), labeled "Last quarter's sales."

If Beta collects 60 percent of its sales in the same quarter, then cash collections from Quarter 1 sales should equal 60 percent of the Quarter 1 sales budget. Thus, in Schedule 2, column 1, collections from this quarter's sales are listed as $825,000 (0.60 × $1,375,000).

The remainder of Schedule 2 is completed similarly. In the second quarter, Beta expects to collect 40 percent of sales from Quarter 1; 60 percent, from Quarter 2. This expectation is represented by the $550,000 for the first quarter's sales (0.40 × $1,375,000) and $900,000 for the second quarter's sales (0.60 × $1,500,000). To obtain total cash collections, the accountant simply adds the amounts in each column.

One final note on the cash collections schedule: later in this chapter a budgeted balance sheet will be prepared for each quarter of 19x9. The end-of-quarter balance of Accounts Receivable will be obtained by calculating *uncollected* sales for the quarter. For the first quarter, uncollected sales will be $550,000 (0.4 × $1,375,000). Notice that this figure appears in Schedule 2, labeled "Last quarter's sales" under Quarter 2.

Production Budget

The sales budget and the desired ending inventories are required to develop the production budget. The **production budget** specifies how many units of each product must be produced to satisfy demand for the product and provide the desired ending finished goods inventory.

Planning the desired finished goods inventory is an important managerial task. Without careful planning of inventories, a company might end up with either too many or too few finished goods. When planning a desired level of inventory, management tries to minimize three costs: (1) the cost of storing excess inventory, (2) the cost of the business lost when customers' orders cannot be filled, and (3) the cost of special-ordered additional inventory. Past experience with these costs, suppliers' schedules, and forecasted demand for products all enter into the process.

With the sales budget completed and the quantity of desired finished goods planned, you can prepare the production budget. The following relationship sums up the basic logic of the budgeting process:

Beginning balance + additions − subtractions = ending balance

That is, the budgeting process is the process of going from beginning balances to ending balances by estimating additions to and subtractions from an account. For example, in preparing the cash collections part of the sales budget, Beta estimated additions (sales) to and subtractions (collections) from Accounts Receivable. Using those estimates plus the beginning balance in Accounts Receivable, its accountants could easily estimate the ending Accounts Receivable balance. For the end of Quarter 1, the computations are

Beginning balance, Accounts Receivable	$ 300,000
Add estimated sales	1,375,000
	$1,675,000
Less total cash collections	1,125,000
Ending balance, Accounts Receivable	$ 550,000

Notice that the figure $550,000 agrees with the figure arrived at earlier (see page 286).

For the production budget, the accountant starts with a unit rather than a dollar figure for ending inventory. The process can be summarized as

$$\text{Beginning units, finished goods inventory} + \text{production in units} - \text{sales in units} = \text{ending units, finished goods inventory}$$

Or, as rearranged:

$$\text{Production in units} = \text{sales in units} + \text{ending units, finished goods inventory} - \text{beginning units, finished goods inventory}$$

The second version of the equation is more convenient for calculating how many units must be produced.

To prepare Beta's production budget, then, the accountant needs (1) estimated sales in units for each quarter, (2) estimated ending units in finished goods inventory, and (3) beginning units in finished goods inventory. The figures for estimated sales in units are obtained from the sales budget (Exhibit 7–2). The figures for ending and beginning units in finished goods inventory depend on managers' estimates of Beta's needs.

Beta's management has decided to plan for an ending finished goods inventory equal to 30 percent of expected sales in the next quarter. They believe that level is high enough to minimize the cost of lost sales, but low enough to prevent excessive holding costs. Thus, in Beta's production budget (Exhibit 7–3), estimated ending finished goods for Quarter 1 is 18,000 units (0.30 × 60,000). Computations for the second, third, and fourth quarters follow the same pattern. Notice that in Quarter 4, the computation is based on estimated sales for Quarter 5 (see page 285).

The figure for beginning finished goods inventory is the same as that for ending finished goods inventory in the prior quarter. For the first quarter the 15,000 figure is obtained from Beta's 19x8 balance sheet. Figures for the second, third, and fourth quarters are repeated from last quarter's ending inventory line. For example, Quarter 2's beginning finished goods inventory of 18,000 is the

Exhibit 7–3
Production Budget for a Manufacturing Company

Beta Corporation
Production Budget
For the Year Ended December 31, 19x9

	Quarter 1	Quarter 2	Quarter 3	Quarter 4	Year
Sales units	55,000	60,000	45,000	50,000	210,000[1]
Add estimated ending finished goods inventory	+18,000	+13,500	+15,000	+15,000	+ 15,000[2]
Total unit requirements	73,000	73,500	60,000	65,000	225,000
Less beginning finished goods inventory	−15,000	−18,000	−13,500	−15,000	− 15,000[3]
Unit production requirements	58,000	55,500	46,500	50,000	210,000

[1]Exhibit 7–2.
[2]Management's estimates: 30% × budgeted sales for following quarter.
[3]Exhibit 7–1; estimated ending finished goods inventory for last quarter.

same as Quarter 1's ending finished goods inventory, two lines above in the Quarter 1 column (Exhibit 7–3).

Once the necessary estimates have been obtained, the production budget is constructed as follows:

1. Budgeted sales units are added to estimated ending finished goods inventory to obtain total unit requirements.
2. Beginning finished goods inventory is deducted from total unit requirements to obtain unit production requirements.
3. The ending finished goods inventory at year-end, in the year column, is added to total sales units for the year. (The end-of-quarter inventory figure is simply repeated from the fourth column.) Notice that the resulting figure, 225,000, is not the sum of quarterly total requirements. Because figures for quarterly ending finished goods inventory represent a balance at a particular point in time rather than for a period, quarterly total requirements cannot be added together to obtain total requirements for the year. Next, the finished goods inventory at the beginning of the year is deducted to obtain the unit production requirements for the year.

Once the production budget is prepared, a series of manufacturing cost budgets must be assembled. These budgets include the direct materials budget, the direct labor budget, and the manufacturing overhead budget.

Review Exercise 7–1

Prepare Sales and Production Budgets

Cynthia Manufacturing Company anticipates sales for the first three months of 19xx as follows:

January	25,000 units
February	30,000 units
March	40,000 units

Cynthia's product sells for $50 per unit. The inventory at the beginning of January amounted to 5,000 units. Cynthia desires to have on hand at the end of each month 30 percent of anticipated sales for the next month. Historically, cash collections have been 70 percent in the month of sale and 30 percent in the following month. The Accounts Receivable balance at January amounts to $375,000.

Required

1. Prepare a sales budget with cash collections for January and February.
2. Prepare a production budget for January and February.

Solution

1. Sales budget prepared:

Cynthia Manufacturing Company
Sales Budget
For the Months of January and February

Schedule 1	**January**	**February**
Sales units	25,000	30,000
Sales price per unit	$ ×50	$ ×50
Total sales	$1,250,000	$1,500,000

Schedule 2		
Cash collections		
Last month's sales	$ 375,000	$ 375,000
This month's sales	+875,000	+1,050,000
Total collections	$1,250,000	$1,425,000

2. Production budget prepared:

Cynthia Manufacturing Company
Production Budget
For the Months of January and February

	January	February
Sales units	25,000	30,000
Add estimated ending finished goods inventory	+9,000	+12,000
Total unit requirements	34,000	42,000
Less beginning finished goods inventory	−5,000	−9,000
Unit production requirements	29,000	33,000

(see Exercises 21, 22)

Direct Materials Budget

The **direct materials budget** includes three parts. The first is a usage budget, which shows the quantity and cost of direct materials needed to meet current production requirements. The second is a **purchases budget.** In a manufacturing company, it shows the quantity and cost of direct materials purchases needed for production and to maintain ending inventory levels. Finally, an expected cash payments schedule shows cash outflows for direct materials purchases, which are usually made on credit.

Exhibit 7–4 shows the direct materials budget for Beta Corporation. Three pieces of information are needed to prepare Schedule 1: (1) unit production (final product output) requirements, (2) direct materials required per unit, and (3) cost per pound of material. The unit production requirements are repeated from the production budget (Exhibit 7–3). The direct materials required per unit and the cost of materials per pound were established early in the planning process (see page 283). These data are shown below:

1 pound of material #103 at $2 per pound

The first step in preparing Schedule 1 is to obtain the figure on direct materials required. This figure is found by multiplying unit production requirements by the amount of direct materials required per unit. To obtain the total cost of direct materials required, multiply the previous figure by the cost per unit of material. Beta will need 58,000 pounds of direct materials in the first quarter of production. At $2 per pound those direct materials will cost $116,000. The final column of the schedule, which shows annual rather than quarterly production requirements, is similarly obtained.

Exhibit 7–4
Direct Materials Budget for a Manufacturing Company

Beta Corporation
Direct Materials Budget
For the Year Ended December 31, 19x9

Schedule 1: Usage budget	Quarter 1	Quarter 2	Quarter 3	Quarter 4	Year
Unit production requirements	58,000	55,500	46,500	50,000	210,000[1]
Direct materials required per unit of output (pounds)	×1	×1	×1	×1	×1[2]
Direct materials required (pounds)	58,000	55,500	46,500	50,000	210,000
Cost per pound of materials	$ ×2	$ ×2	$ ×2	$ ×2	$ ×2[3]
Total cost of direct materials required	$116,000	$111,000	$93,000	$100,000	$420,000
Schedule 2: Purchases budget					
Direct materials required (pounds)	58,000	55,500	46,500	50,000	210,000[4]
Add estimated ending direct materials inventory (pounds)	+5,550	+4,650	+5,000	+5,000	+5,000[5]
Total direct materials required	63,550	60,150	51,500	55,000	215,000
Less beginning direct materials inventory	−5,000	−5,550	−4,650	−5,000	−5,000[6]
Direct materials purchase requirements (pounds)	58,550	54,600	46,850	50,000	210,000
Cost per pound of materials	$ ×2	$ ×2	$ ×2	$ ×2	$ ×2[7]
Total cost of direct materials purchases	$117,100	$109,200	$93,700	$100,000	$420,000
Schedule 3: Expected cash payments for purchases					
Accounts payable	$ 50,000				$ 50,000[8]
Purchases: Quarter 1	81,970	$ 35,130			117,100[9]
Quarter 2		76,440	$32,760		109,200[10]
Quarter 3			65,590	$ 28,110	93,700[11]
Quarter 4				70,000	70,000[12]
Total cash payments for purchases	$131,970	$111,570	$98,350	$ 98,110	$440,000

[1]Exhibit 7–3.
[2]Management's estimates.
[3]Management's estimates.
[4]Schedule 1, Exhibit 7–4
[5]Management's estimates: 10% × direct materials required in next quarter.
[6]Exhibit 7–1; estimating ending direct materials inventory for last quarter.
[7]Management's estimates.
[8]Exhibit 7–1.
[9–12]Management's estimates: 70% in quarter of purchase; 30% in following quarter.

In Schedule 2 of Beta's direct materials budget, the purchases budget, the amount of materials to be purchased, is computed by using the basic budget relationship.

Direct materials purchased	=	direct materials required	+	estimated ending direct materials inventory	−	beginning direct materials inventory

Direct materials required are calculated in Schedule 1. Like ending finished goods inventory, ending direct materials inventory is estimated by management. Beta's managers have decided that an ending inventory of 10 percent of the direct materials needed next quarter will be adequate. For quarters 1, 2, and 3, the calculations are straightforward. Ending direct materials inventory for the fourth quarter is estimated at 5,000 pounds, based on anticipated need for direct materials in the first quarter of the next year, 19x0. The desired ending inventory is added to direct materials required to obtain total direct materials required.

Next, to find the quantity of direct materials purchases requirements, subtract beginning direct materials inventory from total direct materials required. (Beginning direct materials inventory for the first quarter is obtained from Beta's 19x8 balance sheet.) For Quarters 2, 3, and 4, beginning direct materials inventory is the same as estimated ending direct materials inventory for the last quarter.

Finally, the total of direct materials purchases requirements is multiplied by the cost per pound to obtain the total cost of direct materials purchases.

To prepare a cash budget, one needs the computations in Schedule 3, expected cash payments for purchases. Cash payments consist of payments for some of the purchases made in previous periods plus some of the purchases made in the current period. Beta Corporation pays for 70 percent of its purchases in the period of purchase; 30 percent in the period following purchase. Thus, in Quarter 1, Beta must pay for 30 percent of the purchases made in the last quarter of 19x8 and 70 percent of those made in the first quarter of 19x9. In the first quarter, the unpaid purchases from the last quarter need not be figured as a percentage of purchases. Instead, it is taken directly from the balance of Accounts Payable on Beta's 19x8 balance sheet ($50,000). To this is added 70 percent of this quarter's purchases (0.70 × $117,100 = $81,970), for a total of $131,970. In Quarter 2, Beta must pay for 30 percent of purchases made in Quarter 1 (0.30 × $117,100 = $35,130) and 70 percent of those made in Quarter 2 (0.70 × $109,200 = $76,440). Total second quarter payments will be $111,570. The figures in the last column of this schedule were obtained by adding the rows horizontally.

Direct Labor Budget

The **direct labor budget** is a statement showing the quantity cost, and period of payment for labor that can be directly identified with specific products. The direct labor budget is used to plan the size of the work force needed to meet production requirements. Beta Corporation's direct labor budget is shown in Exhibit 7–5. It is calculated by using information from Beta's production budget (Ex-

Exhibit 7–5
Direct Labor Budget for a Manufacturing Company

Beta Corporation
Direct Labor Budget
For the Year Ended December 31, 19x9

	Quarter 1	Quarter 2	Quarter 3	Quarter 4	Year
Unit production requirements	58,000	55,500	46,500	50,000	210,000[1]
Direct labor hours per unit	×0.25	×0.25	×0.25	×0.25	×0.25[2]
Total direct labor hours required	14,500	13,875	11,625	12,500	52,500
Direct labor cost per hour	$ ×20	$ ×20	$ ×20	$ ×20	$ ×20[3]
Total direct labor costs	$290,000	$277,500	$232,500	$250,000	$1,050,000
Cash payments for direct labor	$290,000	$277,500	$232,500	$250,000	$1,050,000

[1]Exhibit 7–3.
[2]Management's estimates.
[3]Management's estimates.

hibit 7–3) as well as figures for direct labor hours per unit and direct labor cost per hour, which were established early in the planning process (see page 283). These data are shown below.

Direct labor hours to produce
one unit of finished product = 0.25 hours
Direct labor cost per hour = $20 per hour

First, the unit production requirements for each quarter are entered from the production budget. These figures are then multiplied by direct labor hours per unit to obtain total direct labor hours required. The last column shows that for the year 19x9, Beta Corporation needs 52,500 direct labor hours to produce 210,000 units of finished product. Note that the number of hours required varies from quarter to quarter. Direct labor hours required are multiplied by the direct labor cost per hour to obtain total direct labor costs for each quarter and for the year. Because cash outflows for direct labor costs usually occur in the period the costs are incurred, cash payments for labor are assumed to be the same as total labor costs.

Manufacturing Overhead Budget

The **manufacturing overhead budget** summarizes all expected manufacturing costs other than direct materials and direct labor costs as well as expected cash payments for those costs. This budget is based on manufacturing overhead costs being

Exhibit 7–6
Manufacturing Overhead Budget for a Manufacturing Company

Beta Corporation
Manufacturing Overhead Budget
For the Year Ended December 31, 19x9

	Quarter 1	Quarter 2	Quarter 3	Quarter 4	Year
Total direct labor costs	$290,000	$277,500	$232,500	$250,000	$1,050,000[1]
Variable overhead rate	×0.80	×0.80	×0.80	×0.80	×0.80[2]
Variable overhead costs	$232,000	$222,000	$186,000	$200,000	$ 840,000
Fixed overhead costs	+150,000	+150,000	+150,000	+150,000	+600,000[3]
Total manufacturing overhead costs	$382,000	$372,000	$336,000	$350,000	$1,440,000
Less depreciation	−50,000	−50,000	−50,000	−50,000	−200,000[4]
Cash payments overhead	$332,000	$322,000	$286,000	$300,000	$1,240,000

[1]Exhibit 7–5.
[2]Management's estimates.
[3]Management's estimates.
[4]Management's estimates.

classified as variable or fixed and on the relationship of variable costs to a suitable activity measure. Beta Corporation's management has chosen direct labor dollars as the activity measure for variable overhead costs. Based on an analysis of historical manufacturing overhead costs, the variable overhead rate is estimated at $0.80 per direct labor dollar. Fixed overhead costs are estimated at $150,000 per quarter. Normally, manufacturing overhead is planned on an item-by-item basis. Costs such as indirect labor, supplies, power, insurance, and property taxes would be shown as separate items in the budget. Manufacturing overhead budgets can contain over twenty different cost items. In order to illustrate the concept of planning manufacturing overhead, we have simplified the budget somewhat, showing only two categories—fixed and variable manufacturing overhead costs.

Using these estimates and estimated direct labor costs from Exhibit 7–5, you can calculate Beta's expected manufacturing overhead costs. Exhibit 7–6 shows Beta's manufacturing overhead budget. First, variable overhead costs are computed by multiplying direct labor costs for each period (from the direct labor budget) by the variable overhead rate. For Quarter 1, Beta Corporation expects to incur $232,000 in variable overhead costs (0.80 × $290,000). Next $150,000 in fixed overhead costs are added to obtain total overhead costs of $382,000.

Finally, to determine cash payments for overhead, you must subtract any depreciation charges from total overhead costs. Remember that depreciation is a noncash cost. That is, there is no cash outflow associated with the annual cost of depreciation. For Beta Corporation, depreciation charges are $50,000 per

Exhibit 7–7
Ending Inventory Budget for a Manufacturing Company

Beta Corporation
Ending Inventory Budget
For the Year Ended December 31, 19x9

		Quarter 1	Quarter 2	Quarter 3	Quarter 4	Year
Estimated ending direct materials inventory, units		5,550	4,650	5,000	5,000	5,000[1]
Cost per unit		$ ×2	$ ×2	$ ×2	$ ×2	$ ×2[2]
Cost of ending direct materials inventory		$ 11,100	$ 9,300	$ 10,000	$ 10,000	$ 10,000
Estimated ending finished goods inventory		18,000	13,500	15,000	15,000	15,000[3]
Variable cost per unit						
Direct materials	$2					
Direct labor	5					
Variable overhead	4	$ ×11	$ ×11	$ ×11	$ ×11	$ ×11[4]
Cost of ending finished goods inventory		$198,000	$148,500	$165,000	$165,000	$165,000

[1]Exhibit 7–4.
[2]Management's estimates.
[3]Exhibit 7–3.
[4]Management's estimates.

quarter. Beta assumes that cash disbursements for overhead are made in the period the costs are incurred. Thus, cash outflow for manufacturing overhead in the first quarter is $332,000 ($382,000 − $50,000).

Ending Inventory Budget

The **ending inventory budget** is a statement showing the cost of ending direct materials, work in process, and finished goods inventories. The ending inventory budget is used to prepare the balance sheet at the end of each budget period. Exhibit 7–7 shows Beta Corporation's ending inventory budget. It begins with the computation of the dollar value of ending direct materials inventory. First, the estimated ending inventory figures (in pounds) for each quarter are copied from Schedule 2 of the direct materials budget (Exhibit 7–4). Then, they are multiplied by the unit cost of direct materials, or $2 per pound. For the first quarter, the value of Beta's ending direct materials inventory is $11,100 (5,550 pounds × $2 per pound).

As noted earlier, Beta Corporation's work in process inventory is so small that they choose to ignore it when preparing their master budget. Furthermore, Beta includes only variable costs in their finished goods inventory.

Next, the cost of finished goods inventory is computed. The number of units in ending finished goods inventory is taken from the production budget (Exhibit 7–3). Recall that Beta's unit costs for direct materials, direct labor, and variable overhead are as follows:

Direct materials		
1 pound @ $2 per pound	=	$ 2 per unit
Direct labor		
0.25 hours @ $20 per hour	=	5 per unit
Variable overhead		
0.80 per direct labor dollar @ $5 per unit	=	4 per unit
Total		$11 per unit

Multiplying the total cost per finished unit by the number of units in finished goods inventory yields the dollar value of ending finished goods inventory. For the first quarter, the value of Beta's ending finished goods inventory is $198,000 (18,000 units × $11 per unit).

Notice that the last column of the ending inventory budget repeats fourth-quarter figures. End-of-year inventory is the same as end-of-quarter inventory for the fourth quarter.

Selling and Administrative Expense Budget

The **selling and administrative expense budget** is a detailed listing of nonmanufacturing expenses during a budget period and expected cash payments for those expenditures. In preparing the selling and administrative expense budget, accountants separate variable from fixed expenses. Variable expenses generally include such items as sales commissions, travel and entertainment, clerical services, and shipping. By analyzing past expenses and adjusting them for inflation and other anticipated changes, the accountant can estimate each variable expense as a percentage of each sales dollar.

Beta Corporation's selling and administrative expense budget is shown in Exhibit 7–8. The first line shows estimated sales revenue for the year by quarter. This information comes from the sales budget (Exhibit 7–2). Beta's accountants have estimated variable expenses as follows:

Sales commissions	7% of sales dollars
Travel	2% of sales dollars
Entertainment	1% of sales dollars

In the selling and administrative expense budget, Beta's variable expenses are calculated by multiplying these percentages by estimated sales revenue for each quarter. In the first quarter, sales commissions are estimated at $96,250 (0.07 × $1,375,000).

Exhibit 7–8
Selling and Administrative Expense Budget for a Manufacturing Company

Beta Corporation
Selling and Administrative Expense Budget
For the Year Ended December 31, 19x9

	Quarter 1	Quarter 2	Quarter 3	Quarter 4	Year
Total sales	$1,375,000	$1,500,000	$1,125,000	$1,250,000	$5,250,000[1]
Selling and administrative expenses					
Variable					
Sales commissions (7% of sales)	$ 96,250	$ 105,000	$ 78,750	$ 87,500	$ 367,500[2]
Travel (2% of sales)	+27,500	+30,000	+22,500	+25,000	+105,000[3]
Entertainment (1% of sales)	+13,750	+15,000	+11,250	+12,500	+52,500[4]
Total variable expenses	$ 137,500	$ 150,000	$ 112,500	$ 125,000	$ 525,000
Fixed					
Salaries	$ 50,000	$ 50,000	$ 50,000	$ 50,000	$ 200,000[5]
Office supplies	+20,000	+20,000	+20,000	+20,000	+80,000[6]
Advertising	+80,000	+80,000	+80,000	+80,000	+320,000[7]
Total fixed expenses	$ 150,000	$ 150,000	$ 150,000	$ 150,000	$ 600,000
Total selling and administrative expenses	$ 287,500	$ 300,000	$ 262,500	$ 275,000	$1,125,000
Cash payments for selling and administrative expenses	$ 287,500	$ 300,000	$ 262,500	$ 275,000	$1,125,000

[1]Exhibit 7–2.
[2–4]Management's estimates.
[5–7]Management's estimates.

Beta's fixed selling and administrative expenses include the cost of salaries, advertising, and office supplies. Again, these amounts are estimated on the basis of historical data and are adjusted for inflation and changes in procedure. Beta's accountants list the following fixed selling and administrative expenses for each quarter:

Salaries	$50,000 per quarter
Supplies	20,000 per quarter
Advertising	80,000 per quarter

These fixed selling and administrative expenses are first totaled then added to Beta's variable selling and administrative expenses. The sum is Beta's total estimated selling and administrative expenses, or $287,500 for the first quarter. In Beta's case, the fixed selling and administrative expenses include no depreciation. It is assumed that selling and administrative expenses are paid in the same period in which they are incurred.

Budgeted Income Statement

The **budgeted income statement** shows estimated revenues and expenses from profit-directed activities for a specific budget period. The budgeted income statement summarizes information from the sales, manufacturing, and selling and administrative expense budgets. Refer back to Figure 7–1. Notice how these operating budgets all feed into the budgeted income statement. The purpose of the budgeted income statement is to estimate a company's after-tax income. Beta Corporation uses the contribution margin format for the income statement, as discussed in Chapter 3. This format facilitates the use of cost-volume-profit analysis to evaluate the financial impact of changes in the basic data used to develop the budget.

Beta Corporation's budgeted income statement is shown in Exhibit 7–9. Sales in units and dollars are obtained from Beta's sales budget (Exhibit 7–2). Then, variable costs of manufacturing are calculated by multiplying sales units by variable manufacturing costs per unit from the ending inventory budget (Ex-

Exhibit 7–9

Budgeted Income Statement for a Manufacturing Company Using the Contribution Margin Format

Beta Corporation
Budgeted Income Statement — Contribution Margin Format
For the Year Ended December 31, 19x9

	Quarter 1	Quarter 2	Quarter 3	Quarter 4	Year
Sales units	55,000	60,000	45,000	50,000	210,000
Sales revenues	$1,375,000	$1,500,000	$1,125,000	$1,250,000	$5,250,000[1]
Less variable costs					
Manufacturing	$ 605,000	$ 660,000	$ 495,000	$ 550,000	$2,310,000[2]
Selling and administrative	137,500	150,000	112,500	125,000	525,000[3]
Total variable costs	$ 742,500	$ 810,000	$ 607,500	$ 675,000	$2,835,000
Contribution margin	$ 632,500	$ 690,000	$ 517,500	$ 575,000	$2,415,000
Less fixed costs					
Manufacturing	$ 150,000	$ 150,000	$ 150,000	$ 150,000	$ 600,000[4]
Selling and administrative	150,000	150,000	150,000	150,000	600,000[5]
Total fixed costs	$ 300,000	$ 300,000	$ 300,000	$ 300,000	$1,200,000
Operating income	$ 332,500	$ 390,000	$ 217,500	$ 275,000	$1,215,000
Income taxes (34%)	113,050	132,600	73,950	93,500	413,100[6]
Net income	$ 219,450	$ 257,400	$ 143,550	$ 181,500	$ 801,900

[1]Schedule 1, Exhibit 7–2.
[2]Exhibit 7–7; $11 × sales units.
[3]Exhibit 7–8.
[4]Exhibit 7–6.
[5]Exhibit 7–8.
[6]Management's estimates.

hibit 7–7). For the first quarter, Beta's variable manufacturing costs are estimated to be $605,000 (55,000 units × $11 per unit).

Next, Beta's variable selling and administrative expenses are calculated. For this computation the accountant uses the sum of the percentages listed in the selling and administrative expense budget, or 0.10 (Exhibit 7–8). That is, total variable selling and administrative expenses are 10 percent of sales dollars. For the first quarter, Beta's variable selling and administrative expenses are $137,500 (0.10 × $1,375,000). Beta's variable expenses are then added together and subtracted from sales revenues to obtain the contribution margin.

Beta's fixed manufacturing costs are obtained from the manufacturing overhead budget (Exhibit 7–6). Fixed selling and administrative expenses are obtained from the selling and administrative expense budget (Exhibit 7–8). These fixed costs are then added together and subtracted from Beta's contribution margin to obtain operating income. Finally, federal income taxes are *estimated* to be 34 percent of operating income, based on current tax rates. This figure is subtracted from operating income to obtain budgeted net income. The budgeted income statement is an important document because it is frequently used to evaluate managerial performance.

Cash Budget

The **cash budget** is a period-by-period statement of: (1) cash on hand at the start of a budget period, (2) expected cash receipts, (3) expected cash disbursements, and (4) the resulting cash balance at the end of the budget period. The cash budget summarizes cash receipts and expenditures provided for in operating budgets. It helps identify periods in which a company might need extra cash so loans can be negotiated in a timely manner. In fact, banks require businesses to plan their cash needs carefully. Businesses that make urgent, last-minute loan requests must generally pay higher interest rates. The cash budget also helps identify periods in which a company may have more cash than necessary. Excess cash can be invested in short-term securities to earn additional income for owners. Depending on their needs, some companies prepare weekly or even daily analyses of their expected cash inflows and outflows. Such preparation facilitates the investment of excess cash.

Beta Corporation's cash budget is shown in Exhibit 7–10. It includes four sections: beginning cash balance, cash receipts, cash payments, and ending cash balance. The beginning cash balance for the first quarter was obtained from Beta's December 31, 19x8, balance sheet. Likewise, the beginning cash balance for any quarter is the ending cash balance from the previous quarter. The figures for cash receipts were cash collections, taken from that line in the sales budget (Exhibit 7–2). They are added to the beginning cash balance to obtain total cash available for the period.

The cash payment section summarizes disbursements for planned purchases and expenses included in the budgets for:

1. Direct materials (Exhibit 7–4)
2. Direct labor (Exhibit 7–5)

Exhibit 7–10
Cash Budget for a Manufacturing Company

Beta Corporation
Cash Budget
For the Year Ended December 31, 19x9

	Quarter 1	Quarter 2	Quarter 3	Quarter 4	Year
Cash balance, beginning	$ 200,000	$ 170,480	$ 476,810	$ 798,510	$ 200,000[1]
Cash receipts	+1,125,000	+1,450,000	+1,275,000	+1,200,000	+5,050,000[2]
Total cash available	$1,325,000	$1,620,480	$1,751,810	$1,998,510	$5,250,000
Cash payments for					
Direct materials purchases	$ 131,970	$ 111,570	$ 98,350	$ 98,110	$ 440,000[3]
Direct labor	290,000	277,500	232,500	250,000	1,050,000[4]
Manufacturing overhead	332,000	322,000	286,000	300,000	1,240,000[5]
Selling and administrative expenses	287,500	300,000	262,500	275,000	1,125,000[6]
Income taxes	113,050	132,600	73,950	93,500	413,100[7]
Total cash payments	$1,154,520	$1,143,670	$ 953,300	$1,016,610	$4,268,100
Cash balance, ending	$ 170,480	$ 476,810	$ 798,510	$ 981,900	$ 981,900

[1]Exhibit 7–1; ending cash balance last quarter.
[2]Schedule 2, Exhibit 7–2.
[3]Schedule 3, Exhibit 7–4.
[4]Exhibit 7–5.
[5]Exhibit 7–6.
[6]Exhibit 7–8.
[7]Exhibit 7–9.

3. Manufacturing overhead (Exhibit 7–6)
4. Selling and administrative expenses (Exhibit 7–8)

It also assumes that income taxes are paid as incurred, as the budgeted income statement (Exhibit 7–9) shows.

Finally, the ending cash balance is found by subtracting total cash payments from total cash available. Notice that in each quarter, the ending cash balance becomes the beginning cash balance for the next quarter. In the last column, all lines except the beginning and ending cash balances are added horizontally. The beginning cash balance for the year is always the same as the beginning cash balance for the first quarter. The ending cash balance is the same as the ending cash balance for the last quarter.

Budgeted Balance Sheet

The **budgeted balance sheet** is an estimate of a firm's financial position at the end of the budget period. It is developed from previous budgets, with beginning

Exhibit 7–11
Budgeted Balance Sheet for a Manufacturing Company

Beta Corporation
Budgeted Balance Sheet by Quarter
December 31, 19x9

	Quarter 1	Quarter 2	Quarter 3	Quarter 4
Assets				
Cash	$ 170,480	$ 476,810	$ 798,510	$ 981,900[1]
Accounts receivable	550,000	600,000	450,000	500,000[2]
Direct materials inventory	11,100	9,300	10,000	10,000[3]
Finished goods inventory	198,000	148,500	165,000	165,000[4]
Plant and equipment	1,000,000	1,000,000	1,000,000	1,000,000[5]
Accumulated depreciation	(400,000)	(450,000)	(500,000)	(550,000)[6]
Total assets	$1,529,580	$1,784,610	$1,923,510	$2,106,900
Liabilities and Equity				
Accounts payable	$ 35,130	$ 32,760	$ 28,110	$ 30,000[7]
Common stock	550,000	550,000	550,000	550,000[8]
Retained earnings	944,450	1,201,850	1,345,400	1,526,900[9]
Total liabilities and equity	$1,529,580	$1,784,610	$1,923,510	$2,106,900

[1]Exhibit 7–10.
[2]40 percent of sales each quarter (Exhibit 7–2.)
[3]Exhibit 7–7.
[4]Exhibit 7–7.
[5]Exhibit 7–1.
[6]Balance, 12/31/x8 + 50,000 each quarter (Exhibits 7–1, 7–6).
[7]30 percent of cost of direct materials purchases (Schedule 2, Exhibit 7–4).
[8]Exhibit 7–1.
[9]Exhibits 7–1, 7–9; beginning retained earnings balance + current quarter's net income.

balances adjusted to include any changes in assets, liabilities, and equity planned for in the operating and financial budgets.

Exhibit 7–11 shows Beta Corporation's budgeted balance sheet for December 31, 19x9. The cash line restates ending cash balances for each quarter, which are taken from the cash budget (Exhibit 7–10). The accounts receivable line represents uncollected credit sales for the last quarter. These figures, which are 40 percent of Beta's quarterly sales revenue, come from the last quarter's sales budget (Exhibit 7–2). For example, accounts receivable for the first quarter are $550,000. In Exhibit 7–2, that is the amount from the first quarter's sales to be collected in the second quarter.

The value of the direct materials and finished goods inventories is obtained from the ending inventory budget (Exhibit 7–7). The value of Beta's plant and equipment is the same as the fixed assets line in Beta's 19x8 balance sheet (Exhibit 7–1), since no purchases are planned for 19x9. Notice from the balance sheet accumulated depreciation was $350,000 on December 31, 19x8. This account is budgeted to increase by $50,000 per quarter (see the manufacturing overhead budget, Exhibit 7–6). Thus, accumulated depreciation at the end of the first quarter of 19x9 is $400,000 on the budgeted balance sheet. It continues to increase by $50,000 each quarter.

Once Beta's assets are totaled, its liabilities are listed. Accounts payable shows amounts still owed for purchases of direct materials in the quarter. Schedule 2 of the direct materials budget (Exhibit 7–4) shows planned purchases of direct materials. If Beta pays for 30 percent of its purchases in the following quarter, then accounts payable will equal 30 percent of planned purchases for the prior quarter. Thus, accounts payable at the end of the first quarter are $35,130 (0.30 × $117,100). This amount can also be found in Schedule 3 of the direct materials budget in the second quarter column, where it is listed as a cash payment for purchases made in the first quarter.

Beta's common stock value is obtained from its December 31, 19x8, balance sheet. It is not expected to change in 19x9. Retained Earnings were $725,000 on December 31, 19x8. This account increases each quarter by the net income earned that quarter because no dividends are planned. Thus, Retained Earnings for the first quarter are $944,450 ($725,000 + $219,450, the first quarter's net income figure on Beta's budgeted income statement in Exhibit 7–9).

Review Exercise 7–2

Prepare Cash Receipts and Disbursements Budget and Budgeted Income Statement

Post Company has budgeted the following activity for the month of July:

Sales are expected to be $600,000. All sales are on credit and are collected during the month of sale. Bad debts are anticipated at 3 percent of sales.

Finished inventory is $80,000 at the beginning of the month and is scheduled to increase $10,000 by the end of the month. All finished inventory is purchased from one supplier. Purchases are paid for during the month of purchase.

All inventory is priced to sell at two times cost.

Estimated selling and administrative expenses for the month are $40,000 plus a 10 percent sales commission. All expenses are paid for in the month incurred.

Depreciation for the month is scheduled at $50,000.

Required

1. Prepare a cash receipts and disbursements budget for the month.
2. Prepare a budgeted income statement for the month.

Solution

1. Cash receipts and disbursements budget prepared:

Post Company
Cash Receipts and Disbursements Budget Computations
For the Month of July

Cash receipts		
$600,000 × 0.97 =		$582,000
Cash disbursements		
Inventory purchases		
Cost of sales (2 × cost = $600,000)	$300,000	
Plus ending inventory ($80,000 + $10,000)	90,000	
Total requirements	$390,000	
Less beginning inventory	80,000	
Purchases		$310,000
Selling and administrative expense disbursements		
Variable ($600,000 × 0.10)	$ 60,000	
Fixed	40,000	100,000
Total disbursements		$410,000
Increase in cash		$172,000

2. Budgeted income statement prepared:

Post Company
Budgeted Income Statement
For the Month of July

Sales		$600,000
Variable expenses		
Variable cost of goods sold	$300,000	
Variable selling expense	60,000	
Bad debt expense ($600,000 × .03)	18,000	378,000
Contribution margin		$222,000
Fixed expenses		
Fixed selling and administrative	$40,000	
Depreciation	50,000	90,000
Operating income		$132,000

(see Exercise 27)

■

The Master Budget in a Merchandising Company

OBJECTIVE 4
Explain the difference between a master budget in a manufacturing company and a master budget in a merchandising company

Until now this discussion has concentrated on preparing a master budget in a manufacturing company. The process is similar in a merchandising company. The major difference is that instead of preparing a production budget and its associated direct materials, direct labor, and manufacturing overhead budgets, one must prepare a purchases budget.

To illustrate this process, master budget documents for Direct Store will be prepared. The store's balance sheet for 19x8 is shown in Exhibit 7–12.

Sales for Direct Store over the past two months of 19x8 and estimated sales for the first five months of 19x9 are given below.

Actual		Estimated	
November 19x8	$120,000	January 19x9	$120,000
December 19x8	100,000	February 19x9	130,000
		March 19x9	115,000
		April 19x9	120,000
		May 19x9	130,000

All sales are credit sales. Fifty percent of collections are made in the month of sale; 40 percent in the month following sale; and 9 percent in the second month following sale. One percent of credit sales are uncollectible.

Exhibit 7–12
Balance Sheet for a Merchandising Company

Direct Store Balance Sheet December 31, 19x8	
Assets	
Cash	$ 50,000
Accounts Receivable	59,800
Inventory	110,000
Fixed Assets (net of accumulated depreciation)	150,000
Total Assets	$369,800
Liabilities and Equity	
Accounts Payable	$ 79,750
Common Stock	100,000
Retained Earnings	190,050
Total Liabilities and Equity	$369,800

OBJECTIVE 5
Prepare a master budget for a merchandising company

At the end of each month, management wants sufficient inventory on hand to satisfy expected demand for the next one and one-half months. Cost of goods sold is expected to be 65 percent of the sales price. Direct Store pays for all inventory in the month following purchase.

Variable selling and administrative expenses are expected to be 10 percent of total sales revenue, excluding uncollectible accounts. Fixed selling and administrative expenses are budgeted at $25,000 per month, including depreciation of $6,000 per month. Selling and administrative expenses are paid in the month they are incurred.

Starting in January 19x9, management wants to maintain a minimum cash balance of $60,000. A local bank must agree to lend cash as needed on a monthly basis. Loans must be made at the beginning of the month and repaid in multiples of $1,000 when the monthly cash balance allows. The interest rate will be 12 percent per year payable quarterly.

For the first three months of 19x9, management at Direct Store requires the following budgets:

- A sales budget
- A purchases budget, including an estimate of ending inventory
- A selling and administrative expense budget
- A cash budget
- A budgeted income statement
- A budgeted balance sheet

Sales Budget

The sales budget for the Direct Store is shown in Exhibit 7–13. Sales for November and December are included for the calculation of cash collections. In January, Direct Store expects to receive 50 percent of revenues from sales made during January ($60,000); 40 percent from sales made during December ($40,000); and 9 percent from sales made during November ($10,800). Notice that the company plans to collect only 99 percent of its sales. The other 1 percent are expected to be uncollectible. This point will come up again later when bad debts will affect the calculation of net income and accounts receivable.

Purchases Budget

Exhibit 7–14 shows the purchases budget for Direct Store. In a merchandising company, the **purchases budget** is a statement showing the cost of merchandise to be purchased to satisfy sales demand and ending inventory needs. It includes estimated sales through May, since ending inventory is calculated on the basis of expected sales for the following month and a half. The cost of goods sold represents the cost of inventory needed to satisfy current month's sales. Management

Exhibit 7–13
Sales Budget for a Merchandising Company

Direct Store
Sales Budget
For the First Quarter, 19x9

	November	December	January	February	March
Sales revenues	$120,000	$100,000	$120,000	$130,000	$115,000[1]
Cash collections					
Month of sale			$ 60,000	$ 65,000	$ 57,500[2]
Previous month			+40,000	+48,000	+52,000[3]
Month before previous month			+10,800	+9,000	10,800[4]
Total cash collections			$110,800	$122,000	$120,300

[1]November–December, actual; January–March, Management's estimates.
[2]50% × Current month's sales.
[3]40% × Last month's sales.
[4]09% × Sales, two months ago.

Exhibit 7–14
Purchases Budget for a Merchandising Company

Direct Store
Purchases Budget
For the First Quarter, 19x9

	January	February	March	April	May
Estimated sales revenues	$120,000	$130,000	$115,000	$120,000	$130,000[1]
Cost of goods sold	$ 78,000	$ 84,500	$ 74,750[2]		
Add planned ending inventory	121,875	113,750	120,250[3]		
Total goods available for sale	$199,875	$198,250	$195,000		
Less beginning inventory	110,000	121,875	113,750[4]		
Purchases	$ 89,875	$ 76,375	$ 81,250		
Cash payments	$ 79,750	$ 89,875	$ 76,375[5]		

[1]Exhibit 7–13, January–March; April–May, management's estimates.
[2]65% × estimated sales.
[3]65% × (next month's sales + 1/2 second month's sales)
Desired ending inventory =
January = 65% [$130,000 + 1/2($115,000)]
February = 65% [$115,000 + 1/2($120,000)]
March = 65% [$120,000 + 1/2($130,000)]
[4]Exhibit 7–12; ending finished goods last quarter.
[5]Accounts payable balance, end of preceding month.

estimated cost of goods sold to be 65 percent of the sales price. The cost of ending inventory is calculated next, at 65 percent of estimated sales for the next month and a half. The cost of goods sold and ending inventory are added together to obtain goods available for sale for the month. Then, the value of the beginning inventory is subtracted to yield the cost of purchases for the month. (Beginning inventory is the same as ending inventory for the past month.) Finally, cash payments for last month's purchases are shown on the last line.

Selling and Administrative Expense Budget

The selling and administrative expense budget for Direct Store is shown in Exhibit 7–15. First, variable selling and administrative expenses are estimated at 10 percent of the month's sales revenues. Fixed selling and administrative expenses of $25,000 per month are added to obtain total monthly selling and administrative expenses. From this total, depreciation expenses of $6,000 per month are deducted to obtain cash payments for selling and administrative expenses.

Cash Budget

Exhibit 7–16 shows the cash budget for Direct Store. The figures for cash receipts are obtained from the last line of the sales budget (Exhibit 7–13). They are added to the beginning cash balance to obtain total cash available to Direct Store. Figures

Exhibit 7–15

Selling and Administrative Expenses Budget for a Merchandising Company

Direct Store
Selling and Administrative Expenses
For the First Quarter, 19x9

	January	February	March
Estimated sales revenues	$120,000	$130,000	$115,000[1]
Selling and administrative expenses			
Variable	$ 12,000	$ 13,000	$ 11,500[2]
Fixed	+25,000	+25,000	+25,000[3]
Total selling and administrative expenses	$ 37,000	$ 38,000	$ 36,500
Less depreciation	6,000	6,000	6,000[4]
Cash payments for selling and administrative expenses	$ 31,000	$ 32,000	$ 30,500

[1]Exhibit 7–13.
[2]10% × estimated sales.
[3]Management's estimate.
[4]Management's estimate.

Exhibit 7–16
Cash Budget for a Merchandising Company Showing Loans and Repayment

Direct Store
Cash Budget
For the First Quarter, 19x9

	January	February	March
Cash balance, beginning	$ 50,000	$ 60,050	$ 60,175[1]
Cash receipts	110,800	122,000	120,300[2]
Total cash available	$160,800	$182,050	$180,475
Cash payments for			
Purchases	$ 79,750	$ 89,875	$ 76,375[3]
Variable selling and administrative expenses	12,000	13,000	11,500[4]
Fixed selling and administrative expenses	19,000	19,000	19,000[5]
Total cash payments	$110,750	$121,875	$106,875
Cash balance before financing	$ 50,050	$ 60,175	$ 73,600
Financing			
Proceeds from loan	$ 10,000[6]		
Loan requirements			(10,000)[7]
Loan interest payments			(300)
Cash balance, ending	$ 60,050	$ 60,175	$ 63,300

[1]Balance sheet, 12/31/x8; ending cash balance for prior month.
[2]Exhibit 7–13.
[3]Exhibit 7–14.
[4]10% × estimated sales (Exhibit 7–13).
[5]$25,000 – $6,000.
[6]Managerial policy.
[7]Managerial policy.

for cash payments for purchases are copied from the purchases budget (Exhibit 7–14). Next, variable and fixed expenses are transferred from the selling and administrative expense budget. Notice that depreciation was deducted from fixed expense figures. Payments are totaled and deducted from total cash available to obtain the cash balance.

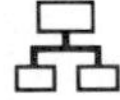

Direct's accountants have included loans and loan payment computations in the cash budget. Management wants a minimum cash balance of $60,000, starting in January. Since the beginning cash balance for January is $50,000, Direct Store must borrow $10,000 to begin the year. This loan is shown at the bottom of the cash budget in the financing section. No loan is needed at the start of February, however. By the end of March, the company's cash balance is $73,600, which is more than $10,000 higher than needed. Thus, the loan is paid off. Loan payments include the principal of $10,000 plus $300 interest, or 1 percent per month for three months.

Exhibit 7–17
Budgeted Income Statement for a Merchandising Company

Direct Store
Budgeted Income Statement
For the First Quarter, 19x9

Sales revenues		$365,000
Cost of goods sold		237,250[1]
Gross margin		$127,750
Operating expenses		
Variable	$36,500[2]	
Fixed	75,000[3]	
Uncollectible accounts	3,650[4]	
Total operating expenses		115,150
Operating income		$ 12,600
Interest expense		300
Income before taxes		$ 12,300

[1]Exhibit 7–14.
[2]Exhibit 7–15.
[3]Exhibit 7–15.
[4]1% × estimated sales (Exhibit 7–13).

Budgeted Income Statement

Exhibit 7–17 shows Direct Store's budgeted income statement for the first quarter of 19x9. Sales and cost of goods sold figures were obtained by totaling monthly figures in the sales and purchases budgets. Variable and fixed expense figures represent three-month totals from the selling and administrative expense budget. Notice that the uncollectible accounts expense equal to 1 percent of credit sales is deducted from gross margin to arrive at operating income. Interest expense of $300 is then deducted to obtain the company's before-tax income.

Budgeted Balance Sheet

Direct Store's budgeted balance sheet for March 31, 19x9, is shown in Exhibit 7–18. The cash balance is the ending cash balance from Direct's cash budget (Exhibit 7–16). The Accounts Receivable figure was computed by totaling uncollected sales for February and March (0.09 × $130,000 = $11,700; 0.49 × $115,000 = $56,350). The balance in the Inventory account is the planned ending inventory for March obtained from the purchases budget (Exhibit 7–14). Fixed assets are shown as net of depreciation, calculated by deducting total depreciation for the first quarter, $18,000, from the $150,000 fixed assets (net) at the beginning of the first quarter from the December 31, 19x8, balance sheet.

Exhibit 7–18
Balance Sheet for a Merchandising Company

Direct Store
Balance Sheet
March 31, 19x9

Assets	
Cash	$ 63,300[1]
Accounts receivable (net)	68,050[2]
Inventory	120,250[3]
Fixed assets (net)	132,000[4]
Total assets	$383,600
Liabilities and Equity	
Accounts payable	$ 81,250[5]
Common stock	100,000[6]
Retained earnings	202,350[7]
Total liabilities and equity	$383,600

[1]Exhibit 7–16.
[2]9% × February sales + 49% × March sales (Exhibit 7–13).
[3]Exhibit 7–14.
[4]Balance sheet, 12/31/x8 − $6,000 depreciation per month (Exhibit 7–12).
[5]March purchases (Exhibit 7–14).
[6]Exhibit 7–12.
[7]Balance sheet, 12/31/x8 + quarterly net income (Exhibit 7–17).

Account payable for purchases are those purchases made on account during March, as shown in the purchases budget (Exhibit 7–14). The balance in capital stock figure comes from the December 31, 19x8, balance sheet. Retained earnings are calculated by adding quarterly income before taxes from the budgeted income statement (Exhibit 7–17) to the balance in Retained Earnings on Direct Store's December 31, 19x8, balance sheet (Exhibit 7–12).

Review Exercise 7–3

Prepare Schedules, Budgets, and Statements

Selected information for Maxvalue Retail Store is given below.

Account balances as of January 1, 19xx:

Assets	
Cash	$ 40,000
Accounts receivable (net)	46,800
Merchandise inventory	113,750
Fixed assets (net)	156,450
Total assets	$357,000

Liabilities and Equity

Current liabilities,	
merchandise purchases	$ 74,750
Common stock	150,000
Retained earnings	132,250
Total liabilities and equity	$357,000

All sales are on account, and collections occur 60 percent in the month of sale and 39 percent in the following month. One percent of the sales are uncollectible. Recent and estimated sales are as follows:

Actual December	$120,000
Estimated January	120,000
Estimated February	110,000
Estimated March	115,000

Management has decided that the inventory level should be equal to the estimated sales for the next one and one-half months. The merchandise inventory costs 65 percent of the sales price. All purchases are paid for in the month following the month of purchase.

All expenses are paid in the month incurred. Variable expenses are expected at 10 percent of sales dollars (exclusive of bad debts). Fixed expenses are anticipated to be $25,000 per month, including $6,000 depreciation.

Required

For the month of January:

1. Prepare a schedule showing cash collections from customers.
2. Prepare a schedule showing merchandise purchases.
3. Prepare a cash budget.
4. Prepare a budgeted income statement.
5. Prepare a budgeted balance sheet as of January 31, 19xx.

Solution

1. Cash collections prepared:

Cash Collection Schedule
Maxvalue Retail Store
For the Month of January 19xx

Sales made in December ($120,000 × 0.39)	$ 46,800
Sales made in January ($120,000 × 0.60)	72,000
Total cash collections in January 19xx	$118,800

2. Merchandise purchases calculated:

Merchandise Purchases
Maxvalue Retail Store
For the Month of January 19xx

Estimated sales	$120,000
Cost of sales (65%)	$ 78,000
Desired inventory*	108,875
Total requirements	$186,875
Beginning inventory	113,750
Purchases	$ 73,125

*Desired inventory = 0.65 ($110,000 + 1/2 ($115,000)).

3. Cash budget prepared:

Cash Budget
Maxvalue Retail Store
For the Month of January 19xx

Cash balance, beginning	$ 40,000
Cash collections	118,800
Total cash available	$158,800
Cash disbursements	
Payments for purchases	$ 74,750
Variable expenses (0.10 of sales)	12,000
Fixed expenses ($25,000 − $6,000)	19,000
Total cash expenditures	$105,750
Cash balance, ending	$ 53,050

4. Budgeted income statement prepared:

Budgeted Income Statement
Maxvalue Retail Store
For the Month of January 19xx

Sales revenues		$120,000
Cost of sales (0.65 × sales)		78,000
Gross margin		$ 42,000
Selling and administrative expenses		
Variable (0.10 × sales)	$12,000	
Fixed	25,000	
Bad debts (0.01 × sales)	1,200	38,200
Operating income		$ 3,800

5. Budgeted balance sheet prepared:

Budgeted Balance Sheet
Maxvalue Retail Store
January 31, 19xx

Assets	
Cash	$ 53,050
Accounts receivable (net) (.39 × $120,000)	46,800
Merchandise inventory	108,875
Fixed assets (net) ($156,450 − $6,000)	150,450
Total assets	$359,175
Liabilities and Equity	
Current liabilities, merchandise purchases	$ 73,125
Common stock	150,000
Retained earnings ($132,250 + $3,800)	136,050
Total liabilities and equity	$359,175

(see Problems 36, 37)

Use of Computerized Financial Planning Models

OBJECTIVE 6
Explain the role of computerized financial planning models in the budgeting process

The budgeting process and the resulting master budget do not always produce a plan acceptable to management. Sometimes managers must adjust their estimates, which means changes in many of the budget documents.

If the budget is prepared using a computer, such changes can be easily made. For example, Beta Corporation's master budget was prepared using a spreadsheet program on a microcomputer. Data from Beta's year-end balance sheet and estimates for the new year were entered into the spreadsheet along with formulas for the interrelationship of the various budgets. The computer then calculated and printed out the complete master budget. To find the effect of an estimate, such as the percentage of sales collected or the cost of materials, the accountant simply enters the change, and the computer recalculates the budget amounts and prints out a new budget. Managers can see the effect of the change on all components of the master budget almost immediately.

New Manufacturing Environment

The United States' manufacturing industry is undergoing major changes in the 1980s and 1990s. Customers are insisting on higher-quality products, and competition is global. **Just in time** (JIT) is a philosophy for designing and operating a manufacturing process that emphasizes higher-quality products and flexible product-oriented flow lines with lower inventories. The fundamental idea behind JIT manufacturing is to produce the needed items at the right time, in the right quantities, and with no defects.

OBJECTIVE 7
Discuss the impact of the new manufacturing environment on production planning

In the Beta Corporation example, materials and finished goods were planned for in the inventory budget. The materials inventory acts as a buffer to absorb the time between the placement of an order with a supplier and the receipt of the order. By carrying materials inventory, Beta Corporation is buffered against disruptions from the supplier on meeting delivery schedules. The materials are on hand so that Beta Corporation's production operation can run smoothly. The work in process inventory for Beta Corporation was considered minimal in our illustration, so we were able to ignore it in preparing the manufacturing budget. However, in some companies the work in process inventory is sizable. The work in process inventory is maintained to stabilize the production rate. To keep the production lines running smoothly, work in process inventories await work at each operation to avoid idle machinery and employees. By maintaining work in process inventories, time is available to rework poor quality parts. The finished goods inventory is maintained as a buffer to meet uneven and unexpected customer demand. This avoids lost sales due to insufficient inventory. With a constant production rate, this generally produces a build-up in finished goods inventory when demand is low and a decrease in finished goods inventory when demand is high. This type of production system is referred to as a "push" approach to manufacturing. The product is pushed through the production system and into finished goods inventory.

In contrast, a JIT inventory system attempts to change this flow by pulling materials and parts into each operation only as needed. Conceptually, shipping one unit of product triggers another unit to move into finished goods inventory, which triggers the final assembly of another unit, which triggers the fabricating of another unit until finally materials and parts are received from suppliers. The goal is to be able to produce one unit of product. This requires a high degree of quality from both the manufacturing operation and the suppliers. The benefit is that inventories are virtually eliminated. Lower inventories free capital and floor space, and reduce costs for storing and moving materials.

Removing inventory as a buffer from the manufacturing process exposes production problems that were unobservable, such as obsolete inventory of poor quality, excessive lead time from suppliers, and poor machine maintenance.

To make JIT inventory systems work, a company needs the cooperation of suppliers, flexibility in the manufacturing process, and a commitment to total quality control.

Suppliers

To successfully implement a JIT inventory system, a company must have only a few suppliers. The suppliers must be bound under long-term contracts and willing to make delivery of the materials and parts more than once per day. In many instances, the production information system of the company and the supplier are tied together to provide constant communication. In some situations, the suppliers locate their facilities adjacent to the manufacturing company. The supplier must be willing to deliver quality materials and parts, since they go directly to the work areas in the manufacturing plant. This eliminates the need to inspect materials and parts upon arrival and thus reduces the amount of time required to convert the materials into finished product.

Flexibility in the Manufacturing Process

Flexible product-oriented flow lines are designed to minimize the amount of time it takes to manufacture a product. The trend is toward designing a different production line for each version of a product. This design has been referred to as manufacturing cells or a factory-within-a-factory. Historically, similar pieces of equipment were grouped together, and products were moved from one group of equipment to another. For example, all milling machines were in one group, and all lathes were in another. Today, equipment is organized in cells by product to minimize the amount of materials handling and inventory. This reduces the distances that parts have to travel, and hence materials-handling costs are reduced.

Machine downtime due to product changeovers is minimized by reducing setup time. Reductions in setup time reduce the total cost of manufacturing a product. In many companies, the same employees that operate the equipment do the setup. Reductions in setup time can also be achieved by using carefully designed and efficient equipment, tools, and work methods. In some cases, additional pieces of equipment may be purchased to reduce setup time; in other instances, simply having a separate tray of tools for each product significantly reduces setup time. In a JIT manufacturing environment, setup is performed off-line ahead of time, to minimize machine downtime.

Labor is not specialized in a JIT manufacturing process, rather it is interdisciplinary. Employees are assigned to manufacturing cells and are trained to perform all tasks within that cell. In some organizations, employees are paid based on how many tasks they can perform rather than seniority. Flexibility is needed in the work force so that if an employee does not report for work, another employee can be substituted.

Quality

A major factor in implementing a JIT inventory system is total quality control (TQC). The goal of TQC is to achieve a zero defect manufacturing environment. This includes suppliers of materials and parts as well as the manufacturing process. The need for TQC is based on the product being pulled rather than pushed through the manufacturing operations. Since final demand initiates the production, one defective part could shut down the entire manufacturing cell. Poor quality cannot be accepted, since the JIT inventory system operates with no work in process inventory.

Once a high level of product quality is established, management can reduce the amount of time devoted to product inspection. With the exception of technically difficult inspections, all inspection is the responsibility of the worker who performed the job. Any rework of defective parts is the worker's responsibility. In stable production processes, a first-and-last inspection system may be used. This system assumes that if the first unit is good and the last unit is good then all units produced in between will also be good. Management today is adopting the concept that in the long run, low cost and high quality go hand in hand.

Benefits of a JIT Inventory System

Obvious benefits to be derived from using a JIT inventory system include:

- Lower inventories
- Higher-quality output
- Faster market response (since materials and work in process inventories are low and product changeover is quicker)
- Less investment in materials-handling equipment
- Smaller manufacturing facilities (since less space is needed to store inventories)
- Lower setup costs

Chapter Review

Review of Learning Objectives

1. **Explain why a company prepares a master budget.**
The master budget is a series of interrelated budgets that quantify management's expectations about a company's revenues, expenses, net income, cash flows, and financial position. As the culmination of the planning process, it provides the basis for (a) reassessing the company's objectives, (b) coordinating the activities of various segments of the organization, (c) communicating management's plans throughout the organization, and (d) evaluating employee performance.

2. **List the components of a master budget and explain their interrelationship.**
In a manufacturing company, the master budget includes an operating budget and a financial budget. The operating budget, which represents expected results of operations, includes the following documents:

- Sales budget
- Production budget
- Direct materials budget
- Direct labor budget
- Manufacturing overhead budget
- Ending inventory budget
- Selling and administrative expense budget
- Budgeted income statement, which summarizes the above documents

The financial budget includes (a) the capital expenditure budget, (b) the cash budget, and (c) the budgeted balance sheet. Figure 7–1 summarizes the interrelationship between components of operating and financial budgets.

3. **Prepare a master budget for a manufacturing company.**
The budgeting process begins with the sales forecast, which states the company's expected sales and sales price per unit. The sales forecast, which is prepared by the sales manager, is based on an analysis of general economic conditions, industry trends, and current prospects for the company. From it the sales budget is developed. Next, the production budget is prepared on the basis of sales prospects and desired inventory levels. These predicted production and sales levels are then used to prepare forecasts of expected costs for direct materials, direct labor, manufacturing overhead, and ending inventory as well as selling and administrative expenses. Expected results of operations are summarized in the budgeted income statement. Finally, financial results of operations are summarized in the cash budget and budgeted balance sheet.
Many computations in the budgeting process can be summarized as follows:
Beginning balance + additions − subtractions = ending balance

4. **Explain the difference between a master budget in a manufacturing company and a master budget in a merchandising company.**
In a merchandising company, a purchases budget replaces the production budget and its associated direct materials, direct labor, and manufacturing overhead budgets.

5. **Prepare a master budget for a merchandising company.**
The budgeting process in a merchandising company is essentially the same as that in a manufacturing company. The only difference is that a purchases budget replaces the production budget.

6. **Explain the role of computerized financial planning models in the budgeting process.**
Budgeting was once an extremely time-consuming process. Today, computerized financial planning programs can do most of the mechanical work of preparing a master budget. These programs relieve managers of the drudgery of budgeting, so they have more time for strategic planning.

7. **Discuss the impact of the new manufacturing environment on production planning.**
In the new manufacturing environment, companies are attempting to minimize inventory through developing cooperation with suppliers, building flexibility into the manufacturing process, and committing to total quality control. Suppliers are required to supply materials and parts several times a day so the manufacturer does not have to carry materials and parts inventory. Flexibility is built into the manufacturing process by organizing product production into small cells capable of starting and finishing the product. Employees are trained to perform all tasks within a cell. Setup times are reduced by performing some of the setup operations off-line. Total quality control is part of the environment. With no

inventories to act as buffers, suppliers and employees must ensure a high level of quality. The benefits being gained by companies include lower inventories, higher-quality output, faster market response, smaller facilities, and lower setup costs.

Review of Key Terms

Budget A document through which management communicates its plans for the organization and later measures its performance. As a quantification of planned revenues and expenses, the budget is used to communicate goals for revenues, expenses, assets, liabilities, and other business activities.

Budgeted balance sheet An estimate of a firm's financial position at the end of the budget period.

Budgeted income statement A statement showing estimated revenues and expenses from profit-directed activities for a specific budget period.

Capital expenditure budget A listing of all approved long-range expenditures planned to improve a firm's operating capacity or efficiency.

Cash budget A period-by-period statement of (1) cash on hand at the start of a budget period, (2) expected cash receipts, (3) expected cash disbursements, and (4) the resulting cash balance at the end of the budget period.

Continuous budget A budget that adds a future time period as the one just ended is completed and dropped. It is revised at the end of each period on the basis of actual results from the previous period. Also called a *rolling budget.*

Direct labor budget A statement showing the quantity, cost, and period of payment for labor that can be directly identified with specific products.

Direct materials budget A statement consisting of three schedules that show (1) the quantity and cost of direct materials needed to meet production requirements; (2) the level of direct materials purchases needed for production and maintenance of ending inventory levels; and (3) the expected cash outflows for direct materials purchases.

Ending inventory budget A statement showing the cost of ending direct materials, work in process, and finished goods inventories for each period.

Financial budget The second part of the master budget, which details capital expenditures and summarizes the effect of operations on a company's cash balances and expected financial position. It contains the capital expenditure budget, the cash budget, and the budgeted balance sheet.

Just in time (JIT) A philosophy for designing and operating a manufacturing process that emphasizes higher-quality products and flexible product-oriented flow lines with lower inventories.

Manufacturing overhead budget A statement summarizing all expected manufacturing costs other than direct materials and direct labor costs as well as expected cash payments for those costs.

Master budget A series of interrelated budgets that quantify management's expectations about revenues, expenses, net income, cash flows, and financial position.

Operating budget The first part of the master budget, representing expected results of operations. Contains the sales, production, direct materials, direct labor, manufacturing overhead, ending inventory, and selling and administrative expense budgets as well as the budgeted income statement.

Planning period The period for which detailed budgets are developed from managerial plans.

Production budget A statement specifying the number of units of each product to be produced to satisfy demand for the product and provide the desired ending finished goods inventory.

Purchases budget (for a manufacturing company) In a manufacturing company, this statement shows the quantity and cost of direct materials purchases needed both for production and maintenance of ending inventory levels.

Purchases budget (for a merchandising company) In a merchandising company, this statement shows the cost of merchandise to be purchased to satisfy sales demand and ending inventory needs.

Sales budget An estimate of the unit sales and sales revenues expected during the budget period as well as an estimate of cash receipts.

Selling and administrative expense budget A detailed listing of nonmanufacturing expenses during a budget period and expected cash payments for those expenditures.

Review Problem

Tech Corporation is preparing its annual budget. The balance sheet at the end of December 19x8 is shown below.

Tech Corporation
Balance Sheet
December 31, 19x8

Assets		
Cash		$ 150,000
Accounts receivable		200,000
Direct materials inventory (15,000 pounds @ $1.00)		15,000
Finished goods inventory (20,000 units @ $13.25)		265,000
Plant and equipment	$1,000,000	
Accumulated depreciation	(350,000)	650,000
Total assets		$1,280,000
Liabilities and Equity		
Accounts payable		$ 50,000
Common stock		600,000
Retained earnings		630,000
Total liabilities and equity		$1,280,000

Tech expects to sell its product for $50 a unit in 19x9. Based on this sales price, estimated unit sales by quarter are:

Quarter	Estimated sales in units
1	40,000
2	45,000
3	50,000
4	40,000
5	40,000

Tech expects to collect 70 percent of its sales revenues in the quarter of sale; 30 percent in the following quarter. It expects to collect on all accounts.

Manufacturing requirements per unit		
Direct materials	2 pounds @ $1 per pound	$ 2.00
Direct labor	0.5 hours @ $15 per hour	7.50
Variable overhead	$0.50 per direct labor dollar	3.75
		$13.25

Total fixed manufacturing overhead is expected to be $100,000 per quarter, $40,000 of which represents depreciation on plant and equipment.

Tech's managers' plan requires that quarterly ending finished goods inventory be 30 percent of expected sales in the following quarter. They also want the ending direct materials inventory to be 30 percent of the materials required in the next quarter. The desired ending direct materials inventory for the fourth quarter is 24,000 pounds. Sixty percent of direct materials purchases are paid for in the quarter of purchase; 40 percent in the quarter following purchase.

An analysis of selling and administrative expenses indicates these variable cost-to-sales ratios:

Sales commissions	10% of sales dollars
Travel	5% of sales dollars
Entertainment	2% of sales dollars

Fixed selling and administrative expenses for each quarter are estimated as follows:

Salaries	$30,000
Supplies	10,000
Advertising	40,000

These expenses are paid in the quarter incurred. Tech Corporation expects its income tax rate to be 34 percent in 19x9.

Required Using these data, prepare a quarterly master budget for Tech. Include the following documents:

1. Sales budget
2. Production budget
3. Direct materials budget
4. Direct labor budget
5. Manufacturing overhead budget

6. Ending inventory budget
7. Selling and administrative expense budget
8. Budgeted income statement using the contribution margin format
9. Cash budget
10. Budgeted balance sheet

Solution to Review Problem

1. Sales budget prepared:

Tech Corporation
Sales Budget
For the Year Ended December 31, 19x9

Schedule 1	Quarter 1	Quarter 2	Quarter 3	Quarter 4	Year
Sales units	40,000	45,000	50,000	40,000	175,000
Sales price per unit	$ ×50	$ ×50	$ ×50	$ ×50	$ ×50
Total sales	$2,000,000	$2,250,000	$2,500,000	$2,000,000	$8,750,000
Schedule 2					
Cash collections					
Last quarter's sales	$ 200,000	$ 600,000	$ 675,000	$ 750,000	$2,225,000
This quarter's sales	+1,400,000	+1,575,000	+1,750,000	+1,400,000	+6,125,000
Total collections	$1,600,000	$2,175,000	$2,425,000	$2,150,000	$8,350,000

2. Production budget prepared:

Tech Corporation
Production Budget
For the Year Ended December 31, 19x9

	Quarter 1	Quarter 2	Quarter 3	Quarter 4	Year
Sales units	40,000	45,000	50,000	40,000	175,000
Add estimated ending finished goods inventory	+13,500	+15,000	+12,000	+12,000	+12,000
Total unit requirements	53,500	60,000	62,000	52,000	187,000
Less beginning finished goods inventory	−20,000	−13,500	−15,000	−12,000	−20,000
Unit production requirements	33,500	46,500	47,000	40,000	167,000

3. Direct materials budget prepared:

Tech Corporation
Direct Materials Budget
For the Year Ended December 31, 19x9

Schedule 1: Usage budget	Quarter 1	Quarter 2	Quarter 3	Quarter 4	Year
Unit production requirements	33,500	46,500	47,000	40,000	167,000
Direct materials required per unit of output (pounds)	×2	×2	×2	×2	×2
Direct materials required (pounds)	67,000	93,000	94,000	80,000	334,000
Cost per unit of materials	$ ×1	$ ×1	$ ×1	$ ×1	$ ×1
Total cost of direct materials required	$67,000	$93,000	$94,000	$80,000	$334,000

Schedule 2: Purchases budget					
Direct materials required	67,000	93,000	94,000	80,000	334,000
Add estimated ending direct materials inventory	+27,900	+28,200	+24,000	+24,000	+24,000
Total direct materials required	94,900	121,200	118,000	104,000	358,000
Less beginning direct materials inventory	−15,000	−27,900	−28,200	−24,000	−15,000
Direct materials purchase requirements	79,900	93,300	89,800	80,000	343,000
Cost per pound of materials	$ ×1	$ ×1	$ ×1	$ ×1	$ ×1
Total cost of direct materials purchases	$79,900	$93,300	$89,800	$80,000	$343,000

Schedule 3: Schedule of expected cash payments for purchases					
Accounts payable	$50,000				$ 50,000
Purchases: Quarter 1	47,940	$31,960			79,900
Quarter 2		55,980	$37,320		93,300
Quarter 3			53,880	$35,920	89,800
Quarter 4				48,000	48,000
Total cash payments for purchases	$97,940	$87,940	$91,200	$83,920	$361,000

4. Direct labor budget prepared:

Tech Corporation
Direct Labor Budget
For the Year Ended December 31, 19x9

	Quarter 1	Quarter 2	Quarter 3	Quarter 4	Year
Unit production requirements	33,500	46,500	47,000	40,000	167,000
Direct labor hours per unit	×0.50	×0.50	×0.50	×0.50	×0.50
Total direct labor hours required	16,750	23,250	23,500	20,000	83,500
Direct labor cost per hour	$ ×15	$ ×15	$ ×15	$ ×15	$ ×15
Total direct labor costs	$251,250	$348,750	$352,500	$300,000	$1,252,500
Cash payments for direct labor	$251,250	$348,750	$352,500	$300,000	$1,252,500

5. Manufacturing overhead budget prepared:

Tech Corporation
Manufacturing Overhead Budget
For the Year Ended December 31, 19x9

	Quarter 1	Quarter 2	Quarter 3	Quarter 4	Year
Total direct labor costs	$251,250	$348,750	$352,500	$300,000	$1,252,500
Variable overhead rate	×0.50	×0.50	×0.50	×0.50	×0.50
Variable overhead costs	$125,625	$174,375	$176,250	$150,000	$ 626,250
Fixed overhead costs	+100,000	+100,000	+100,000	+100,000	+400,000
Total manufacturing overhead costs	$225,625	$274,375	$276,250	$250,000	$1,026,250
Less depreciation	−40,000	−40,000	−40,000	−40,000	−160,000
Cash payments for overhead	$185,625	$234,375	$236,250	$210,000	$ 866,250

6. Ending inventory budget prepared:

Tech Corporation
Ending Inventory Budget
For the Year Ended December 31, 19x9

	Quarter 1	Quarter 2	Quarter 3	Quarter 4	Year
Estimated ending direct materials inventory, pounds	27,900	28,200	24,000	24,000	24,000
Cost per pound	$ ×1	$ ×1	$ ×1	$ ×1	$ ×1
Cost of ending direct materials inventory	$ 27,900	$ 28,200	$ 24,000	$ 24,000	$ 24,000
Estimated ending finished goods inventory	13,500	15,000	12,000	12,000	12,000
Variable costs per unit					
Direct materials	$ 2.00				
Direct labor	7.50				
Variable overhead	3.75				
Total variable costs per unit	$ ×13.25	$ ×13.25	$ ×13.25	$ ×13.25	$ ×13.25
Cost of ending finished goods inventory	$ 178,875	$ 198,750	$ 159,000	$ 159,000	$ 159,000

7. Selling and administrative expense budget prepared:

Tech Corporation
Selling and Administrative Expense Budget
For the Year Ended December 31, 19x9

	Quarter 1	Quarter 2	Quarter 3	Quarter 4	Year
Sales revenues	$2,000,000	$2,250,000	$2,500,000	$2,000,000	$8,750,000
Variable selling and administrative expenses					
Sales commissions, 10%	$ 200,000	$ 225,000	$ 250,000	$ 200,000	$ 875,000
Travel, 5%	+100,000	+112,500	+125,000	+100,000	+437,500
Entertainment, 2%	+40,000	+45,000	+50,000	+40,000	+175,000
Total variable selling and administrative expenses	$ 340,000	$ 382,500	$ 425,000	$ 340,000	$1,487,500
Fixed selling and administrative expenses					
Salaries	$ 30,000	$ 30,000	$ 30,000	$ 30,000	$ 120,000
Supplies	+10,000	+10,000	+10,000	+10,000	+40,000
Advertising	+40,000	+40,000	+40,000	+40,000	+160,000
Total fixed selling and administrative expenses	$ 80,000	$ 80,000	$ 80,000	$ 80,000	$ 320,000
Total selling and administrative expenses	$ 420,000	$ 462,500	$ 505,000	$ 420,000	$1,807,500
Cash payments for selling and administrative expenses	$ 420,000	$ 462,500	$ 505,000	$ 420,000	$1,807,500

8. Budgeted income statement prepared using the contribution margin format:

Tech Corporation
Budgeted Income Statement — Contribution Margin Format
For the Year Ended December 31, 19x9

	Quarter 1	Quarter 2	Quarter 3	Quarter 4	Year
Sales units	40,000	45,000	50,000	40,000	175,000
Sales revenues	$2,000,000	$2,250,000	$2,500,000	$2,000,000	$8,750,000
Less variable costs					
Manufacturing*	$ 530,000	$ 596,250	$ 662,500	$ 530,000	$2,318,750
Selling and administrative	340,000	382,500	425,000	340,000	1,487,500
Total variable costs	$ 870,000	$ 978,750	$1,087,500	$ 870,000	$3,806,250
Contribution margin	$1,130,000	$1,271,250	$1,412,500	$1,130,000	$4,943,750
Less fixed costs					
Manufacturing	$ 100,000	$ 100,000	$ 100,000	$ 100,000	$ 400,000
Selling and administrative	80,000	80,000	80,000	80,000	320,000
Total fixed costs	$ 180,000	$ 180,000	$ 180,000	$ 180,000	$ 720,000
Operating income	$ 950,000	$1,091,250	$1,232,500	$ 950,000	$4,223,750
Income taxes (34%)	323,000	371,025	419,050	323,000	1,436,075
Net income	$ 627,000	$ 720,225	$ 813,450	$ 627,000	$2,787,675

*Calculated by multiplying variable manufacturing costs by sales units.

9. Cash budget prepared:

Tech Corporation
Cash Budget
For the Year Ended December 31, 19x9

	Quarter 1	Quarter 2	Quarter 3	Quarter 4	Year
Cash balance, beginning	$ 150,000	$ 472,185	$1,142,595	$1,963,595	$ 150,000
Cash receipts	+1,600,000	+2,175,000	+2,425,000	+2,150,000	+8,350,000
Total cash available	$1,750,000	$2,647,185	$3,567,595	$4,113,595	$8,500,000
Cash payments for					
Direct materials purchases	$ 97,940	$ 87,940	$ 91,200	$ 83,920	$ 361,000
Direct labor	251,250	348,750	352,500	300,000	1,252,500
Manufacturing overhead	185,625	234,375	236,250	210,000	866,250
Selling and administrative expenses	420,000	462,500	505,000	420,000	1,807,500
Income taxes	323,000	371,025	419,050	323,000	1,436,075
Total cash payments	$1,277,815	$1,504,590	$1,604,000	$1,336,920	$5,723,325
Cash balance, ending	$ 472,185	$1,142,595	$1,963,595	$2,776,675	$2,776,675

10. Budgeted balance sheet prepared:

Tech Corporation Budgeted Balance Sheet by Quarter December 31, 19x9				
	Quarter 1	Quarter 2	Quarter 3	Quarter 4
Assets				
Cash	$ 472,185	$1,142,595	$1,963,595	$2,776,675
Accounts receivable	600,000	675,000	750,000	600,000
Direct materials inventory	27,900	28,200	24,000	24,000
Finished goods inventory	178,875	198,750	159,000	159,000
Plant and equipment	1,000,000	1,000,000	1,000,000	1,000,000
Accumulated depreciation	(390,000)	(430,000)	(470,000)	(510,000)
Total assets	$1,888,960	$2,614,545	$3,426,595	$4,049,675
Liabilities and Equity				
Accounts payable	$ 31,960	$ 37,320	$ 35,920	$ 32,000
Common stock	600,000	600,000	600,000	600,000
Retained earnings	1,257,000	1,977,225	2,790,675	3,417,675
Total liabilities and equity	$1,888,960	$2,614,545	$3,426,595	$4,049,675

Chapter Assignments

Questions

1. (L.O. 1) Why are planning and control important in business, and how are they related to budgeting?
2. (L.O. 2) What is a master budget? Describe its components.
3. (L.O. 1) What are the advantages of budgeting? How can a budget be used to achieve a company's goals?
4. (L.O. 1) Explain how the budgeting process can coordinate an organization's activities.
5. (L.O. 1) How can the budgeting process motivate managers?
6. (L.O. 2) Briefly explain the interrelationship between the components of an operating budget and a financial budget.

7. (L.O. 3) Describe the methods used to develop a sales forecast. What factors would you consider in selecting a particular method?

8. (L.O. 3) How would you compute the number of units to be produced during the budget period? The amount of direct materials to be purchased during the period?

9. (L.O. 3) What are an organization's objectives when preparing a cash budget?

10. (L.O. 3) How are selling and administrative expenses planned?

11. (L.O. 6) What are the major advantages of using computer simulation models to prepare the master budget?

12. (L.O. 7) Briefly explain how the JIT philosophy has changed the manufacturing environment.

13. (L.O. 7) What is needed to make a JIT inventory system work?

14. (L.O. 7) What are the benefits of a JIT inventory system?

Exercises

15. (L.O. 3) Rookwood Company has budgeted for sales of 42,000 clay pots in December 19x8. Each pot requires three pounds of clay. Beginning inventories and desired ending inventories for clay and pots are given below.

	Dec. 1, 19x8	Dec. 31, 19x8
Clay	100,000 pounds	110,000 pounds
Pots	22,000	24,000

Required

1. Prepare a production budget for the pots.
2. Prepare a purchases budget in pounds for the clay.

16. (L.O. 3) Walsh, Inc., is preparing its cash budget for November. The following information is available on finished goods:

Finished goods at the beginning of November	$180,000
Estimated cost of goods sold for November	900,000
Estimated finished goods at the end of November	160,000
Payments in November for purchases before November	210,000
Payments in November for November purchases	80% of November purchases

Required

1. Calculate finished goods purchases in November.
2. What are the estimated cash payments for finished goods in November? (AICPA)

17. (L.O. 3) Bartell Company's projected cost of goods sold is $4,000,000, which includes $800,000 in fixed costs. Variable costs of goods sold is expected to be 75 percent of sales.

Required Calculate expected sales.

18. (L.O. 3) Greco Company wants to decrease its inventory of 25,000 widgets by 40 percent during 19x9.

Required If budgeted sales are 22,000 Gizmos and each Gizmo requires six widgets, how many widgets must be purchased in 19x9, assuming that there is no change in the level of finished goods inventory?

19. **(L.O. 3)** O'Callaghan Corporation expects the following sales for the year ending June 30, 19x8:

Year		
	Quarter	Unit sales
19x8	First	50,000
	Second	40,000
	Third	25,000
	Fourth	60,000
19x9	First	50,000

Projected finished goods inventory at June 30, 19x7, is 10,000 units. The quarterly ending finished goods inventory should equal 25 percent of the next quarter's budgeted sales.

Required Prepare a production budget in units for 19x8.

20. **(L.O. 3)** Dornoff Manufacturing Company, producers of high-quality stereo components, has budgeted for the sale of 25,000 compact disc players for the year ended December 31, 19xx. Each compact disc player is made up of five component parts. The desired beginning and ending inventories for the component parts and the compact disc players are as follows:

	Jan. 1, 19xx	Dec. 31, 19xx
Component parts	200,000	300,000
Compact disc players	5,000	3,000

Required

1. Prepare a production budget for the compact disc players.
2. Prepare a purchases budget for the component parts.

21. **(L.O. 3)** Harlin Corporation sells its merchandise at 20 percent markup over cost. Seventy-five percent of purchases are paid for during the month of purchase, with the remaining 25 percent paid during the month following purchase. Monthly merchandise ending inventory is projected to be 40 percent of the following month's projected sales in sales dollars. The beginning inventory for the months of September and October are $900,000 and $700,000.

Sixty percent of each month's credit sales are collected during the month of the sale, with the remaining 38 percent collected during the month following the sale. Two percent of sales are assumed to be uncollectible.

Projected sales data are as follows:

Month	Cash sales	Credit sales
September	$600,000	$ 900,000
October	500,000	1,000,000
November	850,000	1,500,000
December	950,000	2,500,000
January	750,000	950,000

Required For each month of the fourth quarter (October–December), prepare:

1. A schedule of cash collections

2. A purchases budget
3. A payment schedule for purchases (see Review Exercise 7–1)

22. (L.O. 3) Smith Manufacturing Company has budgeted the sales of its scuba gear over the next four months as follows:

Month	Sales in units
May	30,000
June	40,000
July	60,000
August	50,000

The company is now in the process of preparing a production budget for the summer months. Past experience has shown that monthly ending inventory balances of finished goods must equal 25 percent of the current month's sales. The inventory at the end of April was 10,000 units.

Required Prepare a production budget for the summer months showing the number of units to be produced each month. (see Review Exercise 7–1)

23. (L.O. 3) Burns, Inc., manufactures state of the art radar detectors. Each radar detector requires two small chips. Each chip costs $5 and is purchased from an outside supplier. Burns, Inc., has prepared a production budget for the radar detector by quarters as shown below:

	19x8				19x9
	First	Second	Third	Fourth	First
Budgeted production (number of units)	5,000	8,000	15,000	10,000	5,000

In order to avoid unnecessary production delays as the result of chip stockouts, inventory policies require that at least 25 percent of the following quarter's production needs must be on hand at the end of each quarter. Three thousand chips will be on hand at the beginning of the first quarter.

Required Prepare a materials purchases budget for chips by quarter and in total for 19x8. Show the budget in both dollars and number of chips.

24. (L.O. 3) Reid Company is budgeting sales of 100,000 units of Product R for September. Production of one unit of Product R requires two pounds of Material A and three gallons of Material B. Actual inventory units on September 1 and budgeted inventory units on September 30 are as follows:

	Actual September 1	Budgeted September 30
Product R	20,000 units	10,000 units
Material A	25,000 pounds	18,000 pounds
Material B	22,000 gallons	24,000 gallons

Required

1. Prepare a production budget for Product R for September.
2. Prepare a direct materials budget in pounds for Material A for September.
3. Prepare a direct materials budget in gallons for Material B for September. (AICPA)

25. (L.O. 3) The sales budget at Betz Company shows the following projections for the year ending December 31, 19x5:

Year	Quarter	Unit sales
19x5	First	60,000
	Second	80,000
	Third	45,000
	Fourth	55,000
19x6	First	60,000

Finished goods inventory on December 31, 19x4, is 18,000 units. The quantity of finished goods inventory at the end of each quarter should equal 30 percent of the next quarter's budget for units sold.

Required Prepare a production budget in units for 19x5. (AICPA)

26. (L.O. 5) Patsy Corporation has estimated its activity for December. Total selling and general and administrative expenses will be $35,500 per month plus 15 percent of sales. Selected data follow:

Sales	$350,000
Gross profit as a percentage of sales	30%

Required Prepare a budgeted income statement for December. (AICPA)

27. (L.O. 5) Enquirer Company has budgeted for the following activity in July:

- Sales are expected to be $300,000. All sales are on credit and are collected in the month of sale. Bad debts are anticipated to be 3 percent of sales.
- Merchandise inventory is $70,000 at the beginning of the month. It is scheduled to increase by $10,000 by month end. Purchases are paid for in the month of purchase.
- All merchandise is marked up to sell at cost plus 50 percent.
- Estimated selling and administrative expenses for the month are $40,000. All expenses are paid for in the month they are incurred.
- Depreciation for the month will be $5,000 (not included above).

Required

1. Prepare a cash budget for the month, ignoring the beginning and ending cash balance.
2. Prepare a budgeted income statement for the month.
(see Review Exercise 7–2)

28. (L.O. 5) Fields Corporation projects it will have the following transactions in 19x4, its first year of operations:

Cash proceeds from issuance of common stock	$1,000,000
Credit sales	2,200,000
Collection of credit sales	1,800,000
Cost of goods sold	1,400,000
Payments for purchases of merchandise and expenses	1,200,000
Payments for income taxes	250,000
Payments for purchases of fixed assets	800,000
Depreciation on fixed assets	150,000

Required Calculate the projected cash balance on December 31, 19x4. (AICPA)

29. (L.O. 5) Clark Company is developing a forecast of cash receipts from credit sales for March 19x4. Credit sales for March 19x4 are estimated at $640,000. Credit sales for January and February were $500,000 each. Clark's history of accounts receivable collections is as follows:

In the month of sale	30%
In the first month after the month of sale	40
In the second month after the month of sale	25
Written off as uncollectible	5

Required Calculate Clark's expected cash receipts from credit sales for the month of March 19x4.

30. (L.O. 5) Fish Corporation is preparing a cash budget for the month of May. The following information has been assembled about merchandise inventories and payments for purchases:

Beginning merchandise inventory	$3,000
Estimated cost of goods sold	2,400
Ending merchandise inventory	70% beginning inventory
Accounts payable, May 1	$2,390

Seventy-five percent of purchases are paid for in the month of purchase; 25 percent in the month following purchase.

Required Calculate cash payments for purchases in May.

31. (L.O. 5) Dilly Company sells all merchandise at a 25 percent markup on its purchase price. Normally, 60 percent of each month's purchases are paid in the month of purchase. The other 40 percent are paid for in the first 10 days of the following month. Merchandise inventories at the end of each month are planned to be 30 percent of the next month's projected cost of goods sold. The beginning inventory for December, however, is only $450,000.

Fifty percent of each month's credit sales are collected during the month of sale. Forty-five percent are collected in the succeeding month. The others are uncollectible.

Projected sales data for selected months follow:

Month	Cash sales	Credit sales
December	$400,000	$1,900,000
January	250,000	1,500,000
February	350,000	1,700,000
March	300,000	1,600,000

Required For January and February prepare

1. A schedule of cash collections.
2. A purchases budget.
3. A payment schedule for purchases. (AICPA)

32. (L.O. 5) Rex Corporation is a retailer who makes all sales on credit. Sales are billed at the end of each month. Based on past experience the collection of accounts receivable is as follows:

First month following the sale	75%
Second month following the sale	23
Uncollectible	2

Sales revenues for April and May 19x9 and the forecast for the next four months are as follows:

April, actual	$450,000
May, actual	500,000
June	600,000
July	700,000
August	700,000
September	500,000

Rex's selling price averages 125 percent of the cost of sales. On June 1, 19x9, inventory is $100,000. Accounts payable for May purchases is $200,000.

Rex purchases merchandise for resale to meet sales demand for the current month and to maintain a desired monthly ending inventory of 25 percent of the cost of sales for next month. All purchases are on credit. Rex pays for one-half of a month's purchases in the month of purchase; the other half in the following month.

All sales and purchases occur uniformly throughout the month.

Required For June, July, and August, prepare the following:

1. A purchases budget.
2. A cash collections schedule.
3. A cash payments schedule for purchases.

33. (L.O. 3) Shields Manufacturing Company has hired you to complete its quarterly cash budgets for the year ending 19x9. A partial cash budget has been started and appears below. The company requires a minimum cash balance of at least $15,000 to start each quarter.

	First quarter	Second quarter	Third quarter	Fourth quarter
Cash balance, beginning	$ 15	$?	$?	$15
Add collections	?	85	90	?
Total cash available	$ 70	$?	$105	$80
Less disbursements				
Purchases	$ 35	$ 30	$?	$40
Operating expenses	?	43	25	?
Equipment purchases	10	25	15	10
Dividends	2	2	2	2
Total disbursements	$?	$100	$ 75	$?
Excess of cash over disbursements	$(20)	$ -0-	$?	$ 8
Financing				
Borrowings	$?	$ 15	$ -0-	$?
Repayment	-0-	?	?	-0-
Total financing	?	$?	$?	$?
Cash balance, ending	$ 15	$ 15	$ 15	$15

Required Fill in the missing amounts (000 omitted).

34. (L.O. 5) Maxwell Company has estimated sales dollars for the first four months of 19x9 as follows:

January	$100,000
February	150,000
March	200,000
April	150,000

The selling and administrative expenses are estimated to be:

Fixed — $20,000 per month ($5,000 is depreciation on delivery trucks)
Variable — 10 percent of sales dollars

Maxwell Company pays 60 percent of the selling and administrative expenses in the month incurred and 40 percent the following month. Accounts payable for selling and administrative expenses at January 1 is $8,000.

Required

1. For January, February, and March:
   a. Calculate the estimated selling and administrative expenses.
   b. Calculate the cash payments for selling and administrative expenses.
2. Calculate the accounts payable for selling and administrative expenses at March 31.

Problems

35. (L.O. 5) Tomlinson Retail seeks your assistance in developing cash and other budget information for May, June, and July 19x3. On April 30, 19x3, the company had $115,000 in cash, $373,080 in net accounts receivable, $238,000 in inventories, $100,000 in net fixed assets, $108,928 in accounts payable for materials purchases, $500,000 in capital stock, and $217,152 in retained earnings.

    The budget will be based on the following assumptions:

    A. **Sales**
       1. Each month's sales will be billed on the last day of the month.
       2. Eighty-five percent of sales will be collected in the month following the sale. Nine percent will be collected by the end of the second month. Six percent will prove uncollectible and an adjustment recognizing the expense will be made in the month of sale.
       3. All sales are credit sales.

    B. **Purchases**
       1. Fifty-four percent of all purchases of materials will be paid in the month of purchase; the remainder in the following month. This policy begins in May.
       2. Each month's units of ending inventory will equal the projected units to be sold in the next month.
       3. The cost of each unit of inventory will be $20.
       4. All purchases are on credit.

    C. **Selling and general and administrative expenses**
       1. Variable selling and general and administrative expenses will equal 15 percent of the current month's sales excluding bad debts.
       2. Fixed selling and general and administrative expenses will be $2,000 per month for depreciation of furniture and fixtures.
       3. Variable selling and general and administrative expenses will be paid in the month incurred.

    Actual and projected sales are as follows on page 334.

19x3	Dollars	Units
March (actual)	$354,000	11,800
April (actual)	363,000	12,100
May	357,000	11,900
June	342,000	11,400
July	360,000	12,000
August	366,000	12,200

Required For May, June, and July

1. Prepare a sales and cash collections budget.
2. Prepare a purchases budget with cash disbursements for purchases.
3. Prepare a selling, general, and administrative expense budget.
4. Prepare a cash budget. Ignore income taxes.
5. Prepare a budgeted income statement. Ignore income taxes.
6. Prepare a budgeted balance sheet as of July 31, 19x3. (AICPA)

36. (L.O. 5) Data from the January 31 balance sheet at Shelpat Corporation are given below.

Assets

Cash	$ 8,000
Accounts receivable (net of allowance for uncollectible accounts of $2,000)	38,000
Inventory	16,000
Fixed assets (net of allowance for accumulated depreciation of $60,000)	40,000
Total Assets	$102,000

Liabilities and Equity

Accounts payable (purchases)	$ 82,500
Common stock	50,000
Retained earnings (deficit)	(30,500)
Total liabilities and equity	$102,000

Sales are budgeted as follows:

January (actual)	$100,000
February	110,000
March	120,000

All sales are credit sales, and collections are expected to be 60 percent in the month of sale; 38 percent the next month. Two percent are assumed to be uncollectible, and the expense is recognized in the month of sale. The gross margin rate is 25 percent of sales dollars. Purchases each month are equal to 75 percent of projected sales dollars for the next month. Purchases are paid in full the month following the month of purchase. Selling and administrative expenses for each month are paid in cash. They are expected to be $16,500 per month. In addition, depreciation each month is $5,000.

Required For February, prepare

1. A sales and cash collections budget
2. A purchases budget, showing cash payments

3. A cash budget; ignore income taxes
4. A budgeted income statement; ignore income taxes
5. A budgeted balance sheet (AICPA)

(see Review Exercise 7–3)

37. (L.O. 3) The balance sheet of the Wiley Manufacturing Company appears as follows:

Wiley Manufacturing Company
Balance Sheet
Year Ended December 31, 19x8

Assets	
Cash	$ 500,000
Accounts receivable	950,000
Inventory	250,000
Plant and equipment (net)	700,000
Total assets	$2,400,000
Liabilities and Equity	
Accounts payable	$ 650,000
Capital stock	1,000,000
Retained earnings	750,000
Total liabilities and equity	$2,400,000

Wiley Manufacturing company has hired you to prepare some budgets for the month of January 19x9. The following information for the month of January has been gathered to assist you in your work:

a. January sales are budgeted at $500,000. Of these sales, 10 percent will be for cash, the remainder will be on credit. Sixty percent of credit sales are collected during the month of the sale, with the remainder collected during the month following the sale. All of the December 31, 19x8, ending accounts receivable will be collected during the month of January.
b. Inventory purchases are expected to total $150,000 during the month of January. All of the inventory purchases will be made on account. Forty percent of all purchases made on credit are paid for in the month of the purchase; the remaining balance is paid in full during the month following the purchase. All of the December 31, 19x8, accounts payable will be paid during the month of January.
c. The ending January inventory balance is budgeted at $300,000.
d. Operating expenses for January are budgeted at $250,000, exclusive of depreciation. The expenses will be paid for in cash.
e. Depreciation is budgeted at $50,000 for the month of January.

Required

1. Prepare a cash budget for the month of January.
2. Prepare a budgeted income statement for the month ended January 19x9.
3. Prepare a budgeted balance sheet as of January 19x9.

(see Review Exercise 7–3)

38. (L.O. 5) Standard Mercantile Corporation is a wholesaler. Its fiscal year ends on December 31. You have been requested in early January 19x4 to help prepare a cash budget and budgeted income statement. The following information on company operations is available:

a. Management believes the 19x3 sales pattern is a reasonable estimate of 19x4 and 19x5 sales. Sales in 19x3 were as shown on the next page:

January	$ 360,000
February	420,000
March	600,000
April	540,000
May	480,000
June	400,000
July	350,000
August	550,000
September	500,000
October	400,000
November	600,000
December	800,000
Total	$6,000,000

b. Accounts receivable on December 31 totaled $380,000. Sales collections are generally made as shown below.

During month of sale	60%
In first subsequent month	30
In second subsequent month	9
Uncollectible	1

c. The purchase cost of inventory averages 60 percent of selling price. The cost of inventory on hand on December 31 was $828,000.

The company wants inventory levels at the first of each month to equal the cost of sales for the next three months. All purchases are paid for on the 10th of the month following purchase. Accounts payable for purchases totaled $370,000 on December 31.

d. Recurring fixed expenses at $120,000 per month, including depreciation of $20,000. Variable expenses (other than the cost of goods sold) are 10 percent of sales.

Payments for expenses are made as follows:

	During month incurred	**Following month**
Fixed expenses	55%	45%
Variable expenses	70	30

Accounts payable on December 31, 19x3, is $45,000 for fixed expenses and $24,000 for variable expenses.

e. Annual property taxes are $50,000, and they are paid in equal installments on December 31 and March 31. These taxes are paid in addition to expenses in item d above. They are apportioned equally to each month's income statement.

f. Cash dividends of $20,000 are expected to be paid on the 15th of the third month of the quarter.

g. During the winter, unusual fixed advertising costs will be incurred, requiring cash payments of $10,000 in February and $15,000 in March. Advertising costs are in addition to expenses in item d above.

h. A $60,000 payment on the 19x3 income tax is due on March 15, 19x4.

i. On December 31, 19x3, the company's bank loan had an unpaid balance of $280,000. The loan requires a principal payment of $20,000 on the last day of each month plus interest of 2 percent per month on the unpaid balance. Interest payments are accrued on the first of the month. The entire balance is due on March 31, 19x4.

j. The cash balance on December 31, 19x3, was $100,000.

Required Prepare a cash budget and a budgeted income statement by month for the first quarter of 19x4. Ignore income taxes when preparing the income statement. The statement should show the amount of cash on hand or the cash deficiency at the end of each month. Round cents to the nearest whole dollar. (AICPA)

39. (L.O. 5) United Business Education, Inc., (UBE) is a not-for-profit organization. It sponsors various management seminars throughout the United States. In addition, it is heavily involved in researching methods to better educate and motivate business executives. The seminars are largely supported by fees; the research program, from members' dues.

UBE operates on a calendar-year basis. It is now finalizing its 19x9 budget. The following information has been taken from approved but somewhat flexible plans:

Seminar Program The scheduled programs should produce $12 million in revenue for the year. Each program is budgeted to produce the same amount of revenue, which is collected in the month the program is offered. Programs are scheduled so that 12 percent of the revenue is collected in each of the first five months of the year. The remaining programs, accounting for 40 percent of revenue, are distributed evenly through September, October, and November. No programs are offered in the other four months of the year. Seminar expenses are composed of three segments.

- Instructors' fees are 70 percent of seminar revenue and are paid in the month following the seminar. Instructors are considered independent contractors and, thus, are ineligible for UBE employee benefits.
- Facilities fees total $5,600,000 for the year. They are the same for each program and are paid in the month the program is given.
- Annual promotional costs of $1 million are spent equally to promote specific programs in all months except June and July, when there are no promotions.

Research Program Many projects are near completion. A main research activity this year includes feasibility studies for new projects next year. As a result, total research expenses of $3 million for 19x9 are expected to be paid during the first six months of the year. The rate of payment is $500,000 per month.

Salaries and Other Expenses An annual amount of $240,000 is paid for the office lease. This amount is paid evenly throughout the year with payments due at the beginning of each month. General and administrative expenses, such as those for the telephones, supplies, and postage, are $1,500,000 annually, or $125,000 a month.

Other Expenses Depreciation expenses are $240,000 a year. General UBE promotional costs are $600,000 annually and payments are made monthly. These costs are in addition to the monthly promotions discussed above. Salaries and benefits are as follows:

Number of employees	Annual salary paid monthly	Total annual salaries
1	$50,000	$ 50,000
3	40,000	120,000
4	30,000	120,000
15	25,000	375,000
5	15,000	75,000
22	10,000	220,000
50		$960,000

Employee benefits are $240,000, or 25 percent of annual salaries. Except for pension contributions, benefits are paid for at the same time as salary checks are issued. The annual pension payment of $24,000, which is based on a rate of 2.5 percent of salaries, is due April 15, 19x9. (This amount is included in total benefits costs of $240,000.)

Other Information UBE has 100,000 members, who pay an annual fee of $100. The fee for the calendar year is invoiced in late June. The collection schedule follows:

July	60%
August	30
September	5
October	5
	100%

The capital expenditures program calls for a total of $510,000 in cash payments to be spread evenly over the first five months of 19x9.

Estimated cash on hand at January 1, 19x9, is $750,000.

Required

1. Prepare a budget for annual cash receipts and cash payments for UBE for 19x9.
2. Prepare a cash budget for UBE for January 19x9. (CMA adapted)

40. (L.O. 3) Barby Company is preparing its annual budget for 19x8. The company manufactures a powerful bug spray called Cicadex. The spray is sold in three-gallon containers. The balance sheet at December 31, 19x7, is shown below.

Barby Company expects to sell each unit of Cicadex for $60 in 19x8. Based on this sales price, estimated sales units by quarter are given below.

Quarter	Estimated sales units
1	50,000
2	55,000
3	35,000
4	60,000
5	60,000

The company expects to collect on 80 percent of its sales in the quarter of sale; 20 percent in the following quarter. All sales are on credit, and no bad debts are expected. Manufacturing requirements for direct materials, direct labor, and variable overhead are presented below the balance sheet, on page 339.

Barby Company
Balance Sheet
December 31, 19x7

Assets	
Cash	$ 350,000
Accounts receivable	150,000
Direct materials inventory (12,000 gallons @ $1)	12,000
Finished goods inventory (9,600 units @ $48)	460,800
Plant and equipment	1,500,000
Accumulated depreciation	(500,000)
Total assets	$1,972,800

Liabilities and Equity

Accounts payable	$ 50,000
Common stock	600,000
Retained earnings	1,322,800
Total liabilities and equity	$1,972,800

Direct materials	3 gallons @ $1 per gallon
Direct labor	1.5 hours @ $20 per hour
Variable overhead	$0.50 per direct labor dollar

Total fixed manufacturing overhead is expected to be $50,000 per quarter. Of that amount, $30,000 is for plant and equipment depreciation.

Management plans production so finished goods inventory at the end of each quarter will equal 20 percent of expected sales in the following quarter. The inventory policy for direct materials states that ending direct materials inventory should equal 10 percent of the direct materials required for the next quarter. The desired ending direct materials inventory for the fourth quarter is planned to be the same as at the end of the third quarter. Purchases of direct materials are 70 percent paid for in the quarter of purchase; 30 percent in the following quarter.

An analysis of selling and administrative expenses indicates the following variable costs to sales relationships:

Sales commissions	5% of sales dollars
Travel	2% of sales dollars
Entertainment	1% of sales dollars

Fixed costs for selling and administrative expenses are anticipated as follows:

Salaries	$15,000
Supplies	15,000
Advertising	30,000

All selling and administrative expenses, direct labor, and manufacturing overhead are paid in the quarter incurred.

Required Barby Company expects to have a 34 percent tax rate for 19x8. Using these data, prepare the following quarterly documents for Barby Company for 19x8:

1. Sales budget
2. Production budget
3. Direct materials budget
4. Direct labor budget
5. Manufacturing overhead budget
6. Ending inventory budget
7. Selling and administrative expense budget
8. Budgeted income statement using the contribution margin format
9. Cash budget
10. Budgeted balance sheet

41. (L.O. 5) Voorhees Hospital provides a wide range of health services in its community. Voorhees' board of directors has authorized the following capital expenditures:

Inter-aortic balloon pump	$1,100,000
CT scanner	700,000
X-ray equipment	600,000
Laboratory equipment	1,400,000
	$3,800,000

The expenditures are planned for October 1, 19x4, and the board wishes to know the amount of borrowing, if any, necessary on that date. Marc Kelly, hospital controller, has gathered the following information to be used in preparing an analysis of future cash flows.

- Billings, made in the month of service, for the first six months of 19x4 are listed below.

Month	Actual amount
January	$4,400,000
February	4,400,000
March	4,500,000
April	4,500,000
May	5,000,000
June	5,000,000

Ninety percent of Voorhees' billings are made to third parties such as Blue Cross, federal or state governments, and private insurance companies. The remaining 10 percent of the billings are made directly to patients. Historical patterns of billing collections are presented below.

	Third-party billings	Direct patient billings
Month of service	20%	10%
Month following service	50	40
Second month following service	20	40
Uncollectible	10	10

Estimated billings for the last six months of 19x4 are listed below. The same billing and collection patterns that have been experienced during the first six months of 19x4 are expected to continue during the last six months of the year.

Month	Estimated amount
July	$4,500,000
August	5,000,000
September	5,500,000
October	5,700,000
November	5,800,000
December	5,500,000

- The purchases that have been made during the past three months and the planned purchases for the last six months of 19x4 are presented in the following schedule:

Month	Amount
April	$1,100,000
May	1,200,000
June	1,200,000
July	1,250,000
August	1,500,000
September	1,850,000
October	1,950,000
November	2,250,000
December	1,750,000

All purchases are made on account, and accounts payable are remitted in the month following the purchase.

- Salaries for each month during the remainder of 19x4 are expected to be $1,500,000 per month plus 20 percent of that month's billings. Salaries are paid monthly.
- Voorhees' monthly depreciation charges are $125,000.
- Voorhees incurs interest expense of $150,000 per month and makes interest payments of $450,000 on the last day of each calendar quarter.
- Endowment fund income is expected to continue to total $175,000 per month.
- Voorhees has a cash balance of $300,000 on July 1, 19x4, and has a policy of maintaining a minimum end-of-month cash balance of 10 percent of the current month's purchases.
- Voorhees Hospital employs a calendar-year reporting period.

Required

1. Prepare a schedule of cash receipts by month for the third quarter of 19x4.
2. Prepare a schedule of cash disbursements by month for the third quarter of 19x4.
3. Determine the amount of borrowing, if any, necessary on October 1, 19x4, to acquire the capital items totaling $3,800,000. (CMA adapted)

42. (L.O. 3) Pantex Corporation has gone through a period of rapid expansion to reach its present size of seven divisions. The expansion program has placed strains on its cash resources. Therefore, the need for better cash planning at the corporate level has become very important.

At the present time, each division is responsible for the collection of receivables and the disbursement for all operating expenses and approved capital projects. The corporation does exercise control over division activities but has attempted to coordinate the cash needs of the divisions and the corporation. However, it has not yet developed effective division cash reports from which it can determine the needs and availability of cash in the next budgetary year. As a result of inadequate information, the corporation permitted some divisions to make expenditures for goods and services that need not have been made or could have been postponed until a later time, while other divisions had to delay expenditures that should have had a greater priority.

The 19x8 cash receipts and disbursements plan prepared by the Tapon Division for submission to the corporate office is presented below.

Tapon Division
Budgeted Cash Receipts and Disbursements
For the Year Ended December 31, 19x8
(000 omitted)

Receipts	
Collection on accounts	$9,320
Miscellaneous	36
	$9,356

Disbursements	
Production	
Direct materials	$2,240
Labor and fringe benefits	2,076
Overhead	2,100
Sales	
Commisions	395
Travel and entertainment	600
Other	200
Administrative	
Accounting	80
Personnel	110
General management	350
Capital expenditures	1,240
	$9,391
Excess of receipts over (under) disbursements	$ (35)

The following additional information was used by the Tapon Division to develop the cash receipts and disbursements budget:

a. Receipts — Miscellaneous receipts are estimated proceeds from the sales of unneeded equipment.
b. Sales — Travel and entertainment represents the costs required to produce the sales volume projected for the year. The other sales costs consist of $50,000 for training new sales personnel, $25,000 for attendance by sales personnel at association meetings (not sales shows), and $125,000 for sales management salaries.
c. Administration — The personnel costs include $50,000 for salary and department operating costs, $20,000 for training new personnel, and $40,000 for management training courses for current employees. The general management costs include salaries and office costs for the division management, $310,000, plus $10,000 for officials' travel to Pantex Corporation meetings and $30,000 for industry and association conferences.
d. Capital expenditures — Planned expenditures for capital items during 19x8 are as follows:

Capital programs approved by the corporation:

Items ordered for delivery in 19x8	$300,000
Items to be ordered in 19x8 for delivery in 19x8	700,000
New programs to be submitted to corporation during 19x8	240,000

Required Present a revised budgeted cash receipts and disbursement statement for the Tapon Division. Design the format of the revised statement to include adequate detail so management can distinguish cash flow from normal operations from other cash flows. Such a statement would be submitted by all divisions to provide the basis for overall corporation cash planning. (CMA adapted)

43. (L.O. 3) Modern Products Corporation is a manufacturer of molded plastic containers. In October 19x8, Modern projected a possible need to borrow funds to continue operations. The corporation began negotiating with a local bank for a $110,000 line of credit. The bank requested a projected income statement and November's cash budget.

The following information is available:

a. Sales were budgeted at 120,000 units for October and December 19x8 and January 19x9. For November 19x8, sales were budgeted at 90,000 units.

The selling price is $2 per unit. All sales are on credit. Past experience indicates that sales are evenly distributed throughout the month and that 50 percent of customers pay the entire billed amount during the month of sale. The remainder pay in the following month.

b. Finished goods inventory on October 1 was 24,000 units. The finished goods inventory at the end of each month is to be maintained at 20 percent of anticipated sales for the following month. There is no work in process.

c. Direct materials inventory on October 1 was 22,800 pounds. At the end of each month, direct materials inventory should be no less than 40 percent of production requirements for the following month. Direct materials purchases for each month are paid in the month following purchase.

d. All salaries and wages are paid on the 15th and last day of that month.

e. All manufacturing overhead and selling and administrative expenses are paid on the 10th of the month after the month in which they were incurred. Selling expenses are 10 percent of sales. Administrative expenses, which include $500 in depreciation for office furniture and fixtures per month, total $33,000 per month.

f. The cost of a molded plastic container is as follows:

Direct materials, 1/2 pound	$0.50
Direct labor	0.40
Variable manufacturing overhead	0.20
Total	$1.10

Fixed manufacturing overhead is expected to be $10,000 per month. This amount includes depreciation of factory equipment of $4,000 per month.

g. The cash balance on November 1 is expected to be $10,000.

Required Prepare the following for Modern Products Corporation:

1. Schedules showing budgets by months for
   a. Units of finished goods to be produced in October, November, and December
   b. Materials purchases in pounds for October and November
2. A budgeted income statement for November, using the contribution margin format. Ignore income taxes
3. A cash budget for November, showing the opening balance, receipts, payments, and balance at month end (AICPA)

44. (L.O. 3) Barker Corporation manufactures and distributes souvenir wood baseball bats. The bats are manufactured at its only plant in Mexico, and shipped to the U.S. on a monthly basis. This is a seasonal business with most sales occurring in late winter and early spring. The production schedule for the last quarter of the year is heavy, since inventory must be built up to meet expected sales volume.

The company experiences temporary cash shortages during this heavy production period. Payroll costs rise in the last quarter because overtime is needed to meet increased production needs. At the same time, collections from customers are low because fall sales are modest. This year the company's concern is intensified. Costs will be even greater than last year because of inflation. In addition, the sales department estimates the company will sell less than 1 million bats for the first time in three years. This sales decrease seems to be caused by the popularity of aluminum bats.

The Cash account builds up during the first and second quarters as sales exceed production. The excess cash is invested in U.S. Treasury bills and similar short-term investments. During the last half of the year, these investments are liquidated to meet cash needs. In the company's early years, short-term borrowing supplemented these funds. However, this has been unnecessary in recent years. Because costs are higher this year, the treasurer has asked for a sales forecast for December. He wants to know if the $90,000 in temporary investments will carry the company through the month and maintain a minimum cash balance of $10,000. Should the $90,000 be insufficient, he wants to negotiate a short-term loan.

The unit sales volume for the past two months and estimates for the next four months are:

Actual unit sales		Estimated unit sales	
October	70,000	December	50,000
November	50,000	January	90,000
		February	90,000
		March	120,000

Bats sell for $3 each. All sales are made on account. Half the accounts are collected in the month of sale. Forty percent are collected in the following month. The remaining 10 percent are collected in the second month.

The production schedule for a six-month period, which begins on October 1, reflects the company's policy of maintaining a stable year-round work force and scheduling overtime to meet production schedules. Shown below is the current production schedule.

Actual units		Estimated units	
October	90,000	December	90,000
November	90,000	January	90,000
		February	100,000
		March	100,000

The bats are made from wood blocks that cost $12 each. Ten bats can be produced from one block. All blocks are acquired one year in advance so they can be properly aged. Barker pays the supplier one-twelfth of the cost of the material each month. The monthly payment is $60,000.

The plant is normally scheduled for a 40-hour, five-day workweek. During the busy season, however, the workweek often increases to six 10-hour days. Workers can produce 7.5 bats per hour. Normal monthly output is 75,000 bats. Producing bats above this level requires overtime. Factory employees are paid $8 per hour, an increase of $1.50 per hour over last year, for regular time. Time and a half is paid for overtime. Employees are paid in the month wages are earned.

Other manufacturing costs include variable overhead of $0.30 per unit and annual fixed manufacturing overhead of $280,000. Depreciation charges of $40,000 are included in fixed manufacturing overhead. Selling expenses include variable costs of $0.20 per unit and annual fixed costs of $60,000. Fixed administrative costs are $120,000 annually. All fixed costs are incurred uniformly throughout the year. All overhead selling and administrative costs are paid in the month incurred.

The controller has accumulated the following additional information:

a. The balance of selected accounts as of November 30, 19x4, is as follows:

Cash	$ 12,000
Marketable securities	
(cost and market value are the same)	90,000
Accounts receivable (net)	81,000
Prepaid expenses	4,800
Accounts payable, direct materials purchases	300,000
Equipment note payable	102,000
Accrued income taxes payable	50,000

b. Interest to be received from the company's temporary investments is estimated at $1,000 for December.
c. Prepaid expenses of $3,600 will expire during December, leaving a $4,200 balance in the prepaid account at the end of December.
d. Barker purchased new machinery in 19x4 as part of a plant modernization program. The machinery was financed by a 24-month note of $144,000. The terms call for equal principal payments over the next 24 months. Interest is paid at the rate of 2 percent per month on the unpaid balance on the first of the month. The first payment was made May 1, 19x4.
e. Old equipment, which has a book value of $8,000, is to be sold in December for $7,500.
f. Quarterly dividends of $0.20 per share will be paid on December 15. Barker Corporation has 7,000 shares outstanding.
g. A quarterly income tax payment of $40,000 is due on December 15, 19x4.

Required Prepare a schedule that forecasts the cash position on December 31, 19x4. What action, if any, is required to maintain a $10,000 cash balance? (CMA)

45. (L.O. 5) Mason Agency, a division of General Service Industries, offers consulting services to clients for a fee. The corporate management at General Service is pleased with the performance of the Mason Agency for the first nine months of the current year and has recommended that the division manager of the Mason Agency, Richard Howell, submit a revised forecast for the remaining quarter, as the division has exceeded the annual plan year-to-date by 20 percent of operating income. An unexpected increase in billed hour volume over the original plan is the main reason for this gain in income. The original operating budget for the first three quarters for the Mason Agency is presented on page 346.

When comparing the actuals for the first three quarters to the original plan, Howell analyzed the variances and will reflect the following information in his revised forecast for the fourth quarter:

- The division currently has 25 consultants on staff, 10 for management consulting and 15 for EDP consulting, and has hired three additional management consultants to start work at the beginning of the fourth quarter in order to meet the increased client demand.
- The hourly billing rate for consulting revenues is market acceptable and will remain at $90 per hour for each management consultant and $75 per hour for each EDP consultant. However, due to the favorable increase in billing hour volume when compared to plan, the hours for each consultant will be increased by 50 hours per quarter. There is no learning curve for billable consulting hours for new employees.
- The budgeted annual salaries and actual annual salaries, paid monthly, are the same at $50,000 for a management consultant and 8 percent less for an EDP consultant. Corporate management has approved a merit increase of 10 percent at

the beginning of the fourth quarter for all 25 existing consultants, while the new consultants will be compensated at the planned rate.

- The planned salary expense includes a provision for employee fringe benefits amounting to 30 percent of the annual salaries; however, the improvement of some corporatewide employee programs will increase the fringe benefit allocation to 40 percent.
- The original plan assumes a fixed hourly rate for travel and other related expenses for each billing hour of consulting. These are expenses that are not reimbursed by the client, and the previously determined hourly rate has proven to be adequate to cover these costs.
- Other revenues are derived from temporary rentals and interest income and remain unchanged for the fourth quarter.
- General and administrative expenses have been favorable at 7 percent below the plan; this 7 percent savings on fourth-quarter expenses will be reflected in the revised plan.
- Depreciation for office equipment and microcomputers will stay constant at the projected straight-line rate.
- Due to the favorable experience for the first three quarters and the division's increased ability to absorb costs, the corporate management at General Service Industries has increased the corporate expense allocation by 50 percent.

Required

1. Prepare a revised operating budget for the fourth quarter for the Mason Agency that Richard Howell will present to General Service Industries. Be sure to furnish supporting calculations for all revised revenue and expense amounts.
2. Discuss the reasons why an organization would prepare a revised forecast. (CMA)

Mason Agency
19x8–19x9 Operating Budget

	First quarter	Second quarter	Third quarter	Total nine months
Revenues				
Consulting fees				
Management consulting	$315,000	$315,000	$315,000	$ 945,000
EDP consulting	421,875	421,875	421,875	1,265,625
Total consulting fees	$736,875	$736,875	$736,875	$2,210,625
Other revenues	10,000	10,000	10,000	30,000
Total revenues	$746,875	$746,875	$746,875	$2,240,625
Expenses				
Consultant salary expense	$386,750	$386,750	$386,750	$1,160,250
Travel and related expense	45,625	45,625	45,625	136,875
General and administrative expense	100,000	100,000	100,000	300,000
Depreciation expense	40,000	40,000	40,000	120,000
Corporate allocation	50,000	50,000	50,000	150,000
Total expenses	$622,375	$622,375	$622,375	$1,867,125
Operating income	$124,500	$124,500	$124,500	$ 373,500

Case 1
Mayne Manufacturing Co. (L.O. 3)

Mayne Manufacturing Co. has incurred substantial losses for several years and has become insolvent. On March 31, 19x5, Mayne petitioned the court for protection from creditors, and submitted the following statement of financial position:

Mayne Manufacturing Co.
Statement of Financial Position
March 31, 19x5

	Book value	Liquidation value
Assets		
Accounts receivable	$100,000	$ 50,000
Inventories	90,000	40,000
Plant and equipment	150,000	160,000
Total assets	$340,000	$250,000
Liabilities and Equity		
Accounts payable — general creditors	$600,000	
Common stock outstanding	60,000	
Deficit	(320,000)	
Total liabilities and equity	$340,000	

Mayne's management informed the court that the company has developed a new product, and that a prospective customer is willing to sign a contract for the purchase of 10,000 units of this product during the year ending March 31, 19x6; 12,000 units of this product during the year ending March 31, 19x7; and 15,000 units of this product during the year ending March 31, 19x8, at a price of $90 per unit. This product can be manufactured using Mayne's present facilities. Monthly production with immediate delivery is expected to be uniform within each year. Receivables are expected to be collected during the calendar month following sales.

Unit production costs of the new product are expected to be as follows:

Direct materials	$20
Direct labor	30
Variable overhead	10

Fixed costs (excluding depreciation) will amount to $130,000 per year.

Purchases of direct materials will be paid during the calendar month following purchase. Fixed costs, direct labor, and variable overhead will be paid as incurred. Inventory of direct materials will be equal to 60 days' usage. After the first month of operations, 30 days' usage of direct materials will be ordered each month.

The general creditors have agreed to reduce their total claims to 60 percent of their March 31, 19x5, balances, under the following conditions:

- Existing accounts receivable and inventories are to be liquidated immediately, with the proceeds turned over to the general creditors.
- The balance of reduced accounts payable is to be paid as cash is generated from future operations, but in no event later than March 31, 19x7. No interest will be paid on these obligations.

Under this proposed plan, the general creditors would receive $110,000 more than the current liquidation value of Mayne's assets. The court has engaged you to determine the feasibility of this plan.

Required Ignoring any need to borrow and repay short-term funds for working capital purposes, prepare a cash budget for the years ending March 31, 19x6 and 19x7, showing the cash expected to be available to pay the claims of the general creditors, payments to general creditors, and the cash remaining after payment of claims. (AICPA)

Case 2
Prime Time Court Club (L.O. 5)

Prime Time Court Club (PTCC) has been in business for five years. The club has experienced cash flow problems each year, especially in the summer when court use is quite low and new membership sales are insignificant. Temporary loans have been obtained from the local bank to cover the summer shortages. Additional permanent capital has also been invested by the owners.

The owners and the bank have decided some action needs to be taken at this time to improve PTCC's net cash flow position. They would like to review a quarterly cash budget based upon a revised fee structure that hopefully would increase club revenues. The purpose of the cash budget would be to better anticipate both the timing and amounts of the probable cash flow of the club and to determine if the club can survive.

John Harper, club manager, recommended that the membership dues be increased and that the hourly court time fees be replaced with a monthly charge for unlimited court use. He believes that this plan will increase membership and that the cash flow and timing problem should be reduced. The proposed fee schedule, which is consistent with rates at other clubs, is presented on the next page. In his opinion, the proportions of the different membership categories should not change, but the total number of members will increase by 10 percent.

Court use will also increase an estimated 20 percent as a result of this new program. The pattern of use throughout the year is not expected to change.

The present fee structure, the distribution among membership categories, and the projected 19x3 operating data including membership status, court usage, and estimated operating costs are presented below.

Proposed Fee Schedule

Membership category	Annual membership fees	Monthly court charges
Individual	$ 75	$10
Youth	45	8
Family	150	18

Present Fee Structure

Annual membership dues	
Individual	$ 45
Youth	30
Family	100
Court time fees	
Prime	$10 per hour
Regular	6 per hour

Membership distribution

Individual	50%
Youth	20
Family	30
	100%

Projected Operating Data

Quarter	Membership renewal or new memberships	Court time in hours: Prime	Court time in hours: Regular	Costs: Fixed costs*	Costs: Variable costs
1	600	5,500	6,000	$ 56,500	$ 57,500
2	200	2,000	4,000	56,500	30,000
3	200	1,000	2,000	56,500	15,000
4	600	5,500	6,000	56,500	57,500
	1,600			$226,000	$160,000

*Includes a quarterly depreciation charge of $12,500.

Required

1. Construct a quarterly cash budget for one year for PTCC assuming the new fee structure is adopted and John Harper's estimates of increases in membership and court use occur. Assume a new member increase of 10 percent per quarter. Assume that monthly court charges are based on a total of 1,760 members.
2. Will John Harper's proposal solve the summer cash shortfall problem? Explain your answer.
3. Will John Harper's proposal support a conclusion that the club can become profitable and survive in the long-run? Explain your answer. (CMA)

Case 3
Molid Company (L.O. 3)

Molid Company was founded by Mark Dalid three years ago. The company produces a modulation-demodulation unit (modem) for use with minicomputers and microcomputers. Business has expanded rapidly since the company's inception.

Bob Wells, the company's general accountant, prepared a budget for the fiscal year ending August 31, 19x6. The budget was based on the prior year's sales and production activity because Dalid believed that the sales growth experienced during the prior year would not continue at the same pace. The budgeted statements of income and cost of goods sold that were prepared as part of the budget process are presented below.

Molid Company
Budgeted Statement of Income
For the Year Ending August 31, 19x6
($000 omitted)

Net sales		$31,248
Cost of goods sold		20,765
Gross profit		$10,483
Operating expenses		
Marketing	$3,200	
General and administrative	2,200	5,400
Income from operations before income taxes		$ 5,083

Molid Company
Budgeted Statement of Cost of Goods Sold
For the Year Ending August 31, 19x6
($000 omitted)

Direct materials		
Materials inventory, 9/1/x5	$ 1,360	
Materials purchased	14,476	
Materials available for use	$15,836	
Materials inventory, 8/31/x6	1,628	
Direct materials consumed		$14,208
Direct labor		1,134
Factory overhead		
Indirect materials	$ 1,421	
General factory overhead	3,240	4,661
Cost of goods manufactured		$20,003
Finished goods inventory, 9/1/x5		1,169
Cost of goods available for sale		$21,172
Finished goods inventory, 8/31/x6		407
Cost of goods sold		$20,765

On December 10, 19x5, Dalid and Wells met to discuss the first quarter operating results (i.e., results for the period September 1–November 30, 19x5). Wells believed that several changes should be made to the original budget assumptions that had been used to prepare the budgeted statements. Wells prepared the following notes that summarized the changes that did not become known until the first quarter results had been compiled. The following data was submitted to Dalid:

- The estimated production in units for the fiscal year should be revised upward from 162,000 units to 170,000 units with the balance of production being scheduled in equal segments over the last nine months of the fiscal year. Actual first quarter production was 35,000 units.
- The planned ending inventory for finished goods of 3,300 units at the end of the fiscal year remains unchanged. The finished goods inventory of 9,300 units as of September 1, 19x5, had dropped to 9,000 units by November 30, 19x5. The finished goods inventory at the end of the fiscal year will be valued at the average manufacturing cost for the year.
- The direct labor rate will increase 8 percent as of June 1, 19x6, as a consequence of a new labor agreement that was signed during the first quarter. When the original budgeted statements were prepared, the expected effective date for this new labor agreement had been September 1, 19x6.
- Direct materials purchases are now estimated at $15,576,000 and the ending materials inventory at $1,709,400.
- On the basis of historical data, indirect material cost is projected at 10 percent of the cost of direct materials consumed.
- One-half of general factory overhead and all of marketing and general and administrative expenses are considered fixed.

After an extended discussion, Dalid asked for new budgeted statements for the fiscal year ending August 31, 19x6.

Required

1. Based on the revised data presented by Bob Wells, calculate Molid Company's projected sales for the year ending August 31, 19x6, in:
   a. Number of units to be sold.
   b. Dollar volume of new sales.
2. Prepare the statement of cost of goods sold for the year ending August 31, 19x6, that Mark Dalid has requested. (CMA)

■

8

Relevant Costs and Management Decisions

LEARNING OBJECTIVES

After studying this chapter you should be able to:

1. Distinguish between recurring and nonrecurring decisions
2. Define relevant cost and sunk cost and explain their roles in decision making
3. Estimate changes in operating income if a special order is accepted
4. Calculate and use relevant costs in a make-or-buy decision
5. Calculate the indifference cost volume in a make-or-buy decision
6. Use relevant cost concepts to decide whether a product line should be added or dropped
7. Decide whether a product should be sold at the split-off point or processed further

Managers must constantly make decisions. They must determine which products the company should produce. How much of each product should be scheduled for production? From which suppliers should the company order materials? In making these decisions, managers must estimate how each decision could affect operating income.

The managerial accountant's role in this process is to supply information on changes in costs and revenues to facilitate the decision process. How does the accountant decide which information to present? As you may recall from Chapter 1, information is relevant to a decision if it will affect whether the decision maker's objectives will be met and if the information differs between alternatives.

■

Recurring and Nonrecurring Decisions

In this chapter the principle of relevance will be applied to a special type of managerial decision, called a nonrecurring decision. **Recurring decisions** are made regularly. For example, each month managers must determine the quantity of products to produce based on expected demand and desired inventory levels. **Nonrecurring decisions** concern situations that occur sporadically and unpredictably. For example,

- A discount house will place a large order with a manufacturer if its normal selling price is reduced. Should the order be accepted?
- A company has been purchasing a part from an outside supplier. Because some of the purchaser's facilities are idle, it could fabricate the part itself. Should the company make or buy the part?
- A major company engages in both food processing and toy manufacturing. The company's directors are dissatisfied with recent performance and are considering selling the toy business. Would the company be better off without the toy division?
- A refining company's processing method produces several intermediate products. Should the company sell all the products as is or process some further?

OBJECTIVE 1
Distinguish between recurring and nonrecurring decisions

Nonrecurring decisions represent opportunities, often unexpected, for management to improve a firm's profitability. The managerial accountant plays a vital role in helping managers meet the challenge of these special decisions. In this chapter some typical nonrecurring decisions will be analyzed. Before studying such analyses, however, you should examine two important cost concepts, relevant costs and sunk costs.

■

Relevant Costs

OBJECTIVE 2
Define relevant cost and sunk cost and explain their roles in decision making

Relevant costs are costs that will affect the accomplishment of a decision maker's objectives and that differ between alternatives. Since revenue as well as expenses can affect operating income, changes in revenue must also be included in any definition of relevant costs. In the discussion that follows, the term **relevant cost** is used in the broad sense, that is, for any change, either in revenue or expenses, that will affect a manager's decision. In many situations only expenses will change. In that case, managers should only compare the expenses of one alternative with the expenses of another. The most profitable decision is the one with the lowest expenses. If a decision will change both revenue and expenses, managers must know the amount of each change to estimate the change in operating income.

The second part of the definition of relevant costs — that they differ for each alternative of a decision — can be best explained with an example. Assume management knows two suppliers from whom they can buy direct materials. If the price is the same for both suppliers, then the price of the direct materials is irrelevant. Regardless of which supplier the manager selects, the price will not change. Thus, in this situation the choice depends on considerations other than price, such as a supplier's relative reliability and financial stability. But had one supplier offered a price of $7.80 per liter and the other $8.00 per liter, the direct materials price would have been relevant. Then, the manager's decision will change the materials price. In this case, the manager will have to consider differences in price along with differences in reliability and financial stability.

That relevant costs can be changed by a manager's decision implies that they are future costs, or costs not yet incurred. That is, they are costs based on management's expectations and not on historical fact. A marketing manager who is considering eliminating a product line must base that decision on the predicted demand, predicted selling price, and predicted manufacturing and marketing expenses. Past costs, except when used to estimate future costs, are not relevant to the decision.

■

Sunk Costs

At first you may have difficulty understanding that costs incurred in the past are irrelevant to current decisions. Costs incurred in prior accounting periods that cannot be reversed are referred to as **sunk costs.** This is because from the manager's viewpoint, the costs are past recovery. For example, assume a farmer plants ten acres of corn, incurring labor and seed costs in the process. The farmer incurs these costs based on expected revenue from selling the corn. Later in the season the farmer must decide whether to fertilize the growing corn. Still later, he must

Exhibit 8–1
Sunk Costs for Machine Replacement

Revenues and Costs	Old machine	Proposed new machine
Original cost	$20,000	$30,000
Book value	9,000	
Remaining life	4 years	4 years
Current disposal value	$ 4,000	
Disposal value in 4 years	-0-	$ -0-
Annual variable operating costs	40,000	30,000
Annual sales revenue	50,000	50,000

decide whether to harvest the corn. He will base his decisions on the expected costs of fertilizing and harvesting and revised estimates of the selling price of the corn. The cost of planting is a sunk cost — an expenditure of resources that cannot be reversed. Sunk costs thus have no economic relevance to the decisions.

Another common example of a sunk cost is the book value of old equipment. Many people think that if a firm has invested resources in equipment, the value of those resources must be recovered before the equipment can be replaced. But book value is irrelevant in a replacement decision. Consider the data in Exhibit 8–1. You can see that by purchasing the new machine and disposing of the old, a firm will report a $5,000 loss, as shown below.

Book value of old machine	$9,000
Less current disposal value	4,000
Loss on sale of old machine	$5,000

Reporting this $5,000 loss could cause some managers to decide that the old machine should not be sold until the investment is recovered.

But Exhibit 8–1 shows that the new machine is more efficient than the old one. It will save the company $10,000 a year in operating costs. And although a manager might like to recover an investment in a machine by using it longer, the investment is a sunk cost. It was incurred in a prior accounting period and cannot be changed. As such it is irrelevant to the decision of whether to purchase the new machine.

When all costs of the two alternatives are listed, the tally looks like Exhibit 8–2. Over a four-year period, replacing the old machine will increase the company's operating income by $14,000 ($45,000 − $31,000). Notice that the book value of the old machine, $9,000, is deducted from operating income regardless of management's decision. If the old machine is kept, the $9,000 is written off as a depreciation. If it is sold, the $9,000 is deducted as a lump-sum write-off. Consequently, the book value of the old machine has no effect on the decision; it does not change, regardless of the alternative selected.

In considering only relevant costs, that is, future costs that will change because of a managerial decision, one can eliminate book value from the compu-

Exhibit 8–2
Analysis of Machine Replacement Alternatives

Revenues and Costs over Four Years	Keep old machine	Replace old machine
Sales revenues	$200,000	$200,000
Variable costs	(160,000)	(120,000)
Contribution margin	$ 40,000	$ 80,000
Depreciation, old machine	(9,000)	
Write-off, old machine		(9,000)
Salvage value, old machine		4,000
Depreciation, new machine		(30,000)
Total operating income	$ 31,000	$ 45,000

tations. The $4,000 that is expected to be received if the machine is sold is relevant. This amount will reduce the reported loss from $9,000 to $5,000, and will have a positive effect on income. Thus, the difference between the two alternatives can be summarized as follows:

Decrease in variable costs	+ $40,000
Disposal of old machine	+ 4,000
Depreciation, new machine	− 30,000
Net increase in operating income	+ $14,000

Sales revenues have been excluded in this analysis because they will not change as a result of the equipment decision. Sales revenues will be $200,000 in either case. Notice, however, that even though the book value of the old machine — a sunk cost — is excluded, depreciation on the new machine is included. It is a future cost that will change. The above method can be used to analyze costs that are associated with any nonrecurring decision. In the following sections you will examine several of the most typical nonrecurring decisions and the relevant costs applicable to each.

■

Special Orders and Capacity Utilization

Quite often companies anticipating future increases in customer demand construct new manufacturing facilities. Such investments are usually well advised even if these firms will have excess capacity for a few years. Building only for current needs means haphazard expansion, which can be more expensive in the long run than planned investments. Another common cause of excess capacity is the transfer of production to foreign countries. To take advantage of lower wages else-

Exhibit 8–3
Budgeted Income Statement Before Considering Special Order

Finn Company Budgeted Income Statement For the Year 19x1 (dollars in thousands)	Total
Sales revenues (300,000 units)	$120,000
Variable expenses	
Manufacturing	$ 72,000
Marketing	30,000
Total variable expenses	$102,000
Contribution margin	$ 18,000
Fixed expenses	
Manufacturing	$ 3,000
Marketing	3,000
Total fixed expenses	$ 6,000
Operating income	$ 12,000

where, many manufacturers import parts from outside the United States, leaving U.S. factories underutilized.

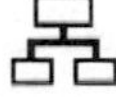

In both cases, managers may be asked to consider accepting a special order for their product at a reduced price to make use of the excess, or idle, facilities. Such orders are worth considering, provided they will not affect regular sales of the same product. To decide whether an order will be profitable at a lower price, managers must isolate its relevant costs.

Consider the position of Finn Company, which has the capacity to manufacture 400,000 videocassette recorders per year. Based on past sales and present trends, Finn expects to manufacture and sell 300,000 VCRs in the coming year at a price of $400 each. Fixed manufacturing costs for the year are expected to be $3 million; variable manufacturing costs, $240 per unit. Annual marketing expenses are expected to be $3 million plus $100 per unit sold. (Exhibit 8–3 summarizes Finn's costs for 19x1).

Projected unit sales for 19x1 leave Finn Company with excess productive capacity of 100,000 units. A discount chain has offered to buy 50,000 recorders if the price is reduced to $300. Because the discount chain approached Finn, Finn has the opportunity to sell many VCRs without time and effort from the marketing staff. Also, the discount chain would pay all shipping expenses. Finn would thus have no variable marketing expenses on this order.

Finn's managers think this special order will not adversely affect sales made through regular marketing channels. The company will sell the 300,000 recorders regardless of whether it accepts the special order. Without the special order, the company expects to earn an operating income of $12 million (Exhibit 8–3). What

Exhibit 8–4
Comparison of Operating Income With and Without Special Order

Finn Company
Comparative Budgeted Income Statements
For the Year 19x1
(dollars in thousands)

	Total without special order	Total with special order	Effect on operating income increase/(decrease)
Sales revenues			
300 × $400	$120,000	$120,000	
50 × $300		15,000	$ 15,000
Total sales revenues	$120,000	$135,000	$ 15,000
Variable expenses			
Manufacturing			
300 × $240	$ 72,000		
350 × $240		$ 84,000	$ (12,000)
Marketing			
300 × $100	30,000	30,000	
Total variable expenses	$102,000	$114,000	$ (12,000)
Contribution margin	$ 18,000	$ 21,000	$ 3,000
Fixed expenses			
Manufacturing	$ 3,000	$ 3,000	
Marketing	3,000	3,000	
Total fixed expenses	$ 6,000	$ 6,000	
Operating income	$ 12,000	$ 15,000	$ 3,000

will be the operating income if the order is accepted? Again, one must ask what the relevant costs are. That is, what revenue and expenses will change because of the special order?

OBJECTIVE 3
Estimate changes in operating income if a special order is accepted

Exhibit 8–4 contains calculations of relevant costs for the special order. In this case, relevant costs are revenues and variable manufacturing costs. Notice that revenues will increase by $15 million (50,000 units × $300 per unit). Variable manufacturing costs will increase by $12 million (50,000 units × $240 per unit). The net result is a $3 million increase in the contribution margin and operating income. Also notice that variable marketing expenses are not relevant. They will be $30 million whether or not management accepts the special order. Fixed expenses are also irrelevant. They are expected to remain unchanged by the special order.

This same information can be shown in abbreviated form by listing only relevant revenues and costs, as in Exhibit 8–5. Only changes in revenues and expenses appear in this type of statement. The choice of which format to use depends on management's preference.

Exhibit 8–5
Effect of a Special Order on Budgeted Operating Income

Finn Company Relevant Revenue and Expenses for Special Order For the Year 19x1 (dollars in thousands)	
Sales revenues (50 units @ $300)	$15,000
Variable manufacturing expenses (50 units @ $240)	12,000
Operating income	$ 3,000

A Common Pitfall: Unit Fixed Costs

As previously stated, total fixed costs were not relevant to Finn Company's decision, since these costs would be the same regardless of the decision. Had Finn's managers been using per unit figures instead of totals, however, they could have been misled, since per unit fixed costs would change.

Without the special order, the fixed manufacturing costs will be $10 per unit ($3,000,000 ÷ 300,000 units). With the special order, the fixed manufacturing costs will be $8.57 per unit ($3,000,000 ÷ 350,000 units). This seeming savings in fixed costs is an illusion, however. Finn Company will incur the same fixed manufacturing costs regardless of the decision. It is the number of units, not the costs, that has changed and that is responsible for the change in per unit costs.

Thus, in analyzing such nonrecurring decisions as special orders, accountants must be careful. They must base their calculations on total rather than unit fixed costs.

Other Factors in a Special-Order Decision

In determining whether to accept or reject a special order, managers must consider factors besides the order's immediate effect on operating income. Finn Company's management believed the special order would have no effect on regular sales. However, were any regular customers to learn of the order, they might demand a similar price. And should some consumers decide to buy from the discount chain instead of Finn's merchandisers, regular sales units would drop.

Federal law prohibits price discrimination, or the quoting of different prices to different customers, unless the difference can be justified by reduced manufacturing or marketing costs to the producer.[1] The law relates only to customers competing for the same product, however. It does not apply to situations in which

[1]The Clayton and Sherman Antitrust Acts and the Robinson Patman Act forbid certain pricing practices unless they are justified by reduced costs. See F. M. Sherer, *Industrial Market Structure and Economic Performance* (Boston: Houghton Mifflin Company, 1980)

idle capacity is used to produce a product in a noncompetitive market or products not regularly produced.

Sometimes companies with idle capacity choose to modify their products slightly so they can be sold under the brand names of discounters. Many durable products sold by national retail chains, from typewriters to washing machines, are manufactured under this type of arrangement.

Review Exercise 8–1

Whether or Not to Accept an Order

Jeri Company manufactures and sells Product J for $40 per unit. At full production capacity, Jeri Company can produce 100,000 units per year. The manufacturing cost per unit at full capacity is shown below.

Direct materials	$ 8	
Direct labor	10	
Manufacturing overhead	12	(50% is fixed)
Total	$30	

Currently Jeri Company is producing and selling 70,000 units of Product J in the domestic market. A foreign distributor has offered to purchase 20,000 units of Product J for $30 per unit. The distribution of the special order would have no impact on the domestic market. There would be no additional selling costs. However, the product would require some modification that would cost $20,000 for the whole order.

Required

Should Jeri Company accept the order?

Solution

Jeri Company
Relevant Revenue and Costs for a Special Order

Sales revenues (20,000 units @ $30)		$600,000
Costs		
Direct materials (20,000 units @ $8)	$160,000	
Direct labor (20,000 units @ $10)	200,000	
Manufacturing overhead (20,000 units @ $6)	120,000*	
Additional modifications	20,000	500,000
Increase in operating income		$100,000

*Manufacturing overhead is 50 percent fixed. The variable portion would be 0.50 × $12 = $6 per unit.

Jeri Company should accept the special order. (see Exercise 23)

■

Make-or-Buy Decisions

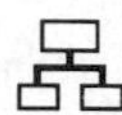

The **make-or-buy decision** is a management decision about whether an item should be made internally or bought from an outside supplier. To put idle capacity to use, firms often consider manufacturing a part or subassembly they are currently purchasing. For example, a major automobile manufacturer might use its idle capacity to manufacture its own bumper shocks instead of buying them from an outside supplier. A watch company might use its idle capacity to produce its own watch bands. Or a company that manufacturers household appliances might fabricate its own electronic components instead of importing them from a Mexican manufacturer.

When these opportunities arise, the managerial accountant is often asked to compare the cost of manufacturing a part internally with the cost of purchasing it. The costs that should be included in such an analysis are relevant costs. For example, assume that Smythe Company is purchasing 20,000 parts from an outside supplier for $17 a part. If the company makes the part internally, the costs will be assigned to the part as follows:

	Cost per part	Total cost, 20,000 parts
Direct materials	$6	$120,000
Direct labor	5	100,000
Variable overhead	3	60,000
Fixed overhead		80,000
Total costs		$360,000

If Smythe's managers simply compare total internal costs of $360,000 with total purchase costs of $340,000 (20,000 parts @ $17), they will undoubtedly decide to buy the part.

OBJECTIVE 4
Calculate and use relevant costs in a make-or-buy decision

Before presenting these costs to management, however, the accountant should look more closely at the individual components and their related amounts that comprise the $80,000 in fixed overhead costs. Assume that $40,000 of the costs represent such fixed costs as depreciation, property taxes, and insurance on the building. The company will incur these costs regardless of whether it makes or buys the part. Thus, these costs are not relevant. The other $40,000 represent costs the firm will incur only if it makes the part. These costs might include supervisors' salaries and other indirect labor costs as well as the cost of special equipment to produce the part. Because these fixed costs are different under each alternative, they are relevant costs.

If you assume the company's only alternatives are to make the part or allow its facilities to remain idle, the accountant's analysis would look like Exhibit 8–6. The relevant cost of making the part is $320,000. This total cost includes direct materials, direct labor, variable overhead, and relevant fixed overhead cost.

In comparison with the $340,000 it would cost to purchase the part, the total manufacturing costs of $320,000 are lower. Careful analysis of the available information shows that Smythe should use its idle facilities to make the part.

Exhibit 8–6
Make-or-Buy Decision — 20,000 Parts Needed

Smythe Company
Make-or-Buy Analysis
For 20,000 Parts

	Make		Buy		
	Cost per part	Total costs	Cost per part	Total costs	Difference make — buy
Direct materials	$ 6	$120,000			$ 120,000
Direct labor	5	100,000			100,000
Variable overhead	3	60,000			60,000
Fixed overhead		40,000			40,000
Outside purchase price	—	———	$17	$340,000	$(340,000)
Total in favor of make	$14	$320,000	$17	$340,000	$ (20,000)

The Effect of Production Volume

The analysis just completed was based on a need for 20,000 parts. Should Smythe's decision change if the needed production level is different? Exhibit 8–7 shows an analysis of Smythe's costs if only 12,000 parts are needed.

Variable costs of producing 12,000 parts are, of course, considerably lower than variable costs of producing 20,000 parts. But relevant fixed costs are the same for 12,000 or 20,000 parts. If only 12,000 parts need to be purchased from an outside supplier, however, the cost of purchasing is significantly reduced. As Exhibit 8–7 shows, the $208,000 cost of making the part exceeds the $204,000 cost of purchasing it. Therefore, Smythe should buy the part if they anticipate a need for only 12,000 parts.

OBJECTIVE 5
Calculate the indifference cost volume in a make-or-buy decision

Since the number of units required is relevant to make-or-buy decisions, an accountant can use cost-volume-profit analysis (see Chapter 6) to determine the production level at which a company will be indifferent to buying or making an item. In other words, he or she can calculate a breakeven volume at which the cost of buying an item equals the cost of making it. This production level is called the **indifference cost volume.**

To find the indifference cost volume, an accountant sets up an equation in which the cost of making a part equals the cost of buying it. In Smythe's case, if the company buys the part from an outside supplier, the purchase cost will be $17X$, with X representing the production volume. The purchase cost per part will be $17. If the company manufactures the part, manufacturing costs will be $40,000 + 14X$.

Exhibit 8–7
Make-or-Buy Decision — 12,000 Parts Needed

Smythe Company
Make-or-Buy Analysis
For 12,000 Parts

	Make		Buy		
	Cost per part	Total costs	Cost per part	Total costs	Relevant cost (difference)
Direct materials	$ 6	$ 72,000			$ 72,000
Direct labor	5	60,000			60,000
Variable overhead	3	36,000			36,000
Fixed overhead		40,000			40,000
Outside purchase price	—	———	$17	$204,000	$(204,000)
Total in favor of buy	$14	$208,000	$17	$204,000	$ 4,000

$40,000 of relevant fixed overhead costs
+ variable manufacturing costs of $14 per part

By equating these two cost functions and solving for X, the accountant gets:

$$\text{Total cost to purchase} = \text{total cost to make}$$
$$\$17X = \$40{,}000 + \$14X$$
$$\$3X = \$40{,}000$$
$$X = 13{,}333$$

The indifference cost volume is 13,333 units.

Figure 8–1 shows Smythe's indifference cost volume graphically. The function for the purchase cost of the part starts at zero and increases at a rate of $17 per unit. The cost function for manufacturing the part starts at fixed cost of $40,000 and increases at a rate of $14 per unit. The two functions intersect at the indifference cost volume of 13,333 units. If expected production volume is below 13,333 units, purchasing the part is the least costly alternative. If expected production volume is above 13,333 units, making the part is less costly.

Other Factors in a Make-or-Buy Decision

Thus far, this chapter has discussed only the quantitative factors in a make-or-buy decision. But as with special orders, qualitative factors sometimes dominate management's thinking. For example, managers may be reluctant to disturb a good relationship with a supplier. Suppliers tend to be more responsive to regular

Figure 8–1

Smythe Company: Indifference Cost Volume

The indifference cost volume is the volume at which Smythe Company is indifferent about making or buying a part because the total cost is the same for either alternative. For Smythe, the equation for the cost to purchase line is Total cost = \$17*X*. The equation for the cost to make line is \$40,000 + \$14*X*.

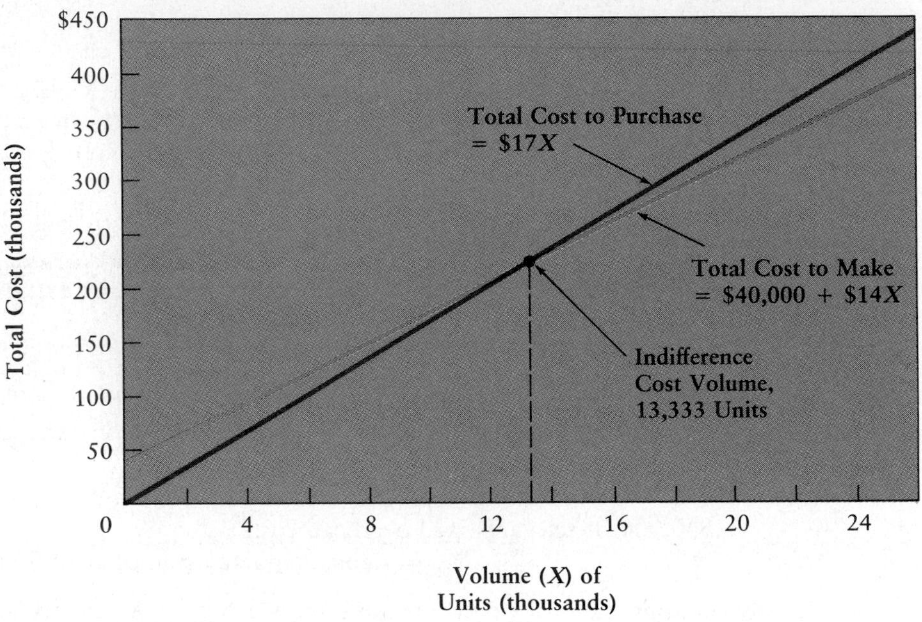

customers. Customers who order parts only when business is good and production levels are high may not get good service. In such cases, buying, even when it is a bit more costly than making the part, may be preferable.

When quality control is the primary concern, the opposite might be true. Managers needing close control over an item's quality might decide to manufacture it regardless of the cost.

Review Exercise 8–2

A Make-or-Buy Decision

Greenspan Company manufactures ten parts for assembly into its final product. A materials supplier, Patterson Company, has offered to provide Part 784 on a daily basis at a price of \$30 per unit. Greenspan Company requires 10,000 units of Part 784 per year. Current costs of manufacturing Part 784 are as follows on page 365.

Direct materials	$ 3
Direct labor	15
Variable overhead	6
Fixed overhead	8
Total	$32

If Greenspan Company accepts the offer from Patterson Company, $5 per unit of fixed overhead can be eliminated.

Required

Should Greenspan Company accept the offer from Patterson Company?

Solution

Greenspan Company
Make-or-Buy Analysis
For 10,000 Units

	Make		Buy	
	Cost per unit	**Total costs**	**Cost per unit**	**Total costs**
Direct materials	$ 3	$ 30,000		
Direct labor	15	150,000		
Variable overhead	6	60,000		
Fixed overhead	5	50,000		
Outside purchase price			$30	$300,000
Total	$29	$290,000	$30	$300,000

Greenspan Company should continue to manufacture Part 784.

(see Exercises 12, 15)

■

Adding and Dropping Products

OBJECTIVE 6
Use relevant cost concepts to decide whether a product line should be added or dropped

Over time, consumers' preferences change. Some products become obsolete and are dropped from product lines. Others are developed to replace them. An important factor in deciding whether to add or drop a product is the decision's effect on operating income. Again, relevant costs are the key to the accountant's analysis.

For example, consider the case of the Burns Drugstore, whose income statement is shown in Exhibit 8–8. Burns carries three product lines: drugs, general merchandise, and cosmetics. Total oper-

Exhibit 8–8
Budgeted Income Statement, Cosmetics Department Included

Burns Drugstore
Budgeted Income Statement
For the Month of January, 19x9

	Drugs	General Merchandise	Cosmetics	Total
Sales revenues	$100,000	$50,000	$50,000	$200,000
Variable expenses	50,000	20,000	24,000	94,000
Contribution margin	$ 50,000	$30,000	$26,000	$106,000
Fixed expenses				
Avoidable	$ 20,000	$16,000	$22,000	$ 58,000
Unavoidable	6,000	6,000	6,000	18,000
Total fixed expenses	$ 26,000	$22,000	$28,000	$ 76,000
Operating income (loss)	$ 24,000	$ 8,000	$ (2,000)	$ 30,000

ating income is $30,000. Cosmetics sales, however, showed a net loss of $2,000. Given the loss on this product line, the owners think it should be dropped.

Perhaps the first question Burns's accountant should ask is which fixed expenses associated with that product line are avoidable and which are unavoidable. An **avoidable cost** is a cost that can be eliminated by ceasing some economic activity or by improving the activity's efficiency. Avoidable costs are relevant costs. For cosmetics, avoidable fixed expenses would include the salaries of employees assigned to that department and advertising expenses specific to that line. These costs are relevant, since they would change if the product line were dropped. **Unavoidable costs** would include such fixed expenses as the store manager's salary, rent, and utilities. These costs are not relevant, for they will continue regardless of whether the line is kept or dropped.

Assume that if cosmetics are dropped, the store space this line now occupies will be idle. No new income will be generated, and $50,000 of sales revenue will be lost. Exhibit 8–9 shows the effects of the decision to drop the cosmetics line. The first column is simply copied from the total column in Exhibit 8–8. It shows the store's operating income if cosmetics are retained. The second column shows financial results if cosmetics are dropped. Figures for total sales revenues, variable expenses, and avoidable fixed expenses in column 1 have been reduced by the amounts specific to cosmetics (column 3 of Exhibit 8–8).

The analysis shows that if cosmetics are dropped, operating income will decrease by $4,000. Although this department showed a loss, it also contributed $26,000 toward payment of its avoidable fixed expenses. Since its avoidable fixed expenses are only $22,000, the remaining $4,000 were used to defray unavoidable fixed costs. That $4,000 will be unavailable if the line is dropped, and it will be

Exhibit 8–9
Decision to Keep or Drop Cosmetics Product Line

Burns Drugstore
Budgeted Income Statement
For the Month of January 19x9

	(1) Keep cosmetics	(2) Drop cosmetics	(1 − 2) Relevant cost (difference)
Sales revenues	$200,000	$150,000	$(50,000)
Variable expenses	94,000	70,000	(24,000)
Contribution margin	$106,000	$ 80,000	$(26,000)
Fixed expenses			
Avoidable	$ 58,000	$ 36,000	$(22,000)
Unavoidable	18,000	18,000	-0-
Total fixed expenses	$ 76,000	$ 54,000	$(22,000)
Operating income (loss)	$ 30,000	$ 26,000	$(4,000)

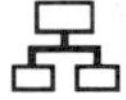

deducted from revenues of the other two lines. For this reason, Burns should not drop the product line unless a more profitable use can be found for the space it now occupies.

■

Sell-or-Process-Further Decisions

In some industries, several products are produced from one material. For example, the cracking of crude oil yields gasoline, kerosene, heating oil, and other oil-based products. Although the relative proportions can be changed by altering how the crude oil is processed, none can be entirely eliminated. Products produced from a common input are referred to as **joint products.**

The point in the manufacturing process at which separate products are identifiable and can be separately processed or sold is called the **split-off point.** Costs incurred before the split-off point benefit all products and are called **joint costs.** Costs incurred after the split-off point for the benefit of only one product are called **separable costs.** For example, in lumber processing, the cost of the trees, the direct labor, and the overhead needed to rough-saw the trees into boards, planks, and beams are joint costs. Once the trees have been processed into separate products, the direct labor and overhead needed to finish processing them are considered separable cost.

Figure 8–2
Joint Costs and Separable Costs in a Lumber Mill
Costs incurred before the split-off point are joint costs for rough sawing the trees into planks and beams. Cost incurred after the split-off point are separable costs traceable to a single product.

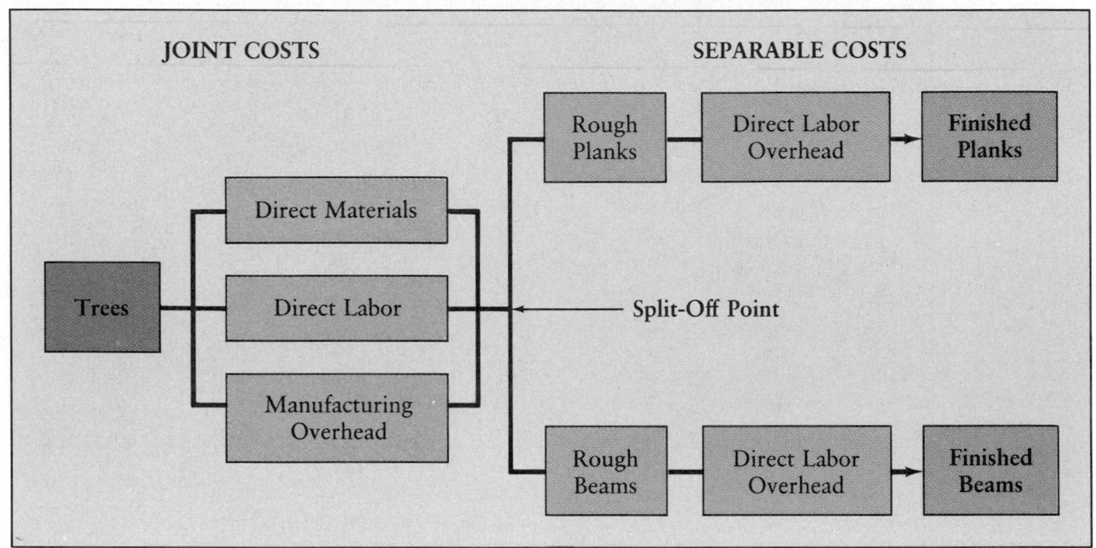

Figure 8–2 summarizes the relationship of joint costs and separable costs. Once materials have been split between the products, managers must decide whether to market each product as is or process it further. The question in this **sell-or-process-further decision** is whether the additional cost of processing can be justified by the greater revenues earned. For example, will the added revenue from selling leather gloves cover the expense of making gloves from the cowhides, rather than selling them to shoe manufacturers? The answer to this question depends on market conditions. If the demand for leather gloves rises or falls, managers should reevaluate their decision.

OBJECTIVE 7
Decide whether a product should be sold at the split-off point or processed further

Relevant costs in such decisions are the cost of processing beyond the split-off point and the resulting added revenues. Joint costs, or costs incurred before the separation point, are not relevant. Consider the following example. Nutt Company incurs joint costs of $5,000 to process 2,000 gallons of material. At the split-off point, the process yields 900 gallons of Product A and 1,100 gallons of Product B. Product A is processed further at a cost of $2 a gallon. It sells for $8 a gallon. Product B requires no additional processing. It sells for $4 a gallon (Figure 8–3).

The total operating income from the two products, $4,800, is shown in the income statement in Exhibit 8–10. Notice that all separable processing costs are deducted from Product A's revenues, whereas joint costs are deducted from com-

Figure 8–3
Joint Costs and Separable Costs for Products A and B at Nutt Company

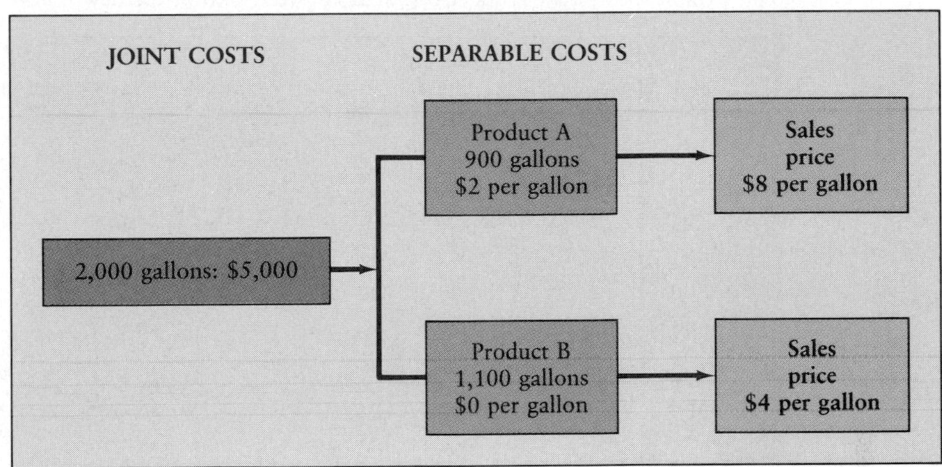

bined revenues. Thus, managers can see the contribution from each product once relevant costs are subtracted.

Now, assume a new market has been identified for Product B. The selling price in this market is $5 a gallon. Additional processing costs are $0.30 a gallon. Should the company enter the new market? Exhibit 8–11 shows that operating income will increase by $770 if Product B is processed further. To reach this conclusion, one must revise the company's income statement or consider only revenues and costs relevant to further processing. Both methods are shown in the

Exhibit 8–10
Income Statement

Nutt Company
Income Statement
For the Month of March 19x9

	Product A	Product B	Total
Sales revenues			
900 gallons × $8	$7,200		
1,100 gallons × $4		$4,400	$11,600
Separable costs			
900 gallons × $2	1,800		1,800
Contribution to joint costs	$5,400	$4,400	$ 9,800
Joint costs			5,000
Operating income			$ 4,800

Exhibit 8–11
Revised Income Statement
This exhibit shows that Product B should be processed for the new market.

Nutt Company
Revised Income Statement
For the Month of March 19x9

	Product A	Product B	Total
Sales revenues			
900 gallons × $8	$7,200		
1,100 gallons × $5		$5,500	$12,700
Separable costs			
900 gallons × $2	1,800		
1,100 gallons × $0.30		330	2,130
Contribution to joint costs	$5,400	$5,170	$10,570
Joint costs			5,000
Operating income			$ 5,570

Additional income from Product B	Per unit	Total (1,100 gallons)
Additional revenues ($5 − $4)	$1.00	$1,100
Separable costs	0.30	330
Additional income	$0.70	$ 770

exhibit. The point to remember is that joint costs are irrelevant in a sell-or-process-further decision. They will not change regardless of what the company does with Product B.

Review Exercise 8–3

A Sell-or-Process-Further Decision

From a joint process, Allen Company produces Products 311, 312, and 313. Each product can be sold at the split-off point or processed further. During 19xx, Allen company processed all of the products beyond the split-off point. The additional processing costs are all variable and traceable to each product. The joint production costs for 19xx amounted to $160,000. The sales value at the split-off point, additional processing costs, and sales value after additional processing are given below.

	Product		
	311	312	313
Units produced	12,000	8,000	4,000
Sales value at split-off	$60,000	$32,000	$40,000
Additional costs and sales value if processed further			
Additional costs	24,000	8,000	12,000
Sales value	78,000	48,000	60,000

Required

To maximize profits, which products should Allen Company process further?

Solution

	Product		
	311	312	313
Sales value with additional processing	$78,000	$48,000	$60,000
Sales value at split-off	60,000	32,000	40,000
Additional revenues	$18,000	$16,000	$20,000
Additional costs	24,000	8,000	12,000
Additional income (loss)	$(6,000)	$ 8,000	$ 8,000

Product 311 should not be processed further, Product 312 should be processed further, and Product 313 should be processed further.

(see Exercises 18, 19)

■

Chapter Review

Review of Learning Objectives

1. **Distinguish between recurring and nonrecurring decisions.**
Recurring decisions are made regularly, whereas nonrecurring decisions are made sporadically. The managerial accountant's role in a nonrecurring decision is to estimate the effect each alternative has on profits by using the concept of relevant cost.

2. **Define relevant cost and sunk cost and explain their roles in decision making.**
   Relevant costs are future costs that will affect whether a decision maker's objectives are met and that differ between alternatives. Here, the term *cost* is used to mean revenue as well as costs that will change with the decision. A sunk cost is a cost incurred in a prior accounting period. Thus, it cannot be reversed. Therefore, sunk costs are irrelevant to managerial decisions, since the costs will remain unchanged regardless of the decision.

3. **Estimate changes in operating income if a special order is accepted.**
   Most nonrecurring decisions concern the use of idle plant capacity. Sometimes managers will accept a special order at a reduced price in order to use idle capacity if regular sales will be unaffected. The relevant costs of accepting or rejecting a special order are the additional revenue from the order and costs of filling the order. Often, some fixed costs and some marketing costs will not be relevant. Relevant costs are deducted from relevant revenue to determine how operating income will change.

4. **Calculate and use relevant costs in a make-or-buy decision.**
   Sometimes companies will consider using idle space to produce parts they usually buy. Again, such decisions should be based on how relevant costs will affect operating income. The managerial accountant should compare the relevant costs of making an item internally with the costs of purchasing it. Often, some fixed costs are not relevant. In addition, qualitative factors must be considered.

5. **Calculate the indifference cost volume in a make-or-buy decision.**
   When a fixed cost is relevant to a make-or-buy decision, the number of units required is a factor. The indifference cost volume is the production level at which the cost of making an item is equal to the cost of buying it. It is found by setting up an equation in which the cost of making an item equals the cost of buying it. The indifference cost volume (production volume) is then calculated.

6. **Use relevant cost concepts to decide whether a product line should be added or dropped.**
   As consumer preferences change, products may be added or dropped from a company's product line. When analyzing the effects of such changes, the managerial accountant must identify the relevant costs of the decision, including fixed costs. Costs may be classified as either avoidable or unavoidable. Avoidable costs are those that will not be incurred if a product line is eliminated. Unavoidable costs are those that will be incurred regardless of whether or not the product line is dropped.

7. **Decide whether a product should be sold at the split-off point or processed further.**
   Some manufacturing processes yield more than one product. At the split-off point, some products may be sold as is, whereas others may be processed further. The relevant costs in a sell-or-process-further decision include the added costs and added revenue of processing further. Joint processing costs, or costs incurred before the split-off point, are not relevant.

Review of Key Terms

Avoidable cost A cost that can be eliminated by ceasing some economic activity or by improving the activity's efficiency. Avoidable costs are relevant costs.

Indifference cost volume The production level at which the cost of making an item equals the cost of buying it.

Joint cost Costs incurred before the split-off point benefit all products.

Joint products Products produced from a common input.

Make-or-buy decision A management decision about whether an item should be made internally or bought from an outside supplier.

Nonrecurring decisions Decisions concerning situations that occur sporadically and unpredictably.

Recurring decisions Decisions made regularly.

Relevant costs Costs that will affect the accomplishment of a decision maker's objectives and that differ between alternatives. Broadly speaking, any change in revenue or expenses that will affect a manager's decision.

Sell-or-process-further decision A decision between selling a product as is or processing it further.

Separable costs Costs incurred after the split-off point for the benefit of only one product.

Split-off point The point in the manufacturing process at which separate products are identifiable and can be separately processed or sold.

Sunk costs Costs incurred in a prior accounting period that cannot be reversed.

Unavoidable costs Costs that will continue regardless of whether the economic activity is eliminated.

Review Problem 1

Bell Company must decide whether to make or buy subassembly XYZ. Although Bell's idle equipment could be used to produce up to 15,000 units of the subassembly, the company presently needs only 10,000 units. A cost analyst has prepared the following estimates on making the subassembly:

Annual additional setup and maintenance costs	$30,000 per year
Allocated general manufacturing overhead	20,000
Depreciation on existing equipment	40,000
Total fixed costs	$90,000 per year
Direct materials costs	$ 4 per unit
Direct labor	6
Variable overhead	6
Total variable costs	$16 per unit

Tracy Manufacturing Company is willing to sell Bell the subassembly for $20 per unit.

Required

1. Should Bell Company make or buy the subassembly?
2. At what volume would Bell Company be indifferent to making or buying the subassembly?

Solution to Review Problem 1

1. First, the relevant cost of each alternative must be determined. To calculate the relevant cost of buying, multiply the $20 per unit by the number of units needed. The variable manufacturing cost per unit multiplied by the number of units needed is a relevant cost. The additional setup and maintenance costs are also relevant. The allocated general manufacturing overhead and the depreciation on current equipment are not relevant, since they will remain unchanged regardless of whether the part is made.

   The calculations are as follows:

Make the Subassembly	
Setup costs	$ 30,000
Variable costs	
$16 × 10,000	160,000
Total	$190,000

Buy the Subassembly	
$20 × 10,000	$200,000

   Bell Company should make the subassembly.

2. Calculation of the indifference cost volume:

$$\text{Total cost to purchase} = \text{total cost to make}$$
$$X = \text{number of units required}$$
$$\$20X = \$30{,}000 + \$16X$$
$$\$4X = \$30{,}000$$
$$X = \underline{\underline{7{,}500}}$$

Review Problem 2

Assume that with Marlo Company's manufacturing process, 5 gallons of input processed in Department A yields 3 gallons of Product X and 2 gallons of Product Y. Only 40,000 gallons of input are available each month.

The fixed operating costs of Department A are $100,000 per month. The variable operating costs in Department A are $1 per gallon processed. This includes the cost of materials.

Product X can be sold at the split-off point for $4 per gallon or processed further in Department B. Processing further costs $3 per gallon, but the product can then be sold for $8 per gallon.

Product Y can be sold for $4 at the split-off point. If processed further in Department C at a cost of $2 per gallon, it can be sold for $5 per gallon.

Required

1. Should Product X or Product Y be sold at the split-off point or processed further and then sold?
2. Based on your answer to *1* above, prepare a monthly income statement for Marlo Company. Remember that only 40,000 gallons of input are available.

Solution to Review Problem 2

1. Calculations for the sell-or-process-further decision are shown below.

Product X

Additional revenue per unit ($8 − $4)	$4
Less separable costs per unit in Department B	3
Equals additional profit per unit	$1

Product X should be processed further, since further processing makes it a more profitable product.

Product Y

Additional revenue per unit ($5 − $4)	$1
Less separable costs per unit in Department C	2
Equals additional losses per unit	$(1)

Product Y should be sold at the split-off point, since further processing will have a negative effect on income.

2. Because only 40,000 gallons of input are available, the maximum yield in department A is 24,000 gallons of X (40,000 × 3/5) and 16,000 gallons of Y (40,000 × 2/5). Calculations for the monthly income statement are as follows:

Marlo Company
Income Statement
For One Month

Product X		Product Y		Total
Sales, 24,000 gallons × $8 =	$192,000	16,000 gallons × $4 =	$64,000	$256,000
Separable costs, 24,000 gallons × $3 =	72,000		-0-	72,000
Contribution to joint costs	$120,000		$64,000	$184,000
Joint costs, $100,000 + ($1 × 40,000 gallons) =				140,000
Operating income				$ 44,000

Notice that nowhere in the analysis were joint costs for Products X and Y relevant. The relevant costs in deciding to sell the products at the split-off point or to process them further included only additional revenue and additional costs. However, joint costs are used when preparing the income statement.

Chapter Assignments

Questions

1. (L.O. 1) What is a nonrecurring decision? Give examples different from those given in the text.
2. (L.O. 2) Define a relevant cost and discuss its two major characteristics.
3. (L.O. 2) Define a sunk cost. When is a sunk cost relevant to a decision?
4. (L.O. 3) How does the cost of idle capacity influence the acceptance or rejection of a special order?
5. (L.O. 3) What qualitative factors influence a special-order decision?
6. (L.O. 5) Explain when production volume can change a make-or-buy decision.
7. (L.O. 4) What qualitative factors influence a make-or-buy decision?
8. (L.O. 6) Distinguish between avoidable and unavoidable costs.
9. (L.O. 7) What is the split-off point for joint products?
10. (L.O. 7) What role do joint costs play in a sell-or-process-further decision?

Exercises

11. (L.O. 2) Lawlwer Company wants to purchase a new production machine to replace the outdated version it currently owns. The new machine will decrease direct materials cost by 20 percent. Other production costs will not change. Listed below are several costs incurred by the Lawlwer Company.

    Direct labor
    Direct materials
    Variable production overhead
    Fixed production overhead
    Variable selling and administrative expenses
    Fixed selling and administrative expenses
    Book value of old machine
    Market value of old machine
    Market value of new machine

Required Indicate which of the costs are relevant for the purchase decision.

12. (L.O. 4) Jones Company manufactures widgets to use in the production of Product X. The cost per 100,000 widgets follows:

Direct materials	$ 2
Direct labor	20
Variable overhead	5
Fixed overhead	10
Total	$37

Jones Company is in the process of accepting bids from outside widget manufacturers. If Jones accepts the best proposal, they will be able to purchase the widgets in lots of 100,000 for $35 each. Outside purchases of the widgets will eliminate all related variable costs. However, 40 percent of total fixed costs will still be incurred.

Required Determine if Jones should accept this proposal and discontinue the manufacturing of widgets or continue to produce the widgets. (see Review Exercise 8–2)

13. (L.O. 1, 2, 3) Lantern Corporation has 1,000 obsolete lanterns. They are carried in inventory at a manufacturing cost of $20,000. If the lanterns are remachined for $5,000, they can be sold for $9,000. If the lanterns are scrapped, they can be sold for $1,000.

Required
1. Which alternative is more desirable?
2. What are the total relevant costs for each alternative? (AICPA)

14. (L.O. 4, 5) Kingston Company needs 10,000 units of a part for one of its products. Kingston will have no other use for the production equipment if it buys the part from Utica Company instead of making it. Sixty percent of fixed overhead will continue regardless of the decision. Kingston's per unit costs of processing 10,000 parts are as follows:

Cost to Kingston to make the part	
Direct materials	$ 6
Direct labor	24
Variable overhead	12
Fixed overhead	15
Total	$57

Utica Company is willing to sell the parts to Kingston Company for $53 each.

Required
1. Should Kingston make or buy the part?
2. Calculate the indifference cost volume for Kingston Company. (AICPA)

15. (L.O. 4) Motor Company manufactures 10,000 units of Part M-1, which is used in its annual production process. The following annual costs are reported:

Direct materials	$ 20,000
Direct labor	55,000
Variable overhead	45,000
Fixed overhead	70,000
Total	$190,000

Valve Company is willing to sell Motor Company 10,000 units of Part M-1 for $18 a unit. If Motor decides to accept the offer, facilities presently used to manufacture Part M-1 will be idle. Additionally, $40,000 of the fixed overhead assigned to Part M-1 will be eliminated.

Required Should Motor accept Valve's offer? Why or why not? (see Review Exercise 8–2) (AICPA)

16. (L.O. 4) Golden, Inc., has been manufacturing 5,000 units of Part 10541, a necessary part for one of its products. At this production level the per unit cost of Part 10541 is as follows:

Direct materials	$ 2
Direct labor	8
Variable overhead	4
Fixed overhead	6
Total	$20

Brown Company is willing to sell Golden 5,000 units of Part 10541 for $19 a unit. Golden has determined that the facilities being used to manufacture Part 10541 could be used to manufacture Product RAC. This product would generate a contribution to profit of $4,000. Golden has also determined that two-thirds of its fixed overhead would continue even if Part 10541 were purchased from Brown.

Required Should Golden, Inc., make or buy Part 10541? (AICPA)

17. (L.O. 4) Reno Company manufactures Part 498 for one of its products. The cost per unit for 20,000 units is as follows:

Direct materials	$ 6
Direct labor	30
Variable overhead	12
Fixed overhead	16
Total	$64

Tray Company is willing to sell Reno 20,000 units of Part 498 for $60 per unit. If Reno accepts Tray's offer, $9 per unit in fixed overhead will be eliminated.

Required Should Reno make or buy the part? (AICPA)

18. (L.O. 7) Rockline Company produces two products from common inputs into the manufacturing process. Joint manufacturing costs are $20,000. The sales value of the products at the separation point is given below.

Rock A	$15,000
Rock B	18,000

Each product may be sold at the split-off point or processed further, using the same manufacturing facilities. The additional processing costs and sales value after further processing are given below.

Product	Additional processing costs	Sales value
Rock A	$ 8,000	$35,000
Rock B	10,000	27,000

Required Which product should be sold at the split-off point? Which product should be processed further? (see Review Exercise 8–3)

19. (L.O. 7) Clairson Company manufactures three products from a common input in a joint processing operation. Joint processing costs total $250,000 up to the split-

off point. Joint costs are allocated on the basis of their total sales value at the split-off point. The sales value of the three products at split-off are as follows:

Product 1	$40,000
Product 2	25,000
Product 3	50,000

Each of the products may be sold at the split-off point or processed further. The additional costs incurred if processed further are as follows:

Product	Additional processing costs	Sales value
1	$100,000	$200,000
2	70,000	130,000
3	55,000	100,000

Required Determine which of the three products should be sold at the split-off and which should be processed further. (see Review Exercise 8–3)

20. (L.O. 7) Rowland Paint Company is a major producer and distributor of paint products. The company has 500 gallons of paint base on hand. Management needs to determine if they should sell the base to other paint manufacturers or process it further into enamel and/or latex paints.

If the paint base is sold as is to other manufacturers, the company will make the following profit per gallon:

Selling price — base/gallon	$ 3
Less joint product costs	(1)
Profit per gallon — base	$ 2

If additional processing is done on the paint base, processing costs incurred per gallon will be $3. The latex and the enamel can be sold for $7 per gallon.

Required

1. Determine the incremental profit per gallon when further processing the paint base.
2. Would you recommend that the paint base be sold in its current form to other paint manufacturers or would you recommend it be processed further?

21. (L.O. 5, 7) Chemed Chemical Company manufactures three products from a common input into the manufacturing process. Joint materials, labor, and overhead costs are $80,000. Each product can be sold at the split-off point or processed further at an additional cost. At the split-off point the products can be sold at the following prices:

Product	Sales price
1	$ 8
2	10
3	13

Typically, 10,000 gallons of each product are produced per month. The cost function for additional processing and the sales price for each product after additional processing are given in the following table.

Product	Additional costs	Sales price
1	$1.00 per gallon	$10 per gallon
2	$10,000 + $0.50 per gallon	12 per gallon
3	5,000 + $0.75 per gallon	14 per gallon

Required

1. Which of the products should receive further processing?
2. Which of the products should be processed further if typical production is 5,000 gallons?
3. Calculate the production volume at which management would be indifferent between processing Products 2 and 3 further or selling them at the separation point.

22. (L.O. 3) Wagner Company sells Product A for $21 per unit. If Wagner operates at full production capacity of 200,000 units, its manufacturing costs per unit are as follows:

Direct materials	$ 4
Direct labor	5
Overhead, 2/3 of which is fixed	6
Total	$15

A special order for 20,000 units was received from a foreign distributor. The only selling costs on this order would be $3 per unit for shipping. Wagner has sufficient capacity to manufacture the additional units.

Required

Calculate the price per unit at which the special order would increase operating income by $20,000. (AICPA)

23. (L.O. 3) Jordan Company's yearly budget calls for sales of 400,000 calculators at $40 per unit. Variable manufacturing costs are budgeted at $16 per unit; fixed manufacturing costs at $10 per unit. In March, Jordan received a special order for 40,000 calculators at $18 each. Jordan has sufficient plant capacity to manufacture the additional quantity. However, the production must be done on overtime at an estimated additional cost of $3 per calculator. Acceptance of the special order would not affect Jordan's normal sales, and no selling expenses would be incurred on the special order.

Required

If the special order were accepted, how would it change operating income? (see Review Exercise 8–1) (AICPA)

24. (L.O. 3) The manufacturing capacity at Grater Company is 30,000 units of finished product per year. A summary of operations results for 19x9 is given below.

Sales revenues (18,000 units @ $100)	$1,800,000
Variable costs	990,000
Contribution margin	$ 810,000
Fixed costs	495,000
Operating income	$ 315,000

A foreign distributor wants to buy 15,000 units at $90 per unit during 19x0. Assume all costs in 19x0 will be the same as those in 19x9. If Grater's management accepts this order, the company must reject some orders from regular customers because of its capacity limits.

Required

1. Prepare an estimated income statement for 19x0. Assume Grater Company accepts the order.
2. Should Grater Company accept the order?
3. Discuss any qualitative reasons for Grater's accepting or not accepting the order.

25. (L.O. 4, 5) Moonlighting Company manufacturers stars for use in one of its products. The cost per unit for 10,000 stars is given below.

Direct materials	$ 3
Direct labor	15
Variable overhead	6
Fixed overhead	8
Total	$32

Venus Company is willing to sell Moonlighting Company 10,000 stars at $30 per unit. If Moonlighting Company accepts this offer from Venus Company, all variable costs of manufacturing the stars can be eliminated. Fifty percent of total fixed costs assigned to the stars can also be eliminated. The remaining 50 percent of fixed costs would be incurred regardless of the decision.

Required

1. Should Moonlighting Company accept Venus Company's offer?
2. What would your answer be if 5,000 stars were to be purchased?
3. At what volume of activity would Moonlighting be indifferent to making or buying the stars?
4. Graphically illustrate your answer to 3 above.

26. (L.O. 6) Greenspan Manufacturing Company produces three products, Products X, Y, and Z. Costs relating to these products are as follows:

	Product		
	X	Y	Z
Selling price	$40	$60	$75
Variable expenses			
Direct materials	$15	$25	$23
Direct labor	5	10	22
Variable overhead	2	5	8
Total variable expenses	$22	$40	$53
Contribution margin	$18	$20	$22
Contribution margin ratio	45%	33%	29%

Due to a temporary fluctuation in demand, demand for Products, X, Y, and Z has far exceeded capacity. Management is trying to determine which product(s) they should concentrate on this week in filling back orders. The direct labor rate is $5 per hour, and only 2,500 hours of labor time are available each week.

Required

1. Compute the amount of contribution margin that will be obtained per hour of labor time spent on each product.
2. Which back orders do you recommend the company work on this week?

27. (L.O. 6) Mallady Company manufactures three types of farm machinery, Tractors

A, B, and C. Data on sales and expenses for each tractor for the past six months are as follows (in thousands):

	Tractor			
	A	B	C	Total
Sales revenues	$300	$100	$150	$550
Variable expenses				
Manufacturing and selling	120	25	70	215
Contribution margin	$180	$ 75	$ 80	$335
Fixed expenses				
Advertising, direct	$ 30	$ 15	$ 20	$ 65
Depreciation	20	10	25	55
Salaries	40	35	45	120
Common costs*	27	9	14	50
Total fixed expenses	$117	$ 69	$104	$290
Operating income (loss)	$ 63	$ 6	$ (24)	$ 45

*Common costs allocated on the basis of sales dollars: Tractor A, (300/550) × $50; Tractor B, (100/550) × $50; and Tractor C, (150/550) × $50.

Required Should the production and sale of tractor C be continued? Show computations to support your answer.

28. (L.O. 5, 7) E-Z Clean Corporation produces various cleaning compounds and solutions for industrial and household use. Although most products are processed independently, a few are produced jointly.

Grit 337 is a coarse cleaning powder with many industrial uses. It costs $1.60 a pound to make, and its selling price is $2 a pound. All the Grit 337 that E-Z Clean produces can be sold.

Annually, a small portion of this product is retained for further processing in the mixing department. There, it is combined with several other ingredients to form a paste. This paste, which is then marketed as a silver polish, sells for $4 per jar. The further processing requires $\frac{1}{4}$ pound of Grit 337 per jar. The other ingredients, labor, and variable overhead associated with this processing cost $2.80 per jar. If production of the silver polish was stopped, $5,600 in fixed costs assigned to the mixing department could be avoided.

Required Calculate how many jars of silver polish must be sold to break even on the further processing of Grit 337. (CMA)

29. (L.O. 3) Bodine Company produces a single product that sells for $5. Fixed costs of $60,000 are expected this year. All variable manufacturing and administrative costs are expected to be $3 per unit. In addition, Bodine has two salesmen, who are paid on commission only. The standard sales commission is 10 percent of each sales dollar generated.

Required

1. If Bodine alters its current plans and spends an additional $5,000 on advertising, increases the selling price of its product to $6 per unit, and sells 60,000 units, what is Bodine's operating income?
2. Sorde Company has just approached Bodine about a special, one-time purchase of

10,000 units. Bodine has the capacity to produce the additional units. These units would not be sold by the salesman, so no commission would be paid. Calculate the per unit price Bodine must charge on this order to earn an additional income of $25,000 per year, assuming regular sales are not affected. (CMA)

30. (L.O. 7) From a joint process, Watkins Company produces three products, X, Y, and Z. Each product can be sold at the split-off point or processed further. Additional processing requires no special facilities. Production costs of further processing are entirely variable and traceable to the products. In 19x3, all three products were processed beyond split-off. Joint production costs for the year were $80,000. Sales values and costs needed to evaluate Watkins' 19x3 production policy follows:

	Product		
	X	Y	Z
Units produced	6,000	4,000	2,000
Sales values at split-off	$25,000	$41,000	$24,000
Additional costs and sales values if processed further			
Sales value	42,000	45,000	33,000
Added costs	9,000	7,000	8,000

Required To maximize profits, which products should Watkins process further? (AICPA)

31. (L.O. 3) Gyro Gear Company produces a special gear for automatic transmissions. Each gear sells for $28. The company sells approximately 500,000 gears per year. Unit cost data for 19x3 are presented below.

Direct materials	$6	
Direct labor	5	
Other costs	**Variable**	**Fixed**
Manufacturing	$2	$7
Distribution	4	3

A foreign manufacturer wants to buy 25,000 gears. Domestic sales would be unaffected by this transaction. Were the order accepted, variable distribution costs would increase by $1.50 per gear for insurance, shipping, and import duties.

Required Calculate the sales price at which Gyro would be indifferent to accepting or rejecting the order. (AICPA)

Problems

32. (L.O. 3) Nubo Manufacturing, Inc., operates at 50 percent of capacity. Its annual production of a patented electronic component is about 50,000 units. A company in Yokohama, Japan, wants to purchase 30,000 components at $6 per unit. Nubo has not previously sold components in Japan. Budgeted production costs for 50,000 and 80,000 units of output follow:

	Units	
	50,000	80,000
Costs		
Direct materials	$ 75,000	$120,000
Direct labor	75,000	120,000
Manufacturing overhead	200,000	260,000
Total costs	$350,000	$500,000
Cost per unit	$7.00	$6.25

The sales manager thinks the order should be accepted, even if it results in a loss of $0.25 per unit. He thinks the order could build future markets. The production manager does not want the order accepted, primarily because of the $0.25 per unit loss ($6.00 less $6.25). According to the treasurer's quick computation, the order would actually increase contribution margin.

Required

1. Explain why the cost seemed to drop from $7.00 per unit to $6.25 per unit when budgeted production increased from 50,000 to 80,000 units. Show supporting computations.
2. Explain how each of the following could affect the decision to accept or reject the special order:
   a. The likelihood of repeat sales and/or that all sales would be made at $6 per unit.
   b. Sales are made to customers operating in two isolated markets or to customers competing in the same market. (AICPA)

33. (L.O. 5) FastQ Company, a specialist in printing, has established 500 convenience copying centers throughout the country. In order to upgrade its services, the company is considering three new models of laser copying machines for use in producing high-quality copies. These high-quality copies would be added to the growing list of products offered in the FastQ shops. The selling price to the customer for each laser copy would be the same, no matter which machine would be installed in the shop.

    The three models of laser copying machines under consideration are 1024S, a small volume model; 1024M, a medium volume model; and 1024G, a large volume model. The annual rental costs and the operating costs vary with the size of each machine. The machine capacities and costs are shown below.

	Copier model		
	1024S	1024M	1024G
Annual capacity (copies)	100,000	350,000	800,000
Costs			
Annual machine rental	$8,000	$11,000	$20,000
Actual product costs	0.02	0.02	0.02
Variable overhead costs	0.12	0.07	0.03

Required Calculate the volume level in copies where FastQ Company would be indifferent to acquiring either the small volume model laser copier, 1024S, or the medium volume model laser copier, 1024M. (CMA)

34. (L.O. 3) George Jackson operates a small machine shop. He manufactures one standard product available from many other similar businesses and he also manufactures

products to customer order. His accountant prepared the annual income statement shown below.

	Custom sales	Standard sales	Total
Sales revenues	$50,000	$25,000	$75,000
Materials	$10,000	$ 8,000	$18,000
Labor	20,000	9,000	29,000
Depreciation	6,300	3,600	9,900
Rent	6,000	1,000	7,000
Heat and light	600	100	700
Other overhead	1,800	300	2,100
Total expenses	$44,700	$22,000	$66,700
Operating income	$ 5,300	$ 3,000	$ 8,300

The depreciation charges are for machines used exclusively in the respective product lines. The rent is for the building space that has been leased for ten years at $7,000 per year. The rent, heat, and light, and other overhead are apportioned to the product lines based on amount of floor space occupied.

A valued custom parts customer has asked Jackson if he would manufacture 5,000 special units for him. Jackson is working at capacity and would have to give up some other business in order to take this business. He cannot refuse to produce custom orders already agreed to but he could reduce the output of his standard product by about one-half for one year while producing the specially requested custom part. The customer is willing to pay $7 for each part. The material cost will be about $2.00 per unit and the labor will be $3.60 per unit. Jackson will have to spend $2,000 for a special device which will be discarded when the job is done.

Required Should Jackson take the order? Explain your answer. (CMA)

35. (L.O. 3) Marx Manufacturing Company produces electronic parts. These parts are sold to producers of electronic consumer products. The company production capacity is 500,000 units per year. The books for the year ended 19x8 reflect the following financial information:

Sale price per unit	$5
Variable costs	
Selling	5%
Manufacturing	?
Contribution margin ratio	60%
Fixed costs per year	$500,000

Four hundred thousand units were manufactured and sold during 19x8. Management anticipates that current year sales will closely match those of 19x8.

Required Note: Each of the following cases is independent.

1. Marx Company is preparing a bid to sell 50,000 units to a major consumer electronics manufacturer. If this proposal is accepted, the company will be able to eliminate the normal selling expense. What sales price will management need to charge in order to maintain the normal contribution margin ratio of 60 percent? The variable cost per unit will not change.
2. Marx Company has received a proposal from a major electronics manufacturer to supply 150,000 electronic components. If this contract is accepted, management

knows they will have to turn away other customers as total capacity is 500,000 units and Marx anticipates regular customer orders of 400,000. If this contract is accepted, selling expenses will be avoided for the 150,000 units. At what sales price per unit will management need to offer the electronic parts in order to increase profits by $300,000?

36. (L.O. 3) E. Berg and Sons build custom-made pleasure boats that range in price from $10,000 to $250,000. For the past 30 years, Mr. Berg, Sr., has determined the selling price of each boat by estimating the costs of materials and labor, allocating a portion of overhead, and adding 20 percent to these estimated costs.

For example, a recent price quotation was determined as follows:

Direct materials	$ 5,000
Direct labor	8,000
Overhead	2,000
	$15,000
Plus 20%	3,000
Selling price	$18,000

The overhead figure was determined by estimating total overhead costs for the year and allocating them at 25 percent of direct labor.

If a customer rejected the price and business was slack, Mr. Berg, Sr. would often be willing to reduce his markup to as little as 5 percent over estimated costs. Thus, average markup for the year is estimated at 15 percent.

Total overhead which includes selling and administrative expenses for the year has been estimated at $150,000 of which $90,000 is fixed and the remainder is variable in direct proportion to direct labor.

Required

Assume the customer in the example rejected the $18,000 quotation and also rejected a $15,750 quotation (5 percent markup) during a slack period. The customer countered with a $15,000 offer.

1. What is the difference in operating income for the year between accepting or rejecting the customer's offer?
2. What is the minimum selling price Mr. Berg, Sr. could have quoted without reducing or increasing operating income? (CMA)

37. (L.O. 6) Officers at Bradshaw Company are reviewing the company's four products' profitability and the potential effects of several proposals for varying the product mix. An excerpt from the income statement and other data follow:

	Product				
	P	Q	R	S	Total
Sales revenues	$10,000	$18,000	$12,600	$22,000	$62,600
Cost of goods sold	4,750	7,056	13,968	18,500	44,274
Gross margin	$ 5,250	$10,944	$ (1,368)	$ 3,500	$18,326
Operating expenses	1,990	2,976	2,826	4,220	12,012
Income before income taxes	$ 3,260	$ 7,968	$ (4,194)	$ (720)	$ 6,314
Units sold	1,000	1,200	1,800	2,000	
Sales price per unit	$10.00	$15.00	$7.00	$11.00	
Variable cost of goods sold per unit	2.50	3.00	6.50	6.00	
Variable operating expenses per unit	1.17	1.25	1.00	1.20	

Required Each of the following questions should be considered independently. Assume that all fixed costs are unavoidable. Consider only the product changes stated in each proposal. The activity of other products remains stable.

1. If Product R is discontinued, calculate the effect on income before income taxes.
2. If Product R is discontinued and a consequent loss of customers causes sales of Q to decrease by 200 units, calculate the effect on income before income taxes.
3. If the sales price of R is increased to $8 and the number of units sold decreases to 1,500, calculate the effect on income before income taxes.
4. The plant that produces R can be used to produce a new product, T. Total variable costs and expenses per unit of T are $8.05, and 1,600 units can be sold for $9.50 each. If T is introduced and R is discontinued, calculate the total effect on income before income taxes.
5. Part of the plant that produces P can easily be adapted to produce S. However, changes in quantities may require changes in sales prices. If production of P is reduced to 500 units (to be sold for $12 each) and production of S is increased to 2,500 units (to be sold for $10.50 each), calculate the effect on income before income taxes.

(AICPA)

38. (L.O. 6) Your client, Ocean Company, manufactures and sells three products, Ex, Why, and Zee. Projected income statements by product line for the year ended December 31, 19x8, are presented below.

	Product			
	Ex	Why	Zee	Total
Units sales	10,000	500,000	125,000	635,000
Sales revenues	$925,000	$1,000,000	$575,000	$2,500,000
Cost of goods sold				
Variable	$285,000	$ 350,000	$150,000	$ 785,000
Fixed	304,200	289,000	166,800	760,000
Total cost of goods sold	$589,200	$ 639,000	$316,800	$1,545,000
Gross margin	$335,800	$ 361,000	$258,200	$ 955,000
General and administrative expenses				
Variable	$270,000	$ 200,000	$ 80,000	$ 550,000
Fixed	125,800	136,000	78,200	340,000
Total general and administrative expenses	$395,800	$ 336,000	$158,200	$ 890,000
Income (loss) before taxes	$ (60,000)	$ 25,000	$100,000	$ 65,000

Production costs are similar for all three products. The total fixed general and administrative expenses are divided among products in proportion to revenues. The fixed cost of units sold is allocated to products by various allocation bases, such as square feet for factory rent and machine-hours for repairs.

Ocean's management is concerned about the operating loss of Product Ex and is considering two alternate courses of action, A and B.

A. Ocean could purchase less expensive direct materials for the production of Ex. This would reduce variable production costs so total variable costs (cost of goods sold + general and administrative expenses) for Product Ex would equal 52 percent of Product Ex's revenues.

B. Ocean would discontinue manufacturing Product Ex. Selling prices of products Why and Zee would remain constant. Management expects production of and revenue from Product Zee to increase by 50 percent. By eliminating Product Ex, fixed manufacturing costs would be reduced by $180,000 per year. The remaining fixed costs allocated to Product Ex would continue to be incurred.

Required Prepare a schedule, analyzing how A and B above would affect total company income before taxes. (AICPA)

39. (L.O. 3) Jenco, Inc., manufactures a combination fertilizer and weed killer under the name "Fertikil." This is the only product Jenco produces. Fertikil is sold nationwide through wholesalers to independent retail nurseries and garden stores.

Taylor Nursery plans to sell a similar fertilizer and weed killer compound through its regional nursery chain under its private label. Taylor has asked Jenco to submit a bid for a 25,000-pound order of the private brand. Although the chemical composition of the Taylor compound differs from Fertikil, the manufacturing process is similar.

The Taylor compound would be produced in 1,000-pound lots. Each lot would require 60 direct labor hours and the following chemicals:

Chemicals	Quantity in pounds
CW-3	400
JX-6	300
MZ-8	200
BE-7	100

The first three chemicals, CW-3, JX-6, and MZ-8, are used to produce Fertikil. BE-7 was used in a compound Jenco discontinued. This chemical was never sold or discarded because it does not deteriorate and storage facilities were adequate. Jenco could sell BE-7 at the prevailing market price.

Jenco also has on hand a chemical called CN-5, which was manufactured for another product no longer being produced. CN-5, which cannot be used in Fertikil, can be substituted for CW-3 on a one-for-one basis without affecting the quality of the Taylor compound.

Inventory and cost data for chemicals that can be used to produce the Taylor compound are shown below.

Direct materials	Pounds in inventory	Current market price per pound
CW-3	22,000	$0.90
JX-6	8,000	0.60
MZ-8	8,000	1.60
BE-7	4,000	0.65
CN-5	5,500	0.10

The current direct labor rate is $7 per hour. A predetermined manufacturing overhead rate is established at the beginning of the year, using direct labor hours as a base.

The overhead rate for the current year, based on a capacity of 400,000 direct labor hours, is as follows:

Variable manufacturing overhead	$2.25 per direct labor hour
Fixed manufacturing overhead	3.75
Combined rate	$6.00 per direct labor hour

Assume that Jenco, Inc., has sufficient capacity to produce the 25,000-pound order and will submit a bid. The order must be delivered by the end of the current month. Taylor has indicated that this is a one-time order.

Required Calculate the bidding price at which Jenco would increase operating profit by $15,000.

(CMA)

40. (L.O. 2, 3) Auer Company received an order for a special machine from Jay Company. Just as Auer had completed the machine, Jay Company (a) declared bankruptcy, (b) defaulted on the order, and (c) forfeited the 10 percent deposit paid on the selling price of $72,500.

Auer's manufacturing manager identified the costs incurred to produce the special machine as follows:

Direct materials used		$16,600
Direct labor incurred		21,400
Manufacturing overhead		
Variable	$10,700	
Fixed	5,350	16,050
Fixed selling and administrative expenses		5,405
Total costs		$59,455

Another company, Kaytell Corporation, is interested in buying the machine if it is reworked to Kaytell's specifications. Auer is considering selling the reworked special machine to Kaytell as a special order for $68,100. The additional direct costs to rework the machine are as follows:

Direct materials	$ 6,200
Direct labor	4,200
	$10,400

A second alternative is to convert the special machine into a standard model. The standard model lists for $61,250. The additional, direct costs to convert the machine into a standard model are as follows:

Direct materials	$2,850
Direct labor	3,300
	$6,150

A third alternative is to sell the machine as is for $52,000.

The following additional information is available on Auer's operations:

- The sales commission rate on standard models is 2 percent, whereas the sales commission rate on special orders is 3 percent. Rates for applying manufacturing overhead and fixed selling and administrative costs are as follows:

Manufacturing	
Variable	50% of direct labor costs
Fixed	25% of direct labor costs

Selling and administrative	
Fixed	10% of total sales price

- The normal time needed for rework is one month. Auer normally sells a sufficient number of standard models to operate at a volume exceeding the breakeven point.

Required

1. Determine the dollar contribution that each alternative will add to Auer's operating income.
2. If Kaytell makes a counteroffer, what is the lowest price Auer should accept for the reworked machine? Explain your answer. (CMA)

41. (L.O. 4) Sarbec Company needs a total of 125 tons of sheet steel, 50 tons of 2-inch width and 75 tons of 4-inch width, for a customer's job. Sarbec can purchase the sheet steel in these widths directly from Jensteel Corporation, a steel manufacturer, or it can purchase sheet steel from Jensteel that is 24 inches wide and have it slit into the desired widths by Precut Inc. Both vendors are local and have previously supplied materials to Sarbec.

The 24-inch wide sheet steel is a regular stock item of Jensteel and can be shipped to Precut within five days after receipt of Sarbec's purchase order. If Jensteel is to do the slitting, shipment to Sarbec would be scheduled for 15 days after receipt of the order. Precut has quoted delivery at ten days after receipt of the sheet steel. In prior dealings, Sarbec has found both Jensteel and Precut to be reliable vendors with high-quality products.

Sarbec has received the following price quotations from Jensteel and Precut:

Jensteel Corporation Rates

Size	Gauge	Quantity	Cost per ton
2″	14	50 tons	$210
4″	14	75 tons	200
24″	14	125 tons	180

Precut Inc. Steel Slitting Rates

Size	Gauge	Quantity	Price per ton
2″	14	50 tons	$18
4″	14	75 tons	15

Freight and Handling Charges

Destination	Cost per ton
Jensteel to Sarbec	$10.00
Jensteel to Precut	5.00
Precut to Sarbec	7.50

Required

1. Prepare an analysis that will show whether Sarbec Company should
   a. Purchase the required slit steel directly from Jensteel Corporation.
   b. Purchase the 24-inch wide sheet steel from Jensteel and have it slit by Precut Inc. into 50 tons 2 inches wide and 75 tons 4 inches wide.

2. Without prejudice to your answer to *1* above, present three qualitative arguments why Sarbec Company may favor the purchase of the slit steel directly from Jensteel Corporation. (CMA)

42. (L.O. 4) Vernom Corporation, which produces and sells to wholesalers a highly successful line of summer lotions and insect repellents, has decided to diversify in order to stabilize sales throughout the year. A natural area for the company to consider is the production of winter lotions and creams to prevent dry and chapped skin.

After considerable research, a winter products line has been developed. However, because of the conservative nature of the company management, Vernom's president has decided to introduce only one of the new products for this coming winter. If the product is a success, further expansion in future years will be initiated.

The product selected (called Chap-off) is a lip balm that will be sold in a lipstick-type tube. The product will be sold to wholesalers in boxes of 24 tubes for $8 per box. Because of available capacity, no additional fixed charges will be incurred to produce the product. However, $100,000 of the company's present fixed costs will be allocated to the new product.

Using the estimated sales and production of 100,000 boxes of Chap-off as the standard volume, the accounting department has developed the following costs:

Direct labor	$2.00 per box
Direct materials	3.00
Overhead (fixed and variable)	1.50
Total	$6.50 per box

Vernom has approached a cosmetics manufacturer to discuss the possibility of purchasing the tubes for Chap-off rather than manufacture their own. The purchase price of the empty tubes from the cosmetics manufacturer would be $.90 per 24 tubes. If the Vernom Corporation accepts the purchase proposal, it is estimated that per unit direct labor and variable overhead costs would be reduced by 10 percent and direct materials costs would be reduced by 20 percent.

Required

1. Should Vernom Corporation make or buy the tubes? Show calculations to support your answer.
2. What would be the maximum purchase price acceptable to the Vernom Corporation for the tubes? Support your answer with an appropriate explanation.
3. Instead of sales of 100,000 boxes, revised estimates show sales volume at 125,000 boxes. At this new volume additional equipment, at an annual rental of $10,000, must be acquired to manufacture the tubes. However, this incremental cost would be the only additional fixed cost required even if sales increased to 300,000 boxes. (The 300,000 level is the goal for the third year of production.) Under these circumstances should the Vernom Corporation make or buy the tubes? Show calculations to support your answer.
4. The company has the option of making and buying at the same time. What would be your answer to *3* above if this alternative were considered? Show calculations to support your answer.
5. What nonquantifiable factors should Vernom Corporation consider in determining whether they should make or buy the lipstick tubes? (CMA)

43. (L.O. 6) Foster Company normally produces and sells 50,000 widgets each month. The widgets sell for $20 per unit, variable expenses are $12 per unit, fixed overhead costs total $100,000 per month, and fixed selling costs total $25,000 per month.

Employment strikes in the industry that purchase the bulk of the widgets have caused sales of the widget to temporarily drop to 15,000 units per month. Foster Company estimates that the strikes will last for about two months. Once the strikes are resolved, sales are expected to return to their normal level.

Due to the current decline in sales, Foster Company is thinking about closing its plant during the periods of the strikes. If Foster does close the plant during this period, it is estimated that fixed overhead costs can be reduced to $75,000 per month and that fixed selling costs can be reduced by 25 percent. Start-up costs at the end of the shutdown period would total $15,000. Foster Company strictly produces to order, therefore, no inventories are kept on hand.

Required

1. Assuming that it is highly probable that the strikes will continue for two months, would you recommend that Foster Company close its plant ?
2. At what sales level (in units) would Foster be indifferent as between closing the plant or keeping it open?

44. (L.O. 3) Anchor Company manufactures several different styles of jewelry cases. Management estimates that during the third quarter of 19x6 the company will be operating at 80 percent of normal capacity. Because the company desires a higher utilization of plant capacity, the company will consider a special order.

Anchor has received special-order inquiries from two companies. The first order is from JCP, Inc., which would like to market a jewelry case similar to one of Anchor's cases. The JCP jewelry case would be marketed under JCP's own label. JCP, Inc., has offered Anchor $5.75 per jewelry case for 20,000 cases to be shipped by October 1, 19x6. The cost data for the Anchor jewelry case which is similar to the specifications of the JCP special order are as follows:

Regular selling price per unit	$9.00
Cost per unit	
Direct materials	$2.50
Direct labor (0.5 hours @ $6)	3.00
Total overhead (0.25 machine-hours @ $4)	1.00
Total costs	$6.50

According to the specifications provided by JCP, Inc., the special-order case requires less expensive direct materials. Consequently, the direct materials will only cost $2.25 per case. Management has estimated that the remaining costs, labor time, and machine time will be the same as the Anchor jewelry case.

The second special order was submitted by Krage Company for 7,500 jewelry cases at $7.50 per case. These jewelry cases, as with the JCP cases, would be marketed under the Krage label and have to be shipped by October 1, 19x6. However, the Krage jewelry case is different from any jewelry case in the Anchor line. The estimated per unit costs of this case are as follows:

Direct materials	$3.25
Direct labor (0.5 hours @ $6)	3.00
Total overhead (0.5 machine-hours @ $4)	2.00
Total costs	$8.25

In addition, for the Krage order, Anchor will incur $1,500 in additional setup costs and will have to purchase a $2,500 special device to manufacture these cases. This device will be discarded once the special order is completed.

The Anchor manufacturing capabilities are limited to the total machine-hours available. The plant capacity under normal operations is 7,500 machine-hours per month. The budgeted fixed overhead per month amounts to $18,000. All manufacturing overhead costs are applied to production on the basis of machine-hours at $4 per hour, calculated using 7,500 monthly machine-hours.

Anchor will have the entire third quarter to work on the special orders. Management does not expect any repeat sales to be generated from either special order. Company practice precludes Anchor from subcontracting any portion of an order when special orders are not expected to generate repeat sales.

Required Should Anchor Company accept either special order? Justify your answer and show your calculations. (CMA)

45. (L.O. 6) Stac Industries is a multiproduct company with several manufacturing plants. The Clinton Plant manufactures and distributes two household cleaning and polishing compounds, Regular Cleen-Brite and Heavy-Duty Cleen Brite. The forecasted operating results for the first six months of 19x2, when 100,000 cases of each compound are expected to be manufactured and sold, are presented in the following statement:

Cleen-Brite Compounds — Clinton Plant
Results of Operations for the
Six-Month Period Ending June 30, 19x2
($000 omitted)

	Regular	Heavy duty	Total
Sales revenues	$2,000	$3,000	$5,000
Cost of sales	1,600	1,900	3,500
Gross margin	$ 400	$1,100	$1,500
Selling and administrative expenses			
Variable	$ 400	$ 700	$1,100
Fixed*	240	360	600
Total selling and administrative expenses	$ 640	$1,060	$1,700
Income (loss) before taxes	$ (240)	$ 40	$ (200)

*The fixed selling and administrative expenses are allocated between the two products on the basis of dollar sales volume.

The regular compound sells for $20 a case and the heavy-duty sells for $30 a case. The manufacturing costs by case of product are presented in the schedule below. Each product is manufactured on a separate production line. Annual normal manufacturing capacity is 200,000 cases of each product. However, the plant is capable of producing 250,000 cases of regular compound and 350,000 cases of heavy-duty compound annually.

	Cost per case	
	Regular	Heavy duty
Direct materials	$ 7	$ 8
Direct labor	4	4
Variable manufacturing overhead	1	2
Fixed manufacturing overhead*	4	5
Total manufacturing cost	$16	$19
Variable selling and administrative expenses	$ 4	$ 7

*Depreciation charges are 50 percent of the fixed manufacturing overhead of each line.

Top management believes the loss for the first six months reflects a light profit margin caused by intense competition. Management also believes that many companies will be forced out of this market by next year and profits should improve.

Assume that for the last six months of 19x2 a selling price of $23 and volume level of 50,000 cases for the regular compound and a selling price of $35 and volume of 35,000 cases for the heavy-duty compound can be expected.

Required

1. Should Stac Industries consider closing down its operations until 19x3 in order to minimize its losses? Support your answer with appropriate calculations.
2. Identify and discuss the qualitative factors that should be considered in deciding whether the Clinton plant should be closed down during the last six months of 19x2. (CMA)

Case 1
GianAuto Corporation (L.O. 2, 4)

GianAuto Corporation manufactures automobiles, vans, and trucks. Among the various GianAuto plants in the United States is the Denver Cover Plant. Coverings made primarily of vinyl and upholstery fabric are sewn at the Denver Cover Plant. The coverings are used on interior seating and other surfaces of GianAuto's products.

Ted Vosilo is plant manager at Denver Cover, the first GianAuto plant in the region. He is also regional manager. Nevertheless, the salary of Vosilo and his budget staff is charged entirely to the Denver Cover plant.

Vosilo has just received a report, indicating that GianAuto could purchase the entire annual output of Denver Cover from outside suppliers for $30 million. Vosilo was astonished at this low price, since Denver Cover's budget for operating costs for the coming year is $52 million. Vosilo believes that GianAuto must close operations at Denver Cover to save the $22 million in annual costs.

Denver Cover's budget for operating costs for the coming year is presented on the next page.

Denver Cover Plant
Budget for Operating Costs
For the Year Ending December 31, 19x9
($000 omitted)

Materials		$12,000
Labor		
Direct	$13,000	
Supervision	3,000	
Indirect plant	4,000	20,000
Overhead		
Depreciation, equipment	$ 5,000	
Depreciation, building	3,000	
Pension expenses	4,000	
Plant manager and staff	2,000	
Corporate allocations	6,000	20,000
Total budgeted costs		$52,000

Additional facts on the plant's operations are as follows:

- Denver Cover is committed to using high-quality fabrics in all products. Thus, the purchasing department has placed blanket purchase orders with major suppliers to ensure receipt of sufficient materials for the coming year. If these orders are canceled because of plant closings, termination charges will be 15 percent of the cost of direct materials.
- Approximately 700 plant employees will lose their jobs if the plant is closed. This number includes all direct laborers and supervisors as well as plumbers, electricians, and other skilled workers classified as indirect plant workers. Some employees could find new jobs, but many others would have difficulty. All employees would have difficulty matching Denver Cover's base pay of $9.40 per hour, which is the highest in the area. A clause in Denver Cover's contract with the union may help some employees. Under this contract the company must provide employment assistance to former employees for 12 months after a plant closing. The estimated cost to administer this service for a year is $1 million.
- Some employees would probably elect early retirement, as GianAuto has an excellent pension plan. In fact, $3 million in 19x9 pension expenses would continue regardless of whether Denver Cover is open.
- Vosilo and his staff would be unaffected by the closing. They would still be responsible for administering three other area plants.

Required

1. Without looking at costs, identify GianAuto's advantages in continuing to obtain covers from its Denver plant.
2. GianAuto Corporation management plans to prepare a numerical analysis to help them decide about closing the Denver Cover plant. Identify the following:
   a. Recurring annual budgeted costs that can be avoided by closing the plant.

b. Recurring annual budgeted costs not relevant to the decision. Explain.
c. Nonrecurring costs that could arise if the plant were closed. Explain how they would affect the decision.
d. Revenues or costs not specifically mentioned in the problem that should be considered. (CMA)

Case 2
Sofak Company (L.O. 6)

Sofak Company manufactures precision sensing equipment. Jerry Adams, a project engineer at Sofak, has developed a prototype of an automatic testing kit. This kit was designed for continual evaluation of water quality and the chemical contents of hot tubs. Adams believes this kit will permit domestic tub owners to better control water quality at substantially reduced costs and in less time. Sofak's management is convinced the kit will be well received in the marketplace. Furthermore, this new equipment uses the same technology as Sofak's employees use in manufacturing other equipment. Thus, Sofak can use existing facilities to produce the product.

Adams is ready to proceed with developing cost and profit plans for the testing kit. He has asked the marketing department to estimate a selling price and sales volume. Sofak contracted the market research to an independent firm.

The market analysis firm considered unit prices ranging from $80 to $120. Within this price range it recommended a price of $100 per kit and estimated annual sales volume of 60,000 units at this price.

Sofak's profit planning department has accumulated the cost data Adams requested. The new product will require direct materials costing $25 per unit, and two hours of direct labor time for manufacturing. The current direct labor cost is $8.80 per direct labor hour.

Sofak's estimated manufacturing overhead for the entire company for 19x9 is given on page 397.

Introducing the new product will require changes in the manufacturing plant. Although the plant is below capacity and current facilities can be used, a new production line, requiring a supervisor, would be opened. The annual cost for the supervisor would be $28,000. In addition, Sofak must obtain an operating lease for a piece of equipment, with an annual cost of $150,000.

Sofak has already paid $132,000 for the marketing study. A distributor has agreed to promote and distribute the new product for a fee of $6 per unit.

Required Determine the annual profit or loss from introducing the new product. (CMA)

Sofak Company
Schedule of Total Budgeted Manufacturing Overhead Costs
For the Fiscal Year Ending November 30, 19x9

	Budgeted annual costs	Costs per direct labor hour
Variable manufacturing overhead costs		
Supplies	$ 360,000	$0.40
Materials handling	315,000	0.35
Heat, light, and power	1,125,000	1.25
Fixed manufacturing overhead costs		
Supervisors' salaries	1,440,000	
Depreciation, building	4,410,000	
Depreciation, equipment	3,420,000	
Property taxes, factory	1,620,000	
Insurance	810,000	
Total budgeted costs	$13,500,000	

■

Part 4

Accounting in Managerial Control Decisions

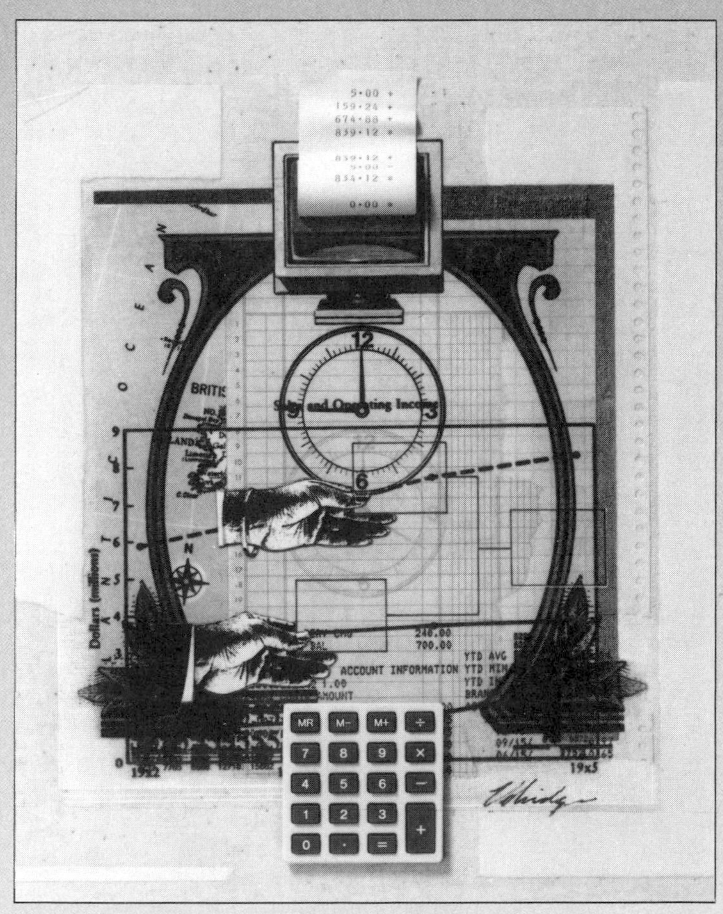

Part 4 explains how to report costs and revenues for use in managerial control decisions. The concept of responsibility accounting is discussed. Then, the ways in which managers use the accounting information to control costs, production, revenues, and profits are illustrated.

■

Chapter 9, Responsibility Accounting: Segmented Reporting and Direct Costing, introduces the guiding principle in reporting for control purposes: that accounting reports should include only those costs and revenues for which each manager is directly responsible.

■

Chapter 10, Standard Costs: Direct Materials and Direct Labor, shows how to calculate standard cost variances and use them to control variable production costs.

■

Chapter 11, Flexible Budgets and Manufacturing Overhead Costs, explains how overhead budgets can be adjusted to changes in the production level and used to report manufacturing overhead variances.

■

Chapter 12, Performance Measurement: Revenue Centers and Profit Centers, covers reporting for managers who are responsible for a firm's revenues or for its profits.

■

Chapter 13, Performance Measurement: Investment Centers, details measures used to evaluate performance of top-level managers, whose responsibility it is to maximize a firm's return on investment by balancing profits and investments.

■

9

Responsibility Accounting: Segmented Reporting and Direct Costing

LEARNING OBJECTIVES

After studying this chapter you should be able to:

1. Explain how managers use responsibility accounting to control an organization's operations
2. Describe the common patterns for delegating decision-making authority
3. Explain the four types of financial responsibility centers
4. Define controllability and explain its importance in responsibility accounting
5. Distinguish between direct and common costs
6. Prepare a segmented report to help managers make control decisions
7. Explain why managers prefer direct costing to absorption costing
8. Use direct costing to calculate the value of inventory and operating income in a manufacturing company

In Chapters 6, 7, and 8, you saw how accounting information is used in the planning process. In this chapter you will see how it is used to control operations, that is, to ensure that planned results are realized.

To control operations, you must make informed decisions. To do so, you must determine from preliminary results which actions will help fulfill your plans in future months. Take a simple example. You are traveling to your brother's home in the next state. Because road conditions are favorable and the speed limit permits, you plan to drive at 55 miles an hour. Halfway there you glance at the speedometer and notice that you are cruising at only 50 miles an hour. To increase your speed, you press on the accelerator pedal and watch the speedometer climb. In a very simple way, you have exercised control. You have compared a plan with actual results and adjusted your driving accordingly.

Although managers need a certain amount of information to make control decisions, unnecessary information causes confusion. The more irrelevant information they are provided with, the more information they must sort through to find the facts they need. Say that you are still driving on the highway. The facts that the speed limit in town is 30 miles an hour and that your car can reach 100 miles an hour are not relevant to your decision to increase your driving speed to 55 miles per hour.

■

Responsibility Accounting

Control is the action that a manager takes to ensure that actual results correspond to planned results. To control a business, managers need information detailing the results of specific activities. If a company offers several product lines in many sales regions, managers must know how much each product is contributing to the profitability of each region. Such information is necessary to determine where special action is needed. To provide managers with this type of information, managerial accountants prepare segmented reports, or detailed reports on particular aspects of a business. Segmented reports will be discussed later in this chapter (pages 411–421).

To ensure that managers receive only necessary information, accountants must understand each manager's responsibilities. That is, the accountant must know what type of control decisions a manager makes. In a **responsibility accounting system**, the accountant reports to each manager only information that is relevant to that manager's responsibility.

Higher-level managers assign responsibilities to their subordinates. In a small organization, perhaps one person can follow operations and make all important decisions. But as a company grows and operations become more complex, some division of responsibility is necessary. Not only is there not enough time for one

OBJECTIVE 1
Explain how managers use responsibility accounting to control an organization's operations

person to make all decisions but some information required for those decisions cannot be reported from lower levels fast enough. Therefore, decision-making authority is delegated to managers who assume responsibility for the financial results of their decisions.

When decision making is delegated to managers, the organization is said to be decentralized. A **decentralized organization** is where managers at different levels within the organization have the authority to make decisions concerning business activities. The managers are held responsible for the financial consequences of their decisions. With the exception of only the smallest organization, all organizations are decentralized to some extent. Most large multinational organizations decentralize the decision-making authority simply because of the geographic dispersion of operations. In large multinational organizations, some managers have few constraints on their authority to make decisions. In centralized organizations, managers have constraints on decisions and must obtain approval from higher-level managers before implementing anything other than minor decisions.

Decentralization provides a number of benefits to an organization as listed below.

1. The managers are in a better position to make decisions, since they have access to more information on a timely basis. The managers are at the focal point of the business activity that requires a decision.
2. By delegating authority to make decisions, top managers are relieved of running the business on a day-to-day basis. This provides top managers with more time for strategic planning and the coordination of the various business segments in the organization.
3. Since the managers have greater control over the business activities that affect their performance, they generally are more motivated to make better decisions.
4. The more authority and responsibility that is delegated to managers, the better their experience as they are promoted to higher levels of management. Managing a business segment is considered excellent training for future promotions.
5. Decentralization provides for a base to measure managers' performance. In a decentralized organization, authority and responsibility are well defined with respect to the business activity and the related financial results.

Decision-making authority is usually divided among managers according to some common pattern. Managerial accountants should be familiar with those patterns to design a financial accounting system.

■

Common Patterns for Dividing Responsibility

OBJECTIVE 2
Describe the common patterns for delegating decision-making authority

There are three major patterns of business activity by which managerial authority is delegated: (a) business function, (b) product line, and (c) geographic region. Most organizations use some combination of the three. Each one will be discussed briefly. Then, you will see why a combination of patterns is sometimes desirable.

Division by Business Function

Many companies are organized primarily according to a form called the **business function organization.** In a functionally organized company, each manager is responsible for a specific business function. The four major business functions are (1) production, which is sometimes called operations; (2) marketing; (3) finance; and (4) human resources. Thus, in a functionally organized company, one manager is responsible for production, another for marketing. Decisions about the company's finances would probably be made by the controller and treasurer. Decisions about hiring, compensation, or training are made by the human resources manager. Although this example illustrates the simplest form of organization, it is the one used most often by small companies. Part A of Figure 9–1 shows an organization chart for a functionally organized company.

In a functionally organized company, the president, who is often called the chief executive officer, has two main tasks: (a) long-range planning and (b) coordination of functional activities. The president must see that a long-range plan is developed to establish the company's direction and objectives. In addition, the president must ensure that the production manager is informed of the marketing manager's new product plans. Otherwise, production resources may not be available to make the new product. Similarly, the finance manager must know of new product plans and new production methods, so he or she can arrange adequate financing. If a new product requires an expanded work force, the human resources manager must develop a new hiring program. Throughout this process, the president must coordinate the flow of information among top management. This form of organization takes advantage of the special skills of each functional manager, but it requires careful coordination by the president.

Division by Product Line

Large companies often organize operations according to a form called the **product-line organization.** In this type of organization, a single manager is responsible for hiring required employees, production, and marketing of a specific product line. For instance, this type of organization is appropriate for a computer company selling both large computers and microcomputers. The manager of the microcomputer division makes production, marketing, and human resource decisions

Figure 9–1

Different Ways of Dividing Responsibility in an Organization

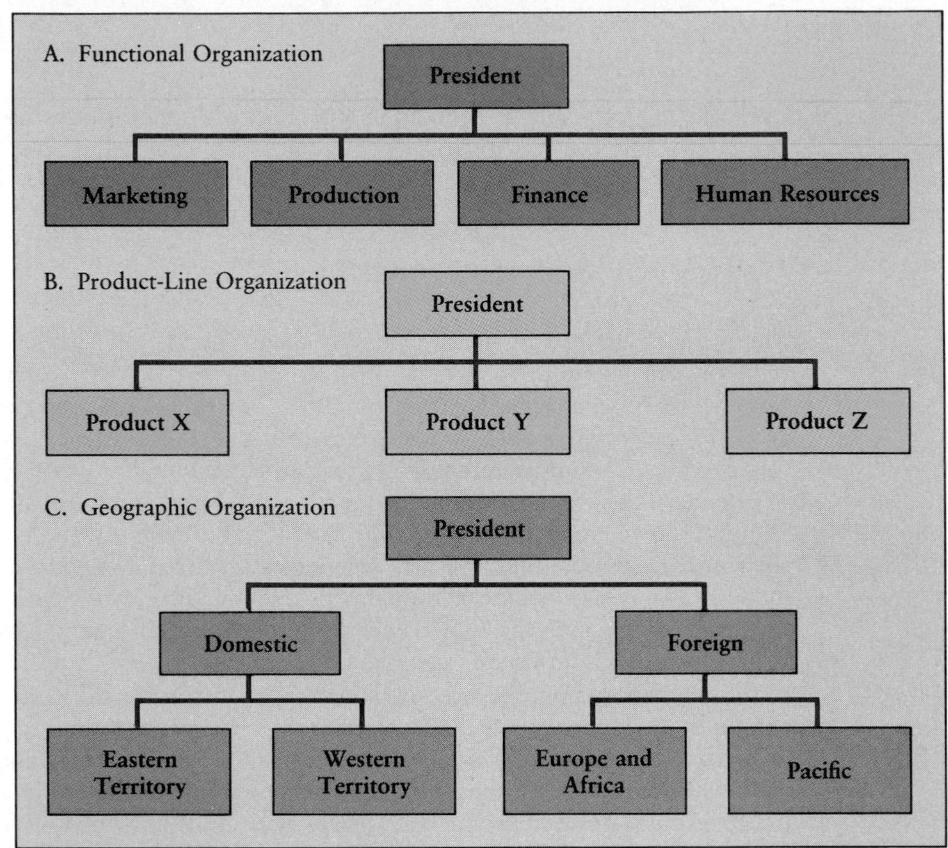

for that division. Another manager does the same for large computers. Part B of Figure 9–1 shows an organization chart for this type of company.

All functions are not necessarily split among product-line managers. Financing decisions are commonly delegated to the vice president of finance, who takes care of financing the entire organization. The reason for this exception is that financing decisions for one product line inevitably affect other product lines. Even the largest organization has a limited borrowing capacity. If funds are borrowed to finance expansion of one product line, expansion of another line might be curtailed. A product-line manager cannot be expected to make objective decisions in such cases.

Other decisions, such as marketing decisions, do not necessarily affect other divisions. Large computers, for example, are marketed to computer specialists; microcomputers to small businesses and home users. When customers differ, a marketing decision affecting one product line will not significantly affect other lines. This form of organization allows better coordination of market demands with product development and manufacturing. However, it requires managers who are knowledgeable in both production and marketing.

Division by Geographic Region

Another common organization structure, **geographic organization,** allows one manager to make functional decisions for a geographic region. In a nation as large as the United States, a company's operations are usually separated into regions, such as the Southeast, Midwest, Northeast, and West. Smaller countries, such as England or France, might form a single region. Where a company does little business, a single manager might be responsible for a huge area, such as Africa or the Middle East. Part C of Figure 9–1 shows an organization chart for a geographically organized firm.

Unlike product-line managers, regional managers of foreign operations often make some financing decisions. This is because companies generally want to obtain some financing in the countries in which they operate. In such cases, financing decisions made by a regional manager in one country will not greatly affect those of a regional manager in another country.

Geographically organized companies may also divide their regions functionally. Thus, each division might have its own production manager and marketing manager. However, in very large companies, regions may be divided into product lines, which are themselves divided functionally. Figure 9–2 illustrates some ways in which a company might divide responsibilities: by product line (A) or geographically (B). This form of organization permits the organization to tailor its products and operations to the needs of different regions or countries. It requires managers who are familiar with the environment and culture in which they operate.

Regardless of how a company is organized — functionally, by product line, or geographically — managers also have specific financial responsibilities. The four types of financial responsibility centers and the accounting needs associated with them are discussed next.

■

Financial Responsibility Centers and Their Accounting Needs

OBJECTIVE 3
Explain the four types of financial responsibility centers

Not all managers have the same type of financial responsibility. Some control only expenses; others, revenues. A few managers control both. And those at the highest levels control a company's revenues, expenses, and investments. In order to make good decisions, however, managers need reliable, timely, and relevant information.

Figure 9–2
Patterns of Dividing Responsibility in Product-Line and Geographic Organizations

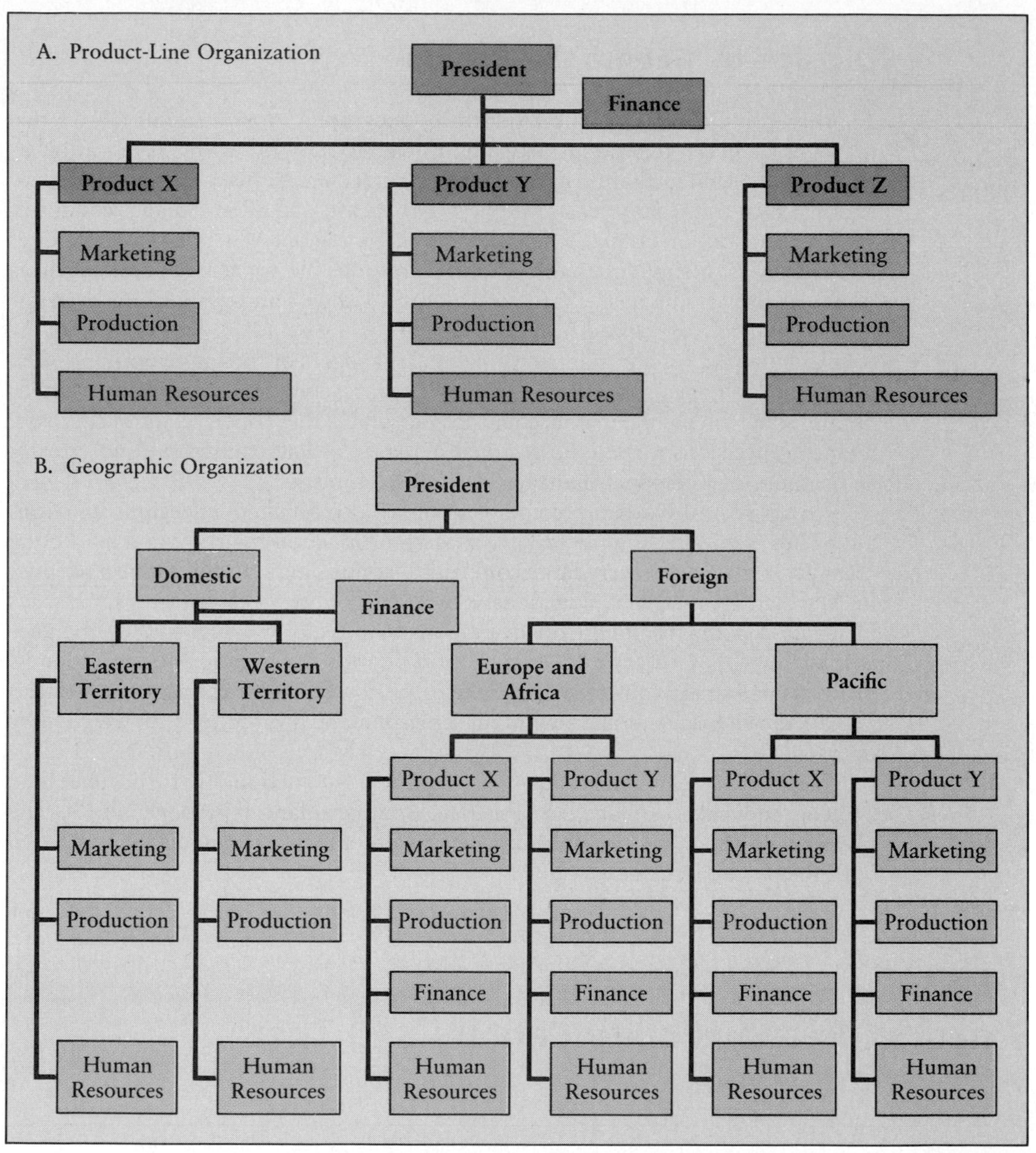

Organizational units are considered centers of financial responsibility, and each unit has its own accounting needs. Financial responsibility falls into four categories — expense centers, revenue centers, profit centers, and investment centers. These categories will now be discussed.

Expense Centers

An **expense center** manager must ensure that assigned tasks are completed within limits allowed by budgets or standard costs. The responsibility accounting system should supply managers with information needed to schedule workers efficiently; avoid wasting materials, supplies, and energy; and use equipment carefully. Expense centers are sometimes called cost centers.

Managers of expense centers use standard costs and flexible budgets to control expenses. (These topics are discussed in detail in Chapters 10 and 11.)

Revenue Centers

The manager of a **revenue center** is responsible for selling budgeted quantities of various products or services at budgeted prices. A sales representative selling bread to grocery stores, a sales manager distributing automobiles to dealers in specific geographic areas, and the manager of a furniture department in a local department store are all managers of revenue centers.

Managers of revenue centers use variances in sales volume, sales price, and sales mix to monitor or control these operations. (Calculation of these variances is discussed in Chapter 12.) Such managers may also be responsible for travel, entertainment, and other marketing expenses. If so, they are likely to use flexible budgets to control these expenses. But expense control is a secondary goal in a revenue center. Since design and operation of an accounting system to report these variances is expensive, the responsibility accounting system must be designed with care.

Profit Centers

The manager of a **profit center** is responsible for controlling both expenses and revenues and balancing them to produce a budgeted profit. (Remember that profit equals total revenues minus total expenses.) The manager of a new-car department for a local automobile dealer is usually a manager of the profit center. He or she controls profits by purchasing the right cars, setting sales commissions to motivate sales representatives, and using advertising and other expenditures to generate sales.

The responsibilities of such managers are broader than those for managers of expense centers or revenue centers. Not only must profit center managers control both expenses and revenues, they must also balance the two. Take the case of the manager at a franchised pizza restaurant. This manager thinks sales will increase by widening the area in which pizzas are delivered. He or she expects this increased service to attract customers not ordinarily buying from the restaurant. If the manager is correct, the contribution margin from increased sales will outweigh the increased delivery expense, and the restaurant's profits will rise. That is, the manager will have manipulated expenses and revenue to achieve a desired profit.

This is just one example of how profit center managers can increase profits. Another way is to increase advertising expenses, expecting that added sales will more than offset added expenses. Or a manager might redesign a product to raise its selling price, again expecting added revenues to more than equal added expenses. The point is that managers of profit centers must control two *related* variables to achieve a more complex goal, control of profits.

The manager of a profit center uses contribution margin analysis, standard costs, flexible budgets, and sales variances to control profits. Ways in which some of these methods can be combined and their results reported are discussed in Chapter 12.

Investment Centers

The manager of an **investment center** is responsible for controlling expenses, revenues, and investments and balancing them to produce a budgeted return on investments. Such managers have the broadest responsibility. A chief executive officer has this responsibility, as do managers of divisions in some large organizations.

In financial terms, a **return on investment (ROI)** is the ratio of profit earned by an investment center to the investment in that center.[1] It is calculated as follows:

$$\text{ROI} = \frac{\text{center's net earnings}}{\text{center's investments}}$$

The center's net earnings and investment figures are usually taken from the center's income statement and balance sheet. The ratio is expressed as a percentage rather than a decimal figure.

If the manager of a franchised pizza restaurant is the manager of an investment center, he or she may make decisions about investments in the restaurant as well as those concerning revenues and expenses. Assume for the sake of illustration that this is the case. If the chain has invested $200,000 in the restaurant and it earned a profit of $30,000 last year, the return on investment would be 15 percent.

$$\text{ROI} = \frac{\text{center's net earnings}}{\text{center's investments}}$$

[1]A center's investment is usually measured using an average of the beginning and end of the year investments.

$$\text{ROI} = \frac{\$30{,}000}{\$200{,}000} = \underline{\underline{15}} \text{ percent}$$

From this calculation you can see that several methods will increase the return on investment. One method is to increase profits while holding investments constant. This can be accomplished by increasing revenues or reducing costs. Another is to reduce investments while holding profits constant. A third method is to change both profits and investments so the return on investment is increased. This third method is the one the restaurant manager will use.

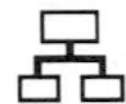

The manager's plan is to increase sales and profits by replacing the restaurant's tables with more comfortable booths. Since customers seem to prefer sitting in booths and competing restaurants do not have booths, sales should increase. The manager has spoken to several suppliers. The lowest bid for removing the tables and installing booths is $20,000. But how does the manager evaluate the plan's potential?

First, the manager should calculate the return on investment. To do so, he or she needs to estimate the increased profit the booths will bring. Suppose he or she estimates that extra sales will increase annual profits by $4,000. The return on the investment in booths will be 20 percent ($4,000 added profit ÷ by $20,000 added investment). Thus, by installing booths, the restaurant's 15 percent return on investment should increase. The new return on the total investment of $220,000 will be approximately 15.5 percent.

$$\text{ROI} = \frac{\$30{,}000 + \$4{,}000}{\$200{,}000 + \$20{,}000} = \underline{\underline{15.5}} \text{ percent}$$

The manager of an investment center uses contribution margin analysis, standard costs, flexible budgets, and sales and investment analysis to control the return on investments. How these methods are combined for use in investment centers is discussed in Chapter 13.

As you know, a responsibility accounting system is one that reports only relevant information to managers, that is, information on operations controlled by the particular managers. As defined, control is an action a manager takes to ensure that actual results correspond to planned results. Now, you will learn about a new concept, controllability. Although the two terms *control* and *controllability* are similar, their meanings differ.

■

The Principle of Controllability

OBJECTIVE 4
Define controllability and explain its importance in responsibility accounting

Managerial control is rarely absolute. Were managers held responsible only for matters over which they have total control, they would be responsible for little. For example, the manager of a computer center can control labor costs by carefully scheduling workers so they are available when needed. But most likely the hourly rates for these workers are determined by the supply of and demand for such skilled people. Thus, the manager has less than total control over labor costs. Still, by controlling the amount of labor used, he or she can significantly influence labor costs. Or, a manager may be able to reduce investment by careful attention to accounts receivable. In this case, the manager is controlling investments.

When a manager has significant influence over the amount of a cost, revenue, or investment, that cost or revenue is called a **controllable item.** Therefore, labor costs in the computer center are a controllable cost.

The concept of controllability is important to the accountant because it helps define what information would be reported to a manager. If a manager can significantly influence the amount of an item, that is, if it is controllable, then control information on that item should be reported to the manager. If uncontrollable items are reported, as sometimes happens, they should be listed separately in the report. For example, the manager of the franchised pizza restaurant should receive information on the investment (cost of replacing the tables with booths) and the change in sales and profits after the investment is implemented.

Controllability varies with the manager's level of authority and the time period in which a decision must be made. The effect of each will be briefly discussed.

Level of Authority and Controllability

Generally, the nearer a manager is to the top, the broader his or her influence over budget items. Managers close to the top of an organization are probably managers of profit or investment centers. Such managers should control expenses, revenues, and investments. Those on lower levels are probably running expense or revenue centers. The managers of these centers can influence only expenses and/or revenues. None of these managers can completely control an item, but they can influence some of the budget items enough for those items to be considered controllable. Top managers can influence all aspects of an operation if given enough time.

Time Period and Controllability

Some budget items cannot be controlled at any managerial level over a short period of time. For example, if you purchase an insurance policy, for all practical purposes you cannot control the cost until the policy expires. (Insurance policies may be canceled before they expire, but usually at great expense to the purchaser.) Thus, the time period also determines controllability. In the short run, few budget items are controllable. In the long run, however, everything is controllable by high-level managers.

Commercial leases, which often run for up to twenty years, are another item that cannot be controlled over a short period. During the lease period, which is part of the legally binding contract, a company's rental expense is basically uncontrollable. Employment contracts and contracts for materials purchases also render a cost uncontrollable for specific periods.

Investments in buildings or equipment are difficult to reverse because their market value tends to depreciate more quickly than their usefulness. When you buy a new car, it loses about 20 percent of its value as soon as you drive it away from the dealer. Were you to try selling your new $10,000 car immediately, you would probably get only $8,000 for it. The same thing happens with equipment, especially if much of the cost was for installation. If a new owner must move the equipment, the original installation cost is wasted. In addition, the warranty might not extend to another owner. Thus, the cost of equipment is generally uncontrollable over the short run. Associated costs, such as property taxes on the equipment, are also uncontrollable over the short run.

In summary, if a manager's decisions can significantly influence the amount of a cost, the cost is controllable. A manager's ability to influence cost depends on (1) the manager's level of authority and (2) the time period involved. Contracts and the economic costs of disposing of assets determine the time period during which an item is uncontrollable.

Now that the basic concepts of reporting for management control have been covered, this chapter will discuss how the accountant implements these concepts. You will study how costs are assigned and how reports for various divisions of an organization are prepared.

■

Assigning Costs to Organizational Segments: Direct Costs Versus Common Costs

A **segment** is any subpart of an organization. Product lines, sales territories, customer groupings, divisions, and manufacturing operations are all segments. Each of these segments contributes separately to a company's objectives, and each must be evaluated on its own merits.

OBJECTIVE 5
Distinguish between direct and common costs

As you have seen, a company's contribution margin is the difference between its sales revenues and its variable costs. The contribution margin for a segment is also the difference between its sales revenues and its variable costs. But calculating a segment's contribution margin involves more than collecting sales data and variable costs for each segment. The accountant must also separate many of the company's expenses into two categories, direct and common costs, and assign them to segments.

In Chapter 2, a direct cost was defined as a cost physically traceable to a product or service. Direct materials and direct labor costs are direct costs to particular products in that sense. A **direct cost to an organizational segment,** however, is a cost that can be physically traced to a segment. For example, in an organization segmented by product line, direct materials and direct labor costs are considered direct costs to the segment. Other costs, including fixed costs incurred for a single product line, are also direct costs to the segment.

Some companies have separate manufacturing plants for each product line. In that case, all manufacturing costs incurred in a plant are direct costs to the plant and to the product line. If each product line does its own advertising, then advertising costs are direct costs to the product line, whether they are fixed or variable. A cost need not be variable to be considered a direct cost.

A **common cost** benefits more than one product, service, or organizational segment at the same time. A common cost is the opposite of a direct cost, which benefits only one product, service, or organizational segment. If an organization is segmented by product line and more than one product line is produced in a manufacturing plant, then depreciation on that plant is a common cost. Likewise, the plant manager's salary is considered a common cost, since it is incurred for the benefit of more than one product line. Advertising expenses to promote the entire organization rather than a product line are common costs, as are the salaries of top management.

If, however, an organization is segmented by sales territory, then national advertising expenditures for even a single product are a common cost. These expenditures benefit all sales territories, even though they promote only one item. The crucial question is, what is the cost objective? Not only advertising expenditures but many other items can be classified as direct costs of a product and common costs for sales territories.

Another example is the salary of a company president. If the cost objective is the entire company, the president's salary is a direct cost. But if the cost objective is product lines or sales territories, then the president's salary is a common cost. Generally, the narrower the cost objective, the fewer costs are considered direct costs. If the cost objective is a sales representative, then probably none of a company's advertising costs would be direct costs. Once a company's costs are separated into direct and common costs, the accountant can prepare a segmented income statement.

■

Preparing Reports for Segments

OBJECTIVE 6
Prepare a segmented report to help managers make control decisions

The basic format of the accounting statement for a segment and the contribution margin income statement are the same. The contribution margin format was used extensively in Chapters 6, 7, and 8. In this chapter you will see how it can be adapted to the needs of segment managers.

Assume Lorharr Corporation produces two cleaning products, Product A and Product B, in a single factory. The two products are sold to industrial firms for use in their factories and to merchandisers for resale to the general public. The sales department is organized by region.

The two major regions are East and West. The selling prices of both products are the same for all customers. Unit prices and variable costs are as follows:

	Product A	Product B
Sales price	$3.00	$5.00
Variable costs		
Cost of goods sold	$1.00	$2.00
Sales commission	0.50	1.00
Total variable costs	$1.50	$3.00
Contribution margin	$1.50	$2.00

Unit sales for June 19x9 were divided by territory and customer type as follows:

Territory/type of customer	Product A (units)	Product B (units)
East		
Industrial	10,000	20,000
Commercial	15,000	25,000
West		
Industrial	20,000	15,000
Commercial	15,000	20,000
Total sales	60,000	80,000

Using this information, the accountant can prepare an income statement segmented by product line, territory, or type of customer.

Product-Line Reports

To prepare a segmented report, the accountant must first separate fixed costs into direct and common costs. For a product-line report, the accountant must know which costs are direct costs of each product. For Lorharr Corporation the breakdown is as follows:

	Direct costs			
Fixed costs	Product A	Product B	Common costs	Total costs
Manufacturing	$20,000	$40,000	$50,000	$110,000
Selling and administrative	10,000	30,000	30,000	70,000
Total	$30,000	$70,000	$80,000	$180,000

Lorharr incurred $180,000 in fixed costs during June 19x9. Fixed manufacturing costs were $110,000, $60,000 ($20,000 + $40,000) of which were direct to Products A and B and $50,000 of which were common to both products. The direct manufacturing costs could be related to supervision for one product or depreciation of equipment used exclusively for one product. The common manufacturing fixed costs could represent depreciation, property taxes, insurance,

Exhibit 9–1
Illustration of Income Statement by Product Line

Loharr Corporation
Income Statement by Product
For the Month of June 19x9

	Product A	Product B	Total
Sales units	60,000	80,000	140,000
Sales revenues	$180,000	$400,000	$580,000
Variable costs			
Cost of goods sold	$ 60,000	$160,000	$220,000
Sales commissions	30,000	80,000	110,000
Total variable costs	$ 90,000	$240,000	$330,000
Contribution margin	$ 90,000	$160,000	$250,000
Direct fixed costs			
Manufacturing	$ 20,000	$ 40,000	$ 60,000
Selling and administrative	10,000	30,000	40,000
Total direct fixed costs	$ 30,000	$ 70,000	$100,000
Segment margin	$ 60,000	$ 90,000	$150,000
Common fixed costs			
Manufacturing			$ 50,000
Selling and administrative			30,000
Total common fixed costs			$ 80,000
Operating income			$ 70,000

general supervision, and maintenance of the building in which the two products were produced.

Total fixed sales and administrative costs were $70,000, $40,000 of which were direct to the two products; $30,000 common. The direct costs could represent advertising or warehouse storage costs for a single product. The common costs could represent salaries of territory managers selling both products, or general data processing and administrative costs.

With this information about direct and common costs, the accountant can develop a product-line income statement. Exhibit 9–1 shows the resulting report, prepared according to the contribution margin format. Sales revenues are listed by product. Then, variable costs are deducted to obtain the contribution margin for each product. Until this point the procedure is the same as that used to find the contribution margin in Chapter 6. Next, direct fixed costs are deducted from the contribution margin to obtain the segment margin for each product. The **segment margin** is the dollar amount contributed by each segment toward covering common fixed costs.

In the long run, all products should produce a positive segment margin. Management may tolerate negative segment margins when demand is low, but eventually each product must cover its direct fixed costs.

Territory Reports

When preparing a product-line income statement or an income statement segmented by territory, the accountant uses the same sales prices and variable costs. The only difference is that fixed costs must be divided by sales territory rather than product line. The breakdown for Lorharr is as follows:

Fixed costs	Direct costs East	Direct costs West	Common costs	Total costs
Manufacturing	$ -0-	$ -0-	$110,000	$110,000
Selling and administrative	20,000	30,000	20,000	70,000
Total	$20,000	$30,000	$130,000	$180,000

Notice that all fixed manufacturing costs are classified as common costs to the territories. All units of both products are produced in a single factory. In companies with regional plants, manufacturing costs might be considered direct to the regions.

Exhibit 9–2
Computing Sales Revenues and Variable Costs by Territory

Lorharr Corporation
Computation of Sales Revenues and Variable Costs by Territory
For the Month of June 19x9

East territory		West territory	
Sales revenues		Sales revenues	
Product A, 25,000 @ $3	= $ 75,000	Product A, 35,000 @ $3	= $105,000
Product B 45,000 @ $5	= 225,000	Product B 35,000 @ $5	= 175,000
	$300,000		$280,000
Variable cost of goods sold		Variable cost of goods sold	
Product A, 25,000 @ $1	= $ 25,000	Product A, 35,000 @ $1	= $ 35,000
Product B, 45,000 @ $2	= 90,000	Product B, 35,000 @ $2	= 70,000
	$115,000		$105,000
Sales commissions		Sales commissions	
Product A, 25,000 @ $0.50	= $ 12,500	Product A, 35,000 @ $0.50	= $ 17,500
Product B, 45,000 @ $1	= 45,000	Product B, 35,000 @ $1	= 35,000
	$ 57,500		$ 52,500

Exhibit 9–3
Income Statement Segmented by Territory

Lorharr Corporation
Income Statement by Territory
For the Month of June 19x9

	East territory	West territory	Total
Sales units			
Product A	25,000	35,000	60,000
Product B	45,000	35,000	80,000
Total sales units	70,000	70,000	140,000
Sales revenues	$300,000	$280,000	$580,000
Variable costs			
Cost of goods sold	$115,000	$105,000	$220,000
Sales commissions	57,500	52,500	110,000
Total variable costs	$172,500	$157,500	$330,000
Contribution margin	$127,500	$122,500	$250,000
Direct fixed costs			
Manufacturing costs	$ -0-	$ -0-	$ -0-
Selling and administrative costs	20,000	30,000	50,000
Total direct fixed costs	$ 20,000	$ 30,000	$ 50,000
Segment margin	$107,500	$ 92,500	$200,000
Common fixed costs			
Manufacturing			$110,000
Selling and administrative			20,000
Total common fixed costs			$130,000
Operating income			$ 70,000

Notice, too, that the same $70,000 fixed selling and administrative costs from Exhibit 9–1 are now segmented by sales territory instead of by product line. The direct costs are salaries of territory managers. While they are common fixed costs in the product-line report, as are regional advertising costs, they are direct to the territories. The common costs include such items as corporate administration, promotion of corporate image, and national advertising programs for selected products.

Preparing an income statement segmented by territory is a bit more complicated than preparing product-line reports. Because sales in each territory are split between two products, each with its own unit price and variable costs per unit, sales revenues and variable costs must be computed by product, then added together to obtain territory figures. The computations are shown in Exhibit 9–2.

Splitting sales between products affects the territory's income statement as well. Exhibit 9–3 shows Lorharr's income statement segmented by sales territory.

Notice that the East territory's contribution margin is slightly larger than the West's ($127,500 as opposed to $122,500). Within territories, the contribution margin is a function of the **sales mix** (proportion of total sales volume contributed by each product) as well as the sales volume, sales price per unit, and variable costs per unit. The East's contribution margin is larger because it sells a larger proportion of Product B than does West. Product B also has a higher contribution margin per unit than Product A ($2.00 per unit for Product B versus $1.50 per unit for Product A).

The segment margin for a territory is calculated by subtracting its direct fixed costs from its contribution margin. This figure tells managers how much operating income they will lose if the sales territory is eliminated. Were the eastern territory eliminated, for instance, operating income would be reduced by $107,500.

By subtracting common fixed costs from the total segment margin, you get Lorharr's operating income for the month. This figure is the same as obtained in Exhibit 9–1. Notice, however, that the division of fixed costs between common and direct is different from the one in Exhibit 9–1. When cost objectives are different — product line versus territory — the direct costs will differ.

Exhibit 9–4
Computing Sales Revenues and Variable Costs by Type of Customer

Lorharr Corporation
Computation of Sales Revenues and Variable Costs by Customer Type
For the Month of June 19x9

Industrial customers		Commercial customers	
Sales revenues		Sales revenues	
Product A, 30,000 @ $3	= $ 90,000	Product A, 30,000 @ $3	= $ 90,000
Product B, 35,000 @ $5	= 175,000	Product B, 45,000 @ $5	= 225,000
	$265,000		$315,000
Variable cost of goods sold		Variable cost of goods sold	
Product A, 30,000 @ $1	= $ 30,000	Product A, 30,000 @ $1	= $ 30,000
Product B, 35,000 @ $2	= 70,000	Product B, 45,000 @ $2	= 90,000
	$100,000		$120,000
Sales commissions		Sales commissions	
Product A, 30,000 @ $0.50	= $ 15,000	Product A, 30,000 @ $0.50	= $ 15,000
Product B, 35,000 @ $1	= 35,000	Product B, 45,000 @ $1	= 45,000
	$ 50,000		$ 60,000

Exhibit 9–5
Income Statement Showing Segment Contribution by Customer Type

Lorhарr Corporation Income Statement by Customer Type For the Month of June 19x9	Industrial	Commercial	Total
Sales units			
Product A	30,000	30,000	60,000
Product B	35,000	45,000	80,000
Total sales units	65,000	75,000	140,000
Sales revenues	$265,000	$315,000	$580,000
Variable costs			
Cost of goods sold	$100,000	$120,000	$220,000
Sales commissions	50,000	60,000	110,000
Total variable costs	$150,000	$180,000	$330,000
Contribution margin	$115,000	$135,000	$250,000
Direct fixed costs			
Manufacturing	$ -0-	$ -0-	$ -0-
Selling and administrative	10,000	20,000	30,000
Total direct fixed costs	$ 10,000	$ 20,000	$ 30,000
Segment margin	$105,000	$115,000	$220,000
Common fixed costs			
Manufacturing			$110,000
Selling and administrative			40,000
Total common fixed costs			$150,000
Operating income			$ 70,000

Reports by Type of Customer

To organize Lorharr's income statement by type of customer, you must redivide fixed costs into direct and common costs. This need must be anticipated when the accounting system is designed so that information by customer type is available. The breakdown by type of customer is shown below.

	Direct costs			
Fixed costs	Industrial	Commercial	Common costs	Total costs
Manufacturing	$ -0-	$ -0-	$110,000	$110,000
Selling and administrative	10,000	20,000	40,000	70,000
Total	$10,000	$20,000	$150,000	$180,000

Lorharr's fixed manufacturing costs are common to both types of customers, since Lorharr has only one factory, which produces both products. If the company had two plants, one supplying industrial customers and the other supplying commercial customers, all fixed manufacturing costs would be direct costs.

Next, sales revenues and variable costs must be calculated by customer type. These computations are shown in Exhibit 9–4 on page 417. Since both products are sold to both types of customers, separate calculations must be made for each product and each type of customer.

Exhibit 9–5 shows recalculated revenues and costs combined into a customer-type income statement. Again, as in a territory statement, the total contribution margin is a function of the sales mix as well as sales volume, sales price, and variable costs. Lorharr's commercial customers provide a larger total contribution margin than industrial customers, partly because they purchase 10,000 more units. Commercial customers also purchase more of Product B, which has a higher contribution margin per unit.

A customer-type segment margin is calculated by deducting total direct fixed costs from the contribution margin. Notice that fewer fixed costs are direct for Lorharr's customer segments than for its territory or product segments (compare Exhibits 9–1 and 9–3). Direct fixed costs by type of customer include advertising in magazines or newspapers targeted to a specific type of customer. For Lorharr, this advertising represents only a small portion of fixed costs.

Review Exercise 9–1

Prepare an Income Statement by Market Segment

Mahaffey Company manufactures a single Product xx that is sold in the domestic market and an international market. To sell the product in the international market, Mahaffey Company incurs additional shipping costs and tariffs, both of which are variable costs. The unit sales price and variable costs for the two markets are given below.

	Product xx	
	Domestic	**International**
Sales price	$10	$12
Variable costs		
Manufacturing	$ 5	$ 5
Selling	2	5
Total variable costs	$ 7	$10
Contribution margin	$ 3	$ 2

Unit sales for product xx for the year 19x0 amounted to 50,000 units in the domestic market and 40,000 units in the international market. All fixed costs are common to the two markets. The manufacturing fixed costs amounted to $100,000. The selling and administrative fixed costs amounted to $60,000.

Required

Prepare an income statement showing the contribution of the two markets toward covering common fixed costs and operating income.

Solution

Mahaffey Company
Income Statement by Market Segment
For the Year 19x0

	Domestic	International	Total
Sales units	50,000	40,000	90,000
Sales revenues	$500,000	$480,000	$980,000
Variable costs			
Manufacturing	$250,000	$200,000	$450,000
Selling	100,000	200,000	300,000
Total variable costs	$350,000	$400,000	$750,000
Contribution margin	$150,000	$ 80,000	$230,000
Common fixed costs			
Manufacturing			$100,000
Selling and administrative			60,000
Total common fixed costs			$160,000
Operating income			$ 70,000

(see Exercises 27, 29, 33)

■

Controllability and Segmented Reporting

An important message of this chapter is that managerial accounting reports should be custom-designed to the needs of managers. Segmented reports fulfill that aim by clearly indicating the revenue and costs within a manager's control.

Take the case of Bruno Sims, manager of the shoe department at Martin Department Store. Sims has organized the department's sales activities by the two major product lines, dress shoes and sports shoes. The budget for Sims's department reflects his organization (Exhibit 9–6). As one would expect, the contribution margin is shown by product line as well as in total. But Martin's accountant has gone even further in recognizing Sims's needs.

In the shoe department, all fixed costs are common to both product lines, so none are assigned to the product lines. But it is helpful to Sims to know which of the department's fixed costs he can control. The accountant has recognized this need by listing uncontrollable items separately. Sims can control clerks' salaries and advertising costs. These expenses are deducted from the total contribution margin to obtain the department's controllable contribution to store income. However, his own salary and depreciation of the department's furniture

Exhibit 9–6
Controllable and Uncontrollable Fixed Expenses

Martin Department Store, Shoe Department
Responsibility Accounting Report
Plan for the Month of April 19x9

Manager: Bruno Sims	Dress shoes	Sports shoes	Total
Sales revenues	$10,000	$15,000	$25,000
Variable costs			
Cost of goods sold	$ 6,000	$10,500	$16,500
Sales commissions	1,000	1,200	2,200
Total variable costs	$ 7,000	$11,700	$18,700
Contribution margin	$ 3,000	$ 3,300	$ 6,300
Direct controllable costs			
Clerks' salaries			$ 2,000
Advertising			700
Total controllable costs			$ 2,700
Controllable departmental contribution			$ 3,600
Direct uncontrollable costs			
Department manager's salary			$ 1,400
Depreciation, furniture and fixtures			600
Total direct uncontrollable costs			$ 2,000
Segment margin			$ 1,600

and fixtures are beyond his control. These items are totaled and deducted from the department's controllable contribution to obtain the department's segment margin, $1,600.

Although the manager's salary and depreciation of furniture and fixtures are uncontrollable by Sims, they are controllable by higher-level managers. Just as the manager of each department is responsible for balancing sales mix and controllable costs to meet the department's contribution target, store managers are responsible for balancing the combined sales and fixed costs of all departments.

For the store managers, the accountant should prepare a statement segmented by department. This report would deduct common fixed costs from the total segment margin of all departments to show operating income for the store. Showing department segment margins and total operating income for the store tells store managers what they really need to know: how well the various departments are doing in comparison with one another.

Just as managers must know the revenues and costs of organizational segments, so must they know how inventory costs can affect operating income. Thus, this chapter will now examine two inventory costing systems, absorption costing and direct costing. As you will see, one system is more useful than the other in controlling operating income.

■

Assigning Costs to Inventory: Direct Costing Versus Absorption Costing

When managers design an accounting system, they must choose a method for inventory valuation. For external reporting, full absorption costing is required. As discussed in Chapters 4 and 5, full absorption costing combines variable and fixed manufacturing costs in the product cost. However, this creates manufacturing cost information that is not appropriate for preparing income statements using the contribution margin format. Because of this, managerial accountants prefer direct costing, which does not combine variable and fixed manufacturing costs. Direct costing is consistent with the contribution margin format. In this section, we will discuss the differences between direct costing and absorption costing.

When **absorption costing** is used, direct materials, direct labor, and manufacturing overhead costs, both fixed and variable, are absorbed into the value of inventory. This method must be used in external financial reporting when preparing cost of goods manufactured and sold statements and in the costing of inventories on the balance sheet. It is required that all costs necessary for production must be assigned to the job or product produced. The rationale behind this requirement is that proper matching of revenues and expenses requires that all expenses related to the revenues must be reported in the same period as the revenues. Since fixed manufacturing costs are necessary for the production of a product, they should be assigned to the product and inventoried until the product is sold. When the product is sold, the cost becomes an expense and is matched with the revenue from the sale of the product. Absorption costing was used in discussing job order costing in Chapter 4 and process costing in Chapter 5.

When a second method, called **direct costing,** is used, only direct materials, direct labor, and variable manufacturing overhead costs are absorbed into the value of inventory. Fixed manufacturing overhead costs are excluded. Instead, they are treated as period expenses, much like fixed selling and administrative costs. Thus, inventory costs include only variable costs of production. The ra-

Exhibit 9–7

Inventoriable Costs: Absorption Costing Versus Direct Costing

The only difference between absorption costing and direct costing is the way in which fixed manufacturing overhead is accounted for.

Absorption costing	Type of cost	Direct costing
Inventory costs	Direct materials Direct labor Variable manufacturing overhead Fixed manufacturing overhead	Inventory costs (Direct materials, Direct labor, Variable manufacturing overhead)
Income statement expenses	Selling and general administrative expenses	Income statement expenses (Fixed manufacturing overhead, Selling and general administrative expenses)

tionale behind this treatment of fixed manufacturing costs is that these costs will be incurred regardless of how many units are produced. Hence, they represent the cost of providing productive capacity for the period. Therefore, their total cost should be expensed in the period in which they provide capacity with no portion assigned to inventory. Exhibit 9–7 illustrates the difference between absorption and direct costing. In addition, absorption costing income statements follow the functional format. Direct costing income statements follow the contribution margin format discussed in Chapter 3.

OBJECTIVE 7
Explain why managers prefer direct costing to absorption costing

Managers generally prefer direct costing to absorption costing for many of the same reasons they favor separate listings of fixed and variable costs on the income statement. Reporting of actual results can be compared more easily to planned results when direct costing is used. With direct costing, fixed costs included in the income statement and per unit inventory costs remain stable even if production volume fluctuates.

An example will illustrate both these points. Verneer Corporation produces a single product. Financial data on the company's 19x9 operations follow:

Number of units expected to be sold		3,800
Number of units expected to be produced		4,000
Beginning inventory, finished units		-0-
Estimated ending inventory, finished units		200
Selling price per unit		$19.00
Variable costs per unit		
Direct materials	$1.00	
Direct labor	4.00	
Variable manufacturing overhead	2.00	
Variable selling and administrative	1.50	8.50
Fixed costs for 19x9		
Manufacturing overhead		$12,000
Selling and administrative		20,000

Depending on the method used to cost Verneer's inventory, the value per unit will be $10 or $7 as shown below.

Absorption Costing

Direct materials	$ 1
Direct labor	4
Variable manufacturing overhead	2
Fixed manufacturing overhead, $12,000 per year ÷ 4,000 units produced	3
Total inventory costs	$10

Direct Costing

Direct materials	$1
Direct labor	4
Variable manufacturing overhead	2
Total inventory costs	$7

Exhibit 9–8
Comparison of Absorption and Direct Costing Net Income with Changing Inventory Levels

Verneer Corporation
Absorption Costing Income Statement
For the Year 19x9

Sales revenues (3,800 units × $19)		$72,200
Cost of goods sold		
Finished goods inventory, beginning	$ -0-	
Add cost of goods manufactured (4,000 units × $10)	40,000	
Cost of goods available for sale	$40,000	
Less finished goods inventory, ending (200 units @ $10)	2,000	
Cost of goods sold		38,000
Gross margin		$34,200
Selling and administrative expenses		
Variable (3,800 units × $1.50)	$ 5,700	
Fixed	20,000	25,700
Operating income		$ 8,500

Verneer Corporation
Direct Costing Income Statement
For the Year 19x9

Sales revenues (3,800 units × $19)			$72,200
Variable costs			
Cost of goods sold			
Finished goods inventory, beginning	$ -0-		
Add variable cost of goods manufactured (4,000 units × $7)	28,000		
Cost of goods available for sale	$28,000		
Less finished goods inventory, ending (200 units @ $7)	1,400		
Cost of goods sold		$26,600	
Selling and administrative (3,800 units × $1.50)		5,700	
Total variable costs			32,300
Contribution margin			$39,900
Fixed costs			
Manufacturing		$12,000	
Selling and administrative		20,000	
Total fixed costs			32,000
Operating income			$ 7,900

OBJECTIVE 8
Use direct costing to calculate the value of inventory and operating income in a manufacturing company

Notice that inventory costs are lower under direct costing since fixed overhead is excluded from the calculations. On Verneer's income statement, cost of goods sold expense will be lower if direct costing is used. Total expenses, however, will be higher because the total of $12,000 fixed manufacturing overhead is included. Direct costing matches variable costs with revenue, and fixed costs with the period in which they are incurred.

Exhibit 9–8 shows two income statements, one prepared using absorption costing, the other, direct costing. Note that operating income is $600 higher by using absorption costing. When using absorption costing, the 200 units of inventory unsold at year-end carry part of the year's fixed manufacturing overhead costs. When the cost of ending inventory is deducted from the cost of goods available for sale, the $600 in fixed costs reduces the cost of goods sold. Thus, operating income is $600 higher. With direct costing the entire $12,000 in fixed manufacturing overhead costs is deducted in a lump sum, regardless of the level of unsold inventory at year-end.

Using cost-volume-profit analysis, you can confirm that operating income should be $7,900. At a sales level of 3,800, the figures are

$$\begin{aligned} OI &= [(SP - VC) \times V] - FC \\ &= [(\$19 - \$8.50) \times 3{,}800] - \$32{,}000 \\ &= \$7{,}900 \end{aligned}$$

Where

OI = operating income VC = variable costs per unit
SP = selling price per unit FC = total fixed costs per year
V = sales volume

The $8.50 in variable costs per unit are the sum of variable manufacturing and variable selling and administrative expenses. The $32,000 in fixed costs are the sum of fixed manufacturing overhead and fixed selling and administrative expenses. Notice that the predicted operating income when cost-volume-profit analysis is used is the same as that obtained when direct costing is used.

With a few additional calculations, you can prove that changes in inventory levels do not change operating income if direct costing is used. Assume that sales remain at 3,800 units as expected but production equals sales. (When units sold equal units produced, inventory remains constant.) Exhibit 9–9 shows both absorption and direct costing income statements for the Verneer Corporation at a production volume of 3,800 units. All other facts are the same as those presented in Exhibit 9–7. Under direct costing, operating income is unchanged when the production level changes.

With absorption costing, however, operating income was reported at $8,500. Using direct costing, income was $7,900. Although production is now 3,800 units, fixed manufacturing overhead remains at $12,000. The result is that fixed overhead costs per unit rise from $3 to $3.158 ($12,000 ÷ 3,800). This higher per unit cost adds $600 to the cost of goods available for sale. Since there is no

Exhibit 9–9
Comparison of Absorption and Direct Costing Net Income when Inventory Levels Are Constant

Verneer Corporation
Absorption Costing Income Statement
For the Year 19x9

Sales revenues (3,800 units × $19)		$72,200
Cost of goods sold		
Finished goods inventory, beginning	$ -0-	
Add cost of goods manufactured (3,800 units × $10.158)	38,600	
Cost of goods available for sale	$38,600	
Less finished goods inventory, ending (0 units @ $10.158)	-0-	
Cost of goods sold		38,600
Gross margin		$33,600
Selling and administrative expenses		
Variable (3,800 units × $1.50)	$ 5,700	
Fixed	20,000	25,700
Operating income		$ 7,900

Verneer Corporation
Direct Costing Income Statement
For the Year 19x9

Sales revenues (3,800 units × $19)			$72,200
Variable costs			
Cost of goods sold			
Finished goods inventory, beginning	$ -0-		
Add variable cost of goods manufactured (3,800 units × $7)	26,600		
Cost of goods available for sale	$26,600		
Less finished goods inventory, ending (0 units @ $7)	-0-		
Cost of goods sold		$26,600	
Selling and administrative (3,800 units × $1.50)		5,700	
Total variable costs			32,300
Contribution margin			$39,900
Fixed costs			
Manufacturing		$12,000	
Selling and administrative		20,000	
Total fixed costs			32,000
Operating income			$ 7,900

ending inventory to absorb any of the fixed manufacturing costs of the period, cost of goods sold also increases by $600. Operating income drops by $600. This can be summarized as follows:

Operating income for direct costing	$7,900
Operating income for absorption costing	8,500
Greater for absorption costing	600
Fixed costs in beginning inventory	$ -0-
Fixed costs in ending inventory (200 × $3)	600
Greater for absorption costing	$ 600

As previously seen, the use of per unit figures for fixed costs can be misleading.

Review Exercise 9–2

Prepare Direct and Absorption Costing Income Statements

Shook Company produces a single product. During the year 19xx, Shook Company produced 50,000 units and sold 45,000 units for $20 per unit. The variable manufacturing cost per unit amounted to $10. Total fixed manufacturing costs for the year were $100,000. The variable selling costs were $5 per unit. Fixed selling and administrative costs amounted to $75,000. There were no beginning inventories.

Required

1. Prepare an income statement using direct costing.
2. Prepare an income statement using absorption costing.
3. Reconcile the difference between the two operating incomes.

Solution

1. Absorption costing income statement prepared:

Shook Company
Absorption Costing Income Statement
For the Year 19xx

Sales revenues (45,000 units × $20)		$900,000
Cost of goods sold		
Finished goods inventory, beginning	$ -0-	
Add cost of goods manufactured (50,000 units × $12)	600,000	

Cost of goods available for sale	$600,000	
Less finished goods inventory, ending (5,000 units × $12)	60,000	
Cost of goods sold		540,000
Gross margin		$360,000
Selling and administrative expenses		
Variable (45,000 units × $5)	$225,000	
Fixed	75,000	300,000
Operating income		$ 60,000

2. Direct costing income statement prepared:

Shook Company
Direct Costing Income Statement
For the Year 19xx

Sales revenues (45,000 units × $20)			$900,000
Variable costs			
Cost of goods sold			
Finished goods inventory, beginning	$ -0-		
Add variable cost of goods manufactured (50,000 units × $10)	500,000		
Cost of goods available for sale	$500,000		
Less finished goods inventory, ending (5,000 units × $10)	50,000		
Cost of goods sold		$450,000	
Selling expense (45,000 units × $5)		225,000	
Total variable costs			675,000
Contribution margin			$225,000
Fixed costs			
Manufacturing		$100,000	
Selling and administrative		75,000	
Total fixed costs			175,000
Operating income			$ 50,000

3. Reconciliation of income:

Finished goods inventory, ending	$ 5,000
Finished goods inventory, beginning	-0-
Increase in finished goods inventory	$ 5,000
Fixed manufacturing cost per unit	2
Increase in operating income, absorption costing	$ 10,000

(see Exercises 23, 26)

■

Chapter Review

Review of Learning Objectives

1. **Explain how managers use responsibility accounting to control an organization's operations.**
Managers use accounting information to monitor expenses and revenues to ensure they are within budget. If actual figures deviate too much from planned figures, managers must take action to bring the organization back within budget so goals will be met.
Since each manager is responsible for only a portion of an organization's operation, he or she needs to know only information relevant to his or her responsibilities. A responsibility accounting system is one that reports only the information a manager needs. To design an effective responsibility accounting system, the managerial accountant must understand which decisions each manager is responsible for.

2. **Describe the common patterns for delegating decision-making authority.**
There are three major patterns by which authority is delegated. One is by *business function,* that is, a manager is responsible for one area, such as production, marketing, finance or human resources. Another is by *product line.* When this pattern is used, managers are responsible for all business functions, such as marketing and production, of a specific product line. In the third pattern, authority is delegated by *geographic region,* that is, by region, country, state, or even continent. Large organizations often use a combination of the three patterns.

3. **Explain the four types of financial responsibility centers.**
The four types of financial responsibility centers are: (1) expense centers, (2) revenue centers, (3) profit centers, and (4) investment centers. The manager of each type of center has a different financial responsibility. The manager of an expense center must ensure that assigned tasks are completed within budgeted or standard cost levels. A revenue center manager is responsible for selling budgeted quantities of products or services at budgeted prices. The manager of a profit center must control both expenses and revenue and balance them to produce a budgeted profit. Finally, the manager of an investment center is responsible for controlling expenses, revenues, and investments and balancing them to produce a budgeted return on investment.

4. **Define controllability and explain its importance in responsibility accounting.**
Managers can control only so many aspects of the activities for which they are responsible. The actions of competitors, government regulations, decisions by higher-level managers, and the general economic climate all affect the results managers achieve. However, managers should be accountable only for those actions within their control. Thus, controllability is the ability to significantly influence the amount of an expense, revenue, or investment. The controllability concept is used in responsibility accounting to determine what information is relevant and should be reported to a manager.
The amount of control a manager possesses depends on his or her level of authority. Upper-level managers can influence or control more items than lower-level managers. Time periods also determine controllability. Expenses that cannot be changed over a short period, such as a week or a month, can often be controlled over a longer period, such as a year or more.

5. **Distinguish between direct and common costs.**
Direct costs are costs that can be physically traced to a cost objective. The cost objective of concern in this chapter is an organizational segment. Common costs are costs that benefit more than one product, service, or organizational segment of an organization.

6. **Prepare a segmented report to help managers make control decisions.**
Accounting reports may be segmented by product line, sales territory, or type of customer. Segmented income statements are prepared using the contribution margin format. First, compute the contribution margin of each segment by deducting variable expenses from sales revenues. Then, calculate the segment margin by deducting direct fixed costs from the segment's contribution margin.

7. **Explain why managers prefer direct costing to absorption costing.**
Managers generally prefer direct costing because it separates fixed from variable costs, just as in cost-volume-profit analysis. As a result, it is easier to compare actual operating income to planned operating income. With absorption costing, actual operating income corresponds well with planned operating income only when inventory levels remain unchanged. With direct costing, income is more closely associated with sales, while absorption costing income is influenced by units produced and units sold.

8. **Use direct costing to calculate the value of inventory and operating income in a manufacturing company.**
In direct costing, only variable manufacturing costs are included in a unit's product costs, and thus in the value of inventory and cost of goods sold. Fixed manufacturing overhead is excluded. It is reported as a separate expense and deducted from the contribution margin along with fixed selling and administrative expenses in determining operating income.

Review of Key Terms

Absorption costing A costing method in which direct materials, direct labor, and manufacturing overhead costs, both fixed and variable, are absorbed into the value of inventory. Contrast with *Direct costing*.

Business function organization A form of organizing in which each manager is responsible for a specific function, such as production, marketing, finance, or human resources.

Common cost A cost that benefits more than one product, service, or organizational segment at the same time.

Control The action that a manager takes to ensure that actual results correspond to planned results.

Controllable item A cost, revenue, or investment item over which a manager has significant influence.

Decentralized organization An organization where managers at different levels within the organization have the authority to make decisions concerning business activities.

Direct cost to an organizational segment A cost is direct to a segment when it can be physically traced to that organizational segment.

Direct costing A cost accounting system that excludes fixed manufacturing overhead costs from the unit cost of inventory and cost of goods sold. Only direct materials, direct labor, and variable manufacturing overhead costs are absorbed into the value of inventory. Fixed manufacturing costs are treated as a period expense. Contrast to *Absorption costing*.

Expense center A responsibility center whose manager is responsible for completing assigned tasks within budgeted or standard cost levels. Also called *cost center*.

Geographic organization A form of organization in which one manager is responsible for several business functions such as marketing and production in a particular geographic region.

Investment center A responsibility center whose manager is responsible for controlling expenses, revenues, and investments and balancing them to produce a budgeted return on investments.

Product-line organization A form of organization in which a single manager is responsible for human resources, production, and marketing of a specific product line.

Profit center A responsibility center whose manager is responsible for controlling both expenses and revenues and balancing them to produce the budgeted profit.

Responsibility accounting system An accounting system in which the accountant reports to each manager only information relevant to that manager's responsibilities.

Return on Investment (ROI) The ratio of profit earned by an investment center to the investment in that center. Calculated by dividing the center's net earnings by its investment.

Revenue center A responsibility center whose manager is responsible for selling budgeted quantities of various products or services at budgeted prices.

Sales mix The proportion of total sales volume contributed by each product. Also called *product mix*.

Segment A subpart of an organization.

Segment margin The dollar amount contributed by a segment toward covering common fixed costs.

Review Problem 1

Malinowski Company is considering introducing two products, A and B, into two sales territories, East and West. Based on an analysis of manufacturing and marketing activities, the following sales prices and variable cost estimates were developed:

	Product A	Product B
Sales price	$5	$8
Variable costs		
Cost of goods sold	$2	$5
Sales commission	1	2
Total variable costs	$3	$7
Contribution margin	$2	$1

Estimated sales units for the two products by territory for June 19x9 are given below.

	Product A	Product B
East	25,000	30,000
West	20,000	15,000
Total unit sales	45,000	45,000

Fixed manufacturing and selling and administrative costs were estimated for June 19x9, then segmented by product and territory. The results of this analysis are given below.

Fixed costs	Direct costs: Product A	Direct costs: Product B	Common costs	Total costs
Manufacturing	$10,000	$15,000	$50,000	$ 75,000
Selling and administrative	15,000	5,000	20,000	40,000
Total	$25,000	$20,000	$70,000	$115,000

Fixed costs	Direct costs: East	Direct costs: West	Common costs	Total costs
Manufacturing	$ -0-	$ -0-	$ 75,000	$ 75,000
Selling and administrative	5,000	5,000	30,000	40,000
Total	$5,000	$5,000	$105,000	$115,000

Required Prepared a budgeted segment income statement segmented by product and another segmented by sales territory for Malinowski Company. For each statement, show the company's budgeted contribution margin, segment margin, and operating income for June 19x9.

Solution to Review Problem 1

Malinowski Company
Budgeted Income Statement by Product
For the Month of June 19x9

	Product A	Product B	Total
Sales units	45,000	45,000	90,000
Sales revenues	$225,000	$360,000	$585,000
Variable costs			
Cost of goods sold	$ 90,000	$225,000	$315,000
Sales commissions	45,000	90,000	135,000
Total variable costs	$135,000	$315,000	$450,000
Contribution margin	$ 90,000	$ 45,000	$135,000
Direct fixed costs			
Manufacturing	$ 10,000	$ 15,000	$ 25,000
Selling and administrative	15,000	5,000	20,000
Total direct fixed costs	$ 25,000	$ 20,000	$ 45,000
Segment margin	$ 65,000	$ 25,000	$ 90,000
Common fixed costs			
Manufacturing ($75,000 − $25,000 of direct costs)			$ 50,000

Selling and administrative ($40,000 – $20,000 of direct costs)	20,000
Total common fixed costs	$ 70,000
Operating income	$ 20,000

Malinowski Company
Budgeted Income Statement by Territories
For the Month of June 19x9

	Territory		
	East	West	Total
Sales units			
Product A	25,000	20,000	45,000
Product B	30,000	15,000	45,000
Total sales units	55,000	35,000	90,000
Sales revenues	$365,000	$220,000	$585,000
Variable costs			
Cost of goods sold	$200,000	$115,000	$315,000
Sales commissions	85,000	50,000	135,000
Total variable costs	$285,000	$165,000	$450,000
Contribution margin	$ 80,000	$ 55,000	$135,000
Direct fixed costs			
Manufacturing	$ -0-	$ -0-	$ -0-
Selling and administrative	5,000	5,000	10,000
Total direct fixed costs	$ 5,000	$ 5,000	$ 10,000
Segment margin	$ 75,000	$ 50,000	$125,000
Common fixed costs			
Manufacturing			75,000
Selling and administrative ($40,000 – $10,000 of direct costs)			30,000
Total common fixed costs			$105,000
Operating income			$ 20,000

Review Problem 2

Miller Company manufactures one product in its Dayton, Ohio, plant. Data on company operations for the year 19x2 are are follows:

Number of units sold		5,000
Number of units produced		6,000
Beginning inventory, finished units		-0-
Ending inventory, finished units		1,000
Selling price per unit		$ 20
Variable costs per unit		
Direct materials	$2	
Direct labor	3	
Variable manufacturing overhead	1	
Variable selling and administrative	2	8

Fixed costs for 19x2	
Manufacturing overhead	$12,000
Selling and administrative	15,000

Required

1. Prepare an income statement using absorption costing.
2. Prepare an income statement using direct costing.
3. Reconcile the difference between your answers *1* and *2* above.

Solution to Review Problem 2

1. Absorption costing income statement prepared:

Miller Company
Absorption Costing Income Statement
For the Year 19x2

Sales revenues (5,000 units × $20)		$100,000
Cost of goods sold		
Finished goods inventory, beginning	$ -0-	
Add cost of goods manufactured (6,000 units × $8*)	48,000	
Cost of goods available for sale	$48,000	
Less finished goods inventory, ending (1,000 units @ $8*)	8,000	40,000
Cost of goods sold		$60,000
Gross margin		
Selling and administrative expenses		
Variable (5,000 units × $2)	$10,000	
Fixed	15,000	25,000
Operating income		$ 35,000

*$6 + ($12,000 ÷ 6,000) = $8

2. Direct costing income statement prepared:

Miller Company
Direct Costing Income Statement
For the Year 19x2

Sales revenues (5,000 units × $20)			$100,000
Variable costs			
Cost of goods sold			
Finished goods inventory, beginning	$ -0-		
Add variable cost of goods manufactured (6,000 units × $6)	36,000		
Cost of goods available for sale	$36,000		
Less finished goods inventory, ending (1,000 units @ $6)	6,000		
Cost of goods sold		$30,000	
Selling and administrative (5,000 units × $2)		10,000	
Total variable costs			40,000
Contribution margin			$ 60,000

Fixed costs		
Manufacturing	$12,000	
Selling and administrative	15,000	
Total fixed costs		27,000
Operating income		$ 33,000

3. Reconciliation of income:

Increase in inventory units	1,000
Finished manufacturing overhead per unit	× $2
Difference in income	$2,000

Chapter Assignments

Questions

1. (L.O. 1) What is control? How do managers use accounting information to control operations?
2. (L.O. 5) What is a segment of an organization? Give examples of different kinds of segments.
3. (L.O. 5) How are costs assigned to organizational segments?
4. (L.O. 2) Discuss the benefits of decentralization.
5. (L.O. 1) Define responsibility accounting.
6. (L.O. 1) With a responsibility accounting system, unnecessary information is avoided. Why?
7. (L.O. 1) Why do managers delegate authority?
8. (L.O. 2) What are the common organizational patterns for delegating authority?
9. (L.O. 3) Describe the four types of financial responsibility centers.
10. (L.O. 4) Distinguish between controllable and uncontrollable aspects of revenue and costs. Can a manager totally control all revenue and costs? Why or why not?
11. (L.O. 4) Discuss how time affects the controllability of costs.
12. (L.O. 6) Why are responsibility reports for profit and investment centers based on contribution margins?
13. (L.O. 7) Explain why direct costing is useful to managers.
14. (L.O. 8) Under the direct and absorption costing columns on page 436, write true or false to indicate whether each statement is true or false for each costing system.

	Direct costing	Absorption costing
a. Fixed factory overhead is a product cost (inventoriable).	____	____
b. Variable selling expenses are period cost (noninventoriable).	____	____
c. Direct labor costs are a deduction when calculating contribution margin or gross margin.	____	____
d. Fixed administrative expenses are product costs.	____	____
e. Variable selling expenses are a deduction when calculating contribution margin or gross margin.	____	____

15. (L.O. 7) Discuss costs that should be included with inventory costs under (a) absorption costing and (b) direct costing.

16. (L.O. 7) A basic principle of direct costing is that fixed manufacturing overhead costs should be expensed as incurred. What is the rationale behind this procedure?

Exercises

17. (L.O. 8) During the year 19x1, Fleet, Inc., manufactured 700 units of Product A, a new product. Product A's variable and fixed manufacturing costs per unit were $6 and $2, respectively. Inventory on December 31 consisted of 100 units of Product A. There was no inventory of Product A on January 1.

Required Calculate the difference in the dollar amount of inventory on December 31 if direct costing had been used instead of absorption costing. (AICPA)

18. (L.O. 8) The following costs were incurred by the ABC Company:

    a. Variable selling expenses
    b. Direct materials
    c. Direct labor
    d. Variable manufacturing overhead
    e. Fixed factory overhead
    f. Fixed selling expenses

Required Classify the costs as components of inventory under absorption costing, direct costing, both or neither.

19. (L.O. 8) Case Company, which manufactures rivets, uses absorption costing. Case's manufacturing costs are as follows:

Direct materials and direct labor	$800,000
Depreciation, machines	100,000
Rent, factory building	60,000
Electricity, machines	35,000

Required What is the dollar amount of costs that should be included in inventory cost computations:

1. Under absorption costing?
2. Under direct costing?

(AICPA)

20. (L.O. 8) Herbson Manufacturing Company produces bicycle frames for several bicycle retailers. The company uses absorption costing. Herbson's manufacturing costs are as follows:

Direct materials	$500,000
Direct labor	250,000
Depreciation, machinery	100,000
Utilities, production	75,000
Rent, production facility	48,000

Required Determine the amount of cost that would be included in inventory cost computations under the following methods:

1. Absorption costing
2. Direct costing

21. (L.O. 8) For the year ended December 31, 19x9, Gorman Corporation produced 100,000 units. During the year, 75,000 of these units were sold for $15 per unit. There were no beginning inventories. Related manufacturing costs incurred were as follows:

Direct materials	$350,000
Direct labor	200,000
Manufacturing overhead	
Fixed	150,000
Variable	100,000
Selling and administrative expenses	75,000

Required Calculate the value of ending inventory using direct and absorption costing.

22. (L.O. 8) Drydon Corporation produces a single product. Year-end information is presented below for 19x8.

Opening inventory (units)	-0-
Units produced during the year	150,000
Units sold during the year	120,000
Variable costs per unit	
Direct materials	$5.00
Direct labor	4.50
Overhead	3.00
Selling and administrative	2.50
Fixed costs per year	
Manufacturing overhead	$300,000
Selling and administrative	100,000

Required

1. Compute unit cost under absorption and direct costing.
2. Determine the cost of ending inventory under absorption costing and direct costing.

23. (L.O. 8) Indiana Corporation began operating on January 1. It produces a single product, which sells for $9 a unit. During the year, 100,000 units were produced, and 90,000 units were sold. Manufacturing costs and selling and administrative expenses for the year were as follows on page 438.

	Fixed costs	Variable costs
Direct materials	$ -0-	$1.75 per unit produced
Direct labor	-0-	1.25 per unit produced
Manufacturing overhead	100,000	0.50 per unit produced
Selling and administrative	70,000	0.60 per unit sold

Required

1. Prepare a direct costing income statement and absorption costing income statement for the year.
2. Calculate the value of ending inventory using direct and absorption costing. (AICPA) (see Review Exercise 9–2)

24. (L.O. 8) The following information for the year ended December 31, 19x8, was obtained from records at Peterson Company:

Units manufactured	70,000
Units sold	60,000
Sales	$1,400,000
Cost of goods manufactured	
Variable	630,000
Fixed	315,000
Operating expenses	
Variable	98,000
Fixed	140,000

There was no finished goods inventory on January 1, 19x8.

Required

1. Calculate the value of ending inventory using absorption and direct costing.
2. What is the difference in operating income under absorption costing and direct costing? (AICPA)

25. (L.O. 8) JV Company produces a single product that sells for $7 per unit. During the year, 100,000 units were produced and 80,000 units were sold. Manufacturing costs and selling and administrative expenses are presented below. JV had no inventory at the beginning of the year.

	Fixed costs	Variable costs
Direct materials	$ -0-	$1.50 per unit produced
Direct labor	-0-	1.00 per unit produced
Manufacturing overhead	150,000	0.50 per unit produced
Selling and administrative expenses	80,000	0.50 per unit sold

Required

Prepare annual income statements using
1. Direct costing
2. Absorption costing

26. (L.O. 8) Information on the new product line at Keller Corporation is given below. There was no inventory at the beginning of the year. During the year, 12,500 units were produced; 10,000 units were sold.

Selling price per unit	$ 15
Variable manufacturing costs per unit of production	8

Total annual fixed manufacturing costs	25,000
Variable selling costs per unit of sales	3
Total annual fixed selling and administration expenses	15,000

Required

1. Prepare an income statement using direct costing.
2. Prepare an income statement using absorption costing.
3. Show what caused any difference between the income statements prepared in *1* and *2* above. (AICPA)

(see Review Exercise 9–2)

27. (L.O. 6) Markezin Company produces two products, X and Y. Both products are sold through either a domestic or foreign sales organization. Based on an analysis of manufacturing and marketing activities, the following sales prices and variable cost estimates were developed:

	Product X	Product Y
Sales price	$6	$9
Variable costs		
Cost of goods sold	$3	$5
Sales commission	1	1
Total variable costs	$4	$6
Contribution margin	$2	$3

Sales units for the two products by segment for 19x9 are given below.

	Product X	Product Y
Domestic	10,000	30,000
Foreign	20,000	20,000
Total	30,000	50,000

Fixed manufacturing and sales and administrative costs for 19x9, segmented by product and by region, are given below.

	Direct costs			
Fixed costs	Product X	Product Y	Common costs	Total costs
Manufacturing	$20,000	$25,000	$60,000	$105,000
Selling and administrative	25,000	10,000	30,000	65,000
Total	$45,000	$35,000	$90,000	$170,000

	Direct costs			
Fixed costs	Domestic	Foreign	Common costs	Total costs
Manufacturing	$ -0-	$ -0-	$105,000	$105,000
Selling and administrative	15,000	25,000	25,000	65,000
Total	$15,000	$25,000	$130,000	$170,000

Required Prepare income statements by product and territory for Markezin Company. Show contribution margin, segment margin, and operating income for 19x9. (see Review Exercise 9–1)

28. (L.O. 8) Vorst Manufacturing Company produces and sells a single product. The following costs relate to its production and sales:

Variable costs per unit	
Direct materials	$12
Direct labor	5
Manufacturing overhead	3
Selling and administration	4
Fixed costs per year	
Manufacturing overhead	$150,000
Selling and administrative	200,000

During last year, 50,000 units were produced and 45,000 units were sold. The Finished Goods Inventory account at the end of the year shows a balance of $100,000 for the 5,000 unsold units.

Required

1. Is the company using absorption costing or direct costing to cost the units in finished goods inventory? (Show computations to support your answer.)
2. Can Vorst Manufacturing Company use the $100,000 ending finished goods inventory amount when preparing external financial statements? Explain.

29. (L.O. 6) Ace Company sells two products, U and C, in two sales territories, East and West. An analysis of manufacturing and marketing activities for May 19x9 revealed the following sales prices and variable costs:

	Product U	Product C
Sales price	$16	$12
Variable costs		
Cost of goods sold	6	4
Sales commission	2	4
Contribution margin	$ 8	$ 4

Sales units for the two products by territory for May 19x9 are given below.

	Product U	Product C
East	60,000	70,000
West	40,000	20,000
Total product sales	100,000	90,000

The fixed manufacturing and sales and administrative costs have been collected for the month of May 19x9 and segmented by product and by territory as shown below.

	Direct costs			
Fixed costs	Product U	Product C	Common costs	Total costs
Manufacturing	$ 80,000	$ 90,000	$300,000	$470,000
Selling and administrative	120,000	60,000	150,000	330,000
Total	$200,000	$150,000	$450,000	$800,000

Fixed costs	Direct costs East	Direct costs West	Common costs	Total costs
Manufacturing	$ -0-	$ -0-	$470,000	$470,000
Selling and administrative	90,000	160,000	80,000	330,000
Total	$ 90,000	$160,000	$550,000	$800,000

Required Prepare segment income statements by product and by sales territory for Ace Company showing the contribution margin, the segment margin, and the operating income for the company for the month of May 19x9. (see Review Exercise 9–1)

30. (L.O. 8) The following information was obtained from the records of the Groovearts Manufacturing Company:

Units manufactured	100,000
Units sold	75,000
Sales	$1,875,000
Cost of goods manufactured	
Variable	225,000
Fixed	150,000
Operating expenses	
Variable	375,000
Fixed	800,000

There was no beginning inventory for the year.

Required

1. Using absorption costing, calculate the value of ending inventory.
2. Using direct costing, calculate the value of ending inventory.
3. Calculate the difference in operating income when using absorption costing versus direct costing.

31. (L.O. 8) Allen Company manufactures and sells a single product. The following costs are available for 19x9:

Variable costs per unit	
Direct materials	$10
Direct labor	7
Manufacturing overhead	4
Selling and administrative	2
Fixed costs per year	
Manufacturing overhead	$250,000
Selling and administrative	150,000

During 19x9, the company produced 25,000 units and sold 15,000 units at a sales price of $50 per unit. There was no beginning inventory at January 1, 19x9.

Required

1. Using absorption costing
   a. Compute the cost of producing one unit.
   b. Prepare an income statement for 19x9.
2. Using direct costing
   a. Compute the cost of producing one unit.
   b. Prepare an income statement for 19x9.

32. (L.O. 8) Weber Company's December 31, 19x8, financial statements, prepared on the basis of absorption costing, are as follows:

Sales revenues (10,000 @ $100/unit)		$1,000,000
Cost of goods sold		
Begining inventory	$ -0-	
Cost of goods manufactured (25,000 @ $10/unit)	250,000	
Goods available for sale	$250,000	
Ending inventory (15,000 @ $10/unit)	150,000	
Cost of goods sold		100,000
Gross margin		$ 900,000
Selling and administrative expenses		
Fixed		300,000
Variable (10,000 @ $3/unit)		30,000
Operating income		$ 570,000

The $10 manufacturing cost per unit is computed as follows:

Direct materials	$ 4
Direct labor	3
Variable manufacturing overhead	2
Fixed manufacturing overhead	1
	$10

Production and cost data are as follows:

Units produced	25,000
Units sold	10,000

Required

1. Prepare a contribution format income statement for the year ended December 31, 19x8, using direct costing.
2. Reconcile the difference between the two incomes.

33. (L.O. 6) Acme Company produces two products, J and W. The sales staff for Acme is segmented between domestic and foreign operations. The management accountants have just completed an analysis of manufacturing and selling costs for the year 19x9. Based on this analysis, the following sales prices and variable cost estimates have been developed:

	Product J	Product W
Sales price	$12	$18
Variable costs		
Cost of goods sold	6	10
Sales commission	2	2
Contribution margin	$ 4	$ 6

The sales units for the two products by segment for 19x9 are given below:

	Product J	Product W
Domestic	20,000	60,000
Foreign	40,000	40,000
Total sales	60,000	100,000

Fixed manufacturing and selling and administrative costs for 19x9 segmented by product and by geographic region are given below.

Fixed costs	Direct: Product J	Direct: Product W	Common costs	Total costs
Manufacturing	$40,000	$50,000	$120,000	$210,000
Selling and administrative	50,000	20,000	60,000	130,000
Total	$90,000	$70,000	$180,000	$340,000

Fixed costs	Direct: Domestic	Direct: Foreign	Common costs	Total costs
Manufacturing	$ -0-	$ -0-	$210,000	$210,000
Selling and administrative	30,000	50,000	50,000	130,000
Total	$30,000	$50,000	$260,000	$340,000

Required Prepare segment income statements by product and by market segment for Acme Company showing the contribution margin, the segment margin, and the operating income for the company for 19x9. (see Review Exercise 9–1)

Problems

34. (L.O. 6) Justa Corporation produces and sells three products, A, B, and C. These products are sold in both the local market and regional market. At the end of the first quarter of the current year, the following income statement was prepared:

	Local	Regional	Total
Sales revenues	$1,000,000	$300,000	$1,300,000
Cost of goods sold	775,000	235,000	1,010,000
Gross margin	$ 225,000	$ 65,000	$ 290,000
Selling expenses	$ 60,000	$ 45,000	$ 105,000
Administrative expenses	40,000	12,000	52,000
Total selling and administrative expenses	$ 100,000	$ 57,000	$ 157,000
Operating income	$ 125,000	$ 8,000	$ 133,000

Management is particularly concerned about the regional market because of its low operating income. This market was entered into a year ago because of excess capacity. Originally, it was thought that operating income would improve with time. But after a year there is no noticeable improvement.

When trying to decide whether to eliminate the regional market, managers received the following additional information about first quarter operations:

	Product		
	A	B	C
Sales revenues	$500,000	$400,000	$400,000
Variable manufacturing expenses as a percentage of sales	60%	70%	60%
Variable selling expenses as a percentage of sales	3	2	2

	Sales by markets	
Product	Local	Regional
A	$400,000	$100,000
B	300,000	100,000
C	300,000	100,000

All administrative expenses are fixed. The fixed administrative and fixed manufacturing expenses are common to the three products and the two markets. Remaining selling expenses are fixed for the year. They are common to the products and are direct costs for each market.

Required

1. Prepare a new income statement for the first quarter showing contribution margins by markets and segment contribution.
2. Prepare another income statement for the first quarter showing contribution margins by products.

(CMA)

35. (L.O. 6) Fauver Company sells two products, T and J, in two sales territories, North and South. Based on an analysis of manufacturing and marketing activities, the following sales prices and variable costs were developed:

	Product T	Product J
Sales price	$8	$6
Variable costs		
Cost of goods sold	$3	$2
Sales commission	1	2
Total variable costs	$4	$4
Contribution margin	$4	$2

Sales units for the two products by territory for May 19x9 are given below.

	Product T	Product J
North	50,000	60,000
South	40,000	30,000
Total	90,000	90,000

Fixed manufacturing and sales and administrative costs were collected for May 19x9 and segmented by products and territory. The results of this analysis are given on page 445.

	Direct costs			
Fixed costs	Product T	Product J	Common costs	Total costs
Manufacturing	$ 40,000	$60,000	$200,000	$300,000
Selling and administrative	60,000	20,000	80,000	160,000
Total	$100,000	$80,000	$280,000	$460,000

	Direct costs			
Fixed costs	North	South	Common costs	Total costs
Manufacturing	$ -0-	$ -0-	$300,000	$300,000
Selling and administrative	80,000	50,000	30,000	160,000
Total	$80,000	$50,000	$330,000	$460,000

Required Prepare segment income statements by product and by sales territory. Show the contribution margin, segment margin, and operating income for May 19x9.

36. (L.O. 8) The following information on operations at Kern Company for the year ended December 31, 19x8, was selected from their accounting records:

Units produced	10,000
Units sold	9,000
Direct materials used	$40,000
Direct labor incurred	20,000
Fixed manufacturing overhead	25,000
Variable manufacturing overhead	12,000
Fixed selling and administrative expenses	30,000
Variable selling and administrative expenses	4,500
Finished goods inventory, January 1, 19x8	None

Required

1. Calculate the value of the finished goods inventory using
   a. Direct costing
   b. Absorption costing
2. Calculate the difference between income when direct costing and absorption costing are used. (AICPA)

37. (L.O. 8) The following annual budget was prepared for managers making decisions about Product X:

Budgeted annual unit sales			200,000
Sales revenues			$1,600,000
Manufacturing costs			
Variable	$600,000		
Fixed	200,000		
Total		$800,000	
Selling and other expenses			
Variable	$400,000		
Fixed	160,000		
Total		560,000	1,360,000
Operating income			$ 240,000

At the end of the first six months, the following information is available:

Production completed	100,000 units
Sales	60,000 units

All fixed costs are budgeted and incurred uniformly throughout the year. Actual costs incurred were as budgeted. Annual sales of Product X have the following seasonal pattern (there is no beginning inventory):

	Portion of annual sales
First quarter	10%
Second quarter	20
Third quarter	30
Fourth quarter	40
	$100%

Required

1. Prepare an absorption costing income statement for the first six months.
2. Prepare a direct costing income statement for the first six months. (AICPA)

38. (L.O. 8) Patsy Corporation produces a single product. The following information relates to a year's budgeted activity:

	Units
Beginning inventory	-0-
Production	125,000
Available units	125,000
Sales	110,000
Ending inventory	15,000

	Per unit
Selling price	$5.00
Variable manufacturing costs	1.00
Variable selling and administrative costs	2.00
Fixed manufacturing costs, based on 100,000 units	0.25
Fixed selling and administrative costs, based on 100,000 units	0.65

Total fixed costs remain unchanged within a relevant range of 25,000 units and 160,000 units, or total capacity.

Required

1. Prepare income statements for the Patsy Corporation using
   a. Direct costing
   b. Absorption costing
2. Calculate the value of ending inventory using
   a. Direct costing
   b. Absorption costing (AICPA)

39. (L.O. 8) The vice president of sales at Huber Corporation has received the income statement for November 19x9. This statement, which was prepared on the basis of

direct costing, is reproduced below. The firm has just adopted a direct costing system for internal reporting.

Huber Corporation
Income Statement
For the Month of November 19x9

Sales revenues		$2,400,000
Variable cost of goods sold		1,200,000
Contribution margin		$1,200,000
Fixed costs		
Manufacturing	$600,000	
Selling and administrative	400,000	1,000,000
Operating income		$ 200,000

The controller attached the following notes to the statements.

- Unit sales price for November averaged $24
- Unit manufacturing costs for the month were:

Variable costs	$12
Fixed costs	$ 4
Total costs	$16

The unit rate for fixed manufacturing costs is based on monthly production of 150,000 units. Production for November was 50,000 units above sales. Inventory on November 30 was 50,000 units.

Required

1. The vice president for sales is uncomfortable with using direct costing and wonders what operating income would have been using absorption costing. Therefore, you have been asked to do the following:
   a. Prepare the November income statement using absorption costing.
   b. Reconcile and explain the difference between income figures when direct costing and absorption costing are used.
2. Provide the vice president of sales with sound reasons for using direct costing for income measurement. (CMA)

40. (L.O. 6, 7) DePaolo Industries manufactures carpets, furniture, and foam in three divisions. DePaolo's operating statement for 19x9 is given below.

DePaolo Industries
Operating Statement
For the Year Ended December 31, 19x9

	Carpet division	Furniture division	Foam division
Sales revenues	$3,000,000	$3,000,000	$4,000,000
Cost of goods sold	2,000,000	1,300,000	3,000,000
Gross margin	$1,000,000	$1,700,000	$1,000,000
Operating expenses			
Administrative	$ 300,000	$ 500,000	$ 400,000
Selling	600,000	600,000	500,000
Total operating expenses	$ 900,000	$1,100,000	$ 900,000
Income from operations	$ 100,000	$ 600,000	$ 100,000

Additional information on DePaolo's operations follows:

	Cost of goods sold		
	Carpet	Furniture	Foam
Direct materials	$ 500,000	$1,000,000	$1,000,000
Direct labor	500,000	200,000	1,000,000
Variable overhead	750,000	50,000	1,000,000
Fixed overhead	250,000	50,000	-0-
Total	$2,000,000	$1,300,000	$3,000,000

	Administrative expenses		
	Carpet	Furniture	Foam
Segment expenses			
Variable	$ 85,000	$140,000	$ 40,000
Fixed	85,000	210,000	120,000
Fixed home office expenses			
Directly traceable	100,000	120,000	200,000
General, allocated on sales dollars	30,000	30,000	40,000
Total	$300,000	$500,000	$400,000

Selling expenses are incurred at the segment level and are 80 percent variable for all segments.

John Sprint, manager of the foam division, is unhappy with DePaolo's operating performance as presented. According to Sprint, the foam division makes a greater contribution to company profits than is shown. He thinks operating statements should be revised for internal purposes. Furthermore, the company should consider using the contribution approach as a reporting format for these internal statements.

Required Using the contribution approach, prepare a revised operating statement by division for 19x9. It should facilitate the evaluation of divisional performance. (CMA)

41. (L.O. 8) BBG Corporation manufactures a synthetic element. For top management's use, BBG's accounting department prepared the comparable income statements presented below.

BBG Corporation
Statements of Operating Income
For the Years Ended November 30, 19x1, and 19x2

	19x2	19x1
Sales revenues	$11,200,000	$9,000,000
Cost of goods sold	8,800,000	7,200,000
Gross margin	$ 2,400,000	$1,800,000
Selling and administrative expenses	1,500,000	1,500,000
Income before taxes	$ 900,000	$ 300,000

The accounting staff also prepared related financial information, which is presented below. This schedule is meant to help management evaluate company performance. BBG uses the LIFO inventory method for finished goods.

BBG Corporation
Selected Operating and Financial Data
For the Years 19x1 and 19x2

	19x2	19x1
Sales volume	1,000,000 kg	900,000 kg
Beginning inventory	100,000 kg	-0-
Production volume	1,000,000 kg	1,000,000 kg
Sales price	$11.20/kg	$10.00/kg
Direct materials costs	1.65/kg	1.50/kg
Direct labor costs	2.75/kg	2.50/kg
Variable manufacturing overhead costs	1.10/kg	1.00/kg
Fixed manufacturing overhead costs	3.30/kg	3.00/kg
Total fixed manufacturing overhead costs	$3,300,000	$3,000,000
Fixed selling and administrative expenses	1,500,000	1,500,000

Required

1. Prepare an operating income statement for the years ended November 30, 19x1, and 19x2 for BBG Corporation. Use the direct costing method.
2. Present a numerical reconciliation of the difference in income before taxes for 19x1 and 19x2 using (a) the absorption costing method and (b) the direct costing method. (CMA)

42. (L.O. 6) Caprice Company manufactures and sells two products, a small, portable office file cabinet, which has been made for more than 15 years, and a home/travel file, which was introduced in 19x1. Caprice has only one manufacturing plant. Actual variable production costs per unit of product for 19x4 follows:

	Office file	Home/travel file
Sheet metal	$ 3.50	$ -0-
Plastic	-0-	3.75
Direct labor, $8 per direct labor hour	4.00	2.00
Variable manufacturing overhead, $9 per direct labor hour	4.50	2.25
Total variable production costs	$12.00	$8.00

Annual fixed manufacturing overhead costs were $120,000. Fifty percent of these costs are directly traceable to the office file department; 22 percent to the home/travel file department. The remaining 28 percent are common to both departments.

Caprice employs two full-time salespeople who sell both products, Pam Price and Robert Flint. Each salesperson receives an annual salary of $14,000 plus a sales commission of 10 percent of his or her total sales.

Caprice's selling and administrative expenses include the following traceable selling expenses:

	Office file	Home/travel file
Packaging expenses per unit	$2.00	$1.50
Promotion	$30,000	$40,000

Data on Caprice's actual sales for the fiscal year ended May 31, 19x4, are presented below. There were no beginning or ending balances of finished goods inventory.

	Office file	Home/travel file
Actual selling price per unit	$29.50	$19.50
Actual unit sales		
Pam Price	10,000	9,500
Robert Flint	5,000	10,500
Total units	15,000	20,000

Selling and administrative expenses other than the compensation of the sales people for the year ended May 31, 19x4, are as follows:

Untraceable administrative expenses		$34,000
Travel and entertainment expenses		
Pam Price	$24,000	
Robert Flint	28,000	52,000
Total		$80,000

Required

1. Prepare a segmented income statement of actual operating income for the fiscal year ended May 31, 19x4. Prepare the report in a contribution margin format by product. Reflect the operating income or losses for the company.
2. Prepare a segment income statement for each salesperson. Show the contribution margin and each salesperson's contribution. (CMA)

Case 1
Stratford Corporation (L.O.6)

Stratford Corporation is a diversified company whose products are marketed both domestically and internationally. The company's major product lines are pharmaceutical products, sports equipment, and household appliances. At a recent meeting of Stratford's board of directors, there was a lengthy discussion on ways to improve overall corporate profitability without new acquisitions as the company is already heavily leveraged. The members of the board decided that they required additional financial information about individual corporate operations in order to target areas for improvement.

Dave Murphy, Stratford's controller, has been asked to provide additional data that would assist the board in its investigation. Stratford is not a public company and, therefore, has not prepared complete income statements by segment. Murphy regularly has prepared an income statement by product line through contribution margin. However, Murphy now believes that income statements prepared through operating income along both product lines and geographic areas would provide the directors with the required insight into corporate operations. Murphy has the following data available to him:

	Product lines			
	Pharmaceutical	Sports	Appliances	Total
Production/sales in units	160,000	180,000	160,000	500,000
Average selling price per unit	$8.00	$20.00	$15.00	
Average variable manufacturing cost per unit	4.00	9.50	8.25	
Average variable selling expense per unit	2.00	2.50	2.25	
Fixed factory overhead excluding depreciation				$ 500,000
Depreciation of plant and equipment				400,000
Administrative and selling expense				1,160,000

Murphy had several discussions with the division managers for each product line and compiled the following information from these meeting:

- The division managers concluded that Murphy should allocate fixed factory overhead on the basis of the ratio of the variable costs expended per product line or per geographic area to total variable costs.
- Each of the division managers agreed that a reasonable basis for the allocation of depreciation on plant and equipment would be the ratio of units produced per product line or per geographical area to the total number of units produced.
- There was little agreement on the allocation of administrative and selling expenses so Murphy decided to allocate only those expenses that were directly traceable to the segment being delineated; i.e., manufacturing staff salaries to product lines and sales staff salaries to geographic areas. Murphy used the following data for this allocation:

Manufacturing staff		Sales staff	
Pharmaceutical	$120,000	U.S.	$ 60,000
Sports	140,000	Canada	100,000
Appliances	80,000	Europe	250,000

- The division managers were able to provide reliable sales percentages for their product lines by geographical area.

	Percentage of unit sales		
	U.S.	Canada	Europe
Pharmaceutical	40%	10%	50%
Sports	40	40	20
Appliances	20	20	60

Murphy prepared the product-line income statement shown below based on the data presented above.

Stratford Corporation
Statement of Income by Product Lines
For the Fiscal Year Ended April 30, 19x7

	Product lines				
	Pharmaceutical	Sports	Appliances	Unallocated	Total
Sales in units	160,000	180,000	160,000		
Sales revenues	$1,280,000	$3,600,000	$2,400,000	$ —	$7,280,000
Variable manufacturing and selling costs	960,000	2,160,000	1,680,000	—	4,800,000
Contribution margin	$ 320,000	$1,440,000	$ 720,000	—	$2,480,000
Fixed costs					
Fixed factory overhead	$ 100,000	$ 225,000	$ 175,000	—	$ 500,000
Depreciation	128,000	144,000	128,000	—	400,000
Administrative and selling expense	120,000	140,000	80,000	820,000	1,160,000
Total fixed costs	$ 348,000	$ 509,000	$ 383,000	$ 820,000	$2,060,000
Operating income (loss)	$ (28,000)	$ 931,000	$ 337,000	$(820,000)	$ 420,000

Required

1. Prepare a segmented income statement for Stratford Corporation based on the company's geographic areas of sales. The statement should be in good form and show the operating income for each statement.
2. As a result of the information disclosed by both segmented income statements (by product line and by geographic area), recommend areas where Stratford Corporation should focus its attention in order to improve corporate profitability.

(CMA)

Case 2
Music Teachers, Inc. (L.O.6)

Music Teachers, Inc. is an educational association for music teachers that had 20,000 members during 19x5. The association operates from a central headquarters but has local membership chapters throughout the United States. Monthly meetings are held by the local chapters to discuss recent developments on topics of interest to music teachers. The association's journal, *Teacher's Forum,* is issued monthly with features about recent developments in the field. The association publishes books and reports and sponsors professional courses that qualify for continuing professional education credit. The statement of revenues and expenses for the current year is presented below.

Music Teachers, Inc.
Statement of Revenues and Expenses
For the Year Ended November 30, 19x5
($000 omitted)

Sales revenues	$3,275
Expenses	
Salaries	$ 920
Personnel costs	230
Occupancy costs	280
Reimbursement to local chapters	600
Other membership services	500
Printing and paper	320
Postage and shipping	176
Instructors fees	80
General and administrative	38
Total expenses	$3,144
Excess of revenues over expenses	$ 131

The board of directors of Music Teachers, Inc. has requested that a segmented statement of operations be prepared showing the contribution of each revenue center (i.e., membership, magazine subscriptions, books and reports, continuing education). Mike Doyle has been assigned this responsibility and has gathered the following data prior to statement preparation.

- Membership dues are $100 per year of which $20 is considered to cover a one-year subscription to the association's journal. Other benefits include membership in the association and chapter affiliation. The portion of the dues covering the magazine subscription ($20) should be assigned to the magazine subscriptions revenue center.
- One-year subscriptions to *Teacher's Forum* were sold to nonmembers and libraries at $30 each. A total of 2,500 of these subscriptions were sold. In addition to subscriptions, the magazine generated $100,000 in advertising revenue. The costs per magazine subscription were $7 for printing and paper and $4 for postage and shipping.
- A total of 28,000 technical reports and professional texts were sold by the books and reports department at an average unit selling price of $25. Average costs per publication were as follows.

Printing and paper	$4
Postage and shipping	2

- The association offers a variety of continuing education courses to both members and nonmembers. The one-day courses cost $75 each and were attended by 2,400 students in 19x5. A total of 1,760 students took two-day courses at a cost of $125 for each course. Outside instructors were paid to teach some courses.
- Salary and occupancy data are as follows:

	Salaries	Square footage
Membership	$210,000	2,000
Magazine subscriptions	150,000	2,000
Books and reports	300,000	3,000
Continuing education	180,000	2,000
Corporate staff	80,000	1,000
	$920,000	10,000

The books and reports department also rents warehouse space at an annual cost of $50,000. Personnel costs are 25 percent of salaries.

- Printing and paper costs other than for magazine subscriptions and books and reports relate to the continuing education department.
- General and administrative expenses include all other costs incurred by the corporate staff to operate the association.

Doyle has decided he will assign all revenues and expenses to the revenue centers that can be

- Traced directly to a revenue center
- Allocated on a reasonable and logical basis to a revenue center

The expenses that can be traced or assigned to corporate staff as well as any other expenses that cannot be assigned to revenue centers will be grouped with the general and administrative expenses and not allocated to the revenue centers. Doyle believes that allocations often tend to be arbitrary and are not useful for management reporting and analysis. He believes that any further allocation of the general and administrative expenses associated with the operation and administration of the association would be arbitrary.

Required

1. Prepare a segmented statement of revenues and expenses that presents the contribution of each revenue center and includes the common costs of the organization that are not allocated to the revenue centers.
2. If segmented reporting is adopted by the association for continuing usage, discuss the ways the information provided by the report can be utilized by the association.
3. Mike Doyle decided not to allocate some indirect or nontraceable expenses to revenue centers because he believes that allocations tend to be arbitrary.
   a. Beside the arbitrary argument, what reasons are often presented for not allocating indirect or nontraceable expenses to revenue centers?
   b. Under what circumstances might the allocation of indirect or nontraceable expenses to revenue centers be acceptable? (CMA)

Case 3

Pralina Products Company (L.O.6)

Pralina Products Company is a regional firm that has three major product lines — cereals, breakfast bars, and dog food. The income statement for the year ended April 30, 19x8 is shown below; the statement was prepared by product line using absorption (full) costing. Explanatory data related to the items presented in the income statement appear after the statement.

Pralina Products Company
Income Statement
For the Year Ended April 30, 19x8
(000 omitted)

	Cereals	Breakfast bars	Dog food	Total
Sales in pounds	2,000	500	500	3,000
Sales revenues	$1,000	$400	$200	$1,600
Cost of sales				
Direct materials	$ 330	$160	$100	$ 590
Direct labor	90	40	20	150
Factory overhead	108	48	24	180
Total cost of sales	$ 528	$248	$144	$ 920
Gross margin	$ 472	$152	$ 56	$ 680
Operating expenses				
Selling expenses				
Advertising	$ 50	$ 30	$ 20	$ 100
Commissions	50	40	20	110
Salaries and related benefits	30	20	10	60
Total selling expenses	$ 130	$ 90	$ 50	$ 270
General and administrative expenses				
Licenses	$ 50	$ 20	$ 15	$ 85
Salaries and related benefits	60	25	15	100
Total general and administrative expenses	$ 110	$ 45	$ 30	$ 185
Total operating expenses	$ 240	$135	$ 80	$ 455
Operating income	$ 232	$ 17	$ (24)	$ 225

a. Cost of sales. The company's inventories of direct materials and finished products do not vary significantly from year to year. The inventories at April 30, 19x8, were essentially identical to those at April 30, 19x7.

The factory overhead costs for the 19x7–19x8 fiscal year were as follows:

Variable indirect labor and supplies	$ 15,000
Variable employee benefits on factory labor	30,000
Supervisory salaries and related benefits	35,000
Plant occupancy costs	100,000
	$180,000

b. Advertising. The company has been unable to determine any direct causal relationship between the level of sales volume and the level of advertising expenditures. However, because management believes advertising is necessary, an annual advertising program is implemented for each product line. Each product line is advertised independently of the others.

c. Commissions. Sales commissions are paid to the sales force at the rate of 5 percent on the cereals and 10 percent on the breakfast bars and dog food.

d. Licenses. Various licenses are required for each product line. These are renewed annually for each product line.

e. Salaries and related benefits. Sales and general and administrative personnel devote time and effort to all product lines. Their salaries and wages are allocated on the basis of management's estimates of time spent on each product line.

Required

1. The controller of Pralina Products Company has recommended that the company do a cost-volume-profit (CVP) analysis of its operations. As a first step the controller has requested that you prepare a revised income statement for Pralina Products Company that employs a product contribution margin format which will be useful in CVP analysis. The statement should show the profit contribution for each product line and the operating income for the company as a whole.
2. Calculate the breakeven point in sales dollars for 19x8.
3. What volume of sales dollars is necessary to achieve a 19x9 operating income 20 percent higher than in 19x8, assuming the revenues, costs, and product mix are the same as in 19x8?
4. What effect, if any, would there be on operating income determined in *1* above if the inventories as of April 30, 19x8, had increased significantly over the inventory levels of April 30, 19x7? Explain your answer. (CMA)

■

10

Standard Costs: Direct Materials and Direct Labor

LEARNING OBJECTIVES

After studying this chapter you should be able to:

1. Identify the two components of a standard cost and use them to calculate standard cost per unit
2. Discuss how standard costs are used
3. Discuss the two philosophies used to establish standard costs and evaluate their usefulness to managers
4. Calculate quantity and price variances for direct materials
5. Prepare a report showing direct materials quantity and price variances
6. Calculate efficiency and rate variances for direct labor
7. Prepare a report showing direct labor efficiency and rate variances
8. List common guidelines for variance investigations and evaluate their usefulness
9. Record standard costs in the general journal

Standards of one type or another are used to evaluate many activities. Universities set minimum grade-point standards for graduating students and for awarding honors. Designers of golf courses set an average score, or par, against which players may compare their scores.

Standards also determine the price you pay for some services. Automotive shops charge for repairs based on a standard time allowed for the work. For example, the standard time allowed for tune-ups might be one hour. In that case, the bill is based on the labor rate for one hour, even if the actual time needed to tune your engine is an hour and 15 minutes. The same standard can be used to evaluate the mechanic's efficiency, or the actual time he or she takes to perform a job.

Standards are used for planning and controlling as well. Manufacturing companies use standards to predict the per unit manufacturing cost of products before they are produced. Such information can be used to monitor costs as products move through production.

■

Uses of Standard Costs

OBJECTIVE 1
Identify the two components of a standard cost and use them to calculate standard cost per unit

In technical terms, a **standard cost per unit** is a predetermined cost consisting of two components:

1. A cost component based on a quantity of input used to produce a standard unit of finished product. The quantity standard is expressed in terms of some measure of input, such as pounds, gallons, board feet, yards, or direct labor hours for one unit of output.
2. A cost component based on a price standard for each measure of the quantity standard. The price standard is expressed in monetary terms per measure of input, such as dollars per pound, per gallon, per board foot, or per direct labor hour of input.

The standard cost is calculated by multiplying the quantity standard for each input by the price standard for that input.

Standard cost = quantity standard × price standard

From a cost accounting perspective, standard costs can simplify the process of assigning inventory a value so the cost of goods sold can be determined. From a managerial accounting perspective, standard costs facilitate the planning and control of operations. Standard costs are used both to prepare budgets (the planning function) and to measure performance (the control function).

Cost Accounting

OBJECTIVE 2
Discuss how standard costs are used

From a cost accounting perspective, the important feature of standard costs is that it is unnecessary to choose between LIFO, FIFO, or average cost to value inventories. With the collection of standard costs, all units are valued at the same standard cost per unit. When all inventory is valued at the same standard cost per unit, the cost of the ending inventory and the cost of goods sold will be the same whether you use LIFO, FIFO, or average costing. This simplifies the accounting procedures for recording the issuance and usage of direct materials and the recording of direct labor costs. If standard costs are revised at reasonable intervals to reflect current conditions, they can be used to value inventories on the balance sheet so long as they approximate actual costs.

Preparing Budgets

Quantity standards specify the quantity of direct materials and hours of direct labor needed to produce one unit of finished product. To prepare a budget, a manager must find the quantities of each direct material and type of direct labor needed to produce the planned level of output. This is done by multiplying the quantity standard for each input by the expected level of output, as shown below.

Standard unit quantity = quantity standard per unit × units of output

Next, the expected cost is determined by multiplying each standard input quantity by its price standard.

Expected cost = standard input quantity × price standard

Assume, for example, that a company plans to produce 1,000 units of product. The quantity standard specifies that 2 pounds of a direct material are needed for each finished unit. The standard input quantity would be calculated as follows:

Standard input quantity = 2 pounds × 1,000 units
= 2,000 pounds

Now, assume the standard price is $4 per pound of direct material. The expected cost would be:

Expected cost = 2,000 pounds × $4
= $8,000

Measuring Performance

Many variables affect the cost of producing a product, and managers are expected to control these variables to the extent that their authority permits. To know whether costs are within bounds, managers need a yardstick for comparing actual costs. Standard costs serve this purpose. They represent the expected cost of producing one unit of product. Thus, by comparing actual cost against standard cost, a manager can see the difference between actual and planned expenditures, or a **variance.** Any significant variance from standard costs indicates that operations are not proceeding as planned and that corrective action may be needed.

Because standard costs are used to measure managerial performance, how they are set is important to department managers and employees. In the next section, this text will examine the philosophy behind two methods of setting cost standards.

■

Bases of Standard Costs

How difficult should it be for managers and employees to meet standard costs? Should standard costs be set at a level rarely attained or a level attainable with a reasonable amount of effort? Opinions differ. Generally standard costs are classified into two categories, depending on the philosophy from which they were developed.

1. Currently attainable standards based on efficient operating conditions
2. Theoretical standards based on perfect operating conditions

Currently Attainable Standards

OBJECTIVE 3
Discuss the two philosophies used to establish standard costs and evaluate their usefulness to managers

Currently attainable standards represent the expected current cost of efficient operations. Because these standards are based on real rather than ideal targets, they include allowances for normal spoilage, idle time caused by equipment breakdowns, and other unavoidable events.

Currently attainable standards are expensive to develop. They are based on engineering estimates, including allowances for normal inefficiencies to the extent they can be anticipated and quantified. But they are also accurate and useful, both in cost accounting and managerial accounting. Throughout this chapter, the term *standards* will mean currently attainable standards.

Theoretical Standards

Theoretical standards represent the lowest possible cost attainable under ideal conditions. Theoretical standards are based on use of the smallest possible amount of materials and labor, purchased at the lowest prices, and used in the most efficient manner. In other words, if everything goes right and nothing goes wrong, theoretical standards can be attained.

Unlike currently attainable standards, theoretical standards make no allowance for normal spoilage, idle time due to equipment breakdowns, or other unplanned events. Like currently attainable standards, theoretical standards are based on engineering estimates. But since no allowance is made for normal inefficiencies, the estimates are less time-consuming and, thus, less expensive to develop. They are also less useful.

Some managers think employees perform more efficiently if they must strive toward high goals. But because theoretical standards represent unreal expectations, they should not be used to value inventory, prepare budgets, or evaluate performance.

■

Direct Materials Variances

Like all standard costs, those for direct materials consist of two components, a quantity standard and a price standard. The **quantity standard** represents the quantity of input—in this case, a direct material—that goes into producing one unit of output. The **price standard** is the price that management expects to pay for a unit of input; again, in this case, a direct material.

Establishing Standards for Direct Materials

Quantity Standards Quantity standards for direct materials are based on specifications from the design or engineering department about how a product should be produced. These specifications cover the types of materials needed, the quantities, and the appropriate production methods. Allowances for normal shrinkage and spoilage are quantified. For example, when liquid detergent is produced, the average shrinkage from evaporation is 0.1 per gallon. Thus, 1.1 gallons of input is needed to produce 1 gallon of output. Here, the quantity standard is 1.1 gallons of input per each gallon of output.

Price Standards The materials price standard is the price a company expects to pay per unit of direct materials in the current budget period. Price standards are usually set after consulting the purchasing department. They allow for discounts on bulk purchases as well as freight and shipping costs and are often controlled by market conditions.

Because materials prices tend to fluctuate, establishing such standards requires an awareness of supply and demand. Good forecasting of the quantities of materials needed and a knowledge of the most economical way of shipping them are also important.

Calculating Variances for Direct Materials

Once quantity and price standards are established, they can be used to evaluate actual costs by calculating variances. Variances from direct materials standards stem from the following two sources:

OBJECTIVE 4
Calculate quantity and price variances for direct materials

1. Differences between the actual quantity of materials used and standard quantities allowed for a given period's actual output
2. Differences between the actual price paid for direct materials and standard prices

The first of these differences is measured by a quantity variance; the second, by a price variance.

Quantity Variances The **direct materials quantity variance** is the difference between the actual quantity of direct materials used and the standard quantity of direct materials allowed, multiplied by the standard price per unit of direct materials. All variances can be either favorable or unfavorable. An unfavorable direct materials quantity variance means more direct materials were used than expected. This situation indicates either abnormal spoilage that may result from low-quality materials purchased from an outside vendor, inefficient use of materials, or both. A favorable direct materials quantity variance means fewer direct materials were used than expected. This situation indicates less than normal spoilage, better than expected efficiency in using the direct materials, or both. This may have resulted from good management of the production department, or perhaps from the purchase of materials of above-average quality.

The first step in calculating a quantity variance for direct materials is to determine the **standard quantity of direct materials allowed.** This computation is done by multiplying the standard quantity of direct materials per unit of output by the actual number of units manufactured during the accounting period. This is the amount of direct materials that should have been used, given the actual output.

$$\text{Standard quantity of direct materials allowed} = \text{standard quantity of direct materials per unit} \times \text{number of units produced}$$

During the accounting period, the standard quantity of direct materials allowed may differ from the budgeted quantity. This is because the number of units produced may differ from planned production levels.

Assume Thompson Company has set the following standards for one of its products:

Standard price per pound of direct materials	$4
Standard quantity of direct materials per unit of product	× 2
Standard direct materials cost per unit	$8

If the company produces 3,000 units in the first quarter, the total standard quantity of direct materials allowed is calculated as follows:

$$\text{Total standard quantity of direct materials allowed} = 2 \text{ pounds} \times 3{,}000 \text{ units} = \underline{\underline{6{,}000}} \text{ pounds}$$

The second step in calculating the quantity variance is to find the difference between the actual quantity of direct materials used and the standard quantity of direct materials allowed. Multiplying this difference by the standard price per unit of direct materials yields the direct materials quantity variance in dollars.

$$\text{Direct materials quantity variance} = \left[\text{actual quantity of direct materials used} - \text{standard quantity of direct materials allowed}\right] \times \text{standard price per unit of direct materials}$$

The standard price per unit of direct materials is the price a company expects to pay per unit of direct materials. When calculating the quantity variance, the standard price is used instead of the actual price to ensure measurement consistency over the year. A standard price usually remains constant over a year, while actual prices may fluctuate. By using a standard price in the calculation, variations in the quantity variance reflect changes in efficiency, not changes in price.

In the case of Thompson Company, assume that 6,100 pounds of direct materials were used. Therefore, the dollar value of the quantity variance is as follows:

$$\text{Direct materials quantity variance} = (6{,}100 \text{ pounds} - 6{,}000 \text{ pounds}) \times \$4$$
$$= \underline{\underline{\$400}} \text{ (unfavorable)}$$

The variance is unfavorable because the actual quantity of direct materials used was greater than the standard quantity allowed. Possibly because of some manufacturing inefficiency, 100 extra pounds of direct materials were needed to produce 3,000 units. The standard cost of those 100 pounds was $400.

The direct materials quantity variance can be shown graphically. In Figure 10–1, the company's unfavorable direct materials quantity variance is indicated by the gray-shaded area. This is the area between the actual quantity used, 6,100 pounds, and the standard quantity allowed, 6,000 pounds, on the horizontal axis, and the standard price per pound, $4, on the vertical axis. The dollar value of the variance is found by multiplying the values of the axes as follows:

$$100 \text{ pounds} \times \$4 \text{ per pound} = \$400 \text{ (unfavorable)}$$

The area to the left represents the cost of standard direct materials allowed for 6,000 pounds, or $24,000 (6,000 pounds × $4 per pound).

Price Variances The **direct materials price variance** is the difference between the actual price per unit of direct materials and the standard price, multiplied by the actual quantity of materials *purchased*. In a just-in-time (JIT) manufacturing environment, the quantity purchased is the same as the quantity used. Suppliers often make deliveries a number of times per day so the manufacturer does not

Figure 10–1

Graphic Illustration of Direct Materials Quantity Variance for Thompson Company

The standard price per pound of direct materials is $4 on the vertical axis. The standard quantity of materials allowed for this period's production is 6,000 pounds. The actual quantity of direct materials used is 6,100 pounds.

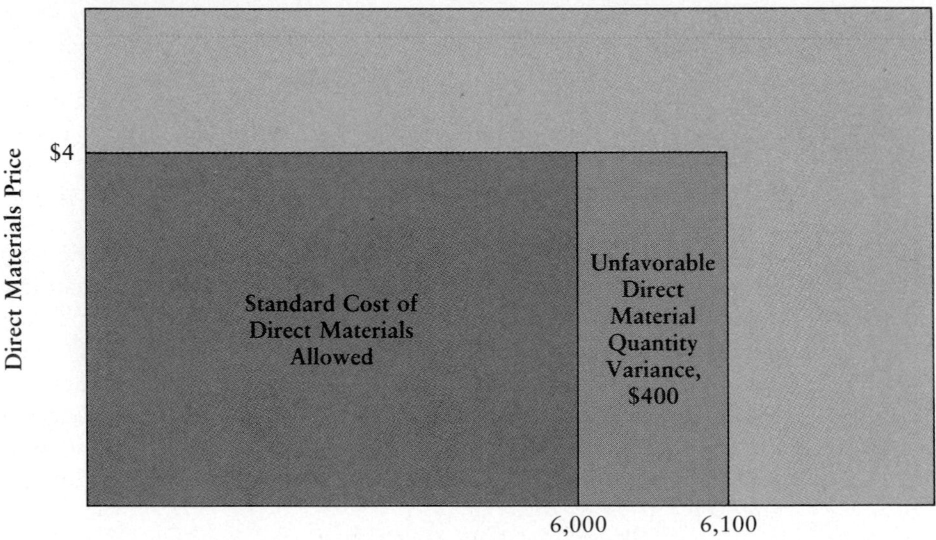

have to carry an inventory of materials. The direct materials price variance is used to determine the total amount of money saved or expended because of price differences. The computation for a price variance, which is sometimes called the purchase price variance for direct materials, is expressed mathematically as follows:

$$\begin{array}{c}\text{Direct}\\\text{materials}\\\text{price}\\\text{variance}\end{array} = \left[\begin{array}{c}\text{actual price}\\\text{per unit}\\\text{of direct}\\\text{materials}\end{array} - \begin{array}{c}\text{standard price}\\\text{per unit}\\\text{of direct}\\\text{materials}\end{array}\right] \times \begin{array}{c}\text{actual quantity}\\\text{of direct}\\\text{materials}\\\text{purchased}\end{array}$$

Remember that the standard price per pound of direct materials is estimated at the beginning of the fiscal year. The quantity of direct materials purchased, on the other hand, is a current figure.

Notice, too, that the price variance is based on the actual quantity *purchased*, not the actual quantity used. There are three reasons for calculating price variances this way. First, this method offers advantages in recordkeeping, which will be illustrated later. Second, and more important, since the purchase of materials precedes their use, a variance based on the quantity purchased can be reported earlier than a variance based on quantity used. The sooner a variance is reported, the sooner management is alerted to problems needing correction. Finally, the direct materials price variance is often regarded as a measure of the purchasing department's performance. Quantity purchased is a better measure of this department's activity than quantity used.

Actual data on direct materials purchased by Thompson Company follow:

Pounds of direct materials purchased	12,000 pounds
Price per pound of direct materials	× $4.20 per pound
Actual cost of purchases	$50,400

Using these data, the accountant calculates the price variance as follows:

$$\text{Direct materials price variance} = (\$4.20 - \$4.00) \times 12{,}000 \text{ pounds}$$
$$= \$2{,}400 \text{ (unfavorable)}$$

This calculation shows that the variance is unfavorable because the actual price exceeds the standard price.

Figure 10–2 shows the direct materials price variance graphically. It is the gray-shaded area between the standard price per pound, $4.00, and the actual price per pound, $4.20, on the vertical axis and the actual quantity purchased, 12,000 pounds, on the horizontal axis. Multiplying the difference of the values

Figure 10–2

Graphic Illustration of Direct Materials Price Variance for Thompson Company

The actual price of direct materials purchased is $4.20 per pound, while the standard price is $4.00 per pound. During this period, 12,000 pounds of direct materials were purchased.

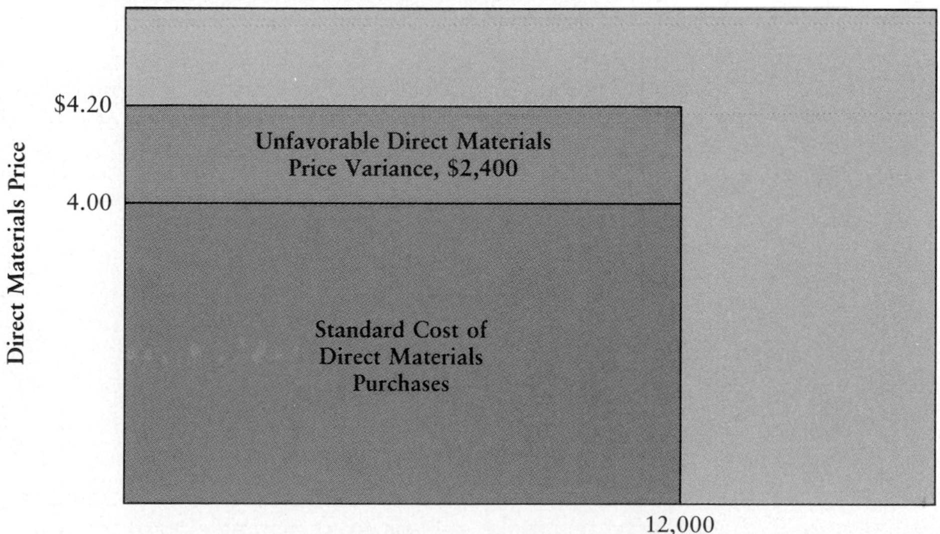

in the axes by the quantity purchased ($0.20 × 12,000 pounds = $2,400) yields the dollar value of the variance, which is an unfavorable $2,400. The area below shows the standard cost of direct materials purchases. This time it is for the actual quantity purchased, or 12,000 pounds.

To find the total variance for direct materials, the accountant simply adds the purchase price variance to the quantity variance. For Thompson Company, the total variance for direct materials is an unfavorable $2,800.

Direct materials price variance	$2,400 (unfavorable)
Direct materials quantity variance	400 (unfavorable)
Total direct materials variance	$2,800 (unfavorable)

Exhibit 10–1 shows an alternative computation of direct materials price and quantity variances that is mathematically equivalent to the above equation. Some people find it easier to visualize the variances using the format Exhibit 10–1 shows.

Review Exercise 10–1

Calculate Quantity and Price Variances

During May, Hasty Company incurred the following costs for direct materials:

Purchases (21,000 gallons @ $4 per gallon) $84,000
Usage 19,000 gallons

The standard requirements call for 2 gallons of direct materials to be used for each unit of output. The standard price per gallon of direct materials is $3.50 per gallon. During May, Hasty Company produced 9,000 units of finished product.

Required

1. Calculate the direct materials quantity variance.
2. Calculate the direct materials price variance.

Solution

1. Direct materials quantity variance

Standard quantity of direct materials allowed	=	standard quantity of direct materials per unit	×	number of units produced

18,000 gallons = 2 gallons × 9,000 units

$$\text{Direct materials quantity variance} = \left[\text{actual quantity of direct materials used} - \text{standard quantity of direct materials allowed}\right] \times \text{standard price per unit of direct materials}$$

$3,500 unfavorable = (19,000 − 18,000) × $3.50

2. Direct materials price variance

$$\text{Direct materials price variance} = \left[\text{actual price per unit of direct materials} - \text{Standard price per unit of direct materials}\right] \times \text{actual quantity of direct materials purchased}$$

$10,500 unfavorable = ($4.00 − $3.50) × 21,000 gallons

(see Exercises 12, 13)

Exhibit 10–1

Alternative Computation of Direct Materials Quantity and Price Variances

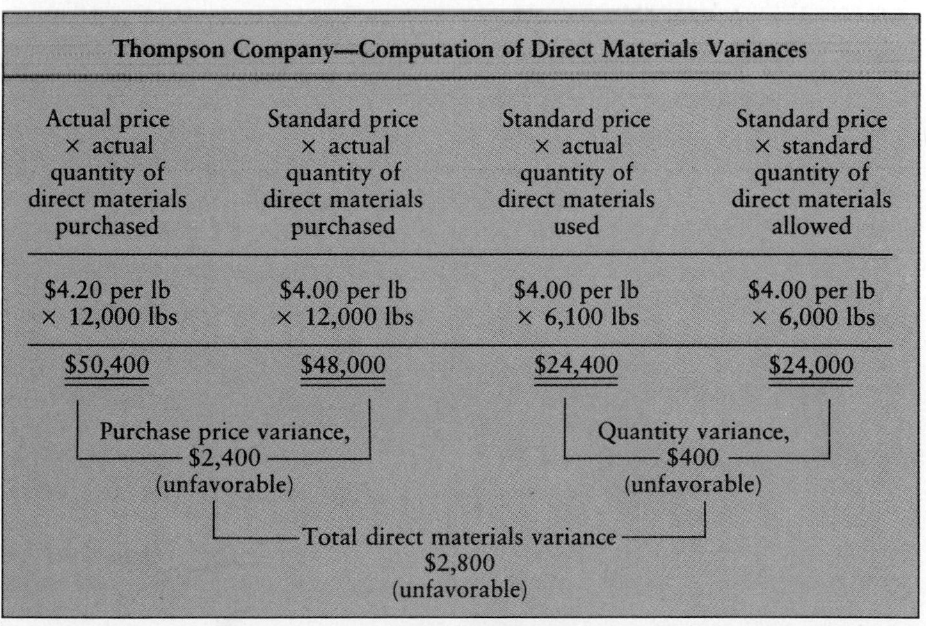

Thompson Company—Computation of Direct Materials Variances

Actual price × actual quantity of direct materials purchased	Standard price × actual quantity of direct materials purchased	Standard price × actual quantity of direct materials used	Standard price × standard quantity of direct materials allowed
$4.20 per lb × 12,000 lbs	$4.00 per lb × 12,000 lbs	$4.00 per lb × 6,100 lbs	$4.00 per lb × 6,000 lbs
$50,400	$48,000	$24,400	$24,000

Purchase price variance, $2,400 (unfavorable)

Quantity variance, $400 (unfavorable)

Total direct materials variance $2,800 (unfavorable)

Reporting Direct Materials Variances to Management

OBJECTIVE 5
Prepare a report showing direct materials quantity and price variances

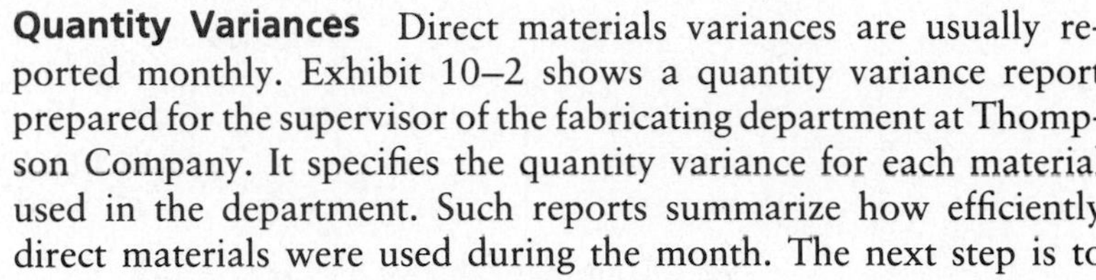

Quantity Variances Direct materials variances are usually reported monthly. Exhibit 10–2 shows a quantity variance report prepared for the supervisor of the fabricating department at Thompson Company. It specifies the quantity variance for each material used in the department. Such reports summarize how efficiently direct materials were used during the month. The next step is to 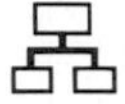 determine whether variances are significant. For significant variances, management must identify causes of that variance. If it is an unfavorable variance, management takes appropriate steps to prevent it from recurring in the future.

For day-to-day control of direct materials usage, department supervisors generally look at the amount of scrap material generated on the production line. Spoiled units are usually identified at inspection points throughout the factory. If spoilage exceeds normal expectations at any point, the supervisor in charge is notified. Machine operators and materials handlers prepare scrap tickets daily. If the quantity of scrap exceeds normal limits, the supervisor will investigate.

Direct materials quantity variances can be caused by various factors, depending on the nature of the manufacturing process. The most common are as follows:

- Inferior materials
- Incorrect machine settings
- Inexperienced personnel
- Incorrect standards
- Changes in the production process

The production supervisor can control only some of these factors. If the purchasing department acquires inferior materials, the production supervisor can only report the resulting quantity variance to upper-level management. The point is that only by investigating the causes of variances can problems be corrected. An unfavorable accounting report simply signals the need for an investigation.

Exhibit 10–2
Departmental Report for Direct Materials Quantity Variance

Thompson Company
Direct Materials Quantity Variance: Fabricating Department
For the Month of June 19x8

Item	Actual quantity used	Standard quantity allowed	Difference	Standard materials price	Quantity variance
Sheet metal (sq ft)	25,000	26,500	1,500	$1.80 per sq ft	$2,700 (F)
Plastic (lbs)	560	500	60	0.90 per lb	54 (U)

Exhibit 10–3
Departmental Report for Direct Materials Price Variance

Thompson Company
Analysis of Materials Purchase Price Variance
For the Month of June 19x8

Item	Supplier	Quantity purchased	Actual price per unit	Standard price per unit	Price difference per unit	Materials purchase price variance
Sheet metal	Xomac Co.	40,000 sq ft	$1.10	$ 1.00	$0.10	$4,000 (U)
Part #1064	Poncho Parts Co.	15,000 units	9.80	10.00	0.20	3,000 (F)
Total						$1,000 (U)

Price Variances Materials price variances are reported every month to the person in charge of purchasing. A large organization might have a purchasing manager overseeing all direct materials purchases. In a small organization, the production manager might make all purchases.

Exhibit 10–3 shows a price variance report for Thompson Company. For each material the report includes:

- A description of the item
- The supplier
- The quantity purchased
- The actual price per unit
- The standard price per unit
- The price difference per unit
- The resulting purchase price variance

Materials price variances are caused by many factors, such as:

- Ordering from the wrong supplier
- Incorrect order size, which affects the quantity discount
- Incorrect quality of materials
- Rush orders, which increase shipping costs
- Incorrect standard prices
- Changes in supply and demand

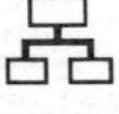

In most companies, a materials price variance is associated with the purchasing department. Thus, the manager of the purchasing department is responsible for identifying the causes of variances. The cause of a variance, however, might not have originated in the purchasing department. A change in production schedules might require a rush order at a higher-than-standard price. This would result in an unfavorable price variance. The appropriate corrective action would then be better production scheduling, which is outside the control of the purchasing department.

In the above discussion, control of direct materials cost is accomplished by comparing the actual cost with the standard cost and investigating important variances. In Chapter 7 we discussed the new manufacturing environment and the concept of a just-in-time (JIT) manufacturing philosophy. When JIT is adopted by an organization, control of direct materials cost is accomplished before the cost is incurred. This is accomplished by negotiating long-term direct materials contracts with suppliers specifying the price, quality of materials, and delivery schedules. An important performance measure for a JIT company is deliveries on time to the manufacturing site. Since the production of a product is initiated by customer demand, it is critical for the supplier to deliver high-quality materials on time to keep the manufacturing process operating. In these companies, price and quantity variances are calculated and reported along with other measures such as returns to suppliers, excess inventory levels, and delivery schedules met by supplier.

■

Direct Labor Variances

Like direct materials standards, direct labor standards can be divided into two components, a quantity standard and a price standard. The quantity standard represents the number of direct labor hours needed to produce one unit of finished product. The price standard represents the labor rate a company expects to pay for one hour of direct labor.

Establishing Standards for Direct Labor

Quantity Standards Since manufacturing most products involves a combination of many tasks, each task requires a direct labor quantity standard stating the amount of direct labor required for each unit of output. In many companies, quantity standards are established by engineering analyses. The condition and type of equipment, working conditions, availability of materials, and other factors possibly influencing the time needed to perform a task are measured quantitatively.

Allowances are then made for normal idle time, that is, time during which workers are paid even though they are not working. Such idle time is caused by fatigue or minor equipment malfunctions. This type of measurement is the most accurate method of setting quantity standards. Other methods management uses to set labor quantity standards include analyses of historical data and intuitive judgments by supervisors or other experienced people.

Price Standards The direct labor price standard is actually a labor rate standard. It represents the hourly rate a company expects to pay for each skill category for the year. The human resources department is usually consulted, as they are familiar with local labor markets. If the labor rate is based on a negotiated union contract, it is fairly accurate. If there is no union contract, the human resources department uses the prevailing market rate for each type of labor. The direct labor price standard generally includes an allowance for fringe benefits such as health care, life insurance, retirement, and employment taxes.

Calculating Variances for Direct Labor

OBJECTIVE 6
Calculate efficiency and rate variances for direct labor

The direct labor variance compares actual direct labor cost with the standard direct labor cost allowed for the units produced. As with the direct materials variance, the direct labor variance can result from the following two sources:

1. Differences between actual quantity of direct labor used and standard quantity of direct labor allowed
2. Differences between actual direct labor rate and standard direct labor rate

Direct labor variances are defined and calculated in exactly the same way as direct materials variances. Although quantities are measured in hours instead of pounds, yards, or gallons, the basic computations are the same.

Efficiency Variances The **direct labor efficiency variance** is the difference between the actual direct labor hours used and the standard direct labor hours allowed, multiplied by the standard rate per direct labor hour. **Standard hours allowed** is the standard quantity of direct labor hours allowed per unit of output, multiplied by the actual number of units produced. The direct labor efficiency variance is calculated in two steps. First, standard hours allowed is calculated as follows:

$$\text{Standard hours allowed} = \text{standard hours allowed per unit of output} \times \text{actual number of units produced}$$

Using this information, you can calculate the direct labor efficiency variance as follows:

$$\text{Direct labor efficiency variance} = \left[\text{actual direct labor hours used} - \text{standard direct labor hours allowed}\right] \times \text{standard rate per direct labor hour}$$

Suppose Thompson Company's labor costs are as follows:

Standard rate per direct labor hour	\$20
Standard hours allowed per unit of product	× 2
Standard direct labor cost per unit	\$40

Also suppose Thompson produces 3,000 units. Standard hours allowed is therefore:

$$\text{Standard hours allowed} = 2 \text{ hours} \times 3{,}000 \text{ units} = \underline{\underline{6{,}000}} \text{ hours}$$

Assume, however, that Thompson used only 5,800 direct labor hours to produce 3,000 units. Thus, its direct labor efficiency variance is as follows:

$$\begin{aligned}\text{Direct labor efficiency variance} &= (5{,}800 \text{ hours} - 6{,}000 \text{ hours}) \times \$20 \text{ per hour} \\ &= \underline{\underline{\$4{,}000}} \text{ (favorable)}\end{aligned}$$

The efficiency variance is favorable because the number of labor hours used was less than the standard quantity allowed. In other words, 200 fewer hours of labor were used in this period than would ordinarily be needed to produce 3,000 units. Since actual cost was less than standard, the result of the equation is a negative number, but by using the word favorable, the minus sign can be eliminated. At a standard rate of $20 per direct labor hour, this favorable variance saves the company $4,000.

Rate Variances The **direct labor rate variance** is the difference between the actual rate per direct labor hour and the standard rate per direct labor hour, multiplied by the actual direct labor hours used. This last number is the same as was used in calculating the efficiency variance. Direct labor is consumed as purchased, and its cost is immediately attached to units of output. This is not true of its materials counterpart, the direct materials price variance. Since the actual quantity of direct materials purchases is an inventoriable cost, it will rarely equal the actual quantity of direct materials used in production, a consumed cost. The direct labor rate variance may be stated as the difference between the actual direct labor rate and the standard direct labor rate, multiplied by the actual direct labor hours worked.

The first step in computing a direct labor rate variance is to find the actual rate (price) per direct labor hour. The formula is as follows:

$$\text{Actual rate per direct labor hour} = \frac{\text{actual direct labor cost}}{\text{actual direct labor hours used}}$$

The rate variance can then be calculated by using the formula below.

$$\text{Direct labor rate variance} = \left[\text{actual rate per direct labor hour} - \text{standard rate per direct labor hour}\right] \times \text{actual direct labor hours used}$$

Thompson paid $113,100 for 5,800 hours of labor used. Therefore, its actual labor rate averaged $19.50 per hour.

$$\frac{\$113{,}100}{5{,}800 \text{ hours}} = \$19.50$$

Thompson's direct labor rate variance is therefore:

$$\begin{aligned}\text{Direct labor rate variance} &= (\$19.50 \text{ per hour} - \$20.00 \text{ per hour}) \times 5{,}800 \text{ hours} \\ &= \underline{\underline{\$2{,}900}} \text{ (favorable)}\end{aligned}$$

In this case, the variance is favorable, since the actual labor rate is less than the standard labor rate.

The total direct labor variance is the sum of the direct labor efficiency variance and the direct labor rate variance. For Thompson Company, it is as shown below:

Direct labor efficiency variance	\$4,000 (favorable)
Direct labor rate variance	2,900 (favorable)
Total direct labor variance	\$6,900 (favorable)

The total direct labor variance is a favorable \$6,900. It is favorable because actual direct labor cost, \$113,100, was less than the standard cost allowed, \$120,000 (6,000 hours × \$20 per hour).

Thompson's direct labor variances are shown in Figure 10–3. Both variances can be illustrated on the same graph, since the hours purchased and the hours used are the same. The efficiency variance is represented by the area between the standard hours allowed, 6,000 hours, and the actual hours used, 5,800 hours, on the horizontal axis, and the standard labor rate, \$20, on the vertical axis. (This area is shaded dark gray.) The efficiency variance is a favorable \$4,000 (200 hours × \$20 per hour).

The direct labor rate variance is represented by the light gray-shaded area between the actual labor rate, \$19.50, and the standard labor rate, \$20.00, on

Figure 10–3
Graphic Illustration of Direct Labor Efficiency and Rate Variances
The standard labor rate is \$20.00 per hour, while the actual average labor rate was \$19.50 per hour. The standard quantity of direct labor hours allowed was 6,000 hours, but the actual quantity was only 5,800 hours.

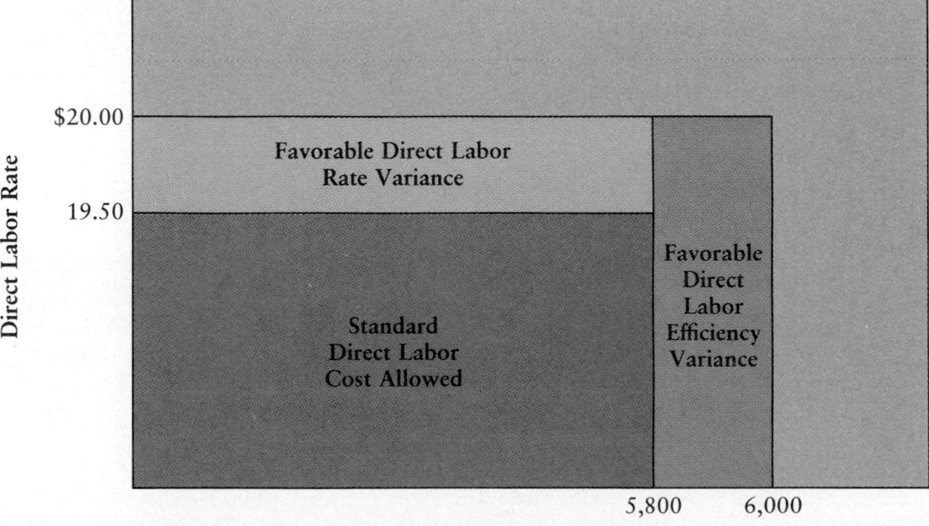

Exhibit 10–4
Alternative Computation of the Direct Labor Rate and Efficiency Variances

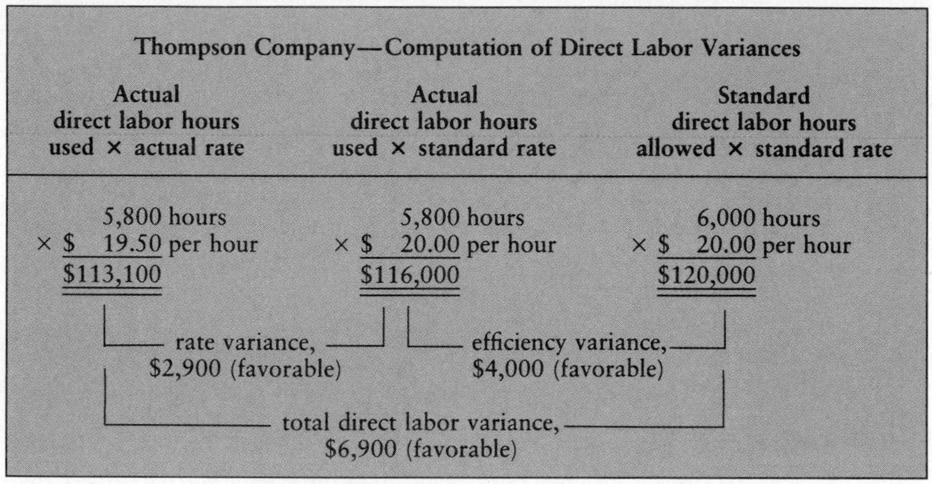

the vertical axis and the actual hours used, 5,800 hours, on the horizontal axis. This variance is a favorable $2,900 ($0.50 per hour × 5,800 hours).

The standard direct labor cost is the total red-shaded area, as well as the light and dark gray sections. This is the area bounded by the standard labor rate, $20, and the standard hours allowed, 6,000. The standard cost allowed is $120,000 (6,000 hours × $20).

Exhibit 10–4 shows an alternative computation of the efficiency and rate variances for direct labor that is mathematically equivalent to the above equation. Some people find it easier to visualize the variances using the format shown in Exhibit 10–4. Notice that only three columns are needed to summarize direct labor variances, as opposed to four for direct materials (Exhibit 10–1). As explained earlier, this is because actual direct labor hours purchased are the same as the actual hours used.

Review Exercise 10–2

Calculate Efficiency and Rate Variances

Case Company has collected the following information concerning their direct labor cost for April:

Actual hours worked	16,000
Actual direct labor rate per hour	$10.75

During April, Case Company produced 5,000 units of a product. The standard direct labor hours and standard direct labor rate are given below.

Standard direct labor hours	3.5 hours per unit
Standard direct labor rate	\$11 per hour

Required

1. Calculate the direct labor efficiency variance.
2. Calculate the direct labor rate variance.

Solution

1. Direct labor efficiency variance

$$\text{Standard hours allowed} = \text{standard hours allowed per unit of output} \times \text{actual number of units produced}$$

$$\underline{\underline{17{,}500 \text{ hours}}} = 3.5 \text{ hours} \times 5{,}000 \text{ units}$$

$$\text{Direct labor efficiency variance} = \left[\text{actual direct labor hours used} - \text{standard direct labor hours allowed}\right] \times \text{standard rate per direct labor hour}$$

$$\underline{\underline{\$16{,}500}} \text{ favorable} = (16{,}000 - 17{,}500) \times \$11 \text{ per hour}$$

2. Direct labor rate variance

$$\text{Direct labor rate variance} = \left[\text{actual rate per direct labor hour} - \text{standard rate per direct labor hour}\right] \times \text{actual direct labor hours used}$$

$$\underline{\underline{\$4{,}000}} \text{ favorable} = (\$10.75 - \$11.00) \times 16{,}000 \text{ hours}$$

(see Exercises 22, 26)

■

Reporting Direct Labor Variances to Management

OBJECTIVE 7
Prepare a report showing direct labor efficiency and rate variances

Efficiency Variances For day-to-day control purposes, a department supervisor relies on a daily direct labor report. This report summarizes information on employees' timecards, which show the number of hours spent on each operation and the number of units completed each day. The cards are collected at the end of each work shift. Actual hours worked are then compared with standard hours allowed for the number of units completed. Next, the information is reported to

Exhibit 10–5
Departmental Report for Daily Direct Labor Efficiency Variance

Thompson Company
Daily Direct Labor Efficiency Report: Fabricating Department
For Wednesday, June 20, 19x8

Employee number	Operation	Units completed	Standard hours allowed	Actual hours worked	Difference	Difference as a percent of standard
6574	Punch press	35	(35 × 0.2 hrs) 7 hrs	8 hrs	1 hr	(1/7) = 14%
8473	Punch press	30	(30 × 0.2 hrs) 6 hrs	8 hrs	2 hrs	(2/6) = 33%

the department supervisor, so any significant variance can be immediately investigated. Exhibit 10–5 shows a daily direct labor report for the fabricating department at Thompson Company.

Daily efficiency variances as well as any rate variance are summarized each month. Exhibit 10–6 shows such a monthly report. An efficiency variance is listed for each operation, such as punch press and folding. This breakdown tells the department supervisor how much each operation contributed to the total efficiency variance. In this case, the $2,000 in total variance is unfavorable because of a $4,000 unfavorable variance in the folding operation. Direct labor efficiency variances can be caused by various factors, including:

- Nonstandard equipment
- Inexperienced personnel
- Machine breakdowns
- Incorrect standards
- Lack of materials
- Inferior materials
- Changes in the production process

The department supervisor is responsible for investigating causes of significant variances and deciding how to correct them.

Rate Variances A direct labor rate variance generally results from the way workers are assigned to tasks and not from differences in labor rates. (Labor rates, which are set by union contract or established locally by supply and demand, change infrequently.) For this reason, rate variances are reported to the department supervisor, who assigns jobs to workers.

Suppose, for example, that a task calls for an unskilled worker but the department supervisor assigns a semiskilled worker to the task. The semiskilled worker would probably be paid a higher wage than an unskilled worker. Thus,

Exhibit 10–6
Departmental Report for Monthly Direct Labor Variances

Thompson Company
Analysis of Direct Labor: Fabricating Department
For the Month of June 19x8

Direct labor efficiency variance

Operation	Actual hours worked	Standard hours allowed	Difference	Standard labor rate	Efficiency variance
Punch press	800	900	100	$20 per hour	$2,000 (F)
Folding	1,500	1,300	200	20 per hour	4,000 (U)
Total	2,300	2,200	100		$2,000 (U)

Direct labor rate variance

Actual direct labor cost	$46,700
Standard direct labor cost allowed for actual hours (2,300 hours × $20 per hour)	46,000
Direct labor rate variance	$ 700 (U)

the assignment of the semiskilled worker to the task creates an unfavorable rate variance. If the worker performs the task more efficiently than an unskilled worker, the unfavorable rate variance could be offset to some extent by a favorable efficiency variance. Of course, the department supervisor may have good reasons for assigning a semiskilled worker to a task normally done by an unskilled worker. Perhaps there is a shortage of unskilled workers. In that case, departing from the standard skill level may be the only way to meet production objectives. Notice that the use of inexperienced personnel at a lower wage rate could cause a *favorable* direct labor *rate* variance while causing an *unfavorable* direct labor *efficiency* variance.

When skilled, semiskilled, and unskilled workers are employed together, the combination is called a **labor mix.** Hence, it is sometimes said that a direct labor rate variance is caused by the labor mix.

In the above discussion, performance of direct laborers was measured primarily through the calculation of efficiency and rate variances. In the new manufacturing environment, nonfinancial indicators are used extensively to measure performance. One need of just-in-time (JIT) manufacturing is multifunctional personnel. Since manufacturing is accomplished in cells for a single product, it is important for employees to know how to perform all the tasks required in the cell. Some manufacturing companies base promotion in part on the number of tasks an employee can perform. Many Japanese companies will display charts in the work area showing a roster of all employees and the tasks for which they are qualified. One of the major objectives of JIT manufacturing is continuous improvement of the process and product. Performance of employees is measured in some organizations by the number of ideas generated and the number of ideas implemented.

■

Investigating Variances

OBJECTIVE 8
List common guidelines for variance investigations and evaluate their usefulness

Direct materials and direct labor variances represent the difference between an expected cost and an actual cost. If a variance is significant, it signals that one of the following two actions should be taken:

1. The cause of the variance should be determined and corrected so the standard cost can be achieved.
2. The standard should be revised as it is no longer attainable.

How large should a variance be before it is investigated? To investigate a variance and take corrective action costs an organization something. That cost should be incurred only when there is reasonable chance that benefits will exceed costs. Variances representing minor deviations from budgeted amounts caused only by random fluctuations in business operations should not be investigated.

For example, if a quantity standard stipulates that one pint of paint should be used to finish a window frame, one expects some frames to take a little more than a pint and others a little less. This variation might be caused by fluctuations in air pressure in the paint gun or differences in paint thickness. Such deviations are part of normal operations. In this case, probably only a costly change in the painting process, such as the purchase of better-quality equipment, could change the deviation. Thus, the cause should not be investigated. The potential benefit is not worth the cost.

Should only unfavorable variances be investigated? Definitely not. Investigating favorable variances might reveal improved operating procedures applicable to other parts of the organization. A favorable variance might also suggest that a standard cost should be changed. Since standard costs are used to estimate variable costs and contribution margins, they should be current.

Two methods for deciding which variances to investigate are (1) statistical quality control and (2) managerial judgment. Both methods attempt to distinguish random variations from those with a correctable cause. Each one will be discussed.

Statistical Quality Control

The basic concept behind **statistical quality control** is that manufacturing and other repetitive processes are subject to some variability because of chance. This method also assumes some stable pattern of variability when measurements of repetitive processes are taken. As long as the measurements are within that pattern, the process is considered to be in a state of statistical control. However, a measurement outside the pattern is a signal that the process is out of control and should be investigated.

Thus, the objective of statistical quality control is to determine whether a process is operating in a state of statistical control. Technically speaking, a process is considered to be in a state of statistical control when the variability of its outputs is confined to chance. For example, a quantity standard specifies an average labor time of 0.5 hour per unit of product. That does not mean each unit of product requires exactly 0.5 hour or a sample of 4 units always averages 0.5 hour per unit to produce. In fact, if employees average 0.55 or 0.45 hour per unit, their variance from the average time of 0.5 hour will probably be considered a chance variation.

At a certain point, however, an observed variance is large enough to be considered statistically abnormal. For example, if employees suddenly begin averaging 0.75 hour a unit, the sharp rise in production time cannot be attributed to chance. Statistical quality control procedures indicate exactly what size variance should be considered normal or abnormal.

Figure 10–4 shows a **control chart,** a graphic representation of the range of random variations one expects in a manufacturing process that is in control. The red- and gray-shaded areas show the range of expected production time, or the range in which variations are considered normal. In this case, management expects average assembly times ranging from 0.3 hours per unit, the lower control limit, to 0.7 hours per unit, the upper control limit. Observed times outside this range

Figure 10–4
Statistical Control Chart

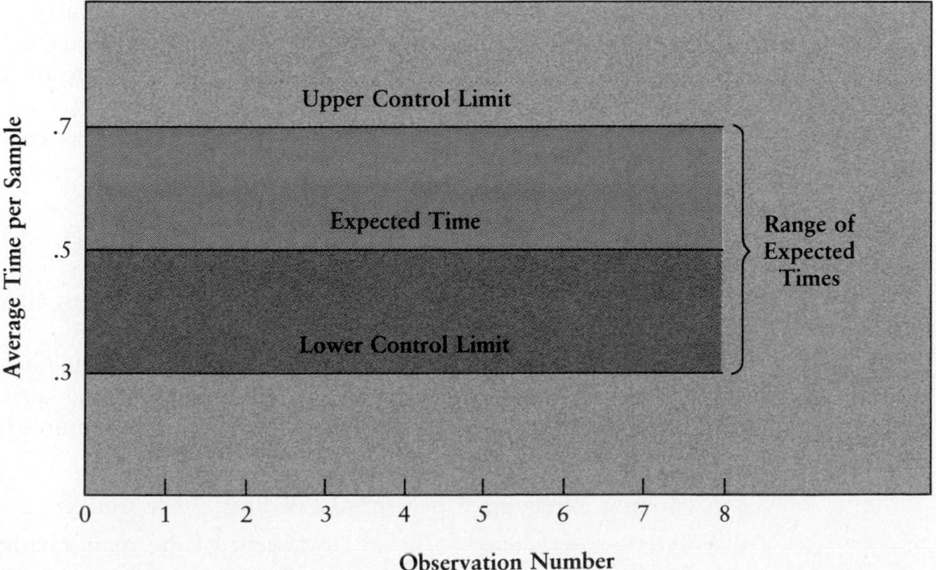

suggest abnormal performance and they should be investigated to see if the benefit from correcting the process outweighs the cost of making the correction.

In setting the control limits, management is balancing the cost of letting the process continue to operate versus the cost of investigating and correcting the cause of the variance.

Managerial Judgment

Managerial judgment is a method of monitoring manufacturing variances by using general guidelines developed by management to evaluate the significance of a variance. Some guidelines are based on the absolute dollar amounts, percentages of budgeted cost, or a combination of these two measures.

Using absolute amounts is simple, and it seems logical at first glance. For example, a manager using absolute amounts might investigate all variances greater than $500. The amount is usually established by comparing the cost of investigating a variance with its potential benefits (savings created by avoiding that variance in the future). Using an absolute dollar amount prevents small variances from being investigated. The savings from such investigations are almost always less than the investigation's cost. The problem is that the probability of an out-of-control process might be fairly high in some situations and fairly low in others, given the same dollar variation.

For example, if an item is budgeted at $1,000 and the variance is $500, common sense tells you there is a high probability something has gone wrong. A process that generates a variance that is 50 percent of the budgeted amount is almost certainly out of control. But if the budgeted amount is $10,000 and the variance is $500, the probability that something has gone wrong is low. A variance of only 5 percent of a budgeted amount is common in some processes.

To overcome the problems involved in using a dollar amount, some firms use percentages to decide whether to investigate variances. Based on experience, managers might decide that any variance greater than 10 percent of a budgeted cost should be investigated. In their judgment, any variance of more than 10 percent means a process is probably out of control.

There are problems with this approach as well, however. For instance, if a process is out of control but the budget item is small, a 10 percent variance may be an insignificant dollar amount. A 10 percent deviation from a $1 million item, however, would certainly be worth investigating. The savings or loss would be $100,000. But a 10 percent deviation from a $100 item is worth only $10. In this instance, the cost of investigating the variance would almost always be greater than the potential savings.

For this reason, many companies use both percentages and absolute amounts to determine the significance of a variance. Some companies also consider the type of budget item causing the variance in question. For example, one company investigates variances for any of the following conditions:

- A variance exceeding 1 percent of the direct labor budget
- A variance exceeding $500 or 10 percent of the manufacturing overhead budget

- A variance exceeding 10 percent of budgeted profit
- A variance exceeding 5 percent of budgeted sales revenue

Although one can criticize such guidelines for their lack of statistical support, they are simple and inexpensive to apply. And the benefits of using a statistical approach may not outweigh development and implementation costs.

■

Standard Costs in the General Ledger

OBJECTIVE 9
Record standard costs in the general journal

Manufacturing costs are usually entered into the general or special journals each week or month from purchase records, materials requisition forms, timecards, and records of the number of units finished. To illustrate the process, the text uses data from Exhibits 10–1 and 10–4.

Materials costs as well as any price variances are entered when purchased. To record the purchase of 12,000 pounds of direct materials at a cost of $4.20 per pound, the accountant makes the following journal entry:

Materials Inventory		
(12,000 pounds × $4 per pound)	48,000	
Direct Materials Purchase Price Variance	2,400	
Accounts Payable		50,400
To record purchase of 12,000 pounds at $4.20 per pound		

Accounts Payable is increased by the actual amount owed for the materials. The Materials Inventory is increased by the quantity of materials purchased times the standard price per unit. To balance the two entries, the accountant enters a price variance account. The accounting is simplified because all items in the Materials Inventory are valued at the same standard price. The accountant need not worry about whether average cost, LIFO, or FIFO is to be used. All inventory is valued equally, regardless of when it was purchased.

Direct materials quantity variances are entered into the general ledger either weekly or monthly from direct materials requisition forms. To record the issue of material from inventory, an accountant makes the following journal entry:

Work in Process Inventory		
(6,000 pounds × $4 per pound)	24,000	
Direct Materials Quantity Variance	400	
Materials Inventory		24,400
To record the use of 6,100 pounds at $4 per pound		

As in the first entry, the unfavorable variance balances the entry.

Direct labor costs as well as any price and quantity variances are entered in a single journal entry.

Work in Process Inventory (6,000 hours × $20 per hour)	120,000	
Direct Labor Efficiency Variance		4,000
Direct Labor Rate Variance		2,900
Payroll		113,100
To record the payroll of 5,800 hours at $19.50 per hour		

Work in Process Inventory is debited for the cost of the standard amount of direct labor hours allowed for 3,000 units of product at the standard rate. The efficiency and rate variances balance the entry after the payroll liability is increased.

Chapter Review

Review of Learning Objectives

1. **Identify the two components of a standard cost and use them to calculate standard cost per unit.**
Standard cost per unit of output is a predetermined cost consisting of two components.

   a. A cost component based on a quantity of input used to produce a standard unit of finished product. The quantity standard is expressed in terms of some measure of input, such as pounds, gallons, board feet, yards, or direct labor hours for one unit of output.

   b. A cost component based on a price standard for each measure of the quantity standard. The price standard is expressed in monetary terms per measure of input, such as dollars per pound, per gallon, per board foot, or per direct labor hour of input.

   To calculate the standard cost, multiply the quantity standard for each input by the price standard for that input (standard cost = quantity standard × price standard).

2. **Discuss how standard costs are used.**
In financial accounting, standard costs are used to simplify the cost accounting process, to value inventories, and to determine the cost of goods sold. In managerial accounting, standard costs are used to prepare budgets and measure performance.
When preparing budgets, you use the quantity standard to calculate standard input quantity, given the expected level of output (standard input quantity = quantity standard per unit × units of output). The price standard is used to calculate the expected cost of the input quantity (expected cost = standard input quantity × price standard).
When evaluating performance, compare actual costs against standard costs. The difference between an actual cost and a standard cost is called a variance. If the variance is large, the cause of that variance should be investigated.

3. **Discuss the two philosophies used to establish standard costs and evaluate their usefulness to managers.**
The two philosophies used to set standard costs are (a) currently attainable standards, which are based on efficient operating conditions; and (b) theoretical standards, which are based on perfect operating conditions. Currently attainable standards include allowances for normal spoilage, idle time, and other unavoidable instances of waste. Based on engineering estimates, currently attainable standards are useful in both cost accounting and managerial accounting. Theoretical standards include no allowance for normal instances of waste. The standards are based on the assumption that nothing will go wrong. Although some managers believe theoretical standards motivate employees to achieve higher levels of production, they are generally not used for planning and control purposes or for preparing financial statements.

4. **Calculate quantity and price variances for direct materials.**
Variances from direct materials standards stem from (a) differences between the actual quantity of direct materials used and standard quantity of direct materials allowed and (b) differences between the actual price per unit paid for direct materials and the standard price. A direct materials quantity variance is calculated as shown below.

$$\text{Standard quantity of direct materials allowed} = \text{standard quantity of direct materials per unit} \times \text{actual number of units produced}$$

$$\text{Direct materials quantity variance} = \left[\text{actual quantity of direct materials used} - \text{standard quantity of direct materials allowed}\right] \times \text{standard price per unit of direct materials}$$

The direct materials price variance is calculated as follows:

$$\text{Direct materials price variance} = \left[\text{actual price per unit of direct materials} - \text{standard price per unit of direct materials}\right] \times \text{actual quantity of direct materials purchased}$$

5. **Prepare a report showing direct materials quantity and price variances.**
To control day-to-day usage of direct materials, department supervisors generally look at the amount of scrap material generated on the production line and recorded on scrap tickets collected from production employees. At the end of each month, a report is prepared for the supervisor of each department. This report shows quantity variances for the materials used. (In Exhibit 10–2 an example of such a report is shown.) The supervisor is expected to follow up on significant variances and take corrective action. A report summarizing direct materials price variances is also prepared for the purchasing manager. This report shows price variances by items and by suppliers (Exhibit 10–3). The purchasing manager follows up on significant price variances.

6. **Calculate efficiency and rate variances for direct labor.**
Variances from direct labor standards stem from (a) differences between the actual direct labor hours used and the standard hours allowed and (b) differences between the actual direct labor rate and the standard direct labor rate. The direct labor efficiency variance is calculated as follows:

$$\text{Standard hours allowed} = \text{standard hours allowed per unit of output} \times \text{number of units produced}$$

$$\text{Direct labor efficiency variance} = \left[\text{actual direct labor hours used} - \text{standard direct labor hours allowed}\right] \times \text{standard rate per direct labor hour}$$

The direct labor rate variance is calculated as follows:

$$\text{Direct labor rate variance} = \left[\text{actual rate per direct labor hour} - \text{standard rate per direct labor hour}\right] \times \text{actual direct labor hours used}$$

7. **Prepare a report showing direct labor efficiency and rate variances.**
To control day-to-day use of direct labor, department supervisors rely on daily reports that show the relationship between actual hours worked and standard hours allowed for each operation (Exhibit 10–5). Each month a report, showing the efficiency variance by operation as well as the rate variance, is prepared for each department's supervisor (Exhibit 10–6). Significant variances are investigated to determine whether corrective action is warranted.

8. **List common guidelines for variance investigations and evaluate their usefulness.**
When a variance is significant, it signals that (a) the variance should be corrected or (b) the standard quantity or price is no longer attainable and should be revised. There are two methods for deciding whether a variance is worth investigating: (a) statistical quality control and (b) managerial judgment. Statistical quality control relies on the concept that repetitive processes are subject to some variability because of chance. This method uses a control chart that graphically represents the range of random variation management expects when a process is under control. Observations outside the range of expected performance indicate the process is out of control and should be investigated.
Managerial judgment, a method of monitoring manufacturing variances, relies on general guidelines developed by managers over the years. These guidelines are based on measures of absolute dollar amounts, percentages of expected costs, or a combination of the two. Although such guidelines may be criticized for lack of statistical support, they are simple and easy to use.

9. **Record standard costs in the general journal.**
Manufacturing costs are usually entered into the general or special journals each week or month from purchase records, materials requisition forms, timecards, and records of the number of units finished. Variances are recorded as resources are purchased and used.

Review of Key Terms

Control chart A graphic representation of the range of random variations one expects in a manufacturing process that is in control. Used in statistical quality control.

Currently attainable standards Standard costs representing the expected current cost of efficient operations.

Direct labor efficiency variance The difference between actual direct labor hours used and standard direct labor hours allowed, multiplied by the standard rate per direct labor hour.

Direct labor rate variance The difference between the actual rate per direct labor hour and the standard rate per direct labor hour, multiplied by the actual direct labor hours used.

Direct materials price variance The difference between the actual price paid per unit of direct materials and the standard price, multiplied by the actual quantity of direct materials purchased.

Direct materials quantity variance The difference between the actual quantity of direct materials used and the standard quantity of direct materials allowed, multiplied by the standard price per unit of direct materials.

Labor mix The combination of skilled, semiskilled, and unskilled workers used.

Managerial judgment A method of monitoring manufacturing variances by using general guidelines developed by management to evaluate the significance of a variance. The guidelines are based on absolute dollar amounts, percentages of budgeted cost, or a combination of these two measures. Used to decide if variances should be investigated.

Price standard The price that management expects to pay for a unit of input.

Quantity standard The quantity of input needed to produce one unit of output. Expressed in terms of pounds, gallons, board feet, yards, direct labor hours, or another measure.

Standard cost per unit A predetermined cost consisting of two components: (1) a cost component based on a quantity of input used to produce a standard unit of finished product and (2) a cost component based on a price standard for each measure of the quantity standard. Calculated by multiplying the quantity standard for each input by the price standard for that input.

Standard hours allowed The standard quantity of direct labor hours allowed per unit of output, multiplied by the actual number of units produced.

Standard quantity of direct materials allowed The standard quantity of direct materials per unit of output multiplied by the actual number of units manufactured during the accounting period.

Statistical quality control A procedure for monitoring manufacturing variances. It is based on statistical estimates of chance variations in a manufacturing process that is under control. Used to decide which variances should be investigated.

Theoretical standards Standard costs representing the lowest possible costs attainable under ideal conditions.

Variance For each type of input, the total difference between actual costs and standard costs.

Review Problem

Bay Company, which manufactures widgets, has developed the following standards for direct materials and direct labor for one widget:

Direct materials	
(12 pounds @ \$4)	\$ 48
Direct labor	
(5 hours @ \$15)	75
Total	\$123

During the year, 15,000 units were completed. However, 16,000 units were budgeted for production. The actual results show the following:

Direct materials	190,000 pounds used
Direct labor	73,000 hours used
Direct labor cost	$1,080,400
Purchases (200,000 pounds of direct materials @ $3.90)	780,000

Required

1. Calculate the direct materials quantity variance.
2. Calculate the direct materials price variance.
3. Calculate the direct labor efficiency variance.
4. Calculate the direct labor rate variance.

Solution to Review Problem

1. Direct materials quantity variance

$$\text{Standard quantity of direct materials allowed} = \text{standard quantity of direct materials per unit} \times \text{number of units produced}$$
$$= 12 \text{ pounds per unit} \times 15{,}000 \text{ units}$$
$$= \underline{\underline{180{,}000}} \text{ pounds}$$

$$\text{Direct materials quantity variance} = \left[\text{actual quantity of direct materials used} - \text{standard quantity of direct materials allowed}\right] \times \text{standard price per unit of direct materials}$$
$$= (190{,}000 \text{ pounds} - 180{,}000 \text{ pounds}) \times \$4 \text{ per pound}$$
$$= \underline{\underline{\$40{,}000}} \text{ (unfavorable)}$$

2. Direct materials price variance

$$\text{Direct materials price variance} = \left[\text{actual price per unit of direct materials} - \text{standard price per unit of direct materials}\right] \times \text{actual quantity of direct materials purchased}$$
$$= (\$3.90 - \$4.00) \times 200{,}000$$
$$= \underline{\underline{\$20{,}000}} \text{ (favorable)}$$

3. Direct labor efficiency variance

$$\text{Standard hours allowed} = \text{standard hours allowed per unit of output} \times \text{number of units produced}$$
$$= 5 \text{ hours per unit} \times 15{,}000 \text{ units}$$
$$= \underline{\underline{75{,}000}} \text{ hours}$$

$$\text{Direct labor efficiency variance} = \left[\text{actual direct labor hours used} - \text{standard direct labor hours allowed}\right] \times \text{standard rate per direct labor hour}$$
$$= (73{,}000 \text{ hours} - 75{,}000 \text{ hours}) \times \$15 \text{ per hour}$$
$$= \underline{\underline{\$30{,}000}} \text{ (favorable)}$$

4. Direct labor rate variance

$$\text{Actual labor rate} = \frac{\$1{,}080{,}400}{73{,}000 \text{ hours}} = \underline{\underline{\$14.80}}$$

$$\begin{aligned}\text{Direct labor rate variance} &= \left[\begin{matrix}\text{actual rate}\\ \text{per direct}\\ \text{labor hour}\end{matrix} - \begin{matrix}\text{standard rate}\\ \text{per direct}\\ \text{labor hour}\end{matrix}\right] \times \begin{matrix}\text{actual}\\ \text{direct labor}\\ \text{hours used}\end{matrix}\\ &= (\$14.80 \text{ per hour} - \$15.00 \text{ per hour}) \times 73{,}000 \text{ hours}\\ &= \underline{\underline{\$14{,}600}} \text{ (favorable)}\end{aligned}$$

Chapter Assignments

Questions

1. (L. O. 1) Define the components of a standard cost.
2. (L.O. 2) Discuss how a standard cost is used.
3. (L.O. 3) Discuss the two philosophies used to decide the levels at which a standard cost should be set.
4. (L.O. 4) How are standards established for direct materials?
5. (L.O. 6) How are standards established for direct labor?
6. (L.O. 5) What are the major causes of direct materials price and quantity variances?
7. (L.O. 7) What are the major causes of direct labor rate and efficiency variances?
8. (L.O. 4) Why is the direct materials price variance generally computed based on quantity purchased?
9. (L.O. 8) Should only unfavorable variances be investigated? Why?
10. (L.O. 8) Discuss the major differences between the statistical quality control approach and the managerial judgment approach to investigating variances.
11. (L.O. 6) Why is the quantity of direct labor purchased always the same as the quantity used? Is this true for direct materials? Discuss.

Exercises

12. (L.O. 4) Home Company manufactures tables with vinyl tops. The standard material cost for the vinyl used for a Type-R table is $7.80. This cost is based on 6 square feet of vinyl at $1.30 per square foot. During January, 7,000 square feet of vinyl

were purchased for $8,610. In January, 1,000 tables were produced and 6,400 square feet of vinyl were used.

Required Calculate direct materials price and quantity variances. (see Review Exercise 10–1)(AICPA)

13. (L.O. 4, 9) During March, direct materials costs for manufacturing Product T at Younger Company were as follows:

Actual price per unit	$6.50
Standard quantity allowed for actual production	2,100
Quantity purchased	2,400
Quantity used for production	2,300
Standard price per unit	$6.25

Required

1. Calculate direct materials price and quantity variances.
2. Prepare journal entries to record the purchase and use of direct materials. (AICPA) (see Review Exercise 10–1)

14. (L.O. 6) Lion Company's direct labor costs for January were as follows:

Actual direct labor hours used	20,000
Standard direct labor hours allowed	21,000
Direct labor rate variance (unfavorable)	$ 3,000
Actual direct labor costs	126,000

Required Calculate Lion's direct labor efficiency variance. (AICPA)

15. (L.O. 4, 9) During the month of June, the books of the Orange Company reflected the following cost data for direct materials:

Actual price per unit	$8.00 per pound
Standard quantity allowed for production	2,500 pounds
Quantity purchased	3,000 pounds
Quantity used for production	2,800 pounds
Standard price per unit	$7.75 per pound

Required

1. Calculate direct materials price and quantity variances.
2. Prepare journal entries to record the purchase and use of direct materials.

16. (L.O. 6) Greenspan Manufacturing Company's books for the month of July reflect the following information regarding direct labor:

Actual direct labor hours used	5,000
Standard direct labor hours allowed	4,500
Direct labor rate variance	$ 2,000 (unfavorable)
Actual direct labor cost	25,000

Required Calculate Greenspan's direct labor efficiency variance.

17. (L.O. 4, 9) Mars Company uses a standard cost system. Information on direct materials for Product M for November is given below.

Standard price per unit	$3.60
Actual purchase price per unit	3.55
Actual quantity purchased	4,000 units
Actual quantity used	3,900 units
Standard quantity allowed for actual output	3,800 units

Required

1. Calculate direct materials price and quantity variances.
2. Prepare journal entries, recording the purchase and use of direct materials.

18. (L.O. 6) Information on direct labor costs at Barber Company for January is as follows:

Actual direct labor hours used	34,500
Standard direct labor hours allowed	35,000
Total direct labor payroll	$241,500
Direct labor efficiency variance (favorable)	3,200

Required Calculate Barber's direct labor price variance. (AICPA)

19. (L.O. 6) Boling Company's direct labor costs for October 19x2 were as follows:

Standard direct labor hours allowed	42,000
Actual direct labor hours	40,000
Direct labor rate variance	$8,400 (favorable)
Standard direct labor rate per hour	$6.30

Required Calculate total actual direct labor cost for October.

20. (L.O. 6) Information on direct labor costs at Baker Meat Packing Company is as follows:

Standard direct labor rate per hour	$3.60
Actual direct labor hours purchased	1,600
Standard direct labor hours allowed	1,450
Direct labor rate variance	$240 (favorable)

Required Calculate the actual direct labor rate per hour.

21. (L.O. 6, 9) Information on direct labor costs at Schlomer Company is as follows:

Standard direct labor rate	$4.75
Actual direct labor rate	4.50
Standard direct labor hours allowed	10,000
Direct labor efficiency variance (unfavorable)	$3,800

Required

1. Calculate actual direct labor hours worked.
2. Prepare a graph similar to Figure 10–3 showing variances in direct labor.
3. Prepare journal entries, recording direct labor costs and variances.

22. (L.O. 6) Boz Corporation uses a standard cost system. Direct labor information on Product B for October is given below.

Standard rate	$12.00 per hour
Actual rate paid	12.10 per hour
Standard hours allowed for production	1,400 hours
Actual hours worked	1,500 hours

Required

1. Calculate rate and efficiency variances for direct labor.
2. Prepare a graph similar to that shown in Figure 10–3 showing direct labor variances. (see Review Exercise 10–2)

23. (L.O. 4, 9) Sugar Company uses a standard cost system. The books for the month of August reflect the following information:

Standard price per pound	$4.00
Actual purchase price per pound	4.50

Actual quantity purchased	5,000 pounds
Actual quantity used	4,750 pounds
Standard quantity allowed for actual output	4,700 pounds

Required

1. Calculate the direct materials price and quantity variances.
2. Prepare journal entries to record the purchase and use of direct materials.

24. (L.O. 6) Clark Company's direct labor costs for January were as follows:

Actual direct labor hours	3,500
Standard direct labor hours allowed	4,000
Direct labor rate variance	$3,000 (unfavorable)
Standard direct labor rate per hour	$5

Required Calculate total actual direct labor cost for January.

25. (L.O. 4) Hyde Park Manufacturing Company manufactures a chemical compound. Each bottle of the mixture requires two items of material, Ren and Reas, as described below.

Ren is purchased in 10-gallon containers at a cost of $60 per container. Reas is purchased in 100-pound boxes at a cost of $50 per box.

Required

1. Compute the standard cost of a quart of Ren.
2. Compute the standard cost of a pound of Reas.
3. Assume that each bottle of compound requires 1.5 quarts of Ren and 0.5 pounds of Reas. Determine the standard cost of the materials in a bottle of the compound.

26. (L.O. 6) Conrad Manufacturing Company produces car parts for the car manufacturing industry. The company uses standards to control its costs. The labor standards that have been set for one very popular automotive part are as follows:

Direct labor per part	10 minutes
Direct labor rate per hour	$6

During the most recent year of production, Conrad Company worked 10,000 hours in order to produce 58,000 of these auto parts. The direct labor cost amounted to $61,000.

Required

1. What direct labor cost should have been incurred in the production of the 58,000 parts?
2. Calculate the labor rate variance and the labor efficiency variance.
(see Review Exercise 10–2)

27. (L.O. 4, 6) Francais International produces fine wine. The direct materials and direct labor standards for one bottle of its most popular wine is as follows:

Direct materials

Standard quantity	16 oz
Standard price	$ 1.20 per oz
Standard cost	19.20 per bottle

Direct labor

Standard hours	0.5 hrs
Standard rate	$8 hr
Standard cost	4 per bottle

During the most recent month, the following activity was recorded:

a. 50,000 ounces of materials were purchased at a cost of $1 per ounce.
b. All of the material was used to produce 3,000 bottles of the fine wine.
c. 1,300 hours of direct labor time were recorded at a total labor cost of $6,500.

Required

1. Compute the direct materials price and quantity variances for the month.
2. Compute the direct labor rate and efficiency variances for the month.

Problems

28. (L.O. 4) Paz Company uses a standard cost system. The following information for June pertains to direct material Q:

Actual number of pounds purchased	2,800
Actual number of pounds used	2,500
Standard number of pounds allowed for production	2,300
Standard cost per pound	$2.00
Actual cost per pound	2.10

Required

1. Calculate price and quantity variances for direct materials.
2. Prepare graphs similar to Figures 10–1 and 10–2 showing direct materials variances.

29. (L.O. 6) Information on direct labor costs at Townsend Company for May is as follows:

Standard direct labor rate	$6.00
Actual direct labor rate	5.80
Standard direct labor hours allowed	20,000
Actual direct labor hours used	21,000
Direct labor rate variance (favorable)	$4,200

Required

1. Calculate the total direct labor payroll for May and the direct labor efficiency variance.
2. Prepare a graph similar to Figure 10–3 showing direct labor variances. (AICPA)

30. (L.O. 6) Information on direct labor costs at Hanley for January is as follows:

Actual direct labor rate	$7.50
Standard direct labor hours allowed	11,000
Actual direct labor hours used	10,000
Direct labor rate variance (favorable)	$5,500

Required Calculate the standard direct labor rate for January. (AICPA)

31. (L.O. 6, 9) Direct labor costs for Goodman Company are presented below.

Standard direct labor hours allowed	30,000
Actual direct labor hours purchased	29,000
Direct labor rate variance (favorable)	$5,800
Total payroll	$220,400

Required

1. Calculate the actual direct labor rate and the standard direct labor rate.
2. Prepare a journal entry, recording direct labor costs and variances. (AICPA)

32. (L.O. 4, 6) Bear Company, located in Hong Kong, manufactures plastic toys for adults. Each toy requires 1 pound of plastic and two hours of direct labor. Variances from standard for the past month of production are given below.

Direct materials price variance	$ 262.50	(favorable)
Direct materials quantity variance	250.00	(unfavorable)
Direct labor rate variance	1,485.00	(unfavorable)
Direct labor efficiency variance	320.00	(favorable)
Total	$1,152.50	(unfavorable)

Unfortunately, the data on which these computations were based was destroyed in a fire. The accountant remembers some facts about the previous month's operations. She remembers that 1,000 units were completed during the month and that 50 extra pounds of plastic from that month's purchases were used in production. All plastic purchased during the month was used, and the actual price was $4.75 per pound. The employees were paid for 1,980 hours. The standard labor rate is $16 per hour.

Required

1. For the direct materials, calculate the standard quantity allowed, the standard price per pound, and the actual pounds purchased.
2. For direct labor, calculate the standard hours allowed and the actual direct labor rate.

33. (L.O. 4, 6, 9) Groomer Company manufactures two products, Florimene and Glyoxide, for use in the plastics industry. The company uses a standard cost system. Data for September are given below.

	Florimene	Glyoxide
Data on standard costs		
Units produced in September	1,000	1,200
Direct materials per unit	3 lbs @ $1 per pound	4 lbs @ $1.10 per pound
Direct labor per unit	5 hrs @ $12 per hour	6 hrs @ $12.50 per hour
Costs incurred for September		
Direct materials purchased and used	3,100 lbs @ $0.90 per pound	4,700 lbs @ $1.15 per pound
Direct labor	4,900 hrs @ $11.95 per hour	7,400 hrs @ $12.55 per hour

Required

1. Calculate direct materials and direct labor variances for each product.
2. Prepare journal entries, recording the purchase and use of direct materials and the use of direct labor for each product. (CMA)

34. (L.O. 4, 6) Creebler Cookie Company produces peanut butter cookies. Standard costs for 1,000 dozen cookies are as follows:

Direct materials	
Flour (300 pounds @ 20¢ per pound)	$ 60.00
Sugar (100 pounds @ 25¢ per pound)	25.00
Peanut butter (25 pounds @ 95¢ per pound)	23.75
Eggs (1,920 eggs @ 58¢ per dozen)	92.80
	$ 201.55
Direct labor (450 elf hours @ $1.90 per elf hour)	855.00
Total	$1,056.55

Results for the company's first month of operation showed the following:

a. 12,000 cookies were produced.
b. One elf quit his job after 3 days (24 hours). The remaining elves worked a total of 396 hours. Actual wages paid were $2 per elf hour.
c. Actual purchases of direct materials during the month were as follows:

Flour	500 pounds @ 18¢ per pound
Sugar	100 pounds @ 29¢ per pound
Peanut butter	30 pounds @ 95¢ per pound
Eggs	2,400 eggs @ 56¢ per dozen

d. Direct materials remaining in inventory at the end of the month were as follows:

Flour	220 pounds
Sugar	None
Peanut butter	5 pounds
Eggs	420

e. There were no cookies in progress at the end of the month.

Required

1. Compute all direct materials and direct labor variances for the first month.
2. Show that the sum of the individual direct labor variances equals the total direct labor variance (difference between total standard cost and total actual cost).

35. (L.O. 4, 6) Dr. Y. Bottoms has recently invented a revolutionary new diaper. Based on the principle of avoidance conditioning, this diaper houses a small moisture-sensitive electric current capable of producing a small shock when wet. Dr. Bottoms' theory is that this diaper will result in the rapid extinction of a form of behavior peculiar to small babies.

In anticipation of tremendous demand for his product (although field testing is still in progress), Dr. Bottoms has developed a standard cost for the production of 10,000 diapers as follows:

Direct materials	
10,000 yards cotton cloth @ $0.30	$ 3,000
15,000 feet copper wire @ $0.27	4,050
10,000 small watch batteries @ $1.25	12,500
Direct labor	
12,500 hours @ $3.40	42,500
Total	$62,050

During the first month of production, Dr. Y. Bottoms Company produced 9,500 diapers.

Actual costs were as follows:

Direct materials	
9,000 yards of cotton cloth @ $0.29	$ 2,610
14,250 feet copper wire @ $0.28	3,990
9,500 batteries @ $0.98	9,310
Direct labor	
12,000 hours @ $3.45	41,400
Total	$57,310

Required

Compute the direct material and direct labor variances.

36. (L.O. 4, 6) Valpo Bows & Knots Company engages in the massive production of shoelaces. The company employs four skilled laborers whose primary tasks are to cut the shoecord into appropriate lengths and apply a molten plastic coating to each end for ease in threading.

Variances for the month of September were as follows:

Materials price variance	$719.20 U
Labor rate variance	26.00 U
Materials quantity variance	
Cord	100.00 F
Plastic	3.00 F
Labor efficiency variance	17.51 F
Total variance	$624.69 U

a. The actual price of the shoelace cord used in September was $0.025.
b. The company actually used 5,000 less feet of cord than the standard allowed.
c. Tip-dippers complained of the complexity of their task and threatened to strike. Consequently, their wages were increased as of September 1. Their hours did not vary from standard.
d. Cordcutters were paid at the standard rate of $3.75 per hour during September. They completed cutting the 100,000 laces in 95 hours, 20 minutes.
e. Standard hours allowed the tip-dippers were 200 at a standard rate of $5.25.
f. The standard cost for molten plastic was $30 per gallon. During September, the company used 2.9 gallons at a total actual cost of $81.20.

Required Given the above information, determine the following:

1. The standard quantity allowed for molten plastic for 100,000 shoelaces
2. The wage increase received by the tip-dippers
3. The standard hours allowed for cordcutters
4. The standard quantity allowed for cord for 100,000 shoelaces

37. (L.O. 4, 6, 9) Eastern Company manufactures special electrical equipment and parts. The company employs a standard cost accounting system with separate standards established for each product.

A special transformer is manufactured in the transformer department. Standard costs for the transformer are determined in September for the coming year. The standard cost of a transformer for the current year is shown below.

Direct materials	
Iron	5 sheets @ $2 = $10
Copper	3 spools @ $3 = $ 9
Direct labor	4 hours @ $7 = $28

During October, 800 transformers were produced. This was below expectations because a work stoppage occurred during contract negotiations with the labor force.

The following costs were incurred in October:

	Materials purchased	Material used
Direct materials		
Iron	5,000 sheets @ $2.00 per sheet	3,900 sheets
Copper	2,700 spools @ $3.10 per spool	2,600 spools
Direct labor	3,400 hours $24,080	

Required

1. Calculate variances for direct materials and direct labor. (Carry the computation of the actual direct labor rate to six decimal places.)
2. Prepare journal entries, recording the purchase and use of direct materials and use of direct labor. (CMA)

38. (L.O. 6, 7) Landeau Manufacturing Company uses a standard cost accounting system. The standard direct labor rates are established each year when the annual plan is formulated. These rates are held constant for the year.

Standard direct labor rates for the fiscal year ending June 30, 19x8, and standard hours allowed for April output are as follows:

	Standard direct labor rate per hour	Standard direct labor hours allowed for output, April
Labor class III	$8.00	500
Labor class II	7.00	500
Labor class I	5.00	500

The wage rates for each class increased on January 1, 19x8, under terms of a union contract negotiated in December 19x7. The standard wage rates were not revised to reflect the new contract.

The actual direct labor hours worked and actual direct labor rates per hour for April follow:

	Actual direct labor rate per hour	Actual direct labor hours
Labor class III	$8.50	550
Labor class II	7.50	650
Labor class I	5.40	375

Required Calculate direct labor variances for each labor class. (CMA)

39. (L.O. 4, 6) On March 1, the Aqua-Seat Company began manufacturing a unique lounge chair based on the principle of the waterbed. The company has established the following standards for direct materials and direct labor:

Direct materials	
7 yards of floral print plastic @ $3.25	$22.75
1 two-way watertight valve @ $1	1.00
6 feet metal tubing @ $0.75	4.50
Direct labor	
6 hours @ $4.25	25.50
Total	$53.75

During March, 1,500 chairs were produced, although the budget had provided for only 1,250.

Direct materials used in March were	
11,000 yards of plastic @ $3.20	$35,200.00
1,499 valves @ $1.02	1,528.98
8,500 feet of metal tubing @ $0.75	6,375.00
Direct labor used in March	
6,000 hours @ $3.75	22,500.00
Total	$65,603.98

There was no work in process at the end of March.

Required

1. Compute all direct materials and direct labor variances.
2. What are the possible implications of the direct labor variance?

40. (L.O. 4, 6, 9) Following extensive market research and feasibility of production studies, Mr. Base has founded the Edible Tableware Company of Kansas, Inc. To spare millions of housepersons from the drudgery of dishwashing and the preparation of nightly desserts, the company manufactures edible tableware in five popular flavors. Final products include plates, forks, spoons, and knives. Standard costs for each four-piece set, as determined by Mr. Base, are as follows:

Direct materials (8 ounces @ $0.04)	$0.32
Direct labor (0.25 hours @ $4)	1.00

In January, the company produced 3,000 sets. This required 1,700 pounds of direct materials and 720 direct labor hours. The direct materials cost $0.035 per ounce for the 1,700 pounds purchased. Direct labor rates were actually $3.85 per hour.

Required

1. Calculate all direct materials and direct labor variances.
2. Prepare journal entries to record the above data.

41. (L.O. 4, 6) Arrow Industries employs a standard cost system in which direct materials inventory is carried at standard cost. The company is located in London, England. Arrow's standards for one unit of product are given below.

	Standard quantity	Standard price	Standard cost
Direct materials	8 grams	£1.80 per gram	£14.40
Direct labor	0.25 hour	£8.00 per hour	2.00
Total			£16.40

During May, Arrow purchased 160,000 grams of direct materials for £304,000. Total direct labor costs for May were £37,800. Arrow manufactured 19,000 units of product during May, using 142,500 grams of direct materials and 5,000 direct labor hours.

Required

1. Calculate all direct materials and direct labor variances.
2. Prepare graphs similar to those in Figures 10–1, 10–2, and 10–3 showing direct labor and direct materials variances. (CMA)

42. (L.O. 4) Energy Products Company produces a gasoline additive, "Gas Gain." This product increases engine efficiency and improves gasoline mileage by creating a more complete burn in the combustion process.

Careful controls are required during the production process to ensure the proper mix of input chemicals and to control evaporation. If the controls are ineffective, a loss in output and efficiency results.

The standard cost of producing a 500-liter batch of Gas Gain is $135. The standard materials mix and related standard cost of each chemical used in a 500-liter batch are as follows:

Chemical	Standard input quantity in liters	Standard price per liter	Total costs
Echol	200	$0.200	$ 40.00
Protex	100	0.425	42.50
Benz	250	0.150	37.50
CT-40	50	0.300	15.00
Total	600		$135.00

The quantities of chemicals purchased and used in the past production period are shown in the schedule below. A total of 140 batches of Gas Gain were manufactured. Energy Products determines cost and chemical use variations at the end of each production period.

Chemical	Quantity purchased	Total purchase price	Quantity used
Echol	25,000 liters	$ 5,365	26,600 liters
Protex	13,000	6,240	12,880
Benz	40,000	5,840	37,800
CT-40	7,500	2,220	7,140
Total	85,500 liters	$19,665	84,420 liters

Required

1. Calculate price variances by chemical.
2. Calculate the materials quantity variance for each chemical used. (CMA)

43. (L.O. 4, 6, 9) Jones Job Shop produces a wide variety of products. Many of the products are produced in sufficient quantities to justify a standard cost system. The standard cost card for one of the products is shown below.

Standard Cost
Product XLX30

Material

Type	Quantity	Price	Standard cost
A	10 pounds	$2.50	$25.00
B	8 pounds	3.00	24.00
C	6 pounds	1.50	9.00
Total material cost			$58.00

Labor

Operation	Hours	Price	Standard cost
1	2.0	$12.00	$ 24.00
3	3.0	12.60	37.80
4	1.5	18.00	27.00
7	2.0	9.00	18.00
Total labor cost			$106.80

During the past year, the company records showed the following materials purchases:

Material	Quantity	Cost
A	100,000 pounds	$258,000
B	70,000 pounds	205,000
C	70,000 pounds	112,500

Jobs 108, 121, and 145 called for the production of 2,000, 3,000, and 2,500 units of product XLX30, respectively. All units were produced, and the job cost sheets revealed the following information:

Actual Usage

	Material units			Labor hours			
Job	A	B	C	1	3	4	7
108	20,580	15,850	12,870	4,150	5,800	3,050	4,250
121	29,700	24,650	18,500	5,850	8,700	4,500	5,900
145	24,650	21,210	14,350	5,150	7,200	3,748	5,000

The actual labor rates for the operations were as follows:

Operation	Labor rate
1	$12.30
3	12.75
4	17.40
7	8.85

Required

1. Calculate the direct materials variances by type of material.
2. Calculate the direct labor variances by operation.

Case 1
Ogwood Company (L.O. 1, 2)

Ogwood Company is a small manufacturer of wooden household items. Al Rivkin, corporate controller, plans to introduce a standard cost system. Several coworkers have given him information helpful in developing standards for Ogwood's products.

One of Ogwood's products is a wooden cutting board. Preparing and cutting lumber for each board requires 1.25 board feet of lumber and 12 minutes of direct labor. The cutting boards are inspected after they are cut. Because the cutting boards are made of a natural material that contains imperfections, one board is normally rejected for each five accepted. Four rubber footpads are attached to each good cutting board. Fifteen minutes of direct labor time are required to attach all four footpads and finish each cutting board. The lumber costs $3 per board foot. Each footpad costs $0.05. Direct labor is paid at the rate of $8 per hour.

Required

1. Develop a standard cost for a cutting board, itemizing the cost of all inputs. The standard cost calculations should identify
   a. Standard quantity
   b. Standard price
   c. Standard cost per unit
2. List the advantages of implementing a standard cost system.
3. Explain the role of each of the following people in developing standards:
   a. Purchasing manager
   b. Industrial engineer
   c. Cost accountant

(CMA)

Case 2
Mountain View Hospital (L.O. 6)

Mountain View Hospital has adopted a standard cost accounting system for evaluation and control of nursing labor. Diagnosis Related Groups (DRGs), instituted by the U.S. government for health insurance reimbursement, are used as the output measure in the standard cost system. A DRG is a patient classification scheme that perceives hospitals to be multiproduct firms where inpatient treatment procedures are related to the numbers and types of patient ailments treated. Mountain View Hospital has developed standard nursing times for the treatment of each DRG classification, and nursing labor hours are assumed to vary with the number of DRGs treated within a time period.

The nursing unit on the fourth floor treats patients with four DRG classifications. The unit is staffed with registered nurses (RNs), licensed practical nurses (LPNs), and aides. The standard nursing hours and salary rates are as follows.

Fourth Floor Nursing Unit
Standard Hours

DRG classification	RN	LPN	Aide
1	6	4	5
2	26	16	10
3	10	5	4
4	12	7	10

Standard Hourly Rates

RN	$12
LPN	8
Aide	6

For the month of May 19x9, the results of operations for the fourth floor nursing unit are presented below.

Actual Number of Patients

DRG 1	250
DRG 2	90
DRG 3	240
DRG 4	140
	720

	RN	LPN	Aide
Actual hours	8,150	4,300	4,400
Actual salary	$100,245	$35,260	$25,300
Actual hourly rate	$12.30	$8.20	$5.75

The accountant for Mountain View Hospital calculated the following standard times for the fourth floor nursing unit for May 19x9.

		Standard hrs/DRG			Total standard hrs		
DRG classification	No. of patients	RN	LPN	Aide	RN	LPN	Aide
1	250	6	4	5	1,500	1,000	1,250
2	90	26	16	10	2,340	1,440	900
3	240	10	5	4	2,400	1,200	960
4	140	12	7	10	1,680	980	1,400
					7,920	4,620	4,510

The hospital calculates labor variances for each reporting period by labor classification (RN, LPN, Aide), since the hospital does not have data to calculate variances by DRG. The variances are used by nursing supervisors and hospital administration to evaluate the performance of nursing labor.

Required Calculate the total labor variance for the fourth-floor nursing unit of Mountain View Hospital for May 19x9, indicating how much of this variance is attributed to:

1. Labor efficiency
2. Rate differences

(CMA)

11

Flexible Budgets and Manufacturing Overhead Costs

LEARNING OBJECTIVES

After studying this chapter you should be able to:

1. Prepare a flexible budget for manufacturing overhead
2. State the criterion for selecting a cost driver when preparing a flexible budget
3. Establish a predetermined overhead rate and explain the necessity for such rates
4. Calculate a standard applied manufacturing overhead cost
5. Calculate a manufacturing overhead budget variance
6. Calculate manufacturing overhead spending and efficiency variances
7. Calculate a manufacturing overhead volume variance
8. List the major causes of manufacturing overhead variances
9. Explain how flexible budgets are used to control nonmanufacturing activities
10. Enter manufacturing overhead costs in the general ledger

In the last chapter you saw how standards are developed and variances calculated for direct materials and direct labor, two of the three components of a product cost. In this chapter you will study flexible budgets and variances associated with the third component, manufacturing overhead.

Unlike direct materials and direct labor costs, manufacturing overhead costs include many items. Thus, an engineering analysis of overhead costs is impractical. Its cost would exceed its value. Instead, a flexible overhead budget is developed by analyzing past overhead costs at various production levels. Such results are reasonably accurate, and the cost is bearable.

Overhead costs also differ from direct materials and direct labor costs because some overhead costs, such as supervisors' salaries, are fixed, whereas others, such as indirect materials, are variable. Still others are partly fixed and partly variable. For example, the cost of electricity used in a factory contains both a fixed and a variable component. The cost of lighting work areas is the same whether the factory is producing at full or partial capacity. Hence, lighting is a fixed cost. But the cost of operating equipment increases as the production level increases. Thus, this cost is variable. Therefore, the total cost of electricity is a mixed cost, with both fixed and variable elements. To help managers control costs that are partly fixed and partly variable, accountants have developed the flexible budget.

■

Flexible Overhead Budgets

A **flexible budget** is a budget that may be adjusted to any activity level to reflect how costs vary with changes in production volume. A flexible overhead budget indicates that as volume increases, total overhead costs increase, but not in proportion to volume. That is, a 10 percent increase in volume may cause only a 7 percent increase in total overhead costs. As volume increases, the variable part of the cost rises, but the fixed part remains the same within the relevant range. Because only part of the total cost increases, the percentage rise in total costs cannot equal the percentage rise in volume.

In flexible budgeting, output is generally measured in direct labor hours or machine-hours instead of units. **Manufacturing overhead** includes all costs needed to manufacture a product *except* direct materials and direct labor costs. Manufacturing overhead benefits many products, but not every product equally. For instance, large complex products require more factory space per unit than small, simple ones. Thus, to divide overhead costs equally among units of product is illogical. However, direct labor hours and machine-hours do provide a good measure of overhead when products differ. A large, complex product generally requires more direct labor hours to assemble than a small, simple product. This greater number of labor hours indicates that more productive effort and, thus, more overhead costs went into that unit of product. The same concept applies to machine-hours, which are most often used as a measure in industries with highly automated production, where machines do much of the work.

Flexible budgets are usually developed for each department of a factory for two reasons. First, the appropriate measure of output may differ between departments. Machining departments tend to use machine-hours; assembly departments, direct labor hours. Second, manufacturing overhead costs are best controlled within departments where variances from expected costs can be spotted quickly, analyzed, and remedied. This follows the principle of responsibility accounting discussed in Chapter 9.

Format for the Flexible Budget

OBJECTIVE 1
Prepare a flexible budget for manufacturing overhead

Exhibit 11–1 shows a flexible budget for the machining department of Dailey Corporation. Dailey expects to produce 3,000 large and 4,000 small disks in June. Each large disk requires one hour of machine time; each small disk, a half hour. The budget lists an estimated **fixed cost** for each cost item as well as the **variable cost** per machine-hour. While a fixed cost's total remains constant over

Exhibit 11–1
Illustration of a Flexible Budget

Dailey Corporation
Flexible Budget for 5,000 Machine-Hours
For the Month of June 19x8

Estimated machine-hours	
3,000 large disks × 1.0 standard machine-hours =	3,000
4,000 small disks × 0.5 standard machine-hours =	2,000
Total planned machine-hours	5,000

	Fixed costs	Variable costs	Total costs for 5,000* machine-hours
A. Controllable			
Indirect labor		$1.50	$ 7,500
Cutting tools		0.50	2,500
Lubricants		0.20	1,000
Power	$ 600	0.30	2,100
B. Allocated			
Maintenance	3,000	0.50	5,500
C. Noncontrollable			
Supervision	6,000		6,000
Depreciation	25,400		25,400
Total	$35,000	$3.00	$50,000

*Because this budget is for a machining department, machine-hours are used to measure production activity. Were the budget for an assembly department, it would be expressed in direct labor hours.

a range of business activity, a variable cost's total changes in direct proportion to changes in business activity. (**Mixed costs** contain elements of both fixed and variable costs.) These costs are estimated from past costs by using the high-low method, the graphic method, or regression analysis (discussed in Chapter 3). The upper part of the exhibit shows how Dailey estimates planned machine-hours for the month. The total costs column in the lower part of the exhibit shows the total cost of producing the 7,000 disks.

Notice that the items included in the budget have been separated into three categories: controllable, allocated, and noncontrollable. **Controllable costs** are those costs over which the department supervisor has significant influence. Typically, they include the cost of indirect labor, cutting tools, machine lubricants, and power for running machines.

Allocated costs are incurred in a separate manufacturing service department. These costs are allocated to the machining department by the accounting department, based on machining's need for maintenance. The fixed maintenance cost of $3,000 represents the expected cost of routine maintenance, such as cleaning, lubricating, and adjusting the machinery. This cost is incurred regardless of the department's level of activity.

The variable maintenance cost of $0.50 per machine-hour represents the expected extra cost of maintenance, which depends on how much the machines are run. This cost includes repair or replacement of moving parts and additional lubrication. Maintenance costs are included in the flexible budget because the department manager can reduce needed maintenance by using the machinery carefully and seeing that routine maintenance is performed regularly.

Noncontrollable costs are costs assigned to the machining department simply because they are incurred there. Salaries and depreciation are direct to the department even though the department supervisor has no control over them. Noncontrollable costs may be included in a flexible budget for two reasons. First, flexible budgets are used not only for control but also for product costing purposes. Second, some managers think department supervisors should know the total cost of operating their departments.

Advantages of the Flexible Budget

Flexible budgets are especially useful for evaluating the performance of department managers. Before flexible budgets, firms used budgets based on the estimated level of production to cost products and evaluate managers' performance. Such budgets, called **static budgets,** were not revised if the actual production level differed from the estimated level. And since production estimates were usually made a year in advance, they rarely matched actual volume.

The production level is significant because variable overhead costs change if production changes. For instance, the total cost of electricity increases with the number of machine-hours. A flexible overhead budget automatically increases the cost allowed for electricity when machine-hours increase. A static budget does not. It provides one amount for electricity, regardless of the production level.

As a result, static budgets are rarely useful for evaluating performance. But a flexible budget tells managers how much manufacturing overhead should have been incurred at the level of production that occurred. Any differences between the actual and flexible budgeted overhead reflect potential cost control problems and may warrant investigation.

Selecting a Cost Driver

To develop a flexible overhead budget, the accountant first selects a suitable measure of production activity. That measure is usually not finished units but direct labor hours, machine-hours, or some other base. Units of product are generally not used because overhead costs usually benefit several products. For example, if several different products are produced on a machine, the cost of maintaining the machine benefits all the products. However, the products may be so different from each other that one product takes considerably more machine time than the other. To measure the machine's total production, one needs an activity measure common to all products produced on it—such as machine-hours. This measure is called the **cost driver** (or activity base or measure).

OBJECTIVE 2
State the criterion for selecting a cost driver when preparing a flexible budget

The cost driver selected should be the one that best relates manufacturing overhead costs to production volume. That is, it should be the one that best measures how manufacturing overhead costs vary with production volume. For example, if the cost of drills depends on how many hours the drill presses run, then the number of machine-hours spent on the drill press is probably the driver for that cost. There is a cause-and-effect relationship between drill costs and drill-press machine-hours.

In many production processes, the best cost driver is difficult to identify. In such cases, the accountant should ask someone familiar with the process, perhaps the production supervisor, to identify measures bearing a cause-and-effect relationship to overhead costs.

In Exhibit 11–1, all of the manufacturing overhead costs were assumed to be driven by machine-hours. A cost formula was developed for each cost element as a function of machine-hours. If the cost items are all associated with machine-hours, the cost estimates will be accurate and provide useful information for planning and control. On the other hand if the cost items are associated with more than one cost driver, the estimates will not be accurate, and the information will not be useful for planning and control.

The solution is to develop a flexible budget with more than one cost driver. Managerial accountants separate the manufacturing overhead into cost pools with each cost pool having a different cost driver. In manufacturing environments where just-in-time (JIT) production policies are implemented, companies are using cost drivers such as number of setups for machine setup costs, number of orders for receiving costs, weight of materials and number of parts for materials-handling costs, and number of inspections for quality control costs. These and other cost drivers are replacing direct labor hours and machine-hours as overhead cost drivers. When multiple cost drivers are used, the additional information is acquired at an additional cost. The managerial accountant and managers will decide if the additional information is worth the cost.

■

Manufacturing Overhead Standards

OBJECTIVE 3
Establish a predetermined overhead rate and explain the necessity for such rates

A **standard applied manufacturing overhead cost** is useful for product costing. In contrast to direct materials and direct labor standards, however, a manufacturing overhead standard is *not* useful for planning and control. This is because a manufacturing overhead standard treats fixed overhead costs as variable. Flexible budgets are used for planning and control of overhead costs. A **predetermined overhead rate** is calculated by dividing estimated manufacturing overhead costs for the year by estimated annual production volume, as discussed in Chapter 4. A predetermined overhead rate based on machine-hours is calculated as follows:

$$\text{Predetermined overhead rate based on machine-hours} = \frac{\text{estimated annual overhead}}{\text{estimated annual machine-hours}}$$

The predetermined overhead rate is used to apply or assign manufacturing overhead costs to each unit of product or to departments. Thus, the assigned standard cost is the standard applied manufacturing overhead cost.

Avoiding Seasonal Variations in Cost and Volume

There are two reasons for using annual figures to establish a predetermined overhead rate. First, manufacturing overhead costs vary from season to season. Second, almost all businesses experience periodic variations in production volume.

When production volume is high one month and low another month, or costs vary from one month to another, the fixed manufacturing overhead cost per unit would differ drastically from month to month without the use of a predetermined overhead rate. Basing the predetermined overhead rate on annual production volume solves the problem of seasonal variation in production volume and its effect on per unit fixed manufacturing overhead cost.

Calculating the Predetermined Overhead Rate

Accountants at Dailey Corporation have gathered the following information for the machining department:

Estimated variable overhead rate	\$3 per machine-hour
Estimated fixed overhead costs	\$420,000 per year
Estimated production volume	60,000 machine-hours per year

To calculate a predetermined overhead rate, the accountant estimates the total overhead cost for the year, calculated by using the flexible budget formula:

$$\begin{aligned}\text{Total cost} &= \text{fixed costs per year} \\ &\quad + (\text{variable costs per cost driver} \times \text{production volume})\end{aligned}$$

$$\text{Estimated annual overhead costs} = \$420{,}000 + (\$3 \times 60{,}000 \text{ machine-hours}) = \underline{\underline{\$600{,}000}}$$

Finally, the predetermined overhead rate is figured:

$$\text{Predetermined overhead rate} = \frac{\text{estimated annual overhead}}{\text{estimated annual machine-hours}} = \frac{\$600{,}000}{60{,}000 \text{ machine-hours}} = \underline{\underline{\$10}} \text{ per machine-hour}$$

For calculating volume variances (discussed later in the chapter), it is useful to break the predetermined overhead rate into its fixed and variable components as follows:[1]

$$\begin{aligned}\text{Predetermined overhead rate} &= \text{fixed overhead rate} + \text{variable overhead rate}\\ &= \frac{\text{estimated annual fixed overhead}}{\text{estimated annual machine-hours}} + \frac{\text{estimated annual variable overhead}}{\text{estimated annual machine-hours}}\\ &= \frac{\$420{,}000}{60{,}000 \text{ machine-hours}} + \frac{\$180{,}000}{60{,}000 \text{ machine-hours}}\\ &= \underline{\underline{\$7}} \text{ per machine-hour} + \underline{\underline{\$3}} \text{ per machine-hour}\end{aligned}$$

Calculating the Standard Applied Manufacturing Overhead Cost per Unit

OBJECTIVE 4
Calculate a standard applied manufacturing overhead cost

By using the combined predetermined overhead rate and standard quantity of cost driver per unit, you can calculate the standard applied manufacturing overhead cost per unit. The formula is as follows:

$$\text{Standard applied manufacturing overhead cost per unit} = \text{predetermined overhead rate} \times \text{standard quantity of cost driver per unit of output}$$

For Dailey Corporation's two products, the computation is:

$$\text{Standard applied manufacturing overhead costs, large disk} = \$10 \text{ per machine-hour} \times 1 \text{ machine-hour} = \underline{\underline{\$10}} \text{ per unit}$$

[1]Some companies base the fixed overhead rate on average monthly fixed costs and average monthly production. This provides the same fixed overhead rate as using annual data.

$$\text{Standard applied manufacturing overhead costs, small disk} = \$10 \text{ per machine-hour} \times 0.5 \text{ machine-hour} = \underline{\underline{\$5}} \text{ per unit}$$

Notice that the standard applied manufacturing overhead cost per unit does not change with month-to-month variations in actual costs and production volume. (As you have seen, costs for standard direct materials and direct labor behave in the same way.)

■

Manufacturing Overhead Variances

Actual overhead costs may vary from standard overhead costs for several reasons. Variances related to specific reasons can be calculated. The budget variance represents that part of total overhead variance that can be attributed to the difference between actual overhead costs and estimated overhead costs. The volume variance represents that part of total overhead variance that can be attributed to the difference between the actual production volume and the average production volume on which the predetermined overhead rate is based.

The Budget Variance

OBJECTIVE 5
Calculate a manufacturing overhead budget variance

A **budget variance** is the difference between actual manufacturing overhead costs, as recorded in the Actual Manufacturing Overhead account in a firm's accounting records, and budgeted costs, based on the standard quantity of machine-hours allowed for the actual number of units produced. It is calculated as follows:

$$\text{Budget variance} = \text{actual manufacturing overhead costs} - \text{flexible budget overhead costs for standard quantity of machine-hours allowed for actual number of units produced}$$

Notice that the standard quantity of machine-hours allowed is calculated just as it was in Chapter 10 for direct labor hours. In fact, were the flexible budget for manufacturing overhead based on direct labor hours, the computations would be identical.

The first step in calculating Dailey's budget variance is to find the standard quantity of machine-hours allowed for the actual production level. Using standard machine-hours per unit from Exhibit 11–1, you get

$$\text{Standard quantity of machine-hours allowed} = \text{standard quantity of machine-hours per unit} \times \text{actual number of units produced}$$

Exhibit 11–2
Actual Overhead Costs from Dailey Corporation's Accounting Records

Dailey Corporation Actual Overhead Costs: Machining Department For the Month of June 19x8	
Production output:	3,000 large disks 3,800 small disks
Actual machine-hours operated	5,100
Actual costs	
Indirect labor	$ 7,595
Cutting tools	2,500
Lubricants	1,029
Power	1,825
Maintenance	5,255
Supervision	6,250
Depreciation	25,400
Total actual costs	$49,854

Large disk	3,000	= 1 × 3,000
Small disk	1,900	= 0.5 × 3,800
Total	4,900	machine hours

In Exhibit 11–1, the estimated hours for June were reported to be 5,000 hours. This number is the estimated average monthly standard machine-hours, calculated by dividing the estimated annual output of 60,000 standard machine-hours by 12. You also know from this exhibit that budgeted fixed costs are $35,000 per month ($420,000 ÷ 12); and variable costs, $3 per machine-hour. Using these costs you can calculate flexible budget overhead costs for 4,900 machine-hours as follows:

Fixed	$35,000
Variable ($3 × 4,900)	14,700
Total	$49,700

Actual manufacturing overhead costs for the machining department for June, given in Exhibit 11–2, totaled $49,854. Thus, the budget variance is as follows:

$$\text{Budget variance} = \text{actual manufacturing overhead costs} - \text{flexible budget overhead costs for standard quantity of machine-hours allowed for actual number of units produced}$$

$$= \$49{,}854 - \$49{,}700$$

$$= \$154 \text{ (unfavorable)}$$

Exhibit 11–3
Sample of an Overhead Budget Variance Report

Dailey Corporation
Budget Variance Report: Machining Department
For the Month of June 19x8

Cost items	Actual overhead costs	Flexible budget overhead costs for 4,900 standard machine-hours	Budget variances
A. Controllable			
Indirect labor	$ 7,595	$ 7,350[1]	$245 (U)
Cutting tools	2,500	2,450[2]	50 (U)
Lubricants	1,029	980[3]	49 (U)
Power	1,825	2,070[4]	245 (F)
B. Allocated			
Maintenance	5,255	5,450[5]	195 (F)
C. Noncontrollable			
Supervision	6,250	6,000	250 (U)
Depreciation	25,400	25,400	-0-
Total	$49,854	$49,700	$154 (U)

[1]$1.50 per machine-hour × 4,900 standard machine-hours.
[2]$0.50 per machine-hour × 4,900 standard machine-hours.
[3]$0.20 per machine-hour × 4,900 standard machine-hours.
[4]$600 + $0.30 per machine-hour × 4,900 standard machine hours.
[5]$3,000 + $0.50 per machine-hour × 4,900 standard machine hours.

The budget variance is unfavorable because actual overhead costs were greater than those allowed by the flexible budget at a production volume of 4,900 standard machine-hours allowed.

The budget variance is usually reported by department, since department managers can control many factors contributing to this variance. For example, a budget variance might be caused by using more than the scheduled number of indirect labor hours or by paying a higher-than-anticipated wage rate for indirect labor. Exhibit 11–3 shows a budget variance report for Dailey's machining department. For each cost item, the report lists the actual costs, the flexible budget costs, and the difference between these costs, which is the budget variance. Flexible budget costs are calculated on the basis of the 4,900 standard machine-hours allowed for Dailey's actual production level. The budget variance report provides management with the detailed information needed to identify and control the source of any favorable or unfavorable variance.

Like direct materials and direct labor variances, manufacturing overhead variances can be shown graphically. The flexible budget line and unfavorable budget variance for Dailey's machining department are shown in Figure 11–1. But unlike direct materials and direct labor variances, a manufacturing overhead budget variance can be further divided into a spending variance and an efficiency variance (shown in Figure 11–2).

Figure 11–1
Dailey Corporation:
Graphic Analysis of a Manufacturing Overhead Budget Variance
The actual overhead cost is $49,854. The flexible budget overhead cost for 4,900 standard machine-hours allowed is $49,700. Thus, the unfavorable budget variance is $154.

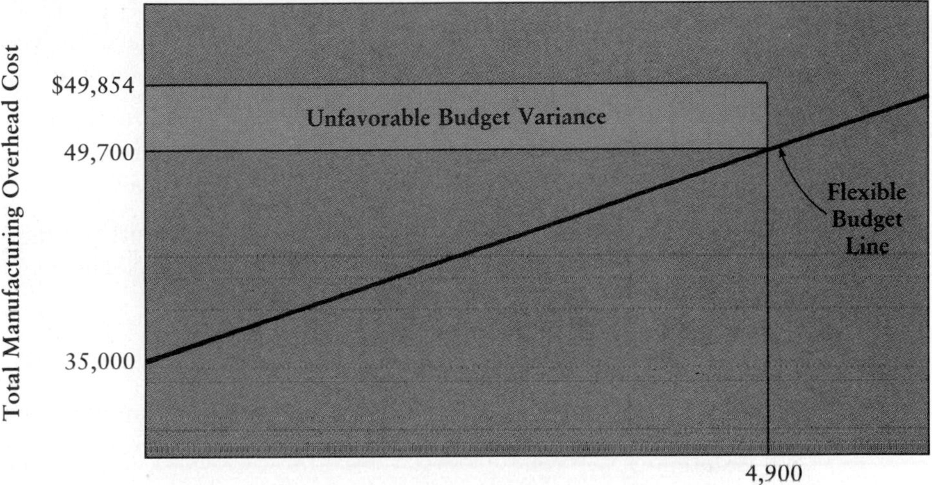

Figure 11–2
Manufacturing Overhead Variances

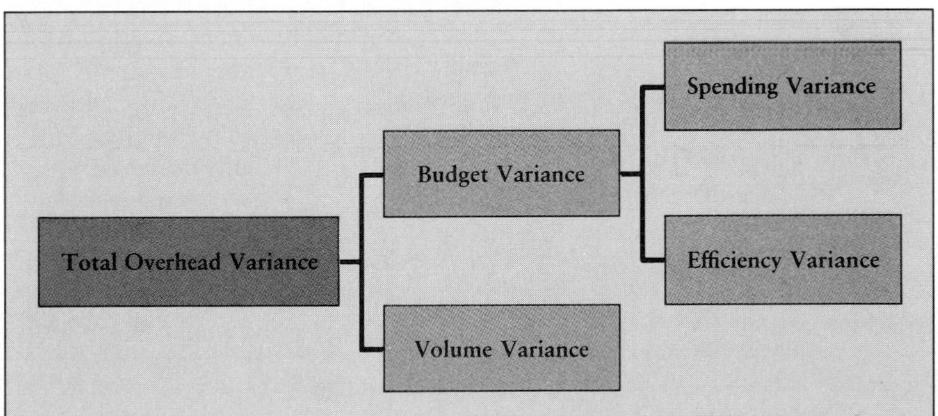

Review Exercise 11–1

Calculate the Budget Variance

The managerial accountants of Schook Company have analyzed the company's historical costs and developed the following flexible budget for the monthly manufacturing overhead costs:

$$\text{Total manufacturing overhead costs} = \text{\$20,000 per month} + \text{\$2 per direct labor hour}$$

Standard direct labor hours are expected to be 2 hours per unit of finished product. During June 19x2, 980 units were produced. The actual manufacturing overhead costs amounted to $25,760.

Required

Calculate the manufacturing overhead budget variance for June.

Solution

$$\begin{aligned}\text{Standard quantity of direct labor hours allowed} &= \text{standard quantity of direct labor hours per unit} \times \text{actual number of units produced} \\ &= 2 \times 980 \\ &= \underline{\underline{1{,}960}} \text{ direct labor hours}\end{aligned}$$

$$\begin{aligned}\text{Budget variance} &= \text{actual manufacturing overhead costs} - \text{flexible budget overhead costs for standard quantity of direct labor hours allowed for actual number of units produced} \\ &= \$25{,}760 - [\$20{,}000 + (\$2 \times 1{,}960)] \\ &= \$25{,}760 - (\$20{,}00 + \$3{,}920) \\ &= \$25{,}760 - \$23{,}920 \\ &= \underline{\underline{\$1{,}840}} \text{ unfavorable}\end{aligned}$$

(see Exercise 16)

OBJECTIVE 6
Calculate manufacturing overhead spending and efficiency variances

The Spending Variance The manufacturing overhead **spending variance** is the difference between actual overhead costs and flexible budget overhead costs for actual activity during the period. This variance is based on one assumption: the best measure of how much money should have been spent on manufacturing overhead is computed by using the *actual,* not the *standard,* number of machine-hours or direct labor hours.

The spending variance is calculated as follows:

$$\text{Spending variance} = \begin{matrix}\text{actual}\\ \text{manufacturing}\\ \text{overhead costs}\end{matrix} - \begin{matrix}\text{flexible budget overhead costs}\\ \text{for actual quantity of}\\ \text{machine-hours used}\end{matrix}$$

Notice that the only difference between this formula and the formula for the budget variance is the use of actual machine-hours rather than standard machine-hours allowed. Flexible budget overhead costs for the actual quantity of machine-hours used can be found by using information in Exhibit 11–1. Dailey's budgeted fixed overhead costs are $35,000 per month; its variable costs, $3 per machine-hour. In addition, accountants report that 5,100 actual machine-hours were used in June. Therefore, flexible budget costs for actual machine-hours are:

Fixed	$35,000
Variable ($3 × 5,100)	15,300
Total	$50,300

You know that actual manufacturing overhead costs were $49,854 (Exhibit 11–2). Therefore, by substituting these last two figures into the spending variance equation, you get:

$$\begin{aligned}\text{Spending variance} &= \begin{matrix}\text{actual}\\ \text{manufacturing}\\ \text{overhead costs}\end{matrix} - \begin{matrix}\text{flexible budget overhead costs}\\ \text{for actual quantity of}\\ \text{machine-hours used}\end{matrix}\\ &= \$49{,}854 - \$50{,}300\\ &= \underline{\underline{\$446}}\ \text{(favorable)}\end{aligned}$$

The spending variance is favorable because actual overhead costs incurred were less than flexible budget overhead costs for the actual number of machine-hours used. In other words, costs were less than expected for the month's cost driver level.

Managers often request that the spending variance be broken down by individual cost item, so the source of the variance can be pinpointed. Exhibit 11–4 shows such a breakdown for Dailey Corporation. As you can see, the three major contributors to the variance are power and maintenance costs (both less than expected) and supervision costs (more than expected).

Efficiency Variance The **efficiency variance** is the difference between flexible budget overhead costs for actual machine-hours used and flexible budget overhead

Exhibit 11–4
Sample Report of Overhead Spending Variance

Dailey Corporation
Spending Variances Report: Machining Department
For the Month of June 19x8

Cost items	Actual overhead costs	Flexible budget overhead costs for 5,100 actual machine-hours	Spending variance
A. Controllable			
Indirect labor	$ 7,595	$ 7,650[1]	$ 55 (F)
Cutting tools	2,500	2,550[2]	50 (F)
Lubricants	1,029	1,020[3]	9 (U)
Power	1,825	2,130[4]	305 (F)
B. Allocated			
Maintenance	5,255	5,550[5]	295 (F)
C. Noncontrollable			
Supervision	6,250	6,000	250 (U)
Depreciation	25,400	25,400	-0-
Total	$49,854	$50,300	$446 (F)

[1]\$1.50 per machine-hour × 5,100 actual machine-hours.
[2]\$0.50 per machine-hour × 5,100 actual machine-hours.
[3]\$0.20 per machine-hour × 5,100 actual machine-hours.
[4]\$600 + \$0.30 per machine-hour × 5,100 actual machine hours.
[5]\$3,000 + \$0.50 per machine-hour × 5,100 actual machine hours.

costs for the standard quantity of machine-hours allowed. It indicates the amount of variable manufacturing overhead costs saved or overspent because of efficient or inefficient use of machine time.

The formula for the efficiency variance is:

$$\text{Efficiency variance} = \text{flexible budget overhead costs for actual quantity of machine-hours used} - \text{flexible budget overhead costs for standard quantity of machine-hours allowed}$$

Both cost figures needed to calculate Dailey's efficiency variance have been computed. Flexible budget overhead costs for 5,100 actual machine-hours were found when the spending variance was calculated.

Fixed	$35,000
Variable ($3 × 5,100)	15,300
Total	$50,300

Flexible budget overhead costs for 4,900 standard machine-hours were found while calculating the budget variance.

Fixed	$35,000
Variable ($3 × 4,900)	14,700
Total	$49,700

The difference between the flexible budget at actual machine-hours and the flexible budget at the standard machine-hours allowed gives the efficiency variance.

Efficiency variance = $50,300 − $49,700
= $600 (unfavorable)

The variance is unfavorable because the actual machine-hours are greater than the standard number of machine-hours allowed.

The efficiency variance can also be stated as the variable overhead rate times the difference between actual machine-hours used and standard machine-hours allowed:

Efficiency variance = variable overhead rate
× (actual machine-hours used − standard machine-hours allowed)

For Dailey Corporation the figures are as follows:

Efficiency variance = $3 × (5,100 − 4,900)
= $600 unfavorable

Notice that this version of the formula yields the same answer as when flexible budgets are used. Using variable cost figures instead of total cost figures yields the same result because budgeted fixed manufacturing overhead costs do not change as production levels change. Only the variable costs change.

The meaning of the efficiency variance is easier to understand if it is calculated by the second method. This method emphasizes the difference between actual quantity and standard quantity of the cost driver. Standard machine-hours allowed represents the number of hours it should have taken to produce the goods according to engineering estimates. If the actual number of machine-hours used is greater than the standard number of hours allowed, the extra machine-hours are presumed to have been wasted. Sometimes such hours are wasted for perfectly valid reasons, such as the use of inferior materials that are difficult to work with or an error in the standard itself. At other times the variance indicates avoidable waste caused by incorrect machine settings or carelessness by operators. But if the actual number of machine-hours used is less than the standard number of hours allowed, operations are presumed to have been more efficient than expected.

Although the efficiency variance can be broken down by cost item in the same way the spending variance is broken down (Exhibit 11–4), such information is useless to management. The efficiency variance is controlled by monitoring the use of machine-hours, not the use of individual cost items such as tools and power.

If the budget variance consists of spending variances and efficiency variances, the sum of the spending and efficiency variances should equal the budget variance. That is the case for Dailey's machining department, whose unfavorable budget variance for June was $154.

Spending variance	$446 (favorable)
Efficiency variance	600 (unfavorable)
Total budget variance	$154 (unfavorable)

The chief reason for computing these extra variances is that they are controlled differently. As you have just seen, the efficiency variance is controlled by regulating use of machine-hours. The spending variance is controlled by monitoring the amount of money spent on and the use of each overhead cost item. If managers are presented with only a budget variance, there is no way of knowing the appropriate action to take in response to the variance. For this reason, reports on overhead costs should always show both spending and efficiency variances, as shown in Exhibit 11–5.

Exhibit 11–5

Sample Report of Overhead Spending and Efficiency Variances

Dailey Corporation
Spending and Efficiency Variance: Machining Department
For the Month of June 19x8

Cost item	(a) Actual overhead costs	(b) Flexible budget overhead costs for 5,100 actual machine-hours	(c) Flexible budget overhead costs for 4,900 standard machine-hours	(a) − (b) Spending variance	(b) − (c) Efficiency variance
A. Controllable					
Indirect labor	$ 7,595	$ 7,650	$ 7,350	$ 55 (F)	
Cutting tools	2,500	2,550	2,450	50 (F)	
Lubricants	1,029	1,020	980	9 (U)	
Power	1,825	2,130	2,070	305 (F)	
B. Allocated					
Maintenance	5,255	5,550	5,450	295 (F)	
C. Noncontrollable					
Supervision	6,250	6,000	6,000	250 (U)	
Depreciation	25,400	25,400	25,400	-0-	
Total	$49,854	$50,300	$49,700	$446 (F)	$600 (U)

Review Exercise 11–2

Calculate the Spending and Efficiency Variances

The managerial accountants of Schook Company have analyzed the company's historical costs and developed the following flexible budget for the monthly manufacturing overhead costs:

$$\text{Total manufacturing overhead costs} = \text{\$20,000 per month} + \text{\$2 per direct labor hour}$$

Standard direct labor hours are expected to be 2 hours per unit of finished product. During June 19x2, 980 units were produced. The actual manufacturing overhead costs amounted to $25,760. The actual direct labor hours worked during June are 1,850.

Required

Calculate the manufacturing overhead spending and efficiency variances for June.

Solution

$$\text{Standard quantity of direct labor hours allowed} = \text{standard quantity of direct labor hours per unit} \times \text{actual number of units produced}$$

$$= 2 \times 980$$

$$= \underline{\underline{1{,}960}} \text{ direct labor hours}$$

$$\text{Spending variance} = \text{actual manufacturing overhead costs} - \text{flexible budget overhead costs for actual quantity of direct labor hours used}$$

$$= \$25{,}760 - [\$20{,}000 + (2 \times 1{,}850)]$$
$$= \$25{,}760 - (\$20{,}000 + \$3{,}700)$$
$$= \$25{,}760 - \$23{,}700$$
$$= \underline{\underline{\$2{,}060}} \text{ unfavorable}$$

$$\text{Efficiency variance} = \text{flexible budget overhead costs for actual quantity of direct labor hours used} - \text{flexible budget overhead costs for standard quantity of direct labor hours allowed}$$

$$= [\$20{,}000 + (\$2 \times 1{,}850)] - [\$20{,}000 + (2 \times 1{,}960)]$$
$$= \$23{,}700 - \$23{,}920$$
$$= \underline{\underline{\$220}} \text{ favorable}$$

An alternate computation of the efficiency variance is given below.

$$\text{Efficiency variance} = \text{variable overhead rate} \times \left(\text{actual direct labor hours used} - \text{standard direct labor hours allowed}\right)$$

$$= \$2 \times (1{,}850 - 1{,}960)$$

$$= \$2 \times 110$$

$$= \underline{\underline{\$220}} \text{ favorable}$$

(see Exercise 19)

The Volume Variance

OBJECTIVE 7
Calculate a manufacturing overhead volume variance

A **volume variance** is a measure of the difference between the actual production volume and the estimated average monthly production volume on which the predetermined overhead rate is based. It can be calculated in two ways. One way is to determine the difference between applied overhead and flexible budget overhead for the actual number of units produced. Standard machine-hours should be used to calculate *both* figures. This is an important point. When applied overhead was calculated for job order costing (Chapter 4), actual hours or dollars, not standard hours, were used in determining the amount of overhead cost applied to units produced. But in standard costing, you use standard hours because overhead costs, like direct materials and direct labor costs, are applied on the basis of what is allowed for each unit produced using the predetermined overhead rate per unit. The volume variance is calculated as follows:

$$\text{Volume variance} = \text{flexible budget overhead costs for standard quantity of machine-hours allowed for actual number of units produced} - \text{applied manufacturing overhead costs for standard quantity of machine-hours allowed for actual number of units produced}$$

As calculated earlier, Dailey Corporation's machining department had 4,900 standard machine-hours allowed for June's actual production level (see page 509). Flexible budget overhead costs for those standard machine-hours are as follows:

Fixed	$35,000
Variable (4,900 × $3)	14,700
Total	$49,700

Applied overhead for those standard machine-hours is calculated by using Dailey's total predetermined overhead rate of $10 per machine-hour, or by using both fixed and variable predetermined overhead rates. The computation below uses the separate fixed and variable overhead rates as computed earlier.

Fixed (4,900 × $7)	$34,300
Variable (4,900 × $3)	14,700
Total	$49,000

By substituting the two total cost figures obtained above into the formula for volume variance, you get:

$$\text{Volume variance} = \$49{,}700 - \$49{,}000$$
$$= \underline{\underline{\$700}} \text{ (unfavorable)}$$

The volume variance is unfavorable because the 4,900 standard machine-hours allowed for the units produced was less than the estimated monthly average of 5,000 standard machine-hours allowed on which the overhead rate was based.

A second way of calculating the volume variance is to multiply the fixed overhead rate by the difference between the estimated average monthly standard quantity of machine-hours allowed and the standard quantity of machine-hours allowed for the number of units produced:

$$\text{Volume variance} = \begin{matrix}\text{fixed}\\\text{overhead}\\\text{rate}\end{matrix} \times \left[\begin{matrix}\text{standard quantity}\\\text{of machine-hours}\\\text{allowed for}\\\text{average monthly}\\\text{production}\end{matrix} - \begin{matrix}\text{standard quantity}\\\text{of machine-hours}\\\text{allowed for}\\\text{actual number}\\\text{of units produced}\end{matrix}\right]$$

For Dailey Corporation the computation is:

$$\$7 \times (5{,}000 - 4{,}900)$$
$$\text{Volume variance} = \underline{\underline{\$700}} \text{ (unfavorable)}$$

This is, of course, the same answer obtained by using the first method.

What was the source of the volume variance? In looking at the calculations, you may have noticed that only fixed overhead figures changed. Variable overhead was the same for both flexible budget and applied overhead costs: 4,900 machine-hours × $3 per machine-hour. Furthermore, the activity level at which fixed costs were calculated did not change. It was 4,900 machine-hours in both cases. A volume variance is caused by the way fixed manufacturing overhead costs are accounted for.

By definition, fixed overhead is constant, that is, independent of production volume over the relevant range. Dailey's fixed manufacturing overhead is expected to be $35,000 per month at all volumes within the relevant range, as shown in Part A of Figure 11–3. But when fixed overhead costs are applied to products, the fixed component of the predetermined overhead rate is multiplied by the quantity of standard machine-hours allowed for that production level. As a result, applied fixed overhead is accounted for as if it were a variable cost. Part B of Figure 11–3 shows the applied fixed overhead curve for Dailey Corporation. If no units are produced, no fixed overhead is applied, even though the company

Figure 11–3
Graphic Analysis of Volume Variance
The gray area is a favorable volume variance. The red area is an unfavorable volume variance.

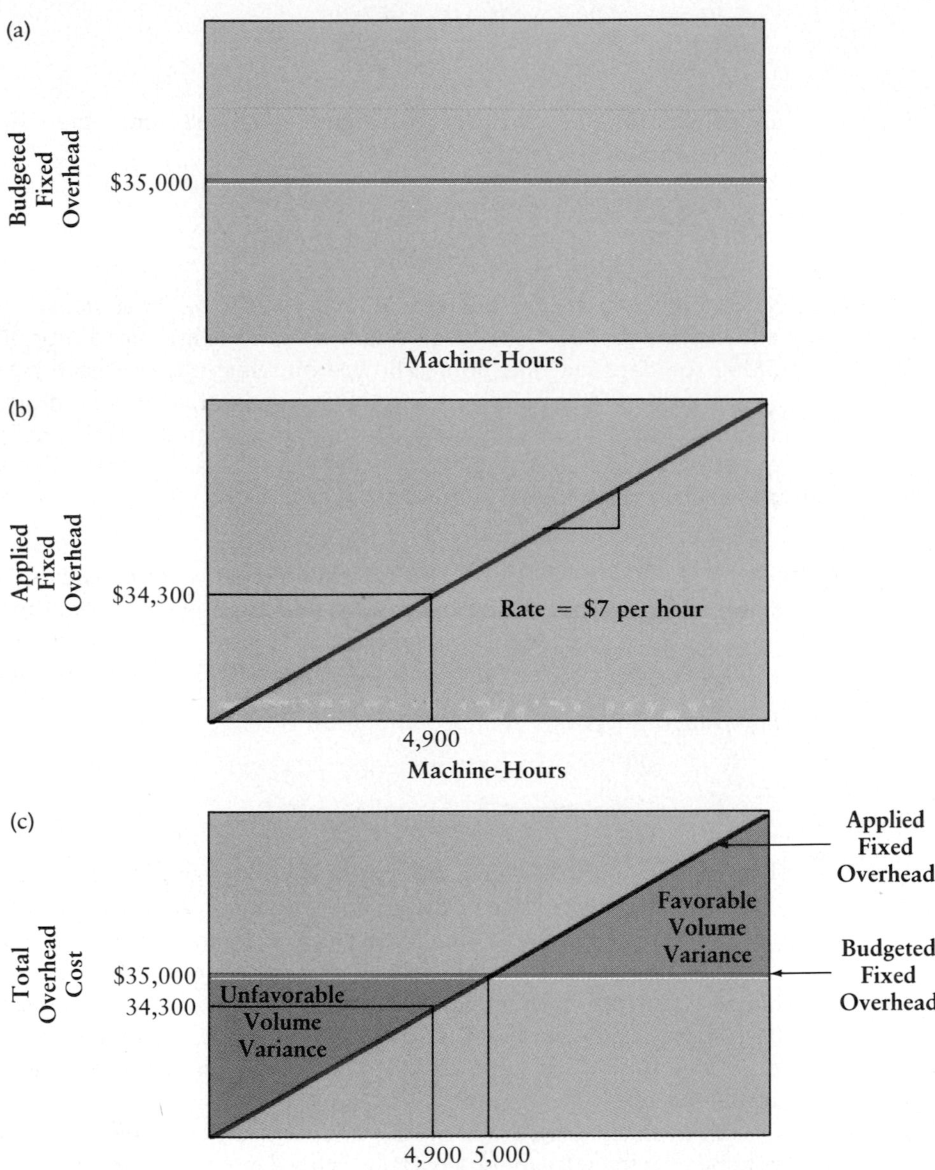

still incurs fixed overhead costs of $35,000. As production volume increases, fixed overhead is applied to products at a rate of $7 per standard machine-hour allowed. For the 4,900 standard machine-hours allowed, $34,300 in fixed overhead is applied.

The volume variance is the difference between the budgeted fixed overhead and the applied fixed overhead, which is shown in the red- and gray-shaded areas of Part C in Figure 11–3. Notice that the applied fixed overhead line intersects the budgeted fixed overhead line at 5,000 machine-hours. This is the point at which the standard machine-hours allowed will equal the monthly average of standard machine-hours allowed for expected production. Since the predetermined fixed overhead rate is based on an estimated quantity of machine-hours, 5,000 hours is the only volume at which applied fixed overhead will exactly equal the estimated fixed overhead budgeted for the month. At any other volume, a variance results. (Recall that Dailey Corporation calculated its predetermined overhead rate on the basis of an estimated annual production volume of 60,000 standard machine-hours and estimated fixed costs $420,000, with a monthly average of 5,000 standard machine-hours allowed and $35,000 in fixed costs.)

The volume variance is a quantity measure, not a cost measure. It indicates whether actual production volume was above or below the estimated average monthly production volume. Dailey Corporation's June production allowed only 4,900 standard machine-hours as opposed to the monthly average of 5,000 machine-hours. This 100 machine-hour difference caused the $700 unfavorable volume variance (the red-shaded area in Part C of Figure 11–3). Had Dailey produced at a level of more than 5,000 machine-hours, its volume variance would have been favorable, as the gray-shaded area in Part C of Figure 11–3 shows.

The total manufacturing overhead variance (also called over- or underapplied overhead cost) is the difference between actual manufacturing overhead costs and applied overhead costs. When a standard cost system is used, overhead costs are applied on the basis of total standard hours allowed for the number of units produced:

$$\begin{array}{c}\text{Total manufacturing}\\ \text{overhead variance}\\ \text{(or under- or}\\ \text{overapplied overhead)}\end{array} = \left[\begin{array}{c}\text{actual}\\ \text{manufacturing}\\ \text{overhead costs}\end{array} - \begin{array}{c}\text{applied manufacturing}\\ \text{overhead costs for}\\ \text{standard machine-hours}\\ \text{allowed for actual number}\\ \text{of units produced}\end{array}\right]$$

Standard machine-hours allowed is calculated just as it is for flexible budget overhead costs (page 509). To review:

Large disk: 1.0 machine-hour × 3,000 =	3,000
Small disk: 0.5 machine-hour × 3,800 =	1,900
Total	4,900 machine hours

For Dailey Corporation, the total overhead variance is as follows:

Total manufacturing overhead variance = $49,854 − $49,000 ($10 × 4,900 hours)

= $854 (underapplied)

Exhibit 11–6
Relationship of Overhead Variances

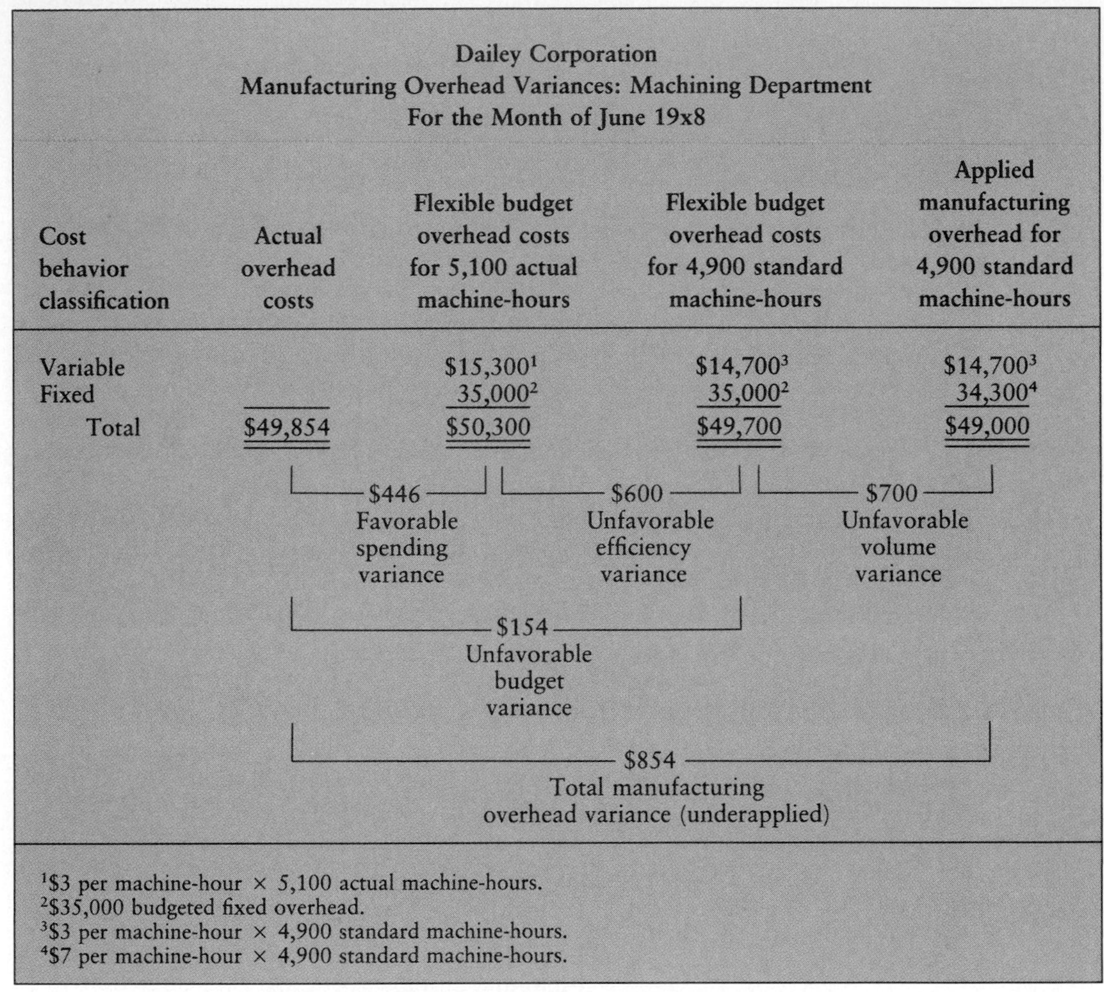

Dailey Corporation
Manufacturing Overhead Variances: Machining Department
For the Month of June 19x8

Cost behavior classification	Actual overhead costs	Flexible budget overhead costs for 5,100 actual machine-hours	Flexible budget overhead costs for 4,900 standard machine-hours	Applied manufacturing overhead for 4,900 standard machine-hours
Variable		\$15,300[1]	\$14,700[3]	\$14,700[3]
Fixed		35,000[2]	35,000[2]	34,300[4]
Total	\$49,854	\$50,300	\$49,700	\$49,000

\$446 Favorable spending variance

\$600 Unfavorable efficiency variance

\$700 Unfavorable volume variance

\$154 Unfavorable budget variance

\$854 Total manufacturing overhead variance (underapplied)

[1]\$3 per machine-hour × 5,100 actual machine-hours.
[2]\$35,000 budgeted fixed overhead.
[3]\$3 per machine-hour × 4,900 standard machine-hours.
[4]\$7 per machine-hour × 4,900 standard machine-hours.

The overhead variance is underapplied because actual overhead costs are more than applied overhead costs.

Exhibit 11–6 summarizes the computation of manufacturing overhead variances. Column 1 shows actual manufacturing overhead costs; column 2, flexible budget overhead costs for actual number of machine-hours used. The difference between columns 1 and 2 is the spending variance. For Dailey Corporation, this variance is a favorable \$446.

Column 3 shows flexible budget overhead costs for standard machine-hours allowed for the units produced in June. The difference between columns 2 and 3 is the efficiency variance. For Dailey Corporation, this variance is an unfavorable \$600. The difference between columns 1 and 3 is the budget variance, which is the sum of the spending and efficiency variances.

Column 4 shows applied manufacturing overhead costs for the standard machine-hours allowed. The difference between columns 3 and 4 is the volume variance, or an unfavorable $700. The difference between columns 1 and 4 is the total manufacturing overhead variance, which is the sum of the budget and volume variances.

Review Exercise 11–3

Calculate the Volume Variance

The managerial accountants of Schook Company have analyzed the company's historical costs and developed the following flexible budget for the monthly manufacturing overhead costs:

$$\text{Total manufacturing overhead costs} = \$20{,}000 \text{ per month} + \$2 \text{ per direct labor hour}$$

Standard direct labor hours are expected to be 2 hours per unit of finished product. During June 19x2, 980 units were produced. The company normally produces 1,000 units per month.

Required

Calculate the manufacturing overhead volume variance for June.

Solution

$$\begin{aligned}\text{Expected direct labor hours} &= 1{,}000 \text{ units} \times 2 \text{ hours per unit}\\ &= \underline{\underline{2{,}000}} \text{ direct labor hours}\end{aligned}$$

$$\begin{aligned}\text{Fixed overhead rate} &= \$20{,}000/2{,}000 \text{ direct labor hours}\\ &= \underline{\underline{\$10}} \text{ per direct labor hour}\end{aligned}$$

$$\begin{aligned}\text{Standard quantity of direct labor hours allowed} &= \text{standard quantity of direct labor hours per unit} \times \text{actual number of units produced}\\ &= 2 \times 980\\ &= \underline{\underline{1{,}960}} \text{ direct labor hours}\end{aligned}$$

$$\text{Volume variance} = \text{fixed overhead rate} \times \left[\text{standard quantity of direct labor hours allowed for average monthly production} - \text{standard quantity of direct labor hours allowed for actual number of units produced}\right]$$

$$\text{Volume variance} = \$10 \times (2{,}000 - 1{,}960)$$
$$= \underline{\underline{\$400}} \text{ unfavorable}$$

(see Exercise 20)

■

Causes of Manufacturing Overhead Variances

OBJECTIVE 8
List the major causes of manufacturing overhead variances

Before managers can investigate overhead variances and take appropriate action, they must understand the causes of these variances. The causes differ, depending on whether the cost involved is controllable, allocated, or noncontrollable. The causes of variances in the first two categories will now be discussed. Noncontrollable costs and variances are beyond the authority of department managers.

Controllable Costs

Recall that controllable costs are those listed in the first part of a flexible overhead budget. Both price and quantity differences can cause spending variances for these items. The actual price paid for an item may differ from the expected price used in establishing the flexible budget. For example, if oil is budgeted at $1.00 per quart but the actual price paid is $1.40 per quart, an unfavorable spending variance will result. Or the actual quantity used may differ from the estimated quantity. For example, the budget might call for 10 gallons of oil per 1,000 units produced. If 11 gallons per 1,000 units are used, an unfavorable spending variance will result.

As with direct materials and direct labor variances, managers must first decide whether a controllable variance is large enough to warrant investigation. Again, as with direct materials and direct labor variances, managers use percentages of the budgeted amount, absolute dollar amounts or some combination of those measures to help them decide what to investigate. If an investigation is needed, a performance report, such as the one shown in Exhibit 11–4, serves as the starting point.

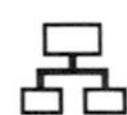

Allocated Costs

Control of allocated costs, such as maintenance, is shared by two or more managers. The manager of the machining department is responsible for controlling the *amount* of maintenance service used in that department. But the manager of the maintenance department is responsible for the *cost* of providing that service. The manager of the machining department can minimize the quantity of maintenance required by seeing that workers use machinery carefully. For example, he or she can see that machines are not run at higher than normal speeds to make up for lost production time. But the manager of the maintenance department is responsible for ensuring that the work is done as carefully and efficiently as possible.

In the case of maintenance, at least, the responsibility for controlling costs is divided. Either manager may be responsible for a spending variance. Other allocated costs are not necessarily controllable by department managers. Part of the cost of maintaining a company cafeteria, for example, might be allocated to the machining department based on the number of workers in that department. But the manager of the machining department can do nothing to control the number of workers in that department who eat in the cafeteria. Since these allocated costs are not controllable by the machining department manager, a strong argument can be made for not allocating such costs to departments on the basis of use. However, because these costs are included in the price of products and because managers should be reminded of all costs associated with a business, these costs are often allocated.

Whether or not these noncontrollable costs are allocated, flexible budgets and performance reports should be prepared for service departments. In this way, actual costs for service departments can be compared with estimated costs for the departments' activity levels. The key to implementing a flexible budget in a service department is to identify some drivers responsible for fluctuations in such costs. Some commonly used cost drivers are given below.

Manufacturing service department	Cost driver
Repairs and maintenance	Repair hours, number of setups, number of machine-hours
Cafeteria	Number of employees served
Power plant	Kilowatt-hours generated
Materials handling	Pounds of material moved, number of vendors, number of parts
Production scheduling	Number of orders processed, engineering change orders
Personnel	Number of employees served

Nonfinancial Measures for Controlling Manufacturing Overhead

In the just-in-time (JIT) manufacturing environment where the emphasis is on quality control, flexible product-oriented flow lines, and lower inventories, nonfinancial measures are used to measure performance and control manufacturing overhead costs.

The implication of JIT manufacturing for the managerial accountant is that performance measurement must include many noncost elements. Specific measures will vary from company to company, but the emphasis should be on the noncost items such as:

- Meeting delivery schedules
- Setup time
- Days in inventory
- Manufacturing time
- Amount of scrap
- Amount of rework
- Quality assurance
- Number of customer complaints
- Machine downtime
- Supplier reliability

Information concerning such noncost items must be collected and reported in a more timely manner than traditional cost variance information. The shorter the manufacturing cycle, the quicker that information is needed. Many of these nonmanufacturing performance measures are to encourage employees to keep inventory moving rather than to keep labor and machines working.

■

Application of Flexible Budgets to Nonmanufacturing Activities

OBJECTIVE 9
Explain how flexible budgets are used to control nonmanufacturing activities

Although flexible budgets have been used to plan and control manufacturing overhead costs for years, managers have only recently begun to rely on them to control nonmanufacturing activities. This extended use is logical, however, since flexible budgets can be developed for any repetitive activity producing a measurable output, including selling and administrative functions.

The first step in establishing a flexible budget for a nonmanufacturing activity is to decide what drives the activity's cost. The criterion for selecting a cost driver is the same as that used in manufacturing departments. That is, you should select the driver most closely related to fluctuations in the activity's costs. Some typical nonmanufacturing activities and their related costs drivers are shown below.

Activity	Cost driver
Warehousing operations	Pounds or crates handled
Packing of finished goods	Units processed
Delivery of products	Number of miles driven
Motor pool	Number of miles driven
Order entry	Number of orders processed
Billing	Number of bills processed
Data entry	Number of forms processed

Once the appropriate cost driver is chosen, the usual procedures for establishing a flexible budget are followed. Service department costs are classified as controllable or noncontrollable, and their fixed and variable components are identified. The accounting system records actual costs for each item and compares them with the flexible budget amount.

The major difference between manufacturing and nonmanufacturing costs is not in budgeting procedures, but in variances. There is no volume variance for nonmanufacturing activities. Remember that the volume variance relates to how fixed manufacturing overhead costs are accounted for. Nonmanufacturing costs are period costs, which are not assigned to products. Therefore, there is no volume variance for nonmanufacturing costs.

Review Exercise 11–4

Prepare a Flexible Budget

Bottom Company has decided to use a flexible budget to develop planning and control information for its warehouse operation. Based on an analysis of the company's historical data, the following costs and cost drivers have been identified for a normal month of operations.

Cost item	Fixed	Variable		Cost driver
Product handling	$5,000	$1.00	per	100 units
Storage pallets		2.00	per	pallet
Utilities	500	1.00	per	100 units
Shipping clerks	500	0.50	per	shipment
Supplies		0.25	per	shipment

During May, the warehousing operation processed 50,000 units using 450 pallets. This activity resulted in 300 shipments to customers. The actual costs for May are given below.

Cost item	Cost
Product handling	$5,450
Storage pallets	930
Utilities	1,010
Shipping clerks	700
Supplies	85
Total	$8,175

Required

Prepare a flexible budget of the warehousing operation and compare it to the actual costs for May.

Solution

Bottom Company
Flexible Budget Report
Warehousing Operation
For the Month of May

Cost item	Actual cost	Flexible budget cost	Variance
Product handling	$5,450	$5,500[1]	$50 (F)
Storage pallets	930	900[2]	30 (U)
Utilities	1,010	1,000[3]	10 (U)
Shipping clerks	700	650[4]	50 (U)
Supplies	85	75[5]	10 (U)
Total	$8,175	$8,125	$50 (U)

[1] $5,000 + ($1 × 500).
[2] $2 × 450.
[3] $500 + ($1 × 500).
[4] $500 + ($0.50 × 300).
[5] $0.25 × 300.

(see Exercise 24)

Manufacturing Overhead Costs in the General Ledger

OBJECTIVE 10
Enter manufacturing overhead costs in the general ledger

Actual manufacturing overhead costs are entered in the general ledger accounts from journal entries. Such entries for the machining department at Dailey Corporation are shown below.

Actual Manufacturing Overhead	49,854	
Wages Payable		13,845
Accounts Payable		10,609
Accumulated Depreciation		25,400
To record actual overhead costs for June		

Overhead is applied to products, based on the quantity of standard machine-hours allowed, and is recorded as follows:

Work in Process Inventory	49,000	
Applied Manufacturing Overhead		49,000
To record the application of manufacturing overhead at a rate of $10 per machine-hour for 4,900 standard machine-hours allowed		

Variances are recorded by closing actual and applied manufacturing overhead accounts to accounts for each variance:

Applied Manufacturing Overhead	49,000	
Efficiency Variance	600	
Volume Variance	700	
Spending Variance		446
Actual Manufacturing Overhead		49,854
To close overhead accounts and record variances		

Chapter Review

Review of Learning Objectives

1. Prepare a flexible budget for manufacturing overhead.
In a flexible budget, expected manufacturing overhead costs are separated into fixed and variable components. They are also categorized as controllable, allocated, or noncontrollable. Controllable costs are production costs that can be significantly affected by a department supervisor. Allocated costs are incurred in a separate manufacturing service department. They are allocated to production departments based on the amount of service used and, as such, are partially controllable by supervisors. Noncontrollable costs are costs, such as the department manager's salary or depreciation, assigned to a department simply because they are incurred there. Because the department supervisor cannot influence these costs, they are sometimes excluded from the budget.
Flexible budgets are superior to static budgets because they can be used to evaluate the efficiency of actual operations. First, a revised budget based on the actual level of production is prepared. This revised budget is used to compute the variances or the difference between actual overhead costs and budgeted costs for that level. Because a static budget is not adjusted to allow for variations between planned and actual production levels, any variance between the static budget and actual costs mixes the effects of volume, spending, and efficiency. Only flexible budgets should be used to evaluate performance.

2. State the criterion for selecting a cost driver when preparing a flexible budget.
The cost driver used to prepare a flexible budget should be the one that best relates manufacturing overhead costs to production volume. Since most departments produce several products, units of output are generally not used to measure production activity Some common cost drivers are direct labor hours and machine-hours.

3. Establish a predetermined overhead rate and explain the necessity for such rates.
A predetermined overhead rate is calculated by dividing estimated manufacturing overhead costs for the year by estimated annual production volume. Using a one-year period avoids seasonal variations in manufacturing overhead costs and production activity. A predetermined overhead rate based on machine-hours, for example, is calculated as follows:

$$\frac{\text{Predetermined overhead rate}}{\text{based on machine-hours}} \text{ (} = \text{) } \frac{\text{estimated annual overhead}}{\text{estimated annual machine-hours}}$$

The predetermined overhead rate is used to assign manufacturing overhead to each unit of product produced.

4. **Calculate a standard applied manufacturing overhead cost.**
The standard applied manufacturing overhead cost per unit is calculated by multiplying the predetermined overhead rate by the standard quantity of cost driver per unit of output.

5. **Calculate a manufacturing overhead budget variance.**
The manufacturing overhead budget variance is calculated by subtracting flexible budget overhead costs for standard quantity of machine-hours or direct labor hours allowed for the actual number of units produced from total actual manufacturing overhead costs. When the company produces more than one product, standard direct labor or machine-hours allowed is used to calculate the flexible budget amount. An unfavorable budget variance represents a loss in the sense that actual costs were higher than budgeted costs.

$$\text{Budget variance} = \text{actual manufacturing overhead costs} - \text{flexible budget overhead costs for standard quantity of cost driver allowed for actual number of units produced}$$

6. **Calculate manufacturing overhead spending and efficiency variances.**
The spending variance shows how effectively manufacturing overhead costs were controlled, both in quantity and price. It is calculated by subtracting flexible budget overhead costs for the actual quantity of machine-hours or direct labor hours used from actual manufacturing overhead costs.

The efficiency variance shows how carefully the cost driver, usually machine-hours or direct labor hours, was controlled. It is calculated by multiplying the variable overhead rate by the difference between the actual number of machine-hours used and standard number of machine-hours allowed.

$$\text{Spending variance} = \text{actual manufacturing overhead costs} - \text{flexible budget overhead costs for actual quantity of cost driver used}$$

$$\text{Efficiency variance} = \text{flexible budget overhead costs for actual quantity of cost driver used} - \text{flexible budget overhead costs for standard quantity of cost driver allowed}$$

7. **Calculate a manufacturing overhead volume variance.**
The volume variance is not a measure of efficiency. Rather, it shows whether actual production was above or below the estimated average monthly production level. It is calculated by multiplying the fixed overhead rate by the difference between the standard quantity of machine-hours allowed for average monthly production and the standard quantity of machine-hours allowed for actual number of units produced.

$$\text{Volume variance} = \text{fixed overhead rate} \times \left[\text{standard quantity of cost driver allowed for expected number of units produced} - \text{standard quantity of cost driver allowed for actual number of units produced}\right]$$

8. **List the major causes of manufacturing overhead variances.**
Manufacturing overhead spending variances are caused by differences between the stan-

dard prices and quantities allowed for overhead items and the actual prices paid and quantities used. Manufacturing overhead efficiency variances are caused by efficient or inefficient use of the cost driver used in the flexible budget. For example, if actual direct labor hours are greater than standard direct labor hours, a manufacturing overhead efficiency variance will result. This variance reflects how much variable overhead was wasted as direct labor hours were wasted. Manufacturing overhead volume variances stem from differences between average monthly expected production volumes and actual production volumes.

9. **Explain how flexible budgets are used to control nonmanufacturing activities.**
Flexible budgets can be used to control the costs of nonmanufacturing departments including selling and administrative functions. Accountants select a cost driver most closely related to the cost variations such as number of miles driven or number of invoices processed.

10. **Enter manufacturing overhead costs in the general ledger.**
Actual manufacturing overhead costs, applied manufacturing overhead, and all overhead variances are entered in the general ledger from journal entries.

Review of Key Terms

Allocated costs Costs incurred in a separate manufacturing service department and allocated to production departments.

Budget variance The difference between actual manufacturing overhead costs, as recorded in a firm's accounting records, and budgeted costs, as based on the standard quantity of cost driver (machine-hours or direct labor hours) allowed for the actual number of units produced. Calculated by subtracting flexible budget overhead costs for the standard quantity of cost driver allowed for the actual number of units produced from actual manufacturing overhead costs.

Controllable costs Costs over which the department supervisor has significant influence.

Cost driver A measure of business or production activity, such as machine-hours or miles driven, that causes a cost to change. Also called activity base or measure.

Efficiency variance The difference between flexible budget overhead costs for actual quantity of cost driver used and flexible budget overhead costs for the standard quantity of cost driver allowed. Calculated by subtracting flexible budget overhead costs for the standard quantity of cost driver allowed from flexible budget overhead costs for actual quantity of cost driver used.

Fixed cost An operating cost whose total remains constant over a wide range of business activity.

Flexible budget A budget that may be adjusted to any activity level to reflect how costs vary with changes in production volume.

Manufacturing overhead All manufacturing costs other than direct materials and direct labor necessary to manufacture a product.

Mixed costs Costs composed of both variable and fixed elements. Also called *semivariable costs.*

Noncontrollable costs Costs over which a manager has no significant influence or control.

Predetermined overhead rate A ratio that relates total estimated manufacturing overhead costs for the year to expected manufacturing activity for the year. Used to assign manufacturing overhead costs to batches of product or to departments. Calculated by dividing estimated manufacturing overhead cost for the year by the estimated amount of cost driver for the year.

Spending variance The difference between actual overhead costs and flexible budget overhead costs for actual quantity of cost driver used during the period. Calculated by subtracting flexible budget overhead costs for the actual quantity of cost driver used from total actual manufacturing overhead costs.

Standard applied manufacturing overhead cost The standard manufacturing overhead cost assigned to each unit of product or department according to a predetermined overhead rate. Calculated by multiplying the standard quantity of cost driver by the predetermined overhead rate.

Static budgets Budgets based on the level of production as estimated at the beginning of the year. They are not revised as actual production levels change.

Variable cost A cost whose total changes in direct proportion to changes in business activity. (Cost per unit remains constant.)

Volume variance A measure of the difference between the actual production volume, computed by using the standard amount of cost driver per unit, and the estimated average monthly production volume on which the predetermined overhead rate is based. Calculated by subtracting applied manufacturing overhead costs for the standard quantity of cost driver allowed for the number of units produced from flexible budget overhead costs for the standard quantity of cost driver allowed for the number of units produced.

Review Problem

Ronald Manufacturing Company manufactures a pesticide effective in controlling beetles. The company uses a flexible budget. The standard direct labor and overhead cost of one gallon of pesticide is as follows:

Direct labor	
(2 hours @ $16)	$32
Manufacturing overhead	
(2 direct labor hours @ $12)	24

The flexible budget system allows $50,000 in fixed manufacturing overhead per month. The average monthly production activity is 10,000 standard direct labor hours allowed. Variable overhead is projected at $7 per direct labor hour. Actual results for the period indicated the following:

Production		5,200 gallons of product
Direct labor		9,800 actual hours worked @ a cost of $158,400
Manufacturing overhead		
Fixed	$ 47,600	
Variable	81,300	
Total overhead	$128,900	

Required Calculate the following variances for manufacturing overhead:

1. Manufacturing overhead spending variance
2. Manufacturing overhead efficiency variance
3. Manufacturing overhead volume variance

Solution to Review Problem

1. Spending variance = actual manufacturing overhead costs − flexible budget overhead costs for 9,800 actual direct labor hours
   = \$128,900 − [\$50,000 + (9,800 × \$7 per hour)]
   = \$128,900 − \$118,600
   = \$10,300 (unfavorable)

2. Standard direct labor hours allowed = 5,200 gallons of output
   × 2 direct labor hours per gallon
   10,400 direct labor hours

   Efficiency variance = flexible budget overhead costs for 9,800 actual direct labor hours − flexible budget overhead costs for 10,400 standard direct labor hours
   = [\$50,000 + (9,800 × \$7 per hour)] − [\$50,000 + (10,400 × \$7 per hour)]
   = \$118,600 − \$122,800
   = \$4,200 (favorable)

   Efficiency variance = variable overhead rate × [actual direct labor hours − standard direct labor hours allowed]
   = \$7 × (9,800 − 10,400)
   = \$4,200 (favorable)

3. Volume variance = flexible budget overhead costs for 10,400 standard direct labor hours allowed − applied manufacturing overhead costs for 10,400 standard direct labor hours allowed
   = [\$50,000 + (10,400 × \$7 per hour)] − (10,400 × \$12 per hour)
   = \$122,800 − \$124,800
   = \$2,000 (favorable)

   Volume variance = fixed overhead rate × [standard direct labor hours allowed for average monthly production − standard direct labor hours allowed for actual production]
   = \$5* × (10,000 − 10,400)
   = \$2,000 (favorable)

*Fixed overhead application rate = fixed overhead budgeted ÷ average monthly production in standard direct labor hours allowed: \$50,000 ÷ 10,000 = \$5 per direct labor hour or \$12–\$7

Chapter Assignments

Questions

1. (L.O. 1) Define the three components of a product cost. Discuss the differences between the three product costs.
2. (L.O. 1) What is a flexible budget? How does a flexible budget differ from a static budget?
3. (L.O. 2) How is production output measured with a flexible budget? How does an accountant select a production cost driver?
4. (L.O. 1) Distinguish between controllable costs, allocated costs, and noncontrollable costs.
5. (L.O. 1) Why are flexible budgets developed on a departmental basis?
6. (L.O. 3) Why is the predetermined overhead rate calculated on an annual basis?
7. (L.O. 5, 6) Why is the budget variance divided into a spending and efficiency variance?
8. (L.O. 8) What are some possible causes of a spending variance?
9. (L.O. 8) What are some possible causes of an efficiency variance?
10. (L.O. 7) What causes a volume variance?
11. (L.O. 9) Are flexible budgets appropriate for nonmanufacturing activity?
12. (L.O. 9) How are outputs measured for nonmanufacturing activities?
13. (L.O. 9) Why is no volume variance calculated for nonmanufacturing activities?

Exercises

14. (L.O. 5, 7) Information on Bond Company's overhead costs is given below:

Actual overhead	$180,000
Budgeted fixed overhead	$ 34,000
Standard direct labor hours allowed for actual production	30,000
Standard variable overhead rate per direct labor hour	$ 5
Standard fixed overhead rate per direct labor hour	$ 1
Monthly average standard direct labor hours allowed	34,000

Required Calculate manufacturing overhead budget and volume variances.

15. (L.O. 6, 7, 10) Ace, Inc., uses a standard cost system. Overhead cost information for Product X for October is as follows:

Total actual overhead incurred	$12,600
Fixed overhead budgeted	$ 3,500
Total standard overhead rate per direct labor hour	$ 3
Variable overhead rate per direct labor hour	$ 2
Standard hours allowed for actual production	3,500
Actual hours worked	3,200
Monthly average standard direct labor hours allowed	3,500

Required

1. Calculate the following variances for manufacturing overhead:
   a. Spending variance
   b. Efficiency variance
   c. Volume variance
2. Prepare journal entries, recording actual and applied manufacturing overhead as well as manufacturing overhead variances.

16. (L.O. 5) The managerial accountants of West Company have analyzed the company's historical costs and developed the following flexible budget for the monthly manufacturing overhead costs:

Total manufacturing overhead costs = $10,000 per month + $4 per direct labor hour

Standard direct labor hours are expected to be 2 hours per unit of finished product. During June 19x2, 870 units were produced. The actual manufacturing overhead costs amounted to $16,100.

Required Calculate the manufacturing overhead budget variance for June. (see Review Exercise 11–1)

17. (L.O. 3, 4) Rahn Company uses a standard cost system. For the year 19x3, total manufacturing overhead is budgeted at $960,000. This figure is based on expected annual activity of 240,000 direct labor hours. The standard cost system allows two direct labor hours for each unit of finished product. The following data are available for November:

Units completed	9,500
Direct labor hours worked	19,500
Actual total overhead incurred	$79,500

Required What is Rahn's applied manufacturing overhead for November?

18. (L.O. 5) Cincinnati Corporation uses a flexible budget system. It prepared the following estimates of planned operations for the year:

Direct labor hours	32,000
Variable manufacturing overhead	$ 64,000
Fixed manufacturing overhead	160,000
Predetermined overhead rate	7 per direct labor hour

Assume Cincinnati operated at 36,000 standard direct labor hours allowed and actual overhead costs for the year were $252,000.

Required Calculate the manufacturing overhead budget variance.

19. (L.O. 6) The managerial accountants of School Company have analyzed the company's historical costs and developed the following flexible budget for the monthly manufacturing overhead costs:

Total manufacturing overhead costs = $40,000 per month + $4 per direct labor hour

Standard direct labor hours are expected to be 2 hours per unit of finished product. During June 19x2, 1,010 units were produced. The actual manufacturing overhead costs amounted to $49,300. The actual direct labor hours worked during June are 2,100.

Required Calculate the manufacturing overhead spending and efficiency variances for June. (see Review Exercise 11–2)

20. (L.O. 7) The managerial accountants of Hathaway Company have analyzed the company's historical costs and developed the following flexible budget for the monthly manufacturing overhead costs:

Total manufacturing overhead costs = $30,000 per month + $3 per direct labor hour

Standard direct labor hours are expected to be 3 hours per unit of finished product. During June 19x2, 990 units were produced. The company normally produces 1,000 units per month.

Required Calculate the manufacturing overhead volume variance for June. (see Review Exercise 11–3)

21. (L.O. 6, 7, 10) Hill Pumps produces pumps for fire departments. They employ a standard cost system. At the end of the current period, the cost accounting department showed the following:

Actual data	
Actual manufacturing overhead	$44,800
Direct labor	
Actual hours worked	38,400
Standard hours allowed	37,600

The predetermined overhead rate is based on expected activity of 36,000 direct labor hours. Budgeted overhead for 36,000 direct labor hours is as follows:

Variable overhead	$30,600
Fixed overhead	12,600
Total	$43,200

Required

1. Calculate manufacturing overhead spending, efficiency, and volume variances.
2. Prepare journal entries to record actual overhead, applied overhead, and spending, efficiency, and volume variances.

22. (L.O. 6, 7) The following information is available from Schloemer Company for June:

Actual manufacturing overhead costs	$30,000
Fixed overhead expenses, budgeted	$14,000
Actual direct labor hours	3,500
Monthly average standard direct labor hours allowed	4,000
Standard direct labor hours allowed for June	3,700
Predetermined variable overhead rate per direct labor hour	$ 5

Required Calculate the following variances for manufacturing overhead:

1. Spending variance
2. Efficiency variance
3. Volume variance

23. (L.O. 6, 7, 10) Universal Company uses a standard cost system. It prepared the following budget on expected activity for January:

Average monthly standard direct labor hours allowed	24,000
Variable manufacturing overhead	$ 48,000
Fixed manufacturing overhead	$108,000
Manufacturing overhead rate per direct labor hour	$ 6.50

Actual data for January were as follows:

Direct labor hours worked	22,000
Total manufacturing overhead incurred	$147,000
Standard direct labor hours allowed for actual output	21,000

Required

1. Calculate the following variances for January:
   a. Spending variance
   b. Efficiency variance
   c. Volume variance
2. Prepare journal entries to record actual manufacturing overhead costs, applied manufacturing overhead costs, and manufacturing overhead variances. (AICPA)

24. (L.O. 9) Patterson Company has decided to use a flexible budget to develop planning and control information for its warehouse operation. Based on an analysis of historical data, the following costs and cost drivers have been identified for a normal month of operations:

Cost item	Fixed	Variable		Cost driver
Product handling	$4,000	$2.00	per	100 units
Storage pallets		3.00	per	pallet
Utilities	600	2.00	per	100 units
Shipping clerks	700	1.50	per	shipment
Supplies		0.50	per	shipment

During May, the warehousing operation processed 60,000 units using 500 pallets. This activity resulted in 400 shipments to customers. The actual costs for May are given below.

Cost item	Cost
Product handling	$5,420
Storage pallets	1,030
Utilities	1,710
Shipping clerks	1,200
Supplies	205
Total	$9,565

Required Prepare a flexible budget of the warehousing operation and compare it to the actual costs for May. (see Review Exercise 11–4)

25. (L.O. 6, 7) King Company estimated that its manufacturing facilities will operate at 800,000 direct labor hours this year. Total budgeted manufacturing overhead was $2 million. The budgeted variable manufacturing overhead rate was $2 per direct labor hour. This rate resulted in standard applied variable manufacturing overhead cost of $6 per unit. Actual data for the year are presented below.

Actual finished units	250,000
Actual direct labor hours	764,000
Actual manufacturing overhead	$2,002,000

Required Calculate the following manufacturing overhead variances for the year:

1. Spending variance
2. Efficiency variance
3. Volume variance

26. (L.O. 6, 7) Burns Company has developed standard manufacturing overhead costs based on estimated average output of 180,000 direct labor hours per month. The standards are as follows:

Standard manufacturing overhead costs per unit		
Variable overhead:	2 hours @ $2 =	$ 4
Fixed overhead:	2 hours @ $5 =	10
Total		$14

During April, 90,000 units were scheduled for production, but only 80,000 units were actually produced. The following data relate to April:

Actual direct labor costs incurred for 165,000 actual direct labor hours	$1,320,000
Actual manufacturing overhead incurred	1,378,000

Required Calculate the following variances in manufacturing overhead costs for April:

1. Spending variance
2. Efficiency variance
3. Volume variance

(CMA)

27. (L.O. 5, 7) Oliver Manufacturing Company produces and sells a single product. Information on the company's overhead costs is given below:

Actual overhead	$250,000
Budgeted fixed overhead	$ 75,000
Standard direct labor hours allowed for actual production	50,000
Standard variable overhead rate per direct labor hour	$ 6
Standard fixed overhead rate per direct labor hour	$ 2
Monthly average standard direct labor hours allowed	55,000

Required Calculate the manufacturing overhead budget and volume variance.

28. (L.O. 6, 7) Vincent Corporation uses a standard costing system. Overhead cost information for June is as follows:

Total actual overhead incurred	$18,000
Fixed overhead budgeted	$ 5,000
Total standard overhead rate per direct labor hour	$ 6
Variable overhead rate per direct labor hour	$ 4
Standard hours allowed for actual production	2,500
Actual hours worked	1,800
Monthly average standard direct labor hours allowed	2,500

Required Calculate the following variances for the Vincent Company's manufacturing overhead:

1. Spending variance
2. Efficiency variance
3. Volume variance

29. (L.O. 6, 7) Cafe Manufacturing Company produces and sells a single product. The company estimates that its manufacturing facility will operate at 500,000 direct labor hours per year. Total budgeted manufacturing overhead was $2,000,000. The budgeted variable manufacturing overhead rate is $3 per direct labor hour. The standard applied manufacturing overhead cost is $8 per unit. Actual data for the year is as follows:

Actual finished units	250,000
Actual direct labor hours	550,000
Actual manufacturing overhead	$2,250,000

Required Calculate the following manufacturing overhead variances for the year:

1. Spending variance
2. Efficiency variance
3. Volume variance

30. (L.O. 4, 5, 7) Kaplan Manufacturing Company's cost information for July is as follows:

Budgeted fixed manufacturing overhead per month	$75,000
Variable manufacturing overhead per direct labor hour	$ 7
Standard direct labor hours allowed for the month	50,000
Unfavorable budget variance for July	$ 5,000
Favorable volume variance for July	8,000

Required Calculate the actual manufacturing overhead incurred and the applied manufacturing overhead for July.

31. (L.O. 6, 7) Beatty Manufacturing Company's manufacturing overhead information for May is as follows:

Actual manufacturing overhead	$992,000
Flexible budget formula	250,000 + $2 per direct labor hour
Predetermined manufacturing overhead rate	2.80 per direct labor hour
Spending variance	6,000 (unfavorable)
Volume variance	7,500 (unfavorable)

Required Compute the actual direct labor hours worked and the standard direct labor hours allowed.

32. (L.O. 3, 4) Seattle Company produces 10,000 units operating at a normal level of 25,000 direct labor hours. The direct labor wage rate is $7.50 per hour. Three pounds of materials go into each unit of product at a cost of $2 per pound. A flexible budget is used to plan and control overhead costs. It is as follows:

Flexible Budget Data

		Direct labor hours		
Overhead costs	Cost formula	20,000	22,500	25,000
Variable costs	$1.50	$30,000	$33,750	$37,500
Fixed costs		60,000	60,000	60,000
Total		$90,000	$93,750	$97,500

Required

1. Using 25,000 direct labor hours as the expected activity, compute the predetermined overhead rate and then break it into fixed and variable elements.
2. Complete the standard cost card below for one unit of product:

Direct materials (3 lbs @ $2)	$6
Direct labor	?
Variable overhead	?
Fixed overhead	?
Total standard cost per unit	?

33. (L.O. 5) Gorman Company's flexible budget is given on page 541.

Overhead costs	Cost formula per unit	Number of units 10,000	12,500	15,000
Supplies	$0.50	$ 5,000	$ 6,250	$ 7,500
Maintenance	0.75	7,500	9,375	11,250
Utilities	0.20	2,000	2,500	3,000
Total overhead costs	$1.45	$14,500	$18,125	$21,750

During the recent period, the company produced 12,000 units. The variable overhead costs incurred were as follows:

Supplies	$7,000
Maintenance	9,500
Utilities	2,800

The production budgeted for the period had been 12,500 units.

Required Prepare a performance report for the period. Indicate whether the variances are favorable or unfavorable.

34. (L.O. 6, 7) Derf Company applies overhead on the basis of direct labor hours. Two direct labor hours are required for each product unit. Planned production for the period was set at 9,000 units. Manufacturing overhead is budgeted at $135,000 for the period, of which 20 percent of this cost is fixed. The 17,200 hours worked during the period resulted in production of 8,500 units. Variable manufacturing overhead cost incurred was $108,500 and fixed manufacturing overhead cost was $28,000.

Required For manufacturing overhead, calculate the following:

1. The spending variance
2. The efficiency variance
3. The volume variance

(CMA)

35. (L.O. 6, 7) Able Control Company, which manufactures electrical switches, uses a standard cost system and carries all inventory at standard. The standard factory overhead costs per switch are based on direct labor hours and are shown below.

Variable overhead (5 hours @ $8 per hour)	$ 40
Fixed overhead (5 hours @ $12* per hour)	60
Total overhead	$100

*Based on capacity of 300,000 direct labor hours per month.

The following information is available for the month of October:

- 56,000 switches were produced, although 60,000 switches were scheduled to be produced.
- 275,000 direct labor hours were worked at a total cost of $2,550,000.
- Variable overhead costs were $2,340,000.
- Fixed overhead costs were $3,750,000.

Required Calculate the following manufacturing overhead variances for October:

1. Spending variance
2. Efficiency variance
3. Volume variance

(CMA)

Problems

36. (L.O. 5, 7) Information on manufacturing overhead costs at Ripley Company for January's production activity follows:

Budgeted fixed overhead	$ 75,000
Standard fixed overhead rate per direct labor hour	$ 3
Standard variable overhead rate per direct labor hour	$ 6
Standard direct labor hours allowed for actual production	24,000
Actual total overhead incurred	$220,000

Required

1. Calculate January's budget and volume variances for manufacturing overhead.
2. Prepare graphs illustrating budget and volume variances. (AICPA)

37. (L.O. 4, 5, 7) Budgeted fixed manufacturing overhead costs at Simon Company are $50,000 per month. Variable manufacturing overhead is budgeted at $8 per direct labor hour. Standard direct labor hours allowed for October's production were 36,000. An analysis of October's manufacturing overhead indicates that Simon had an unfavorable budget variance of $2,000 and a favorable volume variance of $5,000.

Required Calculate the actual manufacturing overhead incurred and the applied manufacturing overhead for October.

38. (L.O. 6, 7) The total manufacturing overhead variance for Herman Company is divided into three variances: spending, efficiency, and volume. The following information is for August:

Actual manufacturing overhead	$178,500
Flexible budget formula	110,000 + $0.50 per direct labor hour
Predetermined manufacturing overhead rate	1.50 per direct labor hour
Spending variance	8,000 (unfavorable)
Volume variance	5,000 (favorable)

Required Compute the actual direct labor hours worked and the standard direct labor hours allowed. (AICPA)

39. (L.O. 5, 7) The following information for April relates to Marilyn, Inc., which uses a standard cost system. Marilyn computes two overhead variances, budget and volume.

Actual direct labor costs	$86,800
Actual direct labor hours worked	14,000
Standard direct labor hours allowed	15,000
Direct labor rate variance (unfavorable)	$ 1,400
Actual manufacturing overhead	$32,000
Budgeted fixed manufacturing overhead costs	$ 9,000
Average monthly standard direct labor hours allowed	12,000
Predetermined manufacturing overhead rate per direct labor hour	$ 2.25

Required Calculate the following variances for Marilyn, Inc.:

1. Direct labor quantity variance
2. Manufacturing overhead budget variance
3. Manufacturing overhead volume variance

(AICPA)

40. (L.O. 6, 7) Milner Manufacturing Company, located in Hong Kong, uses standard costs. It manufactures one product whose standard cost per unit is as follows:

Direct materials	
(20 yards @ $0.90 per yard)	$18
Direct labor	
(4 hours @ $6 per hour)	24
Standard allowed manufacturing overhead	20
Variable selling, general, and administrative expenses	12
Fixed selling, general, and administrative expenses	7
Total unit cost	$81

The standards are based on a monthly average production activity of 2,400 direct labor hours. The predetermined overhead rate is five-sixths of direct labor cost, and the ratio of variable costs to fixed costs is 3 to 1.

Actual activity for October 19x5 was as follows:

Units of product produced		500
Direct materials purchased		
(18,000 yards @ $0.92 per yard)	$16,560	
Direct materials used		9,500 yards
Direct labor		
(2,100 hours @ $6.10 per hour)	$12,810	
Manufacturing overhead costs	11,100	

Required Compute the variances listed below for October 19x5. Indicate whether each variance is favorable or unfavorable.

1. Direct materials price variance
2. Direct materials quantity variance
3. Direct labor rate variance
4. Direct labor efficiency variance
5. Manufacturing overhead spending variance
6. Manufacturing overhead efficiency variance
7. Manufacturing overhead volume variance

(AICPA)

41. (L.O. 6, 7) Carberg Corporation manufactures and sells a single product. The company uses a standard cost system. The standard cost per unit of product is shown below.

Direct materials	
(1 pound plastic @ $2)	$ 2.00
Direct labor	
(1.6 hours @ $8)	12.80
Variable manufacturing overhead costs	
(1.6 direct labor hours @ $3.125)	5.00
Fixed manufacturing overhead costs	
(1.6 direct labor hours @ $0.9375)	1.50
Total unit manufacturing cost	$21.30

The manufacturing overhead cost per unit was calculated from the following annual manufacturing overhead cost budget for 60,000 units of production:

Variable manufacturing overhead costs	
Indirect labor (30,000 hours @ $8)	$240,000
Supplies, oil (60,000 gallons @ $0.50)	30,000
Allocated variable service department costs	30,000
Total variable manufacturing overhead costs	$300,000
Fixed manufacturing overhead costs	
Supervision	$ 30,000
Depreciation	45,000
Other fixed costs	15,000
Total fixed manufacturing overhead costs	$ 90,000
Total budgeted annual manufacturing overhead costs for 60,000 units	$390,000

Actual costs for the manufacturing department for November when 5,000 units were produced are given below.

Direct materials (5,300 pounds @ $2)	$10,600
Direct labor (8,200 hours @ $8.10)	66,420
Indirect labor (2,400 hours @ $8.10)	19,440
Supplies, oil (6,000 gallons @ $0.55)	3,300
Allocated variable service department costs	3,200
Fixed manufacturing overhead costs	
Supervision	2,475
Depreciation	3,750
Other	1,250
Total	$110,435

The purchasing department buys about the same quantity of materials as production uses each month. In November, 5,300 pounds were purchased for $2 per pound.

Required

1. Calculate the following variances from standard costs for the data given:
   a. Direct materials price
   b. Direct materials quantity
   c. Direct labor rate
   d. Direct labor efficiency
   e. Manufacturing overhead spending
   f. Manufacturing overhead efficiency
   g. Manufacturing overhead volume
2. Prepare a performance report showing the spending variance by item and the efficiency variance. Follow the format of Exhibit 11–5. (CMA)

42. (L.O. 5, 7) Eastern Company manufactures special electrical equipment and parts. Eastern employs a standard cost accounting system with separate standards established for each product.

A special transformer is manufactured in the transformer department. Production volume is measured by direct labor hours in this department and a flexible budget system is used to plan and control department overhead.

Standard costs for the special transformer are determined annually in September for the coming year. The standard cost of a transformer for 19x7 was computed at $67 as shown below.

Direct materials	
Iron (5 sheets @ $2)	$10
Copper (3 spools @ $3)	9
Direct labor (4 hours @ $7)	28
Variable overhead (4 hours @ $3)	12
Fixed overhead (4 hours @ $2)	8
Total	$67

Overhead rates were based on normal and expected monthly capacity for 19x7, both of which were 4,000 direct labor hours. Variable overhead costs are expected to vary with the number of direct labor hours actually used.

During October 19x7, 800 transformers were produced. This was below expectations because a work stoppage occurred during contract negotiations with the labor force. Once the contract was settled, the department scheduled overtime in an attempt to catch up to expected production levels.

The following costs were incurred in October 19x7:

Direct materials	Direct materials purchased	Materials used
Iron	5,000 sheets @ $2.00 per sheet	3,900 sheets
Copper	2,200 spools @ $3.10 per spool	2,700 spools
Direct labor		
Regular time	2,000 hours @ $7.00 1,400 hours @ $7.20	
Overtime	600 of the 1,400 hours were subject to overtime premium. The total overtime premium of $2,160 is included in variable overhead in accordance with company accounting practices.	
Variable overhead	$10,000	
Fixed overhead	8,800	

Required

1. Calculate the direct materials variances
2. Calculate the direct labor variances
3. For manufacturing overhead, calculate
   a. Budget variance
   b. Volume variance

(CMA)

43. (L.O. 6, 7) Donner Company produces a single product and uses a standard cost accounting system. The standards and related data are as follows:

Direct materials	
(2 pounds @ $1.30 per pound)	$2.60
Direct labor	
(1 hour @ $8 per hour)	8.00
Manufacturing overhead	?

Average monthly production volume	10,000 units per month
Predetermined overhead rate	$3.10 per direct labor hour
Variable overhead rate	$1.60 per direct labor hour

For May the following data are known:

Units produced	10,600
Total direct labor costs	$87,140
Direct labor efficiency variance	$ 800 (favorable)
Overhead spending variance	$ 700 (unfavorable)
Direct materials purchased	24,200 pounds
Cost of direct materials purchased	$31,702
Direct materials used	22,000 pounds

Required Calculate the following:

1. Direct materials price variance
2. Direct materials quantity variance
3. Budgeted fixed overhead per month
4. Manufacturing overhead volume variance
5. Total manufacturing overhead variance

(AICPA)

44. (L.O. 1, 5) Melcher Company produces farm equipment at several plants. The business is seasonal and cyclical in nature. The company has attempted to use budgeting for planning and controlling activities, but the variable nature of the business has caused some company officials to be skeptical about the usefulness of budgeting to the company. The accountant for the Adrian plant has been using a system he calls "flexible budgeting" to help his plant management control operations.

The company president asks him to explain what the term means, how he applies the system at the Adrian plant, and how it can be applied to the company as a whole. The accountant presents the following data as part of his explanation:

Budget data for 19x3	
Normal monthly capacity of the plant in direct labor hours	10,000 hours
Material costs (6 lbs. @ $1.50)	$9 unit
Labor costs (2 hours @ $6.00)	12 unit
Overhead estimate at normal monthly capacity	
Variable (controllable)	
Indirect labor	$ 6,650
Indirect materials	600
Repairs	750
Total variable	$ 8,000
Fixed (noncontrollable)	
Depreciation	$ 3,250
Supervision	3,000
Total fixed	$ 6,250
Total fixed and variable	$ 14,250
Planned units for January 19x3	4,000
Planned units for February 19x3	6,000
Actual data for January 19x3	
Hours worked	8,400
Units produced	3,800

Costs incurred	
Materials (24,000 lbs)	$ 36,000
Direct labor	50,400
Indirect labor	6,000
Indirect materials	600
Repairs	1,800
Depreciation	3,250
Supervision	3,000
Total	$101,050

Required

1. Prepare a flexible budget for January based on planned units.
2. Prepare an overhead report for January comparing actual and budgeted costs for the actual activity for the month.
3. Can flexible budgeting be applied to the nonmanufacturing activities of the company? Explain your answer.

Case 1

Jones Furniture Company (L.O. 6, 7)

Jones Furniture Company uses a standard cost system to account for production costs. The standard cost of a unit of furniture follows:

Lumber (100 feet @ $150 per 1,000 feet)		$ 15
Direct labor (4 hours @ $12.50 per hour)		50
Manufacturing overhead		
Fixed (30% of direct labor)	$15	
Variable (60% of direct labor)	30	45
Total standard cost per unit		$110

The following flexible monthly overhead budget is in effect:

Direct labor hours	Estimated overhead
20,800	$216,000
19,200	204,000
17,600	192,000
16,000 (expected production)	180,000
14,400	168,000

Actual costs for December when 3,800 units were produced are as follows:

Lumber purchased and used (110 feet @ $120 per 1,000 feet)	$ 13.20 per unit
Direct labor ($4\frac{1}{4}$ hours @ $12.60 per hour)	53.55 per unit
Manufacturing overhead	180,000.00

Required Prepare an analysis of direct materials, direct labor, and manufacturing overhead variances. Calculate the spending, efficiency and volume variance for manufacturing overhead. (AICPA)

Case 2

University of Boyne (L.O. 9)

The University of Boyne offers an extensive continuing education program in many cities throughout the state. For the faculty and administrative staff's convenience and to save costs, the university operates a motor pool. Until February, the motor pool operated with 20 vehicles. However, an additional automobile was acquired in February, which increased the number to 21 vehicles. The motor pool purchases gasoline, oil, and other supplies for the cars in bulk and hires one mechanic for routine maintenance and minor repairs. Major repairs are done at a nearby commercial garage. A supervisor manages operations.

Each year the supervisor prepares an operating budget for the motor pool. The budget informs university management about funds needed to operate the pool. Automobile depreciation is recorded in the budget so each car's total cost per mile can be determined.

The annual budget approved by the university is shown below. The actual costs for March are compared with those for one-twelfth of the annual budget.

The annual budget was based on the following assumptions:

a. 20 automobiles in the pool
b. 30,000 miles per year per automobile
c. 15 miles per gallon per automobile
d. $0.60 per gallon of gas
e. $0.006 per mile for oil, minor repairs, parts, and supplies
f. $135 per automobile in outside repairs

University Motor Pool
Budget Report
For the Month of March 19x6

	Annual budget	One-month budget	March actual	Over*/ under
Gasoline	$24,000	$ 2,000	$2,800	$800*
Oil, minor repairs, parts, and supplies	3,600	300	380	80*
Outside repairs	2,700	225	50	175
Insurance	6,000	500	525	25*
Salaries, benefits	30,000	2,500	2,500	—
Depreciation	26,400	2,200	2,310	110*
Total	$92,700	$ 7,725	$ 8,565	$840*

	Annual budget	One-month budget	March actual	Over*/ under
Total miles	600,000	50,000	63,000	
Cost per mile	$0.1545	$0.1545	$0.1360	
Number of autos	20	20	21	

The supervisor is unhappy with the monthly report comparing budget and actual costs for March. He claims it unfairly represents his performance. His previous employer used flexible budgeting for such comparisons.

Required

1. Employing flexible budgeting techniques, prepare a report showing flexible budgeted amounts, actual costs, and the spending variances for March.
2. Briefly explain the basis for the budget figure for outside repairs. (CMA)

Case 3

Pearsons (L.O. 9)

Pearsons is a successful regional chain of moderately priced restaurants with carryout delicatessens. The chain plans to expand into a nationwide operation. As it grows and the territory covered becomes wider, managerial control and reporting techniques become more important.

Typical Pearsons Restaurant-Deli
Budgeted Income Statement
For the Year Ended December 31, 19x8
(000 omitted)

	Delicatessen	Restaurant	Total
Gross sales	$1,000	$2,500	$3,500
Expenses			
Purchases	$ 600	$1,000	$1,600
Wages	50	875	925
Franchise fees	30	75	105
Advertising	100	200	300
Utilities	70	125	195
Depreciation	50	75	125
Lease expenses	30	50	80
Salaries	30	50	80
Total expenses	$ 960	$2,450	$3,410
Operating income	$ 40	$ 50	$ 90

Management believes a budget program for the entire company as well as each restaurant-deli unit is needed. The budget shown above was prepared for a typical unit in the chain. A new unit, once in operation, is expected to perform according to this budget.

All restaurants are approximately the same size with the same amount of space devoted to carryout service. The facilities and equipment are uniformly styled. Unit operators are expected to carry out the advertising program recommended by the corporation. The corporation charges a franchise fee, which is a percentage of gross sales. This fee is for use of the company name, design of building and facilities, and advertising advice. The Akron, Ohio unit was selected to test the budget program. Below, this unit's performance for the year ended December 31, 19x8, is compared with the typical budget.

Pearsons Restaurant-Deli: Akron, Ohio
Operating Income
For the Year Ended December 31, 19x8

	Actual results				
	Deli	**Restaurant**	**Total**	**Budget**	**Variances**
Gross sales	$1,200	$2,000	$3,200	$3,500	$300 (U)
Expenses					
Purchases	$ 780	$ 800	$1,580	$1,600	$ 20 (F)
Wages	60	700	760	925	165 (F)
Franchise fees	36	60	96	105	9 (F)
Advertising	100	200	300	300	—
Utilities	76	100	176	195	19 (F)
Depreciation	50	75	125	125	—
Lease expenses	30	50	80	80	—
Salaries	30	50	80	80	—
Total expenses	$1,162	$2,035	$3,197	$3,410	$213 (F)
Operating income	$ 38	$ (35)	$ 3	$ 90	$ 87 (U)

The above report was carefully reviewed and discussed by management. Management concluded that the comparison would be more meaningful if a flexible budget analysis was performed for each operation, rather than comparing the two in a single budget.

Required

1. Prepare a schedule, comparing a flexible budget for the deli line at Akron with its actual performance. Use sales dollars as the activity measure.
2. Would a complete report, comparing a flexible budget with the performance of each operation, make Akron's problems easier to identify? Explain, using an example from the problem and your answer to *1* above. (CMA)

■

12

Performance Measurement: Revenue Centers and Profit Centers

LEARNING OBJECTIVES

After studying this chapter you should be able to:

1. Explain how the performance of a revenue center manager is measured
2. Explain how the performance of a profit center manager is measured
3. Explain how revenue center and profit center managers use sales price, sales volume, and sales mix variances
4. Calculate sales price, sales volume, and sales mix variances
5. Explain how profit center managers use expense and revenue variances to achieve their financial goals
6. Calculate manufacturing, marketing, and administrative expense variances
7. Calculate sales variances for sales territories, distribution channels, and products

In Chapter 9 you saw that a manager's financial responsibility is defined by the type of responsibility center he or she manages. Each type of center involves different managerial responsibilities, and each calls for different reporting practices. Reporting systems for expense center managers were covered in Chapters 10 and 11. This chapter discusses reporting systems for managers of revenue and profit centers. Investment center reporting will be discussed in Chapter 13.

■

Performance Measurement in Revenue Centers

Managers of **revenue centers** are responsible for achieving budgeted levels of contribution margin. They do so by selling budgeted quantities of various products or services at budgeted prices. Put another way, managers of revenue centers attempt to control the number of units sold, product mix, and selling prices in order to achieve their contribution margin goal.

Selling the budgeted number of units is important to achieving an organization's net earnings goal. If a record store plans to sell 150,000 records a year, achieving its target profit will be difficult if actual sales are only 120,000. The **product mix,** or the proportion of total sales volume from each product (also called **sales mix**), is equally important. Suppose a record store plans to sell 105,000 CDs and 45,000 albums. This sales plan calls for a sales mix of 70 percent CDs and 30 percent albums. Achieving this planned sales mix is important. The selling price and profitability are higher for CDs than for albums. Even though the store could meet its 150,000 unit sales goal by selling 90,000 CDs and 60,000 albums, this sales mix makes it difficult to meet the contribution margin goal.

OBJECTIVE 1
Explain how the performance of a revenue center manager is measured

The record store must also sell products close to their budgeted selling prices. Suppose the plan is to sell CDs at an average price of $18. If the store achieves its planned sales of 105,000 CDs by selling them at an average price of $16 each, sales revenue at year-end will fall short of budgeted sales revenue. Not every CD must be sold at $18 to meet the sales price goal. Some CDs will be sold for more than $18; others will be discounted. As long as the *average* selling price is $18, the sales price goal will be met.

In seeking to achieve the budgeted average selling price, a revenue center manager may shift emphasis from one product to another. For example, a store manager may decide to emphasize classical CDs, whose average selling price is relatively high, in order to achieve the budgeted average selling price. Thus, revenue center managers trade off sales of one product for another in trying to achieve their revenue goals. If budgeted quantities of products can be sold at the planned average selling price, such trades will be successful, and managers will achieve their total revenue goals.

Three types of variances are useful to revenue center managers in meeting their goals:

1. The sales price variance
2. The sales volume variance
3. The sales mix variance

A responsibility accounting report for a revenue center manager should include these variances. If a revenue center manager bears responsibility for controlling some marketing expenses as well, the accounting report may also include marketing expense variances. The use of **flexible budgets** to control selling and administrative expenses was discussed in Chapter 11.

■

Performance Measurement in Profit Centers

The performance of a profit center manager is measured by whether the center achieves its budgeted profit. The amount of budgeted profit each center must achieve is usually stated in the master budget. It is determined by the following:

1. The amount of capital invested in the center
2. The center's past profits
3. The past profits of competing businesses
4. Any plans for introducing new products or other changes that may alter the center's profitability

OBJECTIVE 2
Explain how the performance of a profit center manager is measured

A **profit center** manager achieves the budgeted profit by selling budgeted quantities of product at budgeted selling prices while also controlling expenses so they do not exceed budgeted amounts. Thus, profit center managers have more responsibilities than revenue center managers. A profit center manager is responsible for purchasing, manufacturing, and administrative expenses as well as for marketing expenses and revenue control.

Profit center managers may incur added expenses if they believe increased sales will offset such expenses. For example, suppose the manager of a profit center that makes nails finds the product is selling poorly because customers cannot read the small type on the boxes. The manager might decide to redesign the box to include a drawing of the nail and to print all lettering in larger type. If the new box costs only slightly more than the old one and sales increase by even a small amount, the added contribution margin from the extra sales should justify the expense.

Profit center managers can afford to incur added expenses because they are responsible for balancing sales and expenses to achieve profit goals. **Expense center** managers have no motivation to incur added expenses, for they would only make the job of meeting expense goals more difficult. Unlike profit center managers, expense center managers reap no benefit from the added contribution margin an extra expense may produce.

■

Uses of Revenue Variances

OBJECTIVE 3
Explain how revenue center and profit center managers use sales price, sales volume, and sales mix variances

As an example of how revenue variances can be useful to both revenue center and profit center managers, suppose Brandow Division has budgeted revenue of $80,000 for April. At the end of April, accountants report actual sales of $88,000. Naturally, the division's manager is pleased. But what caused sales to go over budget? Was some new sales strategy particularly successful? Or was the cause some other factor within the manager's control?

Revenue variances can help managers identify possible causes of differences between budgeted and actual sales. Assume that Brandow's budget for April was based on the expectation that 160,000 units of product would be sold for $0.50 each. The product would then yield revenue of $80,000. The $8,000 increase over planned revenue may have been caused by:

1. A 10 percent increase in unit sales (176,000 units @ $0.50 each = $88,000)
2. A $0.05 increase in selling price (160,000 units at $0.55 each = $88,000)
3. Some combination of change in sales volume and price, such as selling 162,963 units at $0.54 cents per unit

Sales volume and sales price variances will help the manager identify the cause of the difference between budgeted and actual revenues. With that information he or she will be better positioned to decide what action, if any, to take. In this case, if the increased revenue arose from both higher unit sales and a higher selling price, the combination should be continued and, if possible, applied to other products. If the variance resulted from higher unit sales and a lower selling price, the manager may try maintaining the number of units sold while increasing the selling price.

Revenue variances are also useful in evaluating product mix. Product mix is an issue only when a revenue center sells more than one product, as most do. As you have seen, the mix of products sold is important, since products usually have different contribution margins. An organization can achieve its total revenue goals but not its contribution margin goals if the product mix differs from the budgeted mix.

Consider the case of Riverside Services, Inc., an organization that provides microcomputer word processing and bookkeeping services. Assume the price for word processing services is a competitive $8 an hour. Since many people have the training to provide this service, competition limits the planned contribution margin to 25 percent of total revenues. Competition for bookkeeping services is limited by the higher level of education required. The price of bookkeeping services, which is $15 per hour, is therefore higher than the price of word processing

Table 12–1
Riverside Services Budgeted and Actual Hours Billed, Revenues, and Contribution Margin for the Month of October 19xx

	Budget			Actual		
	Word processing	Bookkeeping	Total	Word processing	Bookkeeping	Total
Hours	250	100	350	280	84	364
Revenues	$2,000	$1,500	$3,500	$2,240	$1,260	$3,500
Contribution margin	500	750	1,250	560	630	1,190

services. It is also higher relative to the cost of providing the service. Riverside's planned contribution margin from bookkeeping revenue is 50 percent.

For October, Riverside planned to sell its services in the amounts shown in Table 12–1. Notice that the planned contribution margin *per hour* for word processing is different from the one for bookkeeping:

$$\text{Word processing:} \quad \frac{\$500 \text{ contribution margin}}{250 \text{ hours}} = \underline{\underline{\$2.00}} \text{ per hour}$$

$$\text{Bookkeeping:} \quad \frac{\$750 \text{ contribution margin}}{100 \text{ hours}} = \underline{\underline{\$7.50}} \text{ per hour}$$

At the end of October, accounting records showed that Riverside had provided 280 hours in word processing services but only 84 hours in bookkeeping services. Billing rates (selling prices) and **variable costs** were as planned. Thus, although actual revenues equaled budgeted revenues, the total contribution margin was $60 less than budgeted (Table 12–1).

If **fixed costs** were as planned, this reduced contribution margin means Riverside's October net earnings fell short of budgeted net earnings. The unfavorable product mix caused the shortfall. Although the planned mix of billed hours was 71 percent word processing and 29 percent bookkeeping, the actual mix was 77 percent word processing (280 hours ÷ 364 hours) and 23 percent bookkeeping (84 hours ÷ 364 hours). Since word processing services generate a far lower contribution margin per hour, the shift from bookkeeping to word processing lowered the firm's profits. To correct this trend, Riverside's managers should focus marketing attention on their firm's bookkeeping services. They might also increase word processing services if feasible to help make up the shortfall in contribution margin experienced in October.

Riverside sells only two services, so the change in its product mix was easy to analyze. When a company sells many services or products, analyzing changes in product mix is more difficult. The sales mix variance is useful in such situations. In the next section you will see how it and the two other revenue variances, sales price and sales volume, are calculated.

■

Exhibit 12–1

Data Used to Prepare May Budgets

Budgeted product mix measured in units: 50 percent Able, 50 percent Baker

Artz Company Budget Data For May 19x1 Budgets		Product Able	Product Baker
Sales in units		5,000	5,000
Selling price per unit		$13.00	$10.00
Variable expenses per unit			
Manufacturing		$ 5.00	$ 3.00
Marketing		2.00	2.50
Total variable expenses per unit		$ 7.00	$ 5.50
Contribution margin per unit		$ 6.00	$ 4.50
Fixed expenses per month for both products			
Manufacturing	$18,000		
Marketing	14,000		
Administration	8,000		
Total fixed expenses	$40,000		

Calculation of Revenue Variances

Artz Company's financial records will be used to illustrate how to calculate the three revenue variances. Exhibit 12–1 shows the company's budgeted sales and expense data for May. Using those data, accountants prepared the profit budget shown in Exhibit 12–2. At month end, accounting records revealed that actual results for May were as shown in Exhibit 12–3. Compare Exhibits 12–2 and 12–3. Notice how actual results differ from budgeted estimates.

When comparing actual results with budgeted results, you undoubtedly noticed that actual earnings fell $2,925 short of budgeted earnings ($12,500 − $9,575). To find the causes of that difference so appropriate action may be taken, you start by calculating three revenue variances. Of the three, the sales price variance is easiest to calculate, since it is unaffected by product mix.

Sales Price Variance

A change in sales price will change total revenues, contribution margin, and earnings. The contribution margin must change because, by definition, it is determined by the sales price:

$$\text{Contribution margin per unit} = \left(\text{sales price per unit}\right) - \left(\text{variable expenses per unit}\right)$$

OBJECTIVE 4
Calculate sales price, sales volume, and sales mix variances

If the sales price is reduced \$0.10 and variable expenses remain constant, for example, the contribution margin will fall \$0.10. The **sales price variance** shows how much of the difference between actual and budgeted contribution margin is caused by a difference between actual and budgeted sales prices.

The sales price variance is calculated separately for each product. Exhibit 12–1 shows that Artz planned to sell Product Able for \$13 each. The actual average price was \$12.50 per unit (Exhibit 12–3). The sales price variance is found by multiplying the difference in price by the actual quantity of units sold as shown below.

$$\text{Sales price variance} = \left(\text{actual sales price} - \text{master budget sales price}\right) \times \text{actual unit sales}$$

Since Artz sold 4,800 units of Product Able in May, the sales price variance for Product Able is \$2,400, as shown on page 558.

Exhibit 12–2
Direct Costing Format for a Profit Budget
This budget was prepared by using data contained in Exhibit 12–1. Budgeted selling prices and budgeted variable expenses per unit are multiplied by budgeted unit sales to yield total budgeted revenue, variable expenses, and contribution margin for each product. Then, total fixed expenses are deducted from the total contribution margin *from both products* to arrive at net earnings before taxes.

Artz Company
Profit Budget
For the Month of May 19x1

	Product Able		Product Baker		
	Per unit	Total	Per unit	Total	Total for both products
Sales in units		5,000		5,000	10,000
Sales revenues	\$13.00	\$65,000	\$10.00	\$50,000	\$115,000
Variable expenses					
Manufacturing	\$ 5.00	\$25,000	\$ 3.00	\$15,000	\$ 40,000
Marketing	2.00	10,000	2.50	12,500	22,500
Total variable expenses	\$ 7.00	\$35,000	\$ 5.50	\$27,500	\$ 62,500
Contribution margin	\$ 6.00	\$30,000	\$ 4.50	\$22,500	\$ 52,500
Fixed expenses					
Manufacturing					\$ 18,000
Marketing					14,000
Administration					8,000
Total fixed expenses					\$ 40,000
Operating income					\$ 12,500

Exhibit 12–3
Direct Costing Income Statement

Artz Company
Actual Results
For the Month of May 19x1

	Product Able		Product Baker		
	Per unit	Total	Per unit	Total	Total for both products
Sales in units		4,800		5,300	10,100
Sales revenues	$12.50	$60,000	$10.00	$53,000	$113,000
Variable expenses					
Manufacturing	$ 4.90	$23,520	$ 2.60	$13,780	$ 37,300
Marketing	2.00	9,600	3.05	16,165	25,765
Total variable expenses	$ 6.90	$33,120	$ 5.65	$29,945	$ 63,065
Contribution margin	$ 5.60	$26,880	$ 4.35	$23,055	$ 49,935
Fixed expenses					
Manufacturing					$ 18,130
Marketing					14,280
Administration					7,950
Total fixed expenses					$ 40,360
Operating income					$ 9,575

$$\text{Sales price variance} = (\$12.50 - \$13.00) \times 4{,}800 \text{ units}$$
$$= \$2{,}400 \text{ (unfavorable)}$$

The variance is unfavorable because the actual selling price was lower than the budgeted selling price.

The sales price variance for Product Baker is calculated in the same way:

$$\text{Sales price variance} = (\$10 - \$10) \times 5{,}300 \text{ units}$$
$$= \$0$$

Whenever the actual average selling price exactly equals the budgeted selling price, the sales price variance is zero. (Such equality is rare in practice.)

The **total sales price variance** is the sum of the sales price variances for each product.

Sales price variance, Product Able	$2,400 (unfavorable)
Sales price variance, Product Baker	-0-
Total sales price variance	$2,400 (unfavorable)

This computation of sales price variances shows that Artz may have a pricing problem with Product Able. Following the principle of management by exception, managers will spend less time on Product Baker because its pricing is according to plan.

Sales Volume Variance

The **sales volume variance** is a measure of the difference between actual unit sales and budgeted unit sales. The best measure of how a change in sales volume will affect profitability is the change in contribution margin. Therefore, the accountant multiplies the difference between actual units and master budget unit sales by the master budget average contribution margin per unit. The **master budget average contribution margin per unit** is the total contribution margin as stated in the master budget divided by the total units budgeted to be sold in the master budget.

$$\text{Sales volume variance} = \left(\text{actual unit sales} - \text{master budget unit sales}\right) \times \text{master budget average contribution margin per unit}$$

The master budget average contribution margin per unit is a weighted average that eliminates the effect of variations in sales price, sales mix, and expenses.

Refer back to Exhibit 12–2. Notice that the total budgeted contribution margin for May was $52,500. Sales of 10,000 units were budgeted. Therefore, the master budget average budgeted contribution margin per unit is $5.25 ($52,500 ÷ 10,000). This method of computation gives an average weighted according to the planned product mix, as stated in the master budget (5,000 units of each product).

Using this average contribution margin per unit, you can calculate the sales volume variance. You know that Artz expected to sell 10,000 units in May. Actual sales were 10,100 units. To calculate the variance, multiply the difference between actual and budgeted sales units by the master budget average contribution margin per unit:

$$\begin{aligned}\text{Sales volume variance} &= (10{,}100 \text{ units} - 10{,}000 \text{ units}) \times \$5.25 \text{ per unit} \\ &= \underline{\underline{\$525}} \text{ (favorable)}\end{aligned}$$

The variance is favorable because the actual number of units sold was greater than the budgeted sales volume.

This favorable sales volume variance means the shortfall in Artz's earnings for May was not caused by poor sales volume. In fact, the actual sales volume would have increased profits by $525 had the sales price and product mix been as budgeted. However, you will soon see that variances in sales mix and expenses contribute to Artz's poor showing in May.

Sales Mix Variance

The **sales mix variance** is a measure of the change in contribution margin caused by selling products in proportions different from those that were budgeted. It is calculated by using a flexible budget. Recall that as sales volume changes, total revenues and total variable expenses are expected to change in direct proportion to volume, whereas total fixed expenses remain constant (within the relevant range). That is a basic assumption behind a flexible budget, which shows what total revenues and total variable expenses should have been for the actual sales

Exhibit 12–4

Sample Calculations for a Flexible Budget

This exhibit shows how data in the middle column of Exhibit 12–5 are calculated. Budgeted sales price, variable expenses per unit, and fixed expenses per month are taken from Exhibit 12–1. Actual sales volume for May is taken from Exhibit 12–3.

Artz Company Flexible Budget Calculations For the Month of May 19x1	
Sales revenues: **actual units sold × budgeted sales price**	
Able (4,800 units × $13)	$ 62,400
Baker (5,300 units × $10)	53,000
Total	$115,400
Variable manufacturing expenses: **actual units sold × budgeted variable expenses per unit**	
Able (4,800 units × $5)	$ 24,000
Baker (5,300 units × $3)	15,900
Total	$ 39,900
Variable marketing expenses: **actual units sold × budgeted variable expenses per unit**	
Able (4,800 units × $2)	$ 9,600
Baker (5,300 units × $2.50)	13,250
	$ 22,850
Fixed manufacturing expenses: **amount does not change as volume changes;** **same as master budget for the month**	
Manufacturing	$ 18,000
Marketing	14,000
Administration	8,000
Total	$ 40,000

volume. Since Artz sold only 4,800 units of Product Able—less than the master budget volume of 5,000 units—total revenues and total variable expenses for that product should decrease. Similarly, since sales of Product Baker were above the master budget level, you should expect higher total revenues and total variable expenses for that product.

Exhibit 12–4 shows calculations needed to develop a flexible budget for Artz's actual sales volume. Budgeted sales prices, variable expenses per unit, and

Exhibit 12–5
Comparison of Budgeted Amounts with Actual Results

Artz Company
Master Budget, Flexible Budget, and Actual Results
For the Month of May 19x1

	Master budget	Flexible budget	Actual
Sales in units	10,000	10,100	10,100
Sales revenues	$115,000	$115,400	$113,000
Variable expenses			
Manufacturing	$ 40,000	$ 39,900	$ 37,300
Marketing	22,500	22,850	25,765
Total variable expenses	$ 62,500	$ 62,750	$ 63,065
Contribution margin	$ 52,500	$ 52,650	$ 49,935
Fixed expenses			
Manufacturing	$ 18,000	$ 18,000	$ 18,130
Marketing	14,000	14,000	14,280
Administration	8,000	8,000	7,950
Total fixed expenses	$ 40,000	$ 40,000	$ 40,360
Operating income	$ 12,500	$ 12,650	$ 9,575

budgeted total fixed expenses were taken from Exhibit 12–1; actual unit sales from Exhibit 12–3. Notice that total sales revenues and total variable expenses have been recalculated, since those items vary with changes in volume. As long as sales volume remains within the relevant range, however, fixed expenses need not be recalculated. By definition, fixed expenses remain constant over the relevant range. And since actual volume differs from budgeted volume by only 100 units, you can be confident that actual volume is within the relevant range. Exhibit 12–5 shows flexible budget data in the form of an income statement. These data will soon be used to calculate the sales mix variance.

As seen earlier, the sales mix variance reflects that products may be sold in different proportions than anticipated. Since different products have different contribution margins, changing the product mix will usually change total contribution margin. In the case of the Artz Company, Product Able was budgeted to generate a contribution margin of $6 per unit; Product Baker, a contribution margin of $4.50 per unit (Exhibit 12–1). The budgeted product mix was 50 percent units of Able, 50 percent units of Baker.

The difference between the budgeted contribution margin per unit for the two products is probably caused by different variable costs and selling prices. Since Product Able's contribution margin per unit is higher than Product Baker's, the sales mix variance will be favorable if Able generates more than 50 percent of sales. It will be unfavorable when Able generates less than 50 percent of unit sales. When the sales mix variance for May is calculated, it shows that Artz's sales mix was unfavorable. Although total sales for May were 100 units over budget, only 4,800 units, or 47.5 percent of that total, represented sales of Product Able. The remaining 52.5 percent were of Product Baker. The sales mix variance measures how this change in sales mix will affect total contribution margin and earnings.

The sales mix variance is calculated in the four following steps:

Step 1: Calculate a flexible budget for actual sales volume (See Exhibit 12–4 and the middle column of Exhibit 12–5.)

Step 2: Calculate the **flexible budget average contribution margin per unit** by dividing the flexible budget total contribution by the actual volume of units sold. The middle column of Exhibit 12–5 shows the flexible budget total contribution margin of \$52,650 and the actual sales volume of 10,100 units. Therefore

$$\begin{aligned}\text{Flexible budget average contribution margin per unit} &= \frac{\text{flexible budget total contribution margin}}{\text{actual unit sales}} \\ &= \frac{\$52,650}{10,100} \\ &= \underline{\underline{\$5.21287}} \text{ per unit}\end{aligned}$$

Step 3: Calculate the master budget average contribution margin per unit by dividing the master budget total contribution margin by the total budgeted volume. The master budget for Artz is shown in the first column in Exhibit 12–5. The master budget total contribution margin for May was \$52,500. Ten thousand units were budgeted to be sold. As we calculated before:

$$\begin{aligned}\text{Master budget average contribution margin per unit} &= \frac{\text{master budget total contribution margin}}{\text{master budget sales}} \\ &= \frac{\$52,500}{10,000} \\ &= \underline{\underline{\$5.25}} \text{ per unit}\end{aligned}$$

Step 4: Subtract the master budget average contribution margin per unit (obtained in step 3) from the flexible budget average contribution margin per unit (obtained in step 2). Multiply the difference by the actual units sold to obtain the sales mix variance. For May at Artz Company, the computations would be:

$$\begin{aligned}\text{Sales mix variance} &= \left[\begin{array}{c}\text{flexible budget}\\ \text{average contribution}\\ \text{margin per unit}\end{array} - \begin{array}{c}\text{master budget}\\ \text{average contribution}\\ \text{margin per unit}\end{array}\right] \times \text{actual unit sales} \\ &= (\$5.21287 - \$5.25) \times 10,100 \text{ units} \\ &= \underline{\underline{\$375}} \text{ (unfavorable)}\end{aligned}$$

The sales mix variance is unfavorable because the flexible budget average contribution margin per unit is less than the master budget average contribution margin per unit. (It would be favorable if the flexible budget average contribution margin per unit were greater than the master budget average contribution margin per unit.) The amount of the variance tells Artz's managers that the total contribution margin and total earnings before income taxes were reduced by $375 in May because of an unfavorable sales mix.

Review Exercise 12–1

Calculate Sales Price, Volume, and Mix Variances

Farrington Temporary Help offers temporary employees to organizations. They screen employees for appropriate skills and assign them to organizations who request temporary workers. Temporary assignments can last from one day to several months, depending on the need of the organization. In order to provide the highest quality temporary workers, Farrington concentrates on two types of temporary workers, secretarial and general clerical.

Individual billing rates and employee earnings vary within ranges because employees have different experience and skills. Farrington plans to bill clients an average of $9 per hour for temporary clerical workers and $14 per hour for temporary secretaries. Farrington pays wages, taxes, and fringe benefits averaging $5 per hour for clerical workers and $6.80 per hour for secretaries. These are Farrington's only variable expenses. The difference between the hourly fee paid by clients and the wages, taxes, and benefits of employees covers Farrington's monthly overhead of $35,000 and allows for a profit. Employees are paid only for the hours they actually work for clients.

During April, Farrington's temporary clerical workers worked 4,400 hours and generated $37,708 of revenue. Its secretarial workers worked 3,500 hours and generated $49,350 of revenue. April wages, taxes, and fringe benefits for temporary clerical workers were $22,400. April wages, taxes, and fringe benefits for temporary secretaries were $24,675. Farrington had planned that clerical workers would work 4,100 hours and secretarial workers would work 3,900 hours.

Required

1. Calculate Farrington's sales price variance for April.
2. Calculate Farrington's sales volume variance for April.
3. Calculate Farrington's sales mix variance for April.

Solution

1. The variance is calculated by product line. We must first calculate actual selling prices for April.

$$\text{Actual clerical selling price} = \frac{\text{total revenue}}{\text{actual hours billed}} = \frac{\$37{,}708}{4{,}400 \text{ hours}} = \underline{\underline{\$8.57}} \text{ per hour}$$

$$\text{Actual secretarial selling price} = \frac{\text{total revenue}}{\text{actual hours billed}} = \frac{\$49{,}350}{3{,}500 \text{ hours}} = \underline{\underline{\$14.10}} \text{ per hour}$$

Now we can calculate the sales price variance by product.

Sales price variance = (actual sales price − master budget sales price) × actual unit sales

Clerical
Sales price variance = ($8.57 − $9.00) × 4,400 hours
= $1,892 unfavorable

Secretarial
Sales price variance = ($14.10 − $14.00) × 3,500 hours
= 350 favorable

Total sales price variance $1,542 unfavorable

2. In order to calculate the sales volume variance, we must calculate the master budget average contribution margin per hour. The master budget is based on planned sales volume, selling price, and variable expenses per hour.

Farrington Company
Master Contribution Margin Budget for April

	Product lines				
	Clerical		Secretarial		
	Per hour	Total	Per unit	Total	Total both lines
Sales in units		4,100		3,900	8,000
Sales revenues	$9.00	$36,900	$14.00	$54,600	$91,500
Variable expenses					
Wages, taxes, and fringe benefits	5.00	20,500	6.80	26,520	47,020
Contribution margin	$4.00	$16,400	$ 7.00	$28,080	$44,480

$$\text{Master budget average contribution margin per hour} = \frac{\text{master budget total contribution margin}}{\text{master budget planned total hours billed}}$$

$$= \frac{\$44,480}{8,000 \text{ hours}}$$

$$= \underline{\underline{\$5.56}} \text{ per hour}$$

$$\text{Sales volume variance} = \text{master budget average contribution margin per unit} \times (\text{actual unit sales} - \text{master budget unit sales})$$

$$= \$5.56 \times (7,900 \text{ hours} - 8,000 \text{ hours})$$

$$= \underline{\underline{\$556}} \text{ unfavorable}$$

3. This variance requires the flexible budget average contribution margin per unit. It is calculated as follows:

Farrington Company
Flexible Contribution Margin Budget for April

	Product lines				
	Clerical		Secretarial		
	Per hour	Total	Per unit	Total	Total both lines
Sales in units		4,400		3,500	7,900
Sales revenues	$9.00	$37,708	$14.00	$49,350	$87,058
Variable expenses					
Wages, taxes, and fringe benefits	5.00	22,400	6.80	24,675	47,075
Contribution margin	$4.00	$15,308	$ 7.00	$24,675	$39,983

$$\text{Flexible budget Average contribution margin per hour} = \frac{\text{flexible budget total contribution margin}}{\text{flexible budget planned total hours billed}}$$

$$= \frac{\$39,983}{7,900 \text{ hours}}$$

$$= \underline{\underline{\$5.061}} \text{ per hour}$$

$$\text{Sales mix variance} = (\text{flexible budget average contribution margin per unit} - \text{master budget average contribution margin per unit}) \times \text{actual unit sales}$$

$$= (\$5.061 \text{ per hour} - \$5.560 \text{ per hour}) \times 7,900 \text{ hours}$$

$$= \underline{\underline{\$3,942}} \text{ unfavorable}$$

(see Exercises 14, 15, 17, 18)

■

Calculation of Expense and Revenue Variances for Profit Center Managers

OBJECTIVE 5
Explain how profit center managers use expense and revenue variances to achieve their financial goals

Because managers of profit centers are responsible for both revenues and expenses, they are interested in seeing both revenue and expense variances. Usually, profit center managers do not want detailed standard cost and flexible budget expense variance reports, however. Those reports, illustrated in Chapters 10 and 11, are useful to managers of expense centers, who report to profit center managers. Profit center managers need only a summary of how expenses are being controlled.

Profit center managers receive only summarized revenue information because marketing managers make the day-to-day decisions. Expense and revenue variances are calculated for the center as a whole, using the type of master budget, flexible budget, and actual sales information shown in Exhibit 12–5. Notice from that exhibit that Artz's actual variable marketing expenses for May were $25,765, whereas the master budget allowed only $22,500. This discrepancy does not necessarily represent an expense control problem. Remember that actual sales volume for May was 100 units higher than planned. When actual volume is above budgeted volume, variable expenses are expected to increase. The question is whether variable marketing expenses increased more or less than expected.

The answer is in the flexible budget, which shows the level of variable expenses the company should expect for a product mix of 4,800 units of Able and 5,300 units of Baker. According to the flexible budget, variable marketing expenses should have increased to $22,850. Thus, part of the $3,265 increase in marketing expenses is justified by the increased sales volume. An expense variance quantifies that part of the expense increase that volume increases cannot justify.

Once the master budget, flexible budget, and actual sales and expense data are compared, you can calculate the variances needed by a profit center manager. Recall that the goal of a profit center manager is to ensure that actual earnings equal or exceed master budget earnings. There are four reasons that master budget earnings and actual earnings might differ:

1. Actual sales volume differs from master budget sales volume. This causes differences in revenues, variable expenses, contribution margin, and earnings.
2. Actual sales mix differs from the master budget sales mix. This causes differences in revenues, variable expenses, contribution margin, and earnings.
3. Actual sales price per unit differs from the master budget sales price per unit. This causes differences in revenues, contribution margin, and earnings.
4. Actual expenses differ from flexible budget expenses. This can cause differences in total variable expenses, contribution margin, total fixed expenses, and earnings.

By carefully comparing master budget, flexible budget, and actual sales and expense data, the profit center manager can determine which of these causes might be responsible for an increase or decrease in the center's earnings.

Exhibit 12–6
Control Report for a Profit Center

Artz Company
Volume and Mix Variances and Expense and Price Variances
For the Month of May 19xx

	Master budget (a)	Flexible budget (b)	Actual (c)	Variances: Volume and mix (b − a)	Variances: Price and expense (c − b)
Sales in units	10,000	10,100	10,100	100 (F)	
Sales revenues	$115,000	$115,400	$113,000	$400 (F)	$2,400 (U)
Variable expenses					
Manufacturing	$ 40,000	$ 39,900	$ 37,300	$100 (F)	$2,600 (F)
Marketing	22,500	22,850	25,765	350 (U)	2,915 (U)
Total variable expenses	$ 62,500	$ 62,750	$ 63,065	$250 (U)	$ 315 (U)
Contribution margin	$ 52,500	$ 52,650	$ 49,935	$150 (F)	$2,715 (U)
Fixed expenses					
Manufacturing	$ 18,000	$ 18,000	$ 18,130	$-0-	$ 130 (U)
Marketing	14,000	14,000	14,280	-0-	280 (U)
Administration	8,000	8,000	7,950	-0-	50 (F)
Total fixed expenses	$ 40,000	$ 40,000	$ 40,360	$-0-	$ 360 (U)
Operating income	$ 12,500	$ 12,650	$ 9,575	$150 (F)	$3,075 (U)

OBJECTIVE 6
Calculate manufacturing, marketing, and administrative expense variances

Refer to Exhibit 12–6, which shows the three columns from Exhibit 12–5 as well as two new columns for variances. Managers are not interested in the combined variances shown at the bottom of the last two columns. They are interested in the line-by-line breakdowns. Variances in volume and mix are shown in the second-to-last column. They are found by subtracting figures in the master budget column from corresponding figures in the flexible budget column. These variances cannot reflect differences in price and expenses, since the first two columns are based on budgeted sales prices and expenses. The difference in the first variance column must, therefore, reflect only volume and mix differences.

Price and expense variances are shown in the last column of Exhibit 12–6. They are found by subtracting each figure in the flexible budget column from the corresponding figure in the actual column. Since both the actual column and the flexible budget column are based on actual sales volume and mix, differences between the two columns cannot be caused by volume differences. They must, therefore, be caused by differences between actual sales prices or expenses and the budgeted sales prices and expenses.

A profit center manager using the report in Exhibit 12–6 would probably start at the bottom. He or she would observe that actual earnings for May, $9,575, were significantly below master budget earnings of $12,500. Then, the manager would check the right column, which shows the following variances:

1. A $2,400 unfavorable variance in sales price
2. A $2,600 favorable variance in variable manufacturing expenses
3. A $2,915 unfavorable variance in variable marketing expenses

Next, the profit center manager would ask the revenue center manager to explain the cause of the $2,400 unfavorable sales price variance. The profit center manager would state that future sales price should be increased. The marketing manager would need to investigate the $2,915 unfavorable variance in variable marketing expenses. Similarly, the expense center manager should investigate the $2,600 favorable variance in variable manufacturing expenses. Perhaps whatever caused this variance can be applied elsewhere to produce similar favorable results for other expenses. Because the variances in fixed expenses are 2 percent or less of the budgeted amounts, the profit center manager would probably decide that they are too small to investigate.

The combined sales mix and sales volume variances total only $150 favorable. The profit center manager might ask the revenue center manager to divide the variance into its two components. As you may recall, the sales volume and sales mix variances were calculated on pages 559 and 562. They were $525 favorable and $375 unfavorable, respectively. The amounts are relatively small (sales volume variance is only 1 percent of the master budget contribution margin), so the profit center manager should probably not investigate their causes.

Review Exercise 12–2

Calculate Budgets and Variances by Product

Neverust Marine Products, Inc., sells aluminum boat docks and boat lifts for pleasure boats. The average dock sells for $1,400. The average boat lift sells for $2,300. June plans were based on the following data:

	Docks	Boat lifts
Unit sales	120	40
Cost of goods sold per unit	$600	$1,200
Other variable expenses per unit	150	300
Monthly fixed expenses	$20,000	

Actual June results were as follows:

	Docks	Boat lifts
Unit sales	127	48
Total revenues	$190,500	$108,000
Total cost of goods sold	82,550	52,800
Total other variable expenses	20,320	14,640
Fixed expenses per month	$20,400	

Required

1. Calculate Neverust's master budget for June.
2. Calculate Neverust's flexible budget for June.
3. Prepare a statement similar to Exhibit 12–6 showing volume and mix variances and price and expense variances.

Solution

1. Master budget for June prepared:

Neverust Marine Products, Inc.
Master Budget for June

Sales revenues			
Docks, 120 units @ $1,400		$168,000	
Boat lifts, 40 units @ $2,300		92,000	$260,000
Variable expenses			
Cost of goods sold—docks, 120 @ $600	$72,000		
Cost of goods sold—boat lifts, 40 @ $1,200	48,000	$120,000	
Other—docks, 120 @ $150	$18,000		
Other—boat lifts, 40 @ $300	12,000	30,000	
Total variable expenses			150,000
Total contribution margin			$110,000
Fixed expenses			20,000
Operating income			$ 90,000

2. Flexible budget for June prepared:

Neverust Marine Products, Inc.
Flexible Budget for June

Sales revenues			
Docks, 127 units @ $1,400		$177,800	
Boat lifts, 48 units @ $2,300		110,400	$288,200
Variable expenses			
Cost of goods sold—docks, 127 @ $600	$76,200		
Cost of goods sold—boat lifts, 48 @ $1,200	57,600	$133,800	
Other—docks, 127 @ $150	$19,050		
Other—boat lifts, 48 @ $300	14,400	33,450	
Total variable expenses			167,250
Total contribution margin			$120,950
Fixed expenses			20,000
Operating income			$100,950

3. Statement showing sales volume and mix variances and price and expense variances:

Neverust Marine Products, Inc.
Volume and Mix Variances and Expense and Price Variances
March

	Master budget (a)	Flexible budget (b)	Actual (c)	Variances: Volume and mix (b − a)	Variances: Price and expense (c − b)
Sales in units	160	175	175	15 (F)	
Sales revenues	$260,000	$288,200	$298,500	$28,200 (F)	$10,300 (F)
Variable expenses					
Cost of goods sold	$120,000	$133,800	$135,350	$13,800 (U)	$ 1,550 (U)
Other	30,000	33,450	34,960	3,450 (U)	1,510 (U)
Total variable expenses	$150,000	$167,250	$170,310	$17,250 (U)	$ 3,060 (U)
Contribution margin	$110,000	$120,950	$128,190	$10,950 (F)	$ 7,240 (F)
Fixed expenses	20,000	20,000	20,400	-0-	400 (U)
Operating income	$ 90,000	$100,950	$107,790	$10,950 (F)	$ 6,840 (F)

(see Exercises 19, 21, 22)

■

Performance Analysis by Sales Territory, Distribution Channel, and Product Line

In Chapter 9 you learned that businesses are organized in three major ways: by function, by geography, and by product line. Up to this point you have been looking at performance measurement in a functionally organized company, that is, a company in which one manager is responsible for manufacturing, another for marketing, and so on. This type of structure is found mostly in small- and medium-sized companies with only one revenue center and one profit center, such as the Artz Company. In companies organized by geographic territory or product line, accountants must calculate the variances discussed in this chapter separately for each area or product. Even in functionally organized companies, variances might be reported by territory, distribution channel, or product line to obtain a more precise indication of the source of a variance.

Analysis by Territory

Functionally organized companies are often subdivided by geographic sales territory. That is, the marketing manager has overall responsibility for sales, but responsibility for sales in a particular region is delegated to district managers. In such cases, each district manager is a revenue center manager. Revenue variances are reported as shown in Exhibit 12–6, except that variances and contribution margin for each territory are reported. The revenue center manager is not concerned with manufacturing or administrative expense variances. Only those fixed marketing expenses incurred directly in the territory are deducted from the territory contribution margin. Instead of showing earnings, the bottom line of the revenue center report shows a territory's contribution to overall company earnings before taxes.

OBJECTIVE 7
Calculate sales variances for sales territories, distribution channels, and products

Exhibit 12–7 shows master budget and actual revenues and expenses for the western sales territory of Ryan Company by product. The territory's direct fixed expenses include the territory manager's salary, the cost of advertising in the western territory, and travel expenses within the territory. In reporting this information to the territory manager, accountants must combine the figures on individual products, as was done for the profit center manager at Artz Company in Exhibit 12–6. Exhibit 12–8 shows the result. The territory manager's report is similar to the profit center manager's report (Exhibit 12–6), except for two differences:

1. The territory manager's report does not show expenses applicable to the organization as a whole, only expenses direct to the territory.
2. Budgeted variable manufacturing expenses are shown in both the flexible budget and the actual columns, since the territory manager is not responsible for manufacturing expense variables.

Variable manufacturing expenses must be shown in order to calculate the territory's contribution margin. By reporting *budgeted* variable manufacturing expenses in both the flexible budget and actual columns, no variance will result.

The flexible budget column is calculated as usual. The budgeted selling price and variable expenses per unit are multiplied by actual sales volume. Fixed expenses are the same as those in the master budget column, since fixed expenses are expected to remain unchanged as volume changes.

Like the profit center manager, the territory manager may wish to break the combined sales volume and sales mix variance into separate components. The manager will also want to see a breakdown on the sales price variance to determine whether or not further investigation is necessary. As you can see by examining Exhibit 12–7, the decline in Product Red's sales price has had a serious impact on that product's contribution to earnings. The increase in Product Brown's unit sales price has offset this to some extent. These changes have resulted in Product Brown's actual contribution margin per unit exceeding that of Product Red's. The manager will want to determine if the cause of these variances rests with the sales force or with changes in the market and take appropriate action. Recall that

Exhibit 12–7
Budget and Actual Data for a Sales Territory

Ryan Company
Data for the Western Sales Territory
For the Year Ended December 31, 19x0

	Master budget				
	Red		Brown		Total
Sales in units	60,000		30,000		90,000
	Per unit	Total	Per unit	Total	
Sales revenues	$1.50	$90,000	$1.00	$30,000	$120,000
Variable expenses					
Manufacturing	$0.64	$38,400	$0.40	$12,000	$ 50,400
Marketing	0.15	9,000	0.10	3,000	12,000
Total variable expenses	$0.79	$47,400	$0.50	$15,000	$ 62,400
Contribution margin	$0.71	$42,600	$0.50	$15,000	$ 57,600
Territory direct fixed expenses					27,500
Territory contribution					$ 30,100

the manager's performance is measured on the territory's contribution. The formulas for the three sales variances and the calculations to determine them are shown below.

$$\text{Sales volume variance} = \left(\text{actual unit sales} - \text{master budget unit sales}\right) \times \text{master budget average contribution margin per unit}$$

$$= (100{,}000 \text{ units} - 90{,}000 \text{ units}) \times (\$57{,}600 \div 90{,}000 \text{ units})$$

$$= \underline{\underline{\$6{,}400}} \text{ (favorable)}$$

$$\text{Sales mix variance} = \left[\text{flexible budget average contribution margin per unit} - \text{master budget average contribution margin per unit}\right] \times \text{actual unit sales}$$

$$= \left[\frac{\$63{,}650}{100{,}000 \text{ units}} - \frac{\$57{,}600}{90{,}000 \text{ units}}\right] \times 100{,}000 \text{ units}$$

$$= \underline{\underline{\$350}} \text{ (unfavorable)}$$

$$\text{Total sales volume and sales mix variance} = \$6{,}400 \text{ (favorable)} + \$350 \text{ (unfavorable)}$$

$$= \underline{\underline{\$6{,}050}} \text{ (favorable)}$$

Exhibit 12–7 continued

Actual				
Red		Brown		Total
65,000		35,000		100,000
Per unit	Total	Per unit	Total	
$1.35	$87,750	$1.10	$38,500	$126,250
$0.64	$41,600	$0.40	$14,000	$ 55,600
0.14	9,100	0.12	4,200	13,300
$0.78	$50,700	$0.52	$18,200	$ 68,900
$0.57	$37,050	$0.58	$20,300	$ 57,350
				28,460
				$ 28,890

Exhibit 12–8
Control Report for a Territory

Ryan Company
Control Report for the Western Territory Sales Manager
For the Year Ended December 31, 19x0

	Master budget (a)	Flexible budget (b)	Actual (c)	Variances: Volume and mix (b − a)	Variances: Price and expense (c − b)
Sales in units	90,000	100,000	100,000	10,000 (F)	
Sales revenues	$120,000	$132,500	$126,250	$12,500 (F)	$6,250 (U)
Variable expenses					
Manufacturing	$ 50,400	$ 55,600	$ 55,600	$ 5,200 (U)	$ —
Marketing	12,000	13,250	13,300	1,250 (U)	50 (U)
Total variable expenses	$ 62,400	$ 68,850	$ 68,900	$ 6,450 (U)	$ 50 (U)
Contribution margin	$ 57,600	$ 63,650	$ 57,350	$ 6,050 (F)	$6,300 (U)
Territory direct fixed expenses	27,500	27,500	28,460	—	960 (U)
Territory contribution	$ 30,100	$ 36,150	$ 28,890	$ 6,050 (F)	$7,260 (U)

$$\text{Sales price variance} = \left(\text{actual sales price} - \text{master budget sales price}\right) \times \text{actual unit sales}$$

$$\text{Red} = (\$1.35 - \$1.50) \times 65{,}000$$
$$= \underline{\underline{\$9{,}750}} \text{ (unfavorable)}$$

$$\text{Brown} = (\$1.10 - \$1.00) \times 35{,}000$$
$$= \underline{\underline{\$3{,}500}} \text{ (favorable)}$$

$$\text{Total sales price variance} = \$9{,}750 \text{ (unfavorable)} - 3{,}500 \text{ (favorable)}$$
$$= \underline{\underline{\$6{,}250}} \text{ (unfavorable)}$$

The breakdown shows that the increase in sales volume had an overall favorable impact on the territory's contribution. The small, unfavorable sales mix variance is attributable to slightly higher proportional sales of Product Brown, whose contribution margin per unit is lower than Product Red's.

A comparison of Exhibits 12–7 and 12–8 shows why the territory manager would choose the more useful format of Exhibit 12–8. Exhibit 12–7 provides a large amount of data but no variances. Exhibit 12–7 shows that sales volume has increased and that the territory contribution margin was $1,210 below the master budget contribution. But the causes of the decline are unclear. In Exhibit 12–8, however, revenue and expense variances controllable within the territory are shown, and thus, the source of the problem is indicated. The $6,050 favorable variance in contribution margin, a result of the net effect of the sales volume and sales mix variance, shows that if Ryan had maintained sales prices, the profit for the territory would have been considerably higher than the master budget amount. But on average, sales prices were lower than expected, reducing total revenue and territory contribution by $6,250, which is the amount of the unfavorable price variance.

As explained earlier, flexible budget figures were used when reporting actual variable manufacturing expenses so that no variance resulted, since these expenses cannot be controlled by the revenue center manager. There was only a small unfavorable variance in variable marketing expenses. Overall, the actual territory contribution margin was $1,210 below the master budget contribution margin. The increase in sales volume was more than offset by a lower average sales price of Product Red. In addition to the variance in territory contribution margin, there was an unfavorable variance in territory direct fixed expenses. This variance reduced the territory contribution by $960 below the master budget amount.

Ryan's corporate marketing manager should receive a report showing each territory's variances for sales volume, sales mix, sales price, and marketing expenses. Since the marketing manager is responsible for total sales, he or she would want only a summary of each territory's results.

Analysis by Distribution Channel

A national department store chain might have a manager for each marketing region as well as each distribution channel. For example, catalog sales and retail sales are probably managed separately even if they are both housed in the same building. This is because each department requires different skills. Naturally, each manager would want to see variances pertaining exclusively to his or her distribution channel.

Or suppose one manager is responsible for wholesale, mail order, and telephone sales. If the department experiences a large sales volume variance, the first thing the manager needs to know is which channel produced the discrepancy. If the variance occurred mainly in telephone sales, the manager could direct his attention toward that distribution channel and waste no time on the others.

To meet the needs of this manager, accountants would prepare a variance report similar to the one in Exhibit 12–8. The only difference is that figures are reported by distribution channel rather than territory. The manager could then tell not only the channel to which a variance pertains but whether the problem was one of sales volume, price, or mix. The variances are calculated just as they are for territories.

Review Exercise 12–3

Calculate Budgets and Variances by Channels

Beta Software Company sells computer games through two channels. One is mail order and the other is computer stores. The average program provides $40 revenue if sold through mail order. The average program sold through computer stores brings $25 revenue to Beta because of the discount offered to the computer store.

November plans were based on the following data:

	Mail order	Computer stores
Unit sales	5,000	3,000
Cost of goods sold per unit	$12	$12
Other variable expenses per unit	7	1
Monthly fixed expenses	$98,000	

Actual November results were as follows:

	Mail order	Computer stores
Unit sales	4,800	3,100
Total revenues	$192,000	$74,400
Total cost of goods sold	57,600	37,200
Total other variable expenses	31,200	3,410
Fixed expenses per month	$114,100	

Required

1. Calculate Beta's master budget for November.
2. Calculate Beta's flexible budget for November.
3. Prepare a statement similar to Exhibit 12–6 showing volume and mix variances and price and expense variances.

Solution

1. Master budget for November prepared:

Beta Software Company
Master Budget for November

Sales revenues			
Mail order (5,000 units @ $40)		$200,000	
Computer stores (3,000 units @ $25)		75,000	$275,000
Variable expenses			
Cost of goods sold			
Mail order (5,000 @ $12)	$60,000		
Computer stores (3,000 @ $12)	36,000	$ 96,000	
Other variable expenses			
Mail order (5,000 @ $7)	$35,000		
Computer stores (3,000 @ $1)	3,000	38,000	
Total variable expenses			134,000
Total contribution margin			$141,000
Fixed expenses			98,000
Operating income			$ 43,000

2. Flexible budget for November prepared:

Beta Software Company
Flexible Budget for November

Sales revenues			
Mail order (4,800 units @ $40)		$192,000	
Computer stores (3,100 units @ $25)		77,500	$269,500
Variable expenses			
Cost of goods sold			
Mail order (4,800 @ $12)	$57,600		
Computer stores (3,100 @ $12)	37,200	$ 94,800	
Other variable expenses			
Mail order (4,800 @ $7)	$33,600		
Computer stores (3,100 @ $1)	3,100	36,700	
Total variable expenses			131,500
Total contribution margin			$138,000
Fixed expenses			114,100
Operating income			$ 25,990

3. Statement showing sales volume and mix variances and price and expense variances:

Beta Software Company
Volume and Mix Variances and Expense and Price Variances
November

	Master budget (a)	Flexible budget (b)	Actual (c)	Variances: Volume and mix (b − a)	Variances: Price and expense (c − b)
Sales in units	8,000	7,900	7,900	100 (F)	
Sales revenues	$275,000	$269,500	$269,400	$5,500 (U)	$ 100 (U)
Variable expenses					
Cost of goods sold	$ 96,000	$ 94,800	$ 94,850	$1,200 (F)	$ 50 (U)
Other	38,000	36,700	34,610	1,300 (F)	2,090 (F)
Total variable expenses	$134,000	$131,500	$129,460	$2,500 (U)	$ 2,040 (F)
Contribution margin	$141,000	$138,000	$139,940	$3,000 (U)	$ 1,940 (F)
Fixed expenses	98,000	98,000	114,100	-0-	16,100 (U)
Operating income	$ 43,000	$ 40,000	$ 25,840	$3,000 (U)	$14,160 (U)

(see Exercise 20)

■

Analysis by Product

Revenue center managers are often responsible for more than one product. In such cases, a manager may require a separate variance report for each product. This type of analysis is similar to reports on territories and distribution channels except that there is no sales mix variance. A sales mix variance naturally presupposes the inclusion of more than one product and thus would be inappropriate for single-product reports.

Basic data on sales in Ryan's western region were first presented in Exhibit 12–7. Recall that Ryan sells two products, Red and Brown. To produce a separate report on each product for the western regional sales manager, the accountant must first calculate a flexible budget for Product Red, as shown in Exhibit 12–9. Then, the accountant combines the master budget, flexible budget, and actual sales and expense data, as shown in Exhibit 12–10.

Exhibit 12–10 gives the western regional manager further information on the region's performance. Exhibit 12–8 showed that in the territory as a whole, a favorable sales volume and mix variance had been offset by an unfavorable sales price variance. Exhibit 12–10 showed a $3,550 favorable sales volume

Exhibit 12–9

Sample Calculations for a Product-Line Flexible Budget

To prepare a variance report by product line, the accountant must first prepare a flexible budget for that product line. These flexible budget amounts are needed to calculate variances by product line, as illustrated in Exhibit 12–10.

Ryan Company, Western Region Flexible Budget Calculations for Product Red For the Year Ended December 31, 19x0	
Sales revenues: **actual units sold × budgeted sales price**	
65,000 units × $1.50	$97,500
Variable manufacturing expenses: **actual units sold × budgeted variable manufacturing expenses per unit**	
65,000 units × $0.64	$41,600
Variable marketing expenses: **actual units sold × budgeted variable marketing expenses per unit**	
65,000 units × $0.15	$ 9,750

variance for Product Red (see the contribution margin line). Since the total sales volume and mix variances for the territory was $6,050 favorable (see the contribution margin line in Exhibit 12–8), more than half the total favorable sales volume variance must be caused by sales of Product Red.

The manager can also tell that the unfavorable sales price variance resulted entirely from Product Red without calculating the price variance for Product Brown. Product Brown's price variance must have been favorable to offset Product Red's $9,750 unfavorable price variance and lower it to an overall variance of $6,250 unfavorable (Exhibit 12–8). The manager could use the budgeted and actual unit selling prices in Exhibit 12–7 to double-check these price variances.

The manager should note the favorable variance for variable marketing expenses, as shown in the last column of Exhibit 12–10. This variance means the western region spent less than the flexible budget allowed for Product Red, given the actual sales volume. As in the report on the territory as a whole (Exhibit 12–8), no variance is shown for variable manufacturing expenses. This is because the western regional manager cannot control manufacturing expenses.

The overall variance in Product Red's contribution margin was an unfavorable $5,550 ($9,100 − $3,550). The contribution margin lost from a lower sales

Exhibit 12–10

Control Report for a Single Product

Data taken from Exhibit 12–7 and Exhibit 12–9.

Ryan Company, Western Region
Control Report for Product Red
For the Year Ended December 31, 19x0

	Master budget (a)	Flexible budget (b)	Actual (c)	Variances: Sales Volume* (b − a)	Variances: Price and expense (c − b)
Sales in units	60,000	65,000	65,000	5,000 (F)	
Sales revenues	$90,000	$97,500	$87,750	$7,500 (F)	$9,750 (U)
Variable expenses					
Manufacturing	$38,400	$41,600	$41,600	$3,200 (U)	$ —
Marketing	9,000	9,750	9,100	750 (U)	650 (F)
Total variable expenses	$47,400	$51,350	$50,700	$3,950 (U)	$ 650 (F)
Contribution margin	$42,600	$46,150	$37,050	$3,550 (F)	$9,100 (U)

*There is no sales mix variance since only one product is analyzed.

price was greater than the contribution margin gained from increased sales volume and reduced variable marketing expenses. The manager of the western region must ask whether there is some way of maintaining Product Red's sales volume at the budgeted price. If so, the favorable sales volume variance would bring in high profits for Ryan Company.

Chapter Review

Review of Learning Objectives

1. **Explain how the performance of a revenue center manager is measured.** A revenue center manager's performance is measured by whether the center's actual contribution margin equals or exceeds its target contribution margin, as established by the master budget. A revenue center manager may also be responsible for controlling some marketing expenses.

2. **Explain how the performance of a profit center manager is measured.**
A profit center manager's performance is measured by whether the profit center's actual earnings equal or exceed target earnings, as established by the master budget. A profit center manager may meet this goal by seeing that the center achieves target revenue and does not exceed target expenses. Or he or she may balance revenue and expense changes to equal or exceed budgeted earnings.

3. **Explain how revenue center and profit center managers use sales price, sales volume, and sales mix variances.**
Since both revenue center and profit center managers are responsible for achieving budgeted revenue, both will want to know why actual revenues and contribution margin differ from budgeted levels. The three revenue variances provide an explanation. The sales price variance shows how much of the difference in total revenues and contribution margin was caused by a difference between the actual selling price and budgeted selling price. The sales volume variance shows how much the total contribution margin would have been affected by the change in volume if sales price and mix had remained constant. The sales mix variance shows how much the total contribution margin was altered by a change in the budgeted proportion of products sold. Since different products usually have different per unit contribution margins, a change in sales mix will almost always produce a change in total contribution margin, even if total units sold are as budgeted.

4. **Calculate sales price, sales volume, and sales mix variances.**
The three revenue variances can be calculated by using formulas or by comparing master budget, flexible budget, and actual sales and expense figures in an income statement format. The formulas are shown below.

Sales price variance = (actual sales price − master budget sales price)
× actual unit sales

Sales volume variance = (actual unit sales − master budget unit sales)
× master budget average contribution margin per unit

Sales mix variance = (flexible budget average contribution margin per unit
− master budget average contribution margin per unit)
× actual unit sales

Flexible budgets are calculated by mutliplying the actual unit sales volume by the budgeted sales price and variable expenses per unit shown in the master budget. Fixed expenses are the same as in the master budget. (See Exhibits 12–5 and 12–8.)

5. **Explain how profit center managers use expense and revenue variances to achieve their financial goals.**
Since profit is total revenue minus total expenses, profit center managers control profit by controlling these items. When there is a variance between budgeted and actual profits, the manager must ask if the variance was caused by revenue variances, expense variances, or both. Knowledge of expense and revenue variances helps the profit center manager decide what may have caused the profit variance and which subordinate managers should be consulted.

6. **Calculate manufacturing, marketing, and administrative expense variances.**
These variances are the difference between the flexible, actual, and budget data for each expense category. The flexible budget is prepared by multiplying budgeted variable expense per unit (from the master budget) by actual unit sales. The fixed expenses in the flexible budget are the same as the fixed expenses in the master budget. Actual expense data come from the accounting records. (See Exhibits 12–6 and 12–8.)

7. **Calculate sales variances for sales territories, distribution channels, and products.** Variances can also be calculated and reported by sales territory, distribution channel, or product. The process is essentially the same as the one used in developing a report for a profit center manager, except only those fixed expenses direct to the territory, channel, or product are deducted from the contribution margin. A sales mix variance cannot be calculated for a single product, since, by definition, a sales mix implies the existence of two or more products.

Review of Key Terms

Expense center A responsibility center whose manager is responsible for completing assigned tasks within budgeted or standard cost levels.

Fixed cost An operating cost whose total remains constant over a wide range of business activity.

Flexible budget A budget that may be adjusted to any activity level to reflect how costs vary with changes in production volume.

Flexible budget average contribution margin per unit The total contribution margin as stated in the flexible budget divided by the total actual units sold.

Master budget average contribution margin per unit The total contribution margin as stated in the master budget divided by the total units estimated to be sold in the master budget.

Product mix The proportion of total sales volume contributed by each product. Also called *sales mix*.

Profit center A responsibility center whose manager is responsible for controlling both expenses and revenues and balancing them to produce a budgeted profit.

Revenue center A financial responsibility center whose manager is responsible for selling the budgeted quantities of various products or services at budgeted prices.

Sales mix See *Product mix*.

Sales mix variance A measure of the change in contribution margin produced by a difference between the budgeted and actual sales mix. Algebraically: sales mix variance = (flexible budget average contribution margin per unit − master budget average contribution margin per unit) × actual unit sales.

Sales price variance A measure of the change in contribution margin produced by the difference between actual and budgeted sales prices. Algebraically: sales price variance = (actual sales price − master budget sales price) × actual unit sales.

Sales volume variance A measure of the change in contribution margin produced by the difference between actual unit sales and budgeted unit sales. Algebraically: sales volume variance = (actual unit sales − master budget unit sales) × master budget average contribution margin per unit.

Total sales price variance The sum of sales price variances for each product.

Variable costs Costs whose total changes in direct proportion to changes in business activity. (Cost per unit remains constant.)

Review Problem

In November 19x9, Kim Company prepared the following budgeted income statement as part of its master budget for 19x0:

Kim Company
Master Budget Income Statement
For the Year Ending December 31, 19x0

	Product T	Product U	Total
Sales units	4,000	5,000	9,000
Sales revenues	$60,000	$50,000	$110,000
Variable expenses			
Manufacturing	$24,000	$20,000	$ 44,000
Selling	8,000	5,000	13,000
Total variable expenses	$32,000	$25,000	$ 57,000
Contribution margin	$28,000	$25,000	$ 53,000
Fixed expenses			
Manufacturing			$ 14,000
Selling			9,000
Total fixed expenses			$ 23,000
Operating income			$ 30,000

At year-end, actual data from the accounting records were summarized in the income statement below.

Kim Company
Income Statement
For the Year Ended December 31, 19x0

	Product T	Product U	Total
Sales units	3,750	5,800	9,550
Sales revenues	$52,500	$52,200	$104,700
Variable expenses			
Manufacturing	$25,250	$17,400	$ 43,650
Selling	7,500	8,700	16,200
Total variable expenses	$33,750	$26,100	$ 59,850
Contribution margin	$18,750	$26,100	$ 44,850
Fixed expenses			
Manufacturing			$ 14,000
Selling			9,000
Total fixed expenses			$ 23,000
Operating income			$ 21,850

Required

1. Prepare a flexible budget for 19x0, using the format of the 19x0 income statement.
2. Prepare a statement similar to Exhibit 12–6. This statement should be for the company as a whole.
3. Calculate the sales price variance for each product.

4. Calculate sales volume and sales mix variances for Kim Company as a whole. Carry computations to four decimal places and round answers to the nearest whole dollar.
5. List the expense variances calculated in 2 above.

Solution to Review Problem

1. Flexible budget for 19x0 prepared:

Kim Company
Flexible Budget Income Statement
For the Year Ended December 31, 19x0

	Product T	Product U	Total
Sales units	3,750	5,800	9,550
Sales revenues	$56,250	$58,000	$114,250
Variable expenses			
Manufacturing	$22,500	$23,200	$ 45,700
Selling	7,500	5,800	13,300
Total variable expenses	$30,000	$29,000	$ 59,000
Contribution margin	$26,250	$29,000	$ 55,250
Fixed expenses			
Manufacturing			$ 14,000
Selling			9,000
Total fixed expenses			$ 23,000
Operating income			$ 32,250

2. Statement showing sales volume and mix variances and price and expense variances:

Kim Company
Volume and Mix Variances and Price and Expense Variances
For the Year Ended December 31, 19x0

	Master budget	Flexible budget	Actual	Volume and mix variances	Price and expenses variances
Sales units	9,000	9,550	9,550	500 (F)	
Sales revenues	$110,000	$114,250	$104,700	$4,250 (F)	$ 9,550 (U)
Variable expenses					
Manufacturing	$ 44,000	$ 45,700	$ 43,650	$1,700 (U)	$ 2,050 (F)
Selling	13,000	13,300	16,200	300 (U)	2,900 (U)
Total variable expenses	$ 57,000	$ 59,000	$ 59,850	$2,000 (U)	$ 850 (U)
Contribution margin	$ 53,000	$ 55,520	$ 44,850	$2,250 (F)	$10,400 (U)
Fixed expenses					
Manufacturing	$ 14,000	$ 14,000	$ 14,000	$ -0-	$ -0-
Selling	9,000	9,000	9,000	-0-	-0-
Total fixed expenses	$ 23,000	$ 23,000	$ 23,000	$ -0-	$ -0-
Operating income	$ 30,000	$ 32,250	$ 21,850	$2,250 (F)	$10,400 (U)

3. Sales price variances calculated:

Sales price variance = (actual sales price − master budget sales price) × actual unit sales

$$\text{Sales price variance, Product T} = \left[\frac{\$52{,}500}{3{,}750\text{ units}} - \frac{\$60{,}000}{4{,}000\text{ units}}\right] \times 3{,}750\text{ units}$$
$$= [\$14 - \$15] \times 3{,}750$$
$$= \underline{\underline{\$3{,}750}}\text{ (unfavorable)}$$

$$\text{Sales price variance, Product U} = \left[\frac{\$52{,}200}{5{,}800\text{ units}} - \frac{\$50{,}000}{5{,}000\text{ units}}\right] \times 5{,}800\text{ units}$$
$$= [\$9 - \$10] \times 5{,}800$$
$$= \underline{\underline{\$5{,}800}}\text{ (unfavorable)}$$

Total sales price variance

Product T	$3,750 (unfavorable)
Product R	5,800 (unfavorable)
Total	$9,550 (unfavorable)

4. Sales volume and sales mix variances calculated:

Sales volume variance = (actual sales units − master budget unit sales) × master budget average contribution margin per unit

$$= (9{,}550\text{ units} - 9{,}000\text{ units}) \times \frac{\$53{,}000}{9{,}000\text{ units}}$$
$$= \$5.8889 \times 550\text{ units}$$
$$= \underline{\underline{\$3{,}239}}\text{ (favorable)}$$

$$\text{Sales mix variance} = \left[\begin{matrix}\text{flexible budget}\\ \text{average}\\ \text{contribution}\\ \text{margin per unit}\end{matrix} - \begin{matrix}\text{master budget}\\ \text{average}\\ \text{contribution}\\ \text{margin per unit}\end{matrix}\right] \times \begin{matrix}\text{actual}\\ \text{unit}\\ \text{sales}\end{matrix}$$
$$= \left[\frac{\$55{,}250}{9{,}550\text{ units}}\right] - \left[\frac{\$53{,}000}{9{,}000\text{ units}}\right] \times 9{,}550\text{ units}$$
$$= [\$5.7853 - \$5.8889] \times 9{,}550$$
$$= \underline{\underline{\$989}}\text{ (unfavorable)}$$

Total sales volume and sales mix variance

Volume	$3,239 (favorable)
Mix	989 (unfavorable)
Total	$2,250 (favorable)

5. Expense variances can be read directly from the price and expense column in the comparative income statements. The expense variances in the volume and mix column are not counted, as their differences are part of the volume and mix variances total.

Expense variances

Variable manufacturing	$2,050 (favorable)
Variable selling	2,900 (unfavorable)
Total	$ 850 (unfavorable)

Chapter Assignments

Questions

1. (L.O. 1) Define revenue center.
2. (L.O. 2) Define profit center.
3. (L.O. 4) Define sales mix.
4. (L.O. 3) What variances are useful to managers in controlling the activities of a revenue center?
5. (L.O. 3) What variances are useful to managers in controlling the activities of a profit center?
6. (L.O. 5) Explain the role of the flexible budget in calculating a sales mix variance.
7. (L.O. 4) What is the major cause of a sales price variance?
8. (L.O. 4) What is the major cause of a sales volume variance?
9. (L.O. 4) What is the major cause of a sales mix variance?
10. (L.O. 7) Why are revenue variances sometimes calculated by sales territory or product line?

Exercises

11. (L.O. 4) Johnson Company has been very successful with its single product, Tantal. February is usually a good sales month. Selected data for February are given below.

	Actual	Master budget
Sales in units	85,000	83,000
Selling price per unit	$5.50	$5.60
Contribution margin per unit	1.30	1.40

Required

1. Calculate the sales price variance.
2. Calculate the sales volume variance.

12. (L.O. 4) Home Cleaning Services provides cleaning services to clients on an hourly rate of $10. They have a $50 per day minimum and pay workers $6 per hour. Clients supply all necessary supplies. During November, Home Cleaning expected to provide 700 hours of service. They actually worked 780 hours and billed clients $8,073.

Required

1. Calculate Home Cleaning's sales price variance for November.
2. Calculate Home Cleaning's sales volume variance for November.

13. (L.O. 3, 4) Harlan Company sells a single product, Tace. The revenue center manager is comparing July results with budgeted results. Selected July data are given below.

	Actual	Master budget
Sales in units	12,000	11,000
Sales in dollars	$57,600	$55,000
Budgeted variable expenses		41,800

Required

1. Calculate the sales price variance.
2. Calculate the sales volume variance.
3. Briefly explain what a sales mix variance is. Notice that this question does not require computations.

14. (L.O. 4) MacWay Company sells two products, English and French. Selected data for October are given below.

	Actual		Master budget	
	English	French	English	French
Sales in units	8,000	4,000	9,000	3,500
Sales in dollars	$12,000	$3,000	$12,600	$2,800
Variable expenses per unit			$0.70	$0.30

Required

1. Calculate the sales price variances.
2. Calculate the sales volume variance.
3. Calculate the total contribution margin a flexible budget will show for October.
4. Calculate the sales mix variance. Carry computations to three decimal places.

(see Review Exercise 12–1)

15. (L.O. 4) Sorkin Company sells two products, George and Howard. Early reports from the sales force suggested September sales were strong. Thus, the revenue center manager was anxious to review the first data available for September, which are given below.

	Actual		Master budget	
	George	Howard	George	Howard
Sales in units	34,000	66,000	29,000	71,000
Sales in dollars	$207,400	$627,000	$174,000	$660,300
Contribution margin			$ 58,000	$213,000

Required

1. Calculate the sales price variances.
2. Calculate the sales volume variance.
3. Calculate the total contribution margin a flexible budget will show for September.
4. Calculate the sales mix variance.

(see Review Exercise 12–1)

16. (L.O. 4, 6) Ajax Company sells two products, Alpha and Beta. The following information is the basis for the budget for 19x9.

	Alpha	Beta	
Sales units	10,000	15,000	
Sales price per unit	$15.00	$12.50	
Purchase price per unit	6.00	5.50	
Variable sales expense per unit	2.00	1.00	
Fixed administrative expenses			$30,000

Actual results for 19x9 are given below.

	Alpha	Beta	Total
Sales units	9,500	16,000	25,500
Sales revenues	$133,000	$208,000	$341,000
Variable cost of goods sold	(61,750)	(96,000)	(157,750)
Variable sales expenses	(19,000)	(19,200)	(38,200)
Contribution margin	$ 52,250	$ 92,800	$145,050
Fixed administrative expenses			(28,000)
Operating income			$117,050

Required

1. Calculate the sales price variances.
2. Calculate the sales volume variance.
3. Calculate the sales mix variance. Carry computations to two decimal places.
4. Calculate the expense variances.

17. (L.O. 4) Pleasure Ride repairs bicycles and motorcycles. They have separate departments to work on each type of product. Repair workers are paid a percentage of the labor cost billed to each client. Pleasure Ride makes most of its profit on the margin on repair parts.

The average charge for bicycle repair is $45. The average bicycle repair used parts costing $15 and labor costing $12. The average charge for motorcycle repair is $95. The average motorcycle repair uses repair parts costing $35 and labor costing $40. Parts and labor cost are Pleasure Ride's only variable expenses.

During April, Pleasure Ride did 80 bicycle repairs and 120 motorcycle repairs. Bicycle repairs generated $4,160 in revenues. Motorcycle repairs generated revenues of $10,800. Pleasure Ride used bicycle parts costing $1,600 and paid $1,120 for bicycle repair labor. During April, they used $4,560 of motorcycle parts and paid $5,040 for motorcycle repair labor. Pleasure Ride had planned 75 bicycle repairs and 125 motorcycle repairs during April.

Required

1. Calculate Pleasure Ride's sales price variance for April.
2. Calculate Pleasure Ride's sales volume variance for April.
3. Calculate Pleasure Ride's sales mix variance for April.

(see Review Exercise 12–1)

18. (L.O. 4) Photo Plus provides fast developing of films. To keep the price at a minimum, they do only prints from 35mm film. They have two services, two-hour and two-day. Developing a roll with the two-hour service requires $2.70 of supplies and $1.20 of labor. Two-hour developing sells for $8 per roll. Two-day developing also takes $2.70 of supplies, but only $0.60 of labor since the work can be scheduled for part-time evening workers. Two-day developing sells for $6 per roll. Photo Plus' fixed

expenses are $7,300 per month. During September, Photo Plus expected to process 2,100 rolls on their two-hour service and 3,700 rolls on their two-day service.

During September, they actually processed 1,800 rolls on the two-hour service and 4,600 rolls on the two-day service. Total revenues from two-hour service were $14,220. Total revenues from two-day service were $27,830.

Required

1. Calculate Photo Plus' sales price variance for September.
2. Calculate Photo Plus' sales volume variance for September.
3. Calculate Photo Plus' sales mix variance for September.

(see Review Exercise 12–1)

19. (L.O. 6, 7) Quality Brakes and Mufflers repairs brakes and installs replacement mufflers in automobiles. The average brake repair sells for $140. The average muffler replacement sells for $105. Mechanics are paid a flat rate for each job they do. July plans were based on the following data:

	Brakes	Mufflers
Unit sales	230	140
Cost parts used	$20	$35
Mechanic pay	45	30
Monthly fixed expenses	$14,000	

Actual July results were as follows.

	Brakes	Mufflers
Unit sales	228	144
Total revenues	$33,060	$15,552
Total cost of parts used	4,788	5,328
Total mechanic pay	10,260	4,320
Fixed expenses per month	$12,850	

Required

1. Calculate Quality's master budget for July.
2. Calculate Quality's flexible budget for July.
3. Prepare a statement similar to Exhibit 12–6 showing volume and mix variances and price and expense variances.

(see Review Exercise 12–2)

20. (L.O. 4, 7) Minor Auto Parts sells automobile parts through two channels. One is individual gasoline stations and the other is auto repair parts stores who sell to do-it-yourself people. October plans were based on the following data:

	Gasoline station	Repair parts stores
Unit sales	500	30
Average sale	$140	$3,250
Cost of goods sold per sale	60	1,950
Delivery and other variable expenses per sale	17	61
Monthly fixed expenses	$53,000	

Actual October results were as follows on page 589.

	Gasoline station	Repair parts stores
Unit sales	525	28
Average sale	$150	$3,325
Cost of goods sold per sale	64	1,995
Delivery and other variable expenses per sale	16	65
Monthly fixed expenses	$56,100	

Required

1. Calculate Minor Auto Parts' master budget for October.
2. Calculate Minor Auto Parts' flexible budget for October.
3. Prepare a statement similar to Exhibit 12–6 showing volume and mix variances and price and expense variances.
(see Review Exercise 12–3)

21. (L.O. 6, 7) Campus Printing prints small quantity, high-quality copies and does binding. The average printing job sells for $14. The average binding job sells for $5. The only variable costs are paper and supplies. March plans were based on the following data:

	Printing	Binding
Number of jobs	6,200	1,700
Cost paper and supplies per job	$3	$2
Monthly fixed expenses	$51,700	

Actual March results were as follows:

	Printing	Binding
Unit sales	6,850	1,840
Total revenues	$82,200	$9,568
Total cost of paper and supplies used	19,865	3,772
Fixed expenses for March	$50,800	

Required

1. Calculate Quality's master budget for March.
2. Calculate Quality's flexible budget for March.
3. Prepare a statement similar to Exhibit 12–6 showing volume and mix variances and price and expense variances.
(see Review Exercise 12–2)

22. (L.O. 4, 7) Marine Services repairs pleasure fiberglass boats and boat engines. June plans were based on the following data:

	Boat repairs	Engine repairs
Unit sales	50	140
Planned average billing per repair	$700	$230
Materials cost per repair	150	45
Labor cost per repair	300	95
Monthly fixed expenses	$12,000	

Actual June results were as follows:

	Boat repairs	Engine repairs
Unit sales	45	155
Actual average billing per repair	$825	$210
Materials cost per repair	175	42
Labor cost per repair	380	90
Monthly fixed expenses	$12,700	

Required

1. Calculate Marine Services' master budget for June.
2. Calculate Marine Services' flexible budget for June.
3. Prepare a statement similar to Exhibit 12–6 showing volume and mix variances and price and expense variances.
(see Review Exercise 12–2)

23. (L.O. 4, 6) Patty Company provides typing and receptionist services to companies in the Cincinnati area. In 19x7, Patty expected to provide 4,000 hours of typing services at $25 per hour and 8,000 hours of receptionist services at $15 per hour. Patty expected to pay $15 per hour for typing and $10 per hour for receptionist services. Administrative overhead to operate the company was expected to be $40,000. Actual results of operations for 19x7 are given below.

	Typing	Receptionist	Total
Hours billed	3,800	8,200	12,000
Sales revenues	$98,800	$114,800	$213,600
Cost of labor	60,800	90,200	151,000
Contribution margin	$38,000	$ 24,600	$ 62,600
Administrative overhead			45,000
Operating income			$ 17,600

Required

1. Calculate the sales price variances.
2. Calculate the sales volume variance. Carry computations to two decimal places.
3. Calculate the sales mix variance. Carry computations to two decimal places.
4. Calculate the expense variances.

24. (L.O. 4, 6) Linda Company produces two products, X and Y. Actual and budgeted contribution statements for 19x8 are given below.

Budgeted

Product	Sales units	Sales dollars	Variable expenses	Contribution margin
X	4,000	$100,000	$ 60,000	$40,000
Y	3,100	124,000	108,500	15,500
Total	7,100	$224,000	$168,500	$55,500

Actual

Product	Sales unit	Sales dollars	Variable expenses	Contribution margin
X	3,600	$ 97,200	$ 59,400	$37,800
Y	3,400	122,400	112,200	10,200
Total	7,000	$219,600	$171,600	$48,000

Required

1. Calculate the sales price variances.
2. Calculate the sales volume variance. Carry computations to two decimal places.
3. Calculate the sales mix variance. Carry computations to two decimal places.
4. Calculate the expense variance.

25. (L.O. 4, 5, 6, 7) Houston Security Company provides guard services to industrial and commercial customers. For 19x1, Houston budgeted operating income of $56,000, based on sales of $400,000. The budget by customer type is given below.

	Industrial	Commercial	Total
Sales in hours	10,000	24,000	34,000
Sales revenues	$160,000	$240,000	$400,000
Variable costs	112,000	192,000	304,000
Contribution margin	$ 48,000	$ 48,000	$ 96,000
Fixed costs			40,000
Operating income			$ 56,000

Actual sales were $380,000, but operating income was only $45,600. Actual results by customer type are given below.

	Industrial	Commercial	Total
Sales in hours	10,000	26,000	36,000
Sales revenues	$120,000	$260,000	$380,000
Variable costs	79,200	213,200	292,400
Contribution margin	$ 40,800	$ 46,800	$ 87,600
Fixed costs			42,000
Operating income			$ 45,600

Required Calculate the sales price, sales volume, sales mix, and expense variances. Use these variances to briefly explain why actual operating income differed from budgeted operating income. Carry computations to four decimal places.

Problems

26. (L.O. 4, 5, 6) Garfield Company sells a single product. The following data are from its income statements for the calendar years 19x4 and 19x3:

	19x4
Sales revenues (150,000 units)	$ 750,000
Cost of goods sold	(450,000)
Other variable expenses	(75,000)
Contribution margin	$ 225,000
Fixed expenses	(160,000)
Operating income	$ 65,000

	19x3 (base year)
Sales revenues (180,000 units)	$ 747,000
Cost of goods sold	(531,000)
Other variable expenses	(93,600)
Contribution margin	$ 122,400
Fixed expenses	(120,000)
Operating income	$ 2,400

Required Calculate the variances listed below, and use them to explain the difference in operating income between the two years. Using the 19x3 results as a master budget, calculate:

1. Sales price variance.
2. Sales volume variance.

Then, discuss any disadvantages of using 19x3 as a master budget. (AICPA)

27. (L.O. 4) Moos Restaurant serves breakfast and noon and evening meals. The noon menu is similar to the evening menu except that the portions are smaller and the prices are lower. There are some items on the evening menu that do not appear on the noon menu.

Moos regards the cost of ingredients as variable costs. Other costs, including wages, are regarded as fixed. Moos has a policy of providing a fixed number of hours to workers each week regardless of the number of customers served. If there are more workers than needed to cook for and serve customers, the workers do cleaning and other tasks which need to be done. Planning data are shown below.

	Breakfast	Noon	Evening
Average customer bill	$4.80	$7.40	$12.10
Average cost of ingredients	1.70	2.60	4.00
Planned meals per week	140	280	170
Weekly fixed costs total $1,850			

During the first week in April, the chef experimented with some new menu items in the evening. During this week, Moos served 150 breakfasts generating $705 in revenues, 320 noon meals generating $2,304, and 150 evening meals, generating $2,145 in revenues.

Required

1. Calculate Moos's sales price variance for the first week of April.
2. Calculate Moos's sales volume variance for the first week of April.
3. Calculate Moos's sales mix variance for the first week of April.

28. (L.O. 6, 7) Carpet Art, Inc., retails floor coverings. It has two product lines, carpet and hard coverings. Carpet Art based its plans for October on the following data:

	Carpet	Hard coverings
Monthly unit sales	25,000 square yards	45,000 square yards
Selling price per yard	$18.00	$9.00
Cost of goods sold per yard	10.80	5.75
Other variable expenses per yard	2.10	1.05
Fixed expenses per month	$167,000	

Actual October results were as follows:

	Carpet	Hard coverings
Monthly unit sales	27,000 square yards	48,000 square yards
Average selling price per yard	$17.80	$9.40
Cost of goods sold per yard	10.70	5.60
Other variable expenses per yard	2.30	1.10
Fixed expenses per month	$164,000	

Required

1. Calculate Carpet Art's master budget for October.
2. Calculate Carpet Art's flexible budget for October.
3. Prepare a statement similar to Exhibit 12–6 showing volume and mix variances and price and expense variances.

29. (L.O. 4, 7) Arsco Company makes three grades of indoor-outdoor carpet. Sales volume for the annual budget is determined by estimating total market volume for indoor-outdoor carpet. Then, the prior year's market share, adjusted for planned changes in company programs for the coming year is applied to the new total market volume to estimate Arsco's sales volume. The volume is apportioned between three grades of carpet, based on the prior year's sales mix, again adjusted for planned changes in company programs for the coming year. Shown below are the company budget for 19x3 and the results of operations for 19x3.

	Budget			
	Grade 1	Grade 2	Grade 3	Total
Sales in rolls	1,000	2,000	1,000	4,000
Sales in dollars	$1,000	$3,000	$2,000	$6,000
Variable expenses	700	2,300	1,600	4,600
Contribution margin	$ 300	$ 700	$ 400	$1,400
Direct fixed expenses	200	300	200	700
Product margin	$ 100	$ 400	$ 200	$ 700
Selling and administrative expenses				250
Operating income				$ 450

	Actual			
	Grade 1	Grade 2	Grade 3	Total
Sales in rolls	800	2,100	1,000	3,900
Sales in dollars	$810	$3,000	$2,000	$5,810
Variable expenses	560	2,320	1,610	4,490
Contribution margin	$250	$ 680	$ 390	$1,320
Direct fixed expenses	210	315	220	745
Product margin	$ 40	$ 365	$ 170	$ 575
Selling and administrative expenses				$ 275
Operating income				$ 300

Required

1. Calculate the sales price variance by product. Carry computations to three decimal places and round answers to the nearest whole dollar.
2. Calculate the sales volume variance.
3. Calculate the sales mix variance. Carry average contribution margins per unit to three decimal places. (CMA)

30. (L.O. 4) Mill Company manufactures and sells two types of industrial components, which are so similar they can be substituted for each other. One component is manufactured from plastic; the other, from metal. Both components are manufactured in the same plant but in separate production departments. The budgeted and actual contribution margins for Mill Company for 19x4 are presented below.

Mill Company
Budgeted and Actual Contribution Margins
For the Year Ended December 31, 19x4
(in thousands)

	Budget			Actual		
	Plastic	Metal	Total	Plastic	Metal	Total
Unit sales	300	200	500	260	260	520
Sales revenues	$1,800	$2,000	$3,800	$1,560	$2,470	$4,030
Variable manufacturing expenses	900	1,500	2,400	780	1,950	2,730
Contribution margin	$ 900	$ 500	$1,400	$ 780	$ 520	$1,300

The 19x4 sales mix did not match the budgeted one. More metal components were sold than planned because of reduced availability of plastic components. Some increase in the volume of metal components was caused by the lower than budgeted price. The sales volume of plastic components was down because of lost production.

Required Management at Mill Company would like a detailed explanation of why the contribution margin was $100,000 less than originally budgeted for 19x4. Calculate sales price, sales volume, and sales mix variances to explain the $100,000 difference between budgeted and actual total contribution margin. (There was no variable expense variance.) (CMA)

31. (L.O. 4, 6, 7) Information on Duo, Incorporated, is presented below.

	Product AR-10		Product ZR-7		Total	
	Budget	Actual	Budget	Actual	Budget	Actual
Unit sales	2,000	2,800	6,000	5,600	8,000	8,400
Sales revenues	$6,000	$7,560	$12,000	$11,760	$18,000	$19,320
Expenses						
Variable manufacturing	$2,400	$2,800	$ 6,000	$ 5,880	$ 8,400	$ 8,680
Fixed manufacturing	1,800	1,900	2,400	2,400	4,200	4,300
Total expenses	$4,200	$4,700	$ 8,400	$ 8,280	$12,600	$12,980
Operating income	$1,800	$2,860	$ 3,600	$ 3,480	$ 5,400	$ 6,340

Required

1. Calculate Duo's sales price variances.
2. Calculate Duo's sales volume variance.
3. Calculate Duo's sales mix variance. Carry computations to two decimal places.
4. Calculate Duo's expense variance. (CMA)

32. (L.O. 4) Western Corporation sells bottled water in the western part of the United States. Its sparkling water is a premium product sold in a specially designed bottle, sometimes with flavors added. Its plain water, which is for everyday use, is sold in a simple bottle. The sales territory is divided into a northern region and a southern region. Western's sales manager has been concerned about the June contribution margin, which was less than planned. Revenue and expense data for June are shown below.

Western Corporation
Data on Budgeted and Actual Revenue Results
For the Month of June

	Master budget			Actual		
	Sparkling	Plain	Total	Sparkling	Plain	Total
Sales in units	126,000	66,000	192,000	125,000	69,000	194,000
Sales revenues	$504,000	$132,000	$636,000	$503,250	$132,800	$636,050
Variable expenses						
Manufacturing	$201,600	$ 46,200	$247,800	$200,000	$ 48,300	$249,300
Marketing	63,000	16,500	79,500	68,150	17,610	85,760
Total variable expenses	$264,600	$ 62,700	$327,300	$268,150	$ 65,910	$334,060
Contribution margin	$239,400	$ 69,300	$308,700	$235,100	$ 66,890	$301,990

Required

1. Calculate the sales price variances. Carry computations to three decimal places.
2. Calculate the sales volume variance. Carry computations to three decimal places.
3. Calculate the sales mix variance. Carry computations to three decimal places.

33. (L.O. 4, 6, 7) Assume the same facts as those given in 32 above. Western Corporation's controller has suggested experimenting with an improved reporting system for the territories. Data on June results for the southern territory follow.

Western Corporation
Data for the Southern Sales Territory
For the Month of June

	Master budget					Actual				
	Sparkling		Plain		Total	Sparkling		Plain		Total
Sales in units		70,000		30,000	100,000		65,000		35,000	100,000
	Per unit	Total	Per unit	Total	Total	Per unit	Total	Per unit	Total	
Sales revenues	$4.00	$280,000	$2.00	$60,000	$340,000	$4.05	$263,250	$1.90	$66,500	$329,750
Variable expenses										
Manufacturing	$1.60	$112,000	$0.70	$21,000	$133,000	$1.60	$104,000	$0.70	$24,500	$128,500
Marketing	0.50	35,000	0.25	7,500	42,500	0.55	35,750	0.27	9,450	45,200
Total variable expenses	$2.10	$147,000	$0.95	$28,500	$175,500	$2.15	$139,750	$0.97	$33,950	$173,700
Contribution margin	$1.90	$133,000	$1.05	$31,500	$164,500	$1.90	$123,500	$0.93	$32,550	$156,050
Territory direct fixed expenses					69,000					71,200
Territory contribution					$ 95,500					$ 84,850

Required Carry all computations to three decimal places.

1. Prepare a report similar to Exhibit 12–8 for the territory.
2. Calculate the sales price variance for the territory.
3. Calculate the sales volume variance for the territory.
4. Calculate the sales mix variance for the territory.

34. (L.O. 4, 6, 7) Assume the same facts as in 32 above. Western Corporation's controller has suggested experimenting with an improved reporting system for the territories. Data on June results for the northern territory are presented below.

Western Corporation
Data for the Northern Sales Territory
For the Month of June

	Master budget					Actual				
	Sparkling		Plain		Total	Sparkling		Plain		Total
Sales in units		56,000		36,000	92,000		60,000		34,000	94,000
	Per unit	Total	Per unit	Total	Total	Per unit	Total	Per unit	Total	
Sales revenues	$4.00	$224,000	$2.00	$72,000	$296,000	$4.00	$240,000	$1.95	$66,300	$306,300
Variable expenses										
Manufacturing	$1.60	$ 89,600	$0.70	$25,200	$114,800	$1.60	$ 96,000	$0.70	$23,800	$119,800
Marketing	0.50	28,000	0.25	9,000	37,000	0.54	32,400	0.24	8,160	40,560
Total variable expenses	$2.10	$117,600	$0.95	$34,200	$151,800	$2.14	$128,400	$0.94	$31,960	$160,360

	Master budget					Actual				
	Per unit	Total	Per unit	Total		Per unit	Total	Per unit	Total	
Contribution margin	$1.90	$106,400	$1.05	$37,800	$144,200	$1.86	$111,600	$1.01	$34,340	$145,940
Territory direct fixed expenses					62,000					64,400
Territory contribution					$ 82,200					$ 81,540

Required Carry all computations to three decimal places.

1. Prepare a report similar to Exhibit 12–8 for the territory.
2. Calculate the sales price variance for the territory.
3. Calculate the sales volume variance for the territory.
4. Calculate the sales mix variance for the territory.

Case 1
Resdec Corporation (L.O. 4, 7)

Resdec Corporation sells two types of soap, liquid and powdered. They have marketed these products in North America for many years and have recently begun marketing the products in countries on the Western side of the Pacific Ocean. Two exhibits shown below give planned and actual results for a recent month.

Resdec Corporation
Master Budget Data
For February

	North American region					Pacific region				
	Liquid		Powder		Territory total	Liquid		Powder		Territory total
Sales in tons		540,000		230,000	770,000		120,000		190,000	310,000
	Per unit	Total	Per unit	Total		Per unit	Total	Per unit	Total	
Sales revenues	75	$40,500,000	115	$26,450,000	$66,950,000	95	$11,400,000	110	$20,900,000	$32,300,000
Variable expenses										
Manufacturing	34	$18,360,000	47	$10,810,000	$29,170,000	34	$ 4,080,000	47	$ 8,930,000	$13,010,000
Marketing	8	4,320,000	6	1,380,000	5,700,000	19	2,280,000	9	1,710,000	3,990,000
Total variable expenses		$22,680,000		$12,190,000	$34,870,000		$ 6,360,000		$10,640,000	$17,000,000
Contribution margin		$17,820,000		$14,260,000	$32,080,000		$ 5,040,000		$10,260,000	$15,300,000

Resdec Corporation
Actual Results
For February

	North American region				Territory total	Pacific region				Territory total
	Liquid		Powder			Liquid		Powder		
Sales in tons		545,000		233,000	778,000		108,000		172,000	280,000
	Per unit	Total	Per unit	Total		Per unit	Total	Per unit	Total	
Sales revenues	74	$40,330,000	117	$27,261,000	$67,591,000	93	$10,044,000	110	$18,920,000	$28,964,000
Variable expenses										
Manufacturing	33	$17,985,000	45	$10,485,000	$28,470,000	33	$ 3,564,000	46	$ 7,912,000	$11,476,000
Marketing	9	4,905,000	7	1,631,000	6,536,000	26	2,808,000	16	2,752,000	5,560,000
Total variable expenses		$22,890,000		$12,116,000	$35,006,000		$ 6,372,000		$10,664,000	$17,036,000
Contribution margin		$17,440,000		$15,145,000	$32,585,000		$ 3,672,000		$ 8,256,000	$11,928,000

Required

1. Calculate sales price and volume and mix variances by product. That is, ignore the region in which the products are sold in calculating these three variances.
2. Calculate sales price and volume and mix variances by region. That is, ignore the product and concentrate on variances by region.
3. Write a brief report identifying any concerns that management might want to address as a result of the variances you calculated in *1* and *2* above.

Case 2
Data Storage Products (L.O. 4, 6, 7)

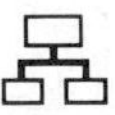

Data Storage Products sells computer hard disk drives and related products in two markets, North America and Europe. One evening, Sue Partin, corporate controller, brought home a report showing volume, mix, price, and expense variances for March. She intended to review the report in the evening to prepare for a morning meeting. After dinner, Sue laid the report on her desk and then remembered that she had to replace a faucet washer in the bathroom. While Sue was replacing the washer, her three-year-old daughter colored on her report. When Sue returned to her desk, the only readable parts of the report were as shown on the next page. She could also read that the volume variance for March was $5,400 favorable.

	Master budget (a)	Flexible budget (b)	Actual (c)	Variances: Volume and mix (b − a)	Variances: Price and expense (c − b)
Sales in units	6,000	xxxxx	xxxxx	xxxxxxx	
Sales revenues	$495,000	$xxxxxxx	$520,000	$xxxxxxxxx	$ xxxxxxxx
Variable expenses					
Cost of goods sold	$397,500	$xxxxxxx	$428,800	$xxxxxxxxx	$ xxxxxxxx
Other	16,500	xxxxxxx	19,200	xxxxxxxxx	xxxxxxxx
Total variable expenses	$414,000	$xxxxxxx	$448,000	$xxxxxxxxx	$ xxxxxxxx
Contribution margin	81,000	$xxxxxxx	$ 72,000	$xxxxxxxxx	$ xxxxxxxx
Fixed expenses	54,000	xxxxxxx	56,240	xxxxxxxxx	xxxxxxxxx
Operating income	$ 27,000	$ xxxxxx	$ 15,760	$xxxxxxxxx	$xxxxxxxxx

Sue found the following March planning data in her briefcase:

	North America	Europe
Unit sales	4,500	1,500
Average selling price	$80	$90
Cost of goods sold per unit	65	70
Other variable expenses per unit	2	5
Monthly fixed expenses	$54,000	

Required

1. Calculate Data Storage Product's actual March unit sales.
2. Calculate the missing amounts shown by x's in the March report and prepare a complete report.
3. According to your complete report, what items should Sue bring to the attention of other managers at tomorrow's meeting? Explain briefly.

■

13

Performance Measurement: Investment Centers

LEARNING OBJECTIVES

After studying this chapter you should be able to:

1. Explain how the financial performance of an investment center manager is measured
2. Calculate return on investment (ROI)
3. Calculate residual income (RI) and explain how it differs from ROI
4. Calculate return on sales and asset turnover, and explain how managers use those ratios to analyze ROI
5. Discuss the problems of measuring earnings for an investment or profit center and the common solutions
6. Discuss the problems of measuring investment for an investment center and the common solutions
7. Explain a market-based transfer price and why it is considered the ideal transfer price
8. Discuss the advantages and disadvantages of cost-based transfer prices

In Chapter 9 you saw that a responsibility accounting system provides information tailored to a manager's responsibilities. Lower-level managers generally receive detailed reports, whereas higher-level managers receive summary reports. You have also studied reporting for three of the four main types of financial responsibility centers: expense centers, revenue centers, and profit centers. In this chapter you will study reporting guidelines for the broadest level of responsibility center, an investment center.

To put investment center reporting into context, this chapter will briefly review the financial responsibilities of expense, revenue, and profit center managers. An expense center manager is responsible for completing assigned tasks within budgeted or standard cost levels. A revenue center manager is responsible for selling budgeted quantities of various products or services at budgeted prices in order to earn the budgeted contribution margin. Revenue center managers may also be responsible for controlling some marketing expenses. Finally, a profit center manager is responsible for achieving budgeted earnings. This manager's responsibilities are broader than those of either an expense or revenue center manager, as he or she controls both expenses and revenues. In fact, a profit center manager must actually balance expenses and revenues so budgeted earnings are achieved.

For example, assume a profit center sells a product whose contribution margin is $3 per unit. The manager of that profit center thinks unit sales will increase by 4,000 units a month if advertising is increased by $10,000 per month. If the manager's estimate is correct, 4,000 additional units will increase the product's contribution margin by $12,000 per month ($3 per unit × 4,000 units). This increase will more than cover the additional advertising expense of $10,000. Profits will then increase by $2,000 a month. Thus, the manager will have balanced expenses and revenues to increase earnings. Only a profit center manager, not an expense or revenue center manager, can make such decisions.

■

Return on Investment (ROI)

OBJECTIVE 1
Explain how the financial performance of an investment center manager is measured.

An investment center manager has even broader responsibilities. **Investment center** managers balance revenues, expenses, *and investments* to achieve a budgeted return on investment or residual income. Chief executive officers and heads of major divisions of large companies are investment center managers. These managers have substantial authority in deciding whether to develop, produce, and market products or services. These decisions may require added investments, as well as adding to revenues and expenses. To help investment center managers gauge their progress toward meeting their financial goals, accountants use various numerical measures. The most common is return on investment.[1] Average investment is used if data for more than one year exist.

Return on Investment (ROI) is the ratio of a center's earnings to its investment as shown below.

$$\text{ROI} = \frac{\text{center's earnings}}{\text{center's average investment}}$$

This ratio is usually expressed as a percentage. Notice the word *center* in the formula: *center's* earnings, *center's* average investment. The distinction between the profit and investment of an investment center and that of a total organization is important. There are some problems in determining the profit and investment of a part of an organization, and those problems will be discussed later in the chapter. For now, simply remember that to be a useful measure of performance, ROI must be calculated by using the proper values for earnings and investment. Also, managers must have control over the center's revenues, expenses, and investments.

Calculating ROI

OBJECTIVE 2
Calculate return on Investment (ROI)

Cedar Theater will be used to illustrate how ROI's is calculated. Cedar Theater, which is part of a theater chain, earned $60,000 last year. The chain's investment in the theater was $400,000. Thus, Cedar Theater's ROI was 15 percent, as calculated below.

$$\text{ROI} = \frac{\$60,000}{\$400,000}$$
$$= \underline{\underline{15}} \text{ percent}$$

By itself Cedar Theater's ROI is not very informative. To be useful it must be compared with the budgeted ROI.

Setting a Budgeted ROI

Companies using ROI to evaluate the performance of investment center managers generally set budgeted (sometimes called target) ROIs a year in advance. When a year's results are in, actual ROIs are compared with budgeted ROIs. Had the budgeted ROI been 12 percent for Cedar Theater, the center's financial performance would have been good, since actual ROI was 15 percent. But had the budgeted ROI been 20 percent, the 15 percent ROI would have reflected poor performance by the manager.

Budgeted ROI is usually based on the following three considerations:

1. The budget for the coming year, which shows (a) expected earnings under expected market conditions and (b) capital available to the center

[1]James S. Reece and William R. Cool, "Measuring Investment Center Performance" (Cambridge, Mass. *Harvard Business Review,* May–June, 1978).

2. The average ROI recently earned by competitors
3. The ROI earned by the investment center in past years

■

Residual Income (RI)

OBJECTIVE 3
Calculate residual income (RI) and explain how it differs from ROI

There is an alternative to ROI: residual income. **Residual income (RI)** relates an investment center's earnings to its average investment and its target rate of return. Unlike the ROI, which is a ratio expressed as a percentage, RI is expressed in dollars. The formula for RI is as follows:

$$\text{RI} = \text{center's earnings} - (\text{center's average investment} \times \text{target rate of return})$$

Calculating RI

Suppose a particular fast-food restaurant has annual earnings of $350,000. The corporation that owns the fast-food restaurant chain has invested an average of $1,600,000 into this particular restaurant. The corporation expects to earn a 20 percent return on its investment. Thus, the restaurant's RI is $30,000, as calculated below.

$$\begin{aligned} \text{RI} &= \$350{,}000 - (\$1{,}600{,}000 \times 20\%) \\ &= \$350{,}000 - \$320{,}000 \\ &= \underline{\underline{\$30{,}000}} \end{aligned}$$

In this case, RI is positive, since the restaurant earned more than its target rate of return ($320,000). When RI is zero, a center has earned its exact target rate of return. If RI is negative, a center has earned less than its target rate of return.

How does a company determine whether ROI or RI should be used to evaluate the activities of an investment center? From the computations of the two measures, you should note that ROI is the *ratio* of a center's net earnings to the center's investment. RI is a *dollar amount* calculated by subtracting a charge for the capital used by the vendor from the centers' net earnings. The choice of ROI (a ratio) or RI (a dollar amount) can influence the investment decisions of a center manager.

For example, assume the manager of the restaurant discussed above has the opportunity to invest in a project that will yield a 21 percent return. If performance is measured using RI, the investment will appear desirable since the capital charge rate is 20 percent. However, the restaurant is currently earning an ROI of 21.88 percent ($350,000 ÷ $1,600,000). If the investment is made at 21 percent, the restaurant's ROI will drop.

What would you do if you were the manager of the restaurant? If your performance was evaluated based on ROI, you would probably reject the investment since the average ROI will drop. But if your performance is based on RI, you would probably accept the investment since the RI will increase. For the company as a whole, the best decision is to accept the investment since its return exceeds the minimum return expected by the company. The use of RI leads to this decision.

Review Exercise 13–1

Calculate ROI and RI

The financial performance of the Mario Division of Ward Corporation is measured as an investment center. The following data are available for Mario Division:

Center's earnings, 19x9	$ 373,176
Center's investment, Jan. 1, 19x9	2,457,000
Center's investment, Dec. 31, 19x9	2,799,000

Ward Corporation has a 12 percent target rate of return for its investment centers.

Required

1. Calculate Mario Division's ROI for 19x9.
2. Calculate Mario Division's RI for 19x9.

Solution

1. Mario Division's ROI for 19x9 is as follows:

Center's investment, Jan. 1, 19x9	$2,457,000
Center's investment, Dec. 31, 19x9	2,799,000
Total	$5,256,000
Average investment, $5,256,000 ÷ 2	2,628,000

$$\text{ROI} = \frac{\text{center's earnings}}{\text{center's total (average) investment}}$$

$$= \frac{\$373{,}176}{2{,}628{,}000}$$

$$= \underline{\underline{14.2}} \text{ percent}$$

2. Mario Division's RI for 19x9 is as follows:

$$\text{RI} = \text{center's earnings} - (\text{center's average investment} \times \text{target rate of return})$$

RI = \$373,176 − (\$2,628,000 × 12%)
= \$373,176 − \$315,360
= \$57,816

(see Exercises 19, 20, 21)

Setting Target Rate of Return

To calculate RI, management must first set a target rate of return. In choosing the rate, management considers the same three factors used to set a target ROI: (1) budgeted earnings and investment, (2) competitor's ROIs, and (3) the center's ROI in past years. Allowances are made for factors peculiar to an investment center. For example, if one fast-food restaurant in a chain is exceptionally well located, management should expect a higher ROI from it than from most other restaurants in that chain. The higher budgeted revenue and budgeted contribution margin for the well-located restaurant would justify the higher rate. On the other hand, a new restaurant might be assigned a lower-than-average target rate of return. The restaurant's high start-up costs for training new employees, for example, and lower-than-average sales would justify the lower rate.

What should a manager do if RI or ROI is lower than anticipated? To find the source of the problem, a manager can analyze a center's performance by using a method called the Du Pont formula.

The Du Pont Formula

The manager of an investment center usually receives monthly reports that include an income statement, a balance sheet, and such selected statistics as the center's ROI and RI. If actual ROI is below budgeted ROI, the manager must find out why financial performance is below expectations so performance can be improved. A method called the Du Pont formula, popularized by the chemical company E. I. du Pont de Nemours, is useful for this purpose. The **Du Pont formula** breaks ROI into two ratios, return on sales and asset turnover:

ROI = return on sales × asset turnover

Return on Sales

Return on sales is the ratio of the center's earnings to its total sales revenues, and it is expressed as a percentage. It is calculated as follows:

$$\text{Return on sales} = \frac{\text{center's earnings}}{\text{center's total sales}}$$

OBJECTIVE 4
Calculate return on sales and asset turnover, and explain how managers use those ratios to analyze ROI

Recall the example of Cedar Theater. If Cedar Theater had total revenues of \$760,000 (its net earnings were \$60,000), its return on sales would be 7.89 percent, as calculated below.

$$\text{Return on sales} = \frac{\$60{,}000}{\$760{,}000}$$
$$= \underline{\underline{7.89}} \text{ percent}$$

Return on sales is a measure of how efficiently a center is generating a profit. It shows how much of each dollar in sales revenues remains as profit after expenses are covered. A high return on sales means management has maintained a good margin between sales and total expenses. A center can keep its return on sales as high as possible by ensuring that sales prices are as high as competition will permit and by controlling expenses.

What constitutes a good margin between sales and expenses? That depends on the industry. A well-managed firm of CPAs should achieve around a 30 percent return on sales. In contrast, a well-managed supermarket might aim for only a 1 percent return on sales. This numerical difference does not mean accounting firms are highly profitable and supermarkets are not. Total profit earned depends on the dollar amount of sales as well as the return on sales ratio.

Asset Turnover

Asset turnover is the ratio of a center's total sales to its total assets or total average assets if data for more than one year exist:

$$\text{Asset turnover} = \frac{\text{center's total sales}}{\text{center's total (average) assets}}$$

It is expressed as a ratio rather than a percentage, as in "The asset turnover is 3 to 1" or "The asset turnover is 3 times." In the case of Cedar Theater, annual sales were \$760,000 and total assets \$400,000. The theater's asset turnover is therefore 1.9 times, as follows:

$$\text{Asset turnover} = \frac{\$760{,}000}{\$400{,}000} = \underline{\underline{1.9}}$$

Asset turnover is a measure of how effectively a unit uses its assets. Cedar Theater's asset turnover tells you the theater generated \$1.90 worth of sales for each invested dollar. Generally, management prefers a high asset turnover. A low asset turnover may mean the center has more assets than necessary.

As with return on sales, the acceptable level of asset turnover depends on the industry. To take an extreme example, an electric power company must make a large investment to operate. Besides investing in the generating plant, it must invest in such items as transformers, towers, and wires. Thus, its asset turnover, even if well managed, would be only about 0.5 percent. In contrast, a person operating an outdoor popcorn stand invests little in equipment, needs only a small inventory, and has no accounts receivable. Hence, an acceptable asset turnover for a popcorn stand might be 150 times.

Calculating ROI with the Du Pont Formula

Now return to the Du Pont formula, which relates asset turnover and return on sales to ROI. You can use the Du Pont formula to compute the Cedar Theater's ROI as follows:

$$\begin{aligned} \text{ROI} &= \text{return on sales} \times \text{asset turnover} \\ &= \$7.89\% \times 1.9 \\ &= \underline{\underline{15}} \text{ percent} \end{aligned}$$

Notice that this answer agrees with earlier computations (page 602).

To see why the Du Pont formula gives the same answer as the ROI formula, you can substitute the formulas for return on sales and asset turnover into the Du Pont formula as follows:

$$\text{ROI} = \frac{\text{center's earnings}}{\text{center's total sales}} \times \frac{\text{center's total sales}}{\text{center's total (average) assets}}$$

Notice that the center's total sales is the denominator of the first fraction and the numerator of the second. If those numbers are canceled, one gets

$$\begin{aligned} \text{ROI} &= \frac{\text{center's earnings}}{\cancel{\text{center's total sales}}} \times \frac{\cancel{\text{center's total sales}}}{\text{center's total (average) assets}} \\ &= \frac{\text{center's earnings}}{\text{center's total (average) assets}} \end{aligned}$$

Since a center's total assets usually equal a center's investment, this formula is the equivalent of the original formula given for ROI.

$$\text{ROI} = \frac{\text{center's earnings}}{\text{center's average investment}}$$

Review Exercise 13–2

Calculate Return on Sales, Asset Turnover, and ROI

The financial performance on the Harold Division of Solli Corporation is measured as an investment center. The following data on page 608 are available for Harold Division:

Center's 19x5 sales	\$1,863,000
Center's earnings, 19x5	139,755
Center's total assets, Jan. 1, 19x5	761,000
Center's total assets, Dec. 31, 19x5	933,000

Required

1. Calculate Harold Division's return on sales for 19x5.
2. Calculate Harold Division's asset turnover for 19x5.
3. Calculate Harold Division's ROI for 19x5 using your results from *1* and *2* above.

Solution

1. Harold Division's return on sales for 19x5 is as follows:

$$\text{Return on sales} = \frac{\text{center's earnings}}{\text{center's total sales}} = \frac{\$139{,}755}{\$1{,}863{,}000} = \underline{\underline{7.5}} \text{ percent}$$

2. Harold Division's asset turnover for 19x5 is as follows:

Center's total assets, Jan. 1, 19x5	\$ 761,000
Center's total assets, Dec. 31, 19x5	933,000
Total	\$1,694,000
Total average assets, \$1,694,000 ÷ 2	847,000

$$\text{Asset turnover} = \frac{\text{center's total sales}}{\text{center's total (average) assets}} = \frac{\$1{,}863{,}000}{\$847{,}000} = \underline{\underline{2.2}} \text{ times}$$

3. Harold Division's ROI for 19x5 is as follows:

$$\begin{aligned} \text{ROI} &= \text{return on sales} \times \text{asset turnover} \\ &= 7.5\% \times 2.2 \text{ times} \\ &= \underline{\underline{16.5}} \text{ percent} \end{aligned}$$

(see Exercises 24, 26)

■

Using the Du Pont Formula

The Du Pont formula is important because it shows two ways to improve a manager's ROI: (1) by increasing return on sales and (2) by increasing asset

Table 13–1
Search Strategy for Locating ROI Problems by Using the Du Pont Formula

Does Actual ROI Equal Planned ROI?	
If actual return on sales differs from planned return on sales:	If actual asset turnover differs from planned asset turnover:
1. Is there a sales price variance? 2. Is there a sales mix variance? 3. Are individual expenses too high?	1. Is there a sales volume variance? 2. Is the investment in individual assets too high?

turnover. If an investment center manager receives a report showing a below-budget ROI, then he or she should first calculate return on sales and asset turnover. If return on sales is lower than expected, the cause can then be investigated. Perhaps the average selling price was low because of unplanned discounts. Or perhaps the sales mix contained more units than expected of products with a low **contribution margin.** If there are no problems with sales price or mix, the manager should then turn to expenses. As a start he or she should probably ask expense center managers working for him or her to examine their flexible budgets and standard cost variances.

If return on sales was not lower than expected, the investment center manager should examine asset turnover. First, he or she should look at sales volume as a possible cause. If total sales were within budget, the turnover for individual assets should be calculated to identify which assets are too high.

In summary, the Du Pont formula is useful because it provides a strategy for locating problems when actual ROI differs from planned ROI. Table 13–1 summarizes that strategy.

■

Problems in Measuring Earnings for an Investment or Profit Center

As suggested earlier, there are some problems in calculating the profits of one portion of a business to evaluate an investment center's performance. Actually, the same problems apply to profit centers. The hardest part is deciding which, if any, corporate costs are to be allocated; then one must also decide on the allocation method. Both of these decisions significantly affect earnings. How prices are established for business that is done between centers of a company is also problematic. These problems must all be resolved in advance, so the way in which budgets are prepared will be consistent with how actual earnings are reported.

Allocation of Corporate Costs

OBJECTIVE 5
Discuss the problems of measuring earnings for an investment or profit center and the common solutions

When accounting for an organization as a whole without profit or investment centers, there is no need to **allocate** costs incurred at the corporate level. There is only one entity to which costs may be charged. But when net earnings for part of an organization are calculated, one must decide if some portion of corporate costs can be justly charged against a center's revenues. If costs incurred at corporate headquarters are allocated to investment and profit centers, they become an expense that reduces both budgeted and actual earnings for the center.

There are two criteria for resolving such allocation problems:

1. What costs can the manager control?
2. What type of allocation will motivate a manager to make decisions in the best interest of the corporation?

The first criterion, controllability, was previously discussed. A cost is a **controllable item** if a manager can *significantly influence* the amount of the cost. Control is never absolute. A manager can never completely or totally control a cost. But if the manager can make decisions that will significantly influence a cost, that cost is controllable.

For example, a supervisor may be unable to control employee wage rates because they are fixed annually by a union contract. However, he or she can influence employee efficiency and productivity, which controls the number of hours employees work. Thus, because the supervisor can influence a worker's productivity, labor costs are considered a controllable cost.

The second criterion, motivation, is important because one purpose of measuring performance is to encourage managers to achieve their goals. Budgeted earnings are determined in advance precisely so managers know what level of achievement is expected from them. If a manager's earnings target is $10,000 for January and accountants report earnings of only $8,500 at month end, that manager will be motivated to make up the $1,500 deficiency during the remaining months of the year.

Corporate administrative expenses can be divided into two categories based on how they affect a manager's motivation. The first includes the cost of the services corporate headquarters provides to investment and profit centers. Accounting, data processing, engineering, and market research all belong in this category. The second includes general administrative expenses, which benefit centers only indirectly. The salaries of the president and vice presidents and the cost of advertising to promote corporate image belong in this second category. Other corporate costs indirectly benefiting profit and investment centers sometimes allocated to those centers include interest expense and income taxes.

A good argument can be made for allocating the costs in the first category. If the services were not provided by corporate headquarters, the center would have to pay for those services from another source. And even though the cost of the services is not controllable, the *amount* of the services requested is controllable. In fact, to motivate profit and investment center managers to use corporate services carefully, a company should charge for those services. Managers who are charged for a service try to keep the use of that service to the minimum needed.

For example, data processing services for billing customers are usually provided for an entire organization through a large central computer. Such an arrangement is more efficient than installing small computers in each profit or investment center to perform this task. In the early years of data processing, companies often provided the service free of charge to encourage computer use. But as managers became familiar with the advantages of data processing, use of the service grew, as did its cost. As a result, companies began charging departments for that service. And managers began weighing the cost and benefit of requesting data processing services. If a manager requests more service than his or her center can effectively use, that excess cost reduces the center's profits. But to the extent that data processing services assist a center's operations, they add to a center's profits. Allocating the cost of services helps ensure that services are not wasted.

The second category of corporate costs, general administrative costs, is not controllable by center managers, in either amount or cost. When budgeted earnings or target ROIs are set, divisions are often compared with independent companies that incur such expenses; some managers believe all corporate costs should be allocated to divisions. Not only does this make earnings more comparable to those of independent companies under such an arrangement, but managers are sometimes more highly motivated when they know what earnings would be if the centers were independent companies.

Table 13–2 summarizes the allocation of corporate costs.

Table 13–2
Allocation of Corporate Costs to Profit and Investment Centers

Category 1: Costs of specific services
Allocated to encourage center managers to control the quantity of services requested. Examples of such costs are: Accounting Data processing Engineering Market research
Category 2: Other corporate costs
Usually not controllable by investment or profit center managers. Allocated so a center's earnings are more comparable to those of independent companies. Examples of such costs are: Salaries of corporate officers Corporate advertising Interest expense Income taxes

Effects of Transfer Prices

Another problem in measuring profits for parts of an organization is accounting for products or services transferred between divisions. Normally, competition determines selling prices. But competition exists only when buyer and seller are free to act in their own best interests. If one part of an organization provides another with a product, the buyer and seller may not be free to act in their own best interests because of policies set by the organization. That is, the price may not be the same as that set by the competitive market.

Sales between two divisions of the same organization result in special prices called transfer prices. The issues involved in setting transfer prices are discussed in some detail in the last section of this chapter. The problem is mentioned here because it can greatly affect the earnings of the centers involved. Naturally, the center selling the product or service wants the highest possible price, since a higher price means higher revenue and higher profits. But the center buying the product or service wants to keep the transfer price as low as possible to reduce its cost. The transfer price is an expense.

■

Problems in Measuring Investment for ROI and RI Computations

To calculate ROI and RI for an investment center, the accountant needs a measure of the amount invested in each center. (Recall that the formulas for both ROI and RI include the value of the center's investment.) To measure a center's investment, accountants must first answer two questions:

1. What is included in the center's investment?
2. How are the included items to be measured (assigned a dollar amount)?

The same criteria for resolving allocation problems apply to investment measurement. Those criteria are:

1. What costs can managers control?
2. What type of allocation will motivate a manager to make decisions in the best interests of the corporation?

What is included in investment and how the included items are measured will be discussed next using these two criteria.

What Is Included in Investment?

To calculate a center's investment, accountants usually start with the assets on a center's balance sheet. Not all assets are necessarily included, however. Often

OBJECTIVE 6
Discuss the problems of measuring investment for an investment center and the common solutions

an investment center's cash is controlled at corporate headquarters, because it is more efficient to administer a single pool of cash. In such a case, cash might be excluded from a center's investment because it is an uncontrollable item. But excluding cash renders a center's ROI less comparable to that of an independent firm. A compromise is to include in both budgets and actual reports an estimate of the amount of cash a center would need were it an independent company. Including this amount in both budgets and actual reports causes no significant differences between actual and budgeted ROI and RI and keeps the center's assets comparable to those of an independent firm.

Idle assets are sometimes excluded from investment when calculating ROI or RI. Suppose an investment center owns a vacant lot next to its plant. The lot is being held for future expansion. Were the lot included in the center's investment, the manager might be motivated to sell it to reduce the denominator in the ROI ratio. No earnings would be lost, and the center's ROI would increase. Excluding idle assets discourages such counterproductive behavior that would greatly increase the cost of future expansion. Organizations including idle assets in a center's investment generally establish safeguards, requiring corporate approval to dispose of large assets.

Should some or all of a center's liabilities be subtracted from assets when calculating investment? In terms of the balance sheet, the question is whether accountants should use the total assets figure or owner's equity (total assets − total liabilities). Owner's equity more realistically represents the amount an organization has invested in an investment center. Nevertheless, liabilities are usually not subtracted from assets, since borrowing is commonly controlled by corporate managers rather than investment center managers. Further, subtracting liabilities from investment might motivate managers to incur too many liabilities (if they could).

How Are Included Items Measured?

The question of how investment items should be measured or what dollar value should be assigned to them is a choice among three alternatives: (1) gross book value, (2) net book value, and (3) estimated current value. Gross book value and net book value are the most common choices, as these figures are easily obtained from a company's accounting records. The only difference between the two methods is that when **net book value** is used, accumulated depreciation is deducted from the cost of plant and equipment. When **gross book value** is used, plant and equipment are valued at the original cost, and there is no reduction for depreciation. Because both methods value assets at their original cost, which may be out-of-date, both may distort the real value of a center's investment. The gross book value method also consistently understates a center's time-adjusted rate of return, which is sometimes called the economic return on investment. The time-adjusted rate of return is discussed in Chapter 14.

An asset's **current value** is the amount for which it can now be purchased. Current value is an appealing method because it represents an organization's investment in an investment center at the time the calculation is made. The current value method is used, however, in only about 2 percent of firms.[2] The main obstacle to its wider use is the difficulty of determining current value at a reasonable cost. Often an appraisal is required, which can be expensive if considerable assets are involved. And even professional appraisals are subject to dispute.

Although there are some difficulties involved in calculating an ROI when net book value is used, about 85 percent of firms prefer that method. Fourteen percent use gross book values.[3] These figures seem to show a strong desire by management to use the same method of valuing assets for ROI computations as is used in preparing balance sheets.

■

Supplementary Measures of Performance

Even when its components have been properly defined, ROI should not be used as the sole criterion of divisional performance. Overemphasis on ROI can cause an investment project whose forecasted returns exceed a firm's cost of capital to be rejected merely because the project's return is less than the division's target ROI. This type of result can be avoided by evaluating divisional performance by various measures, including RI, which emphasizes added profit in dollars (see page 603). Other useful performance measures include profit growth, sales growth, market share, working capital management, new product development, and managerial personnel development. In the long run, the effect of these items is reflected in a division's ROI, but taking them into account individually provides a more immediate view of performance.

Consider the following example. Texon Company[4] is organized into several divisions, each serving a different regional market. Each divisional manager is responsible for sales, cost of operations, acquisition and financing of assets, and management of working capital. Each division's target ROI is 10 percent.

The vice president of general operations will retire in September 19x5. In seeking a replacement, the selection committee has reviewed the performance, attitudes, and skills of several divisional managers as well as outside candidates. The committee has narrowed its choice to the managers of Divisions A and F. Divisions A and F both manufacture and sell all company products in separate regional markets. Both candidates were appointed division managers in late 19x1. The manager of Division A was the division's assistant manager during the preceding five years. The manager of Division F was previously assistant divisional manager of Division B before being appointed manager of Division F when it was formed in 19x1.

[2]Reece and Cool, *op. cit.*

[3]Reece and Cool, *op. cit.* The percentages quoted total 101 percent because a few companies used more than one method.

[4]Adapted from the CMA Exam.

Exhibit 13–1
Data for Measuring Divisional Performance

Comparison of Performance
Texon Company: Divisions A and F
For the Year 19x2–19x4
(dollars in thousands)

	Division A			Division F		
	19x4	19x3	19x2	19x4	19x3	19x2
Estimated total market sales	$13,000	$12,000	$10,000	$6,500	$6,000	$5,000
Division sales	$ 1,210	$ 1,100	$ 1,000	$ 750	$ 600	$ 450
Variable expenses	$ 345	$ 320	$ 300	$ 210	$ 175	$ 135
Fixed expenses	770	730	675	480	400	310
Total expenses	$ 1,115	$ 1,050	$ 975	$ 690	$ 575	$ 445
Net income	$ 95	$ 50	$ 25	$ 60	$ 25	$ 5
Assets employed	$ 360	$ 340	$ 330	$ 300	$ 240	$ 170
Liabilities	115	105	103	130	100	47
Net investment	$ 245	$ 235	$ 227	$ 170	$ 140	$ 123

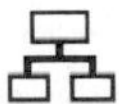

Financial data for the past three years are summarized in Exhibit 13–1. Based on the information given, which manager would you recommend for vice president of general operations?

Good management looks at a variety of measures of performance in selecting a manager for higher positions. We will look at only the financial measures of performance, but you should not forget that things such as product or service quality and development of subordinates are also important.

Evaluating financial performance requires looking at several measures. From the data given for Texon Company, we can look at the following six:

1. ROI
2. RI
3. Sales growth
4. Market share
5. Expenses relative to sales
6. Net income growth

ROI and RI are the broadest measures of performance because they are effected by revenues, expenses, and investment. If we assume that each division manager is responsible for financing divisional assets, we might calculate these two measures using net investment, that is, total assets minus liabilities. Divisional managers exercise control over net investment by decisions to acquire and finance

Exhibit 13–2
Trends in ROI and RI of Two Divisions

Return on Investment and Residual Income
Texon Company: Divisions A and F
For the Years 19x2–19x4
(dollars in thousands)

	Return on Investment					
	Division A			Division F		
	19x4	19x3	19x2	19x4	19x3	19x2
Operating income	$ 95	$ 50	$ 25	$ 60	$ 25	$ 5
Net investment	$245	$235	$227	$170	$140	$123
Return on investment	39%	21%	11%	35%	18%	4%

	Residual Income					
	Division A			Division F		
	19x4	19x3	19x2	19x4	19x3	19x2
Operating income	$95	$50	$25	$60	$25	$ 5
Capital charge (10% × assets employed)	36	34	33	30	24	17
Residual income	$59	$16	$(8)	$30	$ 1	$(12)

divisional assets. Because each division's sales are made in a separate regional market, divisional managers can apparently control all revenues and expenses within the division as well.

Exhibit 13–2 shows the ROI and RI calculations. Notice that the divisions' ROIs are fairly close. RIs are different, but that reflects the fact that Division A is larger than Division F. The trend in ROI and RI in both divisions is favorable. Given the closeness of these measures, the other measures will be important in the promotion decision.

We calculate sales growth by dividing the increase in sales by the last year's sales. Division F had sales growth of 25 percent in 19x4 [($750 − $600) ÷ $600], a year when overall market growth was just 8 percent. For comparison, Division A had 10 percent growth in 19x4 [($1,210 − $1,100) ÷ $1,100]. This was good when compared to market growth of 8 percent [($13,000 − $12,000) ÷ $12,000], but not as good as Division F's growth. Often it is easier to obtain a higher percentage sales growth from a lower base such as the one in Division F, but Division F's dollar amount of sales growth was also higher than Division A's.

You calculate market share by dividing a division's annual sales by the estimated annual total sales in its market. Division A's market share for 19x4 was 9.3 percent ($1,210 ÷ $13,000). Market shares for both divisions for 19x2–19x4 were as follows:

	19x4	19x3	19x2
Division A	9.3%	9.2%	10.0%
Division F	11.5	10.0	9.0

Notice that Division F steadily increased its market share during these years, whereas Division A lost a small share.

Both divisions reduced costs relative to sales. In 19x4, each division incurred total expenses equal to 92 percent of sales ($1,115 ÷ $1,210 in Division A; $690 ÷ $750 in Division F), whereas in 19x2, they were 97.5 percent for Division A and 99 percent for Division F. As a result income as a percentage of sales increased each year in both divisions. But because of better sales growth, Division F's income grew faster than Division A's: 400 percent from 19x2 to 19x3 and 140 percent from 19x3 to 19x4 as compared with 100 percent and 90 percent for the same periods for Division A.

Division F is a new division in a relatively early stage of development. Its manager has obtained sales and profit growth despite the normal difficulties encountered in these early years. This manager also has a more diversified background than the manager of Division A. The manager of Division F has served in two divisions. Still, even though the numerical data give this manager a slight edge, it is possible that subjective considerations such as personality and leadership might recommend the manager of Division A. Performance evaluation is a complex task requiring multiple measures of the different attributes of good management.

■

Transfer Prices

Earlier in this chapter you read that transfer prices can create problems when measuring the earnings of an investment or profit center. A **transfer price** is a special selling price used in interdivisional exchanges to record the selling division's revenues and the buying division's expenses. Transfer prices, therefore, affect the earnings of both the buying and selling division. Since earnings are vital to performance measurement in both profit and investment centers, establishing transfer prices is important to managers. The buying division's manager is concerned about the transfer price because it establishes the cost of items purchased from another division. The selling division's manager is concerned about the transfer price because it establishes the revenue received from selling items to another division.

Top management is also interested in transfer prices. First, it is in a company's interest to avoid unnecessary friction between buying and selling divisions. If a division thinks it is at a disadvantage in doing business in-house, it is unlikely to cooperate in such arrangements, even if they benefit the company as a whole. Second, the capacity of the selling division should be used to maximize a company's overall profitability. If a selling division has idle capacity, that fact should influence the transfer price. Finally, the buying division should know the true marginal cost of the product it buys. From the buying division's point of view, the full transfer price appears to be the marginal cost of the item. Yet, the marginal cost to the selling division (and the corporation as a whole) is usually lower than the transfer price.

In practice, there are two common approaches to establishing transfer prices: market-based transfer prices and cost-based transfer prices. Cost-based transfer prices use either standard variable costs or standard full costs. How each of these approaches is used as well as the advantages and disadvantages of each will be discussed.

Market-Based Transfer Prices

OBJECTIVE 7
Explain a market-based transfer price and why it is considered the ideal transfer price

A **market price** is the price at which a product can be purchased or sold by independent buyers and sellers. A **market-based transfer price** is the outside market price of the product, possibly adjusted for savings in transportation, credit, and other costs avoided by selling to a related division. The market price, if it can be determined, is the ideal transfer price. Generally, if a market price exists for a product or service sold in-house, firms will use it as the basis of their transfer price.

Market-based prices tend to be used when a company's buying divisions are free to buy from outside suppliers and selling divisions are free to sell to outside buyers. Since both divisions can buy and sell on the outside market, no arbitration of prices is necessary. A buyer who thinks the seller's price is higher than the market price can get a price quote from an outside seller. A seller who complains about an inside buyer's unwillingness to pay the outside price can sell to outside customers.

When excess capacity exists in an industry, sellers will probably reduce their selling price. The transfer price offered to internal buyers should reflect that reduction. In extreme cases of excess capacity, suppliers will sell at any price covering marginal costs. Knowing marginal costs, the buying division can adjust its prices and production levels accordingly. If a shortage occurs, market prices will rise. A buying division will buy an item only if it can still make a profit. The selling division will sell an item internally only at the higher outside price. Thus, the market price automatically adjusts to market conditions.

Consider the following data which represent a normal market situation with no shortages or excess capacity. Each division sells its product to outside customers. In addition, the buying division needs one unit of the selling division's product for each unit it makes and sells. The buying division can either buy from an outside supplier or from the selling division.

	Buying division	Selling division
Outside selling price	$6.50	$3.00
Variable expenses	2.00	1.00
Outside demand for item		2,000 units
Buying division's demand for item	1,000 units	
Selling division's productive capacity		3,000 units

Both divisions handle many products. Whether units are sold internally, externally, or not at all, fixed costs are the same.

The selling division will produce 3,000 units, which will sell for $3 a unit. This production level is enough to meet both the outside and inside demand. The product's total contribution margin to the company as a whole is calculated as follows:

Units sold outside by the selling division		
Sales revenues (2,000 units @ $3/unit)	$ 6,000	
Variable expenses (2,000 units @ $1/unit)	(2,000)	
Contribution margin		$4,000
Units sold inside by the selling division		
Sales revenues (1,000 units @ $3/unit)	$ 3,000	
Variable expenses (1,000 units @ $1/unit)	(1,000)	
Contribution margin		$2,000
Units sold outside by the buying division		
Sales revenues (1,000 units @ $6.50/unit)	$ 6,500	
Variable expenses (1,000 units @ $2/unit)	(2,000)	
Transfer price (1,000 units @ $3/unit)	(3,000)	
Contribution margin		1,500
Total contribution margin		$7,500

Notice that at the market price of $3, both divisions earn contribution margin on the 1,000 units sold internally. The company as a whole gains $3,500 because there is no outside demand for the 1,000 units sold inside.

Now, assume outside demand increases for the selling division's item, but demand for the buying division's product remains the same. In the short run, this increased demand for the selling division's item will increase its market price. If the market price increases to $5 and the company uses market-based transfer prices, the transfer price will increase to $5. At this price the buying division will no longer buy the item, since its contribution margin on the item will be negative as shown below.

Buying division's contribution margin at $5 transfer price		
Sales revenues		
(1,000 units @ $6.50)	$ 6,500	
Variable expenses		
(1,000 units @ $2)	(2,000)	
Transfer price		
(1,000 units @ $5)	(5,000)	
Total contribution margin		$(500)

In this case, the selling division will sell its entire production to outside buyers. That is the best solution for the company as a whole, since the selling division will make a contribution margin of $4 per unit ($5 – $1) by selling to outside customers at the market price. Units sold to the buying division would generate a contribution margin of only $3.50 per unit ($6.50 – $2.00 – $1.00). Thus, market-based transfer prices automatically adjust for changes in supply and demand. By doing so, divisions produce and sell in the markets that yield the greatest possible profit for the company as a whole.

A transfer price based on market price can be adjusted to allow for cost savings on sales to inside buyers. For example, when sales are made to an outside buyer, they are usually made on credit. Outside credit sales entail a cost of capital invested in accounts receivable as well as the cost of bad debt losses. Those costs do not exist in internal sales. The transfer is simply a bookkeeping transaction. Shipping and packaging costs may also be lower on internal sales.

Unfortunately, transfer prices cannot always be based on market prices, as market prices do not always exist. If a product is made to a buying division's specifications, a simliar product may not be sold on the outside market. Therefore, there is no market price on which to base a transfer price. Even if a similar product is sold on the outside market, the inside buyer may purchase such large quantities that the outside price is not relevant. Major companies in the steel, automobile, oil, and electrical appliance industries are so large that if a part is bought from an outside instead of an inside supplier, they can create shifts in market demand that change market prices.

Occasionally, a firm insists that a product or service be produced inside to protect trade secrets. The product may use special ingredients or require special technology. In such cases, divisions may be unable to agree on a market price, since the buying division is not free to purchase on the outside. Cost-based transfer prices may be the best solution in such situations.

Review Exercise 13–3

Calculate Contribution Margin

McArthur Corporation has two divisions, Willy and Nilly. Nilly Division makes electric motors. Willy Division makes electric tools. Each division has a separate plant, but they are located beside each other on the same lot. One of Willy's tools, a drill, needs a motor that Nilly makes and sells to outside customers. The following data are available on the two products:

	Willy's drill	Nilly's motor
Selling price	$32.00	$5.25
Variable costs (excluding motor cost for Willy Division)	21.00	3.10
Outside demand for each product	7,000 units	16,000 units
Capacity for this product	10,000 units	30,000 units

Required

1. Calculate the total contribution margin in each division from these two products. Assume that Nilly Division makes 7,000 motors and transfers them to Willy Division at market price. Assume both divisions sell their outside demand for their products.
2. Suppose outside demand for Nilly's motors increases to 25,000 units. Suppose also that as a result of the increased demand, the market price of this motor goes to $6.30. Calculate the contribution margin in each division and McArthur's total contribution margin on these two products if Nilly Division makes 7,000 motors for Willy Division and transfers them at the new market price and sells enough motors outside to use its remaining capacity.
3. Assume the same facts as in 2 above, but that McArthur Corporation continues the $5.25 transfer price. Calculate the contribution margin in each division if Nilly Division makes 7,000 motors for Willy Division and transfers them at the $5.25 market price. Assume that Nilly sells the balance of its capacity to outside customers at $6.30 per unit. Compare the contribution margin in each division and the total contribution margin for McArthur Corporation on these products to your results from 2 above. What do you observe?
4. Assume the same facts as in 2 above. Explain briefly what arguments Willy Division might offer for a transfer price below $6.30 per unit.

Solution

1. Total divisional contribution margins from these products are as follows:

	Willy's drill		Nilly's motor	
Selling price	$32.00		$5.25	
Variable expenses incurred in each division	21.00		3.10	
Transfer price	5.25			
Total variable expenses	$26.25		$3.10	
Contribution margin per unit	$ 5.75		$2.15	
Times total demand for each product	7,000	units	23,000	units*
Total contribution margin from this product	$40,250		$49,450	

*7,000 units to Willy and 16,000 units outside sales.

2. Total divisional contribution margins from these products with the sales demand and new market price are as follows:

	Willy's drill		Nilly's motor	
Selling price	$32.00		$6.30	
Variable costs incurred in each division	21.00		3.10	
Transfer price	6.30			
Total variable expenses	$27.30		$3.10	
Contribution margin per unit	$ 4.70		$3.20	
Times total demand for each product	7,000	units	30,000	units*
Total contribution margin from this product	$32,900		$96,000	

*7,000 units to Willy and balance of capacity to outside sales.

The total corporate contribution margin on these two products is higher than the result in *1* above because the higher outside selling price and higher demand for motors adds to total corporate contribution margin. The total corporate contribution margin is the sum of the contribution margin for each division. You can confirm this with the following computation:

	McArthur Corporation	
Sales revenues		
Willy Division (7,000 units @ $32)	$224,000	
Nilly Division (23,000 units @ $6.30)	144,900	
Total sales revenues		$368,900
Variable expenses		
Willy Division (7,000 units @ $21)	$147,000	
Nilly Division (30,000 units @ $3.10*)	93,000	
Total variable expenses		240,000
Total corporate contribution margin		$128,900

*Nilly incurs variable expense on all 30,000 units whether sold inside or outside.

3. Total divisional contribution margins from these products with the new sales demand but old transfer price.

   The total contribution margin from Willy's Division will be the same as in answer to *1* above, $40,250. Since the transfer price is different from the outside market price, we must calculate Nilly's total contribution margin as follows:

	Outside sales		Inside sales	
Selling price	$6.30		$5.25	
Variable costs incurred	3.10		3.10	
Contribution margin per unit	$3.20		$2.15	
Times total demand for each product	23,000	units	7,000	units*
Total contribution margin from these sales	$73,600		$15,050	
Total contribution margin for Nilly Division		$88,650		

*7,000 units to Willy and balance of capacity to outside sales.

   The total corporate contribution margin on these two products is the same as calculated in *2* above, $128,900 ($40,250 + $88,650). Nilly still sells 23,000 units outside for $6.30 each and transfers 7,000 units to Willy Division. Variable expenses do not change. However, the split of the total contribution margin between divisions changes. The lower transfer price gives Willy Division total contribution margin of $40,250 rather than the $32,900 calculated in *2* above. Nilly Division's total contribution margin is reduced by the same amount from $96,000 in *2* above to $88,650. The change in transfer price simply shifts contribution margin from one division to the other without changing the total as long as total sales and outside selling prices are unchanged.

4. Arguments Willy might use to justify a transfer price lower than $6.30.

   The argument would have to be that Nilly incurs costs selling to outside customers that it does not incur in selling to Willy. If this is true, and the transfer price is not adjusted, sales to Willy would be more profitable than sales to outside customers.

   There is probably a savings on credit losses. There will be no credit losses from selling to Willy. Usually with sales to independent organizations there is a certain percentage of sales which are never collected. In addition, there are probably savings in packaging and transportation since the plants are next to each other. Shipments to outside customers would need to be packaged so that they will not be damaged in shipment. Motors can be moved from one plant to another without much packaging. The closeness to Willy also means transportation savings as compared to a more remote customer. Nilly may be able to deliver motors with a lift truck rather than loading them into a regular truck. Usually there is no sales commission paid on sales to affiliated divisions. Sales are negotiated by top managers, and a sales representative is not involved in the transaction. Finally, if the product produced for Willy is made to the same specifications as outside sales, there should be no difference in production costs. However, if there is a difference in specifications, there could be a difference in production costs which should be considered in setting the transfer price. All of these factors could justify a market-based transfer price that is lower for Willy than the price at which Nilly sells motors to outside customers. (see Exercises 33, 34)

■

Cost-Based Transfer Prices

In almost all cases, **cost-based transfer prices** are based on standard variable or standard full costs (fixed plus variable) of manufacturing. Were they based on actual costs, the selling division could pass along the cost of inefficiencies to the buying division. That would, of course, have the undesirable effect of reducing the selling division's motivation to control costs.

Cost-based transfer prices may be based on standard variable costs or on standard full costs. Each method has its advantages and disadvantages.

OBJECTIVE 8
Discuss the advantages and disadvantages of cost-based transfer prices

Standard Variable Costs The major advantage of basing a transfer price on a standard variable cost is that a standard variable cost is usually equivalent to the marginal cost of a product or service. Thus, a buying division knows the total marginal cost of its product and can make pricing and selling decisions accordingly. The assumption is that selling to an inside customer does not change fixed costs.

Although fixed costs frequently remain unchanged because of inside sales, there are exceptions to the rule. For example, suppose a selling division must purchase a lift truck to deliver a product to the buying division at the other end of the plant. The depreciation, maintenance, and insurance costs of the truck must be considered an incremental cost of the internal sale. Yet, a transfer price based on variable costs alone would not pass that cost on to the buying division. As a result, the buying division would not know the true marginal cost of the product. Thus, its decisions might not serve the company's best interests.

The most important disadvantage of basing transfer prices on standard variable costs is that it produces a zero contribution margin on the selling division's inside sales. (If a selling price equals variable costs, nothing is contributed to profit.) If the selling division adds nothing to its earnings by producing and selling to inside buyers, it has no motivation to make the sale. Indeed, if the selling division has limited production capacity, it will be motivated to sell all its products or services to outside buyers.

Because of this problem, standard variable costs are not widely used as a basis for transfer prices. Most often cost-based transfer prices are based on the full cost.

Standard Full Costs Full-cost transfer prices permit a selling division to add to its earnings. A **full-cost transfer price** equals a product's variable costs plus the fixed manufacturing costs allocated to it. Since a full-cost transfer price exceeds variable costs by the amount of fixed costs, the selling division's contribution margin equals the allocated fixed costs.

As long as a division has available production capacity and no need to give up outside sales, a contribution margin equal to fixed costs is satisfactory. But when demand is high, the outside selling price is normally greater than full cost. In that case, the selling division would prefer to sell outside and earn a higher contribution margin. The problem is that the outside sales may not maximize the firm's contribution margin. This difficulty can be minimized by restricting the selling division from selling outside the company so long as inside needs have not been met. Of course, such a policy creates hard feelings in the selling division.

A more important disadvantage of full-cost transfer prices arises in the buying division. With a standard full-cost transfer price, the buying division does not know the real marginal cost of its final product. To the buying division, a transfer price always appears to be a variable cost. If the division buys one more unit, its cost increases by the amount of the transfer price. But the additional cost to the organization *as a whole* is likely to be just the variable cost. As a result, selling decisions made on the basis of full-cost transfer prices may not maximize profit for the entire firm.

For example, assume the Systems Division of Major Electronics Corporation makes electronic accessories for microcomputers. The division is considering producing and marketing a modem, an electronic device for connecting microcomputers to telephone lines for data transmission. Divisional sales managers believe they can sell 1,000 new modems a month at a wholesale price of $95 per unit. The Systems Division will design, assemble, and market the product. It will buy most of the components from outside suppliers or other divisions of Major Electronics.

A major component of the new modem is an electronic chip designed by the Systems Division and manufactured by the Circuits Division of Major Electronics Corporation. The Circuits Division estimated materials costs of $2.00 per unit and direct labor costs of $7.50 per unit. Each unit requires one-half hour of labor. The division's predetermined overhead rate is $24 per direct labor hour. Although only 10 percent of the division's overhead costs are variable, the Circuits Division bid the following full-cost transfer price for the chip:

Direct materials	$ 2.00
Direct labor	7.50
Applied overhead (1/2 hour)	12.00
Total	$21.50

The Systems Division estimated that materials purchased from outside suppliers would cost $10. Direct labor costs in the Systems Division would total $9 (one hour at $9 per hour). Systems estimated its variable overhead at $4 per direct labor hour. Fixed overhead incurred specifically for the new product would be $30,000 per month. Variable selling expenses were expected to be $10 per modem; fixed advertising costs, $20,000 per month.

Using these data, the Systems Division prepared the following analysis:

Selling price		$95.00
Variable expenses		
Chip	$21.50	
Materials	10.00	
Direct labor	9.00	
Variable manufacturing overhead	4.00	
Selling expenses	10.00	
Total variable expenses		54.50
Contribution margin per unit		$40.50

$$\text{Breakeven volume per month} = \frac{\text{fixed expense per month}}{\text{contribution margin per unit}}$$
$$= \frac{\$30{,}000 + \$20{,}000}{\$40.50}$$
$$= \underline{\underline{1{,}235}} \text{ units per month}$$

Since sales managers projected monthly sales of only 1,000 units a month at a price of $95, divisional management concluded that the modem was not a viable product.

Was the managers' conclusion correct? Not if the Circuits Division has the capacity to produce the chip without adding to its fixed costs. The Systems Division's analysis was correct given the information available to the division. The problem is that to the Systems Division the entire transfer price of $21.50 seemed to be a variable cost. After all, each additional chip purchased by the division cost $21.50. But from the viewpoint of the company as a whole, only $10.70 of the transfer price is variable. The other $10.80 is fixed manufacturing overhead incurred by the Circuits Division ($12 × 90%). So, from a companywide viewpoint, the modem's contribution margin is $51.30 ($95.00 − $10.70 − $10.00 − $9.00 − $4.00 − $10.00).

With these revised data the correct breakeven point can be calculated:

$$\text{Breakeven volume per month} = \frac{\text{fixed expenses per month}}{\text{contribution margin per unit}}$$
$$= \frac{\$30{,}000 + \$20{,}000}{\$51.30}$$
$$= \underline{\underline{975}} \text{ units per month}$$

The new breakeven volume is below the expected sales level of 1,000 units per month. In fact, if 1,000 units can be sold every month, the new modem will generate net earnings before income taxes of more than $1,200 per month.[5]

[5]At breakeven volume all fixed costs have been covered. Therefore, the contribution margin on units sold over the breakeven point represents additional net earnings: (1,000 units sold − 975 units) × $51.30 = $1,282.50.

This example illustrates the major defect in using full-cost-based transfer prices: the buying division does not receive the information it needs to make sound decisions on sales of the final product. Yet, despite this drawback, full cost-based transfer prices are fairly widely used. This is probably because full-cost data are readily available to managers and accountants.

In summary, the ideal transfer price is a market-based transfer price. Market prices change as supply and demand change, permitting firms as a whole to maximize their earnings. When management forces a reduction in transfer price, the decision can potentially have an effect on the morale of division managers. One purpose of a divisional organization is to allow division managers to operate as though their divisions are independent companies. To order a division to reduce its prices on intercompany sales undermines that purpose.

■

Multinational Transfer Pricing

The methods of transfer pricing we have just discussed are also used by multinational businesses that operate in more than one country. We have discussed transfer pricing from the viewpoint of the business's best economic interests. These considerations are equally applicable to multinational businesses. There are, however, two additional issues that must be considered in transfer pricing for multinational businesses. The first is tariffs, and the second is income taxes.

Tariffs are taxes that are applied at national borders when products are imported into a country. The amount of tariff that must be paid is usually a percentage of the value of the product imported. The rates vary from zero to two or three hundred percent. Each country sets its own rates. A high rate is designed to discourage imports by making the imported product very expensive. If a business wants to import a product to a country to sell it in that country, it would like to minimize the tariff so the product can be sold at a competitive price. Since a business cannot change a country's tariff rates, the only possibility of reducing tariff taxes is to reduce the stated value of the product. Oftentimes the tariff is based on the transfer price. This provides businesses with incentives to minimize transfer prices to minimize tariffs.

Income tax rates vary from country to country. Suppose that a company has a manufacturing division in one country and a sales division in another country. Suppose further that the company decides that overall, it is profitable to transfer a product from one country to another. Once the decision to transfer is made, the transfer prices simply determine how much of the total contribution margin and profit on the sale of the product will be assigned to each division. To minimize the total income taxes paid by the company, it would like to have more profit assigned to the division in the country with lower income tax rates. Transfer prices provide a mechanism to do this.

As you might expect, taxing authorities are aware of these transfer pricing issues and try to avoid manipulation of transfer prices to their tax disadvantage. Generally, countries try to establish rules that require use of prices that cannot be manipulated easily. If a well-established world market price exists, organizations usually must use this as the transfer price. For many products, however, no market price exists. This is particularly true of patented products or components that are usually only sold as a part of another product. Lacking a market price, countries accept cost base prices as long as the costs are determined by recognized accounting standards. Sometimes countries try to enforce a "fair" sharing of the total profit that the organization realizes when the end product is finally sold. This is also a matter of judgment.

You cannot become an expert in international transfer pricing in a few paragraphs. The basic ideas of transfer pricing apply to both domestic and international situations. However, it is important to recognize that there are added criteria to consider in international transfer pricing.

Chapter Review

Review of Learning Objectives

1. **Explain how the financial performance of an investment center manager is measured.** The financial performance of an investment center manager is measured by whether the center achieves or exceeds its budgeted ROI or RI.

2. **Calculate return on investment (ROI)** The formula for ROI is

$$\text{ROI} = \frac{\text{center's earnings}}{\text{center's average investment}}$$

The answer is expressed as a percentage.

3. **Calculate residual income (RI) and explain how it differs from ROI.** The formula for RI is

$$\text{RI} = \text{center's earnings} - (\text{center's average investment} \times \text{target rate of return})$$

Unlike ROI, RI is expressed in dollars. It indicates how much income a company will earn over and above its target rate of return.

4. **Calculate return on sales and asset turnover, and explain how managers use those ratios to analyze ROI.** Return on sales is the ratio of profit (net earnings) to total sales revenues. Expressed as a

percentage, it is calculated by dividing a center's earnings by a center's total sales. Asset turnover is the ratio of a center's total sales to total (average) assets.

When return on sales is multiplied by asset turnover, it yields a center's ROI:

ROI = return on sales × asset turnover

This formula, called the Du Pont formula, is particularly helpful in monitoring the performance of an investment center. It means that ROI can be improved by: (1) increasing the return on sales while holding asset turnover constant; (2) increasing asset turnover while holding return on sales constant; or (3) by using some combination of the two strategies. To improve return on sales, a manager must analyze a division's income statement. To improve asset turnover, a manager must examine the relationship between sales and asset levels.

5. **Discuss the problems of measuring earnings for an investment or profit center and the common solutions.**
   When measuring a profit or investment center's earnings, you must decide which, if any, corporate costs to allocate to the center. For some corporate services, divisional management can control the quantity of services requested. The cost of these services should be allocated in order to motivate managers to use them efficiently. But even uncontrollable indirect corporate services are sometimes allocated to make an investment center's earnings more comparable to those of other companies in the same industry. Since these costs are not controllable by divisional management yet reduce a center's earnings, they should be carefully allocated. Another problem in measuring a center's net earnings is establishing transfer prices for sales between divisions. Prices should allow both divisions involved in the transfer to earn their target income.

6. **Discuss the problem of measuring investment for an investment center and the common solutions.**
   When measuring investment for an investment center, one must decide what assets to include in investments and how they will be valued. For example, should such assets as cash, which are not controllable at the center level, be included? What about idle assets? Should liabilities be subtracted? How these questions are answered can affect a manager's motivation. Most often investment is defined as a center's total assets as they appear on the center's balance sheet. These assets may be valued using gross book value, net book value, or estimated current market value. Although book value is often not current, most firms use net book value because the information can be easily and inexpensively obtained.

7. **Explain a market-based transfer price and why it is considered the ideal transfer price.**
   A market-based transfer price is the outside selling price of a product or service sold in-house, adjusted for savings on such items as shipping and credit. A market-based transfer price is the ideal transfer price because it adjusts automatically for changes in supply and demand, motivating managers to make decisions that produce the greatest possible profit for a firm.

8. **Discuss the advantages and disadvantages of cost-based transfer prices.**
   When no market price exists, firms usually base transfer prices on the selling division's standard variable costs or standard full costs. Variable cost transfer prices usually have the advantage of indicating the true marginal cost of a product or service. If fixed costs change with an in-house sale, however, the variable cost price will not be equivalent to marginal cost. More importantly, the selling division can earn no contribution margin if the variable price is used as the transfer price. Full-cost prices frequently overstate the

marginal cost of a product because they are the sum of fixed costs and variable costs. But the transfer price appears as a variable cost to the buying division, thus overstating marginal costs and leading to poor decisions.

Review of Key Terms

Allocate To divide a general cost of production among products, departments, or divisions, using a predetermined ratio. This ratio is based on activity level or use.

Asset turnover The ratio of a center's total sales to its total average assets. Used as a measure of how effectively assets are employed. Algebraically:

$$\text{Asset turnover} = \frac{\text{center's total sales}}{\text{center's total (average) assets}}$$

Contribution margin Sales revenues less variable expenses. Represents the amount sales has contributed toward fixed expenses and operating income.

Controllable item A cost, revenue, or investment item over which a manager has significant influence.

Cost-based transfer prices Transfer prices based either on standard variable or standard full costs (fixed plus variable) of manufacturing.

Current value The amount for which an asset can be presently purchased. Usually determined by an appraisal.

Du Pont formula A formula used to analyze the cause of differences between actual and budgeted ROI. Algebraically:

$$\text{ROI} = \text{return on sales} \times \text{asset turnover}$$

Full-cost transfer price A transfer price based on variable costs plus allocated fixed manufacturing costs.

Gross book value The original cost of an asset with no deduction for accumulated depreciation.

Investment center A responsibility center whose manager is responsible for balancing revenues, expenses, and investments to achieve a budgeted ROI or RI.

Market-based transfer price The outside market price of a product adjusted for savings in transportation, credit, and other costs avoided by selling to a related division.

Market price The price at which a product can be purchased or sold by independent buyers and sellers.

Net book value The original cost of an asset minus accumulated depreciation.

Residual income (RI) A measure of an investment center's earnings in relation to its average investment and its target rate of return. Expressed in dollars. Algebraically:

$$\text{RI} = \text{center's earnings} - (\text{center's average investment} \times \text{target rate of return})$$

Return on investment (ROI) The ratio of an investment center's earnings to its average investments. Expressed as a percentage, it is calculated by dividing a center's net earnings by its average investments.

$$\text{ROI} = \frac{\text{center's earnings}}{\text{center's average investment}}$$

Return on sales The ratio of profit (net earnings) to total sales revenues. Expressed as a percentage, it is used as a measure of how efficiently net earnings was generated. Algebraically:

$$\text{Return on sales} = \frac{\text{center's earnings}}{\text{center's total sales}}$$

Transfer price A special selling price used in interdivisional exchanges to record the selling division's revenues and the buying division's expenses.

Review Problem 1

Seabury Company is evaluating the performance of its two divisions, the Hendel Division and the Boyce Division. Each division is responsible for manufacturing and selling its own products. In addition, each division has considerable latitude in deciding the amount to invest in assets. For these reasons both divisions are considered investment centers.

Selected financial data for the past two years are given below.

Selected Data
Seabury Company: Hendel and Boyce Divisions
For the Years 19x1 and 19x2

	Hendel Division		Boyce Division	
	19x1	19x2	19x1	19x2
Estimated total market sales	$9,200	$10,120	$2,225	$2,700
Division sales	$1,800	$ 1,890	$ 900	$1,085
Variable expenses	480	523	185	255
Fixed expenses	700	888	400	480
Total expenses	$1,180	$ 1,411	$ 585	$ 735
Net income	$ 620	$ 479	$ 315	$ 350
Assets employed	$3,340	$ 3,390	$1,100	$1,320

Required

1. Calculate each division's return on sales for both years.
2. Calculate each division's asset turnover for 19x2.
3. Using the Du Pont formula, calculate each division's ROI for 19x2.
4. Calculate each division's RI for 19x2 using a target rate of return of 15 percent.
5. Calculate each division's market share for both years.
6. Calculate each division's profit growth between 19x1 and 19x2.

Solution to Review Problem 1

1. Return on sales calculated:

	Hendel Division		Boyce Division	
	19x1	19x2	19x1	19x2
Operating income	$ 620	$ 479	$315	$ 350
Division's net sales	$1,800	$1,890	$900	$1,085
Return on sales	34.4%	25.3%	35.0%	32.3%

2. Asset turnover calculated:

	Hendel Division		Boyce Division	
	19x1	19x2	19x1	19x2
Assets employed	$3,340	$3,390	$1,100	$1,320
Average assets employed	$3,365		$1,210	
Division's sales		$1,890		$1,085
Average assets employed		$3,365		$1,210
Asset turnover		0.56 times		0.90 times

3. ROI calculated:

	Hendel Division 19x2	Boyce Division 19x2
	25.3% × 0.56	32.2% × 0.90
ROI	14.2%	28.9%

4. RI calculated:

	Hendel Division 19x2	Boyce Division 19x2
	[$479 – ($3,390 × 15%)]	[$350 – ($1,320 × 15%)]
RI	($29.50)	$152.00

5. Market share calculated:

	Hendel Division		Boyce Division	
	19x1	19x2	19x1	19x2
Division's sales	$1,800	$ 1,890	$ 900	$1,085
Estimated total market sales	$9,200	$10,120	$2,225	$2,700
Market share	19.6%	18.7%	40.5%	40.2%

6. Profit growth calculated:

	Hendel Division		Boyce Division	
	19x1	19x2	19x1	19x2
Operating income	$620	$479	$315	$350
	($479 − $620) / $620		($350 − $315) / $315	
Profit growth	(22.7%)		11.1%	

Review Problem 2

The Pat Division of Sale Company produces an electronic component used by the Lin Division in its finished product. Pat, which is operating at full capacity, sells the electronic component in an active external market for $40 per unit. The current transfer price for the unit is the market price, or $40. Variable costs on the unit are $25.

Lin Division is operating at 75 percent capacity. The division has an opportunity to bid on a special order from a large mail-order house. Accountants have prepared the following cost analysis for Lin's manager:

Variable costs	
Manufacturing	$15
Shipping	5
Electrical component purchased	
Transfer price (from Pat)	40
Total variable costs	$60
Fixed costs (based on 100% capacity)	15
Total costs	$75

The manager considers the total cost too high to allow a competitive bid on the special order. To obtain the order, Lin must bid no more than $65. Accordingly, the manager has asked Pat Division to reduce its transfer price to $30. Pat's manager has refused because the division can sell all its production to external customers at $40 a unit.

Sale Company's management uses ROI to measure the financial performance of divisional managers.

Required

1. Will Sale Company's overall contribution margin per unit increase or decrease if Pat sells its electrical component to Lin for the special order?
2. Should corporate management force the transfer at a price of $30 per unit?

Solution to Review Problem 2

1. If Pat Division sells all electrical components on the outside market, Sale's contribution margin per unit will be the same as Pat's, which follows:

Sales revenues	$40
Variable costs	25
Contribution margin per unit	$15

If Pat Division sells to the Lin Division, Sale's contribution margin per unit will be as follows:

Estimated revenue from special order		$65
Variable costs		
Manufacturing, Lin Division	$15	
Shipping, Lin Division	5	
Electrical component, Pat Division	$25	45
Contribution margin per unit		$20

Sale Corporation's overall contribution margin per unit will be $5 greater if Pat sells to Lin. Notice that fixed costs were excluded from the calculation, as they will not change with the special order and are therefore irrelevant to the decision.

2. No, management should not force the transfer price down to $30 per unit. It should follow the present transfer price policy and transfer at market price. Corporate management should also ensure that Lin Division does not refuse the special order. Even at a transfer price of $40, the order will generate a contribution margin of $5 per unit of Lin. Although the Lin Division would prefer a higher contribution margin, its managers should realize that a $5 contribution margin per unit is better than a zero contribution margin. And that is the amount that would be generated by idle facilities.

   Another reason management should not force Pat to reduce its transfer price is the reduction's potential effect on the morale of Pat's management. The purpose of divisional organization is to allow division managers to operate as though their units were independent businesses. To order a division manager to reduce profits undermines that purpose.

Chapter Assignments

Questions

1. (L.O. 1) Describe the basic financial responsibilities of managers of expense centers, revenue centers, profit centers, and investment centers.
2. (L.O. 2, 3) Define return on investment (ROI) and residual income (RI).
3. (L.O. 3) What factors do corporate management consider when setting a target ROI or RI? What impact can this have on investment decisions by division management?
4. (L.O. 3) What does zero RI indicate? What does negative or positive RI indicate?
5. (L.O. 4) What information does return on sales provide? How can managers improve a return on sales ratio?
6. (L.O. 4) What information does asset turnover provide? How can managers improve asset turnover?

7. (L.O. 5) Discuss the problems of measuring earnings for an investment or profit center.

8. (L.O. 5) Discuss the two criteria for allocating corporate costs to investment centers.

9. (L.O. 6) Discuss the problem of deciding what to include in a division's investment when computing ROI and RI.

10. (L.O. 6) Discuss the advantages and disadvantages of using gross book value to measure divisional investment.

11. (L.O. 7) What is a transfer price? How does it differ from a market price?

12. (L.O. 8) Why should a cost-based transfer price be based on standard costs rather than actual costs?

13. (L.O. 8) What are the advantages and disadvantages of basing transfer prices on standard variable costs? On standard full costs?

14. (L.O. 7) Explain briefly the similarities and differences between domestic and international transfer pricing decisions.

Exercises

15. (L.O. 2) Bocce Company has two divisions, Tiber and Arno. Earnings and investments for each division are shown below.

	Tiber	Arno
Center's net earnings	$ 34,000	$ 88,000
Center's investment	280,000	743,000

Required Calculate ROI for each division.

16. (L.O. 3) Assume the same facts as those given in *15* above. Also assume the target rate of return for both centers is 13 percent.

Required Calculate the RI for each division.

17. (L.O. 2) Schotz Company has two divisions, Rhine and Main. Each division's net earnings and investments are shown below.

	Rhine	Main
Center's net earnings	$ 12,000	$ 8,000
Center's investment	100,000	76,000

Required Calculate ROI for each division.

18. (L.O. 3) Assume the same facts as those given in *17* above. Also assume the target rate of return for both centers is 8 percent.

Required

1. Calculate RI for each division.
2. A $20,000 investment opportunity yielding 11 percent is available to Schotz Company.

Would either division accept the investment if:
a. ROI is used to measure divisional performance?
b. RI is used to measure divisional performance?

19. (L.O. 2, 3) The financial performance of the Lou Division of China Corporation is measured as an investment center. The following data are available for Lou Division:

Center's earnings, 19x3	$ 846,000
Center's investment, Jan 1, 19x3	4,374,000
Center's investment, Dec. 31, 19x3	5,295,000

China Corporation has an 18 percent target rate of return for its investment centers.

Required

1. Calculate Lou Division's ROI for 19x3.
2. Calculate Lou Division's RI for 19x3.
3. How did the large increase in assets during 19x3 affect ROI?

(see Review Exercise 13–1)

20. (L.O. 2, 3) The financial performance of the Peg Division of Wood Corporation is measured as an investment center. The following data are available for Peg Division:

Center's earnings, 19x7	$ 146,000
Center's investment, Jan 1, 19x7	1,397,000
Center's investment, Dec. 31, 19x7	1,053,000

Wood Corporation has a 14 percent target rate of return for its investment centers.

Required

1. Calculate Peg Division's ROI for 19x7.
2. Calculate Peg Division's RI for 19x7.

(see Review Exercise 13–1)

21. (L.O. 2, 3) The financial performance of the Duke Division of Potter Corporation is measured as an investment center. The following data are available for Duke Division:

Center's earnings, 19x5	$346,000
Center's ROI for 19x5	17%

Potter Corporation has a 15 percent target rate of return for its investment centers.

Required

1. Calculate Duke Division's average investment for 19x5.
2. Calculate Duke Division's RI for 19x5.

(see Review Exercise 13–1)

22. (L.O. 2, 4) Dotter Company's accounting system shows the following data for the Norrland Division:

Annual sales	$2,500,000
Net earnings	245,000
Average investment	1,300,000

Required

1. Calculate Norrland's return on sales.
2. Calculate Norrland's asset turnover.
3. Using the Du Pont formula, calculate Norrland's ROI.
4. Calculate Norrland's ROI without using the Du Pont formula.

23. (L.O. 2, 4) Somerville Company's accounting system shows the following data for the Medford Division:

Annual sales	$1,250,000
Net earnings	137,500
Average investment	825,000

Required

1. Calculate Medford's return on sales.
2. Calculate Medford's asset turnover.
3. Using the Du Pont formula, calculate Medford's ROI.
4. Calculate Medford's ROI without using the Du Pont formula to confirm your answer to *3* above.

24. (L.O. 2, 4) The financial performance of the Anderson Division of Connor Corporation is measured as an investment center. The following data are available for Anderson Division:

Center's 19x8 sales	$3,211,000
Center's earnings, 19x8	218,348
Center's total assets, Jan. 1, 19x8	1,244,000
Center's total assets, Dec. 31, 19x8	1,376,000

Required

1. Calculate Anderson Division's return on sales for 19x8.
2. Calculate Anderson Division's asset turnover for 19x8.
3. Calculate Anderson Division's ROI for 19x8 using your results from *1* and *2* above. (see Review Exercise 13–2)

25. (L.O. 2, 4) Letich Corporation evaluates its Ferro Division as an investment center. Data for Ferro Division for the last three years is given below.

	Year 1	Year 2	Year 3
Division earnings	$ 152,880	$ 177,800	$ 226,287
Division sales	1,274,000	1,270,000	1,331,100
Division average net assets	245,000	254,000	261,000

Required

1. Calculate Ferro Division's ROI for each year.
2. Calculate Ferro Division's return on sales for each year.
3. Calculate Ferro Division's asset turnover for each year.
4. How do the returns on sales and asset turnovers help explain the changes in ROI over the years? Use the data to illustrate.

26. (L.O. 2, 4) The financial performance of the Alvin Division of Mead Corporation is measured as an investment center. The following data are available for Alvin Division:

Center's 19x1 sales	$1,034,800
Center's earnings, 19x1	186,264
Center's total assets, Jan. 1, 19x1	767,000
Center's total assets, Dec. 31, 19x1	845,000

Required

1. Calculate Alvin Division's return on sales for 19x1.
2. Calculate Alvin Division's asset turnover for 19x1.
3. Calculate Alvin Division's ROI for 19x1 using your results from *1* and *2* above. (see Review Exercise 13–2)

27. (L.O. 2, 4) Skivor Corporation evaluates its Dugar Factory as an investment center. For 19x0, Skivor based the Dugar Factory's budgeted ROI on budgeted sales of $1,400,000. Dugar expected return on sales for 19x0 to be 6 percent and asset turnover to be three times. In calculating RI for the Dugar Factory, Skivor uses a target rate of return of 15 percent.

During 19x0, Dugar Factory earned operating profit of $77,748 on sales of $1,413,600. Its average net book value of all division assets during 19x0 was $456,000.

Required

1. Calculate Dugar Factory's actual RI for 19x0.
2. How does Dugar Factory's actual RI for 19x0 compare to its budgeted RI?
3. Calculate Dugar Factory's target of return on investment.
4. Use the Du Pont formula to calculate Dugar Factory's actual ROI for 19x0.
5. Explain briefly what insights the Du Pont formula provides on the financial performance of the Dugar Factory for 19x0.

28. (L.O. 2, 4) Outlay Corporation evaluates its Weber Division as an investment center. Data for Weber Division for the last three years are given below.

	Year 1	Year 2	Year 3
Division earnings	$ 175,536	$ 191,899	$ 201,656
Division sales	2,544,000	2,702,800	2,880,800
Division average net assets	795,000	932,000	1,108,000

Required

1. Calculate Weber Division's ROI for each year.
2. Calculate Weber Division's return on sales for each year.
3. Calculate Weber Division's asset turnover for each year.
4. How do the returns on sales and asset turnovers help explain the changes in ROI over the years? Use the data to illustrate.

29. (L.O. 2, 4) Marshall Stores evaluates its Buzzer Branch as an investment center. For 19x6, Marshall based the Buzzer Branch's target rate of return (ROI) on its planned operating income of $251,160 on budgeted sales of $4,680,000. Buzzer expected net book value of Buzzer's assets to average $1,800,000 during 19x6. In calculating RI for the Buzzer Branch, Marshall uses a target rate of return of 20 percent.

During 19x6, Buzzer Branch earned operating profit of $324,800 on sales of $4,640,000. Its average net book value of assets during 19x6 was $1,600,000.

Required

1. Calculate Buzzer Branch's actual RI for 19x6.
2. How does Buzzer Branch's actual RI for 19x6 compare to its budgeted RI?
3. Calculate Buzzer Branch's target rate of ROI.
4. Use the Du Pont formula to calculate Buzzer Branch's actual ROI for 19x6.
5. Explain briefly what insights the Du Pont formula provides on the financial performance of the Buzzer Branch for 19x6.

30. (L.O. 2, 4) Mac Corporation evaluates its Severin Factory as an investment center. For 19x4, Mac based the Severin Factory's target rate of return (ROI) on its planned operating income of $248,400 on budgeted sales of $2,760,000. Severin expected net book value of all division assets to average $920,000 during 19x4. In calculating RI for the Severin Factory, Mac uses a target rate of return of 25 percent.

During 19x4, Severin Factory earned operating profit of $314,600 on sales of $2,860,000. Its average net book value of all division assets during 19x4 was $1,040,000.

Required

1. Calculate Severin Factory's actual RI for 19x4.
2. How does Severin Factory's actual RI for 19x4 compare to its budgeted RI?
3. Calculate Severin Factory's target rate of ROI.
4. Use the Du Pont formula to calculate Severin Factory's actual ROI for 19x4.
5. Explain briefly what insights the Du Pont formula provides on the financial performance of the Severin Factory for 19x4.

31. (L.O. 8) The Rockville Division of Long Island Company sells a machine part to the Deer Park Division. Standard costs for the part are as follows:

Direct materials (1.2 kilograms @ $6 per kilogram)	$7.20
Direct labor (0.5 hour @ $13 per hour)	6.50

The Rockville Division uses a predetermined overhead rate of $22 per direct labor hour. Long Island Company estimates that 20 percent of Rockville's overhead costs are variable.

Required

1. Calculate a transfer price based on standard full costs for the machine part.
2. Calculate a transfer price based on standard variable costs for the machine part.

32. (L.O. 8) The Seneca Division of Fingerlake Company sells an electronic display to the Utica Division. Standard costs of the display are as follows:

Direct materials (2.0 units @ $6.20 per unit)	$12.40
Direct labor (0.2 hour @ $14 per hour)	2.80

The Seneca Division uses a predetermined manufacturing overhead rate of $18 per machine-hour. This display requires 0.6 of a machine-hour to produce. The Seneca Division estimates that 30 percent of its manufacturing overhead costs are variable.

Required

1. Calculate a transfer price based on standard full costs for the display.
2. Calculate a transfer price based on standard variable costs for the display.

33. (L.O. 7) Northwest Produce Corporation has two divisions, Markets and Farms. Farms Division grows various fruits and vegetables. Markets Division operates produce stores. One of Markets Division's stores sells tomatoes which Farms grows. Farms Division sells most of its output to outside customers at $4 per bushel, but sells some to Markets Division at the same price. The following data are available on the two divisions:

	Markets' tomato sales	Farms' tomatoes
Selling price	$11 per bushel	$4 per bushel
Variable costs incurred in each division	6	2
Sales per month	300 bushels	2,900 bushels

Required

1. What is the total contribution margin that Northwest Produce makes on a bushel of tomatoes sold through the Markets Division?
2. Given a $4 per bushel transfer price, what is the contribution margin generated for each division by a bushel of tomatoes sold through the Markets Division?
3. If the transfer price changes to $3.50 per bushel, what is the contribution margin generated for each division by the tomatoes sold through the Markets Division? Assume no change in anything else.

(see Review Exercise 13–3)

34. (L.O. 7) Dakota Corporation has two divisions, Kite and Fabric. Fabric Division makes various high-strength fabrics. Kite Division makes premium quality kites. Each division has a separate plant, but they are located near each other. Company policy is that transfers are made at the market price. One of Kite's new products needs one yard of material that Fabric makes and sells to outside customers. The following data are available on the two products:

	Kite's kite	Fabric's material
Selling price	$3.95	$1.20 per yard
Variable costs (excluding fabric from Fabric Division)	2.30	0.70
Outside demand for each product	60,000 units	240,000 yards
Capacity for this product	80,000 units	400,000 yards

Required

1. Calculate the total contribution margin in each division from these two products. Assume that Fabric Division makes 240,000 yards for the Kite Division and transfers them at market price. Assume both divisions sell their outside demand for their products.
2. Suppose outside demand for Fabric's material increases to 350,000 yards. Suppose also that the increased demand drives the market price of this fabric to $1.40. Calculate the contribution margin in each division and Dakota's total contribution margin on these two products if Fabric Division makes 60,000 yards for Kite Division and transfers them at the new market price and sells enough material outside to use its remaining capacity.
3. Assume the same facts as in 2, above but that Dakota Corporation continues the $1.20 transfer price. Calculate the contribution margin in each division if Fabric Division makes 60,000 yards for Kite Division and transfers them at the $1.20 price. Assume that Fabric sells the balance of its capacity to outside customers at $1.40 per yard. Compare the contribution margin in each division and the total contribution margin for Dakota Corporation on these products to your results from 2 above. What do you observe?

(see Review Exercise 13–3)

Problems

35. (L.O. 2, 4) The following data were selected from the financial statements of three companies:

	Company		
	One	Two	Three
Sales revenues	$200,000	?	?
Income	?	?	$30,000
Investment base	?	$180,000	50,000
Return on sales	2%	20%	6%
Asset turnover	?	6 times	?
ROI	4%	?	?

Required

Calculate the missing figures using the Du Pont formula.

36. (L.O. 2, 3, 5, 6) XYZ Company has three divisions, X, Y, and Z. The divisions were all created when the company was founded. Each division has assets whose expected life is 20 years. The following data were collected for 19x0:

	Division		
	X	Y	Z
Net earnings before taxes	$ 60,000	$ 67,500	$ 75,000
Average investment, net book value	150,000	225,000	300,000

Required

1. Rank the three divisions based on ROI using net book value.
2. Rank the three divisions based on RI using net book value. Use 10 percent as the target rate of return.
3. Based on net earnings before taxes, which division was the most profitable in 19x0? Explain briefly why management should prefer to rank the divisions based on ROI rather than net earnings before taxes.

37. (L.O. 2, 4) National Discount Appliances evaluates its Lyon Store as an investment center. For 19x9, National based the Lyon Store's target rate of return (ROI) on its planned operating income of $251,160 and on average net book value of all division assets of $1,480,000. In addition, Lyon had planned on a return on sales of 7 percent. In calculating RI for the Lyon Store, National uses a target rate of return of 14 percent.

During 19x9, Lyon Store earned operating profit of $298,080 on sales of $4,320,000. Its average net book value of all division assets during 19x9 was $1,600,000.

Required

1. Calculate Lyon Store's actual RI for 19x9.
2. How does Lyon Store's actual RI for 19x9 compare to its budgeted RI?
3. Calculate Lyon Store's target rate of ROI.
4. Use the Du Pont formula to calculate Lyon Store's actual ROI for 19x9.
5. Explain briefly what insights the Du Pont formula provides on the financial performance of the Lyon Store for 19x9.

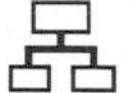

38. (L.O. 7) Whinston Corporation has two divisions, East and West. East is primarily a manufacturing division, although it sells its own products in the eastern region. West Division does some manufacturing. Most of West's activities are designing and marketing products in the western region. West Division manufactures some of its product, buys some product from the East Division, and buys some product from outside suppliers. Whinston evaluates both divisions as investment centers.

West has just designed a new product for which it forecasts demand of 10,000 units per year. West does not have the production skills needed to produce a major component of this product. East Division does have the needed skills. West could either buy the component from East or from an outside supplier.

West's new product will sell for $10 per unit. West will incur $3 in variable expense to assemble and sell the unit (not including the cost of the component it intends to purchase). West will have to incur $12,000 per year additional fixed expense to market the new product. In addition, Whinston's accounting system will allocate $3 per unit of fixed manufacturing expenses to the product. Total fixed manufacturing expense, however will not change.

West can purchase the component from an outside supplier for $6 per unit. East Division can produce the new component without incurring any additional fixed expenses and by incurring $3.75 per unit variable expenses. The accounting system will allocate $2 per unit fixed expense to the product in East Division. East Division would not pay its normal 10 percent sales commission on the sale to West Division.

Most of East Division's products sell for 20 percent more than the sum of variable and allocated fixed expenses.

Neither division has alternate use for the facilities that would be used for this product.

Required

1. From the viewpoint of the corporation as a whole, is the new product likely to add to profit? Support your answer with appropriate computations.
2. If the transfer price is the market price, $6 per unit, will the new product add profit from West Division's viewpoint. Support your answer with appropriate computations.
3. What transfer price would you recommend? Briefly explain your recommendation and its impact on the two divisions.

39. (L.O. 1, 5, 6) ATCO Company purchased Dexter Company three years ago. Before the acquisition Dexter manufactured and sold plastic products to many outside customers. Since becoming a division of ATCO, it only manufactures plastic components for products made at ATCO's Macon Division. Macon sells its products to hardware wholesalers.

ATCO's corporate management allows Dexter's management considerable authority. However, ATCO retains control over capital investments, pricing, and production levels. ATCO evaluates divisional performance largely on the basis of ROI. Corporate general service costs are allocated on the basis of sales dollars. The computer department's actual costs are apportioned among divisions on the basis of use. Divisional investments include divisional fixed assets, valued at net book value (cost less depreciation); divisional inventories; and cash and accounts receivables that are apportioned on the basis of sales dollars. Dexter's income statement is presented below.

Dexter Division
Income Statement
For the Year Ended October 31, 19x0
(dollars in thousands)

Sales revenues		$4,000
Costs and expenses		
Product costs		
Direct materials	$ 450	
Direct labor	900	
Factory overhead	1,200	
Total product costs		$2,550
Engineering and research		120
Shipping and receiving		240
Division's administration		
Manager's office	$ 210	
Cost accounting	40	
Personnel	82	332
Corporate costs		
Computer	$ 48	
General services	230	278
Total costs and expenses		$3,520
Division's operating income		$ 480
Average plant investment		$1,600
Return on investment		30%

Required

1. Discuss ATCO's performance evaluation program in relation to the Dexter Division.
2. Based on your response to *1* above, recommend appropriate revisions to the financial information and reports used to evaluate Dexter's performance. If revisions are unnecessary, explain why. (CMA)

40. (L.O. 7) Mar Company has two decentralized divisions, X and Y. Division X has always purchased some units from Division Y at $75 per unit. Division X incurs additional variable processing and selling costs of $25 per unit before selling these units for $120 each.

Division Y plans to raise the transfer price to $100. Division X thinks it can buy the units from an outside supplier at $75 per unit. Division Y's costs are as follows:

Variable costs per unit	$70
Annual fixed costs allocated to product transferred to Division X	$15,000
Annual production for Division X	1,000 units

If Division X buys from an outside supplier, Division Y's facilities would become idle. Its fixed costs would not change.

Required

1. What will be Mar Company's total contribution margin if Division X buys its usual 1,000 units from an outside supplier for $75 per unit?
2. What will be Mar's total contribution margin if the company enforces a transfer price of $100 per unit?
3. At a $75 transfer price, how is the company's total contribution margin divided between Divisions X and Y?
4. Assume Division Y can sell *all* output to outside customers at $100 per unit. Division X can sell its output at $120 per unit, but it can only buy input units for $100. What should the Mar Company do to maximize profits? Support your answer with calculations.

41. (L.O. 7, 8) The Wilkins Division of Lakeside Manufacturing Company is negotiating a transfer price for fans, which the Flemming Division puts into its electric heaters. Although each division has its own production plant, the plants are within two kilometers of each other. Lakeside requires that transfers be done at market price.

Since the fans are a fairly standard part used in various appliances, Flemming can purchase them from outside suppliers. One outside supplier will sell and deliver the fans for $2.35 per unit. That is the same price Wilkins charges outside customers. Wilkins's other customer is 500 kilometers from the plant, however. Wilkins ships the fans to this customer via a commercial trucking company, which requires careful packing to avoid shipping damage. Packing costs are $0.14 per unit; shipping, $0.06 per unit.

When negotiating the transfer price with Wilkins, Flemming's manager said Wilkins could deliver the fans by Lakeside company trucks. Since the distance is short and company drivers are careful, the fans can be delivered in the same racks in which they come off the assembly line. No packing is necessary. Delivery costs by Lakeside company truck are estimated at no more than $0.03 per unit.

Wilkins's managers find that on average, 5 percent of the selling price covers the cost of capital tied up in accounts receivable and bad debt losses. That ratio is standard in the industry.

Required

1. The manager at Flemming is willing to pay market price for the fans. However, he thinks the price should be adjusted for the savings Wilkins will realize by selling in-house. What transfer price should he propose? Show your calculations.

2. Assume the Wilkins division wants to hold to its $2.35 market price with no adjustments. What arguments can it offer Flemming to justify that price?

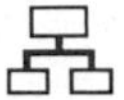

42. **(L.O. 8)** MBR, Inc., has three divisions that were formerly independent manufacturers. Bader Corporation and Roach Corporation merged in 19x5. The new corporation then acquired Mitchell Company in 19x6. All three divisions operate as if they were independent companies. Each has its own sales force and production facilities. Each division's management is responsible for sales, cost of operations, acquisition and financing of divisional assets, and management of working capital. Corporate management evaluates divisional performance on the basis of ROI.

Mitchell has just been awarded a contract whose product uses a component manufactured both by the Roach Division and outside suppliers. Mitchell estimated the cost of the component at $3.80 when preparing its bid for the new product. Roach supplied Mitchell with this figure when the average variable cost of the component was requested. This figure represents standard variable manufacturing costs plus variable selling and distribution expenses.

Roach has an active sales force, which continually solicits new prospects. The regular selling price of the component is $6.50. Sales of the component are expected to increase. Roach's managers are willing to supply the component to Mitchell at the regular selling price minus variable selling and distribution expenses. Mitchell's management has responded by offering to pay standard variable manufacturing costs plus 20 percent.

The two divisions cannot agree on a transfer price. Corporate management has never established a policy on transfer prices, since interdivisional transactions never previously occurred. As a compromise the corporate vice president of finance suggested a price equal to the standard full manufacturing cost (selling and distribution expenses not included) plus a 15 percent markup. Both divisions rejected the suggestion.

The unit cost of the component can be broken down as follows:

Standard variable manufacturing costs	$3.20
Standard fixed manufacturing costs	1.20
Variable selling and distribution expenses	0.60
Total	$5.00

Required

1. Calculate the three proposed transfer prices.
2. What will be Roach's contribution margin per unit on each of the three proposed transfer prices? How likely is the Roach Division to sell at each of the proposed prices?
3. Should corporate management become involved in the controversy? Explain. (CMA)

Case 1
Bio-Grade Products (L.O. 3, 4, 5, 6)

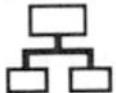

Bio-Grade Products is a multiproduct manufacturer of animal feed and feed supplements. Bio-Grade has a highly decentralized management structure, encompassing eight geographic areas. Each divisional manager is responsible for production and distribution in his or her area.

Divisional managers are evaluated on the basis of RI. RI is a division's contribution to corporate profits before taxes minus a 20 percent return on its investments. A center's investments are the total of its year-end balances in accounts receivable, inventories, and net fixed assets (costs minus accumulated depreciation). Divisional managers are expected to minimize their investments in receivables and inventories. Investments in fixed assets are divisional and corporate management's joint responsibility. Proposals are made by divisional managers and approved on the basis of available corporate funds and general corporate policy.

Alex Williams, manager of the Southeastern Division, prepared his division's 19x7 and preliminary 19x8 budgets in late 19x6. Final approval of the 19x8 budget occurred in late 19x7 after adjustments for recent market trends. Preliminary work on the 19x9 budget also occurred at that time. In October 19x8, Williams asked the divisional controller to prepare a report, showing the division's performance in the first nine months of 19x8. The report is reproduced below. Selected balance sheet data are also shown in this report.

Bio-Grade Products, Southeastern Division
Report for the First Three Quarters
For the Period Ended October 31, 19x8
(dollars in thousands)

	19x8			19x7	
	Annual budget	Nine-month budget	Nine-month actual	Annual budget	Actual
Sales revenues	$2,800	$2,100	$2,200	$2,500	$2,430
Division costs and expenses					
Direct materials and labor	$1,064	$ 798	$ 995	$ 900	$ 890
Supplies	44	33	35	35	43
Maintenance and repairs	200	150	60	175	160
Depreciation	120	90	90	110	110
Administration	120	90	90	90	100
Total division costs and expenses	$1,548	$1,161	$1,270	$1,310	$1,303
Division margin	$1,252	$ 939	$ 930	$1,190	$1,127
Allocated corporate fixed costs	360	270	240	340	320
Division's contribution to corporate profits	$ 892	$ 669	$ 690	$ 850	$ 807

Selected Balance Sheet Data

	19x8			19x7	
	Budgeted balances Dec. 31	Budgeted balances Sept. 30	Actual balances Sept. 30	Budgeted balances Dec. 31	Actual balances Dec. 31
Division's investments					
Accounts receivable	$ 280	$ 290	$ 250	$ 250	$ 250
Inventories	500	500	650	450	475
Net fixed assets	1,320	1,350	1,100	1,150	1,100
Total	$2,100	$2,140	$2,000	$1,850	$1,825

Required

1. Calculate (*a*) budgeted RI for 19x8 and (*b*) budgeted and actual RI for the first nine months of 19x8 and for 19x7.
2. Evaluate Alex Williams's performance for the nine months ending September 19x8. Support your evaluation with calculations and facts from the problem.
3. If Bio-Grade's divisional performance measurement system is to effectively reflect the responsibilities of divisional managers, which features should be revised? (CMA)

Case 2

Staple, Inc. (L.O. 1, 2, 5, 6)

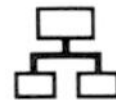

George Johnson was hired on July 1, 19x0, as assistant general manager at Botel, a division of Staple, Inc. On being hired, he was promised the position of divisional general manager when the current general manager retired on January 1, 19x2. In addition to becoming acquainted with the division and the general manager's duties, Mr. Johnson was to develop the 19x1 and 19x2 budgets. When promoted to general manager in 19x2, he became responsible for the 19x3 budget as well.

Staple, Inc., is a highly decentralized multiproduct company. The corporate staff reviews division-prepared budgets but seldom makes major changes. In situations requiring capital investments for expansion or replacement, it makes all final decisions. Divisional management is responsible for implementing the capital investment program.

Staple measures a division's performance mainly by its ROIs. Budget and actual data for 19x0 to 19x3 are presented below. Revision's to the 19x3 budget are considered unnecessary even though the division departed from the approved 19x2 budget.

Botel Division
Budget and Actual Data
For the Years 19x0 to 19x3
(dollars in thousands)

	Actual			Budget	
	19x0	19x1	19x2	19x2	19x3
Sales revenues	$1,000	$1,500	$1,800	$2,000	$2,400
Division expenses					
Variable					
Materials and labor	$ 250	$ 375	$ 450	$ 500	$ 600
Repairs	50	75	50	100	120
Supplies	20	30	36	40	48
Fixed					
Employee training	30	35	25	40	45
Maintenance	50	55	40	60	70
Depreciation	120	160	160	200	200
Rent	80	100	110	140	140
Total	$ 600	$ 830	$ 871	$1,080	$1,223
Division's contribution to earnings	$ 400	$ 670	$ 929	$ 920	$1,177
Division's investments					
Accounts receivable	$ 100	$ 150	$ 180	$ 200	$ 240
Inventory	200	300	270	400	480
Fixed assets	1,590	2,565	2,800	3,380	4,000
Less accounts and wages payable	(150)	(225)	(350)	(300)	(360)
Net investments	$1,740	$2,790	$2,900	$3,680	$4,360

Required

1. Calculate actual ROIs for 19x0–19x2 and budgeted ROIs for 19x2 and 19x3 based on the division's net investments.
2. Identify Johnson's responsibilities under Staple's management and measurement system.
3. Evaluate Johnson's performance in 19x2.
4. Based on your analysis, recommend changes in the responsibilities assigned to managers and/or the methods used to measure and evaluate a division's performance. (CMA)

Case 3
Lorax Electric Company (L.O. 8)

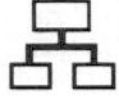

Lorax Electric Company manufactures many systems and components for the electronics industry. The firm's divisional managers have the authority to make virtually all operating decisions. Divisional profits and ROIs are reviewed regularly by top management, which has been pleased with the company's improved profitability over the past few years.

The Devices Division, which manufactures solid state devices, is operating at capacity. The Systems Division has asked the Devices Division to supply it with a large quantity of integrated circuit number IC378. The Devices Division is currently selling this component to regular customers at $40 per hundred.

The Systems Division is operating at about 60 percent capacity. It wants the component for a digital clock system, which it can supply in large quantities to Centonic Electric. Centonic, a major producer of clock radios, has offered to pay $7.50 for the system.

The Systems Division has analyzed the costs of the clock system. Accountants have determined the amount that can be paid for the integrated circuits by working backward from the selling price. The estimated transfer price reflects the highest per unit cost the Systems Division can incur and still realize sufficient margin to show improvement on the division's income statement. These estimates are shown below.

Costs excluding Circuit IC378	
Components purchased from outside suppliers	$2.75
Circuit board etching	
Labor and variable overhead	0.40
Assembly, testing, and packaging	
Labor and variable overhead	1.35
Fixed overhead allocations	1.50

In addition, each clock will require five circuits from the Devices Division. Given these costs, the Systems Division calculates it should earn $0.50 per system.

Because of this analysis the Systems Division offered the Devices Division $20 per hundred for the integrated circuit. The bid was refused by Devices' manager, since it was only half the market price of $40 per hundred paid by regular customers. When Systems found it could not obtain a comparable integrated circuit from outside vendors, the matter was referred to an arbitration committee set up to review such problems.

The arbitration committee prepared the following analysis of the cost of producing the circuits:

Variable manufacturing costs	$0.15
Fixed manufacturing costs	0.13
Normal gross margin	0.07

Normal gross margin is actually the average gross margin on all products sold by the Devices Division.

The manager at Systems reacted to this analysis by stating, "They could sell us that circuit for $0.18 and still earn a positive contribution toward profit. In fact, they should be required to sell to us at their variable cost of $0.15." Lou Belcher, manager of the Devices Division, argued that the Systems Division could pay up to almost $60 per hundred for the circuits and still make a positive contribution toward profit. Both managers rejected the committee's recommendation to set the price at $0.35 per unit, or $35 per hundred, so Devices could earn a "normal" gross margin. The dispute has now come to the attention of the vice president of operations.

Required

1. What would be the immediate economic effect on Lorax as a whole if the Devices Division were required to supply five IC378 circuits to the Systems Division at a price of $0.35 per unit? Compare the *corporate* total contribution margin if the Devices Division sells five circuits to its outside customers at $40 per hundred with the corporate total contribution margin if Devices sells the five circuits to the Systems Division.
2. Assume the circuits are sold to Systems at $0.35 per unit. Calculate Devices' contribution margin from selling five circuits to Systems.
3. Assume the circuits are sold to Systems at $0.35 per unit. Calculate System's earned contribution margin from selling one clock system to Centonic Electric.
4. Discuss the advisability of top management's intervening in the dispute over transfer pricing.
5. Suppose Lorax adopts a policy that all internal transfers must be made at a price equal to the selling division's variable cost per unit. Supplying divisions would be required to sell if buying divisions wanted an item. Discuss how such a policy would affect motivation at the selling division and corporate interests as a whole.

(CMA)

Case 4

A. R. Oma, Inc. (L.O. 8)

A. R. Oma, Inc., manufactures a line of men's colognes and after-shave lotions. The manufacturing process is a series of mixing operations after the addition of certain aromatic and coloring ingredients. When finished, the products are poured into company-produced glass bottles and packed in cases of six bottles each. Because A. R. Oma thinks sales of its products are heavily influenced by the appearance of its bottles, it has devoted considerable attention to developing unique bottle designs.

Over the years the processing and bottle-making operations have evolved into highly autonomous, competitive divisions. Some rivalry has developed between managerial personnel, with each division claiming to be more important to the company. This competitive attitude is partly due to the fact that the bottle plant was an independent company until purchased ten years ago. No real interchange of divisional personnel has occurred since then. All bottle production is now sold in-house to the Processing Division. Each division is considered a separate profit center and is evaluated as such.

As the new corporate controller, you are responsible for defining an appropriate transfer price between the Bottle Division and the packaging center in the Processing Division. At your request the general manager of the Processing Division has asked other bottle manufacturers to quote a price for the quantity and size the division needs. Competitive market prices are shown below.

Volume in cases	Total price	Price per case
2,000,000	$ 4,000,000	$2.00
4,000,000	7,000,000	1.75
6,000,000	10,000,000	1.67*

A cost analysis by the Bottle Division indicates bottles can be produced in-house at the following costs:

Volume in cases	Total cost	Cost per case
2,000,000	$ 3,200,000	$1.60
4,000,000	5,200,000	1.30
6,000,000	7,200,000	1.20

These costs include fixed costs of $1,200,000 per year and variable costs of $1 per case. They have caused considerable corporate discussion about the bottles' proper transfer price. Interest is high because a significant portion of each division manager's income is a bonus based on profits at his or her division.

The Processing Division has budgeted for the following costs in addition to the cost of the bottles:

Sales volume in cases	Total costs	Costs per case
2,000,000	$16,400,000	$8.20
4,000,000	32,400,000	8.10
6,000,000	48,400,000	8.07*

Total costs include variable costs of $8 per case. After considerable analysis the marketing research department has furnished you with these price-demand relationships for Oma's finished products.

Sales volume in cases	Total sales revenues	Sales price per case
2,000,000	$25,000,000	$12.50
4,000,000	45,600,000	11.40
6,000,000	63,900,000	10.65

*Rounded.

Required

1. Oma Company has used market price as a transfer price in the past. Using current costs and market prices and assuming a volume of 6,000,000 cases, calculate the income for:
   a. The Bottle Division
   b. The Processing Division
   c. The corporation as a whole
2. Recalculate *1* above, assuming a transfer price of $1.50 per case for the bottles.
3. Should the Bottle Division be considered a profit center? (CMA)

■

Part 5

Advanced Topics in Managerial Accounting

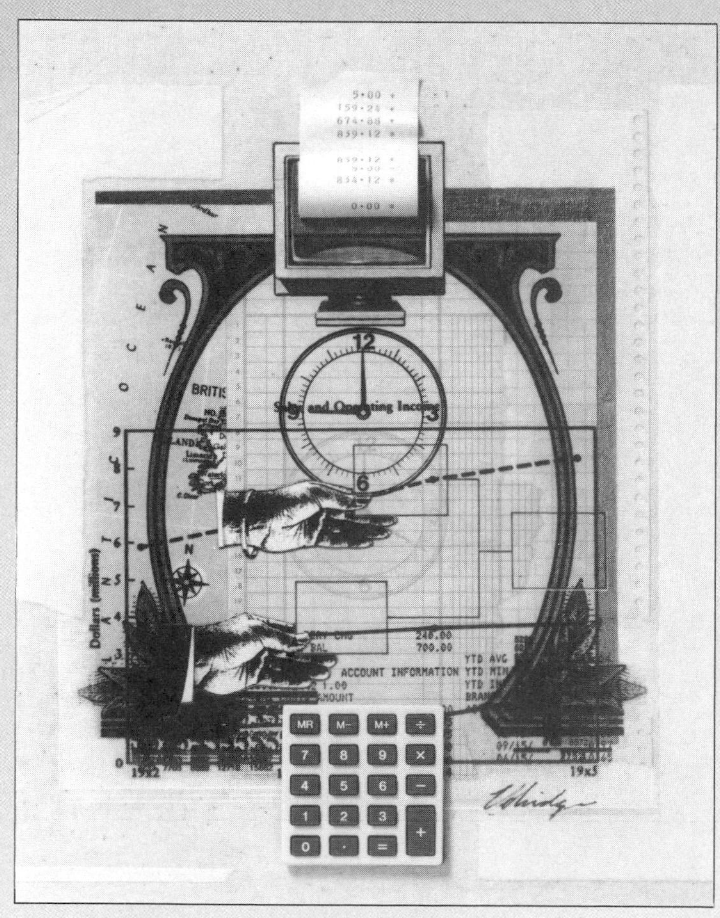

Part 5 covers four advanced topics in managerial accounting: capital expenditure analysis, cost allocation, the analysis of financial statements for managerial use, and the statement of cash flows.

■

Chapters 14 and 15, Introduction to Capital Expenditure Analysis and Further Topics in Capital Expenditure Analysis, explain the complex process by which managers evaluate proposals for investments in plant and equipment.

■

Chapter 16, Cost Allocation, shows how the allocation of overhead costs to particular products or services can be refined by accounting for costs by activity. This method allows different activities to use different predetermined overhead rates and different cost drivers.

■

Chapter 17, Analysis of Financial Statements, explains how managers interpret and use information from the income statement and balance sheet. For the day-to-day planning and control of operations, managers rely mostly on budgets, variance reports, and cost-volume-profit analyses. But they also refer to published income statements, balance sheets, and statements of cash flows.

■

Chapter 18, Statement of Cash Flows, shows how to prepare and use the statement of cash flows. The statement of cash flows shows managers, shareholders, and lenders how the organization generates and uses its cash.

■

14

Introduction to Capital Expenditure Analysis

LEARNING OBJECTIVES

After studying this chapter you should be able to:

1. Define capital expenditures and explain how they relate to long-range plans
2. Define discounted cash flow and explain its usefulness in analyzing capital expenditure proposals
3. Calculate the present value of future cash flows
4. Evaluate capital expenditure proposals for new products and machine replacement
5. Compute the net present value of an incremental cash flow
6. Calculate and use the time-adjusted rate of return to evaluate a capital expenditure proposal
7. Find the time-adjusted rate of return for a project whose present value factor is not listed in a present value table
8. Describe a postaudit of a capital expenditure and explain its uses

Implementing long-range plans usually requires capital expenditures. Expansion plans may call for new production facilities or new products. And new products may require long-range research or special production and distribution facilities. Since all firms have limited capital, managers must often choose between several competing investments. Thus, a manager's skill in selecting investments ultimately determines how well an organization performs over the long run.

This chapter introduces the basic concepts of analyzing these investments, called capital expenditures. It also covers two important methods of capital expenditure analysis, net present value and time-adjusted rate of return. Chapter 15 extends the discussion, covering income tax effects and methods of ranking competing proposals.

■

Capital Expenditures and Long-Range Planning

OBJECTIVE 1
Define capital expenditures and explain how they relate to long-range plans

A **capital expenditure** is an investment in an asset whose useful life is more than one year. In contrast, a **current expenditure** is the purchase of an asset with value only during the current year. The replacement of a machine or an investment to launch a new product are examples of capital expenditures. The purchase of supplies and the payment of monthly rent are current expenditures.

Capital expenditures must be analyzed carefully for two reasons. First, the amounts expended are usually large. Organizations often invest $100,000 or more in a single piece of equipment. The relatively high labor rates in the United States and other industrial nations are an incentive to minimize labor costs by using computers, robots, and other sophisticated but expensive devices. Land and buildings require still larger investments. Even for large corporations, such purchases ought to be analyzed carefully.

Second, capital expenditure decisions are costly to reverse in the short run. If a buyer makes a mistake in purchasing inventory, he or she can usually sell or dispose of the unwanted items in a few months. But the purchase of land entails sales commissions and legal fees. Although these costs are valuable to the purchaser, they have little resale value. If land is resold shortly after its purchase, the value will not have increased enough to offset purchase costs. Only by owning land for several years can purchase costs be recovered. In that time the value of land could have increased or other benefits could have been derived from using the land.

Since buildings are usually sold with the land they occupy, they have the same loss potential as land if sold shortly after purchase. Real estate commissions on buildings are often higher than those on land. And if a building is new, it was probably built to the purchaser's specifications, which will probably not meet the new purchaser's needs.

For example, suppose a firm buys some land and builds a cast-iron foundry. The building will have facilities for receiving and shipping heavy metal parts as well as high ceilings for dispersing heat and operating moving cranes. Special floors and windows may be needed. Now, suppose the location turns out to be poor, making transportation costs high. Or perhaps not enough skilled foundry workers can be hired in the region. If the builder of the foundry cannot operate profitably, probably no one else can either. If he or she tries to sell the foundry, the new buyer will most likely want to use the building for something else. The high ceilings and special floors and windows will be of little value to the new buyer. Hence, the foundry will be sold at a loss.

Both the large amounts of money expended and the difficulty of reversing such decisions over the short run suggest that any capital expenditure should be carefully analyzed.

■

Characteristics of Capital Expenditures

Most of the examples of capital expenditures in this and the next chapter cover proposed purchases of property and equipment. The purchase of stocks and bonds, however, are also capital expenditures. And the principles discussed in this and the next chapter apply to the purchase of stocks and bonds just as much as to the purchase of property and equipment. First, investments in stocks and bonds will be discussed because they are more familiar to most students. Then, investments in property and equipment will be considered.

Capital expenditures involve spending an amount of cash in the present with the expectation of a future cash return. Conceptually, it makes no difference whether the future cash returns are bond interest received, revenue from the sale of a new product, or savings of labor costs.

Return on Investment Versus Return of Investment

All capital expenditures have two characteristics. First, they generate future cash returns, which usually include a mixture of return *on* investment and return *of* investment. Second, the investment is made for a period of more than one year.

Bonds are a good illustration of the difference between return on investment and return of investment. You pay cash to purchase a bond. Later, you receive cash interest payments and eventually repayment of the face amount of the bond. Repayment of the face amount is a return *of* the original investment; interest payments, a return *on* the investment.

The return on a bond is relatively simple to analyze, since the cash returns are stated on the bond. For example, suppose you pay $1,000 to purchase a 20-year bond with an annual interest rate of 11 percent. You can expect to receive annual interest payments of $110 ($1,000 × 11 percent) each year you hold the bond. If you hold the bond for twenty years, the original investment of $1,000 will be returned to you. You receive a return *on* your investment while you own the bond ($110 per year) and a return *of* your investment when it is repaid ($1,000 at the end of twenty years).

Investors in common stock also expect a return on their investments as well as a return of their investments. But evaluating stock investments is more difficult than evaluating bond investments, since no contract specifies annual cash returns or repayment of the original amount. Furthermore, the return on the investment is mixed with the return of the investment. Part of the return on the investment is the cash dividends paid by a company. Dividends may not be paid as regularly as interest payments on bonds, however, and they may be relatively small. Often the main return on a stock investment comes from selling your shares. If the market price of the shares goes up, you will recover the original investment (return *of* the investment).The increase in the market price provides return *on* the investment in addition to the dividends received.

Suppose that you purchase 50 shares of stock in Myco, Inc., for $800. During the next year you receive a cash dividend of $50. At year-end you sell your shares for $900. Your total cash return is $950: $800 is a return *of* your original investment; $150, a return *on* your investment. Since you held the shares for one year, the rate of return on your investment is 18.75 percent ($150 ÷ $800). You receive the return *on* your investment in two parts: the $50 dividend and the $100 increase in the shares' value on sale.

Purchases of property and equipment resemble investment in stocks more than investments in bonds. Usually, the original investment is not repaid at the end of an investment period. The owner receives cash returns over the life of the investment. And those cash returns provide a return of the invested amount as well as a return on the investment.

Thus, analyzing a proposed investment in property or equipment is more difficult than analyzing investments in bonds. To separate the return *of* an investment from the return *on* an investment, a technique called discounting has been developed. Because capital expenditures are made for a year or more, discounting allows for compound interest rather than simple interest on future cash flows.

Discounted Cash Flows

OBJECTIVE 2
Define discounted cash flow and explain its usefulness in analyzing capital expenditure proposals

Discounted cash flows are based on a concept called the **time value of money.** Given a choice between receiving a dollar now or some time in the future, you should prefer to receive a dollar now. There are two reasons for that preference. First, if you receive the dollar now, you can invest it, so you will have more than one dollar later. Second, you may not actually receive the dollar in the future. Whenever payment is postponed, there is the risk that it will not be made.

Discounting reduces the value of future receipts, making them equivalent to present value. **Present value** is the amount that, if invested in the present at a given rate of return, will provide a specified amount in the future.

In capital expenditure analysis, you compute the present value of a set of future cash flows to determine if it is greater than the immediate investment. If the present value of the cash returns is greater than the immediate investment, then these future returns are large enough and provide return of your investment and a satisfactory return on your investment. That is, the expected returns justify the present investment of cash. Discounting does not adjust for the effects of inflation. If inflation is expected, the manager must adjust for that separately.

■

Present Value Analysis

The average person is unfamiliar with discounting. Most people do not often ask themselves what the present value of a future receipt might be. But they are familiar with a closely related concept, future value. Therefore, this study of discounting will begin by calculating future values.

Calculating Future Values

Probably you have had the experience of depositing money into a savings account. You do so because you expect the **future value** on your investment to be higher than its present value. The bank pays interest regularly, so by year-end, you will have your original investment plus interest. Mathematically expressed, the amount you expect to have at year-end is:

$$F_1 = P(1 + r)$$

where

F_1 = future value of an account at the end of the first year
P = present value of the account (deposit)
r = rate of interest paid

If you deposit $100 into an account on which the bank pays 7 percent interest, at year-end you can expect to have:

$$F_1 = \$100 \times (1 + 0.07) = \$107$$

This computation was fairly simple because interest was paid for only one year. Were the money invested for more than a year, interest would be earned on the first year's interest as well as on the original $100 invested. Earning interest on interest is called **compounding.** Compounding may occur daily, monthly, quarterly, or annually. Annual compounding is assumed in most capital expenditure analyses.

At the end of two years, the future value of a $100 investment at 7 percent interest would be:

Original investment	\$100.00
Interest for the first year ($\$100 \times 0.07$)	7.00
Value at the end of the first year	\$107.00
Interest for the second year ($\$107 \times 0.07$)	7.49
Value at the end of the second year	\$114.49

Notice that interest earned in the second year is higher than in the first because of compounding. Rather than calculating interest year by year, however, one can adapt the formula for future value to allow for compounding as follows:

$$F_n = P(1 + r)^n$$

where

n = number of years the money is invested

Thus, the future value of \$100 invested for two years at 7 percent interest would be:

$$F_2 = \$100 \times (1 + 0.07)^2$$
$$= \$100 \times 1.1449$$
$$= \$114.49$$

Figure 14–1 shows how the future value of a \$100 investment increases over a five-year period, assuming a 7 percent interest rate compounded annually.

Figure 14–1
Increase in the Future Value of \$100 Invested for Five Years at a 7 Percent Interest Rate Compounded Annually
The height of each column represents the value of an investment (principal + interest earned to date) at the end of each year. The value at the end of each future year is called the future value.

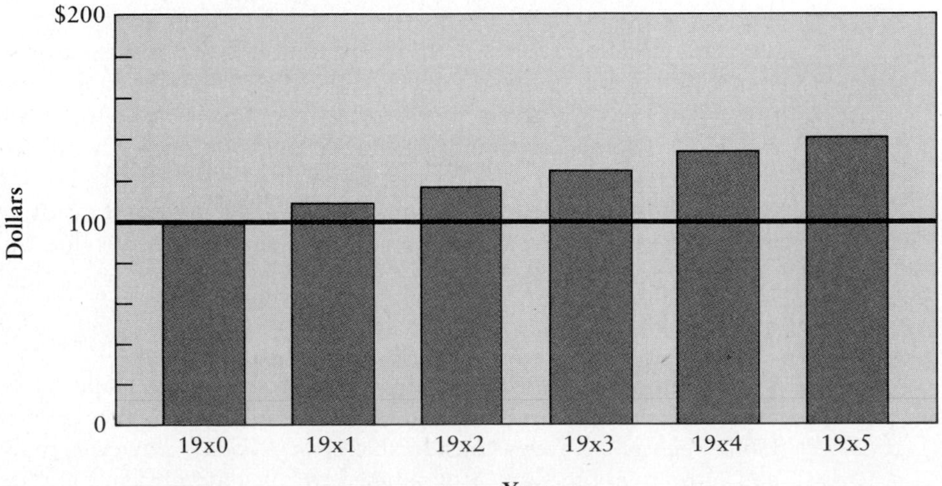

Calculating Present Values (Discounting)

OBJECTIVE 3
Calculate the present value of future cash flows

You have now seen how to calculate the *future* value of an invested amount. To calculate the *present* value of an amount to be received in the future, you simply reverse the process. If you want to have \$1,000 two years from now and can earn a return of 10 percent on the investment, how much money must you invest? You can obtain the answer by solving the future value equation for the present value, P:

$$F_n = P(1 + r)^n$$

$$P = \frac{F_n}{(1 + r)^n}$$

$$P = \frac{\$1,000}{(1 + 0.10)^2}$$

$$= \frac{\$1,000}{1.21}$$

$$= \underline{\underline{\$826.446}}$$

The future value of \$1,000 received two years from now was just discounted to its present value of \$826.446. To confirm the answer, you may calculate the future value of \$826.446 in two years.

Original investment	\$826.4460
Interest for the first year ($826.446 × 0.10)	82.6446
Value at the end of the first year	\$909.0906
Interest for the second year ($909.0906 × 0.10)	90.9091
Value at the end of the second year	\$999.9997

Rounded to a whole number, the answer is \$1,000, the amount desired at the end of two years.

Present value tables, such as the one in Table 14–1, save some work in computing present value. Looking at the top part of the table, you find that the present value of \$1 received two years from now is \$0.8264 when the interest rate is 10 percent compounded annually. Such amounts when listed in a present value table are often referred to as a **present value factor.** To find the present value of \$1,000 received in two years at a 10 percent rate of return, simply multiply \$1,000 by the appropriate factor from the present value table as follows:

$$P = \$1,000 \times 0.8264$$

$$= \underline{\underline{\$826.40}}$$

The small difference between this and the previous calculation of net present value is a result of rounding the factor in the present value table to four digits. Using such tables saves considerable effort. Today, however, many calculators and most computers are programmed to calculate present values easily. (For a more complete table, see Appendix A, Table A–1, at the end of the book.)

Table 14–1
Sample Present Value Tables
These are abbreviated present value tables. Tables with more periods and discount rates are contained in Appendix A at the end of the book.

Present Value of $1					
Discount rate	8%	10%	12%	15%	18%
Period					
1	0.9259	0.9091	0.8929	0.8696	0.8475
2	0.8573	0.8264	0.7972	0.7561	0.7182
3	0.7938	0.7513	0.7118	0.6575	0.6086
4	0.7350	0.6830	0.6355	0.5718	0.5158
5	0.6806	0.6209	0.5674	0.4972	0.4371
6	0.6302	0.5645	0.5066	0.4323	0.3704
7	0.5835	0.5132	0.4523	0.3759	0.3139
8	0.5403	0.4665	0.4039	0.3269	0.2660
9	0.5002	0.4241	0.3606	0.2843	0.2255
10	0.4632	0.3855	0.3220	0.2472	0.1911

Present Value of an Annuity of $1 per Period					
Discount rate	8%	10%	12%	15%	18%
Period					
1	0.9259	0.9091	0.8929	0.8696	0.8475
2	1.7833	1.7355	1.6901	1.6257	1.5656
3	2.5771	2.4869	2.4018	2.2832	2.1743
4	3.3121	3.1699	3.0373	2.8550	2.6901
5	3.9927	3.7908	3.6048	3.3522	3.1272
6	4.6229	4.3553	4.1114	3.7845	3.4976
7	5.2064	4.8684	4.5638	4.1604	3.8115
8	5.7466	5.3349	4.9676	4.4873	4.0776
9	6.2469	5.7590	5.3282	4.7716	4.3030
10	6.7101	6.1446	5.6502	5.0188	4.4941

Calculating the Present Value of an Annuity

A present value table is useful for finding the present value of a single future cash return. But capital expenditures sometimes involve a series of future returns of the same amount with each being received at year-end. The technical term for a series of payments of equal amount received at regular intervals is **annuity.**

Although you could calculate the present value of each future return separately, there is a short cut. The bottom part of Table 14–1 gives the present value of an annuity of $1 for various periods and discount rates. Cash returns are assumed to occur at the end of each year, with annual compounding. The amounts found in a table of the present value of an annuity are also referred to as present value factors. (For a more complete table, see Appendix A, Table A–2, at the end of the book.)

To illustrate how the present value of an annuity is calculated, assume you can invest in a $1,000 note whose return at the end of each year is $90 for three years. At the end of the third year, the borrower will also pay the original $1,000. Also assume that you are willing to invest in the note if you can expect an 8 percent return on the investment. The question is, what is the present value of the note? In other words, what is the highest price you should be willing to pay for the note now if you are satisfied with an 8 percent rate of return?

You might guess that the amount is $1,000. But if you pay $1,000 for the note and receive $90 payments each year, you will be earning a 9 percent return when all you require is an 8 percent return. To adjust the rate of return, you can

Table 14–2
Comparison of Present Value Computations
There are two methods of calculating present value when a problem involves an annuity. The first is to calculate the value of each cash flow separately by using the present value of $1 table. The second is to use the present value of an annuity. The table for the present value of an annuity is used to calculate the present value of the annuity. The table for the present value of $1 is used in this case because a single lump sum is returned at the end.

Both methods give the same answer. (The $0.01 difference is a rounding error that can be ignored). Any problem can be solved by using only the table for the present value of $1. The second method is faster, however, when the problem involves an annuity.

Using Only the Present Value of $1 Table

Year	Amount	Present value factor @ 8%	Present value
1	$ 90	0.9259	$ 83.33
2	90	0.8573	77.16
3	90	0.7938	71.44
3	1,000	0.7938	793.80
Total			$1,025.73

Using Both Present Value Tables

Year	Amount	Present value factor @ 8%	Present value
1–3	$ 90	2.5771	$ 231.94
3	1,000	0.7938	793.80
Total			$1,025.74

adjust the amount you pay for the note. In this case, you should be willing to pay more than $1,000 for the note.

To calculate the exact present value of the note, you can use one or both of the present value tables in Table 14–1. Table 14–2 shows computations both ways. In the first part of Table 14–2, the present value of the note and its returns are figured year by year. The process requires four multiplications and the addition of the four products.

Notice, however, that the three $90 payments are an annuity. They are equal in amount and are received at regular yearly intervals. Therefore, you can use the present value table for annuities to calculate the present value of those three payments in a single operation. Then, you need only add the present value of the $1,000 cash return at the end of three years.

Table 14–2 shows that you can invest $1,025.74 in the $1,000.00 note and still earn a return rate of 8 percent. The **rate of return** expresses the return on an investment as a percentage of the amount invested. Other things being equal, an investor prefers to obtain the highest possible return on an investment. Expressing a return as a percentage facilitates the comparison of returns on investments of differing amounts.

Remember that the annuity table may be used only when cash returns are equal and occur at regular intervals. That is why a separate calculation must be made for the cash return of $1,000 at the end of the third year. Had it been added to the third payment of $90, the series would not have qualified as an annuity. Likewise, annual returns of differing amounts, such as $100, $140, $150, are not annuities. Nor is a return of $100 at the end of one year, followed by another return of $100 at the end of the third and fourth years. The annuity table may be used only when future cash flows meet the strict definition of an annuity.

Review Exercise 14–1

Calculate Present Value

You have just won $34,500 on a popular game quiz show. You intend to spend some of the money immediately, but you want to buy a cruising sailboat five years from now. You project that the sailboat you want will cost $50,000. You also think you can invest money today that will earn 8 percent compounded annually.

Required

1. How much of your winnings can you spend today and still have $50,000 in five years?
2. A friend tells you that he knows of an investment that will return 10 percent compounded annually. Will this permit you to spend $5,000 today and still purchase your sailboat at the end of five years?

3. Assume that you want to be able to spend a little more today. You may be willing to defer the purchase of the sailboat three more years. However, if you wait eight years to purchase the sailboat, you estimate that it will cost $53,000. How much can you spend of your winnings and be able to purchase the sailboat in eight years, still assuming an 8 percent discount rate?

Solution

1. Another way of stating this problem is: What is the present value of $50,000 if the discount rate is 8 percent compounded annually? From the top section of Table 14–1 or Table A–1 in Appendix A, the present value of $1 received after five periods if the discount rate is 8 percent is 0.6806. This means if you invest $0.6806 today at 8 percent compounded annually, you will have $1 in five years. Since you want $50,000 not $1, you must multiply the present value of $1 by $50,000. Then $50,000 × $0.6806 = $34,030. You must invest $34,030 today to have $50,000 in five years at 8 percent compounded annually. This leaves you $470 to spend today, your $34,500 winnings minus the $34,030 you must invest today.
2. A higher discount rate (10 percent) over five years should require less investment today. From the table for the present value of $1, we see the discount factor is 0.6209 for the five-year period and 10 percent. The amount you must invest is therefore 0.6209 × $50,000, or $31,045. You will not be able to spend $5,000 of your $34,500 winnings today and still have enough to invest for your sailboat.
3. Here the problem is to find the present value of $53,000 at the end of eight years. The process is the same as before. Using the 8 percent discount rate and the eight-year period, the table shows that the present value of $1 is 0.5403. Because of the longer waiting period, you need to invest less to have $1. This is moving in the right direction. The sailboat, however, will cost $53,000 at the end of eight years. The present value of $53,000 given the assumptions is $28,635.90. This leaves $5,864.10 of your earnings to spend now. (see Exercises 17, 18, 19)

■

Evaluation of Capital Expenditures

Like stocks and bonds, the essential elements of a capital expenditure on property or equipment are (1) the present amount spent and (2) the future cash returns. To evaluate such an expenditure, the manager must first establish a minimum acceptable rate of return on the investment. (In the example of the three-year note discussed on pages 662–663, 8 percent was the minimum rate of return.) Then, the manager calculates the present value of the future returns and compares it with the amount being invested. If the present value of the future returns is equal to or greater than the amount now being spent, the capital expenditure will yield at least the minimum desired rate of return. (In the example of the three-year note, you saw that up to $1,025.74 could be invested and still achieve the 8 percent minimum rate of return.)

Business organizations must obtain capital from investors. Thus, the cost of capital is based on the rates businesses must pay investors to use their money. No organization can afford to invest capital at a 15 percent rate of return if it must pay investors 20 percent to use that capital. (For a further discussion of how the minimum rate of return is established, see Chapter 15.)

Assume the manager of a restaurant has established a minimum rate of return of 22 percent on equipment purchases. The restaurant has an opportunity to acquire a coin-operated video game that customers may use while waiting to be served. The game will cost $4,800. It is expected to generate $3,200 in revenue the first year and $2,800 the second year. At the end of the second year, the game will no longer be popular. However, the machine can then be sold back to the supplier for $2,000. Assume the machine will require no maintenance and will use an insignificant amount of electricity.

This capital expenditure will require an initial cash outflow of $4,800. Cash returns will occur over the next two years. To keep the computations simple, assume cash returns occur at the end of each year. The return from selling the machine back to the supplier is treated in the same way as cash returns from customers using the machine. To calculate whether the investment will yield at least 22 percent return, you must discount the future cash returns to their present value using 22 percent as the discount rate. If the total present value of the future returns is greater than the initial $4,800 investment, the project will yield more than the 22 percent minimum acceptable return.

The calculations would be:

Year	Amount	Present value factor @ 22%	Present value
1	$3,200	0.8197	$2,623.04
2	2,800	0.6719	1,881.32
2	2,000	0.6719	1,343.80
Total			$5,848.16

Since the present value of the future returns is greater than the $4,800 initial investment, the video game promises a return greater than 22 percent.

By combining the cash received from using the machine with the cash received from its resale, one multiplication step could have been saved. This is because both receipts occur at the end of the second year. Normally, cash flows occurring at the same time are combined in such calculations. However, the factor for the present value of an annuity could not have been used, since unequal amounts were received in the two years.

Exhibit 14–1
Worksheet for a Capital Expenditure Analysis
This worksheet is one format for organizing present value computations for capital expenditures.

Project name ______________________ Department ______________

Item	End of year	Amount of cash flow	Present value factor @ %	Present value of cash flow
________	____	______	____	______
________	____	______	____	______
________	____	______	____	______
________	____	______	____	______
________	____	______	____	______
________	____	______	____	______
________	____	______	____	______
________	____	______	____	______
________	____	______	____	______
________	____	______	____	______
________	____	______	____	______
	____	______	____	______
Net present value of cash flows				======

Capital expenditures typically involve more than one or two cash flows. Many cash flows may occur each year, some inflows and some outflows. This pattern may extend over five or more years. For this reason, most businesses use a standard form to organize inflows and outflows and to calculate their net present value. Exhibit 14–1 shows one such form. The nature of each cash flow is listed as a separate item in the left column. Investment in machinery, working capital, sales revenues, operating expenses, and salvage values should also be listed there. Annuities should be listed once for the series of years they cover. If the amount of an item changes, it must be relisted for each year in which it differs.

The second column of the exhibit shows the time at which each cash flow occurs. Usually, a cash flow is assumed to occur at year-end. A cash flow occurring at the start of a project is listed as occurring at the end of year zero, or "now."

The third column shows the amount of each cash flow, whether a single flow or an annuity. The fourth column lists the appropriate present value factor, which depends on the discount rate, the year the flow occurs, and whether it is a single amount or an annuity. The present value factor of a single cash flow received in the future will always be less than 1. The present value factor of an annuity may be greater than 1. (A comprehensive listing of present value factors is found in Appendix A at the end of this book.) The present value factor for any cash flow occurring at the start of a project is 1.00, since there is no delay in receiving the cash flow. (That is, it does not need to be discounted.)

Finally, annual cash flows are multiplied by their present value factors to obtain the present value of each cash flow, which is shown in the last column.

The total of that column (including the amount of the investment at the start of the project) yields the project's **net present value.**

Now that you have seen how a relatively simple capital expenditure — the purchase of a video game — is evaluated, you will examine two more complicated proposals: introduction of a new product and replacement of an old machine.

New Product Investment

OBJECTIVE 4
Evaluate capital expenditure proposals for new products and machine replacement

Launching a new product often requires various expenditures. Exhibit 14–2 summarizes the cash flows connected with one new product, including the purchase of a new machine for $74,000 and the cost of installing and testing it. Notice that besides the cost of the machine, an additional $6,000 must be invested in working capital for such items as inventory and accounts receivable by the end of the first year. This is an important characteristic of new product proposals. Investing in a machine to produce an old product usually requires no increase in inventory or accounts receivable. Those investments already exist.

Notice also that the machine is expected to produce declining revenues over its five-year life, since competition will reduce the selling price. The cash expenses

Exhibit 14–2

Completed Expenditure Worksheet for a New Product

The project being considered is a new product. Parentheses indicate cash outflows.

Project Name Product Saturn Department Celeste

Item	End of year	Amount of cash flow	Present value factor @ 18%	Present value of cash flow
Cost of machine	0	$(74,000)	1.0000	$(74,000)
Added working capital	1	(6,000)	0.8475	(5,085)
Sales revenues	1	60,000	0.8475	50,850
	2	50,000	0.7182	35,910
	3	40,000	0.6086	24,344
	4	30,000	0.5158	15,474
	5	26,000	0.4371	11,365
Cash operating expenses	1–5	(18,000)	3.1272	(56,290)
Salvage value of machine	5	2,000	0.4371	874
Recovery of working capital investment	5	6,000	0.4371	2,623
Net present value of cash flows				$ 6,065

of operating the machine, such as direct materials, labor, supplies, and electricity, are expected to be a constant $18,000 per year. The machine's salvage value and the recovery of working capital when the product is discontinued are also shown. The working capital will be recovered by using up inventory over the last year and collecting on accounts receivable.

The project summarized in Exhibit 14–2 yields a positive net present value when a discount rate of 18 percent is used. That is, if actual cash flows equal the estimates on the worksheet, the project will yield a return of more than 18 percent. Since the new product is expected to return more than the company's minimum rate of return, management will probably decide to invest in it. The project must meet other long-range organizational objectives, however. For example, management would probably not want to invest in a new product if its product line is scheduled to be discontinued.

Exhibit 14–3

Completed Capital Expenditure Worksheet for a Machine Replacement

This worksheet compares two alternative proposals. Alternative 1 is to keep an existing machine with a current salvage value of $7,000 and relatively high operating costs. Alternative 2 is to buy a new machine for $16,000 and reduce operating costs. Both the existing machine and its replacement will have a useful life of four years. (Parentheses indicate cash outflow).

Project name Milling Machine Department Machining

Item	End of year	Amount of cash flow	Present value factor @ 15%	Present value of cash flow
		Alternative 1: Keep Old Machine		
Salvage value of machine 1	0	$ (7,000)	1.0000	$ (7,000)
Cash operating expenses	1–4	(5,000)	2.8550	(14,275)
Salvage value of machine 1	4	1,000	0.5718	572
Net present value of cash flows				$(20,703)
		Alternative 2: Buy New Machine		
Cost of machine 2	0	$(16,000)	1.0000	$(16,000)
Cash operating expenses	1–4	(3,000)	2.8550	(8,565)
Salvage value of machine 2	4	2,000	0.5718	1,144
Net present value of cash flows				$(23,421)

Machine Replacement

Another common capital expenditure is the replacement of an old machine. Assume a company is considering buying a new machine to replace an old one. The current salvage value of the existing machine is $7,000. Thus, it could now be sold for $7,000. Its annual cash operating expenses are $5,000. Although the new machine requires an investment of $16,000, since it is more efficient than the old machine, it will reduce annual operating expenses to $3,000. Neither machine requires additional working capital. The expected life of the new machine is four years, after which its salvage value will be $2,000. Although the old machine is also expected to last for the next four years, its salvage value at the end of four years will be only $1,000. Both machines can produce the quantity of product demanded, so unit sales will be the same regardless of which machine is used.

Since revenue will be the same in either case, the question is which machine will have the lower present value of cash outflows over the next four years. You must use present value for this comparison because the timing of cash outflows differs for each machine. Exhibit 14–3 shows a comparison of the two alternatives. A discount rate of 15 percent is used. Notice that the old machine's present salvage value is counted as a cash outflow in Alternative 1. If the old machine is not kept, the company will recover its present market value of $7,000. This money can then be used for other purposes, such as paying for a new machine. Deciding to keep the old machine is essentially a decision to forgo recovery of that $7,000.

As you can see, the present value of the firm's cash outflows will be $2,718 lower ($23,421 - $20,703) if the old machine is kept. Thus, managers should decide to keep the old machine as long as it can produce the product when needed and according to acceptable quality standards.

■

The Incremental Approach to Evaluation

When a capital expenditure proposal involves a comparison of two alternatives, as in the replacement of a machine, some people prefer to compare the net present values of incremental cash flows rather than total cash flows. An **incremental cash flow** is the difference between the yearly cash flows of two alternatives. The advantage of the incremental approach is that it reduces the number of computations needed. The incremental approach can be confusing, however, especially if more than two alternatives must be evaluated. Although the total cash flow approach illustrated in Exhibit 14–3 is generally recommended, managers should be familiar with both methods.

Exhibit 14–4 shows present value calculations for the same proposal as Exhibit 14–3, using the incremental approach. In the first part of the exhibit, the

Exhibit 14–4

The Incremental Approach to Present Value Analysis

When two alternate proposals are evaluated, the total cost of each need not be discounted, as in Exhibit 14–3. Instead, the present value of the incremental cash flows can be found.

Computation of Incremental Cash Flows

Item	End of year	Cash flow alternative 2 (buy new machine)	Cash flow alternative 1 (keep old machine)	Incremental cash flow of alternative 2
Cost/salvage of machine	0	$(16,000)	$(7,000)	$(9,000)
Cash operating expenses	1–4	(3,000)	(5,000)	2,000
Salvage value of machine	4	2,000	1,000	1,000

Computation of Present Values of Incremental Cash Flow

Item	End of year	Incremental cash flow	Present value factor @ 15%	Present value of alternative 2 incremental cash flows
Cost/salvage of machine	0	$(9,000)	1.0000	$(9,000)
Cash operating expenses	1–4	2,000	2.8550	5,710
Salvage value of machine	4	1,000	0.5718	572
Net present value of incremental cash flows				$(2,718)

OBJECTIVE 5
Compute the net present value of an incremental cash flow

cash flow of each alternative is computed year by year. In the two columns for cash flow alternatives, parentheses indicate cash outflow just as before. In the last column, the yearly cash flows for Alternative 1 are subtracted from the yearly cash flows for Alternative 2 to obtain incremental cash flows. Parentheses in this last column indicate that Alternative 2 has a disadvantage over Alternative 1. A lack of parentheses means that Alternative 2 has an advantage over Alternative 1. Finally, in the second part of the exhibit, the present values of these incremental cash flows are computed and totaled.

The negative net present value of the total incremental cash flows of Alternative 2 shows that Alternative 1 is better than Alternative 2. The company should keep the old machine as long as it can reliably produce the items needed. Notice that this conclusion matches the one reached in Exhibit 14–3. The net present value of the incremental cash flows shown in Exhibit 14–4 ($2,718) equals the difference between the present values of the total costs of the two alternatives listed in Exhibit 14–3 ($20,703 − $23,421). The two methods should always yield the same conclusion and the same numerical difference in present values.

Review Exercise 14–2

Net Present Value Approach to Evaluating Capital Expenditures

March Restaurant is considering replacing its dishwashing machine. The new machine has a larger capacity. The larger capacity will save labor cost. The machine will use more electricity but save hot water since it has an improved spray. Maintenance cost should also be lower on the new machine. The old machine has an estimated remaining useful life of seven years. The old machine has $1,800 salvage value now but will have no salvage value at the end of seven years.

The new machine is expected to have a useful life of seven years. It will cost $9,000. It will have $2,000 salvage value at the end of seven years.

The annual operating costs of the two machines are estimated as follows:

	Old machine	New machine
Labor	$17,000	$14,000
Utilities	2,000	1,600
Maintenance	1,500	300

Required

Prepare a capital expenditure analysis worksheet for the machine replacement showing the net present value of replacing the dishwashing machine. Assume that March's uses a discount rate of 18 percent.

Solution

March Restaurant

Project name Dishwashing machine replacement

Item	End of year	Amount of cash flow	Present value factor @ 18%	Present value of cash flow
		Alternative 1: Keep Old Machine		
Salvage value of old machine	0	$ (1,800)	1.0000	$ (1,800)
Labor cost	1–7	(17,000)		
Utilities	1–7	(2,000)		
Maintenance	1–7	(1,500)		
Subtotal	1–7	(20,500)	3.8115	(78,136)
Present value of cash flows				$(79,936)
		Alternative 2: Buy New Machine		
Cost of new machine	0	$ (9,000)	1.0000	$ (9,000)
Labor cost	1–7	(14,000)		
Utilities	1–7	(1,600)		
Maintenance	1–7	(300)		
Subtotal	1–7	(15,900)	3.8115	(60,603)
Salvage value of new machine	7	2,000	0.3139	628
Present value of cash flows				$(68,975)

March should buy the new machine because its present value cost is lower than the present value cost of keeping the old machine.

(see Exercises 27, 28, 29)

■

Time-Adjusted Rate of Return: An Alternate Method of Analysis

Earlier in this chapter we considered whether various projects would earn a minimum rate of return. A **minimum rate of return** is the return management thinks it must earn to encourage outside capital investment in its business. The minimum rate of return was used as a discount rate in calculating the present value of future cash flows.

Another way of evaluating capital expenditures is to calculate the time-adjusted rate of return of a proposed investment and to compare it with the minimum rate of return. The **time-adjusted rate of return**, also called the *internal rate of return,* is the discount rate that yields a zero net present value when used to find the present value of a project's cash flows. It can be thought of as a project's economic rate of return. If a project's time-adjusted rate of return is greater than the organization's minimum rate of return, the project is acceptable. If the time-adjusted rate of return is lower than the organization's minimum rate of return, the project is unacceptable as planned and should probably not be considered further.

Calculating the Time-Adjusted Rate of Return

OBJECTIVE 6
Calculate and use the time-adjusted rate of return to evaluate a capital expenditure proposal

The only way of finding the time-adjusted rate of return is by trial and error. First, estimate the project's future cash flows as you would if you were estimating net present value. Then, calculate the net present value of the project's cash flows at an arbitrarily selected discount rate. Often the organization's minimum rate of return is a good starting point. If the resulting net present value is positive, the calculation is repeated with a higher discount rate. If the net present value is negative, the calculation is repeated with a lower discount rate. When a discount rate yielding a net present value of zero is found, that discount rate is the time-adjusted rate of return.

Suppose a firm is considering an $80,000 investment in a new product. Sales of that new product will produce annual net cash inflows of $20,000 a year for the next six years. (The net cash inflows were obtained by subtracting annual cash operating expenses from annual revenue.) First, calculate the net present value of the project, using the organization's minimum rate of return of 10 percent as the discount rate, as shown in Exhibit 14–5. Since the net present value of the

Exhibit 14–5

Completed Capital Expenditure Analysis Worksheet for a New Product

Finding the time-adjusted rate of return on a capital expenditure proposal for a new product is a trial-and-error process. The first trial uses the organization's minimum rate of return of 10 percent as the discount rate. The positive net present value tells you that the time-adjusted rate of return is greater than 10 percent.

Item	End of year	Amount of cash flow	Present value factor @ 10%	Present value of cash flow
Investment	0	$(80,000)	1.00	$(80,000)
Net cash inflows	1–6	20,000	4.3553	87,106
Net present value of cash flows				$ 7,106

Exhibit 14–6

Completed Capital Expenditure Analysis Worksheet for a New Product

The calculations in Exhibit 14–5 showed that the time-adjusted rate of return for this new product is greater than 10 percent. To continue the trial-and-error process, you should redo the calculations, using a higher discount rate of, say, 15 percent. The negative net present value tells you the time-adjusted rate of return is less than 15 percent.

Item	End of year	Amount of cash flow	Present value factor @ 15%	Present value of cash flow
Investment	0	$(80,000)	1.00	$(80,000)
Net cash inflows	1–6	20,000	3.7845	75,690
Net present value of cash flows				$ (4,310)

project is positive, the time-adjusted rate of return must be more than 10 percent. Thus, a higher discount rate of 15 percent is tried, as shown in Exhibit 14–6.

This time the net present value is negative by $4,310. Thus, the time adjusted rate of return must be between 10 and 15 percent. It should be closer to 15 percent, since the net present value was closer to zero when a 15 percent discount rate was used. Another trial, using 13 percent as the discount rate, is shown in Exhibit 14–7. As you can see, for all practical purposes the net present value is zero at 13 percent. (The negative present value of $50 is small compared with the $80,000 investment in the project.) Therefore, the time-adjusted rate of return on this project is 13 percent. Since the firm's minimum rate of return is 10 percent, the project should be accepted.

Finding the time-adjusted rate of return is always a trial-and-error process. There is a short cut, however, when future cash inflows are equal for each year,

Exhibit 14–7

Completed Capital Expenditure Analysis Worksheet for a New Product

The calculations in Exhibit 14–5 and Exhibit 14–6 show that the time-adjusted rate of return for this new product is greater than 10 percent but less than 15 percent. Since the net present value is closest to zero when the 15 percent discount rate was used, the time-adjusted rate of return must be closer to 15 percent than to 10 percent. To continue the trial-and-error processes, you should redo the calculations using 13 percent as the discount rate. The near zero net present value tells you the time-adjusted rate of return in close to 13 percent.

Item	End of year	Amount of cash flow	Present value factor @ 13%	Present value of cash flow
Investment	0	$(80,000)	1.00	$(80,000)
Net cash inflows	1–6	20,000	3.9975	79,950
Net present value of cash flows				$ (50)

as in the example. Future cash flows of an equal amount each year are an annuity. Appendix A, Table A–2, at the end of the book gives the present value for an annuity of $1 per year. To find the time-adjusted rate of return, you must go through two steps. In step 1 you must find the amount the firm is paying for each dollar of future annuities. To do so, divide the initial cash outflow by annual net cash inflow. In step 2 you must search the row in the annuity table corresponding to the last year of the project's life to find the amount closest to that found in step 1. You should read up the column to the discount rate at the top.

In the example just given, the firm paid $80,000 for an annuity of $20,000 per year. That is equivalent to paying $4 for an annuity of $1 per year ($80,000 ÷ $20,000). In the period 6 row in Appendix A, Table A–2, the numbers closest to 4 are 3.8887 and 4.1114. In fact, 4 is almost exactly halfway between 3.8887 and 4.1114. Reading up, you see that the discount rates for those amounts are 14 percent and 12 percent, respectively. It therefore follows that a six-year annuity worth $4 on every dollar has a time-adjusted rate of return of approximately 13 percent. This is the same conclusion reached by using the trial-and-error method (Exhibit 14–7). Remember that this short cut can only be used if future cash flows are equal for all years of a project's life.

Interpolating to Find the Time-Adjusted Rate of Return

OBJECTIVE 7
Find the time-adjusted rate of return for a project whose present value factor is not listed in a present value table

Interpolation is the process of estimating a number between two adjacent numbers in a table. This process was done informally in the last section by noting that for six years the present value factor of 4 was almost exactly halfway between factors for the discount rates of 12 percent and 14 percent. The time-adjusted rate of return was therefore estimated at 13 percent. Usually, a factor will not be exactly halfway between two listed factors. Therefore, some calculations must be made to find the appropriate discount rate.

Suppose a project requiring an initial investment of $12,000 is being considered. The project will return equal annual net cash flows of $2,843 for ten years. By dividing the $12,000 initial investment by the $2,843 in annual net cash inflows, you find that each $1.00 in annuity costs $4.2209. Next, you go to the annuity table and look for 4.2209 in the ten-period row. You find a value of 4.4941 in the 18 percent column and 4.1925 in the 20 percent column. This investment's value of 4.2209 is between these two numbers, although it is closer to 4.1925 than to 4.4941. Hence, you know that the time-adjusted rate of return is between 18 and 20 percent and that it is closer to 20 percent than 18 percent.

The percentage rate can be more closely estimated by interpolating. To do so:

1. Find the difference between the calculated value for the project, 4.2209, and the larger present value factor that surrounds the calculated amount (18 percent column). For our example, 4.4941 − 4.2209 = 0.2732.
2. Next, find the difference between the two factors in the same row of the table that surrounds the calculated present value. For our example, 4.4941 − 4.1925 = 0.3016.

3. Then divide the difference found in step *1* by the difference found in step *2* and multiply the result by the difference in the rates at the top of the two columns surrounding your value. For our example, (0.2732 ÷ 0.3016) × 2 percent = 1.8 percent.
4. Finally, add the result of step *3* to the rate at the top of the column that is larger than the calculated amount. This is the interpolated time-adjusted rate of return. For our example, 18 percent + 1.8 percent = 19.8 percent.

The calculations just illustrated are shown in more compact form below.

	Present value factors	
18% factor	4.4941	4.4941
Project factor	4.2209	
20% factor		4.1925
Difference	0.2732	0.3016

$$\frac{0.2732}{0.3016} \times 2\% = 1.8\%$$

Time-adjusted rate = 18% + 1.8%
= 19.8%

■

Postaudit of Capital Expenditures

OBJECTIVE 8
Describe a postaudit of a capital expenditure and explain its uses

Once a capital expenditure has been made, management will want to see whether actual results correspond to expected results. Such a comparison usually requires a special study called a **postaudit** of capital expenditures.

A postaudit serves two main purposes. First, it helps ensure that capital expenditure proposals are realistic. Postaudits identify future cash flow projections that have proved inaccurate over time. A firm can then improve or change its projection techniques. Also, managers tend to be more careful in making projections if they know their accuracy will be checked.

Second, a postaudit signals the need for corrective action in capital expenditure projects not meeting management's expectations. Corrective action often improves implementation of a project so it can meet expectations. In some cases, however, a project is simply bad and should be canceled before further resources are committed.

Accountants perform postaudits by collecting data on actual cash flows. Results are then compared with the projections on which the original proposal was based. If the proposal involves cash inflows from future sales revenues, accountants compare actual revenue over the first few years with projected revenue for those years. If the proposal projected cash benefits from labor savings, accountants try to determine the actual amount of labor savings realized.

The main difficulty in performing a postaudit is that accounting records usually show only combined revenues, expenses, and cash flows for an organization or division as a whole. Capital expenditures, however, are approved as single projects, which may be only a small part of a department's activity. A project may also span several departments. Accounting records may show the total labor costs incurred in a department, but not the labor costs incurred on a particular machine. And they do not normally show savings in labor costs. To find labor savings, accountants must do a thorough search of such original documents as time tickets and cost records that predate a capital expenditure.

Chapter Review

Review of Learning Objectives

1. **Define capital expenditures and explain how they relate to long-range plans.**
A capital expenditure is an investment in an asset whose useful life is more than one year. Long-range plans for new products and new production and distribution facilities usually require capital expenditures. If such expenditures are not carefully evaluated, they may interfere with rather than aid in accomplishing long-range objectives.

2. **Define discounted cash flow and explain its usefulness in analyzing capital expenditure proposals.**
Other things being equal, people prefer to receive cash payments now rather than in the future. A cash payment received or paid in the future has a lower value than one received or paid now. Discounted cash flows are a way of putting future cash flows on a basis equivalent with present cash flows. They reduce the value of future cash flows to an equivalent present value, so flows occurring at different future times may be compared. Thus, discounted cash flows are useful in analyzing the value of capital expenditure proposals and the relative value of competing capital expenditure proposals.

3. **Calculate the present value of future cash flows.**
Present value is the amount that if invested in the present at a given rate of return will provide a specified amount in the future. The process of calculating the present value of a future amount, called discounting, can be summarized in the formula:

$$P = \frac{F_n}{(1 + r)^n}$$

However, tables such as those in Appendix A are usually used.

4. **Evaluate capital expenditure proposals for new products and machine replacement.**
Capital expenditures are evaluated by projecting the future cash flows they will generate and calculating their present value at some minimum rate of return. For a new product to meet the minimum rate of return, the net present value of all cash flows must be equal to or greater than zero. When deciding whether to replace a machine, the objective is to

minimize the present value of cash outflows. Cash flows from keeping an old machine and buying a new one are both estimated. The present value of the net outflow of each machine is then calculated. The better alternative is the one with the lower present value.

5. **Compute the net present value of an incremental cash flow.**
When two alternatives are proposed, the incremental cash flow is the difference between the net present value of each alternative for each year. The cash flows of both alternatives must be projected and subtracted from each other. Then, the incremental cash flows are discounted to their present value. This method can become confusing, especially if more than two alternatives are being considered.

6. **Calculate and use the time-adjusted rate of return to evaluate a capital expenditure proposal.**
The time-adjusted rate of return is an alternative to the net present value method of evaluating capital expenditures. The time-adjusted rate of return is the discount rate that yields a net present value of zero when used to find the present value of a project's cash flows. First, cash inflows and outflows are listed for each year. Then, various discount rates are tried until one yields a net present value close to zero. If the resulting rate is greater than a firm's minimum rate of return, the project is acceptable. If the rate is lower, the project should probably be rejected.

7. **Find the time-adjusted rate of return for a project whose present value factor is not listed in a present value table.**
Interpolation is the process of estimating a number between two adjacent numbers in a table. To determine this number, first search the row which equals the life of the project. Find the two values in the row that surround the calculated value for the project. Then find the difference between the value of the rate you are seeking and the present value factor of the discount rate just below that. Next, find the difference between the two factors surrounding the present value factor of the project in the table. Then, divide one difference by the other and multiply by the difference between the two discount rates. This yields the position of the factor between the two rates as a percentage. Last, add the result to the lower of the two rates. (See pages 675 and 676 for an example of this calculation.)

8. **Describe a postaudit of a capital expenditure and explain its uses.**
A postaudit of a capital expenditure compares actual results of a capital expenditure with results expected when the project was approved. Postaudits are used to improve projection techniques, to encourage managers to make realistic projections, and to uncover projects not proceeding according to plan. Such projects may need corrective action. The main difficulty in performing a postaudit is that accounting records show revenues, expenses, and cash flows for an organization or division as a whole, while capital expenditures are approved and must be audited as projects.

Review of Key Terms

Annuity A series of payments of equal amount received at regular intervals.

Capital expenditure Investment in an asset whose useful life is more than one year.

Compounding Earning interest on interest.

Current expenditure Purchase of an asset of value only during the current year.

Discounting A technique for reducing the value of future receipts to an equivalent present value.

Future value An amount available at some specific time in the future because a specific amount was invested today at a specified rate of return. Includes both principal and interest.

Incremental cash flow The difference between the yearly cash flows of two alternate investments.

Interpolation The process of estimating a number between two adjacent numbers in a table.

Minimum rate of return Return that management thinks it must earn to encourage investors to invest capital in a business. Often used as a discount rate in calculating present value of future cash flows.

Net present value Total value of a project's future cash returns discounted to their present value at the minimum rate of return minus the required initial investment (cash outflows). A project with a zero or positive net present value can be expected to earn at least the minimum rate of return. A project with a negative net present value will probably earn less than the minimum rate of return.

Postaudit A special study done after a capital expenditure has been made to see whether actual results correspond to expected results.

Present value Amount that if invested now at a given rate of return will provide a specified future amount.

Present value factor In a present value table, an amount showing the present value of $1 or of an annuity of $1 received at some specified future time or times at a specified discount rate. (See Appendix A at the end of the book.)

Rate of return Return on an investment expressed as a percentage of the amount invested.

Time-adjusted rate of return Discount rate yielding a zero net present value when used to find the present value of a project's cash flows. Also called *internal rate of return.*

Time value of money Preference for receipt of payment immediately rather than at some future time. It is the basis for discounting cash flows.

Review Problem

Berryman Company's internal auditor is reviewing a request to purchase a machine to produce a new product. Data related to the proposal are as follows:

Annual revenue	$41,400
Annual cash expenses	30,500
Cost of machine	32,000
Machine installation and testing	3,000
Project's life	5 years
Minimum rate of return	16%
Expected salvage value of the machine	$0

Required

1. Calculate the project's net present value.
2. Calculate the project's time-adjusted rate of return.

3. The internal auditor has discovered that the original proposal neglected to include a $4,000 investment in working capital at the end of year 1. It will be recovered at the end of year 5. Can the project still be expected to earn the minimum rate of return of 16 percent?

Solution to Review Problem

1. The project's net present value is best calculated by using a capital expenditure analysis worksheet similar to Exhibit 14–1. The completed worksheet for Berryman Company is shown below. Since future cash flows are equal and occur every year, they may be considered an annuity.

Berryman Company
Capital Expenditure Analysis Worksheet for a New Product

Item	End of year	Amount of cash flow	Present value factor @ 16%	Present value of cash flow
Cost of machine	0	$(32,000)		
Installation and testing	0	(3,000)		
Subtotal	0	$(35,000)	1.0	$(35,000)
Sales revenues	1–5	$ 41,400		
Cash expenses	1–5	(30,500)		
Subtotal		$ 10,900	3.2743	35,690
Net present value				$ 690

Since the net present value is positive, this analysis shows that the machine's return on investment will be more than 16 percent.

2. Since annual cash inflows are constant, you can take the short cut to finding the time-adjusted rate of return as follows:

$$\frac{\text{Initial cash outflow}}{\text{Net annual cash inflow}} = \frac{\$32{,}000 + \$3{,}000}{\$41{,}400 - \$30{,}500} = \frac{\$35{,}000}{\$10{,}900} = \underline{\underline{\$3.2110}}$$

Berryman is paying $3.2110 per $1.00 of annuity. By searching the five-period row in the annuity table looking for 3.2110, you find that the project is between 3.2743, the present value factor for a discount rate of 16 percent, and 3.1272, the factor for 18 percent. To find the estimated time-adjusted rate, you interpolate as follows.

	Present value factors	
16% factor	3.2743	3.2743
Project factor	3.2110	
18% factor		3.1272
Difference	0.0633	0.1471

$$\frac{0.0633}{0.1471} \times 2\% = 0.0086$$

Time-adjusted rate of return = 16% + 0.86% = <u>16.86%</u>

3. The easiest way of finding the answer is to redo the project's capital expenditure analysis worksheet, found in *1* above, so it includes the new information. (See the modified worksheet below.) With the new information included, you see that the project will not earn Berryman's 16 percent minimum rate of return.

Berryman Company
Capital Expenditure Analysis Worksheet for a New Product
(omission of working capital investment corrected)

Item	End of year	Amount of cash flow	Present value factor @ 16%	Present value of cash flow
Cost of machine	0	$(32,000)		
Installation and testing	0	(3,000)		
Subtotal	0	$(35,000)	1.0	$(35,000)
Working capital	1	$ (4,000)	0.8621	$ (3,448)
Revenues	1–5	$ 41,400		
Cash expenses	1–5	(30,500)		
Subtotal		$ 10,900	3.2743	35,690
Recovery of working capital	5	4,000	0.4761	1,904
Net present value				$ (854)

Notice that the lines in color are the only difference between this worksheet and the one completed in *1* above. All other lines except net present value are identical to *1* above.

Chapter Assignments

Questions

1. (L.O. 1) Define a capital expenditure.
2. (L.O. 1) Why must capital expenditures be carefully analyzed?
3. (L.O. 1) Distinguish between return *on* investment and return *of* investment.
4. (L.O. 1) List the two most important characteristics of capital expenditures.
5. (L.O. 2) What individual preference gives rise to the time value of money?
6. (L.O. 2) What is meant by the term *discounted cash flow*?
7. (L.O. 2) Define future value. State a problem that could be solved by using the concept of future value.

8. (L.O. 3) Define present value. How is the concept used to evaluate capital expenditures?

9. (L.O. 3) Distinguish between the present value of an annuity and the present value of $1.

10. (L.O. 4) What specific management decisions require present value analysis?

11. (L.O. 5) What is the incremental approach to present value analysis? Can it be used for all capital expenditure decisions?

12. (L.O. 5) What is the disadvantage of using the incremental approach when three machines are being considered as a replacement for one machine?

13. (L.O. 6) Define time-adjusted rate of return.

14. (L.O. 7) How is the time-adjusted rate of return calculated?

15. (L.O. 8) List the objectives of a postaudit of capital expenditures.

16. (L.O. 8) How are postaudits of capital expenditures performed?

Exercises

17. (L.O. 3) You have just received a $24,913 bonus from your company for an invention. The company will either pay you the money immediately or will invest it for you and guarantee a 12 percent return compounded annually. You would like to buy a $35,000 automobile.

Required

1. If you allow the company to invest the money for you, how long will you have to wait before you can buy your $35,000 automobile?
2. If you are willing to settle for a car costing $31,250, how long must you wait?

(see Review Exercise 14–1)

18. (L.O. 3) You are 45 years old and intend to retire at age 62. You want to take a trip around the world when you retire. You estimate that the trip will cost $11,000 when you retire.

Required

1. How much must you invest now to finance your trip if you can invest at 8 percent compounded annually?
2. How much must you invest now to finance your trip if you can invest at 12 percent compounded annually?

(see Review Exercise 14–1)

19. (L.O. 3) Your parents have decided that they would like to put aside money for your child's college education. Your child will begin college in 12 years. You estimate that $32,000 will be required for your child's education.

Required

1. How much must be invested today if you can invest the funds at 8 percent compounded annually? Ten percent?
2. You are expecting another baby. Assume that this baby will not start college for 19 years. How much must be invested today to have $40,000 at the end of 19 years? Assume an 8 percent return on investment compounded annually.

(see Review Exercise 14–1)

20. (L.O. 3) You are now 55 years old and intend to retire at age 65. You are selling your house and moving into a retirement apartment building. You will receive $70,000 proceeds from selling your house. You intend to invest these proceeds to have as a fund when you retire.

Required

1. How much will you have in your fund if you invest the house proceeds at 8 percent compounded annually?
2. How much will you have in your fund if you invest the house proceeds at 10 percent compounded annually?

21. (L.O. 3, 4, 6, 7) Heslin, Inc., is considering investing $3,000 in a machine whose useful life is five years and whose salvage value is zero. Annual cash inflow from operations is expected to be $1,200.

Required

1. If Heslin's minimum rate of return is 20 percent, calculate the net present value of the machine.
2. Calculate the time-adjusted rate of return on Heslin's machine. (AICPA)

22. (L.O. 3, 4, 6, 7) Scott, Inc., is planning to invest $120,000 in a ten-year project. Scott estimates that annual cash inflow from this project will be $20,000. Scott's desired rate of return on such investments is 10 percent.

Required

1. Calculate the net present value of this project.
2. Calculate the time-adjusted rate of return on Scott's project. (AICPA)

23. (L.O. 3, 4, 6, 7) Herman Company bought an asset whose estimated life is ten years. The cost of the asset was $46,600. Annual net cash benefits are estimated at $10,000. They occur at the end of each year.

Required

1. Can the asset be expected to return Herman's minimum rate of return of 18 percent? Should the project be accepted?
2. Calculate the time-adjusted rate of return on Herman's project. (AICPA)

24. (L.O. 3, 4) Gene, Inc., is considering investing $8,000 in a machine whose useful life is six years and whose salvage value is $500. The machine is expected to produce annual cash inflows of $2,000.

Required

Using a discount rate of 20 percent, calculate the net present value of the investment. (AICPA)

25. (L.O. 3, 4) Jenkins, Inc., is considering buying a new machine for $520,000. The machine's useful life is eight years, and its salvage value at the end of eight years, $10,000. The machine is expected to produce annual cash inflows from operations of $120,000.

Required

If Jenkins's minimum rate of return is 15 percent, what is the machine's net present value? (AICPA)

26. (L.O. 3, 4) Heller Company is considering buying a machine for $500,000 to produce a new product. The machine's useful life is five years. Its salvage value at the end of five years is $30,000. The new product will produce revenue of $450,000 per year for each of the five years. Cash operating expenses for five years will be $300,000 per year.

Required

If Heller uses a minimum rate of return of 15 percent to evaluate capital expenditures, what is the machine's net present value? (AICPA)

27. (L.O. 3, 4) Ace Distribution Service delivers advertising leaflets to homes. Until now, they have used people on foot carrying a shoulder bag. The number of leaflets that could be delivered depended on the number of leaflets that a person could carry. Ace is considering buying motor scooters for use by the delivery people. This would make delivery more rapid where the houses are widely separated. More importantly, the motor scooters would permit a delivery person to carry a much larger supply of leaflets.

 Ace expects the motor scooters to have a four-year useful life. They will cost $3,500 each and will have $500 salvage value at the end of four years.

 The yearly costs of delivering a fixed number of leaflets by each method is as follows:

	Old method	Use of scooter
Labor	$24,000	$17,000
Fuel		60
Maintenance		400

Required Prepare a capital expenditure analysis worksheet for the two delivery methods showing the present value of each alternative. Assume that Ace's discount rate is 18 percent. Which alternative should Ace select? (see Review Exercise 14–2)

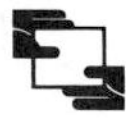

28. (L.O. 3, 4) Avril Corporation uses personal computers for typing letters and other documents. They are considering replacing some machines that are four years old with new machines. The new machines will have a faster central processing unit and will have large hard disks. The old computers used only floppy disks for data storage. Workers would spend a great deal of time searching for disks with previous letters that could be changed and then changing disks. Sometimes, a worker would retype an entire letter because he or she could not find the earlier version to be revised.

 With continued maintenance, Avril thinks that the old machines could continue to be used. Their salvage value is presently $800 each but would be no more than $200 in three years. Avril expects the new computers to have a three-year useful life. They will cost $5,500 each and will have $500 salvage value at the end of three years.

 The yearly costs of preparing a certain number of letters using the old and new computers are as follows:

	Old computer	New computer
Labor	$30,000	$24,000
Disks and supplies	800	200
Maintenance	300	100

Required Prepare a capital expenditure analysis worksheet for the two computers showing the present value of each alternative. Assume that Avril's discount rate is 20 percent. Which alternative should Avril select? (see Review Exercise 14–2)

29. (L.O. 3, 4) Fred Jones is considering purchasing a snow blower for removing snow from his driveway and sidewalks. Until now, he has hired a plowing company that comes after each snowfall and removes the snow. Fred thinks using a snow blower might be fun. With it, he could help his neighbors. He could also clear his sidewalks more quickly than the plowing company can.

The cost of the plowing company has averaged $140 per year. The snow blower would cost $800. It would use $5 worth of gasoline each year and would require an average of $40 per year maintenance. Fred expects its useful life would be seven years, at which time the snow blower would have a salvage value of $50.

Required Prepare a capital expenditure analysis worksheet for the two alternatives showing the present value of each alternative. Assume Fred's discount rate is 8 percent. Which alternative should Fred select? (see Review Exercise 14–2)

Problems

30. (L.O. 3, 4) Sant Company plans to invest $40,000 in a machine with a useful life of five years and a $5,000 salvage value. In addition, $4,000 must be invested in working capital by the end of the first year. It will be recovered at the end of the fifth year. Sant estimates that annual revenue will be $21,000. Cash operating expenses from operations will be $10,800. Sant's minimum rate of return on this type of investment is 10 percent.

Required Calculate this project's net present value. (AICPA)

31. (L.O. 3, 4) Roberts, Inc., is considering buying a machine for $240,000. The machine has a useful life of six years and no salvage value at the end of six years. The machine will be used to produce a new product that is expected to generate revenue of $150,000 per year. Cash operating expenses from operations are expected to be $80,000 in each of the six years. By the end of year 1, $10,000 will be invested in working capital. It will be recovered at the end of the year 6. Roberts's minimum rate of return is 15 percent.

Required What is the project's net present value? (AICPA)

32. (L.O. 3, 4) Virginia Company invested $13,000 in a four-year project. Virginia's expected rate of return is 12 percent. Additional information on the project is as follows:

Year	Cash inflow from operations
1	$4,000
2	4,400
3	4,800
4	5,200

The project will have a salvage value of $500 at the end of the fourth year.

Required Calculate the net present value of the project. (AICPA)

33. (L.O. 3, 4) Kipling Company invested a single amount in an eight-year project. Its expected annual cash flow is $20,000. Kipling's analysis of the project showed that it would earn a rate of return on investment of exactly 20 percent

Required How much did Kipling invest in the project? (AICPA)

34. (L.O. 3, 4) Garwood Company has purchased a machine whose estimated useful life is seven years. The machine has no salvage value. The machine is expected to

generate cash inflows of $80,000 from operations in each of the seven years. Garwood's expected rate of return is 20 percent.

Required If Garwood's analysis shows a positive net present value of $12,700, how much did the machine cost? (AICPA)

35. (L.O. 3, 4) Tracy Corporation plans to invest $80,000 in a three-year project. Tracy's minimum rate of return is 10 percent. Cash inflow will be $30,000 for the first year; $36,000 for the second year.

Required Assume the rate of return on this project is exactly 10 percent. What must cash inflow be in the third year? (AICPA)

36. (L.O. 3, 4) Hilltop Company invested $100,000 in a two-year project. Cash inflow was $40,000 for the first year.

Required Assume the rate of return on this project is exactly 15 percent. What must cash inflow be for the second year of the project? (AICPA)

37. (L.O. 3, 4, 5) Maxwell Company has the opportunity to acquire a new machine that would replace a present machine. The new machine would cost $90,000 and have a five-year life. The estimated salvage value at the end of five years if $10,000. Cash operating costs of the new machine will be $100,000 per year. The present machine's remaining life is five years. Its present salvage value is $5,000. After five years the salvage value will be zero. Cash operating costs of the old machine will be $130,000 per year. Maxwell's minimum rate of return is 20 percent.

Required

1. Calculate the net present value of cash outflows separately for each machine over the next five years. Should Maxwell Company replace its present machine?
2. Using the incremental approach as shown in Exhibit 14–4 to make your calculations, determine if Maxwell Company should purchase the new machine. (AICPA)

38. (L.O. 3, 4, 5) The production manager at Morgan Company has proposed buying a new machine to replace a present one. The new machine would cost $40,000 and have a six-year life. The estimated salvage value at the end of six years is $2,000. Cash operating costs of the new machine will be $30,000 per year. The present machine's remaining life is six years. Its salvage value now is $1,000. The salvage value will be zero after six years. Cash operating costs of the old machine will be $42,000 per year. Morgan's minimum rate of return is 16 percent.

Required

1. Calculate the net present value of cash outflows separately for each machine over the next six years. Should the Morgan Company replace its present machine?
2. Using the incremental approach shown in Exhibit 14–4, determine if Morgan Company should purchase the new machine.

39. (L.O. 3, 4) Rockyford Company is considering replacing a machine. The machine's current market value is $2,800. Its remaining useful life is estimated to be four years. Its annual cash operating costs will be $22,500. After four years the old machine's salvage value will be zero. The new machine will cost $40,000. Its estimated annual cash operating costs will be $10,000, and its estimated useful life will be four years. The salvage value will be $2,000 at the end of four years. This new machine will require an additional $3,000 investment in inventory by the end of the first year. The inventory investment will be recovered at the end of the fourth year. Rockyford's minimum rate of return on investments of this type is 15 percent.

Required Should Rockyford Company replace its current machine?

40. (L.O. 3, 4, 5) Tackless Company is considering two new machines to replace an existing one. One new machine costs $20,000 and has a four-year life. Its estimated salvage value at the end of four years is $5,000 Cash operating costs of this new machine will be $30,000 per year.

    The second machine being considered costs $40,000 and has a four-year life. Its estimated salvage value at the end of four years is $8,000. Cash operating costs of this new machine will be $21,000 per year.

    The present machine has a remaining useful life of four years. Its salvage value now is $3,000. It will be zero after four years. Cash operating costs on the old machine will be $37,000 per year. Tackless Company's minimum rate of return is 24 percent.

Required

1. Calculate the net present value of cash outflows separately for each machine over the next four years. Should Tackless purchase either of the new machines?
2. Use the incremental approach to determine if Tackless Company should purchase either of the new machines. Two capital expenditure analysis worksheets similar to the one in Exhibit 14–4 will be needed.

41. (L.O. 3, 4) Amex Company is considering introducing a new product to be manufactured in an existing plant. New equipment, costing $150,000 with a useful life of five years and no salvage value, will be necessary. The space in the existing plant to be used for the new product is currently being used as a warehouse. When production of the new product begins, Amex plans to rent more warehouse space at an annual cost of $25,000. The new product will require a working capital investment of $70,000 by the end of the first year, which will be recovered at the end of the fifth year.

    An accounting study produced the following estimates of annual revenues and expenses:

Sales revenues	$500,000
Manufacturing expenses, excluding rent	385,000
Marketing expenses	10,000

The company requires a minimum rate of return of 15 percent on investment proposals.

Required

1. Calculate the net cash inflows for years 1 through 5. Include all amounts received, invested, or expended in each year except zero.
2. Should Amex produce the new product?

42. (L.O. 3, 4) Baxter Company manufactures toys and other short-lived products. The research and development department came up with a good promotional gift for office equipment dealers. Aggressive and effective efforts by Baxter's sales personnel have resulted in orders for this product for the next three years, which is the product's expected useful life.

    To produce the quantity demanded, Baxter needs to buy additional machinery and rent additional space. A total of 25,000 square feet of space is needed. Some time ago Baxter leased 12,500 square feet of space. Because of changes in operations, this space is unused and available. Baxter's present lease has ten remaining years. The space costs $3 per square foot. Another 12,500 square feet adjoining Baxter Company's facility can be rented for three years at $4 per square foot per year.

The new product will require equipment costing $900,000. In addition, the machine will require $30,000 in modifications, $60,000 for installation, and $90,000 for testing. All work will be done by a firm of engineers hired by Baxter. All expenditures will be paid for on January 1, 19x3.

The equipment should have a salvage value of about $180,000 at the end of the third year. No additional general overhead costs are expected to be incurred even though the company's accounting system allocates a share of total overhead to all products. The company estimates it will have the following amounts invested in working capital at the end of each year of the product's life:

19x3	$50,000
19x4	80,000
19x5	-0-

The following estimates of revenue and cash expenses for this product for three years were developed by the accounting department:

	19x3	19x4	19x5
Sales revenues	$1,000,000	$1,600,000	$800,000
Direct materials, labor, and overhead	400,000	750,000	350,000
Rent	87,500	87,500	87,500
Overhead	20,000	37,500	17,500

Required

1. Prepare a schedule showing relevant net cash inflows for this project for each of the next three years. Include all amounts received, invested, or expended in each year except zero. (Present value computations are not required to answer this question.)
2. A newly hired business school graduate has recommended use of the net present value method to evaluate this project. Will the project earn the company's minimum rate of return of 25 percent?

(CMA)

Case 1
Collins Company (L.O. 4, 8)

Collins Company is a publisher of books that relate personal histories of a family or an era. Most books are sold in low volume, but occasionally a book does much better than expected.

Two years ago, Collins approved spending $10,000 to publish a new book by the noted author, Bruno, because it fit the company objectives and it promised to yield return on investment of more than the company's minimum rate of 15 percent. One year after publication, Collins auditor, Lionel, is doing a postaudit of this decision.

Lionel does the postaudit by comparing results to date to the projections that were made at the time of the original decision. The company also makes new projections for the remaining life of the book to re-estimate its net present value.

Lionel has gathered the following data to use in the postaudit:

	Original forecast	Current actual or forecast
Selling price	$8.95	$8.95
Author royalties	0.60	0.60
Printing and binding costs	2.65	2.85
Advertising and distribution costs		
Year 1	$8,000	$7,500
Year 2	1,000	1,400*
Years 3–5	600	800*
Unit sales		
Year 1	3,000	4,500
Year 2	1,100	1,600*
Years 3–5	200	300*

*Indicates revised forecast made at the time of the postaudit.

No sales are expected after the fifth year. Actual development costs were $12,325.

Required

1. Prepare a capital expenditure analysis worksheet calculating the net present value of the book using the original forecast data. What was the book's projected net present value?
2. Prepare another capital expenditure analysis worksheet calculating the net present value using the current actual and forecast data. What is the book's projected net present value at the time of the postaudit?
3. What factors have contributed to the difference between the originally projected net present value and the current net present value? Use the data as appropriate in answering this question.

Case 2
Malleret College (L.O. 4, 8)

Malleret college makes many photocopies of teaching materials. Malleret presently contracts with Duplicopy, Inc., to do this photocopying. Duplicopy has set up a copy center on campus in space provided by Malleret. Duplicopy hires and pays staff of the copying center and owns the copy machines. Malleret pays for utilities and the copying paper used. Duplicopy charges Malleret 2.1 cents per copy for its services.

The head of Malleret's administrative services department has proposed that Malleret not renew its contract with Duplicopy. She has proposed that her department purchase machines and hire staff to do the necessary photocopying. The machines would cost $43,000 and would have $2,800 salvage value at the end of their five-year useful lives. She has estimated the cost of operating the department as follows on page 690, assuming that they make 3,875,000 copies per year.

Cost of copy machines	$43,000
Annual maintenance contract on machines	3,000
Salaries of supervisors	34,000
Wages of student workers to make copies	17,825
Cost of paper	15,500
Cost of electricity and utilities	3,100

In her analysis, the supervisor assumed that the wages of student workers and the cost of paper, electricity, and utilities were variable costs. She assumed that all other costs were fixed. The trustees of the college estimate Malleret's cost of capital to be 8 percent.

Required

1. Prepare a capital expenditure analysis worksheet to evaluate the proposal of the administrative services department head.
2. If you found that the proposal has a negative net present value, by how much would volume of copies need to increase to justify the change? If you found a positive net present value, by how much could the volume of copies fall and still justify the change?

■

15

Further Topics in Capital Expenditure Analysis

LEARNING OBJECTIVES

After studying this chapter you should be able to:

1. Calculate the after-tax benefit of a cash receipt and the after-tax cost of a cash expenditure
2. Calculate the depreciation tax shield using both accelerated and straight-line methods
3. Include the effects of income taxes in a capital expenditure analysis
4. Define cost of capital and explain how it relates to the choice between capital expenditure proposals
5. Calculate the profitability index and use it to rank capital expenditure proposals
6. Calculate the payback period for a capital expenditure proposal and discuss its limitations
7. Calculate the accounting rate of return for a capital expenditure proposal and discuss its limitations

Each time you receive a paycheck, you are reminded that income taxes are cash flows. You receive less than you earned because an amount was deducted for taxes. A business organization must also pay income taxes on its earnings, or profits. So when it makes a capital expenditure, it must consider how that expenditure will change income taxes as well as other aspects of cash flow.

Capital expenditure analysis was introduced in Chapter 14. In this chapter several additional topics will be covered. Those topics are: (1) the effect of income taxes on capital expenditures; (2) the determination of an organization's minimum rate of return; and (3) the ranking of capital expenditure proposals by profitability index, payback period, and accounting rate of return. Of these topics, the effect of income taxes is the most complex.

■

The Effect of Income Taxes on Capital Expenditures

In Chapter 14 you were introduced to the concepts of capital expenditure analysis, but the effects of income taxes were omitted to simplify your initial exposure to this topic. All organizations except not-for-profit organizations pay income taxes. Although income taxes do not change the basic concepts or procedures of capital expenditure analysis, they do add an income tax cash flow, which is complicated to calculate. If you understood the discussion of cash flow, present value, and discounting in Chapter 14, allowing for the effect of income taxes should be relatively easy.

Some cash flows associated with capital expenditure proposals are taxable; others are not. For instance, income from the sale of a machine for any amount other than the machine's book value affects income taxes, whereas the price of a machine and its installation costs do not. Taxable items will be discussed in the following sections of this chapter. Even though investment in and recovery of working capital affect cash flows, they do not affect taxes. Therefore, working capital is not included in the following discussion.

Gain or Loss from Selling Old Equipment

Generally, when a business asset is sold for more than its book value, the gain is taxable. A **gain** is the amount by which the selling price of an asset exceeds its book value. If the selling price is less than book value, the **loss** reduces income taxes. **Book value** is defined as the original cost less accumulated depreciation.

Book value = original cost of asset − accumulated depreciation

Suppose, for example, Cadam Company wants to buy a new desk and can sell an old one for $110. Accounting records show that the old desk was purchased for $400 and that its accumulated depreciation is $350. The desk's book value is therefore $50:

Original cost of $400 − accumulated depreciation of $350

Since the desk's $110 selling price is greater than its $50 book value, the company will realize a taxable gain of $60.

A gain from selling a business asset is taxed at the same rate as other income. If Cadam Company's regular income tax rate is 34 percent, then it must pay an additional $20.40 in income tax ($60 × 34%) on the gain. Thus, the cash inflow of $110.00 from selling the desk is partially offset by the cash outflow of $20.40 for income taxes. Net cash inflow is thus $89.60.

Now, consider a different situation. Suppose accumulated depreciation on the desk is only $250. In that case, the book value is $150 ($400 − $250). And its sale for $110 produces a tax loss of $40 ($150 − $110). By deducting the $40 loss, the company saves $13.60 in income taxes ($40 × 34%). Thus, selling the old desk creates a cash inflow of $110 plus a tax savings equivalent to a cash inflow of $13.60. The cash inflow plus the tax savings produce a net cash inflow of $123.60.

Next, assume the new desk costs $1,000 plus a $40 delivery charge. The buyer of the old desk picked it up, so there was no delivery charge on that sale. Now, if you return to the original assumption that the book value of the old desk was $50, cash flows at the time of purchase and sale would be as follows:

Purchase of new desk	$(1,000.00)
Delivery of new desk	(40.00)
Sale of old desk	110.00
Tax on gain from selling old desk	(20.40)
Net cash outflows	$ (950.40)

The net cash outflow from replacing the old desk is $950.40. This amount will appear as an immediate cash outflow (year 0) on the capital expenditure analysis worksheet.

Increased Revenues and Expenses

OBJECTIVE 1
Calculate the after-tax benefit of a cash receipt and the after-tax cost of a cash expenditure

Were you to ask the librarian at your college the cost of a reference book just purchased, he or she would probably tell you the purchase price, $50. But the manager of a profit-making business might respond with a lower amount. For income tax purposes, reference books are a deductible business expense. And that tax deduction changes the effective cost of the book. For this reason, business managers often think of costs on an after-tax basis. Because business expenses are usually deductible, expenses create two cash flows: an outflow to pay for the purchase and an inflow from income tax savings. In the example just given, if the income tax rate is 34 percent, the after-tax cost of the book is $33:

$$\$50 - (34\% \times \$50) = \$33$$

The $17 decrease in taxes is called the **expense tax effect.**

The same concept applies to added revenues, but the effect is the opposite. Increased revenues add to a business's cash flow and to its taxable income. Some of the cash inflow from revenues, however, is offset by a tax cash outflow. The amount by which taxes reduce revenues, is called the **revenue tax effect.**

Income taxes can significantly affect the cost of business expenses. For example, suppose a company is considering an employee training program that will cost $5,000. The company's income tax rate is 34 percent. Although the training program should increase company profitability over the long run, it is not expected to immediately affect income.

Exhibit 15–1 shows two projected monthly income statements for this company. One includes the expense of the training program; the other excludes it. Notice that although the program costs $5,000, the company's after-tax income will be reduced by only $3,300 if management decides to adopt the program.

Remember that this tax effect applies only to taxable items for profit-making organizations. The effect of taxes on revenues and expenses is calculated as follows:

$$\text{Tax effect on revenues} = \text{revenues} \times \text{tax rate}$$

$$\text{Tax effect on expenses} = \text{cash expenses} \times \text{tax rate}$$

Exhibit 15–1

Projected Income Statements With and Without Training Program

This exhibit shows how the deduction for training expenses will reduce the cost of that training. If $5,000 is spent on training, the difference in net income will only be $3,300. The $5,000 deduction will reduce income taxes by $1,700, making the after-tax cost $3,300.

	Without training	Difference	With training
Sales revenues	$150,000	—	$150,000
Cost of goods sold	$ 90,000	—	$ 90,000
Selling expenses	30,000	—	30,000
Training expenses	—	5,000	5,000
Other expenses	10,000	—	10,000
Total expenses	$130,000	5,000	$135,000
Income before taxes	$ 20,000	5,000	$ 15,000
Income taxes (34%)	6,800	(1,700)	5,100
Net income	$ 13,200		$ 9,900
Difference in net income		$ 3,300	

The Depreciation Tax Shield

OBJECTIVE 2
Calculate the depreciation tax shield using both accelerated and straight-line methods

Depreciation by itself does not enter into capital expenditure calculations, since annual depreciation is not a cash flow. But depreciation's effect on tax payments does need to be taken into account as tax payments are made in cash.

Since depreciation is deductible for income tax purposes, it reduces income tax payments. As a result, depreciation is sometimes referred to as a tax shield. Formally defined, a **depreciation tax shield** is the amount by which income taxes are reduced because of depreciation deductions. Calculating it is similar to calculating the tax effect of a deductible expense.

Depreciation tax shield = annual depreciation deduction × tax rate

For assets placed in service after 1986, accountants calculate depreciation deductions for income tax purposes using the **Modified Accelerated Cost Recovery System (MACRS)**. MACRS applies to assets placed in service after 1986. MACRS classifies all depreciable property by groups. The U.S. government publishes tables showing class lives for different kinds of assets. Class lives place the property in one of the categories listed below. If the asset is not listed in the table, you consider it seven-year property. The categories and examples of property in each are as follows:

- 3-year property: Property with class life of 4 years or less—over-the-road truck tractors and any race horse that was two years old when placed in service.
- 5-year property: Property with class life of more than 4 years but less than 10 years—taxis, buses, light and heavy-duty trucks, computers, office machinery, and property used in connection with research.
- 7-year property: Property with class life of 10 years or more but less than 16 years—office furniture and property not designated as belonging to another class.
- 10-year property: Property with class life of 16 years or more but less than 20 years—barges, tugs, single-purpose agricultural structures, and fruit- or nut-bearing trees and vines.
- 15-year property: Property with class life of 20 years or more but less than 25 years—roads, shrubbery, and wharves.
- 20-year property: Property with a class life of 25 years or more—farm buildings and municipal sewers.
- Nonresidential real property: Any real estate that is not residential property. This property is depreciated over 31.5 years.
- Residential rental property: Any real estate (including mobile homes) for which 80 percent or more of the gross rental income is from dwelling units. This property is depreciated over 28.5 years.

Do not try to memorize all these classes. They are covered in detail in income tax courses. What is important is remembering that the first step in computing

Exhibit 15–2

Calculating the Depreciation Tax Shield Under Accelerated MACRS, Half-Year Convention

Since depreciation is not a cash flow, it does not directly enter into capital expenditure analysis. However, because it alters cash payments for income taxes, it enters capital expenditure analysis indirectly. This example shows the annual tax savings on an asset that cost $1,040. The asset is a seven-year property under MACRS. Most profitable companies would elect to use accelerated depreciation, as this company did.

Year	Asset cost	Cost recovery rate	Annual depreciation	Tax rate	Depreciation tax shield
1	$1,040	14.29%	$ 148.62	34%	$ 50.53
2	1,040	24.49	254.70	34	86.60
3	1,040	17.49	181.90	34	61.85
4	1,040	12.49	129.90	34	44.17
5	1,040	8.93	92.87*	34	31.58
6	1,040	8.92	92.77	34	31.54
7	1,040	8.93	92.87	34	31.58
8	1,040	4.46	46.37	34	15.75
Total			$1,040.00		$353.60

*Change to straight-line depreciation occurs at this point.

an annual income tax deduction is to determine a property's class, which determines its useful life for tax depreciation. To simplify the following discussions, we will concentrate on the seven-year class, since most equipment falls into that category.

Now, suppose the desk whose purchase was considered on page 693 was depreciated according to MACRS accelerated depreciation tables. Recall that the desk was purchased for $1,000 plus a $40 delivery charge. The basis for depreciation is therefore $1,040, since salvage value is ignored. Desks are in the seven-year class. Exhibit 15–2 gives the cost recovery percentages established by the U.S. Internal Revenue Code. It also shows how the tax deduction for depreciation on the desk is calculated using the MACRS accelerated depreciation schedule for seven-year property.[1] Notice that in the MACRS accelerated system most of the depreciation deduction is taken in the early years. The right-hand column of Exhibit 15–2 shows the income tax savings for each year of the desk's life if the income tax rate is 34 percent. In a capital expenditure analysis, the tax savings from the deduction would be treated as a cash inflow, just as any other cash savings.

Straight-line depreciation is allowed as an alternative to the MACRS accelerated method. When the straight-line method is used, a constant percentage of an asset's cost is deducted each year except for the first and last year until the total cost is recovered. Depreciation percentage for each year except the first and

[1]The illustration assumes half-year convention. Under some circumstances, a company must follow a midquarter convention. You need not be concerned with the midquarter convention.

last is found by dividing one by the number of years over which the property is depreciated. That result is then multiplied by the asset's cost. For property in the seven-year class, the computation would be:

$$\frac{1}{7} \times \text{ the asset's cost (for each year except the first and last)}$$

For the first and last year, companies must follow what is called the **half-year convention.** This convention requires that firms deduct only one-half of the year's depreciation during the first year of an asset's life. The other half is deducted in the year after an asset's life ends. For example, assume a company has paid $8,000 for an asset in the seven-year class. Even though accelerated depreciation is allowed, the company elects to use the straight-line method. During years two through seven, the company deducts one-seventh (1/7) of the $8,000 each year. Again, salvage value is ignored. The half-year rule permits the company to claim half of one-seventh, or one-fourteenth, the first year; the other one-fourteenth in the eighth year. At first deducting depreciation for a seven-year asset in the eighth year may seem strange. But the useful lives in tax laws are usually shorter than the actual lives of equipment. Therefore, the equipment will probably be in use in the eighth year as well as in later years. In the list on page 695, the seven-year class is for equipment with useful lives of more than ten but less than sixteen years. Exhibit 15–3 shows how the depreciation deductions for this equipment was calculated under both the straight-line and the accelerated methods.

Most companies choose the accelerated depreciation method, since it yields larger deductions and tax savings than the straight-line method in the early years of an asset's life. The earlier a cash savings is received, the greater its (present)

Exhibit 15–3

Comparison of MACRS Accelerated and Straight-Line Depreciation Methods, Half-Year Convention

MACRS accelerated depreciation deductions exceed those for straight line in the first three years, whereas the situation reverses in later years.

	Accelerated depreciation		Straight-line depreciation	
Year	Percentage	Annual depreciation	Percentage	Annual depreciation
1	14.29%	$1,143.20	7.14%	$ 571.20
2	24.49	1,959.20	14.29	1,143.20
3	17.49	1,399.20	14.29	1,143.20
4	12.49	999.20	14.28*	1,142.40
5	8.93	714.40	14.29	1,143.20
6	8.92	713.60	14.28	1,142.40
7	8.93	714.40	14.29	1,143.20
8	4.46	356.80	7.14	571.20
Total		$8,000.00		$8,000.00

*For ease of calculation you may use 14.29 for years 2–7. We use both methods in the illustrations.

value will be. Thus, early deductions are preferred. Usually, when the straight-line method is preferred, it is because there is a lack of taxable *income* in the early years of an asset's life. To benefit from tax deductions, companies must of course have some taxable income from which to deduct them.

You have now seen the effect of income taxes on cash flow and the effect of the depreciation tax shield. In the next section you will see how items affect a typical capital expenditure analysis.

Review Exercise 15–1

Calculate the Depreciation Tax Shield

Mervin's Hair Salon is considering purchasing new chairs. They will cost $20,000 and be seven-year class property. Mr. Mervin is wondering how the depreciation tax shield would be different between MACRS accelerated depreciation and straight-line depreciation. In either case, the half-year convention would apply. Mervin's tax rate is 28 percent.

Required

1. Calculate the depreciation tax shield for each year using MACRS accelerated depreciation.
2. Calculate the depreciation tax shield for each year using straight-line depreciation.

Solution

1. The depreciation tax shield for each year using the MACRS accelerated method is as follows:

Asset cost, $20,000
Depreciation method, MACRS—accelerated
Tax rate, 28%
Asset class, 7-year, half-year convention

Year	Asset cost	Cost recovery rate	Annual depreciation	Tax rate	Depreciation tax shield
1	$20,000	14.29%	$ 2,858.00	28%	$ 800.24
2	20,000	24.49	4,898.00	28	1,371.44
3	20,000	17.49	3,498.00	28	979.44
4	20,000	12.49	2,498.00	28	699.44
5	20,000	8.93	1,786.00	28	500.08
6	20,000	8.92	1,784.00	28	499.52
7	20,000	8.93	1,786.00	28	500.08
8	20,000	4.46	892.00	28	249.76
		100.00%	$20,000.00		$5,600.00

2. The depreciation tax shield for each year using the straight-line method is as follows:

Asset cost, $20,000
Depreciation method, MACRS—straight line
Tax rate, 28%
Asset class, 7-year, half-year convention

Year	Asset cost	Cost recovery rate	Annual depreciation	Tax rate	Depreciation tax shield
1	$20,000	7.14%	$ 1,428.00	28%	$ 399.84
2	20,000	14.29	2,858.00	28	800.24
3	20,000	14.29	2,858.00	28	800.24
4	20,000	14.28	2,856.00	28	799.68
5	20,000	14.29	2,858.00	28	800.24
6	20,000	14.28	2,856.00	28	799.68
7	20,000	14.29	2,858.00	28	800.24
8	20,000	7.14	1,428.00	28	399.84
		100.00%	$20,000.00		$5,600.00

(see Exercises 13, 14, 15, 16, 17, 18, 19, 20, 21, 22)

■

Including Income Tax Effects in a Capital Expenditure Analysis

OBJECTIVE 3
Include the effects of income taxes in a capital expenditure analysis

Morrison Gift Shop is considering adding a new line of gift cards to its collection. To sell the cards, the store needs a special display rack. Introducing the new cards will probably reduce sales of existing cards, but the owner believes the new cards will increase sales of other products by attracting new customers to the store. Thus, the net effect on revenues from existing products should be negligible.

Installing the rack will require some rearrangement of existing displays. The rack's useful life should be ten years. After that time a new style of display will probably be needed. Salvage value is expected to be zero. The rack is in the seven-year class. Cash outflows and inflows from the new product are projected to be as follows:

Purchase price of new rack	$4,500
Installation costs	1,000
Working capital	
Investment at end of year 1	1,100
Recovery of investment at end of year 10	1,100

Expected annual sales revenues	
Year 1: 2,000 units at $1.50	3,000
Years 2–10: 2,800 units at $1.50	4,200
Cash expenses	
Year 1: 2,000 units at $0.70	1,400
Years 2–10: 2,800 units at $0.70	1,960

The new line is not expected to increase other operating expenses.

Morrison's income tax rate is 34 percent. The store uses the accelerated depreciation method. The **minimum rate of return** required on new investments is 16 percent after taxes. Should the store add the new line?

To answer the question, Morrison's accountant prepared the capital expenditure worksheet shown in Exhibit 15–4. The tax effect of the added revenues and variable expenses is the difference between added sales revenues or variable expenses times the income tax rate of 34 percent. In year one, taxes

Exhibit 15–4

Capital Expenditure Analysis Worksheet, Morrison Gift Shop

Item	End of year	Amount of cash flow	Present value factor @ 16%	Present value of cash flow
Purchase of rack	0	$(4,500)		
Installation of rack	0	(1,000)		
Net cash outflows	0	$(5,500)	1.0000	$(5,500)
Investment in working capital	1	(1,100)	0.8621	(948)
Added sales revenues	1	$ 3,000		
Added variable expenses	1	(1,400)		
Tax effect of the above at 34%	1	(544)		
Net cash inflows		$ 1,056	0.8621	910
Added sales revenues	2–10	$ 4,200		
Added variable expenses	2–10	(1,960)		
Tax effect of the above at 34%	2–10	(762)		
Net cash inflows		$ 1,478	3.9711*	5,869
Depreciation tax shield, $5,500, 7-year accelerated	1	$ 267.22	0.8621	$ 230**
	2	457.96	0.7432	340
	3	327.06	0.6407	210
	4	233.56	0.5523	129
	5	166.99	0.4761	80
	6	166.80	0.4104	68
	7	166.99	0.3538	59
	8	83.40	0.3050	25
Subtotal				$ 1,141
Recovery of working capital investment	10	1,100	0.2267	$ 249
Net present value of cash flows				$ 1,721

*Present value factor: 2–10 years at 16% = 4.8332 − 0.8621 = 3.9711.

**Figures are rounded.

Exhibit 15–5
Depreciation Tax Shield Schedule, MACRS Accelerated

Year	Asset cost	Cost recovery rate	Annual depreciation	Tax rate	Depreciation tax shield
1	$5,500	14.29%	$ 785.95	34%	$ 267.22
2	5,500	24.49	1,346.95	34	457.96
3	5,500	17.49	961.95	34	327.06
4	5,500	12.49	686.95	34	233.56
5	5,500	8.93	491.15	34	166.99
6	5,500	8.92	490.60	34	166.80
7	5,500	8.93	491.15	34	166.99
8	5,500	4.46	245.30	34	83.40
Total			$5,500.00		$1,869.98

on the $3,000 in additional sales revenues will subtract $1,020 from Morrison's income. Added variable expenses of $1,400 will yield a $476 savings on taxes, however ($1,400 × 34%). The net effect of these four items is that after-tax cash flow will increase by $1,056 in year one. The same type of calculation is done for years two through ten.

The lower portion of the worksheet shows how the present value of the depreciation tax shield resulting from purchase of the rack was calculated. (The tax shield itself is calculated in Exhibit 15–5.) Annual cash savings from the tax shield (column 2) are multiplied by the appropriate present value factors to obtain the present value of each annual cash inflow. Each year's savings could have been included in the calculation of that year's net cash inflow prior to discounting.

The positive **net present value** shown on the last line of Morrison's capital expenditure worksheet (Exhibit 15–4) indicates that investment in the display rack is expected to return more than Morrison's minimum rate of return. Notice that once the tax effects of the cash flows are calculated and included in the worksheet, the procedure for analyzing the investment is the same as that presented in Chapter 14. Income taxes are simply one more cash flow to consider when making a capital expenditure decision.

Review Exercise 15–2

Calculate After-Tax Net Present Value

Corner Store has been losing a lot of profitable film developing business to companies that can provide two-hour service. An element of Corner Store's strategy is to provide good customer service. Corner Store is therefore considering the purchase of its own developing machine. There is existing space in which to install the machine. The developing machine will cost $39,000 and will be seven-year class property. With the machine, the store anticipates added annual cash sales of $45,000. Its added cash operating expenses will be $32,000 annually. The machine would require investment of $6,750 in supplies by the end of the first year of operation. This investment would be recovered at the end of the machine's seven-year useful life.

The machine would be seven-year class property for income tax purposes, and Corner Store would use straight-line depreciation. The half-year convention would apply. Corner Store's tax rate is 34 percent. Corner Store requires a 16 percent after-tax return on investments.

Required

1. Prepare a capital expenditure analysis worksheet calculating the machine's after-tax net present value.
2. Should Corner Store expect the machine to return its minimum rate of return?

Solution

1. The capital expenditure analysis worksheet for this proposal is as follows:

Corner Store
Capital Expenditure Analysis
Worksheet—Film Developing Machine

Item	End of year	Amount of cash flow	Present value factor @ 16%	Present value of cash flow
Investment		$(39,000)	1.0000	$(39,000)
Added sales revenues	1	45,000		
Added cash expenses	1	(32,000)		
Subtotal		$ 13,000		
Tax effect of the above at 34%	1	(4,420)		
Depreciation tax shield at 34%	1	947		
Net cash inflows	1	$ 9,527	0.8621	8,213
Investment in working capital	1	(6,750)	0.8621	(5,819)
Added sales revenues	2–7	45,000		
Added cash expenses	2–7	(32,000)		
Subtotal	2–7	$ 13,000		
Tax effect of the above at 34%	2–7	(4,420)		
Depreciation tax shield at 34%	2–7	1,894		
Net cash inflows	2–7	$ 10,474	3.1765	33,271
Recovery of working capital	7	6,750	0.3538	2,388
Depreciation tax shield at 34%	8	947	0.3050	289

Net present value of cash flows	$ (658)

2. The net present value is negative, meaning the project will not return Corner Store's minimum rate of return. The negative amount is small, however, less than 2 percent of the investment. If the service the machine provides is important to Corner Store's strategy of service, the store might make the investment anyway. (see Exercises 23, 24, 25, 26)

■

The Cost of Capital and the Minimum Rate of Return

A dynamic organization generates many capital expenditure proposals. Managers are always developing ideas for new products or devising better ways of producing existing ones. These new products and new production methods usually require long-term investments.

Because of limited resources, however, management usually cannot accept all capital expenditure proposals. For example, a chain of dress stores might reject a proposal to open another store because it lacks a qualified manager to run it. Or a suitable building might not be available. In the first case, the store lacks human resources; in the second, a physical resource. Just as often, however, a decision not to expand is made because of lack of capital. In this case, the new store requires an added investment in the form of racks and shelves, inventory, and accounts receivable.

OBJECTIVE 4
Define cost of capital and explain how it relates to the choice between capital expenditure proposals

The limited availability of capital is not generally a matter of physical shortages, although all resources are finite. Usually a firm can obtain additional capital, but at a cost. The **cost of capital** is the amount an organization must pay to induce a lender or potential owner to invest in the organization. Whether borrowed or obtained from owners through the issue of stock, capital has a price. With borrowed capital, the cost is interest payments. With capital provided by owners, the cost is dividends and anticipated increases in share value made possible by increased earnings.

A problem arises when the cost of capital is higher than the return a firm can earn on its capital. For example, a company might be able to borrow capital at an interest rate of 25 percent. But the company would be unwise to make an investment that returns less than its cost of capital. If management cannot satisfy investors with the return earned by the investment, investors will withdraw their capital at the earliest opportunity.

The law of supply and demand suggests that more of an item will be supplied at higher prices and increased demand will increase prices. If a firm demands more and more capital, its cost of capital is likely to increase. The graph shown

Figure 15–1
Marginal Cost of Capital
Increased demand for an item increases the price of that item. Notice that in this example the cost of capital rises as demand rises.

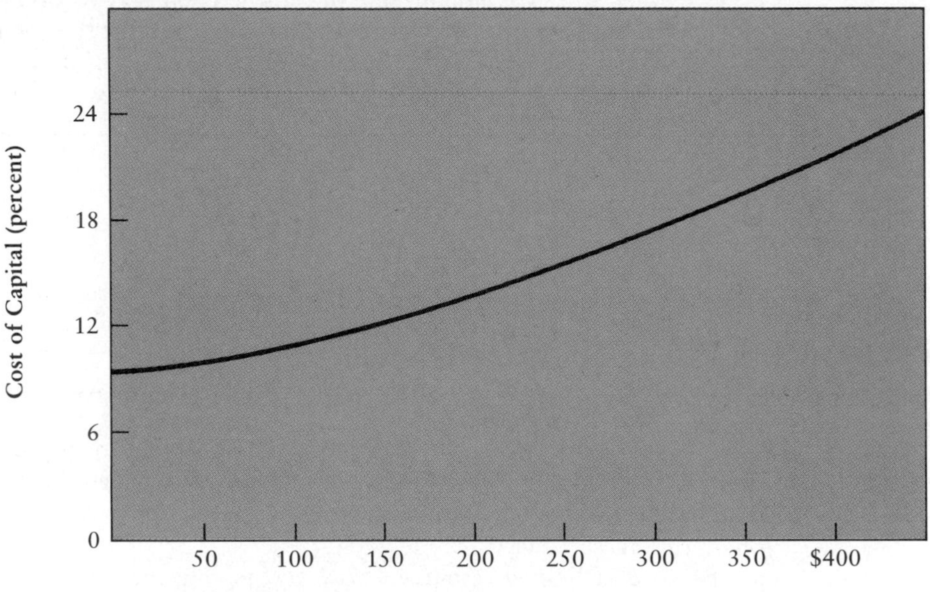

in Figure 15–1 shows how the cost of capital (vertical axis) rises with demand (horizontal axis). Of course, the graph is hypothetical, representing the cost of capital in a particular market at a particular time. At other times or in other markets, the curve might be steeper or flatter, higher or lower, depending on the total supply of capital and other firms' demand for it. Should investors believe that the economy is weakening or strengthening, the curve might shift up or down to compensate for the increased or decreased risk.

As noted earlier, a dynamic organization generates many investment proposals each year. Each proposal requires a certain amount of capital and promises some rate of return. Were you to graph the amount of capital required and the return expected on each proposed project in a firm, the result might look like Figure 15–2. Each bar represents an investment project. The width of the bar indicates the amount of capital required; the height, the expected rate of return. The project with the highest return is shown at the left. The others follow in decending order of return. The marginal cost of capital curve shown in Figure 15–1 cuts across the bars, indicating the cost of capital required by the projects.

Which investment projects should management accept? By comparing the marginal cost of capital with the various projects shown, you can see that only the first five projects on the left are acceptable. The combined effect of the rising cost of capital and the lower return on investment eliminates the desirability of the remaining three projects.

When capital is scarce, as it almost always is, management must rank projects in their order of desirability. The **time-adjusted rate of return** was first discussed

Figure 15–2

Ranking Investment Projects According to Their Time-Adjusted Rate of Return
The bars in this graph represent the amount of capital required by investment proposals (width of bars) and their time-adjusted rate of return (height of bars). Their relation to the marginal cost of capital curve shows their desirability. In this case, the firm considering these proposals should probably accept the first five on the left and reject the other three.

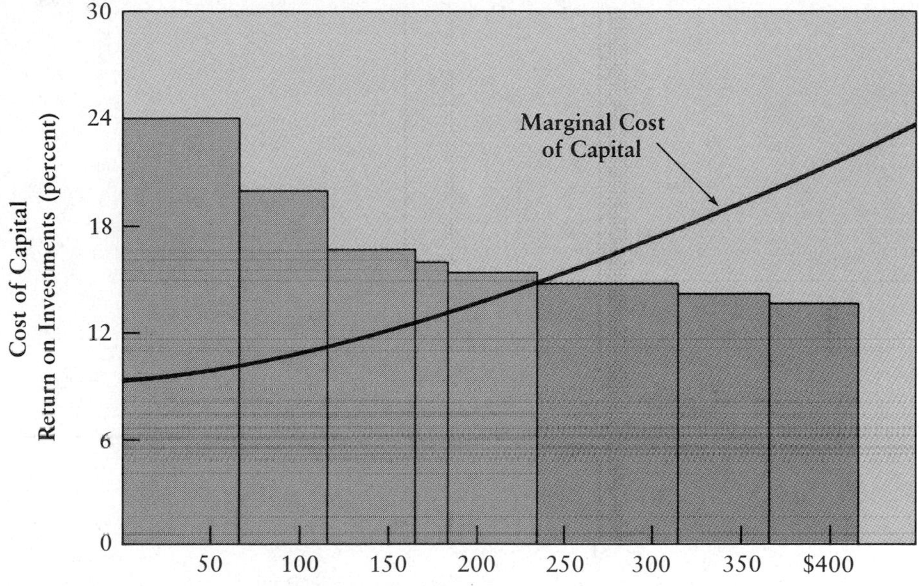

in Chapter 14. It is a popular gauge for ranking. With this method, projects not promising a rate of return equal to or above the cost of capital may be immediately eliminated. Projects with the highest time-adjusted rate of return are the most desirable.

The time-adjusted rate of return appeals to managers because they are accustomed to thinking in terms of rates of return. There are some technical problems with the time-adjusted rate of return, but they are beyond the scope of this book. Three other gauges for ranking projects are: (1) the profitability index, (2) the payback period, and (3) the accounting rate of return. Each one will now be covered separately, starting with the profitability index.

■

Ranking Projects by Profitability Index

Net present value is a measure of how much value a particular investment will add to an organization. Other things being equal, managers prefer projects promising to add the greatest value to the firm. Nevertheless, although net present

Exhibit 15–6

Net Present Value of Three Investment Projects

This exhibit shows the computation of the present value of the future cash flows used in the capital rationing and profitability index computation. The company has $80,000 to invest and cannot, therefore, invest in all three projects. The company's income tax rate is 34 percent. Each project has a useful life of seven years and is depreciated on a straight-line basis with no salvage value.

Item	End of year	Amount of cash flow	Present value factor @ 12%	Present value of cash flow
		Project 1		
Investment	0	$(70,000)	1.0000	$(70,000)
Added sales revenues	1	60,660		
Added cash expenses	1	(46,529)		
Subtotal		$ 14,131		
Tax effect of the above at 34%	1	(4,805)		
Depreciation tax shield at 34%	1	1,700*		
Net cash inflows	1	$ 11,026	0.8929	9,845
Investment in working capital	1	(15,000)	0.8929	(13,393)
Added sales revenues	2–7	90,990		
Added cash expenses	2–7	(68,043)		
Subtotal		$ 22,947		
Tax effect of the above at 34%	2–7	(7,802)		
Depreciation tax shield at 34%	2–7	3,400		
Net cash inflows	2–7	$ 18,545	3.6709	68,077
Recovery of working capital	7	15,000	0.4523	6,785
Depreciation tax shield at 34%	8	1,700*	0.4039	687
Net present value of Project 1 cash flows				$ 2,000

*Rounded to make total depreciation tax shield = $70,000 × 34%.

Item	End of year	Amount of cash flow	Present value factor @ 12%	Present value of cash flow
		Project 2		
Investment	0	$(28,000)	1.0000	$(28,000)
Added sales revenues	1	$ 9,500		
Added cash expenses	1	(4,496)		
Subtotal		$ 5,004		
Tax effect of the above at 34%	1	(1,701)		
Depreciation tax shield at 34%	1	680		
Net cash inflows	1	$ 3,983	0.8929	3,556
Investment in working capital	1	(3,000)	0.8929	(2,679)
Added sales revenues	2–7	18,000		
Added cash expenses	2–7	(8,714)		
Subtotal		$ 9,286		
Tax effect of the above at 34%	2–7	(3,157)		
Depreciation tax shield at 34%	2–7	1,360		
Net cash inflows	2–7	$ 7,489	3.6709	27,491
Recovery of working capital	7	3,000	0.4523	1,357
Depreciation tax shield at 34%	8	680	0.4039	275
Net present value of Project 2 cash flows				$ 2,000

Exhibit 15–6
Continued

Project 3				
Investment	0	$(42,000)	1.0000	$(42,000)
Added sales revenues	1	18,000		
Added cash expenses	1	(8,869)		
Subtotal		$ 9,131		
Tax effect of the above at 34%	1	(3,105)		
Depreciation tax shield at 34%	1	1,020		
Net cash inflows	1	$ 7,046	0.8929	6,292
Investment in working capital	1	(7,000)	0.8929	(6,250)
Added sales revenues	2–7	24,000		
Added cash expenses	2–7	(10,424)		
Subtotal		$ 13,576		
Tax effect of the above at 34%	2–7	(4,616)		
Depreciation tax shield at 34%	2–7	2,040		
Net cash inflows	2–7	$ 11,000	3.6709	40,380
Recovery of working capital	7	7,000	0.4523	3,166
Depreciation tax shield at 34%	8	1,020	0.4039	412
Net present value of Project 3 cash flows				$ 2,000

value is conceptually the soundest way to evaluate capital expenditures, it cannot be used to rank competing projects when capital is limited. This is because net present value by itself does not reflect the size of the project being considered.

OBJECTIVE 5
Calculate the profitability index and use it to rank capital expenditure proposals

For example, suppose a company has $70,000 capital to invest in new projects. Three proposals are under consideration. Complete data on each one are shown in the capital expenditure analysis worksheet reproduced in Exhibit 15–6.

Notice that each project has a positive net present value of $2,000. Thus, each one returns more than the firm's minimum rate of return. But are the three projects equally desirable? Project 1 requires the entire amount of capital available to the firm, or $70,000, to generate $2,000 worth of net present value. The firm could use the $70,000 to invest in Projects 2 and 3 and generate $4,000 in net present value. If an organization has only a limited amount of capital to invest, it would choose the combination of projects that will produce the greatest total net present value.

To reflect the different amounts of capital required by competing investment projects, accountants have developed a measure called the profitability index. The **profitability index** is the ratio of the present value of a project's future net cash inflows to its immediate cash outflows as shown below.

$$\text{Profitability index} = \frac{\text{present value of future net cash inflows}}{\text{immediate cash outflows}}$$

Any project with a profitability index greater than one has a positive net present value. The higher the index, the more desirable the project. Profitability indices for the three projects shown in Exhibit 15–6 appear in Exhibit 15–7.

Exhibit 15–7

Ranking Competing Investment Proposals by Profitability Index

If limited capital is available, Project 2 is preferred over Projects 3 and 1 even though all have the same net present value. This is because Project 2 provides more net present value per dollar invested.

	Project 1	Project 2	Project 3
Immediate cash outflows	$(70,000)	$(28,000)	$(42,000)
Present value of future net cash inflows	72,000	30,000	44,000
Net present value	$ 2,000	$ 2,000	$ 2,000
Profitability index	$ 72,000 / $ 70,000 = 1.029	$ 30,000 / $ 28,000 = 1.071	$ 44,000 / $ 42,000 = 1.048

The profitability indexes for the three projects being discussed are calculated as follows:

Project 1	Project 2	Project 3
$72,000 / $70,000	$30,000 / $28,000	$44,000 / $42,000
= 1.029	= 1.071	= 1.048

The results show that Project 2 is the most desirable; Project 3, the next most desirable. Although Project 1 is the least desirable, it still has a positive net present value, since its profitability index is greater than one. If the organization had $140,000 to invest, all three projects would be good investments. With only $70,000 to invest, however, the firm is better off with Projects 2 and 3.

By relating the present value of future cash flows to the amount invested, the profitability index overcomes the limitation of net present value as a method of ranking competing projects. It is a reliable way of ranking capital expenditure proposals.

Review Exercise 15–3

Calculate Profitability Index

Environmental Control Corporation performs a variety of air and water quality tests. The company is considering adding equipment that will permit it to test automobile emissions as automobiles are driven on public highways. The company believes that there would be substantial demand from governmental units for this kind of service. The test equipment would be fitted into a large van that would be parked along the road to make the tests. The testing equipment will cost $170,000 and have a seven-year useful life. Environmental Control anticipates added annual sales of $88,000. Its cash operating expenses will be $46,000 annually.

The machine would be seven-year class property for income tax purposes, and Environmental Control would use straight-line depreciation. The half-year convention would apply. Environmental Control's tax rate is 34 percent. Management requires a 12 percent after-tax return on investments.

Required

1. Prepare a capital expenditure analysis worksheet for this proposal and calculate the investment's profitability index.
2. Should Environmental Control expect the machine to return its minimum rate of return?

Solution

1. The capital expenditure analysis worksheet for this proposal and the profitability index are as follows:

Item	End of year	Amount of cash flow	Present value factor @ 12%	Present value of cash flow
Investment		$(170,000)	1.0000	$(170,000)
Added sales revenues	1	88,000		
Added cash expenses	1	(46,000)		
Subtotal		$ 42,000		
Tax effect of the above at 34%	1	(14,280)		
Depreciation tax shield at 34%	1	4,127		
Net cash inflows	1	$ 31,847	0.8929	28,436
Added sales revenues	2–7	88,000		
Added cash expenses	2–7	(46,000)		
Subtotal	2–7	$ 42,000		
Tax effect of the above at 34%	2–7	(14,280)		
Depreciation tax shield at 34%	2–7	8,257		
Net cash inflows	2–7	$ 35,977	3.6709	132,068
Depreciation tax shield at 34%	8	4,127	0.4039	1,667
Net present value of cash flows				$ (7,829)

Present value of future net cash inflows	$162,170
Immediate cash outflows	170,000
Profitability index	0.95

2. The profitability index is less than one. This means that the investment will not return Environmental Control's minimum rate of return.

(see Exercises 27, 28, 29, 30, 31, 32, 33)

■

Ranking Projects by Payback Period

OBJECTIVE 6
Calculate the payback period for a capital expenditure proposal and discuss its limitations

An alternate method for ranking projects is by their payback period. The **payback period** is the number of years needed for an investment project to return its original investment. A payback period does not indicate an investment's rate of return. In fact, it ignores the concept of time value of money. Instead of distinguishing between return *on* investment and return *of* investment, the payback method assumes all cash inflows are a return *of* investment until the total investment is recovered. Any cash inflows occurring after the payback period are considered a return *on* investment.

Calculating the Payback Period

Suppose a manager is considering investing in an industrial floor-cleaning machine. The main attraction of the machine is that it saves the labor costs of having someone scrub and mop the floor by hand. The machine costs $29,540, including delivery. Although it should save $19,500 a year in labor costs, it will require $800 worth of electricity and $2,033 of maintenance per year. The company uses straight-line depreciation, and the machine's expected useful life is seven years. Its salvage value will be $8,540 after seven years. The company's income tax rate is 34 percent. The annual net after-tax savings from buying the machine are calculated as follows:

	Savings during year 1	Savings during years 2–6	Savings during year 7	Savings during year 8
Labor savings	$19,500	$19,500	$19,500	
Electricity costs	(800)	(800)	(800)	
Maintenance costs	(2,033)	(2,033)	(2,033)	
Net savings before income taxes	$16,667	$16,667	$16,667	
Tax increase on net savings at 34%	(5,667)	(5,667)	(5,667)	
Depreciation tax shield at 34%	717	1,435	1,435	$717
Salvage value			8,540	
Annual net after-tax savings	$11,717	$12,435	$20,975	$717

The company may deduct $29,540 × 7.14% = $2,109 depreciation in the first year, and the depreciation tax shield for that year is $717 ($2,109 × 34%). In years two through seven, the company may deduct $4,220 per year ($29,540 × 14.29%), making the depreciation tax shield $1,435 ($4,220 × 34%). Thus, the machine promises an annual net cash inflow of $11,717 in the first year and $12,435 per year in years two through six. In year seven, the cash inflow will be $20,975 ($12,435 net after-tax savings as in years two through six + the $8,540 salvage value of the machine). Finally, in year eight, the company will benefit from a $717 depreciation tax shield from the remaining half year's depreciation.

By comparing the cost of the machine, $29,540, with its annual net cash inflow, you can see that the payback period is less than three years as shown below:

Year	Remaining investment to be recovered at beginning of year	Annual net cash inflow
1	$29,540	$11,717
2	17,823	12,435
3	5,388	12,435

Notice that at the start of the third year, only $5,388 of the original $29,540 remains to be recovered. The annual net cash inflow in year three will be $12,435. Thus, the remaining $5,388 will be recovered before the middle of the third year.

$$\$5{,}388 \div \$12{,}435 = 0.4$$

Thus, the payback period is 2.4 years.

When net cash inflows are of equal amounts throughout the payback period, that period can be determined by dividing the initial investment by annual net cash inflows as shown below.

$$\text{Payback period (when future cash flows are equal)} = \frac{\text{initial investment}}{\text{annual net cash inflow}}$$

This formula cannot be used in this example, however, since the annual net cash inflows change from year to year. When annual net cash inflows differ, the payback period must be computed from a table of yearly cash flows, as was illustrated with the floor-cleaning machine.

If the proposal requires an investment in working capital, the investment and recovery of the working capital should be included in cash flow calculations. In fact, estimated cash flows needed to calculate the payback period are the same as for the net present value or profitability index.

Once the payback period has been calculated, what does it tell you? Although the payback period does not measure how profitable an investment project is, it does measure how long a firm must wait to recover an initial investment. When the payback period is used for ranking, the shorter the payback period, the better the investment. A method of ranking that emphasizes early return of an investment may be useful, particularly for firms short on cash. And if the estimates of future cash inflows are uncertain, a method emphasizing early cash flows, which are usually more certain, may be helpful.

Weaknesses of the Payback Method

For several reasons, the payback period is a bad method for ranking or evaluating capital expenditures. First, it ignores the timing of cash flows within the payback period. For example, suppose that in addition to the floor-cleaning machine, the company is considering another $29,540 investment. That investment will produce no cash inflows until the end of the fifth month of the third year when a cash flow of $29,540 is recorded. Notice that this assumes the entire amount of the investment will be recovered at that time. (Additional cash flows will be received after the third year, but they do not change the payback period.) Since the original investment is recovered after 0.4 of the third year, the payback period for this investment is 2.4 years, just as for the floor-cleaning machine. But as you know, the earlier a cash inflow is received, the more valuable it is. If total cash flows are equal over the life of the investment, management should prefer the floor-cleaning machine, even though both investments have the same payback period.

To confirm this conclusion, calculate the net present value of both investments. Examine the following comparison of the two cash flows:

	Cash flows	
End of year	Floor-cleaning machine	Other investment
0	$(29,540)	$(29,540)
1	11,717	-0-
2	12,435	-0-
3	12,435	29,540
4	12,435	16,000
5	12,435	16,000
6	12,435	16,000
7	20,975	18,044
8	717	-0-
Total	$ 66,044	$ 66,044

Notice that both projects have the same payback period and both promise the same *total* cash inflow. The higher cash inflow for the floor-cleaning machine in year seven includes its $8,540 salvage value. Its $717 inflow in year eight represents its depreciation tax shield in that year.

Exhibit 15–8 shows the computation of the net present value of these two machines. At a discount rate of 18 percent, the floor cleaner's net present value is $20,119. The other investment is worth only $15,275. Although both projects have the same payback period and can be expected to yield more than the minimum return rate, the cleaning machine's higher net present value makes it a

Exhibit 15–8

Capital Expenditure Analysis Worksheet for a Floor-Cleaning Machine and a Competing Investment Proposal

The cash flows for each investment are taken from the table on page 712. The higher net present value of the cleaning machine shows that it is preferable to the alternate investment even though the payback periods are the same.

Item	End of year	Amount of cash flow	Present value factor @ 18%	Present value of cash flow
Floor-Cleaning Machine				
Cost of investment	0	$(29,540)	1.0000	$(29,540)
Net cash inflows	1	11,717	0.8475	9,930
	2–6	12,435	2.6501	32,954
	7	20,975	0.3139	6,584
	8	717	0.2660	191
Total net present value of cash flows				$ 20,119
Present value factor for years 2–6 at 18% = 3.4976 − 0.8475 = 2.6501				
Alternative Investment				
Cost of investment	0	$(29,540)	1.0000	$(29,540)
Net cash inflows	1	-0-		
	2	-0-		
	3	29,540	0.6086	17,978
	4–6	16,000	1.3233	21,173
	7	18,044	0.3139	5,664
	8	-0-		
Total net present value of cash flows				$ 15,275
Present value factor for years 4–6 at 18% = 3.4976 − 2.1743 = 1.3233				

better investment. However, the payback period shows them both as equivalent investments.

The second weakness of the payback method is that it ignores cash flows occurring after the payback period. The estimated useful life of the two projects just considered was seven years. But what if the firm were presented with a third investment proposal, requiring the same initial investment and offering the same annual cash inflows as the floor-cleaning machine? However, its useful life would be only four years. The payback period would be the same, 2.4 years. Should the firm prefer the project promising cash inflows for a longer period? Of course, the answer is yes.

As the following comparison shows, the floor-cleaning machine promises total net cash inflows of $66,044, whereas the alternate investment offers net cash inflows totaling only $19,482. The cash flows are identical for the first four years. The alternate investment simply has a shorter life. Although both investments have the same payback period, the floor-cleaning machine is clearly a better investment.

	Cash flows	
End of year	Floor-cleaning machine	Alternate investment
0	$(29,540)	$(29,540)
1	11,717	11,717
2	12,435	12,435
3	12,435	12,435
4	12,435	12,435
5	12,435	-0-
6	12,435	-0-
7	20,975	-0-
8	717	-0-
Total	$ 66,044	$ 19,482

To summarize, the payback period indicates the time needed to recover an initial investment in a capital expenditure project. Although that information may interest an organization short of cash whose investments must be recovered as soon as possible, it does not indicate a project's profitability. A firm ranking investments solely on the basis of payback periods risks making investments with a low rate of return and ignoring investments whose rate of return is higher but earned over longer periods.

Review Exercise 15–4

Calculate Payback Period

Berry Photo Shop is thinking of replacing its old photo processing equipment with a new automated machine. The new machine would cost $33,100 and have a useful life of seven years. Berry's manager has estimated the following annual before-tax cash flows:

	Savings during year 1	Savings during years 2–6	Savings during year 7
Labor savings	$24,500	$24,500	$24,500
Electricity costs	(800)	(800)	(800)
Maintenance costs	(2,033)	(2,033)	(2,033)
Net savings before income taxes	$21,667	$21,667	$21,667

Berry's income tax rate is 34 percent. The equipment would be seven-year class property for income tax purposes, and Berry would use straight-line depreciation. The half-year convention would apply.

Required

1. Calculate after-tax cash flows for the periods shown in the table above.
2. Calculate the investment's payback period.

Solution

	Savings during year 1	Savings during years 2–6	Savings during year 7	Savings during year 8
Labor savings	$24,500	$24,500	$24,500	
Electricity costs	(800)	(800)	(800)	
Maintenance costs	(2,033)	(2,033)	(2,033)	
Net savings before income taxes	$21,667	$21,667	$21,667	
Tax increase on net savings at 34%	(7,367)	(7,367)	(7,367)	
Depreciation tax shield at 34%	804	1,608	1,608	$804
Salvage value	—	—	—	—
Annual net after-tax savings	$15,104	$15,908	$24,448	$804
Machine cost			$33,100	

Year	Remaining investment to be recovered at beginning of year
1	$ 33,100
2	17,996
3	2,088

$$\text{Payback period} = 2 + \frac{\$\ 2{,}088}{\$15{,}908} = 2.13 \text{ years}$$

■

Ranking Projects by Accounting Rate of Return

OBJECTIVE 7
Calculate the accounting rate of return for a capital expenditure proposal and discuss its limitations

Before net present value and the time-adjusted rate of return came into general use, the accounting rate of return was often used to rank capital expenditure proposals. The **accounting rate of return** is the ratio of a project's average added after-tax net income to its average added assets expressed as a percentage. It is calculated by using the same methods accountants use to prepare income statements and balance sheets. For that reason, it includes depreciation, unlike any other method of evaluating capital expenditures. The main advantage of the accounting rate of return is that anyone familiar with financial accounting can easily understand it.

To find the accounting rate of return for a proposed capital expenditure, an accountant calculates the average amount the proposal will add to the firm's annual net income and the assets to be invested in the project. He or she then divides the first figure by the second as follows:

$$\text{Accounting rate of return} = \frac{\text{average added after-tax net income}}{\text{average added assets}}$$

To arrive at the figure for average added after-tax net income, the accountant estimates average annual revenues the project will generate. The next step is to estimate average annual expenses, including depreciation and income taxes, for the project. Subtracting average added expenses from average added revenues yields added net income as shown below.

$$\begin{matrix}\text{Average added}\\\text{after-tax net income}\end{matrix} = \begin{matrix}\text{average added}\\\text{annual revenues}\end{matrix} - \begin{matrix}\text{average added}\\\text{annual expenses}\end{matrix}$$

Notice that amounts are not discounted to their present value.

Average added assets are simply the initial amount of capital invested in the project, divided by 2 and adjusted for the expected salvage value and added working capital. The following formula is useful:

$$\begin{matrix}\text{Average}\\\text{added}\\\text{assets}\end{matrix} = \frac{(\text{initial cost} - \text{salvage value})}{2} + \begin{matrix}\text{salvage}\\\text{value}\end{matrix} + \begin{matrix}\text{added working}\\\text{capital}\end{matrix}$$

As when calculating the payback period, cash flows are not discounted.

As an example, suppose River City Restaurant is thinking of buying an oven for baking fresh pies. Currently, the restaurant serves pies from a local bakery. However, the manager believes that fresh-baked pies will increase sales by \$6,250 per year. He estimates that baking costs will be \$13,750 a year. He will save \$10,000 a year by not purchasing the pies. The oven, including installation, will cost \$10,000. Its estimated useful life is ten years. At the end of its useful life, the oven will have no salvage value. River City's income tax rate is 25 percent.

The restaurant will depreciate the oven over a ten-year period using the straight-line method. Because this calculation is to determine net income according to GAAP, as opposed to taxable income for IRS reporting, the restaurant need not follow such MACRS rules as the half-year convention.

The added after-tax net income would be calculated as follows:

Added sales revenues	$ 6,250
Cost of baking the pies	(13,750)
Savings by not purchasing the pies	10,000
Depreciation ($10,000 × 10%)	(1,000)
Net increase in income	$ 1,500
Income taxes ($1,500 × 25%)	(375)
Increase in after-tax net income	$ 1,125

Since there is no salvage value to consider, the average added assets are simply $10,000 ÷ 2, or $5,000. Therefore,

$$\text{Accounting rate of return} = \frac{\$1{,}125}{\$5{,}000}$$

$$= \underline{\underline{22.5}} \text{ percent}$$

Although it is easily understood, the accounting rate of return has several serious deficiencies. Its major drawback is that it ignores the fact that a dollar received today is worth more than a dollar received later. By averaging revenues and expenses, it also eliminates differences in the timing of cash flows. Finally, since it uses financial accounting methods, it depends on accounting choices such as depreciation method and inventory method. As accounting methods differ, the accounting rate of return differs. In contrast, calculating cash flows requires no choice of accounting method. Thus, the time-adjusted rate of return does not vary on the basis of choice of accounting methods.

To see the effect of ignoring the time value of money, you can calculate the after-tax time-adjusted rate of return on River City's oven. The depreciation tax shield must be calculated following MACRS rules. The oven is seven-year property and the straight-line method with half-year convention will be used. However, depreciation itself is not subtracted in calculating the time-adjusted rate of return because it is not a cash flow. Exhibit 15–9 shows these computations, using a 20 percent discount rate as the starting point. (As always, you must find the exact time-adjusted rate of return by trial and error.) The resulting negative net present value shows the oven will return less than 20 percent.

Were you to carry the computations further, you would find that the time-adjusted rate of return is about 17.3 percent. Thus, the accounting rate of return overestimated the time-adjusted rate of return by about 5 percent (22.5% − 17.3%), a sizable margin. In fact, the accounting rate of return frequently overestimates time-adjusted rate of return on an investment by varying amounts, depending on the pattern of future cash returns and the life of the project. The time-adjusted rate of return is much more reliable, and it should always be preferred to the accounting rate of return.

Exhibit 15–9
Capital Expenditure Analysis Worksheet for Oven Purchase by River City Restaurant

Item	End of year	Amount of cash flow	Present value factor @ 20%	Present value of cash flow
Purchase of oven	0	$(10,000)	1.0000	$(10,000)
Added sales revenues	1	$ 6,250		
Added baking expenses	1	(13,750)		
Reduced pie purchases	1	10,000		
Subtotal	1	$ 2,500		
Added taxes on above at 25%	1	(625)		
Depreciation tax shield at 25%	1	243		
Subtotal	1	$ 2,118	0.8333	1,765
Added sales revenues	2–7	$ 6,250		
Added baking expenses	2–7	(13,750)		
Reduced pie purchases	2–7	10,000		
Subtotal	2–7	$ 2,500		
Added taxes on above at 25%	2–7	(625)		
Depreciation tax shield at 25%	2–7	357		
Subtotal	2–7	$ 2,232	2.7713	6,186
Added sales revenues	8	$ 6,250		
Added baking expenses	8	(13,750)		
Reduced pie purchases	8	10,000		
Subtotal	8	$ 2,500		
Added taxes on above @ 25%	8	(625)		
Depreciation tax shield @ 25%	8	243		
Subtotal	8	$ 2,118	0.2326	493
Added sales revenues	9–10	$ 6,250		
Added baking expenses	9–10	(13,750)		
Reduced pie purchases	9–10	10,000		
Subtotal	9–10	$ 2,500		
Added taxes on above @ 25%	9–10	(625)		
Subtotal	9–10	$ 1,875	0.3553	666
Net present value				$ (890)

The present value of an annuity for years 2 through 7 is 3.6046 – 0.8333.
The present value of an annuity for years 9 through 10 is 4.1925 – 3.8372.

Chapter Review

Review of Learning Objectives

1. **Calculate the after-tax benefit of a cash receipt and the after-tax cost of a cash expenditure.**
The after-tax benefit of revenues is lower than the gross amount received, since revenues increase income taxes. Similarly, the after-tax cost of a deductible expense is lower than

the amount paid, since deductions reduce income taxes. Thus, managers of profit-making organizations often think in terms of after-tax amounts. The after-tax benefit or cost of a cash receipt or expenditure is calculated by deducting the tax effect from the cash receipt or expenditure. The tax effect equals the revenues or expenses multiplied by the tax rate.

2. **Calculate the depreciation tax shield using both accelerated and straight-line methods.**
Income taxes are reduced by the annual depreciation deduction even though depreciation is not a current cash flow. The amount by which taxes are reduced is called the depreciation tax shield. Most organizations prefer to use the accelerated method for income tax purposes because of the time value of money.

   The first step in calculating the deduction is to find the property class of the asset according to government guidelines. Each class has a prescribed rate of depreciation over a prescribed number of years. Once the annual depreciation deduction is calculated, the depreciation tax shield is calculated as follows:

   Depreciation tax shield = annual depreciation deduction × tax rate

   Salvage value is ignored in tax computations, and companies must follow the half-year convention. Under that convention, only one-half of the first-year's depreciation may be deducted in the year the asset is placed into service. The other half is deducted in the year after the asset's useful life ends. MACRS depreciation tables such as Exhibit 15–3 reflect the half-year convention.

3. **Include the effects of income taxes in a capital expenditure analysis.**
Because a proposed capital expenditure often alters a firm's tax payments, income taxes must be considered in capital expenditure analyses of profit-making organizations. Tax payments may affect the initial cash investment because of gains or losses on the replaced equipment. Future income tax payments are also changed by increases in revenue and increases or decreases in operating expenses. All these changes in tax payments must be estimated and entered onto the capital expenditure analysis worksheet.

   Depreciation expense does not directly affect capital expenditure analysis, since it is not a cash flow. Depreciation is, however, deductible for income tax purposes. If a capital expenditure proposal will increase future depreciation deductions, it will also reduce income tax payments. The resulting change in cash flows (depreciation tax shield) must be entered onto the capital expenditure analysis worksheet directly or indirectly by its inclusion in the calculation of net cash inflow.

4. **Define cost of capital and explain how it relates to the choice between capital expenditure proposals.**
The cost of capital is the amount an organization must pay to lenders or owners to induce them to invest capital in that organization. As the company increases its demand for capital, its cost is likely to rise. The organization must rank capital expenditures to select the projects promising the highest return while avoiding projects that will return less than the organization's cost of capital.

5. **Calculate the profitability index and use it to rank capital expenditure proposals.**
The profitability index is the ratio of the present value of a project's future net cash inflows to immediate cash outflows. It is calculated by dividing the total present value of future cash inflows by immediate cash outflows needed at the start of a project.

6. **Calculate the payback period for a capital expenditure proposal and discuss its limitations.**
The payback period is the number of years needed for an investment to return its original investment. It is not a measure of profitability. The first step in calculating a payback

period is to calculate annual after-tax cash flows, as is done in calculating net present value or the time-adjusted rate of return. Next, the accountant must prepare a table similar to the one shown on page 711. The year in which the annual cash inflow (shown in the right column) exceeds the investment amount still to be recovered (middle column) is the year in which the investment is paid back. To find the exact point in the year, divide the amount to be recovered by the annual cash flow for that year. The payback period is the total number of years up to that point, including the fraction of the last year. In the rare case in which annual cash flows are equal, the payback period may be calculated by using the following formula:

$$\text{Payback period} = \frac{\text{initial investment}}{\text{annual net cash inflow}}$$

The payback period is not a measure of a project's profitability. It ignores the time value of money and the effect of cash flows occurring beyond the payback period.

7. **Calculate the accounting rate of return for a capital expenditure proposal and discuss its limitations.**
The accounting rate of return is found by dividing a project's average after-tax net income by its average assets. For a proposed project the accountant calculates the average amount the project will add to the firm's annual net income and to its assets. He or she then applies the following formula:

$$\text{Accounting rate of return} = \frac{\text{average added after-tax net income}}{\text{average added assets}}$$

When this method is used, amounts are not discounted to their present value and net income is determined according to generally accepted accounting principles (GAAP).

Like the payback period, the accounting rate of return ignores the time value of money. It also distorts return on investment by averaging future cash flows.

Review of Key Terms

Accounting rate of return Ratio of a project's average added after-tax net income to its average added assets. Expressed as a percentage.

Book value Original cost less accumulated depreciation

Cost of capital Amount an organization must pay lenders or owners to induce them to invest capital in the organization. The cost of borrowed capital is the interest payments made on a loan. The cost of capital provided by owners is the dividends paid to those owners plus anticipated increases in share value.

Depreciation tax shield Amount by which income taxes are reduced because of depreciation deductions. Calculated by multiplying the annual depreciation deduction by the tax rate.

Expense tax effect Amount by which deductible expenses decrease taxes in a profit-making organization. Calculated by multiplying cash expenses by the tax rate.

Gain (loss) Difference between the book value of an asset and the amount it is sold for. A gain usually increases income taxes; a loss usually reduces them.

Half-year convention A tax requirement that firms deduct only one-half of the first year's depreciation during the first year of an asset's life and the remaining half in the year after the asset's useful life ends.

Loss See *Gain (loss).*

Minimum rate of return Return that management thinks it must earn to encourage investors to invest capital in a business. Often used as a discount rate in calculating present value of future cash flows.

Modified Accelerated Cost Recovery System (MACRS) Method of calculating depreciation deductions for income taxes. The accelerated method allows most of an asset's cost to be depreciated in the first half of its useful life. For tax purposes it is usually preferred to the straight-line method because of the time value of money.

Net present value Total value of a project's future cash returns discounted to their present value at the minimum rate of return minus the required initial investment (cash outflows). A project with a zero or positive net present value can be expected to earn at least the minimum rate of return. A project with a negative net present value will probably earn less than the minimum rate of return.

Payback period Number of years needed for an investment project to return its original investment. Does not indicate an investment's rate of return.

Profitability index Ratio of the present value of a project's future net cash inflows to its immediate cash outflows. Calculated by dividing the present value of future net cash inflows by immediate cash outflows. Any project with a profitability index greater than one has a positive net present value. The higher the index, the more desirable the project.

Revenue tax effect Amount by which taxes reduce revenues in a profit-making organization. Calculated by multiplying an organization's revenue by its tax rate.

Straight-line depreciation Method of calculating depreciation deductions. For income tax purposes, a constant percentage of an asset's cost is deducted each year of the asset's life, except during the first and last years, until the total cost is recovered. An alternative to the MACRS accelerated method.

Time-adjusted rate of return Discount rate yielding a zero present value when used to find the present value of a project's cash flows.

Review Problem

Harlan Company is reviewing a proposal to produce a new product whose estimated life is seven years. It will require the following investment:

Production equipment	$80,000
Installation and testing	15,000
Working capital	30,000

The equipment is specialized and cannot be used for other products. The equipment's salvage value will be $10,000 at the end of seven years. Installation and testing will be done by independent engineers. Investment in working capital will be made by the end of the first year. It will be recovered at the end of the seventh year.

A market research study, which cost $10,000, indicates the product should be well-accepted. Expected revenues and cash expenses are as follows:

Year	Revenue	Cash expenses
1	$220,000	$175,000
2	245,000	195,000
3	260,000	200,000
4	200,000	160,000
5	180,000	145,000
6	150,000	125,000
7	100,000	85,000

The new equipment is in the seven-year class under MACRS rules. Harlan's income tax rate is 34 percent. Its minimum rate of return is 16 percent.

Required

1. Calculate the depreciation tax shield on the new equipment.
2. Calculate the proposal's net present value.
3. Calculate the proposal's profitability index.
4. Calculate the proposal's payback period.
5. Calculate:
   a. The average added net income
   b. The average added investment
   c. The proposal's accounting rate of return

Solution to Review Problem

1. Depreciation tax shield calculated:

Harlan Company
Depreciation Tax Shield Schedule

Year	Asset costs	Cost recovery rate	Annual depreciation	Tax rate	Depreciation tax shield
1	$95,000	14.29%	$13,576	34%	$ 4,616
2	95,000	24.49	23,266	34	7,910
3	95,000	17.49	16,616	34	5,649
4	95,000	12.49	11,866	34	4,034
5	95,000	8.93	8,484	34	2,885
6	95,000	8.92	8,474	34	2,881
7	95,000	8.93	8,484	34	2,885
8	95,000	4.46	4,234*	34	1,440
Total			$95,000		$32,300

*Rounded to total $95,000.

2. Net present value calculated:

Harlan Company
Capital Expenditure Analysis Worksheet

Item	End of year	Amount of cash flow	Present value factor @ 16%	Present value of cash flow
Purchase of equipment	0	$ (80,000)	1.0000	$(80,000)
Installation and testing	0	(15,000)	1.0000	(15,000)
Sales revenues	1	$ 220,000		
Cash expenses	1	(175,000)		
Tax effect of above	1	(15,300)		
Depreciation tax shield	1	4,616		
Working capital investment	1	(30,000)		
Total, year 1	1	$ 4,316	0.8621	3,721
Sales revenues	2	$ 245,000		
Cash expenses	2	(195,000)		
Tax effect of above	2	(17,000)		
Depreciation tax shield	2	7,910		
Total, year 2	2	$ 40,910	0.7432	30,404
Sales revenues	3	$ 260,000		
Cash expenses	3	(200,000)		
Tax effect of above	3	(20,400)		
Depreciation tax shield	3	5,649		
Total, year 3	3	$ 45,249	0.6407	28,991
Sales revenues	4	$ 200,000		
Cash expenses	4	(160,000)		
Tax effect of above	4	(13,600)		
Depreciation tax shield	4	4,034		
Total, year 4	4	$ 30,434	0.5523	16,809
Sales revenues	5	$ 180,000		
Cash expenses	5	(145,000)		
Tax effect of above	5	(11,900)		
Depreciation tax shield	5	2,885		
Total, year 5	5	$ 25,985	0.4761	12,371
Sales revenues	6	$ 150,000		
Cash expenses	6	(125,000)		
Tax effect of above	6	(8,500)		
Depreciation tax shield	6	2,881		
Total, year 6	6	$ 19,381	0.4104	7,954
Sales revenues	7	$ 100,000		
Cash expenses	7	(85,000)		
Tax effect of above	7	(5,100)		
Depreciation tax shield	7	2,885		
Recovery of working capital investment	7	30,000		
Salvage value of equipment	7	10,000		
Tax, gain on salvage of equipment	7	(3,400)		
Total, year 7	7	$ 49,385	0.3538	17,472
Depreciation tax shield	8	1,440	0.3050	439
Total net present value				$23,161

3. Profitability index calculated:

$$\text{Profitability index} = \frac{\text{present value of future net cash inflows}}{\text{immediate cash outflows}}$$

Present value of future net cash inflows

$$= \$3{,}721 + \$30{,}404 + \$28{,}991 + \$16{,}809 + \$12{,}371 + \$7{,}954 + \$17{,}472 + \$439$$

$$= \$118{,}161$$

Immediate cash outflows

$$= \$80{,}000 + \$15{,}000 = \$95{,}000$$

(Figures for the above calculations taken from the capital expenditure worksheet on page 723.)

$$\text{Profitability index} = \frac{\$118{,}161}{\$95{,}000} = \underline{\underline{1.2438}}$$

4. Payback period calculated:

Year	Remaining investment to be recovered at beginning of year	Annual net cash inflows
1	$95,000	$ 4,316
2	90,684	40,910
3	49,774	45,249
4	4,525	30,434

$$\frac{\$4{,}525}{\$30{,}434} = 0.15$$

$$\text{Payback period} = \underline{\underline{3.15}} \text{ years}$$

Annual net cash inflow figures were taken from the amount of cash flow column in the capital expenditure worksheet in 2 above. Inflows or outflows for working capital and/or salvage value are included in calculating annual net cash inflow. (Remember that the payback period is based on *undiscounted* cash flows.)

5. *a.* Average added net income calculated:

The easiest way to calculate average added after-tax net income is to calculate the total revenues, cash expenses, and depreciation. Total revenues and cash expenses are the same as the total revenues and expenses for the seven-year life of the product. Total depreciation is $85,000 (cost + installation and testing − salvage value). Total net income after taxes is calculated using a tax rate of 34 percent. The average added net income is calculated by dividing the total net income by seven.

$$\begin{array}{c}\text{Average added}\\ \text{after-tax}\\ \text{net income}\end{array} = \begin{array}{c}\text{average added}\\ \text{annual revenue}\end{array} - \begin{array}{c}\text{average added}\\ \text{annual expenses}\end{array}$$

Harlan Company Projected Added Income: New Product Investment

	Total	Average (total ÷ 7)
Sales revenues	$1,355,000	$193,571
Cash expenses	$1,085,000	$155,000
Depreciation	85,000	12,143
Total expenses	$1,170,000	$167,143
Income before taxes	$ 185,000	$ 26,428
Income tax (34%)	62,900	8,986
Net income	$ 122,100	$ 17,442

5. *b.* Average added investment calculated:

The equation for the average added assets must be modified for this problem to include the investment in working capital. Since the working capital is invested for the duration of the project, it is added at the end of the equation.

$$\text{Average added assets} = \frac{(\text{initial costs} - \text{salvage value})}{2} + \text{salvage value} + \text{working capital}$$

$$= \frac{(\$95{,}000 - \$10{,}000)}{2} + \$10{,}000 + \$30{,}000$$

$$= \$42{,}500 + \$10{,}000 + \$30{,}000$$

$$= \underline{\underline{\$82{,}500}}$$

5. *c.* Accounting rate of return calculated:

$$\text{Accounting rate of return} = \frac{\text{average added after-tax net income}}{\text{average added assets}}$$

$$= \frac{\$17{,}442}{\$82{,}500}$$

$$= \underline{\underline{21.1}} \text{ percent}$$

Chapter Assignments

Questions

1. (L.O. 3) Discuss the role of income taxes in capital expenditure analysis.
2. (L.O. 1) How does added revenue affect income tax payments?
3. (L.O. 1) How do added expenses affect income tax payments?

4. (L.O. 2) Explain the depreciation tax shield.

5. (L.O. 2) How can depreciation affect capital expenditures if it is not a cash flow?

6. (L.O. 4) What is the minimum rate of return? How is it used?

7. (L.O. 4) How is the cost of capital used to eliminate some investment proposals?

8. (L.O. 4) Why must management rank capital investment projects?

9. (L.O. 5, 6, 7) List three methods of ranking investment projects. Which do you prefer? Why?

10. (L.O. 6) What is a payback period? How is it used to rank capital investment projects?

11. (L.O. 6) What are the advantages and disadvantages of the payback method?

12. (L.O. 7) What is the accounting rate of return? What are its advantages and disadvantages?

Exercises

13. (L.O. 2) Rebecca Company purchased production equipment for $10,000. The company's income tax rate is 25 percent. The machine is in the seven-year class.

Required Calculate the depreciation for each year on the equipment using the MACRS accelerated method and calculate the applicable amount of depreciation tax shield. (see Review Exercise 15–1)

14. (L.O. 2) Barton Company purchased office equipment for $20,000. The company's income tax rate is 34 percent. The machine is in the seven-year class.

Required Calculate the depreciation for each year on the equipment using the MACRS accelerated method and calculate the applicable amount of depreciation tax shield. (see Review Exercise 15–1)

15. (L.O. 2) Arbee Company purchased office equipment for $15,000. The company's tax rate is 25 percent. Salvage value is zero.

Required Calculate the depreciation for each year on the equipment using the optional straight-line method with a seven-year life and calculate the applicable amount of depreciation tax shield. (see Review Exercise 15–1)

16. (L.O. 2) Polly Company paid $14,500 for an oven, which will be used in its business. The company's income tax rate is 34 percent. The oven is in the seven-year class.

Required Calculate the depreciation for each year on the oven using the MACRS accelerated method, and calculate the applicable amount of depreciation tax shield. (see Review Exercise 15–1)

17. (L.O. 2) City Vegetarian Restaurant is considering buying new tables. They will cost $70,000 and will be seven-year class property. The worker-owners want to know how the depreciation tax shield will differ if they use MACRS accelerated depreciation rather than straight-line depreciation. The half-year convention will apply. The restaurant's combined federal and state income tax rate is 40 percent.

Required

1. Calculate the depreciation tax shield for each year using MACRS accelerated depreciation.
2. Calculate the depreciation tax shield for each year using straight-line depreciation. (see Review Exercise 15–1)

18. (L.O. 2) Millet Bakery is considering the purchase of a new oven. The oven will cost $30,000 and will be seven-year class property. The half-year convention will apply. Millet's income tax rate is 34 percent.

Required

Prepare a table like Exhibit 15–5 calculating the depreciation tax shield for each year using MACRS accelerated depreciation. (see Review Exercise 15–1)

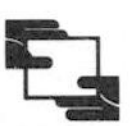

19. (L.O. 2) Tom's Garage is considering the purchase of a new engine diagnostic machine. The machine will cost $30,000 and will be seven-year class property. The half-year convention will apply. Tom's income tax rate is 34 percent.

Required

Prepare a table like Exhibit 15–5 calculating the depreciation tax shield for each year using straight-line depreciation. Use the straight-line cost recovery percentages. (see Review Exercise 15–1)

20. (L.O. 2) Convenience Grocery Store is considering purchasing new cash registers. They will cost $14,000 and will be seven-year class property. The manager wants to know how the depreciation tax shield will differ if they use MACRS accelerated depreciation rather than straight-line depreciation. The half-year convention will apply. The store's combined federal and state income tax rate is 35 percent.

Required

1. Calculate the depreciation tax shield for each year using MACRS accelerated depreciation.
2. Calculate the depreciation tax shield for each year using straight-line depreciation. (see Review Exercise 15–1)

21. (L.O. 2) Winner Wholesale Auto Supply Company is considering new lift trucks. They will cost $80,000. The lift trucks will be seven-year class property. Mr. Winner wants to know how the depreciation tax shield will differ depending on whether they use MACRS accelerated depreciation or straight-line depreciation. The half-year convention will apply. Winner's tax rate is 34 percent.

Required

1. Calculate the depreciation tax shield for each year using MACRS accelerated depreciation.
2. Calculate the depreciation tax shield for each year using straight-line depreciation. (see Review Exercise 15–1)

22. (L.O. 2) Lucky Pet Store is establishing a pet shampooing service. It will cost $12,000 for needed equipment. The equipment will be seven-year class property. Lucky's accountant decided to calculate the depreciation tax shield two ways, MACRS accelerated depreciation and straight-line depreciation, before deciding what to recommend to the owner. In either case, the half-year convention would apply. Lucky's tax rate is 34 percent.

Required

1. Calculate the depreciation tax shield for each year using MACRS accelerated depreciation.
2. Calculate the depreciation tax shield for each year using straight-line depreciation. (see Review Exercise 15–1)

23. (L.O. 3) Pot-o-Gold Food Stores is facing new competition. Pot-o-Gold offers a full range of groceries. It particularly emphasizes its gourmet foods, in-store bakery, and

quality meats. In order to meet the new competition, the store is considering adding a fresh fish department. They have existing space in which to install the new department. The equipment will cost $98,000 and be seven-year class property. The store anticipates the department would add sales of $78,000 per year. Its annual cash operating expenses will be $42,000. The department would require investment of $11,700 in working capital by the end of the first year of operation. This investment would be recovered if the department were discontinued at the end of the equipment's seven-year useful life.

The equipment would be seven-year class property for income tax purposes, and Pot-o-Gold would use straight-line depreciation. The half-year convention would apply. Pot-o-Gold's tax rate is 34 percent. Management requires an 18 percent after-tax return on investments.

Required

1. Prepare a capital expenditure analysis worksheet calculating the department's after-tax net present value.
2. Should Pot-o-Gold expect the machine to return its minimum rate of return? (see Review Exercise 15–2)

24. (L.O. 3) Wheeler's Bike Shop is thinking of setting up a do-it-yourself bike repair station as an experiment. They expect increased sales of small parts as a result of having people work on their bikes in the shop. The work station would require $600 of equipment but no increase in working capital. The equipment will have a seven-year life. Wheeler's expects that the new system would increase revenues by $200 per year. Its annual cash operating expenses will be $40.

The equipment would be seven-year class property for income tax purposes, and Wheeler would use straight-line depreciation. The half-year convention would apply. Wheeler's income tax rate is 34 percent. Management requires a 12 percent after-tax return on investments.

Required

1. Prepare a capital expenditure analysis worksheet calculating the station's after-tax net present value.
2. Should Wheeler expect the system to return its minimum rate of return? (see Review Exercise 15–2)

25. (L.O. 3) Penny's Pizza Parlor is thinking of replacing its old juke box with a new compact disk music system. The system would have improved speakers and a greater variety of recordings. The system would require an investment of $8,000 in equipment and $960 in working capital, mainly for a collection of disks. The equipment will have a seven-year life. Penny estimates that the new system would increase revenues by $8,000 per year. Its annual cash operating expenses will be $5,400. The working capital will be recovered at the end of year seven.

The equipment would be seven-year class property for income tax purposes, and Penny would use straight-line depreciation. The half-year convention would apply. Penny's tax rate is 34 percent. Management requires a 14 percent after-tax return on investments.

Required

1. Prepare a capital expenditure analysis worksheet calculating the new system's after-tax net present value.
2. Should Penny expect the system to return its minimum rate of return? (see Review Exercise 15–2)

26. (L.O. 3) Cutright Discount Store thinks it might be profitable to add a toy department. Cutright expects toy sales might add $155,000 annual revenue to the store. It would require $114,000 investment in displays and a $32,550 increase in working

capital. The displays will have a seven-year life. The toy department's annual cash operating expenses would be $103,000. The working capital will be recovered at the end of year seven.

The equipment would be seven-year class property for income tax purposes, and Cutright would use straight-line depreciation. The half-year convention would apply. Cutright's tax rate is 34 percent. Management requires a 24 percent after-tax return on investments.

Required

1. Prepare a capital expenditure analysis worksheet calculating the investment's after-tax net present value.
2. Will the investment yield Cutright's minimum rate of return?

(see Review Exercise 15–2)

27. (L.O. 5) Bernie's Restaurant is considering replacing some tables with booths. Bernie's believes that this will upgrade the image of the restaurant and increase sales. The new seating will cost $40,000 and will have a seven-year useful life. Bernie's expects added annual revenue of $63,000. It expects added annual cash operating expenses of $46,500.

The seating would be seven-year class property for income tax purposes, and Bernie's would use straight-line depreciation. The half-year convention would apply. Bernie's income tax rate is 34 percent. Management requires a 16 percent after-tax return on investments.

Required

1. Prepare a capital expenditure analysis worksheet and calculate the investment's profitability index.
2. Will the new seating yield a 16 percent rate of return?

(see Review Exercise 15–3)

28. (L.O. 5) Brian's Fishing Shop sells all kinds of sports fishing equipment. Many customers have asked Brian to add a line of live bait. Keeping the bait would require some large tanks and some refrigerators that would have seven-year useful lives. Brian is responsive to his customers' needs and is, therefore, seriously considering the new product line. The equipment would cost $19,000. Because of his cost of capital, Brian can make investments only when he expects them to earn a 16 percent rate of return. Brian estimates that the new product line would add $14,700 annual revenue. He estimates that the line would add $9,200 to annual cash operating expenses.

The tanks and refrigerators would be seven-year class property for income tax purposes, and Brian would use straight-line depreciation. The half-year convention would apply. Brian's tax rate is 34 percent.

Required

1. Prepare a capital expenditure analysis worksheet and calculate the investment's profitability index.
2. Will the investment yield a 16 percent rate of return?

(see Review Exercise 15–3)

29. (L.O. 5) Campus Copy Shop makes photocopies for students and faculty. One of Campus Copy's student employees has explained developments in desk-top publishing computer software to the store manager. Campus Copy now is thinking of adding a computer and software that would permit customers to prepare their own materials for photocopying. The equipment could be fitted into existing space. The equipment will cost $20,000 and have a seven-year useful life. Campus Copy expects added annual sales of $14,500. Its cash operating expenses will be $8,900 annually.

The equipment would be seven-year class property for income tax purposes, and Campus Copy would use straight-line depreciation. The half-year convention would apply. Campus Copy's tax rate is 34 percent. Management requires a 12 percent after-tax return on investments.

Required

1. Prepare a capital expenditure analysis worksheet and calculate the investment's profitability index.
2. Should Campus Copy expect the machine to earn a 12 percent rate of return?
(see Review Exercise 15–3)

30. (L.O. 5) Carter Entertainment Company has an old-style movie theater that has one screen. It has been only marginally profitable. Carter is thinking of remodeling the theater into a three-screen building that would be more profitable. The remodeling could be done so that all of the investment could be considered equipment rather than real estate improvements. The investment would total $250,000 and have a seven-year useful life. Carter would expect added annual revenue of $130,000. Its cash operating expenses would be $39,000 annually.

The equipment would be seven-year class property for income tax purposes, and Carter would use straight-line depreciation. The half-year convention would apply. Carter's income tax rate is 34 percent. Management requires an 18 percent after-tax return on investments.

Required

1. Prepare a capital expenditure analysis worksheet and calculate the investment's profitability index.
2. Will the remodeling yield an 18 percent rate of return?
(see Review Exercise 15–3)

31. (L.O. 5) The manager of Peco's Restaurant wants to add a bakery section to the restaurant. Peco's believes that it will attract more people to the restaurant along with providing a new product line for people wishing to buy bakery items to eat at home. To go into the bakery business, Peco's will have to buy some new baking equipment as well as adding a display case. This equipment and display case will cost $75,000 and have a seven-year useful life. Peco's expects added annual revenue of $84,000. It expects added annual cash operating expenses of $56,300.

The equipment and display cases would be seven-year class property for income tax purposes, and Peco's would use straight-line depreciation. The half-year convention would apply. Peco's tax rate is 34 percent. Management requires a 16 percent after-tax return on investments.

Required

1. Prepare a capital expenditure analysis worksheet and calculate the investment's profitability index.
2. Will the new bakery yield a 16 percent rate of return?
(see Review Exercise 15–3)

32. (L.O. 5) Heller Card and Gift Store is considering replacing some old greeting card displays with new display cases. The design of the cases will encourage customers to browse through the cards and purchase more. Heller will also be able to display more cards than presently possible. The investment in the cases will be $30,000 and have a seven-year useful life. Heller expects added annual revenue of $41,500. Its cash operating expenses would be $31,200 annually.

The display cases would be seven-year class property for income tax purposes, and Heller would use straight-line depreciation. The half-year convention would apply. Heller's tax rate is 34 percent. Management requires a 16 percent after-tax return on investments.

Required

1. Prepare a capital expenditure analysis worksheet and calculate the investment's profitability index.

2. Will the remodeling yield a 16 percent rate of return?
(see Review Exercise 15–3)

33. (L.O. 5) Engineering Support Consultants (ESC) offers engineering consulting to architects and building contractors. The company is considering offering a new consulting service. ESC has people who are qualified to work in the new area, but they would need a piece of equipment. The equipment will cost $8,000 and have a seven-year useful life. ESC expects added annual revenue of $8,100 from this service. Its cash operating expenses will be $5,800 annually.

The equipment would be seven-year class property for income tax purposes, and ESC would use straight-line depreciation. The half-year convention would apply. ESC's tax rate is 34 percent. Management requires a 10 percent after-tax return on investments.

Required

1. Prepare a capital expenditure analysis worksheet and calculate the investment's profitability index.
2. Should ESC expect the machine to earn a 10 percent rate of return?
(see Review Exercise 15–3)

34. (L.O. 6) Chuck's Placement Service is considering replacing its old photocopying machine with a new machine that will collate and staple the output. The new machine would cost $8,300 and have a useful life of seven years. Its salvage value would be $500. Chuck estimates the following annual before-tax cash flows:

	Savings during year 1	Savings during years 2–6	Savings during year 7
Labor savings	$8,190	$8,190	$8,190
Electricity costs	(200)	(200)	(200)
Maintenance costs	(500)	(500)	(500)
Net savings before income taxes	$7,490	$7,490	$7,490

Chuck's income tax rate is 34 percent. The machine would be seven-year class property for income tax purposes, and the company would use straight-line depreciation. The half-year convention would apply.

Required

1. Calculate after-tax cash flows for the periods shown in the table above.
2. Calculate the investment's payback period.

35. (L.O. 6) Margo's Fashions makes dresses that Margo designs in limited copies. The production manager is considering replacing some old cutting machines with a new laser cutter that would permit one person to do the work of several on the old cutting machines. The new machine would cost $54,600 and would have a useful life of seven years. The machine's estimated salvage value will be $8,540 at the end of 7 years. The production manager estimates the following annual before-tax cash flows:

	Savings during year 1	Savings during years 2–6	Savings during year 7
Labor savings	$34,580	$34,580	$34,580
Electricity costs	(250)	(250)	(250)
Maintenance costs	(540)	(540)	(540)
Net savings before income taxes	$33,790	$33,790	$33,790

Margo's income tax rate is 34 percent. The equipment would be seven-year class property for income tax purposes, and the company would use straight-line depreciation. The half-year convention would apply.

Required

1. Calculate after-tax cash flows for the periods shown in the table above.
2. Calculate the investment's payback period.

36. (L.O. 6) Lynn's Bakery is considering replacing a packaging machine with an automated machine that automatically makes the right size package for the item. The new machine would cost $19,200 and its salvage value will be $1,200 at the end of its 7 year useful life. The manager estimates the following annual before-tax cash flows:

	Savings during year 1	Savings during years 2–6	Savings during year 7
Labor savings	$18,800	$18,800	$18,800
Electricity costs	(300)	(300)	(300)
Maintenance costs	(700)	(700)	(700)
Net savings before income taxes	$17,800	$17,800	$17,800

Lynn's income tax rate is 34 percent. The machine would be seven-year class property for income tax purposes, and the company would use straight-line depreciation. The half-year convention would apply.

Required

1. Calculate after-tax cash flows for the periods shown in the table above.
2. Calculate the investment's payback period.

37. (L. O. 6) Tornado Car Wash wants to buy a new machine that will do part of the drying of an automobile at the end of the wash process. Presently, Tornado does all drying with hand labor. The new machine would cost $118,700 and would have a useful life of seven years. It will have no salvage value at that time. The manager estimates the following annual before-tax cash flows:

	Savings during year 1	Savings during years 2–6	Savings during year 7
Labor savings	$72,000	$72,000	$72,000
Electricity costs	(4,100)	(4,100)	(4,100)
Maintenance costs	(2,800)	(2,800)	(2,800)
Net savings before income taxes	$65,100	$65,100	$65,100

Tornado's income tax rate is 34 percent. The machine would be seven-year class property for income tax purposes, and the company would use straight-line depreciation. The half-year convention would apply.

Required

1. Calculate after-tax cash flows for the periods shown in the table above.
2. Calculate the investment's payback period.

38. (L. O. 6) The *Star Journal* delivers its newspapers to a number of drop stations throughout the metropolitan area it serves. The route carriers pick up the papers at each drop station and deliver the newspapers to the customers. One day when the

business manager was taking an airline flight, she noticed that most of the air cargo was loaded into containers and then the containers were loaded into the airplanes. This saved much baggage handling. She wondered if the same process could be used in delivering newspapers to the drop stations. The *Star Journal's* present delivery process requires much human effort to load paper bundles into trucks at the printing plant and then unload them at the drop stations. A little investigation showed that containers could be designed that could be rolled into the delivery trucks. The papers could be bundled at the end of the printing process and loaded automatically into each container.

After deciding that the container idea could be adapted to newspaper delivery, the business manager undertook an economic study. She found that the containers and related equipment would cost $234,900 and would have a useful life of seven years. It will have no salvage value at that time. She also estimated the following annual before-tax cash flows:

	Savings during year 1	Savings during years 2–6	Savings during year 7
Labor savings	$133,400	$133,400	$133,400
Electricity costs	(2,100)	(2,100)	(2,100)
Maintenance costs	(1,300)	(1,300)	(1,300)
Net savings before income taxes	$130,000	$130,000	$130,000

The *Star Journal's* income tax rate is 34 percent. The equipment would be seven-year class property for income tax purposes, and the company would use straight-line depreciation. The half-year convention would apply.

Required

1. Calculate after-tax cash flows for the periods shown in the table above.
2. Calculate the investment's payback period.

39. (L.O. 2, 3, 5, 6, 7) On January 1, Studley Company purchased a new machine for $100,000 to produce a new product. The new product's expected useful life is seven years. The machine is in the seven-year class and has no salvage value. The machine will be depreciated according to the straight-line method. Estimated revenue is $110,000 per year. Estimated cash expenses, excluding income taxes, are $70,000 per year. Assume Studley's minimum rate of return is 12 percent and its income tax rate is 34 percent for all years.

Required

1. Calculate the depreciation tax shield.
2. Calculate the project's net present value.
3. Calculate the project's profitability index.
4. Calculate the project's payback period.
5. Calculate the project's average added net income. Use income tax depreciation amounts.
6. Calculate the accounting rate of return. (AICPA)

40. (L.O. 2, 3, 6) Fleming, Inc., plans to acquire a new machine for a total cost of $35,000. The machine is in the seven-year class and has no salvage value. Straight-line depreciation will be used for tax purposes. Fleming estimates that before income taxes its annual cash flow from operations from this machine will be $9,000. Fleming's cost of capital is 8 percent; its income tax rate, 34 percent.

Required

1. Calculate the payback period.
2. Calculate net present value. (AICPA)

41. (L.O. 2, 3, 6) Bernie Company is considering buying a new machine for $45,000. The machine is in the seven-year class. Its useful life is seven years, and it will have no salvage value. Bernie demands a 20 percent minimum rate of return on investments. The machine is expected to save on cash expenses of the following amounts (excluding income taxes):

1st year	$12,000
2nd year	16,000
3rd year	20,000
4th year	12,000
5th year	10,000
6th year	7,000
7th year	3,000

Bernie's income tax rate is 25 percent. It will use the MACRS accelerated method to depreciate the new machine.

Required

1. Calculate the payback period.
2. If Bernie's minimum rate of return is 20 percent, calculate net present value.
3. Should Bernie Company purchase the new machine?

42. (L.O. 2, 3, 5, 6, 7) George Company plans to acquire a new machine at a total cost of $30,600. The machine's estimated life is seven years. It is in the seven-year class and has no salvage value. George Company estimates its annual before-tax labor savings from using this machine will be $8,000. The company's minimum rate of return is 12 percent; its income tax rate, 25 percent. The company will use MACRS accelerated depreciation for income tax purposes.

Required

1. Calculate the machine's net present value.
2. Does your answer to *1* above justify purchasing the machine?
3. Calculate the project's profitability index.
4. Calculate the project's payback period.
5. Calculate added average net income for this project. Use income tax depreciation amounts.
6. Calculate the accounting rate of return. (AICPA)

Problems

43. (L.O. 3, 6) Denver Company is considering replacing some machinery. The machinery's book value is zero, but the current market value is $2,800. The machinery is usable for another four years, but its salvage value will be zero at that time.

Denver is considering a new machine costing $40,000. This machine would produce an estimated pretax operating cash savings of $12,500 annually. The machinery's estimated useful life is seven years. Denver uses MACRS accelerated depreciation for tax purposes. The new machinery's estimated salvage value is $2,000 at the end of seven years. Investing in this new machinery would require an additional working capital investment of $3,000 by the end of the first year. This investment would be recovered at the end of the seventh year.

Denver Company is subject to a 34 percent income tax rate. Its minimum rate of return after taxes is 10 percent.

Required

1. Calculate the machine's net present value. Assume that the old machinery will be sold for market value.
2. Calculate the machine's payback period.
3. Should Denver Company replace its current machine?

44. (L.O. 5, 6) Netherlands Company wants to introduce a new product, which will be manufactured in an existing plant. New equipment, whose cost is $150,000 and whose useful life is seven years, will be necessary. The equipment will have no salvage value. Space currently being used as a warehouse in the existing plant will be used to produce the new product. Annual depreciation on the space is $15,000. Netherlands will rent new warehouse space for $25,000 a year. An accounting study produced the following estimates of added annual revenue and expenses:

Sales	$500,000
Cost of merchandise sold, excluding depreciation	385,000
Administrative expenses	30,000
Marketing expenses	10,000

Netherlands will use MACRS accelerated depreciation for the seven-year class property. The company requires a minimum rate of return of 14 percent after income taxes on investment proposals. The income tax rate is 34 percent.

Required

1. Calculate the payback period.
2. Calculate the profitability index.
3. Should Netherlands produce the new product?

45. (L.O. 3, 6) Hanley Company bought a machine for $125,000. Its useful life is seven years, and it has no expected salvage value. The company will depreciate the machine by using MACRS accelerated depreciation. Cash flow from operations (cash revenue less cash expenses) before income taxes is expected to be $60,000 a year. Assume Hanley's effective income tax rate is 25 percent for all years.

Required

1. Calculate the payback period.
2. If Hanley's minimum rate of return is 25 percent, what is the machine's net present value?

46. (L.O. 6) Solar Company plans to buy a new machine for $40,000. Solar's analysis shows that the payback period is expected to be exactly five years. The new machine is expected to produce a net cash inflow before taxes of $10,000 a year in each of the first three years and $7,800 in the fourth year. Solar will depreciate the machine according to the straight-line method for tax purposes. The machine is in the seven-year class. Solar's income tax rate is 25 percent.

Required

What amount of annual net cash inflow is the new machine expected to produce in the last (fifth) year of the payback period?

47. (L.O. 3, 5, 6) Cartie Company plans to replace a piece of obsolete equipment. The equipment is fully depreciated, and its salvage value is zero.

The equipment being considered will provide annual cash, labor, and maintenance savings of $7,000 before income taxes. The equipment will cost $18,000. Its estimated useful life is seven years. The equipment is expected to have no salvage value at the end of seven years.

Cartie will use the alternate straight-line depreciation method for tax purposes. The company's tax rate is 34 percent. Cartie's minimum after-tax rate of return is 14 percent.

Required

1. Calculate the payback period for the proposed new equipment.
2. Calculate the net present value for the proposed new equipment.
3. Calculate the profitability index for the proposed new equipment.

48. (L.O. 3, 6) Greenwood Company manufactures short-lived electronic items. The research department has developed a new product that would be a good accessory for office equipment dealers. According to Greenwood's salespeople, projected sales for the next five years are good. The product is expected to be obsolete at the end of five years.

To produce the quantity demanded, Greenwood needs to buy additional machinery and rent additional space. About 5,000 square feet of space are needed. There are 5,000 square feet adjoining Greenwood's manufacturing facility. Greenwood will rent that space for five years at $2 per square foot per year if it decides to make the product.

To produce the product, Greenwood must buy $90,000 worth of equipment. The equipment will require modifications costing $4,000. Installation will cost $5,000; testing, $9,000. These activities will be done by a firm of engineers hired by Greenwood. The equipment should have a salvage value of about $ 18,000 after five years. It is seven-year class property, so depreciation for the five years must follow the seven-year pattern even though the product's life is only five years. The company will use straight-line depreciation for tax purposes.

No additional general overhead costs will be incurred on this product. However, the accounting system will allocate some existing overhead to this product.

The following revenue and expense estimates for this product for the five years were developed:

	19x3	19x4	19x5–19x7
Sales	$100,000	$160,000	$80,000
Materials, labor, and incurred overhead, excluding depreciation	40,000	54,000	32,000
Allocated general overhead	4,000	6,400	3,200
Rent	10,000	10,000	10,000

Required

1. Prepare a schedule, showing the project's annual cash inflows. Greenwood's income tax rate is 34 percent.
2. If the company needs a two-year payback period for the investment, should it undertake the project? Show supporting calculations clearly.
3. If the company requires a return rate of 20 percent after taxes, should this project be accepted? Show supporting calculations clearly.

49. (L.O. 3) L-O Company makes cookies for its chain of snack food stores. L-O is considering buying a newer, more efficient machine. L-O expects to sell 300,000 dozen cookies in each of the next seven years. The selling price of the cookies is expected to average $0.50 per dozen. The old machine has seven years of useful life remaining and a book value of $63,625. The old machine's cost, less $10,000 salvage value, is depreciated over ten years following the half-year convention. L-O uses

straight-line depreciation. The following information was assembled for those making the decision:

	Old machine	New machine
Original cost of machine at acquisition	$81,500	$120,000
Expected annual cash operating expenses		
Variable costs per dozen	0.20	0.14
Total fixed costs per year	15,000	14,000
Estimated salvage value of machines		
At present	63,625	—
After seven years	10,000	20,000

L-O Company's income tax rate is 34 percent.

Required Use the net present value method to determine whether L-O Company should retain the old machine or acquire the new machine. L-O requires an after-tax return of 16 percent. (CMA)

Case 1

Mass Products Company (L.O. 3)

Mass Products Company manufactures several products. One of the firm's principal products sells for $20 per unit. The sales manager has repeatedly said he could sell more units if they were available. In trying to substantiate his claim, the sales manager conducted a market research study to determine potential demand for this product. The study, which cost $44,000, indicated that Mass Products could sell 18,000 units annually over the next seven years.

The equipment being used can produce 11,000 units annually. Variable production costs are $9 per unit. The equipment's market value is 0. The equipment's cost is $85,700. Its book value is $64,275. The machine is depreciated over ten years using the straight-line method and the half-year convention. It has no salvage value.

A new machine that can produce 20,000 units annually costs $300,000. Its estimated useful life is seven years, and it will have no salvage value at the end of that time. Mass Products' production manager has estimated that the new equipment will increase production and reduce variable production costs to $7 per unit. Mass Products uses straight-line depreciation on all equipment for tax purposes. The firm's tax rate is 34 percent.

The sales manager firmly believed additional capacity was needed. As a result, he tried to prepare an economic justification for buying the equipment even though this was not his responsibility. His analysis, which is presented on page 738, was disappointing, as it did not justify buying the equipment.

Required Investment

Purchase price of new equipment		$300,000
Disposal of existing equipment		
Loss on disposal	$64,275	
Less tax benefit, 34%	21,854	42,421
Cost of market research study		44,000
Total investment		$386,421

Annual returns

Contribution margin from product	
Using the new equipment (18,000 × [$20 − 7])	$234,000
Using the existing equipment (11,000 × [$20 − 9])	121,000
Increase in contribution margin	$113,000
Less average increased depreciation	34,330
Increase in before-tax income	$ 78,670
Income tax, 34%	26,748
Increase in net income	$ 51,922
Less 15% cost of capital on the additional investment required (0.15 × $383,600)	57,540
Net annual return of proposed investment in new equipment	$ (5,618)

Required

1. The controller of Mass Products has agreed to prepare a present value analysis for the investment proposal. The controller has asked you to prepare corrected calculations for the following:
   a. Required after-tax investment cost of the new equipment.
   b. Recurring annual net cash inflows.
   Explain how you treated any items in your calculations that were treated differently in the original analysis prepared by the sales manager.
2. Calculate the net present value of the proposed investment. (CMA)

Case 2

Bravo Corporation (L.O. 3)

Bravo Corporation manufactures office equipment and distributes its products through wholesale distributors. The corporation recently heard about a patent on a semiautomatic paper copier. The patent can be obtained for $1,600,000 cash. The semiautomatic copier is vastly superior to the manual one the corporation produces. For $400,000, present equipment could be modified to accommodate production of the semiautomatic model. Such modifications would not affect the equipment's remaining useful life of seven years or its $10,000 salvage value at the end of that time. However, variable costs would increase by $40 per unit. Fixed costs other than depreciation and patent charges would be unaffected. If the equipment is modified, the manual model cannot be produced.

The current income statement covering the manual copier follows:

Sales revenues (10,000 units @ $400)		$4,000,000
Variable costs (10,000 units @ $180)	$1,800,000	
Fixed costs*	1,200,000	
Total costs		3,000,000
Net income before income taxes		$1,000,000
Income taxes, 34%		340,000
Net income after income taxes		$ 660,000

*All current fixed costs are directly traceable to production of the manual copier. These costs include $200,000 in equipment depreciation, calculated according to the straight-line method and using the half-year convention. The equipment's original cost was $2,010,000, and its salvage value is $10,000.

Market research has disclosed three important findings. First, a competitor will certainly purchase the patent if Bravo does not. Were this to happen, Bravo's sales of the manual copier would fall to 7,000 units per year. Second, at the same selling price as the manual model, Bravo can sell approximately 19,000 units of the semiautomatic model each year. Third, because of advances being made in this field, the patent will be worthless at the end of seven years.

Required

1. Prepare a schedule, showing annual net cash inflows for the two alternatives. Assume the corporation will use the straight-line method to depreciate the cost of equipment modifications. The $1,600,000 patent cost will be paid at the start of the project and can be deducted for income tax purposes in seven equal annual installments. (**Note:** This part does not require present value computations.)
2. Should Bravo make the investment if its required rate of return is 18 percent?

(CMA)

■

16

Cost Allocation

LEARNING OBJECTIVES

After studying this chapter you should be able to:

1. List the advantages of activity-based predetermined overhead rates
2. Calculate activity-based predetermined overhead rates and show when they are preferred to plantwide rates
3. Define a service activity and explain why its costs are assigned to production activities
4. List the three steps for assigning service activity costs to production activities
5. Use the direct method to assign service activity costs to production activities
6. Use the step method to assign service activity costs to production activities
7. Assign fixed and variable service activity costs separately

Products benefit indirectly rather than directly from manufacturing overhead costs. Because benefits are indirect, the manufacturing overhead costs of producing one unit of product cannot be measured. For example, factory accounting indirectly benefits all products by providing management with records of production levels and costs. But there is no way to *measure* how much of the accountant's salary should be charged to each unit of product.

Because accountants cannot measure the amount of overhead cost belonging to each product, they allocate overhead costs to products by using predetermined overhead rates. Allocation is based on reasonable measures of production activity such as direct labor costs, material costs, or machine-hours. We call these measures of production activity cost drivers. In Chapters 4 and 5, you saw how a single, plantwide predetermined overhead rate was used to allocate overhead costs to jobs or to individual products. In this chapter you will see how activity-based rates are used to allocate overhead costs more precisely. You will also see how service costs are assigned to production activities. Finally, you will learn the advantages of the procedures for assigning fixed and variable costs separately.

■

Shortcomings of Plantwide Predetermined Overhead Rates

In Chapter 4, plantwide predetermined overhead rates were used to **allocate** manufacturing overhead costs to jobs. **Plantwide predetermined overhead rates** were calculated by dividing total estimated manufacturing overhead by the total estimated amount of a cost driver. The company uses these rates to cost products produced. Plantwide overhead rates are the simplest means of allocating overhead cost to products. And often they are quite satisfactory for financial statements. They may not, however, be satisfactory for management decisions.

In companies manufacturing more than one product, using a plantwide rate may allocate overhead costs inaccurately. This is particularly true when different products require different production facilities. In such cases, the cost differences will probably be noticeable. For example, one product may use the foundry and fabrication activities extensively but use the assembly activity very little. Another product may make no use of the foundry and little use of the fabricating but place heavy demands on the assembly.

In these situations, using a plantwide overhead rate creates two problems. First, a plantwide overhead rate allocates a share of each activity's overhead costs to each product, even if no part of the product used that activity. Thus, a product making no use of the foundry is still allocated some of the foundry's costs. Second, a single cost driver is used to assign overhead costs to products regardless of the production methods. For instance, direct labor costs might be used as the cost driver for allocating overhead costs when in reality those costs fluctuate with machine-hours.

To illustrate, assume Steel Products Company manufactures four products with two activities, welding and assembly. Products 1 and 2 require use of an expensive robotic welding machine. Products 3 and 4 require no welding. Annual costs of using the robotic welding machine are as follows:

Depreciation	$100,000
Insurance	10,000
Property taxes	7,000
Electricity	12,000
Supplies	26,000
Maintenance	8,000
Total annual costs of welding machine	$163,000

Although the machine is costly to operate, its use is justified by labor cost savings and improved product quality. In addition to costs of the welding machine, Steel Products spends $300,000 on supervision, supplies, and other costs.

Steel Products allocates overhead costs to products using machine-hours as cost driver. Estimated total machine-hours in all departments for the year are shown below.

Product 1 (1 hour per unit × 10,000 units)	10,000 hours
Product 2 (3 hours per unit × 6,667 units)	20,000
Product 3 (1 hour per unit × 5,000 units)	5,000
Product 4 (2 hours per unit × 7,500 units)	15,000
Total machine-hours for the year	50,000 hours

Total estimated overhead costs for the company are $463,000 ($163,000 welding machine costs and $300,000 other costs).

If Steel Products uses a plantwide predetermined overhead rate, it will be $9.26 per machine-hour:

($163,000 + $300,000) ÷ 50,000 machine-hours

Overhead costs will be allocated to each of the four products as follows:

Product 1: 1 hour @ $9.26	$ 9.26
Product 2: 3 hours @ $9.26	27.78
Product 3: 1 hour @ $9.26	9.26
Product 4: 2 hours @ $9.26	18.52

Notice that since the plantwide rate includes the $163,000 cost of the robotic welding machine, some of that cost is assigned to all four products. In this example, using a plantwide predetermined overhead rate distorts the cost of each product. Only Products 1 and 2 should bear the cost of the robotic welding machine.

■

Advantages of Activity-Based Predetermined Overhead Rates

OBJECTIVE 1
List the advantages of activity-based predetermined overhead rates

To allocate overhead costs more precisely, accountants use activity-based overhead rates. An **activity-based predetermined overhead rate** is found by separating manufacturing overhead costs by activity and developing a predetermined overhead rate for each activity.

Activity-based overhead rates have two advantages over plant-wide overhead rates. First, with activity-based rates, only products using an activity are charged for its use. Second, each activity uses the cost driver that best relates its costs to its production activity.

To develop separate activity overhead rates, accountants trace manufacturing overhead costs to the activities in which those costs were incurred.

Costs traceable to an activity can be measured rather than allocated. Measurement is more precise than allocation. Once overhead costs have been separated by activity, accountants then develop a predetermined overhead rate for each activity. That rate is used to allocate overhead to products produced using those activities.

Now, return to the example of Steel Products Company. Assume Steel Products has decided that rather than using a plantwide rate, it will use activity-based overhead rates for its two activities, welding and assembly. Accountants start by dividing the company's overhead costs between welding and assembly. To do so, they first trace all costs of the robotic welding machine to the welding activity. They can also trace some of the remaining \$300,000 in overhead for supervision, supplies, and other items directly to welding. Assume, therefore, that \$100,000 of the \$300,000 in overhead goes to welding and \$200,000 to assembly.

Welding's cost driver is machine-hours. Steel Products expects to incur 30,000 machine-hours in welding next year. Assembly, which is less automated than welding, will use direct labor cost as cost-driver. Steel Products has forecasted total annual direct labor costs of \$100,000 for assembly. Thus, the two activity-based overhead rates are calculated as follows:

Welding

$$\text{Predetermined overhead rate} = \frac{\text{total activity overhead costs}}{\text{total machine-hours in welding}}$$

$$= \frac{\$163{,}000 + \$100{,}000}{30{,}000 \text{ machine-hours}}$$

$$= \underline{\underline{\$8.77}} \text{ per machine-hour}$$

Assembly

$$\text{Predetermined overhead rate} = \frac{\text{total activity overhead costs}}{\text{total direct labor costs in assembly}}$$

$$\text{Predetermined overhead rate} = \frac{\$200{,}000}{\$100{,}000}$$

$$= 200 \text{ percent of direct labor costs}$$

To allocate overhead costs to individual products, you must know (1) the number of welding machine-hours each product uses and (2) the amount of assembly direct labor costs for each product. Steel Products estimated these amounts in their budget at the beginning of the year.

Product 1	1 machine-hour in welding $10 direct labor costs in assembly
Product 2	3 machine-hours in welding $10 direct labor costs in assembly
Product 3	No machine-hours in welding $4 direct labor costs in assembly
Product 4	No machine-hours in welding $5 direct labor costs in assembly

Using the two activity-based rates and the data just given, you can calculate the overhead costs allocated to each product as shown below.

Product 1		
1 machine-hour @ $8.77	$ 8.77	
$10 in direct labor costs × 200%	20.00	$28.77
Product 2		
3 machine-hours @ $8.77	$26.31	
$10 in direct labor costs × 200%	20.00	$46.31
Product 3		
$4 in direct labor costs × 200%		$ 8.00
Product 4		
$5 in direct labor costs × 200%		$10.00

Compare these overhead costs with those calculated using the single plantwide rate (page 742). As you can see, by using the more precise activity-based rates that reflect use of the more expensive robotic welding equipment, Products 1 and 2 are more costly to produce. Products 3 and 4 are less expensive to produce than the plantwide rate showed, since they do not use the robotic welding equipment.

OBJECTIVE 2
Calculate activity-based predetermined overhead rates and show when they are preferred to plantwide rates

Although plantwide rates can produce dramatically different results than can activity-based rates, activity-based overhead rates do not always make a significant difference in the overhead allocated to various products. Not every company needs activity-based overhead rates to allocate costs equitably. How then does an accountant decide when to use activity-based overhead rather than plantwide rates? The answer is that activity-based rates should be used only when they will significantly change managerial decisions. When plantwide rates yield approximately the same results as activity-based rates, plantwide rates should be used because they are less expensive to administer.

Table 16–1

Plantwide Versus Activity-Based Allocation of Overhead Costs

Allocation of overhead costs is more precise when activity-based predetermined overhead rates are used. The process is more complicated and costly, however.

Plantwide Overhead Allocation	Activity-Based Overhead Allocation
1. All factory overhead costs in a single pool	1. Overhead costs traced to particular service and production activities 2. Service activity costs assigned to production activities
2. Overhead costs allocated to products by using a single predetermined overhead rate	3. Overhead costs allocated to products by using a separate predetermined overhead rate for each production activity

Reaching a consensus on what constitutes a significant change in managerial decisions might seem like a problem at first. But in practice, managers and accountants usually agree quickly.

Suppose, for example that an organization experiments with both activity-based and plantwide rates. Activity-based rates yield a $10 product cost; the plantwide rate, a $9.90 cost. This small difference should make no difference in management's decision to produce or discontinue the product. Therefore, to minimize accounting costs, accountants should choose a plantwide rate. However, if activity-based overhead rates had yielded a product cost of $2.25 and the plantwide rate a cost of $3.25, the 44 percent difference ([$3.25 − $2.25] ÷ $2.25) might change management's decisions about the product. Thus, activity-based rates should be used. Table 16–1 summarizes the differences between plantwide and activity-based allocation of overhead costs.

Review Exercise 16–1

Calculate Predetermined Overhead Rate

San Juan car rental company has three car rental centers. It has two major cost drivers, number of rental centers and days of car rental. For the coming year, San Juan has made the following estimates:

	Centers		
	Candado	Carolina	Ponce
Estimated overhead	$89,240	$73,600	$34,300
Estimated rental days	4,400	6,800	2,000

Required

1. Calculate an overall (plantwide) overhead rate using rental days as the cost driver.

2. Calculate activity-based overhead rates (one for each center) using rental days as the cost driver.

Solution

1.

	Estimated overhead	Estimated rental days
Candado	$ 89,240	4,400
Carolina	73,600	6,800
Ponce	34,300	2,000
Totals	$197,140	13,200

$$\text{Plantwide rate} = \frac{\text{total estimated overhead}}{\text{total estimated rental days}}$$

$$= \frac{\$197,140}{13,200} = \$14.93$$

2. Activity-based overhead rates

$$\text{Overhead rate} = \frac{\text{total estimated overhead}}{\text{total estimated rental days}}$$

$$\text{Candado} = \frac{\$89,240}{4,400 \text{ days}} = \$20.28$$

$$\text{Carolina} = \frac{\$73,600}{6,800 \text{ days}} = \$10.82$$

$$\text{Ponce} = \frac{\$34,300}{2,000 \text{ days}} = \$17.15$$

(see Exercises 18, 19, 20)

■

Assigning Service Activity Costs to Production Activities

Until now you have been dealing with overhead costs incurred within **production activities**—that is, activities performed directly on products sold to customers. But in many organizations, significant overhead costs are incurred outside production activities, and those costs are not directly traceable to them. In the example of Steel Products Company, management divided $300,000 in overhead costs between welding and assembly. Some of that $300,000 was directly traceable to these activities. Some, however, was not. Here, the concern is with that untraceable portion.

For example, take the factory manager's salary. The factory manager does not work in any production activity, but his or her efforts benefit all production activities. Nevertheless, the manager's time is fundamentally different from electricity, which can be measured in each activity with a meter. Therefore, since tracing portions of the factory manager's time to particular activities is impossible, accountants must assign each production activity a portion of this manager's cost.

OBJECTIVE 3
Define a service activity and explain why its costs are assigned to production activities

Some activities produce nothing but services to support other activities. Food service, maintenance, data processing, and quality control are common examples. **Service activities** do not work directly on a firm's products. Instead, they provide support. Salaries, supplies, equipment, and other costs can be directly traced to service activities. They cannot, however, be allocated directly to *products* from service activities because the service activities have no contact with the products. Therefore, in order to allocate those costs to products, accountants must first **assign** them to production activities for inclusion in their predetermined overhead rates. Then, the rates are used to allocate predetermined overhead costs to units produced.

Service activity costs are assigned to production activities according to the amount of service used. A production activity that uses more service than others should bear a larger amount of the service's costs. For example, activities with many employees use the factory cafeteria more while activities with many machines use the maintenance activity more. Therefore, each should be allocated a greater portion of the cafeteria and maintenance service costs, respectively.

After determining the cost of providing each type of service, that is, the cost of operating each service activity, the accountant assigns a cost to other activities according to their use of the service. This assigned cost is eventually included in each production activity's predetermined overhead rate.

When assigning service activity costs to production activities, one should follow the three steps listed below.

OBJECTIVE 4
List the three steps for assigning service activity costs to production activities

1. Identify service and production activities.
2. Trace all overhead costs to the service or production activity in which the costs will be incurred.
3. Assign overhead costs incurred in service activities to each production activity according to its use of the service.

Identifying Service Activities

A factory has only two types of activities, production and service. Production activities work on products. Service activities do not. They provide services so production activities can operate more efficiently. Janitorial and human resources are service activities. Both exist solely to support the production activities.

Tracing Overhead Costs to Activities in Which They Were Incurred

If an organization has properly defined its activities, an accountant should be able to trace all overhead costs directly to a service activity or a production activity. The costs of the robotic welding machine discussed earlier are easily traced to the welding activity, the only activity that uses the equipment. The salaries of the factory manager, secretaries, and cost accountants are traceable to a service activity called factory administration. Likewise, the cost of food and related labor is traceable to the cafeteria, another service activity. Depreciation of stoves and other cafeteria equipment is also charged to that activity, along with the cost of supplies and utilities used there. If the service and production activities are properly chosen, it should be fairly easy to trace all costs to an activity.

Assigning Service Activity Costs to User Production Activities

Once overhead costs have been traced directly to a service or production activity, service activity costs must be assigned to other activities. The two most common methods of assigning these costs are the direct method and the step method.

The **direct method** assigns service activity costs *only* to production activities. Services performed by one service activity for another service activity are ignored. This is the simpler method.

Table 16-2

Cost Drivers Commonly Used to Assign Service Costs to Production Activities
Service costs are assigned to other activities by using a measure of the service used. Some are more closely tied to the service than others. Some common cost drivers are listed below.

Service department	Cost driver
Building and grounds	Square feet occupied
Cafeteria	Number of employees
Cost accounting	Labor hours
Electrical power	Metered or machine capacity
Engineering	Number of change requests or time records
Factory administration	Number of employees or labor hours
Inspection	Labor hours or product complexity
Maintenance	Service hours or machine-hours if service hours are unavailable
Personnel and employment	Number of employees or time records
Production planning and control	Number of different products or time records (employees)
Receiving, shipping, and storage	Units handled or cubic feet processed

The **step method** assigns service activity costs to other service activities as well as to production activities. Costs of one service activity assigned to another service activity are reassigned to production activities. Although this method is more precise, it is also more complicated to use than the direct method.

Both methods assign costs by using a measure of the service provided to other activities. To use an earlier example, take cafeteria costs, which are usually assigned according to the number of employees in each activity. The assumption is that activities with more employees receive greater service from the cafeteria. Maintenance costs are often assigned on the basis of number of hours of service provided. An activity using 10 percent of total maintenance time would be assigned 10 percent of maintenance costs. Factory administration costs include supervision, training, and employee benefits. They are often assigned according to the number of employees in the activity. Table 16–2 lists cost drivers commonly used to assign service activity costs.

Because the assignment system must be easy to use, data on the chosen cost driver must be readily available in company records. Also, the cost driver should seem fair to department managers. Once a cost driver is chosen, costs may be assigned by using either the direct method or the step method.

OBJECTIVE 5
Use the direct method to assign service activity costs to production activities

The Direct Method To illustrate the direct method, the Mibelle Company data will be used. Mibelle has three service activities and two production activities, machining and assembly. The cost drivers used to assign service costs are as follows:

Service activities	Cost driver
Factory administration	Number of employees
Maintenance	Service hours
Buildings and grounds	Square feet occupied

Over the next year, Mibelle expects its two production activities to have the following amounts in each cost driver:

Cost driver	Machining	Assembly	Total
Number of employees	25	50	75
Service hours required	3,000	1,000	4,000
Square feet occupied	4,000	5,500	9,500

Exhibit 16–1 shows budgeted overhead costs for each of Mibelle's five activities for the next year. The costs shown in the exhibit are direct (traceable) to each activity. The amounts budgeted for supplies used by each activity were based on materials specifications for expected production. The amounts for power, heating, and lighting were based on electric and gas meter readings in previous years. Indirect labor shows expected labor costs indirect to products but direct to the activity. Finally, depreciation and property taxes are for the equipment used in each activity. Mibelle's accountants have estimated these costs based on past experience and budgeted activity levels.

For the accountants at Mibelle, the problem is to assign service costs (columns 2, 3, and 4 in Exhibit 16–1) to production activities (columns 4 and 5).

Exhibit 16–1
Budgeted Overhead Costs Needed to Develop Activity-Based Overhead Rates

Mibelle Company
Budgeted Overhead Costs by Activity
For the Year Ending December 31, 19x1

	Factory administration	Maintenance	Buildings and grounds	Machining	Assembly	Total
Variable overhead costs						
Supplies	$ 3,000	$ 8,000	$ 4,000	$ 5,000	$ 4,500	$ 24,500
Power	1,000	2,000	1,500	4,000	1,200	9,700
Fixed overhead costs						
Indirect labor	80,000	25,000	20,000	30,000	25,000	180,000
Depreciation	2,000	4,000	3,000	50,000	10,000	69,000
Heating and lighting	800	500	300	2,000	2,800	6,400
Property taxes	400	800	600	10,000	2,000	13,800
Total overhead	$87,200	$40,300	$29,400	$101,000	$45,500	$303,400

Exhibit 16–2 shows how this is done when the direct method is used. The $87,200 worth of factory administration costs are assigned to the two production activities based on the number of employees in each activity. Machining is expected to have 25 employees; assembly, 50. Therefore, one-third of the cost (25 ÷ 75), or $29,067, is assigned to machining. The remaining two-thirds, or $58,133 ($87,200 × $^2/_3$), is assigned to the assembly activity. Notice that with the direct method no costs are assigned to other service activities.

Exhibit 16–2
Assigning Service Activity Costs at Mibelle Company by Using Direct Method

	Factory administration	Maintenance	Buildings and grounds	Machining	Assembly	Total
Costs incurred directly in the activity	$ 87,200	$ 40,300	$ 29,400	$101,000	$ 45,500	$303,400
Factory administration	(87,200)			29,067	58,133	
Maintenance		(40,300)		30,225	10,075	
Buildings and grounds			(29,400)	12,379	17,021	
Total activity overhead	$ -0-	$ -0-	$ -0-	$172,671	$130,729	$303,400

Maintenance costs are assigned by using the same procedure. Mibelle assigns maintenance costs based on service hours. The machining activity, which will use 3,000 of the 4,000 hours used in production, is assigned three-fourths of the \$40,300 in maintenance costs, or \$30,225 (\$40,300 × 0.75). The assembly activity uses only 25 percent of the hours provided. Therefore, it is assigned \$10,075 of the costs (\$40,300 × 0.25). Finally, buildings and grounds costs of \$29,400 are split between the two production activities based on square feet occupied: 4,000 square feet in machining and 5,500 square feet in assembly. Machining is assigned 40/95 worth of the costs (4,000 ÷ 9,500), or \$12,379. The balance, \$17,021, is assigned to assembly. Notice that when the process is finished, all service costs have been assigned to the two production activities.

The Step Method The major drawback of the direct method is that it does not recognize services performed for other service activities. The step method does to some extent. Although it does not recognize *all* services performed for other service activities, it does recognize the major ones. Recognition of all services requires a more complex method called reciprocal assignment, which is beyond the scope of this book. For practical purposes, the step method produces results close enough to the reciprocal method to be useful.

When using the step method, one must first select the sequence for assigning service activity costs. Then, the costs of the first service activity are assigned to the other service and production activities. Next, the costs of the second service activity (including costs received from the first service activity) are assigned to the remaining service activities and the production activities. This process continues until all service activity costs are assigned to the production activities. Once the costs of a service activity are assigned to other activities, you never assign any more costs to this service activity.

When using the step method, one must choose a sequence for assigning service costs. The following order is recommended: first, assign the costs of the service activity that serves the largest number of other activities. Then, assign the costs of the service activity that serves the next largest number of activities, and so forth. When two service activities serve an equal number of activities, assign the costs of the activity with the highest costs first.

OBJECTIVE 6
Use the step method to assign service activity costs to production activities

For Mibelle Company the process begins by noting the amount of each cost driver occurring in each activity. Exhibit 16–3 shows this information. Notice that all service activities serve each other. Thus, one cannot choose the sequence for assigning costs based on the number of activities served. Therefore, the order is based on the amount of costs incurred in each service activity. Factory administration costs are assigned first because they are the highest. Next comes maintenance costs, and finally buildings and grounds costs.

When assigning costs by using the step method, two important rules must be followed. First, when calculating the percentage of a cost driver required by each activity, do not include the base amount used in the activity whose cost is being assigned. For example, in determining the percentage of factory administration services used, ignore the 15 employees served in factory administration. Second, after assigning a service activity's costs, ignore that activity's cost driver in subsequent assignments. For example, after the factory administration costs

Exhibit 16–3
Bases for Assigning Service Activity Costs at Mibelle Company

	Factory administration	Maintenance	Buildings and grounds	Machining	Assembly	Total
Costs incurred directly in an activity	$87,200	$40,300	$29,400	$101,000	$45,500	$303,400
Number of employees	15	10	5	25	50	105
Service hours	300	50	150	3,000	1,000	4,500
Square feet occupied	1,500	1,000	600	4,000	5,500	12,600

have been assigned, exclude the service hours that maintenance provides to factory administration when assigning maintenance costs.

First, the costs of factory administration will be assigned. Exhibit 16–3 shows 105 employees served by factory administration. Of that amount, the 15 in factory administration will be ignored. Thus, calculations will be based on the 90 employees in the remaining activities. Since 10 of those 90 employees work in maintenance, 10/90 of factory administration costs, or $9,689, will be assigned to that activity. Buildings and grounds has 5 employees served, so 5/90 of the costs, or $4,844, will be assigned to buildings and grounds. Machining will receive 25/90 ($24,222); and assembly, 50/90 ($48,444). To check the calculations, add the fractions. Notice that they add up to 1. However, the amounts discussed above are $1 short of $87,200. This is due to rounding. Since assembly's cost is largest at $48,444.44, the additional dollar will be allocated to this activity for a total of $48,445.

Maintenance now has total costs of $49,989 assigned to it: $40,300 in direct costs plus $9,689 in factory administration costs. This amount will now be assigned to buildings and grounds, machining, and assembly. In calculating the cost driver for these activities, the 350 service hours provided to maintenance and factory administration are excluded. That leaves 4,150 service hours. Since buildings and grounds uses 150 service hours, it receives 150/4,150 of maintenance costs, or $1,807 (150/4,150 × $49,989). Likewise, machining receives 3,000/4,150 of the total costs, or $36,137 (3,000/4,150 × $49,989). Assembly receives 1,000/4,150, or $12,046 (1,000/4,150 × $49,989). Again, the fractions total 1. Since in this instance costs would be overassigned by $1, assembly is arbitrarily assigned only $12,045.

Buildings and grounds costs can now be reassigned only to the machining and assembly activities, since the costs of the other two service activities are closed out. Total building and grounds costs to be assigned include: (1) costs traced directly to building and grounds, $29,400; (2) costs assigned from factory administration, $4,844; and (3) costs assigned from maintenance, $1,807. These costs total $36,051. Since the space occupied by buildings and grounds must be ignored

Exhibit 16–4
Assigning Service Activity Costs at Mibelle Company by Using the Step Method

	From service activities			To production activities		
	Factory administration	Maintenance	Buildings and grounds	Machining	Assembly	Total
Costs incurred directly in the activity	$ 87,200	$ 40,300	$ 29,400	$101,000	$ 45,500	$303,400
Factory administration	(87,200)	9,689	4,844	24,222	48,445	
		$ 49,989				
Maintenance		(49,989)	1,807	36,137	12,045	
			$ 36,051			
			(36,051)	15,179	20,872	
Total activity overhead	$ -0-	$ -0-	$ -0-	$176,538	$126,862	$303,400

in calculating the total cost driver, the square feet for assigning buildings and grounds costs total 9,500 (total for the two remaining activities). Because the machining activity occupies 4,000 square feet, it is assigned 40/95 of building and grounds costs, or $15,179 (40/95 × $36,051). The assembly activity is assigned $20,872 (55/95 × $36,051). Here, no rounding problem exists.

Exhibit 16–4 summarizes the results of these calculations. Notice that once a service activity's costs are assigned, that activity is not assigned costs from other activities. This is true even if the activity received services from an activity whose costs are assigned later. Although this procedure is arbitrary, it ensures that all service overhead costs are eventually assigned to a production activity for inclusion in its predetermined overhead rate.

■

Calculating Activity-Based Predetermined Overhead Rates

Once service costs are assigned to production activities, activity-based predetermined overhead rates may be calculated. These predetermined overhead rates will be used to allocate overhead costs to products for each production activity. In Mibelle Company, the machining activity assigns overhead costs by machine-hours. The assembly activity uses direct labor hours. Budgeted activity levels for these activities for the coming year are 18,000 machine-hours and 40,000 direct labor hours. Using the data calculated in Exhibit 16–2 (under the direct method), predetermined overhead rates for these two activities are calculated as follows:

$$\text{Predetermined overhead rate, machining} = \frac{\$172{,}671}{18{,}000 \text{ machine-hours}} = \underline{\underline{\$9.59}} \text{ per machine-hour}$$

$$\text{Predetermined overhead rate, assembly} = \frac{\$130{,}729}{40{,}000 \text{ labor hours}} = \underline{\underline{\$3.27}} \text{ per labor hour}$$

Thus, predetermined overhead rates include overhead costs direct to the activity as well as the activity's share of service costs. Using the data computed in Exhibit 16–4 (under the step method), the calculations are:

$$\text{Predetermined overhead rate, machining} = \frac{\$176{,}538}{18{,}000 \text{ machine-hours}} = \underline{\underline{\$9.81}} \text{ per machine-hour}$$

$$\text{Predetermined overhead rate, assembly} = \frac{\$126{,}862}{40{,}000 \text{ labor hours}} = \underline{\underline{\$3.17}} \text{ per labor hour}$$

With the small difference in the rates, Mibelle would probably choose the simpler direct method.

Once activity-based predetermined overhead rates are calculated, they can be used to allocate overhead costs to products, as described in Chapters 4, 5, and 11. Products processed in only one production activity should be charged for overhead costs according to the rate for that activity only. Products processed in more than one production activity should be charged for overhead according to predetermined overhead rates for each activity involved.

Allocation of overhead costs to products will not be explained here, since it was covered in earlier chapters. For further information on this subject, review Chapter 4, pages 126–130.

Review Exercise 16–2

Allocate Administration and Fund-Raising Costs

The Literacy Institute provides English language lessons to immigrants and reading and writing lessons to illiterate adults. The Institute is a not-for-profit organization and offers the lessons at no charge to students. The lessons are taught by a few professional teachers supplemented by a core of dedicated volunteers.

Funding for the Institute comes from several foundations. One of the questions asked by the foundations is the cost of educating one student. Education for emigres focuses first on spoken English and then on reading and writing. Lessons for illiterate adults start directly with reading and then continue with writing.

The Literacy Institute believes that lessons provided to the two different kinds of students have different costs, since they use more volunteers with emigres. The Institute traces as many of the costs as possible directly to each type of student. However, some costs remain to be allocated. The Institute has been trying to decide if the step method of allocating costs would be better than the direct method. An accounting student at a nearby university has volunteered to allocate the costs both ways to see what difference results. The accounting student will allocate administration costs first on the basis of the total budget for the other activities before allocation. Fund-raising costs are allocated on the basis of number of students in each program. There are 1,200 emigre and 800 adult students. The accounting student will then divide the allocated costs by the number of students to obtain the cost per student. The accounting student will carry calculations to three decimal points. The table below gives the basic data.

Literacy Institute
Budgeted Overhead Costs by Activity
For the Year Ended December 31, 19x5

	Adminis-tration	Fund raising	Emigres	Adults	Total
Variable overhead costs					
Books			$ 48,000	$ 64,000	$112,000
Supplies	$18,000	$24,875	7,000	9,125	59,000
Teacher salaries			72,000	96,000	168,000
Fixed overhead costs					
Other salaries	54,000	33,000			87,000
Rent	3,000	4,000	5,000	12,000	24,000
Utilities	2,400				2,400
Professional services	9,000				9,000
Total overhead	$86,400	$61,875	$132,000	$181,125	$461,400

Required

1. Allocate administration and fund-raising costs to the two student categories by the direct method and calculate the costs per student.
2. Allocate administration and fund-raising costs to the two student categories by the step method and calculate the costs per student.
3. What justification do you see for using each method?

Solution

1. Direct method

	Adminis-tration	Fund raising	Emigres	Adults	Total
Costs incurred directly by the activity	$86,400	$ 61,875	$132,000	$181,125	$461,400
Administration	(86,400)		36,423	49,977	-0-
Fund raising		(61,875)	37,125	24,750	-0-
Total activity overhead	$ -0-	$ -0-	$205,548	$255,852	$461,400
Number of students			1,200	800	
Cost per student			$171.290	$319.815	

2. Step method, administration first

	Adminis-tration	Fund raising	Emigres	Adults	Total
Costs incurred directly by the activity	$86,400	$ 61,875	$132,000	$181,125	$461,400
Administration	(86,400)	14,256	30,413	41,731	-0-
Fund raising		(76,131)	45,679	30,452	-0-
Total activity overhead	$ -0-	$ -0-	$208,092	$253,308	$461,400
Number of students			1,200	800	
Cost per student			$173.410	$316.636	

3. The difference between the costs per student is about 1 percent. It is doubtful if a difference this small would affect anyone's decision. This would favor using the simpler direct method. However, since the number is being used as part of a fund-raising request, it might be desirable to use the most accurate method available. This would favor using the step method. (see Exercises 22, 23, 24, 25)

■

Assigning Fixed and Variable Costs Separately

Most companies assign service costs in total; that is, they combine fixed and variable costs. That is what we have done in illustrating the direct and step methods. There are, however, some advantages to assigning these costs separately. Separate assignment provides better data for planning and control. Since variable costs vary in proportion to the amount of service provided, they can be thought of as the cost of providing services once a company has facilities. Fixed costs are the costs of the facilities themselves. Generally these costs change only when the facilities change. A company needs fixed and variable cost data when estimating the costs of different levels of services.

Assigning variable costs is relatively simple, since these costs fluctuate in proportion to the level of service provided. The maintenance activity's variable costs are determined by the hours of maintenance work each activity requires. If company records do not show the number of maintenance-hours performed, it can often be approximated by using the number of machine-hours in each activity. Food costs in a cafeteria vary with the number of meals served.

In both examples, the user activities are free to ask for as much service as they need. They are limited only by the knowledge that they will be charged for the variable expenses of providing those services. Managers usually think assigning costs on this basis is fair and understandable, since the base is the activity causing the cost of such items as maintenance and meals to vary.

Assignment of fixed costs is based on the capacity to provide services, not on the use of those services, in any one year. For example, a cafeteria may have the capacity to provide 500 meals per day so all employees can be served during bad weather. But on most days, only 400 meals are served. However, when assigning fixed costs, one does so on the basis of the maximum number of meals needed by each activity, based on capacity provided, not on services used.

Notice that fixed costs are assigned as fixed charges. That procedure is quite different from the combined assignment of fixed and variable charges discussed earlier. Combined assignment almost always assigns fixed costs as if they were variable.

The total capacity required is usually determined by peak needs rather than average needs. Take for example a large factory that generates its own electricity. Suppose the business of one user activity is seasonal. Although its average monthly use is 10,000 kilowatt-hours, it uses as much as 15,000 kilowatt-hours in peak season. To meet peak needs, the factory's generator must be large enough to supply the activity with 15,000 kilowatt-hours. Here, the size of the generator determines the level of many fixed costs, such as generator depreciation. Thus, the 15,000 kilowatt-hour capacity provided to the user activity should determine its share of fixed generating costs. The average use of 10,000 kilowatt-hours is relevant only to the variable costs of generating electricity.

Assigning fixed and variable service costs separately recognizes this difference in cost behavior. User activities pay a fixed charge for fixed services and a variable charge for variable services. Because charges accurately reflect cost-volume behavior, managers of user activities can make better decisions about using services.

OBJECTIVE 7
Assign fixed and variable service activity costs separately

To illustrate the process of separate assignment, suppose a company cafeteria incurs estimated annual costs of $150,000 plus $1 per meal. The cafeteria is expected to provide 168,000 meals a year. For the sake of simplicity, assume employees in only two activities use the cafeteria. Activity A has a stable work force of

Exhibit 16–5
Basis for Allocating Fixed and Variable Service Costs Separately for Cafeteria Activity

	Basis for fixed costs		
	Maximum number served	Fraction of total	Basis for variable costs
Activity A	400	4/10	$1 per meal
Activity B	600	6/10	1 per meal
Total	1,000	10/10	

400 employees. Activity B averages 300 workers a year, but its work force doubles during the busy summer months. As a result, the cafeteria was built to accommodate 1,000 workers. Employees in Activity A are expected to have 95,928 meals during the year while employees in Activity B will have 72,072.

Fixed and variable cafeteria costs are assigned on the bases shown in Exhibit 16–5. Total variable costs for the year equal the 168,000 expected meals multiplied by $1 cost per meal. By using the fractions for fixed costs obtained in Exhibit 16–5 and the estimated variable cost per meal, you get the cost assignments shown in Exhibit 16–6.

Had the company not separated its fixed and variable cafeteria costs, those costs would probably have been assigned according to the average number of employees in each activity. That basis would have caused 4/7 of the total cost, or $181,714, to be assigned to Activity A. Activity B's share would have been $136,286. But with fixed costs separated, Activity B bears the cost of the extra capacity required by the seasonal nature of its business. Assigning costs in this way is more equitable. Furthermore, managers understand that the added cost of an additional employee is only the variable cost of $1 per meal served to that employee.

Exhibit 16–6
Separate Allocation of Fixed and Variable Service Costs for Cafeteria Service

	Activity A	Activity B	Total
Fixed	$ 60,000	$ 90,000	$150,000
Variable	95,928	72,072	168,000
Total	$155,928	$162,072	$318,000

Chapter Review

Review of Learning Objectives

1. **List the advantages of activity-based predetermined overhead rates.**
With activity-based overhead rates, only those products produced in an activity are charged for that activity's costs. Thus, the cost of specialized equipment or processes in one activity is allocated more equitably than with plantwide rates. Another advantage of activity-based rates is that each production activity can use a different cost driver to allocate its costs. For example, a highly mechanized activity might choose machine-hours; an assembly activity, where much of the work is done manually, direct labor hours.

2. **Calculate activity-based predetermined overhead rates and show when they are preferred to plantwide rates.**
To calculate an activity-based predetermined overhead rate, you first identify the major activities of the organization. You then find the cost driver for each activity, the thing that causes this activity's total overhead to change. Then you estimate the amount of the cost driver for next year and estimate next year's total overhead cost for this activity. Finally, you calculate the activity-based predetermined overhead rate by dividing the total estimated overhead for this activity by its estimated cost driver.
Activity-based predetermined overhead rates should be used only when they will significantly change managerial decisions. Otherwise, the extra accounting costs cannot be justified. Usually, this situation occurs when one activity has costly specialized equipment and only some products are processed in that activity.

3. **Define a service activity and explain why its costs are assigned to production activities.**
Service activities do not work on a firm's products. Instead, they provide services to activities that do. Maintenance, factory administration, and buildings and grounds are examples of service activities.
Although service activities do not work directly on a firm's products, their costs need to be included in the cost of those products. This is done by assigning service costs to production activities, where they are included in each production activity's predetermined overhead rate.

4. **List the three steps for assigning service costs to production activities.**
The three steps for assigning service costs are: (1) identify service and production activities; (2) trace all overhead costs to the service or production in which the costs will be incurred; (3) assign overhead costs incurred in service activities to each production activity according to its use of the service. Once service costs are assigned, a separate predetermined overhead rate can be calculated for each production activity.

5. **Use the direct method to assign service activity costs to production activities.**
Using the direct method, you assign all service costs directly to production activities according to each activity's use of the service. Services that one service activity performs for another are ignored. Exhibit 16–2 illustrates this process.

6. **Use the step method to assign service activity costs to production activities.**
Using the step method, you assign the cost of the most important service activity to the

other service and production activities according to their use of the services. The costs of the next most important activity, including costs received from the first service activity, are then assigned to the remaining service and production activities. This process of assigning costs is repeated until all service costs are assigned to production activities. Once a service activity's costs are assigned, no other costs are added to that department from other service activities.

When using the step method, the sequence of assigning service costs is significant. One recommended order is to assign the costs of the service activity serving the greatest number of activities first. If all service departments serve the same number of activities, you should assign costs by beginning with the service activity with the highest direct costs and ending with the service activity with the lowest direct costs. Exhibit 16–4 illustrates this process.

7. **Assign fixed and variable service activity costs separately.**
Fixed service costs are assigned separately in a lump based on peak capacity demanded by each user activity. Variable costs are assigned on the basis of services used. Thus, each type of cost is assigned according to its behavior. Fixed costs are assigned as a lump and do not change with volume; variable costs are assigned as a sum that varies with volume. Exhibits 16–5 and 16–6 illustrate this process.

Review of Key Terms

Activity-based predetermined overhead rate A ratio for allocating manufacturing overhead costs of a single activity to products processed by that activity. Found by separating manufacturing overhead costs for each production activity and developing a predetermined overhead rate for each of those activities. See also *Plantwide predetermined overhead rate.*

Allocate To divide a general cost of production among products, activities, or divisions.

Assign To apportion service costs among production activities for inclusion in the predetermined overhead rates. Assignment is based on the amount of service used.

Direct method Method for assigning service activity costs *only* to production activities. Services performed by one service activity for another service activity are ignored. See also *Step method.*

Plantwide predetermined overhead rate A ratio for assigning all of the manufacturing overhead costs of a plant to products using a single rate. Found by dividing total estimated manufacturing overhead for the entire plant by total estimated cost driver for the entire plant. See also *Activity-based predetermined overhead rate.*

Production activities Activities performed directly on products sold to customers. See also *Service activities.*

Service activities Activities not performed on products but providing support to production activities so they can operate more efficiently. Maintenance and human resources are examples of service activities. See also *Production activities.*

Step method Method for assigning service activity costs to other service activities according to a predefined sequence before being reassigned to production activities. See also *Direct method.*

Review Problem

The Acme Plastic Company has two service activities and two production activities to manufacture plastic components for radio and television manufacturers. The costs expected to be incurred in each activity and selected cost drivers are given below.

	Scheduling	Maintenance	Molding	Assembly
Total direct overhead costs	$200,000	$375,000	$189,000	$138,000
Machine-hours (MH)			40,000	10,000
Direct labor hours (DLH)			10,000	50,000
Number of employees	2	5	15	30

Maintenance costs are assigned to the production activities based on machine-hours. Costs of scheduling are assigned based on the number of employees in each activity. The predetermined overhead rate is calculated by using machine-hours in the molding activity; direct labor hours are used in assembly.

Required

1. Using the direct method, assign service costs to the production activities and calculate a predetermined overhead rate for each production activity.
2. Using the step method, assign service costs to production activities and calculate a predetermined overhead rate for each production activity. See Table 16–2 for help in selecting cost drivers used to assign service cost.
3. Calculate a plantwide overhead rate, using direct labor hours as the cost driver.
4. Assume that two products manufactured by Acme Plastic require the following machine-hours and direct labor hours:

	Products	
	X1	X2
Molding, machine-hours	4	1
Assembly, direct labor hours	1	4
Molding, direct labor hours	1	0.25

Calculate overhead costs allocated to each product using (a) the activity-based overhead rate from 2 above (step method) and (b) the plantwide overhead rate from 3 above.

Solution to Review Problem

1. Acme Plastic Company
Assignment of Service Activity Costs
Direct Method

	Service		Production		
	Scheduling	Maintenance	Molding	Assembly	Total
Costs incurred directly by the activity	$ 200,000	$ 375,000	$189,000	$138,000	$902,000
Scheduling	(200,000)*		66,667	133,333	
Maintenance		(375,000)†	300,000	75,000	
Total production activity overhead	$ -0-	$ -0-	$555,667	$346,333	$902,000
Cost driver for predetermined overhead rate			40,000 MH	50,000 DLH	
Predetermined overhead rate			$13.89 per MH	$6.93 per DLH	

*Assigned based on number of employees: 15/45 and 30/45.
†Assigned based on machine-hours: 4/5 and 1/5.

2. Acme Plastic Company
Assignment of Service Activity Costs
Step Method

	Service		Production		
	Scheduling	Maintenance	Molding	Assembly	Total
Costs incurred directly by the activity	$ 200,000	$ 375,000	$189,000	$138,000	$902,000
Scheduling	(200,000)*	20,000	60,000	120,000	
		$ 395,000			
Maintenance		(395,000)†	316,000	79,000	
Total production activity overhead	$ -0-	$ -0-	$565,000	$337,000	$902,000
Cost driver for predetermined overhead rate			40,000 MH	50,000 DLH	
Predetermined overhead rate			$14.13 per MH	$6.74 per DLH	

*Assigned based on number of employees: 5/50, 15/50, and 30/50.
†Assigned based on machine-hours: 4/5 and 1/5.

3. Total direct labor hours

Molding	10,000
Assembly	50,000
	60,000

Plantwide overhead rate = \$902,000/60,000 direct labor hours
= \$15.03 per direct labor hour

4. *a.* Overhead costs for Products X1 and X2 step allocation

Product X1 = (\$14.13 × 4 machine-hours) + (\$6.74 × 1 direct labor hour)
= \$63.26

Product X2 = (\$14.13 × 1 machine-hour) + (\$6.74 × 4 direct labor hours)
= \$41.09

b. Overhead costs for Products X1 and X2 plantwide allocation

Product X1 = \$15.03 × 2 direct labor hours = \$30.06

Product X2 = \$15.03 × 4.25 direct labor hours = \$63.88

Chapter Assignments

Questions

1. (L.O. 1) List the advantages and disadvantages of plantwide overhead rates. Give examples of costs causing problems when plantwide rates are used.
2. (L.O. 2) Explain how accountants decide whether to use activity-based or plantwide predetermined overhead rates.
3. (L.O. 3) Distinguish between service activities and production activities. Give examples of each in a food processing company.
4. (L.O. 3) Give examples of service activities in a hospital.
5. (L.O. 4) How are service costs assigned to a production activity? Give an example.
6. (L.O. 4) Describe how one selects a cost driver for assigning service costs.
7. (L.O. 5) Describe the direct method of assigning service costs.
8. (L.O. 6) Describe the step method of assigning service costs.
9. (L.O. 6) How does the reciprocal method of assigning service costs differ from the step method?

10. (L.O. 6) What are the generally preferred sequences for assigning service costs when using the step method?
11. (L.O. 7) Why are fixed and variable service costs sometimes assigned separately?
12. (L.O. 7) Why is it beneficial to assign fixed costs and variable service costs separately?
13. (L.O. 7) What are the cost drivers commonly used to assign fixed service costs? To assign variable service costs?
14. (L.O. 4) How do service costs eventually become part of a product's total cost?

Exercises

15. (L.O. 1) Holder Company has estimated the following costs and activity levels for 19x9:

	Fabricating	Assembly
Manufacturing overhead costs	$400,000	$200,000
Machine-hours	100,000	80,000
Direct labor hours	25,000	50,000

The company uses activity-based predetermined overhead rates to apply manufacturing overhead to products. The rate for fabricating is based on machine-hours; for assembly, direct labor hours.

Required

1. Calculate predetermined overhead rates for the fabricating and assembly activities.
2. Assume Holder Company is considering using a plantwide overhead rate. Calculate a plantwide overhead rate for Holder based on machine-hours.

16. (L.O. 1) Acme Company manufactures two products, A and B, in two manufacturing activities, fabricating and assembly. Expected overhead costs and cost drivers are as follows:

	Fabricating	Assembly
Overhead costs	$350,000	$500,000
Machine-hours	50,000	10,000
Direct labor hours	20,000	50,000

Required

1. Calculate activity-based overhead rates. Use machine-hours for the fabricating activity; direct labor hours for the assembly activity.
2. Calculate a plantwide overhead rate using direct labor hours as the cost driver.
3. Assume Product A requires three machine-hours and one direct labor hour in fabricating; one machine-hour and three direct labor hours in assembly. Allocate overhead costs to Product A using (a) activity-based overhead rates and (b) a plantwide overhead rate.

17. (L.O. 5, 6) Center Company has two service activities and two production activities. The overhead costs and some cost drivers are as follows on page 765.

	Factory administration	Maintenance	Fabricating	Assembly
Total overhead costs	$80,000	$60,000	$150,000	$200,000
Number of employees	10	20	30	50
Machine-hours			10,000	5,000

Factory administration costs are assigned to other activities according to the number of employees in each activity. Maintenance activity costs are assigned by machine-hours.

Required

1. Using the direct method, assign service costs to production activities.
2. Assume Center Company assigns service costs according to the step method rather than the direct method. Using the step method, assign service costs to production activities.

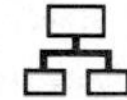

18. (L.O. 2) Domino Supermarket has five departments: meats, produce, bakery, canned goods, and paper products. Until now, it has used a storewide overhead rate based on dollars of sales for determining the profit of different products. A new accounting graduate has suggested that the storewide rate may be overstating the profit of some products and understating the profit of other products. To correct this, she has suggested activity-based predetermined overhead rates using each as a separate activity.

Domino's controller is interested in the idea. He has suggested that the new accountant take the current year's data and show how the activity-based rates would differ from the storewide rate. Fortunately, the store budgets on a departmental basis, so the data needed for activity-based predetermined overhead rates are available. The budget data for the current year are as follows:

	Budgeted sales	Budgeted overhead
Meats	$ 33,000,000	$2,100,000
Produce	12,000,000	600,000
Bakery	6,000,000	150,000
Canned goods	40,000,000	1,800,000
Paper products	9,000,000	360,000
Total	$100,000,000	$5,010,000

Required

1. Calculate a storewide overhead rate using dollar sales as the cost driver.
2. Calculate activity-based overhead rates (one for each department) using dollar sales as the cost driver.
3. Assume August bakery sales of $525,000. What is the amount of overhead that would be allocated to August bakery sales under each method? What does this suggest about the new accountant's proposal? Explain briefly.

(see Review Exercise 16–1)

19. (L.O. 2) Super Burger sells sandwiches to customers who wish to eat in the restaurant and to people who pick up food to eat at home. All food is prepared in a single kitchen. Eat-in customers use the dining room while take-out customers use the drive-up window. The budgeted overhead cost of operating the three activities is listed on the following page along with the cost driver for each area.

Activity	Budgeted overhead	Cost driver	
Kitchen	$200,000	500,000	pounds of food
Eat in	100,000	$1,200,000	of sales
Drive up	75,000	1,000,000	of sales

Super Burger has been considering using activity-based predetermined overhead rates with the cost drivers listed above. The store manager is not convinced that the activity-based system is worth the effort of keeping track of the pounds of food processed in the kitchen. She is considering using a restaurantwide predetermined overhead rate with dollars of sales as the cost driver. To compare the alternatives, she will make calculations to three decimal points.

A typical drive-up order sells for $9.50 and weighs 1.2 pounds.

Required

1. Calculate activity-based overhead rates.
2. Calculate a restaurantwide overhead rate using dollar sales as the cost driver.
3. Calculate the overhead cost of the typical drive-up order using both systems. Does the extra effort of the activity-based system seem to be justified? Explain briefly.

(see Review Exercise 16–1)

20. (**L.O. 2**) Resort Vehicle Rentals rents motorcycles and automobiles. Motorcycles rent for $5 per hour. The average automobile rental is $45 per day. The two types of vehicles are serviced and rented from separate locations. The schedule below shows the budgeted overhead and estimated annual cost driver per year.

Rental activity	Budgeted overhead	Cost driver	
Motorcycles	$120,000	80,000	rental hours
Automobiles	600,000	20,000	rental days

Resort Vehicles has been considering using activity-based predetermined overhead rates with the cost drivers listed above. The manager has asked you as accountant if an activity-based system is worthwhile. You have decided to make some calculations to compare the results of an activity-based system to a companywide system. Make calculations to three decimal points.

Required

1. Calculate activity-based overhead rates.
2. Calculate a companywide overhead rate using dollar sales as the cost driver.
3. Calculate the cost of one hour of motorcycle rental and one day of car rental using both methods. Does the extra effort of the activity-based system seem to be justified? Explain briefly.

(see Review Exercise 16–1)

21. (**L.O. 1, 2**) Andy Company produces two products, Y1 and Y2, in two manufacturing activities. For 19x9, the following estimated costs and operating statistics were prepared:

	Machining	Assembly
Estimated overhead costs	$200,000	$50,000
Estimated direct labor hours	50,000	50,000

Required

1. Calculate a plantwide overhead rate using direct labor hours.
2. Calculate activity-based overhead rates using direct labor hours.
3. Assume that the direct labor hours to produce each product in 19x9 are as follows:

	Machining	Assembly
Product Y1	15	5
Product Y2	5	15

   Allocate the manufacturing overhead costs to each product using (a) the plantwide rate and (b) activity-based rates.
4. Which of the predetermined overhead rates would you choose for calculating the cost of the two products? Why?

22. (L.O. 5, 6) Metro Lawn Care offers lawn-care services such as mowing, trimming, and fertilizing lawns. The company also offers a landscaping service that involves moving earth and stones and planting bushes and trees. Metro likes to know the cost per hour of each service offered for purposes of making sure each type of service is profitable.

Metro budgets costs in four categories: administration, marketing, lawn care, and landscaping. Metro then allocates administration and marketing costs to the two productive activities, lawn care and landscaping, by the direct method. Administration is allocated on the basis of activity budget before allocation. Marketing is allocated according to Metro's estimate of the relative amount of marketing for each activity, 60 percent for lawn care and 40 percent for landscaping. Budget data for each activity is given below.

Metro Lawn Care
Budgeted Overhead Costs by Activity
For the Year Ended December 31, 19x3

	Administration	Marketing	Lawn care	Landscaping	Total
Variable overhead costs					
Fuel and maintenance	$ 800		$13,000	$ 9,700	$ 23,500
Supplies	3,000	$ 5,110	10,030	12,000	30,140
Part-time workers			24,000	15,000	39,000
Fixed overhead costs					
Other salaries	35,000	21,000	28,000	22,000	106,000
Depreciation	3,000	1,500	7,000	12,000	23,500
Utilities	6,000				6,000
Property taxes	1,000	500	2,300	4,400	8,200
Total overhead	$48,800	$28,110	$84,330	$75,100	$236,340
Hours of activity			18,000	9,000	

The president of Metro Lawn Care recently attended a seminar on strategic costing where the step method of allocation was mentioned. He is wondering if Metro should consider using the step method. Metro carries allocation calculations to three decimal points.

Required

1. Allocate the service activity costs to the production activities using the direct method and calculate the hourly rate for lawn care and landscaping.

2. Allocate the service activity costs to the production activities using the step method and calculate the hourly rate for lawn care and landscaping.
(see Review Exercise 16–2)

23. (L.O. 5, 6) Rainbow Painting Contractors does both interior and exterior painting. Rainbow bids on painting jobs and includes all labor, paint, and materials in the bids. Rainbow is growing and becoming more professional in its management. The president was recently discussing management with a friend who is a heating contractor. The heating contractor mentioned using the step method for allocating the cost of service activities to their productive activities. Now Rainbow's president is wondering if Rainbow should be using the step method.

Rainbow budgets costs in four categories: administration, marketing, interior, and exterior. Rainbow then allocates administration and marketing costs to the two productive activities by the direct method. Administration is allocated on the basis of the activity budget before allocations. Marketing is allocated according to Rainbow's estimate of the relative amount of marketing for each activity, 70 percent for interior and 30 percent for exterior. Budget data for each activity is given below.

Rainbow Painting Contractors
Budgeted Overhead Costs by Activity
For the Year Ended December 31, 19x4

	Administration	Marketing	Interior	Exterior	Total
Variable overhead costs					
Paint			$120,000	$121,500	$241,500
Supplies	$2,500	$ 3,954	22,137	26,909	55,500
Permits			12,000	18,000	30,000
Fixed overhead costs					
Advertising		6,000			6,000
Depreciation	800	300	3,000	5,000	9,100
Utilities and fuel	900		1,800	1,200	3,900
Licenses and taxes	2,000				2,000
Total overhead	$6,200	$10,254	$158,937	$172,609	$348,000
Hours of activity			24,000	18,000	

As an experiment, Rainbow's president asked the accountant to allocate the current year's overhead by the direct and step methods and compare the resulting cost per hour of painting activity. The president said that allocation calculations to three decimal points would surely be sufficient.

Required

1. Allocate the service activity costs to the production activities using the direct method. Calculate the overhead cost per hour for interior and exterior work.
2. Allocate the service activity costs to the production activities using the step method with administration allocated first. Calculate the overhead cost per hour for interior and exterior work.
3. Should the accountant recommend a change to the step method? Explain briefly.
(see Review Exercise 16–2)

24. (L.O. 5, 6) Metropolitan Art Center is a small not-for-profit art museum. They have two main collections: paintings and sculptures. The trustees would like to operate the museum at a breakeven point so that donated funds can be used solely for

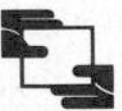

acquisitions. Metropolitan therefore tries to set admission prices so that they cover all of Metropolitan's operating costs. There is a separate admission for each part of the museum or a combined ticket for both parts.

Metropolitan budgets costs in four categories: administration, fund raising, paintings, and sculpture. Metropolitan then allocates administration and fund-raising costs to paintings and sculptures activities by the direct method. Administration is allocated on the basis of the activity budget before allocations. Fund raising is divided equally between the paintings and sculptures activities. Budget data for each activity is given below.

Metropolitan Art Center
Budgeted Overhead Costs by Activity
For the Year Ended December 31, 19x6

	Adminis-tration	Fund raising	Paintings	Sculptures
Variable overhead costs				
Catalogs			$ 65,000	$ 88,000
Supplies	$13,000	$48,000	4,000	6,000
Exhibit setup and maintenance			30,000	50,000
Fixed overhead costs				
Salaries	54,000	33,000	45,000	60,000
Utilities	2,400			
Professional services	9,000			
Total overhead	$78,400	$81,000	$144,000	$204,000
Number of visitors			400,000	350,000

Metropolitan's new accountant has decided to experiment with overhead allocations comparing the step method to the direct method. She is also interested in whether the methods would give a different cost per visitor and possible different ticket pricing. She felt that carrying calculations to the nearest dollar would be satisfactory for allocating costs to paintings and sculptures, but that the overhead rates should be carried to three decimal points.

Required

1. Allocate the service activity costs to paintings and sculptures using the direct method. Calculate the cost per visitor.
2. Allocate the service activity costs to the production activities using the step method with administration allocated first. Calculate the cost per visitor.

(see Review Exercise 16–2)

25. (L.O. 5, 6) Budget Travel Service provides both domestic and international travel services. Agents make transportation, hotel, and entertainment reservations. The largest part of the company's revenue, however, comes from airline ticket reservations where the airlines pay Budget Travel a percentage of the ticket price. Budget Travel tries to assure customer loyalty by finding the lowest airfares available that meet customer travel needs. Since airlines have many different airfares to the same location, finding the lowest possible airfares requires considerable time searching fare tables with computers.

Budget Travel budgets costs in four categories: administration, marketing, domestic, and international. Administration and marketing costs are then allocated to the two productive activities, domestic and international, by the direct method. Administration is allocated on the basis of number of people working in the other activities. Domestic and international share one person, so domestic has 3.5 people and international has 1.5 people. In addition, there is one person in marketing. Marketing is allocated according to Budget Travel's estimate of the relative amount of marketing for each activity, 60 percent for domestic and 40 percent for international. Budget data for each activity is given below.

Budget Travel Service
Budgeted Overhead Costs by Activity
For the Year Ended December 31, 19x4

	Administration	Marketing	Domestic	International	Total
Variable overhead costs					
Promotional brochures		$27,000			$ 27,000
Supplies	$ 4,000	12,000	$ 6,000	$ 8,000	30,000
Computer connect charges	3,000		18,000	14,000	35,000
Fixed overhead costs					
Salaries	35,000	21,000	66,000	44,000	166,000
Depreciation	2,000	3,000	8,000	6,000	19,000
Telephone and utilities	1,000	2,000	5,000	6,500	14,500
Other expenses	3,000	4,000	1,000	1,500	9,500
Total overhead	$48,000	$69,000	$104,000	$80,000	$301,000
Tickets issued			45,000	16,000	

Budget Travel's accountant recently attended a seminar on costing methods. She began to wonder if Budget Travel should be using the step method of allocation. She decided to allocate the current year's overhead by the direct and step methods and compare the resulting cost per ticket issued. She will carry allocation calculations to three decimal points.

Required

1. Allocate the service activity costs to the production activities using the direct method. Calculate the overhead cost of issuing each type of ticket.
2. Allocate the service activity costs to the production activities using the step method with administration allocated first. Calculate the overhead cost of issuing each type of ticket.
3. Should the accountant recommend a change to the step method? Explain briefly.

(see Review Exercise 16–2)

26. (L.O. 7) The university computer center serves both research and academic computing needs. The main computer costs $5,000,000 per year to operate plus $20 per hour. Research computing is fairly steady throughout the year, but use of academic computing has several peaks during the year. When the computer was purchased, the university anticipated average monthly use of 417 hours for research and 250 hours for academic computing. However, when purchasing the computer, they allowed for maximum monthly use of 442 hours for research computing and 408 hours for academic computing.

Required

1. Assume that during May, the university used 420 computer hours for research and 400 hours for academic computing. Separately assign the fixed and variable costs to each type of computing use for May.

2. Assume that the university does not assign fixed and variable costs separately. Assign computer costs to each activity for May.

27. (L.O. 7) A hotel in a major tourist center has agreed to build an air conditioning center to be shared with a major office building. In designing the air conditioning center, the hotel recognized that its peak monthly load would be for 5,000,000 British thermal units (btu's) of cooling capacity while its average use would be 3,600,000 btu's per month. The office building requires a monthly maximum of 4,200,000 btu's and an average of 3,570,000 btu's per month. Budgeted fixed costs of operating the air conditioning center is $552,000 per year. Variable costs are expected to be $0.02 per btu.

During October, the hotel used 3,000,000 btu's and the office building used 3,200,000 btu's.

Required

1. Separately assign the fixed and variable costs to the hotel and the office building for October.
2. Assume that the air conditioning center does not assign fixed and variable costs separately. Assign air conditioning costs to each activity for October.

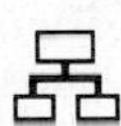

28. (L.O. 1, 7) Bonham Company cafeteria has estimated annual fixed costs of $250,000 and estimated variable costs of $2 per meal. The company expects to provide 200,000 meals during the year. Assume only two activities' employees use the cafeteria. Activity A has a stable work force of 500 employees. Activity B averages 400 workers per year but employs additional workers during the busy season, bringing the work force to 500 during the summer. The company cafeteria was built to serve 1,000 workers, since demand is that high during the summer.

Required

1. Calculate the total cost of the cafeteria for the year. Then, assign costs to Activities A and B using the average number of workers in each activity as a base.
2. Assign fixed cafeteria costs based on maximum activity needs and the variable cafeteria costs based on the average number of employees in each activity.
3. Which procedure provides a "fair" allocation?

Problems

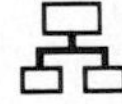

29. (L.O. 2) Better Buy Department Store, Inc., is a department store with only four departments: women's clothing, men's clothing, small appliances, and bargain basement. The bargain basement sells discontinued items and items purchased from insurance companies. Better Buy is able to sell quality merchandise at very low prices in their bargain basement. Of course, the selection and amount of items is limited, but the bargain basement brings customers into the store. Often when customers cannot find what they want in the bargain basement, they purchase items in the other departments that have a good selection of merchandise. Department managers watch their department's profits carefully.

In calculating department profitability, overhead has been allocated to departments based on total sales in each department. The bargain basement manager, however, objects to this system. She points out that the bargain basement sells large volumes at low prices to attract customers to the store. However, the low prices mean low margins, making it harder to cover the allocated overhead. She proposed activity-based overhead rates regarding each department as a separate activity. She also points out that each department could use a different cost driver. The small appliance department manager supported the idea because it permits more careful evaluation of the profitability of individual products within a department. Annual information about the departments is as follows:

Activity	Budgeted overhead	Budgeted sales	Possible cost driver
Women's clothing	$140,000	$2,000,000	Sales dollars
Men's clothing	90,000	1,000,000	Sales dollars
Small appliances	60,000	600,000	10,000 units sold
Bargain basement	110,000	990,000	1,100,000 items sold

Required

1. Calculate the storewide predetermined overhead rate using the present system.
2. Calculate activity-based overhead rates using the cost drivers shown in the table.
3. Does the extra effort of the activity-based system seem to be justified? Explain briefly.

30. (L.O. 6) Westend Hotel has three service activities: administration, building and grounds, and cleaning and laundry. It also has three operating centers or production activities: guest rooms, restaurant, and meeting rooms. The administration activity hires and trains new employees, processes all personnel records, and prepares the monthly payroll. The cost of administration is assigned based on number of employees in each activity. The building and grounds activity performs all maintenance for the hotel, both inside and outside. That activity's costs are assigned on the basis of square feet. The cleaning and laundry activity is responsible for cleaning all guest rooms, the restaurant, and the meeting rooms as well as doing the laundry. The costs for that activity are assigned on the basis of labor hours in each operating center.

    Costs and operating data for the Westend Hotel are as follows:

	Adminis-tration	Building and grounds	Cleaning and laundry	Guest rooms	Restaurant	Meeting rooms
Direct overhead costs ($000)	$100	$120	$ 80	$ 240	$ 80	$ 60
Number of employees	5	8	18	7	20	5
Square feet (000)	20	8	50	600	100	150
Cleaning hours spent	130	520	260	5,200	520	260

Required Using the step method, assign service costs to operating centers and calculate the total costs for each center.

31. (L.O. 1, 5, 6) Sold Manufacturing Company has two production activities and two service activities. Cost data and relevant statistics for a normal year are summarized below.

	Production activities	
	Fabrication	Assembly
Direct labor hours	50,000	100,000
Direct labor costs	$412,500	$645,000
Overhead costs	$820,000	$467,000
Number of employees	20	50
Machine-hours	75,000	25,000

	Service activities	
	Factory maintenance	Factory administration
Indirect labor hours	20,000	5,000
Indirect labor costs	$186,000	$49,000
Other overhead costs	$210,000	$70,000
Number of employees	10	2
Machine-hours	—	—

Factory maintenance is assigned based on machine-hours, and factory administration costs are assigned based on number of employees. Overhead in both production activities is assigned to products on the basis of direct labor hours.

Required

1. Using the direct method to assign service costs, compute predetermined overhead rates for the two production activities.
2. Using the step method to assign service costs and assigning factory administration costs first, compute the predetermined overhead rates for both production activities.

32. (L.O. 1, 5, 6) Hogan Company produces a complete line of plastic toys in three production activities: molding, cutting, and assembly. These activities are supported by two service activities, maintenance and human resources. For the coming year, direct overhead costs traceable to each activity were estimated as follows:

Activity	Estimated overhead
Human resources	$ 20,000
Maintenance	50,000
Molding	175,000
Cutting	120,000
Assembly	75,000

Service costs are assigned to production activities on the basis of machine-hours for maintenance and number of employees in each activity for human resources. Overhead is then allocated to the products, using machine-hours for molding and cutting and direct labor hours for assembly. Data for assigning service costs to products are shown below.

Activity	Number of employees	Machine-hours	Direct labor hours
Human resources	5	—	—
Maintenance	50	—	—
Molding	50	50,000	20,000
Cutting	50	40,000	20,000
Assembly	100	10,000	60,000

Required

1. Assign service costs to production activities using the direct method.
2. Calculate the predetermined overhead rate for each production activity.
3. Answer *1* and *2* above using the step method. Assign human resources activity costs first.

33. (L.O. 1, 5) Gundahl Manufacturing Company has two service (S) and three production (P) activities. A schedule showing the percentage of service activity (S1 and S2) resources provided to each user is shown below.

	To					
	S1	S2	P1	P2	P3	Total
From S1	—	40%	20%	10%	30%	100%
From S2	20%	—	30	40	10	100

Overhead was estimated and traced to activities for the following year as shown below.

Activity	Overhead
Service	
S1	$126,000
S2	200,000
Production	
P1	350,000
P2	215,000
P3	240,000

Overhead is allocated to products on the basis of machine-hours in P1 and direct labor hours in P2 and P3.

Estimated annual activity for all three production activities in both machine-hours and labor hours is shown below.

	Estimated	
Activity	Machine-hours	Direct labor hours
P1	100,000	40,000
P2	30,000	85,000
P3	15,000	120,000

Required

1. Using the direct method, assign service costs to production activities.
2. Compute predetermined overhead rates for the production activities.

34. (L.O. 6) Assume the same facts as those given in *33* above. In addition, assume Gundahl is considering using the step method for assigning service costs to production activities.

Required

1. Using the step method, assign service costs to production activities. Assign S1 costs first.
2. Compute the predetermined overhead rate for each production activity.

35. (L.O. 6) Parker Manufacturing Company has two production activities, fabrication and assembly. Its three service activities are general factory administration, factory maintenance, and factory cafeteria. A summary of the year's costs and other data prior to assigning service costs follows on page 775.

	Fabrication	Assembly	General factory administration	Factory maintenance	Factory cafeteria
Labor costs	$1,950,000	$2,050,000	$90,000	$82,000	$87,000
Materials costs	$3,130,000	$ 950,000	—	$65,000	$91,000
Manufacturing overhead	$1,650,000	$1,850,000	$70,000	$56,000	$62,000
Direct labor hours	562,500	437,500	31,000	27,000	42,000
Number of employees	280	200	12	8	20
Square footage occupied	88,000	72,000	1,750	2,000	4,800

General factory administration, factory maintenance, and factory cafeteria costs are assigned on the basis of direct labor hours, square footage occupied, and number of employees in each activity, respectively.

Required Using the step method, assign service costs to production activities in the following order: (a) administration, (b) maintenance, and (c) cafeteria. (AICPA)

36. (L.O. 6, 7) XYZ Company has two main products, Y and Z. Product Y is produced in Activity A; Product Z, in Activity B. To produce these products, the production activities use the services of two service activities, P and Q. An analysis of work done by the service activities yields the following data:

	Units of service activity transferred to				
	P	Q	A	B	Total
From Activity P	0	30	70	100	200
From Activity Q	20	0	40	40	100

Total costs incurred by Activity P are $100,000; by Activity Q, $200,000.

Required

1. Using the step method, assign service costs to Activities A and B. Assign Activity P's costs first.
2. Rework the problem using the step method. However, Activity Q's costs should be assigned first. Compare your two answers.

37. (L.O. 5, 6) Wall Production Company manufactures components for radio and television satellites. Wall has two service activities and two production activities. Service relationships and estimated overhead costs are shown below.

	Percentage of service provided to			
	Maintenance	Scheduling	Molding	Assembly
From maintenance	—	10%	40%	50%
From scheduling	20%	—	50%	30%
Direct overhead costs	$750,000	$400,000	$378,000	$276,000

Required

1. Use the direct method to assign service costs to production activities. Show total overhead costs for molding and assembly.
2. Rework *1* above using the step method. Assign maintenance costs first.
3. Rework *2* above assigning scheduling costs first.

Case 1
Ace Company (L.O. 1, 5, 6)

Ace Company manufactures components for major automotive companies. Ace has two service activities and two production activities. Expected costs for each activity and data on selected cost drivers are as follows:

	Maintenance	Scheduling	Molding	Assembly
Total direct overhead costs	$300,000	$200,000	$400,000	$200,000
Machine-hours			50,000	20,000
Direct labor hours			20,000	60,000
Number of employees	40	3	60	100

Maintenance costs are assigned to production activities on the basis of machine-hours; scheduling costs according to the number of employees in each activity. The predetermined overhead rate is calculated using machine-hours for molding and direct labor hours for assembly.

Required

1. Using the direct method, assign service costs to production activities. Then, calculate a predetermined overhead rate for each production activity.
2. Using the step method, assign service costs to production activities. Then, calculate a predetermined overhead rate for each production activity. Assign scheduling activity costs first.
3. Assume that two products manufactured by Ace Company require the following machine-hours and direct labor hours to produce:

	Products	
	Y1	Y2
Molding, machine-hours	8	2
Assembly, direct labor hours	2	8

Allocate overhead costs to each product using activity-based overhead rates from *1* and *2* above. (Notice that you must allocate the overhead cost to each product twice, using both direct and step rates.) (AICPA)

Case 2

ABC Manufacturing Firm (L.O. 7)

ABC Manufacturing Firm recently constructed its own power plant. It can now supply electricity to its three production activities: A, B, and C. Activity A is the major user of electricity during June, July, and August, a period of high product demand. Activity A runs two production shifts during those months. Activities B and C consume a consistent amount of electricity. The kilowatt-hours expected to be consumed by each activity for the coming year are as follows:

Month	Activity A	Activity B	Activity C
January	100,000	100,000	100,000
February	100,000	100,000	100,000
March	100,000	100,000	100,000
April	100,000	100,000	100,000
May	100,000	100,000	100,000
June	200,000	100,000	100,000
July	200,000	100,000	100,000
August	200,000	100,000	100,000
September	100,000	100,000	100,000
October	100,000	100,000	100,000
November	100,000	100,000	100,000
December	100,000	100,000	100,000
Total	1,500,000 kwh	1,200,000 kwh	1,200,000 kwh

The power plant was constructed to handle 400,000 kilowatt-hours, the amount required by all activities during the summer. Fixed annual costs for operating the plant are $240,000. Variable costs are $0.05 per kilowatt-hour. ABC assigns fixed costs separately from variable costs.

Required Prepare a schedule assigning fixed and variable costs for the power plant to the three production activities.

■

17

Analysis of Financial Statements

LEARNING OBJECTIVES

After studying this chapter you should be able to:

1. Explain how analysis of financial statements assists in financial predictions
2. List and discuss the three standards of comparison used in financial analysis
3. Calculate and present year-to-year comparisons and trends
4. Prepare and interpret common-size financial statements
5. Calculate the seven earning-power ratios and explain their significance
6. Define financial leverage and explain how its effects are measured
7. Calculate the ten debt-paying-ability ratios and explain their significance

In past chapters this text concentrated on preparing special reports for managers and other in-house personnel. In this chapter the focus shifts to using income statements and balance sheets prepared according to generally accepted principles of financial accounting. Income statements and balance sheets provide a historical record of an organization's past activities. As such, they are a useful starting point when predicting a company's future financial performance.

Still, past experience tells only part of the story and cannot by itself indicate future performance. For example, suppose you want to predict how long it will take you to jog from your home to the college. Knowing that your friend next door jogs this same distance every day, you might ask how long it takes him or her to make the trip. Although your friend's time may be the best indicator of how long the trip will take, you will probably want to modify that time to allow for your own circumstances. For instance, you may think your friend is a better runner than you. Or if his or her preferred route is closed for repairs, you may modify your friend's time to allow for a detour. As you acquire running experience, you may notice your time gradually dropping. As a result you may predict that next month the trip will take even less time.

■

Standards for Financial Comparison

Managers, investors, and lenders analyze financial statements to identify an organization's financial strengths and weaknesses. Using financial statements to predict a firm's future performance is similar to using a past running time to predict next month's running time. Income statements and balance sheets from the past few years indicate an organization's recent track record. They do not, however, guarantee that next year's income will be the same as last year's. Last year's income must be adjusted for recent trends and changes in the firm and general business conditions.

Financial analysis is an analysis performed to identify an organization's major financial strengths and weaknesses. Shareholders are interested in predicting future dividends and growth in market value, the two components of a shareholder's return on investment. Lenders are interested in predicting whether an organization will have resources to repay debts when they fall due.

For example, financial analysis indicates whether a company

OBJECTIVE 1
Explain how analysis of financial statements assists in financial predictions

1. Has enough cash to pay bills on time
2. Is collecting on accounts receivable when they fall due
3. Is managing its inventory efficiently
4. Has sufficient plant and equipment
5. Has an adequate balance between permanent capital and short-term debt
6. Is generating an adequate profit margin

All these conditions are necessary to achieve a maximum possible return for shareholders. To determine whether such conditions exist, one must establish some standard of comparison against which a firm's actual circumstances may be measured.

The most important aspect of financial analysis is the comparison of actual financial conditions with expected financial conditions. Expected conditions may be represented by (1) predetermined standards, (2) past performance, or (3) competitors' performance.

Comparison with Predetermined Standards

OBJECTIVE 2
List and discuss the three standards of comparison used in financial analysis

The best basis for comparison, if available, is a standard predetermined by management. This is because **predetermined standards** represent the best performance one can realistically expect given the environment and resources. Standard costs, as discussed in Chapter 10, are a good example of predetermined standards. These costs, which are determined in advance, represent the lowest costs one can realistically expect given a firm's production resources. Other common standards include the expected collection period for accounts receivable, for example, 45 days, and the expected return on assets, such as 18 percent. Standards of this type are the best basis of comparison, for they incorporate the effects of both past and current conditions. In the example of running time, you had to develop a standard time appropriate to the circumstances. You had to consider the runner's ability, expected detours, weather conditions, and any other factors that could influence a runner's time.

Comparison with Past Performance

Comparing current results with past results is particularly helpful in identifying trends. Trends are useful because they provide an early warning about developing problems or early confirmation that problems are being solved. For example, accounts receivable may be taking an average of 60 days to collect, more than the targeted 45 days. If accounts receivable last year took 70 days to collect, then the trend is favorable. Although collection of accounts receivable is above the 45-day standard, the company is making progress.

Comparisons with past results are particularly helpful to investors and lenders, who are not part of an organization's day-to-day management. Lacking inside knowledge of an organization's standards, these analysts must usually rely on historical comparisons. An outsider may not know whether materials should cost 30 or 35 percent of a product's selling price. But if a firm has reduced the cost of materials from 30 percent of sales to 27 percent without reducing product quality, clearly some improvement occurred.

Comparison with Competitors

Managers often compare a company's results with those of competitors or with industry averages. Looking at competitors' performance may help managers establish standards for their own performance. There may, of course, be good reasons for one organization's performance to differ from anothers', but managers should know and understand those reasons. Differences in performance may also stimulate managers to ask how their firms can perform better.

Investors and creditors use industry averages for the same reasons they use past performance. They do not have the detailed knowledge needed to establish performance standards, so they look at how one organization compares to others in the industry.

Industry averages can often be obtained from trade associations. For example, Dun & Bradstreet, the credit rating company, publishes 14 key ratios for 800 lines of business in three size categories. Robert Morris Associates, an association of bank loan officers, compiles 16 ratios for over 250 lines of business by using information from loan applications. The United States Federal Trade Commission and the Securities and Exchange Commission publish a joint quarterly report, showing manufacturers' financial statements in ratio form. Financial Research Associates publish *Financial Studies of Small Business,* a book of ratios particularly applicable to small businesses.

■

Preparing Comparative Statements

Regardless of the standard of comparison, financial analysis uses financial statements. Such statements are easier to interpret if they are prepared with the analyst's needs in mind. For example, including comparative financial statements, which show the amount and percentage of change in each item from one year to the next, helps analysts understand changes in dollar amounts. Also adjustments that allow for differences in the relative size of organizations can facilitate comparisons of competing firms.

Showing Amount and Percentage of Change

OBJECTIVE 3
Calculate and present year-to-year comparisons and trends

Year-to-year comparisons for the same company are useful, especially if reported changes are expressed in percentages. Analysts can then see whether sales and expenses are increasing at the same rate or whether total liabilities are increasing more rapidly than owners' equity. For example, consider the comparative balance sheets shown in Exhibit 17–1. Annual reports generally present only comparative financial statements. However, this balance sheet for Fashion Clothing Stores includes two extra columns that show dollar and percentage changes from one year to the next.

According to the balance sheets, accounts receivable and inventories increased substantially. When sales increase, some increase in these assets is expected. But as you will see when the company's income statements are examined,

Exhibit 17–1

Comparative Balance Sheets Showing Year-to-Year Changes in Dollar Amounts and Percentages

Fashion Clothing Stores Comparative Balance Sheets December 31, 19x3, and 19x2			Increase (decrease)	
	19x3	19x2	Amount	Percent
Assets				
Current assets				
Cash	$ 70,392	$ 68,250	$ 2,142	3.1
Accounts receivable (net)	218,549	184,978	33,571	18.1
Inventory	223,242	197,097	26,145	13.3
Prepaid expenses	67,710	76,542	(8,832)	(11.5)
Total current assets	$579,893	$526,867	$ 53,026	10.1
Plant and equipment				
Plant and equipment (net)	90,503	110,987	(20,484)	(18.5)
Total assets	$670,396	$637,854	$ 32,542	5.1
Liabilities and shareholders' equity				
Current liabilities				
Accounts payable	$158,214	$139,135	$ 19,079	13.7
Bank loans and other payables	71,672	56,769	14,903	26.3
Current portion of notes payable	30,000	30,000	-0-	0.0
Total current liabilities	$259,886	$225,904	$ 33,982	15.0
Long-term liabilities				
Notes payable (11%)	139,000	169,000	(30,000)	(17.8)
Total liabilities	$398,886	$394,904	$ 3,982	1.0
Shareholders' equity				
Preferred shares, $8 dividend, $100 par	$ 70,000	$ 70,000	$ -0-	0.0
Common shares, $1 par value	10,000	10,000	-0-	0.0
Additional paid-in capital	90,000	90,000	-0-	0.0
Total paid-in capital	$170,000	$170,000	$ -0-	0.0
Retained earnings	101,510	72,950	28,560	39.2
Total shareholders' equity	$271,510	$242,950	$ 28,560	11.8
Total liabilities and shareholders' equity	$670,396	$637,854	$ 32,542	5.1

those assets increased by a greater percentage than sales.. The value of property and equipment declined, probably because equipment was depreciated. Accounts payable and bank loans increased significantly. But since the company paid off $30,000 worth of long-term notes, total liabilities changed little. Shareholders' equity increased because of retained earnings, which is explained in more detail in the income statements in Exhibit 17–2. Notice that total liabilities increased

Exhibit 17–2
Comparative Income Statements Showing Year-to-Year Changes in Dollar Amounts and Percentages

Fashion Clothing Stores
Comparative Income Statements
For the Years Ended December 31, 19x3, and 19x2

			Increase (decrease)	
	19x3	19x2	Amount	Percentage
Sales revenues	$2,000,000	$1,801,802	$198,198	11.0
Expenses				
Cost of goods sold	$1,472,000	$1,309,910	$162,090	12.4
Selling	248,000	230,000	18,000	7.8
Administrative	138,000	142,000	(4,000)	2.8
Total expenses	$1,858,000	$1,681,910	$176,090	10.5
Operating income	$ 142,000	$ 119,892	$ 22,108	18.4
Interest expense	27,907	29,270	(1,363)	4.7
Income before taxes	$ 114,093	$ 90,622	$ 23,471	25.9
Income taxes (35%)	39,933	31,718	8,215	25.9
Net income	$ 74,160	$ 58,904	$ 15,256	25.9
Dividends to preferred shareholders	5,600	5,600		
Net income remaining for common shareholders	$ 68,560	$ 53,304		
Dividends to common shareholders	40,000	32,000		
Net income added to retained earnings	$ 28,560	$ 21,304		
Retained earnings, beginning of year	72,950	51,646		
Retained earnings, end of year	$ 101,510	$ 72,950		

by only 1 percent, whereas shareholders' equity increased by 11.8 percent. Thus, the company's financial structure shifted slightly away from borrowing and toward capital provided by owners.

Exhibit 17–2 shows a comparative income statement for Fashion Clothing Stores. Again, two extra columns show dollar and percentage changes from year to year. From this document you can see that an 11 percent increase in sales was accompanied by a 10.5 percent increase in expenses. This situation produced an 18.4 percent increase in operating income. Repayment of $30,000 worth of notes payable reduced interest expense by 4.7 percent. Reduced interest expense together with higher operating income increased income before taxes by 25.9 percent.

Although two-year comparisons are useful, longer-term comparisons are better since special circumstances can distort a two-year comparison. For instance, short-term borrowing just before year-end will increase current assets and current liabilities. But if the borrowing is temporary, it may be insignificant to long-term investors. Examining trends over a period of five to ten years is usually more revealing. Of course, analyzing too many items over too many years can become confusing.

For instance, suppose sales and net income for Fashion Clothing Stores over the past seven years (in thousands) were as follows:

	19x3	19x2	19x1	19x0	19x9	19x8	19x7
Sales	$2,000	$1,802	$1,653	$1,503	$1,342	$1,177	$1,023
Net income	74.16	58.90	48.28	39.57	34.41	30.72	28.44

Sales and earnings grew significantly over the past seven years. The growth between 19x2 and 19x3 was not an isolated incident. Nevertheless, you might also want to ask what the percentage of growth was from year to year. Did net income grow more rapidly or more slowly than sales?

To answer those questions, you can express the same data as an index, that is, as a percentage of the first year's figures, as follows:

	19x3	19x2	19x1	19x0	19x9	19x8	19x7
Sales	196%	176%	162%	147%	131%	115%	100%
Net income	261	207	170	139	121	108	100

These numbers were found by dividing each year's amounts by the 19x7 amount and expressing the result as a percentage. Thus, the index of sales for 19x8 is $1,177 ÷ $1,023 = 115 percent. Expressed this way, the data show that sales growth was fairly steady over the years, with a larger-than-average jump in 19x3. Net income lagged behind sales in the early years, but in 19x1 its growth began exceeding sales growth. Management probably gained better control over expenses in later years.

If precise dollar amounts or percentages are not crucial, a graph can show growth in sales and net income even more clearly. (If precise amounts are needed, tables are better than graphs.) Figure 17–1 shows Fashion Clothing's growth graphically. As you can see, the steady upward trend is visible at a glance.

OBJECTIVE 4
Prepare and interpret common-size financial statements

Year-to-year comparisons and trend analyses are useful in understanding an organization's performance. But as the size of an organization changes, year-to-year comparisons of dollar amounts can be misleading. Comparisons with competing organizations of different size are also difficult to interpret with only dollar amounts. Thus, to adjust for size differences, analysts and accountants have developed common-size financial statements.

Figure 17–1
Fashion Clothing Stores: Sales and Net Income Growth from 19x7 to 19x3
This graph shows sales and net income for Fashion Clothing Stores over a seven-year period. The steady growth can be seen more easily in a graph than in a table.

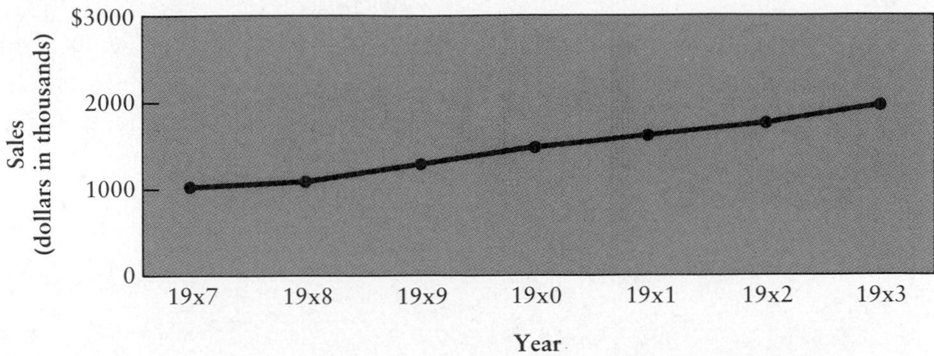

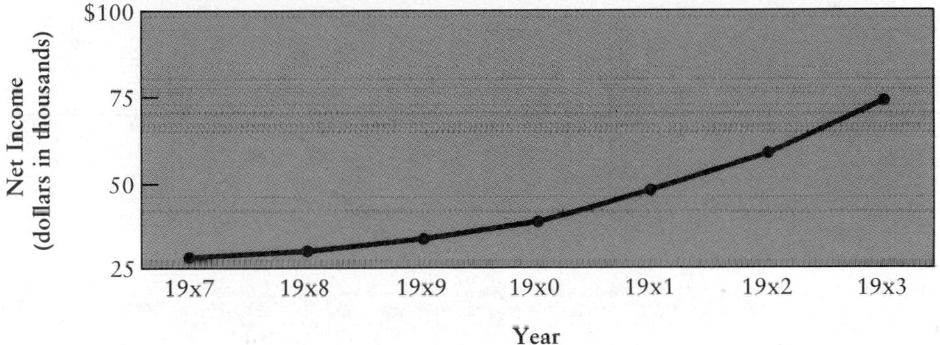

Adjusting for Differences in Size: Common-Size Financial Statements

Common-size financial statements translate dollar amounts into percentages, which indicate the relative size of an item in proportion to the whole. *Common-size balance sheets* show assets, liabilities, and owners' equity as a percentage of total assets. *Common-size income statements* express revenue and expenses as a percentage of sales revenues. Exhibit 17–3 shows that balance sheet for Fashion Clothing Stores redone in common-size format. Common-size percentages are shown in the two right columns. Compare Exhibits 17–3 and 17–1. Make sure you understand the differences in the percentages shown.

Most of Fashion's assets, like those of other retailers, are current assets. Retail businesses usually rent buildings or space in shopping malls. And most of the equipment used by such businesses is unsophisticated. Examples include clothing racks and displays. In fact, retailers' most valuable equipment is probably

Exhibit 17–3
Comparative Balance Sheets in Common-Size Format

Fashion Clothing Stores
Common-Size Comparative Balance Sheets
December 31, 19x3, and 19x2

			Common-size percentages*	
	19x3	19x2	19x3	19x2
Assets				
Current assets				
Cash	$ 70,392	$ 68,250	10.5%	10.7%
Accounts receivable (net)	218,549	184,978	32.6	29.0
Inventory	223,242	197,097	33.3	30.9
Prepaid expenses	67,710	76,542	10.1	12.0
Total current assets	$579,893	$526,867	86.5%	82.6%
Plant and equipment				
Plant and equipment (net)	90,503	110,987	13.5	17.4
Total assets	$670,396	$637,854	100.0%	100.0%
Liabilities and shareholders' equity				
Current liabilities				
Accounts payable	$158,214	$139,135	23.6%	21.8%
Bank loans and other payables	71,672	56,769	10.7	8.9
Current portion of notes payable	30,000	30,000	4.5	4.7
Total current liabilities	$259,886	$225,904	38.8%	35.4%
Long-term liabilities				
Notes payable (11%)	139,000	169,000	20.7	26.5
Total liabilities	$398,886	$394,904	59.5%	61.9%
Shareholders' equity				
Preferred shares, $8 dividend, $100 par	$ 70,000	$ 70,000	10.4%	11.0%
Common shares, $1 par value	10,000	10,000	1.5	1.6
Additional paid-in capital	90,000	90,000	13.4	14.1
Total paid-in capital	$170,000	$170,000	25.4%	26.7%
Retained earnings	101,510	72,950	15.1	11.4
Total shareholders' equity	$271,510	$242,950	40.5%	38.1%
Total liabilities and shareholders' equity	$670,396	$637,854	100.0%	100.0%

*The addition and subtraction on common-size statements is often inexact due to rounding.

Figure 17–2

Fashion Clothing Stores: Relative Size of Balance Sheet Items on December 31, 19x3

These two pie charts show the relative size of Fashion's assets and liabilities as well as owners' equity on December 31, 19x3. The slices correspond to the common-size percentages shown in Exhibit 17–3. To avoid showing too many slices, balance sheet categories are sometimes combined. In this case, common shares and additional paid-in capital were combined.

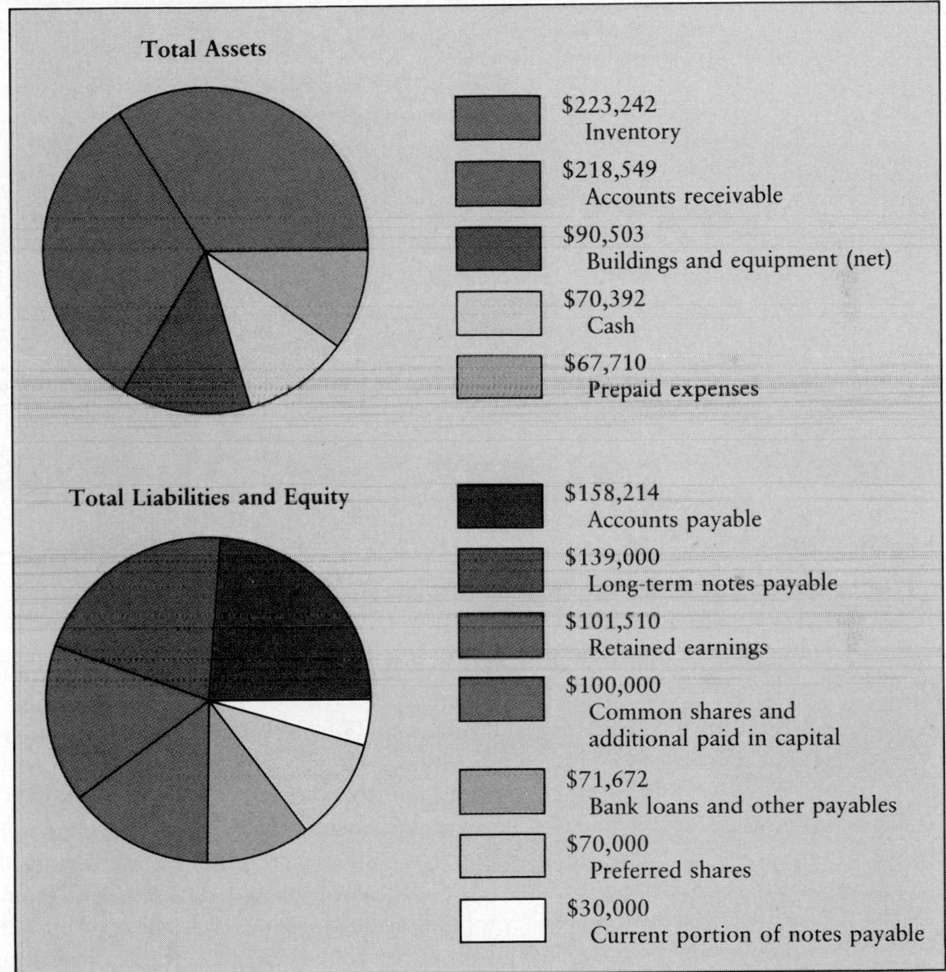

their cash registers and computers. Because this type of equipment is depreciated over much shorter lives than buildings and heavy equipment, the fall in Fashion's investments in equipment from 17.4 percent to 13.5 percent of total assets from 19x2–19x3 is not alarming. You should notice also that accounts receivable and inventory both rose to a slightly higher percentage of total assets during 19x3.

The liabilities and owners' equity section of the balance sheet shows that Fashion obtains about 60 percent of its capital by borrowing (see total liabilities).

Exhibit 17–4

Comparative Income Statements with Common-Size Percentages

Fashion Clothing Stores
Common-Size Comparative Income Statements
For the Years Ended December 31, 19x3, and 19x2

			Common-size percentages*	
	19x3	19x2	19x3	19x2
Sales revenues	$2,000,000	$1,801,802	100.0%	100.0%
Expenses				
Cost of goods sold	$1,472,000	$1,309,910	73.6%	72.7%
Selling	248,000	230,000	12.4	12.7
Administrative	138,000	142,000	6.9	7.9
Total expenses	$1,858,000	$1,681,910	92.9%	93.3%
Operating income	$ 142,000	$ 119,892	7.1%	6.6%
Interest expense	27,907	29,270	1.4	1.6
Income before taxes	$ 114,093	$ 90,622	5.7%	5.0%
Income taxes (35%)	39,933	31,718	2.0	1.7
Net income	$ 74,160	$ 58,904	3.7%	3.3%

*The addition and subtraction on common-size statements is often off by a small amount due to rounding.

The percentage of debt fell slightly from 19x2–19x3 because retained earnings increased more than borrowing. In 19x3, accounts payable, which arises naturally as a store purchases inventory, was 23.6 percent of liabilities. The remainder of the borrowing financed other needs.

The relative importance of Fashion's assets and liabilities as well as its shareholders' equity can be shown even more effectively in pie charts. Figure 17–2 shows the composition of Fashion's assets and liabilities and shareholders' equity for 19x3. As you can see, the pie charts show at a glance the information covered in the last two paragraphs. The problem is that such charts are limited to about six segments. Further division makes them hard to read. If a balance sheet shows more than six major categories, some categories should probably be combined when you prepare a pie chart.

Exhibit 17–4 shows income statements for Fashion Clothing Stores redone in common-size format. In this case, the percentages show how expenses and profits compare to sales revenues. In 19x3, Fashion's after-tax net income was 3.7 percent of sales, a small improvement over 19x2. In other words, 3.7 cents of every dollar in sales revenues was available for dividends or retained earnings. Net income as a percentage of sales improved from 19x2 to 19x3, mainly because selling, administrative, and interest expenses were reduced. The cost of goods

Figure 17–3
Fashion Clothing Stores: Relative Size of Expenses and Net Income
This pie chart shows the relative importance of Fashion's expenses and net income as a percentage of total revenue for 19x3. It can also be thought of as a picture of how each sales dollar was divided.

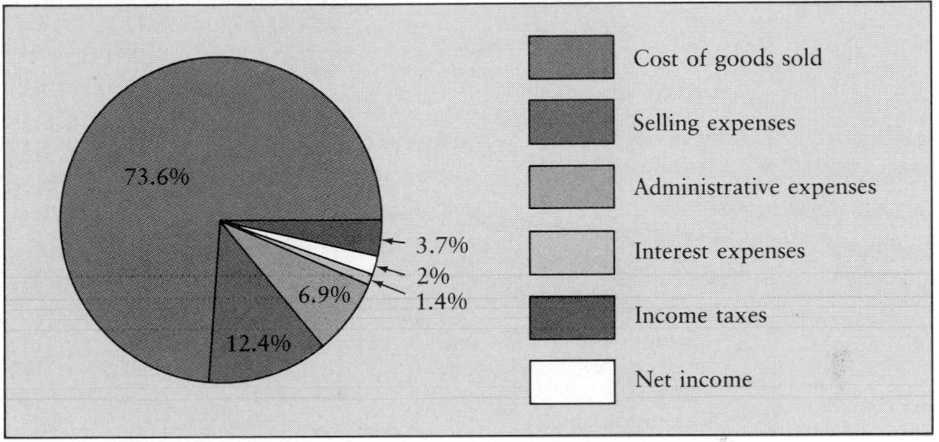

sold as a percentage of sales increased slightly. This fact means the cost of merchandise sold increased more rapidly than sales prices.

Again, a pie chart is useful for showing how sales dollars were distributed between expenses and net income (Figure 17–3). Common-size financial statements are not the only device useful in comparing organizations of different size. Other ratios, the subject of the rest of this chapter, were developed for just that purpose.

Review Exercise 17–1

Prepare Graphs and Comparative Income Statement

Eastland Manufacturing Corporation manufactures both casual and dressy women's clothing. The company prides itself on its market and product research which permits it to offer quality products that meet customer needs.

Eastland's new president has just proposed a 19x5 income budget to the board of directors for their review and approval. As a board member, you are studying the budget. In addition to judging whether it is realistic, you think it may provide insights into the philosophy of the new president. To help you in your analysis, you have the last three years' income statements along with the proposed budget. They are shown on the following page.

Eastland Manufacturing Corporation
Comparative Income Statements
For the Years Ended December 31, 19x5–19x2
(in thousands)

	Budget for 19x5	19x4	19x3	19x2
Sales revenues				
Casual clothing	$ 8,149	$ 7,616	$ 6,680	$5,860
Dress clothing	3,700	3,627	3,455	3,290
Total sales revenues	$11,849	$11,243	$10,135	$9,150
Expenses				
Cost of goods sold				
Casual clothing	$ 3,015	$ 3,046	$ 2,672	$2,344
Dress clothing	1,554	1,632	1,555	1,481
Marketing				
Salaries and commissions	2,027	1,906	1,730	1,573
Advertising	1,016	968	880	800
Research	178	225	203	183
Administration				
Salaries	750	640	600	540
Human resources development	136	151	138	125
Facilities	798	753	710	670
Product research	474	675	608	548
Total expenses	$ 9,948	$ 9,996	$ 9,096	$8,264
Operating income	$ 1,901	$ 1,247	$ 1,039	$ 886

Required

1. Prepare a single graph showing the trend in the following items for 19x2 to 19x4 and the budget for 19x5. After drawing the graph, explain briefly any insights you find in:
   a. Casual clothing sales
   b. Dress clothing sales
   c. Operating income
2. Prepare a single graph showing the trend in the following items for 19x2 to 19x4 and the budget for 19x5. After drawing the graph, explain why the director might be interested in these items and briefly explain any insights shown from the graph.
   a. Market research
   b. Product research
   c. Human resources development
3. Prepare common-size income statements for 19x3, 19x4, and the 19x5 budget. Comment on any changes you observe.

Solution

1. The graph shows steady growth in actual sales for 19x2 through 19x4. The new president is projecting reduced sales growth for the budget

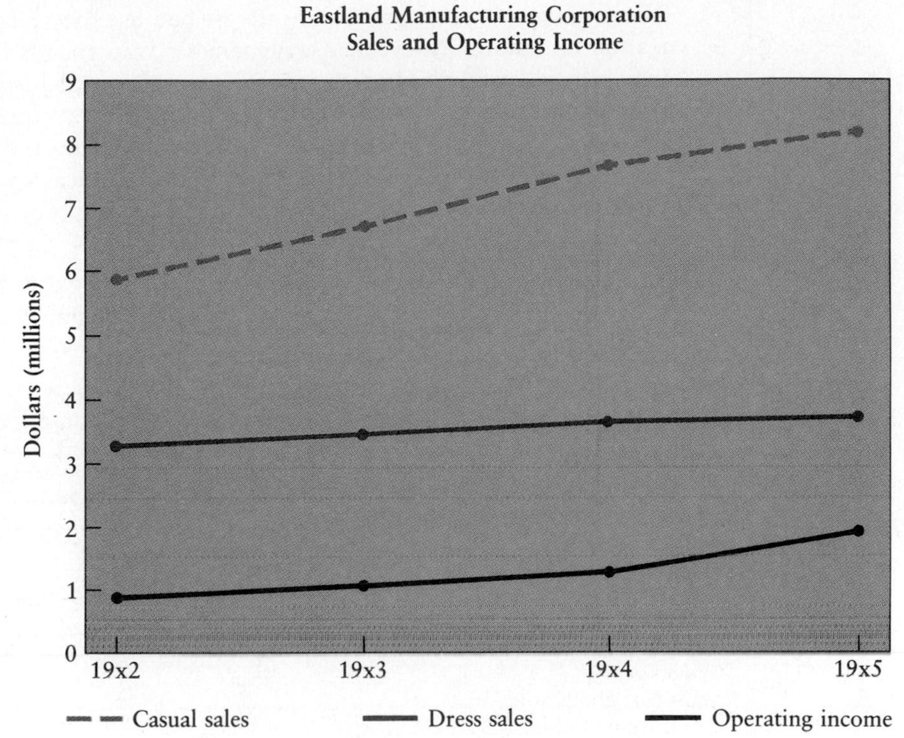

year, particularly for casual clothing. The budgeted operating income growth increases at a higher rate in the budget year. This must be due to expense reductions. The important question is which expenses are being reduced.

2.

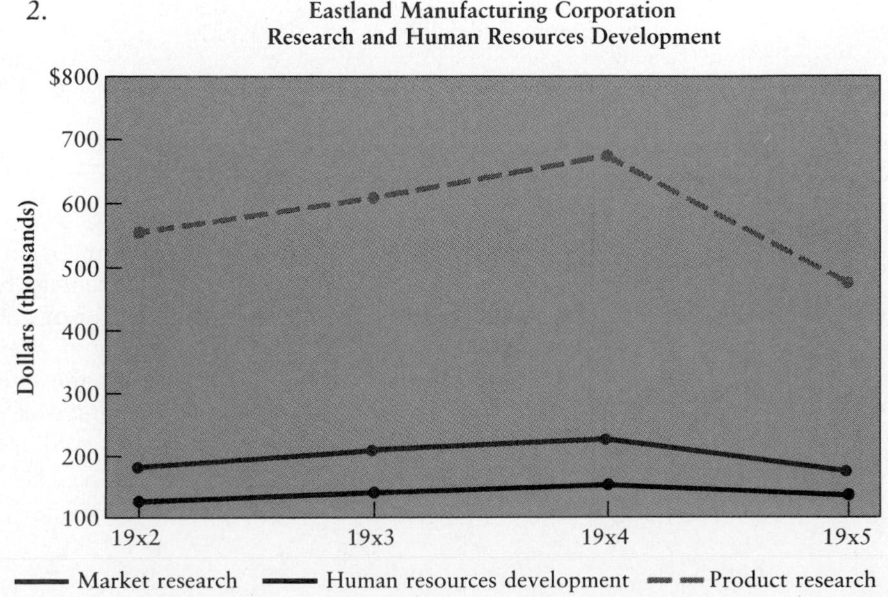

These expenses are of particular interest because they build the organization for future achievements. A manager who spends in these areas may reduce current operating income to prepare for higher future income. Conversely, a manager who fails to spend adequately in these areas will look good in next year's performance but may damage the organization's future. In this case, the budget reduces spending on all three areas, suggesting that the new president may be trying to look good next year at the expense of future years.

3. The common-size income statements are shown below. If sales grow faster than expenses, we would expect these percentages to drop.

Eastland Manufacturing Corporation
Common-Size Comparative Income Statements
For the Years Ended December 31, 19x5–19x3

	Budget for 19x5	19x4	19x3
Sales revenues			
Casual clothing	68.8%	67.7%	65.9%
Dress clothing	31.2	32.3	34.1
Total sales revenues	100.0	100.0	100.0
Expenses			
Cost of goods sold			
Casual clothing	25.5*	27.1	26.4
Dress clothing	13.1	14.5	15.3
Total cost of goods sold	38.5	41.6	41.7
Marketing			
Salaries and commissions	17.1	17.0	17.1
Advertising	8.6	8.6	8.7
Research	1.5	2.0	2.0
Administration			
Salaries	6.3	5.7	5.9
Human resources development	1.2*	1.3	1.4
Facilities	6.7	6.7	7.0
Product research	4.0	6.0	6.0
Total expenses	84.0	88.9	89.7
Operating income	16.0	11.1	10.3

*Numbers are rounded.

Notice that casual clothing is becoming a more important part of total sales. Cost of goods sold is decreasing as a percentage of total sales. However, we must look at each product line's cost of goods sold as a percentage of sales to understand what is happening. We divided each year's cost of goods sold for a product line by the line's sales. For example, 19x3 cost of goods sold for casual clothing was \$2,344, while casual clothing sales were \$5,860. Cost of goods sold as a percentage of sales is 40 percent (\$2,344 ÷ \$5,860).

	Budget for 19x5	19x4	19x3
Cost of goods sold as percentage of sales			
Casual	37.0%	40.0%	40.0%
Dress	42.0	45.0	45.0

Cost of goods sold as a percentage of sales had been steady. For the budget year, it is expected to drop. If this is a result of expense control, this is good. If it is a result of substituting lower quality material or poorer work, this is undesirable.

In 2 above, we saw the trend of lower spending on research and human resources development for the budget year. This is probably not a good place to reduce expenses. Salaries seem to be increasing more rapidly than sales. The director would want to investigate the rationale for this plan.

The net effect is increased salaries, lower sales growth, offset by savings in research and human resources development. This plan seems to emphasize short-term profits while potentially damaging long-run position. The director should question this philosophy.

(see Exercises 20, 24, 33)

■

Use of Ratios

When you see a set of financial statements in a textbook, do you always study them carefully? Or do you skip over them, hoping the text will direct your attention to the important aspects? In fact, financial statements are so complex that people tend to look for an easier way to obtain the necessary information. Even managers, who are strongly motivated to understand these statements, prefer to have their attention directed to the major points. And that is just what ratios do.

A **ratio** is simply a relationship between the two numbers expressed either as a percentage or an absolute number. For example, if you talk about an 18 percent return on assets or an average selling period of 90 days for inventory, you are using ratios. Managers are interested in many ratios. Two additional examples are the average collection period for accounts receivable and the relationship between current assets and current liabilities. The **current ratio** shows the relationship between current assets and current liabilities. Both ratios highlight two items from the financial statements. Such attention on selected items can be both helpful and potentially misleading, and thus must be interpreted carefully. By focusing attention on only two items, you ignore others. And some of those items may be just as important, or more so, as the ones selected.

As suggested earlier, ratios help analysts adjust for differences in a company's size over the years. For example, the following data were taken from one company's income statements over a three-year period. The data are used to compute net earnings as a percentage of sales revenue.

	19x3	19x2	19x1
Sales revenues	$1,500	$1,200	$1,100
Net earnings	140	130	100
Net earnings as a percentage of sales	9.3%	10.8%	9.1%

The data also show that although sales and net earnings increased from year to year, net earnings as a percentage of sales increased only in 19x2. In fact, in 19x3, net earnings as a percentage of sales dropped significantly. In other words, between 19x1 and 19x2, net earnings grew more rapidly than sales. But between 19x2 and 19x3, the trend reversed. Managers should investigate the reversal.

As an example of how ratios correct for differences in size on balance sheets, consider the following comparisons of two companies' current assets and current liabilities. As previously stated, the relationship between a company's current assets and current liabilities is called the current ratio. This ratio will be discussed in more detail later in the chapter. For now you must only know that the current ratio is found by dividing total current assets by total current liabilities as shown:

	Company A	Company B
Total current assets	$12,000	$95,000
Total current liabilities	6,500	42,000
Current ratio	1.85	2.26

Notice that Company B has greater current liabilities than Company A. But when its current assets, which may be used to pay off current liabilities, are considered, Company B appears as the stronger company. Company B has $2.26 in current assets for every dollar of current liabilities, whereas Company A has only $1.85. Thus, the current ratio adjusts for the difference in the two companies' size. It does so by showing that Company B has a proportionately larger pool of liquid assets for paying off debts.

As mentioned earlier, however, ratios must be carefully interpreted. If most of Company B's current assets are invested in inventory and its current liabilities are due next month, it might have difficulty paying these debts on time. If Company A's current assets consist mostly of cash and accounts receivable and most of its current liabilities are not due for six months, it is in a strong position to pay off its debts when due. Hence, the current ratio does not tell the entire story about a company's ability to pay its bills when due. It does not distinguish between different types of current assets or the due dates of current liabilities.

As defined, ratios are the relationship between two numbers. Accordingly, trend percentages and common-size percentages discussed earlier are ratios. Other useful ratios may be calculated by using information from financial statements. In the next sections of this chapter, you will look at examples of two categories of ratios, ratios indicating an organization's earning power and ratios indicating an organization's ability to pay debts.

■

Earning-Power Ratios

OBJECTIVE 5
Calculate the seven earning-power ratios and explain their significance

Earning-power ratios are a group of ratios that help analysts assess the adequacy of a firm's net income. A company's earning power is of interest primarily to its shareholders, whose dividends are paid from net income, and to long-term lenders, who require some assurance the company will be able to repay its debts.

A firm's present assets are no assurance a loan can be repaid in twenty years. Assets owned twenty years from now will probably be quite different from those owned today. Today's accounts receivable will have been collected and the inventory sold and replaced. Most of the present equipment will have worn out or become obsolete. Hence, long-term lenders look instead for some assurance that an organization will continue to operate profitably, so that in twenty years it will have new assets for paying off the loan. In other words, the organization must have good earning power.

The seven ratios most commonly used to evaluate earning power are as follows:

1. Earnings per share
2. Fully diluted earnings per share
3. Price-earnings ratio
4. Dividend payout ratio
5. Dividend yield ratio
6. Return on total assets ratio
7. Return on common shareholders' equity.

Earnings per Share

Earnings per share (EPS) is the net income available to common shareholders divided by the number of common shares outstanding. (Preferred shareholders' earnings are the dividends on preferred shares.) Because common shareholders own a portion of a corporation, they are interested in knowing their share of net income. Earnings per share indicates how much of a company's net income can be paid as dividends or retained for growth to increase each share's value. Dividends and growth in the value of the shares comprise the shareholders' total return.

Earnings per share is calculated as follows:

$$\text{Earnings per share} = \frac{(\text{net income} - \text{preferred dividends})}{\text{number of common shares outstanding}}$$

Using data from Exhibits 17–1 and 17–2, you can calculate Fashion's earnings per share in 19x3 as follows on page 796.

$$\text{Earnings per share} = \frac{(\$74{,}160 - \$5{,}600)}{10{,}000 \text{ shares}} = \underline{\underline{\$6.86}} \text{ per share}$$

Preferred dividends must always be subtracted from net income, even when they are not paid. Preferred shareholders usually have a cumulative claim on unpaid past dividends, which means that all previously unpaid preferred dividends must be paid before paying common share dividends. If the firm does not have preferred shares, zero is inserted for preferred dividends.

By itself earnings per share does not tell an analyst much about a company's performance. It must be interpreted in the context of long-term company trends.

Two complications may arise in calculating earnings per share. The first occurs whenever net income includes extraordinary gains or losses. Extraordinary gains or losses require that earnings per share be separated into two parts, one for normal continuing operations, the other for extraordinary items. By definition, **extraordinary gains and losses** are not expected to repeat themselves. Therefore, they should be excluded from financial predictions.

Extraordinary items are reported after adding or subtracting their income tax effect. Most extraordinary gains are taxable and increase a firm's income taxes. Were the total income taxes charged against normal earnings, the extra tax on the extraordinary gain would reduce net income and earnings per share below normal levels. Conversely, an extraordinary loss would reduce income taxes. Reporting the tax effect of the extraordinary loss deduction as part of income from continuing operations would exaggerate a company's net income and earnings per share. Thus, the amount of an extraordinary item must be reported with the tax effect of that extraordinary item, and not as a part of income from continuing operations. To do so, a firm adjusts the extraordinary item in much the same way that cash flows of capital expenditures are adjusted to after-tax revenue and expenses (see Chapter 15).

For example, suppose Courier Corporation has sustained a fire loss of $50,000. Because the loss is not covered by insurance, Courier must bear the loss but is entitled to a tax deduction. The loss deduction reduces Courier's taxable income by $50,000. If Courier's income tax rate is 34 percent, the $50,000 reduction in taxable income will save Courier $17,000 in income taxes ($50,000 × 34%). Therefore, the economic effect of this loss is $33,000, not $50,000. This $33,000 loss would be shown as an extraordinary item in earnings per share computations.

Next, suppose Courier's income statement is as shown in Exhibit 17–5. The company has 50,000 shares outstanding. Under these circumstances, its earnings per share would be calculated as follows:

Earnings per share	
Net earnings from continuing operations, $88,492 ÷ 50,000 shares	$ 1.77
Extraordinary fire loss (net of tax savings), $33,000 ÷ 50,000 shares	(0.66)
Net earnings per share	$ 1.11

As you can see, this two-part computation properly reports the economic effect of the extraordinary item. The $1.77 is a better indicator of the organization's continuing earning power than one including the extraordinary loss.

Exhibit 17–5

Income Statements Illustrating Correct and Incorrect Reporting of an Extraordinary Loss

These two income statements illustrate the correct and incorrect methods of reporting an extraordinary loss and its associated income tax effect. The correct method reports income from continuing operations, whereas the incorrect method does not show it.

Courier Company
Income Statement
For the Year Ended December 31, 19x6

Incorrect Method		Correct Method	
Sales revenues	$2,805,000	Sales revenues	$2,805,000
Expenses		Expenses	
Cost of goods sold	$1,991,550	Cost of goods sold	$1,991,550
Selling	329,027	Selling	329,027
Administrative	350,345	Administrative	350,345
Fire loss	50,000	Total expenses	$2,670,922
Total expenses	$2,720,922	Net earnings before taxes	$ 134,078
Earnings before taxes	$ 84,078	Income taxes (34%)	45,586
Income taxes (34%)	28,586	Net earnings from	
Net earnings	$ 55,492	continuing operations	$ 88,492
		Extraordinary loss	
		Fire loss (net of tax	
		savings of $17,000)	33,000
		Net earnings	$ 55,492

The second complication that may arise in calculating earnings per share is the existence of convertible securities. This complication is dealt with by using a special ratio called fully diluted earnings per share.

Fully Diluted Earnings per Share

Convertible securities are shares, often debt or preferred shares, that may be converted into common shares at some future time according to a fixed ratio. Convertible securities appeal to investors because they provide security of repayment before conversion, plus gains resulting from anticipated strong future earnings after conversion. That is, if the earnings and market value of common shares increase enough, holders of convertible securities will find it profitable to convert them into common shares. When these securities are converted into common shares, they can change an organization's future earnings per share. Remember, the number of common shares is the denominator in the earnings per share ratio. And preferred dividends or interest expense pertaining to convertible debt are subtracted from the numerator in that ratio.

Generally accepted accounting principles require companies that have convertible securities to report earnings per share two ways.

1. Based on the assumption that they are not converted
2. Based on the assumption that they are converted

Assume a company has convertible preferred shares outstanding. In the first calculation, the dividends on the preferred shares are deducted as usual from net income. Earnings per share on the common shares is then calculated as described in the last section, based on the number of shares actually outstanding. In the second calculation, fully diluted earnings per share is calculated by using the following formula:

$$\text{Fully diluted earnings per share} = \frac{\text{net income}}{\text{original common shares outstanding} + \text{converted shares}}$$

Preferred share dividends are not subtracted in the second calculation and potential new common shares are included.

Suppose, for instance, that Fashion Clothing's 700 preferred shares are convertible to 1,400 shares of common stock. Also, preferred shares have a market value of $100 per share, as stated in Exhibit 17–1. Therefore, preferred shareholders should be interested in converting their shares when the market value of the common shares exceeds $50 per share. At that price, the value of the two common shares received for conversion of one preferred share is greater than the $100 market value of each preferred share.

Conversion of the preferred shares has two effects. First, there are no more preferred dividends to deduct from net income in the earnings per share computation. Second, it adds 1,400 common shares to the denominator. When earnings per share is calculated as if all shares were converted to common stock, the resulting ratio is called **fully diluted earnings per share.** That calculation for Fashion Clothing would be as follows:

$$\text{Fully diluted earnings earnings per share} = \frac{\$74{,}160 \text{ net income}}{10{,}000 \text{ original shares} + 1{,}400 \text{ converted shares}}$$

$$= \frac{\$74{,}160}{11{,}400} = \underline{\underline{\$6.51}} \text{ per share}$$

By comparing this figure for fully diluted earnings per share with the figure for earnings per share (page 796), you can see that earnings dropped $0.35 per share. The amount of difference between the two ratios will vary, depending on the conversion ratio and the amount of the dividend previously paid on converted preferred shares.

Price-Earnings Ratio

Besides earnings per share, shareholders are interested in the return on the market value of their shares. The **price-earnings ratio** is the ratio of the market price of a share to its earnings per share. For example, assume the market price of Fashion

Clothing's stock was $47 per share at the end of 19x3. Given that fact and the figure for earnings per share, you can calculate the price-earnings ratio as follows:

$$\text{Price-earnings ratio} = \frac{\text{current market price per share}}{\text{earnings per share}}$$

$$= \frac{\$47}{\$6.86} = \underline{\underline{6.85}}$$

Since retail clothing is not a high-growth industry, price-earnings ratios at clothing stores tend to be relatively low. Price-earnings ratios of companies with high growth potential are often 20 or more.

Dividend Payout Ratio

The **dividend payout ratio** is the ratio of dividends per share of stock to earnings per share expressed as a percentage. It is a measure of how much of the common shareholders' net earnings were paid out as dividends. Earnings not paid out as dividends are retained to provide a broader base for future growth. The formula for the dividend payout ratio is as follows:

$$\text{Dividend payout ratio} = \frac{\text{dividends per share}}{\text{earnings per share}}$$

For Fashion Clothing Stores the computation for 19x3 would be

$$\text{Dividends per share} = \frac{\$40{,}000}{10{,}000 \text{ shares}}$$

$$= \$4.00$$

$$\text{Dividend payout ratio} = \frac{\$4.00}{\$6.86} = \underline{\underline{58.3}} \text{ percent}$$

As stated earlier, retail clothing stores tend to have relatively low price-earnings ratios because of their low growth prospects. That tendency is consistent with Fashion Clothing's paying out more than half its earnings per share as dividends. Should the managers of Fashion Clothing see good prospects for future growth, they might pay low dividends and retain most of the company's earnings to help finance future growth.

Dividend-Yield Ratio

The **dividend-yield ratio** is the ratio of the dividend per share of stock to its market value per share expressed as a percentage. Shareholders expect a return on their investments, either in dividends or by growth in the market value of their shares. The dividend yield shows how much return on investment was received as dividends. Dividend yield is particularly important to retired people, who may need the income from their shares to pay living expenses.

Market price per share is used to calculate dividend yield because an investor dissatisfied with his investment will receive the market price if he or she sells those shares and makes another investment. The formula is as follows:

$$\text{Dividend-yield ratio} = \frac{\text{dividends per share}}{\text{market price per share}}$$

For Fashion Clothing Stores, the computation would be

$$\text{Dividend-yield ratio} = \frac{\$4}{\$47} = \underline{\underline{8.5}} \text{ percent}$$

Fashion Clothing has quite a high dividend yield. Often dividend yields are below 5 percent, depending on a company's growth prospects.

Return on Total Assets Ratio

Two important managerial responsibilities consist of using assets wisely and acquiring assets economically. The **return on total assets** is a ratio that measures how wisely management is using assets. It is calculated by dividing net income *before* interest but *after* taxes by average total assets. Notice that the value of the numerator is not shown on a company's financial statements. It must be calculated. Interest expense is excluded so the ratio will not be affected by the use of debt financing. As stated, this ratio measures how wisely management is using assets, not whether they were obtained in the most economical way.

In the earlier illustration of extraordinary gains and losses, you saw how a gain or loss is adjusted for its income tax effects. You must do the same with interest expense when calculating return on total assets. Thus, you must take net income after taxes and add back interest expense less the tax savings resulting from the tax deductibility. The formula is as follows:

$$\text{Return on total assets} = \frac{\text{net income} + [\text{interest expense} \times (1 - \text{tax rate})]}{\text{average total assets}}$$

Average total assets is preferred as the denominator because a firm's assets fluctuate during the year. Were total assets on a single date used, the ratio might be distorted by an unusual asset balance at year-end.

When calculating return on total assets for Fashion Clothing, one must first calculate the numerator, the net income before interest but after taxes. For 19x3, the computation would be

Net income	$74,160
After-tax interest expense	
[$27,907 × (1 − 35%)]	18,140
Total numerator	$92,300

This is the amount net income would have been if the company had no interest expense. Average asset is calculated by using the balance sheet figures for total assets at the beginning and end of the year, as shown below.

Total assets, end of 19x3	$ 670,396
Total assets, end of 19x2	637,854
Total	$1,308,250

$$\text{Average total assets} = \frac{\$1,308,250}{2} = \$654,125$$

$$\text{Return on total assets} = \frac{\$92,300}{\$654,125} = 14.1 \text{ percent}$$

Return on Common Shareholders' Equity

Earlier, the dividend-yield ratio for Fashion Clothing Stores was calculated. As noted, dividends are only a portion of a shareholder's return. However, the **return on common shareholders' equity** is defined as the net income available to common shareholders after subtracting preferred dividends divided by the book value of the common shareholders' equity. (This ratio is not strictly comparable to the dividend-yield ratio, since that ratio is based on the market value, not the book value, of common shareholders' equity.)

The return on common shareholders' equity is expressed as a percentage. It is calculated as follows:

$$\text{Return on common shareholders' equity} = \frac{\text{net income} - \text{preferred dividends}}{\text{average common shareholders' equity}}$$

For Fashion Clothing Stores the numerator would be

Net income	$74,160
Preferred dividends	5,600
Total numerator	$68,560

Average common shareholders' equity would be computed using data from the balance sheets at the beginning and end of the year, as follows:

	December 31	
	19x3	19x2
Par value	$ 10,000	$ 10,000
Additional paid-in capital	90,000	90,000
Retained earnings	101,510	72,950
Total	$201,510	$172,950

$$\text{Average common shareholders' equity} = \frac{\$201,510 + \$172,950}{2}$$

$$= \$187,230$$

Return on common shareholders' equity

$$= \frac{\$68{,}560}{\$187{,}230} = \underline{\underline{36.6}} \text{ percent}$$

Like most ratios, return on common shareholders' equity must be evaluated according to what is normal for the industry. But notice that Fashion Clothing's return on common shareholder's equity is more than twice as high as its return on total assets. This phenomenon is called financial leverage, and it will be examined in the next section.

Review Exercise 17–2

Calculate Earning-Power Ratios

B & A Management is a family owned company that designs and produces designer clothing. Through careful management and the use of financial leverage, B & A has been very profitable. Management is beginning its planning for next year and would like an analysis of their profitability for 19x2. Financial statements for the last two years are given below.

B & A Management Company
Comparative Balance Sheet
December 31, 19x2, and 19x1

	19x2	19x1
Assets		
Current assets		
Cash	$ 8,000	$ 10,000
Accounts receivable	93,380	72,953
Inventory	40,576	42,267
Prepaid expenses	650	500
Total current assets	$ 142,606	$ 125,720
Plant and equipment (cost)	$ 695,878	$ 570,600
Accumulated depreciation	(347,939)	(313,830)
Net plant and equipment	$ 347,939	$ 256,770
Total assets	$ 490,545	$ 382,490
Equities		
Current liabilities		
Accounts payable	$ 23,669	$ 21,133
Notes payable	10,000	10,000
Total current liabilities	$ 33,669	$ 31,133
Long-term notes	240,000	205,000
Common stock	$ 50,000	$ 50,000
Retained earnings	166,876	96,357
Owners' equity	$ 216,876	$ 146,357
Total equities	$ 490,545	$ 382,490

B & A Management Company
Comparative Income Statements
Years Ended December 31, 19x2, and 19x1

	19x2	19x1
Sales revenues	$710,080	$634,000
Expenses		
Cost of goods sold	$284,032	$253,600
Salaries	192,050	167,000
Advertising	70,400	64,000
Other and income taxes	70,975	61,185
Total expenses	$617,457	$545,785
Net income	$ 92,623	$ 88,215

Required

1. B & A has 50,000 shares outstanding. Calculate B & A's earnings per share for 19x1 and 19x2.
2. At December 31, 19x2, the market price of B & A's shares is $22. Calculate B & A's price-earnings ratio at December 31, 19x2.
3. Calculate B & A's dividend payout ratio for 19x2. Dividends and earnings were the only events affecting their retained earnings during the year.
4. Calculate B & A's dividend yield for 19x2.
5. Calculate B & A's return on total assets for 19x2.

Solution

1. Earnings per share (EPS)

$$\text{EPS} = \frac{\text{Net income} - \text{preferred dividends}}{\text{Number of common shares outstanding}}$$

$$\text{19x1 EPS} = \frac{\$88{,}215 - \$0}{\$50{,}000} = \underline{\underline{\$1.76}} \text{ per share}$$

$$\text{19x2 EPS} = \frac{\$92{,}623 - \$0}{50{,}000} = \underline{\underline{\$1.85}} \text{ per share}$$

2. 19x2 price-earnings ratio

$$\text{Price-earnings ratio} = \frac{\text{current market price per share}}{\text{earnings per share}}$$

$$= \frac{\$22}{\$1.85} = \underline{\underline{11.9}}$$

3. 19x2 dividend payout

Beginning retained earnings	$ 96,357
Net income	92,623
	$188,980
Ending retained earnings	166,876
19x2 dividends	$ 22,104

$$\text{Dividend per share} = \frac{\$22{,}104}{50{,}000 \text{ shares}} = \$0.44208$$

$$\text{Dividend payout ratio} = \frac{\text{dividends per share}}{\text{earnings per share}}$$

$$= \frac{\$0.44208}{\$1.85} = \underline{\underline{22.7}} \text{ percent}$$

4. 19x2 dividend yield

$$\text{Dividend yield} = \frac{\text{dividends per share}}{\text{market price per share}}$$

$$= \frac{\$0.44208}{\$22.00} = \underline{\underline{2.0}} \text{ percent}$$

5. 19x2 return on owner's equity

$$\text{Return on owner's equity} = \frac{\text{net income} - \text{preferred dividends}}{\text{Average common shareholders' equity}}$$

Beginning owners' equity	$146,357.00
Ending owners' equity	216,876.00
Total	$363,233.00
Average	$181,616.50

$$\text{Return on owner's equity} = \frac{\$92{,}623 - \$0}{\$181{,}616.50} = \underline{\underline{51.0}} \text{ percent}$$

(see Exercises 21, 31, 34)

■

Financial Leverage

OBJECTIVE 6
Define financial leverage and explain how its effects are measured

As noted earlier, two important managerial responsibilities are to use assets wisely and to acquire assets economically. A return on total assets measures how wisely or efficiently managers have used assets. A return on common shareholders' equity reflects not only how well assets were used but how they were obtained. **Financial leverage** is the result of obtaining capital from debt or preferred shares and using the capital to earn a return by investing in assets.

Generally, assets are either borrowed from creditors or obtained from owners (shareholders). Some borrowing, such as accounts payable, can be obtained at no interest cost simply because of business custom. But usually borrowed capital has an explicit cost, expressed as an interest rate. Because the risk to lenders is generally lower than the risk to equity investors, the cost of debt capital is usually lower than the cost of equity capital. And being allowed to deduct interest in income tax calculations reduces the cost of borrowed capital still further. In the example, Fashion Clothing obtained most of its assets at a relatively low cost by borrowing.

Fashion also obtained some relatively low-cost capital by issuing shares of preferred stock. The cost of the preferred dividends was only $8 per $100 share or 8 percent. And its return on total assets in 19x3 was 14.1 percent. But what happens to the difference between the 14.1 percent return on assets and the cost of the borrowed and preferred share capital? It accrues to the benefit of the common shareholders, increasing their return to 36.6 percent, Fashion's return on shareholder's equity.

Fashion Clothing is an example of *favorable financial leverage,* or the ability to invest borrowed capital to earn more than it costs. Because a fairly large portion of Fashion's capital is provided by debt, the positive effect of its favorable financial leverage is magnified.

However, financial leverage can also work against shareholders. If return on total assets falls below the average after-tax cost of debt, the common shareholders' return suffers. And interest on the debt must be paid regardless of a firm's earnings. Such fixed interest payments may reduce the amount of net income available for the common shareholders. This situation then depresses the return on stockholders' equity below the return on total assets. Since dividends on preferred shares must usually be paid before paying dividends on common shares, these dividends have the same effect as debt on return on common shareholders' equity.

Leverage is a boon to stockholders as long as return on assets is high and it does not make repayment of debts difficult. Managers can create favorable financial leverage by using (1) current liabilities, (2) long-term debt, and (3) preferred stock. With such current liabilities as accounts and wages payable, on which there is customarily no interest charge, any positive rate of return will produce favorable leverage. Other current liabilities, such as short-term bank loans, will produce favorable leverage if return on total assets is greater than the after-tax interest rate. Since interest expense is deductible, its true cost to the organization is reduced by its tax effect. The formula for the after-tax interest rate, which was used previously, is shown below.

$$\text{After-tax interest rate} = \text{before-tax interest rate} \times (1 - \text{income tax rate})$$

The same rule applies to long-term debt: leverage will be favorable when the return on total assets is greater than the after-tax interest rate.

Preferred stock can be used to create favorable leverage if the return on total assets is greater than the preferred dividend rate. The dividend rate is not adjusted for taxes, since dividends are not tax deductible. Fashion Clothing issued preferred shares, which is sold for $100 per share. On those shares the store paid an $8 dividend. Thus, the dividend rate is 8 percent ($8 ÷ $100). On some preferred shares, dividend rates are stated as a percentage of par value rather than as a dollar amount.

Debt has a high priority in liquidation proceedings, and interest payments are required by contract even when a corporation does not earn a profit. In liquidation proceedings, preferred shares have higher priority than common shares but lower priority than debt. Hence, ownership risks are higher for preferred shareholders than for lenders. To compensate preferred shareholders for this additional risk, firms promise a rate of return higher than the rate on debt. But one must also consider that those dividends are not tax deductible, which makes the cost of preferred shares considerably higher than the cost of debt. Therefore, preferred shares create less leverage than debt.

■

Debt-Paying-Ability Ratios

The ratios just discussed are helpful in evaluating a corporation's earning power. Listed below is another group of ratios. These ratios focus on a firm's ability to pay debts when due.

1. Working capital
2. Current ratio
3. Acid-test ratio
4. Accounts receivable turnover
5. Average collection period
6. Inventory turnover
7. Average selling period
8. Times-interest-earned ratio
9. Debt-to-equity ratio
10. Book value per share

OBJECTIVE 7
Calculate the ten debt-paying-ability ratios and explain their significance

The first seven of these ratios concern the ability to pay short-term debts. As such they are of primary interest to short-term creditors, who expect to be paid from existing current assets. The eighth and ninth ratios concern the ability to pay long-term debt. As noted earlier, the interests of long-term creditors more closely resemble those of shareholders than short-term creditors. Should a lender make a ten- or twenty-year loan to a firm, most of the firm's present assets will not be available when the loan comes due. The long-term creditor's major protection is the firm's ability to operate at a profit and to generate cash inflows from operations. Thus, long-term creditors are interested in the earning-power ratios discussed earlier as well as trends in sales and net income. The times-interest-earned and debt-to-equity ratios supplement these measures of earning power.

The tenth ratio, book value per share, has limited value. It is included here because it is sometimes mentioned in financial discussions.

Working Capital

Working capital is a pool of liquid assets financed by long-term capital sources. Therefore, there are no short-run claims on working capital, and management has considerable discretion in its use. Expressed mathematically, working capital is a firm's total current assets minus its total current liabilities.

Working capital = total current assets − total current liabilities

By using information from the company's balance sheets (Exhibit 17–1), you can calculate Fashion Clothing Stores' working capital on December 31, 19x3, and 19x2, as shown below.

	December 31	
	19x3	19x2
Current assets		
Cash	$ 70,392	$ 68,250
Accounts receivable	218,549	184,978
Inventory	223,242	197,097
Prepaid expenses	67,710	76,542
Total current assets	$579,893	$526,867
Current liabilities		
Accounts payable	$158,214	$139,135
Bank loans and other payables	71,672	56,769
Current portion of notes payable	30,000	30,000
Total current liabilities	$259,886	$225,904
Working capital	$320,007	$300,963

Working capital interests short-term creditors because it represents assets convertible to cash within the next year. Inventories are converted to cash by selling them. Accounts receivable are converted to cash by collecting them. Prepaid expenses are not directly converted to cash, but will increase the organization's cash balance because they save a cash payment. Likewise, current liabilities must be paid within the next year[1] Fashion Clothing's working capital at December 31, 19x3, suggests the company could pay off all current liabilities and still have

[1]Working capital is current assets minus current liabilities. *Statement on Management Number 2, Management Accounting Terminology* (Copyright © 1983 by the National Association of Accountants, Montvale, NJ. All rights reserved.), defines current assets as "cash and other assets that are expected to be sold, converted into cash, or otherwise consumed during the normal operating cycle of a business or within one year, whichever is longer." Current liabilities are "liabilities expected to be discharged by using current assets within one year or the operating cycle, whichever is longer, or transferred to income in a relatively short period of time." Operating cycle is defined as "the period between the acquisition of raw materials or finished goods by the expenditure of cash or its equivalent and the recovery of related amounts of cash through the sale of inventory for cash or receivables and the conversion of those receivables into cash." For most organizations, the operating cycle is less than one year so the one-year rule applies.

$320,007 worth of current assets left. Put another way, the company could pay off all current liabilities by converting less than half its current assets to cash.

Prudent financial management usually requires a company to maintain more current assets than liabilities in order to allow for differences in the timing of payments and the lag time involved in converting accounts receivable and inventory to cash. Having current assets greater than current liabilities also ensures against the possibility that some accounts receivable or inventory may never be converted to cash. Inventory may become obsolete and lose all or most of its value. Customers owing accounts receivable may encounter financial difficulties and go bankrupt, making their accounts uncollectible.

After providing a reserve fund for these contingencies, management has considerable discretion in using the remaining working capital. These excess funds are important because management can do many things with them. After providing for payment of current liabilities, the remaining current assets are available for repaying long-term debt, investing in plant and equipment, or paying dividends. The significance of this flexibility can be seen when you consider other assets on the balance sheet. Besides current assets a firm's main assets are land, buildings, and equipment. Although these assets can be sold and converted to cash, doing so is usually not economical. The market for buildings and equipment may be limited, and a firm can only spare so much of its land, plant, and equipment. Even a company operating at 50 percent capacity could probably not sell 50 percent of its plant and continue to operate. In the long run, keeping the partially idle plant and equipment is more economical than selling them and replacing them later when business picks up.

Again, notice the difference between inventory, a current asset, and equipment. When sales and production are down, inventories can be reduced by cutting back on purchases. When sales and production rise, those inventories are easy to replace. Equipment does not provide such flexibility.

Current Ratio

The **current ratio** is another useful way of looking at working capital. Current ratio is defined as total current assets divided by total current liabilities:

$$\text{Current ratio} = \frac{\text{total current assets}}{\text{total current liabilities}}$$

Using data from the balance sheet in Exhibit 17–1, you can compute Fashion Clothing's current ratio on December 31, 19x3, as follows:

$$\text{Current ratio} = \frac{\$579{,}893}{\$259{,}886}$$

$$= \underline{\underline{2.2 \text{ to } 1}}$$

Like working capital, current ratio is an indicator of a company's ability to pay current liabilities. Fashion Clothing's current ratio of 2.2 to 1 shows that at the end of 19x3, the company had $2.20 in current assets for every $1.00 in current liabilities. Short-term creditors often consider a current ratio of 2 to 1 as reasonable. However, the appropriate ratio varies from company to company.

When two companies of different size are being compared, current ratio is more informative than working capital. Suppose, for example, you wanted to compare Fashion Clothing with a larger chain called Widespread Retail Stores. Because Widespread is larger, you would expect it to have more working capital than Fashion. But how much more would indicate a stronger financial position? To answer that question, you must look at more than a comparison of working capital for the two stores, which is shown below.

	Fashion	Widespread
Current assets		
Cash	$ 70,392	$ 192,079
Accounts receivable	218,549	565,367
Inventory	223,242	723,015
Prepaid expenses	67,710	132,429
Total current assets	$579,893	$1,612,890
Total current liabilities	259,886	929,869
Working capital	$320,007	$ 683,021

As expected, Widespread's working capital is substantially higher than Fashion's. But to find out which chain is in the stronger financial position, you must look at the current ratio.

	Fashion	Widespread
Current ratio =	$\frac{\$579,893}{\$259,886}$	$\frac{\$1,612,890}{\$929,869}$
=	2.2 to 1	1.7 to 1

Because current ratio is a *relationship* between two figures rather than an absolute amount, it eliminates the effect of Widespread's larger size. As you can see, in relative terms Fashion's short-term financial position is stronger.

Figure 17–4 graphs the relationship between current assets and current liabilities, and working capital for the two stores. Widespread's lower current ratio does not necessarily mean it will have difficulty paying current liabilities. Rather, Fashion's higher current ratio compared with its larger competitor suggests its working capital position is stronger.

On the other hand, even with its relatively strong current ratio, Fashion Clothing might have difficulty paying debts if they fall due at the wrong time. Were all current liabilities to fall due in January (an unlikely event), the company would only have on hand its cash and whatever accounts receivable it could collect immediately. Fashion's December 31, 19x3, balance sheet shows only $70,392 in cash plus $218,549 worth of accounts receivable, not all of which could be collected at once. Fashion could probably not collect enough of its accounts to pay all liabilities that month. Of course, the store might arrange some new bank loans for that purpose. Whatever the situation, the point is that a firm's

Figure 17–4

Comparison of Current Assets and Current Liabilities of Two Clothing Stores

This comparison of Widespread Retail Stores and Fashion Clothing Stores shows Fashion to be in the stronger financial position. This is true even though Widespread has more working capital. The total area of each circle represents total current assets. The gray shaded area represents total current liabilities. The red shaded area represents the working capital of each company.

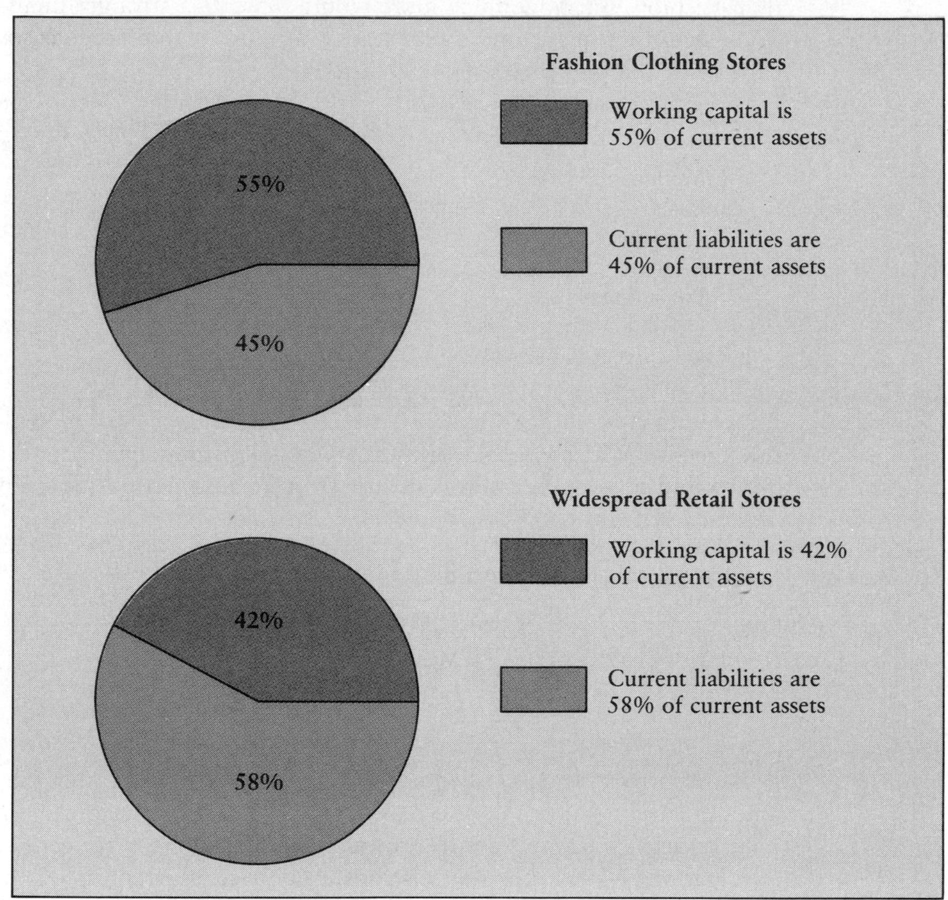

ability to pay its debts depends on timing as well as on the amount of working capital available.

Since the usefulness of working capital depends on its availability for paying short-term debts, it is important to ensure that current assets are convertible to cash in normal business operations. If inventories are excessive or obsolete, they will be difficult to sell and convert to cash. Similarly, if accounts receivable are long past due, they will probably be difficult to collect. Five additional ratios are helpful in analyzing liquidity of assets. They are the acid-test ratio, accounts receivable turnover, average collection period, inventory turnover, and average selling period.

Acid-Test Ratio

The **acid-test ratio**, sometimes called the quick ratio, is a stricter test of an organization's ability to pay its current liabilities than is the current ratio. The acid-test ratio is similar to current ratio, but it includes in the calculation only the most liquid assets, such as cash, marketable securities, and accounts receivable. Thus, it eliminates the effect of inventories and prepaid expenses. The formula for the acid-test ratio is shown below.

$$\text{Acid-test ratio} = \frac{\text{cash} + \text{marketable securities} + \text{accounts receivable}}{\text{total current liabilities}}$$

Fashion Clothing's acid-test ratios on December 31, 19x3, and 19x2, would be calculated as follows:

	December 31	
	19x3	19x2
Cash	$ 70,392	$ 68,250
Accounts receivable	218,549	184,978
Marketable securities	-0-	-0-
Total quick assets	$288,941	$253,228
Total current liabilities	$259,886	$225,904
Acid-test ratio =	$\frac{\$288,941}{\$259,886}$	$\frac{\$253,228}{\$225,904}$
=	1.11 to 1	1.12 to 1

Notice that Fashion Clothing had no marketable securities at the end of either 19x3 or 19x2. (If it had, they would have been shown on the balance sheet between cash and accounts receivable.)

Fashion Clothing's acid-test ratio has been stable from year to year and is above 1 to 1. A ratio of 1 to 1 or above is often thought to be the acceptable acid-test level. Thus, Fashion Clothing passes even this stricter test.

Accounts Receivable Turnover

The **accounts receivable turnover** indicates how rapidly accounts receivable are being collected and turned into cash. It is found by dividing total annual credit sales by the average balance in accounts receivable.

$$\text{Accounts receivable turnover} = \frac{\text{total annual credit sales}}{\text{average balance in accounts receivable}}$$

Assume that 75 percent of Fashion Clothing's 19x3 sales, or $1,500,000, were made on credit. Then, calculate the average accounts receivable balance by adding together the balances in accounts receivable at the beginning and end of the year and dividing by 2.

Accounts Receivable	
Beginning of 19x3	$184,978
End of 19x3	218,549
Total	$403,527

$$\text{Average balance} = \frac{\$403,527}{2} = \$201,764$$

The calculation of accounts receivable turnover would then be

$$\text{Accounts receivable turnover} = \frac{\$1,500,000}{\$201,764} = 7.4 \text{ times}$$

The meaning of the accounts receivable turnover is clearer when converted into an average collection period.

Average Collection Period

An accounts receivable turnover may also be expressed as the average time taken to collect on accounts receivable. That time is called the **average collection period.** The average collection period is found by dividing the number of days in the year by the accounts receivable turnover.

$$\text{Average collection period} = \frac{365}{\text{accounts receivable turnover}}$$

For Fashion Clothing Stores, the average collection period would be calculated as follows:

$$\text{Average collection period} = \frac{365}{7.4} = 49.3 \text{ days}$$

A company's average collection period is evaluated by comparing it with the credit terms offered customers. If Fashion asks customers to pay accounts within 30 days, an average collection period of 49.3 days indicates minor collection problems. Since not all customers pay within the stated terms, one cannot expect an average collection period of exactly 30 days. But for 30-day terms, an average collection period of 40–45 days is normal.

Fashion Clothing has two credit plans. One requires payment within 30 days. The other allows customers to put a third down and pay the remaining balance in two equal installments. Those installments are due 30 and 60 days after the original one-third payment. Without knowing how many customers choose each plan, you cannot determine an acceptable average collection period. If customers on the second plan pay exactly as expected, then they pay half their balances after 30 days; the other half after 60. Such a situation would produce an average collection period of 45 days. But you cannot expect that everyone on the second plan will pay exactly on time either. Even so, as long as some of Fashion's sales are made on the second plan, the 49.3-day average collection period suggests that customers are paying accounts fairly promptly. Therefore, Fashion does not appear to have significant collection problems or to be at risk of having excessive bad debts.

Inventory Turnover

Inventory turnover is a measure of inventory liquidity. It is defined as the annual cost of goods sold divided by the average balance in inventory:

$$\text{Inventory turnover} = \frac{\text{cost of goods sold}}{\text{average balance in inventory}}$$

To calculate inventory turnover, one must first find the average annual inventory level. For Fashion Clothing the computations are as follows:

Inventory	
Beginning of 19x3	$197,097
End of 19x3	223,242
Total	$420,339

$$\text{Average balance} = \frac{\$420{,}339}{2} = \$210{,}170$$

$$\text{Inventory turnover} = \frac{\$1{,}472{,}000}{\$210{,}170} = 7.0 \text{ times}$$

Generally, a high inventory turnover is preferred to a low one, since a high turnover means inventory is being sold soon after it arrives. However, an extremely high turnover might mean a company has too little inventory on hand to fill customers' orders and is risking lost sales. In the clothing business, for example, if a store does not have a blouse to display as well as several to deliver to customers, it will probably not sell blouses. This is particularly true if customers can go to another store to find the blouses they want. On the other hand, a below-average inventory turnover might indicate that inventory remains on hand long enough to become obsolete and that it may never be sold above cost. A store with summer blouses still in stock in September will probably have to reduce prices well below cost to sell that inventory.

Average Selling Period

Like accounts receivable turnover, inventory turnover is easier to understand when converted into an average time period. The **average selling period** is the time required to sell inventory or the average time stock remains in inventory. It is calculated by dividing the number of days in a year by inventory turnover.

$$\text{Average selling period} = \frac{365}{\text{inventory turnover}}$$

For Fashion Clothing Stores, the average selling period would be:

$$\text{Average selling period} = \frac{365}{7}$$

$$= \underline{\underline{52.1}} \text{ days}$$

Fashion Clothing Stores' average selling period indicates that inventory items are in stock an average of 52.1 days, or just a little less than 8 weeks. For a fashion-oriented business, such as a clothing store, that is probably an appropriate selling period. For a butcher shop, however, the appropriate period is probably three days. For an automobile parts store, which must stock parts for new cars as well as for those 10 or 15 years old, the average selling period might be 180 days or longer.

The debt-paying ability ratios just discussed are mostly of interest to short-term creditors. The next two ratios, times-interest-earned and debt-to-equity ratios, are of more interest to long-term creditors and shareholders.

Times-Interest-Earned Ratio

Times-interest-earned is the ratio of a firm's net earnings to its interest expenses. It is found by dividing annual earnings before interest and income taxes, often called operating income, by annual interest expenses.

$$\text{Times-interest-earned ratio} = \frac{\text{annual earnings before interest expense and income taxes}}{\text{annual interest expense}}$$

Fashion Clothing's operating income and interest expenses for 19x3 are found on its income statement (Exhibit 17–2). The calculation is as follows:

$$\text{Times-interest-earned ratio} = \frac{\$142{,}000}{\$27{,}907}$$

$$= \underline{\underline{5.1}} \text{ times}$$

Fashion Clothing's times-interest-earned ratio shows the store to be currently earning more than five times its interest charges. In other words, operating income could drop by more than four-fifths, and the company would still earn enough money to pay its interest charges. Notice that this ratio is based on earnings *before* interest expense and income taxes. Were a company earning just enough to cover interest expense, it would have no taxable income and would pay no income taxes.

Although an operating income of 5.1 times a company's interest expense is very strong, a long-term creditor should examine the historical pattern of the ratio. The historical pattern shows whether Fashion Clothing can maintain its earnings in poor economic times as well as good. Shareholders are also interested in that information. When a company regularly earns more than its interest charges, it will have funds available for return on shareholders' equity as well as for protecting long-term creditors. The adequacy of shareholders' return should be judged by the return on common shareholders' equity (pages 801 and 802). A company earning a satisfactory return on common shareholders' equity should be able to issue additional shares of capital for expanding operations or repaying long-term debt.

Debt-to-Equity Ratio

The **debt-to-equity ratio** is a measure of the balance between an organization's debt and equity. It is found by dividing total liabilities by total shareholders' equity.

$$\text{Debt-to-equity ratio} = \frac{\text{total liabilities}}{\text{total shareholders' equity}}$$

Fashion Clothing's total liabilities and total shareholders' equity are shown on its balance sheet (Exhibit 17–1). At the end of 19x3 and 19x2, Fashion's debt-to-equity ratios were as follows:

	December 31	
	19x3	**19x2**
Debt-to-equity ratio	$= \frac{\$398,886}{\$271,510}$	$= \frac{\$394,904}{\$242,950}$
	= 1.47 to 1	= 1.63 to 1

This ratio shows that on December 31, 19x3, Fashion Clothing's creditors provided $1.47 worth of capital for every $1.00 of capital provided by shareholders. For many businesses, that would be a high debt-to-equity ratio. But it is a normal ratio for retailing, a business in which investment in plant and equipment is relatively low, and large inventories are financed by accounts payable. Fashion reduced its debt-to-equity ratio slightly during 19x3, mainly by paying off some long-term debt and adding to shareholders' equity through retained earnings (Exhibit 17–1).

Long-term creditors prefer low debt-to-equity ratios. The lower a firm's debt, the lower its interest and principal payments. In such situations, firms can probably pay their creditors. But if a firm's financial leverage is favorable, common shareholders prefer a high debt-to-equity ratio, since leverage increases their return on investment. Fashion's high debt relative to owners' equity is the reason its return on common shareholders' equity is 36.6 percent when return on total assets is only 14.1 percent (see pages 801 and 802).

Book Value per Share

Book value per share is the book value of a firm's assets divided by the number of its common shares outstanding. Expressed in dollars per share, book value per share is calculated as follows:

$$\text{Book value per share} = \frac{\text{average common shareholder's equity}}{\text{number of common shares outstanding}}$$

The book value per share for Fashion Clothing would be computed as follows:

	December 31		
	19x3	**19x2**	**Average**
Common shares	$ 10,000	$ 10,000	$ 10,000
Additional paid-in capital	90,000	90,000	90,000
Retained earnings	101,510	72,950	87,230
Total	$201,510	$172,950	$187,230

$$\text{Book value per share} = \frac{\$187{,}230}{10{,}000 \text{ shares}} = \underline{\underline{\$18.72}} \text{ per share}$$

Book value per share is sometimes viewed as the rock-bottom value of common shares. The idea is that if a corporation is liquidated—that is, if all assets are sold, all debts paid, and the remaining cash returned to shareholders—shareholders would receive close to the firm's book value per share.

There are two flaws in this idea. First, corporations rarely liquidate. Even when a firm is unprofitable, management usually tries to correct the situation rather than shut down. Second, the book value of common shareholders' equity depends on the book value of the firm's assets, which is based on their original cost. But the cost paid to acquire assets may be quite different from the amounts for which they could be sold in liquidation. This is particularly true if an asset has been owned for a long time. The book value of buildings and equipment is usually quite different from their liquidation value.

In special cases in which assets are mostly marketable or liquid, book value per share may be a useful ratio. But generally it has little meaning.

Chapter Review

Review of Learning Objectives

1. **Explain how analysis of financial statements assists in financial predictions.**
Managers, investors, and lenders analyze financial statements to identify an organization's strengths and weaknesses. Shareholders are interested in predicting future dividends and

growth in market value, the two components of a shareholder's return on investment. Lenders are interested in predicting whether an organization will have resources to repay debts when they fall due. Analysis of financial statements provides an understanding of past performance and is a useful starting point for making these predictions.

2. **List and discuss the three standards of comparison used in financial analysis.**
The three types of standards for financial comparison are: (a) predetermined standards, (b) past performance, and (c) competitors' performance. Standard costs are a good example of predetermined standards. They are based on an analysis of the best performance one can expect under the circumstances. Predetermined standards are costly to establish, however. And analysts outside an organization lack the inside knowledge needed to establish such standards.

Lacking predetermined standards, analysts must compare present performance with either past performance or the performance of competitors. Comparisons with past performance help identify trends, both good and bad. Comparisons with industry averages are based on the assumption that an organization should be able to do as well as others in its industry. However, there may be good reasons for a particular company's performance to differ from industry averages.

3. **Calculate and present year-to-year comparisons and trends.**
Income statements and balance sheets comparing the current year's data with the previous year's are more useful if two columns are added showing the amount of change in dollars and percentages.

Even more useful than two-year comparisons are year-to-year comparisons over periods of five to ten years. Long-term trends become apparent in such comparisons and are often best presented in line graphs.

4. **Prepare and interpret common-size financial statements.**
Common-size statements show percentages, indicating the relative proportion of a dollar amount to the whole. Such statements provide a perspective for an organization whose size changes over time or for comparing organizations of different size. Common-size financial statements present the dollar amounts shown on income statements as percentages of total sales and the amounts shown on balance sheets as percentages of total assets. Common-size income statements indicate which expenses are most important and how a firm's sales dollars are divided between expenses and profit. Common-size balance sheets show the relative composition of a firm's assets, liabilities, and owners' equity. Information from these statements may often be effectively presented in pie charts.

5. **Calculate the seven earning-power ratios and explain their significance.**
The seven earning-power ratios are as follows:

1. Earnings per share $= \dfrac{\text{(net income} - \text{preferred dividends)}}{\text{number of common shares outstanding}}$

2. Fully diluted earnings per share =

$$\frac{\text{net income}}{\text{original common shares outstanding} + \text{converted shares}}$$

3. Price-earnings ratio $= \dfrac{\text{current market price per share}}{\text{earnings per share}}$

4. Dividend payout ratio $= \dfrac{\text{dividends per share}}{\text{earnings per share}}$

5. Dividend-yield ratio $= \dfrac{\text{dividends per share}}{\text{market price per share}}$

6. Return on total assets $= \dfrac{\text{net income} + [\text{interest expense} \times (1 - \text{tax rate})]}{\text{average total assets}}$

7. Return on common shareholders' equity $= \dfrac{\text{net income} - \text{preferred dividends}}{\text{average common shareholders' equity}}$

Owners, lenders, and managers are all interested in an organization's earnings power. Owners are interested because their return is based on that earning power. Lenders are interested because their chances of being repaid are better when an organization operates profitably. And finally, managers are interested for two reasons: first, because of owners' and lenders' concern about an organization's earning power; second, because earning power influences how much an organization can grow from retained earnings.

Earnings per share shows how much earnings benefit each share of common stock. The price-earnings ratio indicates how the market values net income. Dividend payout and dividend yield show how much of the owner's return is received as dividends. Return on total assets shows how effectively managers are using available assets. Return on common shareholders' equity is a similar measure, but it also takes into account the effects of financial leverage.

6. **Define financial leverage and explain how its effects are measured.**
Financial leverage, when favorable, is the ability to earn more on capital than must be paid for its use. If a firm can earn a return on total assets of 15 percent and can borrow capital at an after-tax interest rate of only 6 percent, the 9 percent difference benefits common shareholders by increasing earnings per share and their return on investment. The effects of favorable leverage can be seen by comparing a firm's return on total assets with return on common shareholders' equity.

Financial leverage can become unfavorable when a firm's return on total assets falls below its after-tax interest rate on borrowed capital or the dividend rate on preferred shares. In such cases, common shareholders' earnings are reduced or eliminated.

7. **Calculate the ten debt-paying-ability ratios and explain their significance.**
The ten debt-paying-ability ratios are as follows:

1. Working capital = total current assets − total current liabilities

2. Current ratio $= \dfrac{\text{total current assets}}{\text{total current liabilities}}$

3. Acid-test ratio $= \dfrac{\text{cash} + \text{marketable securities} + \text{accounts receivable}}{\text{total current liabilities}}$

4. Accounts receivable turnover $= \dfrac{\text{total annual credit sales}}{\text{average balance in accounts receivable}}$

5. Average collection period $= \dfrac{365}{\text{accounts receivable turnover}}$

6. Inventory turnover $= \dfrac{\text{cost of goods sold}}{\text{average balance in inventory}}$

7. Average selling period $= \dfrac{365}{\text{inventory turnover}}$

8. Times-interest-earned ratio $= \dfrac{\text{annual earnings before interest expense and income taxes}}{\text{annual interest expense}}$

9. Debt-to-equity ratio $= \dfrac{\text{total liabilities}}{\text{total shareholders' equity}}$

10. Book value per share $= \dfrac{\text{average common shareholders' equity}}{\text{number of common shares outstanding}}$

Debt-paying ability is of interest to lenders, owners, and managers, all of whom want an organization to pay its debts on time. Short-term creditors generally focus on working capital, or the difference between total current assets and total current liabilities. Current assets are a firm's most liquid assets. Current liabilities are debts falling due within one year. Thus, working capital is the pool of liquid assets on which there are no short-run claims. Management has considerable discretion in using those assets.

The current ratio also deals with the balance between current assets and current liabilities. It is a convenient way of comparing organizations of different size. For a stricter measure of a company's ability to pay short-term debt, analysts use the acid-test ratio. An organization generates cash by collecting accounts receivable and selling inventory. Turnover ratios are a useful indicator of how long it will take to convert accounts receivable and inventory to cash.

When an organization is profitable, it generates enough cash to replace assets and repay long-term debts as they fall due. Therefore, long-term creditors are more concerned about a firm's earning-power ratios than its working capital. Long-term creditors are also concerned about the times-interest-earned and debt-to-equity ratios, which indicate how a firm obtains its capital.

Analyses of financial statements involve much more than calculating ratios. Although ratios are helpful, they are only a tool for the careful evaluation of a firm's future financial prospects.

Review of Key Terms

Accounts receivable turnover An indicator of how rapidly accounts receivable are being collected and turned into cash. Found by dividing total annual credit sales by average balance in accounts receivable.

Acid-test ratio Total cash, marketable securities, and accounts receivable divided by total current liabilities. A measure of debt-paying ability.

Average collection period The average time taken to collect on accounts receivable. Another way of expressing the accounts receivable turnover. Found by dividing number of days in a year by accounts receivable turnover.

Average selling period The time required to sell inventory or the average time stock remains in inventory. Calculated by dividing number of days in a year by inventory turnover.

Book value per share Book value of a firm's assets divided by the number of its common shares outstanding. In most cases, it has little meaning.

Common-size financial statements Statements that translate the dollar amounts on financial statements into percentages that indicate the relative size of an item in proportion to the whole. *Common-size balance sheets* show assets, liabilities, and owners' equity as a percentage of total assets. *Common-size income statements* express revenue, expenses, and income as a percentage of sales revenues.

Current ratio A firm's total current assets divided by its total current liabilities. A measure of a firm's debt-paying ability.

Debt-to-equity ratio A measure of the balance between an organization's debt and equity. Found by dividing total liabilities by total shareholders' equity.

Dividend payout ratio The ratio of dividends per share of stock to earnings per share expressed as a percentage.

Dividend-yield ratio The ratio of dividend per share of stock to market value per share expressed as a percentage.

Earning-power ratios A group of ratios that help analysts assess the adequacy of a firm's net income.

Earnings per share (EPS) Net income available to common shareholders divided by the number of common shares outstanding.

Extraordinary gains or losses Unusual gains or losses occurring in one year that are not expected to be repeated. They are reported in a separate section of the income statement net of their income tax effect. An uninsured loss is an example.

Financial analysis An analysis performed to identify an organization's major financial strengths and weaknesses.

Financial leverage Obtaining capital from debt or preferred shares and using the capital to earn a return by investing in assets. Financial leverage is favorable when the return on assets is greater than after-tax interest expense or the preferred dividend rate.

Fully diluted earnings per share Earnings per share calculated on the assumption that all convertible debt or preferred shares are converted into common shares. The number of common shares after conversion is the denominator of the earnings per share ratio. In the numerator, net income is adjusted to eliminate the effect of interest or dividends on debt or preferred shares assumed to be converted.

Inventory turnover A measure of inventory liquidity. Defined as annual cost of goods sold divided by average balance in inventory.

Predetermined standards Standards determined in advance. They represent the best performance one can realistically expect given the environment and resources.

Price-earnings ratio Ratio of the market price of a share to its earnings per share.

Ratios A relationship between two numbers expressed either as a percentage or as an absolute number.

Return on common shareholders' equity A percentage measuring the total return earned by common shareholders. It is the net income available to common shareholders after subtracting preferred dividends divided by the book value of common shareholders' equity.

Return on total assets A ratio that measures how wisely management is using assets. It is calculated by dividing net income *before* interest but *after* taxes by average total assets.

Times-interest-earned Ratio of a firm's net earnings to its interest expenses. It is found by dividing annual earnings before interest and income taxes, often called operating income, by annual interest expenses.

Working capital A pool of liquid assets financed by long-term capital sources. Working capital is the firm's total current assets minus its total current liabilities.

Review Problem

The financial statements for Small Change, Inc., are reproduced below. Additional data include the following:

	19x3	19x2
Market price of shares	$91	$84
Average collection period, 19x2		33.2 days
Inventory turnover, 19x2		8 times
Return on total assets, 19x2		11.0%
Return on common shareholders' equity, 19x2		15.2%

All sales are made on credit.

Small Change, Inc.
Comparative Balance Sheets
December 31, 19x3, and 19x2

	19x3	19x2
Assets		
Current assets		
Cash	$ 270,000	$ 380,000
Accounts receivable	225,000	201,000
Inventory	258,000	142,000
Prepaid expenses	21,500	22,000
Total current assets	$ 774,500	$ 745,000
Plant and equipment		
Land	$ 100,000	$ 100,000
Plant and equipment (net)	1,630,000	1,400,000
Total plant and equipment	$1,730,000	$1,500,000
Total assets	$2,504,500	$2,245,000
Liabilities and shareholders' equity		
Current liabilities		
Accounts payable	$ 333,169	$ 323,000
Other payables	12,500	22,000
Total current liabilities	$ 345,669	$ 345,000
Long-term liabilities		
Notes payable (11%)	700,000	600,000
Total liabilities	$1,045,669	$ 945,000
Shareholders' equity		
Common shares (20,000 shares)	$ 500,000	$ 500,000
Retained earnings	958,831	800,000
Total shareholders' equity	$1,458,831	$1,300,000
Total liabilities and shareholders' equity	$2,504,500	$2,245,000

Small Change, Inc. Comparative Statements of Income and Retained Earnings For the Years Ended December 31, 19x3, and 19x2	19x3	19x2
Sales revenues	$2,152,000	$1,801,802
Expenses		
Cost of goods sold	$1,299,808	$1,018,018
Selling	288,368	269,000
Administrative	170,008	174,312
Total expenses	$1,758,184	$1,461,330
Operating income	$ 393,816	$ 340,472
Interest expenses	81,200	69,100
Income before taxes	$ 312,616	$ 271,372
Income taxes (30%)	93,785	81,412
Net income	$ 218,831	$ 189,960
Dividends to common shareholders	60,000	60,000
Net income added to retained earnings	$ 158,831	$ 129,960
Retained earnings, beginning of year	800,000	670,040
Retained earnings, end of year	$ 958,831	$ 800,000

Required

1. Review Small Change's working capital position. To do so,
   a. Calculate working capital on December 31, 19x2, and 19x3.
   b. Calculate current ratio on December 31, 19x2, and 19x3.
   c. Calculate the acid-test ratio on December 31, 19x2, and 19x3.
   d. Calculate the average collection period for accounts receivable for 19x3.
   e. Calculate inventory turnover for 19x3.
   f. Comment on the meaning of the ratios calculated above.
2. Review the situation of Small Change's long-term creditors. To do so,
   a. Calculate the times-interest-earned ratio for 19x2 and 19x3.
   b. Calculate the debt-to-equity ratio on December 31, 19x2, and 19x3.
   c. Calculate return on total assets for 19x3.
   d. Comment on the ratios calculated above.
3. Review the situation of Small Change's common shareholders. To do so,
   a. Calculate return on common shareholders' equity for 19x3.
   b. Calculate earnings per share for 19x2 and 19x3.
   c. Calculate the dividend payout for 19x2 and 19x3.
   d. Calculate the dividend yield for 19x2 and 19x3.
   e. Calculate the price-earnings ratio for 19x2 and 19x3.
   f. Summarize the common shareholders' situation, using the ratios calculated above.

Solution to Review Problem

1. *a.* Working capital = total current assets − total current liabilities

	19x3	19x2
Total current assets	$774,500	$745,000
Total current liabilities	345,669	345,000
Working capital	$428,831	$400,000

b. Current ratio $= \dfrac{\text{total current assets}}{\text{total current liabilities}}$

	19x3	19x2
=	$\dfrac{\$774{,}500}{\$345{,}669}$	$\dfrac{\$745{,}000}{\$345{,}000}$
=	2.2 to 1	2.2 to 1

c. Acid-test ratio $= \dfrac{\text{cash + marketable securities + accounts receivable}}{\text{total current liabilities}}$

	19x3	19x2
Cash	$270,000	$380,000
Marketable securities	-0-	-0-
Accounts receivable	225,000	201,000
Total	$495,000	$581,000
Total current liabilities	$345,669	$345,000
Acid-test ratio =	$\dfrac{\$495{,}000}{\$345{,}669}$	$\dfrac{\$581{,}000}{\$345{,}000}$
=	1.4 to 1	1.7 to 1

d. To calculate the average collection period for accounts receivable, you first find the accounts receivable turnover.

Accounts receivable turnover $= \dfrac{\text{total credit sales}}{\text{average balance in accounts receivable}}$

Since all sales are made on credit, total credit sales equal total sales.

	Accounts receivable
Beginning of 19x3	$201,000
End of 19x3	225,000
Total	$426,000

Average balance $= \dfrac{\$426{,}000}{2} = \$213{,}000$

Accounts receivable turnover $= \dfrac{\$2{,}152{,}000}{\$213{,}000}$

$= 10.1$ times

$$\text{Average collection period} = \frac{365}{\text{accounts receivable turnover}}$$

$$= \frac{365}{10.1}$$

$$= \underline{\underline{36.1}} \text{ days}$$

e. $\text{Inventory turnover} = \dfrac{\text{cost of goods sold}}{\text{average balance inventory}}$

Inventory	
Beginning of 19x3	$142,000
End of 19x3	258,000
Total	$400,000

$$\text{Average balance} = \frac{\$400{,}000}{2} = \$200{,}000$$

$$\text{Inventory turnover} = \frac{\$1{,}299{,}808}{\$200{,}000}$$

$$= \underline{\underline{6.5}} \text{ times}$$

f. Working capital focuses on the difference between liquid assets and liabilities falling due within one year. At December 31, 19x2, Small Change's current assets exceeded its current liabilities by $400,000; and at December 31, 19x3, by $428,831, providing a reasonable safety margin in both years. Its current ratio was the same in both years: current assets were 2.2 times the total current liabilities. Both these indicators show a strong, stable short-term financial position.

Small Change's acid-test ratio declined slightly from 19x2 to 19x3, but remains strong. Considerable cash is available for paying current liabilities. Since accounts receivable can be collected in about 36 days, Small Change can raise enough cash in just over five weeks to pay off all current debts. Of course, Small Change will probably also need cash for other purposes, such as the payroll, during that period. But it is also unlikely that *all* current liabilities will require payment in 36 days. Thus, Small Change should have little difficulty paying debts when they fall due.

The average collection period increased from 33.2 days in 19x2 (given) to 36.1 days in 19x3. Although a three-day increase is not great, it may indicate that Small Change is doing a poorer job of collecting accounts receivable than in the past. Management and creditors should watch this ratio to ensure that it becomes no worse.

Finally, inventory turnover has fallen from 8.0 (given) to 6.5. This trend could concern short-term creditors, since funds invested in inventory are taking longer to convert to cash. Large inventories are also more prone to obsolescence. For this reason, management may want to increase inventory turnover, and short-term creditors may want to monitor it.

2. *a.* $\text{Times-interest-earned ratio} = \dfrac{\text{annual earnings before interest expense and income taxes}}{\text{annual interest expense}}$

	19x3	19x2
Times-interest-earned ratio =	$\frac{\$393{,}816}{\$81{,}200}$	$\frac{\$340{,}472}{\$69{,}100}$
=	4.8 times	4.9 times

b. Debt-to-equity ratio = $\frac{\text{total liabilities}}{\text{total shareholders' equity}}$

	19x3	19x2
=	$\frac{\$1{,}045{,}669}{\$1{,}458{,}831}$	$\frac{\$945{,}000}{\$1{,}300{,}000}$
=	0.717 to 1	0.727 to 1

c. Return on total assets = $\frac{\text{net income} + [\text{interest expense} \times (1 - \text{tax rate})]}{\text{average total assets}}$

Net income	$ 218,831
After-tax interest expenses, $81,200 × (1 − 30%)	56,840
	$ 275,671

Total assets, end of 19x3	$2,504,500
Total assets, beginning of 19x3	2,245,000
Total	$4,749,500

Average total assets = $\frac{\$4{,}749{,}500}{2}$ = $2,374,750

Return on total assets = $\frac{\$275{,}671}{\$2{,}374{,}750}$ = 11.6 percent

d. The times-interest-earned ratio shows the amount of a company's operating income can drop before threatening payment of interest expenses. In 19x3, Small Change's times-interest-earned ratio was 4.8 times, meaning that its operating income could drop 79 percent [(4.8 − 1.0) ÷ 4.8] before its ability to pay interest charges was endangered. That is a reasonable margin of safety for long-term creditors.

The debt-to-equity ratio shows the amount of capital provided by lenders and the amount provided by investors. Small Change's debt is about 72 percent of its equity, although this amount has decreased slightly over the year. Seventy-two percent is higher than the average for all industries, but as long as Small Change is not in an industry suffering wide sales fluctuations, that amount of debt probably poses no problems for long-term creditors.

Small Change's return on total assets is 11.6 percent for 19x3. Its after-tax interest rate is 7.7 percent [11% × (1 − 30%)]. The before-tax interest rate of 11 percent is found on the balance sheet under notes payable. The company's return on assets is sufficient to provide favorable leverage. Overall, these three ratios suggest that Small Change has the earning power to protect the interests of long-term creditors.

3. *a.* Return on common shareholders' equity

$$= \frac{\text{net income} - \text{preferred dividends}}{\text{average common shareholders' equity}}$$

Since Small Change has no preferred shares, the numerator can be taken directly from the income statement. The average common shareholder's equity must be calculated.

	19x3	**19x2**
Common shareholders' equity	$1,458,831	$1,300,000

$$\text{Average balance} = \frac{(\$1,458,831 + \$1,300,000)}{2} = \$1,379,415.50$$

$$\text{Return on shareholders' equity} = \frac{\$218,831}{\$1,379,415.50}$$

$$= \underline{\underline{15.9}} \text{ percent}$$

b. Earnings per share $= \dfrac{(\text{net income} - \text{preferred dividends})}{\text{number of common shares outstanding}}$

The number of common shares outstanding is shown on Small Change's balance sheet.

	19x3	**19x2**
Earnings per share	$= \dfrac{\$218,831}{20,000}$	$\dfrac{\$189,960}{20,000}$
	= $\underline{\underline{\$10.94}}$ per share	$\underline{\underline{\$9.50}}$ per share

c. Dividend payout ratio $= \dfrac{\text{dividends per share}}{\text{earnings per share}}$

Number of shares was taken from the balance sheet. Dividends are shown at the bottom of the income statement. Small Change's dividends were $60,000 in both 19x2 and 19x3; the number of common shares outstanding, a constant 20,000. Therefore, for both years:

$$\text{Dividends per share} = \frac{\$60,000}{20,000}$$

$$= \underline{\underline{\$3}} \text{ per share}$$

	19x3	**19x2**
Dividend payout	$= \dfrac{\$3.00}{\$10.94}$	$\dfrac{\$3.00}{\$9.50}$
	= $\underline{\underline{27.4\%}}$	$\underline{\underline{31.6\%}}$

d. Dividend yield $= \dfrac{\text{dividends per share}}{\text{market price per share}}$

	19x3	19x2
Dividends per share	$3	$3
Market price per share	$91	$84
Dividend yield	3.3%	3.6%

e. Price-earnings ratio $= \dfrac{\text{current market price per share}}{\text{earnings per share}}$

	19x3	19x2
Market price per share	$91.00	$84.00
Earnings per share	$10.94	$9.50
Price-earnings ratio	8.3	8.8

f. Return on common shareholders' equity is difficult to judge without some background information on business and industry conditions. Small Change's return on common shareholders' equity increased slightly from 19x2 to 19x3, which is, of course, positive. Earnings per share, by itself, tells an analyst little. Still, its increase from 19x2 to 19x3 is a good sign.

The dividend payout ratio has fallen, however. This is because dividends remained constant and net income increased. This situation is understandable, since companies are reluctant to increase dividends unless they think higher dividends can also be paid in future years. Thus, Small Change retained a larger proportion of the assets generated by its 19x3 earnings. Since the company earned a return on common shareholders' equity of 15.9 percent in 19x3, shareholders should ask themselves if they could invest their money at a higher rate elsewhere. If not, allowing Small Change to retain the earnings is probably best for the shareholders.

Small Change's dividend yield is average for many businesses. Only part of the shareholders' return is received in the form of dividends. The other part comes from growth in the shares' market value, which will occur if Small Change invests assets from retained earnings wisely.

The drop in Small Change's price-earnings ratio from 19x2 to 19x3 may indicate a lack of investor confidence in Small Change's ability to maintain its earnings growth. Companies with a strong record of earnings growth often have a price-earnings ratio of 20 or more. Shares with modest growth records have price-earnings ratios similar to Small Change's. From the shareholders' viewpoint, a high price-earnings ratio is preferable because the higher the ratio, the higher the market value of their shares at any given earnings level.

Overall, Small Change's record is about average. Its return on shareholders' equity is 15.9 percent, and that percentage has grown slightly over the past year. The company has retained earnings for reinvestment. However, investors probably lack confidence in Small Change's ability to use those retained earnings well, since the price-earnings ratio is more comparable to those of stable companies than of growth companies.

Chapter Assignments

Questions

1. (L.O. 1) What are the objectives of financial statement analysis?
2. (L.O. 2) What measurement standards can a company use to evaluate its current financial position? Which one do you prefer?
3. (L.O. 5) What is a ratio? How are ratios expressed? Give examples.
4. (L.O. 3) How are ratios used in year-to-year financial comparisons?
5. (L.O. 4) Why must ratios be interpreted with care?
6. (L.O. 4) What are common-size statements? How are they used?
7. (L.O. 5, 7) What are the two major categories of financial statement ratios?
8. (L.O. 5) List the earning-power ratios.
9. (L.O. 5) Who is interested in earning-power ratios? Why?
10. (L.O. 5) What is the difference between earnings per share and fully diluted earnings per share?
11. (L.O. 5) What adjustments must one make in calculating earnings per share when a firm has extraordinary gains or losses?
12. (L.O. 5) In calculating fully diluted earnings per share, what adjustments must be made to net income? To the number of shares?
13. (L.O. 6) What is favorable financial leverage? How is it created?
14. (L.O. 7) List the ratios used to analyze debt-paying ability. Divide your list into two categories: those ratios of interest primarily to short-term creditors, and those of interest primarily to long-term creditors.
15. (L.O. 7) Why are short-term creditors interested in working capital?
16. (L.O. 7) Why are managers interested in working capital?
17. (L.O. 7) Explain why long-term creditors are interested in different ratios than short-term creditors.

Exercises

18. (L.O. 4) The manager of C & S Book Store has been told that common-size income statements help understand the operation of a business. She is particularly interested in understanding how operating income increased between 19x7 and 19x8. Income statements for the two years are shown on the following page.

C & S Book Store Comparative Income Statements For the Years Ended December 31, 19x8, and 19x7	19x8	19x7
Sales revenues	$605,330	$550,300
Expenses		
Cost of goods sold	$472,157	$434,737
Salaries and commissions	78,960	75,200
Advertising	3,000	3,000
Other	31,620	31,000
Total expenses	$585,737	$543,937
Operating income	$ 19,593	$ 6,363

Required

1. Prepare common-size income statements for the two years.
2. How do they explain the increase in profit of C & S?

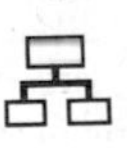

19. (L.O. 4) Logan Lotion Company uses common-size financial statements to help it understand changes from year to year. Logan's financial statements for the last two years are shown below.

Logan Lotion Company Comparative Balance Sheet December 31, 19x8, and 19x7	19x8	19x7
Assets		
Current assets		
Cash	$ 8,000	$ 10,000
Accounts receivable	54,247	46,233
Inventory	44,688	27,083
Prepaid expenses	5,000	4,500
Total current assets	$111,934	$ 87,816
Plant and equipment (cost)	$783,750	$562,500
Accumulated depreciation	(431,063)	(292,500)
Net plant and equipment	$352,688	$270,000
Total assets	$464,622	$357,816
Equities		
Current liabilities		
Accounts payable	$ 22,344	$ 20,313
Notes payable	15,000	10,000
Total current liabilities	$ 37,344	$ 30,313
Long-term notes	298,178	213,204
Common stock	$ 50,000	$ 50,000
Retained earnings	79,100	64,300
Total owners' equity	$129,100	$114,300
Total equities	$464,622	$357,816

Logan Lotion Company Comparative Income Statements For the Years Ended December 31, 19x8, and 19x7	19x8	19x7
Sales revenues	$412,500	$375,000
Expenses		
Cost of goods sold	$268,125	$243,750
Salaries and commissions	78,960	75,200
Advertising	3,000	3,000
Other	31,620	31,000
Total expenses	$381,705	$352,950
Operating income	$ 30,795	$ 22,050

Required

1. Prepare common-size income statements for Logan for both years.
2. Prepare common-size balance sheets for Logan for both years.
3. Explain the increase in operating income from 19x7 to 19x8.

20. (L.O. 4) In 19x5, Barry Mills purchased Comfort Shoe Store. Mills was an experienced manager. He decided to change his marketing strategy by temporarily cutting sales margins and increasing marketing efforts. The immediate effect of Mills' strategy was to reduce operating income. By 19x7, however, the results of the program were showing. Financial statements of Comfort Shoe Store are shown below.

Comfort Shoe Store Comparative Income Statements For the Years Ended December 31, 19x7–19x4	19x7	19x6	19x5	19x4
Sales revenues	$326,634	$296,940	$272,422	$254,600
Expenses				
Cost of goods sold	$182,915	$169,255	$149,833	$140,030
Sales commissions	48,995	44,541	29,966	28,006
Advertising	5,034	4,576	3,520	3,200
Administration	57,411	56,286	55,182	54,100
Total expenses	$294,355	$274,658	$238,501	$225,336
Operating income	$ 32,279	$ 22,282	$ 33,921	$ 29,264

Required

1. Prepare common-size income statements for the four years.
2. How do they reflect Mills' strategy? Explain briefly.
(see Review Exercise 17–1)

21. (L.O. 5) Candado Graphics are commercial artists. They are known for their creativity. Each year, Candado's owners review their financial statements. This year their review is particularly important because they are considering issuing some shares to an outside investor to provide capital to open a new branch. An outside investor has offered to pay $46 per share. Financial statements for the last two years are given on page 831.

Candado Graphics Company
Comparative Income Statements
Years Ended December 31, 19x6, and 19x5

	19x6	19x5
Sales revenues	$311,360	$278,000
Expenses		
Supplies	$ 34,250	$ 27,800
Salaries	183,060	169,500
Advertising	15,400	14,000
Other and income taxes	24,575	21,185
Total expenses	$257,284	$232,485
Net income	$ 54,076	$ 45,515

Candado Graphics Company
Comparative Balance Sheets
December 31, 19x6, and 19x5

	19x6	19x5
Assets		
Current assets		
Cash	$ 6,000	$ 5,400
Accounts receivable	3,412	3,808
Inventory	4,893	4,633
Prepaid expenses	1,950	1,800
Total current assets	$ 16,255	$ 15,642
Plant and equipment (cost)	$ 47,900	$ 45,200
Accumulated depreciation	(23,950)	(24,860)
Net plant and equipment	$ 23,950	$ 20,340
Total assets	$ 40,205	$ 35,982
Equities		
Current liabilities		
Accounts payable	$ 1,408	$ 2,317
Notes payable	7,000	5,000
Total current liabilities	$ 8,408	$ 7,317
Common stock	$ 10,000	$ 10,000
Retained earnings	21,797	18,665
Owners' equity	$ 31,797	$ 28,665
Total equities	$ 40,205	$ 35,982

Required

1. Candado's has 10,000 shares outstanding. Calculate Candado's earnings per share for 19x5 and 19x6.
2. Assume the outside investor's offer of $46 per share represents a fair market price at December 31, 19x6. Calculate Candado's price earnings ratio at December 31, 19x6.

3. Calculate Candado's dividend payout for 19x6. Dividends and earnings were the only events affecting their retained earnings during the year.
4. Calculate Candado's dividend yield for 19x6, assuming a $46 per share market price.
5. Calculate Candado's return on total assets for 19x6. Candado had $650 of interest expense in 19x6. It was included in the income statement in "Other and income taxes." Candado's income tax rate was 34 percent.
(see Review Exercise 17–2)

22. (**L.O. 2, 4, 7**) The manager of C & S Book Store has been told that common-size income statements help understand the operation of a business. After seeing the common-size income statements, she asked for a common-size balance sheet at December 31, 19x8. The balance sheet of C & S is shown below. C & S's income statement is given in **18**.

C & S Book Store
Balance Sheet
December 31, 19x8

Assets		Equities	
Current assets		Current liabilities	
Cash	$ 8,000	Accounts payable	$ 39,346
Accounts receivable	74,630	Notes payable	15,000
Inventory	78,693	Total current liabilities	$ 54,346
Prepaid expenses	5,000	Long-term notes	$200,000
Total current assets	$166,323	Common stock	$ 50,000
Plant and equipment (cost)	$907,995	Retained earnings	270,574
Accumulated depreciation	(499,397)	Total owners' equity	$320,574
Net plant and equipment	$408,598	Total equities	$574,920
Total assets	$574,920		

Required

1. Prepare a common-size balance sheet at December 31, 19x8.
2. Assume that all of the bookstore's sales were credit sales. Assume also that the store's average collection period of accounts receivable was 40 days and its inventory turnover was nine times. Assume that the assets released would be applied to reduce the long-term notes. Prepare a revised balance sheet. (Hint: Calculate the new ending inventory by dividing the cost of goods sold by the inventory turnover. Calculate the ending accounts receivable using a similar procedure.)
3. Prepare a revised common-size balance sheet based on your changes in 2 above.

23. (**L.O. 4**) Comparative income statements of Burden Company are given on page 833.

Burden Company Comparative Income Statements For the Years Ended December 31, 19x5, and 19x4	19x5	19x4
Net sales	$800,000	$650,000
Expenses		
Cost of goods sold	$510,000	$400,000
Selling and administrative	55,000	46,500
Interest	18,000	19,500
Total expenses	$583,000	$466,000
Income before taxes	$217,000	$184,000
Income taxes	65,100	82,800
Net income	$151,900	$101,200

Required

1. Express Burden's income statements in common-size percentages.
2. Comment on how well the company may have controlled expenses.

24. (L.O. 3) Selected data from income statements at Forsberg Company are given below, (000 omitted).

	19x4	19x3	19x2	19x1
Sales	$290	$255	$233	$210
Cost of goods sold	171	152	140	126
Net income	65	62	59	55

Required

1. Express the data as trend percentages, with 19x1 as 100 percent, for each item. Carry computations to one decimal place.
2. Show the actual data graphically, plotting all three lines on one graph.
3. Comment on the results of your analysis.
(see Review Exercise 17–1)

25. (L.O. 7) Selected data from the balance sheet of Coffman Company is shown below (000 omitted).

	December 31	
	19x3	19x2
Current assets		
Cash	$ 44	$ 62
Accounts receivable	121	153
Inventories	498	311
Prepaid expenses	32	24
Total current assets	$695	$550
Current liabilities	$302	$290

Required

1. Calculate the current ratio for each year.
2. Calculate the acid-test ratio for each year.

3. Explain briefly why the above ratios are moving in different directions. What significance does this have for management?

26. (L.O. 5, 6) Selected data from financial statements of Berger Company are given below.

	Beginning of year	During the year	Year-end
Net income		$180,000	
Interest expense		38,000	
Preferred dividends		36,000	
Total assets	$2,750,000		$2,825,000
Long-term debt, 10% interest rate	350,000		400,000
Preferred shares	600,000		600,000
Common shareholders' equity	1,200,000		1,545,000

The company's income tax rate is 30 percent.

Required

1. Calculate return on total assets.
2. Calculate return on common shareholders' equity.
3. Is financial leverage favorable or unfavorable?

27. (L.O. 4, 5) Comparative income statements for Murphy Company are given below. Included in selling and administrative expenses was an uninsured fire loss of $12,000 during 19x7.

Murphy Company
Comparative Income Statements
For the Years Ended December 31, 19x8, and 19x7

	19x8	19x7
Net sales	$596,000	$501,000
Expenses		
Cost of goods sold	$380,000	$319,400
Selling and administrative	41,000	46,500
Other	13,000	11,000
Total expenses	$434,000	$376,900
Income before taxes	$162,000	$124,100
Income taxes (30%)	48,600	37,230
Net income	$113,400	$ 86,870

Required

1. Calculate common-size percentages for both income statements.
2. Revise the 19x7 income statement to properly account for the extraordinary fire loss.
3. Recalculate common-size percentages for the 19x7 income statement.
4. Compare your impressions of operating results as originally presented with the revised results where the fire loss is properly reported. Comment on how the correct reporting affects your conclusion.
5. Assume the company has 40,000 common shares outstanding in both years. No preferred shares are outstanding. Calculate earnings per share for both years as it should appear in Murphy's financial statements.

28. (L.O. 5, 7) The following balance sheet, income statement, and related information pertains to the Brief Company:

Brief Company Balance Sheet December 31, 19x1	
Assets	
Cash	$ 106,000
Accounts receivable	566,000
Inventories	320,000
Prepaid expenses	40,000
Plant and equipment (net)	740,000
Total assets	$1,772,000
Liabilities and owners' equity	
Accounts payable	$ 208,000
Federal income taxes payable	32,000
Bonds payable (8%, due 20x2)	300,000
Preferred stock ($100 par, 10%)	200,000
Common stock (60,000 shares)	400,000
Retained earnings	632,000
Total liabilities and owners' equity	$1,772,000

Brief Company Income Statement For the Year Ended December 31, 19x1	
Net sales	$1,500,000
Cost of goods sold	900,000
Gross margin on sales	$ 600,000
Operating expenses, including bond interest expenses	498,000
Income before taxes	$ 102,000
Income taxes	37,000
Net income	$ 65,000

Also assume no preferred dividends are in arrears. The balances in accounts receivable and inventory are unchanged from January 1, 19x1. There were no changes in the Bonds Payable, Preferred Stock, or Common Stock accounts during 19x1.

Required

1. Calculate the current ratio at December 31, 19x1.
2. Calculate how many times bond interest was earned in 19x1. (Hint: Information on bonds payable on the balance sheet will help you calculate bond interest expenses.)
3. Calculate the average selling period for inventory.
4. Calculate the book value per share of common stock on December 31, 19x1.
5. Calculate the return on common shareholder's equity at year-end. (Hint: Use the

formula given in the text, but substitute year-end shareholders' equity for average common shareholders' equity.)

6. Calculate earnings per share.
7. Assume the preferred shares are convertible to common shares at a ratio of two common shares for every one preferred share. Calculate fully diluted earnings per share.
8. Calculate Brief's working capital on December 31, 19x1. (AICPA)

29. (L.O. 7) Financial statements for Johanson Company are reproduced at the bottom of this page and top of page 837.

Required

1. Calculate the acid-test ratio on December 31, 19x9.
2. Calculate the average collection period for accounts receivable in 19x9. Assume all sales are credit sales.
3. Calculate the times-interest-earned ratio for 19x9.
4. Calculate the debt-to-equity ratio on December 31, 19x9.
5. Calculate the inventory turnover for 19x9. (CMA)

Johanson Company
Comparative Balance Sheets
December 31, 19x9, and 19x8
($000 omitted)

	19x9	19x8
Assets		
Current assets		
Cash	$ 400	$ 380
Accounts receivable	1,700	1,500
Inventory	2,200	2,120
Total current assets	$4,300	$4,000
Long-term assets		
Land	$ 500	$ 500
Plant and equipment (net)	4,700	4,000
Total long-term assets	$5,200	$4,500
Total assets	$9,500	$8,500
Liabilities and shareholders' equity		
Current liabilities		
Accounts payable	$1,400	$ 700
Current portion of long-term debt	1,000	500
Total current liabilities	$2,400	$1,200
Long-term debt	3,000	4,000
Total liabilities	$5,400	$5,200
Shareholders' equity		
Common stock (100,000 shares)	$3,000	$3,000
Retained earnings	1,100	300
Total shareholders' equity	$4,100	$3,300
Total liabilities and shareholders' equity	$9,500	$8,500

Johanson Company, Inc. Statements of Income and Retained Earnings For the Year Ended December 31, 19x9 ($000 omitted)		
Net sales		$28,800
Less expenses		
Cost of goods sold	$15,120	
Selling expenses	7,180	
Administrative expenses	4,100	
Interest	400	26,800
Income before taxes		$ 2,000
Income taxes		800
Net income		$ 1,200
Retained earnings, January 1, 19x9		300
Subtotal		$ 1,500
Cash dividends declared and paid		400
Retained earnings, December 31, 19x9		$ 1,100

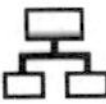

30. (L.O. 5, 6,) Assume the same facts as those given in Exercise 29.

Required

1. Calculate return on total assets for 19x9.
2. Calculate return on common shareholders' equity for 19x9.
3. Explain why you got different answers to *1* and *2* above. (CMA)

31. (L.O. 5) Assume the same facts as those given in Exercise 29.

Required

1. Calculate earnings per share for 19x9.
2. Calculate dividend payout for 19x9.
3. Assume the shares were selling for $108 per share. Calculate the price-earnings ratio for 19x9. (CMA)

(see Review Exercise 17–2)

32. (L.O. 7) Assume the same facts as those given in Exercise 29.

Required

1. Calculate Johanson's working capital on December 31, 19x8, and 19x9.
2. Calculate the change in working capital during 19x9. How are short-term creditors likely to feel about this change? Briefly explain. (CMA)

Problems

33. (L.O. 3, 4) Dexter Manufacturing Company is a mature slow-growing company. The quality of Dexter's product is better than most competitors. For several years, management tried to make the best profit they could with sales growing at the same rate as the industry as a whole. In 19x4, they decided that with aggressive, high quality advertising they might be able to grow more rapidly than the industry. Here are their income statements for the last four years.

Dexter Manufacturing Company Comparative Income Statements For the Years Ended December 31, 19x6–19x3	19x6	19x5	19x4	19x3
Sales revenues	$4,152	$3,881	$3,805	$3,730
Expenses				
Cost of goods sold	$2,408	$2,290	$2,246	$2,238
Salaries and commissions	515	488	480	473
Advertising	714	649	590	590
Research	83	78	76	75
Administration	159	156	153	150
Total expenses	$3,879	$3,661	$3,545	$3,526
Operating income	$ 273	$ 220	$ 260	$ 204

Required

1. Graph the level of sales over the last four years. Does it appear that the increase in advertising in 19x5 has produced favorable results?
2. Prepare common-size income statements for the four years. What do the common-size income statements reveal? Explain briefly.
(see Review Exercise 17–1)

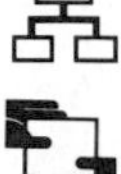

34. (L.O. 2, 5) Martin Local Moving Company started many years ago as a part-time job for a college student with a pickup truck. Bob Martin is the sole owner. Because of his bank loans, Martin's bank asks for comparative financial statements each year. Martin reviews the statements each year before delivering them to the bank to prepare for any questions the banker might have. Financial statements for the last two years are given below.

Martin Local Moving Company Comparative Income Statements For the Years Ended December 31, 19x4, and 19x3	19x4	19x3
Sales revenues	$530,208	$473,400
Expenses		
Supplies	$ 58,323	$ 47,340
Salaries	315,099	274,000
Advertising	70,400	64,000
Other and income taxes	70,975	61,185
Total expenses	$514,797	$446,525
Net income	$ 15,411	$ 26,875

Martin Local Moving Company Comparative Balance Sheets December 31, 19x4, and 19x3	19x4	19x3
Assets		
Current assets		
Cash	$ 8,000	$ 10,000
Accounts receivable	5,810	6,485
Inventory	8,332	7,890
Prepaid expenses	1,950	1,800
Total current assets	$ 24,092	$ 26,175
Plant and equipment (cost)	201,479	189,360
Accumulated depreciation	(100,739)	(104,148)
Net plant and equipment	$ 100,740	$ 85,212
Total assets	$ 124,832	$ 111,387
Equities		
Current liabilities		
Accounts payable	$ 3,414	$ 3,945
Notes payable	13,565	10,000
Total current liabilities	$ 16,979	$ 13,945
Common stock	$ 10,000	$ 10,000
Retained earnings	97,853	87,442
Total owners' equity	$ 107,853	$ 97,442
Total equities	$ 124,832	$ 111,387

Required

1. Martin's has 10,000 shares outstanding. Calculate Martin's earnings per share for 19x3 and 19x4.
2. At December 31, 19x4, Bob estimates that if the shares were traded the market price would be $22. Calculate Martin's price-earnings ratio at December 31, 19x4.
3. Calculate Martin's dividend payout for 19x4. Dividends and earnings were the only events affecting retained earnings during the year.
4. Calculate Martin's dividend yield for 19x4.
5. Calculate Martin's return on total assets for 19x4. Their tax rate was 25 percent. The income statement included $1,200 interest under the heading "Other and income taxes."
6. Calculate common-size income statements for Martin for 19x3 and 19x4. What questions might Bob's banker ask about the decrease in net income? (see Review Exercise 17–2)

35. (L.O. 2, 4, 6) Tom's Hardware Store competes with Bert's Hardware Company. Financial statements for both companies are given below. Bert is wondering why Tom's store seems more profitable.

Comparative Income Statements
For the Year Ended December 31, 19x5

	Tom's	Bert's
Sales revenues	$895,000	$1,163,500
Expenses		
Cost of goods sold	$358,000	$ 465,400
Salaries	345,000	396,750
Advertising	64,000	70,400
Interest at 13%	41,185	167,700
Total expenses	$808,185	$1,100,250
Operating income	$ 86,815	$ 63,250

Comparative Balance Sheets
December 31, 19x5

	Tom's	Bert's
Assets		
Current assets		
Cash	$ 10,000	$ 8,000
Accounts receivable	24,520	35,064
Inventory	23,867	38,783
Prepaid expenses	500	650
Total current assets	$ 58,887	$ 82,497
Plant and equipment (cost)	$ 1,700,500	$ 2,501,525
Accumulated depreciation	(1,156,340)	(1,125,686)
Net plant and equipment	$ 544,160	$ 1,375,839
Total assets	$ 603,047	$ 1,458,336
Equities		
Current liabilities		
Accounts payable	$ 29,833	$ 38,783
Notes payable	10,000	7,000
Total current liabilities	$ 39,833	$ 45,783
Long-term notes	316,814	1,392,191
Common stock	$ 50,000	$ 2,000
Retained earnings	196,400	18,362
Total owners' equity	$ 246,400	$ 20,362
Total equities	$ 603,047	$ 1,458,336

Required

1. Prepare common-size income statements for both Tom's and Bert's. Use the statements to explain the difference in profitability of the two companies.
2. Prepare common-size balance sheets for both Tom's and Bert's.
3. What is financial leverage and how does it differ between the two companies?

36. (L.O. 7) Printing Company is listed on the New York Stock Exchange. The market value of its common stock was quoted at $10 per share on December 31, 19x5, and 19x4. Printing's balance sheet and statement of income and retained earnings on December 31, 19x4, and 19x5 are presented on pages 841 and 842.

Printing Company
Comparative Balance Sheets
December 31, 19x5, and 19x4

	19x5	19x4
Assets		
Current assets		
Cash	$ 3,500,000	$ 3,600,000
Marketable securities	13,000,000	11,000,000
Accounts receivable	105,000,000	95,000,000
Inventories	126,000,000	154,000,000
Prepaid expenses	2,500,000	2,400,000
Total current assets	$250,000,000	$266,000,000
Long-term assets		
Plant and equipment (net)	$311,000,000	$308,000,000
Investments (at equity)	2,000,000	3,000,000
Long-term receivables	14,000,000	16,000,000
Goodwill and patents	6,000,000	6,500,000
Other assets	7,000,000	8,500,000
Total long-term assets	$340,000,000	$342,000,000
Total assets	$590,000,000	$608,000,000
Liabilities and shareholders' equity		
Current liabilities		
Notes payable	$ 5,000,000	$ 15,000,000
Accounts payable	38,000,000	48,000,000
Accrued expenses	24,500,000	27,000,000
Income taxes payable	1,000,000	1,000,000
Current portion of long-term debt	6,500,000	7,000,000
Total current liabilities	$ 75,000,000	$ 98,000,000
Long-term liabilities		
Long-term debt	$169,000,000	$180,000,000
Deferred income taxes	74,000,000	67,000,000
Other liabilities	9,000,000	8,000,000
Total long-term liabilities	$252,000,000	$255,000,000
Total liabilities	$327,000,000	$353,000,000
Shareholders' equity		
10,000,000 common shares outstanding	$ 10,000,000	$ 10,000,000
Preferred stock, par value $100, 5%	4,000,000	4,000,000
Additional paid-in capital	107,000,000	107,000,000
Retained earnings	142,000,000	134,000,000
Total shareholders' equity	$263,000,000	$255,000,000
Total liabilities and shareholders' equity	$590,000,000	$608,000,000

Printing Company Statement of Income and Retained Earnings For the Years Ended December 31, 19x5, and 19x4	19x5	19x4
Net sales	$600,000,000	$500,000,000
Expenses		
Cost of goods sold	$490,000,000	$400,000,000
Selling and administrative	55,000,000	46,500,000
Interest	18,000,000	19,500,000
Total expenses	$563,000,000	$466,000,000
Income before taxes	$ 37,000,000	$ 34,000,000
Income taxes	16,800,000	15,800,000
Net income	$ 20,200,000	$ 18,200,000
Beginning retained earnings	134,000,000	126,000,000
Subtotal	$154,200,000	$144,200,000
Dividends on common shares	12,000,000	10,000,000
Dividends on preferred shares	200,000	200,000
Ending retained earnings	$142,000,000	$134,000,000

Required

1. Compute the current ratio on December 31, 19x5.
2. Compute the acid-test ratio on December 31, 19x5.
3. Compute the average collection period for 19x5. Assume all sales are credit sales.
4. Compute inventory turnover for 19x5.
5. Compute working capital at the end of 19x4 and 19x5.

37. (L.O. 5, 7) Assume the same facts as those given in Problem 36.

Required

1. Calculate book value per share on December 31, 19x5.
2. Calculate earnings per share for 19x5.
3. Calculate the price-earnings ratio on December 31, 19x5. Market price is $10 per share.
4. Calculate dividend payout for 19x5.
5. Calculate dividend yield for 19x5.

38. (L.O. 5) Assume the same facts as those given in Problem 36.

Required

1. Calculate return on total assets for 19x5. Assume a 45 percent tax rate.
2. Calculate return on common shareholders' equity for 19x5.

Case 1
Warford Corporation (L.O. 3, 5, 7)

Warford Corporation was formed five years ago by a public issue of common stock. Lucinda Street, who owns 15 percent of the common stock, was an organizer of Warford. She is also its president. Although the company has been successful, it experienced a shortage of funds in 19x0. On June 10, 19x0, Street approached Bell National Bank. She asked for a 24-month extension on two $30,000 notes, which are due on June 30, 19x0, and September 30, 19x0. Another note for $7,000 is due on December 31, 19x0. She expects no difficulty in paying this note on its due date, however. Street explained that Warford's cash flow problems are primarily caused by the company's desire to finance a $300,000 plant expansion over the next two fiscal years through internally generated funds.

The Commercial Loan Officer at Bell National Bank requested financial statements for the past two fiscal years. These reports are reproduced below and on page 844.

Required

1. Calculate the following items for Warford Corporation:
   a. Current ratio at March 31, 19x9, and 19x0.
   b. Acid-test ratio at March 31, 19x9, and 19x0.
   c. Inventory turnover for fiscal year 19x0.
   d. Return on total assets at March 31, 19x9, and 19x0. Total assets on March 31, 19x8, were $812,000.
   e. Percentage change in sales, cost of goods sold, gross margin, and net income from fiscal year 19x9 to 19x0.

Warford Corporation
Statement of Financial Position
March 31, 19x0, and 19x9

	19x0	19x9
Assets		
Cash	$ 16,400	$ 12,500
Notes receivable	112,000	104,000
Accounts receivable	81,600	68,500
Inventories	80,000	50,000
Plant and equipment (net)	680,000	646,000
Total assets	$970,000	$881,000
Liabilities and owners' equity		
Accounts payable	$ 69,000	$ 72,000
Notes payable	67,000	54,000
Accrued liabilities	9,000	6,500
Common stock (60,000 shares)	600,000	600,000
Retained earnings*	225,000	148,500
Total liabilities and owners' equity	$970,000	$881,000

*Cash dividends were paid at the rate of $1.00 per share during fiscal year 19x9 and $1.25 per share during fiscal year 19x0.

Warford Corporation
Income Statements
For the Years Ended March 31, 19x0, and 19x9

	19x0	19x9
Sales revenues	$1,000,000	$700,000
Expenses		
Cost of goods sold*	$ 552,000	$350,000
Selling and administrative	186,000	142,000
Interest	9,500	8,000
Total expenses	$ 747,500	$500,000
Net income before taxes	$ 252,500	$200,000
Income taxes (40%)	101,000	80,000
Net income	$ 151,500	$120,000

*Depreciation charges of $50,000 and $62,500 on plant and equipment for fiscal years ended March 31, 19x9, and 19x0, respectively, are included in cost of goods sold.

2. Identify and explain what other financial information or financial analyses might be helpful to the commercial loan officer at Bell National Bank.

Case 2
Ratio, Inc. (L.O. 7)

The December 31, 19x5, balance sheet for Ratio, Inc., is presented on page 845. These are the only accounts on Ratio's balance sheet. Amounts indicated by a question mark can be calculated from the additional information given below.

Additional information	
Current ratio at year-end	1.5 to 1
Debt to equity ratio	0.8
Inventory turnover based on cost of goods sold and ending inventory	10.5 times
Total sales for 19x5	$1,050,000
Gross margin for 19x5	$ 315,000

Required

1. Calculate Ratio's total current assets on December 31, 19x5.
2. Calculate Ratio's total current liabilities on December 31, 19x5.
3. Calculate Ratio's December 31, 19x5, inventory balance. (Note: The formula for inventory turnover when using a year-end balance is the same as the

Ratio, Inc. Balance Sheet December 31, 19x5	
Assets	
Cash	$ 25,000
Accounts receivable	?
Inventory	?
Plant and equipment (net)	294,000
Total assets	$432,000
Liabilities and shareholders' equity	
Accounts payable	$?
Income taxes payable (current)	25,000
Long-term debt	?
Common stock	200,000
Retained earnings	?
Total liabilities and shareholders' equity	$432,000

formula given in the text, except the year-end inventory balance is substituted for the average annual inventory balance.)

4. Calculate Ratio's December 31, 19x5, accounts receivable balance.
5. Calculate Ratio's December 31, 19x5, accounts payable balance.
6. Calculate Ratio's total liabilities on December 31, 19x5.
7. Calculate Ratio's December 31, 19x5, balance in retained earnings.
8. Calculate Ratio's long-term debt on December 31, 19x5. (AICPA)

Case 3
Academic Services, Inc. (L.O. 2, 5, 7)

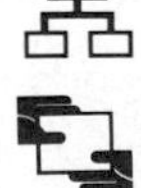

You are controller of Academic Services, Inc. The president has requested the ratios given below from your staff. This information will be used to convince creditors that the business is financially sound. The president wants to save time by concentrating on only these important data.

The data requested and the computations taken from financial statements follows on page 846.

	This year	Last year
Current ratio	2.5 to 1	2.0 to 1
Acid-test ratio	0.7 to 1	1.2 to 1
Debt-to-equity ratio	2.6 to 1	2.3 to 1
Book value per share	$31.50	$27.50
Net income	Up 30%	Down 10%
Earnings per share	$3.12	$2.40
Return on total assets	11.7%	8.9%

Required

1. The president has asked you for a list of brief comments on each item to support the case that the business is financially sound. At the same time you were also asked to draft a paragraph, explaining the overall message conveyed by the ratios. Please fulfill these requests.
2. Having done as the president requested in *1* above, prepare a brief list of additional ratios creditors might request. Explain why you think each additional ratio will help creditors evaluate the company's financial position.
3. What are the limitations of ratio analysis that the creditors face in this instance, and how can they be overcome?

Case 4
Chrysler Corporation and Ford Motor Company (L.O. 4)

The earnings statements for Chrysler Corporation and Ford Motor Company are shown below and on page 848.

Consolidated Statement of Earnings
Chrysler Corporation and Consolidated Subsidiaries

	Year Ended December 31		
	1988	1987	1986
	(In millions of dollars)		
Sales and service of manufactured products	$ 31,884.2	$ 26,279.1	$ 22,588.5
Financial services and other income	3,588.5	2,978.8	2,631.7
Total Sales and Revenues	35,472.7	29,257.9	25,220.2
Costs, other than items below (Note 3)	27,019.1	21,531.6	18,796.7
Depreciation of property and equipment	616.5	488.0	258.1
Amortization of special tools	539.8	411.5	306.8
Selling and administrative expenses	2,501.4	2,109.0	1,728.1
Pension expense (Note 15)	585.3	476.2	239.8
Interest expense (Notes 9 and 16)	2,453.2	2,061.9	1,737.8
Gain on equity investment transactions (Notes 6 and 19)	(85.0)	—	(144.3)
Special provision for plant closings (Note 20)	150.2	—	—
Total Costs and Expenses	33,780.5	27,078.2	22,923.0
Earnings Before Income Taxes	1,692.2	2,179.7	2,297.2
Provision for income taxes (Note 10)	642.0	890.0	908.0
Net Earnings	$ 1,050.2	$ 1,289.7	$ 1,389.2
		(In dollars or shares)	
Per Share Data (Note 18):			
Net earnings per common share	$ 4.66	$ 5.90	$ 6.25
Average number of common and equivalent shares outstanding (in thousands)	225,112	218,612	222,324
Common stock dividends declared	$ 1.00	$ 1.00	$ 0.80

See notes to consolidated financial statements.

Consolidated Statement of Income

For the Years Ended December 31, 1988, 1987, and 1986 (in millions)
Ford Motor Company and Subsidiaries

	1988	1987	1986
AUTOMOTIVE			
Sales	$82,193.0	$71,797.2	$62,868.3
Costs and Expenses (Note 1)			
Costs, excluding items listed below	68,233.3	58,572.7	51,931.5
Depreciation	1,914.9	1,827.7	1,679.9
Amortization of special tools	1,334.7	1,353.2	1,293.2
Selling and administrative	3,452.0	3,289.3	3,109.8
Employee retirement plans (Note 2)	646.2	498.4	711.7
Total costs and expenses (Note 3)	75,581.1	65,541.3	58,726.1
Operating Income	6,611.9	6,255.9	4,142.2
Interest income	885.2	823.5	671.7
Interest expense	354.0	452.9	490.1
Net interest income	531.2	370.6	181.6
Equity in net income/(loss) of affiliated companies	147.8	(136.6)	11.6
Net revenue/(expense) from transactions with Financial Services (Note 14)	21.1	9.4	(35.9)
Income Before Income Taxes—Automotive	7,312.0	6,499.3	4,299.5
FINANCIAL SERVICES			
Revenues (Note 1)	10,252.6	8,095.8	6,826.3
Costs and Expenses			
Interest expense	5,784.0	4,298.1	3,650.1
Operating and other expenses	1,625.4	1,259.6	985.7
Provision for credit and insurance losses (Note 7)	1,248.9	864.3	726.7
Depreciation (Note 6)	542.7	279.0	178.8
Total costs and expenses	9,201.0	6,701.0	5,541.3
Net revenue/(expense) from transactions with Automotive (Note 14)	(21.1)	(9.4)	35.9
Income Before Income Taxes—Financial Services	1,030.5	1,385.4	1,320.9
TOTAL COMPANY			
Income Before Income Taxes	8,342.5	7,884.7	5,620.4
Provision for income taxes (Note 4)	2,998.7	3,226.0	2,323.6
Income Before Minority Interests	5,343.8	4,658.7	3,296.8
Minority interests in net income of consolidated subsidiaries	43.6	33.5	11.7
Net Income	$ 5,300.2	$ 4,625.2	$ 3,285.1
Average number of shares of capital stock outstanding	483.8	511.0	533.1
Net Income a Share (Note 1)	$ 10.96	$ 9.05	$ 6.16
Cash Dividends a Share	$ 2.30	$ 1.58	$ 1.11

The accompanying notes are part of the financial statements.

Used by permission of Ford Motor Company.

Required

1. Revise the income statement for the Ford Motor Company to combine the results of automotive operations and financial services operations. Follow the format of the Chrysler Corporation income statement, and do the following:
   a. List financial services revenues as financial services and other income as on the Chrysler report.

   b. Include "Equity in net income of affiliated companies" in financial services and other income.
   c. Omit the offsetting $21,100,000 in both automotive and financial services.
   d. Deduct the provision for credit and insurance losses from the category financial services and other income.
   e. Add a line to report "Minority interests in new income of consolidated subsidiaries" as it is in the Ford report.
   f. Combine the remaining financial services expenses with the corresponding automotive expenses. (Hint: This should result in Financial Services and other income of $10,036.1 million and Total sales and revenues of $92,229.7 millions for Ford.)
2. Prepare common-size income statements for both companies for 1988.
3. Use your common-size income statements to compare 1988 operations for both companies. What seem to be the important differences in their operations?

■

18

Statement of Cash Flows

LEARNING OBJECTIVES

After studying this chapter you should be able to:

1. List the uses for a statement of cash flows
2. Explain how to identify cash flows from the balance sheet
3. Prepare a simple statement of cash flows using only balance sheet changes
4. Organize a statement of cash flows into the format preferred by the FASB
5. Use T accounts to double-check and refine a statement of cash flows
6. Use T accounts to prepare a statement of cash flows

The published annual reports of business firms include three major statements: (1) the income statement, (2) the balance sheet, and (3) the statement of cash flows. This chapter focuses on the third statement, the statement of cash flows, formerly called the funds statement or statement of changes in financial position.

You studied the balance sheet and income statement in a financial accounting course. The balance sheet reports an organization's financial position at a particular point in time. It does not show how the organization arrived at the financial position. Both the income statement and the statement of cash flows report what occurred during a period of time. The statement of cash flows reports the inflows and outflows of cash.

Cash outflows usually relate to the flows of other resources. For example, a purchase of equipment creates an *out*flow of cash resulting in an *in*flow of the resource called equipment. Therefore, the statement of cash flows provides insight into how the total resources of an organization changed during a particular time period.

■

Uses for Statements of Cash Flows

Alan H. Seed III listed the uses of the **statement of cash flows** by external and internal users.[1] External users, that is, shareholders, lenders, and government and regulatory authorities, use statements of cash flows for the following purposes:

OBJECTIVE 1
List the uses for a statement of cash flows

1. To assess a company's ability to finance operations from internal sources
2. To assess a company's ability to service its debts
3. To identify the relationship between a company's income and its cash flows

Internal users, who are mostly managers, use statements of cash flows for these purposes:

1. To forecast a company's cash needs and plan its finances
2. To monitor a company's cash flows and liquidity

Seed found that statements of cash flows are generally not used in performance evaluations.

A company's ability to finance operations, service its debt, and monitor cash flows and liquidity is important to both investors and managers. Generally, an

[1]Alan H. Seed III, *The Funds Statement Structure and Uses* (Morristown, N.J.: Financial Executives Research Foundation, 1984), p. 5.

Seed's findings were based on a review of the literature, an examination of annual reports, an analysis of 749 responses to questionnaires, and interviews with 105 users and preparers of funds statements.

organization's past ability to generate cash is an indication of its future ability to do so. To test how well a firm is accomplishing this task, investors and managers often use measures such as the current ratio. However, a statement of cash flows provides a more complete picture. In fact, the Financial Accounting Standards Board (FASB) considers statements of cash flows so important to investors that such statements are required in audited annual reports. Cash flows are also important to managers, since managers have greater discretion in using cash than other resources.

In a 1987 *Statement,* the FASB described the purpose of a statement of cash flows slightly differently. According to the FASB *Statement of Financial Standards No. 95,* the purpose is to assess:

1. A company's ability to generate positive future net cash flows
2. A company's ability to meet its obligations and pay dividends as well as its need for external financing
3. The reasons for differences between income and associated cash receipts and payments
4. Both the cash and noncash aspects of a company's investing and financing transactions[2]

This list of uses is important because it is the basis of the FASB's recommended format for cash flow statements. The preferred format will be discussed later in this chapter.

■

Definition of Cash

Before the FASB's 1987 *Statement of Financial Standards No. 95,* funds could be defined either as cash or working capital. In the 1987 *Statement,* however, only the cash definition is allowed. But as Figure 18–1 shows, cash was quickly gaining favor as the preferred definition anyway.

The term **cash** includes cash and cash equivalents. Cash equivalents include United States Treasury bills, commercial paper,[3] and money market funds. Usually, an organization with cash in excess of its immediate needs will put that cash into short-term, secure investments, sometimes investing for only one to three days. Cash equivalents are such investments. And because management can recover cash whenever needed, such investments are, for all practical purposes, the

[2]*Statement of Financial Accounting Standards No. 95,* "Statement of Cash Flows," (Stamford, Conn.: Financial Accounting Standards Board, 1987).

[3]Commercial paper is a short-term loan to an organization of very high credit rating. Because of the high credit rating and the short maturity, the risk of these investments is very low, and the commercial paper can be sold for cash at any time.

Figure 18–1
Trends in Defining Funds
Cash was quickly becoming the preferred definition of funds, even before 1987 when the Financial Accounting Standards Board required that definition. *Source:* Alan H. Seed III, *The Funds Statement, Structure and Use* (Morristown, N.J.: Financial Executives Research Foundation, 1984), p. 27. Used with permission.

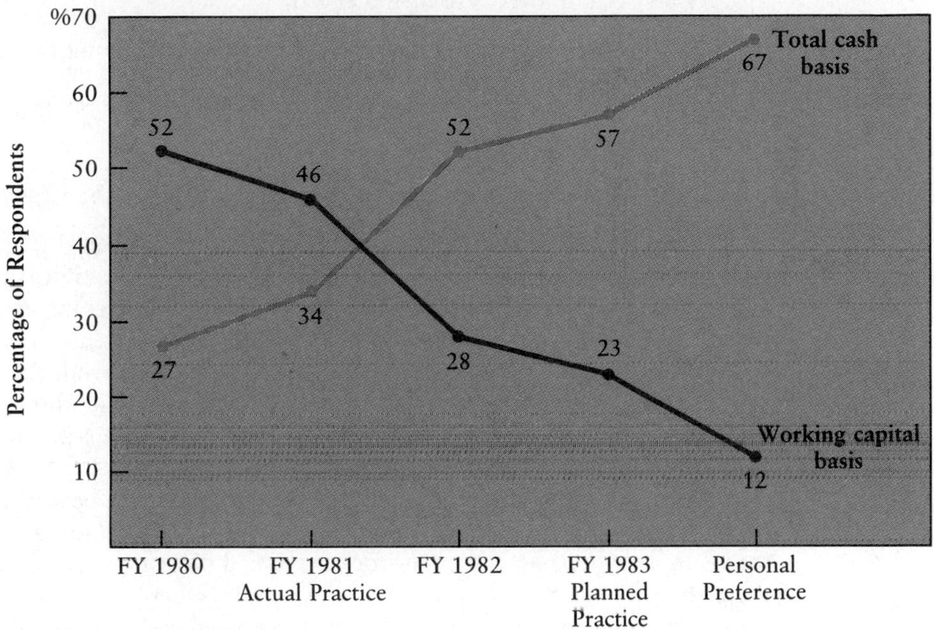

same as having cash. A statement of cash flows shows events that changed the amount of cash and cash equivalents available to the organization.

■

Identifying Cash Flows

OBJECTIVE 2
Explain how to identify cash flows from the balance sheet

As a rule, any change in a balance sheet item *other than cash* is a potential cash flow. Therefore, any change in a liability, asset, or equity account other than cash is potentially a cash flow.

Whether a change is a cash inflow or cash outflow depends on its nature. If the equipment account increased, cash was probably used to purchase new equipment. Therefore, an increase in equipment represents a cash outflow. If the long-term debt account increased, the company probably borrowed additional cash. Therefore, an increase in long-term debt is a cash inflow.

This concept may be easier to grasp by thinking in terms of the relationship between assets, liabilities, and owners' equity on the balance sheet.[4] As you know, total assets must always equal total liabilities plus owners' equity on a balance sheet. Otherwise, the balance sheet does not balance. This relationship may be expressed algebraically as the balance sheet equation:

Assets = liabilities + owners' equity

To highlight cash, you can restate the assets side of the equation as follows:

Cash + assets other than cash = liabilities + owners' equity

Rearranged, this equation reads

Cash = liabilities + owners' equity − assets other than cash

From this equation you can see that if only one item on the right side of the equals sign changes, there must be an equal change on the left side, that is, the cash side. Thus, an increase in liabilities produces an increase in cash. Because cash has increased, this increase in liabilities represents a cash inflow. Likewise, with other items held constant, a decrease in liabilities produces a decrease in cash. Because the cash balance is reduced, a decrease in liabilities must be cash outflow. Liabilities decrease because they are repaid, and repayment uses cash. Borrowing increases liabilities and increases cash.

The other items on the right side of the equation may be similarly analyzed. When owners' equity increases, there should be a corresponding cash inflow, as, for example, when new shares of stock are issued. When owners' equity decreases, there should be a cash outflow, as, for example, when paying a dividend.

Notice that in the equation, "assets other than cash" is preceded by a minus sign. In others words, changes in assets other than cash have the opposite effect from changes in liabilities and owners' equity. An increase in assets other than cash results in a cash outflow. If a firm purchases inventory without increasing liabilities, it must pay cash, a cash outflow. Conversely, if a firm collects some accounts receivable, decreasing that asset's balance, the firm adds to its cash balance. Thus, a decrease in assets other than cash is a cash inflow.

To test your understanding of this concept, check the appropriate blanks in the following table:

	Cash inflow	Cash outflow
Purchasing equipment	______	______
Paying accounts payable	______	______
Borrowing from a bank	______	______
Earning a profit	______	______
Paying dividends	______	______
Selling inventory for cash	______	______

[4]This approach was suggested by Daniel Pearl in his article, "Teaching the Statements of Changes in Financial Position Without Worksheets and T-Accounts," *Issues in Accounting Education 1986* (Sarasota, Fla.: American Accounting Association, Spring 1986), pp. 132–142.

You can check your answers against the answers shown on page 875.

In summary, there are three general sources of cash inflows: (1) the sale of assets other than cash, (2) an increase in liabilities, and (3) an increase in owners' equity. There are also three corresponding cash outflows: (1) the purchase of assets other than cash, (2) a decrease in liabilities, and (3) a decrease in owners' equity.

■

Preparing a Simple Statement of Cash Flows from the Balance Sheet

OBJECTIVE 3
Prepare a simple statement of cash flows using only balance sheet changes

Exhibits 18–1, 18–2, and 18–3 (pages 856 and 857) show Brian Company's comparative balance sheet, income statement, and statement of retained earnings. Together, these statements make up the basic data required to prepare a statement of cash flows.

The first step in preparing a statement of cash flows is to add two extra columns to the balance sheet. These columns will reflect changes from the past year, as shown in Exhibit 18–4 (page 858). As you can see, no changes are shown for subtotals and totals, only for individual items.

The changes may then be incorporated into a **simple statement of cash flows,** as shown in Exhibit 18–5 (page 859). Notice that in each column, cash flows are divided into three categories: (1) owners' equity, (2) liabilities, and (3) other assets. These categories correspond to the three items on the right side of the equation shown on page 854. In addition, a proof is shown at the bottom of the statement. Preparing the statement of cash flows is simply a matter of transferring changes in balance sheet items (except for cash) as shown on the worksheet (Exhibit 18–4) to the appropriate column and category in the statement of cash flows. (Later, the format required by the FASB will be discussed. But first, you should understand how to identify cash inflows and outflows.)

Notice that the $494 increase retained earnings shown in Exhibit 18–4 is divided between net income, a cash inflow, and dividends, a cash outflow, on the statement of cash flows. The net income and dividend amount are taken from Brian's statement of retained earnings (Exhibit 18–3). The increase in retained earnings is the change in that account from December 31, 19x8, to December 31, 19x9 ($1,750 − $1,256). Finally, notice that the increase in accumulated depreciation shown in Exhibit 18–4 appears as a *decrease* in assets on the statement of cash flows (Exhibit 18–5).

The bottom section of Exhibit 18–5 is a proof to check the difference between the total cash inflows and outflows to ensure that it equals the change in cash balance from the beginning balance sheet to the ending balance sheet. Change in cash for the year is shown at the bottom of the statement of cash flows by subtracting cash outflows from cash inflows. The statement of cash flows shows that cash increased by $155 during the year. This figure can be confirmed by

Exhibit 18–1
Balance Sheet Used to Prepare a Statement of Cash Flows

Brian Company Comparative Balance Sheet December 31, 19x9, and 19x8	19x9	19x8
Assets		
Current assets		
Cash	$ 476	$ 321
Accounts receivable	286	208
Inventory	1,660	1,682
Total current assets	$ 2,422	$ 2,211
Investment in shares of supplier	$ 200	$ 200
Plant and equipment	$ 5,290	$ 4,784
Accumulated depreciation	(1,587)	(1,375)
Net plant and equipment	$ 3,703	$ 3,409
Total assets	$ 6,325	$ 5,820
Liabilities and shareholders' equity		
Current liabilities		
Accounts payable	$ 1,865	$ 1,848
Taxes payable	20	19
Wages payable	190	197
Total current liabilities	$ 2,075	$ 2,064
Bonds payable	1,500	1,500
Total liabilities	$ 3,575	$ 3,564
Shareholders' equity		
Paid-in capital	$ 1,000	$ 1,000
Retained earnings	1,750	1,256
Total shareholders' equity	$ 2,750	$ 2,256
Total liabilities and shareholders' equity	$ 6,325	$ 5,820

looking at the difference between the beginning and ending cash balances from the comparative balance sheet in Exhibit 18–1. The balance sheet differences are shown at the bottom right of Exhibit 18–5. In practice, this proof is not usually shown on a statement of cash flows. The balance is simply assumed to have been checked. It is shown here because it is useful for double-checking answers to problems.

Format for a Statement of Cash Flows

In previous sections of this chapter, you learned to identify cash inflows and outflows by using comparative balance sheets and a statement of changes in

Exhibit 18–2
Income Statement Used in Statement of Cash Flows Example

Brian Company
Income Statement
For the Year Ended December 31, 19x9

Sales revenues	$4,070
Expenses	
Cost of goods sold	$2,290
Selling	206
Administrative	191
Depreciation	212
Interest	15
Income taxes	462
Total expenses	$3,376
Net income	$ 694

Exhibit 18–3
Statement of Retained Earnings Used in Example

Brian Company
Statement of Retained Earnings
For the Year Ended December 31, 19x9

Retained earnings, December 31, 19x8	$1,256
Add net income	694
Subtotal	$1,950
Less dividends declared	(200)
Retained earnings, December 31, 19x9	$1,750

OBJECTIVE 4
Organize a statement of cash flows into the format preferred by the FASB

retained earnings. Such identification is fundamental to preparing a statement of changes in cash flows. However, the simple statement illustrated in Exhibit 18–5 is more useful when cash inflows and outflows are grouped according to several major management activities. These activities interest both managers and investors.

Statement 95 of the FASB requires a format that fulfills the purposes outlined for the statement of cash flows on page 852. According to the FASB format, cash flows are divided into three categories:

1. **Operating activities,** which include all transactions other than investment and financing activities, as defined in 2 and 3, below. Operating activities include delivering or producing goods for sale and providing services. These activities are mainly transactions related to dealing with customers.

Exhibit 18–4

Worksheet for Statement of Cash Flows

The first step in preparing a statement of cash flows is to add two extra columns to the balance sheet. These columns will show the amount of change in each item and the direction of the change from the previous year. Notice that changes are not entered for subtotals and totals, only for individual items.

Brian Company
Balance Sheet
December 31, 19x9 and 19x8

	19x9	19x8	Change	Direction of change
Assets				
Current assets				
Cash	$ 476	$ 321	$155	Increase
Accounts receivable	286	208	78	Increase
Inventory	1,660	1,682	(22)	Decrease
Total current assets	$2,422	$2,211		
Investment in shares of supplier	$ 200	$ 200	—	
Plant and equipment	$5,290	$4,784	506	Increase
Accumulated depreciation	(1,587)	(1,375)	212	Increase
Net plant and equipment	$3,703	$3,409		
Total assets	$6,325	$5,820		
Liabilities and shareholders' equity				
Current liabilities				
Accounts payable	$1,865	$1,848	17	Increase
Taxes payable	20	19	1	Increase
Wages payable	190	197	(7)	Decrease
Total current liabilities	$2,075	$2,064		
Bonds payable	1,500	1,500	—	
Total liabilities	$3,575	$3,564		
Shareholders' equity				
Paid-in capital	$1,000	$1,000	—	
Retained earnings	1,750	1,256	494	Increase
Total shareholders' equity	$2,750	$2,256		
Total liabilities and shareholders' equity	$6,325	$5,820		

2. **Investing activities,** which include lending money and collecting loans, acquiring and selling securities that are not cash equivalents, and buying and selling plant and equipment.
3. **Financing activities,** which include raising capital from shareholders, paying dividends, and borrowing or repaying long-term debts.

Producing a statement of cash flows in the FASB recommended format is merely a matter of rearranging cash flows into the three categories listed above.

Exhibit 18–5

Simple Statement of Cash Flows

This statement is based on the increases and decreases in assets other than cash, liabilities, and owners' equity shown in Exhibit 18–4. Notice that decreases in an asset other than cash and increases in liabilities are listed as cash inflows. Increases in assets other than cash and decreases in liabilities and owners' equity are listed as cash outflows.

Brian Company
Statement of Cash Flows
For the Year Ended December 31, 19x9

Cash inflows		Cash outflows	
Owners' equity increases		Owners' equity decreases	
Net income	$694	Dividends	$200
Liability increases		Liability decreases	
Accounts payable	17	Wages payable	7
Taxes payable	1		
Other asset decreases		Other asset increases	
Inventory	22	Accounts receivable	78
Accumulated depreciation	212	Plant and equipment	506
Total cash inflows	$946	Total cash outflows	$791

Proof

From statement of cash flows		From balance sheet	
Total cash inflows	$946	Ending cash	$476
Total cash outflows	791	Less beginning cash	321
Cash increase	$155	Cash increase	$155

This procedure will be illustrated by changing the statement of cash flows in Exhibit 18–5 to the format recommended by the FASB.

For most firms, operating activities are the prime source of cash. There are two reasons for this situation. First, the amount of cash derived from these activities is usually larger than amounts from other sources. Second, unlike most other sources, operating activities recur each year. If a firm cannot generate cash from operating activities, it will have difficulty paying bills in a few years. Because of the importance of operating activities to total cash inflows, many managers and investors think this figure is the primary indicator of financial health.

Many of the cash flows shown in Exhibit 18–5 are from operating activities. Generally, cash received from customers, cash paid to suppliers and employees, and interest and taxes paid are operating items.

There are two ways of reporting cash flows from operating activities, the direct method and the indirect method. The direct method has some theoretical advantages over the indirect method and is favored by the FASB. The indirect method is easier to calculate from income statement and balance sheet changes. The **direct method** classifies operating cash flows into cash received from customers, dividends received, cash paid to suppliers and employees, and cash payment for interest and taxes for the purpose of determining cash flows from operating activities. The **indirect method** starts with the organization's net income based on accrual accounting and makes four types of adjustments to find cash flows from operating activities, which is net income according to the cash basis of accounting. The only difference between the two methods is the approach to calculating cash flows from operating activities. Both methods calculate cash flows from financing and investing activities in exactly the same way. We shall discuss both the direct and indirect methods.

The indirect method makes the following four adjustments to net income to determine cash flows from operating activities:

1. Adding back any noncash expenses deducted in the income statement. The most common example is depreciation expense, although amortization of patent costs, amortization of bond premiums or discounts, and gains or losses on sale of equipment are other examples.
2. Adjusting for the change in the accounts receivable balance to indicate that cash collected from customers is different from the amount of sales shown in the income statement.
3. Adjusting for changes in inventories to indicate that the purchase of inventory items is different from the cost of goods sold on the income statement.
4. Adjusting for changes in the balances of accounts payable, wages payable, taxes payable, prepayment, and similar current liabilities to show that the actual cash disbursed during the year is different from expenses reported on the income statement. These adjustments are shown on the simple statement of cash flows. They are not grouped together under the heading of operating activities.

Now look at the simple statement of cash flows shown in Exhibit 18–5. This statement will be revised to conform to the more useful format recommended by the FASB, but using the indirect method of calculating cash flows from operating activities. The revised statement is shown as Exhibit 18–6. In the revised statement, the first category is cash flows from operating activities. This section starts by adding the annual depreciation to the 19x9 net income. Annual depreciation expense is added because it does not involve a cash outflow. Because of this, it must be added back to net income when using the indirect method to calculate cash flows from operating activities. Depreciation is a legitimate expense in 19x9, but not a cash outflow. This adjustment is shown just below net income in the statement of cash flows in Exhibit 18–6.

The next adjustment is for the change in the accounts receivable balance. During the year, the accounts receivable balance increased by $78. This means cash collections from customers during 19x9 were less than 19x9 sales by $78. Thus, cash flows from operating activities must be reduced $78 as shown in Exhibit 18–6.

Next, adjustments must be made for the change in inventory. Exhibit 18–5 as well as the worksheet in Exhibit 18–4 show an inventory decrease of $22. This means the amount purchased was less than the amount sold. Since purchases were less than the cost of goods sold, less cash was used in operating activities.

Exhibit 18–6

Statement of Cash Flows in the FASB Format, Indirect Method

This statement of cash flows is identical to the one in Exhibit 18–5 except that it follows the FASB format by grouping cash flows into three categories: (1) operating activities, (2) investing activities, and (3) financing activities. Cash flows from operating activities are listed prominently at the top of the statement because they are a large recurring source. As such they are extremely important.

Brian Company
Statement of Cash Flows
For the Year Ended December 31, 19x9

Cash flows from operating activities		
Net income	$694	
Add (deduct) cash adjustments to net income		
Annual depreciation	212	
Increase in accounts receivable	(78)	
Decrease in inventory	22	
Increase in accounts payable	17	
Increase in taxes payable	1	
Decrease in wages payable	(7)	
Cash flows from operating activities		$861
Cash flows from investing activities		
Purchases of plant and equipment		(506)
Cash flows from financing activities		
Dividends paid		(200)
Increase (decrease) in cash		$ 155

Proof

From balance sheet	
Ending cash	$476
Less beginning cash	321
Cash increase	$155

Thus, this decrease in inventory is added to cash flows from operating activities. Notice in Exhibit 18–5 that the decrease in inventory was reported as a cash inflow. The inventory decrease has the same effect in Exhibit 18–6 by adding cash flows from operating activities.

Finally, notice from the simple statement in Exhibit 18–5 that accounts payable and taxes payable have increased, whereas wages payable decreased. These changes affect the amount of cash paid for expenses. The increases in accounts and taxes payable show Brian company paid less than the related income statement amounts. Otherwise, these liabilities would not have increased. The decrease in wages payable means Brian paid an amount equal to wages expense plus an added amount to reduce this liability during the year. These adjustments are shown in Exhibit 18–6 in calculating funds from operating activities.

A second major category in the FASB format is cash flows from investing activities. This category represents such additional investments as new plant and equipment or long-term loans made. It can also represent reductions in those investments. In the case of Brian Company, the only investing activity during 19x9 was a cash flow resulting from the purchase of equipment for $506.

The final category in the FASB format is cash flows from financing activities. If the company borrowed cash or issued more shares of stock, this activity would be a financing cash inflow. Conversely, loan payments and the repurchase of shares of stock or the payment of dividends represent financing cash outflows. In Brian's case, the only financing cash flow was a $200 dividend. It is shown as the last item on Exhibit 18–6 before the proof.

By adding cash flows from each of the three categories, you find the increase or decrease in cash during the period. For Brian Company, the cash flows statement shows cash increases of $155 during 19x9. To confirm this figure, compare the cash balances on the balance sheets at the beginning and end of the year. Such proof is shown at the bottom of Exhibit 18–6, even though it is not normally included in the FASB format. When working problems, it is always a good idea to calculate a proof to ensure that no arithmetic mistakes were made.

The direct method of calculating cash flows from operating activities makes adjustments to separate income statement items directly rather than making adjustments to the net income figure alone. The direct method lists cash flows from operating activities in three categories:[5]

1. Cash receipts from customers
2. Cash payments to suppliers and employees
3. Cash payments for taxes

No adjustment is needed for depreciation, since it is not a cash outflow. Cash receipts from customers is the revenue for the year, adjusted for the change in the accounts receivable balance. If accounts receivable increased during the year, then cash received from customers was less than revenue. If accounts receivable decreased, then cash received from customers was more than revenue.

Calculating cash paid to suppliers and employees requires adjusting cost of goods sold and selling and administrative expenses for changes in inventory, accounts payable, and wages payable. If inventory increased, purchases were more than the cost of goods sold, and cash paid out was greater than cost of goods sold as well. If inventory decreased, purchases were less than cost of goods sold. Similarly, if accounts payable and wages payable increased, cash payments were less than reported for purchases and wages. If accounts payable and wages payable decreased, the payments for inventory and wages must have been greater than reported. These expense amounts are therefore adjusted accordingly to obtain cash payments. Finally, interest and taxes must be adjusted for any changes in their associated current liabilities.

A statement of cash flows for Brian Company in the FASB format using the direct method for calculating cash flows is shown in Exhibit 18–7. By comparing

[5]If the organization receives cash dividends from its investments, dividends received is a fourth category. It is not used here since Brian Company did not receive any cash dividends.

Exhibit 18–7

Statement of Cash Flows, FASB Format, Direct Method

This statement of cash flows is the same as the one in Exhibit 18–6 except that it uses the direct rather than the indirect method of presenting cash flows from operating activities.

Brian Company
Statement of Cash Flows
For the Year Ended December 31, 19x9

Cash flows from operating activities			
Cash receipts from customers		$3,992	
Cash payments			
Suppliers and employees	$2,655		
Increase in income taxes	476	3,131	
Net cash flows from operating activities			$ 861
Cash flows from investing activities			
Purchases of plant and equipment			(506)
Cash flows from financing activities			
Dividends paid			(200)
Increase (decrease) in cash			$ 155

Proof

From balance sheet	
Ending cash	$476
Less beginning cash	321
Cash increase	$155

this to Exhibit 18–6, you can see that only the format of reporting cash flows from operating activities has changed. The total amount of cash flows from operating activities is the same, and the other two sections are exactly the same as before.

In Exhibit 18–7, cash received from customers consists of sales of $4,070, reduced for the $78 increase in accounts receivable. The cash paid to suppliers and employees is calculated as follows:

Cost of goods sold	$2,290
Selling expenses	206
Administrative expenses	191
Subtotal	$2,687
Add (deduct) cash adjustments	
Decrease in inventory	(22)
Increase in accounts payable	(17)
Decrease in wages payable	7
Cash payments to suppliers and employees	$2,655

Finally, the payments for interest and income taxes is the sum of $15 in interest expense and the $462 in income tax expense reduced by the $1 increase in taxes payable. As expected, the cash flows from operating activities is $861, the same amount found earlier by the indirect method.

Review Exercise 18–1

Prepare Statements Using Direct and Indirect Methods

The accountant for Barb's Hair Salon has prepared an income statement for the year ended 19x3 and balance sheets at the beginning and end of the year. The cash flow statement for 19x3 must still be prepared.

Barb's Hair Salon
Income Statement
For the Year Ended December 31, 19x3

Sales revenues	$99,000
Expenses	
Cost of goods sold	$19,800
Salaries and commissions	15,960
Advertising	13,000
Other cash expenses	28,133
Depreciation	3,487
Total expenses	$80,380
Operating income	$18,620
Income taxes @ 15%	2,793
Net income	$15,827
Dividend	$ 5,000

Barb's Hair Salon
Comparative Balance Sheets
December 31, 19x3, and 19x2

	19x3	19x2
Assets		
Current assets		
Cash	$ 8,000	$10,000
Accounts receivable	4,068	3,699
Inventory	3,300	2,000
Prepaid expenses	650	500
Total current assets	$16,018	$16,199
Plant and equipment (cost)	$14,850	$ 9,000
Accumulated depreciation	(8,167)	(4,680)
Net plant and equipment	$ 6,683	$ 4,320
Total assets	$22,701	$20,519

	19x3	19x2
Equities		
Current liabilities		
Accounts payable	$ 1,650	$ 1,500
Income taxes payable	279	192
Total current liabilities	$ 1,929	$ 1,692
Long-term notes	400	9,282
Total liabilities	$ 2,329	$10,974
Common stock	$ 2,000	$ 2,000
Retained earnings	18,372	7,545
Owners' equity	$20,372	$ 9,545
Total equities	$22,701	$20,519

Required

1. Prepare a cash flow statement for Barb's Hair Salon following the FASB format and using the *direct* method of calculating funds from operations.
2. Prepare a cash flow statement for Barb's Hair Salon following the FASB format and using the *indirect* method of calculating funds from operations.

Solution

1. Cash flow statement using the direct method of calculating funds from operations

Barb's Hair Salon
Statement of Cash Flows
For the Year Ended December 31, 19x3

		Receivables/payables adjustments			Cash flow
Funds from operations—direct method					
Sales	$99,000	+$3,699	−$4,068	$98,630	
Cost of goods sold	19,800				
+ ending inventory	3,300				
− beginning inventory	(2,000)				
Purchases of inventory	21,100	+1,500	−1,650	20,950	
Remaining expenses	57,093	+650	−500	57,243	
Income taxes	2,793	+192	−279	2,706	
Funds from operations					$17,732
Investing activities					
Purchase of plant and equipment					(5,850)
Financing activities					
Long-term note repayment					(8,882)
Cash dividend					(5,000)
Change in cash balance					$(2,000)

2. Cash flow statement using the indirect method of calculating funds from operations

Barb's Hair Salon
Statement of Cash Flows
For the Year Ended December 31, 19x3

Funds from operations — indirect method		
Net income	$15,827	
Depreciation	3,487	
Changes in current assets other than cash	(1,819)	
Changes in current liabilities	237	
Funds from operations		$17,732
Investing activities		
Purchase of plant and equipment		(5,850)
Financing activities		
Note repayment		(8,882)
Cash dividend		(5,000)
Change in cash balance		$ (2,000)

(see Exercises 12, 14, 16, 35, 36)

■

T Accounts as an Aid in Preparing a Statement of Cash Flows

The method outlined thus far may be used to prepare any statement of cash flows. However, some people prefer an alternate method based on T accounts, primarily because calculating cash flows from operating activities can seem complex. The **T account method** helps ensure that all information affecting cash flows is included.

Another important advantage of T accounts is that they may reveal relevant information not shown on the balance sheet. For example, the change in retained earnings often reflects the difference between an increase in cash from net income and a decrease in cash caused by payment of dividends. For the Brian Company, those items were reported separately in the cash flows statement. But information from the statement of retained earnings was needed. Net income was shown as part of cash flows from operating activities. Dividends were shown as cash flows from financing activities.

Other accounts, such as Plant and Equipment and Accumulated Depreciation, may be similarly complicated. Just as organizations buy equipment during the year, they also sell or dispose of it. A statement of cash flows showing only overall changes in the Plant and Equipment account (cost of equipment purchased less cost of equipment sold) omits equipment sales as a cash inflow and understates the cash outflow for equipment purchased. If equipment sales are small, as they often are, such understatement of purchases is not serious. To be accurate, however, accountants should adjust for offsetting sales and purchases. The T account method does just that.

T accounts may be used to supplement the balance sheet method for preparing statements of cash flows. In that case, the accountant must look at only selected accounts, such as retained earnings, plant and equipment, and accumulated depreciation. T accounts may also be used as the primary document from which a statement of cash flows is prepared. Each approach will be discussed separately.

Using T Accounts to Double-Check and Refine Statements of Cash Flows

OBJECTIVE 5
Use T accounts to double-check and refine a statement of cash flows

Suppose you have prepared a statement of cash flows by using comparative balance sheets. You wish to check the Plant and Equipment T account to ensure that no significant changes were overlooked. The most important change in the Accumulated Depreciation account is usually annual depreciation expense. Depreciation expense increases accumulated depreciation for the year. But if the equipment is sold during the year, accumulated depreciation on that equipment is deducted from the total in the Accumulated Depreciation account. Thus, by using only the balance sheet change in accumulated depreciation to calculate cash flows from operating activities, you may understate those cash flows.

Annual statements for a new sample firm, Bard Company, are shown in Exhibits 18–8, 18–9, and 18–10. During 19x9, Bard Company sold production equipment for \$1,000. The equipment's original cost was \$1,619. Accumulated depreciation was \$619. T accounts for Plant and Equipment and Accumulated Depreciation are shown in Exhibit 18–11. Notice that except for the cost of equipment purchased, all figures in the T accounts are given in Exhibit 18–8 and 18–9. The beginning and ending balances in both equipment cost and accumulated depreciation are shown on the balance sheet (Exhibit 18–8). The cost of equipment sold and its accumulated depreciation are shown in the explanatory material at the top of Exhibit 18–8. Annual depreciation expense is shown on the income statement (Exhibit 18–9). The cost of equipment purchased was calculated as shown below.

$$\text{Beginning balance} + \text{cost of equipment purchased} - \text{cost of equipment sold} = \text{ending balance}$$

$$\text{Cost of equipment purchased} = \text{ending balance} - \text{beginning balance} + \text{cost of equipment sold}$$

$$\text{Cost of equipment purchased} = \$25{,}778 - \$23{,}628 + \$1{,}619$$

$$= \underline{\underline{\$3{,}769}}$$

Exhibit 18–8

Sample Balance Sheet for Preparing a Statement of Cash Flows

During 19x9 Bard Company sold production equipment for $1,000. The equipment's original cost was $1,619. Accumulated depreciation was $619.

Bard Company
Comparative Balance Sheets
December 31, 19x9, and 19x8

	19x9	19x8	Change increase (decrease)
Assets			
Current assets			
Cash	$ 5,341	$ 5,597	$ (256)
Accounts receivable	7,263	8,841	(1,578)
Inventory	12,994	15,322	(2,328)
Total current assets	$25,598	$29,760	
Investment in shares of printing company	$ 6,000	$ 4,000	2,000
Plant and equipment	$25,778	$23,628	2,150
Accumulated depreciation	(11,385)	(10,139)	1,246
Net plant and equipment	$14,393	$13,489	
Total assets	$45,991	$47,249	
Liabilities and Shareholders' Equity			
Current liabilities			
Accounts payable	$10,138	$11,724	(1,586)
Taxes payable	2,337	2,187	150
Wages payable	894	952	(58)
Total current liabilities	$13,369	$14,863	
Bonds payable, due 20x0	10,000	12,000	(2,000)
Total liabilities	$23,369	$26,863	
Shareholders' equity			
Paid-in capital	$ 5,000	$ 4,800	200
Retained earnings	17,622	15,586	2,036
Total shareholders' equity	$22,622	$20,386	
Total liabilities and shareholders' equity	$45,991	$47,249	

As you can see, by using T accounts three facts were discovered that might have been missed by using only balance sheet changes. First, the amount of equipment purchased during the year was $3,769, not $2,150, as suggested by the change in the balance sheet item plant and equipment. Second, an additional cash inflow of $1,000, the amount received from selling the old equipment, was discovered. (Notice that a cash inflow from the sale of an asset is always the amount received from the sale, not its book value unless the sale is for that

Exhibit 18–9
Sample Income Statements for Preparing a Statement of Cash Flows

Bard Company Comparative Income Statements For the Years Ended December 31, 19x9, and 19x8	19x9	19x8
Sales revenues	$71,942	$62,388
Expenses		
Cost of goods sold	$26,733	$25,891
Selling	21,120	16,524
Administrative	13,601	11,606
Depreciation	1,865	1,638
Income taxes	2,587	2,019
Total expenses	$65,906	$57,678
Net income	$ 6,036	$ 4,710

amount.) Third, it was discovered that annual depreciation expenses was $1,865, not $1,246, as shown by a change in accumulated depreciation on the balance sheets. (Annual depreciation expenses are also shown on Bard's income statement.) Thus, when calculating cash flows from operating activities, you must add back $1,865 as a noncash flow. Adding back $1,865 reports cash flows from operations more accurately.

With this information you can now prepare a statement of cash flows, as illustrated earlier in the chapter, by supplementing the balance sheet information with T accounts as necessary. You might also start from scratch, however, using T accounts as a major document. Such an approach is discussed next.

Exhibit 18–10
Sample Statements of Retained Earnings for Preparing a Statement of Cash Flows

Bard Company Comparative Statements of Retained Earnings For the Years Ended December 31, 19x9, and 19x8	19x9	19x8
Retained earnings, beginning of year	$15,586	$13,876
Add net income	6,036	4,710
Subtotal	$21,622	$18,586
Less dividends declared	4,000	3,000
Retained earnings, end of year	$17,622	$15,586

Exhibit 18–11
Bard Company Selected T Accounts for the Year 19x9

Plant and Equipment

Beginning balance	23,628		
Cost of equipment purchased	3,769	Cost of equipment sold	1,619
Ending balance	25,778		

Accumulated Depreciation

		Beginning balance	10,139
Accumulated depreciation on equipment sold	619	19x9 annual depreciation expenses	1,865
		Ending balance	11,385

Using T Accounts to Prepare a Statement of Cash Flows

OBJECTIVE 6
Use T accounts to prepare a statement of cash flows

To prepare a complete statement of cash flows using T accounts, the accountant must first establish a T account for each balance sheet item. Next, he or she records summary entries to explain changes in each account. Exhibit 18–12 shows a full T account analysis for Bard Company. Notice that the Cash account, at the top, is divided into cash inflows on the left and cash outflows on the right. The Cash account is then further divided into operating activities, investing activities, and financing activities. This division will be useful in preparing the statement in the FASB format.

To begin preparing Bard's statement of cash flows, one takes the balance sheet accounts shown in Exhibit 18–8 and enters the beginning and ending balances, except for cash, into each T account. Next, any additional information, such as equipment sales and dividends, are entered onto the appropriate side of the relevant T account. If an item affects cash, it is entered into the Cash account as well. The order in which the T accounts are filled is unimportant. It is only important that each entry balance.

Now, suppose that after entering beginning and ending balances in all T accounts except Cash, additional information on net income and dividends is entered into Retained Earnings (entries **1** and **2**). This information is taken from Bard's comparative statements of retained earnings (Exhibit 18–10).

Next, trace entries **1** and **2** from the T account for Retained Earnings, at the bottom of Exhibit 18–12, to the T account for Cash, at the top. Notice that net

Exhibit 18–12

Bard Company — T Account Analysis of Cash Flows for the Year Ended December 31, 19x9

Changes in balance sheet items are recorded in individual T accounts at the bottom of the exhibit. The corresponding entry to the T account for Cash, at the top, shows either a cash inflow or cash outflow.

Cash

Cash Inflows		Debit		Credit	Cash Outflows
From Operating Activities					
Net income	(1)	6,036	(9)	1,586	Decrease in accounts payable
Decrease in accounts receivable	(3)	1,578	(11)	58	Decrease in wages payable
Decrease in inventory	(4)	2,328			
Annual depreciation	(8)	1,865			
Increase in taxes payable	(10)	150			
Cash flows from operations		10,313			
From Investing Activities					
From sale of equipment	(6)	1,000	(5)	2,000	To increase investment in printing company shares
			(7)	3,769	To purchase new equipment
From Financing Activities					
Issue of additional common shares	(13)	200	(2)	4,000	To pay cash dividend
			(12)	2,000	Payment on bonds payable
				256	Decrease in cash balance

Accounts Receivable

	Debit		Credit
Balance	8,841		
		(3)	1,578
Balance	7,263		

Inventory

	Debit		Credit
Balance	15,322		
		(4)	2,328
Balance	12,994		

Investment in Shares of Printer

	Debit		Credit
Balance	4,000		
(5)	2,000		
Balance	6,000		

Plant and Equipment

	Debit		Credit
Balance	23,628		
(7)	3,769	(6)	1,619
Balance	25,778		

Accumulated Depreciation

	Debit		Credit
		Balance	10,139
(6)	619	(8)	1,865
		Balance	11,385

Accounts Payable

	Debit		Credit
		Balance	11,724
(9)	1,586		
		Balance	10,138

Taxes Payable

	Debit		Credit
		Balance	2,187
		(10)	150
		Balance	2,337

Wages Payable

	Debit		Credit
		Balance	952
(11)	58		
		Balance	894

Bonds Payable

	Debit		Credit
		Balance	12,000
(12)	2,000		
		Balance	10,000

Paid-in Capital

	Debit		Credit
		Balance	4,800
		(13)	200
		Balance	5,000

Retained Earnings

	Debit		Credit
		Balance	15,586
(2)	4,000	(1)	6,036
		Balance	17,622

earnings are recorded as a cash inflow from operating activities; dividends as a cash outflow from financing activities.

To continue the analysis, start at the top of the balance sheet and work down. Cash may be skipped, since this analysis concerns only the change in the cash balance, which will be explained by examining changes in all other accounts. Skipping cash, the next item on the balance sheet is accounts receivable, which declined by $1,578 during the year. Since collections on accounts receivable exceeded credit sales by $1,578, the cash collected from customers must have exceeded revenue by $1,578. Therefore, $1,578 is entered onto the credit, or right, side of the Accounts Receivable T account to reduce its balance (see entry **3**). That amount is also recorded on the left side of the Cash account, since it is a cash inflow. Also, an entry on the left is required to balance the entry on the right. If this were shown as a journal entry, it would appear as follows:

(3) Cash (inflow from operating activities)	1,578	
Accounts receivable		1,578
To summarize the effect of the net change in accounts receivable during 19x9		

The next item on the balance sheet is inventory, which decreased by $2,328 during the year. Reduced inventory means less cash was spent because purchases were less than the cost of goods sold. This increased the company's cash balance. That is, the reduced inventory has the effect of a cash inflow. Thus, $2,328 is entered onto the credit, or right, side of the Inventory account as well as onto the debit, or left, side of the Cash account (see entry **4**). A summary of the journal entry is as follows:

(4) Cash (inflow from operating activities)	2,328	
Inventory		2,328
To summarize the effect of the net change in inventory during 19x9		

Next on the balance sheet is a $2,000 increase in the investment in shares of a printing company affiliated with Bard. Without further information you must assume that Bard paid cash for the additional shares. This transaction is recorded in entry **5**.

Plant and equipment and accumulated depreciation were discussed in the previous section. Entry **6** shows the $1,619 decrease in the Plant and Equipment account, which resulted from selling the equipment in 19x9. On the equipment sold, annual depreciation had accumulated to $619 during the years Bard owned it. Therefore, an entry must be made to reduce the balance in accumulated depreciation by $619. (Remember that the Accumulated Depreciation account works in the opposite direction of an asset. An entry on the left *reduces* the account balance; an entry on the *right* increases it.) The $1,000 in cash received from the sale is entered as a cash inflow in the Cash account. Notice that the entry of the $1,000 balances the entry, as follows:

(6) Cash (inflow from investing activities)	1,000	
Accumulated depreciation	619	
Plant and equipment		1,619
To record sale of equipment during 19x9		

Entry 7 records the purchase of equipment worth $3,769. And entry 8 records annual depreciation expense, which is recorded as an adjustment to cash inflows from operating activities in the Cash account. Such recording is done because these expenses are a noncash deduction from income.

This completes the asset side of the balance sheet. The entries into liability accounts are similar to those for asset accounts, except liabilities are reduced by entries on the *left* and increased by entries on the *right*. Entries **9**, **10**, and **11** represent changes in current liabilities and are part of the operating activities. Entry **12** represents a $2,000 payment on long-term bonds and is financing activity. Notice entry **13** in the T accounts, a $200 increase in paid-in capital. Lacking information to the contrary, you must assume this increase resulted from the issue of additional common shares for cash. Thus, this issue is recorded as a cash inflow from financing activities in the Cash account at the top of Exhibit 18–12.

Dividing the Cash account into cash flows from operating activities, investing activities, and financing activities makes it easier to use the FASB format. Cash flows from operating activities, such as net income, accounts receivable, inventory, and current liabilities, are likely to recur. Annual depreciation is also a recurring item. Although the amounts in these accounts may change from year to year, as long as the organization continues to operate, it will generate net income (or a loss), accumulate depreciation, maintain accounts receivable and inventories, and incur current liabilities.

In contrast, although dividends are often paid each year, they need not be paid regularly. In fact, if a company's year was bad, they will probably not be paid. Likewise, changes in investments and in plant and equipment are made irregularly. Thus, these investments cannot be used to predict future changes in those amounts. Should a firm invest heavily in plant and equipment one year, there is no reason to assume it will make a similar investment the next. Nor are the issue of additional common shares and the payment of bonds payable an annual occurrence.

Generally, a cash flow item fitting into neither the investing nor financing category is a cash flow from operating activities. You can also think about cash flows from operating activities as being related to the income statement, whereas investing and financing activities are more closely related to the balance sheet.

Now examine the Cash account at the top of Exhibit 18–12. Notice that net income and annual depreciation are income statement items. Accounts receivable is directly related to sales revenue, another income statement item, and inventory is directly related to the cost of goods sold. Taxes payable is related to taxes expense. And accounts payable and wages payable are usually related to the purchase of inventory and the accrual of wages expense. Together, these items make up the normal operations summarized in the income statement. In

Exhibit 18–13
Statement of Cash Flows Completed from T Account Information, Indirect Method

Bard Company
Statement of Cash Flows
For the Year Ended December 31, 19x9

Cash flows from operating activities		
Net income	$ 6,036	
Annual depreciation	1,865	
Add (deduct) cash adjustments to net income		
Decrease in accounts receivable	1,578	
Decrease in inventory	2,328	
Decrease in accounts payable	(1,586)	
Increase in taxes payable	150	
Decrease in wages payable	(58)	
Cash flows from operating activities		$10,313
Cash flows from investing activities		
Purchase of new equipment	$(3,769)	
Proceeds from sale of equipment	1,000	
Purchase of additional shares of printing company	(2,000)	
Cash flows from investing activities		(4,769)
Cash flows from financing activities		
Dividends paid	$(4,000)	
Issue of additional common shares	200	
Payment of bonds payable	(2,000)	
Cash flows from financing activities		(5,800)
Increase (decrease) in cash		$ (256)

Proof

From balance sheet	
Ending cash	$5,341
Less beginning cash	5,597
Cash decrease	$ (256)

contrast, both the purchase and the sale of equipment are balance sheet items, as are investments in shares of an affiliated company, issuance of common shares, payment of dividends, and payment of bonds.

Once the T account analysis is finished, preparing the statement of cash flows is simple. Exhibit 18–13 shows Bard Company's statement of cash flows. This statement is simply a rearrangement of numbers in the Cash account, shown in Exhibit 18–12, according to the FASB format.

In this chapter you have learned to identify cash flows and present them in a statement of cash flows using the FASB format. You can prepare a simple statement using balance sheet data. A more complete statement requires analysis of activities in accounts, especially in retained earnings, plant and equipment, and accumulated depreciation. T accounts help in this analysis if the transactions are complex.

Solution to Self Test on page 854

	Cash inflow	Cash outflow
Purchasing equipment		✓
Paying accounts payable		✓
Borrowing from a bank	✓	
Earning a profit	✓	
Paying dividends		✓
Selling inventory for cash	✓	

Chapter Review

Review of Learning Objectives

1. **List the uses for a statement of cash flows.**
Management, outside shareholders, and long-term lenders are all concerned about how much cash an organization generates and how that cash is used. If an organization is to grow and repay long-term debts, it must generate cash from operations. If not, the organization will probably continue to borrow until additional borrowing becomes impossible. At that point the organization will stop operations. A statement of cash flows identifies the types and amounts of cash flows.

2. **Explain how to identify cash flows from the balance sheet.**
Cash inflows are transactions that increase available cash. Cash outflows are transactions that decrease available cash. Statements of cash flows are prepared by using two balance sheets, one at the start of the year and one at the end of the year. A statement of changes in retained earnings is also useful, since it shows net income and dividends paid during the year. Increases or decreases in any asset (other than cash), liabilities, or owners' equity reflect either cash inflows or outflows.

3. **Prepare a simple statement of cash flows using only balance sheet changes.**
The first step in preparing a simple statement of cash flows is to add two columns to the comparative balance sheets. These columns will represent changes in each asset or liability category. They will also indicate whether a change is an increase or a decrease. These increases and decreases must then be classified as either cash inflows or outflows and put into the appropriate part of the statement.

4. **Organize a statement of cash flows into the format preferred by the FASB.**
The FASB prefers statements that divide cash flows into three categories: (a) operating activities, (b) investing activities, and (c) financing activities. These categories match uses for the statement listed in FASB *Statement of Financial Standards No. 95* in 1987.
Investing activities include lending money and collecting on those loans as well as acquiring and selling long-term investments, such as shares in affiliated companies. Acquiring plant and equipment is also an investing activity. Financing activities include transactions with the company's shareholders, borrowing, and repayment of loans.
Operating activities include all transactions affecting cash except investment and financing activities. There are two ways of reporting cash flows from operating activities, the direct method and the indirect method. The direct method classifies cash flows from operations into cash received from customers, dividends received, cash paid to suppliers and employees, and interest and taxes paid. The indirect method starts with the organization's net income and makes four adjustments to find cash flows from operating activities. The only difference between the two methods is in the treatment of cash flows from operating activities. Financing and investing activities are treated the same regardless of which method is used.
Balance sheet changes are grouped into these three categories to produce a statement of cash flows in the FASB format.

5. **Use T accounts to double-check and refine a statement of cash flows.**
A cash flows statement reporting only changes in balance sheet items may fail to report certain offsetting changes. For example, the Retained Earnings account is affected by net income as well as dividends paid. Were only the change in retained earnings reported, dividend amounts would not be reported as a financing activity, and cash flows from operating activities would be understated. Similarly, equipment purchases are offset by any equipment sold during the year.
A way to find offsetting changes is to prepare a T account for a balance sheet account and make summary entries for transactions that occurred during the year. This is illustrated in Exhibit 18–11.

6. **Use T accounts to prepare a statement of cash flows.**
T accounts may be used to analyze transactions that affected one particular balance sheet account or all balance sheet accounts. When used for all accounts, the T account for cash contains all cash inflow and outflow items for the period. The statement of cash flows may then be prepared by arranging entries in the cash account into the statement of cash flows format. This process is illustrated for the Bard Company in Exhibit 18–12.

Review of Key Terms

Cash Cash and cash equivalents. Cash equivalents include United States Treasury bills, commercial paper, and money market funds.

Direct method (of reporting cash flows from operating activities) This method divides cash flows into cash received from customers, dividends received, cash payments to suppliers and employees, and cash payment for interest and taxes for the purpose of determining cash flows from operating activities.

Financing activities Raising capital from shareholders, paying dividends, and borrowing or repaying of long-term debt.

Indirect method (of reporting cash flows from operating activities) This method starts with the organization's net income based on accrual accounting, adds back annual depreciation and any other noncash expenses, and adjusts for changes in accounts receivable, inventories, and current liabilities to determine net income according to the cash basis of accounting, which is the amount of cash flows from the operating activities.

Investing activities Lending money and collecting loans, acquiring and selling securities that are not cash equivalents, and buying and selling plant and equipment.

Operating activities Delivering or producing goods for sale and providing services. These are mainly transactions related to dealing with customers. All transactions that are not investing or financing activities are operating activities.

Simple statement of cash flows A report that classifies the changes between the beginning and ending balance sheet amounts according to whether they represent cash inflows or cash outflows. It does not attempt to identify offsetting changes.

Statement of cash flows A report of the inflows and outflows of cash during a period. The FASB recommends classifying cash inflows and outflows into operating activities, investing activities, and financing activities.

T account method Analyzing cash flows by setting up T accounts for all balance sheet accounts and entering summary entries explaining the balance sheet changes. Helps ensure that no information affecting cash flows is omitted and that all offsetting items are discovered. See Exhibit 18–12.

Review Problem

Shore Company, whose management is somewhat confused by past variations in statements of cash flows, has asked you to prepare a statement of cash flows for 19x9. A comparative balance sheet for 19x8 and 19x9 is shown on page 878. A statement of income and retained earnings for the same years appears below.

Shore Company
Comparative Statements of Income and Retained Earnings
For the Years Ended December 31, 19x9, and 19x8

	19x9	19x8
Sales revenues	$21,451	$18,472
Expenses		
Cost of goods sold	$12,871	$11,098
Selling	3,558	2,946
Administrative	1,080	940
Depreciation	621	547
Income taxes, 30%	996	882
Total expenses	$19,126	$16,413
Net income	$ 2,325	$ 2,059
Retained earnings, beginning of year	5,722	4,353
Subtotal	$ 8,047	$ 6,412
Dividends	775	690
Retained earnings, year-end	$ 7,272	$ 5,722

Shore Company
Comparative Balance Sheets
December 31, 19x9, and 19x8

	19x9	19x8	Change increase (decrease)
Assets			
Current assets			
Cash	$3,229	$ 2,878	$ 351
Accounts receivable	4,331	4,852	(521)
Inventory	3,227	3,116	111
Total current assets	$10,787	$10,846	
Investment in shares of distributing company	$ 6,000	$ 5,000	1,000
Plant and equipment	$ 7,881	$ 7,344	537
Accumulated depreciation	3,286	2,868	418
Net plant and equipment	$ 4,595	$ 4,476	
Total assets	$21,382	$20,322	
Liabilities and shareholders' equity			
Current liabilities			
Accounts payable	$ 3,224	$ 3,251	(27)
Taxes payable	1,435	1,342	93
Other current liabilities	451	307	144
Total current liabilities	$ 5,110	$ 4,900	
Notes payable, due 20x9	5,000	5,500	(500)
Total liabilities	$10,110	$10,400	
Shareholders' equity			
Paid-in capital	$ 4,000	$ 4,200	(200)
Retained earnings	7,272	5,722	1,550
Total shareholders' equity	$11,272	$ 9,922	
Total liabilities and shareholders' equity	$21,382	$20,322	

During 19x9, Shore sold production equipment for $400 cash whose original cost was $603. Accumulated depreciation on this equipment was $203.

Required

1. Prepare a simple statement of cash flows using only data contained in the comparative balance sheet. Do not use the income statement.
2. Prepare three T accounts showing changes in retained earnings, plant and equipment, and accumulated depreciation. Using data from these three accounts, revise your statement of cash flows prepared in *1* above. Also, put the statement in the format recommended by the FASB. Use the indirect method of reporting cash flows from operating activities.

Solution to Review Problem

1.

Shore Company
Simple Statement of Cash Flows
For the Year Ended December 31, 19x9

Cash inflows		Cash outflows	
Owners' equity increases		Owners' equity decreases	
Retained earnings	$1,550	Paid-in capital	$ 200
Liability increases		Liability decreases	
Taxes payable	93	Accounts payable	27
Other current liabilities	144	Notes payable	500
Asset decreases		Asset increases	
Accounts receivable	521	Inventory	111
Accumulated depreciation	418	Shares of distributing company	1,000
		Plant and equipment	537
Total cash inflows	$2,726	Total cash outflows	$2,375

Proof

From statement of cash flows		From balance sheet	
Total cash inflows	$2,726	Ending cash	$3,229
Total cash outflows	2,375	Less beginning cash	2,878
Cash increase	$ 351	Cash increase	$ 351

Cash inflow less cash outflow equals the change in cash from the balance sheet.

2.

Shore Company — Retained Earnings

19x9 dividends	775	Beginning balance	5,722
		19x9 net income	2,325
		Ending balance	7,272

Plant and Equipment

Beginning balance	7,344	Cost of equipment sold	603
19x9 purchases	1,140		
Ending balance	7,881		

Accumulated Depreciation

Accumulated depreciation on equipment sold	203	Beginning balance	2,868
		19x9 annual depreciation expenses	621
		Ending balance	3,286

From these T accounts you can see that $2,325 in net income should be reported as a cash inflow and the $775 payment of dividends should be reported as a cash outflow. The cash outflow for an equipment purchase should be reported as $1,140 rather than $537. The sale of equipment should be reported as a $400 cash inflow ($603 cost of equipment minus $203 in accumulated depreciation). Finally, cash inflows from operating activities should be adjusted for $621 of depreciation rather than $418.

Once these changes are incorporated into the simple statement of cash flows shown in *1* above, the revised statement will appear as follows:

Shore Company
Statement of Cash Flows (FASB Format)
Indirect Method of Reporting Cash Flows from Operating Activities
For the Year Ended December 31, 19x9

Cash flows from operating activities		
Net income	$ 2,325	
Add (deduct) cash adjustments to net income		
Annual depreciation	621	
Decrease in accounts receivable	521	
Increase in inventory	(111)	
Decrease in accounts payable	(27)	
Increase in taxes payable	93	
Increase in other current liabilities	144	
Cash flows from operating activities		$ 3,566
Cash flows from investing activities		
Sale of equipment	$ 400	
Plant and equipment purchases	(1,140)	
Purchase of shares of distributing company	(1,000)	
Cash flows from investment activities		(1,740)
Cash flows from financing activities		
Payment on notes payable	$ (500)	
Decrease in paid-in capital	(200)	
Dividends paid	(775)	
Cash flows from financing activities		(1,475)
Increase in cash		$ 351

Proof

From balance sheet	
Ending cash balance	$3,229
Less beginning cash balance	2,878
Cash increase	$ 351

Chapter Assignments

Questions

1. (L.O. 1) Who are the external users of statements of cash flows? List three major uses they have for statements of cash flows.
2. (L.O. 1) Who are the internal users of statements of cash flows? List two major uses they have for a statement of cash flows.
3. (L.O. 4) Explain why dividing cash flows into operating activities, investing activities, and financing activities is useful to managers.
4. (L.O. 1) Before 1987 there were two possible definitions of funds. What were they?
5. (L.O. 2) Explain how you determine whether a change in inventory or accounts receivable is a cash inflow or a cash outflow.
6. (L.O. 5) What added information can be found from analysis of T accounts that is not evident from changes in balance sheet accounts?
7. (L.O. 2) Write the balance sheet equation showing only cash on the left side. Then, use it to show which changes increase or decrease an organization's cash balance.
8. (L.O. 4) Explain the terms *investing, financing activities,* and *operating activities* in relation to statements of cash flows.
9. (L.O. 5) Which financial statement is used to prepare simple statements of cash flows? What information is added by the statement of retained earnings?

Exercises

10. (L.O. 2) The table below shows some transactions for Bane Company for 19x3.

	Cash inflow	Cash outflow
a. Purchase of land for a parking lot	____	____
b. Payment of wages payable	____	____
c. Borrowing money; note payable in three years	____	____
d. Payment of insurance premium for the next year	____	____
e. Declaration and payment of dividends	____	____
f. Sale of inventory for cash	____	____

Required Show how each transaction affects Bane's cash by placing a check mark in the appropriate blank.

11. (L.O. 2) The table below shows some transactions for Date Company for 19x2.

	Cash inflow	Cash outflow
a. Collection of accounts receivable	_____	_____
b. Purchase of inventory	_____	_____
c. Repayment of six-month bank loan	_____	_____
d. Purchase of equipment	_____	_____
e. Prepayment of one year's rent	_____	_____
f. Sale of equipment	_____	_____

Required Show how each transaction affects Date's cash by placing a check mark in the appropriate blank.

12. (L.O. 4) Morton Motors has prepared an income statement for 19x5. Morton's president, Amos Morton, wants to know why the balance sheets show an increase in cash of only $6,000 for the year when net income for the year was $187,000. The income statement and beginning and ending balance sheets are as follows.

Morton Motors
Comparative Balance Sheets
December 31, 19x5, and 19x4
(000 omitted)

	19x5	19x4
Assets		
Current assets		
Cash	$ 41	$ 35
Accounts receivable	759	690
Inventory	1,602	1,493
Prepaid expenses	7	4
Total current assets	$2,409	$2,222
Plant and equipment (cost)	$ 924	$ 620
Accumulated depreciation	(508)	(322)
Net plant and equipment	$ 416	$ 298
Total assets	$2,825	$2,520
Equities		
Current liabilities		
Accounts payable	$ 400	$ 373
Income taxes payable	10	5
Total current liabilities	$ 410	$ 378
Long-term notes	1,083	997
Total liabilities	$1,493	$1,375
Common stock	$ 300	$ 300
Retained earnings	1,032	845
Owners' equity	$1,332	$1,145
Total equities	$2,825	$2,520

Morton Motors Income Statement For the Year Ended December 31, 19x5 (000 omitted)	
Sales revenues	$6,160
Expenses	
Cost of goods sold	$4,805
Salaries and commissions	546
Advertising	150
Other cash expenses	190
Depreciation	186
Total expenses	$5,877
Operating income	$ 283
Income taxes @ 34%	96
Net income	$ 187

Required

1. Prepare a cash flow statement for Morton Motors for 19x5. Use the direct method for calculating cash flows from operations.
2. Prepare a cash flow statement for Morton Motors for 19x5. Use the indirect method for calculating cash flows from operations.
(see Review Exercise 18–1)

13. (L.O. 4) The manager of Lilly Garden Center was happy to see that the company could pay its regular dividend in a year in which it had purchased quite a bit of equipment. Her controller suggested it was not that simple, pointing out that Lilly had to increase long-term loans during the year. Lilly's manager asked for a cash flow statement which would summarize what happened to the cash flow situation during 19x9.

Lilly Garden Center Income Statement For the Year Ended December 31, 19x9 (000 omitted)	
Sales revenues	$524
Expenses	
Cost of goods sold	$225
Salaries and commissions	88
Advertising	25
Other cash expenses	63
Depreciation	44
Total expenses	$445
Operating income	$ 79
Income taxes @ 25%	20
Net income	$ 59
Dividend	$ 20

Lilly Garden Center Comparative Balance Sheets December 31, 19x9, and 19x8 (000 omitted)	19x9	19x8
Assets		
Current assets		
Cash	$ 17	$ 14
Accounts receivable	65	56
Inventory	38	34
Prepaid expenses	1	3
Total current assets	$ 121	$ 107
Plant and equipment (cost)	$ 288	$ 205
Accumulated depreciation	(130)	(86)
Net plant and equipment	$ 158	$ 119
Total assets	$ 279	$ 226
Equities		
Current liabilities		
Accounts payable	$ 19	$ 17
Income taxes payable	2	2
Total current liabilities	$ 21	$ 19
Long-term notes	39	27
Total liabilities	$ 60	$ 46
Common stock	$ 35	$ 35
Retained earnings	184	145
Owners' equity	$ 219	$ 180
Total equities	$ 279	$ 226

Required

1. Prepare a cash flow statement for 19x9 in the FASB format using the indirect method of calculating cash flow from operations.
2. Prepare a cash flow statement for 19x9 in the FASB format using the direct method of calculating cash flow from operations.
3. Explain why it is useful to management to have the cash flow statement in three sections, showing whether Lilly generated enough cash flow from operations to cover its dividend and part of its equipment purchases.

14. (L.O. 4) Hakon Gift Shop is located in a center booth in a shopping center that attracts many shoppers. Hakon has been able to do well without any advertising. Results for 19x2 are given in the income statement and the comparative balance sheet shown on page 885.

Hakon Gift Shop
Income Statement
For the Year Ended December 31, 19x2
(000 omitted)

Sales revenues	$190
Expenses	
Cost of goods sold	$ 78
Salaries and commissions	35
Rent	10
Other cash expenses	8
Depreciation	6
Total expenses	$137
Operating income	$ 53
Income taxes @ 15%	8
Net income	$ 45
Dividend	$ 20

Hakon Gift Shop
Comparative Balance Sheets
December 31, 19x2, and 19x1

	19x2	19x1
Assets		
Current assets		
Cash	$ 8	$ 6
Accounts receivable	8	7
Inventory	26	22
Prepaid expenses	2	1
Total current assets	$ 44	$ 36
Plant and equipment (cost)	$ 66	$ 58
Accumulated depreciation	(30)	(24)
Net plant and equipment	$ 36	$ 34
Total assets	$ 80	$ 70
Equities		
Current liabilities		
Accounts payable	$ 6	$ 6
Income taxes payable	1	1
Total current liabilities	$ 7	$ 7
Long-term notes	24	39
Total liabilities	$ 31	$ 46
Common stock	$ 10	$ 10
Retained earnings	39	14
Owners' equity	$ 49	$ 24
Total equities	$ 80	$ 70

Required

1. Prepare a cash flow statement in the FASB format using the direct method of calculating cash flows from operations.
2. Prepare a cash flow statement in the FASB format using the indirect method of calculating cash flows from operations.

(see Review Exercise 18–1)

15. (L.O. 4) Lewis Schools has a solid place in its market. The management of Lewis is quite conservative and had a vigorous debate about paying the regular dividend in 19x4. They made a major investment in new microcomputers. The computer purchase and the dividend forced them to increase their long-term borrowing. Lewis Schools has a number of retired investors who depend on their dividends for living expenses. Management believed a cash flow statement would help them understand Lewis Schools' cash position.

Lewis Schools
Income Statement
For the Year Ended December 31, 19x4
(000 omitted)

Sales revenues	$907
Expenses	
Supplies	$100
Salaries and commissions	336
Advertising	30
Other cash expenses	127
Depreciation	65
Total expenses	$658
Operating income	$249
Income taxes @ 34%	85
Net income	$164
Dividend	$120

Lewis Schools
Comparative Balance Sheets
December 31, 19x4, and 19x3

	19x4	19x3
Assets		
Current assets		
Cash	$ 55	$ 45
Accounts receivable	40	22
Supplies inventory	33	26
Prepaid expenses	5	7
Total current assets	$ 133	$ 100
Plant and equipment (cost)	$ 771	$ 671
Accumulated depreciation	(347)	(282)
Net plant and equipment	$ 424	$ 389
Total assets	$ 557	$ 489

	19x4	19x3
Equities		
Current liabilities		
Accounts payable	$ 8	$ 7
Income taxes payable	9	12
Total current liabilities	$ 17	$ 19
Long-term notes	252	226
Total liabilities	$ 269	$ 245
Common stock	$ 100	$ 100
Retained earnings	188	144
Owners' equity	$ 288	$ 244
Total equities	$ 557	$ 489

Required

1. Prepare a cash flow statement in the FASB format using the direct method of calculating cash flows from operating activities.
2. Prepare a cash flow statement in the FASB format using the indirect method of calculating cash flows from operating activities.
3. Why did Lewis Schools have to increase long-term borrowing during 19x4?

16. (L.O. 4) The president of Mead Book Store was wondering if she should be concerned about the decrease in cash last year. The company accountant thought the cash flow statement would explain what had happened.

Mead Book Store Income Statement For the Year Ended December 31, 19x7 (000 omitted)	
Sales revenues	$944
Expenses	
Cost of goods sold	$746
Salaries and commissions	57
Advertising	14
Other cash expenses	28
Depreciation	13
Total expenses	$858
Operating income	$ 86
Income taxes @ 25%	22
Net income	$ 64
Dividend	$ 20

Mead Book Store Comparative Balance Sheets December 31, 19x7, and 19x6	19x7	19x6
Assets		
Current assets		
Cash	$ 5	$ 10
Accounts receivable	16	11
Inventory	186	164
Prepaid expenses	2	3
Total current assets	$ 209	$ 188
Plant and equipment (cost)	$ 142	$ 123
Accumulated depreciation	(102)	(89)
Net plant and equipment	$ 40	$ 34
Total assets	$ 249	$ 222
Equities		
Current liabilities		
Accounts payable	$ 62	$ 55
Income taxes payable	4	3
Total current liabilities	$ 66	$ 58
Long-term notes	115	140
Total liabilities	$ 181	$ 198
Common stock	$ 10	$ 10
Retained earnings	58	14
Owners' equity	$ 68	$ 24
Total equities	$ 249	$ 222

Required

1. Prepare a cash flow statement in the FASB format calculating operating cash flows by the direct method.
2. Prepare a cash flow statement in the FASB format calculating operating cash flows by the indirect method.
   (see Review Exercise 18–1)

17. (L.O. 5) Shown below are data on Lincoln Company. Assume the statement of retained earnings shows 19x5 dividends as $200 and net income as $942. Also assume that during the year equipment costing $1,500, with accumulated depreciation of $600, was sold for $900 cash.

Lincoln Company
Comparative Balance Sheets
December 31, 19x5, and 19x4

	19x5	19x4
Assets		
Current assets		
Cash	$ 321	$ 195
Accounts receivable	1,324	1,494
Inventory	1,406	2,236
Total current assets	$ 3,051	$ 3,925
Investment in shares of subsidiary	$ 5,000	$ 5,000
Plant and equipment	$19,561	$17,699
Accumulated depreciation	12,743	11,399
Net plant and equipment	$ 6,818	$ 6,300
Total assets	$14,869	$15,225
Liabilities and shareholders' equity		
Current liabilities		
Accounts payable	$ 1,634	$ 2,637
Taxes payable	345	500
Other current liabilities	189	129
Total current liabilities	$ 2,168	$ 3,266
Long-term notes payable	5,600	5,600
Total liabilities	$ 7,768	$ 8,866
Shareholders' equity		
Paid-in capital	$ 5,000	$ 5,000
Retained earnings	2,101	1,359
Total shareholders' equity	$ 7,101	$ 6,359
Total liabilities and shareholders' equity	$14,869	$15,225

Required Prepare T accounts for Retained Earnings, Plant and Equipment, and Accumulated Depreciation. (This exercise does not require you to prepare a statement of cash flows.)

18. (L.O. 5) Shown below are data on Truman Company. Assume the statement of retained earnings shows 19x6 dividends as $50 and net income as $1,971. Also assume that during the year equipment that cost $4,500, with accumulated depreciation of $3,700, was sold for $800 cash.

Truman Company
Comparative Balance Sheets
December 31, 19x6, and 19x5

	19x6	19x5
Assets		
Current assets		
Cash	$ 706	$ 429
Accounts receivable	2,913	3,287
Inventory	3,093	4,919
Total current assets	$ 6,712	$ 8,635
Investment in shares of subsidiary	$11,000	$11,000
Plant and equipment	$43,034	$38,938
Less accumulated depreciation	25,446	22,779
Net plant and equipment	$17,588	$16,159
Total assets	$35,300	$35,794
Liabilities and shareholders' equity		
Current liabilities		
Accounts payable	$ 3,595	$ 5,801
Taxes payable	759	1,100
Other current liabilities	416	284
Total current liabilities	$ 4,770	$ 7,185
Long-term notes payable	12,000	12,000
Total liabilities	$16,770	$19,185
Shareholders' equity		
Paid-in capital	$10,000	$10,000
Retained earnings	8,530	6,609
Total shareholders' equity	$18,530	$16,609
Total liabilities and shareholders' equity	$35,300	$35,794

Required Prepare T accounts for Retained Earnings, Plant and Equipment, and Accumulated Depreciation. (This exercise does not require you to prepare a statement of cash flows.)

19. (L.O. 4, 5) Shown below are data on Kennedy Company. Assume the statement of retained earnings shows 19x1 dividends as $100 and net income as $13. Also assume that during the year equipment that cost $3,000, with accumulated depreciation of $2,500, was sold for $500 cash.

Kennedy Company
Comparative Balance Sheets
December 31, 19x1, and 19x0

	19x1	19x0
Assets		
Current assets		
Cash	$ 459	$ 278
Accounts receivable	2,137	1,893
Inventory	3,197	2,010
Total current assets	$ 5,793	$ 4,181
Investment in shares of subsidiary	$ 7,000	$ 7,000
Plant and equipment	$25,310	$27,972
Accumulated depreciation	14,806	15,540
Net plant and equipment	$10,504	$12,432
Total assets	$23,297	$23,613
Liabilities and shareholders' equity		
Current liabilities		
Accounts payable	$ 2,771	$ 2,337
Taxes payable	715	493
Other current liabilities	185	270
Total current liabilities	$ 3,671	$ 3,100
Long-term notes payable	7,000	7,800
Total liabilities	$10,671	$10,900
Shareholders' equity		
Paid-in capital	$ 6,500	$ 6,500
Retained earnings	6,126	6,213
Total shareholders' equity	$12,626	$12,713
Total liabilities and shareholders' equity	$23,297	$23,613

Required

1. Prepare T accounts for Retained Earnings, Plant and Equipment, and Accumulated Depreciation.
2. Prepare a statement of cash flows following the FASB format. Use the indirect method of reporting cash flows from operating activities.

20. (L.O. 3, 6) Shown below are data on the Charles Company. Assume dividends for 19x9 were $1,000, and net income was $3,435. No equipment was sold.

Charles Company
Comparative Balance Sheets
December 31, 19x9, and 19x8

	19x9	19x8	Change	Direction of change
Assets				
Current assets				
Cash	$ 789	$ 823	$ (34)	Decrease
Accounts receivable	1,449	1,254	195	Increase
Inventory	5,621	3,497	2,124	Increase
Total current assets	$ 7,859	$5,574		
Investment in shares of AC Company stock	$ 6,000	$ 8,000	(2,000)	Decrease
Plant and equipment	$53,900	$48,600	5,300	Increase
Accumulated depreciation	25,800	21,100	4,700	Increase
Net plant and equipment	$28,100	$27,500		
Total assets	$41,959	$41,074		
Liabilities and shareholders' equity				
Current liabilities				
Accounts payable	$ 3,460	$ 2,990	470	Increase
Taxes payable	400	210	190	Increase
Other current liabilities	1,230	1,440	(210)	Decrease
Total current liabilities	$ 5,090	$ 4,640		
Bond payable	17,000	19,000	(2,000)	Decrease
Total liabilities	$22,090	$23,640		
Shareholders' equity				
Paid-in capital	$10,000	$10,000		
Retained earnings	9,869	7,434	2,435	Increase
Total shareholders' equity	$19,869	$17,434		
Total liabilities and shareholders' equity	$41,959	$41,074		

Required

1. Prepare a full T account analysis of Charles's cash flow similar to Exhibit 18–12.
2. Prepare a simple statement of cash flows.

21. (L.O. 4) Assume the same data as given in Exercise 20.

Required

Prepare a statement of cash flows in the format recommended by the FASB. Use the indirect method of reporting cash flows from operating activities.

22. (L.O. 3, 6) Shown below are data on Shirley Company. Assume dividends for 19x9 were $3,500, and net income was $5,994.

Shirley Company
Comparative Balance Sheets
December 31, 19x9, and 19x8

	19x9	19x8	Change	Direction of change
Assets				
Current assets				
Cash	$ 789	$ 625	$ 164	Increase
Accounts receivable	2,997	2,554	443	Increase
Inventory	5,772	5,873	(101)	Decrease
Total current assets	$ 9,558	$ 9,052		
Investment in shares of subsidiary	$10,500	$ 7,000	3,500	Increase
Plant and equipment	$36,644	$34,700	1,944	Increase
Accumulated depreciation	11,110	8,220	2,890	Increase
Net plant and equipment	$25,534	$26,480		
Total assets	$45,592	$42,532		
Liabilities and shareholders' equity				
Current liabilities				
Accounts payable	$ 4,020	$ 4,435	(415)	Decrease
Taxes payable	530	500	30	Increase
Other current liabilities	95	144	(49)	Decrease
Total current liabilities	$ 4,645	$ 5,079		
Long-term notes payable	$ 7,000	$ 8,000	(1,000)	Decrease
Total liabilities	$11,645	$13,079		
Shareholders' equity				
Paid-in capital	$11,000	$ 9,000	2,000	Increase
Retained earnings	22,947	20,453	2,494	Increase
Total shareholders' equity	$33,947	$29,453		
Total liabilities and shareholders' equity	$45,592	$42,532		

Required

1. Assume that equipment with an original cost of $7,000 and $7,000 in accumulated depreciation was disposed of with no salvage value. Prepare a T account analysis of Shirley's cash flows similar to that shown in Exhibit 18–12.
2. Prepare a simple statement of cash flows.

23. (L.O. 4, 5) Assume the same data as given in Exercise 22. Also assume that equipment that cost $7,000 with $7,000 accumulated depreciation was disposed of during 19x9 with no salvage value.

Required

Prepare a statement of cash flows for Shirley Company for 19x9 using the format recommended by the FASB. Use the indirect method of reporting cash flows from operating activities.

24. **(L.O. 4)** The income statement and comparative balance sheets for Hamlin, Inc., are shown below. Hamlin paid no dividends during the year. No equipment was sold in 19x8.

Hamlin, Inc.
Comparative Balance Sheets
December 31, 19x8, and 19x7

	19x8	19x7
Assets		
Current assets		
Cash	$ 8,000	$ 10,000
Accounts receivable	22,000	21,000
Inventory	18,000	19,000
Total current assets	$ 48,000	$ 50,000
Plant and equipment	$148,000	$139,000
Accumulated depreciation	75,000	68,000
Net plant and equipment	$ 73,000	$ 71,000
Total assets	$121,000	$121,000
Liabilities and shareholders' equity		
Current liabilities		
Accounts payable	$ 15,300	$ 15,779
Wages payable	2,383	2,084
Taxes payable	3,145	2,385
Total current liabilities	$ 20,828	$ 20,248
Long-term notes payable	-0-	25,000
Total liabilities	$ 20,828	$ 45,248
Shareholders' equity		
Paid-in capital	$ 20,000	$ 20,000
Retained earnings	80,172	55,752
Total shareholders' equity	$100,172	$ 75,752
Total liabilities and shareholders' equity	$121,000	$121,000

Hamlin, Inc.
Income Statement
For the Year Ended December 31, 19x8

Sales revenues	$200,000
Expenses	
Cost of goods sold	$ 90,000
Selling	26,000
Administrative	30,000
Depreciation	7,000
Interest	10,000
Income taxes	12,580
Total expenses	$175,580
Net income	$ 24,420

Required Prepare a statement of cash flows for Hamlin, Inc., for 19x8 using the FASB recommended format and the direct method of calculating cash flows from operating activities.

25. (L.O. 4) The income statement and comparative balance sheets for Catherine Company are shown on page 896 and below. In addition to the data in the statements, records show that dividends of $10,000 were paid during the year. During the year, equipment that cost $5,000, with accumulated depreciation of $5,000, was disposed of with no salvage value.

Catherine Company
Comparative Balance Sheets
December 31, 19x7, and 19x6

	19x7	19x6
Assets		
Current assets		
Cash	$ 12,000	$ 10,000
Accounts receivable	33,000	29,000
Inventory	27,000	24,000
Total current assets	$ 72,000	$ 63,000
Plant and equipment	$188,000	$165,000
Accumulated depreciation	70,000	64,000
Net plant and equipment	$118,000	$101,000
Total assets	$190,000	$164,000
Liabilities and shareholders' equity		
Current liabilities		
Accounts payable	$ 22,950	$ 37,031
Wages payable	3,575	2,084
Taxes payable	4,675	2,385
Total current liabilities	$ 31,200	$ 41,500
Long-term notes payable	10,000	-0-
Total liabilities	$ 41,200	$ 41,500
Shareholders' equity		
Paid-in capital	$ 30,000	$ 30,000
Retained earnings	118,800	92,500
Total shareholders' equity	$148,800	$122,500
Total liabilities and shareholders' equity	$190,000	$164,000

Catherine Company Income Statement For the Year Ended December 31, 19x7		
Sales revenues		$300,000
Expenses		
Cost of goods sold	$135,000	
Selling	39,000	
Administrative	45,000	
Depreciation	11,000	
Interest	15,000	
Income taxes	18,700	
Total expenses		$263,700
Net income		$ 36,300

Required Prepare a statement of cash flows for Catherine Company for 19x7 using the FASB recommended format and the direct method of calculating cash flows from operating activities.

26. **(L.O. 4)** The income statement and comparative balance sheets for Bethel, Inc., are shown on the following page. In addition to the data in the statements, records show that dividends of $15,000 were paid during the year. During the year, equipment that cost $18,000, with accumulated depreciation of $18,000, was disposed of with no salvage value.

Bethel, Inc.
Comparative Balance Sheets
December 31, 19x6, and 19x5

	19x6	19x5
Assets		
Current assets		
Cash	$ 16,000	$ 10,000
Accounts receivable	44,000	39,000
Inventory	36,800	34,000
Total current assets	$ 96,800	$ 83,000
Plant and equipment	$214,000	$200,000
Accumulated depreciation	85,000	77,000
Net plant and equipment	$129,000	$123,000
Total assets	$225,800	$206,000
Liabilities and shareholders' equity		
Current liabilities		
Accounts payable	$ 31,280	$ 27,208
Wages payable	4,858	4,300
Taxes payable	5,100	4,530
Total current liabilities	$ 41,238	$ 36,038
Long-term notes payable	10,000	20,000
Total liabilities	$ 51,238	$ 56,038
Shareholders' equity		
Paid-in capital	$ 40,000	$ 40,000
Retained earnings	134,562	109,962
Total shareholders' equity	$174,562	$149,962
Total liabilities and shareholders' equity	$225,800	$206,000

Bethel, Inc.
Income Statement
For the Year Ended December 31, 19x6

Sales revenues	$400,000
Expenses	
Cost of goods sold	$184,000
Selling	56,000
Administrative	58,000
Depreciation	26,000
Interest	16,000
Income taxes	20,400
Total expenses	$360,400
Net income	$ 39,600

Required Prepare a statement of cash flows for Bethel, Inc., for 19x6 using the FASB recommended format and the direct method of calculating cash flows from operating activities.

27. (L.O. 4) The income statement and comparative balance sheets for Norman Company are shown below. In addition to the data in the statements, records show that dividends of $12,000 were paid during the year. During the year, equipment that cost $13,000, with accumulated depreciation of $9,000, was sold for $4,000.

Norman Company
Comparative Balance Sheets
December 31, 19x4, and 19x3

	19x4	19x3
Assets		
Current assets		
Cash	$ 10,000	$ 14,000
Accounts receivable	27,500	26,000
Inventory	24,500	24,000
Total current assets	$ 62,000	$ 64,000
Plant and equipment	$113,000	$ 98,000
Accumulated depreciation	45,000	44,000
Net plant and equipment	$ 68,000	$ 54,000
Total assets	$130,000	$118,000
Liabilities and shareholders' equity		
Current liabilities		
Accounts payable	$ 20,825	$ 13,772
Wages payable	3,427	4,300
Taxes payable	2,550	4,530
Total current liabilities	$ 26,802	$ 22,602
Shareholders' equity		
Paid-in capital	$ 25,000	$ 25,000
Retained earnings	78,198	70,398
Total shareholders' equity	$103,198	$ 95,398
Total liabilities and shareholders' equity	$130,000	$118,000

Norman Company
Income Statement
For the Year Ended December 31, 19x4

Sales revenues	$250,000
Expenses	
Cost of goods sold	$122,500
Selling	42,500
Administrative	40,000
Depreciation	10,000
Interest	5,000
Income taxes	10,200
Total expenses	$230,200
Net income	$ 19,800

Required Prepare a statement of cash flows for Norman Company for 19x4 using the FASB recommended format and the direct method of calculating cash flows from operating activities.

28. (L.O. 4) The income statement and comparative balance sheets for Ramsey, Inc., are shown on page 900 and below. Ramsey paid no dividends during the year. During 19x3, equipment that cost $11,000, with accumulated depreciation of $7,000, was sold for $4,000.

Ramsey, Inc.
Comparative Balance Sheets
December 31, 19x3, and 19x2

	19x3	19x2
Assets		
Current assets		
Cash	$ 9,000	$ 8,000
Accounts receivable	16,500	16,000
Inventory	14,700	14,000
Total current assets	$ 40,200	$ 38,000
Plant and equipment	$134,000	$118,000
Accumulated depreciation	48,000	44,000
Net plant and equipment	$ 86,000	$ 74,000
Total assets	$126,200	$112,000
Liabilities and shareholders' equity		
Current liabilities		
Accounts payable	$ 12,495	$ 16,836
Wages payable	2,056	1,900
Taxes payable	1,105	1,300
Total current liabilities	$ 15,656	$ 20,036
Long-term notes payable	10,000	-0-
Total liabilities	$ 25,656	$ 20,036
Shareholders' equity		
Paid-in capital	$ 15,000	$ 15,000
Retained earnings	85,544	76,964
Total shareholders' equity	$100,544	$ 91,964
Total liabilities and shareholders' equity	$126,200	$112,000

Ramsey, Inc. Income Statement For the Year Ended December 31, 19x3	
Sales revenues	$150,000
Expenses	
Cost of goods sold	$ 73,500
Selling	25,500
Administrative	24,000
Depreciation	11,000
Interest	3,000
Income taxes	4,420
Total expenses	$141,420
Net income	$ 8,580

Required Prepare a statement of cash flows for Ramsey, Inc., for 19x3 using the FASB recommended format and the direct method of calculating cash flows from operating activities.

Problems

29. (L.O. 3, 6) Shown below are data on Thomas Company. Assume dividends for 19x9 were $100; and net income was $62.

Thomas Company
Comparative Balance Sheets
December 31, 19x9, and 19x8

	19x9	19x8	Change	Direction of change
Assets				
Current assets				
Cash	$ 541	$ 345	$ 196	Increase
Accounts receivable	2,219	2,453	(234)	Decrease
Inventory	2,348	3,664	(1,316)	Decrease
Total current assets	$ 5,108	$ 6,462		
Investment in shares of subsidiary	$ -0-	$ 5,000	(5,000)	Decrease
Plant and equipment	$32,610	$32,610		
Accumulated depreciation	21,110	18,220	2,890	Increase
Net plant and equipment	$11,500	$14,390		
Total assets	$16,608	$25,852		
Liabilities and shareholders' equity				
Current liabilities				
Accounts payable	$ 2,720	$ 4,465	(1,745)	Decrease
Taxes payable	-0-	500	(500)	Decrease
Other current liabilities	278	239	39	Increase
Total current liabilities	$ 2,998	$ 5,204		
Long-term notes payable	5,000	12,000	(7,000)	Decrease
Total liabilities	$ 7,998	$17,204		
Shareholders' equity				
Paid-in capital	$ 5,000	$ 5,000		
Retained earnings	3,610	3,648	(38)	Decrease
Total shareholders' equity	$ 8,610	$ 8,648		
Total liabilities and shareholders' equity	$16,608	$25,852		

Required

1. Assume that equipment that cost $5,000, with $3,700 in accumulated depreciation, was sold for $1,300. Prepare a full T account analysis of Thomas's cash flows similar to that shown in Exhibit 18–11.
2. Prepare a simple statement of cash flows.

(AICPA)

30. (L.O. 3, 4, 6) Shown below are data on Jenna Company. Assume dividends for 19x9 were $2,000.

Jenna Company Comparative Balance Sheets December 31, 19x9, and 19x8	19x9	19x8
Assets		
Current assets		
Cash	$ 544	$ 956
Accounts receivable	4,003	3,455
Inventory	5,334	4,866
Total current assets	$ 9,881	$ 9,277
Investment in shares of subsidiary	$10,000	$ 9,000
Plant and equipment	$54,770	$44,695
Less accumulated depreciation	14,110	9,335
Net plant and equipment	$40,660	$35,360
Total assets	$60,541	$53,637
Liabilities and shareholders' equity		
Current liabilities		
Accounts payable	$ 6,228	$ 5,773
Taxes payable	1,200	500
Other current liabilities	325	144
Total current liabilities	$ 7,753	$ 6,417
Long-term notes payable	14,000	15,000
Total liabilities	$21,753	$21,417
Shareholders' equity		
Paid-in capital	$15,000	$12,000
Retained earnings	23,788	20,220
Total shareholders' equity	$38,788	$32,220
Total liabilities and shareholders' equity	$60,541	$53,637

Required

1. Assume that during the year equipment that cost $17,000, with accumulated depreciation of $14,000, was sold for $3,000. Prepare a full T account analysis of Jenna's cash flow similar to that shown in Exhibit 18–12. (You are not required to prepare a cash flow statement for this part—only the T accounts.)
2. Prepare a simple statement of cash flows.
3. During the year, equipment that cost $17,000, with accumulated depreciation of $14,000, was sold for $3,000. Prepare a statement of cash flows. Use the format recommended by the FASB and use the indirect method of reporting cash flows from operating activities.

31. (L.O. 4) The income statement and comparative balance sheets for Mac Company are shown opposite. In addition to the data in the statements, records show that dividends of $3,000 were paid during the year. During the year, equipment that cost $10,000, with accumulated depreciation of $8,000, was sold for $2,000.

Mac Company
Comparative Balance Sheets
December 31, 19x5, and 19x4

	19x5	19x4
Assets		
Current assets		
Cash	$ 7,530	$ 6,678
Accounts receivable	15,813	12,973
Inventory	15,437	15,488
Total current assets	$ 38,780	$ 35,139
Investment in shares of subsidary	$ 45,000	$ 35,000
Plant and equipment	$105,700	$101,300
Accumulated depreciation	32,200	26,150
Net plant and equipment	$ 73,500	$ 75,150
Total assets	$157,280	$145,289
Liabilities and shareholders' equity		
Current liabilities		
Accounts payable	$ 13,121	$ 9,784
Wages payable	1,921	2,084
Taxes payable	2,006	2,385
Total current liabilities	$ 17,048	$ 14,253
Long-term notes payable	30,120	33,500
Total liabilities	$ 47,168	$ 47,753
Shareholders' equity		
Paid-in capital	$ 15,000	$ 15,000
Retained earnings	95,112	82,536
Total shareholders' equity	$110,112	$ 97,536
Total liabilities and shareholders' equity	$157,280	$145,289

Mac Company
Income Statement
For the Year Ended December 31, 19x5

Sales revenues	$150,600
Expenses	
Cost of goods sold	$ 61,746
Selling	27,108
Administrative	21,084
Depreciation	14,050
Interest	3,012
Income taxes	8,024
Total expenses	$135,024
Net income	$ 15,576

Required Prepare a statement of cash flows for Mac Company for 19x5 using the FASB recommended format and the direct method of calculating cash flows from operating activities.

August Company
Comparative Balance Sheets
December 31, 19x2, and 19x1

	19x2	19x1
Assets		
Current assets		
Cash	$ 20,417	$ 16,678
Accounts receivable	42,877	44,332
Inventory	61,253	61,898
Total current assets	$124,547	$122,908
Investment in shares of subsidiary	$150,000	$130,000
Plant and equipment	$309,900	$278,000
Accumulated depreciation	123,400	98,500
Net plant and equipment	$186,500	$179,500
Total assets	$461,047	$432,408
Liabilities and shareholders' equity		
Current liabilities		
Accounts payable	$ 52,065	$ 47,482
Wages payable	4,305	4,900
Taxes payable	3,883	2,385
Total current liabilities	$ 60,253	$ 54,767
Long-term notes payable	81,670	88,670
Total liabilities	$141,923	$143,437
Shareholders' equity		
Paid-in capital	$ 45,000	$ 40,000
Retained earnings	274,124	248,971
Total shareholders' equity	$319,124	$288,971
Total liabilities and shareholders' equity	$461,047	$432,408

August Company
Income Statement
For the Year Ended December 31, 19x2

Sales revenues	$408,350
Expenses	
Cost of goods sold	$245,010
Selling	53,086
Administrative	24,501
Depreciation	31,900
Interest	8,167
Income taxes	15,533
Total expenses	$378,197
Net income	$ 30,153

32. (L.O. 4) The income statement and comparative balance sheets for August Company are shown on page 904. In addition to the data in the statements, records show that dividends of $5,000 were paid during the year. During the year, equipment that cost $13,000, with accumulated depreciation of $7,000, was sold for $6,000.

Required Prepare a statement of cash flows for August Company for 19x2 using the FASB recommended format and the direct method of calculating cash flows from operating activities.

33. (L.O. 4) The income statement and comparative balance sheets for Carleton Company are as follows. In addition to the data in the statements, records show that dividends of $15,000 were paid during the year. During the year, equipment that cost $40,000 and with accumulated depreciation of $30,000 was sold for $10,000.

Carleton Company
Comparative Balance Sheets
December 31, 19x4, and 19x3

	19x4	19x3
Assets		
Current assets		
Cash	$ 12,030	$ 15,700
Accounts receivable	33,083	30,451
Inventory	26,466	34,692
Total current assets	$ 71,579	$ 80,843
Investment in shares of subsidiary	$ 75,000	$ 50,000
Plant and equipment	$238,600	$232,690
Accumulated depreciation	78,400	84,600
Net plant and equipment	$160,200	$148,090
Total assets	$306,779	$278,933
Liabilities and shareholders' equity		
Current liabilities		
Accounts payable	$ 22,496	$ 9,871
Wages payable	3,647	2,084
Taxes payable	4,112	2,385
Total current liabilities	$ 30,255	$ 14,340
Long-term notes payable	90,225	95,225
Total liabilities	$120,480	$109,565
Shareholders' equity		
Paid-in capital	$ 60,000	$ 60,000
Retained earnings	126,299	109,368
Total shareholders' equity	$186,299	$169,368
Total liabilities and shareholders' equity	$306,779	$278,933

Carleton Company Income Statement For the Year Ended December 31, 19x4	
Sales revenues	$300,751
Expenses	
Cost of goods sold	$132,330
Selling	36,090
Administrative	51,128
Depreciation	23,800
Interest	9,023
Income taxes	16,449
Total expenses	$268,820
Net income	$ 31,931

Required Prepare a statement of cash flows for Carleton Company for 19x4 using the FASB recommended format and the direct method of calculating cash flows from operating activities.

34. (L.O. 4) The income statement and comparative balance sheets for Norpine Company are shown opposite. In addition to the data in the statements, records show that dividends of $12,000 were paid during the year. During the year, equipment costing $32,000 and with accumulated depreciation of $21,000 was sold for $11,000.

Required Prepare a statement of cash flows for Norpine Company for 19x9 using the FASB recommended format and the direct method of calculating cash flows from operating activities.

35. (L.O. 4) Matthews Furniture Store is a full-service store. To improve delivery service, they have just purchased new equipment. They replaced equipment costing $85,000, and sold the old equipment for $5,000. Its accumulated depreciation was $55,000. Matthews' income statement for 19x8 and the beginning and ending balance sheets are shown on page 908.

Required

1. Prepare a cash flow statement in the FASB format using the direct method of calculating operating cash flows.
2. Prepare a cash flow statement in the FASB format using the indirect method of calculating operating cash flows.
(see Review Exercise 18–1)

36. (L.O. 4) The owner of Medan Grocery Store had just received the preliminary income statement and balance sheet at the end of 19x6. He was concerned that the long-term borrowing had increased by more than $400,000 during the year. The company had paid its regular $200,000 dividend. It had also replaced some equipment which had cost $45,000. This equipment was sold for $8,000 and had accumulated depreciation at the time of sale of $35,000. He felt that a cash flow statement would help him see if cash flows from operations were enough to cover the dividend and the small increase in cash balance. The income statement and balance sheets are on page 909.

Required

1. Prepare a cash flow statement in the FASB format using the direct method of calculating funds from operations.
2. Prepare a short explanation for the owner of the causes of the increased borrowing.
(see Review Exercise 18–1)

Norpine Company
Comparative Balance Sheets
December 31, 19x9, and 19x8

	19x9	19x8
Assets		
Current assets		
Cash	$ 12,295	$ 16,678
Accounts receivable	25,820	24,887
Inventory	29,508	35,112
Total current assets	$ 67,623	$ 76,677
Investment in shares of subsidiary	$ -0-	$ 20,000
Plant and equipment	$550,300	$525,700
Accumulated depreciation	221,600	201,670
Net plant and equipment	$328,700	$324,030
Total assets	$396,323	$420,707
Liabilities and shareholders' equity		
Current liabilities		
Accounts payable	$ 25,082	$ 33,825
Wages payable	2,346	4,900
Taxes payable	3,001	2,385
Total current liabilities	$ 30,429	$ 41,110
Long-term notes payable	75,000	100,000
Total liabilities	$105,429	$141,110
Shareholders' equity		
Paid-in capital	$ 50,000	$ 50,000
Retained earnings	240,894	229,597
Total shareholders' equity	$290,894	$279,597
Total liabilities and shareholders' equity	$396,323	$420,707

Norpine Company
Income Statement
For the Year Ended December 31, 19x4

Sales revenues	$245,900
Expenses	
Cost of goods sold	$118,032
Selling	31,967
Administrative	14,754
Depreciation	40,930
Interest	4,918
Income taxes	12,002
Total expenses	$222,603
Net income	$ 23,297

35.

Matthews Furniture Store
Income Statement
For the Year Ended December 31, 19x8
(000 omitted)

Sales revenues	$1,117
Expenses	
Cost of goods sold	$ 570
Salaries and commissions	292
Other cash expenses	115
Depreciation	33
Total expenses	$1,010
Operating income	$ 107
Loss on disposal of equipment	25
Income before income tax	$ 82
Income taxes @ 34%	28
Net income	$ 54
Dividend	$ 10

Matthew's Furniture Store
Comparative Balance Sheets
December 31, 19x8, and 19x7

	19x8	19x7
Assets		
Current assets		
Cash	$ 18	$ 34
Accounts receivable	110	89
Inventory	142	119
Prepaid expenses	7	5
Total current assets	$ 277	$ 247
Plant and equipment (cost)	$ 290	$ 233
Accumulated depreciation	(99)	(121)
Net plant and equipment	$ 191	$ 112
Total assets	$ 468	$ 359
Equities		
Current liabilities		
Accounts payable	$ 47	$ 40
Income taxes payable	5	3
Total current liabilities	$ 52	$ 43
Long-term notes	177	121
Total liabilities	$ 229	$ 164
Common stock	$ 100	$ 100
Retained earnings	139	95
Owners' equity	$ 239	$ 195
Total equities	$ 468	$ 359

36.

Medan Grocery Store
Income Statement
For the Year Ended December 31, 19x6
(000 omitted)

Sales revenues	$6,768
Expenses	
Cost of goods sold	$5,414
Salaries	282
Utilities	118
Other expenses	253
Loss on disposal of equipment	2
Depreciation	180
Total expenses	$6,249
Operating income	$ 519
Income taxes @ 34%	176
Net income	$ 343

Medan Grocery Store
Comparative Balance Sheets
December 31, 19x6, and 19x5
(000 omitted)

	19x6	19x5
Assets		
Current assets		
Cash	$ 80	$ 45
Accounts receivable	-0-	-0-
Inventory	1,354	1,142
Prepaid expenses	18	15
Total current assets	$1,452	$1,202
Plant and equipment (cost)	$1,760	$1,241
Accumulated depreciation	(790)	(645)
Net plant and equipment	$ 970	$ 596
Total assets	$2,422	$1,798
Equities		
Current liabilities		
Accounts payable	$ 451	$ 381
Income taxes payable	32	24
Total current liabilities	$ 483	$ 405
Long-term notes	1,401	998
Total liabilities	$1,884	$1,403
Common stock	$ 100	$ 100
Retained earnings	438	295
Owners' equity	$ 538	$ 395
Total equities	$2,422	$1,798

Dilly Legal Services
Income Statement
For the Year Ended December 31, 19x8
(000 omitted)

Sales revenues	$774
Expenses	
Supplies	$101
Salaries	228
Utilities	47
Other expenses	146
Loss on disposal of equipment	4
Depreciation	56
Total expenses	$582
Operating income	$192
Income taxes @ 34%	65
Net income	$127
Dividend declared and paid	50
Addition to retained earnings	$ 77

Dilly Legal Services
Comparative Balance Sheets
December 31, 19x8, and 19x7

	19x8	19x7
Assets		
Current assets		
Cash	$ 15	$ 25
Accounts receivable	117	106
Supplies inventory	25	18
Prepaid expenses	16	12
Total current assets	$ 173	$ 161
Plant and equipment (cost)	$ 271	$ 142
Accumulated depreciation	(115)	(74)
Net plant and equipment	$ 156	$ 68
Total assets	$ 329	$ 229
Equities		
Current liabilities		
Accounts payable	$ 8	$ 6
Income taxes payable	12	9
Total current liabilities	$ 20	$ 15
Long-term notes	23	5
Total liabilities	$ 43	$ 20
Common stock	$ 115	$ 115
Retained earnings	171	94
Owners' equity	$ 286	$ 209
Total equities	$ 329	$ 229

37. (L.O. 4) Dilly Legal Services opened a new office during 19x8. Normally, Dilly's operating cash flows were enough to cover equipment purchases and the small dividend paid to the shareholders. With the higher than normal investment resulting from the new office, Dilly had to increase its long-term debt and reduce its cash balance. The owner was wondering how best to explain the changes in the company's cash position. She decided that she needed a cash flow statement, but wasn't sure whether to use the direct or indirect method of calculating cash flow from operating activities. During the year, Dilly sold equipment that cost $25,000 for $6,000. At the time of sale, the equipment's accumulated depreciation was $15,000. The income statement and balance sheets are shown opposite.

Required

1. Prepare a cash flow statement in the FASB format using the direct method of calculating operating cash flows.
2. Prepare a cash flow statement in the FASB format using the indirect method of calculating operating cash flows.
3. How close did Dilly come to financing its investing activities from operating cash flows? If they operate at the same level in 19x9 and have to make investments of $80,000 in equipment, should they be able to return their cash balance to $25,000?

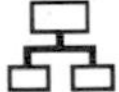

38. (L.O. 4) The statement of cash flows presented below was adapted from the statement of a major company, called here XXX Company. It was prepared before 1987 and therefore did not follow the FASB recommended format exactly. The data given are in millions of dollars.

XXX Company
Statement of Cash Flows
For the Years Ended December 31, 19x4, and 19x3

	19x4	19x3
Cash provided by (used for) operations		
Net earnings	$ 6.9	$ 224.9
Noncash items affecting earnings		
Depreciation	281.3	323.8
Other items	66.4	174.2
Cash provided by operations	$ 354.6	$ 722.9
Cash provided by (used for) financing		
Increase in accounts payable and accrued liabilities	$ 63.3	$ (47.9)
Increase in short-term debt	1,124.6	(63.7)
Preferred and common share dividends	(87.7)	(31.0)
Cash provided by financing	$ 1,100.2	$(142.6)
Cash used for (provided by) investments		
Increase in accounts receivable	$ 1,036.5	$ 120.5
Increase in inventories	208.0	(61.8)
Purchase of plant and equipment	274.0	378.0
Increase in investment in subsidiary	295.0	43.2
Marketable securities	(274.7)	177.6
Cash used for investments	$ 1,538.8	$ 657.5
Decrease in cash	$ (84.0)	$ (77.2)

Required

1. Redo the 19x4 statement in the format recommended by the FASB using the indirect method of calculating cash flows from operations.
2. What was the company's most important source of funds in 19x4? In 19x3?
3. Is the change in this source a good sign? Explain briefly.

Case 1
Dart & Kraft, Inc. (L.O. 1, 4)

The 1985 annual report for Dart & Kraft, Inc., included the Consolidated Statement of Changes in Financial Position shown below.

Consolidated Statement of Changes in Financial Position
Dart & Kraft, Inc. and Subsidiaries

(In millions) Years Ended	Dec. 28, 1985	Dec. 29, 1984	Dec. 31, 1983
Cash provided from operations			
Net income	$ 466.1	$ 455.8	$ 435.1
Items not resulting in cash flow:			
Depreciation and amortization	191.4	182.2	178.6
Deferred income taxes	49.2	42.6	58.9
(Increase) decrease in working capital (except cash, temporary investments and borrowings) adjusted for translation	52.3	(98.2)	245.8
Cash provided from operations	759.0	582.4	918.4
Dividends paid	(219.3)	(208.5)	(210.4)
Investments			
Capital expenditures	(261.9)	(268.7)	(211.9)
Book value of properties sold	25.0	44.8	42.1
Business acquisitions and divestitures, net	(82.1)	(34.9)	(2.5)
(Increase) decrease in investments and long-term receivables	(70.2)	35.5	(41.8)
(Increase) decrease in prepaid employee benefit and pension costs	13.0	6.9	(86.1)
Other	7.6	(2.3)	(11.1)
Cash used for investments	(368.6)	(218.7)	(311.3)
Financing			
Purchase of treasury stock	–	(531.7)	–
Decrease in long-term debt	(69.6)	(34.3)	(55.9)
Increase (decrease) in short-term borrowings	(143.4)	162.7	6.2
Cash used for financing	(213.0)	(403.3)	(49.7)
Increase (decrease) in cash and temporary investments	$(41.9)	$(248.1)	$ 347.0

See Notes to the Consolidated Financial Statements.

Used by permission of Kraft, Inc.

Required

1. How must Dart & Kraft's 1985 statement be changed to conform to the FASB's 1987 format recommendations?
2. What was Dart & Kraft's most important source of funds in 1985?
3. Was enough cash generated from operating activities in 1985 to cover investments and dividends? If so, is that a good sign? Explain. What happened to the balance of cash inflow?

Consolidated Statement of Cash Flows
Hewlett-Packard Company and Subsidiaries

For the years ended October 31 In millions	1989	1988	1987
Cash flows from operating activities:			
Net earnings	$ 829	$ 816	$ 644
Adjustments to reconcile net earnings to cash provided by operating activities:			
Depreciation and amortization	462	373	342
U.S. federal deferred taxes on earnings	(6)	(189)	97
Changes in assets and liabilities:			
Accounts and notes receivable	(385)	(305)	(230)
Inventories	(324)	(361)	(136)
Accounts payable	134	118	76
Taxes on earnings	(130)	192	65
Other current assets and liabilities	97	218	175
Other, net	(181)	(39)	(12)
	496	823	1,021
Cash flows from investing activities:			
Investment in property, plant and equipment	(857)	(648)	(507)
Disposition of property, plant and equipment	120	107	73
Purchase of short-term investments	(58)	(57)	(427)
Maturities of short-term investments	174	466	469
Purchase of Apollo Computer Inc., net of cash acquired	(486)	–	–
Other, net	(45)	(139)	6
	(1,152)	(271)	(386)
Cash flows from financing activities:			
Increase (decrease) in notes payable and short-term borrowings	799	(465)	682
Issuance of long-term debt	31	30	42
Repayment of current maturities of long-term debt	(95)	(117)	(66)
Issuance of common stock under employee stock plans	223	211	191
Repurchase of common stock	(140)	(1,569)	(220)
Dividends	(85)	(69)	(60)
Other, net	15	10	7
	748	(1,969)	576
Increase (decrease) in cash and cash equivalents	92	(1,417)	1,211
Cash and cash equivalents at beginning of year	814	2,231	1,020
Cash and cash equivalents at end of year	$ 906	$ 814	$2,231

The accompanying notes are an integral part of these financial statements.

From Hewlett-Packard Company. Reprinted by permission.

Case 2
Hewlett-Packard Company (L.O. 1)

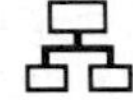

Hewlett-Packard's cash flow statement, shown opposite, is from their 1989 Annual Report. You are to answer the following questions, using the statement.

Required

1. Does Hewlett-Packard use the direct or indirect method of calculating cash flow from operating activities? Briefly explain the difference.
2. From 1987 to 1989, Hewlett-Packard's annual net earnings increased by $185 million. During the same time period, their annual cash flow from operating activities fell from $1,021 million $496 million. What are the main explanations for cash flow from operations falling while net earnings rose?
3. In 1987, what was Hewlett-Packard's two main uses of cash?
4. In 1989, Hewlett-Packard invested $857 million in property, plant and equipment, and spent $486 million to acquire Apollo Computer, Inc. What were the two main sources of cash for financing these investments?

Case 3
Pillsbury Company (L.O. 4)

The 1985 annual report for Pillsbury Company included the Consolidated Statement of Changes in Financial Position shown on page 916. On their statement, the word *funds* is used for *cash*.

Required

1. How does Pillsbury's 1985 definition of funds from operations differ from FASB's 1987 definition? Following the FASB definition of operating activities, what were Pillsbury's 1985 funds from operating activities?
2. What category of FASB's 1987 recommended format would include the items Pillsbury labeled "Funds from conversion of noncurrent assets" on its 1985 statement?
3. What were Pillsbury's three most important sources of funds in 1985?
4. In 1985, Pillsbury did not generate as much funds from operating activities as it used for investment. How did management make up for the difference?

The Pillsbury Company and Subsidiaries

Consolidated Statements of Changes in Financial Position

	Year ended May 31		
	1985	1984	1983
		(In millions)	
Funds provided from operations:			
Net earnings	**$191.8**	$169.8	$138.9
Charges to income not requiring working capital:			
Depreciation	**133.9**	114.6	105.5
Amortization of intangibles	**8.8**	6.2	3.3
Deferred taxes on income	**26.1**	21.9	(4.3)
	360.6	312.5	243.4
Funds from (used for) changes in working capital employed:			
(Increase) decrease in receivables	**(27.7)**	(5.2)	22.9
(Increase) decrease in inventories	**7.4**	(49.5)	(1.0)
(Increase) decrease in other current assets	**87.8**	17.4	39.5
Increase (decrease) in trade accounts payable	**(22.0)**	89.6	(18.5)
Increase (decrease) in advances on sales	**(101.6)**	(.7)	(51.3)
Increase (decrease) in taxes on income	**11.9**	(4.3)	(30.6)
Increase (decrease) in other current liabilities	**28.9**	28.6	16.5
	(15.3)	75.9	(22.5)
Funds from conversion of noncurrent assets:			
Disposals of property, plant and equipment	**33.1**	30.9	66.5
Proceeds from sale of notes with recourse	**22.3**	33.7	
Other proceeds from investments and other assets	**21.9**	22.2	25.4
Other, net	**11.5**	4.5	16.6
	88.8	91.3	108.5
Total funds generated internally	**434.1**	479.7	329.4
Funds utilized for investment activities:			
Capital expenditures	**(327.1)**	(282.4)	(243.9)
Additions to other noncurrent assets	**(78.0)**	(50.7)	(36.0)
Noncurrent assets of acquired companies:			
Property, plant and equipment	**(67.6)**	(23.9)	
Intangibles	**(86.6)**	(61.0)	
	(559.3)	(418.0)	(279.9)
Net funds generated (used) before financing activities	**(125.2)**	61.7	49.5
Funds from (used for) financing activities:			
Issuance of long-term debt	**219.3**	54.2	30.2
Long-term debt of acquired companies	**5.2**	3.6	
Retirement of long-term debt	**(132.5)**	(65.1)	(73.7)
Increase (decrease) in notes payable	**(6.0)**	6.8	(9.6)
Investment in tax lease			(24.7)
Income tax benefits from tax lease	**17.0**	19.0	33.6
Issuance (purchase) of common stock, net	**5.2**	(8.4)	(2.8)
Cash dividends	**(65.8)**	(58.9)	(52.5)
	42.4	(48.8)	(99.5)
Increase (decrease) in cash and equivalents	**$(82.8)**	$ 12.9	$(50.0)

Notes to Consolidated Financial Statements are an integral part of this statement.

Used by permission of the Pillsbury Company from the 1985 Annual Report.

Appendix A
Present Value Tables

This appendix contains two present value tables. Table A–1, Present Value of \$1, shows the present value of a single payment of \$1 paid or received at the end of the number of periods listed in the far left column. This table can be used to work any present value problem. Table A–2, Present Value of an Annuity of \$1, is used to find the present value of an annuity. An annuity is a series of payments of equal amount paid or received at regular time intervals. Using both tables sometimes saves computations.

■

Using Present Value Tables

Although the tables specify the present value of one dollar, both tables can be used to find the present value of any amount by multiplying the factor in the table by the amount of the payment. Although the tables can be used for time periods of months, quarters, or any other period, in most problems the time period given will be in years. The interest payment must be matched to the length of the period. That is, an annual interest rate of 12 percent would translate to 6 percent if the periods were six months long. The following discussion assumes a period of one year.

Table A–1 is used to find the present value of a single amount to be received or paid at some time in the future. To use the table you must know (1) the dollar amount to be received or paid, (2) the discount rate per year, and (3) number of years until the amount will be received or paid.

Table A–1
Present Value of $1

Discount rate	8%	10%	12%	14%	15%	16%	18%	20%
Period 1	0.9259	0.9091	0.8929	0.8772	0.8696	0.8621	0.8475	0.8333
2	0.8573	0.8264	0.7972	0.7695	0.7561	0.7432	0.7182	0.6944
3	0.7938	0.7513	0.7118	0.6750	0.6575	0.6407	0.6086	0.5787
4	0.7350	0.6830	0.6355	0.5921	0.5718	0.5523	0.5158	0.4823
5	0.6806	0.6209	0.5674	0.5194	0.4972	0.4761	0.4371	0.4019
6	0.6302	0.5645	0.5066	0.4556	0.4323	0.4104	0.3704	0.3349
7	0.5835	0.5132	0.4523	0.3996	0.3759	0.3538	0.3139	0.2791
8	0.5403	0.4665	0.4039	0.3506	0.3269	0.3050	0.2660	0.2326
9	0.5002	0.4241	0.3606	0.3075	0.2843	0.2630	0.2255	0.1938
10	0.4632	0.3855	0.3220	0.2697	0.2472	0.2267	0.1911	0.1615
11	0.4289	0.3505	0.2875	0.2366	0.2149	0.1954	0.1619	0.1346
12	0.3971	0.3186	0.2567	0.2076	0.1869	0.1685	0.1372	0.1122
13	0.3677	0.2897	0.2292	0.1821	0.1625	0.1452	0.1163	0.0935
14	0.3405	0.2633	0.2046	0.1597	0.1413	0.1252	0.0985	0.0779
15	0.3152	0.2394	0.1827	0.1401	0.1229	0.1079	0.0835	0.0649
16	0.2919	0.2176	0.1631	0.1229	0.1069	0.0930	0.0708	0.0541
17	0.2703	0.1978	0.1456	0.1078	0.0929	0.0802	0.0600	0.0451
18	0.2502	0.1799	0.1300	0.0946	0.0808	0.0691	0.0508	0.0376
19	0.2317	0.1635	0.1161	0.0829	0.0703	0.0596	0.0431	0.0313
20	0.2145	0.1486	0.1037	0.0728	0.0611	0.0514	0.0365	0.0261
21	0.1987	0.1351	0.0926	0.0638	0.0531	0.0443	0.0309	0.0217
22	0.1839	0.1228	0.0826	0.0560	0.0462	0.0382	0.0262	0.0181
23	0.1703	0.1117	0.0738	0.0491	0.0402	0.0329	0.0222	0.0151
24	0.1577	0.1015	0.0659	0.0431	0.0349	0.0284	0.0188	0.0126
25	0.1460	0.0923	0.0588	0.0378	0.0304	0.0245	0.0160	0.0105
26	0.1352	0.0839	0.0525	0.0331	0.0264	0.0211	0.0135	0.0087
27	0.1252	0.0763	0.0469	0.0291	0.0230	0.0182	0.0115	0.0073
28	0.1159	0.0693	0.0419	0.0255	0.0200	0.0157	0.0097	0.0061
29	0.1073	0.0630	0.0374	0.0224	0.0174	0.0135	0.0082	0.0051
30	0.0994	0.0573	0.0334	0.0196	0.0151	0.0116	0.0070	0.0042

22%	24%	25%	26%	28%	30%	32%	35%	40%
0.8197	0.8065	0.8000	0.7937	0.7813	0.7692	0.7576	0.7407	0.7143
0.6719	0.6504	0.6400	0.6299	0.6104	0.5917	0.5739	0.5487	0.5102
0.5507	0.5245	0.5120	0.4999	0.4768	0.4552	0.4348	0.4064	0.3644
0.4514	0.4230	0.4096	0.3968	0.3725	0.3501	0.3294	0.3011	0.2603
0.3700	0.3411	0.3277	0.3149	0.2910	0.2693	0.2495	0.2230	0.1859
0.3033	0.2751	0.2621	0.2499	0.2274	0.2072	0.1890	0.1652	0.1328
0.2486	0.2218	0.2097	0.1983	0.1776	0.1594	0.1432	0.1224	0.0949
0.2038	0.1789	0.1678	0.1574	0.1388	0.1226	0.1085	0.0906	0.0678
0.1670	0.1443	0.1342	0.1249	0.1084	0.0943	0.0822	0.0671	0.0484
0.1369	0.1164	0.1074	0.0992	0.0847	0.0725	0.0623	0.0497	0.0346
0.1122	0.0938	0.0859	0.0787	0.0662	0.0558	0.0472	0.0368	0.0247
0.0920	0.0757	0.0687	0.0625	0.0517	0.0429	0.0357	0.0273	0.0176
0.0754	0.0610	0.0550	0.0496	0.0404	0.0330	0.0271	0.0202	0.0126
0.0618	0.0492	0.0440	0.0393	0.0316	0.0254	0.0205	0.0150	0.0090
0.0507	0.0397	0.0352	0.0312	0.0247	0.0195	0.0155	0.0111	0.0064
0.0415	0.0320	0.0281	0.0248	0.0193	0.0150	0.0118	0.0082	0.0046
0.0340	0.0258	0.0225	0.0197	0.0150	0.0116	0.0089	0.0061	0.0033
0.0279	0.0208	0.0180	0.0156	0.0118	0.0089	0.0068	0.0045	0.0023
0.0229	0.0168	0.0144	0.0124	0.0092	0.0068	0.0051	0.0033	0.0017
0.0187	0.0135	0.0115	0.0098	0.0072	0.0053	0.0039	0.0025	0.0012
0.0154	0.0109	0.0092	0.0078	0.0056	0.0040	0.0029	0.0018	0.0009
0.0126	0.0088	0.0074	0.0062	0.0044	0.0031	0.0022	0.0014	0.0006
0.0103	0.0071	0.0059	0.0049	0.0034	0.0024	0.0017	0.0010	0.0004
0.0085	0.0057	0.0047	0.0039	0.0027	0.0018	0.0013	0.0007	0.0003
0.0069	0.0046	0.0038	0.0031	0.0021	0.0014	0.0010	0.0006	0.0002
0.0057	0.0037	0.0030	0.0025	0.0016	0.0011	0.0007	0.0004	0.0002
0.0047	0.0030	0.0024	0.0019	0.0013	0.0008	0.0006	0.0003	0.0001
0.0038	0.0024	0.0019	0.0015	0.0010	0.0006	0.0004	0.0002	0.0001
0.0031	0.0020	0.0015	0.0012	0.0008	0.0005	0.0003	0.0002	0.0001
0.0026	0.0016	0.0012	0.0010	0.0006	0.0004	0.0002	0.0001	0.0000

Table A–2
Present Value of an Annuity of $1

Discount rate	8%	10%	12%	14%	15%	16%	18%	20%
Period 1	0.9259	0.9091	0.8929	0.8772	0.8696	0.8621	0.8475	0.8333
2	1.7833	1.7355	1.6901	1.6467	1.6257	1.6052	1.5656	1.5278
3	2.5771	2.4869	2.4018	2.3216	2.2832	2.2459	2.1743	2.1065
4	3.3121	3.1699	3.0373	2.9137	2.8550	2.7982	2.6901	2.5887
5	3.9927	3.7908	3.6048	3.4331	3.3522	3.2743	3.1272	2.9906
6	4.6229	4.3553	4.1114	3.8887	3.7845	3.6847	3.4976	3.3255
7	5.2064	4.8684	4.5638	4.2883	4.1604	4.0386	3.8115	3.6046
8	5.7466	5.3349	4.9676	4.6389	4.4873	4.3436	4.0776	3.8372
9	6.2469	5.7590	5.3282	4.9464	4.7716	4.6065	4.3030	4.0310
10	6.7101	6.1446	5.6502	5.2161	5.0188	4.8332	4.4941	4.1925
11	7.1390	6.4951	5.9377	5.4527	5.2337	5.0286	4.6560	4.3271
12	7.5361	6.8137	6.1944	5.6603	5.4206	5.1971	4.7932	4.4392
13	7.9038	7.1034	6.4235	5.8424	5.5831	5.3423	4.9095	4.5327
14	8.2442	7.3667	6.6282	6.0021	5.7245	5.4675	5.0081	4.6106
15	8.5595	7.6061	6.8109	6.1422	5.8474	5.5755	5.0916	4.6755
16	8.8514	7.8237	6.9740	6.2651	5.9542	5.6685	5.1624	4.7296
17	9.1216	8.0216	7.1196	6.3729	6.0472	5.7487	5.2223	4.7746
18	9.3719	8.2014	7.2497	6.4674	6.1280	5.8178	5.2732	4.8122
19	9.6036	8.3649	7.3658	6.5504	6.1982	5.8775	5.3162	4.8435
20	9.8181	8.5136	7.4694	6.6231	6.2593	5.9288	5.3527	4.8696
21	10.0168	8.6487	7.5620	6.6870	6.3125	5.9731	5.3837	4.8913
22	10.2007	8.7715	7.6446	6.7429	6.3587	6.0113	5.4099	4.9094
23	10.3711	8.8832	7.7184	6.7921	6.3988	6.0442	5.4321	4.9245
24	10.5288	8.9847	7.7843	6.8351	6.4338	6.0726	5.4509	4.9371
25	10.6748	9.0770	7.8431	6.8729	6.4641	6.0971	5.4669	4.9476
26	10.8100	9.1609	7.8957	6.9061	6.4906	6.1182	5.4804	4.9563
27	10.9352	9.2372	7.9426	6.9352	6.5135	6.1364	5.4919	4.9636
28	11.0511	9.3066	7.9844	6.9607	6.5335	6.1520	5.5016	4.9697
29	11.1584	9.3696	8.0218	6.9830	6.5509	6.1656	5.5098	4.9747
30	11.2578	9.4269	8.0552	7.0027	6.5660	6.1772	5.5168	4.9789

22%	24%	25%	26%	28%	30%	32%	35%	40%
0.8197	0.8065	0.8000	0.7937	0.7813	0.7692	0.7576	0.7407	0.7143
1.4915	1.4568	1.4400	1.4235	1.3916	1.3609	1.3315	1.2894	1.2245
2.0422	1.9813	1.9520	1.9234	1.8684	1.8161	1.7663	1.6959	1.5889
2.4936	2.4043	2.3616	2.3202	2.2410	2.1662	2.0957	1.9969	1.8492
2.8636	2.7454	2.6893	2.6351	2.5320	2.4356	2.3452	2.2200	2.0352
3.1669	3.0205	2.9514	2.8850	2.7594	2.6427	2.5342	2.3852	2.1680
3.4155	3.2423	3.1611	3.0833	2.9370	2.8021	2.6775	2.5075	2.2628
3.6193	3.4212	3.3289	3.2407	3.0758	2.9247	2.7860	2.5982	2.3306
3.7863	3.5655	3.4631	3.3657	3.1842	3.0190	2.8681	2.6653	2.3790
3.9232	3.6819	3.5705	3.4648	3.2689	3.0915	2.9304	2.7150	2.4136
4.0354	3.7757	3.6564	3.5435	3.3351	3.1473	2.9776	2.7519	2.4383
4.1274	3.8514	3.7251	3.6059	3.3868	3.1903	3.0133	2.7792	2.4559
4.2028	3.9124	3.7801	3.6555	3.4272	3.2233	3.0404	2.7994	2.4685
4.2646	3.9616	3.8241	3.6949	3.4587	3.2487	3.0609	2.8144	2.4775
4.3152	4.0013	3.8593	3.7261	3.4834	3.2682	3.0764	2.8255	2.4839
4.3567	4.0333	3.8874	3.7509	3.5026	3.2832	3.0882	2.8337	2.4885
4.3908	4.0591	3.9099	3.7705	3.5177	3.2948	3.0971	2.8398	2.4918
4.4187	4.0799	3.9279	3.7861	3.5294	3.3037	3.1039	2.8443	2.4941
4.4415	4.0967	3.9424	3.7985	3.5386	3.3105	3.1090	2.8476	2.4958
4.4603	4.1103	3.9539	3.8083	3.5458	3.3158	3.1129	2.8501	2.4970
4.4756	4.1212	3.9631	3.8161	3.5514	3.3198	3.1158	2.8519	2.4979
4.4882	4.1300	3.9705	3.8223	3.5558	3.3230	3.1180	2.8533	2.4985
4.4985	4.1371	3.9764	3.8273	3.5592	3.3254	3.1197	2.8543	2.4989
4.5070	4.1428	3.9811	3.8312	3.5619	3.3272	3.1210	2.8550	2.4492
4.5139	4.1474	3.9849	3.8342	3.5640	3.3286	3.1220	2.8556	2.4994
4.5196	4.1511	3.9879	3.8367	3.5656	3.3297	3.1227	2.8560	2.4996
4.5243	4.1542	3.9903	3.8387	3.5669	3.3305	3.1233	2.8563	2.4997
4.5281	4.1566	3.9923	3.8402	3.5679	3.3312	3.1237	2.8565	2.4998
4.5312	4.1585	3.9938	3.8414	3.5687	3.3317	3.1240	2.8567	2.4999
4.5338	4.1601	3.9950	3.8424	3.5693	3.3321	3.1242	2.8568	2.4999

Example of Use of Table A–1

A friend owes you \$5,000, due on December 31, 19x2. Several months before the due date, your friend asks you to extend the loan for two years so it would instead be due on December 31, 19x4. To induce you to extend one loan, your friend offers to pay you \$7,000 at the end of the additional two years rather than the \$5,000 that will soon be due (no interest will be paid on the additional \$2,000). You have been considering making a similar loan to another friend for which you would receive 10 percent interest. From an economic viewpoint, should you extend the loan to your friend to December 31, 19x4?

The economic question is whether present value of the payment of \$7,000 received two years is greater than the \$5,000 that could be received now assuming a 10 percent discount rate. From Table A–1, you can determine that the present value of \$1 received at the end of two years is 0.8264 if the discount rate is 10 percent. Look at the table in the Period 2 row and the 10 percent column to make sure that you see how to use the table to find a present value factor. The present value factor is used to calculate the present value of \$7,000 as follows:

$$\text{Present value of \$7,000 received in 2 years at 10\%} = \$7,000 \times 0.8264$$
$$= \underline{\underline{\$5,784.80}}$$

Since the present value of the future payment is greater than the \$5,000 to be received now, the sensible economic decision would be to extend the loan.

Example of Use of Table A–2

On January 1, 19x7 an executive of a small company had earned a bonus of \$10,000, payable immediately. However, since the company was a little short of cash it offered to substitute five annual payments of \$3,000 each beginning on December 31, 19x7. The executive liked the idea of receiving a total of \$15,000 (5 × \$3,000) rather than \$10,000, but realized that he could expect to earn 12 percent return on the \$10,000 if he received it in full on January 1, 19x7. Ignoring possible income tax differences, which bonus is preferable?

Since the \$3,000 payments are equal in amount and will be received at regular intervals of one year, they represent an annuity. Table A–2 can be used to calculate its present value. According to Table A–2, the present value of \$1 received annually for five years at 12 percent per year is 3.6048. The present value of the \$3,000 payments are calculated as follows:

$$\text{Present value of a 5 year annuity of \$3,000 at 12\%} = \$3,000 \times 3.6048$$
$$= \underline{\underline{\$10,814.40}}$$

If the executive is confident that the company will pay the bonus over the five years, the 5-year payments have a somewhat higher present value than the \$10,000 payments and are therefore preferable.

■

Glossary

Absorption costing: A costing method in which direct materials, direct labor, and manufacturing overhead costs, both fixed and variable, are absorbed into the value of inventory. Contrast with *Direct costing.* (9)

Accounting rate of return: Ratio of a project's average added after-tax net income to its average added assets. Expressed as a percentage. (15)

Accounts receivable turnover: An indicator of how rapidly accounts receivable are being collected and turned into cash. Found by dividing total annual credit sales by average balance in accounts receivable. (17)

Acid-test ratio: Total cash, marketable securities, and accounts receivable divided by total current liabilities. A measure of debt-paying ability. (17)

Activity-based predetermined overhead rate: A ratio for allocating manufacturing overhead costs of a single activity to products processed by that activity. Found by separating manufacturing overhead costs for each production activity and developing a predetermined overhead rate for each of those activities. See also *Plantwide predetermined overhead rate.* (16)

Actual manufacturing overhead costs: All manufacturing costs except direct labor and direct materials costs necessary for the manufacture of a product. Includes the cost of indirect materials, indirect labor, expired factory insurance, depreciation on factory equipment, utilities, and other costs of operating the factory. (4, 5)

Allocate: To divide a general cost of production among products, activities, or divisions, using a predetermined ratio. This ratio is based on activity level or use. (4, 13, 16)

Allocated costs: Costs incurred in a separate manufacturing service activity and allocated to production activities. (11)

Annuity: A series of payments of equal amount received at regular intervals. (14)

Applied manufacturing overhead costs: The estimated total manufacturing overhead costs assigned to a job or product. Calculated by using a predetermined overhead rate. (4, 5)

Apply: To divide the manufacturing overhead cost of production among products, using a predetermined rate based on activity measure or usage. (4)

Area of feasible solutions: On a linear program graph, the area bounded by constraint equations. (App6)

Asset turnover: The ratio of a center's total sales to its total assets or total average assets if data for more than one year exist. Used as a measure of how effectively assets are employed. Algebraically:

$$\text{Asset turnover} = \frac{\text{center's total sales}}{\text{center's total (average assets)}} \quad (13)$$

Assign: To apportion service costs among production activities for inclusion in the predetermined overhead rates. Assignment is based on the amount of service used. (16)

Average collection period: The average time taken to collect on accounts receivable. Another way of expressing the accounts receivable turnover. Found by dividing number of days in a year by accounts receivable turnover. (17)

Average cost per unit: The unit manufacturing cost of a product; used in valuing inventory on the balance sheet. In a job order costing system, average cost per unit is calculated by dividing total costs of the job by number of units in the job. In a process costing system, calculated by dividing the total cost of processing in an activity by the number of units processed in a particular month. (4, 5)

Average selling period: The time required to sell inventory or the average time stock remains in inventory. Calculated by dividing number of days in a year by inventory turnover. (17)

Avoidable cost: A cost that can be eliminated by ceasing some economic activity or by improving the activity's efficiency. Avoidable costs are relevant costs. (8)

Book value: Original cost less accumulated depreciation. (15)

Book value per share: Book value of a firm's assets divided by the number of its common shares outstanding. In most cases, it has little meaning. (17)

Breakeven point: The sales volume at which total sales revenues equal total expenses and there is no profit or loss. (6)

Budget: A document through which management communicates its plans for the organization and measures the organization's performance. As a quantification of planned revenues and expenses, the budget is used to communicate goals for revenues, expenses, assets, liabilities, and other business activities. (1, 7)

Budget variance: The difference between actual manufacturing overhead costs, as recorded in a firm's accounting records, and budgeted costs, as based on the standard quantity of cost driver (machine-hours or direct labor hours) allowed for the actual number of units produced. Calculated by subtracting flexible budget overhead costs for the standard quantity of cost driver allowed for the actual number of units produced from actual manufacturing overhead costs. (11)

Budgeted balance sheet: An estimate of a firm's financial position at the end of the budget period. (7)

Budgeted income statement: A statement showing estimated revenues and expenses from profit-directed activities for a specific budget period. (7)

Budgeting: The quantification of plans to guide future operations and measure performance. (1)

Business function organization: A form of organizing in which each manager is responsible for a specific function, such as production, marketing, finance, or human resources. (9)

Capital expenditure: Investment in an asset whose useful life is more than one year. (14)

Capital expenditure budget: A listing of all approved long-range expenditures planned to improve a firm's operating capacity or efficiency. (7)

Cash: Cash and cash equivalents. Cash equivalents include United States Treasury bills, commercial paper, and money market funds. (18)

Cash budget: A period-by-period statement of (1) cash on hand at the start of a budget period, (2) expected cash receipts, (3) expected cash payments, and (4) the resulting cash balance at the end of the budget period. (7)

Certified management accountant (CMA): One who holds a certificate of professional competence obtained by passing a four-part exam given by the Institute of Certified Management Accountants. (1)

Committed fixed costs: The cost of the basic facilities and organizational structure needed for a business. (3)

Common cost: A cost that benefits more than one product, service, or organizational segment at the same time. (9)

Common-size financial statements: Statements that translate the dollar amounts on financial statements into percentages that indicate the relative size of an item in proportion to the whole. *Common-size balance sheets* show assets, liabilities, and owners' equity as a percentage of total assets. *Common-size income statements* express revenue and expenses as a percentage of sales revenues. (17)

Compounding: Earning interest on interest. (14)

Constraint equation: An equation representing a limitation on the production, distribution, or demand for a company's product. Used in linear programming. (App6)

Continuous budget: A budget that adds a future time period as the one just ended is completed and dropped. It is revised at the end of each period on the basis of actual results from the previous period. Also called a *rolling budget.* (7)

Contribution format income statement: An income statement in which expenses are grouped by cost behavior. Variable expenses are totaled and deducted from sales revenue to obtain the contribution margin. Fixed expenses are then totaled and deducted from the contribution margin to obtain operating income. (3)

Contribution margin: Sales revenues less variable expenses. Represents the amount sales has contributed toward fixed expenses and operating income. (3, 13)

Contribution margin per unit: The dollar amount contributed by the sale of one unit to cover fixed costs and, after covering fixed costs, to the company's operating income. Calculated by subtracting the variable cost per unit from the sales price. (6)

Contribution margin per unit of scarce resource: For each product, the contribution margin generated by one unit of the scarce resource. Calculated by dividing the contribution margin per unit by the quantity of scarce resource required to produce one unit of product. (6)

Contribution margin ratio: The percentage of each sales dollar contributed toward fixed costs and, after covering fixed costs, to the company's operating income. Calculated by dividing contribution margin by revenues. (6)

Control: The action that a manager takes to ensure that actual results correspond to planned results. (9)

Control chart: A graphic representation of the range of random variations one expects in a manufacturing process that is in control. Also used in statistical quality control. (10)

Controllable costs: Costs over which a manager has significant influence. (11)

Controllable item: A cost, revenue, or investment item over which a manager has significant influence. (9, 13)

Controller: The person in charge of all accounting services in an organization. (1)

Controlling: The process of ensuring that management's plan is successfully implemented. (1)

Conversion costs: The sum of direct labor and applied manufacturing overhead costs. (2, 5)

Cost behavior pattern: The relationship between a cost and the level of business activity. (3)

Cost driver: A measure of business or production activity, such as direct labor cost, machine-hours, or miles driven, that causes changes in the manufacturing overhead cost. Also called *activity base* or *measure.* (3, 4, 11)

Cost formula: A mathematical equation describing the fixed and variable components of a cost. The cost formula is generally expressed as $Y = a + bX$, that is, total costs = fixed costs + variable costs × activity measure. (3)

Cost of capital: Amount an organization must pay lenders or owners to induce them to invest capital in the organization. The cost of borrowed capital is the interest payments made on a loan. The cost of capital provided by owners is the dividends paid to those owners plus anticipated increases in share value. (15)

Cost of goods manufactured: In a manufacturing company, the total cost of all good units completed during a period and transferred from Work in Process Inventory to Finished Goods Inventory. Obtained after adjusting total manufacturing costs by beginning and ending work in process inventories. Equivalent to purchases in a merchandising company. (2, 4)

Cost of Goods Sold: An account that represents the total cost of all products sold during the accounting period. In a manufacturing company, the cost of goods sold is obtained by adjusting the cost of goods manufactured for the beginning and ending finished goods inventories. (2, 4)

Cost-based transfer prices: Transfer price based either on standard variable or standard full costs (fixed plus variable) of manufacturing. (13)

Cost-benefit analysis: A comparison of the benefits of an action with its cost. (1)

Cost-volume-profit analysis: A method used to estimate how changes in the following variables will affect profit: fixed costs, unit sales price, sales volume, unit variable costs, and sales mix. (6)

Cost-volume-profit graph: A graph showing the relationship between revenues, costs, profit, and volume over a range of sales activity. At any volume, profit or loss is the vertical distance between the total revenues and total costs lines. (6)

Costs accounted for: In process costing, section 4 of the cost summary, which shows the cost of units completed and transferred out of the activity and the cost of units in the ending inventory. The sum of these costs should equal the month's costs to account for (see section 3 of the cost summary). (5)

Costs to account for: In process costing, section 3 of the cost summary, which shows the cost of the activity's beginning inventory and the cost of units started or transferred into the activity during the month. The sum of these costs should equal the month's costs accounted for (see section 4 of the cost summary). (5)

Current expenditure: Purchase of an asset of value during the current period only. (14)

Current ratio: A firm's total current assets divided by its total current liabilities. A measure of a firm's debt-paying ability. (17)

Current value: The amount for which an asset can be presently purchased. Usually determined by an appraisal. (13)

Currently attainable standards: Standard costs representing the expected current cost of efficient operations. (10)

Debt-to-equity-ratio: A measure of the balance between an organization's debt and equity. Found by dividing total liabilities by total shareholders' equity. (17)

Decentralized organization: An organization where managers at different levels within the organization have the authority to make decisions concerning business activities. (9)

Depreciation tax shield: Amount by which income taxes are reduced because of depreciation deductions. Calculated by multiplying the annual depreciation deduction by the tax rate. (15)

Direct cost to an organizational segment: A cost is direct to a segment when it can be physically traced to that organizational segment. (9)

Direct costing: A cost accounting system that excludes fixed manufacturing overhead costs from the unit cost of inventory and cost of goods sold. Only direct materials, direct labor, and variable manufacturing overhead costs are absorbed into the value of inventory. Fixed manufacturing costs are treated as a period expense. Contrast to *Absorption costing.* (9)

Direct costs: Costs physically traceable to a specific product or service. (2)

Direct labor: Work that can be physically traced to a particular product. (2, 4)

Direct labor budget: A statement showing the quantity, cost, and period of payment for labor that can be directly identified with specific products. (7)

Direct labor cost: The cost of work that can be physically traced to a particular job or product. (5)

Direct labor efficiency variance: The difference between actual direct labor hours used and standard direct labor hours allowed, multiplied by the standard rate per direct labor hour. (10)

Direct labor rate variance: The difference between the actual rate per direct labor hour and the standard rate per direct labor hour, multiplied by the actual direct labor hours used. (10)

Direct materials: Materials that can be physically traced to a particular job or product. (2, 4, 5)

Direct materials budget: A statement consisting of three schedules that show (1) the quantity and cost of direct materials needed to meet production requirements; (2) the level of direct materials purchases needed for production and maintenance of ending inventory levels; and (3) the expected cash outflows for direct materials purchases. (7)

Direct materials cost: The cost of materials that can be physically traced to a job or product. (5)

Direct materials price variance: The difference between the actual price paid per unit of direct materials and the standard price, multiplied by the actual quantity of direct materials purchased. (10)

Direct materials quantity variance: The difference between the actual quantity of direct materials used and the standard quantity of direct materials allowed, multiplied by the standard price per unit of direct materials. (10)

Direct method: Method for assigning service costs *only* to production activities. Services performed by one service activity for another service activity are ignored. See also *Step Method.* (16)

Direct method (of reporting cash flows from operating activities)**:** This method divides cash flows into cash received from customers, dividends received, cash payments to suppliers and employees, and cash payments for interest and taxes for the purpose of determining cash flows from operating activities. (18)

Discounting: A technique for reducing the value of future receipts to an equivalent present value. (14)

Discretionary fixed costs: Fixed costs over which management can exercise some control at any time during the fiscal year. (3)

Dividend payout ratio: The ratio of dividends per share of stock to earnings per share expressed as a percentage. (17)

Dividend-yield ratio: The ratio of dividend per share of stock to market value per share expressed as a percentage. (17)

Du Pont formula: A formula used to analyze the cause of differences between actual and budgeted return on investment (ROI). Algebraically:

$$\text{ROI} = \begin{pmatrix}\text{return on}\\ \text{sales}\end{pmatrix} \times \begin{pmatrix}\text{asset}\\ \text{turnover}\end{pmatrix} \qquad (13)$$

Earning-power ratios: A group of ratios that help analysts assess the adequacy of a firm's net income. (17)

Earnings per share: Net income available to common shareholders divided by the number of common shares outstanding. (17)

Efficiency variance: The difference between flexible budget overhead costs for actual quantity of cost driver used and flexible budget overhead costs for the standard quantity of activity base allowed. Calculated by subtracting flexible budget overhead costs for the standard quantity of activity base allowed from flexible budget overhead costs for actual quantity of cost driver used. (11)

Ending inventory budget: A statement showing the cost of ending direct materials, work in process, and finished goods inventories for each period. (7)

Engineering approach to cost estimation: A cost estimate based on the physical relationship between manufacturing activity and costs, as measured by time and motion studies and materials estimates. (3)

Equation approach: An approach to analyzing cost-volume-profit relationships based on this equation:

$$\begin{pmatrix}\text{Sales}\\ \text{revenues}\end{pmatrix} - \begin{pmatrix}\text{variable}\\ \text{costs}\end{pmatrix} - \begin{pmatrix}\text{fixed}\\ \text{costs}\end{pmatrix} = \text{profit} \quad (6)$$

Equivalent units: See *Total equivalent units.* (5)

Expense center: A responsibility center whose manager is responsible for completing assigned tasks within budgeted or standard cost levels. Also called *cost center.* (9, 12)

Expense tax effect: Amount by which deductible expenses decrease taxes in a profit-making organization. Calculated by multiplying cash expenses by the tax rate. (15)

Extraordinary items: Unusual gains or losses occurring in one year that are not expected to be repeated. They are reported in a separate section of the income statement net of their income tax effect. An uninsured loss is an example. (17)

FIFO cost flow assumption: In process costing, a method of accounting for beginning work in process inventories. The cost of beginning work in process is separated from the cost of units started and completed during the period. For contrast, see *Moving average cost flow assumption.* (5)

Financial accounting: The branch of accounting that deals with information reported to people outside an organization. (1)

Financial analysis: An analysis performed to identify an organization's major financial strengths and weaknesses. (17)

Financial budget: The second part of the master budget, which details capital expenditures and summarizes the effect of operations on a company's cash balances and expected financial position. It contains the capital expenditure budget, the cash budget, and the budgeted balance sheet. (7)

Financial leverage: Obtaining capital from debt or preferred shares and using the capital to earn a return by investing in assets. Financial leverage is favorable when the return on assets is greater than after-tax interest expense or the preferred dividend rate. (17)

Financing activities: Raising capital from shareholders, paying dividends, and borrowing or repayment of long-term debt. (18)

Finished Goods Inventory: In a manufacturing company, an account that represents the cost of products finished but not sold by the end of the accounting period. Equivalent to merchandise inventory in a merchandising firm. (2, 4)

Fixed cost: An operating cost whose total remains constant over a wide range of business activity. (3, 11, 12)

Flexible budget: A budget that may be adjusted

to any activity level to reflect how costs vary with changes in production volume. (11, 12)

Flexible budget average contribution margin per unit: The total contribution margin as stated in the flexible budget divided by the total actual units sold. (12)

Full absorption costing: A cost accounting system that includes fixed manufacturing overhead costs in the unit cost of inventory. (4)

Full-cost transfer price: A transfer price based on variable costs plus allocated fixed manufacturing costs. (13)

Fully diluted earnings per share: Earnings per share calculated on the assumption that all convertible debt or preferred shares are converted into common shares. The number of common shares after conversion is the denominator of the earnings per share ratio. In the numerator, net income is adjusted to eliminate the effect of interest or dividends on debt or preferred shares assumed to be converted. (17)

Functional income statement: Income statements in which expenses are grouped by business functions. Fixed and variable costs are not listed separately under each functional expense category. (3)

Future value: An amount available at some specific time in the future because a specific amount was invested today at a specified rate of return. Includes both principal and interest. (14)

Gain (loss): Differences between the book value of an asset and the amount it is sold for. A gain usually increases income taxes; a loss usually reduces them. (15)

Geographic organization: A form of organization in which each manager is responsible for several business functions such as marketing and production in a particular geographic region. (9)

Goals: Concrete targets to be achieved within a definite time period. (1)

Graphic approach: A method of estimating costs by plotting historical cost and activity data onto a graph. A line is then fitted visually onto the data. Also called the *scattegraph method.* (3)

Gross book value: The original cost of an asset with no deduction for accumulated depreciation. (13)

Half-year convention: A tax requirement that firms deduct only one-half of the first year's depreciation during the first year of an asset's life and remaining one-half in the year after the asset's useful life ends. (15)

High-low approach: A method of estimating costs by using only the high and low points of historical costs and activity data. (3)

Historical costs: Actual costs incurred in the past. (4)

Historical data approach: An approach to estimating costs that is based on historical data for costs and business activity. (3)

Implementing: The process of motivating people to work together efficiently and effectively to achieve an organization's objectives and goals. (1)

Incremental cash flow: The difference between the yearly cash flows of two alternate investments. (14)

Indifference cost volume: The production level at which the cost of making an item equals the cost of buying it. (8)

Indirect costs: Costs not directly traceable to a product or service. (2)

Indirect labor: Factory work that is not performed directly on a particular product. Accounted for as a part of manufacturing overhead. (2, 4, 5)

Indirect materials: Miscellaneous materials of small value used in a factory. Accounted for as part of manufacturing overhead. (2, 4, 5)

Indirect method (of reporting cash flows from operating activities): This method starts with the organization's net income based on accrual accounting, adds back annual depreciation and any other noncash expenses, and adjusts for changes in accounts receivable, inventories, and current liabilities to determine net income according to the cash basis of accounting, which is the amount of cash flows from operating activities. (18)

Inequality: A relationship between two numbers that indicates those numbers to be of unequal value. (App6)

Internal control system: An organizational plan plus all methods and measures taken to safeguard assets, verify the accuracy and reliability of records, encourage efficiency, and ensure compliance with company policy. An internal control system is generally evaluated through internal audits. (1)

Interpolation: The process of estimating a number between two adjacent numbers in a table. (14)

Inventoriable costs: Costs incurred to acquire or

manufacture finished goods inventory for sale. Also called *product costs*. (2)

Inventory turnover: A measure of inventory liquidity. Defined as annual cost of goods sold divided by average balance in inventory. (17)

Investing activities: Lending money and collecting loans, acquiring and selling securities that are not cash equivalents, and buying and selling plant and equipment. (18)

Investment center: A responsibility center whose manager is responsible for controlling expenses, revenues, and investments and balancing them to produce a budgeted return on investments or residual income. (9, 13)

Job: A batch of products with a definite starting and completion point and with a distinct separation from other batches. May consist of one or more units of product. (4)

Job cost sheet: A form for recording the direct materials, direct labor, and applied manufacturing overhead costs of a job as well as the number of units produced. (4)

Job order costing (cost accounting system): A cost accounting system designed for companies whose products or services are produced in distinct batches, often to customer specifications. See *Job*. Each job has a clear starting and completion point. (2, 4, 5)

Joint costs: Costs incurred before the split-off point that benefit all products. (8)

Joint products: Products produced from a common input. (8)

Just in time (JIT): A philosophy for designing and operating a manufacturing process that emphasizes higher-quality products and flexible product-oriented flow lines with lower inventories. (7)

Labor mix: The combination of skilled, semiskilled, and unskilled workers used. (10)

Least squares line: A line fitted to a series of plotted points by means of statistical analysis. Also called a *regression line*. (3)

Line position: An employment position with direct responsibility for creating and delivering an organization's goods and services to customers. Sales and production management are line positions. (1)

Linear programming: A method for determining the quantity of each product that should be produced and sold in order to maximize or minimize some objective. In this chapter, the objective is to maximize total contribution margin. Used when more than one resource is limited. (App6)

Loss: See *Gain (loss)*.

Make-or-buy decision: A management decision about whether an item should be made by the organization itself or bought from an outside supplier. (8)

Managerial accounting: The branch of accounting concerned with reporting information to people inside an organization for planning and control decisions. (1)

Managerial judgment: A method of monitoring manufacturing variances by using general guidelines developed by management to evaluate the significance of a variance. The guidelines are based on absolute dollar amounts, percentages of budgeted cost, or a combination of these two measures. Used to decide if variances should be investigated. (10)

Manufacturing company: An organization that converts direct materials into products for sale. (2, 7)

Manufacturing overhead: All manufacturing costs other than direct materials and direct labor necessary to manufacture a product. Also called *factory overhead*. (2, 4, 5, 11)

Manufacturing overhead budget: A statement summarizing all expected manufacturing costs other than direct materials and direct labor costs as well as expected cash payments for those costs. (7)

Margin of safety: The difference between the expected sales volume and the breakeven point in units divided by expected sales volume. Expressed as a percentage of expected sales volume, it is used as a measure of the risk inherent in a sales plan. (6)

Market price: The price at which a product can be purchased or sold by independent buyers and sellers. (13)

Market-based transfer price: The outside market price of a product adjusted for savings in transportation, credit, and other costs avoided by selling to a related division. See also *Transfer price*. (13)

Master budget: A series of interrelated budgets that quantify management's expectations about revenues, expenses, net income, cash flows, and financial position. (7)

Master budget average contribution margin per unit: The total contribution margin as stated in the master budget divided by the total units estimated to be sold in the master budget. (12)

Matching: The process of associating product costs with the period in which a product is sold and period costs with the time period in which the costs expire. (2)

Materials inventory: A balance sheet asset account that shows the value of direct and indirect materials on hand for use in production. (2, 4)

Materials requisition forms: Forms used to request materials for use in production. Indicates where materials were used in the factory and for what purpose, either job or overhead. (4)

Materials stock cards: Cards used to record the quantity and cost of materials used in production. A separate card is maintained on each type of material used. Includes receipts for the materials, issues of the materials to production, and the balance of materials available for production. (4)

Merchandise Inventory: A merchandising company account that includes all goods purchased for resale that were not sold by the end of the accounting period. Equivalent to Finished Goods Inventory in a manufacturing company. (2)

Merchandising companies: Companies that purchase merchandise for resale. (2, 7)

Minimum rate of return: Return that management thinks it must earn to encourage investors to invest capital in a business. Often used as a discount rate in calculating present value of future cash flows. (14, 15)

Mixed costs: Costs composed of both variable and fixed elements. Also called *semivariable costs.* (3, 11)

Modified Accelerated Cost Recovery System (MACRS): Method of calculating depreciation deductions for income taxes. The accelerated method allows most of an asset's cost to be depreciated in the first half of its useful life. For tax purposes it is usually preferred to the straight-line method because of the time value of money. (15)

Moving average: In process costing, a weighted average of the cost of the beginning inventory (partially completed in the last period) and costs from the current period. (5)

Moving average cost flow assumption: In process costing, a method of accounting for beginning work in process inventories. The cost of beginning inventories is averaged with the cost of other units worked on during the period. For contrast, see *FIFO cost flow assumption.* (5)

Multiple regression analysis: A statistical approach to estimating costs by using more than one independent variable. (3)

Multiple regression equations: Regression equations with more than one independent variable. (3)

Net book value: The original cost of an asset minus accumulated depreciation. (13)

Net present value: Total of a project's future cash returns discounted to their present value at the minimum rate of return minus the required initial investment (cash outflows). A project with a zero or positive net present value can be expected to earn at least the minimum rate of return. A project with a negative net present value will probably earn less than the minimum rate of return. (14, 15)

Noncontrollable costs: Costs over which a manager has no significant influence or control. (11)

Nonrecurring decisions: Decisions concerning situations that occur sporadically and unpredictably. (8)

Normative approach: An approach to estimating costs that prescribes what future costs ideally should be based on engineering estimates. (3)

Objective function: An algebraic representation of a company goal that is to be maximized or minimized by a linear program. An example is to maximize total contribution margin. (App6)

Objectives: Guidelines prepared by top management to establish the long-range direction of an organization. (1)

Operating activities: Delivering or producing goods for sale and providing services. These are mainly transactions related to dealing with customers. All transactions that are not investing or financing activities are operating activities. (18)

Operating budget: The first part of the master budget, representing expected results of operations. Contains the sales, production, direct materials, direct labor, manufacturing overhead, ending inventory, and selling and administrative expense budgets as well as the budgeted income statement. (7)

Optimal solution: In linear programming, the solution that maximizes the program's objective function. Generally found at one corner of the area of feasible solutions. (App6)

Organization: A group of people working together to achieve a common goal. (1)

Organizing: The process by which managers del-

egate responsibility for using an organization's human, financial, and physical resources. (1)
Outlier: A cost observation that is influenced by unusual events and, thus, is nonrepresentative of the true cost of business activity. (3)
Overapplied overhead: The amount by which applied overhead for a period is greater than actual manufacturing overhead. (4)

Payback period: Number of years needed for an investment project to return its original investment. Does not indicate an investment's rate of return. (15)
Period costs: Selling and administrative costs that usually cannot be associated with a product or sale. (2)
Planning: The process of identifying alternate courses of action, evaluating those alternatives, and deciding which one will best achieve an organization's objectives and goals. (1)
Planning period: The period for which detailed budgets are developed from managerial plans. (7)
Plantwide predetermined overhead rate: A ratio for assigning all of the manufacturing overhead costs of a plant to products using a single rate. Found by dividing total estimated manufacturing overhead for the entire plant by total estimated cost driver for the entire plant. See also *Activity-based predetermined overhead rate.* (16)
Postaudit: A special study done after a capital expenditure has been made to see whether actual results correspond to expected results. (14)
Predetermined overhead rate: A ratio that relates total estimated manufacturing overhead costs for the year to expected manufacturing activity for the year. Used to assign manufacturing overhead costs to batches of product or to activities. Calculated by dividing estimated total manufacturing overhead costs for the year by estimated amount of cost driver for the year. (4, 5, 11)
Predetermined standards: Standards determined in advance. They represent the best performance one can realistically expect given the environment and resources. (17)
Prepaid expense: An unconsumed or unexpired period cost classified as an asset on the balance sheet. (2)
Present value: Amount that if invested now at a given rate of return will provide a specified future amount. (14)
Present value factor: In a present value table, an amount showing the present value of $1 or of an annuity of $1 received at some specified future time or times at a specified discount rate. (14)
Price-earnings ratio: Ratio of the market price of a share to its earnings per share. (17)
Price standard: The price that management expects to pay for a unit of input. (10)
Prime costs: The sum of direct materials and direct labor costs. (2)
Prior department costs: Costs assigned to a product by activities through which it was processed earlier. (5)
Process costing (cost accounting system): A cost accounting system designed for companies that mass-produce identical products on a continuous assembly line. (2, 4, 5)
Product cost: A cost incurred to acquire or manufacture finished goods inventory. Also called *inventoriable cost.* (2)
Product mix: See *Sales mix.* (6, 9, 12)
Product-line organization: A form of organization in which a single manager is responsible for human resources, production, and marketing of a specific product line. (9).
Production activities: Activities performed directly on products sold to customers. See also *Service activities.* (16)
Production budget: A statement specifying the number of units of each product to be produced to satisfy demand for the product and provide the desired ending finished goods inventory. (7)
Profitability index: Ratio of the present value of a project's future net cash inflows to its immediate cash outflows. Calculated by dividing the present value of future net cash inflows by immediate cash outflows. Any project with a profitability index greater than one has a positive net present value. The higher the index, the more desirable the project. (15)
Profit center: A responsibility center whose manager is responsible for controlling both expenses and revenues and balancing them to produce the budgeted profit. (9, 12)
Profit-volume graph: A graph showing the relationship between profits and volume. Profits are shown by a profit line, which intersects the horizontal axis at the breakeven point. (6)
Purchases budget: In a manufacturing company, this statement shows the quantity and cost of direct materials purchases needed both for production and maintenance of ending inventory levels. In a merchandising company, this statement shows

the cost of merchandise to be purchased to satisfy sales demand and ending inventory needs. (7)
Purchases of inventory: In a merchandising company, the cost of inventory purchases made during a specific accounting period. Equivalent to cost of goods manufactured in a manufacturing company. (2)

Quantity standard: The quantity of input needed to produce one unit of output. Expressed in terms of pounds, gallons, board feet, yards, direct labor hours, or another measure. (10)

Rate of return: Return on an investment expressed as a percentage of the amount invested. (14)
Ratio: A relationship between two numbers expressed either as a percentage or as an absolute number. (17)
Recurring decisions: Decisions made regularly. (8)
Regression analysis: A more accurate version of the graphic approach to estimating costs. Using this approach, one fits a line to cost and activity data by means of statistical analysis. (3)
Regression line: A line fitted to a series of plotted points by means of statistical analysis. Also called a *least squares line.* (3)
Relevant costs: Costs that will affect the accomplishment of a decision maker's objectives and that differ between alternatives. Broadly speaking, any change in revenues or expenses that will affect a manager's decision. (8)
Relevant information: Information that affects the accomplishment of objectives and that differs between alternatives. (1)
Relevant range: The range of business activity over which fixed costs do not change and costs estimates are valid. (3)
Residual income (RI): A measure of an investment center's earnings in relation to its average investment and its target rate of return. Expressed in dollars. Algebraically:

$$\text{RI} = \frac{\text{center's}}{\text{earning}} - \left(\begin{array}{c}\text{center's}\\ \text{average}\\ \text{investment}\end{array} \times \begin{array}{c}\text{target rate}\\ \text{of return}\end{array} \right) \qquad (13)$$

Responsibility accounting system: An accounting system in which the accountant reports to each manager only information relevant to that manager's responsibilities. (9)
Return on common shareholders' equity: A percentage measuring the total return earned by common shareholders. It is the net income available to common shareholders after subtracting preferred dividends divided by the book value of common shareholders' equity. (17)
Return on investment (ROI): The ratio of an investment center's earnings to its average investments. Expressed as a percentage, it is calculated by dividing a center's net earnings by its average investments.

$$\text{ROI} = \frac{\text{center's earnings}}{\text{center's average investment}} \qquad (9, 13)$$

Return on sales: The ratio of profit (net earnings) to total sales revenues. Expressed as a percentage, it is used as a measure of how efficiently net earnings was generated. Algebraically:

$$\text{Return on sales} = \frac{\text{center's earnings}}{\text{center's total sales}} \qquad (13)$$

Return on total assets: A ratio that measures how wisely management is using assets. It is calculated by dividing net income *before* interest but *after* taxes by average total assets. (17)
Revenue center: A responsibility center whose manager is responsible for selling the budgeted quantities of various products or services at budgeted prices. (9, 12)
Revenue tax effect: Amount by which taxes reduce revenues in a profit-making organization. Calculated by multiplying an organization's revenue by its income tax rate. (15)

Sales budget: An estimate of the unit sales and sales revenues expected during the budget period as well as an estimate of cash receipts. (7)
Sales mix: The proportion of total sales volume contributed by each product. Also called *product mix.* (6, 9, 12)
Sales mix variance: A measure of the change in contribution margin produced by a difference between the budgeted and actual sales mix. Algebraically: sales mix variance = (flexible budget average contribution margin per unit − master

budget average contribution margin per unit) × actual unit sales. (12)
Sales price variance: A measure of the change in contribution margin produced by the difference between actual and budgeted sales prices. Algebraically: sales price variance = (actual sales price − master budget sales price) × actual unit sales. (12)
Sales volume variance: A measure of the change in contribution margin produced by the difference between actual unit sales and budgeted unit sales. Algebraically: sales volume variance = (actual unit sales − master budget unit sales) × master budget average contribution margin per unit. (12)
Scattergraph method: See *Graphic approach.* (3)
Segment: A subpart of an organization. (9)
Segment margin: The dollar amount contributed by a segment toward covering common fixed costs. (9)
Sell-or-process-further decision: A decision between selling a product as is or processing it further. (8)
Selling and administrative expense budget: A detailed listing of nonmanufacturing expenses during a budget period and expected cash payments for those expenditures. (7)
Semivariable costs: Costs composed of both variable and fixed elements. Also called *mixed costs.* (3)
Separable costs: Costs incurred after the split-off point for the benefit of only one product. (8)
Service activities: Activities not performed on products but providing support to production activities so they can operate more efficiently. Maintenance and human resources are examples of service activities. See also *Production activities.* (16)
Service company: A company that provides services rather than products to customers. Accounting firms are service companies. (2)
Simple regression analysis: A statistical approach to estimating costs by using only one independent variable. (3)
Simple statement of cash flows: A report that classifies the changes between the beginning and ending balance sheet amounts according to whether they represent cash inflows or cash outflows. It does not attempt to identify offsetting changes. (18)
Spending variance: The difference between actual overhead costs and flexible budget overhead costs for actual quantity of cost driver during the period. Calculated by subtracting flexible budget overhead costs for the actual quantity of cost driver used from total actual manufacturing overhead costs. (11)
Split-off point: The point in the manufacturing process at which separate products are identifiable and can be separately processed or sold. (8)
Staff position: A position that indirectly supports creation and delivery of goods and services to customers. Jobs in purchasing, market research, and financial and managerial accounting services are staff positions. (1)
Standard applied manufacturing overhead cost: The standard manufacturing overhead cost assigned to each unit of product or activity according to a predetermined overhead rate. Calculated by multiplying the standard activity measure by the predetermined overhead rate. (11)
Standard cost per unit: A predetermined cost consisting of two components: (1) a cost component based on a quantity of input used to produce one unit of finished product and (2) a cost component based on a price standard for each measure of the quantity standard. Calculated by multiplying the quantity standard for each input by the price standard for that input. (10)
Standard costs: Estimates of what unit costs should be, based on past costs and engineering estimates. (4)
Standard hours allowed: The standard quantity of direct labor hours allowed per unit of output, multiplied by the actual number of units produced. (10)
Standard quantity of direct materials allowed: The standard quantity of direct materials per unit of output multiplied by the actual number produced. (10)
Statement of cash flows: A report of the inflows and outflows of cash during a period. The FASB recommends classifying cash inflows and outflows into operating activities, investing activities, and financing activities. (18)
Static budgets: Budgets based on the level of production as estimated at the beginning of the year. They are not revised as actual production levels change. (11)
Statistical quality control: A procedure for monitoring manufacturing variances. It is based on statistical estimates of chance variations in a manufacturing process that is under control. Used to decide which variances should be investigated. (10)

Step cost: A cost that is fixed over a short range of business activity, then rises abruptly and remains fixed over another short range. (3)
Step method: Method for assigning service activity costs to other service activities according to a predefined sequence before being reassigned to production activities. See also *Direct method.* (16)
Straight-line depreciation: Method of calculating depreciation deductions. For income tax purposes, a constant percentage of an asset's cost is deducted each year of the asset's life, except during the first and last years, until the total cost is recovered. An alternative to the MACRS accelerated method. (15)
Sunk costs: Costs incurred in a prior accounting period that cannot be reversed. (8)

T account method: Analyzing cash flows by setting up T accounts for all balance sheet accounts and entering summary entries explaining the balance sheet changes. Helps ensure that no information affecting cash flows is omitted and that all offsetting items are discovered. See Exhibit 18–12. (18)
Target profit: The amount of profit expected by investors in a business. (6)
Theoretical standards: Standard costs representing the lowest possible costs attainable under ideal conditions. (10)
Time value of money: Preference for receipt of payment immediately rather than at some future time. It is the basis for discounting cash flows. (14)
Time-adjusted rate of return: Discount rate yielding a zero net present value when used to find the present value of a project's net cash flows. Also called *Internal rate of return.* (14, 15)
Timecard: A record of the total hours an employee worked on any one day and how those hours were spent. (4)
Times-interest-earned ratio: Ratio of a firm's net earnings to its interest expenses. It is found by dividing annual earnings before interest and income taxes, often called operating income, by annual interest expenses. (17)
Total equivalent units: A measure of the effort and cost put into both partially completed and fully completed units processed during an accounting period. (5)
Total manufacturing cost: The sum of direct materials, direct labor, and manufacturing overhead costs incurred during an accounting period. (2, 4)
Total sales price variance: The sum of sales price variances for each product. (12)
Transfer price: A special selling price used in interdivisional exchanges to record the selling division's revenues and the buying division's expenses. (13)
Treasurer: The person responsible for a company's financing activities, including financing, cash management, establishing sound credit policy, and investment of funds. (1)

Unavoidable costs: Costs that will continue regardless of whether the economic activity is eliminated. (8)
Underapplied overhead: The amount by which applied overhead for a period is less than actual manufacturing overhead. (4)
Unit manufacturing costs: The average manufacturing cost per unit found by dividing total manufacturing costs by the number of units manufactured. Also called *average cost per unit.* (2)
Units accounted for: Section 2 of the cost summary, which shows the number of physical units completed and transferred out of the activity and the number of units in the ending inventory. The sum of these units should equal the month's units to account for (see section 1 of the cost summary). (5)
Units to account for: Section 1 of the cost summary, which shows the number of physical units in an activity's beginning inventory and the number of units started or transferred into the activity during the month. The sum of these units should equal units accounted for (see section 2 of the cost summary). (5)

Variable costs: Costs whose total changes in direct proportion to changes in business activity. (Cost per unit remains constant.) (3, 11, 12)
Variance: The difference between actual revenues, costs, and profits and planned, or budgeted, results, expressed numerically. For each type of input, the total difference between actual costs and standard costs. (1, 10)
Volume variance: A measure of the difference between the actual production volume, computed by using the standard amount of cost driver per

unit, and the estimated average monthly production volume on which the predetermined overhead rate is based. Expressed in dollars, it is calculated by subtracting applied manufacturing overhead costs for the standard quantity of cost driver allowed for the number of units produced from flexible budget overhead costs for the standard quantity of cost driver allowed for the number of units produced. (11)

Work in Process Inventory: An account that represents the cost of direct materials, direct labor, and manufacturing overhead invested in the manufacture of products not yet finished. (2, 4)

Working capital: A pool of liquid assets financed by long-term capital sources. Working capital is the organization's total current assets minus its total current liabilities. (17)

Index